CONTENTS

D0300973

THE NATIONWIDE
FOOTBALL ANNUAL
2019–2020

Published by SportsBooks Limited, 9 St Aubyns Place, York, YO24 1EQ
First published in 1887

A CIP catalogue record for this book is available from the British Library.

Editorial compilation by Stuart Barnes

ISBN-13 9781907524592

Front cover shows Liverpool celebrating their European Champions League victory over
Tottenham. Back cover has Manchester City celebrating their English treble. Photos from
PA Images.

Printed and bound in the UK by CPI Group (UK) Ltd, Croydon CRO 4YY

COMMENT

By Stuart Barnes

Will a memorable season be talked about for years to come, not just for a titanic title race and a clean sweep in Europe but also for how the women's game picked up the baton during the summer and demanded the right to be recognised as mainstream sport? It made steady progress in recent years with a fully-professional Super League, third place at the 2015 World Cup in Canada and players treated as not just names on a team sheet but also stars in their own right. Modest attendances and sporadic media coverage hampered greater strides. Now all that could change after the performance of Steph Houghton and her team, under the guidance of Phil Neville, generated unprecedented attention at this World Cup. The former Manchester United and England defender's appointment in January 2018 was accompanied by a degree of scepticism in some quarters. Neville himself admitted to having little experience of this level. But he spotted the potential, forged an immediate bond with his players and predicted ahead of the tournament: 'We can take women's football to a level nobody ever dreamed of.' What happened in France probably exceeded even his own expectation. There was no fairytale finish, with the United States too strong and too streetwise on their way to a record fourth title. Instead, the likes of Houghton, Lucy Bronze and Ellen White became household names, blanket coverage of matches included record peak viewing figures of 11.7m on the BBC and a dramatic semi-final was the lead story on *News at Ten*. England ensured a Great Britain women's team at the 2020 Tokyo Olympics, which Neville will manage, and he is contracted through to the 2021 European Championship, for which England qualify automatically as hosts. Meanwhile, Wembley can expect a bumper crowd for an international against Germany in November, the team's first appearance at the national stadium since 2014. Off the field, too, there have been significant developments. The Super League has attracted a record £10m sponsorship from Barclays, with annual prize money of £500,000. Manchester United and Tottenham have been promoted to the top division, delivering extra appeal. And perhaps most significantly, there are moves for the league to be taken over by the Premier League, with the FA seeing England teams and grassroots participation as it own long-term priorities. The future certainly looks rosy.

***

It would be too much to expect a repeat of the way Manchester City and Liverpool stood toe-to-toe throughout a classic Premier League season. Even so, it is difficult to see beyond a third successive title for City, or a first since 1990 for Jurgen Klopp's Champions League winners, with the remainder of the big-six in their wake. If there is to be a sustained challenge, Tottenham look the best equipped to deliver it from the club's first full campaign in their new stadium. Europa League champions Chelsea are sure to miss Eden Hazard, Arsenal need to stiffen defensively and Ole Gunnar Solksjaer admits Manchester United still have some way to go to recapture past glories. Frank Lampard's return as manager to Stamford Bridge, where he spent 13 years as a player, is the summer's most fascinating appointment. Lampard, the 12th incumbent since Roman Abramovich bought the club in 2003, is one of four English managers new to the top flight, alongside Aston Villa's Dean Smith, Brighton's Graham Potter and Sheffield United's Chris Wilder. Saddest sight is that of Rafael Benitez leaving Newcastle for China after a long-running disagreement over investment with owner Mike Ashley. 'Shambolic,' fumed Newcastle legend Alan Shearer, summing up the loss of a world-class manager to one of the game's outposts, albeit at a reported annual salary of £12m.

DUTCH TOO MUCH FOR ENGLAND

Victory in one European tournament unwittingly conspired against success in another as England were found lacking in the semi-finals of the inaugural UEFA Nations League. Liverpool's Champions League triumph against Tottenham presented Gareth Southgate with a dilemma for the match against Holland five days later. Conscious of the demands on players from both those teams, and restricted to two full training sessions in preparation, he decided to gamble. No Jordan Henderson, Dele Alli or Trent Alexander-Arnold. Instead, a starting midfield of two players who had not been regulars for their clubs during the season, Fabian Delph and Ross Barkley, alongside the relatively inexperienced Declan Rice. The gamble did not pay off. Marcus Rashford's penalty put England ahead, but they were second best overall, with the eventual introduction of Henderson and Alli, along with a rusty Harry Kane, unable to compensate for two costly mistakes by John Stones and a Kyle Walker own goal which could define Southgate's defensive strategy for the European Championship campaign ahead. A fourth semi-final defeat for an England side, the previous one against Croatia in the World Cup, meant that a penalty shootout win over Switzerland in the third-place match meant little, apart from the novelty of goalkeeper Jordan Pickford scoring one of them as well as producing the decisive save. Portugal followed their Euro 2016 success by beating Holland 1-0 in the final with a 60th minute goal scored by Goncalo Guedes and created by Manchester City's Bernardo Silva, who was named the player of the tournament. Portugal defeated the Swiss 3-1 in their semi-final, courtesy of Cristiano Ronaldo's hat-trick on his 157th international appearance. The 34-year-old, now playing his club football with Juventus, took his tally as Europe's leading international marksman to 88, four more than Ferenc Puskas scored for Hungary and Spain.

EUROPEAN NATIONS LEAGUE FINALS – PORTUGAL

SEMI-FINALS

PORTUGAL 3 (Ronaldo 25, 88, 90) SWITZERLAND 1 (Rodriguez 57)
Porto (42,415); Wednesday, June 5, 2019)
Portugal (4-3-1-2): Rui Patricio, Nelson Semedo, Pepe (Jose Fonte 63), Ruben Dias, Raphael Guerrero, Bruno Fernandes (Joao Moutinho 90+1), Ruben Neves, William Carvalho, Bernardo Silva, Joao Felix (Goncalo Guedes 70), Ronaldo.
Switzerland (3-5-1-1): Sommer, Schar, Akanji, Rodriguez, Mbabu. Zakaria (Fernandes 71), Xhaka, Freuler (Drmic 89), Zuber (Steffen 83), Shaqiri, Seferovic. **Booked**: Xhaka, Schar, Shaqiri
Referee: F Brych (Germany). **Half-time**: 1-0

HOLLAND 3 (De Ligt 73, Walker 97 og, Promes 114) ENGLAND 1 (Rashford 32 pen) – aet
Guimaraes (25,711); Thursday, June 6, 2019
Holland (4-2-3-1): Cillessen, Dumfries, De Ligt, Van Dijk, Blind, De Roon (Van de Beek 68), F de Jong (Strootman 114), Bergwijn (Propper 90), Wijnaldum, Babel (Promes 68), Depay
Booked: De Ligt, Dumfries, Van de Beek
England (4-3-3): Pickford, Walker, Stones, Maguire, Chilwell, Rice (Alli 105), Delph (Henderson 77), Barkley, Sancho (Lingard 61), Rashford (Kane 46), Sterling. **Booked**: Kane
Referee: C Turpin (France). **Half-time**: 0-1

THIRD PLACE PLAY-OFF

SWITZERLAND 0 ENGLAND 0 – aet, England won 6-5 on pens
Guimaraes (15,642); Sunday, June 9, 2019
Switzerland (3-5-1-1): Sommer, Elvedi, Schar, Akanji, Mbabu, Fernandes (Zakaria 61), Xhaka, Freuler, Rodriguez (Drmic 87), Shaqiri (Zuber 65), Seferovic (Okaor 113). **Booked**: Xhaka,
England (4-3-3): Pickford, Alexander-Arnold, Gomez, Maguire, Rose, Lingard (Sancho 106), Dier, Delph (Barkley 106), Alli, Kane (Wilson 75), Sterling. **Booked**: Rose, Lingard
Referee: O Hategan (Romania)

FINAL

PORTUGAL 1 (Goncarlo Guedes 60) HOLLAND 0
Porto (43,199); Sunday, June 9, 2019

Portugal (4-3-1-2): Rui Patricio, Nelson Semedo, Jose Fonte, Ruben Dias, Raphael Guerrero, Bruno Fernandes (Joao Moutinho 81), Danilo, William Carvalho (Ruben Neves 90+3) Bernardo Silva, Ronaldo (capt), Goncalo Guedes (Rafa Silva 75). **Coach:** Fernando Santos
Holland (4-3-3): Cillessen, Dumfries, De Ligt, Van Dijk (capt), Blind, De Roon (L de Jong 88), F de Jong, Wijnaldum, Bergwijn (Van der Beek 60), Babel (Promes 46), Depay. **Booked:** Dumfries, Van Dijk. **Coach:** Ronald Koeman
Referee: A Undiano (Spain). **Half-time:** 0-0

England squad: Butland (Stoke), Heaton (Burnley), Pickford (Everton); Alexander-Arnold (Liverpool), Chilwell (Leicester), Gomez (Liverpool), Keane (Everton), Maguire (Leicester), Rose (Tottenham), Stones (Manchester City), Walker (Manchester City); Alli (Tottenham), Barkley (Chelsea), Delph (Manchester City), Dier (Tottenham), Henderson (Liverpool), Rice (West Ham); Kane (Tottenham), Lingard (Manchester Utd), Rashford (Manchester Utd), Sancho (Borussia Dortmund), Sterling (Manchester City), Wilson (Bournemouth)

LEAGUE A

Group 1

	P	W	D	L	F	A	Pts
Holland Q	4	2	1	1	8	4	7
France	4	2	1	1	4	4	7
Germany R	4	0	2	2	3	7	2

Group 2

Switzerland Q	4	3	0	1	14	5	9
Belgium	4	3	0	1	9	6	9
Iceland R	4	0	0	4	1	13	0

Group 3

Portugal Q	4	2	2	0	5	3	8
Italy	4	1	2	1	2	2	5
Poland R	4	0	2	2	4	6	2

Group 4

England Q	4	2	1	1	8	5	7
Spain	4	2	0	2	12	7	6
Croatia R	4	1	1	2	4	10	4

LEAGUE B

Group 1

Ukraine P	4	3	0	1	5	5	9
Czech Republic	4	2	0	2	4	4	6
Slovakia R	4	1	0	3	5	5	3

Group 2

Sweden P	4	2	1	1	5	3	7
Russia	4	2	1	1	4	3	7
Turkey R	4	1	0	3	4	7	3

Group 3

Bosnia-Herz P	4	3	1	0	5	1	10
Austria	4	2	1	1	3	2	7
Northern Ireland R	4	0	0	4	2	7	0

Group 4

Denmark P	4	2	2	0	4	1	8
Wales	4	2	0	2	6	5	6
Rep of Ireland R	4	0	2	2	1	5	2

LEAGUE C

Group 1

Scotland P	4	3	0	1	10	4	9
Israel	4	2	0	2	6	5	6
Albania R	4	1	0	3	1	8	3

Group 2

Finland P	6	4	0	2	5	3	12
Hungary	6	3	1	2	9	6	10
Greece	6	3	0	3	4	5	9
Estonia R	6	1	1	4	4	8	4

Group 3

Norway P	6	4	1	1	7	2	13
Bulgaria	6	3	2	1	7	5	11
Cyprus	6	1	2	3	5	9	5
Slovenia R	6	0	3	3	5	8	3

Group 4

Serbia P	6	4	2	0	11	4	14
Romania	6	3	3	0	8	3	12
Montenegro	6	2	1	3	7	6	7
Lithuania R	6	0	0	6	3	16	0

LEAGUE D

Group 1

Georgia P	6	5	1	0	12	2	16
Kazakhstan	6	1	3	2	8	7	6
Latvia	4	0	4	2	2	6	4
Andorra	6	0	4	2	2	9	4

Group 2

Belarus P	6	4	2	0	10	0-	14
Luxembourg	6	3	1	2	11	4	10
Moldova	6	2	3	1	4	5	9
San Marino	6	0	0	6	0	16	0

Group 3

Kosovo P	6	4	2	0	15	2	14
Azerbaijan	6	2	3	1	7	6	9
Faroe Is	6	1	2	3	5	10	5
Malta	6	0	3	3	5	14	3

Group 4

Macedonia P	6	5	0	1	14	5	15
Armenia	6	3	1	2	14	8	10
Gibraltar	6	2	0	4	5	15	6
Liechtenstein	6	1	1	4	7	12	4

Q – Qualified for finals; P – Promoted; R – Relegated

HOME COMFORTS FOR EURO 2020

England have every incentive to maintain a successful start to qualification for Euro 2020 – and to make a real impact in the tournament proper. Gareth Southgate's side will have home advantage if they reach the semi-final and again if they make the final, with Wembley staging both matches as part of UEFA's decision to spread venues across the continent for the first time. The national stadium will also host the other semi-final – along with three group games and a last-16 tie which were taken away from Brussels because of delays in building a new arena in the Belgian capital. Hampden Park and the Aviva Stadium in Dublin will also stage those four games. Cardiff's bid for the Principality Stadium was unsuccessful. England have so far played only two qualifiers because of participation in the finals of UEFA's Nations League. But they top the group after scoring five goals in successive games for the first time since 1984, defeating the Czech Republic 5-0, with a hat-trick by Raheem Sterling, and Montenegro 5-1. They should comfortably build on those victories in September's games against Bulgaria and, for the first time, against Kosovo, who were affiliated to UEFA and the world governing body FIFA in 2016. That fixture will be played at St Mary's in Southampton, the first senior international since Sven-Goran Eriksson's team, played Macedonia there in 2002. Northern Ireland also lead their group after winning four successive qualifiers at the start of a campaign for the first time – two each against Belarus and Estonia. They have still to face Germany and Holland in a group manager Michael O'Neill described as 'cruel – the worst we could have.' The Republic of Ireland, with Mick McCarthy in charge for the second time, have also made a good start with ten points from four matches. Scotland, under their new manager Steve Clarke, look set to contest second-place with Russia behind Belgium, but Ryan Giggs admits it will be tough for Wales to go through after successive defeats by Croatia and Hungary. The first match of the finals is on June 12 in Rome, with the final on July 12. Venues and capacities: Amsterdam, Holland (54,000), Baku, Azerbaijan (65,000), Bilbao, Spain (53,000), Bucharest, Romania (56,000), Budapest, Hungary (68,000), Copenhagen, Denmark (38,000), Dublin (50,000), Glasgow (52,000), London (90,000), Munich, Germany, (75,000), Rome, Italy (73,000), Saint Petersburg, Russia (56,000).

QUALIFYING TABLES
(Winners and runners-up qualify; four places decided by play-offs)

GROUP A

	P	W	D	L	F	A	Pts
England	2	2	0	0	10	1	6
Czech Republic	3	2	0	1	5	6	6
Kosovo	3	1	2	0	5	4	5
Bulgaria	4	0	2	2	5	7	2
Montenegro	4	0	2	2	3	10	2

GROUP B

	P	W	D	L	F	A	Pts
Ukraine	4	3	1	0	8	1	10
Luxembourg	4	1	1	2	4	5	4
Serbia	3	1	1	1	5	7	4
Portugal	2	0	2	0	1	1	2
Lithuania	3	0	1	2	3	7	1

GROUP C

	P	W	D	L	F	A	Pts
Northern Ireland	4	4	0	0	7	2	12
Germany	3	3	0	0	13	2	9
Holland	2	1	0	1	6	3	3
Belarus	4	0	0	4	1	9	0
Estonia	3	0	0	3	1	12	0

GROUP D

	P	W	D	L	F	A	Pts
Republic of Ireland	4	3	1	0	5	1	10
Denmark	3	1	2	0	9	5	5
Switzerland	2	1	1	0	5	3	4
Georgia	4	1	0	3	4	8	3
Gibraltar	3	0	0	3	0	6	0

GROUP F

	P	W	D	L	F	A	Pts
Hungary	4	3	0	1	6	4	9
Slovakia	3	2	0	1	7	2	6
Croatia	3	2	0	1	5	4	6
Wales	3	1	0	2	2	3	3
Azerbaijan	3	0	0	3	3	10	0

GROUP F

	P	W	D	L	F	A	Pts
Spain	4	4	0	0	11	2	12
Romania	4	2	1	1	11	5	7
Sweden	4	2	1	1	8	7	7
Norway	4	1	2	1	8	7	5
Malta	4	1	0	3	2	10	3
Faroe Is	4	0	0	4	3	12	0

GROUP G

	P	W	D	L	F	A	Pts
Poland	4	4	0	0	8	0	12
Israel	4	2	1	1	8	7	7
Austria	4	2	0	2	7	6	6
Slovenia	4	1	2	1	7	3	5
Macedonia	4	1	1	2	5	7	4
Latvia	4	0	0	4	1	13	0

GROUP H

	P	W	D	L	F	A	Pts
France	4	3	0	1	12	3	9
Turkey	4	3	0	1	9	2	9
Iceland	4	3	0	1	5	5	9
Albania	4	2	0	2	5	3	6
Moldova	4	1	0	3	2	10	3

GROUP I

	P	W	D	L	F	A	Pts
Belgium	4	4	0	0	11	1	12
Russia	4	3	0	1	15	3	9
Kazakhstan	4	2	0	2	7	7	6
Scotland	4	2	0	2	4	7	6
Cyprus	4	1	0	3	6	5	3
San Marino	4	0	0	4	0	20	0

GROUP J

	P	W	D	L	F	A	Pts
Italy	4	4	0	0	13	1	12
Finland	4	3	0	1	6	2	9
Amenia	4	2	0	2	7	6	6

	P	W	D	L	F	A	Pts
Greece	4	1	1	2	6	8	4
Bosnia-Herz	4	1	1	2	5	7	4
Liechtenstein	4	0	0	4	0	13	0

YOUNG ENGLAND OUT ON A LIMB

England Under-21 manager Aidy Boothroyd admitted his side lacked 'steel' and were not 'streetwise enough' after a miserable European Championship hosted by Italy and San Marino. 'We have issues to address with a new team into the next season,' Boothroyd said after a single point gained in their group. 'We've clearly got the talent, but talent needs some structure.' His squad was weakened by the absence, though injuries, of Chelsea's Callum Hudson-Odoi, Everton's Tom Davies and Newcastle's Sean Longstaff. But there was still sufficient talent and experience to guard against the failure to hold on to leads, a lack of discipline and the individual errors which littered the closing stages of all three games. Phil Foden, Manchester City's gifted midfielder, put England ahead and Dean Henderson saved a penalty in the opening match against France. But Hamza Choudhury was shown a straight red card, on VAR evidence for a poorly-timed tackle, and although the subsequent second spot-kick struck a post, France levelled in the 89th minute and were gifted the winner by Aaron Wan-Bissaka's own goal in the fifth minute of stoppage time. Controversially, Boothroyd omitted Foden from the starting line-up against Romania, who cancelled out strikes from Demarai Gray and Tammy Abraham and won 4-2 with further goals after 88 and 93 minutes. That put paid to England's chances of qualifying for the semi-finals and there no consolation in the dead rubber, despite leading three times through Reiss Nelson's penalty, James Maddison and Jonjoe Kenny. Croatia cancelled out each one, their third equaliser coming eight minutes from the end of normal time for a 3-3 draw.
● There was disappointment, too, for other England youth teams. The Under-17s failed to qualify from their group at the European Championship, held in the Republic of Ireland, and will not defend the World Cup in Brazil in October-November 2019. The Under-20 side lost all three group matches at the Toulon Tournament.

GROUP A

	P	W	D	L	F	A	Pts
Spain Q	3	2	0	1	8	4	6
Italy	3	2	0	1	6	3	6
Poland	3	2	0	1	4	7	6
Belgium	3	0	0	3	4	8	0

Results: Poland 3 Belgium 2, Italy 3 Spain 1, Spain 2 Belgium 1, Italy 0 Poland 1, Belgium 1 Italy 3, Spain 6 Belgium 0

GROUP B

	P	W	D	L	F	A	Pts
Germany Q	3	2	1	0	10	3	7
Denmark	3	2	0	1	6	4	6
Austria	3	1	1	1	4	4	4
Serbia	3	0	0	3	1	10	0

Results: Serbia 0 Austria 2, Germany 3 Denmark 1, Denmark 3 Austria 1, Germany 6 Serbia 1, Austria 1 Germany 1, Denmark 2 Serbia 0

GROUP C

	P	W	D	L	F	A	Pts
Romania Q	3	2	1	0	8	3	7
France Q	3	2	1	0	3	1	7
England	3	0	1	2	6	9	1
Croatia	3	0	1	2	4	8	1

Match-day 1

England 1 (Foden 54) **France** 2 (Ikone 89, Wan-Bissaka 90+5 og). Att: 11,211 (Cesena)
England (4-3-3): Henderson, Wan-Bissaka, Clarke-Salter, Tomori, Dasilva, Maddison, Choudhury, Foden, Sessegnon (Calvert-Lewin 75), Solanke (Mount 71), Gray (Abraham 75),. **Booked**: Maddison, Wan-Bissaka. **Sent off**: Choudhury (63)
Other result: Romania 4 Croatia 1

Match-day 2

England 2 (Gray 79, Abraham 87) **Romania** 4 (Puscas 76 pen, Hagi 85, Coman 88, 90+3). Att: 8,440 (Cesena)
England (4-3-3): Henderson, Kenny, Clarke-Salter, Tomori, Dasilva (Abraham 77), Maddison, Dowell, Mount, Gray, Calvert-Lewin, Barnes (Sessegnon 46, Foden 57). **Booked**: Tomori
Other result: France 1 Croatia 0

Match-day 3

Croatia 3 (Brekalo 39, 82, Vlasic 62) **England** 3 (Nelson 11 pen, Maddison 48, Kenny 70). Att: 3,512 (Serravalle)
England (4-3-3): Henderson, Kenny, Clarke-Salter (Konsa 49), Tomori, Kelly, Maddison (Gibbs-White 73), Dowell (Mount 56), Foden, Nelson, Abraham, Gray. **Booked**: Dowell, Kenny
Other result: France 0 Romania 0

SEMI-FINALS

Germany 4 Romania 2; Spain 4 France 1

FINAL

Spain 2 (Ruiz 7, Olmo 69) **Germany** (Amiri 88). Att: 23,232 (Udine, Italy), June 30, 2019

England squad: Gunn (Southampton), Henderson (Manchester Utd), Woodman (Newcastle); Clarke-Salter (Chelsea), Dasilva (Chelsea), Kelly (Bournemouth), Kenny (Everton), Konsa (Brentford), Tomori (Chelsea), Wan-Bissaka (Crystal Palace); Barnes (Leicester), Choudhury (Leicester), Dowell (Everton), Foden (Manchester City), Gibbs-White (Wolves), Maddison (Leicester), Mount (Chelsea), Sessegnon (Fulham); Abraham (Chelsea), Calvert-Lewin (Everton), Gray (Leicester), Nelson (Arsenal), Solanke (Bournemouth)

THE THINGS THEY SAY ...

'Do you think I deserve to have this type of question the day we won the treble?' – **Pep Guardiola**, Manchester City manager, angry at being asked about Financial Fair Play and alleged irregular payments after the FA Cup Final.

'It was an intense season with the most beautiful finish I could ever have imagined' – **Jurgen Klopp**, Liverpool manager, on his side's Champions League success and Premier League near miss.

'I have loved every moment at Chelsea and I would not have left for any other club' – **Eden Hazard** on fulfilling his dream to play for Real Madrid.

'I've lost one of my best friends' – **Pele** on the death of England's Gordon Banks, who miraculously saved the Brazil legend's header in the 1970 World Cup.

SO NEAR YET SO FAR FOR LIONESSES

Phil Neville acclaimed his players for committing 'heart and soul' to the tournament, 'touching the hearts of the nation' – and attracting an unprecedented television audience. But once again it all ended in tears as England bowed out of the Women's World Cup in heartbreaking fashion at the semi-final stage. Four years previously in Canada, Laura Bassett's own goal in the second minute of stoppage-time condemned her side to a 2-1 defeat by Japan in the last four. This time, it was captain Steph Houghton left distraught in her 111th international after missing an 84th minute penalty which enabled the United States to hold on to their 2-1 lead. The Manchester City player was given the responsibility after Nikita Parris twice failed from the spot, but a poor strike was comfortably saved   and Millie Bright's second yellow card two minutes later meant England had to throw caution to the wind with ten players against a team with vast experience of closing the game out. Prior to Houghton's dismissal in an enthralling match, watched by a 53,000 crowd in Lyon and delivering peak BBC viewing figures of 11.7m, another VAR decision deprived Ellen White of an equaliser by a matter of inches. The offside verdict was accepted by Neville and his players without complaint. There was also a consensus that, overall, the United States deserved to win. England, who also lost in the semi-finals of the 2017 European Championship, continued to make great strides, without displaying the consistency and control needed to win the big tournaments. That took nothing away from Houghton's inspirational leadership – which had earned her the Professional Footballers' Association's 2019 Merit Award – White's predatory instincts in front of goal and the sheer quality of Lucy Bronze, highlighted by a stunning strike against Norway in the quarter-finals.

All round, England were good value for guaranteeing Great Britain a women's team at the 2020 Olympics by finishing in the top three European in France. More importantly, perhaps, they have taken women's football in this country to a new level. White had another effort ruled out by VAR, this time for handball, in the 2-1 defeat by Sweden in the play-off for third-place. Sloppy defending cost two goals in the opening 22 minutes, which meant England failed to match the bronze medal four years previously. Midfielder Karen Carney's 144th international appearance was her last before retiring. The United States were champions for a record fourth time, beating Holland 2-0 in the final.

Scotland, playing in their first World Cup finals, also bade a tearful farewell to the tournament after a VAR-awarded penalty. But their players were left kicking themselves for surrendering a three-goal lead against Argentina and missing out on going through as one of the best third-placed teams. They wilted after Kim Little, Jennifer Beattie and Erin Cuthbert established a commanding position with 20 minutes of normal time remaining. Two goals were lost in a five-minute spell and another followed a third spot-kick conceded in three matches. Lee Alexander saved the first attempt, but was ruled to have been off her line and was beaten by the second in the fourth minute of added time.

GROUP A

	P	W	D	L	F	A	Pts
France Q	3	3	0	0	7	1	9
Norway Q	3	2	0	1	6	3	6
Nigeria Q	3	1	0	2	2	4	3
South Korea	3	0	0	3	1	8	0

Results: France 4 South Korea 0; Norway 3 Nigeria 0; Nigeria 2 South Korea 0; France 2 Norway 1; Nigeria 0 France 1; South Korea 1 Norway 2

GROUP B

	P	W	D	L	F	A	Pts
Germany Q	3	3	0	0	6	0	9
Spain Q	3	1	1	1	3	2	4
China Q	3	1	1	1	1	1	4
South Africa	3	0	0	3	1	8	0

Results: Germany 1 China 0; Spain 3 South Africa 1; Germany 1 Spain 0; South Africa 0 China 1; South Africa 0 Germany 4; China 0 Spain 0

GROUP C

	P	W	D	L	F	A	Pts
Italy Q	3	2	0	1	7	2	6
Australia Q	3	2	0	1	8	5	6
Brazil Q	3	2	0	1	6	3	6
Jamaica	3	0	0	3	1	12	0

Results: Australia 1 Italy 2; Brazil 3 Jamaica 0; Australia 3 Brazil 2; Jamaica 0 Italy 5; Jamaica 1 Australia 4; Italy 0 Brazil 1

GROUP D

	P	W	D	L	F	A	Pts
England Q	3	3	0	0	5	1	9
Japan Q	3	1	1	1	2	3	4
Argentina	3	0	2	1	3	4	2
Scotland	3	0	1	2	5	7	1

Match-day 1
England 2 (Parris 14 pen, White 40) **Scotland** 1 (Emslie 79). Att: 13,188 (Nice)
England (4-2-3-1): Bardsley, Bronze, Houghton, Bright (McManus 55), Greenwood, Walsh, Parris, Scott, Kirby (Stanway 82), Mead (Carney 70), White
Scotland (4-2-3-1): Alexander, Howard (Arthur 74), Corsie, Beattie, Docherty (Smith 55), Murray (Arnot 86), Weir, Emslie, Little, Evans, Cuthbert. **Booked**: Beattie, Docherty
Other result: Argentina 0 Japan 0

Match-day 2
England 1 (Taylor 61) **Argentina** 0. Att: 20,294 (Le Havre)
England (4-2-3-1): Telford, Bronze, Houghton, McManus, Greenwood, Moore, Parris (Daly 87), Scott, Kirby (Carney 89), Mead (Stanway 81)), Taylor

Japan 2 (Iwabuchi 23, Sugasawa 37 pen) **Scotland** 1 (Clelland 88). Att: 13,201 (Rennes)
Scotland (4-4-2): Alexander, Smith, Corsie, Beattie, Lauder, Evans (Brown 85), Little, Weir, Arnot (Emslie 60), Cuthbert, Ross (Clelland 76). **Booked**: Corsie

Match-day 3
Japan 0 **England** 2 (White 14, 84). Att: 14,319 (Nice)
England (4-2-3-1): Bardsley, Bronze, Houghton, Bright, Stokes, Walsh (Moore 72), Daly, Scott, Stanway (Carney 74), Duggan (Parris 83), White

Scotland 3 (Little 19, Beattie 49, Cuthbert 69) **Argentina** 3 (Menendez 74, Alexander 79 og, Bonsegundo 90+4 pen). Att: 28,205 (Paris).
Scotland (4-2-3-1): Alexander, Smith (Howard 86), Corsie, Beattie, Docherty, Crichton, Weir, Evans (Brown 86), Little, Emslie, Cuthbert. **Booked**: Weir, Cuthbert, Alexander

GROUP E

	P	W	D	L	F	A	Pts
Holland Q	3	3	0	0	6	2	9
Canada Q	3	2	0	1	4	2	6
Cameroon Q	3	1	0	2	3	5	3
New Zealand	3	0	0	3	1	5	0

Results: Canada 1 Cameroon 0; New Zealand 0 Holland 1; Holland 3 Cameroon 1; Canada 2 New Zealand 0; Cameroon 2 New Zealand 1; Holland 2 Canada 1

GROUP F

	P	W	D	L	F	A	Pts
USA Q	3	3	0	0	18	0	9
Sweden Q	3	2	0	1	7	3	6
Chile	3	1	0	2	2	5	3
Thailand	3	0	0	3	1	20	0

Results: Chile 0 Sweden 2; USA 13 Thailand 0 (record); Sweden 5 Thailand 1; USA 3 Chile 0; Sweden 0 USA 2; Thailand 0 Chile 2

ROUND OF 16

England 3 (Houghton 14, White 45, Greenwood 58) **Cameroon** 0. Att: 20,148 (Valenciennes)
England (4-2-3-1): Bardsley, Bronze, Houghton, Bright, Greenwood, Walsh, Parris (Williamson 84), Scott (Staniforth 78), Kirby, Duggan, White (Taylor 63)
Other results: Norway 1 Australia 1 (aet, Norway won 4-1 on pens); Germany 3 Nigeria 0; France 2 Brazil 1 (aet); Sweden 1 Canada 0; Spain 1 USA 2; Italy 2 China 0; Holland 2 Japan 1

QUARTER-FINALS

Norway 0 **England** 3 (Scott 3, White 40, Bronze 57). Att: 21,111 (Le Havre)
England (4-2-3-1): Bardsley, Bronze, Houghton, Bright, Stokes, Walsh, Parris (Daly 88), Scott Kirby (Stanway 74), Duggan (Mead 54), White
Other results: France 1 USA 2; Italy 0 Holland 2; Germany 1 Sweden 2

SEMI-FINALS

England 1 (White 19) **USA** 2 (Press 10, Morgan 31). Att: 53,512 (Lyon)
England (4-4-2): Telford, Bronze, Houghton, Bright, Stokes, Daly (Stanway 89), Scott, Walsh (Moore 71), Mead (Kirby 58), White, Parris. **Booked**: Bright, Parris. **Sent off**: Bright (86)
Other result: Holland 1 Sweden 0 (aet)

THIRD PLACE PLAY-OFF

England 1 (Kirby 31) **Sweden** 2 (Asllani 11, Jakobsson 22). Att: 20,316 (Nice)
England (4-3-3): Telford, Bronze, Houghton, McManus (Daly 83), Greenwood, Moore, Parris (Carney 75), Scott, Kirby, Mead (Taylor 50), White. **Booked**: Moore

FINAL

USA 2 (Rapinoe 61 pen, Lavelle 69) **Holland** 0. Att: 57,900 (Lyon) – Sunday, July 7, 2017

England squad: Bardsley (Manchester City), Earps (Wolfsburg), Telford (Chelsea); Bright (Chelsea), Bronze (Lyon), Daly (Houston), Greenwood (Manchester Utd), Houghton (Manchester City), McManus (Manchester City), Stokes (Manchester City), Williamson (Arsenal); Carney (Chelsea), Moore (Reading), Scott (Manchester City), Staniforth (Birmingham), Stanway (Manchester City), Walsh (Manchester City), Duggan (Barcelona), Kirby (Chelsea), Mead (Arsenal), Parris (Manchester City), Taylor (Seattle), White (Birmingham)

Scotland squad: Alexander (Glasgow), Fife (Hibernian), Lynn (Vittsjo); Arthur (Birmingham), Beattie (Manchester City), Corsie (Utah), Docherty (Glasgow), Howard (Reading), Lauder (Glasgow), Murray (Hibernian), Smith (Manchester Utd); Arnot (Manchester Utd), Crichton (Glasgow), Littler (Arsenal), Love (Glasgow), Murray (Liverpool), Weir (Manchester City); Brown (Rosengard), Clelland (Fiorentina), Cuthbert (Chelsea), Emslie (Manchester City), Evans (Arsenal), Ross (West Ham)

THE THINGS THEY SAY ...

● 'I've let the team down. I didn't connect with it (the penalty) properly and the goalkeeper guessed the right way. I hold myself to high standards. I'm heartbroken. We were so close' – **Steph Houghton**, England captain.

● 'No blame should be attached to Steph. She has had probably the best season of her career and had the courage to take the penalty. My players gave me everything against the best team in the world. They left their hearts and souls out on the pitch. I am so proud of them' – **Phil Neville**, England manager.

● 'All I feel is pride for my team-mates. It was devastating not to get to the final. We had so much belief, but we just couldn't do it on the day' – **Ellen White**, England striker.

● 'The officiating was really poor, but it doesn't take away from the fact that we were comfortable in the game. The bottom line is we conceded three goals. I'm gutted for the players'- **Shelley Kerr**, Scotland manager, after her side surrendered a three-goal lead to Argentina.

Leading scorers: 6 Morgan (USA), Rapinoe (USA), White (England); 5 Kerr (Australia); 4 Cristiane (Brazil), Renard (France)
Golden Ball: Megan Rapinoe USA) – 6 goals, 3 assists
Golden Boot: Megan Rapinoe; runner-up Lucy Bronze (England)

HOW ENGLAND AND SCOTLAND QUALIFIED FOR THE FINALS

GROUP 1

	P	W	D	L	F	A	Pts
England Q	8	7	1	0	29	1	22
Wales	8	5	2	1	7	3	17
Russia	8	4	1	3	16	13	13
Bosnia & Herz	8	1	0	7	3	19	3
Kazakhstan	8	1	0	7	2	21	3

GROUP 2

Scotland Q	8	7	0	1	19	7	21
Switzerland	8	6	1	1	21	5	19
Poland	8	3	2	3	16	12	11
Albania	8	1	1	6	6	22	4
Belarus	8	1	0	7	5	21	3

GROUP 5

Norway Q	8	7	0	1	22	4	21
Holland Q	8	6	1	1	22	2	19
Republic of Ireland	8	4	1	3	10	6	13
Northern Ireland	8	1	0	7	4	27	3
Slovakia	8	1	0	7	4	23	3

DAY BY DAY DIARY 2018–19

JULY 2018

17 The FA promise a 'full and open process' if selling Wembley Stadium is considered viable.

18 Alex Oxlade-Chamberlain is ruled out for most of the 2018-19 season after the full extent of his knee injury is revealed as multiple ligament damage. Celtic are 6-0 aggregate winners over the Armenian side Alashkert in the Champions League first qualifying round.

19 Brazil international Alisson signs for Liverpool from Roma for a world-record fee for a goalkeeper of £66.8m.

20 Billionaire businessmen Nassef Sawiris and Wes Edens take over ownership of Aston Villa from Tony Xia.

21 Son Heung-min and Erik Lamela sign new contracts with Tottenham through to 2023 and 2022 respectively.

22 Arsenal's Mesut Ozil announces his retirement from international football after 92 caps for Germany.

23 Hearts are fined £10,000 – £8,000 of which is suspended – and deducted two points by the Scottish PFL for fielding an ineligible player in their League Cup group tie against Cove Rangers.

24 Watford receive a club-record £40m from Everton for their Brazilian striker Richarlison. Huddersfield bank a record £10m for Tom Ince's move to Stoke.

25 Brighton pay a club record £17m for Alkmaar's Iran winger Alireza Jahanbakhsh. Manager Steve Bruce is given a vote of confidence by Aston Villa's new owners.

26 Speaking publicly for the first time since undergoing emergency surgery for a brain haemorrhage in May, Sir Alex Ferguson praises hospital staff for saving his life and says he will return to Old Trafford in the new season.

27 Queens Park Rangers agree a settlement of almost £42m with the Football League for a breach of spending limits in season 2013-14 after their claim that Financial Fair Play rules are unlawful is dismissed by an arbitration panel. The club also accept a transfer ban in January.

28 Wolves goalkeeper Carl Ikeme, 32, retires on medical advice following successful treatment for leukaemia.

29 Riyad Mahrez, Manchester City's record-signing, is given the all-clear to return to training after limping off with an ankle injury in a pre-season friendly against Bayern Munich.

30 Burnley's Nick Pope suffers a dislocated shoulder in a Europa League qualifier against Aberdeen and is ruled out for four months.

31 The FA announce the introduction for the new season of yellow and red cards for misbehaving managers and coaches in Football League matches and cup ties. There will be verbal warnings in the Premier League.

AUGUST 2018

1 Celtic defeat Rosenborg 3-1 on aggregate to reach the third qualifying round of the Champions League.

2 Burnley overcome Aberdeen 4-2 on aggregate after extra-time in the second qualifying round of the Europa League. Watford's Abdoulaye Doucoure signs a new five-year contract.

3 The Football League season gets under way with Frank Lampard making a successful start to his managerial career as Derby win 2-1 at Reading.

4 Celtic open their defence of the Scottish Premiership title with a 3-1 victory over promoted Livingston. Two teams returning to the Football League have mixed fortunes. Tranmere retrieve a two-goal deficit to draw 2-2 at Stevenage. Macclesfield concede two stoppage-time penalties and lose 3-2 at Swindon.

5 Sergio Aguero scores twice to pass 200 goals for the club as Manchester City defeat Chelsea 2-0 in the FA Community Shield.

6 Blackpool manager Gary Bowyer resigns after one match of the new season, having lost the core of his squad during the summer.

7 American billionaire Stan Kroenke, owner of 67 per cent of Arsenal, takes full control of the club by paying £550m for the 30 per cent stake of Russian businessman Alisher Usmanov.

8 Bournemouth pay a club-record £25m for Levante's Colombia World Cup midfielder Jefferson Lerma. Wolves break their record with the £18m signing of Middlesbrough's Adama Traore.

9 The world record fee for a goalkeeper is broken for the second time in three weeks as Chelsea sign Kepa Arrizabalaga from Athletic Bilbao for £71.6m. He replaces Thibaut Courtois, who joins Real Madrid for £38m. The summer transfer window closes with Premier League clubs having spent £1.2bn, down from £1.4bn in 2017. Everton's £27.2m purchase of Barcelona's Colombia World Cup defender Yerry Mina is the biggest on deadline day

10 Crystal Palace manager Roy Hodgson agrees a one-year contract extension through to 2020. Jamie Vardy signs a new four-year deal with Leicester.

11 The three promoted teams gain a single point between them on the first full day of the Premier League season. Cardiff and Fulham lose 2-0 to Bournemouth and Crystal Palace respectively. Wolves draw 2-2 with Everton.

12 Manchester City open their defence of the title with a 2-0 away win over Arsenal.

13 Tottenham's move to their new £1bn stadium is delayed over problems with the safety system, forcing two more Premier League games against Liverpool and Cardiff to be switched to Wembley. Manchester City's David Silva retires from international football after 125 appearances for Spain.

14 Celtic are beaten 3-2 on aggregate by AEK Athens in the third qualifying round of the Champions League.

15 Wilfried Zaha signs a new five-year contract with Crystal Palace. Manchester City's Kevin De Bruyne is ruled out for two months with a knee injury sustained in training.

16 Burnley and Rangers reach the qualifying play-offs for the group stage of the Europa League. Hibernian, New Saints and Cork are beaten. Bobby Madley resigns from the panel of Premier League referees ahead of a move to Norway.

17 Victor Moses retires from international football to concentrate on his Chelsea career after 37 appearances for Nigeria.

19 Former Rangers striker Kenny Miller leaves Livingston after seven weeks as player-manager.

20 West Bromwich Albion's Chris Brunt retires from international football after 65 Northern Ireland caps. Preston's Paul Gallagher receives a three-match ban from the FA for violent conduct after his clash with Stoke's Joe Allen is caught on camera.

21 Cheltenham manager Gary Johnson is sacked after a single point from the opening four fixtures.

22 Former Falkirk manager Gary Holt takes over at Livingston.

23 Nick Daws, manager of Scunthorpe for three months, is sacked following a 5-0 home defeat by Fleetwood. Brentford's Neal Maupay is banned for three matches by the FA after being caught on camera stamping on Aston Villa's John McGinn.

26 Notts County dismiss manager Kevin Nolan after his side gain a single point from their opening five matches.

27 Former Bradford manager Stuart McCall takes over at Scunthorpe.

28 Gary Cahill (61 caps) and Jamie Vardy (26 caps) call time on their international careers with England.

29 Plymouth manager Derek Adams is banned for two matches by the FA for a touchline clash with Southend's Chris Powell, who receives a one game ban. The FA submit a bid for England to host the 2021 Women's European Championship. Hal Robson-Kanu, capped 44 times by Wales, retires from international football.

30 Rangers reach the Europa League group stage with a 2-1 aggregate win over Russian side Ufa, despite having Alfredo Morelos and Jon Flanagan sent off in the second leg. Leigh Griffiths scores his 100th goal for Celtic in their 4-1 aggregate victory over Suduva of Lithuania. Burnley lose 4-2 to Olympiacos over the two legs of their play-off tie. Oxford manager Karl Robinson receives a two-match touchline ban from the FA for improper comments after their game against Accrington.

31 Harry Kewell leves Crawley to become Notts County's new manager. England qualify for the 2019 Women's World Cup Finals with a 3-0 group win over Wales.

SEPTEMBER 2018

1 Bury manager Ryan Lowe receives a two-match stadium ban and £1,500 fine from the FA for abusive language towards anti-doping officials.

2 Steven Gerrard loses for the first time in 13 matches as Rangers manager – 1-0 to Celtic in the Old Firm derby.

3 Two managers are sacked after three months in charge – Bradford's Michael Collins following four defeats in five league games and Alan Stubbs with St Mirren second from bottom of the Scottish Premiership. Liverpool's Jordan Henderson signs a new contract through to 2023. Team-mate Andrew Robertson is named Scotland's new captain.

4 Scotland top their group to reach the Women's World Cup for the first time. Wales, Northern Ireland and the Republic of Ireland miss out. David Hopkin, formerly in charge of Livingston, becomes Bradford's fourth manager of 2018.

5 Manchester United manager Jose Mourinho is ordered to pay a £1.78m fine to settle a tax evasion case in Spain. Lee Bowyer, in charge at Charlton on a caretaker basis for five months, is appointed manager until the end of the season. Ian Lenagan steps down as chairman of the Football League because of increased business interests.

6 Connor Roberts scores his first goal for Wales in a 4-1 victory over the Republic of Ireland in their opening UEFA Nations League match. Shaun Williams nets his first for the Irish. Sheffield Wednesday's Fernando Forestieri is fined £25,000 and banned for three games for fighting in a pre-season friendly. Mansfield's Jacob Mellis is also suspended for three matches, in addition to a £1,500 fine. Wednesday are fined £20,000 and Mansfield £3,000 for the brawl.

7 Scotland suffer their biggest home defeat for 45 years – 4-0 by World Cup semi-finalists Belgium in a friendly international. Former Birmingham coach Gabriele Cioffi is appointed Crawley's new manager. Oran Kearney, manager of the Northern Ireland club Coleraine, takes charge at St Mirren.

8 England lose 2-1 to Spain in their first Nations League game. Northern Ireland are beaten 2-1 by Bosnia Herzegovina.

9 Wales lose 2-0 away to Denmark in their second game of the tournament. Harry Maguire signs a new five-year contract with Leicester.

10 In their first group match, Scotland defeat Albania 2-0. Michael Duff, Burnley's under-23 head coach, is appointed manager of Cheltenham, where he spent eight years as a player.

11 Oxford's Gavin Whyte comes off the bench and scores with his first touch in international football to complete Northern Ireland's 3-0 win over Israel. Millwall's Aiden O'Brien also scores on his debut to give the Republic of Ireland a 1-1 draw with Poland. In another friendly, England return to winning ways after three successive defeats, beating Switzerland 1-0 at Leicester. The Scottish FA agree to buy Hampden Park from Queen's Park for £5m. Charlton manager Lee Bowyer is fined £1,500 for criticising referee James Linington after the game against Peterborough.

12 Bolton avoid going into administration after agreeing a deal to pay the club's main creditor. The club are fined £8,000 and Preston £12,500 by the FA for a players' brawl.

13 Manchester City become the second club in English football, after Manchester United, to reach an annual turnover of £500m.

14 UEFA order the upgrading of floodlights at Wembley to satisfy the requirements of hosting seven games at Euro 2000.

15 Manchester City are led out for the home match against Fulham by two special mascots – long-time supporters Vera Cohen (102) and her sister Olga Halon (98).

16 Wayne Rooney sets his sights on becoming a manager at the end of a three-and-a-half-year contract with DC United.

17 Arsenal's chief executive, Ivan Gazidis, leaves the club to take up the same role with AC Milan.

18 Derby manager Frank Lampard is fined £2,000 by the FA after being sent off for arguing with officials in the match against Rotherham. Stephen Darby, Bolton's former Liverpool defender, announces his retirement at 29 after being diagnosed with motor neurone disease.

19 Manchester City lose their opening group game at home to Lyon and Cristiano Ronaldo is sent off on his first appearance in the competition for new club Juventus against Valencia on an eventful night of Champions League action.

20 Eden Hazard is rested from Chelsea's Europa League match in Greece against PAOK Salonica after complaining of tiredness.

21 Forest Green manager Mark Cooper is given a three-match touchline ban by the FA for abusive language after the game against Port Vale.

22 Sir Alex Ferguson makes his first appearance at Old Trafford since undergoing surgery for a brain haemorrhage, watching Manchester United against Wolves. The League One match between Barnsley and Burton is postponed after a matchday volunteer suffers a cardiac arrest and an air ambulance lands on the Oakwell pitch with medical staff to attend to him.

23 A 2-1 defeat by Kilmarnock leaves defending champions Celtic with their poorest start to a season for 20 years – ten points from six matches.

24 Middlesbrough's Marvin Johnson is fined £12,000 by the FA for abusive comments on social media. Manchester United's David de Gea and Chelsea's N'Golo Kante and Eden Hazard are named in FIFA's World X1 for 2018.

25 Manchester United are knocked out of the League Cup, on penalties, by Frank Lampard's Derby in a third-round tie. Exeter are fined £15,000 by the FA for the behaviour of spectators after their play-off semi-final against Lincoln.

26 England manager Gareth Southgate agrees terms for a new four-year contract through to the 2022 World Cup.

27 Dan Ashworth resigns as the FA's technical director to join Premier League Brighton in the same position.

28 England goalkeeper Jordan Pickford commits his future to Everton by signing a new six-year contract.

29 Germany defeat Turkey in a vote by UEFA's executive committee for the right to stage the 2024 European Championship.

30 Northampton manager Dean Austin is dismissed after a single victory in the opening ten League Two games. UEFA announce that video assistant referees will be used in next season's Champions League and in the Europa League from 2020-21.

OCTOBER 2018

1 Team GB are set for a return to Olympic women's football after England strike a deal with Scotland, Wales and Northern Ireland.

2 Former Carlisle manager Keith Curle takes over at Northampton.

3 Steve Bruce becomes the Championship's first managerial casualty of the season, sacked by Aston Villa after a single win in nine matches.

4 Jadon Sancho becomes the first player born this century to be called up to an England squad, Gareth Southgate naming the 18-year-old Borussia Dortmund winger for Nations League matches against Croatia and Spain.

5 Newcastle manager Rafael Benitez is fined £60,000 for breaking FA rules by talking about the appointed referee ahead of his side's Premier League fixture against Crystal Palace.

7 John Terry, former Chelsea and England captain, announces his retirement as a player.

8 Mark Yates is sacked after four months as Macclesfield manager with his side bottom of League Two.

9 Kevin Long, Burnley's longest-serving player, signs a new contract through to 2021.

10 Brentford's Dean Smith is appointed Aston Villa's new manager with John Terry as his assistant. Paul Gascoigne's nomination for a place in Scottish football's Hall of Fame is withdrawn amid criticism of the former Rangers player and concerns about his health.

11 John Souttar is sent off for a second yellow card as Scotland lose 2-1 in Israel in the Nations League. Wales, playing at the Principality Stadium for the first time since 2011, go down 4-1 to Spain in a friendly. England seal a place in the European Under-21 Championship with a 7-0 qualifying group win over Andorra.

12 England rue missed chances in a goalless Nations League draw against Croatia, played behind closed doors in Rijeka because of previous crowd trouble. Northern Ireland lose 1-0 in Austria. Promoted Macclesfield equal the English league record of 36 successive games without a victory – 13 this season and 23 up to the end of the club's relegation season of 2011-12.

13 The Republic of Ireland share a goalless draw with Denmark in their group. Arsenal legend Thierry Henry is appointed Monaco's new head coach.

14 Scotland suffer their sixth defeat in eight matches under Alex McLeish – 3-1 at home against Portugal in a friendly.

15 Two goals by Raheem Sterling, ending a two-year drought, and one from Marcus Rashford give England their finest win for many years. They defeat Spain 3-2 in Seville with the national side's youngest starting line-up – 23 years and 359 days – since 1959. Northern Ireland face relegation from their group after a third successive defeat – 2-0 against Bosnia-Herzegovina.

16 Wales complete the double over the Republic of Ireland in their group, winning 1-0 in Dublin. Coach Thomas Frank is appointed Brentford's new manager. Dundee manager Neil McCann is sacked with his side bottom of the Scottish Premiership.

17 Fulham owner Shahid Khan withdraws his £600m offer to buy Wembley Stadium from the FA, stating that it was 'more divisive than expected.' Jim McIntyre, former Ross County and Dunfermline manager, takes over at Dundee.

18 Luke Shaw, back in favour at Manchester United after being publicly criticised by manager Jose Mourinho, signs a new five-year contract. Former Manchester City goalkeeper Joe Hart is invited back for a presentation to mark his 12 years at the club and to have a training pitch named after him.

19 Manchester United are fined £13,200 by UEFA for a late start to their Champions League group match against Valencia caused by a traffic jam delaying the team coach on the way to Old Trafford.

20 Macclesfield end the club's run of 36 successive games without a league win by beating Carlisle 2-1.

21 Ben Chilwell, Leicester's new England cap, signs a new contract with the club through to 2024.

22 Stoke manager Gary Rowett admits an FA misconduct charge and receives a one-match touchline ban and £2,000 fine after being sent off in the defeat by former club Birmingham.

23 Cristiano Ronaldo enjoys a successful return to Old Trafford with his new club Juventus, setting up the only goal for Paulo Dybala in a Champions League group match against Manchester United.

24 Liverpool earned £72m for reaching the 2017 Champions League Final, according to UEFA figures. Marcos Alonso signs a new deal with Chelsea through to 2023.

25 Ipswich manager Paul Hurst is sacked after a single victory in his 14 games in charge.

26 Former Norwich manager Paul Lambert replaces Paul Hurst, becoming the first to take charge of both east Anglian clubs. Sam Vokes signs a new three-year contract with Burnley.

27 Leicester owner Vichai Srivaddhanaprabha dies in a helicopter crash following the club's Premier League match against West Ham. The pilot and three others on board are also killed in the crash outside the King Power Stadium, seconds after the helicopter's take-off from the pitch. Glenn Hoddle, former Tottenham midfielder and England manager, suffers a heart attack on his 61st birthday.

28 Thousands of people lay flowers, team shirts and scarves at the stadium in tribute to the Thai billionaire, the man behind Leicester's remarkable title win in 2016. The team's midweek League Cup tie against Southampton is postponed. Celtic beat Hearts 3-0 and Aberdeen defeat Rangers 1-0 in the semi-finals of the Scottish League Cup.

29 Leicester cancel plans fly to Cardiff for their next Premier League fixture, deeming it to be insensitive, and decide to travel by road.

30 Chelsea assistant coach Marco Ianni is fined £6,000 after admitting an FA charge of improper conduct – taunting Jose Mourinho over his team's equaliser at Stamford Bridge. The Manchester United manager is 'reminded of his responsibilities' for his reaction on the touchline. Tottenham's Dele Alli signs a new contract keeping him at the club until 2024.

31 Newcastle captain Jamaal Lascelles commits his future to the club until 2024 with a new contract.

NOVEMBER 2018

1 Raheem Sterling agrees a new five-year contract with Manchester City, making him one of the best paid English players at a salary of up to £300,000 a week.

2 Leading Premier League clubs are reported to be discussing with top Continental clubs a breakaway European super league.

3 On an emotional afternoon, Leicester win 1-0 at Cardiff in their first match since the death of the club's owner. Afterwards, players and staff fly to Bangkok for the funeral of Vichai Srivaddhanaprabha.

4 The FA are revealed to be planning to mark Wayne Rooney's international career with a place in England's squad for a friendly international against the USA.

5 Manchester City are alleged to have cheated by overvaluing sponsorship deals to meet UEFA's Financial Fair Play rules, according to a report in German newspaper.

6 Spain's top league, La Liga, calls for Manchester City – and Paris Saint-Germain – to be punished.

7 Raheem Sterling apologises for winning a penalty after tripping himself up in Manchester City's club-record 6-0 Champions League win over Shakhtar Donetsk. The Whelan family, owners of the club for 23 years, sell Wigan to Hong Kong-based International Entertainment Corporation for £22m.

8 Everton are fined £500,000 and banned from signing academy players for two years for breaking Premier League recruitment rules. Arsenal and Chelsea qualify for the knockout stage of the Europa League.

9 Arsenal's Danny Welbeck faces a long lay-off after surgery on a broken ankle sustained against Sporting Lisbon.

10 Tottenham agree a contingency plan with the FA to play home games for the whole season if delays continue with their new stadium.

11 Swindon sack manager Phil Brown after a single win in eight league matches. England women's captain Steph Houghton wins her 100th cap.

12 Two League One managers pay the price for poor results. Neal Ardley, in charge of AFC Wimbledon for six years, goes after seven successive defeats. John Askey, manager of Shrewsbury for five months, leaves following four wins in 16 matches. Former West Ham and Chelsea midfielder Joe Cole, winner of 56 England caps, retires at 37.

13 Susanna Dinnage, 51, a senior executive at the US television network Discovery, is appointed the first female chief executive of the Premier League. Harry Kewell is dismissed ten weeks into a three-year contract as Notts County manager after seven league and cup matches without a win. Former Oldham manager Richie Wellens takes over at Swindon.

14 Slavisa Jokanovic becomes the first Premier League managerial casualty of the season, sacked with Fulham bottom after 12 matches. He is replaced immediately by Claudio Ranieri, architect of Leicester's remarkable title win in 2016.

15 Wayne Rooney makes his 120th and final England appearance as a 58th minute substitute in a 3-0 win over the United States at Wembley. Callum Wilson scores on his debut and Trent Alexander-Arnold is on the mark for the first time. In another friendly, the Republic of Ireland and Northern Ireland share a goalless draw. Premier League clubs agree in principle to introduce video assistant referees in the 2019-20 season.

16 Wales are denied promotion from their Nations League group by a 2-1 defeat by Denmark. A £5m bonus for outgoing Premier League chief Richard Scudamore is criticised by supporters' groups.

17 Scotland overcome nine withdrawals from the squad with a 4-0 away win over Albania. James Forrest (2) and Ryan Fraser score their first international goals.

18 England come from behind to beat Croatia 2-1 with goals from Jesse Lingard (78) and Harry Kane (85) to top their group and qualify for the finals. Northern Ireland complete a miserable tournament with another defeat – 2-1 by Austria.

19 Liverpool's Virgil van Dijk scores a 90th minute equaliser against Germany to send Holland through to the finals. The Republic of Ireland, already relegated from their group, end with a goalless draw against Denmark. The Football League sign a new £595m five-year TV rights deal with Sky.

20 James Forrest scores a hat-trick as Scotland defeat Israel 3-2 to top their group, gain promotion and book a place in the play-offs for Euro 2020. Chris Gunter overtakes Neville Southall to win a record 93rd cap for Wales in a 1-0 friendly international defeat by Albania. Leading Championship clubs criticise the new TV deal, claiming it gives more matches for less money.

21 Republic of Ireland manager Martin O'Neill and assistant Roy Keane are sacked after relegation from the team's Nations League group. Chief executive Gordon Taylor, under scrutiny for the way he runs the PFA, agrees to an independent review of the players' union. Manchester City manager Pep Guardiola is warned by the FA for discussing referee Anthony Taylor before the victory over Manchester United.

22 Didier Drogba, winner of four Premier League titles, four FA Cups, three League Cups and the Champions League with Chelsea, retires at 40. UEFA fine Manchester United £7,000 for pitch invasions at their Champions League game against Juventus.

23 Glenn Hoddle leaves hospital and returns home to recuperate after his heart attack last month. Neal Ardley makes a rapid return to management, taking over at Notts County 11 days after leaving AFC Wimbledon.

24 Sadio Mané signs a new five-year contract with Liverpool.

25 The Republic of Ireland name their new manager – and his successor. Mick McCarthy is appointed for the second time, having been in charge from 1996-2002, with under-21 manager Stephen Kenny replacing him after the finals of Euro 2020.

26 Peterborough's Steve Evans becomes the first manager to receive a one-match touchline ban from the FA after four yellow cards for misconduct.

27 A 91st minute winner by Marouane Fellaini against Young Boys sends Manchester United through to the knockout stage of the Champions League. Manchester City confirm their place with an 83rd minute equaliser by Sergio Aguero against Lyon. Sol Campbell, former Tottenham, Arsenal and England defender, takes his first step in management at bottom-of-the-table Macclesfield.

28 Watford manager Javi Gracia signs a new four and a half year contract. Aston Villa and Nottingham Forest equal the Championship's record aggregate scoreline, drawing 5-5.

29 Manchester United trigger a 12-month option to extend David de Gea's contract until 2020 in an effort to keep the Spain goalkeeper. Watford's Isaac Success signs a new five-year contract.

30 Derby midfielder Bradley Johnson is banned for four matches by the FA after being caught on camera biting Stoke's Joe Allen

DECEMBER 2018

1 Cesar Azpilicueta signs a new four-year contract with Chelsea. Cambridge, fourth from bottom of League Two, dismiss Joe Dunne after seven months as manager.

2 Celtic win a seventh domestic trophy in a row, beating Aberdeen 1-0 in the League Cup Final with a goal by Ryan Christie. Liverpool manager Jurgen Klopp apologises for running on to the Anfield pitch to celebrate Divock Origi's 96th minute winner against Everton. Luka Modric, Real Madrid and Croatia midfielder, is voted the world's best player, the first time since 2007 the award has not gone to Cristiano Ronaldo or Lionel Messi.

3 Mark Hughes is sacked after nine months as Southampton manager with his side third from bottom. Formerly with Stoke, he becomes the first to be fired by two Premier League clubs in the same calendar year. Sam Ricketts leaves National League club Wrexham to become Shrewsbury's new manager.

4 Jurgen Klopp accepts an FA misconduct charge and is fined £8,000. Wally Downes, former Brentford manager and a player with the old Wimbledon club, takes charge at AFC Wimbledon. UEFA choose England to host the 2021 European Women's Championship finals.

5 Former Leipzig coach Ralph Hasenhuttl succeeds Mark Hughes at St Mary's and becomes the Premier League's first Austrian manager. With Celtic and Rangers dropping points, Kilmarnock go top of the Scottish Premiership for the first time since 1998.

6   Paul Clement, manager of Reading for eight months, is sacked with his side fourth from bottom.

7   Two players are ruled out for the rest of the season with cruciate ligament injuries – Arsenal's Rob Holding and Bournemouth's Lewis Cook.

8   After being abused during Manchester City's game against Chelsea at Stamford Bridge, Raheem Sterling says black players and white players are not treated equally by the media.

9   River Plate are crowned champions of South America – 6,000 miles away. They defeat Buenos Aires rivals Boca Juniors 5-3 on aggregate, with the second leg moved to Madrid on safety grounds after an attack by their fans on the Boca team bus.

10   The Football Supporters' Federation claim the 'magic' of the FA Cup has been threatened by only ten of the 32 third round ties scheduled for a Saturday 3pm kick-off. Liverpool's Joe Gomez and Manchester City's 18-year-old Phil Foden sign new six-year contracts.

11   Liverpool and Tottenham join Manchester City and Manchester United in the knockout stage of the Champions League. At Anfield, a fine save in stoppage-time by Alisson preserves his side's lead over Napoli, At the Nou Camp, an 85th minute equaliser by Lucas Moura against Barcelona sends Tottenham through.

12   Mark Noble will end his career as a one-club player after extending his contract with West Ham until 2021. Businessman Steve Dale becomes Bury's new owner, taking over from Stewart Day.

13   Chelsea condemn their own supporters involved in anti-semitic chants during a Europa League game against MOL Vidi in Budapest. The FA announce that Martin Glenn, chief executive for four years, will step down at the end of the season. Darrell Clark, manager of Bristol Rovers for four-and-a-half-years, is sacked, with his team fourth from bottom.

14   The Premier League take the unprecedented step of urging supporters to report any incidents of racism at the weekend's matches. Bolton chairman Ken Anderson pays the outstanding November wages of players and coaching staff. Liverpool's Mohamed Salah is voted BBC African Footballer of the Year for the second successive year.

15   Chris Smalling signs a new contract with Manchester United through to 2022.

16   England manager Gareth Southgate is named Coach of the Year at the BBC Sports Personality awards night.

17   Pressure intensifies on Manchester United manager Jose Mourinho after a 3-1 defeat by arch-rivals Liverpool.

18   Jose Mourinho, in charge for two-and-a-half-years, is sacked. The club blames poor results and a breakdown in the relationship between the manager and players. Mourinho leaves with a reported pay-off of £15m. League One Burton reach the League Cup semi-finals with a 1-0 win at Middlesbrough. To ease fixture congestion, FA Cup replays are scrapped with immediate effect – a season earlier than planned. A Tottenham fan who threw a banana skin towards Arsenal's Pierre-Emerick Aubameyang is banned from attending matches for four years by magistrates.

19   Former Manchester United striker Ole Gunnar Solskjaer is named caretaker-manager at Old Trafford for the remainder of the season under a loan agreement with his Norwegian club Molde. Mike Phelan, Sir Alex Ferguson's former No 2, is appointed his assistant. Former Nottingham Forest and Hibernian manager Colin Calderwood takes charge at Cambridge.

20   The FA fine Tottenham £50,000 and Arsenal £40,000 for a players' melee in the north London derby. Motherwell manager Stephen Robinson is given a five-match touchline ban, with two suspended, by the Scottish FA for criticising match officials after a 7-1 defeat by Rangers. Rangers are fined £6,000 for comments about referee Wille Collum after the game against St Mirren.

21   Jos Luhukay, manager of Sheffield Wednesday for 11 months, is sacked with his team 18th after a single win in ten matches. Les Reed, former head of football at Southampton, is appointed the FA's new technical director. The FA fine Charlton £6,000 and Portsmouth £2,500 for a players' confrontation. Stoke are fined £5,000 for misbehaving players against Aston Villa.

22   Real Madrid win the Club World Cup for a third successive year, beating Abu Dhabi side Al Ain 4-1 in the final in the United Arab Emirates.

23 Jose Gomes, coach of the Portuguese club Rio Ave, is appointed Reading's new manager.

25 Liverpool top the Premier League at Christmas with a four-point lead after Manchester City suffer two defeats in three matches. In Scotland, Celtic lead Rangers by one point.

26 A record League One crowd of 46,039 see Sunderland defeat Bradford at the Stadium of Light.

27 Bournemouth captain Simon Francis becomes the club's second player in three weeks to be ruled out for the remainder of the season with a cruciate ligament injury. Oldham sack Frankie Bunn, manager for six months, following a 6-0 defeat by Carlisle.

28 Joe Cole, winner of three Premier League titles with Chelsea, is appointed a technical academy coach at the club. Declan Rice, 19-year-old West Ham defender, signs a new contract through to 2024. The FA fine Sheffield United and Derby £5,000 each for a players' confrontation. Stoke are fined £10,000 for misbehaviour by their players against Birmingham.

29 England manager Gareth Southgate (OBE) and World Cup Golden Boot winner Harry Kane (MBE) are honoured in the New Year honours list. There are also awards for Premier League executive chairman Richard Scudamore (CBE), former Manchester United and England goalkeeper Harry Gregg (OBE), former Arsenal and FA vice-chairman David Dein (MBE) and Rangers and Northern Ireland defender Gareth McAuley (MBE).

30 Susanna Dinnage decides not to become the Premier League's new chief executive – six weeks after accepting the position. John Still, 68, retires after 42 years in management, including spells at Luton, Peterborough, Barnet and Dagenham.

31 Arsenal manager Unai Emery is fined £8,000 by the FA for improper conduct – kicking a water bottle which hit a Brighton fan.

JANUARY 2019

1 In the first big-money deal of the winter transfer window, Chelsea pay £58m for Borussia Dortmund's USA international midfielder Christian Pulisic, who is loaned back to the German club for the remainder of the season.

2 Steve Bruce is named Sheffield Wednesday's new manager – his ninth club appointment.

3 The FA give Fleetwood manager Joey Barton a two-match touchline ban and £2,000 fine for abusive language towards referee Brett Huxtable after the game against Bristol Rovers.

4 John Sheridan resigns after seven months as Carlisle manager, with his side in a play-off position, to succeed Martin Allen at National League Chesterfield.

5 League One Gillingham deliver the main upset in the first batch of FA Cup third-round ties, defeating Cardiff.

6 There are three surprises in the second series of ties. League Two sides Oldham and Newport overcome Fulham and Leicester respectively, while non-league Barnet knock out Sheffield United.

7 Graham Coughlan is appointed the new Bristol Rovers manager after winning three of his five matches as caretaker. Hearts manager Craig Levein receives a one-match touchline ban from the Scottish FA, with a second suspended, for criticising referee Bobby Madden after the game against Rangers.

8 Gary Rowett is sacked after eight months as Stoke manager, with his side in the bottom half of the table, and replaced by Luton's Nathan Jones. The FA ban Fleetwood's Ched Evans for two matches and fine him £2,500 for abusive language towards referee Brett Huxtable during the game against Bristol Rovers.

9 Three days after a 7-0 win over Rotherham in the third-round of the FA Cup, Manchester City defeat Burton 9-0 in the first leg of their League Cup semi-final – the first English league team since Don Revie's Leeds in 1967 to score seven or more in successive matches. Tottenham announce that their new stadium will not be open until March at the earliest.

10 The FA reach a settlement with Mark Sampson ahead of the former England women's manager's case for unfair dismissal in 2017. Southampton's Charlie Austin is banned for two matches by the FA for an offensive gesture towards Manchester City supporters.

11 Nottingham Forest manager Aitor Karanka resigns after weeks of speculation about his future. Leeds offer a formal apology to Derby for manager Marcelo Bielsa sending a member of staff to watch Derby in training ahead of the teams' Championship match.

12 Charlie Kelman, 17, scores from inside his own half on his debut for Southend against Plymouth.

13 Petr Cech, 36, Arsenal's former Chelsea goalkeeper, announces his intention to retire at the end of the season.

14 Manager David Wagner leaves Huddersfield by mutual consent with his side eight points adrift at the bottom of the table.

15 Former Republic of Ireland manager Martin O'Neill takes charge at Nottingham Forest, where he was twice in successive seasons a European Cup winner as a player.

16 Carlisle appoint Steven Pressley, formerly in charge of Fleetwood and Coventry, as their new manager. Fleetwood manager Joey Barton is fined another £2,000 by the FA, this time for describing referee Brett Huxtable 'as bad as I have seen in my life.'

17 The FA fine Watford captain Troy Deeney £20,000 for saying referee David Coote 'bottled' decisions during the match against Bournemouth. Liverpool's Andrew Robertson signs a new five-year contract.

18 Leeds manager Marcelo Bielsa admits to having every Championship opponent watched in training. BBC executive Tim Davie turns down the chance to become the Premier League's new chief executive. The FA fine Nottingham Forest £10,000 and Reading £5,000 for a players' melee. Marc Albrighton signs a new four-year contract with Leicester.

19 A proposed £35m transfer taking West Ham's Marko Arnautovic to Guangzhou Evergrande falls through. Tottenham's Mousa Dembele completes an £11m move to another Chinese Super League Club, Guangzhou R & F.

20 Former Chelsea and Liverpool defender Glen Johnson, 34, winner of 54 England caps, announces his retirement.

21 Two days after Nantes striker Emiliano Sala signs for Cardiff for a club-record £15m, the 28-year-old Argentinian dies in a plane crash in the English Channel. The pilot of the light aircraft en route from Nantes to Cardiff, is also killed. Huddersfield choose another German coach as their new manager – Jan Siewert from Borussia Dortmund, who at 36 becomes the youngest in the Premier League. Scott McTominay signs a new contract with Manchester United through to 2023.

22 The FA fine West Ham £100,000 for pitch invasions during the home defeat by Burnley. Wolves manager Nuno Espirito Santo is fined £8,000 for running on to the pitch to celebrate his side's stoppage-time winner against Leicester.

23 Ashley Cole, former Arsenal and Chelsea full-back and winner of 107 England caps, announces he will retire at the end of the season after completing a spell with Derby. Burton restrict Manchester City to a 1-0 win in the second leg of their League Cup semi-final.

24 Chelsea beat Tottenham on penalties in the second semi-final. Thierry Henry is sacked by Monaco after 104 days as manager of the French club. David Beckham joins five former Manchester United team-mates by buying a stake in the Salford City club. Accrington's Sam Finley is banned for five matches after being caught on camera stamping on AFC Wimbledon's Lyle Taylor, the FA ruling as insufficient the standard three game

25 Cardiff's request to conduct transfer business beyond the closure of the winter window following the loss of Emiliano Sala is turned down by the Premier League. Marko Arnautovic signs a contract extension through to 2023 with West Ham. Hibernian suspend Neil Lennon following heated exchanges between the manager and club employees.

26 Steve Evans is sacked as Peterborough manager, with his side in a play-off place, and replaced immediately by Darren Ferguson for a third spell in charge of the club. West Ham are knocked out of the FA Cup in the fourth round by AFC Wimbledon, bottom of League One.

28 Roy Keane joins Nottingham Forest as assistant manager, resuming the partnership he had alongside Martin O'Neill with the Republic of Ireland.

29 Martin Canning, manager of Scottish Premiership club Hamilton for four years, leaves by mutual agreement with his side third from bottom.

30 Anthony Martial signs a new contract with Manchester United through to 2014. Port Vale manager Neil Aspin resigns after a single victory in 12 games in all competitions. Barry Fry,

Peterborough'a director of football, is banned for four months – three of them suspended – and fined £35,000 by the FA for breaching betting rules. Neil Lennon leaves Hibernian by 'mutual consent,' according to the club.

31 Newcastle break their 14-year-old transfer record – £16m for Michael Owen – by paying £20.5m for Paraguay midfielder Miguel Almiron from United States club Atlanta. Surprise signing on deadline day takes Stoke's 38-year-old striker Peter Crouch back to the Premier League with Burnley.

FEBRUARY 2019

1 Premier League clubs spend £180m in a subdued winter transfer window, compared to £430m in 2018.

2 Rangers are awarded four penalties in their 4-0 Scottish Premiership win over St Mirren, converting three of them.

3 John Askey, formerly in charge of Macclesfield and Shrewsbury, is appointed Port Vale's new manager.

4 Hull City's name is restored on a new club crest after unsuccessful moves by the owners to rebrand the club as Hull Tigers.

5 Jose Mourinho accepts a one-year prison sentence for tax fraud in Spain – but will not serve time. Instead, he pays £160,000 on top of a previous fine of £1.7m.

6 Wilfried Zaha is given an additional one-match ban and fined £10,000 by the FA for improper conduct – sarcastically applauding referee Andre Marriner after being sent off in Crystal Palace's match against Southampton.

7 Everton manager Marco Silva, under pressure after poor results, is given a vote of confidence by majority shareholder Farhad Moshiri. The FA fine Queens Park Rangers £12,500 and Portsmouth £4,000 for a players' confrontation in their FA Cup tie.

8 Liverpool post a world-record annual net profit of £106m after the sale of Philippe Coutinho to Barcelona and reaching the Champions League Final. Premier League clubs vote unanimously to extend the £30 cap on away tickets for three more seasons. Florin Andone is banned for three matches by the FA after being caught on camera elbowing Sam Field in Brighton's FA Cup tie against West Bromwich Albion. Charlton are fined £12,000 and Accrington £5,000 for a players' confrontation.

10 Manchester City record the biggest win of the Premier League season – 6-0 against Chelsea.

11 Paul Scholes, former Manchester United and England midfielder, takes his first step into management with Oldham. Millwall and Rotherham are both fined £5,000 by the FA for a players' confrontation.

12 Gordon Banks, England's World Cup-winning goalkeeper in 1966 and rated one of the best ever in his position, dies aged 81. Arsenal's Aaron Ramsey signs a pre-contract with Juventus at a reported £400,000 a week.

13 Blackpool are placed into receivership by the High Court, forcing owner Owen Oyston to pay former director Valeri Belokon the £25m he is owed. Former Barnsley and Leeds manager Paul Heckingbottom, takes charge at Hibernian following Neil Lennon's departure. Rangers call on the Scottish FA to review their disciplinary system after goalkeeper Allan McGregor's appeal against a two-match ban for an incident with Aberdeen's Lewis Ferguson is rejected.

14 Manchester United reveal a payment of £19.6m to Jose Mourinho and his backroom staff, with about £15m going to the sacked manager. Dwight Gayle, on loan at West Bromwich Albion from Newcastle, receives a two-match retrospective ban from the FA for diving against Nottingham Forest.

15 West Ham's Declan Rice switches allegiance to England after three appearances for the Republic of Ireland in friendly internationals. Wolves defenders Conor Coady and Matt Doherty sign new contracts through to 2023.

16 Cardiff manager Neil Warnock and chief executive Ken Choo attend the funeral of Emiliano Sala in the player's home town of Progreso, Argentina.

18 Leeds are fined £200,000 by the Football League for spying on rivals' training sessions, deeming the club's actions a breach of 'good faith' rules towards other teams.

19 The Football League announce that Shaun Harvey, chief executive since 2013, will leave his position at the end of the season.

20 Manchester City's owners buy a stake in the Chinese club Sichuan Jiuniu, following investments in clubs in the United States, Australia, Spain, Uruguay and Japan.

21 Jurgen Klopp is fined £45,000 for comments after Liverpool's match against West Ham which the FA rule questioned the integrity of referee Kevin Friend. The governing body gives Ipswich manager Paul Lambert a two-match touchline ban and £3,000 fine after a touchline clash with Norwich staff. Ipswich are fined £25,000 and Norwich £20,000 for a players' melee. Arsenal and Chelsea reach the last 16 of the Europa League with aggregate victories over DATE Borisov and Malmo respectively. Celtic are beaten by Valencia.

22 Chelsea are banned from signing players in the next two transfer windows and fined £460,000 by FIFA for breaching regulations relating to foreign under-18 players. The FA are fined £390,000 for failing to police the recruitment of young players at a club under their jurisdiction.

23 Everton resolve a long-running dispute with Watford by agreeing compensation for their appointment of Marco Silva as manager.

24 Manchester City retain the League Cup on penalties after a goalless draw with Chelsea. Leicester manager Claude Puel is sacked after four successive home defeats.

25 Owen Oyston is removed as Blackpool owner by order of the High Court, ending his family's controversial control of the club. A new four-man board takes over. David Hopkin resigns after six months as Bradford manager with his side second from bottom of League One.

26 Brendan Rodgers leaves Celtic to become Leicester's new manager. Neil Lennon, Celtic manager from 2010-14, returns to takes charge until the end of the season. Chelsea goalkeeper Kepa Arrizabalaga is fined a week's wages by the club for refusing to be substituted in the League Cup Final. Peterborough sack Josh Yorwerth after the defender is banned for four years by the FA for evading an anti-doping test and taking cocaine. Charlton manager Lee Bowyer is given a three-match touchline ban and £1,750 fine for twice abusing referee Chris Kavanagh in the match against AFC Wimbledon.

27 Manchester City sign a kit deal with Puma, reported to be worth £650m over ten years.

28 Claudio Ranieri is sacked after 106 days as Fulham manager with his side ten points from safety in the Premier League.

MARCH 2019

1 UEFA fine Manchester United £13,700 and Paris Saint-Germain £35,000 for crowd trouble at their Champions League game at Old Trafford.

2 Billy Bonds, who made a record 799 appearances for West Ham, cuts the ribbon at a stand named after him at the London Stadium.

3 The International FA Board rule that from next season goals scored from accidental handball will be disallowed.

4 Rochdale's Keith Hill, second longest-serving manager in League One, is sacked after six years in the job with his side third from bottom. Gary Bowyer, former Blackburn and Blackpool manager, takes charge at Bradford.

5 Tottenham reach the last eight of the Champions League with a 4-0 aggregate win over Borussia Dortmund. Holders Real Madrid are knocked out after a 4-1 home defeat by Ajax. Wolves post a £57m loss for the period covering their Championship-winning season.

6 Manchester United, missing ten players through injury and suspension, deliver one of the finest comebacks in European club history to reach the quarter-finals. Trailing Paris Saint-Germain 2-0 from the first leg at Old Trafford, United win the return 3-1 to go through on away goals, two of them from Romelu Lukaku and a decisive stoppage-time penalty by Marcus Rashford, his first spot-kick for the club. Tottenham manager Mauricio Pochettino is given a two-match touchline ban and £10,000 fine by the FA for confronting referee Mike Dean after the defeat at Burnley. Peter Beardsley, Newcastle's under-23 coach, leaves the club following an investigation into allegations of racism and bullying. The England women's team win a pre-

World Cup four-nation tournament in the United States.

7 The FA fine Bolton £8,000 and Leeds £5,000 for a touchline brawl at Elland Road. Bolton manager Phil Parkinson is banned for two matches and fined £3,000. Barnsley's Cameron McGeehan is banned for three match for a stamping offence caught on camera in the match at Southend.

8 Chelsea are refused permission by FIFA to freeze their transfer ban, pending the club's appeal. A pitch invader confronts Rangers captain James Tavernier during the game against Hibernian. Eight days after being sacked by Fulham, Claudio Ranieri is appointed Roma coach until the end of the season.

9 Darren Moore is dismissed as West Bromwich Albion manager after a 1-1 draw with bottom side Ipswich – even though his side remain fourth. Blackpool supporters end their long-standing boycott of the club following the removal of owner Owen Oyston. A crowd of nearly 16,000 – four times bigger than for the previous home match – watch the team play Southend.

10 Aston Villa captain Jack Grealish is knocked to the ground by a Birmingham supporter at St Andrew's. Grealish later scores the only goal of the match.

11 Appearing before magistrates, the offender admits assault, is jailed for 14 weeks, banned from attending matches for ten years and ordered to pay Jack Grealish £100 compensation. Speculation about Mauricio Pochettino or Jose Mourinho becoming Real Madrid's new manager ends with the appointment of Zinedine Zidane for a second spell in charge.

12 Manchester City swamp Schalke 7-0 in the second leg of their Champions League match, completing the biggest-ever aggregate win by an English side in a knockout tie – 10-2.

13 Liverpool join Manchester City, Manchester United and Tottenham in the quarter-finals with another outstanding performance – a 3-1 victory over Bayern Munich after a goalless first leg at Anfield. West Ham's Declan Rice receives a first England call up – 24 hours after being named the Republic of Ireland's Young Player of the Year – having switched to the country of his birth after playing for the Republic in friendly matches. Manchester City's Bernardo Silva signs a three-year contract extension until 2025.

14 Paul Scholes resigns after 31 days as Oldham manager, claiming broken promises about no interference with team selection. Arsenal retrieve a 3-1 deficit from the first leg to beat Rennes 4-3 on aggregate and reach the quarter-finals of the Europa League. Chelsea defeat Dynamo Kiev 8-0 on aggregate.

15 Oldham owner Abdallah Lemsagam refutes the claim of interference made by Paul Scholes in his resignation statement. Wycombe are fined £7,250 and Sunderland £6,000 by the FA for a touchline brawl at Adams Park. Doncaster manager Grant McCann receives a one-match ban and £1,000 fine for abusive behaviour against Charlton.

16 Burnley's Stephen Ward retires from international football after winning 50 Republic of Ireland caps.

17 Tottenham confirm that their new stadium will stage its first Premier League fixture on April 3 against Crystal Palace.

18 Birmingham and Aston Villa are both fined £5,000 by the FA for a players' melee. Leicester captain Wes Morgan signs a new one-year contract. After receiving a suspended sentence for sexual assault, defender Niall Mason is sacked by Doncaster.

19 Everton manager Marco Silva is fined £12,000 by the FA for confronting match officials after the defeat at Newcastle. The FA sign a new four-year deal with the BBC to show FA Cup ties until 2025.

20 The High Court gives Bolton two weeks to settle debts and avoid a winding-up order. In a three-year deal worth more than £10m, Barclays become the first title-sponsor of the Women's Super League. The biggest-ever investment in women's sport in the UK includes annual prize-money of £500,000. A stoppage-time goal by Ben Woodburn gives an experimental Wales team a 1-0 friendly match win over Trinidad and Tobago in their first international at Wrexham since 2008.

21 Scotland's Euro 2020 qualifying campaign gets off to a nightmare start with a 3-0 away defeat by Kazakhstan. Northern Ireland defeat Estonia 2-0 in their opening match. England newcomer Declan Rice apologises for a social media post, apparently about the IRA, while a Republic of Ireland youth player.

22 Birmingham are deducted nine points by the Football League for breaching profitability and sustainability rules. Raheem Sterling, in the form of his life for club and country, scores a hat-trick as England defeat the Czech Republic 5-0 in their first fixture.

23 Mick McCarthy begins his second spell as Republic of Ireland manager with a laboured 1-0 win in Gibraltar which he describes as a 'horrible game.'

24 Daniel James, scoring his first international goal on his competitive debut, gives Wales victory over Slovakia by the same scoreline in their opening qualifier. Kenny McLean nets his first for Scotland, who defeat the world's lowest-ranked side, San Marino, 2-0 with another unimpressive performance. Northern Ireland beat Belarus 2-1 with an 87th minute goal from Josh Magennis. Two managers of relegation-threatened clubs are sacked – Stuart McCall after seven months at League One Scunthorpe and Yeovil's Darren Way, appointed in December 2015 and the second longest-serving manager in League Two. Tottenham stage the first of two test events at their new stadium, the club's under-18 team playing Southampton in front of a crowd of 29,000.

25 Michael Keane heads his first international goal as England win 5-1 in Montenegro – the first time the national side have scored at least five goals in successive games since 1984. The performance is overshadowed by racial abuse directed at England's black players.

26 Conor Hourihane scores his first goal for the Republic of Ireland for a 1-0 win over Georgia. Southend sack manager Chris Powell after 11 games without a victory. An unbeaten 18-match run built by England's under-21 side is ended by a 2-1 defeat by Germany in a friendly international.

27 A power struggle at the players' union, the PFA, results in Gordon Taylor's decision to step down after 38 years as chief executive on completion of an independent review into the organisation.

28 Ole Gunnar Solskjaer is appointed Manchester United's permanent manager, with a three-year contract, after winning 14 of his 19 games in all competitions as caretaker.

29 Mark Bullingham, the FA's chief commercial and football development officer, is named the governing body's new chief executive.

30 Huddersfield become the first side to be relegated, returning to the Championship after a single season in the Premier League.

31 Rangers striker Alfredo Morelos is shown a fifth red card of the season – one of them rescinded – in the 2-1 defeat by Celtic, who extend their lead at the top to 13 points with seven games remaining. Morelos is later fined by the club and banned for four matches by the Scottish FA. Portsmouth beat Sunderland on penalties after a 2-2 draw in the Checkatrade Trophy Final, watched by a record crowd for the competition of 85,021.

APRIL 2019

1 Queens Park Rangers manager Steve McClaren is sacked after a single win in 15 matches.

2 Fulham are relegated from the Premier League. Mike Dean becomes the first referee to show 100 red cards in the Premier League when dismissing Manchester United's Ashley Young against Wolves.

3 Tottenham's first competitive match in their new £1bn stadium, a 2-0 win over Crystal Palace, is watched by a crowd of 59,215. Wolves pay a club record £30m for Benfica's Raul Jimenez after a season's loan. Brian Barry-Murphy, a former player and first-team coach at the club, is appointed Rochdale's permanent manager after eight points from four games as caretaker.

4 Danny Rose, Tottenham and England defender, hits out at racism in the game and says he longs for the day he retires. Figures show Premier League clubs paying £261m to agents during 2018-19 – up from £211m in the previous 12 months. Liverpool (£43m), Chelsea (£26m) and Manchester City (£24m) top the spending list. Tottenham post a world-record annual profit of £113m.

5 All 20 Premier League clubs reject proposed changes to the Champions League format from eight groups of four teams to four groups of eight.

6 Manchester City defeat Brighton 1-0 in the first FA Cup-semi-final. Dean Keates, manager of

relegation-threatened Walsall, is sacked after a fifth successive defeat.

7 Watford deliver one of the great Wembley comebacks, transforming a 2-0 deficit to beat Wolves 3-2 in the second semi-final.

8 Scotland enjoy a morale-boosting win ahead of the Women's World Cup by beating Brazil 1-0 in a warm-up match.

9 Hugo Lloris saves Sergio Aguero's penalty as Tottenham beat Manchester City 1-0 in the first leg of their Champions League quarter final. Liverpool overcome Porto 2-0.

10 Luke Shaw's own goal costs Manchester United a 1-0 defeat by Barcelona in their last-eight tie.

11 Harry Kane is ruled out for the remainder of the Premier League season with an ankle injury sustained in Tottenham's Champions League win.

13 Fourth Division Lincoln become the first Football League side to be promoted. Ipswich are the first to be relegated, ending 17 successive seasons in the second tier. Hearts beat Inverness 3-0 in the first Scottish Cup semi-final.

14 Celtic defeat Aberdeen 3-0 in the second semi-final.

15 Andre Gomes is banned for three matches by the FA after being caught on camera stamping on Aleksandar Mitrovic in Everton's defeat by Fulham. West Ham's Robert Snodgrass receives a one match ban and £30,000 fine for verbally abusing drug testers. Leicester are fined £20,000 for protecting players surrounding referee David Coote during the match against Huddersfield. Derby receive a £7,500 fine for their players' behaviour against Brentford.

16 Manchester United lose the second leg of their Champions League quarter-final 3-0 to a Lionel Messi-inspired Barcelona, watched by a crowd of 96,000 at the Nou Camp, and go out 4-0 on aggregate.

17 Manchester City win a pulsating second leg 4-3, but it's Tottenham who go through on away goals after the tie ends 4-4 on aggregate. Liverpool beat Porto 4-1 to reach the last four 6-1 over the two legs.

18 Alex McLeish is sacked after 12 games of his second spell as Scotland manager. Arsenal, 3-0 aggregate winners against Napoli, and Chelsea, who defeat Slavia Prague 5-3, reach the semi-finals of the Europa League.

19 Premier League players support a PFA campaign against racial abuse by boycotting social media for 24 hours.

20 The Premier League give Liverpool and Tottenham more time to prepare for midweek Champions League semi-finals against Barcelona and Ajax respectively by bringing forward their domestic fixtures prior to the second legs.

22 Billy McNeill, captain of Britain's first European Cup-winning side Celtic, dies aged 79. League Two Lincoln become the first divisional champions.

23 Southampton's Shane Long scores the fastest-ever Premier League goal, timed at 7.69 sec, in the 1-1 draw at Watford. Chelsea's Callum Hudson-Odoi is ruled out for the rest of the season with a ruptured achilles tendon.

25 Chelsea manager Maurizio Sarri is fined £8,000 by the FA for misconduct after being sent off for leaving his technical area during the game against Burnley.

26 UEFA order Montenegro to play their next home match behind closed doors and issue a £17,250 fine for the racist abuse of England's players in the Euro 2020 qualifier in Podgorica. Gillingham manager Steve Lovell is sacked, despite leading his side away from the League One relegation zone. Bristol City are fined £7,500 by the FA for disorderly conduct by their players against Aston Villa. Ross County return to the Scottish Premiership at the first attempt as Championship title winners.

27 Norwich are promoted to the Premier League. The Football League call off Bolton's home match against Brentford after their players refuse to play because of unpaid wages. Yeovil are relegated to the National League. Leyton Orient return to the Football League as National League champions.

28 Sheffield United's promotion to the Premier League is confirmed after Leeds drop points against Aston Villa. Liverpool's Virgil van Dijk is named Player of the Year by the Professional Footballers' Association – the first defender to win the award since John Terry in 2005.

Plymouth manager Derek Adams is sacked after a 5-1 defeat at Accrington and ahead of the club's possible relegation decider against Scunthorpe.

29 Raheem Sterling wins the football writers' annual award, the first Manchester City player since Tony Book, who shared it with Dave Mackay in 1969. A week after the death of Billy McNeill, Stevie Chalmers, scorer of Celtic's winning goal in the 2-1 win over Inter Milan, passes away aged 83. Derby manager Frank Lampard is fined £2,500 by the FA for improper conduct after the game against Birmingham.

30 Tottenham lose 1-0 at home to Ajax in the first leg of their Champions League semi-final. The FA fine Leeds £12,500 and Aston Villa £10,000 for a players' confrontation.

MAY 2019

1 Liverpool are beaten 3-0 in their first leg in the Nou Camp by Barcelona, for whom Lionel Messi scores twice. The FA fine Cardiff manager Neil Warnock £20,000 for branding Premier League match officials 'the worst in the world.'

2 Celtic and Rangers are both fined £7,500 by the Scottish FA for a players' confrontation. Leeds striker Patrick Bamford is banned for two matches by the FA for pretending to be caught in the face by Aston Villa's Anwar El Ghazi, whose red card is later rescinded

3 Bolton face disciplinary action from the Football League for the failure to fulfil their final fixture against Brentford, who are awarded the points. Fulham captain Tom Cairney signs a new five-year contract.

4 Celtic become Scottish champions for the eighth successive season. Cardiff are relegated from the Premier League. Notts County, the oldest professional football club in the world, are relegated to the National League. Luton win the League One title. Manchester City beat West Ham 3-0 in the Women's FA Cup Final.

5 Norwich are crowned champions of the Championship. Celtic's James Forrest is named PFA Scotland Player of the Year. Steve Clarke wins the Manager of the Year award after leading Kilmarnock to a record points total for the second successive season.

6 A winning goal by Manchester City captain Vincent Kompany against Leicester takes the Premier League title race to the final day, with his side a point ahead of Liverpool.

7 Liverpool produce arguably the greatest comeback in the club's history, defeating Barcelona 4-0 in the second leg to reach the Champions League Final, despite missing injured strikers Mohamed Salah and Roberto Firmino. Port Vale owner Norman Smurthwaite sells the club to local business coupler Carol and Kevin Shanahan.

8 Tottenham, trailing Ajax 3-0 on aggregate at half-time in their second leg, match Liverpool's feat with a hat-trick by Lucas Moura to go through on away goals.

9 Arsenal, 7-3 winners over Valencia on aggregate, and Chelsea, who defeat Eintracht Frankfurt on penalties, complete an unprecedent clearn sweep of English teams in the finals of both Champions League and Europa League.

10 Scott Parker is appointed Fulham's permanent manager after impressing as caretaker. Former Bristol Rovers manager Darrell Clarke fills the vacant position at Walsall. Leicester's Hamza Choudhury is fined £5,000 by the FA for offensive comments on social media in 2013-14.

11 Salford City, the club co-owned by six former Manchester United team-mates, win promotion to the Football League by defeating AFC Fylde 3-0 in the National League Play-off Final at Wembley.

12 Manchester City are crowned champions for the second successive season, finishing one point ahead of Liverpool after the Premiership League's most enthralling title race. Dundee sack manager Jim McIntyre following relegation from the Scottish Premiership.

13 Chris Hughton, Brighton manager for four-and-a-half years, is sacked after his side's narrow escape from relegation. Bolton go into administration and have 12 points deducted from the start of the 2019-20 season. Paul Hurst, former Ipswich and Shrewsbury manager, takes charge at relegated Scunthorpe.

14 Watford's Jose Holebas is cleared to play in the FA Cup Final against Manchester City after his red card against West Ham is rescinded.

16 Chelsea's Ruben Loftus-Cheek is ruled out for up to a year with a ruptured achilles sustained in a match in the United States.

17 Kevin Bond becomes permanent manager at Southend after leading the club away from the threat of relegation.

18 Berwick, the only English-based club in the Scottish League, are relegated after 68 years, losing a play-off to Highland League Cove Rangers, who are promoted to senior football for the first time.

19 Manchester City, Premier League champions and League Cup winners, complete an unprecedented domestic treble by beating Watford 6-0 in the FA Cup Final – the biggest win for 116 years. AFC Fylde defeat Leyton Orient 1-0 in the FA Trophy Final.

20 Vincent Kompany, Manchester City's captain, announces he is leaving the club to become player-manager of the Belgian side Anderlecht. Brighton appoint Swansea's Graham Potter as their new manager. Celtic's James Forrest adds the Scottish football writers' Player of the Year award to his PFA accolade.

21 Steve Clarke, Scotland's Manager of the Year, leaves Kilmarnock to take charge of the national team. Steve Evans is appointed Gillingham's new manager, his seventh Football League appointment.

22 Arsenal announce that Henrikh Mkhitaryan, their Armenia midfielder, will not play in the Europa League Final against Chelsea in Baku, Azerbaijan, because of fears for his safety over political tension between the two countries. Olivier Giroud signs a new one-year contract with Chelsea.

23 Oxford United have a winding up order, served by the landlords of their stadium, dismissed after settling a reported £204,000 debt.

24 FIFA scrap plans to expand the 2022 World Cup in Qatar, admitting that an increase from 32 to 48 teams is impractical.

25 Celtic achieve an unprecedented third successive domestic treble by coming from behind to defeat Hearts 2-1 in the Scottish Cup Final with two goals from Odsonne Edouard, the first a penalty. Tranmere beat Newport 1-0 in the League Two Play-off Final with a goal by Connor Jennings in the final minute of extra time.

26 Charlton captain Patrick Bauer scores in the final seconds for a 2-1 victory over Sunderland in the League One Play-off Final. St Mirren retain Scottish Premiership status with a 2-0 win on penalties against Dundee United in their Play-off Final.

27 Aston Villa defeat Derby 2-1 in the Championship Play-off Final to return to the Premier League after an absence of three years.

28 Scotland complete preparations for the Women's World Cup with a 3-2 victory over Jamaica in front of a crowd of 18,555 at Hampden Park, four times more than the previous biggest for a home international.

29 Chelsea score four times in 23 minutes in the second-half to beat Arsenal 4-1 in the Europa League Final.

30 Goalkeeper Robert Green, who played for Norwich, West Ham, Queens Park Rangers and Leeds, winning 12 England caps, announces his retirement.

JUNE 2019

1 Liverpool defeat Tottenham 2-0 in the Champions League Final in Madrid with Mohamed Salah's second-minute penalty and a goal by substitute Divock Origi two minutes from the end of normal time. Jose Antonio Reyes, 35, part of Arsenal's 'Invincibles' side that went through the 2003-04 season unbeaten, dies in a car crash in Spain.

2 A crowd estimated at 750,000 see Liverpool parade the Champions League trophy through the city.

3 The FA sign a five-year deal worth about £50m with BT as lead sponsor of the governing body.

4 FIFA admit that the gulf between World Cup prize money for men and women needs to be addressed.

5 Cristiano Ronaldo's hat-trick gives Portugal a 3-1 win over Switzerland in the semi-finals of the European Nations League. Ryan Lowe leaves promoted Bury to become manager of relegated Plymouth.

6 England lead Holland through Marcus Rashford's penalty in the second semi-final, but defensive mistakes result in a 3-1 extra-time defeat.

7 Chelsea's Eden Hazard secures his dream move to Real Madrid in a deal that could rise considerably from the initial £88m transfer fee. The Football League give Coventry permission to play home games at Birmingham's St Andrew's Stadium in the 2019-20 season after the club fail to agree a deal to continue at the Ricoh Arena.

8 Justin Edinburgh, 49, the Leyton Orient manager who led the club back to the Football League, dies five days after suffering a cardiac arrest. Oliver Burke comes off the bench to score his first Scotland goal after 89 minutes for a 2-1 win over Cyprus in Steve Clarke's first match as manager. David Brooks nets his first for Wales in a 2-1 defeat by Croatia. In another European Championship qualifier, Northern Ireland defeat Estonia by the same scoreline. Hull manager Nigel Adkins turns down a new contract and leaves the club.

9 Portugal defeat Holland 1-0 in the Nations League Final. England goalkeeper Jordan Pickford scores one of their penalties in a 6-5 shoot-out victory after the third-place play-off match against Switzerland ends goalless. England's women defeat Scotland 2-1 in the teams' first group match at the World Cup Finals in France.

10 The Republic of Ireland make hard work beating of Gibraltar 2-0 in a European Championship qualifier.

11 Northern Ireland win a fourth successive qualifier at the start of a campaign for the first time, thanks to Paddy McNair's first international goal in the 86th minute against Belarus. Manager Ryan Giggs admits it will be hard for Wales to reach the Euro 2020 finals after another defeat – 1-0 by Hungary. Scotland lose 3-0 to Belgium, with Romelu Lukaku scoring twice.

12 Harvey Barnes signs a new-five year contact with Leicester. Former Monaco coach Laurent Banide is appointed Oldham's new manager.

13 Former West Ham manager Slaven Bilic takes over at West Bromwich Albion. Steve Cooper, who led England's youngster to the World Under-17 Cup in 2017, is appointed Swansea's new manager. Aston Villa pay a club-record £22m for Brazilian striker Wesley from Club Bruges. Blackpool-born Simon Sadler, chief executive of an asset management company, buys the club which has been run by receivers since the end of the Oyston family's controversial ownership.

14 Jonathan Woodgate, who started his career with Middlesbrough and had two spells as a player, is appointed the club's new manager. England women reach the knockout stage by beating Argentina 1-0. Scotland lose 2-1 to Japan.

15 Maurizio Sarri leaves Chelsea after one season as manager to take over at Serie A champions Juventus.

16 Angelo Alessio, former assistant to Antonio Conte at Chelsea and Juventus, succeeds Steve Clarke as Kilmarnock manager.

18 Garry Monk, who was sacked by Swansea and Middlesbrough and resigned at Leeds, is fired by Birmingham after a breakdown in his relationship with the club's owners. England concede goals in the 89th and 95th minutes and lose 2-1 to France in their opening group match at the European Under-21 Championship.

19 Paul Scholes, former Manchester United and England midfielder, is fined £8,000 for breaking FA betting rules.

20 Scotland women surrender a three-goal lead, draw 3-3 with Argentina and fail to reach the knockout stage. The equaliser comes from a 90th minute, twice-taken penalty after VAR rules that goalkeeper Lee Alexander moved off her line saving the first. England complete a 100 per cent record by defeating Japan 2-0 with two goals from Ellen White.

21 England Under 21s are knocked out after conceding three goals in the last eight minutes and lose 4-2 to Romania. Grant McCann leaves Doncaster to become Hull's new manager. Manchester City's Kyle Walker and Oleksandr Zinchenko and Manchester United's Juan Mata sign contract extensions. Justin Edinburgh's assistant, Ross Embleton, succeeds him on an interim basis.

22 Petr Cech returns to Chelsea, where he spent 11 years as a player, as the club's technical and performance advisor.

23 England women reach the quarter-finals with a 3-0 victory over Cameroon, whose behaviour leads to FIFA opening disciplinary proceedings. Roy Keane leaves his role as Martin O'Neill's assistant at Nottingham Forest.

24 Newcastle announce that Rafael Benitez, manager for three years, will leave the club at the end of his contact on June 30, having failed to agree a new one.

25 David Silva says he will leave Manchester City at the end of the new season, his tenth at the club.

26 Oran Kearney is replaced as manager of St Mirren by Jim Goodwin, who spent five years at the club as a player. Kearney rejoins the Northern Ireland side Coleraine.

27 Jill Scott scores the quickest goal of the tournament, after 126 seconds, to put England on the way to a 3-0 win over Norway and a place in the last four.

28 Nottingham Forest sack Martin O'Neill after five months as manager and replace him immediately with former Rennes and Ivory Coast coach Sabri Lamouchi. Manchester United sign Crystal Palace right-back Aaron Wan-Bissaka for £50m, a record fee for the London club. Great Britain are guaranteed a women's team at the 2020 Olympics after France lose 2-1 to the USA in the World Cup, ensuring England will be among the top three European sides at the tournament.

29 Christopher Jullien becomes Scottish football's most expensive defender when joining Celtic from Toulouse for £7m.

30 Watford goalkeeper Heurelho Gomes changes his mind about retiring and signs a new one-year contract.

JULY 2019

1 Manchester United's Marcus Rashford signs a new contract extension through to June, 2023.

2 Captain Steph Houghton has a penalty saved and Mollie Bright is sent off for a second yellow card as England lose 2-1 to the United States in the semi-finals. Tottenham break their transfer record with the £54m signing of France midfielder Tanguy Ndombele from Lyon. Two days after the end of his contract at Newcastle, Rafael Benitez becomes manager of the Chinese side Dalian Yifang at a reported annual salary of £12m.

3 Promoted Sheffield United pay an undisclosed club-record fee, thought to be £5m, for midfielder Luke Freeman from Queens Park Rangers. Teemu Pukki and Todd Cantwell sign new three-year contracts with another promoted club, Norwich. Bury appoint former Everton striker Paul Wilkinson as their new manager.

4 Frank Lampard leaves Derby to become manager of Chelsea, where he spent 13 years as a player. Manchester City sign Spain midfielder Rodri from Atletico Madrid for a club-record £62.8m.

5 Terry McPhillips resigns after one season as Blackpool manager and is replaced by Simon Grayson, who was in charge from 2006-08.

6 England lose their third-place play-off match 2-1 to Sweden. Ruben Loftus-Cheek signs a new contract with Chelsea through to 2024.

7 Ben Davies and Harry Winks sign new five-year contracts with Tottenham.

8 Leicester break their transfer record with the £40m signing of Belgium midfielder Youri Tielemans from Monaco.

9 Chris Wilder, manager of promoted Sheffield United, signs a new three-year contract.

10 Divock Origi signs a new five-year contract with Liverpool. Aberdeen manager Derek McInnes extends his contract to 2022. Darren Moore, sacked by West Bromwich Albion, is appointed Doncaster's new manager.

11 Club captain Laurent Koscielny refuses to travel on Arsenal's pre-season tour of the United States. Sam Allardyce is reported to have turned down the chance to manager Newcastle for the second time.

12 Sheffield United break their transfer record for the second time in a month with the £8m signing of Preston's Callum Robinson. Peter Crouch, who played for nine clubs and won 42 England caps, retires at the age of 38.

15 Steve Bruce resigns after six months as Sheffield Wednesday manager ahead of taking over at Newcastle – his tenth club appointment.

ENGLISH TABLES 2018–2019

PREMIER LEAGUE

				Home				Away						
		P	W	D	L	F	A	W	D	L	F	A	GD	Pts
1	Man City	38	18	0	1	57	12	14	2	3	38	11	+72	98
2	Liverpool	38	17	2	0	55	10	13	5	1	34	12	+67	97
3	Chelsea	38	12	6	1	39	12	9	3	7	24	27	+24	72
4	Tottenham	38	12	2	5	34	16	11	0	8	33	23	+28	71
5	Arsenal	38	14	3	2	42	16	7	4	8	31	35	+22	70
6	Man Utd	38	10	6	3	33	25	9	3	7	32	29	+11	66
7	Wolves	38	10	4	5	28	21	6	5	8	19	25	+1	57
8	Everton	38	10	4	5	30	21	5	5	9	24	25	+8	54
9	Leicester	38	8	3	8	24	20	7	4	8	27	28	+3	52
10	West Ham	38	9	4	6	32	27	6	3	10	20	28	-3	52
11	Watford	38	8	3	8	26	28	6	5	8	26	31	-7	50
12	Crystal Palace	38	5	5	9	19	23	9	2	8	32	30	-2	49
13	Newcastle	38	8	1	10	24	25	4	8	7	18	23	-6	45
14	Bournemouth	38	8	5	6	30	25	5	1	13	26	45	-14	45
15	Burnley	38	7	2	10	24	32	4	5	10	21	36	-23	40
16	Southampton	38	5	8	6	27	30	4	4	11	18	35	-20	39
17	Brighton	38	6	5	8	19	28	3	4	12	16	32	-25	36
18	Cardiff	38	6	2	11	21	38	4	2	13	13	31	-35	34
19	Fulham	38	6	3	10	22	36	1	2	16	12	45	-47	26
20	Huddersfield	38	2	3	14	10	31	1	4	14	12	45	-54	16

Manchester City, Liverpool, Chelsea, Tottenham into Champions League group stage; Arsenal, Manchester Utd into Europa League group stage; Wolves into second qualifying round
Prize money (league position = amount received): 1 £150.9m, 2 £152.4m, 3 £146m, 4 £142.2m, 5 £142.2m, 6 £142.5m, 7 £127.1m, 8 £128.6m, 9 £123.3m, 10 £122.5m, 11 £113.9m, 12 £114.2m, 13 £120.1m, 14 £108.1m, 15 £107.3m, 16 £104.3m, 17 £105.7m, 18 £102.7m, 19 £101.9m, 20 £96.6m
Biggest win: Manchester City 6 Chelsea 0
Highest aggregate score: Everton 2 Tottenham 6
Highest attendance: 81,332 (Tottenham v Arsenal)
Lowest attendance: 9,980 (Bournemouth v Huddersfield)
Player of Year: Virgil van Dijk (Liverpool)
Manager of Year: Pep Guardiola (Manchester City)
Golden Boot: 22 Pierre-Emerick Aubameyang (Arsenal) Sadio Mane (Liverpool), Mohamed Salah (Liverpool)
Golden Glove: 21 clean sheets Alisson (Liverpool)
PFA Team of Year: Ederson (Manchester City), Alexander-Arnold (Liverpool), Van Dijk (Liverpool), Laporte (Manchester City), Robertson (Liverpool), Pogba (Manchester Utd), Bernardo Silva (Manchester City), Fernandinho (Manchester City), Aguero (Manchester City), Sterling (Manchester City), Mane (Liverpool)
Leading league scorers: 22 Aubameyang (Arsenal), Mane (Liverpool), Salah (Liverpool); 21 Aguero (Manchester City); 18 Vardy (Leicester); 17 Kane (Tottenham), Sterling (Manchester City); 16 Hazard (Chelsea); 14 Wilson (Bournemouth); 13 Lacazette (Arsenal), Murray (Brighton), Pogba (Manchester Utd), Raul Jimenez (Wolves), Richarlison (Everton), Sigurdsson (Everton); 12 Ayoze Perez (Newcastle), Barnes (Burnley), King (Bournemouth), Lukaku (Manchester Utd), Milivojevic (Crystal Palace), Firmino (Liverpool), Son Heung-min (Tottenham)

SKY BET CHAMPIONSHIP

			Home					Away						
		P	W	D	L	F	A	W	D	L	F	A	GD	Pts
1	Norwich	46	15	4	4	51	34	12	9	2	42	23	+36	94
2	Sheff Utd	46	15	4	4	42	17	11	7	5	36	21	+37	89
3	Leeds	46	14	4	5	38	21	11	4	8	35	29	+23	83
4	West Brom	46	12	7	4	53	31	11	4	8	34	31	+25	80
5	Aston Villa*	46	11	8	4	50	36	9	8	6	32	25	+21	76
6	Derby	46	13	7	3	40	20	7	7	9	29	34	+15	74
7	Middlesbrough	46	10	6	7	23	17	10	7	6	26	24	+8	73
8	Bristol City	46	8	8	7	28	26	11	5	7	31	27	+6	70
9	Nottm Forest	46	13	4	6	34	21	4	11	8	27	33	+7	66
10	Swansea	46	12	6	5	42	28	6	5	12	23	34	+3	65
11	Brentford	46	14	4	5	50	23	3	9	11	23	36	+14	64
12	Sheff Wed	46	10	8	5	34	27	6	8	9	26	35	-2	64
13	Hull	46	11	6	6	37	24	6	5	12	29	44	-2	62
14	Preston	46	8	10	5	41	30	8	3	12	26	37	+0	61
15	Blackburn	46	10	7	6	32	21	6	5	12	32	48	-5	60
16	Stoke	46	8	9	6	26	24	3	13	7	19	28	-7	55
17	Birmingham**	46	7	11	5	31	24	7	8	8	33	34	16	52
18	Wigan	46	11	8	4	29	20	2	5	16	22	44	-13	52
19	QPR	46	9	3	11	33	31	5	6	12	20	40	-18	51
20	Reading	46	8	6	9	29	31	2	11	10	20	35	-17	47
21	Millwall	46	7	9	7	26	27	3	5	15	22	37	-16	44
22	Rotherham	46	7	8	8	32	38	1	8	14	20	45	-31	40
23	Bolton	46	4	4	15	13	35	4	4	15	16	43	-49	32
24	Ipswich	46	3	11	9	22	31	2	5	16	14	46	-41	31

*Also promoted **Deducted 9pts for breaking financial rules

Biggest win: WBA 7 QPR 1
Highest aggregate score: Aston Villa 5 Nottm Forest 5
Highest attendance: 41,696 (Aston Villa v Norwich)
Lowest attendance: 8,018 (Rotherham v QPR)
Player of Year: Teemu Pukki (Norwich)
Manager of Year: Chris Wilder (Sheffield Utd)
PFA Team of Year: Randolph (Middlesbrough), Aarons (Norwich), Cooper (Leeds), Jansson (Leeds), Lewis (Norwich), Hernandez (Leeds), Norwood (Sheffield Utd), Grealish (Aston Villa), Pukki (Norwich), Abraham (Aston Villa), Sharp (Sheffield Utd)
Leading league scorers: 29 Pukki (Norwich); 25 Abraham (Aston Villa), Maupay (Brentford); 23 Gayle (WBA), Sharp (Sheffield Utd); 22 Adams (Birmingham), Bowen (Hull), McBurnie (Swansea), Rodriguez (WBA); 16 Grabban (Nottm Forest); 15 Dack (Blackburn), Graham (Blackburn), McGoldrick (Sheffield Utd), Wilson (Derby); 14 Assombalonga (Middlesbrough), Jutkiewicz (Birmingham), Roofe (Leeds); 13 Diedhiou (Bristol City), 12 Browne (Preston), Campbell (Hull), Meite (Reading), Hernandez (Leeds), Robinson (Preston)

SKY BET LEAGUE ONE

		P	W	D	L	F	A	W	D	L	F	A	GD	Pts
				Home						Away				
1	Luton	46	16	7	0	57	19	11	6	6	33	23	+48	94
2	Barnsley	46	15	8	0	40	16	11	5	7	40	23	+41	91
3	Charlton*	46	16	5	2	41	15	10	5	8	32	25	+33	88
4	Portsmouth	46	12	7	4	42	22	13	6	4	41	29	+32	88
5	Sunderland	46	12	10	1	46	25	10	9	4	34	22	+33	85
6	Doncaster	46	13	7	3	45	21	7	6	10	31	37	+18	73
7	Peterborough	46	9	7	7	31	28	11	5	7	40	34	+9	72
8	Coventry	46	9	7	7	24	20	9	4	10	30	34	+0	65
9	Burton	46	11	5	7	35	23	6	7	10	31	34	+9	63
10	Blackpool	46	8	8	7	28	26	7	9	7	22	26	-2	62
11	Fleetwood	46	9	9	5	33	27	7	4	12	25	25	+6	61
12	Oxford Utd	46	11	4	8	34	27	4	11	8	24	37	-6	60
13	Gillingham	46	7	4	12	27	36	8	6	9	34	36	-11	55
14	Accrington	46	7	6	10	26	33	7	7	9	25	34	-16	55
15	Bristol Rov	46	6	6	11	24	28	7	9	7	23	22	-3	54
16	Rochdale	46	8	4	11	25	37	7	5	11	29	50	-33	54
17	Wycombe	46	10	5	8	28	26	4	6	13	27	41	-12	53
18	Shrewsbury	46	8	9	6	25	25	4	7	12	26	34	-8	52
19	Southend	46	8	2	13	32	34	6	6	11	23	34	-13	50
20	AFC Wimbledon	46	6	5	12	24	37	7	6	10	18	26	-21	50
21	Plymouth	46	9	6	8	36	38	4	5	14	20	42	-24	50
22	Walsall	46	7	5	11	30	37	5	6	12	19	34	-22	47
23	Scunthorpe	46	6	7	10	31	42	6	3	14	22	41	-30	46
24	Bradford	46	7	4	12	25	31	4	4	15	24	46	-28	41

*Also promoted

Biggest win: Doncaster 5 Rochdale 0; Scunthorpe 0 Fleetwood 5
Highest aggregate score: Sunderland 4 Coventry 5
Highest attendance: 46,039 (Sunderland v Bradford)
Lowest attendance: 1,732 (Accrington v AFC Wimbledon)
Player of Year: James Collins (Luton)
Manager of Year: Mick Harford (Luton)
PFA Team of Year: Davies (Barnsley), Cavare (Barnsley), Pinnock (Barnsley), Clarke (Portsmouth), Justin (Luton), McGeady (Sunderland), Mowatt (Barnsley), Lowe (Portsmouth), Collins (Luton), Marquis (Doncaster), Moore (Barnsley)
Leading league scorers: 25 Collins (Luton); 21 Eaves (Gillingham), Marquis (Doncaster), Taylor (AFC Wimbledon); 20 Henderson (Rochdale); 18 Ladapo (Plymouth); 17 Evans (Fleetwood), Moore (Barnsley); 16 Clarke-Harris (11 Bristol Rov, 5 Coventry) Toney (Peterborough), Woodrow (Barnsley); 15 Cox (Southend), Lowe (Portsmouth), Madden (Fleetwood), Maja (Sunderland), McConville (Accrington), Pigott (AFC Wimbledon); 14 Godden (Peterborough), Grant (Charlton), Madden (Fleetwood), Wilks (Doncaster)

SKY BET LEAGUE TWO

				Home					Away					
		P	W	D	L	F	A	W	D	L	F	A	GD	Pts
1	Lincoln	46	11	10	2	35	23	12	6	5	38	20	+30	85
2	Bury	46	14	6	3	52	26	8	7	8	30	30	+26	79
3	MK Dons	46	14	5	4	35	14	9	5	9	36	35	+22	79
4	Mansfield	46	14	5	4	38	15	6	11	6	31	26	+28	76
5	Forest Green	46	8	9	6	28	20	12	5	6	40	27	+21	74
6	Tranmere*	46	14	5	4	33	13	6	8	9	30	37	+13	73
7	Newport	46	14	6	3	32	22	6	5	12	27	37	-1	71
8	Colchester	46	12	4	7	39	23	8	6	9	26	30	+12	70
9	Exeter	46	12	3	8	34	25	7	10	6	26	24	+11	70
10	Stevenage	46	12	3	8	28	23	8	7	8	31	32	+4	70
11	Carlisle	46	12	3	8	42	31	8	5	10	25	31	+5	68
12	Crewe	46	15	2	6	45	25	4	6	13	15	34	+1	65
13	Swindon	46	8	9	6	31	27	8	7	8	28	29	+3	64
14	Oldham	46	10	6	7	42	33	6	8	9	25	27	+7	62
15	Northampton	46	7	12	4	30	27	7	7	9	34	36	+1	61
16	Cheltenham	46	10	7	6	34	29	5	5	13	23	39	-11	57
17	Grimsby	46	11	4	8	26	21	5	4	14	19	35	-11	56
18	Morecambe	46	8	5	10	33	31	6	7	10	21	39	-16	54
19	Crawley Town	46	10	5	8	34	31	5	3	15	17	37	-17	53
20	Port Vale	46	7	3	13	24	36	5	10	8	15	19	-16	49
21	Cambridge Utd	46	7	7	9	21	26	5	4	14	19	40	-26	47
22	Macclesfield	46	5	11	7	26	35	5	3	15	22	39	-26	44
23	Notts Co	46	5	9	9	23	34	4	5	14	25	50	-36	41
24	Yeovil	46	4	9	10	20	34	5	4	14	21	32	-25	40

*Also promoted

Biggest win: Carlisle 6 Oldham 0; Colchester 6 Crewe 0; Crewe 6 Morecambe 0; MK Dons 6 Cambridge 0; Newport 0 Yeovil 6

Highest aggregate score: Port Vale 2 Lincoln 6

Highest attendance: 15,851 (MK Dons v Lincoln)

Lowest attendance: 1,355 (Morecambe v Mansfield)

Player of Year: James Norwood (Tranmere)

Manager of Year: Danny Cowley (Lincoln)

PFA Team of Year: Murphy (Bury), Eardley (Lincoln), Shackell (Lincoln), Pearce (Mansfield), Toffolo (Lincoln), Mayor (Bury), O'Shea (Bury), Brown (Forest Green), Norwood (Tranmere), Akinde (Lincoln), Walker (Mansfield)

Leading league scorers: 29 Norwood (Tranmere); 22 Walker (Mansfield); 21 Maynard (Bury), 20 Agard (MK Dons); 17 Aneke (MK Dons); 16 O'Shea (Bury), Stockley (Exeter); 15 Akinde (Lincoln); 14 Amond (Newport), Doidge (Forest Green), Hemmings (Notts Co), Hope (Carlisle), Mall (Newport), Palmer (Crawley), Szmodics (Colchester), Varney (Cheltenham); 13 Doughty (Swindon), Lang (Oldham), Porter (Crewe)

PREMIER LEAGUE RESULTS 2018-2019

Home \ Away	Arsenal	Bournemouth	Brighton	Burnley	Cardiff	Chelsea	Crystal Palace	Everton	Fulham	Huddersfield	Leicester	Liverpool	Man City	Man Utd	Newcastle	Southampton	Tottenham	Watford	West Ham	Wolves
Arsenal	–	5-1	1-1	3-1	2-1	2-0	2-3	2-0	4-1	1-0	3-1	1-1	0-2	2-0	2-0	2-0	4-2	2-0	3-1	1-1
Bournemouth	1-2	–	2-0	1-3	2-0	4-0	2-1	2-2	0-1	2-1	4-2	0-4	0-1	1-2	2-2	0-0	1-0	3-3	2-0	1-1
Brighton	1-1	2-0	–	1-3	0-2	1-2	3-1	1-0	2-2	1-0	1-1	0-1	1-4	3-2	1-1	0-1	1-2	0-0	1-0	1-0
Burnley	1-3	4-0	1-3	–	2-0	0-4	1-3	1-5	2-1	1-1	1-2	1-3	0-1	0-2	2-0	1-1	2-1	1-3	2-0	2-0
Cardiff	2-3	2-0	2-1	1-2	–	1-2	2-3	0-3	4-2	0-0	0-1	0-2	0-5	1-5	3-0	1-2	0-3	1-5	2-0	2-1
Chelsea	3-2	2-0	3-0	2-2	2-1	–	3-1	0-0	2-0	5-0	0-1	1-1	2-0	0-0	2-1	0-0	0-1	3-0	2-0	1-1
Crystal Palace	2-2	5-3	1-2	2-0	3-1	1-0	–	0-0	2-0	2-0	1-0	0-0	1-3	3-1	0-1	1-1	2-0	1-2	1-1	0-1
Everton	1-0	2-0	3-1	2-0	1-0	2-0	0-0	–	3-0	1-1	1-0	0-0	0-2	2-1	3-2	2-1	2-6	2-2	1-3	1-3
Fulham	1-5	0-3	4-2	2-1	1-0	2-0	2-0	3-0	–	1-0	1-1	1-2	0-2	0-1	0-0	3-2	1-2	1-1	0-2	1-1
Huddersfield	1-2	0-2	1-2	1-2	0-0	0-0	0-2	2-0	1-0	–	1-4	0-1	0-3	3-1	0-1	1-1	0-2	1-2	1-1	1-0
Leicester	3-0	2-0	2-1	2-0	0-0	0-0	1-4	1-0	3-1	3-1	–	1-2	2-1	2-1	2-0	1-2	2-1	2-0	1-1	2-0
Liverpool	5-1	3-0	1-0	4-2	4-1	2-0	4-3	1-0	2-0	5-0	1-1	–	0-0	3-1	4-0	3-0	2-1	5-0	4-0	2-0
Man City	3-1	3-1	2-0	5-0	2-0	6-0	2-3	3-1	3-0	6-1	2-1	2-1	–	3-1	2-1	3-1	2-1	3-1	1-0	3-0
Man Utd	2-2	4-1	2-1	2-2	0-2	1-1	0-0	2-1	4-1	3-1	2-1	0-0	0-2	–	0-0	3-2	1-0	2-1	2-1	1-1
Newcastle	2-0	2-2	1-1	2-0	3-0	1-2	0-1	3-2	0-0	2-0	0-2	1-3	1-0	0-0	–	3-1	1-0	1-1	3-0	1-2
Southampton	3-2	3-3	2-2	0-0	1-2	0-3	1-1	2-1	2-0	1-1	1-2	1-3	3-1	3-2	3-1	–	1-2	1-1	1-2	3-1
Tottenham	1-1	5-0	1-0	1-0	1-0	3-1	2-0	2-2	3-1	4-0	3-1	0-3	1-0	0-1	1-0	3-2	–	2-1	0-1	1-3
Watford	0-1	0-4	2-0	0-0	3-2	1-2	3-2	1-0	4-1	3-0	2-1	2-1	0-2	2-1	1-0	1-1	2-1	–	1-4	1-2
West Ham	1-0	1-2	2-2	4-2	3-1	0-0	3-2	1-0	0-2	1-1	1-1	1-1	0-1	3-1	2-0	2-1	0-1	1-0	–	0-1
Wolves	...	...	...	...	...	...	...	...	...	...	...	...	...	...	...	...	...	...	...	–

SKY BET CHAMPIONSHIP RESULTS 2018–2019

	Aston Villa	Birmingham	Blackburn	Bolton	Brentford	Bristol City	Derby	Hull	Ipswich	Leeds	Middlesbrough	Millwall	Norwich	Nottm Forest	Preston	QPR	Reading	Rotherham	Sheff Utd	Sheff Wed	Stoke	Swansea	WBA	Wigan
Aston Villa	–	4-2	2-1	2-0	2-2	2-1	4-0	2-2	2-1	2-3	3-0	1-0	1-2	5-5	3-3	2-2	1-1	2-0	3-3	1-2	2-2	1-0	0-2	3-2
Birmingham	0-1	–	2-2	0-1	0-0	0-1	2-2	3-3	2-1	1-0	1-2	0-2	2-2	2-0	3-0	0-0	2-1	3-1	1-1	3-1	2-0	0-0	1-1	1-1
Blackburn	1-1	2-0	–	2-0	2-0	0-1	2-2	3-0	2-2	2-1	2-1	0-0	2-2	2-2	1-2	1-0	2-1	1-1	0-0	4-2	0-3	2-2	2-1	3-0
Bolton	1-1	2-0	0-1	–	0-1	2-2	1-0	2-0	2-0	2-1	0-1	0-0	0-4	2-2	1-2	1-0	2-1	1-1	0-3	0-0	0-0	0-2	2-1	3-0
Brentford	1-0	1-1	5-2	1-0	–	0-1	3-3	5-1	2-0	2-0	0-2	2-1	0-1	2-0	1-2	3-0	2-2	5-1	2-3	2-0	3-1	2-3	2-1	2-0
Bristol City	1-1	1-2	4-1	2-1	1-1	–	0-2	1-0	1-1	0-1	0-2	1-1	2-2	1-1	0-1	2-1	2-1	1-0	1-0	1-1	0-1	2-0	3-2	2-2
Derby	0-3	3-1	0-0	2-1	3-1	1-1	–	2-0	2-0	1-4	0-2	1-0	2-2	0-0	0-1	2-1	2-1	6-1	1-0	1-1	0-1	3-2	3-2	2-1
Hull	1-3	0-1	2-0	6-0	2-0	0-2	1-2	–	2-0	0-1	1-1	2-1	0-0	0-2	0-3	2-2	3-1	2-2	0-3	3-0	3-2	3-2	1-0	1-0
Ipswich	1-1	1-1	2-2	2-1	1-1	0-1	1-1	1-1	–	2-3	0-2	2-3	0-0	0-2	2-2	2-2	3-1	2-2	0-2	1-1	0-1	3-2	1-0	2-2
Leeds	1-1	1-2	3-2	2-1	1-1	2-0	2-2	0-1	3-0	–	0-0	3-2	1-1	1-1	1-0	2-1	2-0	2-0	1-0	1-1	3-1	2-1	4-0	1-2
Middlesbrough	0-3	0-2	1-1	2-0	1-2	0-1	1-1	0-2	2-0	0-0	–	2-2	1-0	3-3	0-0	0-1	0-0	2-0	0-1	2-2	0-0	1-0	3-4	2-0
Millwall	2-1	0-2	0-2	2-0	1-2	1-2	2-4	1-1	2-1	2-1	0-0	–	1-3	1-0	0-0	0-0	1-0	1-1	3-0	2-1	1-0	1-2	2-0	2-0
Norwich	2-1	3-1	2-1	5-2	3-2	0-1	3-4	2-2	3-0	4-2	1-0	4-3	–	3-3	1-0	4-0	2-2	3-1	2-2	2-2	1-0	1-0	3-4	2-1
Nottm Forest	1-3	2-2	1-2	1-0	2-1	0-2	1-2	1-1	2-0	1-1	1-2	2-2	1-2	–	1-4	1-0	0-0	1-0	1-1	1-2	2-2	1-0	1-1	4-0
Preston	1-1	1-0	4-1	2-2	1-1	3-0	0-0	2-3	3-0	0-2	2-1	2-0	3-1	0-1	–	1-0	1-4	2-2	1-1	3-3	2-2	4-0	2-3	4-0
QPR	1-0	3-4	1-2	2-2	4-3	0-3	1-2	2-3	3-0	0-1	2-1	2-0	3-1	0-1	1-4	–	0-0	3-2	0-2	1-2	2-1	4-0	2-3	3-2
Reading	0-0	1-3	2-1	0-1	2-1	3-2	1-2	2-0	2-2	0-3	0-1	3-1	2-0	2-0	2-1	0-1	–	1-1	0-2	1-2	2-2	1-4	0-0	3-2
Rotherham	1-2	1-3	3-2	2-0	2-4	2-3	1-0	1-2	1-0	1-2	0-1	1-1	2-1	2-1	2-1	2-2	1-1	–	2-2	0-0	2-2	2-1	0-4	1-1
Sheff Utd	4-1	1-0	3-0	2-0	2-3	3-1	3-1	3-0	2-0	1-0	1-0	2-1	1-2	3-0	3-2	1-0	4-0	2-0	–	0-0	1-1	1-2	1-2	4-2
Sheff Wed	1-3	0-1	4-2	1-0	2-1	0-2	1-2	1-2	2-0	1-1	1-2	2-1	0-4	3-0	1-0	1-2	0-0	2-2	2-2	–	2-2	1-0	2-2	1-1
Stoke	1-1	0-1	2-3	1-1	0-2	0-2	1-2	2-1	2-0	2-1	0-0	1-0	0-1	2-0	0-2	2-2	0-0	2-2	0-2	3-1	–	1-0	0-1	0-3
Swansea	0-1	3-3	3-1	2-0	3-0	0-1	1-1	2-1	2-3	2-2	3-1	1-0	1-4	0-0	1-0	3-0	2-0	4-3	1-0	2-1	3-1	–	1-2	2-2
WBA	2-2	3-2	1-1	1-2	2-1	4-2	1-4	3-3	3-2	4-1	2-3	2-0	1-1	2-2	4-1	7-1	4-1	2-1	1-0	2-1	2-1	3-0	–	2-0
Wigan	3-0	0-3	3-1	5-2	1-3	1-3	0-1	3-2	1-1	1-2	0-0	1-0	2-2	2-2	2-1	2-0	0-0	1-0	0-3	3-2	0-0	0-0	1-0	–

SKY BET LEAGUE ONE RESULTS 2018–2019

Home \ Away	Accrington	Barnsley	Blackpool	Bradford	Bristol Rov	Burton	Charlton	Coventry	Doncaster	Fleetwood	Gillingham	Luton	Oxford	Peterborough	Plymouth	Portsmouth	Rochdale	Scunthorpe	Shrewsbury	Southend	Sunderland	Walsall	Wimbledon	Wycombe
Accrington	–	0-2	1-2	3-1	0-0	1-0	1-1	0-1	1-0	1-1	1-1	0-3	4-2	0-4	0-3	1-1	1-0	1-1	2-1	1-1	2-0	0-1	2-1	1-2
Barnsley	2-0	–	2-1	3-0	1-0	3-1	2-0	1-1	0-1	1-3	0-0	3-2	4-0	2-0	0-1	5-1	2-2	0-4	2-1	3-1	3-1	0-4	0-0	2-1
Blackpool	1-1	0-1	–	3-2	0-3	0-1	2-0	2-0	2-1	3-2	0-1	0-0	0-1	0-1	0-0	5-1	1-0	1-0	0-0	3-2	1-2	1-1	0-0	2-2
Bradford	3-0	0-2	1-4	–	0-0	2-0	2-3	4-1	2-1	2-1	4-0	2-2	1-0	0-1	2-3	1-1	0-0	3-1	2-1	1-1	2-0	4-0	0-0	0-0
Bristol Rov	1-2	2-1	0-3	0-0	–	3-1	0-0	2-4	0-4	0-1	2-1	1-0	2-2	3-1	0-0	0-1	4-2	1-2	1-1	1-1	2-0	0-1	2-0	0-1
Burton	5-2	3-1	3-0	1-1	1-0	–	1-2	1-0	1-0	0-0	2-3	2-1	1-1	1-2	0-0	1-2	1-2	0-0	2-1	1-2	0-2	0-0	2-0	3-1
Charlton	1-0	2-0	1-2	2-0	1-2	1-2	–	1-2	2-1	2-1	3-3	3-1	1-1	1-2	3-1	2-1	1-2	0-0	2-1	2-0	2-0	0-0	2-0	3-2
Coventry	1-1	1-0	0-0	0-2	4-1	2-0	1-2	–	2-1	1-1	1-1	2-1	1-1	1-1	0-2	2-1	0-1	4-0	1-1	1-0	2-1	0-0	1-1	1-0
Doncaster	1-2	0-0	0-2	2-0	0-4	2-0	1-2	2-0	–	0-4	3-3	3-1	1-1	1-1	2-0	0-0	0-1	0-0	0-2	1-2	2-3	3-0	1-1	3-0
Fleetwood	1-1	2-1	3-2	2-1	1-0	0-4	1-0	2-0	2-1	–	1-1	0-1	2-2	1-1	0-2	2-5	4-0	3-0	0-2	0-2	2-3	3-1	1-1	3-0
Gillingham	0-0	1-4	2-1	4-0	0-1	1-1	0-2	1-1	3-0	1-3	–	1-3	3-1	2-4	2-2	1-3	4-2	2-1	2-1	0-2	0-2	0-3	2-2	1-1
Luton	4-1	0-0	5-1	2-2	1-0	3-1	0-2	2-1	1-1	2-0	2-0	–	2-2	0-1	3-0	0-0	1-0	0-1	1-0	3-0	2-1	2-0	1-1	3-0
Oxford	2-3	2-2	2-0	1-0	0-2	3-1	0-2	2-1	2-2	1-2	2-0	3-1	–	0-1	3-1	3-1	3-3	0-3	0-2	1-1	0-3	0-1	1-2	2-1
Peterborough	0-1	0-3	0-1	1-2	2-1	1-0	1-2	1-1	2-2	0-1	2-0	2-3	2-2	–	1-0	2-3	2-1	1-1	2-2	1-0	0-3	2-0	1-2	4-2
Plymouth	0-3	0-3	1-0	3-0	1-1	2-3	1-0	0-1	1-1	1-1	3-0	0-0	3-0	1-5	–	2-3	5-1	3-2	2-0	0-2	1-0	2-0	1-2	1-1
Portsmouth	1-1	0-0	5-1	0-1	2-3	2-2	2-0	0-2	0-0	0-3	3-0	1-2	3-0	2-3	1-3	–	4-1	3-1	0-0	2-3	3-3	2-0	2-1	2-2
Rochdale	1-0	0-4	0-0	0-0	2-3	1-1	1-0	2-0	0-1	1-1	3-0	0-0	1-4	1-4	1-1	1-3	–	3-1	1-0	0-2	4-1	1-2	0-0	1-0
Scunthorpe	2-0	3-1	1-2	2-3	1-1	2-1	5-3	2-1	2-3	1-1	4-2	0-2	2-1	1-4	2-2	1-1	3-1	–	2-1	1-1	1-2	0-2	2-3	3-2
Shrewsbury	1-0	3-1	1-2	1-0	1-0	0-2	0-3	1-1	1-0	1-0	2-2	2-0	2-2	0-2	1-1	2-0	0-2	1-1	–	1-0	0-2	1-0	1-2	2-1
Southend Utd	3-0	0-3	1-0	3-2	2-1	1-2	0-3	1-2	2-3	1-1	0-2	2-3	2-3	2-3	1-2	3-3	1-2	0-0	0-2	–	1-1	3-0	0-1	1-1
Sunderland	2-2	4-2	1-1	1-0	2-1	2-1	1-1	4-2	2-1	1-1	4-2	2-1	2-1	2-3	2-0	1-1	4-1	3-0	1-0	3-0	–	2-1	1-0	2-1
Walsall	0-1	0-1	0-0	3-2	1-3	2-1	0-2	1-1	1-4	2-0	2-4	2-2	1-3	3-0	2-1	1-2	1-2	2-3	0-2	2-1	1-1	–	0-1	1-3
Wimbledon	1-4	1-4	0-0	0-1	1-1	0-0	1-1	1-2	0-3	0-2	1-1	2-1	1-1	1-0	1-0	2-3	2-0	2-3	1-1	2-2	3-0	1-3	–	1-2
Wycombe	1-2	2-1	2-2	1-2	0-1	3-1	3-2	1-0	3-0	1-1	2-2	3-0	2-1	4-2	1-1	1-2	1-0	1-0	2-1	1-1	0-2	2-1	2-1	–

SKY BET LEAGUE TWO RESULTS 2018–2019

	Bury	Cambridge	Carlisle	Cheltenham	Colchester	Crawley	Crewe	Exeter	Forest Green	Grimsby	Lincoln	Macclesfield	Mansfield	MK Dons	Morecambe	Newport	Northampton	Notts Co	Oldham	Port Vale	Stevenage	Swindon	Tranmere	Yeovil
Bury	–	0-3	0-1	4-1	2-0	1-2	1-4	2-0	0-1	0-0	2-1	1-4	2-1	1-0	2-3	5-1	0-0	0-0	4-2	1-0	0-1	1-2	1-1	0-1
Cambridge	2-2	–	1-2	0-1	2-3	2-0	0-2	1-0	0-2	1-0	1-2	1-0	1-1	0-2	1-2	4-3	3-2	3-2	1-1	1-0	0-1	0-3	2-1	0-0
Carlisle	3-2	2-0	–	2-0	4-2	4-2	0-3	0-3	0-2	0-1	2-1	1-1	3-2	2-3	2-2	3-1	3-1	1-3	6-0	1-0	0-1	1-3	0-2	1-0
Cheltenham	1-1	0-1	0-1	–	3-0	0-2	1-2	0-0	2-1	2-0	2-0	1-0	0-2	0-1	3-1	1-0	3-1	2-0	1-1	2-0	1-2	1-0	0-2	1-4
Colchester	1-2	3-0	1-1	2-0	–	3-1	1-1	1-2	1-2	1-0	1-0	3-2	2-3	0-4	2-0	2-2	1-2	1-1	0-2	2-0	1-2	1-0	0-2	3-1
Crawley	3-2	2-0	2-3	4-2	3-1	–	1-0	0-3	4-3	2-0	3-0	1-0	0-0	0-4	1-0	2-5	2-1	1-1	1-1	2-0	1-4	2-2	0-2	3-1
Crewe	1-1	2-0	2-1	0-2	1-1	1-0	–	1-2	1-2	2-0	1-2	1-2	0-0	4-2	1-1	1-0	0-2	0-2	0-3	0-1	1-3	2-2	3-1	2-0
Exeter	0-1	1-0	3-1	0-3	1-2	0-3	6-1	–	1-2	2-0	1-2	1-1	1-4	3-1	0-0	1-1	2-2	5-1	0-1	2-0	1-0	0-1	0-1	2-1
Forest Green	1-2	0-2	1-1	0-3	1-2	4-3	1-3	1-2	–	1-2	4-1	3-0	1-4	1-0	0-0	1-1	2-1	1-2	1-1	2-0	1-0	0-0	0-1	3-0
Grimsby	0-0	1-1	2-0	1-1	1-2	2-1	1-3	0-1	1-4	–	2-0	0-2	1-1	1-0	1-0	0-0	2-1	4-0	0-2	1-2	1-1	1-1	3-1	1-1
Lincoln	2-1	1-1	2-1	1-1	1-2	1-0	2-1	1-1	1-0	1-1	–	2-0	0-1	0-2	3-1	0-1	0-0	4-0	0-3	2-2	0-2	4-1	5-2	1-0
Macclesfield	1-4	2-2	2-1	1-1	2-0	0-1	2-0	1-4	2-1	1-2	1-1	–	1-1	1-3	3-1	0-0	0-5	3-1	2-0	2-2	2-2	4-1	1-1	1-0
Mansfield	2-1	1-0	1-0	4-2	1-1	2-0	3-3	2-1	1-0	2-1	0-1	1-1	–	1-0	1-1	1-0	4-0	2-1	2-1	1-1	1-2	3-0	3-0	2-0
MK Dons	1-0	6-0	1-0	3-2	0-1	2-0	4-2	1-0	2-3	3-0	1-1	1-1	1-0	–	2-0	1-2	1-0	2-1	2-1	1-1	1-2	0-0	3-0	2-0
Morecambe	2-3	3-0	2-0	0-1	0-4	0-0	1-1	0-0	0-0	1-0	1-1	1-3	0-0	1-1	–	1-1	3-1	2-1	2-1	1-0	2-2	3-1	0-0	2-2
Newport	5-1	2-0	2-0	0-0	2-2	2-5	1-0	1-1	1-1	0-0	0-2	4-2	1-0	2-1	4-0	–	3-1	1-1	0-2	0-0	1-2	0-1	0-0	0-6
Northampton	0-0	2-2	3-0	1-3	1-2	2-1	0-2	2-2	2-1	2-1	1-1	0-5	4-0	1-0	3-1	3-1	–	2-0	2-1	0-0	1-1	3-1	0-0	2-1
Notts Co	0-0	0-1	1-3	1-0	1-1	1-1	0-2	5-1	1-2	4-0	1-0	3-1	2-1	2-1	2-1	1-1	2-2	–	2-1	1-2	1-1	0-1	3-2	2-0
Oldham	4-2	2-1	1-3	0-0	0-2	3-3	0-3	0-1	1-1	0-2	2-1	2-0	2-1	2-1	2-1	0-2	2-5	0-0	–	0-0	1-4	1-2	3-2	1-0
Port Vale	1-0	3-0	1-0	3-0	2-0	1-0	0-1	2-0	2-0	1-2	0-1	1-4	1-3	1-1	1-0	0-1	2-2	0-0	1-4	–	2-2	0-1	1-2	1-0
Stevenage	0-1	0-1	0-1	2-0	0-1	1-0	1-3	2-1	1-4	1-0	2-6	1-0	0-1	1-0	1-0	0-2	2-5	2-2	1-4	3-2	–	0-3	2-2	2-0
Swindon	1-2	3-2	0-4	3-2	0-1	2-1	2-2	2-0	0-1	1-1	2-2	0-0	3-2	0-0	4-0	1-4	3-1	1-0	0-0	1-1	0-0	–	3-2	2-0
Tranmere	1-1	–	0-1	1-0	1-1	5-1	3-1	3-1	1-0	3-0	1-0	3-2	3-1	3-4	0-0	1-1	1-1	3-2	1-1	1-0	2-2	–	–	0-0
Yeovil	0-1	1-0	0-0	1-0	3-1	3-1	2-1	3-0	0-1	1-0	0-1	1-0	2-0	1-1	2-2	1-2	1-1	1-1	0-0	1-0	2-0	0-3	0-0	–

HIGHLIGHTS OF THE PREMIER LEAGUE SEASON 2018–19

AUGUST 2018

10 Luke Shaw scores his first career goal as Manchester United defeat Leicester 2-1 in the season's opening fixture.

11 Summer signings feature prominently in the first full programme. Richarlison nets both goals for Everton in a 2-2 draw away to promoted Wolves, whose second equaliser is scored by on-loan Raul Jimenez. Everton, under new manager Marco Silva, have Phil Jagielka shown a straight red card for a dangerous challenge on Diogo Jota. Maurizio Sarri makes a successful start as Chelsea manager – 3-0 at Huddersfield with Jorginho marking his debut with a penalty. Jeffrey Schlupp opens his account for Crystal Palace at the start of his third season at the club to pave the way for a 2-0 victory at Fulham, while the other promoted side, Cardiff, lose by the same scoreline at Bournemouth, despite Neil Etheridge saving Callum Wilson's penalty. A brace by Roberto Pereyra delivers a third 2-0 result, this one for Watford against Brighton. Tottenham's 2-1 success at Newcastle is notable for goal-line technology confirming Jan Vertonghen's goal by just nine millimetres.

12 Manchester City open their title defence with a 2-0 win at Arsenal in Unai Emery's first match in charge after replacing Arsene Wenger at the Emirates. Sadio Mane is on the mark twice for Liverpool, who register their biggest opening-day win at Anfield since 1932 – 4-0 in Manuel Pellegrini's first game in charge of West Ham. Southampton and Burnley share a goalless draw, with Burnley's Joe Hart one of eight goalkeepers making Premier League debuts for new clubs over the weekend.

18 Harry Kane breaks his summer scoring jinx with a goal for the first time in the month of August, while Kieran Trippier reproduces his free-kick for England against Croatia in the World Cup as Tottenham overcome Fulham 3-1. Neil Etheridge saves another penalty, from Kenedy, and this time Cardiff take something from the match – a goalless draw against Newcastle, who have substitute Isaac Hayden sent off for going through the back of Josh Murphy. Jamie Vardy is also shown a straight red card, for a dangerous challenge on Matt Doherty, but Leicester hold on for a 2-0 win over Wolves in which James Maddison scores on his home debut. Chelsea lead Arsenal 2-0, are pegged back against the run of play, then have the final say with an 81st minute strike from Marcos Alonso. A fine solo goal by Callum Wilson sparks Bournemouth's recovery from a goal down at the London Stadium, where West Ham's 2-1 defeat is compounded by six bookings and a £25,000 fine. A first for Danny Ings for Southampton is not enough to prevent a 2-1 defeat at Everton.

19 Sergio Aguero scores his 13th hat-trick, nine of them in the Premier League, for Manchester City in the 6-1 defeat of Huddersfield, whose consolation from Jon Gorenc Stankovic is his first for the club. Glenn Murray marks his 200th league appearance for Brighton with the opening goal in a 3-2 success against Manchester United. Andre Gray registers Watford's first away goal since January to put them on the way to a 3-1 victory over Burnley, who have James Tarkowski on the scoresheet for the first time.

20 Crystal Palace defender Aaron Wan-Bissaka receives a straight red card for bringing down Mohamed Salah in a 2-0 home defeat by Liverpool.

25 Bournemouth's capacity for retrieving losing positions – a league record 25 points salvaged since the start of the previous season – earns a 2-2 draw after they trail Everton 2-0 in a match of two sendings-off. Eddie Howe's team lose Adam Smith for pulling back Theo Walcott, with the defender also involved in the earlier dismissal of Everton's Richarlison for an attempted headbutt. Huddersfield's Jonathan Hogg is shown another straight red card, for a scuffle with Harry Arter, in a goalless draw against Cardiff, while Southampton's Pierre-Emile Hojbjerg receives a second yellow in a 2-1 home defeat by Leicester. Harry Maguire's 25-yard shot in stoppage-time settles this game. Liverpool maintain a 100 per cent record, thanks to the only goal of the game from Mohamed Salah against Brighton, but Aymeric

Laporte's first for Manchester City is not enough for victory against Wolves, who deserve their 1-1 draw. Jack Wilshere has a frustrating return to his former club as Arsenal come from behind to see off West Ham 3-1.

26 Fulham are up and running with a 4-2 success against Burnley, delivered by a brace from Aleksandar Mitrovic and first goals for Jean Michael Seri and on-loan Andre Schurrle. Chelsea, with a 2-1 victory at Newcastle, and Watford, winners by the same scoreline against Crystal Palace, join Liverpool on maximum points from three games.

27 Tottenham also end the month with nine points after a 3-0 victory over Manchester United at Old Trafford, Lucas Moura scoring twice.

SEPTEMBER 2018

1 Kyle Walker opens his account for Manchester City in style – a 30-yard drive delivering a 2-1 win over Newcastle. Record-signing Adama Traore also celebrates after his first for Wolves in stoppage time breaks the deadlock at West Ham and gives his new side their first three points. Liverpool goalkeeper Alisson, however, is left red-faced despite a 2-1 win at Leicester, the £67m signing conceding their first goal of the season to Rachid Ghezzal after being dispossessed trying to execute a 'Cruyff turn.' Brighton are in trouble at home to Fulham when Pascal Gross has a penalty saved by Marcus Bettinelli and their opponents take a 2-0 lead. But Glenn Murray pulls one back, then earns a point by converting their second spot-kick of the afternoon. Southampton go one better at Crystal Palace with a 2-0 success, despite Charlie Austin having his penalty kept out by Wayne Hennessey. Chelsea record a fourth straight victory – 2-0 against Bournemouth.

2 Sir Elton John, the club's honorary life-president, sees Watford overcome Tottenham in the league for the first time since 1987, thanks to headers from Troy Deeney and Craig Cathcart for a 2-1 scoreline. Substitute Marcus Rashford is shown a straight red card for pushing his head into Phil Bardsley's face and Paul Pogba has a penalty saved by Joe Hart. But Manchester United still return to winning ways – 2-0 at Burnley with two goals from Romelu Lukaku. Cardiff's hopes rise when loanee Victor Camarasa scores his and his team's first goal on the stroke of half-time, then fade as Arsenal prevail 3-2 with an 81st minute Alexandre Lacazette strike.

15 An Eden Hazard hat-trick – his third goal a penalty – enables Chelsea to come from behind and defeat Cardiff 4-1. His side keep pace with Liverpool, who deliver their best start since the 1990-91 season by beating Tottenham 2-1 in front of a Wembley crowd of 80,000-plus. Manchester United end Watford's 100 per cent opening by the same scoreline at Vicarage Road, where central defender Chris Smalling finishes like a striker with a hooked volley for their second goal. United have Nemanja Matic dismissed in added time and Leicester captain Wes Morgan is also shown a second yellow card in the 4-2 defeat at Bournemouth, who have Ryan Fraser on the mark twice. Mathias Jorgensen's first Huddersfield goal comes in a 3-1 defeat at Leicester. Manchester City treat two special mascots for the day – Vera Cohen (102) and sister Olga Halon (98) – to a 3-0 win over Fulham.

16 Manuel Pellegrini celebrates his 65th birthday with a first victory as West Ham manager – 3-1 at Everton as Andriy Yarmolenko's first start brings the Ukraine winger his first two goals for the club.

17 Brighton retrieve a two-goal deficit for a 2-2 draw at Southampton, Glenn Murray equalising with a stoppage-time penalty.

22 Record-signing Riyad Mahrez scores his first two goals for the club and record-marksman Sergio Aguero takes his tally to 205 on his 300th appearance as Manchester City sweep aside Cardiff 5-0 away from home. Liverpool also set a new mark, beating Southampton 3-0 for a seventh successive victory – in Premier League and Champions League matches – to start the season. Burnley are up and running as Aaron Lennon opens his account and substitute Ashley Barnes nets twice to see off Bournemouth 4-0. There is also a first goal for Manchester United's Brazilian striker Fred and for Joao Moutinho which earns Wolves a 1-1 draw at Old Trafford, underlining their enterprising start after winning promotion.

23 Liverpool are left as the only team with maximum points after Chelsea are held to a goalless draw at West Ham.

29 Record-signing Felipe Anderson opens his account as West Ham add to Manchester United's early season problems with a 3-1 victory. In contrast, Manchester City beat Brighton 2-0 to return to the top of the table on goal difference ahead of Liverpool, who salvage a 1-1 draw at Chelsea with an 89th minute equaliser struck from 25 yards by Daniel Sturridge. Chelsea are two points behind the leaders. Jonny Otto is also on the mark for his new club, completing a 2-0 victory for Wolves against Southampton. Harry Kane's brace, his second a penalty, delivers Tottenham's 2-0 win at Huddersfield, while two for Gylfi Sigurdsson in Everton's 3-0 defeat of Fulham come after he strikes the bar with a spot-kick.

OCTOBER 2018

1 David Brooks puts Bournemouth on the way to a 2-1 win over Crystal Palace with his first goal for the club.

6 Pressure builds on Jose Mourinho as Newcastle score twice in the first ten minutes at Old Trafford, the second goal from Yoshinori Muto his first for the club. But it eases as Manchester United rally in the second-half to win 3-2 with a 90th minute Alexis Sanchez header. Wolves set a Premier League record with an eighth successive unchanged starting line-up and maintain their impressive opening by beating Crystal Palace 1-0. Joshua King nets twice as Bournemouth record their biggest away success, 4-0 against Watford after the home side have Christian Kabasele sent off for conceding the penalty which King converts for his first goal. Leicester's Wes Morgan also receives a second yellow – his second dismissal in three games – and despite a first goal for Ricardo Pereira on his 25th birthday, they are beaten 2-1 at home by Gylfi Sigurdsson's fourth in four games for Everton. Joe Ralls is shown a straight red for scything down Lucas Moura in Cardiff's 1-0 defeat by Tottenham.

7 Liverpool and Manchester City finish goalless after City's Riyad Mahrez misses the chance to settle the biggest game of the season so far by firing an 85th minute penalty over the bar. Ross Barkley scores his first goal for Chelsea in their 3-0 victory at Southampton, whose six bookings incur a £25,000 fine. Arsenal overwhelm Fulham 5-1 at Craven Cottage, with Alexandre Lacazette and Pierre-Emerick Aubameyang both on the mark twice.

20 Ross Barkley comes off the bench to preserve Chelsea's unbeaten record with a 96th minute goal after two from Anthony Martial put Manchester United 2-1 ahead at Stamford Bridge. The equaliser provokes a touchline skirmish, assistant Chelsea coach Marco Ianni taunting the United bench and Jose Mourinho having to be restrained by a steward. Kevin De Bruyne, out for two months with a knee injury, returns for Manchester City, who make Joe Hart's return to the Etihad an unhappy one by winning 5-0 against the goalkeeper's new club Burnley. Cardiff double their goals tally for the season with their first success – 4-2 against Fulham. But Newcastle are still looking after going down 1-0 to Brighton, the first time the club have lost their opening five home games. West Ham's Andriy Yarmolenko sustains an achilles tendon injury in the 1-0 defeat by Tottenham and is ruled out for the season.

21 Jordan Pickford's penalty save from Luka Milivojevic, followed by manager Marco Silva's triple substitution, deliver Everton's 2-0 victory over Crystal Palace. Dominic Calvert-Lewin breaks the deadlock by heading in Ademola Lookman's cross after 87 minutes and Cenk Tosun strikes two minutes later.

22 Unai Emery also backs a winner in Pierre Emerick-Aubameyang, who comes off the bench to score twice in three minutes to give Arsenal a 3-1 win over Leicester.

27 Tragedy follows Leicester's 1-1 draw against West Ham. Club owner Vichai Srivaddhanaprabha and four others die when their helicopter crashes outside the King Power Stadium seconds after taking off from the pitch. Liverpool concede their first Premier League goal at Anfield since February, but by then are on the way to beating Cardiff 4-1 with two from Sadio Mane and Xherdan Shaqiri's first for the club. Glenn Murray's 100th for Brighton brings a third successive top-flight victory for the first time since 1981 – 1-0 against Wolves, who change their starting line-up for the first time in ten games. Watford's Roberto Pereyra beats five men to score one of the season's outstanding solo goals when putting Watford on the way to a

3-0 success against Huddersfield. Fulham's Kevin McDonald is sent off for two yellow cards in the 3-0 home defeat by Bournemouth, for whom Callum Wilson scores two goals, one a penalty. Mark Noble's straight red comes for a lunging tackle on Leicester's Wilfred Ndidi, whose 89th minute equaliser cancels out Fabian Balburna's first West Ham goal.

28 Crystal Palace captain Luka Milivojevic converts two penalties – their first goals of the season at Selhurst Park – for a 2-2 draw which ends Arsenal's run of 11 successive wins in all competitions. Paul Pogba has his spot-kick saved by Jordan Pickford, but puts away the rebound from the goalkeeper as Manchester United overcome Everton 2-1. Chelsea make light of the absence of Eden Hazard, out with a back complaint, to defeat Burnley 4-0 at Turf Moor.

29 Riyad Mahrez, a member of Leicester's title-winning side in 2016, dedicates his winning goal for Manchester City against Tottenham, to Vichai Srivaddhanaprabha. For the first time in the Premier League era, the three leading teams are all unbeaten after ten matches, with City top on goal difference ahead of Liverpool and Chelsea two points behind on 24.

NOVEMBER 2018

3 Leicester put their emotions to one side to win 1-0 at Cardiff. Goalscorer Demarai Gray is booked by Lee Probert after removing his shirt to reveal a personal tribute to the late chairman and the referee is criticised in some quarters. But manager Claude Puel has no complaint about Probert sticking to the letter of the law. Newcastle put an end to their worst start to a top-flight season since 1898, ten games without a win, by beating Watford 1-0 with a goal by Ayoze Perez. Felipe Anderson nets two in West Ham's 4-2 defeat of Burnley. So does Richarlison as Everton see off Brighton 3-1. Tottenham's third match in six days – one in the Champions League – brings a 3-2 victory at Wolves, while the day's big match, Arsenal against Liverpool, ends 1-1.

4 Raheem Sterling, in Manchester City's 6-1 victory over Southampton, and Alvaro Morata, as Chelsea beat Crystal Palace 3-1, are also two-goal marksmen.

5 Huddersfield's first goal at home brings their first three points. They come courtesy of a header into his own net by Fulham's Timothy Fosu-Mensah for a 1-0 scoreline.

10 What a difference a week makes. After conceding two penalties on his Premier League debut against Wolves, Tottenham's 20-year-old Argentine defender Juan Foyth heads the only goal at Crystal Palace. On-loan Salomon Rondon opens his account for Newcastle with a brace for a 2-1 success against Bournemouth, who have Jefferson Lerma on the mark for the first time. Sol Bamba's 90th minute goal enables Cardiff to edge out Brighton 2-1 in Neil Warnock's 100th game in charge. Unlike Leicester's Demarai Gray, Bamba is not booked by Martin Atkinson for removing his shirt in celebration. Brighton have Dale Stephens shown a straight red for a dangerous tackle on Greg Cunningham. Another emotional afternoon for Leicester, their first home game since the helicopter tragedy, ends in a goalless draw against Burnley.

11 Manchester City complete a 3-1 win over Manchester United through Ilkay Gundogan at the end of a move spanning 44 passes and involving every outfield player The results leaves United 12 points adrift and effectively out of the title reckoning. Another eye-catching goal puts Liverpool on the way to a 2-0 win over Fulham, Mohamed Salah scoring it in a lightening counter-attack 14 seconds after Aleksandar Mitrovic has a header disallowed at the other end. Fulham manager Slavisa Jokanovic is sacked three days later after seven successive league and cup defeats. Chelsea's Maurizio Sarri sets a new record for the longest unbeaten run at the start of a Premier League managerial career – 12 games after a goalless draw against Everton.

24 Claudio Ranieri, Leicester's title-winning manager in 2016, makes a successful start as the new appointment at Craven Cottage. Two goals by Aleksandar Mitrovic, his first for two months, set up Fulham's 3-2 victory over Southampton, for whom Stuart Armstrong opens his account with a brace. Leroy Sane also gets two as Manchester City sweep aside West Ham 4-0, while a 25-yard free-kick from Trent Alexander Arnold highlights Liverpool's 3-0 success at Watford. But Chelsea surrender their unbeaten record, going down 3-1 away to

Tottenham, whose third is a fine solo goal by Son Heung-min, his first of the season in the league. Liverpool's result is clouded by the dismissal of captain Jordan Henderson, who misses the Merseyside derby. Leicester's James Maddison is also sent off for two yellow cards – the second for diving – in a 1-1 draw at Brighton. City end the month on 35 points, two ahead of Liverpool, with Tottenham up to third on 30.

25 Aaron Mooy scores both goals in Huddersfield's 2-0 victory away to Wolves.

26 Newcastle overcome one of the misses of the season – Matt Ritchie from three yards – to score a third successive win – 2-1 at Burnley.

DECEMBER 2018

1 The fastest goal of the season so far, Mathias Jorgensen's header after 54 seconds, boosts Huddersfield's chances of another three points. But they lose Steve Mounie, for scraping Yves Bissouma's shin, and Brighton take advantage to edge the points 2-1, their second goal from Florin Androne his first for the club. Watford's Etienne Capoue also receives a straight red card, for a two-footed challenge on Kelechi Iheanacho in a 2-0 defeat at Leicester. Andros Townsend clinches a first home win of the season for Crystal Palace, 2-0 against Burnley, with a 30-yard drive. Javier Hernandez scores twice at St James' Park as West Ham end Newcastle's successful sequence 3-0, while Manchester United salvage a point after trailing 2-0 at struggling Southampton, whose manager Mark Hughes is sacked two days later. At the top, Manchester City see off Bournemouth 3-1.

2 Derby-day drama at Anfield and the Emirates. Liverpool and Everton are deadlocked going into the sixth minute of added time when substitute Divock Origi punishes a mistake by Jordan Pickford to give the home side a record fifth Premier League victory at the death against their Merseyside rivals. Arsenal take the honours in north London in a match of six goals, two of them penalties, seven yellow cards, a sending-off and a touchline clash between rival players. Pierre-Emerick Aubameyang nets twice, one a spot-kick, and Lucas Torreira scores his first for the club in the 4-2 success against Tottenham, who have Jan Vertonghen dismissed for a second yellow card.

4 Despite playing with ten men for more than an hour after Shane Duffy's dismissal for butting Patrick van Aanholt, Brighton are 3-1 winners over Crystal Palace, helped by Leon Balogun's first goal for the club, scored with his first touch after coming off the bench. Terence Kongolo's first is not enough for Huddersfield, who go down 2-1 at Bournemouth. Manchester City continue to force the pace with victory by the same scoreline at Watford. Lucas Perez becomes the first West Ham player since Paulo Wanchope in 2000 to score twice from the bench in the Premier League, his goals setting up a 3-1 victory over Cardiff after Lukasz Fabianski saves a Joe Ralls penalty at 0-0.

5 Substitute Roberto Firmino scores with his first touch as Liverpool come from behind to win 3-1 at Burnley and keep the pressure on Manchester City. With Chelsea and Arsenal dropping points, the prospect of a three-horse title race emerges. Chelsea go down 2-1 at Molineux, where 18-year-old Morgan Gibbs-White makes his first Wolves start in the Premier League, plays in Raul Jimenez for their equaliser and offers more evidence of his enormous potential. Arsenal are twice pegged back by Manchester United in a 2-2 draw at Old Trafford – the first match between the teams since 1986 not to involve Sir Alex Ferguson or Arsene Wenger. Southampton's new manager, Ralph Hasenhuttl, watches from the stands as his side lose 3-1 to Tottenham after hitting the woodwork three times and being denied further by fine Hugo Lloris saves. The attendance of 33,000 is Tottenham's lowest for a Premier League fixture at Wembley. Fulham and Leicester also finish all square, 1-1, in new Fulham manager Claudio Ranieri's first meeting with the club he turned into champions.

8 Manchester City are beaten for the first time, 2-0 at Chelsea by goals from N'Golo Kante and David Luiz. The result leaves Liverpool as the only undefeated team after Mohamed Salah's hat-trick in a 4-0 success at Bournemouth. Burnley end a run of eight games without a win, thanks to the only goal from James Tarkowski against Brighton. But Southampton remain with a single victory all season after going down by the same scoreline at Cardiff in Ralph Hasenhuttl's first match in charge. West Ham celebrate a third top-flight victory in eight days, with three goals in each one, for the first time since 1982 – 3-2 against Crystal Palace. Felipe Anderson's strike is one of three in the day's programme to catch the eye, alongside Tottenham's Son Heung min (2-0 at Leicester) and Manchester United's Ashley Young (4-1 against Fulham). Claudio Ranieri's side have Andre-Frank Zambo Anguissa sent off for a second yellow card.

9 Newcastle's DeAndre Yedlin is shown a straight red for pulling back Diogo Jota in a seventh defeat in nine home games – 2-1 against Wolves, whose winner from Matt Doherty comes in the fifth minute of stoppage-time.

10 Lucas Digne's 96th minute free-kick, his first goal for the club, earns Everton a 2-2 draw with Watford, for whom Ben Foster saves a penalty from Gylfi Sigurdsson.

15 Gabriel Jesus, with a single goal all season, scores twice as Manchester City overcome Everton 3-1. Tottenham stay in touch, thanks to a 90th minute Christian Eriksen strike against Burnley. Captain Luka Milivojevic, from 30 yards, also gives Crystal Palace a 1-0 victory, over Leicester – their first three points without Wilfried Zaha in the side for two years. West Ham move into the top half of the table by beating Fulham 2-0 at Craven Cottage – their fourth straight victory with 11 goals scored. Wolves defeat Bournemouth by the same scoreline for a third successive top-flight win for the first time since 1980. A good day, too, for 19-year-old Domingos Quina, who becomes Watford's youngest Premier League scorer in their 3-2 success against Cardiff.

16 Xherdan Shaqiri comes off the bench to score twice with the aid of deflected shots and give Liverpool a 3-1 win over Manchester United, a result followed by the sacking of United manager Jose Mourinho with his side 19 points behind their arch-rivals. Another substitute, Charlie Austin, heads an 85th winner for Southampton against Arsenal in Ralph Hasenhuttl's first home game. It follows two headed goals by team-mate Danny Ings, two equalisers from Henrikh Mkhitaryan and brings to an end of Arsenal's 22-match unbeaten run in all competitions.

21 Virgil van Dijk scores his first Premier League goal for Liverpool in a 2-0 away victory over Wolves.

22 Pep Guardiola's gamble in putting Sergio Aguero and Kevin De Bruyne on the bench and playing John Stones in midfield backfires. Crystal Palace take advantage to win 3-2 at the Etihad, with Andros Townsend's stunning 30-yard volley a strong contender for goal of the season. Ole Gunnar Solskjaer enjoys immediate success as Jose Mourinho's interim replacement – 5-1 at Cardiff in which Jesse Lingard's brace includes a penalty. United score five for the first time in the league since Sir Alex Ferguson's last match in charge against West Bromwich Albion in 2013. Also on the mark twice are Arsenal's Pierre Emerick Aubameyang (3-1 v Burnley) and Bournemouth's David Brooks (2-0 v Brighton). Brighton have Lewis Dunk dismissed for two yellow cards. Michael Obafemi, 18, becomes Southampton's youngest Premier League scorer – and the league's youngest marksman from the Republic of Ireland – when wrapping up a 3-1 success at Huddersfield.

23 Tottenham come from behind to inflict a crushing defeat on Everton at Goodison Park. Harry Kane and Son-Heung-min are both on the mark twice in a 6-2 scoreline which suggests their side may have a say who becomes champions.

26 The top of the table takes on an entirely different complexion after Manchester City lose for the third time in four games. Again missing the influential Fernandinho, they go down 2-1 at Leicester and have Fabian Delph shown a straight red card for a late challenge on Ricardo Pereira, scorer of his side's winning goal. Liverpool, meanwhile, put four without reply past Newcastle, a scoreline completed by Fabinho's first goal for the club. And Tottenham overwhelm Bournemouth 5-0, with Son-Heung-min again netting twice. Yerry Mina's first for Everton is followed by two from Lucas Digne in a 5-1 victory at Burnley, whose consolation comes from Ben Gibson on his first Premier League appearance. Eden Hazard scores his 100th goal for Chelsea, then adds a second from the penalty spot to deliver a 2-1 win at Watford. Paul Pogba, like his team revitalised after Jose Mourinho's departure, also gets two as Huddersfield are seen off 3-1.

29 Rampant Liverpool extend their lead at the top to nine points as Roberto Firmino scores a hat-trick, completed with a penalty, in the 5-1 drubbing of Arsenal, who are overwhelmed after taking the lead though Ainsley Maitland-Niles's first goal for the club. Tottenham also lead, through Harry Kane on the day he receives an MBE in the New Year honours. But Kane is later booked for diving and his side are swept aside in the second-half by three Wolves goals in 15 minutes. Claudio Ranieri rages on the touchline at his French striker Aboubakar Kamara for defying team orders by taking a penalty – and having it kept out by Huddersfield's Jonas Lossl. The Fulham manager's annoyance is still evident after Aleksandar Mitrovic gives his side a 1-0 victory in stoppage-time. Spot-kick drama, too, at Leicester, where Cardiff's Neil Etheridge denies James Maddison – his third such save of the season – then sees team-mate Victor Camarasa strike the only goal from 25 yards in added time.

30 Manchester City, with Fernandinho back, close the gap by winning 3-1 at Southampton, who have their scorer Pierre-Emile Hogbjerg sent off for a lunging tackle on the Brazilian. Eric Bailly also receives a straight red for scything down Bournemouth's Ryan Fraser, but Manchester United's revival continues with a 4-1 success and two more goals for Paul Pogba. Dwight McNeil, 19, scores his first goal for Burnley, who defeat West Ham 2-0.

JANUARY 2019

1 Harry Kane puts Tottenham on the way to a 3-0 victory at Cardiff and has now scored against all 28 of the top-flight teams he has faced.

2 Huddersfield suffer a club-record eighth straight defeat, despite leading Burnley through Steve Mounie, their first striker to score this season. They have Christopher Schindler sent off for a second bookable offence and go down 2-1 to their fellow-strugglers, who lose substitute Robbie Brady to a straight red for a tackle from behind on Isaac Mbenza. On-loan Jordan Ayew nets for the first time for Crystal Palace, 2-0 winners away to Wolves, while Romelu Lukaku scores with his first touch after coming off the bench as Manchester United prevail 2-0 at Newcastle. West Ham retrieve a 2-0 deficit for a point against Brighton, thanks to a brace from Marko Arnautovic. Troy Deeney also gets two for Watford, who share six goals at Bournemouth, all coming in a madcap first-half.

3 Liverpool surrender the only unbeaten record, losing 2-1 to goals from Sergio Aguero and Leroy Sane for Manchester City at the Etihad. They still lead the defending champions by four points, with Tottenham a further two points behind in third position.

12 A controversial penalty incident proves to be the final straw for Huddersfield manager David Wagner. Referee Lee Mason points to the spot for a challenge by Cardiff's Joe Bennett on Florent Hadergjonaj, then reverses the decision after consulting his assistant. A goalless draw ends Huddersfield's losing streak, but two days later Wagner leaves the club by mutual consent. There is more woe for Claudio Ranieri as Joe Bryan and Denis Odoi concede own goals in the space of three minutes as Fulham go down 2-1 at Burnley. Craig Cathcart also puts through his own goal at Crystal Palace. But the defender makes amends with the equaliser and substitute Tom Cleverley, out for the best part of a year with an achilles injury, volleys Watford's winner. Declan Rice gives West Ham victory over Arsenal with his first for the club, while Liverpool are also 1-0 winners, courtesy of Mohamed Salah's penalty at Brighton. Southampton overcome the dismissal of Yan Valery for a second yellow card to move out of the bottom three with a 2-1 win at Leicester, earned by first goals of the season from James Ward-Prowse (pen) and Shane Long – each of Long's last four goals for the club having come under different managers.

13 Marcus Rashford puts Manchester United ahead at Wembley, David de Gea defies every Tottenham attempt to equalise and Ole Gunnar Solskjaer's winning start extends to six matches in all competitions – a club record. Tottenham lose Harry Kane to an ankle injury and face a potential striking crisis with Son Heung-min away on international duty at the Asian Cup. On-loan Kurt Zouma heads his first goal for Everton, who defeat Bournemouth 2-0.

14 Gabriel Jesus makes it seven in three appearances in all competitions with two goals, one a penalty, in Manchester City's 3-0 victory over Wolves, who have Willy Boly shown a straight red card for a follow-through on Bernardo Silva.

19 In a contender for game of the season, Diogo Jota completes a hat-trick in stoppage-time to give Wolves a 4-3 win over Leicester. Manager Nuno Espirito Santo celebrates on the pitch with his players and is sent to the stands. Drama, too, at Anfield, where Liverpool concede as many goals as in all ten previous home games – and finish with ten men after James Milner is shown a second yellow card. But they, too, prevail 4-3, with Mohamed Salah on the mark twice. Newcastle score three in the league, without replay, for the first time this season as centre-back Fabian Schar opens his account for the club with two of them. Everton's Lucas Digne scores one of the season's most bizarre goals, directing the ball into his own net from 20 yards while chasing down Nathan Redmond in a 2-1 defeat at Southampton. The race for Champions League places hots up, with Arsenal beating Chelsea 2-0 and Manchester United defeating Brighton 2-1. Arsenal's performance is clouded by a ruptured ligament sustained by Hector Bellerin, ruling him out for the rest of the season.

20 Harry Winks scores in stoppage-time to give Tottenham a 2-1 victory at Fulham, but there is another injury blow for his side as Dele Alli limps off with a damaged hamstring. Danilo's first goal of the season sets Manchester City on the way to 3-0 success at Huddersfield.

29 An eventful night at the top and bottom of the table. Sergio Aguero scores the Premier League's fastest goal of the season so far, after 24 seconds at St James' Park, but Manchester City's title hopes are damaged as Salomon Rondon and Matt Ritchie with a penalty give Newcastle a priceless win in their bid to avoid the drop. Fellow strugglers Fulham come from behind even more dramatically. They overhaul Brighton's 2-0 lead, established by Glenn Murray, with a brace from Aleksandar Mitrovic and first goals for the club by loanees Calum Chambers and Luciano Vietto for a 4-2 success. Manchester United also trail 2-0, with three minutes of regulation time remaining against Burnley, before rallying for a point through Paul Pogba's penalty and Victor Lindelof's first for the club. The result ends Ole Gunnar Solskjaer's eight-match winning start in all competitions. Poignantly, record-signing Emiliano Sala is listed as a Cardiff player on the match-day programme at the Emirates following the tragic loss of the striker in a plane crash. The side he never played for lose 2-1 to Arsenal, but manager Neil Warnock praises the commitment of his players in difficult circumstances. Jan Siewert sees Huddersfield slip closer to a return to the Championship in his first match as manager – a 1-0 defeat by Everton, who have substitute Lucas Digne shown a straight red card for tripping Adama Diakhaby.

30 Liverpool also drop points after scoring quickly, Harry McGuire cancelling out Sadio Mane's third-minute strike. But they move five points clear of Manchester City on 61 points, with Tottenham third on 54 after Son Heung-min scores on his return from international duty in the 2-1 defeat of Watford. Chelsea suffer their heaviest Premier League loss since 1996, and drop out of the top-four for the first time, going down 4-0 at Bournemouth, for whom Joshua King nets twice. Wilfried Zaha issues an apology for his dismissal in Crystal Palace's 1-1 draw against Southampton – a yellow card followed immediately by a red for sarcastically applauding referee Andre Marriner.

FEBRUARY 2019

2 Cardiff display admirable resolve on an emotional afternoon when Emiliano Sala should have been making his home debut for the club. Bobby Reid, on his 26th birthday, scores both goals against Bournemouth – the first a penalty, the second 15 seconds into the second-half with manager Neil Warnock still in the tunnel – to double his tally for the season. Afterwards, Warnock is in tears amid a crescendo of noise from supporters. Son Heung-min keeps Tottenham's title hopes alive with his ninth goal in ten games in all competitions for a 1-0 victory over Newcastle. Chelsea's new striker, Gonzalo Higuain, opens his account with a brace and Eden Hazard also nets twice, the first a penalty, in a 5-0 win over Huddersfield. Burnley are awarded their first spot-kick in 68 Premier League matches, won by 38-year-old new-signing Peter Crouch and converted in stoppage-time by Ashley Barnes for a 1-1 draw against Southampton. Two on-loan players score their first goals at Goodison Park, Andre Gomes for Everton and Leander Dendoncker, who completes an impressive 3-1 success for Wolves.

3 Sergio Aguero scores his 14th hat-trick for the club, ten in the Premier League, as Manchester City defeat Arsenal 3-1. Marcus Rashford marks his 100th Premier League appearance for Manchester United with the only goal at Leicester.

4 Liverpool are held 1-1 at West Ham – and learn that Joe Gomez, out for two months with a fractured leg, may not return for another six weeks after surgery.

5 Manchester City complete a hard-earned 2-0 victory at Everton with a goal by Gabriel Jesus in the seventh minute of stoppage-time.

9 Burnley's resurgence brings with it a club-record seventh Premier League match unbeaten – a 3-1 victory at Brighton achieved by two-goal Chris Wood and another penalty from Ashley Barnes. Delight, too, for Cardiff, who secure back-to-back top-flight wins for the first time since 1962 when beating Southampton 2-1 at St Mary's with a stoppage-time goal by Kenneth Zohore, two minutes after his side concede an equaliser. Sadio Mane, on the mark for the fourth successive game, puts Liverpool on the way to defeating Bournemouth 3-0, while two goals by Paul Pogba, the second a penalty, points Manchester United to a top-four place for the first time after a 3-0 success at Fulham. Everton's Kurt Zouma is sent off for two yellow cards for dissent after the 1-0 defeat at Watford. The Premier League credit Karlan Grant with his first Huddersfield goal on his home debut in a 2-1 defeat by Arsenal after it is initially given as a Saed Kolasinac own goal.

10 Sergio Aguero equals Alan Shearer's record of 11 Premier League hat-tricks as Manchester City overwhelm Chelsea 6-0 – the biggest win of the season. He becomes City's all-time top league scorer on 160 goals. Chelsea's defeat is their heaviest for 28 years. Jamie Vardy is summoned from the bench to take a penalty with Leicester trailing to a Davinson Sanchez header for Tottenham – his first goal for the club. Hugo Lloris saves the spot-kick, Vardy is then on the mark to cut Tottenham's lead to 2-1, but his side finish 3-1 down.

22 Gerard Deulofeu inspires a landmark 5-1 victory for Watford at Cardiff, scoring the club's first top-flight hat-trick since Mark Falco in 1986. Troy Deeney's brace completes Watford's first five-goal performance in the top division since that same year. Fulham are out of luck after Ryan Babel opens his account for the club. West Ham's equaliser, put in with his arm by Javier Hernandez, is allowed to stand and they go on to win 3-1.

23 Crystal Palace's Roy Hodgson celebrates becoming the Premier League's oldest-ever manager, at 71 years and 198 days, with a 4-1 success at Leicester. Hodgson, overtaking Sir Bobby Robson's record, sees Wilfried Zaha score twice and on-loan Michy Batshuayi open his account for the club. Leicester, whose consolation is a first for Johnny Evans, have Claude Puel in charge for the final time before his dismissal. Roger East awards three penalties in Bournemouth's 1-1 draw with Wolves. Joshua King scores one and misses one for the home side, while Raul Jimenez is on the mark for Wolves. Harry Kane, out for five weeks with an ankle injury, scores on his return at Burnley. But Tottenham's title hopes are undermined when Ashley Barnes and Chris Wood are both on the mark for the fourth successive game to stretch resurgent Burnley's unbeaten league run to eight games – the club's longest in the top-flight since 1966. Newcastle's record buy, Miguel Almiron, receives a standing ovation for an impressive home debut in a 2-0 win over Huddersfield, who have Tommy Smith shown a straight red card for a shin-high challenge on the Paraguayan.

24 Manchester United lose Ander Herrera, Juan Mata and Jesse Lingard to first-half injuries, but hold on for a goalless draw against Liverpool.

26 New manager Brendan Rodgers watches from the stands as Leicester end a run of four successive home defeats with a 2-1 win over Brighton, for whom Davy Propper scores for the first time. Huddersfield end a run of 13 defeats and a draw with a stoppage-time winner from Steve Mounie against Wolves, but remain 11 points adrift. Everton also return to winning ways, 3-0 at Cardiff with Gylfi Sigurdsson on the mark twice.

27 The top two have sharply-contrasting victories. Sadio Mane and Virgil van Dijk both score twice as Liverpool sweep aside Watford 5-0. Manchester City need a disputed Sergio Aguero penalty to overcome West Ham 1-0. With ten games remaining, Liverpool lead their rivals by one point. Tottenham are a further eight points back after losing 2-0 at Chelsea and manager Mauricio Pochettino concedes the title. Chelsea goalkeeper Kepa Arrizabalaga is dropped for the match after refusing to be substituted in the League Cup Final against Manchester

City. Manchester United have eight first-teamers out through injury at Selhurst Park, but still register another club-record under Ole Gunnar Solskjaer – eight successive away wins in all competitions after two Romelu Lukaku goals point the way to a 3-1 success against Crystal Palace. Arsenal are also among the goals – 5-1 against Bournemouth, who lose a ninth away game in a row for the first time since 1934 when the club were in the Third Division South. Fulham manager Claudio Ranieri looks resigned to his side's fate after a seventh defeat in eight matches – 2-0 at Southampton – and is sacked the following day.

MARCH 2019

2   Arsenal's bid for a Champions League place is undermined when Pierre-Emerick Aubameyang has an 89th minute penalty saved by Hugo Lloris and they have to be satisfied with a 1-1 draw against Tottenham in front of an 81,000 crowd at Wembley. In stoppage-time, Arsenal have Lucas Torreira sent off for reckless challenge on Danny Rose. Earlier, Aaron Ramsey scores in his final north London derby before joining Juventus in the summer. Tottenham draw in the Premier League for the first time in 29 games. Paul Pogba has a spot-kick saved by Angus Gunn, but Manchester United take over fourth spot by beating Southampton 3-2 in a match of stunning goals. Yan Valery and James Ward-Prowse strike from distance for the visitors and Andreas Pereira does the same for United, who eventually prevail with two goals delivered by Romelu Lukaku's supposedly weaker right boot. One goal from Riyad Mahrez is enough to put Manchester City back on top, although victory at Bournemouth is clouded when Kevin De Bruyne and John Stones join Fernandinho on the injured list. Wilfried Zaha's fifth in four games, this one after a mazy dribble, highlights a 3-1 success for Crystal Palace at Burnley. Brighton's slide, seven games without a win, is halted by substitute Florin Andone's header, the only goal of the game against Huddersfield.

3   Liverpool's fourth draw in six matches comes in the Merseyside derby at Goodison Park. Brendan Rodgers loses his first game as Leicester manager, 2-1 at Watford to a stoppage-time Andre Gray strike.

9   Raheem Sterling and Jordan Pickford are both involved in controversial refereeing decisions. The first goal of Sterling's 13-minute hat-trick in Manchester City's 3-1 win over Watford is allowed to stand by Paul Tierney, who overrules his assistant's offside flag. Pickford escapes with a yellow card from Lee Mason after bringing down Newcastle's Salomon Rondon with a rugby tackle – and saves Matt Ritchie's subsequent penalty. Everton break immediately to extend their lead to 2-0, but Newcastle hit back after the interval to win 3-2, with Ayoze Perez on the mark twice. Two players reach 100 goals for their clubs. Jamie Vardy scores twice – and on-loan Youri Tielemans nets his first for the club – as Leicester defeat Fulham 3-1 in Brendan Rodgers's first home game in charge. Glenn Murray's century comes up in Brighton's 2-1 away success against Crystal Palace. Tottenham manager Mauricio Pochettino accuses his side of arrogance after a 2-1 defeat at Southampton, whose winner from James Ward-Prowse is his second successful 25-yard free-kick in successive matches. Bournemouth end their four-month losing streak away from home - 2-0 against Huddersfield.

10   Liverpool come from behind to beat Burnley 4-2 with two goals each for Roberto Firmino and Sadio Mane. The race for the remaining two Champions League places takes a new twist as Manchester United suffer their first Premier League defeat under Ole Gunnar Solskjaer, 2-0 at Arsenal. Chelsea salvage a point through Eden Hazard's stoppage-time equaliser against Wolves. With Tottenham's loss of form, it means that four points cover the four teams in contention with eight fixtures remaining.

16   Two Karlan Grant goals and a first for the club by Juninho Bacuna look to have secured the points for Huddersfield, 3-1 up against West Ham. Instead, the home side hit back to win 4-3, with substitute Javier Hernandez scoring twice in the final six minutes of normal time. Wes Morgan and Matt Ritchie also make their mark late on in away matches. Morgan, brought on after Harry Maguire's fourth minute straight red card for bringing down Johann Berg Gudmundsson, gives Leicester a 2-1 win at Burnley with a 90th minute header. Ritchie's spectacular stoppage-time half-volley earns Newcastle a 2-2 draw after Joshua King's two goals for Bournemouth, one a penalty.

17 A mix-up between Virgil van Dijk and Alisson presents Ryan Babel with a Fulham equaliser at Craven Cottage. But another goalkeeping error, by Sergio Rico, gives substitute James Milner the opportunity to win it for Liverpool from the penalty spot after 81 minutes.

30 Huddersfield's relegation is confirmed at Selhurst Park, where their Premier League adventure started 18 months ago. They go down with six games still to play after Luka Milivojevic puts Crystal Palace on the way to a 2-0 victory with his ninth successful penalty in a row. Palace move eight points clear of trouble and two other sides boost their chances of staying up. Southampton win a 'six-pointer' at Brighton with the only goal of the game from Pierre-Emile Hoibjerg. Dwight McNeil, Burnley's rapidly maturing 19-year-old midfielder, seals a 2-0 success against Wolves in Sean Dyche's 300th game as manager. At the top, Manchester City ease to a 2-0 win at Fulham, while Manchester United defeat Watford 2-1 in Ole Gunnar Solskjaer's first match as permanent manager after being second-best for much of the afternoon.

31 A 90th minute own goal by Toby Alderweireld delivers a 2-1 victory for Liverpool over Tottenham, putting them two points ahead of Manchester City from an extra game played. Cardiff manager Neil Warnock rages after a 2-1 defeat by Chelsea, whose equaliser by Cesar Azpilicueta is shown to be two yards offside.

APRIL 2019

2 Fulham are relegated after a 4-1 defeat by Watford, who secure their highest-ever Premier League points total, 46, with six fixtures still remaining. Scott McTominay puts Manchester United ahead at Molineux, but his side are beaten by Wolves for the second time in 17 days and have Ashley Young sent off for a second yellow card in a 2-1 scoreline.

3 Son Heung-min scores the first competitive goal in Tottenham's new £1bn stadium, paving the way for a 2-0 victory over Crystal Palace. Manchester City regain top spot by defeating Cardiff 2-0. **5** Naby Keita registers his first goal for the club as Liverpool come from behind to win 3-1 at Southampton.

6 Ashley Barnes makes amends for a fourth minute own goal at Bournemouth by sealing Burnley's recovery for a 3-1 victory which puts his side within sight of safety. Crystal Palace are also nearly three after another Luka Milivojevic penalty, the only goal at Newcastle. Jamie Vardy's brace in Leicester's 4-1 success at Huddersfield takes him past Gary Lineker's 103 goals for the club.

8 Eden Hazard leaves five West Ham players in his wake to score one of the goals of the season and adds a second in Chelsea's 2-0 victory.

12 Any lingering doubts about Newcastle surviving the drop are ended when Ayoze Perez nets the only goal of the game at Leicester.

13 Lucas Moura scores a hat-trick and Paul Pogba converts two penalties to keep Tottenham and Manchester United in the thick of the race for Champions League places. Spurs, with Harry Kane out for the remainder of the season with an ankle injury and Dele Alli nursing a broken hand, ease past Huddersfield 4-0. United record a fortuitous 2-1 win over West Ham, who have a legitimate goal ruled for offside, hit the bar at 1-1 and are denied by David de Gea's world-class save from Michail Antonio. Cardiff are also justifiably aggrieved by a 2-0 defeat at Burnley, where Mike Dean reverses his decision to award a spot-kick for hands against Ben Mee after consulting his assistant referee. Chris Wood's brace effectively makes Burnley safe, along with Southampton, for whom Nathan Redmond is on the mark twice in the 3-1 defeat of Wolves. But Brighton are still sweating, crashing 5-0 at home to Bournemouth and losing Anthony Knockaert to a straight red card for a dangerous challenge on Adam Smith. Fulham's 2-0 victory over Everton ends a run of nine successive defeats and gives Scott Parker his first success as caretaker-manager.

14 Liverpool and Manchester City continue to go toe-to-toe at the top of the table. Mohamed Salah fires a 30-yard angled drive into the top corner for the leaders, who defeat Chelsea 2-0 in Jurgen Klopp's 200th game as manager. Raheem Sterling scores twice in City's 3-1 victory away to Crystal Palace.

15 Watford captain Troy Deeney is shown a straight red card for a forearm into the face of

Lucas Torreira in the 11th minute of a 1-0 home defeat by Arsenal, who revive their top-four chances after losing at Everton.

16 A 2-0 away win over struggling Brighton offers Cardiff a glimmer of hope of beating the drop.

20 Manchester City and Tottenham reconvene at the Etihad, three days after their Champions League thriller, and this time City come out on top by the only goal of the game from Phil Foden, his first in the Premier League. Ayoze Perez, whose goals have been crucial in Newcastle's move away from the danger zone, scores a hat-trick in their 3-1 victory over Southampton. Brighton are goalless for the fifth successive league match, but grind out a point at Wolves, thanks largely to the work of goalkeeper Mat Ryan. Gerard Deulofeu, two-goal hero of Watford's FA Cup semi-final win over Wolves, nets another brace for a 2-1 success at Huddersfield. Harvey Barnes opens his account for Leicester in stoppage time to earn a 2-2 draw at West Ham, while Fulham win away for the first time, 1-0 at Bournemouth courtesy of a penalty from Aleksandar Mitrovic which spoils Eddie Howe's 500th game in management.

21 Liverpool move on to 88 points, eclipsing their previous Premier League best of 86, with a -0 victory at Cardiff in front of a record crowd for a club match at the Cardiff City Stadium of 33,082. Ole Gunnar Solskjaer apologises to Manchester United supporters for a 4-0 defeat at Everton. Arsenal are beaten 3-2 at home by Crystal Palace, for whom Christian Benteke scores for the first time in a year.

22 Manager Maurizio Sarri is sent to the stands for his involvement in a touchline dispute with Burnley's coaching staff as Chelsea, like their rivals for Champions League places, drop points in a 2-2 draw.

23 Southampton's Shane Long scores the fastest-ever Premier League goal, timed at 7.69 sec, in the 1-1 draw at Watford. It overtakes Ledley King's 9.82 sec goal for Tottenham against Bradford in 2000. Brighton fail to score for the seventh time in league and cup games, a club-record, losing 1-0 to Christian Eriksen's 88th minute goal for Tottenham.

24 Manchester City step up the pressure on Liverpool by beating Manchester United 2-0 at Old Trafford with goals from Bernardo Silva and Leroy Sane. Arsenal falter for the third time in four games, beaten 2-1 at Wolves.

27 Matt Targett comes off the bench to score his first goal for the club as Southampton make sure of staying up with a 3-3 draw against Bournemouth, for whom Callum Wilson nets twice. Pascal Gross ends Brighton's goal drought to earn a point against Newcastle, taking his side close to surviving after Cardiff's defeat at Craven Cottage, where Fulham complete a hat-trick of victories with a 30 yard drive by Ryan Babel. West Ham's Michail Antonio sets up another 1-0 scoreline to inflict Tottenham's first defeat in their new stadium.

28 In keeping with the tightest of title races, goalline technology confirms Sergio Aguero's winner for 1-0 at Burnley by a matter of millimeter, leaving Manchester City a point ahead of Liverpool with two to play. Arsenal's slide continues at Leicester, where Ainsley Maitland-Niles is sent off for a second yellow card in a 3-0 defeat, Jamie Vardy scoring two of the goals. After high-profile errors against Arsenal, Barcelona in the Champions League and Manchester City, David de Gea is again at fault for a goal by Marcos Alonso in Chelsea's 1-1 draw at Old Trafford which leaves Manchester United on the outside of the chase for the two remaining Champions League places. They have 65 points, Arsenal 66, Chelsea 68 and Tottenham 70.

MAY 2019

4 Divock Origi, substituting for the injured Mohamed Salah, scores with an 86th minute header to give Liverpool a 3-2 win at Newcastle. Cardiff lose by the same scoreline against Crystal Palace and are relegated. Tottenham have two players sent off in a 1-0 defeat at Bournemouth, inflicted by Nathan Ake's 91st minute goal. Son Heung-min is dismissed for lashing out at Jefferson Lerma and Juan Foyth is also shown a straight red card for a studs-up challenge on Jack Simpson two minutes after coming off the bench. Two goals by Marko Arnautovic point West Ham to a 3-1 victory over Southampton.

5 Chelsea clinch a Champions League place by beating Watford 3-0. Manchester United miss out after a 1-1 draw at Huddersfield, who have Isaac Mbenza on the mark for the first time. And Arsenal are left to rely on the Europa League for entry after being held 1-1 by Brighton, who stay up following Cardiff's defeat.

6   Vincent Kompany plays a captain's role to leave Manchester City a point ahead of Liverpool going into the final day of the season, firing a 28-yard shot into the top corner for a 1-0 victory over Leicester.

12 Manchester City are champions again after a 14th successive win climaxes a title race that will be remembered for many years to come. They trail at Brighton to Glenn Murray's header, but finish on top for the fourth time in eight years with an equaliser a minute later from Sergio Aguero, followed by goals from Aymeric Laporte, Riyad Mahrez and Ilkay Gundogan. Liverpool, beaten only once in the campaign, defeat Wolves 2-0 with two from Sadio Mane, who shares the Golden Boot with team-mate Mohamed Salah and Pierre-Emerick Aubameyang on 22 goals. The Arsenal striker can claim the award outright, but is off target with a late chance to complete a hat-trick in a 3-1 scoreline at Burnley. Michy Batshuayi and Mark Noble also score twice on a day of 36 goals, one fewer than the Premier League record for the final day of a 38-match programme. Batshuayi puts Crystal Palace on the way to beating Bournemouth 5-3. Noble is instrumental in West Ham's 4-1 win at Watford, who have Jose Holebas shown a straight red card for bringing down Michail Antonio. The club appeal and Holebas is cleared to play in the FA Cup Final against Manchester City. Newcastle are 4-0 winners at Fulham, but Manchester United's falter again, losing 2-0 at home to Cardiff.

HOW CITY WON A TITLE THRILLER

AUGUST 2018

12 Arsenal 0 Manchester City 2 (Sterling 14. Bernardo Silva 64). Att: 59,934
19 Manchester City 6 (Aguero 25, 35, 75, Gabriel Jesus 31, David Silva 48, Kongolo 84 og) Huddersfield 1 (Stankovic 43). Att: 54,021
25 Wolves 1 (Boly 57) Manchester City 1 (Laporte 69). Att: 31,322

SEPTEMBER 2018

1   Manchester City 2 (Sterling 8, Walker 52) Newcastle 1 (Yedlin 30). Att: 53,946
15 Manchester City 3 (Sane 2, David Silva 21, Sterling 47) Fulham 0. Att: 53,307
22 Cardiff 0 Manchester City 5 (Aguero 32, Bernardo Silva 35, Gundogan 44, Mahrez 67, 89). Att: 32,321
29 Manchester City 2 (Sterling 29, Aguero 65) Brighton 0. Att: 54,152

OCTOBER 2018

7   Liverpool 0 Manchester City 0. Att: 52,117
20 Manchester City 5 (Aguero 17, Bernardo Silva 54, Fernandinho 56, Mahrez 83, Sane 90) Burnley 0. Att: 54,094
29 Tottenham 0 Manchester City 1 (Mahrez 6). Att: 56,854

NOVEMBER 2018

4   Manchester City 6 (Hoedt 6 og, Aguero 12, David Silva 18, Sterling 45+2, 67, Sane 90+1) Southampton 1 (Ings 30 pen). Att: 53,916
11 Manchester City 3 (David Silva 12, Aguero 48, Gundogan 86) Manchester Utd 1 (Martial 58 pen). Att: 54,316
24 West Ham 0 Manchester City 4 (David Silva 11, Sterling 19, Sane 34, 90+3). Att: 56,886

DECEMBER 2018

1   Manchester City 3 (Bernardo Silva 16, Sterling 57, Gundogan 79) Bournemouth 1 (Wilson 44). Att: 54,409

4	Watford 1 (Doucoure 85) Manchester City 2 (Sane 40, Mahrez 51). Att: 20,389
8	Chelsea 2 (Kante 45, Luiz 78) Manchester City 0. Att: 40,571
15	Manchester City 3 (Gabriel Jesus 22, 50, Sterling 69) Everton 1 (Calvert-Lewin 65). Att: 54,17322
22	Manchester City 2 (Gundogan 27, De Bruyne 85) Crystal Palace 3 (Schlupp 33, Townsend 35, Milivojevic 52 pen). Att: 54,210
26	Leicester 2 (Albrighton 19, Pereira 81) Manchester City 1 (Bernardo Silva 14). Att: 32,090
30	Southampton 1 (Hojbjerg 37) Manchester City 3 (David Silva 10, Ward-Prowse 45 og, Aguero 45). Att: 31,381

JANUARY 2019

3	Manchester City 2 (Aguero 40, Sane 70) Liverpool 1 (Firmino 64). Att: 54,511
14	Manchester City 3 (Gabriel Jesus 10, 39 pen, Coady 78 og) Wolves 0. Att: 54,171
20	Huddersfield 0 Manchester City 3 (Danilo 18, Sterling 54, Sane 56). Att: 24,807
29	Newcastle 2 (Rondon 66, Ritchie 80 pen) Manchester City 1 (Aguero 1). Att: 50,861

FEBRUARY 2019

2	Manchester City 3 (Aguero 1, 44, 61) Arsenal 1 (Koscielny 11). Att: 54,483
6	Everton 0 Manchester City 2 (Laporte 45, Gabriel Jesus 90+7). Att: 39,322
10	Manchester City 6 (Sterling 4, 80, Aguero 13, 19, 56 pen, Gundogan 25) Chelsea 0. Att: 54,452
27	Manchester City 1 (Aguero 59 pen) West Ham 0. Att: 53,528

MARCH 2019

2	Bournemouth 0 Manchester City 1 (Mahrez 55). Att: 10,699
9	Manchester City 3 (Sterling 46, 50, 59) Watford 1 (Deulofeu 66). Att: 54,104
30	Fulham 0 Manchester City 2 (Bernardo Silva 5, Aguero 27). Att: 25,001

APRIL 2019

3	Manchester City 2 (De Bruyne 6, Sane 44) Cardiff 0. Att: 53,559
14	Crystal Palace 1 (Milivojevic 81) Manchester City 3 (Sterling 15, 63, Gabriel Jesus 90). Att: 25,721
20	Manchester City 1 (Foden 5) Tottenham 0. Att: 54,489
24	Manchester Utd 0 Manchester City 2 (Bernardo Silva 54, Sane 66). Att: 74,431
28	Burnley 0 Manchester City 1 (Aguero 63). Att: 21,605

MAY 2019

| 6 | Manchester City 1 (Kompany 70) Leicester 0. Att: 54,506 |
| 12 | Brighton 1 (Murray 27) Manchester City 4 (Aguero 28, Laporte 38, Mahrez 63, Gundogan 72). Att: 30,662 – (Manchester City clinched title) |

... AND HOW LIVERPOOL WENT SO CLOSE

AUGUST 2018

12	Liverpool 4 (Salah 19, Mane 45, 53, Sturridge 88) West Ham 0. Att: 53,235
20	Crystal Palace 0 Liverpool 2 (Milner 45 pen, Mane 90+3). Att: 25,750
25	Liverpool 1 (Salah 23) Brighton 0. Att: 53,294

SEPTEMBER 2018

1	Leicester 1 (Ghezzal 63) Liverpool 2 (Mane 10, Firmino 45). Att: 32,149
15	Tottenham 1 (Lamela 90+3) Liverpool 2 (Wijnaldum 39, Firmino 54). Att: 80,188
22	Liverpool 3 (Hoedt 10 og, Matip 21, Salah 45) Southampton 0. Att: 50,965
29	Chelsea 1 (Hazard 25) Liverpool 1 (Sturridge 89). Att: 40,625

OCTOBER 2018

7   Liverpool 0 Manchester City 0. Att: 52,117
20   Huddersfield 0 Liverpool 1 (Salah 24). Att: 24,263
27   Liverpool 4 (Salah 10, Mane 66, 87, Shaqiri 84) Cardiff 1 (Paterson 77). Att: 53,373

NOVEMBER 2018

3   Arsenal 1 (Lacazette 82) Liverpool 1 (Milner 61). Att: 59,993
11   Liverpool 2 (Salah 41, Shaqiri 53). Fulham 0. Att: 53,120
24   Watford 0 Liverpool 3 (Salah 67, Alexander-Arnold 76, Firmino 89). Att: 20,540

DECEMBER 2018

2   Liverpool 1 (Origi 90+6) Everton 0. Att: 53,195
5   Burnley 1 (Cork 54) Liverpool 3 (Milner 62, Firmino 69, Shaqiri 90). Att: 21,741
8   Bournemouth 0 Liverpool 4 (Salah 25, 48, 77, Cook 68 og). Att: 10,752
16   Liverpool 3 (Mane 24, Shaqiri 73, 80) Manchester Utd 1 (Lingard 33). Att: 52,908
21   Wolves 0 Liverpool 2 (Salah 18, Van Dijk 68). Att: 31,358
26   Liverpool 4 (Lovren 11, Salah 47 pen, Shaqiri 79, Fabinho 85) Newcastle 0.
         Att: 53,318
29   Liverpool 5 (Firmino 14, 16, 65 pen, Mane 32, Salah 45 pen) Arsenal 1
         (Maitland-Niles 11). Att: 53,326

JANUARY 2019

3   Manchester City 2 (Aguero 40, Sane 70) Liverpool 1 (Firmino 64). Att: 54,511
12   Brighton 0 Liverpool 1 (Salah 50 pen). Att: 30,682
19   Liverpool 4 (Salah 46, 75, Firmino 53, Mane 90+4) Crystal Palace 3 (Townsend 34,
         Tomkins 65, Meyer 90+5). Att: 53,171
30   Liverpool 1 (Mane 3) Leicester 1 (Maguire 45). Att: 53,092

FEBRUARY 2019

4   West Ham 1 (Antonio 28) Liverpool 1 (Mane 22). Att: 59,903
9   Liverpool 3 (Mane 24, Wijnaldum 34, Salah 48) Bournemouth 0. Att: 53,178
23   Manchester Utd 0 Liverpool 0. Att: 74,519
27   Liverpool 5 (Mane 9, 20, Origi 66, Van Dijk 79, 82) Watford 0. Att: 53,316

MARCH 2019

3   Everton 0 Liverpool 0. Att: 39,335
10   Liverpool 4 (Firmino 19, 67, Mane 29, 90+3) Burnley 2 (Westwood 6,
         Gudmundsson 90+1). Att: 53,310
17   Fulham 1 (Babel 74) Liverpool 2 (Mane 26, Milner 81 pen). Att: 25,043
31   Liverpool 2 (Firmino 16, Alderweireld 90 og) Tottenham 1 (Lucas Moura 70).
         Att: 53,322

APRIL 2019

5   Southampton 1 (Long 9) Liverpool 3 (Keita 36, Salah 80, Henderson 86). Att: 31,797
14   Liverpool 2 (Mane 51, Salah 53) Chelsea 0. Att: 53,279
21   Cardiff 0 Liverpool 2 (Wijnaldum 57, Milner 81 pen). Att: 33,082
26   Liverpool 5 (Keita 1, Mane 23, 66, Salah 45, 83) Huddersfield 0. Att: 53,249

MAY 2019

4   Newcastle 2 (Atsu 20, Rondon 54) Liverpool 3 (Van Dijk 13, Salah 28, Origi 86).
         Att: 52,206
12   Liverpool 2 (Mane 17, 81) Wolves 0. Att: 53,331

ENGLISH FOOTBALL LEAGUE PLAY-OFFS 2019

Aston Villa returned to the Premier League after a three-year exile – earning an estimated windfall of £170m – by beating Derby 2-1 in front of a crowd of nearly 86,000. Prince William, a supporter of the club, joined the celebrations at Wembley after loanee Anwar El Ghazi and bargain-buy John McGinn scored the goals to complete the club's renaissance under Dean Smith. The former Brentford manager took over the hot-seat two months into the season, after Steve Bruce was sacked, and breathed new life into a team who successfully reconnected with their huge fan-base. El Ghazi, borrowed from French club Lille, scored a minute before half-time and had a hand in the second goal. His shot took a deflection which goalkeeper Kelle Roos misjudged, allowing McGinn, an influential £2.7m signing from Hibernian and Villa's Player of the year, to head in. Jack Marriott, two-goal match-winner in Derby's semi-final win over Leeds but surprisingly starting on the bench, had a shot deflected in by fellow-substitute Martyn Waghorn to reduce the arrears. It was not enough to end their 11 year absence from the top-flight, although Frank Lampard's first season of management was rated a success after a sixth-place finish. Late goals settled the other divisional finals. **Charlton** recovered from Naby Sarr's bizarre fifth-minute own goal against Sunderland – a back-pass missed by goalkeeper Dillon Phillips, who chased back in vain as the ball rolled in. Ben Purrington equalised with his first for the club and captain Patrick Bauer scrambled the winner seconds from the end. **Tranmere** made a successful return to Wembley after winning the National League decider in 2018, with Connor Jennings heading in Jake Caprice's cross in the 119th minute for the only goal against Newport. **Salford**, co-owned by six former Manchester United players, reached the Football League for the first time after a fourth promotion in five years. Managed by Graham Alexander, formerly at Scunthorpe and Fleetwood, they defeated Fylde 3-0 in the National League Final with goals from Emmanuel Dieseruvwe, Carl Piergianni and Ibou Touray.

QUARTER-FINALS (one match)

NATIONAL LEAGUE
AFC Fylde 3(Croasdale 10, Bond 15, Bradley 90) **Harrogate** 1 (Burke 53 og). Att: 1,560.
Wrexham 0 **Eastleigh** 1 (Hollands 109). Att: 6,723 (aet)

SEMI-FINALS (one match)

NATIONAL LEAGUE
Salford 1(Piergianni 43) **Eastleigh** 1 (McCallum 57). Att: 2,963 (aet, Salford won 4-3 on pens). **Solihull** 0 **Fylde** 1 (Philliskirk 2). Att: 3,681

SEMI-FINALS, FIRST LEG

CHAMPIONSHIP
Aston Villa 2 (Hourihane 76, Abraham 79 pen) **WBA** 1 (Gayle 16). Att: 40,754. **Derby** 0 **Leeds** 1 (Roofe 55). Att: 31,723

LEAGUE ONE
Doncaster 1 (Blair 87) **Charlton** 2 (Taylor 32, Aribo 34). Att: 11,140. **Sunderland** 1 (Maguire 62) **Portsmouth** 0. Att: 26,210

LEAGUE TWO
Newport 1 (Amond 83) **Mansfield** 1 (Hamilton 12). Att: 6,035. **Tranmere** 1 (Banks 26) **Forest Green** 0. Att: 9,579

SEMI-FINALS, SECOND LEG

CHAMPIONSHIP
Leeds 2 (Dallas 24, 62) **Derby** 4 (Marriott 45, 85, Mount 46, Wilson 58 pen). Att: 36,326

(Derby won 4-3 on agg). **WBA** 1 (Dawson 29) **Aston Villa** 0. Att: 25,702 (aet, agg 2-2, Aston Villa won 4-3 on pens)

LEAGUE ONE
Charlton 2 (Bielik 2, Pratley 101) **Doncaster** 3 (Rowe 11, Butler 88, Marquis 100). Att: 25,428 (aet, agg 4-4, Charlton won 4-3 on pens)

LEAGUE TWO
Forest Green 1 (Mills 12) **Tranmere** 1 (Norwood 27). Att: 4,492 (Tranmere won 2-1 on agg). **Mansfield** 0 **Newport** 0. Att: 7,361 (aet, agg 1-1, Newport won 5-3 on pens)

FINALS

CHAMPIONSHIP – MONDAY, MAY 27, 2019
Aston Villa 2 (El Ginn 44, McGinn 59) **Derby County**1 (Waghorn 81). Att: 85,826 (Wembley)
Aston Villa (4-3-3): Steer, Elmohamady, Tuanzebe, Mings (Hause 86), Taylor, McGinn, Hourihane, Grealish (capt), Adomah (Green 73), Abraham, El Ghazi. **Subs not used:** Kalinic, Jedinak, Whelan, Lansbury, Kodjia. **Booked:** El Ghazi, Hourihane. **Manager:** Dean Smith
Derby County (4-3-1-2): Roos, Bogle, Keogh (capt), Tomori, Cole, Mount, Huddlestone (Marriott 63), Johnson, Wilson, Lawrence (Jozefzoon 73), Bennett (Waghorn 69). **Subs not used:** Carson, Knight, MacDonald, Evans. **Booked:** Bennett, Tomori, Wilson. **Manager:** Frank Lampard
Referee: P Tierney (Lancs). **Half-time:** 1-0

LEAGUE ONE – SUNDAY, MAY 26, 2019
Charlton Athletic 2 (Purrington 35, Bauer 90+4) **Sunderland** 1 (Sarr 5 og). Att: 76,155 (Wembley)
Charlton Athletic (3-5-2): Phillips, Bielik, Bauer (capt), Sarr (Pearce 46), Dijksteel, Aribo, Cullen, Pratley (Williams 71), Purrington, Taylor, Parker. **Subs not used:** Maxwell, Solly, Lapslie, Forster-Caskey, Reeves. **Booked:** Sarr. **Manager:** Lee Bowyer
Sunderland (4-4-1-1): McLaughlin, O'Nien, Flanagan, Ozturk, Oviedo, Power (Morgan 9), Cattermole, Leadbitter, Maguire (Grigg 57), Honeyman, Wyke (McGeady72). **Subs not used:** Stryjek, Dunne, Matthews, Gooch. **Booked:** Grigg, O'Nien, Leadbitter, Flanagan. **Manager:** Jack Ross
Referee: A Madley (West Yorks). **Half-time:** 1-1

LEAGUE TWO – SATURDAY, MAY 25, 2019 – aet
Newport County 0 **Tranmere Rovers** 1 (Jennings 119). Att: 25,217 (Wembley) – aet
Newport County (3-5-2): Day, Poole, O'Brien (capt), Demetriou, Butler, Labadie (Dolan 72), Bennett, Sheehan (Bakinson 90), Willmott (Marsh-Brown 105), Amond, Matt (Azeez 103). **Subs not used:** Pipe, Crofts, McKirdy. **Booked:** Matt, O'Brien, Poole. **Sent off:** O'Brien (89). **Manager:** Mike Flynn
Tranmere Rovers (4-1-4-1): Davies, Caprice, Nelson (Buxton 115), Monthe, Ridehalgh, Banks, Morris (McNulty, capt, 82), Harris (Pringle 53), Perkins, Jennings, Norwood. **Booked:** Perkins. **Subs not used:** Pilling, Dagnall, Mullin, Gilmour. **Manager:** Micky Mellon
Referee: R Joyce (North Yorks). **Half-time:** 0-0

NATIONAL LEAGUE –SATURDAY, MAY 11, 2019
AFC Fylde 0 **Salford City**3 (Dieseruvwe 15, Piergianni 53, Touray 61). Att: 8,049 (Wembley)
AFC Fylde (4-2-3-1): Lynch, Burke (Haughton 20), Byrne (capt), Tunnicliffe, Francis-Angol, Croasdale, Philliskirk, Reid (Hardy 58), Bond (Crawford 73), Bradley, Rowe. **Subs not used:** Griffiths, Odusina. **Manager:** Dave Challinor
Salford City (4-2-3-1): Neal, Pond, Hogan (capt), Pergianni, Touray, Mafuta (Rodney 54), Maynard, Wiseman, Redmond, Whitehead (Shelton 68), Dieseruvwe (Gaffney 77). **Subs not used:** Crocombe, Walker. **Booked:** Pond. **Manager:** Graham Alexander
Referee: J Oldham (Derbys). **Half-time:** 0-1

PLAY-OFF FINALS – HOME & AWAY

1987: Divs 1/2: Charlton beat Leeds 2-1 in replay (Birmingham) after 1-1 agg (1-0h, 0-1a). Charlton remained in Div 1 Losing semi-finalists: Ipswich and Oldham. **Divs 2/3: Swindon** beat Gillingham 2-0 in replay (Crystal Palace) after 2-2 agg (0-1a, 2-1h). Swindon promoted to Div 2. Losing semi-finalists: Sunderland and Wigan; Sunderland relegated to Div 3. **Divs 3/4: Aldershot** beat Wolves 3-0 on agg (2-0h, 1-0a) and promoted to Div 3. Losing semi-finalists: Bolton and Colchester; Bolton relegated to Div 4

1988: Divs 1/2: Middlesbrough beat Chelsea 2-1 on agg (2-0h, 0-1a) and promoted to Div 1; Chelsea relegated to Div 2. Losing semi-finalists: Blackburn and Bradford City. **Divs 2/3: Walsall** beat Bristol City 4-0 in replay (h) after 3-3 agg (3-1a, 0-2h) and promoted to Div 2. Losing semi-finalists: Sheffield Utd and Notts County; Sheffield Utd relegated to Div 3. **Divs 3/4: Swansea** beat Torquay 5-4 on agg (2-1h, 3-3a) and promoted to Div 3. Losing semi-finalists: Rotherham and Scunthorpe.; Rotherham relegated to Div 4

1989: Div 2: Crystal Palace beat Blackburn 4-3 on agg (1-3a, 3-0h). Losing semi-finalists: Watford and Swindon. **Div 3: Port Vale** beat Bristol Rovers 2-1 on agg (1-1a, 1-0h). Losing semi-finalists: Fulham and Preston **Div.4: Leyton Orient** beat Wrexham 2-1 on agg (0-0a, 2-1h). Losing semi-finalists: Scarborough and Scunthorpe

PLAY-OFF FINALS AT WEMBLEY

1990: Div 2: Swindon 1 Sunderland 0 (att: 72,873). Swindon promoted, then demoted for financial irregularities; Sunderland promoted. Losing semi-finalists: Blackburn and Newcastle Utd **Div 3: Notts County** 2 Tranmere 0 (att: 29,252). Losing semi finalists: Bolton and Bury. **Div 4: Cambridge Utd** 1 Chesterfield 0 (att: 26,404). Losing semi-finalists: Maidstone and Stockport County

1991: Div 2: Notts County 3 Brighton 1 (att: 59,940). Losing semi-finalists: Middlesbrough and Millwall. **Div 3: Tranmere** 1 Bolton 0 (att. 30,217). Losing semi-finalists: Brentford and Bury. **Div 4: Torquay** 2 Blackpool 2 – Torquay won 5-4 on pens (att: 21,615). Losing semi-finalists: Burnley and Scunthorpe

1992: Div 2: Blackburn 1 Leicester 0 (att: 68,147) Losing semi-finalists: Derby and Cambridge Utd. **Div 3: Peterborough** 2 Stockport 1 (att: 35,087). Losing semi finalists: Huddersfield and Stoke. **Div 4: Blackpool** 1 Scunthorpe 1 aet, Blackpool won 4-3 on pens (att: 22,741). Losing semi-finalists: Barnet and Crewe

1993: Div 1: Swindon 4 Leicester 3 (att: 73,802). Losing semi-finalists. Portsmouth and Tranmere **Div 2: WBA** 3 Port Vale 0 (att: 53,471). Losing semi finalists: Stockport and Swansea. **Div 3: York** 1 Crewe 1 aet, York won 5-3 on pens (att: 22,416). Losing semi finalists: Bury and Walsall

1994: Div 1: Leicester 2 Derby 1 (att: 73,671). Losing semi-finalists: Millwall and Tranmere. **Div 2: Burnley** 2 Stockport 1 (att: 44,806). Losing semi-finalists: Plymouth Argyle and York. **Div 3: Wycombe** 4 Preston 2 (att: 40,109). Losing semi finalists: Carlisle and Torquay

1995: Div 1: Bolton 4 Reading 3 (att: 64,107). Losing semi-finalists: Tranmere and Wolves. **Div 2: Huddersfield** 2 Bristol Rov 1 (att: 59,175). Losing semi-finalists: Brentford and Crewe. **Div 3: Chesterfield** 2 Bury 0 (att: 22,814). Losing semi-finalists: Mansfield and Preston

1996: Div 1: Leicester 2 Crystal Palace 1 aet (att: 73,573). Losing semi-finalists: Charlton and Stoke. **Div 2: Bradford City** 2 Notts Co 0 (att: 39,972). Losing semi-finalists: Blackpool and Crewe. **Div 3: Plymouth Argyle** 1 Darlington 0 (att: 43,431). Losing semi-finalists: Colchester and Hereford

1997: Div 1: Crystal Palace 1 Sheffield Utd 0 (att: 64,383). Losing semi-finalists: Ipswich and Wolves. **Div 2: Crewe** 1 Brentford 0 (att: 34,149). Losing semi-finalists: Bristol City and Luton. **Div 3: Northampton** 1 Swansea 0 (att: 46,804). Losing semi-finalists: Cardiff and Chester

1998: Div 1: Charlton 4 Sunderland 4 aet, Charlton won 7-6 on pens (att: 77, 739). Losing semi-finalists: Ipswich and Sheffield Utd. **Div 2: Grimsby** 1 Northampton 0 (att: 62,988). Losing semi-finalists: Bristol Rov and Fulham. **Div 3: Colchester** 1 Torquay 0 (att: 19,486). Losing semi-finalists: Barnet and Scarborough

1999: Div 1: Watford 2 Bolton 0 (att: 70,343). Losing semi-finalists: Ipswich and Birmingham. **Div 2: Manchester City** 2 Gillingham 2 aet, Manchester City won 3-1 on pens (att: 76,935). Losing semi-finalists: Preston and Wigan. **Div 3: Scunthorpe** 1 Leyton Orient 0 (att: 36,985). Losing semi-finalists: Rotherham and Swansea

2000: Div 1: Ipswich 4 Barnsley 2 (att: 73,427). Losing semi-finalists: Birmingham and Bolton. **Div 2: Gillingham** 3 Wigan 2 aet (att: 53,764). Losing semi-finalists: Millwall and Stoke. **Div 3: Peterborough** 1 Darlington 0 (att: 33,383). Losing semi-finalists: Barnet and Hartlepool

PLAY-OFF FINALS AT MILLENNIUM STADIUM

2001: Div 1: Bolton 3 Preston 0 (att: 54,328). Losing semi-finalists: Birmingham and WBA. **Div 2: Walsall** 3 Reading 2 aet (att: 50,496). Losing semi-finalists: Stoke and Wigan. **Div 3: Blackpool** 4 Leyton Orient 2 (att: 23,600). Losing semi-finalists: Hartlepool and Hull

2002: Div 1: Birmingham 1 Norwich 1 aet, Birmingham won 4-2 on pens, (att: 71,597). Losing semi-finalists: Millwall and Wolves. **Div 2: Stoke** 2 Brentford 0 (att: 42,523). Losing semi-finalists: Cardiff and Huddersfield. **Div 3: Cheltenham** 3 Rushden & Diamonds 1 (att: 24,368). Losing semi-finalists: Hartlepool and Rochdale

2003: Div 1: Wolves 3 Sheffield Utd 0 (att: 69,473). Losing semi-finalists: Nott'm Forest and Reading. **Div 2: Cardiff** 1 QPR. 0 aet (att: 66,096). Losing semi-finalists: Bristol City and Oldham. **Div 3: Bournemouth** 5 Lincoln 2 (att: 32,148). Losing semi-finalists: Bury and Scunthorpe

2004: Div 1: Crystal Palace 1 West Ham 0 (att: 72,523). Losing semi-finalists: Ipswich and Sunderland. **Div 2: Brighton** 1 Bristol City 0 (att: 65,167). Losing semi-finalists: Hartlepool and Swindon. **Div 3: Huddersfield** 0 Mansfield 0 aet, Huddersfield won 4-1 on pens (att: 37,298). Losing semi-finalists: Lincoln and Northampton

2005: Championship: West Ham 1 Preston 0 (att: 70,275). Losing semifinalists: Derby Co and Ipswich. **League 1: Sheffield Wed** 4 Hartlepool 2 aet (att: 59,808). Losing semi-finalists: Brentford and Tranmere **League 2: Southend** 2 Lincoln 0 aet (att: 19532). Losing semi-finalists: Macclesfield and Northampton

2006: Championship: Watford 3 Leeds 0 (att: 64,736). Losing semi-finalists: Crystal Palace and Preston. **League 1: Barnsley** 2 Swansea 2 aet (att: 55,419), Barnsley won 4-3 on pens. Losing semi-finalists: Huddersfield and Brentford. **League 2: Cheltenham** 1 Grimsby 0 (att: 29,196). Losing semi-finalists: Wycombe and Lincoln

PLAY-OFF FINALS AT WEMBLEY

2007: Championship: Derby 1 WBA 0 (att: 74,993). Losing semi-finalists: Southampton and Wolves. **League 1: Blackpool** 2 Yeovil 0 (att: 59,313). Losing semi-finalists: Nottm Forest and Oldham. **League 2: Bristol Rov** 3 Shrewsbury 1 (att: 61,589). Losing semi-finalists: Lincoln and MK Dons

2008: Championship: Hull 1 Bristol City 0 (att: 86,703). Losing semi-finalists: Crystal Palace and Watford. **League 1: Doncaster** 1 Leeds 0 (att: 75,132). Losing semi-finalists: Carlisle and Southend. **League 2: Stockport** 3 Rochdale 2 (att: 35,715). Losing semi-finalists: Darlington and Wycombe

2009: Championship: Burnley 1 Sheffield Utd 0 (att: 80,518). Losing semi-finalists: Preston and Reading. **League 1: Scunthorpe** 3 Millwall 2 (att: 59,661). Losing semi-finalists: Leeds and MK Dons. **League 2: Gillingham** 1 Shrewsbury 0 (att: 53,706). Losing semi-finalists: Bury and Rochdale

2010: Championship: Blackpool 3 Cardiff 2 (att: 82,244). Losing semi-finalists: Leicester and Nottm Forest. **League 1: Millwall** 1 Swindon 0 (att:73,108). Losing semi-finalists: Charlton and Huddersfield. **League 2: Dagenham & Redbridge** 3 Rotherham 2 (all: 32,054). Losing semi-finalists: Aldershot and Morecambe

2011: Championship: Swansea 4 Reading 2 (att: 86,581). Losing semi-finalists: Cardiff and Nottm Forest. **League 1: Peterborough** 3 Huddersfield 0 (Old Trafford, att:48,410). Losing semi-finalists: Bournemouth and MK Dons. **League 2: Stevenage** 1 Torquay 0 (Old Trafford, att: 11,484. Losing semi-finalists: Accrington and Shrewsbury

2012: Championship: West Ham 2 Blackpool 1 (att: 78,523). Losing semi-finalists: Birmingham and Cardiff. **League 1: Huddersfield** 0 Sheffield Utd 0 aet, Huddersfield won 8-7 on pens (att: 52,100). Losing semi-finalists: MK Dons and Stevenage. **League 2: Crewe** 2 Cheltenham 0 (att: 24,029). Losing semi-finalists: Southend and Torquay

2013: Championship: Crystal Palace 1 Watford 0 (att: 82,025). Losing semi-finalists: Brighton and Leicester. **League 1: Yeovil** 2 Brentford 1 (att: 41,955). Losing semi-finalists: Sheffield Utd and Swindon. **League 2: Bradford** 3 Northampton 0 (att: 47,127). Losing semi-finalists: Burton and Cheltenham

2014: Championship: QPR 1 Derby 0 (att: 87,348). Losing semi-finalists: Brighton and Wigan. **League 1: Rotherham** 2 Leyton Orient 2 aet, Rotherham won 4-3 on pens (att: 43,401). Losing semi-finalists: Peterborough and Preston. **League 2: Fleetwood** 1 Burton 0 (att: 14,007). Losing semi-finalists: Southend and York

2015: Championship: Norwich 2 Middlesbrough 0 (att: 85,656). Losing semi-finalists: Brentford and Ipswich. **League 1: Preston** 4 Swindon 0 (att: 48,236). Losing semi-finalists: Chesterfield and Sheffield Utd. **League 2: Southend** 1 Wycombe 1 aet, Southend won 7-6 on pens (att: 38,252). Losing semi-finalists: Stevenage and Plymouth

2016: Championship: Hull 1 Sheffield Wed 0 (att 70,189). Losing semi-finalists: Brighton and Derby. **League 1: Barnsley** 3 Millwall 1 (att 51,277). Losing semi-finalists: Bradford and Walsall. **League 2: AFC Wimbledon** 2 Plymouth 0 (att 57,956). Losing semi-finalists: Accrington and Portsmouth)

2017: Championship: Huddersfield 0 Reading 0 aet, Huddersfield won 4-3 on pens (att 76,682). Losing semi-finalists: Fulham and Sheffield Wed. **League 1: Millwall** 1 Bradford 0 (att 53,320. Losing semi-finals: Fleetwood and Scunthorpe. **League 2: Blackpool** 2 Exeter 1 (att 23,380). Losing semi-finalists: Carlisle and Luton

2018: Championship: Fulham 1 Aston Villa 0 (att 85,243). Losing semi-finalists: Derby and Middlesbrough. **League 1: Rotherham** 2 Shrewsbury 1 (att 26,218). Losing semi-finalists: Charlton and Scunthorpe. **League 2: Coventry** 3 Exeter 1. Losing semi-finalists: Lincoln and Notts Co

HISTORY OF THE PLAY-OFFS

Play-off matches were introduced by the Football League to decide final promotion and relegation issues at the end of season 1986-87. A similar series styled 'Test Matches' had operated between Divisions One and Two for six seasons from 1893-98, and was abolished when both divisions were increased from 16 to 18 clubs.

Eighty-eight years later, the play-offs were back in vogue. In the first three seasons (1987-88-89), the Finals were played home-and-away, and since they were made one-off matches in 1990, they have featured regularly in Wembley's spring calendar, until the old stadium closed its doors and the action switched to the Millennium Stadium in Cardiff in 2001.

Through the years, these have been the ups and downs of the play-offs:

1987: Initially, the 12 clubs involved comprised the one that finished directly above those relegated in Divisions One, Two and Three and the three who followed the sides automatically promoted in each section. Two of the home-and-away Finals went to neutral-ground replays, in which **Charlton** clung to First Division status by denying Leeds promotion while **Swindon** beat Gillingham to complete their climb from Fourth Division to Second in successive seasons, via the play-offs, Sunderland fell into the Third and Bolton into Division Four, both for the first time. **Aldershot** went up after finishing only sixth in Division Four; in their Final, they beat Wolves, who had finished nine points higher and missed automatic promotion by one point.

1988: Chelsea were relegated from the First Division after losing on aggregate to **Middlesbrough**, who had finished third in Division Two. So Middlesbrough, managed by Bruce Rioch, completed the rise from Third Division to First in successive seasons, only two years after their very existence had been threatened by the bailiffs. Also promoted via the play-offs: **Walsall** from Division Three and **Swansea** from the Fourth. Relegated, besides Chelsea: Sheffield Utd (to Division Three) and Rotherham (to Division Four).

1989: After two seasons of promotion-relegation play-offs, the system was changed to involve the four clubs who had just missed automatic promotion. That format has remained. Steve Coppell's **Crystal Palace**, third in Division Two, returned to the top flight after eight years, beating Blackburn 4-3 on aggregate after extra time. Similarly, **Port Vale** confirmed third place in Division Three with promotion via the play-offs. For **Leyton Orient**, promotion seemed out of the question in Division Four when they stood 15th on March 1. But eight wins and a draw in the last nine home games swept them to sixth in the final table, and two more home victories in the play-offs completed their season in triumph.

1990: The play-off Finals now moved to Wembley over three days of the Spring Holiday week-end. On successive afternoons, **Cambridge Utd** won promotion from Division Four and **Notts Co** from the Third. Then, on Bank Holiday Monday, the biggest crowd for years at a Football League fixture (72,873) saw Ossie Ardiles' **Swindon** beat Sunderland 1-0 to reach the First Division for the first time. A few weeks later, however, Wembley losers **Sunderland** were promoted instead, by default; Swindon were found guilty of "financial irregularities" and stayed in Division Two.

1991: Again, the season's biggest League crowd (59,940) gathered at Wembley for the First Division Final in which **Notts Co** (having missed promotion by one point) still fulfilled their ambition, beating Brighton 3-1. In successive years, County had climbed from Third Division to First via the play-offs – the first club to achieve double promotion by this route. Bolton were denied automatic promotion in Division Three on goal difference, and lost at Wembley to an extra-time goal by **Tranmere**. The Fourth Division Final made history, with Blackpool beaten 5-4 on penalties by **Torquay** – first instance of promotion being decided by a shoot-out. In the table, Blackpool had finished seven points ahead of Torquay.

1992: Wembley that Spring Bank Holiday was the turning point in the history of **Blackburn**. Bolstered by Kenny Dalglish's return to management and owner Jack Walker's millions, they beat Leicester 1-0 by Mike Newell's 45th-minute penalty to achieve their objective – a place in the new Premier League. Newell, who also missed a second-half penalty, had recovered from a broken leg just in time for the play-offs. In the Fourth Division Final **Blackpool** (denied by penalties the previous year) this time won a shoot-out 4-3 against Scunthorpe., who were unlucky in the play-offs for the fourth time in five years. **Peterborough** climbed out of the Third Division for the first time, beating Stockport County 2-1 at Wembley.

1993: The crowd of 73,802 at Wembley to see **Swindon** beat Leicester 4-3 in the First Division Final was 11,000 bigger than that for the FA Cup Final replay between Arsenal and Sheffield Wed. Leicester rallied from three down to 3-3 before Paul Bodin's late penalty wiped away **Swindon**'s bitter memories of three years earlier, when they were denied promotion after winning at Wembley. In the Third Division Final, **York** beat Crewe 5-3 in a shoot-out after a 1-1 draw, and in the Second Division decider, **WBA** beat Port Vale 3-0. That was tough on Vale, who had finished third in the table with 89 points – highest total never to earn promotion in any division. They had beaten Albion twice in the League, too.

1994: Wembley's record turn-out of 158,586 spectators at the three Finals started with a crowd of 40,109 to see Martin O'Neill's **Wycombe** beat Preston 4-2. They thus climbed from Conference to Second Division with successive promotions. **Burnley**'s 2-1 victory in the Second Division Final was marred by the sending-off of two Stockport players, and in the First Division decider **Leicester** came from behind to beat Derby Co and end the worst Wembley record of any club. They had lost on all six previous appearances there – four times in the FA Cup Final and in the play-offs of 1992 and 1993.

1995: Two months after losing the Coca-Cola Cup Final to Liverpool, Bruce Rioch's **Bolton** were back at Wembley for the First Division play-off Final. From two goals down to Reading in front of a crowd of 64,107, they returned to the top company after 15 years, winning 4-3 with two extra-time goals. **Huddersfield** ended the first season at their new £15m. home with promotion to the First Division via a 2-1 victory against Bristol Rov manager Neil Warnock's third play-off success (after two with Notts Co). Of the three clubs who missed automatic promotion by one place, only **Chesterfield** achieved it in the play-offs, comfortably beating Bury 2-0.

1996: Under new manager Martin O'Neill (a Wembley play-off winner with Wycombe in 1994), **Leicester** returned to the Premiership a year after leaving it. They had finished fifth in the table, but in the Final came from behind to beat third-placed Crystal Palace by Steve Claridge's shot in the last seconds of extra time. In the Second Division **Bradford City** came sixth, nine points behind Blackpool (3rd), but beat them (from two down in the semi-final first leg) and then clinched promotion by 2-0 v Notts County at Wembley. It was City's greatest day since they won the Cup in 1911. **Plymouth Argyle** beat Darlington in the Third Division Final to earn promotion a year after being relegated. It was manager Neil Warnock's fourth play-off triumph in seven seasons after two with Notts County (1990 and 1991) and a third with Huddersfield in 1995.

1997: High drama at Wembley as **Crystal Palace** left it late against Sheffield Utd in the First Division play-off final. The match was scoreless until the last 10 seconds when David Hopkin lobbed Blades' keeper Simon Tracey from 25 yards to send the Eagles back to the Premiership after two seasons of Nationwide action. In the Second Division play-off final, **Crewe** beat Brentford 1-0 courtesy of a Shaun Smith goal. **Northampton** celebrated their first Wembley appearance with a 1-0 victory over Swansea thanks to John Frain's injury time free kick in the Third Division play-off final.

1998: In one of the finest games ever seen at Wembley, **Charlton** eventually triumphed 7-6 on penalties over Sunderland. For Charlton, Wearside-born Clive Mendonca scored a hat-trick and Richard Rufus his first career goal in a match that lurched between joy and despair for both sides as it ended 4-4. Sunderland defender Michael Gray's superb performance ill deserved to end with his weakly struck spot kick being saved by Sasa Ilic. In the Third Division, the penalty spot also had a role to play, as **Colchester**'s David Gregory scored the only goal to defeat Torquay, while in the Second Division a Kevin Donovan goal gave **Grimsby** victory over Northampton.

1999: Elton John, watching via a personal satellite link in Seattle, saw his **Watford** side overcome Bolton 2-0 to reach the Premiership. Against technically superior opponents, Watford prevailed with application and teamwork. They also gave Bolton a lesson in finishing through match-winners by Nick Wright and Allan Smart. **Manchester City** staged a remarkable comeback to win the Second Division Final after trailing by goals by Carl Asaba and Robert Taylor for Gillingham. Kevin Horlock and Paul Dickov scored in stoppage time and City went on to win on penalties. A goal by Spaniard Alex Calvo-Garcia earned **Scunthorpe** a 1-0 success against Leyton Orient in the Third Division Final.

2000: After three successive play-off failures, **Ipswich** finally secured a place in the Premiership. They overcame the injury loss of leading scorer David Johnson to beat Barnsley 4-2 with goals by 36-year-old Tony Mowbray, Marcus Stewart and substitutes Richard Naylor and Martijn Reuser. With six minutes left of extra-time in the Second Division Final, **Gillingham** trailed Wigan 2-1. But headers by 38-year-old player-coach Steve Butler and fellow substitute Andy Thomson gave them a 3-2 victory. Andy Clarke, approaching his 33rd birthday, scored the only goal of the Third Division decider for **Peterborough** against Darlington.

2001: **Bolton**, unsuccessful play-off contenders in the two previous seasons, made no mistake at the third attempt. They flourished in the new surroundings of the Millennium Stadium to beat Preston 3-0 with goals by Gareth Farrelly, Michael Ricketts – his 24th of the season – and Ricardo Gardner to reach the Premiership. **Walsall**, relegated 12 months earlier, scored twice in a three-minute spell of extra time to win 3-2 against Reading in the Second Division Final, while **Blackpool** capped a marked improvement in the second half of the season by overcoming Leyton Orient 4-2 in the Third Division Final.

2002: Holding their nerve to win a penalty shoot-out 4-2, **Birmingham** wiped away the memory of three successive defeats in the semi-finals of the play-offs to return to the top division after an absence of 16 years. Substitute Darren Carter completed a fairy-tale first season as a professional by scoring the fourth spot-kick against Norwich. **Stoke** became the first successful team to come from the south dressing room in 12 finals since football was adopted by the home of Welsh rugby, beating Brentford 2-0 in the Second Division Final with Deon Burton's strike and a Ben Burgess own goal. Julian Alsop's 26th goal of the season helped **Cheltenham** defeat League newcomers Rushden & Diamonds 3-1 in the Third Division decider.

2003: **Wolves** benefactor Sir Jack Hayward finally saw his £60m investment pay dividends when the club he first supported as a boy returned to the top flight after an absence of 19 years by beating Sheffield Utd 3-0. It was also a moment to savour for manager Dave Jones, who was forced to leave his previous club Southampton because of child abuse allegations, which were later found to be groundless. **Cardiff**, away from the game's second tier for 18 years, returned with an extra-time winner from substitute Andy Campbell against QPR after a goalless 90 minutes in the Division Two Final. **Bournemouth**, relegated 12 months earlier, became the first team to score five in the end-of-season deciders, beating Lincoln 5-2 in the Division Three Final.

2004: Three tight, tense Finals produced only two goals, the lowest number since the Play-offs were introduced. One of them, scored by Neil Shipperley, gave **Crystal Palace** victory over West Ham, the much-travelled striker tapping in a rebound after Stephen Bywater parried Andy Johnson's shot. It completed a remarkable transformation for Crystal Palace, who were 19th in the table when Iain Dowie left Oldham to become their manager. **Brighton** made an immediate return to Division One in a poor game against Bristol City which looked set for extra-time until Leon Knight netted his 27th goal of the campaign from the penalty spot after 84 minutes. **Huddersfield** also went back up at the first attempt, winning the Division Three Final in a penalty shoot-out after a goalless 120 minutes against Mansfield.

2005: Goals were few and far between for Bobby Zamora during **West Ham**'s Championship season – but what a difference in the Play-offs. The former Brighton and Tottenham striker scored three times in the 4-2 aggregate win over Ipswich in the semi-finals and was on the mark again with the only goal against Preston at the Millennium Stadium. **Sheffield Wed** were eight minute away from defeat against Hartlepool in the League One decider when Steven MacLean made it 2-2 from the penalty spot and they went on to win 4-2 in extra-time. **Southend**, edged out of an automatic promotion place, won the League Two Final 2-0 against Lincoln, Freddy Eastwood scoring their first in extra-time and making the second for Duncan Jupp. **Carlisle** beat Stevenage 1-0 with a goal by Peter Murphy in the Conference Final to regain their League place 12 months after being relegated.

2006: From the moment Marlon King scored his 22nd goal of the season to set up a 3-0 win over Crystal Palace in the semi-final first leg, **Watford** had the conviction of a team going places. Sure enough, they went on to beat Leeds just as comfortably in the final. Jay DeMerit, who was playing non-league football 18 months earlier, headed his side in front. James Chambers fired in a shot that hit a post and went in off goalkeeper Neil Sullivan. Then Darius Henderson put away a penalty after King was brought down by Shaun Derry, the man whose tackle had ended Boothroyd's playing career at the age of 26. **Barnsley** beat Swansea on penalties in the League One Final, Nick Colgan making the vital save from Alan Tate, while Steve Guinan's goal earned **Cheltenham** a 1-0 win over Grimsby in the League Two Final. **Hereford** returned to the Football League after a nine-year absence with Ryan Green's extra-time winner against Halifax in the Conference Final.

2007: Record crowds, plenty of goals and a return to Wembley for the finals made for some eventful and entertaining matches. Stephen Pearson, signed from Celtic for £650,000 in the January transfer window, took **Derby** back to the Premier League after an absence of five seasons with a 61st minute winner, his first goal for the club, against accounted for West Bromwich Albion. It was third time lucky for manager Billy Davies, who had led Preston into the play-offs, without success, in the two previous seasons. **Blackpool** claimed a place in the game's second tier for the first time for 30 years by beating Yeovil 2-0 – their tenth successive victory in a remarkable end-of-season run. Richard Walker took his tally for the season to 23 with two goals for **Bristol Rov**, who beat Shrewsbury 3-1 in the League Two Final. Sammy McIlroy, who led Macclesfield into the league in 1997, saw his Morecambe side fall behind in the Conference Final against Exeter, but they recovered to win 2-1.

2008: Wembley has produced some unlikely heroes down the years, but rarely one to match 39-year-old Dean Windass. The **Hull** striker took his home-town club into the top-flight for the first time with the only goal of the Championship Final against Bristol City – and it was a goal fit to grace any game. In front of a record crowd for the final of 86,703, Fraizer Campbell, his 20-year-old partner up front, picked out Windass on the edge of the penalty box and a sweetly-struck volley flew into the net. **Doncaster**, who like Hull faced an uncertain future a few years earlier, beat Leeds 1-0 in the League One Final with a header by James Hayer from Brian Stock's corner. Jim Gannon had lost four Wembley finals with **Stockport** as a player, but his first as manager brought a 3-2 win against Rochdale in the League Two Final with goals by Anthony Pilkington and Liam Dickinson and a Nathan Stanton own goal. Exeter's 1-0 win over Cambridge United in the Conference Final took them back into the Football League after an absence of five years.

2009: Delight for Burnley, back in the big time after 33 years thanks to a fine goal from 20 yards by Wade Elliott, and for their town which became the smallest to host Premier League football. Despair for Sheffield Utd, whose bid to regain a top-flight place ended with two players, Jamie Ward and Lee Hendrie, sent off by referee Mike Dean. Martyn Woolford capped a man-of-the-match performance with an 85th minute winner for Scunthorpe, who beat Millwall 3-2 to make an immediate return to the Championship, Matt Sparrow having scored their first two goals. Gillingham also went back up at the first attempt, beating Shrewsbury with Simeon Jackson's header seconds from the end of normal time in the League Two Final. Torquay returned to the Football League after a two-year absence by beating Cambridge United 2-0 in the Conference Final.

2010: Blackpool, under the eccentric yet shrewd Ian Holloway, claimed the big prize two years almost to the day after the manager was sacked from his previous job at Leicester. On a scorching afternoon, with temperatures reaching 106 degrees, they twice came back from a goal down to draw level against Cardiff through Charlie Adam and Gary Taylor-Fletcher, then scored what proved to be the winner through Brett Ormerod at the end of a pulsating first half. **Millwall**, beaten in five previous play-offs, reached the Championship with the only goal of the game against Swindon from captain Paul Robinson. **Dagenham & Redbridge** defeated Rotherham 3-2 in the League Two Final, Jon Nurse scoring the winner 20 minutes from the end. **Oxford** returned to the Football League after an absence of four years with a 3-1 over York in the Conference Final.

2011: Scott Sinclair scored a hat-trick as **Swansea** reached the top flight, just eight years after almost going out of the Football League. Two of his goals came from the penalty spot as Reading were beaten 4-2 in the Championship Final, with Stephen Dobbie netting their other goal. The day after his father's side lost to Barcelona in the Champions League Final, Darren Ferguson led **Peterborough** back to the Championship at the first attempt with goals by Tommy Rowe, Craig Mackail Smith and Grant McCann in the final 12 minutes against Huddersfield. John Mousinho scored the only one of the League Two Final for **Stevenage**, who won a second successive promotion by beating Torquay. **AFC Wimbledon**, formed by supporters in 2002 after the former FA Cup winning club relocated to Milton Keynes, completed their rise from the Combined Counties to the Football League by winning a penalty shoot-out against Luton after a goalless draw in the Conference Final.

2012: West Ham were third in the Championship and second best to Blackpool in the final. But they passed the post first at Wembley, thanks to an 87th minute goal from Ricardo Vaz Te which gave Sam Allardyce's side a 2-1 victory. Allardyce brought the Portuguese striker to Upton Park from Barnsley for £500,000 – a fee dwarfed by the millions his goal was worth to the club. Goalkeepers took centre stage in the League One Final, with **Huddersfield** and Sheffield United still locked in a marathon shoot-out after a goalless 120 minutes. Alex Smithies put the 21st penalty past his opposite number Steve Simonsen, who then drove over the crossbar to give Huddersfield victory by 8-7. Nick Powell, 18, lit up the League Two Final with a spectacular volley as **Crewe** beat Cheltenham 2-0. **York** regained a Football League place after an absence of eight years by beating Luton 2-1 in the Conference decider.

2013: Veteran Kevin Phillips, a loser in three previous finals, came off the bench to fire **Crystal**

Palace into the Premier League with an extra-time penalty. Wilfried Zaha was brought down by Marco Cassetti and 39-year-old Phillips showed nerves of steel to convert the spot-kick. A goalline clearance by Joel Ward then denied Fernando Forestieri as Watford sought an equaliser. **Yeovil** upset the odds by reaching the Championship for the first time. They defeated Brentford 2-1, Paddy Madden scoring his 23rd goal of the season and on-loan Dan Burn adding the second. **Bradford**, back at Wembley three months after their Capital One Cup adventure, swept aside Northampton 3-0 in the League Two Final with goals from James Hanson, Rory McArdle and Nahki Wells. **Newport** returned to the Football League after a 25-year absence by defeating Wrexham 2-0 in the Conference Final.

2014: An immediate return to the Premier League for **Queens Park Rangers** seemed unlikely when Gary O'Neil was sent off for bringing down Derby's Johnny Russell. There was still more than half-an-hour to go of a match Derby had dominated. But Rangers held on and with 90 minutes nearly up Bobby Zamora punished a mistake by captain Richard Keogh to score the only goal. **Rotherham** retrieved a 2-0 deficit against Leyton Orient with two goals by Alex Revell in the League One Final and won the eventual penalty shoot-out 4-3 for a second successive promotion. **Fleetwood** achieved their sixth promotion in ten seasons with a 1-0 victory over Burton, courtesy of a free-kick from Antoni Sarcevic in the League Two Final. Liam Hughes and Ryan Donaldson were on the mark as **Cambridge United** returned to the Football League after a nine-year absence by beating Gateshead 2-1 in the Conference Final, two months after winning the FA Trophy at Wembley.

2015: **Norwich** were rewarded for a flying start with a return to the Premier League at the first attempt. Cameron Jerome put them ahead against Middlesbrough after 12 minutes of the Championship Final and Nathan Redmond made it 2-0 three minutes later, a scoreline they maintained without too many problems. Jermaine Beckford's hat-trick put **Preston** on the way to a record 4-0 victory over Swindon in the League One Final. **Southend**, who like Preston were denied automatic promotion on the final day of the regular season, beat Wycombe 7-6 on penalties after the League Two Final ended 1-1. **Bristol Rovers** were also penalty winners, by 5-3 against Grimsby in the Conference decider, so making an immediate return to the Football League.

2016: A goal worthy of winning any game took Hull back to the Premier League at the first attempt. Mohamed Diame, their French-born Senegal international midfielder, curled a 25-yard shot into the top corner after 72 minutes for a 1-0 win over Sheffield Wednesday. Another spectacular goal, by Adam Hammill, helped Barnsley beat Millwall 3-1 on their return to Wembley for the League One Final after winning the Johnstone's Paint Trophy. AFC Wimbledon achieved their sixth promotion since being formed by supporters in 2002, defeating favourites Plymouth 2-0 in the League Two Final. Grimsby ended a six-year absence from the Football League with a 3-1 victory over Forest Green in the National League decider.

2017: David Wagner transformed **Huddersfield** from relegation candidates into a Premier League club – with the help of German penalty-taking expertise. After a goalless Championship Play-off Final, they beat Reading 4-3 in a shoot-out clinched by Christopher Schindler'spot-kick. Steve Morison followed up his two goals in **Millwall**'s League One semi-final against Scunthorpe with the only one against Bradford, in the 85th minute at Wembley. Brad Potts and Mark Cullen were on the mark to give **Blackpool** a 2-1 victory over Exeter in the League Two Final. **Forest Green** beat Tranmere 3-1 in the National League Final, on-loan Kaiyne Woolery scoring twice.

2018: **Fulham** overcame the sending-off of central defender Denis Odoi after 70 minutes for a second yellow card to reach the Premier League. They protected the lead established by a goal from captain Tom Cairney, set up by the Championship's Player of the Year, 18-year-old Ryan Sessegnon, to defeat Aston Villa 1-0. There was another captain's performance in the League One Final, Richard Wood scoring both goals in **Rotherham**'s 2-1 win over Shrewsbury. **Coventry** ended years of decline by beating Exeter 3-1 in the League Two Final with goals from Jordan Willis, Jordan Shipley and Jack Grimmer. **Tranmere** had Liam Ridehalgh dismissed after 48 seconds for a two-footed challenge, but were 2-1 winners over Boreham Wood in the National League Final (Andy Cook and James Norwood).

Play-off attendances

Year		Attendance	Year		Attendance
1987	20	310,000	2004	15	388,675
1988	19	305,817	2005	15	353,330
1989	18	234,393	2006	15	340,804
1990	15	291,428	2007	15	405,278
1991	15	266,442	2008	15	382,032
1992	15	277,684	2009	15	380,329
1993	15	319,907	2010	15	370,055
1994	15	314,817	2011	15	310,998
1995	15	295,317	2012	15	332,930
1996	15	308,515	2013	15	346,062
1997	15	309,085	2014	15	307,011
1998	15	320,795	2015	15	367,374
1999	15	372,969	2016	15	393,145
2000	15	333,999	2017	15	323,727
2001	15	317,745	2018	15	373,295
2002	15	327,894	2019	15	430,025 (record)
2003	15	374,461			

THE THINGS THEY SAY ABOUT TRAGEDY ...

'It is difficult to put into words how much you have meant to this football club and to the city of Leicester. We all know about the investment in the club. But this is about so much more. You also cared for the entire community. Your contribution to Leicester's hospitals and charities will never be forgotten' – **Kasper Schmeichel**, Leicester goalkeeper, with words which captured the many tributes to owner Vichai Srivaddhanaprabha, who died, along with four others, in a helicopter crash.

'I have received a very big mission and legacy to pass on. I intend to do just that' – **Aiywatt Srivaddhanaprabha**, the owner's son, pledges his commitment to the club.

'Football can often get this wrong, but Leicester City football club has honoured Vichai with total class and total respect' – **Alan Shearer**, Match of the Day pundit.

'I wasn't really thinking about stuff like that. I'm happy I did it. We all know why' – **Demarai Gray**, Leicester winger, on the yellow card for removing his shirt to reveal a tribute after scoring the winning goal in his side's first match, against Cardiff, since the tragedy

'We were professional and it was important for the referee to be professional. We know the rules' – **Claude Puel**, Leicester manager, has no complaint about refereeing Lee Probert's decision which drew some strong criticism throughout football.

'I've been in football management for 40 years and it's by far the most difficult week in my career by an absolute mile' – **Neil Warnock**, Cardiff manager, on the death in a plane crash of the club's record-signing Emiliano Sala.

'We are completely heartbroken. The success he brought to the club will be his legacy' – **Nigel Travis**, chairman of Leyton Orient, on the death of manager **Justin Edinburgh**, six weeks after leading them back to the Football League.

ENGLISH HONOURS LIST

PREMIER LEAGUE

	First	Pts	Second	Pts	Third	Pts
1992–3a	Manchester Utd	84	Aston Villa	74	Norwich	72
1993–4a	Manchester Utd	92	Blackburn	84	Newcastle	77
1994–5a	Blackburn	89	Manchester Utd	88	Nottm Forest	77
1995–6b	Manchester Utd	82	Newcastle	78	Liverpool	71
1996–7b	Manchester Utd	75	Newcastle	68	Arsenal	68
1997–8b	Arsenal	78	Manchester Utd	77	Liverpool	65
1998–9b	Manchester Utd	79	Arsenal	78	Chelsea	75
1999–00b	Manchester Utd	91	Arsenal	73	Leeds	69
2000–01b	Manchester Utd	80	Arsenal	70	Liverpool	69
2001–02b	Arsenal	87	Liverpool	80	Manchester Utd	77
2002–03b	Manchester Utd	83	Arsenal	78	Newcastle	69
2003–04b	Arsenal	90	Chelsea	79	Manchester Utd	75
2004–05b	Chelsea	95	Arsenal	83	Manchester Utd	77
2005–06b	Chelsea	91	Manchester Utd	83	Liverpool	82
2006–07b	Manchester Utd	89	Chelsea	83	Liverpool	68
2007–08b	Manchester Utd	87	Chelsea	85	Arsenal	83
2008–09b	Manchester Utd	90	Liverpool	86	Chelsea	83
2009–10b	Chelsea	86	Manchester Utd	85	Arsenal	75
2010–11b	Manchester Utd	80	Chelsea	71	Manchester City	71
2011–12b	*Manchester City	89	Manchester Ud	89	Arsenal	70
2012–13b	Manchester Utd	89	Manchester City	78	Chelsea	75
2013–14b	Manchester City	86	Liverpool	84	Chelsea	82
2014–15b	Chelsea	87	Manchester City	79	Arsenal	75
2015–16b	Leicester	81	Arsenal	71	Tottenham	70
2016–17b	Chelsea	93	Tottenham	86	Manchester City	78
2017–18b	Manchester City	100	Manchester Utd	81	Tottenham	77
2018–19b	Manchester City	98	Liverpool	97	Chelsea	72

* won on goal difference. Maximum points: a, 126; b, 114

FOOTBALL LEAGUE
FIRST DIVISION

1992–3	Newcastle	96	West Ham	88	††Portsmouth	88
1993–4	Crystal Palace	90	Nottm Forest	83	††Millwall	74
1994–5	Middlesbrough	82	††Reading	79	Bolton	77
1995–6	Sunderland	83	Derby	79	††Crystal Palace	75
1996–7	Bolton	98	Barnsley	80	††Wolves	76
1997–8	Nottm Forest	94	Middlesbrough	91	††Sunderland	90
1998–9	Sunderland	105	Bradford City	87	††Ipswich	86
1999–00	Charlton	91	Manchester City	89	Ipswich	87
2000–01	Fulham	101	Blackburn	91	Bolton	87
2001–02	Manchester City	99	WBA	89	††Wolves	86
2002–03	Portsmouth	98	Leicester	92	††Sheffield Utd	80
2003–04	Norwich	94	WBA	86	††Sunderland	79

CHAMPIONSHIP

2004–05	Sunderland	94	Wigan	87	††Ipswich	85
2005–06	Reading	106	Sheffield Utd	90	Watford	81
2006–07	Sunderland	88	Birmingham	86	Derby	84
2007–08	WBA	81	Stoke	79	Hull	75
2008–09	Wolves	90	Birmingham	83	††Sheffield Utd	80
2009–10	Newcastle	102	WBA	91	††Nottm Forest	79

2010–11	QPR	88	Norwich	84		Swansea 80
2011–12	Reading	89	Southampton	88	West Ham	86
2012–13	Cardiff	87	Hull	79	††Watford	77
2013–14	Leicester	102	Burnley	93	††Derby	85
2014–15	Bournemouth	90	Watford	89	Norwich	86
2015–16	Burnley	93	Middlesbrough	89	††Brighton	89
2016–17	Newcastle	94	Brighton	93	††Reading	85
2017 18	Wolves	99	Cardiff	90	Fulham	88
2018–19	Norwich	94	Sheffield Utd	89	††Leeds	83

Maximum points: 138 ††Not promoted after play-offs

SECOND DIVISION

1992–3	Stoke	93	Bolton	90	††Port Vale	89
1993–4	Reading	89	Port Vale	88	††Plymouth Argyle	85
1994 5	Birmingham	89	††Brentford	85	††Crewe	83
1995–6	Swindon	92	Oxford Utd	83	††Blackpool	82
1996–7	Bury	84	Stockport	82	††Luton	78
1997 8	Watford	88	Bristol City	85	Grimsby	72
1998–9	Fulham	101	Walsall	87	Manchester City	82
1999–00	Preston	95	Burnley	88	Gillingham	85
2000 01	Millwall	93	Rotherham	91	††Reading	86
2001–02	Brighton	90	Reading	84	††Brentford	83
2002–03	Wigan	100	Crewe	86	††Bristol City	83
2003–04	Plymouth Argyle	90	QPR	83	††Bristol City	82

LEAGUE ONE

2004–05	Luton	98	Hull	86	††Tranmere	79
2005–06	Southend	82	Colchester	79	††Brentford	76
2006–07	Scunthorpe	91	Bristol City	85	Blackpool	83
2007–08	Swansea	92	Nottm Forest	82	Doncaster	80
2008–09	Leicester	96	Peterborough	89	††MK Dons	87
2009–10	Norwich	95	Leeds	86	Millwall	85
2010 11	Brighton	95	Southampton	92	††Huddersfield	87
2011–12	Charlton	101	Sheffield Wed	93	††Sheffield Utd	90
2012 13	Doncaster	84	Bournemouth	83	††Brentford	79
2013–14	Wolves	103	Brentford	94	††Leyton Orient	86
2014 15	Bristol City	99	MK Dons	91	Preston	89
2015–16	Wigan	87	Burton	85	††Walsall	84
2016–17	Sheffield Utd	100	Bolton	86	††Scunthorpe	82
2017–18	Wigan	98	Blackburn	96	††Shrewsbury	87
2018–19	Luton	94	Barnsley	91	Charlton	88

Maximum points: 138 †† Not promoted after play-offs

THIRD DIVISION

1992–3a	Cardiff	83	Wrexham	80	Barnet	79
1993–4a	Shrewsbury	79	Chester	74	Crewe	73
1994–5a	Carlisle	91	Walsall	83	Chesterfield	81
1995–6b	Preston	86	Gillingham	83	Bury	79
1996 7b	Wigan	87	Fulham	87	Carlisle	84
1997–8b	Notts Co	99	Macclesfield	82	Lincoln	75
1998–9b	Brentford	85	Cambridge Utd	81	Cardiff	80
1999–00b	Swansea	85	Rotherham	84	Northampton	82
2000–01b	Brighton	92	Cardiff	82	*Chesterfield	80
2001–02b	Plymouth Argyle	102	Luton	97	Mansfield	79
2002–03b	Rushden & D	87	Hartlepool Utd	85	Wrexham	84
2003–04b	Doncaster	92	Hull	88	Torquay	81
2018–19b	Lincoln	85	Bury	79	MK Dons	79

* Deducted 9 points for financial irregularities

LEAGUE TWO

2004–05b	Yeovil	83	Scunthorpe	80	Swansea	80
2005–06b	Carlisle	86	Northampton	83	Leyton Orient	81
2006–07b	Walsall	89	Hartlepool	88	Swindon	85
2007–08b	MK Dons	97	Peterborough	92	Hereford	88
2008–09b	Brentford	85	Exeter	79	Wycombe	78
2009–10b	Notts Co	93	Bournemouth	83	Rochdale	82
2010–11b	Chesterfield	86	Bury	81	Wycombe	80
2011–12b	Swindon	93	Shrewsbury	88	Crawley	84
2012–13b	Gillingham	83	Rotherham	79	Port Vale	78
2013–14b	Chesterfield	84	Scunthorpe	81	Rochdale	81
2014–15b	Burton	94	Shrewsbury	89	Bury	85
2015–16b	Northampton	99	Oxford	86	Bristol Rov	85
2016–17b	Portsmouth	87	Plymouth	87	Doncaster	85
2017–18b	Accrington	93	Luton	88	Wycombe	84
2018–19b	Lincoln	85	Bury	79	MK Dons	79

Maximum points: a, 126; b, 138;

FOOTBALL LEAGUE 1888–1992

1888–89a	Preston	40	Aston Villa	29	Wolves	28
1889–90a	Preston	33	Everton	31	Blackburn	27
1890–1a	Everton	29	Preston	27	Notts Co	26
1891–2b	Sunderland	42	Preston	37	Bolton	36

OLD FIRST DIVISION

1892–3c	Sunderland	48	Preston	37	Everton	36
1893–4c	Aston Villa	44	Sunderland	38	Derby	36
1894–5c	Sunderland	47	Everton	42	Aston Villa	39
1895–6c	Aston Villa	45	Derby	41	Everton	39
1896–7c	Aston Villa	47	Sheffield Utd	36	Derby	36
1897–8c	Sheffield Utd	42	Sunderland	39	Wolves	35
1898–9d	Aston Villa	45	Liverpool	43	Burnley	39
1899–1900d	Aston Villa	50	Sheffield Utd	48	Sunderland	41
1900–1d	Liverpool	45	Sunderland	43	Notts Co	40
1901–2d	Sunderland	44	Everton	41	Newcastle	37
1902–3d	The Wednesday	42	Aston Villa	41	Sunderland	41
1903–4d	The Wednesday	47	Manchester City	44	Everton	43
1904–5d	Newcastle	48	Everton	47	Manchester City	46
1905–6e	Liverpool	51	Preston	47	The Wednesday	44
1906–7e	Newcastle	51	Bristol City	48	Everton	45
1907–8e	Manchester Utd	52	Aston Villa	43	Manchester City	43
1908–9e	Newcastle	53	Everton	46	Sunderland	44
1909–10e	Aston Villa	53	Liverpool	48	Blackburn	45
1910–11e	Manchester Utd	52	Aston Villa	51	Sunderland	45
1911–12e	Blackburn	49	Everton	46	Newcastle	44
1912–13e	Sunderland	54	Aston Villa	50	Sheffield Wed	49
1913–14e	Blackburn	51	Aston Villa	44	Middlesbrough	43
1914–15e	Everton	46	Oldham	45	Blackburn	43
1919–20f	WBA	60	Burnley	51	Chelsea	49
1920–1f	Burnley	59	Manchester City	54	Bolton	52
1921–2f	Liverpool	57	Tottenham	51	Burnley	49
1922–3f	Liverpool	60	Sunderland	54	Huddersfield	53
1923–4f	*Huddersfield	57	Cardiff	57	Sunderland	53
1924–5f	Huddersfield	58	WBA	56	Bolton	55
1925–6f	Huddersfield	57	Arsenal	52	Sunderland	48

1926–7f	Newcastle	56	Huddersfield	51	Sunderland	49
1927–8f	Everton	53	Huddersfield	51	Leicester	48
1928–9f	Sheffield Wed	52	Leicester	51	Aston Villa	50
1929–30f	Sheffield Wed	60	Derby	50	Manchester City	47
1930–1f	Arsenal	66	Aston Villa	59	Sheffield Wed	52
1931–2f	Everton	56	Arsenal	54	Sheffield Wed	50
1932–3f	Arsenal	58	Aston Villa	54	Sheffield Wed	51
1933–4f	Arsenal	59	Huddersfield	56	Tottenham	49
1934–5f	Arsenal	58	Sunderland	54	Sheffield Wed	49
1935–6f	Sunderland	56	Derby	48	Huddersfield	48
1936–7f	Manchester City	57	Charlton	54	Arsenal	52
1937–8f	Arsenal	52	Wolves	51	Preston	49
1938–9f	Everton	59	Wolves	55	Charlton	50
1946–7f	Liverpool	57	Manchester Utd	56	Wolves	56
1947–8f	Arsenal	59	Manchester Utd	52	Burnley	52
1948–9f	Portsmouth	58	Manchester Utd	53	Derby	53
1949–50f	*Portsmouth	53	Wolves	53	Sunderland	52
1950–1f	Tottenham	60	Manchester Utd	56	Blackpool	50
1951–2f	Manchester Utd	57	Tottenham	53	Arsenal	53
1952–3f	*Arsenal	54	Preston	54	Wolves	51
1953–4f	Wolves	57	WBA	53	Huddersfield	51
1954–5f	Chelsea	52	Wolves	48	Portsmouth	48
1955–6f	Manchester Utd	60	Blackpool	49	Wolves	49
1956–7f	Manchester Utd	64	Tottenham	56	Preston	56
1957–8f	Wolves	64	Preston	59	Tottenham	51
1958–9f	Wolves	61	Manchester Utd	55	Arsenal	50
1959–60f	Burnley	55	Wolves	54	Tottenham	53
1960–1f	Tottenham	66	Sheffield Wed	58	Wolves	57
1961–2f	Ipswich	56	Burnley	53	Tottenham	52
1962–3f	Everton	61	Tottenham	55	Burnley	54
1963–4f	Liverpool	57	Manchester Utd	53	Everton	52
1964–5f	*Manchester Utd	61	Leeds	61	Chelsea	56
1965–6f	Liverpool	61	Leeds	55	Burnley	55
1966–7f	Manchester Utd	60	Nottm Forest	56	Tottenham	56
1967–8f	Manchester City	58	Manchester Utd	56	Liverpool	55
1968–9f	Leeds	67	Liverpool	61	Everton	57
1969–70f	Everton	66	Leeds	57	Chelsea	55
1970–1f	Arsenal	65	Leeds	64	Tottenham	52
1971–2f	Derby	58	Leeds	57	Liverpool	57
1972–3f	Liverpool	60	Arsenal	57	Leeds	53
1973–4f	Leeds	62	Liverpool	57	Derby	48
1974–5f	Derby	53	Liverpool	51	Ipswich	51
1975–6f	Liverpool	60	QPR	59	Manchester Utd	56
1976–7f	Liverpool	57	Manchester City	56	Ipswich	52
1977–8f	Nottm Forest	64	Liverpool	57	Everton	55
1978–9f	Liverpool	68	Nottm Forest	60	WBA	59
1979–80f	Liverpool	60	Manchester Utd	58	Ipswich	53
1980–1f	Aston Villa	60	Ipswich	56	Arsenal	53
1981–2g	Liverpool	87	Ipswich	83	Manchester Utd	78
1982–3g	Liverpool	82	Watford	71	Manchester Utd	70
1983–4g	Liverpool	80	Southampton	77	Nottm Forest	74
1984–5g	Everton	90	Liverpool	77	Tottenham	77
1985–6g	Liverpool	88	Everton	86	West Ham	84
1986–7g	Everton	86	Liverpool	77	Tottenham	71

1987–8h	Liverpool	90	Manchester Utd	81	Nottm Forest	73
1988–9j	††Arsenal	76	Liverpool	76	Nottm Forest	64
1989–90j	Liverpool	79	Aston Villa	70	Tottenham	63
1990–1j	Arsenal	83	Liverpool	76	Crystal Palace	69
1991–2g	Leeds	82	Manchester Utd	78	Sheffield Wed	75

Maximum points: *a*, 44; *b*, 52; *c*, 60; *d*, 68; *e*, 76; *f*, 84; *g*, 126; *h*, 120; *j*, 114

*Won on goal average †Won on goal diff ††Won on goals scored No comp 1915–19 –1939–46

OLD SECOND DIVISION 1892–1992

1892–3a	Small Heath	36	Sheffield Utd	35	Darwen	30
1893–4b	Liverpool	50	Small Heath	42	Notts Co	39
1894–5c	Bury	48	Notts Co	39	Newton Heath	38
1895–6c	*Liverpool	46	Manchester City	46	Grimsby	42
1896–7c	Notts Co	42	Newton Heath	39	Grimsby	38
1897–8c	Burnley	48	Newcastle	45	Manchester City	39
1898–9d	Manchester City	52	Glossop	46	Leicester Fosse	45
1899–1900d	The Wednesday	54	Bolton	52	Small Heath	46
1900–1d	Grimsby	49	Small Heath	48	Burnley	44
1901–2d	WBA	55	Middlesbrough	51	Preston	42
1902–3d	Manchester City	54	Small Heath	51	Woolwich Arsenal	48
1903–4d	Preston	50	Woolwich Arsenal	49	Manchester Utd	48
1904–5d	Liverpool	58	Bolton	56	Manchester Utd	53
1905–6e	Bristol City	66	Manchester Utd	62	Chelsea	53
1906–7e	Nottm Forest	60	Chelsea	57	Leicester Fosse	48
1907–8e	Bradford City	54	Leicester Fosse	52	Oldham	50
1908–9e	Bolton	52	Tottenham	51	WBA	51
1909–10e	Manchester City	54	Oldham	53	Hull	53
1910–11e	WBA	53	Bolton	51	Chelsea	49
1911–12e	*Derby	54	Chelsea	54	Burnley	52
1912–13e	Preston	53	Burnley	50	Birmingham	46
1913–14e	Notts Co	53	Bradford PA	49	Woolwich Arsenal	49
1914–15e	Derby	53	Preston	50	Barnsley	47
1919–20f	Tottenham	70	Huddersfield	64	Birmingham	56
1920–1f	*Birmingham	58	Cardiff	58	Bristol City	51
1921–2f	Nottm Forest	56	Stoke	52	Barnsley	52
1922–3f	Notts Co	53	West Ham	51	Leicester	51
1923–4f	Leeds	54	Bury	51	Derby	51
1924–5f	Leicester	59	Manchester Utd	57	Derby	55
1925–6f	Sheffield Wed	60	Derby	57	Chelsea	52
1926–7f	Middlesbrough	62	Portsmouth	54	Manchester City	54
1927–8f	Manchester City	59	Leeds	57	Chelsea	54
1928–9f	Middlesbrough	55	Grimsby	53	Bradford City	48
1929–30f	Blackpool	58	Chelsea	55	Oldham	53
1930–1f	Everton	61	WBA	54	Tottenham	51
1931–2f	Wolves	56	Leeds	54	Stoke	52
1932–3f	Stoke	56	Tottenham	55	Fulham	50
1933–4f	Grimsby	59	Preston	52	Bolton	51
1934–5f	Brentford	61	Bolton	56	West Ham	56
1935–6f	Manchester Utd	56	Charlton	55	Sheffield Utd	52
1936–7f	Leicester	56	Blackpool	55	Bury	52
1937–8f	Aston Villa	57	Manchester Utd	53	Sheffield Utd	53
1938–9f	Blackburn	55	Sheffield Utd	54	Sheffield Wed	53
1946–7f	Manchester City	62	Burnley	58	Birmingham	55
1947–8f	Birmingham	59	Newcastle	56	Southampton	52
1948–9f	Fulham	57	WBA	56	Southampton	55

Season	First	Pts	Second	Pts	Third	Pts
1949–50f	Tottenham	61	Sheffield Wed	52	Sheffield Utd	52
1950–1f	Preston	57	Manchester City	52	Cardiff	50
1951–2f	Sheffield Wed	53	Cardiff	51	Birmingham	51
1952–3f	Sheffield Utd	60	Huddersfield	58	Luton	52
1953–4f	*Leicester	56	Everton	56	Blackburn	55
1954–5f	*Birmingham	54	Luton	54	Rotherham	54
1955–6f	Sheffield Wed	55	Leeds	52	Liverpool	48
1956–7f	Leicester	61	Nottm Forest	54	Liverpool	53
1957–8f	West Ham	57	Blackburn	56	Charlton	55
1958–9f	Sheffield Wed	62	Fulham	60	Sheffield Utd	53
1959–60f	Aston Villa	59	Cardiff	58	Liverpool	50
1960–1f	Ipswich	59	Sheffield Utd	58	Liverpool	52
1961–2f	Liverpool	62	Leyton Orient	54	Sunderland	53
1962–3f	Stoke	53	Chelsea	52	Sunderland	52
1963–4f	Leeds	63	Sunderland	61	Preston	56
1964–5f	Newcastle	57	Northampton	56	Bolton	50
1965–6f	Manchester City	59	Southampton	54	Coventry	53
1966–7f	Coventry	59	Wolves	58	Carlisle	52
1967–8f	Ipswich	59	QPR	58	Blackpool	58
1968–9f	Derby	63	Crystal Palace	56	Charlton	50
1969–70f	Huddersfield	60	Blackpool	53	Leicester	51
1970–1f	Leicester	59	Sheffield Utd	56	Cardiff	53
1971–2f	Norwich	57	Birmingham	56	Millwall	55
1972–3f	Burnley	62	QPR	61	Aston Villa	50
1973–4f	Middlesbrough	65	Luton	50	Carlisle	49
1974–5f	Manchester Utd	61	Aston Villa	58	Norwich	53
1975–6f	Sunderland	56	Bristol City	53	WBA	53
1976–7f	Wolves	57	Chelsea	55	Nottm Forest	52
1977–8f	Bolton	58	Southampton	57	Tottenham	56
1978–9f	Crystal Palace	57	Brighton	56	Stoke	56
1979–80f	Leicester	55	Sunderland	54	Birmingham	53
1980–1f	West Ham	66	Notts Co	53	Swansea	50
1981–2g	Luton	88	Watford	80	Norwich	71
1982–3g	QPR	85	Wolves	75	Leicester	70
1983–4g	†Chelsea	88	Sheffield Wed	88	Newcastle	80
1984–5g	Oxford Utd	84	Birmingham	82	Manchester City	74
1985–6g	Norwich	84	Charlton	77	Wimbledon	76
1986–7g	Derby	84	Portsmouth	78	††Oldham	75
1987–8h	Millwall	82	Aston Villa	78	Middlesbrough	78
1988–9j	Chelsea	99	Manchester City	82	Crystal Palace	81
1989–90j	†Leeds	85	Sheffield Utd	85	†† Newcastle	80
1990–1j	Oldham	88	West Ham	87	Sheffield Wed	82
1991–2j	Ipswich	84	Middlesbrough	80	†† Derby	78

Maximum points: a, 44; b, 56; c, 60; d, 68; e, 76; f, 84; g, 126; h, 132; j, 138 * Won on goal average † Won on goal difference †† Not promoted after play-offs

THIRD DIVISION 1958–92

Season	First	Pts	Second	Pts	Third	Pts
1958–9	Plymouth Argyle	62	Hull	61	Brentford	57
1959–60	Southampton	61	Norwich	59	Shrewsbury	52
1960–1	Bury	68	Walsall	62	QPR	60
1961–2	Portsmouth	65	Grimsby	62	Bournemouth	59
1962–3	Northampton	62	Swindon	58	Port Vale	54
1963–4	*Coventry	60	Crystal Palace	60	Watford	58
1964–5	Carlisle	60	Bristol City	59	Mansfield	59
1965–6	Hull	69	Millwall	65	QPR	57

73

1966–7	QPR	67	Middlesbrough	55	Watford	54
1967–8	Oxford Utd	57	Bury	56	Shrewsbury	55
1968–9	*Watford	64	Swindon	64	Luton	61
1969–70	Orient	62	Luton	60	Bristol Rov	56
1970–1	Preston	61	Fulham	60	Halifax	56
1971–2	Aston Villa	70	Brighton	65	Bournemouth	62
1972–3	Bolton	61	Notts Co	57	Blackburn	55
1973–4	Oldham	62	Bristol Rov	61	York	61
1974–5	Blackburn	60	Plymouth Argyle	59	Charlton	55
1975–6	Hereford	63	Cardiff	57	Millwall	56
1976–7	Mansfield	64	Brighton	61	Crystal Palace	59
1977–8	Wrexham	61	Cambridge Utd	58	Preston	56
1978–9	Shrewsbury	61	Watford	60	Swansea	60
1979–80	Grimsby	62	Blackburn	59	Sheffield Wed	58
1980–1	Rotherham	61	Barnsley	59	Charlton	59
†1981–2	**Burnley	80	Carlisle	80	Fulham	78
†1982–3	Portsmouth	91	Cardiff	86	Huddersfield	82
†1983–4	Oxford Utd	95	Wimbledon	87	Sheffield Utd	83
†1984–5	Bradford City	94	Millwall	90	Hull	87
†1985–6	Reading	94	Plymouth Argyle	87	Derby	84
†1986–7	Bournemouth	97	Middlesbrough	94	Swindon	87
†1987–8	Sunderland	93	Brighton	84	Walsall	82
†1988–9	Wolves	92	Sheffield Utd	84	Port Vale	84
†1989–90	Bristol Rov	93	Bristol City	91	Notts Co	87
†1990–1	Cambridge Utd	86	Southend	85	Grimsby	83
†1991–2	Brentford	82	Birmingham	81	††Huddersfield	78

* Won on goal average ** Won on goal difference † Maximum points 138 (previously 92) †† Not promoted after play–offs

FOURTH DIVISION 1958–92

1958–9	Port Vale	64	Coventry	60	York	60	Shrewsbury	58
1959–60	Walsall	65	Notts Co	60	Torquay	60	Watford	57
1960–1	Peterborough	66	Crystal Palace	64	Northampton	60	Bradford PA	60
1961–2	Millwall	56	Colchester	55	Wrexham	53	Carlisle	52
1962–3	Brentford	62	Oldham	59	Crewe	59	Mansfield	57
1963–4	*Gillingham	60	Carlisle	60	Workington	59	Exeter	58
1964–5	Brighton	63	Millwall	62	York	62	Oxford Utd	61
1965–6	*Doncaster	59	Darlington	59	Torquay	58	Colchester	56
1966–7	Stockport	64	Southport	59	Barrow	59	Tranmere	58
1967–8	Luton	66	Barnsley	61	Hartlepool Utd	60	Crewe	58
1968–9	Doncaster	59	Halifax	57	Rochdale	56	Bradford City	56
1969–70	Chesterfield	64	Wrexham	61	Swansea	60	Port Vale	59
1970–1	Notts Co	69	Bournemouth	60	Oldham	59	York	56
1971–2	Grimsby	63	Southend	60	Brentford	59	Scunthorpe	57
1972–3	Southport	62	Hereford	58	Cambridge Utd	57	Aldershot	56
1973–4	Peterborough	65	Gillingham	62	Colchester	60	Bury	59
1974–5	Mansfield	68	Shrewsbury	62	Rotherham	58	Chester	57
1975–6	Lincoln	74	Northampton	68	Reading	60	Tranmere	58
1976–7	Cambridge Utd	65	Exeter	62	Colchester	59	Bradford City	59
1977–8	Watford	71	Southend	60	Swansea	56	Brentford	59
1978–9	Reading	65	Grimsby	61	Wimbledon	61	Barnsley	61
1979–80	Huddersfield	66	Walsall	64	Newport	61	Portsmouth	60
1980–1	Southend	67	Lincoln	65	Doncaster	56	Wimbledon	55
†1981–2	Sheffield Utd	96	Bradford City	91	Wigan	91	Bournemouth	88
†1982–3	Wimbledon	98	Hull	90	Port Vale	88	Scunthorpe	83
†1983–4	York	101	Doncaster	85	Reading	82	Bristol City	82
†1984–5	Chesterfield	91	Blackpool	86	Darlington	85	Bury	84
†1985–6	Swindon	102	Chester	84	Mansfield	81	Port Vale	79
†1986–7	Northampton	99	Preston	90	Southend	80	††Wolves	79
†1987–8	Wolves	90	Cardiff	85	Bolton	78	††Scunthorpe	77

†1988–9	Rotherham	82	Tranmere	80	Crewe	78	††Scunthorpe	77
†1989–90	Exeter	89	Grimsby	79	Southend	75	††Stockport	74
†1990–1	Darlington	83	Stockport	82	Hartlepool Utd	82	Peterborough	80
1991–2a	Burnley	83	Rotherham	77	Mansfield	77	Blackpool	76

* Won on goal average Maximum points: †, 138; a, 126; previously 92 †† Not promoted after play–offs

THIRD DIVISION SOUTH 1920–58

1920–1a	Crystal Palace	59	Southampton	54	QPR	53
1921–2a	*Southampton	61	Plymouth Argyle	61	Portsmouth	53
1922–3a	Bristol City	59	Plymouth Argyle	53	Swansea	53
1923–4a	Portsmouth	59	Plymouth Argyle	55	Millwall	54
1924–5a	Swansea	57	Plymouth Argyle	56	Bristol City	53
1925–6a	Reading	57	Plymouth Argyle	56	Millwall	53
1926–7a	Bristol City	62	Plymouth Argyle	60	Millwall	56
1927–8a	Millwall	65	Northampton	55	Plymouth Argyle	53
1928–9a	*Charlton	54	Crystal Palace	54	Northampton	52
1929–30a	Plymouth Argyle	68	Brentford	61	QPR	51
1930–31a	Notts Co	59	Crystal Palace	51	Brentford	50
1931–2a	Fulham	57	Reading	55	Southend	53
1932–3a	Brentford	62	Exeter	58	Norwich	57
1933–4a	Norwich	61	Coventry	54	Reading	54
1934–5a	Charlton	61	Reading	53	Coventry	51
1935–6a	Coventry	57	Luton	56	Reading	54
1936–7a	Luton	58	Notts Co	56	Brighton	53
1937–8a	Millwall	56	Bristol City	55	QPR	53
1938–9a	Newport	55	Crystal Palace	52	Brighton	49
1946–7a	Cardiff	66	QPR	57	Bristol City	51
1947–8a	QPR	61	Bournemouth	57	Walsall	51
1948–9a	Swansea	62	Reading	55	Bournemouth	52
1949–50a	Notts Co	58	Northampton	51	Southend	51
1950–1d	Nottm Forest	70	Norwich	64	Reading	57
1951–2d	Plymouth Argyle	66	Reading	61	Norwich	61
1952–3d	Bristol Rov	64	Millwall	62	Northampton	62
1953–4d	Ipswich	64	Brighton	61	Bristol City	56
1954–5d	Bristol City	70	Leyton Orient	61	Southampton	59
1955–6d	Leyton Orient	66	Brighton	65	Ipswich	64
1956–7d	*Ipswich	59	Torquay	59	Colchester	58
1957–8d	Brighton	60	Brentford	58	Plymouth Argyle	58

THIRD DIVISION – NORTH 1921–58

1921–2b	Stockport	56	Darlington	50	Grimsby	50
1922–3b	Nelson	51	Bradford PA	47	Walsall	46
1923–4a	Wolves	63	Rochdale	62	Chesterfield	54
1924–5a	Darlington	58	Nelson	53	New Brighton	53
1925–6a	Grimsby	61	Bradford PA	60	Rochdale	59
1926–7a	Stoke	63	Rochdale	58	Bradford PA	57
1927–8a	Bradford PA	63	Lincoln	55	Stockport	54
1928–9a	Bradford City	63	Stockport	62	Wrexham	52
1929–30a	Port Vale	67	Stockport	63	Darlington	50
1930–1a	Chesterfield	58	Lincoln	57	Wrexham	54
1931–2c	*Lincoln	57	Gateshead	57	Chester	50
1932–3a	Hull	59	Wrexham	57	Stockport	54
1933–4a	Barnsley	62	Chesterfield	61	Stockport	59
1934–5a	Doncaster	57	Halifax	55	Chester	54
1935–6a	Chesterfield	60	Chester	55	Tranmere	54
1936–7a	Stockport	60	Lincoln	57	Chester	53
1937–8a	Tranmere	56	Doncaster	54	Hull	53
1938–9a	Barnsley	67	Doncaster	56	Bradford City	52
1946–7a	Doncaster	72	Rotherham	64	Chester	56

1947–8a	Lincoln	60	Rotherham	59	Wrexham	50
1948–9a	Hull	65	Rotherham	62	Doncaster	50
1949–50a	Doncaster	55	Gateshead	53	Rochdale	51
1950–1d	Rotherham	71	Mansfield	64	Carlisle	62
1951 2d	Lincoln	69	Grimsby	66	Stockport	59
1952–3d	Oldham	59	Port Vale	58	Wrexham	56
1953–4d	Port Vale	69	Barnsley	58	Scunthorpe	57
1954–5d	Barnsley	65	Accrington	61	Scunthorpe	58
1955–6d	Grimsby	68	Derby	63	Accrington	59
1956 7d	Derby	63	Hartlepool Utd	60	Accrington	59
1957–8d	Scunthorpe	66	Accrington	59	Bradford City	57

Maximum points: a, 84; b, 76; c, 80; d, 92 * Won on goal average

TITLE WINNERS

PREMIER LEAGUE

Manchester Utd	13
Chelsea	5
Manchester City	4
Arsenal	3
Blackburn	1
Leicester	1

FOOTBALL LEAGUE CHAMPIONSHIP

Newcastle	2
Reading	2
Sunderland	2
Wolves	2
Bournemouth	1
Burnley	1
Cardiff	1
Leicester	1
Norwich	1
QPR	1
WBA	1

DIV 1 (NEW)

Sunderland	2
Bolton	1
Charlton	1
Crystal Palace	1
Fulham	1
Manchester City	1
Middlesbrough	1
Newcastle	1
Norwich	1
Nottm Forest	1
Portsmouth	1

DIV 1 (ORIGINAL)

Liverpool	18
Arsenal	10
Everton	9
Aston Villa	7
Manchester Utd	7
Sunderland	6
Newcastle	4
Sheffield Wed	4
Huddersfield	3
Leeds	3
Wolves	3

Blackburn	2
Burnley	2
Derby	2
Manchester City	2
Portsmouth	2
Preston	2
Tottenham	2
Chelsea	1
Ipswich	1
Nottm Forest	1
Sheffield Utd	1
WBA	1

LEAGUE ONE

Luton	2
Wigan	2
Brighton	1
Bristol City	1
Charlton	1
Doncaster	1
Leicester	1
Norwich	1
Scunthorpe	1
Sheffield Utd	1
Southend	1
Swansea	1
Wolves	1

DIV 2 (NEW)

Birmingham	1
Brighton	1
Bury	1
Chesterfield	1
Fulham	1
Lincoln	1
Millwall	1
Plymouth	1
Preston	1
Reading	1
Stoke	1
Swindon	1
Watford	1
Wigan	1
Notts Co	1

DIV 2 (ORIGINAL)

Leicester	6
Manchester City	6

Sheffield Wed	5
Birmingham	4
Derby	4
Liverpool	4
Ipswich	3
Leeds	3
Middlesbrough	3
Notts County	3
Preston	3
Aston Villa	2
Bolton	2
Burnley	2
Chelsea	2
Grimsby	2
Manchester Utd	2
Norwich	2
Nottm Forest	2
Stoke	2
Tottenham	2
WBA	2
West Ham	2
Wolves	2
Blackburn	1
Blackpool	1
Bradford City	1
Brentford	1
Bristol City	1
Bury	1
Coventry	1
Crystal Palace	1
Everton	1
Fulham	1
Huddersfield	1
Luton	1
Millwall	1
Newcastle	1
Oldham	1
Oxford Utd	1
QPR	1
Sheffield Utd	1
Sunderland	1

LEAGUE TWO

Chesterfield	2
Accrington	1
Brentford	1
Burton	1

Carlisle	1	Northampton	1	Walsall	1
Gillingham	1	Notts County	1	Yeovil	1
Lincoln	1	Portsmouth	1		
MK Dons	1	Swindon	1		

APPLICATIONS FOR RE–ELECTION (System discontinued 1987)

14	Hartlepool	4	Norwich	2	Oldham
12	Halifax	3	Aldershot	2	QPR
11	Barrow	3	Bradford City	2	Rotherham
11	Southport	3	Crystal Palace	2	Scunthorpe
10	Crewe	3	Doncaster	2	Southend
10	Newport	3	Hereford	2	Watford
10	Rochdale	3	Merthyr	1	Blackpool
8	Darlington	3	Swindon	1	Brighton
8	Exeter	3	Torquay	1	Bristol Rov
7	Chester	3	Tranmere	1	Cambridge Utd
7	Walsall	2	Aberdare	1	Cardiff
7	Workington	2	Ashington	1	Carlisle
7	York	2	Bournemouth	1	Charlton
6	Stockport	2	Brentford	1	Mansfield
5	Accrington	2	Colchester	1	Port Vale
5	Gillingham	2	Durham	1	Preston
5	Lincoln	2	Gateshead	1	Shrewsbury
5	New Brighton	2	Grimsby	1	Swansea
4	Bradford PA	2	Millwall	1	Thames
4	Northampton	2	Nelson	1	Wrexham

RELEGATED CLUBS (TO 1992)

1892–3	In Test matches, Darwen and Sheffield Utd won promotion in place of Accrington and Notts Co
1893–4	Tests, Liverpool and Small Heath won promotion Darwen and Newton Heath relegated
1894–5	After Tests, Bury promoted, Liverpool relegated
1895–6	After Tests, Liverpool promoted, Small Heath relegated
1896–7	After Tests, Notts Co promoted, Burnley relegated
1897–8	Test system abolished after success of Burnley and Stoke, League extended Blackburn and Newcastle elected to First Division

Automatic promotion and relegation introduced

FIRST DIVISION TO SECOND DIVISION

1898–9	Bolton, Sheffield Wed	1919–20	Notts Co, Sheffield Wed
1899–00	Burnley, Glossop	1920–1	Derby, Bradford PA
1900–1	Preston, WBA	1921–2	Bradford City, Manchester Utd
1901–2	Small Heath, Manchester City	1922–3	Stoke, Oldham
1902–3	Grimsby, Bolton	1923–4	Chelsea, Middlesbrough
1903–4	Liverpool, WBA	1924–5	Preston, Nottm Forest
1904–5	League extended Bury and Notts Co, two bottom clubs in First Division, re-elected	1925–6	Manchester City, Notts Co
		1926–7	Leeds, WBA
		1927–8	Tottenham, Middlesbrough
1905–6	Nottm Forest, Wolves	1928–9	Bury, Cardiff
1906–7	Derby, Stoke	1929–30	Burnley, Everton
1907–8	Bolton, Birmingham	1930–1	Leeds, Manchester Utd
1908–9	Manchester City, Leicester Fosse	1931–2	Grimsby, West Ham
1909–10	Bolton, Chelsea	1932–3	Bolton, Blackpool
1910–11	Bristol City, Nottm Forest	1933–4	Newcastle, Sheffield Utd
1911–12	Preston, Bury	1934–5	Leicester, Tottenham
1912–13	Notts Co, Woolwich Arsenal	1935–6	Aston Villa, Blackburn
1913–14	Preston, Derby	1936–7	Manchester Utd, Sheffield Wed
1914–15	Tottenham, *Chelsea	1937–8	Manchester City, WBA
		1938–9	Birmingham, Leicester
		1946–7	Brentford, Leeds
		1947–8	Blackburn, Grimsby

1948–9	Preston, Sheffield Utd
1949–50	Manchester City, Birmingham
1950–1	Sheffield Wed, Everton
1951–2	Huddersfield, Fulham
1952–3	Stoke, Derby
1953–4	Middlesbrough, Liverpool
1954–5	Leicester, Sheffield Wed
1955–6	Huddersfield, Sheffield Utd
1956–7	Charlton, Cardiff
1957–8	Sheffield Wed, Sunderland
1958–9	Portsmouth, Aston Villa
1959–60	Luton, Leeds
1960–61	Preston, Newcastle
1961–2	Chelsea, Cardiff
1962–3	Manchester City, Leyton Orient
1963–4	Bolton, Ipswich
1964–5	Wolves, Birmingham
1965–6	Northampton, Blackburn
1966–7	Aston Villa, Blackpool
1967–8	Fulham, Sheffield Utd
1968–9	Leicester, QPR
1969–70	Sheffield Wed, Sunderland
1970–1	Burnley, Blackpool
1971–2	Nottm Forest, Huddersfield
1972–3	WBA, Crystal Palace
1973–4	Norwich, Manchester Utd, Southampton
1974–5	Chelsea, Luton, Carlisle
1975–6	Sheffield Utd, Burnley, Wolves
1976–7	Tottenham, Stoke, Sunderland
1977–8	Leicester, West Ham, Newcastle
1978–9	QPR, Birmingham, Chelsea
1979–80	Bristol City, Derby, Bolton
1980–1	Norwich, Leicester, Crystal Palace
1981–2	Leeds, Wolves, Middlesbrough
1982–3	Manchester City, Swansea, Brighton
1983–4	Birmingham, Notts Co, Wolves
1984–5	Norwich, Sunderland, Stoke
1985–6	Ipswich, Birmingham, WBA
1986–7	Leicester, Manchester City, Aston Villa
1987–8	Chelsea**, Portsmouth, Watford, Oxford Utd
1988–9	Middlesbrough, West Ham, Newcastle
1989–90	Sheffield Wed, Charlton, Millwall
1990–1	Sunderland, Derby
1991–2	Luton, Notts Co, West Ham

* Subsequently re-elected to First Division when League extended after the war
** Relegated after play-offs

SECOND DIVISION TO THIRD DIVISION

1920–1	Stockport
1921–2	Bradford City, Bristol City
1922–3	Rotherham, Wolves
1923–4	Nelson, Bristol City
1924–5	Crystal Palace, Coventry
1925–6	Stoke, Stockport
1926–7	Darlington, Bradford City
1927–8	Fulham, South Shields
1928–9	Port Vale, Clapton Orient

1929–30	Hull, Notts County
1930–1	Reading, Cardiff
1931–2	Barnsley, Bristol City
1932–3	Chesterfield, Charlton
1933–4	Millwall, Lincoln
1934–5	Oldham, Notts Co
1935–6	Port Vale, Hull
1936–7	Doncaster, Bradford City
1937–8	Barnsley, Stockport
1938–9	Norwich, Tranmere
1946–7	Swansea, Newport
1947–8	Doncaster, Millwall
1948–9	Nottm Forest, Lincoln
1949–50	Plymouth Argyle, Bradford PA
1950–1	Grimsby, Chesterfield
1951–2	Coventry, QPR
1952–3	Southampton, Barnsley
1953–4	Brentford, Oldham
1954–5	Ipswich, Derby
1955–6	Plymouth Argyle, Hull
1956–7	Port Vale, Bury
1957–8	Doncaster, Notts Co
1958–9	Barnsley, Grimsby
1959–60	Bristol City, Hull
1960–1	Lincoln, Portsmouth
1961–2	Brighton, Bristol Rov
1962–3	Walsall, Luton
1963–4	Grimsby, Scunthorpe
1964–5	Swindon, Swansea
1965–6	Middlesbrough, Leyton Orient
1966–7	Northampton, Bury
1967–8	Plymouth Argyle, Rotherham
1968–9	Fulham, Bury
1969–70	Preston, Aston Villa
1970–1	Blackburn, Bolton
1971–2	Charlton, Watford
1972–3	Huddersfield, Brighton
1973–4	Crystal Palace, Preston, Swindon
1974–5	Millwall, Cardiff, Sheffield Wed
1975–6	Portsmouth, Oxford Utd, York
1976–7	Carlisle, Plymouth Argyle, Hereford
1977–8	Hull, Mansfield, Blackpool
1978–9	Sheffield Utd, Millwall, Blackburn
1979–80	Fulham, Burnley, Bolton
1980–1	Preston, Bristol City, Bristol Rov
1981–2	Cardiff, Wrexham, Orient
1982–3	Rotherham, Burnley, Bolton
1983–4	Derby, Swansea, Cambridge Utd
1984–5	Notts Co, Cardiff, Wolves
1985–6	Carlisle, Middlesbrough, Fulham
1986–7	Sunderland**, Grimsby, Brighton
1987–8	Sheffield Utd**, Reading, Huddersfield
1988–9	Shrewsbury, Birmingham, Walsall
1989–90	Bournemouth, Bradford City, Stoke
1990–1	WBA, Hull
1991–2	Plymouth Argyle, Brighton, Port Vale

** Relegated after play-offs

THIRD DIVISION TO FOURTH DIVISION

1958–9	Rochdale, Notts Co, Doncaster, Stockport
1959–60	Accrington, Wrexham, Mansfield, York
1960–1	Chesterfield, Colchester, Bradford City, Tranmere
1961–2	Newport, Brentford, Lincoln, Torquay
1962–3	Bradford PA, Brighton, Carlisle, Halifax
1963–4	Millwall, Crewe, Wrexham, Notts Co
1964–5	Luton, Port Vale, Colchester, Barnsley
1965–6	Southend, Exeter, Brentford, York
1966–7	Doncaster, Workington, Darlington, Swansea
1967–8	Scunthorpe, Colchester, Grimsby, Peterborough (demoted)
1968–9	Oldham, Crewe, Hartlepool Utd, Northampton
1969–70	Bournemouth, Southport, Barrow, Stockport
1970–1	Gillingham, Doncaster, Bury, Reading
1971–2	Mansfield, Barnsley, Torquay, Bradford City
1972–3	Scunthorpe, Swansea, Brentford, Rotherham
1973–4	Cambridge Utd, Shrewsbury, Rochdale, Southport
1974–5	Bournemouth, Watford, Tranmere, Huddersfield
1975–6	Aldershot, Colchester, Southend, Halifax
1976–7	Reading, Northampton, Grimsby, York
1977–8	Port Vale, Bradford City, Hereford, Portsmouth
1978–9	Peterborough, Walsall, Tranmere, Lincoln
1979–80	Bury, Southend, Mansfield, Wimbledon
1980–1	Sheffield Utd, Colchester, Blackpool, Hull
1981–2	Wimbledon, Swindon, Bristol City, Chester
1982–3	Reading, Wrexham, Doncaster, Chesterfield
1983–4	Scunthorpe, Southend, Port Vale, Exeter
1984–5	Burnley, Orient, Preston, Cambridge Utd
1985–6	Lincoln, Cardiff, Wolves, Swansea
1986–7	Bolton**, Carlisle, Darlington, Newport
1987–8	Doncaster, York, Grimsby, Rotherham**
1988–9	Southend, Chesterfield, Gillingham, Aldershot

1989–90	Cardiff, Northampton, Blackpool, Walsall
1990–1	Crewe, Rotherham, Mansfield
1991–2	Bury, Shrewsbury, Torquay, Darlington
**	Relegated after plays–offs

DEMOTED FROM FOURTH DIVISION TO CONFERENCE

1987	Lincoln
1988	Newport
1989	Darlington
1990	Colchester
1991	No demotion
1992	No demotion

DEMOTED FROM THIRD DIVISION TO CONFERENCE

1993	Halifax
1994–6	No demotion
1997	Hereford
1998	Doncaster
1999	Scarborough
2000	Chester
2001	Barnet
2002	Halifax
2003	Exeter, Shrewsbury
2004	Carlisle, York

DEMOTED FROM LEAGUE TWO TO CONFERENCE/NATIONAL LEAGUE

2005	Kidderminster, Cambridge Utd
2006	Oxford Utd, Rushden & Diamonds
2007	Boston, Torquay
2008	Mansfield, Wrexham
2009	Chester Luton
2010	Grimsby, Darlington
2011	Lincoln, Stockport
2012	Hereford, Macclesfield
2013	Barnet, Aldershot
2014	Bristol Rov, Torquay
2015	Cheltenham, Tranmere
2016	Dagenham, York
2017	Hartlepool, Leyton Orient
2018	Barnet, Chesterfield
2019	Notts Co, Yeovil

RELEGATED CLUBS (SINCE 1993)

1993
Premier League to Div 1: Crystal Palace, Middlesbrough, Nottm Forest
Div 1 to Div 2: Brentford, Cambridge Utd, Bristol Rov
Div 2 to Div 3: Preston, Mansfield, Wigan, Chester

1994
Premier League to Div 1: Sheffield Utd, Oldham, Swindon
Div 1 to Div 2: Birmingham, Oxford Utd, Peterborough
Div 2 to Div 3: Fulham, Exeter, Hartlepool Utd, Barnet

1995
Premier League to Div 1: Crystal Palace, Norwich, Leicester, Ipswich
Div 1 to Div 2: Swindon, Burnley, Bristol City, Notts Co
Div 2 to Div 3: Cambridge Utd, Plymouth Argyle, Cardiff, Chester, Leyton Orient

1996
Premier League to Div 1: Manchester City, QPR, Bolton
Div 1 to Div 2: Millwall, Watford, Luton
Div 2 to Div 3: Carlisle, Swansea, Brighton, Hull

1997
Premier League to Div 1: Sunderland, Middlesbrough, Nottm Forest
Div 1 to Div 2: Grimsby, Oldham, Southend
Div 2 to Div 3: Peterborough, Shrewsbury, Rotherham, Notts Co

1998
Premier League to Div 1: Bolton, Barnsley, Crystal Palace
Div 1 to Div 2: Manchester City, Stoke, Reading
Div 2 to Div 3: Brentford, Plymouth Argyle, Carlisle, Southend

1999
Premier League to Div 1: Charlton, Blackburn, Nottm Forest
Div 1 to Div 2: Bury, Oxford Utd, Bristol City
Div 2 to Div 3: York, Northampton, Lincoln, Macclesfield

2000
Premier League to Div 1: Wimbledon, Sheffield Wed, Watford
Div 1 to Div 2: Walsall, Port Vale, Swindon
Div 2 to Div 3: Cardiff, Blackpool, Scunthorpe, Chesterfield

2001
Premier League to Div 1: Manchester City, Coventry, Bradford City
Div 1 to Div 2: Huddersfield, QPR, Tranmere
Div 2 to Div 3: Bristol Rov, Luton, Swansea, Oxford Utd

2002
Premier League to Div 1: Ipswich, Derby, Leicester
Div 1 to Div 2: Crewe, Barnsley, Stockport
Div 2 to Div 3: Bournemouth, Bury, Wrexham, Cambridge Utd

2003
Premier League to Div 1: West Ham, WBA, Sunderland
Div 1 to Div 2: Sheffield Wed, Brighton, Grimsby
Div 2 to Div 3: Cheltenham, Huddersfield, Mansfield, Northampton

2004
Premier League to Div 1: Leicester, Leeds, Wolves
Div 1 to Div 2: Walsall, Bradford City, Wimbledon
Div 2 to Div 3: Grimsby, Rushden & Diamonds, Notts Co, Wycombe

2005
Premier League to Championship: Crystal Palace, Norwich, Southampton
Championship to League 1: Gillingham, Nottm Forest, Rotherham
League 1 to League 2: Torquay, Wrexham, Peterborough, Stockport

2006
Premier League to Championship: Birmingham, WBA, Sunderland
Championship to League 1: Crewe, Millwall, Brighton
League 1 to League 2: Hartlepool Utd, MK Dons, Swindon, Walsall

2007
Premier League to Championship: Sheffield Utd, Charlton, Watford
Championship to League 1: Southend, Luton, Leeds
League 1 to League 2: Chesterfield, Bradford City, Rotherham, Brentford

2008
Premier League to Championship: Reading, Birmingham, Derby
Championship to League 1: Leicester, Scunthorpe, Colchester
League 1 to League 2: Bournemouth, Gillingham, Port Vale, Luton

2009
Premier League to Championship: Newcastle, Middlesbrough, WBA
Championship to League 1: Norwich, Southampton, Charlton
League 1 to League 2: Northampton, Crewe, Cheltenham, Hereford

2010
Premier League to Championship: Burnley, Hull, Portsmouth
Championship to League 1: Sheffield Wed, Plymouth, Peterborough
League 1 to League 2: Gillingham, Wycombe, Southend, Stockport

2011
Premier League to Championship: Birmingham, Blackpool, West Ham
Championship to League 1: Preston, Sheffield Utd, Scunthorpe
League 1 to League 2: Dagenham & Redbridge, Bristol Rov, Plymouth, Swindon

2012
Premier League to Championship: Bolton, Blackburn, Wolves
Championship to League 1: Portsmouth, Coventry, Doncaster
League 1 to League 2: Wycombe, Chesterfield, Exeter, Rochdale

2013
Premier League to Championship: Wigan, Reading, QPR
Championship to League 1: Peterborough, Wolves, Bristol City
League 1 to League 2: Scunthorpe, Bury, Hartlepool, Portsmouth

2014
Premier League to Championship: Norwich, Fulham, Cardiff
Championship to League 1: Doncaster, Barnsley, Yeovil
League 1 to League 2: Tranmere, Carlisle, Shrewsbury, Stevenage

2015
Premier League to Championship: Hull, Burnley QPR
Championship to League 1: Millwall, Wigan, Blackpool
League 1 to League 2: Notts Co, Crawley, Leyton Orient Yeovil

2016
Premier League to Championship: Newcastle, Norwich, Aston Villa
Championship to League 1: Charlton, MK Dons, Bolton
League 1 to League 2: Doncaster, Blackpool, Colchester, Crewe

2017
Premier League to Championship: Hull, Middlesbrough, Sunderland
Championship to League 1: Blackburn, Wigan, Rotherham
League 1 to League 2: Port Vale, Swindon, Coventry, Chesterfield

2018
Premier League to Championship: Swansea, Stoke, WBA
Championship to League 1: Barnsley, Burton, Sunderland
League 1 to League 2: Oldham, Northampton, MK Dons, Bury

2019
Premier League to Championship: Cardiff, Fulham, Huddersfield
Championship to League 1: Rotherham, Bolton, Ipswich
League 1 to League 2: Plymouth, Walsall, Scunthorpe, Bradford

ANNUAL AWARDS

FOOTBALL WRITERS' ASSOCIATION

Footballer of the Year: 1948 Stanley Matthews (Blackpool); **1949** Johnny Carey (Manchester Utd); **1950** Joe Mercer (Arsenal); **1951** Harry Johnston (Blackpool); **1952** Billy Wright (Wolves); **1953** Nat Lofthouse (Bolton); **1954** Tom Finney (Preston); **1955** Don Revie (Manchester City); **1956** Bert Trautmann (Manchester City); **1957** Tom Finney (Preston); **1958** Danny Blanchflower (Tottenham); **1959** Syd Owen (Luton); **1960** Bill Slater (Wolves); **1961** Danny Blanchflower (Tottenham); **1962** Jimmy Adamson (Burnley); **1963** Stanley Matthews (Stoke); **1964** Bobby Moore (West Ham); **1965** Bobby Collins (Leeds); **1966** Bobby Charlton (Manchester Utd); **1967** Jack Charlton (Leeds); **1968** George Best (Manchester Utd); **1969** Tony Book (Manchester City) & Dave Mackay (Derby) – shared; **1970** Billy Bremner (Leeds); **1971** Frank McLintock (Arsenal); **1972** Gordon Banks (Stoke); **1973** Pat Jennings (Tottenham); **1974** Ian Callaghan (Liverpool); **1975** Alan Mullery (Fulham); **1976** Kevin Keegan (Liverpool); **1977** Emlyn Hughes (Liverpool); **1978** Kenny Burns (Nott'm Forest); **1979** Kenny Dalglish (Liverpool); **1980** Terry McDermott (Liverpool); **1981** Frans Thijssen (Ipswich); **1982** Steve Perryman (Tottenham); **1983** Kenny Dalglish (Liverpool); **1984** Ian Rush (Liverpool); **1985** Neville Southall (Everton); **1986** Gary Lineker (Everton); **1987** Clive Allen (Tottenham); **1988** John Barnes (Liverpool); **1989** Steve Nicol (Liverpool); **Special award to the Liverpool players for the compassion shown to bereaved families after the Hillsborough Disaster; 1990** John Barnes (Liverpool); **1991** Gordon Strachan (Leeds); **1992** Gary Lineker (Tottenham); **1993** Chris Waddle (Sheffield Wed); **1994** Alan Shearer (Blackburn); **1995** Jurgen Klinsmann (Tottenham); **1996** Eric Cantona (Manchester Utd); **1997** Gianfranco Zola (Chelsea); **1998** Dennis Bergkamp (Arsenal); **1999** David Ginola (Tottenham); **2000** Roy Keane (Manchester Utd); **2001** Teddy Sheringham (Manchester Utd); **2002** Robert Pires (Arsenal); **2003** Thierry Henry (Arsenal); **2004** Thierry Henry (Arsenal); **2005** Frank Lampard (Chelsea); **2006** Thierry Henry (Arsenal); **2007** Cristiano Ronaldo (Manchester Utd); **2008** Cristiano Ronaldo (Manchester Utd); **2009** Steven Gerrard (Liverpool); **2010** Wayne Rooney (Manchester Utd); **2011** Scott Parker (West Ham); **2012** Robin van Persie (Arsenal); **2013** Gareth Bale (Tottenham); **2014** Luis Suarez (Liverpool); **2015** Eden Hazard (Chelsea); **2016** Jamie Vardy (Leicester); **2017** N'Golo Kante (Chelsea); **2018** Mohamed Salah (Liverpool); **2019** Raheem Sterling (Manchester City)

PROFESSIONAL FOOTBALLERS' ASSOCIATION

Player of the Year: 1974 Norman Hunter (Leeds); **1975** Colin Todd (Derby); **1976** Pat Jennings (Tottenham); **1977** Andy Gray (Aston Villa); **1978** Peter Shilton (Nott'm Forest); **1979** Liam Brady (Arsenal); **1980** Terry McDermott (Liverpool); **1981** John Wark (Ipswich); **1982** Kevin Keegan (Southampton); **1983** Kenny Dalglish (Liverpool); **1984** Ian Rush (Liverpool); **1985** Peter Reid (Everton); **1986** Gary Lineker (Everton); **1987** Clive Allen (Tottenham); **1988** John Barnes (Liverpool); **1989** Mark Hughes (Manchester Utd); **1990** David Platt (Aston Villa); **1991** Mark Hughes (Manchester Utd); **1992** Gary Pallister (Manchester Utd); **1993** Paul McGrath (Aston Villa); **1994** Eric Cantona (Manchester Utd); **1995** Alan Shearer (Blackburn); **1996** Les Ferdinand (Newcastle); **1997** Alan Shearer (Newcastle); **1998** Dennis Bergkamp (Arsenal); **1999** David Ginola (Tottenham); **2000** Roy Keane (Manchester Utd); **2001** Teddy Sheringham (Manchester Utd); **2002** Ruud van Nistelrooy (Manchester Utd); **2003** Thierry Henry (Arsenal); **2004** Thierry Henry (Arsenal); **2005** John Terry (Chelsea); **2006** Steven Gerrard (Liverpool); **2007** Cristiano Ronaldo (Manchester Utd); **2008** Cristiano Ronaldo (Manchester Utd); **2009** Ryan Giggs (Manchester Utd); **2010** Wayne Rooney (Manchester Utd); **2011** Gareth Bale (Tottenham); **2012** Robin van Persie (Arsenal); **2013** Gareth Bale (Tottenham); **2014** Luis Suarez (Liverpool); **2015** Eden Hazard (Chelsea); **2016** Riyad Mahrez (Leicester); **2017** N'Golo Kante (Chelsea); **2018** Mohamed Salah (Liverpool); **2019** Virgin van Dijk (Liverpool)

Young Player of the Year: 1974 Kevin Beattie (Ipswich); **1975** Mervyn Day (West Ham); **1976** Peter Barnes (Manchester City); **1977** Andy Gray (Aston Villa); **1978** Tony Woodcock (Nott'm Forest); **1979** Cyrille Regis (WBA); **1980** Glenn Hoddle (Tottenham); **1981** Gary Shaw (Aston Villa); **1982** Steve Moran (Southampton); **1983** Ian Rush (Liverpool); **1984** Paul Walsh (Luton); **1985** Mark Hughes (Manchester Utd); **1986** Tony Cottee (West Ham); **1987** Tony Adams

(Arsenal); **1988** Paul Gascoigne (Newcastle); **1989** Paul Merson (Arsenal); **1990** Matthew Le Tissier (Southampton); **1991** Lee Sharpe (Manchester Utd); **1992** Ryan Giggs (Manchester Utd); **1993** Ryan Giggs (Manchester Utd); **1994** Andy Cole (Newcastle); **1995** Robbie Fowler (Liverpool); **1996** Robbie Fowler (Liverpool); **1997** David Beckham (Manchester Utd); **1998** Michael Owen (Liverpool); **1999** Nicolas Anelka (Arsenal); **2000** Harry Kewell (Leeds); **2001** Steven Gerrard (Liverpool); **2002** Craig Bellamy (Newcastle); **2003** Jermaine Jenas (Newcastle); **2004** Scott Parker (Chelsea); **2005** Wayne Rooney (Manchester Utd); **2006** Wayne Rooney (Manchester Utd); **2007** Cristiano Ronaldo (Manchester Utd); **2008** Cesc Fabregas (Arsenal); **2009** Ashley Young (Aston Villa); **2010** James Milner (Aston Villa); **2011** Jack Wilshere (Arsenal); **2012** Kyle Walker (Tottenham); **2013** Gareth Bale (Tottenham); **2014** Eden Hazard (Chelsea); **2015** Harry Kane (Tottenham); **2016** Dele Alli (Tottenham); **2017** Dele Alli (Tottenham); **2018** Leroy Sane (Manchester City); **2019** Raheem Sterling (Manchester City)

Merit Awards: 1974 Bobby Charlton & Cliff Lloyd; **1975** Denis Law; **1976** George Eastham; **1977** Jack Taylor; **1978** Bill Shankly; **1979** Tom Finney; **1980** Sir Matt Busby; **1981** John Trollope; **1982** Joe Mercer; **1983** Bob Paisley; **1984** Bill Nicholson; **1985** Ron Greenwood; **1986** England 1966 World Cup–winning team; **1987** Sir Stanley Matthews; **1988** Billy Bonds; **1989** Nat Lofthouse; **1990** Peter Shilton; **1991** Tommy Hutchison; **1992** Brian Clough; **1993** Manchester Utd; 1968 European Champions: Eusebio; **1994** Billy Bingham; **1995** Gordon Strachan; **1996** Pele; **1997** Peter Beardsley; **1998** Steve Ogrizovic; **1999** Tony Ford; **2000** Gary Mabbutt; **2001** Jimmy Hill; **2002** Niall Quinn; **2003** Sir Bobby Robson; **2004** Dario Gradi; **2005** Shaka Hislop; **2006** George Best; **2007** Sir Alex Ferguson; **2008** Jimmy Armfield; **2009** John McDermott; **2010** Lucas Radebe; **2011** Howard Webb; **2012** Graham Alexander; **2013** Eric Harrison/Manchester Utd Class of '92; **2014** Donald Bell (posthumously; only footballer to win Victoria Cross; World War 1); **2015** Steven Gerrard & Frank Lampard; **2016** Ryan Giggs; **2017** David Beckham; **2018** Cyrille Regis (posthumously); **2019** Steph Houghton

MANAGER OF THE YEAR 1 (chosen by media and sponsors)

1966 Jock Stein (Celtic); **1967** Jock Stein (Celtic); **1968** Matt Busby (Manchester Utd); **1969** Don Revie (Leeds); **1970** Don Revie (Leeds); **1971** Bertie Mee (Arsenal); **1972** Don Revie (Leeds); **1973** Bill Shankly (Liverpool); **1974** Jack Charlton (Middlesbrough); **1975** Ron Saunders (Aston Villa); **1976** Bob Paisley (Liverpool); **1977** Bob Paisley (Liverpool); **1978** Brian Clough (Nott'm Forest); **1979** Bob Paisley (Liverpool); **1980** Bob Paisley (Liverpool); **1981** Ron Saunders (Aston Villa); **1982** Bob Paisley (Liverpool); **1983** Bob Paisley (Liverpool); **1984** Joe Fagan (Liverpool); **1985** Howard Kendall (Everton); **1986** Kenny Dalglish (Liverpool); **1987** Howard Kendall (Everton); **1988** Kenny Dalglish (Liverpool); **1989** George Graham (Arsenal); **1990** Kenny Dalglish (Liverpool); **1991** George Graham (Arsenal); **1992** Howard Wilkinson (Leeds); **1993** Alex Ferguson (Manchester Utd); **1994** Alex Ferguson (Manchester Utd); **1995** Kenny Dalglish (Blackburn); **1996** Alex Ferguson (Manchester Utd); **1997** Alex Ferguson (Manchester Utd); **1998** Arsene Wenger (Arsenal); **1999** Alex Ferguson (Manchester Utd); **2000** Sir Alex Ferguson (Manchester Utd); **2001** George Burley (Ipswich); **2002** Arsene Wenger (Arsenal); **2003** Sir Alex Ferguson (Manchester Utd); **2004** Arsene Wenger (Arsenal); **2005** Jose Mourinho (Chelsea); **2006** Jose Mourinho (Chelsea); **2007** Sir Alex Ferguson (Manchester Utd); **2008** Sir Alex Ferguson (Manchester Utd); **2009** Sir Alex Ferguson (Manchester Utd); **2010** Harry Redknapp (Tottenham); **2011** Sir Alex Ferguson (Manchester Utd); **2012** Alan Pardew (Newcastle); **2013** Sir Alex Ferguson (Manchester Utd); **2014** Tony Pulis (Crystal Palace); **2015** Jose Mourinho (Chelsea); **2016** Claudio Ranieri (Leicester); **2017** Antonio Conte (Chelsea); **2018** Pep Guardiola (Manchester City); **2019** Pep Guardiola (Manchester City)

MANAGER OF THE YEAR 2 (Chosen by the League Managers' Association)

1993 Dave Bassett (Sheffield Utd); **1994** Joe Kinnear (Wimbledon); **1995** Frank Clark (Nott'm Forest); **1996** Peter Reid (Sunderland); **1997** Danny Wilson (Barnsley); **1998** David Jones (Southampton); **1999** Alex Ferguson (Manchester Utd); **2000** Alan Curbishley (Charlton Athletic); **2001** George Burley (Ipswich); **2002** Arsene Wenger (Arsenal); **2003** David Moyes (Everton); **2004** Arsene Wenger (Arsenal); **2005** David Moyes (Everton); **2006** Steve Coppell (Reading); **2007** Steve Coppell (Reading); **2008** Sir Alex Ferguson (Manchester Utd); **2009** David Moyes (Everton); **2010** Roy Hodgson (Fulham); **2011** Sir Alex Ferguson (Manchester Utd); **2012** Alan

Pardew (Newcastle); **2013** Sir Alex Ferguson (Manchester Utd); **2014** Brendan Rodgers (Liverpool); **2015** Eddie Howe (Bournemouth); **2016** Claudio Ranieri (Leicester); **2017** Antonio Conte (Chelsea); **2018** Pep Guardiola (Manchester City); **2019** Chris Wilder (Sheffield Utd)

SCOTTISH FOOTBALL WRITERS' ASSOCIATION
Footballer of the Year: 1965 Billy McNeill (Celtic); **1966** John Greig (Rangers); **1967** Ronnie Simpson (Celtic); **1968** Gordon Wallace (Raith); **1969** Bobby Murdoch (Celtic); **1970** Pat Stanton (Hibernian); **1971** Martin Buchan (Aberdeen); **1972** David Smith (Rangers); **1973** George Connelly (Celtic); **1974** World Cup Squad; **1975** Sandy Jardine (Rangers); **1976** John Greig (Rangers); **1977** Danny McGrain (Celtic); **1978** Derek Johnstone (Rangers); **1979** Andy Ritchie (Morton); **1980** Gordon Strachan (Aberdeen); **1981** Alan Rough (Partick Thistle); **1982** Paul Sturrock (Dundee Utd); **1983** Charlie Nicholas (Celtic); **1984** Willie Miller (Aberdeen); **1985** Hamish McAlpine (Dundee Utd); **1986** Sandy Jardine (Hearts); **1987** Brian McClair (Celtic); **1988** Paul McStay (Celtic); **1989** Richard Gough (Rangers); **1990** Alex McLeish (Aberdeen); **1991** Maurice Malpas (Dundee Utd); **1992** Ally McCoist (Rangers); **1993** Andy Goram (Rangers); **1994** Mark Hateley (Rangers); **1995** Brian Laudrup (Rangers); **1996** Paul Gascoigne (Rangers); **1997** Brian Laudrup (Rangers); **1998** Craig Burley (Celtic); **1999** Henrik Larsson (Celtic); **2000** Barry Ferguson (Rangers); **2001** Henrik Larsson (Celtic); **2002** Paul Lambert (Celtic); **2003** Barry Ferguson (Rangers); **2004** Jackie McNamara (Celtic); **2005** John Hartson (Celtic); **2006** Craig Gordon (Hearts); **2007** Shunsuke Nakamura (Celtic); **2008** Carlos Cuellar (Rangers); **2009** Gary Caldwell (Celtic); **2010** David Weir (Rangers); **2011** Emilio Izaguirre (Celtic); **2012** Charlie Mulgrew (Celtic); **2013** Leigh Griffiths (Hibernian); **2014** Kris Commons (Celtic); **2015** Craig Gordon (Celtic); **2016** Leigh Griffiths (Celtic); **2017** Scott Sinclair (Celtic); **2018** Scott Brown (Celtic); **2019** James Forrest (Celtic)

PROFESSIONAL FOOTBALLERS' ASSOCIATION SCOTLAND
Player of the Year: 1978 Derek Johnstone (Rangers); **1979** Paul Hegarty (Dundee Utd); **1980** Davie Provan (Celtic); **1981** Mark McGhee (Aberdeen); **1982** Sandy Clarke (Airdrieonians); **1983** Charlie Nicholas (Celtic); **1984** Willie Miller (Aberdeen); **1985** Jim Duffy (Morton); **1986** Richard Gough (Dundee Utd); **1987** Brian McClair (Celtic); **1988** Paul McStay (Celtic); **1989** Theo Snelders (Aberdeen); **1990** Jim Bett (Aberdeen); **1991** Paul Elliott (Celtic); **1992** Ally McCoist (Rangers); **1993** Andy Goram (Rangers); **1994** Mark Hateley (Rangers); **1995** Brian Laudrup (Rangers); **1996** Paul Gascoigne (Rangers); **1997** Paolo Di Canio (Celtic) **1998** Jackie McNamara (Celtic); **1999** Henrik Larsson (Celtic); **2000** Mark Viduka (Celtic); **2001** Henrik Larsson (Celtic); **2002** Lorenzo Amoruso (Rangers); **2003** Barry Ferguson (Rangers); **2004** Chris Sutton (Celtic); **2005** John Hartson (Celtic) and Fernando Ricksen (Rangers); **2006** Shaun Maloney (Celtic); **2007** Shunsuke Nakamura (Celtic); **2008** Aiden McGeady (Celtic); **2009** Scott Brown (Celtic); **2010** Steven Davis (Rangers); **2011** Emilio Izaguirre (Celtic); **2012** Charlie Mulgrew (Celtic); **2013** Michael Higdon (Motherwell); **2014** Kris Commons (Celtic); **2015** Stefan Johansen (Celtic); **2016** Leigh Griffiths (Celtic); **2017** Scott Sinclair (Celtic); **2018** Scott Brown (Celtic); **2019** James Forrest (Celtic)

Young Player of the Year: 1978 Graeme Payne (Dundee Utd); **1979** Ray Stewart (Dundee Utd); **1980** John McDonald (Rangers); **1981** Charlie Nicholas (Celtic); **1982** Frank McAvennie (St Mirren); **1983** Paul McStay (Celtic); **1984** John Robertson (Hearts); **1985** Craig Levein (Hearts); **1986** Craig Levein (Hearts); **1987** Robert Fleck (Rangers); **1988** John Collins (Hibernian); **1989** Billy McKinlay (Dundee Utd); **1990** Scott Crabbe (Hearts); **1991** Eoin Jess (Aberdeen); **1992** Phil O'Donnell (Motherwell); **1993** Eoin Jess (Aberdeen); **1994** Phil O'Donnell (Motherwell); **1995** Charlie Miller (Rangers); **1996** Jackie McNamara (Celtic); **1997** Robbie Winters (Dundee Utd); **1998** Gary Naysmith (Hearts); **1999** Barry Ferguson (Rangers); **2000** Kenny Miller (Hibernian); **2001** Stilian Petrov (Celtic); **2002** Kevin McNaughton (Aberdeen); **2003** James McFadden (Motherwell); **2004** Stephen Pearson (Celtic); **2005** Derek Riordan (Hibernian); **2006** Shaun Maloney (Celtic); **2007** Steven Naismith (Kilmarnock); **2008** Aiden McGeady (Celtic); **2009** James McCarthy (Hamilton); **2010** Danny Wilson (Rangers); **2011:** David Goodwillie (Dundee Utd); **2012** James Forrest (Celtic); **2013** Leigh Griffiths (Hibernian); **2014** Andy Robertson (Dundee Utd); **2015** Jason Denayer (Celtic); **2016** Kieran Tierney (Celtic); **2017** Kieran Tierney (CelticI); **2018** Kieran Tierney (Celtic); **2019** Ryan Kent (Rangers)

SCOTTISH MANAGER OF THE YEAR
1987 Jim McLean (Dundee Utd); **1988** Billy McNeill (Celtic); **1989** Graeme Souness (Rangers);

1990 Andy Roxburgh (Scotland); 1991 Alex Totten (St Johnstone); 1992 Walter Smith (Rangers); 1993 Walter Smith (Rangers); 1994 Walter Smith (Rangers); 1995 Jimmy Nicholl (Raith); 1996 Walter Smith (Rangers); 1997 Walter Smith (Rangers); 1998 Wim Jansen (Celtic); 1999 Dick Advocaat (Rangers); 2000 Dick Advocaat (Rangers); 2001 Martin O'Neill (Celtic); 2002 John Lambie (Partick Thistle); 2003 Alex McLeish (Rangers); 2004 Martin O'Neill (Celtic); 2005 Alex McLeish (Rangers); 2006 Gordon Strachan (Celtic); 2007 Gordon Strachan (Celtic); 2008 Billy Reid (Hamilton); 2009 Csaba Laszlo (Hearts); 2010 Walter Smith (Rangers); 2011: Mixu Paatelainen (Kilmarnock); 2012 Neil Lennon (Celtic); 2013 Neil Lennon (Celtic); 2014 Derek McInnes (Aberdeen); 2015 John Hughes (Inverness); 2016 Mark Warburton (Rangers); 2017 Brendan Rodgers (Celtic); 2018 Jack Ross (St Mirren); 2019 Steve Clarke (Kilmarnock)

EUROPEAN FOOTBALLER OF THE YEAR

1956 Stanley Matthews (Blackpool); 1957 Alfredo di Stefano (Real Madrid); 1958 Raymond Kopa (Real Madrid); 1959 Alfredo di Stefano (Real Madrid); 1960 Luis Suarez (Barcelona); 1961 Omar Sivori (Juventus); 1962 Josef Masopust (Dukla Prague); 1963 Lev Yashin (Moscow Dynamo); 1964 Denis Law (Manchester Utd); 1965 Eusebio (Benfica); 1966 Bobby Charlton (Manchester Utd); 1967 Florian Albert (Ferencvaros); 1968 George Best (Manchester Utd); 1969 Gianni Rivera (AC Milan); 1970 Gerd Muller (Bayern Munich); 1971 Johan Cruyff (Ajax); 1972 Franz Beckenbauer (Bayern Munich); 1973 Johan Cruyff (Barcelona); 1974 Johan Cruyff (Barcelona); 1975 Oleg Blokhin (Dynamo Kiev); 1976 Franz Beckenbauer (Bayern Munich); 1977 Allan Simonsen (Borussia Moenchengladbach); 1978 Kevin Keegan (SV Hamburg); 1979 Kevin Keegan (SV Hamburg); 1980 Karl-Heinz Rummenigge (Bayern Munich); 1981 Karl-Heinz Rummenigge (Bayern Munich); 1982 Paolo Rossi (Juventus); 1983 Michel Platini (Juventus); 1984 Michel Platini (Juventus); 1985 Michel Platini (Juventus); 1986 Igor Belanov (Dynamo Kiev); 1987 Ruud Gullit (AC Milan); 1988 Marco van Basten (AC Milan); 1989 Marco van Basten (AC Milan); 1990 Lothar Matthaus (Inter Milan); 1991 Jean-Pierre Papin (Marseille); 1992 Marco van Basten (AC Milan); 1993 Roberto Baggio (Juventus); 1994 Hristo Stoichkov (Barcelona); 1995 George Weah (AC Milan); 1996 Matthias Sammer (Borussia Dortmund); 1997 Ronaldo (Inter Milan); 1998 Zinedine Zidane (Juventus); 1999 Rivaldo (Barcelona); 2000 Luis Figo (Real Madrid); 2001 Michael Owen (Liverpool); 2002 Ronaldo (Real Madrid); 2003 Pavel Nedved (Juventus); 2004 Andriy Shevchenko (AC Milan); 2005 Ronaldinho (Barcelona); 2006 Fabio Cannavaro (Real Madrid); 2007 Kaka (AC Milan); 2008 Cristiano Ronaldo (Manchester United); 2009 Lionel Messi (Barcelona)

WORLD FOOTBALLER OF YEAR

1991 Lothar Matthaus (Inter Milan and Germany); 1992 Marco van Basten (AC Milan and Holland); 1993 Roberto Baggio (Juventus and Italy); 1994 Romario (Barcelona and Brazil); 1995 George Weah (AC Milan and Liberia); 1996 Ronaldo (Barcelona and Brazil); 1997 Ronaldo (Inter Milan and Brazil); 1998 Zinedine Zidane (Juventus and France); 1999 Rivaldo (Barcelona and Brazil); 2000 Zinedine Zidane (Juventus and France); 2001 Luis Figo (Real Madrid and Portugal); 2002 Ronaldo (Real Madrid and Brazil); 2003 Zinedine Zidane (Real Madrid and France); 2004 Ronaldinho (Barcelona and Brazil); 2005 Ronaldinho (Barcelona and Brazil); 2006 Fabio Cannavaro (Real Madrid and Italy); 2007 Kaka (AC Milan and Brazil); 2008 Cristiano Ronaldo (Manchester United and Portugal); 2009 Lionel Messi (Barcelona and Argentina)

FIFA BALLON D'OR (replaces European and World Footballer of the Year)

2010: Lionel Messi (Barcelona). 2011 Lionel Messi (Barcelona); 2012 Lionel Messi (Barcelona); 2013 Cristiano Ronaldo (Real Madrid); 2014: Cristiano Ronaldo (Real Madrid); 2015 Lionel Messi (Barcelona)

FIFA BEST PLAYER

2016 Cristiano Ronaldo (Real Madrid); 2017 Cristiano Ronaldo (Real Madrid); 2018 Luka Modric (Real Madrid)

FIFA WORLD COACH OF THE YEAR

2010: Jose Mourinho (Inter Milan). 2011 Pep Guardiola (Barcelona); 2012 Vicente del Bosque (Spain); 2013 Jupp Heynckes (Bayern Munich); 2014 Joachim Low (Germany); 2015 Luis Enrique (Barcelona); 2016 Claudio Ranieri (Leicester); 2017 Zinedine Zidane (Real Madrid); 2018 Didier Deschamps (France)

(figures in brackets denote appearances as substitute)

PREMIER LEAGUE

ARSENAL

Unai Emery faced having to rebuild his side after two golden opportunities to regain a place in the Champions League were wasted. They surrendered a top-four place with a dreadful finish to the Premier League season and were then overwhelmed by Chelsea in the Europa League Final. A title challenge in his first season after succeeding Arsene Wenger was never on the cards for Emery once Manchester City or Liverpool were in full flow. Pierre-Emerick Aubameyang and Alexandre Lacazette delivered plenty of goals, but Arsenal never had the same conviction in defence and were exposed at the business end of the campaign. In the space of eight days, they were beaten by Crystal Palace, Wolves and Leicester, conceding three goals each time, were held at the Emirates by struggling Brighton and surrendered fourth place. By the time Aubameyang scored twice in the final match against Burnley to share the Golden Boot with Liverpool's Sadio Mane and Mohamed Salah, it was too late, with Tottenham having held on to the final spot despite their own dodgy finish. Salvation beckoned in Europe where Arsenal had shown some consistency in overcoming Napoli and Valencia on the way to the final in distant Baku. But after a goalless first-half, they conceded four goals in 23 minutes, with Arsenal old boy Olivier Giroud rubbing it in with one of them, along with an assist in a 4-1 success.

Aubameyang P-E	30 (6)	Lacazette A	27 (8)	Ramsey A	14 (14)
Bellerin H	18 (1)	Leno B	31 (1)	Saka B	- (1)
Cech P	7	Lichtsteiner S	10 (4)	Sokratis	25
Elneny M	5 (3)	Maitland-Niles A	11 (5)	Suarez D	- (4)
Guendouzi M	23 (10)	Mavropanos K	3 (1)	Torreira L	24 (10)
Holding R	9 (1)	Mkhitaryan H	19 (6)	Welbeck D	1 (7)
Iwobi A	22 (13)	Monreal N	21 (1)	Willock J	1 (1)
Jenkinson C	2 (1)	Mustafi S	31	Xhaka G	29
Kolasinac S	22 (2)	Nketiah E	- (5)		
Koscielny L	13 (4)	Ozil M	20 (4)		

League goals (73): Aubameyang 22, Lacazette 13, Mkhitaryan 6, Ozil 5, Ramsey 4, Xhaka 3, Iwobi 3, Koscielny 3, Mustafi 2, Torreira 2, Maitland-Niles 1, Monreal 1, Nketiah 1, Sokratis 1, Welbeck 1, Opponents 4
FA Cup goals (4): Willock 2, Aubameyang 1, Iwobi 1. **League Cup goals** (5): Welbeck 2, Lacazette 1, Lichtsteiner 1, Smith Rowe E 1
Europa League goals (30): Aubameyang 8, Lacazette 5, Iwobi 2, Ramsey 2, Smith Rowe 2, Sokratis 2, Welbeck 2, Guendouzi 1, Maitland-Niles 1, Mustafi 1, Ozil 1, Willock 1, Opponents 2
Average home league attendance: 59,899. **Player of Year**: Alexandre Lacazette

BOURNEMOUTH

A decade after Eddie Howe led the club away from the threat of non-league football after starting on minus-17 points for entering administration, Bournemouth overcame long-term injuries and a late wobble to ensure a fifth successive Premier League season. Their progress was underlined during the summer with £47.7m spent on three players, including Colombia World Cup midfielder Jefferson Lerma for a record £25m. And a solid start brought sixth place after ten matches before the loss of captain Simon Francis and Lewis Cook with cruciate ligament injuries. Both were ruled out for the rest of the season, contributing to a loss of momentum and 20 goals conceded in seven games. The slide was arrested by victory over West Ham and handsome

4-0 success against Chelsea. But again progress was checked by a single win in the next nine matches. Bournemouth still had points to spare over teams below them and made absolutely sure of staying up with a 5-0 win at Brighton, matching their best in the top division.

Ake N	38	Fraser R	35 (3)	Simpson J	4 (2)
Begovic A	24	Gosling D	19 (6)	Smith A	25
Boruc A	12	Hyndman E	(1)	Solanke D	2 (8)
Brooks D	29 (1)	Ibe J	9 (10)	Stanislas J	11 (12)
Clyne N	13 (1)	King J	34 (1)	Surman A	16 (2)
Cook L	8 (5)	Lerma J	29 (1)	Surridge S	(2)
Cook S	31	Mepham C	10 (3)	Travers M	2
Daniels C	17 (4)	Mings T	2 (3)	Wilson C	29 (1)
Defoe J	- (4)	Mousset L	1 (23)		
Francis S	13 (4)	Rico D	5 (7)		

League goals (56): Wilson 14, King 12, Brooks 7, Fraser 7, Ake 4, Gosling 2, Lerma 2, Stanislas 2, Cook S 1, Daniels 1, Ibe 1, Mousset 1, Smith 1, Opponents 1
FA Cup goals (1): Pugh M 1. **League Cup goals** (8): Ibe 2, Stanislas 2, Cook S 1, Fraser 1, Mousset 1, Wilson 1
Average home league attendance: 10,532. **Player of Year**: Ryan Fraser

BRIGHTON AND HOVE ALBION

Chris Hughton's side ran out of goals and into a relegation struggle after looking to be on the way to mid-table security. Back-to-back victories over Huddersfield and Crystal Palace delivered a five-point cushion, along with a game in hand over all the teams around them. But a club-record six successive matches without scoring – and another against Manchester City in the semi-finals of the FA Cup – left them sweating. Two defeats in the space of four days at the Amex, were particularly worrying – a 5-0 drubbing by Bournemouth followed by Cardiff's 2-0 victory which boosted their chances of survival. Brighton also faced a demanding run-in, with fixtures against Tottenham, Arsenal and a City team looking to clinch the Premier League title on the final day of them season. But salvation came with Cardiff's defeat by relegated Fulham and the point secured against Newcastle with a header from Pascal Gross which ended their goal drought. Brighton then held Arsenal courtesy of Murray's penalty, ending their hosts' chances of an automatic Champions League place in the process, while Cardiff went down after losing to Palace. Hughton was sacked at the end of the season and replaced by Swansea's Graham Potter.

Andone F	8 (15)	Duffy S	35	Locadia J	12 (14)
Balogun L	5 (3)	Dunk L	36	March S	30 (5)
Bernardo	19 (3)	Gross P	24 (1)	Montoya M	24 (1)
Bissouma Y	17 (11)	Izquierdo J	9 (6)	Murray G	30 (8)
Bong G	19 (3)	Jahanbakhsh A	12 (7)	Propper D	30
Bruno	14	Kayal B	9 (9)	Ryan M	34
Button D	4	Knockaert A	18 (12)	Stephens D	29 (1)

League goals (35): Murray 13, Duffy 5, Andone 3, Gross 3, Dunk 2, Knockaert 2, Locadia 2, Balogun 1, Kayal 1, March 1, Propper 1, Stephens 1
FA Cup goals (10): Andone 2, Knockaert 2, Locadia 2, Murray 2, Bissouma 1, March 1. **League Cup goals**: None
Average home league attendance: 30,426. **Player of Year**: Shane Duffy

BURNLEY

Burnley overcame the threat of falling victim to their own success in a testing season. The extra workload of qualifying for Europe for the first time for half-a-century cast a long shadow and it needed a rousing finish to guarantee their Premier League status. Sean Dyche's side overcame Aberdeen and the Turkish side Basaksehir in qualifying rounds, before losing to Olympiacos in the Europa League's play-offs. They subsequently experienced a miserable first-half of the domestic campaign with 41 goals conceded – five to Manchester City and Everton, four to Fulham, Chelsea and West Ham and three to Watford, Liverpool and Arsenal. The New Year, with Tom Heaton back in goal after a lengthy absence, brought a new-found spirit and a move out of the bottom three, Ashley Barnes and Chris Wood striking a rich seam of goals in an unbeaten run of eight games – the club's longest in the top-flight since 1966. But alarm bells were ringing again when four successive defeats left them just three points ahead of Cardiff from an extra match played. Then, with an anxious run-in looming, they defeated Wolves, Bournemouth and Cardiff, with Wood again among the goals, to relieve the pressure.

Bardsley P 19	Hart J 19	Tarkowski J.................... 35
Barnes A.............. 26 (11)	Heaton T.........................19	Taylor C....................35 (3)
Brady R 6 (10)	Hendrick J............... 25 (7)	Vokes S................10 (10)
Cork J............................37	Lennon A 14 (2)	Vydra M....................3 (10)
Crouch P...................- (6)	Long K....................... 5 (1)	Ward S.............................. 3
Defour S..........................6	Lowton M 19 (2)	Westwoood A 31 (3)
Gibson B..........................1	McNeil D.................. 19 (2)	Wood C 29 (9)
Gudmundsson J B... 19 (10)	Mee B............................38	

League goals (45): Barnes 12, Wood 10, Gudmundsson 3, Hendrick 3, McNeil 3, Tarkowski 3, Vokes 3, Westwood 2, Cork 1, Gibson 1, Lennon 1, Vydra 1, Opponents 2
FA Cup goals (1): Wood 1. **League Cup goals** (1): Long 1. **Europa League goals** (7): Wood 2, Cork 2, Barnes 1, Vokes 1, Vydra 1
Average home league attendance: 20,534. **Player of Year**: Ashley Westwood

CARDIFF CITY

Cardiff's season was overshadowed by the death in a plane crash of Emiliano Sala, two days after his record signing from Nantes. It put the struggle to avoid an immediate return to the Championship into perspective and will be felt by the club and supporters for a long time to come. Sala never had the chance to justify Neil Warnock's belief that the 28-year-old Argentine striker had the potential to cure a lack of goals which plagued his side throughout the season. His players showed admirable resolve on an emotional afternoon when Sala should have been making his home debut, with Bobby Reid, on his 26th birthday, scoring both goals against Bournemouth. Cardiff then secured back-to-back top-flight wins for the first time since 1962, beating Southampton 2-1 with a stoppage-time goal by Kenneth Zohore. But eight goals conceded in successive home games against Watford and Everton set them back, along with a knee ligament injury which put defensive stalwart Sol Bamba out for the remainder of the season. And despite a lifeline offered by Brighton's goal drought, along with a 2-0 win over their rivals at the Amex Stadium, defeat by relegated Fulham proved a crushing blow. Another at home to Crystal Palace in the penultimate fixture sealed their fate.

Arter H 24 (1)	Gunnarsson A 27 (1)	Paterson C................21 (6)
Bacuna L.................... 4 (7)	Harris K 3 (10)	Peltier L...................17 (3)
Bamba S........................28	Healey R .... - (3)	Ralls J 22 (6)
Bennett J......................30	Hoilett J.................... 23 (9)	Reid B 16 (11)
Camarasa V.............. 31 (1)	Madine G .... - (5)	Richards A ....- (4)
Cunningham G 7	Mendez-Laing N........ 11 (9)	Ward D....................4 (10)
Damour L.................... - (2)	Morrison S....................34	Zohore K..................7 (12)
Ecuele Manga B 37 (1)	Murphy J.................. 22 (7)	
Etheridge N...................38	Niasse O 12 (1)	

League goals (34): Camarasa 5, Reid 5, Bamba 4, Mendez-Laing 4, Paterson 4, Hoilett 3,

Murphy 3, Gunnarsson 1, Harris 1, Morrison 1, Ward 1, Zohore 1, Opponents 1
FA Cup goals: None. **League Cup goals** (1): Ecuele Manga 1
Average home league attendance: 31,413. **Player of Year**: Neil Etheridge

CHELSEA

Maurizio Sarri kept faith with his players during a demanding season of highs and lows and reaped a double reward. Chelsea regained a Champions League place and went on to win the Europa League, delivering the first trophy of the Italian's coaching career. Four goals in a 23-minute spell in the second-half overwhelmed Arsenal in the final in Baku, the first from their former striker Olivier Giroud, who also won the penalty which provided the first of Eden Hazard's brace. Hazard later hinted strongly that this would be his final game – ahead of a move to Real Madrid – after seven seasons at the club. Sarri's first season after succeeding Antonio Conte began well – five successive wins on the way to 18 matches in all competitions without defeat. They reached the League Cup Final, losing to Manchester City on penalties, and remained unbeaten in Europe, but hit a low point in the Premier League with successive defeats by Arsenal and, Bournemouth, after which Sarri accused his team of lacking motivation and fight. There was also a 6-0 drubbing by City, the club's worst for 28 years, and a fall to seventh. Chelsea regrouped and climbed back into the top four with successive wins over Cardiff, Brighton and West Ham, holding on to finish ahead of Tottenham, Arsenal and Manchester United. But Sarri decided to return to Italy to take over at Serie A champions Juventus after one season at Stamford Bridge – the ninth full-time manager to leave Chelsea under owner Roman Abramovich. Hazard also secured his 'dream' move to the Bernabeu. Frank Lampard, who played for Chelsea for 13 years, returned to the club after 13 months as Derby manager.

Arrizabalaga K	36	Giroud O	7 (20)	Luiz D	36
Azpilicueta C	38	Hazard E	32 (5)	Marcos Alonso	31
Barkley R	13 (14)	Higuain G	13 (1)	Morata A	11 (5)
Caballero W	2	Hudson Odoi C	4 (6)	Moses V	- (2)
Cahill G	- (2)	Jorginho	37	Pedro	21 (10)
Christensen A	6 (2)	Kante N	38	Rudiger A	33
Emerson	7 (3)	Kovacic M	21 (11)	Willian	26 (6)
Fabregas C	1 (5)	Loftus-Cheek R	6 (18)	Zappacosta D	1 (3)

League goals (63): Hazard 16, Pedro 8, Loftus-Cheek 6, Higuain 5, Morata 5, Kante 4, Barkley 3, Luiz 3, Willian 3, Giroud 2, Jorginho 2, Marcos Alonso 2, Azpilicueta 1, Rudiger 1, Opponents 2
FA Cup goals (5): Morata 2, Willian 2, Hudson-Odoi 1. **League Cup goals** (8): Hazard 3, Emerson 1, Fabregas 1, Kante 1, Opponents 2
Europa League goals (36): Giroud 11, Pedro 5, Hudson-Odoi 4, Loftus-Cheek 4, Willian 3, Barkley 2, Hazard 2, Marcos Alonso 2, Morata 2, Opponents 1
Average home league attendance: 40,437. **Player of Year**: Eden Hazard

CRYSTAL PALACE

Roy Hodgson celebrated becoming the Premier League's oldest-ever manager by steering his side away from the threat of relegation. Palace were one six teams caught up in the struggle to avoid the drop alongside Huddersfield and Fulham until an impressive surge in the final third of the season. Hodgson, at 71 years and 198 days, overtook Sir Bobby Robson's record, by engineering a 4-1 win at Leicester in which Wilfried Zaha scored twice and on-loan Michy Batshuayi opened his account for the club. It was followed by wins over Burnley, Huddersfield and Newcastle, the latter secured by a tenth penalty in a row converted by Luka Milivojevic. Palace then passed the recognised safety mark of 40 points by beating Arsenal 3-2 at the Emirates with Christian Benteke scoring for the first time in a year. For good measure, Palace rounded off the campaign with eight goals against Cardiff and Bournemouth to complete a run of seven wins in 12 games and a club-best 49 points for a 38-game campaign. They had previously inflicted a rare defeat, 3-2, on Manchester City at the Etihad – described by Hodgson as 'one of those bonanza days' – and threatened to do the same at Anfield until Liverpool edged clear 4-3.

Ayew J 14 (6)	Meyer M 15 (14)	Tomkins J 29
Batshuayi M 9 (2)	Milivojevic L 38	Townsend A 34 (4)
Benteke C 9 (7)	Puncheon J .... - (5)	Van Aanholt P 36
Dann S 7 (3)	Sakho M 27	Wan-Bissaka A 35
Guaita V 20	Sako B .... - (4)	Ward J 6 (1)
Hennessey W 17 (1)	Schlupp J 18 (12)	Wickham C .... - (6)
Kelly M 12 (1)	Sorloth A .... - (12)	Zaha W 34
Kouyate C 21 (10)	Souare P .... - (1)	
McArthur J 36 (2)	Speroni J 1	

League goals (51): Milivojevic 12, Zaha 10, Townsend 6, Batshuayi 5, Schlupp 4, McArthur 3, Van Aanholt 3, Ayew 1, Benteke 1, Meyer 1, Tomkins 1, Ward 1, Opponents 3
FA Cup goals (6): Ayew 1, Batshuayi 1, Meyer 1, Schlupp 1, Townsend 1, Wickham 1. **League Cup goals** (4): Townsend 2, Sorloth 1, Van Aanholt 1
Average home league attendance: 25,455. **Player of Year**: Aaron Wan-Bissaka

EVERTON

In terms of where they finished, nothing much had changed for Everton – another eighth place reflecting another modest season. A 6-2 home defeat by Tottenham followed immediately by a 5-1 victory at Burnley seemed par for the course; no sign of consistency and not much of prospect of it in the New Year. Yet the longer Marco Silva's first campaign in charge went on, the more pronounced his influence became and the more his side began to look capable of bridging the gap to the top-six. Chelsea, West Ham Arsenal were beaten without a goal conceded, an improvement interrupted by a poor performance against relegated Fulham. Manchester United were put to the sword, a 4-0 victory representing one of the most emphatic performances Goodson Park has witnessed in recent seasons. Another win, over Burnley, in the final home match, meant six out of seven clean sheets, a sign that Everton's vulnerability against set-pieces – 16 Premier League goals were conceded during the season – was being addressed. The final eight matches yielded 17 points, enough to overtake Leicester, West Ham and Watford, although not sufficient to prevent Wolves claiming the final Europa League spot.

Andre Gomes 24 (3)	Holgate M 4 (1)	Pickford J 38
Baines L 5 (1)	Jagielka P 4 (3)	Richarlison 32 (3)
Bernard 25 (9)	Keane M 33	Schneiderlin M 10 (4)
Calvert-Lewin D 19 (16)	Kenny J 8 (2)	Sigurdsson G 36 (2)
Coleman S 29	Lookman A 3 (18)	Tosun C 10 (15)
Davies T 10 (6)	McCarthy J .... - (1)	Walcott T 24 (13)
Digne L 33 (2)	Mina Y 10 (3)	Zouma K 29 (3)
Gueye I 32 (1)	Niasse O .... - (5)	

League goals (54): Richarlison 13, Sigurdsson 13, Calvert-Lewin 6, Walcott 5, Digne 4, Tosun 3, Coleman 2, Zouma 2, Andre Gomes 1, Bernard 1, Jagielka 1, Keane 1, Mina 1, Opponents 1
FA Cup goals (4): Bernard 1, Lookman 1, Richarlison 1, Tosun 1. **League Cup goals** (4): Calvert-Lewin 2, Sigurdsson 1, Walcott 1
Average home league attendance: 38,780. **Player of Year**: Lucas Digne

FULHAM

Not even a record spending spree, nor the appointment of 'miracle man' Claudio Ranieri could prevent an immediate return to the Championship. Fulham banked heavily on an influx of new players to meet the demands of the Premier League, becoming the first newly-promoted club to splash out £100m. Instead, 12 summer signings, five of them on transfer deadline represented poor value. Just as significant, the team that went up via the play-offs lost their identity and struggled from the start. Slavisa Jokanovic became the division's first managerial casualty of the season, sacked with his side bottom after 12 matches. He was replaced by Ranieri, architect of Leicester's remarkable title win in 2016, whose immediate task was to plug a defence which had already conceded 31 goals. The Italian was unable to do so, lasting 106 days before he too was dismissed with Fulham now ten points from safety with ten matches remaining. Coach Scott Parker, who had four years as a player at Craven Cottage, could do little in a caretaker role, apart from salvaging some self-respect for his players and breaking a losing sequence which had reached nine matches when a 4-1 defeat at Watford confirmed the drop, with five fixtures remaining. There were back to back victories over Everton, Bournemouth and Cardiff, but a 4-0 drubbing by Newcastle summed up the campaign. Parker was given the job on a permanent basis.

Ayite F	3 (13)	Fosu-Mensah T	10 (2)	Nordtveit H	4 (1)
Babel R	15 (1)	Seri J	27 (5)	Odoi D	29 (2)
Bettinelli M	7	Johansen S	4 (8)	Ream T	25 (1)
Bryan J	27 (1)	Kamara A	5 (8)	Rico S	29
Cairney T	24 (7)	Kebano N	- (7)	Schurrle A	21 (3)
Chambers C	29 (2)	Le Marchand M	25 (1)	Sessegnon R	26 (9)
Christie C	19 (9)	Markovic L	- (1)	Vietto L	10 (10)
Cisse I	1 (2)	Mawson A	13 (2)	Zambo F	16 (6)
Elliott H	- (2)	McDonald K	10 (5)		
Fabri	2	Mitrovic A	37		

League goals (34): Mitrovic 11, Schurrle 6, Babel 5, Kamara 3, Chambers 2, Sessegnon 2, Ayite 1, Cairney 1, Seri 1, Vietto 1, Opponents 1

FA Cup goals (1): Odoi 1. **League Cup goals (5):** Kamara 2, Bryan 1, Christie 1, De la Torre L 1
Average home league attendance: 24,371. **Player of Year:** Calum Chambers

HUDDERSFIELD TOWN

The club's Premier League adventure started with a victory at Selhurst Park and stretched all season against all the odds. It ended, 18 months later, with a defeat on the same ground, where those odds finally caught up with a side who could not score goals and went down with six games still to play. David Wagner tried every permutation to find a solution without response from his strikers. Only once did his side look capable of making a fight of it — a three-match run bringing goals from midfielders Aaron Mooy and Alex Pritchard, victories over Fulham and Wolves, a point against West Ham and brief respite from the bottom three. A club-record eighth straight defeat into the New Year proved the final straw for the manager, along with a controversial penalty incident when Lee Mason pointed to the spot for a challenge by Cardiff's Joe Bennett on Florent Hadergjonaj, then reversed the decision after consulting his assistant. Two days later, Wagner left by mutual consent, to be succeeded by another German coach, Jan Siewert from Borussia Dortmund, who at 36 became the youngest manager in the Premier League. With Huddersfield ten points from safety, Siewert had next to no chance of turning the tide and won just once in his 15 matches — 1-0 against Wolves.

Bacuna J	16 (5)	Hogg J	29	Quaner C	- (2)
Billing P	25 (2)	Jorgensen M	24	Rowe A	1 (1)
Coleman J	1	Kachunga E	13 (7)	Sabiri A	1 (1)
Daly M	- (2)	Kongolo T	32	Schindler C	37
Depoitre L	10 (13)	Lossl J	30 (1)	Smith T	13 (2)
Diakhaby A	6 (6)	Lowe C	23 (6)	Sobhi A	- (4)
Duhaney D	1	Mbenza J	10 (12)	Stankovic J	9 (2)
Durm E	21 (7)	Mooy A	25 (4)	Van La Parra R	5
Grant K	9 (4)	Mounie S	19 (12)	Williams D	1 (4)
Hadergjonaj F	19 (5)	Pritchard A	26 (4)		
Hamer B	7	Puncheon J	5 (1)		

League goals (22): Grant 4, Jorgensen 3, Mooy 3, Billing 2, Mounie 2, Pritchard 2, Bacuna 1, Stankovic 1, Kongolo 1, Mbenza 1, Schindler 1, Opponents 1
FA Cup goals: None. **League Cup goals**: None
Average home league attendance: 23,201. **Player of Year**: Christopher Schindler

LEICESTER CITY

A season scarred by the death of owner Vichai Srivaddhanaprabha and four others in a helicopter crash outside the King Power Stadium following the match against West Ham began to take on a new lease of life following a change of manager. Claude Puel led his players and staff with great dignity in dealing with the aftermath of the tragedy, while at the same time having to concentrate on a continuation of the Premier League season. But supporters' growing frustration with some of his tactics spilled over during a run of four successive home defeats, culminating in a 4-1 reversal against Crystal Palace. Puel was replaced by Celtic's Brendan Rodgers, who in the remaining 11 fixtures had the team playing with greater freedom and fluency – no more so than Jamie Vardy, who scored ten goals, two of them in a 3-0 win over Arsenal. His side also won four in succession, against Fulham, Burnley, Bournemouth and Huddersfield, scoring 11 times in the process. And had Kelechi Iheanacho showed greater composure with a golden opportunity late on at the Etihad, Manchester City might not have been celebrating Vincent Kompany's spectacular strike as another step towards retaining the title. Leicester repeated their 2018 finish of ninth, while looking forward with some confidence to going higher in the new season.

Adrien Silva 1 (1)	Ghezzal R 8 (11)	Okazaki S 1 (20)
Albrighton M 18 (9)	Gray D 23 (11)	Pereira R 35
Amartey D................. 7 (2)	Iborra V 3 (5)	Schmeichel K 38
Barnes H 11 (5)	Iheanacho K 9 (21)	Simpson D 3 (3)
Chilwell B 36	Maddison J 35 (1)	Soyuncu C 4 (2)
Choudhury H 7 (2)	Maguire H 31	Tielemans Y 13
Diabate F........................1	Mendy N 23 (8)	Vardy J................... 30 (4)
Evans J................. 21 (3)	Morgan W................. 21 (1)	
Fuchs C 2 (1)	Ndidi W 37 (1)	

League goals (51): Vardy 18, Maddison 7, Gray 4, Maguire 3, Morgan 3, Tielemans 3, Albrighton 2, Ndidi 2, Pereira 2, Barnes 1, Evans 1, Ghezzal 1, Iheanacho 1, Opponents 3
FA Cup goals (1): Ghezzal 1. **League Cup goals** (5): Albrighton 1, Fuchs 1, Ghezzal 1, Iborra 1, Iheanacho 1
Average home league attendance: 31,851. **Player of Year**: Ricardo Pereira

LIVERPOOL

Not so much a silver lining, more a golden fleece. Liverpool were crestfallen at missing out on the club's first league title since 1990, despite accumulating 97 points. Three weeks later, that despair turned to delight as an equally absorbing Champions League campaign ended with victory over Tottenham in the final in Madrid. Put together, the achievements showed that Jurgen Klopp and his players could prove an even bigger force in the new season. Klopp had already gone some way to curing his side's defensive failings with the acquisition of Virgil van Dijk in January 2018. He followed that up in the summer by signing Brazil goalkeeper Alisson and the imposing pair immediately provided an extra dimension, alongside the formidable strike force of Mohamed Salah, Roberto Firmino and Sadio Mane. In any normal season, that points total would have made them champions. Instead, they came up against a Manchester City side who won the last 14 matches to finish a point ahead after looking to be out of the running with three defeats in four games in December. Liverpool then enjoyed a seven-point cushion, but lost their unbeaten record at the Etihad and were further undermined by dropping points to Leicester, West Ham and Manchester United. Alongside a goalless Merseyside derby, the sequence contributed to the leadership changing 32 times in all before City's 4-1 win at Brighton in the final round of matches kept them in front. Three days before that came arguably the finest comeback in Liverpool's history – a 4-0 win over Barcelona, achieved without the injured Salah and Firmino, overturning a 3-0 defeat in the first leg of their semi-final

Alexander-Arnold T ... 27 (2)	Lallana A.................... 5 (8)	Firmino R 31 (3)
Alisson 38	Lovren D 11 (2)	Robertson A................36
Camacho R .... - (1)	Mane S 35 (1)	Salah M 37 (1)
Clyne N 1 (3)	Matip J 17 (5)	Shaqiri X 11 (13)
Fabinho 21 (7)	Milner J 19 (12)	Sturridge D...............4 (14)
Gomez J 12 (4)	Moreno A 2	Van Dijk V 38
Henderson J 21 (11)	Origi D 4 (8)	Wijnaldum G.............32 (3)
Keita N 16 (9)	Oxlade-Chamberlain A .. - (2)	

League goals (89): Mane 22, Salah 22, Firmino 12, Shaqiri 6, Milner 5, Van Dijk 4, Origi 3, Wijnaldum 3, Keita 2, Sturridge 2, Alexander-Arnold 1, Fabinho 1, Henderson 1, Lovren 1, Matip 1, Opponents 3
FA Cup goals (1): Origi 1. **League Cup goals** (1): Sturridge 1
Champions League goals (24)): Salah 5, Firmino 4, Mane 4, Origi 3, Milner 2, Wijnaldum 2, Van Dijk 2, Keita 1, Sturridge 1
Average home league attendance: 52,983. **Player of Year**: Virgil van Dijk

MANCHESTER CITY

Manchester City continued to rewrite the record books in a remarkable season of high-performance and at times nerve-shredding football. It brought an unprecedented domestic treble of Premier League, FA Cup and League Cup. If Jose Mourinho had been in charge, he would also have included the Community Shield, traditional curtain-raiser to the campaign. There has never been a title race to match it. The lead changed hands 32 times before Pep Guardiola's side had the final say, a point ahead of Liverpool after showing nerves of steel to come from behind for a 4-1 clincher at Brighton in the last game. It was their 14th successive win and City needed every one after twice looking as if they might not last the pace. Three defeats in December, against Chelsea, Crystal Palace and Leicester, left them seven points behind Jurgen Klopp's team – and also trailing Tottenham. Later, defeat at Newcastle threatened to tip the balance. Instead, a 6-0 rout of Chelsea, in which Sergio Aguero equalled Alan Shearer's record of 11 Premier League hat-tricks, recharged some batteries and City never blinked after that. Vincent Kompany's 30-yard strike against Leicester was also special as they came within two points of matching the 2018 tally of 100. Captain Kompany went on to lift the FA Cup before announcing his departure to become player-manager of his first club, Anderlecht. A 6-0 success against Watford in that final, the biggest for 116 years, took their tally for the campaign to a record 169 goals in all competitions. Victory on penalties against Chelsea in the Carabao Cup completed the full set. The one that got away was the Champions League, with Tottenham prevailing in a pulsating quarter-final.

Aguero S.................. 31 (2)	Fernandinho 27 (2)	Mendy B 10
Bernardo Silva.......... 31 (5)	Foden P 3 (10)	Otamendi N.............. 14 (4)
Danilo 9 (2)	Gabriel Jesus............ 8 (21)	Sane L..................21 (10)
David Silva............... 28 (5)	Gundogan I............... 23 (8)	Sterling R.................31 (3)
De Bruyne K............ 11 (8)	Kompany V............... 13 (4)	Stones J...................20 (4)
Delph F 8 (3)	Laporte A 34 (1)	Walker K 30 (3)
Ederson 38	Mahrez R 14 (13)	Zinchenko A 14

League goals (95): Aguero 21, Sterling 17, Sane 10, Gabriel Jesus 7, Bernardo Silva 7, Mahrez 7, David Silva 6, Gundogan 6, Laporte 3, De Bruyne 2, Danilo 1, Fernandinho 1, Foden 1, Kompany 1, Walker 1, Opponents 4

FA Cup goals (26): Gabriel Jesus 5, Foden 3, Sterling 3, Aguero 2, Bernardo Silva 2, De Bruyne 2, Mahrez 2, Sane 2, David Silva 1, Otamendi 1, Opponents 3
League Cup goals (16): Gabriel Jesus 5, De Bruyne 2, Diaz B 2, Foden 2, Mahrez 2, Aguero 1, Walker 1, Zinchenko 1. **Community Shield goals** (2): Aguero 2
Champions League goals (30): Aguero 6, Sterling 5, Bernardo Silva 4, Gabriel Jesus 4, Sane 4, David Silva 3, Laporte 2, Foden 1, Mahrez 1
Average home league attendance: 54,130. **Player of Year**: Bernardo Silva

MANCHESTER UNITED

Ole Gunnar Solskjaer couldn't put a foot wrong as caretaker-manager. He could barely put one right after being confirmed in the job with a three-year contract. The change of fortune left United out of the top four and Solskjaer admitting they did not deserve to be in the Champions League. He also conceded that his squad were not up to competing for the Premier League title and needed major surgery in the summer. Following on from the dismissal of Jose Mourinho, it was an uncomfortable season all-round at Old Trafford. Despite the club's worst start in 29 years, Mourinho targeted a top-four place by the end of 2018. They missed it by eight points and by then he had gone, following a 3-1 defeat by Liverpool. Former United striker Solskjaer, who brought in Sir Alex Ferguson's former No 2, Mike Phelan, as his assistant, enjoyed immediate success – a 5-1 victory at Cardiff and five goals scored for the first time in the league since Ferguson's last match against West Bromwich Albion in 2013. Solskjaer's winning start extended to eight matches in all competitions, a club record. His stock rose with a famous Champions League performance against Paris Saint-Germain and he was given the job on a permanent basis after winning 14 of 19 games. United were then two points off the top four. Then it all went wrong – outclassed by Barcelona, embarrassed by a 4-0 defeat at Everton and beaten at home by Manchester City. The final straw was a 1-1 draw with relegated Huddersfield which meant Europa League football in the new season.

Bailly E...................... 8 (4)	Herrera A 16 (6)	Pogba P 34 (1)
Chong T...................... - (2)	Jones P 15 (3)	Rashford M...............26 (7)
Darmian M................. 5 (1)	Lindelof V................ 29 (1)	Rojo M 2 (3)
Dalot D 12 (4)	Lingard J 19 (8)	Sanchez A 9 (11)
De Gea D 38	Lukaku R 22 (10)	Shaw L........................... 29
Fellaini M 6 (8)	Martial A 18 (9)	Smalling C 24
Fred 13 (4)	Mata J 16 (6)	Valencia A 5 (1)
Garner J...................... - (1)	Matic N.........................28	Young A 28 (2)
Gomes A..................... - (2)	McTominay S.............. 9 (7)	
Greenwood M 1 (2)	Pereira A.................... 6 (9)	

League goals (65): Pogba 13, Lukaku 12, Martial 10, Rashford 10, Lingard 4, Mata 3, Herrera 2, McTominay 2, Young 2, Fred 1, Lindelof 1, Matic 1, Pereira 1, Sanchez 1, Shaw 1, Smalling 1
FA Cup goals (8): Herrera 1, Lingard 1, Lukaku 1, Martial 1, Mata 1, Pogba 1, Rashford 1, Sanchez 1. **League Cup goals** (2): Fellaini 1, Mata 1
Champions League goals (10): Lukaku 2, Pogba 2, Rashford 2, Fellaini 1, Martial 1, Mata 1, Opponents 1
Average home league attendance: 74,498. **Player of Year**: Luke Shaw

NEWCASTLE UNITED

Rafael Benitez made no bones about the task ahead after five successive home defeats to start the season for the first time in the club's history and still no wins overall with ten matches played. Turning things round, he declared, was the biggest challenge of his career. Benitez went even further at Christmas, despite his side having climbed five points clear of the relegation zone. It would be 'a miracle' to keep them up, he admitted. Over the top perhaps, but the response from the players and owner Mike Ashley, proved illuminating. With Swiss international Fabian Schar an increasing defensive influence, 21-year-old Sean Longstaff a revelation in midfield and Ashley sanctioning the club-record £20m purchase of Paraguayan Miguel Almiron, Newcastle won four times in six matches – one of them against Manchester City. Most important of all, Ayoze Perez scored seven goals in nine games, including a hat-trick against Southampton, which took them beyond the 40-point 'survival' point. A 4-0 success at Fulham rounded things off nicely, 11 points clear of the bottom three, and offered some optimism about better times ahead. That, however, was dampened when Benitez left the club after three seasons in charge, unable to agree a new contract. Two days later, he was appointed manager of the Chinese club Dalian Yifang on a reported £12m a year salary. Sam Allardyce reportedly turned down the chance to take over. Steve Bruce jumped at the chance, leaving Sheffield Wednesday after six months in charge.

Almiron M	9 (1)	Fernandez F	17 (2)	Longstaff S	8 (1)
Atsu C	15 (13)	Hayden I	21 (4)	Murphy J	3 (6)
Perez A	34 (3)	Manquillo J	12 (6)	Muto Y	5 (12)
Barreca A	- (1)	Joselu	5 (11)	Ritchie M	35 (1)
Clark C	9 (2)	Kenedy	14 (11)	Rondon S	30 (2)
Diame M	24 (5)	Ki Sung-Yueng	14 (4)	Schar F	22 (2)
Dubravka M	38	Lascelles J	32	Shelvey J	10 (6)
Dummett P	21 (5)	Lejeune F	12	Yedlin D	28 (1)

League goals (42): Perez 12, Rondon 11, Schar 4, Clark 3, Joselu 2, Ritchie 2, Atsu 1, Hayden 1, Kenedy 1, Longstaff 1, Muto 1, Shelvey 1, Yedlin 1, Opponents 1
FA Cup goals (5): Joselu 1, Longstaff 1, Perez 1, Ritchie 1, Roberts C 1. **League Cup goals (1):** Rondon 1
Average home league attendance: 51,121. **Player of Year:** Salomon Rondon

SOUTHAMPTON

Ralph Hasenhuttl punched the air in delight after his side beat the drop on a dramatic afternoon at St Mary's – and no wonder. Many questioned the appointment of the unknown Premier League quantity following the dismissal of Mark Hughes. The league's first Austrian manager, a rising coach in German football, latterly with Leipzig, also admitted taking a risk with a club facing a struggle to survive after a single win in 15 matches, having dropped 12 points from winning positions. He watched from the stands as Southampton lost 3-1 at Tottenham, then went down by the only goal at Cardiff in his first match in charge. His second laid the foundation for a major improvement in the second half of the season – substitute Charlie Austin heading an 85th winner to end Arsenal's 22-match unbeaten run in all competitions. Nathan Redmond, without a goal all season, began to flourish, James Ward-Prowse scored important goals, while Sean Long rediscovered his scoring form with four in five games. His fourth came in a 2-2 draw with Bournemouth which took Southampton to safety on 38 points – 29 of which had been accumulated since the change of manager.

Armstrong S	16 (13)	Hoedt W	13	Romeu O	25 (6)
Austin C	11 (14)	Hojbjerg P	31	Sims J	2 (5)
Bednarek J	24 (1)	Ings D	23 (1)	Slattery J	1 (2)
Bertrand R	24	Johnson T	- (1)	Soares C	16 (2)
Davis S	1 (2)	Lemina M	18 (3)	Stephens J	19 (5)
Elyounoussi M	8 (8)	Long S	12 (14)	Targett M	13 (3)
Forster F	1	McCarthy A	25	Valery Y	20 (3)
Gabbiadini M	4 (8)	Obafemi M	1 (5)	Vestergaard J	23
Gallagher S	- (4)	Ramsay K		Ward-Prowse J	21 (6)
Gunn A	12	Redmond N	36 (2)	Yoshida M	17

League goals (45): Ings 7, Ward-Prowse 7, Redmond 6, Long 5, Hojbjerg 4, Armstrong 3, Austin 2, Valery 2, Bertrand 1, Gabbiadini 1, Lemina 1, Obafemi 1, Romeu 1, Soares 1, Stephens 1, Targett 1, Opponents 1
FA Cup goals (4): Redmond 3, Armstrong 1. **League Cup goals (2):** Austin 1, Ings 1
Average home league attendance: 30,139. **Player of Year:** Nathan Redmond

TOTTENHAM HOTSPUR

Another season without a trophy, but this time a magnificent new stadium to show for it, along with a first-ever appearance in the final of Europe's premier club competion. Tottenham fell at the final hurdle of the Champions League in Madrid, conceding a controversial penalty within two minutes and a second goal to Liverpool two minutes from the end of normal time. Despite the defeat, the manner in which they made it all the way – and may now be in a position to release funds to strengthen the squad – offered the prospect of ending more than a decade's wait for some silverware Mauricio Pochettino's team finished second to Barcelona in a tough group, which also included Inter Milan, after gaining a single point from their first three matches. They knocked out Borussia Dortmund, followed by Manchester City in a seven-goal thriller at the Eithad. Tottenham then overturned a 3-0 half-time aggregate deficit against Ajax in the semi-finals with a hat-trick from Lucas Moura and went through on away goals. Pochettino managed this without signing a single player because of the club's financial commitment to the new ground. This eventually caught up with them in the Premier League when a comfortable top-four place became anything but when the final five matches yielded a single win and Arsenal came within a point of securing fourth place.

Alderweireld T 33 (1)	Janssen V .... - (3)	Skipp O 2 (6)
Alli D 22 (3)	Kane H 27 (1)	Son Heung-min 23 (8)
Amos L .... - (1)	Lamela E 9 (10)	Trippier K 26 (1)
Aurier S 6 (2)	Llorente F 6 (14)	Vertonghen J 22
Davies B 20 (7)	Lloris H 33	Vorm M 2
Dembele M 7 (3)	Lucas Moura 25 (7)	Walker-Peters K 4 (2)
Dier E 18 (2)	Nkoudou G-K .... - (1)	Wanyama V 4 (9)
Eriksen C 30 (5)	Rose D 20 (6)	Winks H 17 (9)
Foyth J 10 (2)	Sanchez D 22 (1)	
Gazzaniga P 3	Sissoko M 27 (2)	

League goals (67): Kane 17, Son Heung-min 12, Lucas Moura 10, Eriksen 8, Alli 5, Lamela 4, Dier 3, Foyth 1, Llorente 1, Sanchez 1, Trippier 1, Vertonghen 1, Wanyama 1, Winks 1, Opponents 1
FA Cup goals (7): Llorente 3, Aurier 2, Kane 1, Son Heung-min 1. **League Cup goals** (9): Son Heung-min 3, Alli 2, Llorente 2, Kane 1, Lamela 1.
Champions League goals (20): Kane 5, Lucas Moura 5, Son Heung-min 4, Eriksen 2, Llorente 2, Lamera 1, Vertonghen 1
Average home league attendance: 54,216. **Player of Year**: Son Heung-min

WATFORD

Watford were taught a harsh lesson in the FA Cup Final, but it did nothing to detract from passing their Premier League examination with flying colours. A 4-1 win over Fulham secured the club's best-ever points total, 46, with six matches still to play, and was followed by their highest finishing position of 11th. Both achievements would have been even better had that level of performance extended to the end of the season. Instead, Javi Gracia's side won only once more, against Huddersfield, after Gerard Deulofeu engineered one of the great Wembley comebacks with two goals in a 3-2 semi-final victory over Wolves after trailing 2-0 approaching the 80th minute. Particularly disappointing was a final-day 4-1 defeat by West Ham in front of their own supporters, who a fortnight later displayed admirable loyalty when turning the national stadium into a blaze of yellow even as Manchester City's score mounted in the final. Gracia, himself, set a new mark in the away fixture against Brighton with a 39th Premier League game in charge. No-one had previously gone beyond 38 at a club with a reputation for a rapid turnover of managers. In that same month, Deulofeu's hat-trick in a 5-1 win at Cardiff was Watford's first in the top-flight since Mark Falco in 1986. Troy Deeney's brace completed the club's first five-goal performance in the top division since the same year.

Britos M	2 (1)	Gray A	13 (16)	Okaka S	- (2)
Capoue E	33	Holebas J	27 (1)	Pereyra R	33
Cathcart C	35 (1)	Hughes W	31 (1)	Prodl S	- (1)
Chalobah N	3 (6)	Janmaat D	17 (1)	Quina	3 (5)
Cleverley T	4 (9)	Kabasele C	19 (2)	Sema K	9 (8)
Deeney T	28 (4)	Kiko	22 (7)	Success I	9 (21)
Deulofeu G	26 (4)	Navarro M	1 (1)	Wilmot B	- (2)
Doucoure A	34 (1)	Mariappa A	20 (6)		
Foster B	38	Masina A	11 (3)		

League goals (52): Deulofeu 10, Deeney 9, Gray 7, Pereyra 6, Doucoure 5, Cathcart 3, Holebas 3, Hughes 2, Capoue 1, Cleverley 1, Success 1, Kiko 1, Quina 1, Sema 1, Opponents 1
FA Cup goals (10): Capoue 2, Deeney 2, Deulofeu 2, Gray 2, Hughes 1, Success 1. **League Cup goals** (4): Success 2, Capoue 1, Quina 1
Average home league attendance: 20,016. **Player of Year**: Etienne Capoue

WEST HAM UNITED

A worrying start to the season gave way to mid table consolidation and finally to an eye-catching finale which brought a place in the top-half. Manuel Pellegrini asked supporters 'to trust me' after a 4-0 drubbing at Liverpool in his first match in charge was followed immediately by defeats against Bournemouth, Arsenal and Wolves. They started to believe with 3-1 wins over Everton and Manchester United as successive club record signings Issa Diop and Felipe Anderson settled in. Then, three-goal performances against Newcastle, Cardiff and Crystal Palace in successive matches took West Ham comfortably clear of trouble, raising expectation levels among the fans for the second-half of the campaign. In fact, there was little further movement until Michail Antonio's sublime finish delivered the first defeat for Tottenham in their new stadium. Marko Arnautovich came out of his shell to score twice as Southampton were seen off 3-0, while Mark Noble's brace rounded things off nicely with a 4-1 success at Vicarage Road which enabled his side to move above FA Cup finalists Watford and into tenth place.

Antonio M	22 (11)	Fredericks R	12 (3)	Ogbonna A	20 (4)
Arnautovic M	24 (4)	Hernandez J	14 (11)	Rice D	34
Balbuena F	23	Johnson B	1	Sanchez C	2 (5)
Carroll A	3 (9)	Lanzini M	8 (2)	Silva X	- (1)
Cresswell A	18 (2)	Lucas Perez	4 (11)	Snodgrass R	25 (8)
Diangana Q	6 (11)	Masuaku A	19 (4)	Wilshere I	4 (4)
Diop I	33	Nasri S	3 (2)	Yarmolenko A	5 (4)
Fabianski L	38	Noble M	29 (2)	Zabaleta P	23 (3)
Felipe Anderson	36	Obiang P	12 (12)		

League goals (52): Arnautovic 10, Felipe Anderson 9, Hernandez 7, Antonio 6, Noble 5, Lucas Perez 3, Rice 2, Snodgrass 2, Yarmolenko 2, Balbuena 1, Diop 1, Fredericks 1, Lanzini 1, Ogbonna 1, Opponents 1
FA Cup goals (4): Arnautovic 1, Carroll 1, Felipe Anderson 1, Lucas Perez 1. **League Cup goals** (12): Diangana 2, Lucas Perez 2, Ogbonna 2, Snodgrass 2, Antonio 1, Diop 1, Fredericks 1, Hernandez 1
Average home league attendance: 58,336. **Player of Year**: Lukasz Fabianski

WOLVERHAMPTON WANDERERS

Nuno Espirito Santo and his players were applauded throughout football for one of the best-ever performances by a newly-promoted Premier League side. It took the club into Europe for the first time since 1980 and earned their Portuguese coach a place on the short-list for Manager of the Year alongside Jurgen Klopp, Mauricio Pochettino and winner Pep Guardiola. Nuno retained the bulk of the squad that won the Championship with 99 points, confident it could cope with the extra demands of top-flight football. He was proved spot-on, notably in the way Wolves performed against the division's big guns, displaying no fear and attacking with pace and precision. They took four points off Arsenal, Chelsea and Manchester United, three off Spurs and held Manchester City at Molineux, succumbing twice only to Liverpool. The reward was seventh place, along with a Europa League spot secured after City's FA Cup Final victory over Watford. Wolves also knocked United and Liverpool out of the FA Cup on the way to the semi-finals, where a 3-2 defeat represented the season's major disappointment. They led 2-0 through goals from Matt Doherty and Raul Jimenez with the 90th minute approaching. But Watford replied to take the tie to extra-time and won it with Gerard Deulofeu's second goal.

Bennett R 34	Helder Costa 16 (9)	Raul Jimenez 36 (2)
Boly W...........................36	Ivan Cavaleiro 6 (17)	Ruben Neves 34 (1)
Coady C 38	Joao Moutinho 35 (3)	Ruben Vinagre 7 (10)
Dendoncker L...........17 (2)	Jonny 32 (1)	Ruddy J 1
Diogo Jota................29 (4)	Kilman M .... - (1)	Rui Patricio 37
Doherty M 35 (3)	Leo Bonatini .... - (7)	Saiss R 12 (7)
Gibbs-White M 5 (21)	Norris W..................... - (1)	Traore A 8 (21)

League goals (47): Raul Jimenez 13, Diogo Jota 9, Boly 4, Doherty 4, Ruben Neves 4, Ivan Cavaleiro 3, Dendoncker 2, Saiss 2, Bennett 1, Helder Costa 1, Joao Moutinho 1, Jonny 1, Traore 1, Opponents 1
FA Cup goals (12): Doherty 4, Raul Jimenez 4, Ivan Cavaleiro 2, Diogo Jota 1, Ruben Neves 1.
League Cup goals (2): Helder Costa 1, Leo Bonatini 1
Average home league attendance: 31,030. **Player of Year**: Joao Moutinho

THE THINGS THEY SAY ...

'It's the job I always dreamed of doing' – **Ole Gunnar Solskjaer** on being appointed permanent manager at Old Trafford after three successful months as caretaker.

'A different attitude and a different mentality is needed at this club' – **Ole Gunnar Solskjaer** after his initial run of success turned sour.

'Moments like these remind you why we started to play football, why we love it so much. It's not about bonuses, contracts or even promotion. It's about scoring goals like that and putting smiles on the faces of fans' – **Daniel Farke**, Norwich manager, after his Championship-winning side retrieved a three goal deficit to draw 3-3 against Nottingham Forest with two in stoppage-time.

'You can have great relationships with your clubs, and I did with mine, but emotionally the national team has always been the biggest thing with me' – **Gareth Southgate**, England manager, on signing a new contract through to the 2022 World Cup.

'Before the game I asked him to present me with the award because I think he will beat my goalscoring record and I look forward to presenting him with the trophy' – **Wayne Rooney**, on his 120th and final international appearance, predicts Harry Kane will eventually overtake his 53 England goals.

'We are World Cup winners in facilities. Now we need to be on the same level on the pitch' – **Mauricio Pochettino**, Tottenham manager, after the opening of the club's new £1bn stadium.

SKY BET CHAMPIONSHIP

ASTON VILLA

Villa regained Premier League status by royal assent, a side transformed by an 'unfashionable' manager, key loan players and the return from injury of their influential captain. On the way to winning the Play-off Final, celebrated in the stands by the Duke of Cambridge, they provided great entertainment, with bulging goals for and against columns. The choice of Brentford's Dean Smith to replace Steve Bruce, sacked after a run of nine games producing a single victory, proved an inspired one. With John Terry alongside him, Smith took his new side out of the bottom half of the table with adventurous, attacking football which delivered wins over Derby, Birmingham and Middlesbrough, along with a crazy 5-5 draw against Nottingham Forest in which Chelsea loanee Tammy Abraham scored four times. Villa lost some of their momentum in the New Year, struggling to overcome the absence of Jack Grealish with a shin injury. The skipper's return after three months sparked a club-record ten successive victories to seal a top-six place. They edged past West Bromwich Albion on penalties in the semi-finals, then overcame Derby 2-1 at Wembley with goals from Anwar El Ghazi, another of their loanees, and Scotland midfielder John McGinn, a £2.7m signing from Hibernian and the club's Player of the Year.

Abraham T	37	Elphick T	11	Lansbury H	1 (2)
Adomah A	22 (14)	Grealish J	31	McGinn J	39 (1)
Bjarnason B	11 (6)	Green A	8 (10)	Mings T	15
Bolasie Y	9 (12)	Hause K	10 (1)	Nyland O	23
Bree J	6 (2)	Hepburn-Murphy R	- (5)	Ramsey J	- (1)
Bunn M	1	Hogan S	- (6)	Steer J	15 (1)
Carroll T	- (2)	Hourihane C	33 (10)	Taylor N	20 (3)
Chester J	28	Hutton A	33	Tuanzebe A	24 (1)
Davis K	- (5)	Jedinak M	12 (5)	Whelan G	23 (12)
El Ghazi A	25 (6)	Kalinic L	7		
Elmohamady A	32 (6)	Kodjia J	22 (17)		

Play-offs – appearances: Elmohamady 3, El Ghazi 3, Grealish 3, McGinn 3, Mings 3, Steer 3, Taylor 3, Tuanzebe 3, Adomah 2 (1), Hourihane 2 (1), **Abraham** 2, Green 1 (2), Whelan 1, Kodjia – (2), Davis – (1), Hause – (1), Jedinak – (1)
League goals (82): Abraham 25, Kodjia 9, Hourihane 7, Grealish 6, McGinn 6, Chester 5, El Ghazi 5, Adomah 4, Bjarnason 2, Bolasie 2, Elmohamady 2, Hutton 2, Mings 2, Elphick 1, Green 1, Hause 1, Whelan 1, Opponents 1. **Play-offs – goals** (4): Abraham 1, El Ghazi 1, Hourihane 1, McGinn 1
FA Cup goals: None. **League Cup goals** (1): Hourihane 1
Average home league attendance: 36,029. **Player of Year:** John McGinn

BIRMINGHAM CITY

A nine-point deduction for breaching profitability and sustainability rules threatened a third successive tense finish at St Andrew's. Together with five successive defeats in March, the penalty dropped Birmingham from mid-table security to the fringes of relegation. But Garry Monk's side responded admirably, becoming the only side to complete the double over Leeds, thanks to a goal from Che Adams to add to the brace he scored at Elland Road earlier in the season. They held two more promotion-minded clubs, Sheffield United and Derby, defeated Rotherham and extended an unbeaten run following the sanction to seven matches to finish well clear of trouble. This proved a sharp contrast with their start to the campaign – one victory in the first 11 fixtures before Adams began to make his mark. He scored hat-tricks against Hull and QPR as Birmingham climbed to within three points of a play-off place before tailing off. Monk was sacked in the summer after a breakdown in his relationship with the club's owners. His assistant, Pep Clotet, was appointed caretaker.

Adams C 43 (3)	Harding W 13 (15)	Mrabti K 6 (6)
Bogle O 3 (12)	Jota 33 (7)	Ndoye C 1 (1)
Camp L 44	Jutkiewicz L 44 (2)	Pedersen K 39
Colin M 43	Kieftenbeld M 34 (2)	Roberts M 3 (5)
Dacres-Cogley J .... - (1)	Lakin C 5 (5)	Solomon-Otabor V ....- (8)
Davis D 8 (3)	Lubala B .... - (3)	Trueman C 2
Dean H 44	Maghoma J 35 (7)	Vassell I 2 (12)
Gardner C 5 (16)	Mahoney C 17 (13)	
Gardner G 39 (1)	Morrison M 43	

League goals (64): Adams 22, Jutkiewicz 14, Morrison 7, Maghoma 6, Jota 3, Gardner G 2, Mahoney 2, Bogle 1, Dean 1, Gardner 1, Gardner C 1, Kieftenbeld 1, Mrabti 1, Pedersen 1, Solomon-Otabor 1, Opponents 1
FA Cup goals: None. **League Cup goals**: None
Average home league attendance: 22,483. **Player of Year**: Che Adams

BLACKBURN ROVERS

Tony Mowbray had mixed feelings about his side's return to the Championship. The manager was satisfied with the way they competed, but frustrated about the failure to build on a promising position established by successive wins over West Bromwich Albion, Millwall, Ipswich and Hull – with a single goal conceded – early in the New Year. The run left them three points away from a play-off place and looking to go higher. But a 5-2 defeat at Brentford, along with the manner in which it was conceded, brought a complete change of direction, Blackburn surrendering a two-goal lead established by Bradley Dack and Danny Graham in the first seven mutes. They took a single point from the next six matches before Graham scored twice to stem the tide against Wigan (3-0). Three further loses finally a provoked a response – successive wins against Derby, Nottingham Forest, Queens Park Rangers and Bolton restoring some much-needed momentum. Rovers also made Norwich work for a win which guaranteed promotion They closed with a 2-2 draw against Swansea and finished 15th.

Armstrong A 31 (13)	Downing P 3	Raya D 41
Bell A 35 (3)	Evans C 33 (2)	Reed H 28 (5)
Bennett E 38 (2)	Graham D 37 (6)	Rodwell J 16 (5)
Brereton B 4 (21)	Lenihan D 34	Rothwell J 13 (20)
Buckley J .... - (2)	Leutwiler J 5	Samuel D 1 (1)
Butterworth D .... - (1)	Magloire T 2	Smallwood R 29 (3)
Chapman H .... - (2)	Mulgrew C 28 (1)	Travis L 19 (7)
Conway C 9 (12)	Nuttall J 2 (13)	Williams D 23 (4)
Dack B 40 (2)	Nyambe R 25 (4)	
Davenport J .... - (1)	Palmer K 10 (4)	

League goals (64): Dack 15, Graham 15, Mulgrew 10, Armstrong 5, Bell 3, Reed 3, Lenihan 2, Nuttall 2, Rothwell 2, Bennett 1, Brereton 1, Conway 1, Palmer 1, Rodwell 1, Travis 1, Opponents 1
FA Cup goals (3): Armstrong 1, Dack 1, Lenihan 1. **League Cup goals** (11): Armstrong 3, Dack 2, Palmer 2, Conway 1, Downing 1, Graham 1, Nuttall 1
Average home league attendance: 14,552. **Player of Year**: Danny Graham

BOLTON WANDERERS

One crisis after another pursued the club, culminating in relegation, administration and a 12-point deduction imposed for the start of the new season. A winding-up petition over unpaid taxes was then suspended, pending a possible takeover. In the build-up to this fall from grace, staff went unpaid, players boycotted training and points were awarded to Brentford for the failure to fulfil an-end-of-season fixture. Bolton finished second from bottom, having escaped the drop on the final day of the previous season. They offered a hint of brighter times by winning three of the opening four games, against West Bromwich Albion, Reading and Birmingham, and drawing the other with Bristol City. Derby, among the promotion favourites, were also beaten before a run of 13 matches without a victory set the tone for the remainder of the campaign. Phil Parkinson was given a vote of confidence, but his team slipped deeper into trouble against a background of gloom and never really looked like escaping the drop zone. They lost to rock-bottom Ipswich and another home defeat, by Aston Villa, confirmed the drop with three matches remaining – one of them the Brentford fixture.

Alnwick B 27	Earing J .... (1)	O'Neil G..................24 (5)
Ameobi S............. 26 (4)	Grounds J 12 (1)	Olkowski P 34 (3)
Beevers M.............. 31 (1)	Hobbs J 24 (1)	Oztumer E................8 (9)
Brockbank H 3	Le Fondre A .... - (1)	Pritchard J 1 (3)
Buckley W............. 23 (10)	Little M.................... 1 (1)	Taylor A......................26
Connell L 8 (2)	Lowe J.......................35	Vela J..................12 (5)
Connolly C 15 (1)	Magenniss J............ 29 (13)	Wheater D 32 (1)
Darcy R .... - (1)	Matthews R 18	Wildschut Y 4 (12)
Doidge C................ 8 (9)	Murphy L 7 (4)	Williams J 29 (1)
Donaldson C..........18 (13)	Muscatt J .... - (1)	Wilson M................13 (3)
Dyer L 2 (5)	Noone C 25 (11)	

League goals (29): Ameobi 4, Buckley 4, Magennis 4, Beevers 3, O'Neil 3, Connolly 2, Olkowski 2, Wildschut 2, Doidge 1, Donaldson 1, Hobbs 1, Noone 1, Opponents 1
FA Cup goals (6): Magennis 3, Beevers 1, Donaldson 1, Opponents 1. **League Cup goals** (1): Oztumer 1
Average home league attendance: 14,636. **Player of Year**: Gary O'Neil

BRENTFORD

Brentford faltered after losing manager Dean Smith, then regrouped under Thomas Frank and narrowly missed a top-ten finish for the fifth successive year. Smith's work in consolidating Championship status on a limited budget at Griffin Park earned him the opportunity to restore Premier League football at Villa Park. Not surprisingly, there was a reaction from the team he left behind, with a promising start to the season giving way to some uncertainly and a slide from fourth into the bottom half of the table. The promoted Frank won just once in his first ten matches in charge before a change to a back-three helped restore the team's appetite for the bright, attacking football Smith had fostered. Neal Maupay's goal brought a modest revival, 1-0 against Bolton. Then, it gathered pace in the New Year with 12 goals scored in successive wins over Stoke, Rotherham and Blackburn. There was a particularly satisfying success against Villa, courtesy of a stoppage time strike from Maupay, who went on to accumulate 25 in the league, plus three in FA Cup ties. Late on, his side were awarded the points for crisis-club Bolton failing to fulfil their fixture, while a 3-0 flourish against Preston in the final match delivered 11th place.

Barbet Y 30 (2)	Gunnarsson P .... (1)	Mepham C....................22
Sorensen M................ 7 (1)	Henry R 13 (1)	Mokotjo K..............25 (10)
Benrahma S 29 (9)	Jeanvier J................ 23 (1)	Odubajo M 22 (8)
Bentley D......................33	Da Silva J................ 5 (12)	Ogbene C ....- (4)
Canos S 25 (19)	Judge A 4 (16)	Oksanen J ....- (1)
Clarke J .... - (1)	Konsa E......................42	Racic L 1 (1)
Dalsgaard H 40	MacLeod L 12 (5)	Sawyers R 41 (1)
Daniels L......................12	Marcondes E............ 3 (10)	Watkins O..............35 (6)
Field T........................ - (1)	Maupay N......................43	Yennaris N..............9 (8)
Forss M 1 (5)	McEachran J........... 19 (5)	Zamburek J ....- (1)

League goals (73): Maupay 25, Benrahma 10, Watkins 10, Canos 7, MacLeod 3, Mokotjo 3, Dalsgaard 2, Jeanvier 2, Barbet 1, Forss 1, Henry 1, Da Silva 1, Judge 1, Konsa 1, McEachran 1, Opponents 4
FA Cup goals (8): Maupay 3, Canos 2, Watkins 2, Jeanvier 1. **League Cup goals** (6): Jeanvier 2, Benrahma 1, Forss 1, Judge 1, Mokotjo 1
Average home league attendance: 10,257. **Player of Year**: Neal Maupay

BRISTOL CITY

Lee Johnson's reshaped side fell just short of a play-off place after faltering at the business end of the season. The manager rebuilt successfully after losing three of his best players, Bobby Reid, Joe Bryan and Aden Flint, and City came through strongly in the second half of the campaign, initially through seven successive wins, alongside two more in the FA Cup. After five without a victory, they picked up the pace again by twice coming from behind to defeat Sheffield United 3-2 at Bramall Lane with Andreas Weimann's first hat-trick of his career. Four days later, they won at Middlesbrough, then overcame another fancied team, West Bromwich Albion, thanks to three goals in the opening 19 minutes. That took them into the top-six, with a game in hand. But City dropped points against Reading and Sheffield Wednesday and were unlucky to lose to Derby after dominating the match with ten men after the dismissal of Antoine Semenyo. They needed to win at Hull in their final match, for Derby to lose and Middlesbrough to drop points. None of this happened, so they finished eighth, four points adrift.

Adelakun H 3 (2)	Kalas T 38	Pisano E................... 11 (4)
Baker N 12 (4)	Kelly L 26 (6)	Semenyo A 1 (3)
Brownhill J.....................45	Maenpaa N.....................26	Smith K 3 (2)
Bryan J............................1	Marinovic S 1	Taylor M 10 (23)
Diedhiou F 35 (6)	Morrell J..................... - (1)	Walsh L.......................4 (5)
Eisa M .... - (5)	O'Dowda C 20 (11)	Watkins M 5 (11)
Eliasson N 21 (12)	O'Leary M 14 (1)	Webster A................43 (1)
Fielding F 5	Pack M 46	Weimann A...............40 (4)
Hunt J 32 (1)	Palmer K 2 (13)	Wright B................10 (2)
Da Silva J 21 (7)	Paterson J 31 (10)	

League goals (59): Diedhiou 13, Weimann 10, Brownhill 5, Paterson 5, O'Dowda 4, Taylor 4, Webster 3, Eliasson 2, Pack 2, Palmer 2, Pisano 2, Watkins 2, Hunt 1, Kelly 1, Opponents 3
FA Cup goals (3): Brownhill 1, Eliasson 1, O'Dowda 1. **League Cup goals**: None
Average home league attendance: 21,080. **Player of Year**: Adam Webster

DERBY COUNTY

Frank Lampard was left cursing the timing and nature of the goals which condemned Derby to another play-off defeat, this time by Aston Villa, and undermined his first venture into management. The first came in the last minute of the first-half in which there was little to choose between the teams; the second stemmed from a mistake by goalkeeper Kelle Roos. Substitute Martyn Waghorn pulled one back, but it was not enough to deny the club's fourth defeat in six seasons of closing in on a return to the Premier League. Consolation for Lampard came with the knowledge that he had adapted well to the demands of a new career which he believed was 'ahead of schedule.' There was even speculation about a return to Stamford Bridge, if the manager's job there came on the market. Derby had conceded seven goals in two defeats by Villa during the regular campaign, the second at a time when they under pressure to secure a top-six place. Waghorn's hat-trick in a 6-1 win over Rotherham helped and a strong finish, culminating in a 3-1 victory over West Bromwich Albion, made sure of sixth place. A single goal defeat by Leeds in the first semi-final looked ominous, but it was overturned by a thrilling 4-2 success at Elland Road in which substitute Jack Marriott scored twice. His omission from the starting line-up at Wembley was something of a surprise. Lampard left after 18 months to become Chelsea's new manager. He was replaced immediately by former Fenerbahce and PSV Eindhoven coach Phillip Cocu.

Bennett M................. 9 (21)	Huddlestone T 21 (3)	Mitchell-Lawson J ....- (1)
Bird M....................... 1 (3)	Johnson B 22 (6)	Mount M 35
Bogle J 39 (1)	Jozefzoon F 13 (14)	Nugent D 11 (20)
Bryson C 25 (3)	Keogh R 46	Pearce A ....- (1)
Carson S 30	King A 2 (2)	Roos K 16
Cole A 6 (3)	Lawrence T................ 28 (5)	Tomori F.................43 (1)
Davies C 3 (2)	Ledley J 3 (1)	Waghorn M 29 (7)
Evans G 6 (5)	Lowe M.........................3	Wilson H 37 (3)
Forsyth C 10 (3)	Malone S................. 24 (3)	Wisdom K.................9 (2)
Holmes D................ 16 (9)	Marriott J 19 (14)	

Play-offs – appearances: Bogle 3, Johnson 3, Keogh 3, Lawrence 3, Mount 3, Roos 3, Tomori 3, Wilson 3, Bennett 2 (1), Holmes 2, Malone 2, Huddlestone 1 (2), Cole 1 (1), Nugent 1, Marriott – (3), Jozefzoon – (1), Waghorn – (1)
League goals (69): Wilson 15, Waghorn 9, Mount 8, Marriott 7, Lawrence 6, Bennett 3, Bryson 3, Keogh 3, Bogle 2, Holmes 2, Johnson 2, Jozefzoon 2, Malone 2, Nugent 2, Ledley 1, Tomori 1, Opponents 1. **Play-offs – goals (5)**: Marriott 2, Mount 1, Waghorn 1, Wilson 1
FA Cup goals (6): Waghorn 2, Cole 1, Lawrence 1, Marriott 1, Wilson 1. **League Cup goals (10)**: Marriott 2, Mount 2, Waghorn 2, Jozefzoon 1, Tomori 1, Wilson 1, Opponents 1
Average home league attendance: 26,850. **Player of Year**: Fikayo Tomori

HULL CITY

Jarrod Bowen enhanced his standing as one of the Championship's most prized players as Hull climbed from the relegation places to within reach of a play-off challenge, before having to settle for a mid-table slot. The 22-year-old broke a 60-year-old club record set by Bill Bradbury in 1958-59 by scoring in eight successive home games on the way to 22 goals for the season. Bowen was on the mark twice on six occasions, most impressively in his side's 2-0 win over Leeds at Elland Road. That performance came as they were building up a head of steam after dropping to second from bottom with 18 games completed. Hull reeled off six successive wins for the first time in the game's second tier since 1910, including a 6-0 drubbing of Bolton, which took them to within striking distance of the top-six. The sequence would have been even more impressive had they not surrendered a 2-0 lead at Villa Park and come away with just a point. After that, Hull lost some momentum against the top teams, particularly in the run in when losing Middlesbrough, West Bromwich Albion and Sheffield United in succession. Manager Nigel Adkins turned down a new contract and was replaced by Doncaster's Grant McCann.

Bally D.................... 22 (5)	Henriksen M...................39	Mazuch O....................9 (3)
Bowen J.................. 45 (1)	Irvine J....................... 36 (2)	McKenzie R 10 (8)
Burke R 32 (2)	Kane I 36 (3)	Milinkovic M.................- (8)
Campbell F 31 (8)	Keane W 1 (7)	Pugh M....................10 (4)
De Wijs J 30 (2)	Kingsley S 25 (1)	Ridgewell L 4 (3)
Dicko N 1 (15)	Lichaj E 35 (4)	Sheaf M ....- (1)
Ephick T.......................18	Long G 3 (1)	Stewart K 16 (11)
Fleming B.................. 1 (3)	MacDonald A...................1	Toral J-M ....- (8)
Evandro 14 (9)	Marshall D...................43	
Grosicki K.............. 35 (4)	Martin C.............. 15 (15)	

League goals (66): Bowen 22, Campbell 12, Grosicki 9, Irvine 6, Evandro 3, Kane 3, Pugh 3, Dicko 2, Henriksen 2, Martin 2, De Wijs 1, Elphick 1
FA Cup goals (1): Toral 1. **League Cup goals (1)**: Toral 1
Average home league attendance: 12,165. **Player of Year**: Jarrod Bowen

IPSWICH TOWN

Relegation and a place in football's third tier for the first time since 1957 was bad enough, watching their bitter rivals Norwich promoted to the Premier League was rubbing it in. Portman Road had a new young manager, Paul Hurst from Shrewsbury, ten new players and. renewed optimism among supporters. It didn't last long and neither did Hurst, sacked after a single victory, 3-2 against Swansea, in 14 games. Former Norwich manager Paul Lambert replaced him, becoming the first to take charge of both east Anglian clubs, and had a harsh introduction to the job, watching from the stands as his new team lost 3-0 at Millwall to remain rooted to the bottom of the table with just nine points on the board. Lambert had to wait another seven matches for his first win, 1-0 against Wigan. By the New Year, Ipswich were ten points from safety, having developed a costly habit of failing to hold on to the lead in matches. An FA Cup defeat by Accrington provided further embarrassment, prompting Lambert to admit the club needed rebuilding. All hope of surviving disappeared in a run of 12 games without a victory and the drop was confirmed with four remaining. Ipswich were the first Football League club to go down, finished 13 points adrift and Lambert had another relegation to ponder, having tried unsuccessfully to pick up the pieces at Stoke the previous season.

Bialkowski B 28	Emmanuel J 4	Nydam T ....- (1)
Bishop E................. 13 (5)	Gerken D........................18	Pennington M 30
Bree J................... 13 (1)	Graham J 3 (1)	Quaner C.................13 (3)
Chalobah T 35 (8)	Harrison E................. 9 (7)	Roberts J....................6 (6)
Chambers L................43	Jackson K............. 14 (22)	Rowe D ....- (3)
Collins J 6	Judge A.....................19	Sears F 21 (3)
Dawkins S.................. - (2)	Keane W 9 (2)	Skuse C 32 (3)
Donacien J............... 9 (1)	Kenlock M 18 (1)	Spence J 16 (1)
Downes F 21 (9)	Knudsen J 27 (1)	Tayo Edun 3 (3)
Dozzell A 10 (10)	Lankester J................. 5 (6)	Walters J 2 (1)
Edwards G 24 (9)	Morris B .... - (1)	Ward G.................11 (3)
El Mizouni I 1 (3)	Nolan J 23 (3)	Woolfenden L...............- (1)
Elder C 3 (1)	Nsiala A 17 (5)	

League goals (36): Edwards 6, Sears 6, Quaner 4, Jackson 3, Keane 3, Nolan 3, Chalobah 2, Downes 1, Dozzell 1, Harrison 1, Lankester 1, Nsiala 1, Pennington 1, Tayo Edun 1, Opponents 2
FA Cup goals: None. **League Cup goals** (1): Jackson 1
Average home league attendance: 17,765. **Player of Year**: Luke Chambers

LEEDS UNITED

Leeds twice surrendered the chance to end a 15-year absence from the Premier League under their controversial manager Marcelo Bielsa. With a month of the regular season remaining, his side were a good bet for automatic promotion with a three-point cushion in second place and a facing a non-too-demanding run-in. Instead, they lost twice over Easter, to ten-man Wigan at Elland Road and away to Brentford, enabling Sheffield United to come through. Bielsa, who sparked a club fine of £200,000 from the Football League after admitting sending staff to spy on opponents' training sessions, then ordered his players to let Aston Villa equalise after Mateusz Klich ignored an injured Villa player to put them ahead. Leeds closed with a defeat by relegated Ipswich, but took a grip on their play-off semi-final against Derby, with Kemar Roofe scoring the only goal of the first leg at Pride Park and Stuart Dallas establishing a 2-0 aggregate lead in the return match. But they fell apart again – a mistake by former Real Madrid goalkeeper Kiko Casilla allowing Derby back into contention and a second conceded 40 seconds into the second-half. Gaetano Berardi was sent off and despite a second from Dallas, his side lost 4-3 on aggregate.

Alioski E 44	Berardi G 9 (3)	Dallas S.................10 (16)
Ayling L 38	Brown I........................- (1)	Davis L 1 (3)
Baker L......................... 2 (9)	Clarke J 4 (18)	Douglas B 21 (6)
Bamford P 15 (7)	Cooper L.........................37	Edmondson R..............- (1)

Forshaw A.............. 19 (11)	Klich M 46	Roofe K 27 (5)
Halme A 1 (3)	Kiko Casilla................17	Saiz S........................ 15 (4)
Harrison J 32 (5)	Peacock-Farrell B 28	Shackleton J 3 (16)
Hernandez P 37 (2)	Pearce T .... - (2)	Stevens J .... - (1)
Huffer W..........................1	Phillips K......................42	
Jansson P 37 (2)	Roberts T................ 20 (8)	

Play offs appearances: Ayling 2, Berardi 2, Dallas 2, Cooper 2, Harrison 2, Hernandez 2, Kiko Casilla 2, Klich 2, Phillips 2, Shackleton 1 (1), Bamford 1, Forshaw 1, Roofe 1, Clarke – (2), Brown 1
League goals (73): Roofe 14, Hernandez 12, Klich 10, Bamford 9, Alioski 7, Harrison 4, Cooper 3, Jansson 3, Roberts 3, Ayling 2, Clarke 2, Dallas 2, Phillips 1, Opponents 1. **Play-offs – goals:** (3) Dallas 2, Roofe 1
FA Cup goals (1): Halme 1 **League Cup goals** (2): Bamford 1, Saiz 1
Average home league attendance: 34,033. **Player of Year:** Pablo Hernandez

MIDDLESBROUGH

A run of six successive defeats spoiled the chance of a return to the Premier League and cost manager Tony Pulis his job. The run, the club's worst for 19 years, came as Middlesdbrough looked a solid bet for the play-offs with a seven-point cushion in fifth place entering the final third of the season. Four of the defeats, against Brentford, Preston, Norwich and Bristol City, were at the Riverside. Two more came against Aston Villa and Swansea, with just three goals scored in the sequence, underlining the team's poor strike rate over the course of the season. Their tally of 49 was beaten by relegated Rotherham, with no player managing double figures to support leading marksman Britt Assombalonga. Ashley Fletcher returned his side to winning ways by netting twice at Bolton and they made up sufficient ground in the final month of the campaign to go into the final fixture at Rotherham still in with a shout. But despite John Obi Mikel's first goal and Assombalonga's 14th, Derby's victory over West Bromwich Albion saw them through by a point. Jonathan Woodgate, born in Middlesbrough, a coach under Pulis and twice a player with the club, was appointed the new manager.

Assombalonga B 28 (14)	Flint A 39	McQueen S................... 1 (4)
Ayala D.................... 32 (1)	Friend G.................. 37 (1)	Mikel J O.......................18
Batth D.......................... 8 (2)	Fry D 33 (1)	Randolph D 46
Besic M 30 (7)	Gestede R 1 (3)	Saville A....................28 (6)
Braithwaite M........... 12 (5)	Howson J 44 (2)	Shotton R 33 (1)
Clayton A................. 29 (7)	Hugill J 20 (17)	Tavernier M 2 (18)
Downing S 24 (14)	Ledbitter G 1 (1)	Van La Parra R.............. - (3)
Fletcher A................. 14 (7)	McNair P.................. 7 (9)	Wing L 19 (9)

League goals (49): Assombalonga 14, Hugill 6, Fletcher 5, Saville 4, Braithwaite 3, Tavernier 3, Wing 3, Besic 2, Downing 2, Friend 2, Ayala 2, Flint 1, Howson 1, Mikel 1, Opponents 1
FA Cup goals (6): Assombalonga 2, Ayala 1, Fletcher 1, Friend 1, Wing 1. **League Cup goals** (8): Fletcher 3, Hugill 1, Johnson M 1, Mahmutovic E 1, Tavernier 1, Wing 1
Average home league attendance: 23,217. **Player of Year:** Darren Randolph

MILLWALL

Neil Harris admitted his squad needed a 'major overhaul' after fending off the threat of relegation. After finishing three points away from a play-place on their return to the second tier the previous season, Millwall spent most of this one looking over their shoulder. They were third from bottom at the midway point after eight matches without a win before back-to-back victories over Reading, Nottingham Forest and Ipswich eased the pressure. But goals were hard to come by amid an exceptional FA Cup run which ended with the team back in trouble and facing five promotion-chasing opponents in the final eight games. Millwall overcame one of them, West

Bromwich Albion, and took a point off another, Sheffield United, with Jake Cooper's goal in the fourth minute of stoppage-time. Then, a goalless draw with Stoke was enough to close out Rotherham's survival bid. In the Cup, Millwall knocked out Everton on the way to the sixth round, where they surrendered a 2-0 lead against Brighton with two minutes of normal time remaining, had one of their penalty takers, Shane Ferguson, dismissed in extra-time and subsequently lost in the spot-kick shootout.

Alexander G .... - (1)	Leonard R 37	Romeo M 40 (1)
Amos D............................12	Marshall D................. 13 (3)	Caville Q 4
Archer J.........................24	Martin D.........................10	Skalak J....................4 (10)
Bradshaw T............... 2 (8)	McLaughlin C 6 (2)	Thompson B 12 (1)
Cooper J.........................46	Meredith J.................. 33 (3)	Tunnicliffe R............22 (5)
Elliott T 16 (17)	Mitchell B .... - (1)	Wallace J..................41 (1)
Ferguson S............... 26 (9)	Morison S.............. 15 (26)	Wallace M 19 (2)
Gregory L 42 (2)	O'Brien A 15 (20)	Webster B 2 (2)
Hutchinson S 24 (2)	Onyedinma F .... - (1)	Williams S...............30 (1)
Karacan J .... - (4)	Pearce A 11	

League goals (48): Gregory 10, Cooper 6, Wallace J 5, Williams 5, Thompson 4, Elliott 3, Tunnicliffe 3, Ferguson 2, Leonard 2, O'Brien 2, Wallace M 2, Hutchinson 1, Marshall 1, Morison 1, Opponents 1
FA Cup goals (8): Ferguson 2, Wallace M 2, Cooper 1, Gregory 1, O'Brien 1, Pearce 1. **League Cup goals** (4): Gregory 2, O'Brien 1, Williams 1
Average home league attendance: 13,624. **Player of Year:** Lee Gregory

NORWICH CITY

Daniel Farke's exciting side upset all the odds to regain Premier League status in a memorable season. They were given little chance of going up, let alone becoming champions, after finishing nowhere in the previous campaign, then losing two of their best players, James Maddison and Josh Murphy. Even among supporters, rated among the most loyal in the country, it was difficult to detect much optimism when the first six fixtures yielded a single victory. Instead, the young players began to show remarkable maturity in this toughest of divisions. Max Aarons and Jamal Lewis developed into the Championship's premier pairing at full-back, alongside Ben Godfrey in central defence and Todd Cantwell in midfield. The manager also struck free transfer gold in Finnish striker Teemu Pukki, the leading light in a 93-goal total which made Norwich not only the best but the most entertaining in the division. They also displayed a never-say-die attitude which pulled so many points out of the fire when all seemed lost, notably when coming back from 3-0 down against Nottingham Forest for a point with Onel Hernandez scoring twice in stoppage-time. A run of eight successive wins enabled Norwich to approach the run-in eight points clear of third-place Leeds. They clinched promotion by beating Blackburn 2-1 in the penultimate fixture with typical long-range strikes from Marco Stiepermann and Mario Vrancic and claimed the title with victory by the same scoreline at Villa Park, where Pukki, voted the division's Player of the Year, netted his 29th goal.

Aarons M 41	Klose T 23 (8)	Rhodes J 9 (27)
Buendia E............... 35 (3)	Krul T 46	Srbeny D .... - (15)
Cantwell T............... 18 (6)	Leitner M 19 (10)	Stiepermann M 39 (4)
Godfrey B 26 (5)	Lewis J.........................42	Tettey A....................26 (4)
Hanley G................ 6 (3)	Marshall B.....................4	Thompson L 1 (5)
Hernandez O 34 (6)	McLean K 15 (5)	Trybull T...................22 (9)
Husband J 1	Passlack F .... - (1)	Vrancic M...............14 (22)
Pinto I 3	Pukki T 43	Zimmermann C 39 (1)

League goals (93): Pukki 29, Vrancic 10, Stiepermann 9, Buendia 8, Hernandez 8, Rhodes

106

6, Godfrey 4, Klose 4, McLean 3, Aarons 2, Leitner 2, Zimmermann 2, Cantwell 1, Hanley 1, Srbeny 1, Tettey 1, Trybull 1, Opponents 1
FA Cup goals: None. **League Cup goals** (11): Rhodes 3, Srbeny 2, Aarons 1, Hernandez 1, Pukki 1, Stiepermann 1, Trybull 1, Zimmermann 1
Average home league attendance: 26,014. **Player of Year**: Teemu Pukki

NOTTINGHAM FOREST

Martin O'Neill declared he had 'realised a lifetime dream' when taking charge of the club where was he twice a European Cup winner as a player. The former Republic of Ireland manager, who was joined by his assistant Roy Keane, promised to go if he had not taken Forest into the Premier League in 18 months. And with his new side on the fringes of a play-off place with a month of the season remaining, there seemed every possibility he would have the chance at the first time of asking. Instead, successive defeats by struggling Rotherham, Sheffield Wednesday, Blackburn and Sheffield United, rendered a return to form against Middlesbrough (3-0) irrelevant. Forest also defeated Queens Park Rangers and Bolton, but finished eight points adrift. O'Neill replaced Aitor Karanka, who signed 12 new players in the summer, including Benfica midfielder Joao Carvalho for a club-record £13.2m. Lewis Grabban scored 15 goals in a run of 15 league and cup games, including two in a crazy 5-5 draw with Aston Villa. But after weeks of speculation about his position, Karanka resigned, the club's tenth successive manager not to have been in charge for a full season. O'Neill became the 11th when he was sacked after five months and replaced by former Rennes coach Sabri Lamouchi

Ansarifard K	3 (9)	Gil Dias	10 (11)	Molla Wague	9 (2)
Appiah A	2 (4)	Goncalves D	1 (6)	Murphy D	17 (11)
Benalouane Y	14	Grabban L	29 (10)	Osborn B	29 (10)
Bridcutt L	- (1)	Guedioura A	18 (9)	Pantilimon C	44
Byram S	6	Hefele M	13 (2)	Pele	6 (3)
Cash M	27 (9)	Hillel Soudani	1 (5)	Robinson J	36 (2)
Colback J	38	Janko S	13 (2)	Steele L	2
Darikwa T	28	Joao Carvalho	28 (10)	Watson B	14 (3)
Dawson M	8 (2)	Leo Bonatini	2 (3)	Yacob C	11 (5)
Figueiredo T	11 (2)	Lolley J	42 (4)	Yates R	15 (1)
Fox D	18	Milosevic A	11 (1)		

League goals (61): Grabban 16, Lolley 11, Cash 6, Joao Carvalho 4, Murphy 4, Colback 3, Molla Wague 3, Ansarifard 2, Guedioura 2, Hillel Soudani 2, Robinson 2, Benalouane 1, Milosevic 1, Osborn 1, Yates 1, Opponents 2
FA Cup goals: None. **League Cup goals** (9): Cash 2, Murphy 2, Appiah 1, Grabban 1, Gil Dias 1, Lolley 1, Osborn 1
Average home league attendance: 28,144. **Player of Year**: Joe Lolley

PRESTON NORTH END

Alex Neil kept faith with his side after a wretched start to the season which left them bottom with a single win in the opening 11 fixtures in which 24 goals were conceded. He predicted they were capable of challenging for a play-off place and that belief was borne out by a recovery launched with a 4-0 victory over Wigan. Preston also scored four against Brentford, Blackburn and Queens Park Rangers, along with three against champions-to-be Norwich on the way to joining sixth-place Aston Villa on 57 points with eight games remaining. At that point they looked a good bet to go higher. Instead, four successive defeats, three of them to top-flight opposition, pushed them back, with Neil blaming speculation linking him with the vacant West Bromwich Albion job. A fifth four-goal haul, against Ipswich, brought a return to winning ways, albeit not enough to make up for lost ground. Preston finished in mid-table after Neil ended the speculation by signing a new three-year contract and looking forward to further developing his young squad at Deepdale.

Barker B 6 (10	Horgan D .... - (1)	Potts B 10
Barkhuizen T 26 (8)	Hughes A 31 (1)	Rafferty J 4 (2)
Browne A 36 (2)	Huntington P 21 (1)	Ripley C 2
Burke G 6 (6)	Johnson D 26 (9)	Robinson C 24 (3)
Clarke T 21	Ledson N 14 (10)	Rudd D 36
Davies B 39 (1)	Maguire S 21 (5)	Stockley J 8 (9)
Earl J 12 (2)	Maxwell C 8	Storey J 27 (1)
Fisher D 32 (3)	Moult L 8 (16)	Walker E ....- (1)
Gallagher D 30 (10)	Nmecha L 24 (17)	Woods C .... - (1)
Ginnelly J .... - (5)	O'Reilly A .... - (1)	
Harrop J 4 (4)	Pearson B 30	

League goals (67): Browne 12, Robinson 12, Barkhuizen 6, Gallagher 6, Johnson 6, Moult 4, Nmecha 4, Stockley 4, Hughes 3, Maguire 3, Potts 2, Burke 1, Clarke 1, Davies 1 Storey 1, Opponents 1
FA Cup goals (1): Hughes 1. **League Cup goals** (7): Barker 2, Barkhuizen 1, Burke 1, Johnson 1, Moult 1, Robinson 1
Average home league attendance: 14,160. **Player of Year**: Ben Davies

QUEENS PARK RANGERS

Steve McClaren, like his predecessor Ian Holloway, felt the full force of the club's penalty for breaking spending limits under the Football League's Financial Fair Play rules. A £42m settlement and transfer embargo meant he had to work under a tight budget, with loan signings the only option to boost a young squad. The former England manager, appointed at the end of the previous season, did well in that respect after losing his first four games, including a 7-1 hammering by West Bromwich Albion, the clubs' biggest for 31 years. He brought in strikers Tomer Hemed and Nahki Wells with instant results – a move up the table and McLaren named Manager of the Month for October after 13 points from five games. A subsequent 3-2 win over Brentford lifted them to within two points of a play-off place. They were still there after beating Ipswich on Boxing Day, then went downhill – a single win in 15 games leading to the sacking of McClaren with a month of the season remaining. Rangers had enough points in the bank to stay clear of trouble, the 4-0 win against Swansea under caretaker John Eustace making absolutely sure.

Baptiste A.................. 3 (1)	Ingram M 4	Scowen J.................23 (12)
Bidwell J........................40	Kakay O 3	Shodipo O 1 (3)
Cameron G............... 17 (2)	Leistner T 40 (3)	Smith M.....................7 (28)
Chair I .... - (4)	Lumley J 42	Smyth P.................... 1 (2)
Cousins J 23 (5)	Luongo M.......................41	Sylla I 1 (2)
Eze E 37 (5)	Lynch J 35	Walker L 1 (3)
Freeman L 43	Manning R 7 (2)	Washington C............. 1 (3)
Furlong D 23 (2)	Osayi-Samuel B 9 (18)	Wells N 32 (8)
Hall G..................... 7 (5)	Oteh A .... - (2)	Wszolek P................. 29 (9)
Hemed T................ 16 (11)	Rangel A 20	

League goals (53): Freeman 7, Hemed 7, Wells 7, Smith 6, Eze 4, Wszolek 4, Luongo 3, Lynch 3, Leistner 2, Osayi-Samuel 2, Rangel 2, Scowen 2, Cameron 1, Cousins 1, Furlong 1, Opponents 1
FA Cup goals (5): Wells 2, Bidwell 1, Oteh 1, Smith 1. **League Cup goals** (5): Wszolek 2, Freeman 1, Osayi-Samuel 1, Smith 1
Average home league attendance: 13,866. **Player of Year**: Luke Freeman

READING

Another disappointing season for Reading, but at least no repeat of 2018 when survival depended on results in the final round of fixtures. For that they could thank Ivory Coast international Yakou

Meite's goals at a time when his side were one of four caught up in a struggle to avoid the third relegation place alongside Bolton and Ipswich. Meite was on the mark in a 2-1 victory over Preston and a 2-2 draw at champions-to-be Norwich. He netted both against Brentford (2-1) and the one which earned a point against Bristol City. The goals left Reading five points clear of the drop, sufficient to compensate for a disappointing finish under Portuguese coach Jose Gomes, who took over when Paul Clement, manager for eight months, was sacked with his side fourth from bottom approaching the midway point of the campaign. His first match was a 1-0 defeat by Millwall in which Tyler Blackett and Leandro Bacuna were both sent off; his first win 2-0 against Nottingham Forest, who had two players dismissed.

Aluko S.................. 13 (6)	Howe T .... (1)	Miazga M 18
Bacuna L................. 23 (3)	Ilori T.......................19	Moore L 38
Baker L.................. 17 (2)	Jaakkola A....................15	Nelson Oliveira 9 (1)
Baldock S 15 (6)	Kelly L................. 17 (3)	O'Shea J 7 (2)
Barrett J 1 (1)	Loader D 8 (13)	Olise M 2 (2)
Barrow M 25 (10)	Mannone V...................6	Osho G........................ 1 (1)
Blackett T 29 (2)	Martinez E...................18	Popa A.........................- (1)
Bodvarsson J D........ 9 (11)	McCleary G 14 (17)	Richards O 8 (2)
East R 1	McIntyre T.................. 1 (1)	Rinomhota A.............24 (2)
Ejaria O 16	McNulty M 4 (9)	Sims J 5 (12)
Ezatolahi S 4	McShane P 4 (1)	Swift J..................... 28 (6)
Gunter C................. 17 (5)	Meite Y................... 31 (6)	Walker S 7
Harriott C.............. 2 (10)	Meyler D 5	Yiadom A.....................45

League goals (49): Meite 12, Bodvarsson 7, Baldock 5, Barrow 4, Bacuna 3, Nelson Oliveira 3, Swift 3, Aluko 1, Baker 1, Harriott 1, Ilori 1, Kelly 1, Loader 1, McNulty 1, Moore 1, Ejaria 1, Rinomhota 1, Yiadom 1, Opponents 1
FA Cup goals: None. **League Cup goals** (2): Meite 1, Swift 1
Average home league attendance: 14,991. **Player of Year**: Andy Rinomhota

ROTHERHAM UNITED

Paul Warne was the first to admit that his side's relegation from the Championship with 23 points in 2017/18 was 'embarrassing.' This time, the manager was full of praise for his players for taking their bid to stay up almost to the wire – and even West Bromwich Albion supporters applauded their efforts at the end of the penultimate match at The Hawthorns which finally cast them adrift. They were still alive after Clark Robertson's opening goal before Albion replied with two in two minutes to seal fourth place. Rotherham got off on the wrong foot after regaining second-tier status at the first attempt via the play-offs, losing 5-1 at Brentford. But for the most part they were competitive, with a decent scoring record for a side in their position. With a month of the season remaining they were within touching distance of three other teams struggling for survival – Reading, Millwall and Wigan – after victories over Blackburn, Queens Park Rangers and Nottingham Forest in the space of six matches. Goals by Michael Smith and Matt Crooks sparked a recovery from 2-0 down for a point at Stoke, but twice surrendering the lead at Swansea proved costly and a 4-3 defeat hard to take.

Ajayi S..............................46	Palmer M 8 (2)	Towell R 28 (6)
Ball D................................1	Potter D .... - (1)	Vassell K 9 (14)
Crooks M 7 (9)	Price L...........................1	Vaulks W 41
Forde A.................. 17 (11)	Proctor J 2 (14)	Vyner Z 28 (3)
Ihiekwe M....................15	Raggett S 6 (1)	Wiles S 9 (11)
Jones B 19 (2)	Robertson C............. 25 (3)	Williams R.............24 (15)
Manning R 13 (5)	Rodak M 45	Wood R 23 (3)
Mattock J........................44	Smith M 44 (1)	Yates J 3 (4)
Newell J 18 (13)	Taylor J 30 (1)	

League goals (52): Smith 8, Ajayi 7, Vaulks 7, Manning 4, Taylor 4, Towell 4, Crooks 3, Robertson 3, Ihiekwe 2, Proctor 2, Wood 2, Forde 1, Mattock 1, Raggett 1, Williams 1, Opponents 2
FA Cup goals: None. **League Cup goals** (4): Proctor 2, Ajayi 1, Vaulks 1
Average home league attendance: 9,880. **Player of Year**: Michael Smith

SHEFFIELD UNITED

Chris Wilder was born in Sheffield, had two spells as a player at Bramall Lane and retained a great affinity with the club. Now he will lead them back to the Premier League after a 12-year absence, having outsmarted and outpaced a clutch of more fancied teams on one of the Championship's more modest budgets to claim the runners-up spot. United had no stand-out big names; instead an abundance of players who had plied their trade in the lower leagues and who relished the opportunity to feed into Wilder's call for boundless effort, energy and organisation. Captain Billy Sharp, also born in the city, led by example, forming a productive strike partnership with David McGoldrick, who impressed Wilder while on a pre-season trial. It was not all plain sailing. United lost their opening two matches and the season was played out amid a dispute between co-owners Kevin McCabe and Prince Abdullah of Saudi Arabia. But once into their stride, they were never out of the top-six. Three days after turning 33, Sharp scored his second hat-trick of the campaign in a 3-3 draw at Villa Park to pass 100 goals for the club. After that, seven successive clean sheets confirmed their challenge and a superior goal difference meant that promotion was effectively sealed courtesy of goals from Scott Hogan and Jack O'Connell in the final home game against Ipswich. The title went to Norwich – the League Managers' Association Manager of the Year award to Wilder.

Baldock G	26 (1)	Fleck J	45	McGoldrick D	36 (9)
Basham C	39 (2)	Freeman K	20	Norwood O	43
Clarke L	9 (15)	Henderson D	46	O'Connell J	41
Coutts P	1 (12)	Hogan S	5 (3)	Sharp B	34 (6)
Cranie M	9 (6)	Johnson M	3 (8)	Stearman R	3 (13)
Dowell K	8 (8)	Lafferty D	- (1)	Stevens E	45
Duffy M	32 (4)	Leonard R	- (3)	Washington C	3 (12)
Egan J	44	Lundstram J	5 (5)	Woodburn B	1 (6)
Evans J	2	Madine G	6 (10)		

League goals (78): Sharp 23, McGoldrick 15, Duffy 6, Basham 4, Stevens 4, Clarke 3, Madine 3, Norwood 3, O'Connell 3, Dowell 2, Fleck 2, Freeman 2, Hogan 2, Baldock 1, Egan 1, Stearman 1, Opponents 3
FA Cup goals: None. **League Cup goals** (1): Sharp 1
Average home league attendance: 26,175. **Player of Year**: David McGoldrick

SHEFFIELD WEDNESDAY

Steve Bruce breathed new life into Wednesday's season after taking up his ninth managerial appointment at Hillsborough. It wasn't enough to burnish an impressive record of leading clubs into the Premier League. But he had the satisfaction of lifting this one from the lower reaches of the division to within striking distance of a play-off place. Wednesday were 11 points adrift when Bruce eventually replaced Jos Luhukay, sacked after 11 months in charge, having fulfilled holiday commitments. Two months later, they had moved to within two points of sixth-place Aston Villa, Bruce's former club, on the back of an unbeaten run of 11 matches. The run came to an end with a 3-1 home defeat by Villa, who scored twice in stoppage-time, and was followed by a 1-0 loss at Leeds. Wednesday, facing two more promotion-chasing sides, were denied victory at Norwich by a 97th minute equaliser, then defeated Bristol City. Another stoppage-time goal brought defeat by Queens Park Rangers on the final day, pushing them down three places to 12th. Bruce resigned after six months at the club to succeed Rafael Benitez at Newcastle.

Aarons R 6 (3)	Iorfa D 9 (3)	Pelupessy J 26 (7)
Baker A 11	Jones D ..... - (1)	Penney M 12 (4)
Bannan B 40 (1)	Kirby C ..... - (1)	Preston F 1 (2)
Boyd G 14 (6)	Lazaar A 3 (1)	Pudil D 9 (2)
Dawson C 26	Lee K 1 (1)	Reach A 42
Fletcher S 32 (8)	Lees T 42	Thorniley J 17 (3)
Forestieri F 15 (10)	Lucas Joao 18 (13)	Van Aken J 1
Fox M 21 (4)	Matias M 20 (11)	Westwood K 20
Hector M 36 (1)	Nuhiu A 13 (21)	Winnall S 1 (6)
Hooper G 4 (2)	Onomah J 10 (5)	
Hutchinson S 22 (2)	Palmer L 34 (1)	

League goals (60): Fletcher 11, Lucas Joao 10, Reach 8, Forestieri 6, Matias 6, Bannan 5, Nuhiu 4, Iorfa 3, Hector 2, Lees 2, Aarons 1, Boyd 1, Hooper 1
FA Cup goals (1): Nuhiu 1. **League Cup goals** (2): Matias 1, Reach 1.
Average home league attendance: 24,429. **Player of Year**: Michael Hector

STOKE CITY

A change of manager and some major signings in both transfer windows failed to rescue a disappointing season for a club who fell well short of an immediate return to the Premier League. They were strong favourites for promotion, but never threatened a top-six place and finished in the bottom half of the table after drawing 22 matches, more than any side in the four divisions. Stoke's failure to consolidate winning positions, along with a continuation of the club's poor record from the penalty spot, proved major factors. Over this season, six out of eight spot-kicks were missed. Gary Rowett was sacked after eight months as manager early in the New Year and replaced by Nathan Jones on the strength of his work in leading Luton on the road to promotion from League One. His first match was a 3-1 loss at Brentford; his second an FA Cup home defeat by Shrewsbury with 2-0 lead surrendered; the third a victory over top-of-the-table Leeds. That success, earned with goals from Sam Clucas and Joe Allen, looked as if it might be the springboard for better times ahead. Instead, it proved to be one of only three victories in his 21 games in charge, a sequence which included four successive goalless draws. Stoke finished 16th.

Adam C 4 (8)	Collins N 1 (2)	Ndiaye B 1
Afobe B 32 (13)	Crouch P 2 (21)	Oghenekaro E 29 (5)
Allen J 46	Edwards T 22 (5)	Pieters E 21
Batth D 17	Federici A 1	Shawcross R 33 (3)
Bauer M 6 (2)	Fletcher D 4 (7)	Sorensen L ..... - (1)
Berahino S 16 (7)	Ince I 36 (2)	Tymon J 1
Biram Diouf M 6 (8)	Krkic B 8 (13)	Vorlinden T 2 (3)
Butland J 45	Martina C 17	Vokes S 10 (2)
Campbell T 2 (1)	Martins Indi B 36 (1)	Williams A 27 (6)
Clucas S 23 (3)	McClean J 32 (10)	Woods R 26 (1)

League goals (45): Afobe 8, Allen 6, Ince 6, Berahino 3, Clucas 3, McClean 3, Vokes 3, Oghenekaro 2, Pieters 2, Crouch 1, Edwards 1, Fletcher 1, Krkic 1, Martins Indi 1, Shawcross 1, Williams 1, Opponents 2
FA Cup goals (3): Campbell 2, Crouch 1. **League Cup goals** (4): Berahino 2, Afobe 1, Opponents 1
Average home league attendance: 25,200. **Player of Year**: Jack Butland

SWANSEA CITY

Relegation was accompanied by the departure of several senior players, forcing new manager Graham Potter to put his faith in a youthful squad. It meant there was never a realistic chance of an immediate return to the Premier League. Instead, the emergence of new Wales cap Daniel James, central defender Joe Rodon and midfielder George Byers helped produce a strong finish to the season for a top-ten place, alongside an eye-catching FA Cup run which threatened a major upset against Manchester City There was also the development of Oliver McBurnie, who took his tally for the season to 24 in both competitions as Swansea gained 18 points from their final nine matches, scoring three goals against Brentford, Middlesborough and Stoke and beating Rotherham 4-3. In the Cup, they scored 11 in knocking out Aston Villa, Gillingham and Brentford to reach the sixth round. Swansea then took a 2-0 lead through a Matt Grimes penalty and Bersant Celina against City, whose comeback brought an 00th Sergio Aguero winner which replays showed was marginally offside. Potter left at the end of the season to succeed Chris Hughton at Brighton. He was replaced by Steve Cooper, who led England to the World Under-17 Cup in 2017.

Asoro J	4 (10)	Fernandez F	1	Narsingh L	- (2)
Baker-Richardson C	6 (11)	Fulton J	21 (12)	Naughton K	31 (4)
Bony W	1 (6)	Grimes M	40 (5)	Nordfeldt K	22
Byers G	20 (1)	Harries C	2	Olsson M	13 (4)
Carroll T	8 (4)	James D	28 (5)	Roberts C	44 (1)
Carter-Vickers C	23 (7)	John D	7 (3)	Rodon J	23 (4)
Celina B	33 (5)	McBurnie O	37 (5)	Routledge W	22 (2)
Dhanda Y	1 (4)	McKay B	16 (14)	Van der Hoorn M	46
Dyer N	18 (4)	Montero J	- (12)		
Fer L	15 (10)	Mulder E	24 (1)		

League goals (65): McBurnie 22, Celina 5, Roberts 5, Routledge 5, James 4, Baker-Richardson 3, Van der Hoorn 3, Byers 2, Dyer 2, Fulton 2, McKay 2, Bony 1, Dhanda 1, Fer 1, Grimes 1, Naughton 1, Opponents 5
FA Cup goals (13): Celina 3, McBurnie 2, Baker-Richardson 1, Byers 1, Dyer 1, Fulton 1, Grimes 1, James 1, McKay 1, Opponents 1. **League Cup goals**: None
Average home league attendance: 18,737. **Player of Year**: Matt Grimes

WEST BROMWICH ALBION

Red cards in both legs of their play-off semi-final against Aston Villa undermined Albion's bid for an immediate return to the Premier League. Dwight Gayle's goals had been a feature of their season and he put them ahead after 16 minutes of the first leg at Villa Park. His side held the lead until the final quarter-of-an-hour when they conceded twice and had Gayle sent off for a second yellow card. It ruled him out of the return match in which Chris Brunt saw red after 80 minutes with Albion leading through Craig Dawson. That dismissal reduced options in the subsequent penalty shootout which Villa won 4-3 after Mason Holgate and Ahmed Hegazi had spot-kicks saved. Albion were handily placed for a challenge for automatic promotion at the midway point of the season, three points behind second-place Norwich after topping 50 goals, including seven against Queens Park Rangers and four against Norwich, Bristol City and Leeds. But six successive games without a win at The Hawthorns left them trailing. Manager Darren Moore was sacked immediately after a 1-1 draw with bottom-of-the-table Ipswich. And coach Jimmy Shan appointed caretaker for the remainder of the season. Former West Ham manager Slaven Bilic took over in June.

Adarabioyo T	21 (8)	Gibbs K	35 (1)	Montero J	1 (3)
Barnes H	26	Harper R	13 (3)	Morrison J	11 (8)
Barry G	15 (9)	Hegazi A	38	Murphy J	8 (5)
Bartley K	24 (4)	Holgate M	19	Nyom A-R	2
Brunt C	22 (10)	Hoolahan W	- (6)	Phillips M	23 (7)
Burke O	- (3)	Johansen S	11 (1)	Robson-Kanu H	14 (21)
Dawson K	40 (1)	Johnsone S	46	Rodriguez J	45
Edwards K	3 (3)	Leko J	- (2)	Sako B	2 (3)
Field S	4 (8)	Livermore J	36 (3)	Townsend C	10 (2)
Gayle D	33 (6)	Mears T	4 (5)		

Play-offs – appearances: Bartley 2, Brunt 2, Dawson 2, Gibbs 2, Hegazi 2, Holgate 2, Johansen 2, Johnstone 2, Phillips 2, Rodriguez 2, Murphy 1 (1), Gayle 1, Morrison – (2), Adarabioyo – (1), Harper – (1), Leko – (1), Mears – (1)
League goals (87): Gayle 23, Rodriguez 22, Barnes 9, Phillips 5, Gibbs 4, Robson-Kanu 4, Brunt 2, Dawson 2, Johansen 2, Livermore 2, Murphy 2, Barry 1, Bartley 1, Edwards 1, Field 1, Harper 1, Hegazi 1, Holgate 1, Montero 1, Opponents 2. **Play-offs scorers:** Gayle 1, Dawson 1
FA Cup goals (2): Bartley 1, Sako 1. **League Cup goals** (3): Burke 1, Edwards 1, Leko 1
Average home league attendance: 24,148. **Player of Year:** Dwight Gayle

WIGAN ATHLETIC

With the worst away record in the division, Wigan were heading towards the drop zone when trailing Leeds on Good Friday at Elland Road, They were down to ten men when Cedric Kipre was sent off after 14 minutes for handling on the line and looked to be in for a long afternoon. Instead, two goals either side of half-time by Gavin Massey, along with fine goalkeeping by Christian Walton, delivered a shock win. Three days later, their side completed a productive Easter by defeating Preston 2-0, thanks to goals from Leon Clarke and Lee Evans to ensure survival. Wigan's return to the Championship had started well with five victories in the opening nine fixtures and a healthy fifth place in the table. Goals then became increasingly hard to come by – a run of five defeats in six games without scoring going into the New Year sending alarm bells ringing. A succession of hamstring injuries added to Paul Cook's problems before a handsome 3-0 win over Aston Villa offered some breathing space. Then came a dozen more matches producing a single success, 5-2 against Bolton, to leave them two points off the bottom three.

Raninime R 1	Gibson D 11 (7)	Olsson J 4 (2)
Burn D 13 (1)	Grigg W 10 (7)	Pilkington A 7 (3)
Byrne N 26 (4)	Jacobs M 19 (3)	Powell N 25 (7)
Clark L 9 (6)	James R 44 (1)	Power M .... (1)
Connolly C 7 (10)	Jolley C .... - (1)	Roberts G 12 (4)
Da Silva Lopes L .... - (1)	Jones J 12	Robinson A 26
Dunkley C 37 (1)	Kipre C 37 (1)	Vaughan J 6 (13)
Evans L 31 (3)	Massey G 15 (5)	Walton C 34
Fox D 10	McManaman C 1 (21)	Weir J .... (1)
Garner J 17 (16)	Morsy S 40	Windass J 30 (9)
Gelhardt J .... - (1)	Naismith K 22 (8)	

League goals (51): Garner 8, Powell 8, Massey 5, Windass 5, Grigg 4, Jacobs 4, Clarke 3, James 3, Roberts 3, Vaughan 2, Byrne 1, Connolly 1, Evans 1, McManaman 1, Morsy 1, Naismith 1, Opponents 1
FA Cup goals: None. **League Cup goals** (1): Vaughan 1
Average home league attendance: 11,663. **Player of Year:** Reece James

THE THINGS THEY SAY ...

'I have five or six years left it football and I just can't wait to see the back of it' – **Danny Rose**, Tottenham and England defender, says he has had enough of racism in the game.

'You're watching the results come in on a Saturday afternoon and you think you want to be involved in that' – **Paul Scholes**, former Manchester United stalwart, after his appointment as Oldham manager – one that lasted 31 days.

'You have to start somewhere. The opportunity came up and there was no messing about' – **Sol Campbell**, former England defender, on becoming Macclesfield manager – then leading the club away from the threat of non-league football.

SKY BET LEAGUE ONE

ACCRINGTON STANLEY

Long-serving manager John Coleman admitted to 'the longest season of my life' after his side delivered a rousing finish to avoid a swift return to League Two. Accrington, with the lowest budget in the division, were ticking over nicely in the top half of the table after Boxing Day's 2-1 win over Shrewsbury. But seven goals conceded in the next two fixtures against Peterborough and Bradford set in motion a slump which produced just two victories in 18 games. It landed them in the middle of a ten-club scramble for safety, two points off a place in the bottom four. Salvation came with two goals from Ross Sykes against fellow-strugglers, Walsall, followed by 2-1 away to promotion-chasing Doncaster with leading marksman Sean McConville and Paul Smyth on the mark. McConville's hat-trick in a 5-1 win over Plymouth, another threatened team, confirmed safety, rendering irrelevant a potential hazardous final day fixture at Portsmouth. Coleman looked ahead to a 'radical overhaul' of his squad during the summer.

Anderton N 20 (2)	Hall C 1 (12)	Nolan L..........................- (2)
Armstrong L 8 (8)	Hughes M.......................46	Richards-Everton B ... 13 (3)
Barlaser D............... 33 (6)	Ihiekwe M 20	Ripley C 21
Brown S................. 18 (11)	Jackson K.........................1	Rodgers H 5 (1)
Clark J.............................43	Johnson C 40 (1)	Smyth P 11 (4)
Conneely S 25 (2)	Kee B 42 (2)	Sousa E ....- (4)
Donacien J.....................19	Mangan A................... - (3)	Sykes R................... 19 (1)
Evtimov D 9 (2)	Maxted J 16 (3)	Williams D...................- (1)
Finley S 32 (5)	McConville S 45	Wood W.......................- 1 (3)
Gibson L.................... 4 (1)	Mingoia P.................. 2 (2)	Zanzala O............. 12 (15)

League goals (51): McConville 15, Kee 13, Clark 5, Zanzala 4, Armstrong 3, Smyth 3, Sykes 3, Barlaser 1, Conneely 1, Finley 1, Hughes 1, Ihiekwe 1.
FA Cup goals (5): Kee 2, Barlaser 1, Clark 1, Zanzala 1. **League Cup goals** (1): Finley 1. **League Trophy goals** (12): Clark 3, Hall 2, Barlaser 1, Brown 1, Finley 1, Kee 1, Sykes 1, Zanzala 1, Opponents 1
Average home league attendance: 2,764. **Player of Year**: Jordan Clark

AFC WIMBLEDON

Wally Downes, a driving force behind the Crazy Gang culture at the old Wimbledon, led the modern-day version to safety against all the odds. Downes took over what looked increasingly like an impossible job after seven successive defeats cost Neal Ardley his job after six years as manager. By the midway point of the season, Wimbledon were bottom, there was little sign of improvement in the New Year and after a 2-0 home defeat by Burton they were ten points adrift. Joe Pigott's hat-trick at Rochdale, completed with a stoppage-time winner from the penalty spot, breathed new life into the campaign – and his goals were to prove crucial as Wimbledon closed the gap. One of them, away to champions-to-be Luton, was followed by Steve Seddon's stoppage-time header for a 2-2 draw. Pigott then netted twice for a victory in the penultimate match against Wycombe which took his side out of the bottom four for the first time in six months. Finally, a goalless draw at Bradford enabled Wimbledon to complete the recovery with a superior goal difference, having accumulated 27 points from their last 15 fixtures.

Appiah K 18 (8)	Egan A .... - (1)	Hartigan A 27 (4)
Barcham A............... 21 (6)	Folivi M 8 (2)	Jervis J 12 (11)
Burey T...................... - (3)	Garrett T 1 (5)	Kalambayi P...................17
Connolly D 2 (10)	Hanson J 18 (11)	King T 12

McDonald R 22 (1)	Pinnock M 19 (15)	Thomas T 20 (3)
McDonnell J 14	Purrington B 26	Trotter L 17 (2)
McLoughlin S 5 (5)	Ramsdale A 20	Wagstaff S 28 (7)
Nightingale W 37 (2)	Seddon S 18	Watson T 22 (2)
Oshilaja A 25	Sibbick T 18 (5)	Wood T .... - (1)
Pigott J 31 (9)	Soares I 19 (4)	Wordsworth A 29 (8)

League goals (42): Pigott 15, Hanson 5, Appiah 4, Pinnock 3, Seddon 3, Folivi 2, Jervis 2, Wagstaff 2, Wordsworth 2, Barcham 1, McLoughlin 1, Oshilaja 1, Trotter 1
FA Cup goals (11). Appiah 2, Wagstaff 2, Barcham 1, Hartigan 1, Pigott 1, Pinnock 1, Purrington 1, Sibbick 1, Wordsworth 1. **League Cup goals** (3): Pigott 2, Opponents 1. **League Trophy goals** (7): Wordsworth 2, Appiah 1, Egan 1, Garrett 1, Hartigan 1, Soares 1
Average home league attendance: 4,254. **Player of Year**: Will Nightingale

BARNSLEY

Barnsley bounced straight back to the Championship in former Hannover coach Daniel Stendel's first season as manager. They overcame the potentially damaging loss of leading scorer Kieffer Moore at a crucial time of the season to hold off the challenge of the big two, Sunderland and Portsmouth, and finish runners-up to Luton. Moore, whose hat-trick against Rochdale came in one of two early season confidence-boosting 4-0 victories, missed two-months after a clash of heads at Gillingham. In his absence, former Fulham striker Cauley Woodrow averaged a goal every two games to keep the promotion pot boiling, one of them at Fleetwood where Stendel was involved in a much-publicised alleged post-match altercation with rival manager Joey Barton, sustaining facial injuries. After a run of 20 unbeaten matches came to an end at Burton, Barnsley won four in succession, scoring 11 goals, to stay ahead of their rivals. They were able to savour promotion without kicking a ball when Portsmouth and Sunderland both lost most midweek matches in hand, but were denied the title on the final day by Luton's win over Oxford and their own defeat away to Bristol Rovers.

Adeboyejo V 2 (23)	Hedges R 5 (16)	Pinnock E 46
Bahre M-S 23 (12)	Isgrove L .... - (2)	Potts B 20 (2)
Bradshaw T 4	Jackson A 5 (1)	Smith J 1
Brown J 22 (10)	Lindsay L 41	Styles C .... - (7)
Cavare D 40 (1)	McGeehan C 32 (7)	Thiam M 36 (10)
Davies A 42	Moncur G 10 (11)	Walton J 3
Dougall K 19 (8)	Moore K 26 (5)	Williams B 11
Fryers E 3 (2)	Mowatt A 46	Williams J 6 (5)
Green J 2 (8)	Pinillos D 32 (3)	Woodrow C 29 (2)

League goals (80): Moore 17, Woodrow 16, Brown 8, Mowatt 8, Thiam 7, McGeehan 6, Potts 6, Adeboyejo 2, Cavare 2, Bahre 1, Bradshaw 1, Green 1, Lindsay 1, Moncur 1, Pinnock 1, Opponents 2
FA Cup goals (8): Woodrow 3, Moore 2, Bahre 1, Fryers 1, Potts 1. **League Cup goals** (1): Moncur 1. **League Trophy goals** (8): Moncur 3, Adeboyejo 2, Hedges 1, Lindsay 1, Williams J 1
Average home league attendance: 12,527. **Player of Year**: Ethan Pinnock

BLACKPOOL

Supporters flooded back to Bloomfield Road after four years boycotting the club in protest against Owen Oyston. Nearly 16,000, four times more than the previous home match, watched a 2-2 draw with Southend following the removal of the controversial owner by order of the High Court which ended his family's control of the club. The fans celebrated when a 96th minute own goal by Taylor Moore earned a point to consolidate a mid-table position under Terry McPhillips, who took over when Gary Bowyer resigned as manager two days after the first game of the season.

Bowyer led Blackpool back to League One, then to a top-half finish the following season but ran out of patience with Oyston, having lost the core of his squad during the summer. McPhillips, Bowyer's assistant, earned a 12-month rolling contract after an eight-match unbeaten run as caretaker, but resigned after a single season and former manager Simon Grayson returned.

Anderton N 10	Gnanduillet A 35 (8)	O'Sullivan J 4 (9)
Bola M 35	Guy C......................... 13 (3)	Pritchard H............. 17 (20)
Boney M .... - (1)	Heneghan B 41 (1)	Ryan J ....- (1)
Burnley J 4 (1)	Howard M....................30	Sorensen E .... (1)
Cullen M.................... 8 (4)	Thompson J 31 (7)	Spearing J 42
Daniels D................. 21 (3)	Kirby N 6 (5)	Taylor C........................ 7 (5)
Davies S .... - (2)	Long C 8 (9)	Tilt C............................... 37
Delfouneso N 32 (7)	Mafoumbi C...................14	Turton O........................ 32
Dodoo J................... 10 (8)	McLaughlin R 1 (5)	Virtue M...................11 (2)
Evans A 9 (3)	Nottingham M......... 15 (14)	
Feeney L................. 24 (10)	O'Connor P................. 7 (3)	

League goals (50): Gnanduillet 10, Delfouneso 7, Spearing 4, Tilt 4, Cullen 3, Thompson 3, Pritchard 3, Virtue 3, Bola 2, Dodoo 2, Long 2, Nottingham 2, Heneghan 1, Kirby 1, Taylor 1, Turton 1, Opponents 1
FA Cup goals (6): Dodoo 2, Cullen 1, Gnanduillet 1, Pritchard 1, Spearing 1. **League Cup goals (8):** Gnanduillet 2, Nottingham 2, Pritchard 2, O'Connor 1, Spearing 1. **League Trophy goals (7):** Dodoo 2, Davies 1, Gnanduuillet 1, Guy 1, O'Connor 1, O'Sullivan 1
Average home league attendance: 5,517. **Player of Year:** Marc Bola

BRADFORD CITY

Three managers tried and failed to arrest the demise of one of the division's best supported clubs. Michael Collins was sacked a month into the season after four defeats in five games. David Hopkin, formerly in charge of Livingston and a former player at Valley Parade, also had a hard time of it before three wins in five matches suggested he might be the man put things right. One of those, 2-0 against Scunthorpe, led by former manager Stuart McCall, took Bradford out of the bottom four. They then scored seven goals in beating Rochdale and Accrington to go into the New Year on a high. But a run of one win in eight led to Hopkin resigning and the appointment of Gary Bowyer, former Blackburn and Blackpool manager, who had 11 games to beat the drop, Bradford, then second from bottom six points from safety, delivered his first win, 3-1 against Peterborough, with three goals in 16 second-half minutes. But their fate was sealed by six successive defeats, the last at Coventry, which sent them down with three fixtures remaining. They finished bottom, nine points adrift.

Akpan H 24 (4)	Gibson J..................... 1 (10)	O'Donnell R.................... 42
Jones A...................... - (2)	Goldthorp E .... - (2)	Omari P ....- (1)
Anderson J................. 9 (4)	Henry K 3 (1)	Payne J....................33 (6)
Ball D....................... 30 (5)	Isherwood T 1 (2)	Riley R 5 (1)
Brunker K 4 (13)	Knight-Percival N...... 34 (1)	Robinson T...................- (2)
Butterfield J 11 (4)	McGowan R 22 (1)	Scannell S................ 15 (1)
Caddis P 25 (2)	Mellor R 17 (3)	Seedorf S 1 (5)
Chicksen A 26 (2)	Miller G................... 18 (21)	Wilson B 4
Clarke B 6 (8)	O'Brien J................... 5 (6)	Wood C................... 18 (4)
Colville L 3 (8)	O'Brien L 38 (2)	Woods C 5 (1)
Devine D................... 2 (1)	O'Connor A 41 (1)	Wright J 15 (3)
Doyle E................... 40 (4)	O'Connor P................. 8 (1)	

League goals (49): Doyle 11, Payne 9, O'Connor A 6, Ball 5, O'Brien L 4, Miller 3, Akpan 2, Knight-Percival 2, Anderson 1, Butterfield 1, Caddis 1, Clarke 1, Colville 1, Mellor 1, Wood 1

FA Cup goals (8): Miller 2, Ball 1, Caddis 1, Colville 1, Knight-Percival 1, Mellor 1, Opponents 1.
League Cup goals (1): Colville 1. League Trophy goals (3): Ball 1, Brunker 1, Miller 1
Average home league attendance: 16,130

BRISTOL ROVERS

Jonson Clarke-Harris rescued Rovers from the threat of relegation. The winter transfer window signing from Coventry scored 11 goals in 11 games, including a hat-trick in the 4-0 win over Blackpool which launched his new side's revival under Graham Coughlan. Clarke-Harris then netted the winner in back-to-back victories over fellow-strugglers Scunthorpe and Gillingham. And a stoppage-time goal delivered a 3-2 success against Bradford which virtually ensured they stayed up. Coughlan was appointed when Darrell Clarke, manager for four-and-a-half-years, was sacked following the club's worst start for 26 years, one win in seven games, then five successive defeats approaching the midway point of the season. The former Plymouth and Sheffield Wednesday defender won three of his five matches to earn a two-and-a-half-year contract as permanent manager. Rovers completed their recovery by coming from behind to beat promoted Barnsley with a stoppage-time Alex Rodman goal, his second of the game.

Bennett K	Kilgour A	Partington J
12 (7)	1 (3)	13 (1)
Bonham J	Leadbitter D	Payne S
40	11	14 (6)
Broadbent T	Lines C	Reilly G
4 (3)	12 (7)	16 (14)
Clarke J	Lockyer T	Rodman A
38 (4)	40	18 (9)
Clarke O	Martin J	Sercombe L
40	8 (2)	33 (6)
Clarke-Harris J	Matthews S	Sinclair S
14 (2)	5 (11)	9 (9)
Craig T	Mensah B	Slocombe S
46	- (1)	2
Holmes-Dennis T	Moore D	Smith A
18	(1)	4 (1)
Jakubiak A	Nichols J	Upson E
12 (26)	26 (10)	34 (1)
Kelly M	Ogogo A	
20 (1)	16	

League goals (47): Clarke-Harris 11, Clarke O 6, Rodman 5, Reilly 4, Sercombe 4, Lockyer 3, Clarke J 2, Craig 2, Jakubiak 2, Payne 2, Holmes Dennis 1, Lines 1, Martin 1, Nichols 1, Upson 1, Opponents 1
FA Cup goals (2): Lines 1, Nichols 1. League Cup goals (3): Bennett 1, Clarke O 1, Upson 1
League Trophy goals (11): Jakubiak 3, Rodman 2, Broadbent 1, Clarke O 1, Craig 1, Lockyer 1, Nichols 1, Payne 1
Average home league attendance: 8,320. Player of Year: Ollie Clarke

BURTON ALBION

Burton broke new ground by reaching the semi-finals of the League Cup for the first time and earning a tribute from Pep Guardiola. Nigel Clough led them into the last four of a competition he twice won as a player with Nottingham Forest when his father Brian was manager. Northern Ireland striker Liam Boyce scored the only goal of ties against Aston Villa and Burnley. Jake Hesketh rounded off a 3-2 success against Forest, then netted the winner at Middlesbrough which earned a two-leg tie against Manchester City. Burton chased shadows at The Etihad, losing 9-0, but restricted the eventual winners to 1-0 in the return and Guardiola said afterwards: 'Burton had an incredible tournament. They have to be so proud.' In the league, Clough's relegated side had a worrying start, losing four of the first five matches, stabilised in mid-season with the help of a hat-trick by Marcus Harness against Rochdale and reached ninth with a strong finish which brought wins over the two automatically promoted clubs, Luton and Barnsley.

Akins L	Bradley A	Campbell H
46	- (7)	- (1)
Allen J	Brayford J	Clarke J
41 (1)	38 (3)	3 (3)
Beardsley C	Buxton J	Cole D
- (1)	21 (9)	6 (7)
Boyce L	Bywater S	Collins B
33 (4)	8	31

Daniel C 17	Hodge E .... - (2)	Sbarra J...................... 2 (7)
Evtimov D 7	Hutchinson R 16 (9)	Sordell M.................. 10 (2)
Fox B 14 (13)	McCrory D................ 10 (5)	Templeton D........... 17 (11)
Fraser S 39 (3)	McFadzean K 35	Turner B 18 (1)
Harness M 21 (11)	Miller W................ 10 (12)	Wallace K 8 (14)
Hesketh J 14 (2)	Quinn S 41 (1)	

League goals (66): Akins 13, Boyce 11, Allen 7, Fraser 6, Harness 5, Templeton 5, McFadzean 4, Drayford 3, Oole 2, Oordell 2, Dradley 1, Fox 1, Hooktoth 1, Millor 1, Quinn 1, Wallace 1, Opponents 2
FA Cup goals: (1): Boyce 1. **League Cup goals** (9): Boyce 2, Hesketh 2, Akins 1, Allen 1, Fraser 1, Templeton 1, Opponents 1. **League Trophy goals** (1): Harness 1
Average home league attendance: 3,351. **Player of Year**: Lucas Akins

CHARLTON ATHLETIC

A club riven by relegation, managerial upheaval and long-standing protests against the owner enjoyed much-needed success with a return to the Championship in dramatic fashion at Wembley. The Play-off Final against Sunderland looked to heading for extra-time, echoing the teams' epic match in 1998 which Charlton won 7-6 on penalties after a 4-4 scoreline. Naby Sarr's fifth-minute own goal had been cancelled out by Ben Purrington's first for Lee Bowyer's team and that's how it remained until defender Patrick Bauer scrambled in the rebound from his initial header with seconds left. Charlton also did it the hard way in the semi-finals, winning a shootout against Doncaster after a rare defeat at The Valley in the second leg. Their place in the top-six previously came under threat with the loss of leading scorer Karlan Grant to Huddersfield in the winter transfer window. But with Lyle Taylor relishing the extra responsibility, they built up a head of steam to take into the knockout phase by winning ten out of 13 games. The run included a 3-1 success over champions-to-be Luton, Taylor scoring twice, and four-goal performances against Scunthorpe and Rochdale to finish third behind Luton and Barnsley. Bowyer had been given the the given the manager's job after five months as caretaker.

Ajose N......................... 6 (3)	Lapslie G................ 11 (16)	Reeves B......................22 (7)
Aribo J..................... 35 (1)	Maloney T .... - (1)	Sarr N......................31 (5)
Bauer P 35	Marshall M 6 (16)	Solly C 36 (1)
Bielik K 30 (1)	Morgan A 6 (2)	Steer J 19
Cullen J 29	Page L.........................11	Stevenson T................ 2 (1)
Dijksteel A 21 (9)	Parker J 3 (7)	Taylor L...........................41
Forster-Caskey J .... - (1)	Pearce J 25 (1)	Vetokele I 12 (11)
Fosu-Henry T............ 14 (13)	Phillips D 27	Ward J 6 (3)
Grant K....................... 25 (3)	Pratley D 20 (8)	Williams J 14 (2)
Hackett-Fairchild R....... 1 (6)	Purrington B..............18	

Play-offs – appearances: Aribo 3, Bauer 3, Bielik 3, Cullen 3, Dijksteel 3, Parker 3, Phillips 3, Purrington 3, Sarr 3, Taylor 3, Morgan 2, Pratley 1 (2), Williams – (2), Pearce – (1), Solly – (1)
League goals (73): Taylor 21, Grant 14, Aribo 9, Reeves 4, Bielik 3, Vetokele 3, Fosu-Henry 2, Pearce 2, Pratley 2, Sarr 2, Ajose 1, Cullen 1, Dijksteel 1, Marshall 1, Solly 1, Ward 1, Opponents 5. **Play-offs – goals** (6): Aribo 1, Bauer 1, Bielik 1, Purrington 1, Pratley 1, Taylor 1
FA Cup goals (6): Taylor 3, Ajose 1, Marshall 1, Stevenson 1. **League Cup goals** None. **League Trophy goals** (10): Stevenson 3, Vetokele 2, Ajose 1, Lapslie 1, Mascoll J 1, Pratley 1, Sarr 1
Average home league attendance: 11,827. **Player of Year**: Lyle Taylor

COVENTRY CITY

Victory in League One's most remarkable match of the season maintained a place on the fringes of the play-offs. A 5-4 success at the Stadium of Light, courtesy of a 78th minute goal from substitute Conor Chaplin, also undermined Sunderland's chance of automatic promotion.

Coventry then condemned ten-man Bradford to the drop, but lost out to an 83rd minute Portsmouth goal at sold-out Fratton Park which effectively ended their bid to close the gap. Even so, eighth place represented a solid campaign of consolidation following promotion via the play-offs, highlighted by results against some of the division's leading lights. They completed the double over Charlton and took four points off Sunderland, Barnsley and Peterborough. There was also a run of five successive league wins in October for the first time since 1998. The downside was inconsistent home form and too many points dropped against teams in the lower reaches of the table.

Allassani R................ - (5)	Enobakhare R 18	Ponticelli J .... (5)
Andreu T....................... 6 (4)	Grimmer J 8 (3)	Shipley J.................. 22 (11)
Bakayoko A.......... 18 (13)	Hiwula J.................. 35 (4)	Sterling D.............. 37 (1)
Bayliss T................. 37 (1)	Hyam D.................. 37 (1)	Stockdale D................... 2
Biamou M.................. 2 (2)	Jones L .... - (8)	Thomas L 41 (2)
Brown J................. 17 (5)	Kelly L 25 (5)	Thompson J..........1 (3)
Burge L 40	Mason B...............25	Wakefield C .... - (8)
Chaplin C.............. 22 (9)	McCallum S.............. 3 (4)	Westbrooke Z.......... 3 (4)
Clarke-Harris J.......... 18 (9)	Meyler D 2 (3)	Williams M 1
Davies T 19 (4)	O'Brien L 4	Willis J.................. 36 (2)
Doyle M 21 (2)	Ogogo A 6 (4)	

League goals (54): Hiwula 12, Chaplin 8, Bakayoko 7, Enobakhare 6, Clarke-Harris 5, Thomas 4, Bayliss 3, Shipley 3, Andreu 1, Doyle 1, Hyam 1, Jones 1, Willis 1, Opponents 1
FA Cup goals (2): Clarke-Harris 1, Thomas 1. **League Cup goals:** None. **League Trophy goals (1):** Hiwula 1.
Average home league attendance: 12,363. **Player of Year:** Dom Hyam

DONCASTER ROVERS

Grant McCann told his players to hold their heads high after losing a promotion bid on penalties at The Valley. His side finished 15 points behind Charlton, lost the first leg of their play-off semi-final 2-1 and were 3-1 down on aggregate in the second minute of the return. They looked to have little chance against opponents unbeaten at home in 17 league matches. Instead, Doncaster rose to the challenge in an absorbing game to level through captain Tommy Rowe and Andy Butler. Leading scorer John Marquis then put them ahead in extra-time, but the lead lasted just 86 seconds and Rowe's spot-kick fired wide in the penalty shootout settled the issue. Doncaster's long-standing grip on the final play-off place came under threat during a run of seven games without a win, culminating in a 4-0 defeat by champions-to-be Luton. The pressure eased with successive victories over Bristol Rovers, Walsall, Bradford and Plymouth, but it remained touch-and-go until the final day of the regular season when goals from Marquis and Kieran Sadlier against Coventry maintained a single point advantage over McCann's former club Peterborough. The manager moved on after a year in charge to take over at Hull. Darren Moore, sacked by West Bromwich Albion, replaced him. Darren Moore, sacked by West Bromwich Albion, replaced him.

Amos D........................ - (1)	Cummings S...................4	May A 8 (26)
Anderson J................. 1 (8)	Downing P................. 1/ (1)	Rowe T.................. 18 (14)
Anderson T 21 (2)	Hasani L .... - (2)	Sadlier K.................... 6 (8)
Andrew D.......................46	Kane H 37 (1)	Smith T..................2 (12)
Beestin A................ - (5)	Kiwomya A 1 (2)	Taylor P.................. 1 (13)
Blair M................. 31 (11)	Lawlor I..........................10	Whiteman B 39 (1)
Boocock R .... - (1)	Lewis A..........................7	Wilks M.................. 42 (4)
Butler A.................. 39 (1)	Marosi M.......................36	Wright J 14
Coppinger J.............. 38 (5)	Marquis J 44	
Crawford A............. 25 (10)	Mason N 19 (1)	

Play-offs – appearances: Andrew 2, Blair 2, Butler 2, Coppinger 2, Downing 2, Kane 2, Marosi 2, Marquis 2, Whiteman 2, Wilks 2, Rowe 1 (1), Sadlier 1 (1), May – (2), Crawford -) 1, Wright – (1) **League goals (76):** Marquis 21, Wilks 14, Andrew 5, Rowe 5, Coppinger 4, Kane 4, Blair 3, Crawford 3, Sadlier 3, Whiteman 3, May 2, Smith 2, Wright 2, Anderson J 1, Anderson T 1, Butler 1, Taylor 1, Opponents 1. **Play-offs – goals (4):** Blair 1, Butler 1, Marquis 1, Rowe 1. **FA Cup goals (16):** May 4, Kane 3, Marquis 3, Whiteman 2. Anderson T 1, Blair 1, Butler 1, Wilks 1. **League Cup goals (3):** Andrew 1, May 1, Wilks 1. **League Trophy goals (5):** May 4, Marquis 1
Average home league attendance. 8,008. **Player of Year:** Ben Whiteman

FLEETWOOD TOWN

It's not just big clubs like Manchester City and Sunderland allowing in the cameras for a fly-on-the-wall documentary. Joey Barton's first taste of management was filmed for a series called 'A Season on the Edge' which chronicled the former City player's training sessions and team talks, together with board meetings and transfer negotiations. Chairman Andy Pilley said the club wanted to reveal 'the true story of the season.' Whether it will include footage of its most controversial moments, an alleged confrontation between Barton and Barnsley manager Daniel Stendel after their teams' match at Oakwell, remains to be seen. Barnsley won it 4-2 on their way to promotion to the Championship. Fleetwood's campaign ended in 11th place, an improvement of three on 2018. Highlight was a 5-0 away win over Scunthorpe, their biggest in seven seasons in the Football League. Another significant success came in the final home match when a 95th minute header by Ashley Eastham ended Sunderland's chance of going up automatically.

Baggley B .... - (3)	Grant R 2 (2)	Morgan C 21 (2)
Biggins H................... 8 (15)	Hill J 1 (1)	Nadesan A................. 12 (8)
Bolger C 5 (6)	Holt J...................... 29 (4)	Rydel R........................ 3 (3)
Burns W 34 (5)	Hunter A 29 (14)	Sheron N................... 17 (9)
Cairns A..........................46	Husband J................. 32 (1)	Southam M................ - (1)
Clarke E 2	Jones G............................3	Souttar H 11
Coyle L...........................41	Long C 1 (7)	Sowerby J................. 10 (5)
Dempsey K 5 (9)	Madden P................. 38 (6)	Spurr T 2 (2)
Eastham A 43 (2)	Marney D 15 (1)	Taylor R........................8 (2)
Evans C 37 (2)	McAleny C................. 6 (8)	Wallace J................... 11 (7)
Garner G .... - (1)	Mooney D .... - (1)	Wallace R................. 34 (2)

League goals (58): Evans 17, Madden 15, Hunter 8, Burns 7, Eastham 2, Biggins 1, Bolger 1, Holt 1, Husband 1, Marney 1, Nadesan 1, Souttar 1, Wallace J 1, Wallace R 1
FA Cup goals (8): Madden 4, Burns 1, Evans 1, Garner 1, Hunter 1. **League Cup goals (1):** Holt 1. **League Trophy goals (3):** Dempsey 1, Long 1, McAleny 1
Average home league attendance: 3,165. **Player of Year:** Wes Burns

GILLINGHAM

Steve Lovell steered his side away from the threat of relegation for the second successive season – and was then sacked. Owner Paul Scally dismissed his manager in a meeting with two games of the season remaining. Lovell, a prolific scorer in five seasons at Priestfield, had been in charge for 18 months. The club thanked him for his work, but made no further comment. Former Republic of Ireland international Tony Cascarino, who began his career at the club, called the decision 'disgraceful.' Gillingham knocked Cardiff out of the FA Cup, but were caught up in a scramble to beat the drop after indifferent home form. They came through it with two resilient performances which took them beyond the 50-point safety mark. Tom Eaves scored his 19th goal of the season as his side came from behind to beat AFC Wimbledon 4-2. They also trailed Plymouth before two second-half goals in two minutes from Regan Charles-Cook and Mark Byrne sparked a 3-1 victory. Lovell was succeeded by former Peterborough and Leeds manager Steve Evans.

Ringham B............... 15 (6)
Burke G 12
Byrne M...........................45
Campbell T 2 (4)
Charles-Cook R........ 16 (10)
Da Silva Lopes L....... 12 (2)
Eaves T.................... 35 (8)
Ehmer M................... 39 (1)
Fuller B 37 (2)

Garmston B 13 (6)
Hanlan B.................... 36 (4)
Holy T...........................46
King B 1 (2)
Lacey A 13 (2)
List E 17 (20)
Mbo N .... - (1)
Nasseri N .... - (4)
O'Neill L 33 (5)

Ogilvie C 29 (2)
Oldaker D 11 (2)
Parker J 19 (2)
Parrett D 19 (8)
Rees J....................... 7 (11)
Reilly C 18 (7)
Stevenson B 1 (2)
Wilkinson C 2 (5)
Zakuani G....................29

League goals (61): Eaves 21, Hanlan 9, List 5, Reilly 5, Byrne 4, Parker 4, Charles-Cook 3, O'Neill 3, Burke 1, Da Silva Lopes 1, Ehmer 1, Fuller 1, Lacey 1, Parrett 1, Rees 1
FA Cup goals (7): List 2, Eaves 1, Ehmer 1, O'Neill 1, Oldaker 1, Rees 1. **League Cup goals:** None. **League Trophy goals** (2): List 1, Stevenson 1
Average home league attendance: 5,128. **Player of Year:** Barry Fuller

LUTON TOWN

Mick Harford picked up the baton from Nathan Jones and carried it all the way into the Championship as Luton recorded back-to-back promotions, this time as champions. Twice a player with the club and a League Cup winner, Harford took over when Jones became Stoke's new manager early in the New Year – and the transition proved seamless. His side displaced Portsmouth at the top, extended their unbeaten league run to a club-record 20 league games and Harford was appointed to stay in charge for the rest of the season. The run reached 28 matches, longest in one season in the game's third tier, before coming to an end in a 3-1 defeat at Charlton. By then, Luton were seven points clear of third place. The gap closed after another defeat, by Burton, but promotion was assured when Portsmouth and Sunderland, favourites to go up automatically, both lost their games in hand. That brought a title decider on the final day of the season in which George Moncur scored twice in a 3-1 win over Oxford. James Collins was named League One Player of the Year for 25 goals, which included hat-tricks against Plymouth and Peterborough. Harford took the manager's accolade, then stepped aside for the permanent appointment of Graeme Jones, former assistant manager at West Bromwich Albion.

Baptiste A................... - (2)
Berry L 12 (9)
Bradley S 44 (1)
Collins J 42 (2)
Connolly A .... - (2)
Cornick H 14 (18)
Cummings J .... - (5)
Grant J 13 (4)
Hylton D 18 (7)
Jarvis A..................... - (4)

Jervis J........................ - (2)
Jones L .... (1)
Justin J 35 (8)
Lee E 36 (2)
LuaLua K 10 (12)
McCormack A 17 (2)
Moncur G 4 (10)
O'Kane E.................. - (3)
Pearson M.....................46
Potts D..................... 15 (9)

Rea G 20 (2)
Ruddock D 46
Shea J 41
Sheehan A................4 (13)
Shinnie A 39 (2)
Stacey J 45
Stech M 5
Thorne G................... - (3)

League goals (90): Collins 25, Lee 12, Hylton 8, Cornick 6, Moncur 6, Pearson 6, Ruddock 5, Shinnie 4, Stacey 4, Berry 3, Justin 3, Grant 2, LuaLua 2, Cummings 1, Potts 1, Rea 1, Opponents 1
FA Cup goals (3): Cornick 2, Shinnie 1. **League Cup goals:** None. **League Trophy goals** (7): Grant 2, Jarvis 1, LuaLua 1, Read A 1, Sheehan 1, Opponents 1
Average home league attendance: 9,516. **Player of Year:** Jack Stacey

OXFORD UNITED

An impressive finish removed the shadow of relegation which hung over the Kassam Stadium for much of the season. Four straight wins, three of them against teams also threatened with the drop, eased all the pressure and Karl Robinson's side kept on climbing for an eventual finish in the top half of the table. It contrasted sharply with four straight defeats and 13 goals conceded at the start of the campaign, then a single win in the first 12 games which left Oxford bottom. They were subsequently stuck for months on the fringes of the drop zone until sparked by a stoppage-time winner from Jamie Mackie against Bradford. Another in added time came from Josh Ruffels against Wycombe and their ten men prevailed 3-1 at Walsall following the dismissal of Marcus Browne. For good measure, Gavin Whyte's hat-trick delivered a 3-2 success at Shrewsbury, despite another red card, this time for Ahmed Kashi.

Baptiste S.................. 7 (2)	Holmes R 13 (3)	Raglan C ....- (1)
Bradbury H ....- (1)	Jones N....................... 2 (1)	Ruffels J 40 (4)
Brannagan C 40 (1)	Kashi A 7 (4)	Shearer S 1
Browne M 25 (9)	Little A.......................- (1)	Sinclair J................. 10 (6)
Carruthers S.............. 3 (7)	Long S 16 (2)	Smith J.......................- (1)
Dickie R 36 (1)	Mackie J 28 (14)	Smith S 5 (9)
Eastwood S 34	McMahon T 10	Spasov S ....- (1)
Garbutt L 18 (7)	Mitchell J....................10	Stephens J 1 (1)
Graham J 13 (3)	Mousinho J............... 32 (3)	Sykes M ....- 7 (2)
Hall R........................ 1 (3)	Nelson C 46	Whyte G 29 (7)
Hanson J 22 (8)	Norman C...................... 6 (1)	
Henry J 39 (5)	Obika J 5 (6)	

League goals (58): Henry 11, Whyte 7, Browne 6, Mackie 5, Garbutt 4, Nelson 4, Ruffels 4, Sinclair 4, Brannagan 3, Holmes 3, Mousinho 2, Dickie 1, Graham 1, Obika 1, Opponents 2
FA Cup goals (5): Henry 2, Brannagan 1, Browne 1, Mackie 1. **League Cup goals** (5). Whyte 2, Baptiste 1, Browne 1, Opponents 1. **League Trophy goals** (13): Smith S 3, Brannagan 2, Henry 2, Browne 1, Carruthers 1, Holmes 1, McMahon 1, Raglan 1, Spasov 1
Average home league attendance: 7,315. **Player of Year**: Josh Ruffels

PETERBOROUGH UNITED

A flying start under Steve Evans and a frustrating finish with Darren Ferguson in charge for the third time summed up Peterborough's season. They closed a point behind Doncaster for the final play-off place which the two sides had contested t throughout the second part of the campaign. Ferguson was left to reflect on the points that got away in the final fortnight. His side conceded a 94th minute equaliser at Fleetwood and lost 3-0 at relegation-threatened Walsall, matches which previously productive away form suggested they might have relished. Two goals by Ivan Toney then ended Portsmouth's automatic promotion chances at Fratton Park and two more came in the last fixture against Burton. But both wins proved in vain, with Doncaster overcoming Coventry to maintain the upper hand in their final game. Ferguson returned to the club when Evans was sacked in late January, even though his side were sixth at the time. He had carried out his promise to assemble a new-look squad, with a dozen summer signings, and for the first time the club won the opening five games, scoring 15 goals in the process.

Bennett R 36 (1)	Godden M 29 (9)	Stevens M ....- (3)
Chapman A....................32	Knight J 6 (2)	Tafazolli R 35 (2)
Cooke C 10 (3)	Lafferty D.......................18	Tomlin L....................14 (5)
Cooper G................... 4 (17)	Lyon D ....- (2)	Toney I....................31 (13)
Cummings J............ 11 (11)	Maddison M 31 (9)	Walker J..................... 6 (6)
Daniel C 20	Naismith J.............. 42 (1)	Ward J 34 (9)
Dembele S 30 (8)	O'Hara M 14 (8)	White B....................14 (1)
Dempsey K 6 (5)	O'Malley C....................14	Woodyard A 41 (2)
Denton T.................... 9 (1)	Reed L 19 (9)	Yorwerth J ....- (2)

League goals (71): Toney 16, Godden 14, Maddison 8, Cummings 6, Dembele 5, Bennett 4,

122

O'Hara 4, Ward 4, Cooper 2, Tomlin 2, Cooke 1, Naismith 1, Reed 1, Tafazolli 1, Walker 1, White 1

FA Cup goals (9): Toney 4, Godden 2, Dembele 1, Maddison 1, Ward 1. **League Cup goals:** None. **League Trophy goals (12):** Toney 3, Cummings 2, Godden 2, Cooper 1, Daniel 1, Dembele 1, Maddison 1, Walker 1

Average home league attendance: 7,315. **Player of Year:** Marcus Maddison

PLYMOUTH ARGYLE

Derek Adams led Plymouth away from the threat of relegation with one of the previous season's great recovery acts. This time, the manager and his club both went under in a bizarre climax to the campaign. Adams, in charge for four years, was sacked following a 5-1 defeat at Accrington, which left his side in the bottom four ahead of a make-or-break final match at home to Scunthorpe. Neither party explained the reasoning behind the decision. Despite winning the game 3-2, they went down on goal difference after finishing on 50 points alongside Southend and AFC Wimbledon. Plymouth won just once in the first 14 games, an identical record to 12 months earlier. But whereas that improvement almost secured a play-off place, this time they continued to find it hard going. They conceded five goals at home to Peterborough and Luton and were bottom going into the New Year. Five wins out of six, with Ruben Lameiras scoring six times, lifted them towards mid-table, while a 5-1 victory over Rochdale, opened a seven-point safety cushion. But eight games without a win at the business end of the season proved costly. Adams was replaced by Bury's Ryan Lowe.

Ainsworth L	- (1)	Grant P	5 (1)	Sarcevic A	37
Anderson P	- (4)	Jephcott L	2 (7)	Sawyer G	29 (4)
Canavan N	30 (3)	Jones L	4 (5)	Smith-Brown A	30 (1)
Carey G	42 (2)	Ladapo F	42 (3)	Songo'o Y	38 (4)
Cooper M	- (1)	Lameiras R	31 (10)	Moore T	14
Edwards R	35 (1)	Letheren K	13	Taylor R	6 (27)
Fletcher A	- (4)	Macey M	33 (1)	Threlkeld O	7 (5)
Fox D	40 (3)	Ness J	17 (7)	Wootton S	6 (3)
Grant C	10	O'Keefe S	6 (5)	Wylde G	1 (6)
Grant J	14 (3)	Riley J	14 (4)		

League goals (56): Ladapo 18, Lameiras 11, Carey 6, Edwards 5, Grant 4, Sarcevic 3, Canavan 2, Fox 1, Jones 1, Smith-Brown 1, Threlkeld 1, Opponents 3

FA Cup goals (2): Lameiras 1, Sarcevic 1. **League Cup goals (3):** Ladapo 1, Ness 1, Songo'o 1. **League Trophy goals:** None

Average home league attendance: 9,052. **Player of Year:** Ruben Lameiras

PORTSMOUTH

A season rich in promise ended in bitter disappointment. Portsmouth had one Wembley success in the bag against Sunderland, four points gained from two league encounters with their rivals and carried the greater momentum going into the play-offs. But they failed to take advantage in the first leg of playing against ten men for the final 25 minutes after the dismissal of Turkish defender Alim Ozturk and lost it 1-0. In the goalless return at Fratton Park, Kenny Jackett's side were unable to break down opponents set up to protect their advantage, with Gareth Evans, Oliver Hawkins and James Vaughan all denied by saves from Jon McLaughlin amid constant pressure. Portsmouth were left to reflect on the failure to nail down an automatic promotion place after a superb record of eight wins and two draws from the first ten away matches. They went top with a seven-point cushion over third place. Then, eight matches without a win – including a 3-3 draw at Southend after leading 3-0 – proved costly, with a strong finish not enough to repair the damage. Victory on penalties in the Checkatrade Trophy was watched by a crowd of 85,021, a record for the competition.

Bogle O 7 (5)	Evans G 34 (8)	Pitman B............... 16 (16)
Brown L..................... 44	Green A 2 (4)	Rose D .... - (1)
Burgess C 20 (5)	Haunstrup B 2 (3)	Solomon-Otabor V 5 (2)
Cannon A...................... 1 (1)	Hawkins O............... 30 (9)	Thompson B 19 (4)
Clarke M..................... 46	Lowe J 44 (1)	Thompson N 30 (1)
Close B................... 25 (9)	MacGillivray C................. 46	Vaughan J 2 (8)
Curtis R 36 (5)	Mason J .... - (1)	Walkes A 17 (7)
Dennis L................... - (1)	Morris B 5 (2)	Whatmough J............... 26
Donohue D 5 (5)	Naylor T 43	Wheeler D 1 (10)

ROCHDALE

Brian Barry-Murphy, a former player and first-team coach at the club, had a successful introduction to management. He took over as caretaker when Keith Hill, second longest-serving manager in League One behind Wycombe's Gareth Ainsworth, was sacked after six years in the job with his side third from bottom after a run of one win in 11 games and 31 goals conceded. Eight points accumulated from four games earned him the job on a permanent basis and with Ian Henderson continuing to score vital goals, Rochdale moved clear of trouble with 1-0 wins over four other threatened teams – Accrington, Wycombe, Bristol Rovers and Southend – in the space five games. They finished four points clear, despite losing the final fixture 4-0 at Charlton. Henderson scored his 100th for the club in the FA Cup win over Gateshead and finished with 21 for the season, including a hat-trick against Gillingham.

Adshead D 8 (2)	Hart S............................ 11	Norman M 6 (1)
Andrew C 13 (25)	Henderson I.................... 45	Ntlhe K 14 (5)
Bradley L .... - (1)	Holden R................... 5 (1)	Perkins D 11 (6)
Bunney J 12 (4)	Inman B 16 (13)	Pyke R 3 (3)
Camps C 40 (1)	Keohane J 4 (4)	Rafferty J 26 (1)
Cannon A 4 (8)	Lillis J 26 (1)	Randall C 1
Clough Z 4 (5)	Lonergan A..................... 7	Rathbone O 26 (2)
Delaney R 29 (1)	Matheson L .... - (3)	Thompson J................... - (1)
Done M 27 (9)	McGahey H...................... 21	Wilbraham A............. 16 (7)
Dooley S 16 (6)	McLaughlin R............... 13	Williams J 22 (6)
Ebanks-Landell E...... 15 (1)	McNulty J....................... 25	Williams J L 12 (7)
Gillam M 6 (4)	Moore L 7 (1)	
Hamilton E 13 (1)	Morley A.................... 2 (1)	

SCUNTHORPE UNITED

Three managers were unable to halt the slide towards relegation. A fourth will try to pick up the pieces. Scunthorpe lost five influential players from the side that reached back-to-back top-six places and a 5-0 drubbing by Fleetwood in the second home match set more alarm bells ringing. Nick Daws, in charge for three months, was replaced by Stuart McCall, formerly at Bradford, who generated some optimism, notably through a 5-3 victory over Charlton and a recovery from 3-0 down against Oxford for a point. That was followed by the club's worst run for 20 years, six successive defeats, then, bizarrely, four straight wins which brought McCall the January Manager of the Month award. Six signings in the winter transfer window had no lasting effect, with basic defensive errors contributing to another lean run, one win in 13 during which McCall was dismissed and coach Andy Dawson put in charge for the remainder of the season. Three goals conceded in 15 minutes to Bradford in the final home match, followed by defeat at Plymouth, confirmed the drop. Paul Hurst, formerly at Ipswich and Shrewsbury, was the new appointment.

Alnwick J 41	Hammill A 10 (5)	Ojo F 37 (2)
Borthwick-Jackson C 29	Holmes D .... - (1)	Olomola, O 2 (4)
Burgess C 33 (3)	Horsfield J 5 (6)	Pearce T 9
Butroid L .... ? (4)	Humphrys S 10 (6)	Perch J 39 (2)
Clarke J 15	Lewis C 3 (12)	Sutton L 16 (2)
Colclough R 12 (5)	Lund M 16 (6)	Thomas G 28 (9)
Dales A 11 (9)	McArdle R 37 (1)	Ugbo I 7 (8)
El-Mhanni Y 2 (3)	McGahey H 8 (2)	Van Veen K 6 (7)
Flatt J .... - (1)	McMahon T 14	Watson N 5
Goode C 21	Morris J 17 (2)	Webster B 8 (1)
Hallam J 4 (3)	Novak L 39 (4)	Wootton K 20 (6)

League goals (53): Novak 12, Wootton 6, Morris 5, Humphrys 4, Goode 3, Thomas 3, Borthwick-Jackson 2, Colclough 2, Lund 2, Perch 2, Burgess 1, Clarke 1, Dales 1, Hallam 1, Hammill 1, McMahon 1, Ojo 1, Pearce 1, Sutton 1, Ugbo 1, Van Veen 1, Opponents 1
FA Cup goals (2): Novak 1, Perch 1. **League Cup goals** (1): Humphrys 1. **League Trophy goals** (3): Colclough 1, Dales 1, El-Mhanni 1
Average home league attendance: 4,227. **Player of Year:** Lee Novak

SHREWSBURY TOWN

League form suffered at the expense of a pleasing FA Cup run and Shrewsbury needed to regroup to prevent being caught up in a relegation dogfight. They won a replay 3-2 at Stoke after transforming a two goal deficit with goals from James Bolton, Fejiri Okenabirhie (pen) and Josh Laurent in the space of ten minutes. Sam Ricketts then saw his side denied a fourth round upset against Wolves by Matt Doherty's stoppage-time equaliser. Shrewsbury also performed well in the replay at Molineux before going down 3-2, but failed to win in nine league games before, during and immediately after the four ties and slipped into the bottom four. Victories over play-off contenders Peterborough and Doncaster, with Tyrese Campbell on the mark in both games, eased the pressure. Shrewsbury then defeated fellow-strugglers Wycombe and Southend to go clear. Ricketts left National League club Wrexham to replace John Askey, manager for five months, who was sacked following four wins in his 17 matches.

Angol L 10 (7)	Colkett C 1	Golbourne S 15
Arnold S 23	Docherty G 34 (7)	Grant A 40 (2)
Barnett R .... - (1)	Edwards D 3 (3)	Haynes R 15 (1)
Beckles O 34 (2)	Eisa A .... - (4)	Holloway A 17 (13)
Bolton J 30 (1)	Emmanuel J 13 (1)	John-Lewis L 5 (12)
Campbell T 13 (2)	Gilliead A 16 (11)	Kennedy K 1
Coleman J 16	Gnahoua A .... - (1)	Laurent J 29 (13)

Loft D.............................1	Payne S....................2 (4)	Vincelot R.................1 (2)
Mitchell J.................7 (2)	Sadler M...................28 (1)	Waterfall L......................44
Norburn O...............39 (2)	Sears R....................2 (3)	Whalley S...............28 (4)
Okenabirhie F.........23 (15)	Smith S......................- (3)	Williams S.....................16

League goals (51): Okenabirhie 10, Norburn 9, Docherty 7, Campbell 5, Waterfall 5, Angol 3, Holloway 2, Laurent 2, Whalley 2, Beckles 1, Bolton 1, Gilliead 1, John-Lewis 1, Opponents 2
FA Cup goals (13): Okenabirhie 3, Bolton 2, Docherty 2, Laurent 2, Norburn 2, Holloway 1, Waterfall 1. **League Cup goals** (1): Whalley 1. **League Trophy goals** (12): Okenabirhie 5, Gilliead 2, Angol 1, Beckles 1, Docherty 1, John-Lewis 1, Loft 1, Sears 1, Opponents 1
Average home league attendance: 6,407. **Player of Year**: Greg Docherty

SOUTHEND UNITED

Masked man Stephen Humphrys saved Southend from relegation with a dramatic late goal on the final day of the season. They were on the way down when the 21-year-old striker came off the bench following Sunderland's equaliser at Roots Hall. Humphrys, wearing a mask to protect facial injuries, struck in the 87th minute for a 2-1 victory which kept his side out of the bottom four on goal difference under Kevin Bond, the caretaker-manager. Bond, who previously spent most of his career as assistant to Harry Redknapp at Portsmouth, Southampton, Tottenham and Birmingham, was rewarded with a two-year contract. He came in with a month remaining, Southend having plunged from a seemingly secure position in the top half of the table. Chris Powell was sacked after 11 games without a victory and the run extended to 15 before a 3-2 victory over Burton in Bond's fourth stint in charge took them out of the bottom four. But they were back in trouble after a single-goal defeat in the penultimate round of fixtures against Rochdale, one of six sides still threatened with the drop.

Acauah E...................1 (2)	Hendrie S................13 (6)	Mantom S.....................43
Barratt S......................- (1)	Hopper T..................13 (1)	McCoulsky S..............- (15)
Bishop N........................18	Humphrys S..............8 (2)	McLaughlin S...........20 (9)
Bunn H................17 (7)	Hutchinson I..............2 (6)	Moore T....................33 (1)
Bwomono E..............27 (3)	Hyam L....................11 (7)	Oxley M..........................25
Clifford T....................- (1)	Kelman C...................2 (8)	Robinson T............13 (11)
Coker B.........................16	Kiernan R......................10	Stockdale D......................3
Cox S......................42 (3)	Kightly M...............15 (16)	Turner M..................33 (3)
Demetriou J...............22 (2)	Klass M....................3 (7)	Wabo N.......................- (2)
Dieng T...................38 (5)	Kyprianou H...................1	White J....................31 (2)
Hart S.............................18	Lennon H..................7 (2)	Yearwood D..............21 (6)

League goals (55): Cox 15, Hopper 7, Humphrys 5, Mantom 5, Bunn 4, Robinson 4, Dieng 3, Demetriou 2, White 2, Hyam 1, Kelman 1, Kiernan 1, Kightly 1, McLaughlin 1, Moore 1, Turner 1, Opponents 1
FA Cup goals (9): Cox 2, Mantom 2, Bunn 2, Dieng 1, Kightly 1, McLaughlin 1, White 1. **League Cup goals** (2): McCoulsky 2. **League Trophy goals** (7): McCloulsky 2, Bunn 1, Bwomono 1, Hutchinson 1, Kyprianou 1, McLaughlin 1
Average home league attendance: 6,932. **Player of Year**: Simon Cox

SUNDERLAND

Sunderland lost momentum at a crucial time, missed out on automatic promotion, then conceded a goal seconds from the end to lose the Play-off Final against Charlton. It was a bitter finish to the season for a club who were firm favourites for an immediate return to the Championship, backed by huge support not just at the Stadium of Light but wherever they travelled. The Boxing Day fixture against Bradford drew a League One record attendance of more than 46,000. An amazing

126

home game against Coventry set in motion their slide from second place behind Luton in the final month of the campaign. Sunderland were beaten 5-4 and also dropped points to Peterborough, Portsmouth, Fleetwood and Southend, finishing fifth after drawing 19 matches. They held on to a single-goal advantage, secured by Chris Maguire, from the first leg of the semi-final against old rivals Portsmouth and went ahead at Wembley through Naby Sarr's own goal. But Charlton survived penalty appeals for hands against Patrick Bauer to level through Ben Purrington and won it with Bauer's scrambled effort. Sunderland also lost in the Checkatrade Trophy at Wembley to Portsmouth, in front of a record crowd for the competition of more than 85,000, after Aiden McGeady's second goal in the 119th minute sent the final to a penalty shootout.

Baldwin J.	34	Loovens G	11	O'Nien L	24 (13)
Cattermole L	28 (1)	Love D	4	Oviedo B	15 (8)
Dunne J.	12	Maguire C	24 (9)	Ozturk A	7 (3)
Flanagan T	30 (2)	Maja J	22 (2)	Power M	29 (6)
Gooch L	31 (8)	Matthews A	20 (3)	Ruiter R	- (1)
Grigg W	15 (13)	McGeady A	29 (5)	Sinclair J	7 (6)
Honeyman G	31 (4)	McGeouch D	14 (8)	Sterling K	- (8)
Hume D	6 (2)	McLaughlin J	46	Watmore D	3 (8)
James R	23 (4)	Molyneux L	- (2)	Wyke C	14 (10)
Kimpioka B	- (4)	Morgan L	12 (5)		
Leadbitter G	13 (2)	Mumba B	2 (2)		

Play-offs-appearances: Cattermole 3, Flanagan 3, Honeyman 3, McLaughlin 3, O'Nien 3, Oviedo 3, Ozturk 3, Power 3, Wyke 3, Maguire 2 (1), Leadbitter 2, Morgan 1 (2), Gooch 1 (1), Grigg – (2), Dunne – (1), McGeady – (1)
League goals (80): Maja 15, McGeady 11, Cattermole 7, Maguire 7, Honeyman 6, Gooch 5, O'Nien 5, Grigg 4, Power 4, Wyke 4, Baldwin 3, Flanagan 2, Dunne 1, Matthews 1, Morgan 1, Sinclair 1, Sterling 1, Watmore 1, Opponents 1. **Play-off goals** (2): Maguire 1, Opponents 1
FA Cup goals (3): Gooch 1, Honeyman 1, McGeady 1. **League Cup goals**: None. **League Trophy goals** (16): Kimpioka 2, McGeady 2, Gooch 1, Grigg 1, Honeyman 1, Maguire 1, Maja 1, Morgan 1, Robson E 1, Sinclair 1, Watmore 1, Wyke 1, Opponents 2
Average home league attendance: 32,157. **Player of Year**: Aiden McGeady

WALSALL

Walsall flirted with the drop the previous season, but there was no escape this time after failing to build on a bright start. Former captain Martin O'Connor couldn't arrest the slide after taking over as interim manager with five matches remaining when Dean Keates was sacked following a 3-1 home loss to ten-man Oxford. Another defeat, by Accrington, came in O'Connor's first match in charge and points were also dropped against two more sides caught up in the division's mass relegation scramble, Southend and Wycombe. A ray of hope accompanied a 3-0 victory over promotion-chasing Peterborough. Instead, a goalless draw at Shrewsbury in the final fixture was not enough for survival. Walsall netted 15 points from the first seven games, rewarded with a place among the early pacemakers, and they were still in touch until late October. The slump started with a single win 12 going into the New Year. Andy Cook's hat-trick at Gillingham brought relief. But five successive defeats left his side facing an uphill struggle. Former Bristol Rovers manager Darrell Clarke took over in the summer.

Chambers A	1	Fitzwater J	21	Kinsella L	24 (7)
Cook A	34 (9)	Ginnelly J	18 (3)	Laird S	5 (2)
Devlin N	42 (1)	Gordon J	28 (9)	Leahy L	44
Dobson G	35 (4)	Guthrie J	41 (1)	Martin R	8
Dunn C	4	Ismail Z	22 (10)	Morris K	11 (6)
Edwards J	18 (2)	Jarvis M	8 (1)	Mussa O	- (1)
Ferrier M	25 (8)	Johnson C	7	Norman C	6 (3)

Isbourne I	27 (5)	Ronan C	4 (7)	Wilson K	5 (9)
Oteh A	4 (9)	Scarr D	17		
Roberts L	42	Taylor C	5 (5)		

League goals (49): Cook 13, Gordon 7, Ferrier 5, Ismail 3, Leahy 3, Osbourne 3, Devlin 2, Edwards 2, Ginnelly 2, Guthrie 2, Morris 2, Oteh 1, Scarr 1, Opponents 3
FA Cup goals (7)): Cook 3, Devlin 1. Ginnelly 1, Kinsella 1, Opponents 1. **League Cup goals** (6): Cook 1, Ferrier 1, Ginnelly 1, Ismail 1, Morris 1. **League Trophy goals** (7): Morris 2, Cook 1, Fitzwater 1, Gordon 1, Johnson 1, Kouhyar 0 1
Average home league attendance: 4,927. **Player of Year**: Andy Cook

WYCOMBE WANDERERS

Wycombe emerged from a relegation scramble involving ten teams with their League One status intact after a see-saw season. Gareth Ainsworth's promoted side overcame an uncomfortable first two months of the campaign to move away from the bottom four and within striking distance of a play-off place with six wins in eight matches. A mid-winter slump knocked them back before a stirring performance against Doncaster restored some momentum. Trailing 2-0, they pulled a goal back through Paris Cowan-Hall, levelled through Curtis Thompson on 90 minutes and won it four minutes into stoppage-time with Cowan-Hall's second. Wycombe then edged out Bristol Rovers and Plymouth to climb back into the top-half, but faltered again, this time falling back into the pack after a dozen games without a victory. But they held their nerve against two fellow-strugglers, with Adebayo Akinfenwa scoring twice in four minutes at Southend and Jason McCarthy delivering a sublime free-kick to see off Walsall – performances which brought up the 50-point mark.

Akinfenwa A	26 (10)	Gape D	41 (2)	Morris B	15 (4)
Allsop R	38	Harriman M	20 (4)	Onyedinma F	16 (5)
Bean M	7 (2)	Henderson S	3	Owens C	- (2)
Bloomfield M	22 (6)	Ingram M	1	Samuel A	26 (4)
Bolton L	4 (6)	Jacobson J	36	Saunders S	2 (2)
Charles D	5	Jombati S	31 (2)	Stewart A	16 (1)
Cowan-Hall P	15 (18)	Kashket S	11 (16)	Stockdale D	2
El-Abd A	34	Mackail-Smith C	13 (8)	Thompson C	33 (6)
Freeman N	18 (9)	Makaba-Makalamby Y	2 (1)	Tyson N	10 (9)
Frempah B	- (1)	McCarthy J	44	Williams R	15 (5)

League goals (55): Akinfenwa 8, Jacobson 7, Samuel 5, Cowan-Hall 4, Onyedinma 4, El-Abd 3, Kashket 3, Mackail-Smith 3, Morris 3, Bloomfield 2, McCarthy 2, Williams 2, Bean 1, Gape 1, Jombati 1, Thompson 1, Tyson 1, Opponents 4
FA Cup goals: None. **League Cup goals** (6): Akinfenwa 1, Cowan-Hall 1, Kashket 1, Saunders 1, Stewart 1, Williams 1. **League Trophy goals** (3): Kashket 2, Samuel 1
Average home league attendance: 5,389. **Player of Year**: Jason McCarthy

THE THINGS THEY SAY ...

'I might not be able to speak English, but I can speak about the 24 teams of the Championship' – **Marcelo Bielsa**, Leeds manager, admitting he sent a member of staff to watch every opponent in training.

'When you have jet-washed the jet-wash you realise you have been out of work long enough' – **Mick McCarthy** on his appointment as Republic of Ireland manager.

'When fear comes into performances, it's like losing the eye of the tiger' – **Sean Dyche**, Burnley manager, on his side's slump – and eventual improvement.

SKY BET LEAGUE TWO

BURY

Ryan Lowe's high-scoring side made an immediate return to League One amid acute financial problems at the club. His players had to contend with delays in wages being paid on time – and a second winding-up order for 'historical' debts – to finish a creditable runners-up to Lincoln. Nicky Maynard led the way as Bury scored four goals on six occasions to finish top of the division's scoring table with 82. It included a 4-3 victory over promotion rivals MK Dons after trailing 3-1 with 20 minutes remaining. A single win in the opening five fixtures gave way to big performances against Grimsby, Notts County, Macclesfield, Stevenage and Cheltenham, rewarded with a climb to fifth. Then, a run of 14 matches unbeaten, starting in the New Year, provided the foundation for a final push. It was undermined by nine goals conceded in successive defeats by Swindon, Cambridge and Carlisle in eight days. But two goals by Dom Telford sparked a return to winning ways against Colchester, they came from behind to beat Northampton and Danny Mayor's goal for a point in the penultimate fixture at Tranmere made sure of going up. Lowe left to manage Plymouth and several players moved on. Paul Wilkinson was appointed the new manager.

Adams J	- (1)	Dawson S	4 (1)	O'Connell E	18 (13)
Adams N	44 (2)	Hulme C	- (1)	O'Shea J	42 (2)
Aimson W	36 (1)	Lavery C	9 (14)	Omotayo G	2 (11)
Barjonas J	- (4)	Maynard N	34 (3)	Rossiter J	15 (1)
Beckford J	- (1)	Mayor D	38 (1)	Stokes C	36 (1)
Bunn H	- (1)	McFadzean C	36 (4)	Styles C	8 (8)
Cooney R	2 (7)	Miller T	3 (4)	Telford D	16 (22)
Dagnall C	12 (5)	Moore B	18 (18)	Thompson A	44
Danns N	28 (6)	Murphy J	46	Wharton S	15

League goals (82): Maynard 21, O'Shea 15, Mayor 8, Telford 6, Lavery 5, Moore 5, Aimson 4, Stokes 4, Adams N 2, Dagnall 2, Danns 2, O'Connell 2, Wharton 2, Omotayo 1, Rossiter 1, Thompson 1, Opponents 1

FA Cup goals (5): Moore 2, Mayor 1, O'Shea 1, Telford 1. **League Cup goals** (1): O'Connell. **League Trophy goals** (16): Telford 7, Mayor 3, Adams 1, Dagnall 1, Lavery 1, Maynard 1, Moore 1, Thompson 1

Average home league attendance: 4,044. **Player of Year:** Jay O'Shea

CAMBRIDGE UNITED

Cambridge finished in their lowest position since regaining Football League status in 2014 following £500,000 in budgets cuts ordered by Paul Barry, the owner. Barry, who took over in February 2018, said the club was 'living in a bubble' because of previous overspending. Two wins in first 14 games set the tone for the season. A modest improvement, lifting them out of the bottom two, was not enough for Joe Dunne, who was replaced by former Nottingham Forest and Hibernian manager Colin Calderwood. A 6-0 drubbing by MK Dons was followed by the team's best run, four wins in five games, which delivered sufficient points to guard against dropping back into relegation trouble. It was just as well. Despite a 3-0 away win over promotion-chasing Bury, achieved by goals from Alex Jones, David Amoo and George Maris, Cambridge failed to win any of their final seven home games, finishing fourth from bottom.

Jones A	5 (7)	Coulson H	6 (8)	Forde D	25
Amoo D	25 (18)	Darling H	12	Halliday B	37 (1)
Azeez A	12 (14)	Davies L	5 (1)	Hepburn-Murphy R	10 (6)
Brown J	40 (3)	Deegan G	40 (1)	Ibehre J	32 (4)
Carroll J	31 (1)	Doyle-Hayes J	4 (2)	John L	17 (5)
Corr B	1 (8)	Dunk H	15 (11)	Knowles T	- (3)

Lambe R................. 27 (5)	Mitov D......................21	Taft G 35 (2)
Lewis P................. 12 (11)	O'Neil L 15 (4)	Taylor G 39
Maris G..........................39	Osadebe E 1 (11)	Worman B................... - (1)

League goals (40): Brown 7, Amoo 5, Maris 5, Ibehre 4, Lewis 4, Lambe 3, Azeez 2, Hepburn-Murphy 2, Taft 2, Taylor 2, Jones 1, Corr 1, Deegan 1, Knowles 1
FA Cup goals (3): Ibehre 2, Maris 1. **League Cup goals** (1): Azeez 1. **League Trophy goals** (9): Azeez 5, Brown 1, Lambe 1, Maris 1, Osadebe 1
Average home league attendance: 4,366 **Player of Year**: Jeavni Brown

CARLISLE UNITED

Carlisle struck a purple patch midway through the season to raise hopes of a serious promotion challenge. They scored 20 goals in six successive victories, including a 6-0 drubbing of John Sheridan's former club Oldham on Boxing Day. But accompanying that run, which took them up to fifth, was the loss of Sheridan, who resigned after seven months in charge to become manager for the second time of Chesterfield, relegated from the Football League the previous season. Under Steven Pressley, formerly at Fleetwood and Coventry, Carlisle lost ground and were caught up in a scramble for the final play-off place involving five teams. Their ten men overcame Bury 3-2 with an 89th minute Hallam Hope goal after Mike Jones was sent off. Then, Jones scored the only goal against eventual champions Lincoln. But those points, along with a 4-2 victory over Crawley in the final home game, were not enough, Carlisle finished three points adrift of Newport, whose greater consistency over the final stretch proved decisive.

Adewusi S.................. - (1)	Gillesphrey M 20 (4)	Miller G.................... 17 (1)
Bennett R 13 (8)	Glendon G 5 (11)	Nadesan A................. 23 (2)
Brown M..................... - (1)	Gnahoua A .... - (1)	O'Hare C 16
Campbell A.............. 2 (11)	Grainger D..................23	Parkes T................... 37 (2)
Collin A 41 (1)	Grant P 4	Scougall S................ 10 (5)
Cullen M.................. 3 (6)	Hope H 39 (1)	Simpson C................. 1 (7)
Devitt J................ 32 (3)	Jones M 19 (5)	Slater R 24 (1)
Etuhu K................ 34 (5)	Kennedy J .... - (6)	Sowerby J................. 22 (3)
Fryer J.........................5	Liddle G................ 38 (1)	Thomas N............. 11 (5)
Gerrard A......................41	McCarron L............. 3 (13)	Yates J 23

League goals (67): Hope 14, Devitt 11, Nadesan 8, Yates 6, Grainger 5, Bennett 4, Sowerby 4, Thomas 4, O'Hare 3, Slater 2, Jones 1, Liddle 1, Miller 1, Parkes 1, Scougall 1, Simpson 1
FA Cup goals (1): Devitt 1. **League Cup goals** (1): Hope 1. **League Trophy goals** (5): Gillesphey 1 Glendon 1, Nadesan 1, Sowerby 1, Yates 1
Average home league attendance: 4,712. **Player of Year**: Adam Collin

CHELTENHAM TOWN

Michael Duff experienced a tough start to his first managerial appointment after leaving Burnley's coaching staff for the club where he spent eight years as a player, winning the FA Trophy, National League title and promotion via the League Two play-offs. Duff had to wait two months for his first league win after replacing Gary Johnson, sacked after a single point from the opening four fixtures. It came with two goals from Luke Varney in a 3-0 success away to Notts County and proved the start of a nine-match run which took his new side from second from bottom to comfortably clear of the drop zone on the back of 18 points accumulated. Another productive sequence, ten goals scored when completing the double over County, as well as defeating Northampton and Crewe offered the opportunity of a move into mid-table. But a win over Swindon aside, Cheltenham's run-in to the end of the season proved disappointing and they had to be satisfied with 16th, an improvement one place on 2018.

ddai A	10 (11)	Duku I	6 (5)	McAlinden L	4 (2)
lcock K	6 (2)	Field T	5 (1)	Mooney K	3 (6)
tangana N	25 (1)	Flinders S	46	Mullins J	18 (1)
aldwin A	3 (1)	Forster J	23 (3)	Pring C	7 (1)
arnett T	19 (11)	Hussey C	31 (3)	Raglan C	19
ingham R	4 (6)	Jones S	6 (6)	Thomas C	26 (6)
ower M	1 (1)	Debayo J	4 (1)	Tillson J	12 (12)
oyle W	36 (2)	Kalala K	1 (6)	Tozer B	34 (3)
room R	33 (6)	Lloyd G	3 (4)	Varney L	30 (5)
ements C	26 (4)	Long S	4 (1)	Waters B	10 (8)
awson K	22 (10)	Maddox J	29 (9)		

eague goals (57): Varney 14, Barnett 6, Thomas 6, Boyle 4, Dawson 4, Waters 4, Atangana 2, room 2, Clements 2, Jones 2, Raglan 2, Duku 1, Forster 1, Hussey 1, Lloyd 1, Maddox 1, ooney 1, Tozer 1, Opponents 2

A Cup goals (3): Addai 2, Barnett 1. **League Cup goals** (2): Broom 1, Thomas 1. **League Trophy als** (10): Maddox 3, Boyle 2, Addai 1, Broom 1, Clements 1, Dawson 1, Mooney 1

verage home league attendance: 3,134. **Player of Year**: Luke Varney

OLCHESTER UNITED

o near, yet so far. Colchester were within touching distance of a place in the play-offs with an utstanding performance against champions Lincoln in the final match of the regular season at ncil Bank. Two goals from Sammie Szmodics and one from Brennan Dickenson – all in the st half – delivered a 3-0 victory which put them on course to overtake Exeter and Newport for venth spot. But while it left them ahead of Exeter on goal difference, the Welsh side equalised ter 87 minutes at Morecambe to finish a single point ahead. It was the second time in three asons they had gone so close, having finished a point behind Blackpool in 2017. This time, lchester spent most of the campaign in the loading group before faltering approaching the n-in and losing five games out of six. Frank Nouble scored the only goal of the game against imsby, then Szmodics was on the mark after 95 seconds against MK Dons and Frankie Kent ded a second to resurrect their chances of going up.

arnes D	22	Kensdale O	1 (1)	Roberts C	- (3)
ilvers N	- (2)	Kent F	39 (1)	Ross E	2 (1)
llins A	1 (6)	Lapslie T	34 (1)	Saunders S	5 (1)
mloy B	5 (8)	Mandron M	16 (25)	Senior C	37 (5)
ckenson B	19 (23)	Millor T	(1)	Stevenson D	11 (3)
stman T	22 (9)	Norris L	21 (13)	Szmodics S	43
sa A	8 (6)	Nouble F	42 (1)	Vincent-Young K	38 (2)
dmartin R	22	Ogedi-Uzokwe J	(1)	Wright D	4 (5)
ndoh R	- (4)	Pell H	30 (1)		
ckson R	46	Prosser L	38		

ague goals (65): Szmodics 14, Nouble 9, Norris 7, Pell 6, Senior 6, Kent 4, Dickenson 3, stman 3, Vincent-Young 3, Eisa 2, Jackson 2, Mandron 2, Prosser 2, Lapslie 1, Opponents 1

Cup goals: None. **League Cup goals** (2): Norris 1, Szmodics 1. **League Trophy goals** (3): llins 1, Kent 1, Pell 1

erage home league attendance: 3,522. **Player of Year**: Frankie Kent

RAWLEY TOWN

strong finish to the season removed nagging doubts about being sucked into a relegation uggle. Crawley were comfortably clear of trouble and looking to consolidate in mid-table ter back-to-back wins over Colchester and Cheltenham early in the New Year. But the next

15 matches yielded just two more victories, leaving them on the periphery of the drop zone. The sequence included a 6-1 drubbing at Crewe, followed immediately by defeats by Lincoln, Morecambe and Forest Green. Filipe Morais, with the only goal of the game against Yeovil restored stability and was on the mark again in the 3-1 defeat of promotion-minded Exeter alongside Reece Gregor-Cox, who opened his account for the club with a brace. Gabriele Cioffi's team then finished on a high by beating play-off qualifiers Tranmere, although 19th place represented a fall of five places on the previous season. Former Birmingham coach Cioffi came in when Harry Kewell took over as Notts County's new manager, an appointment lasting ten weeks before his dismissal by a club on the way out of the league.

Allarakhia T................. - (5)	Grego-Cox R 15 (13)	Payne J 24 (3)
Bulman D 29 (7)	Maguire J 24 (3)	Poloen D 21 (9)
Camara P............... 34 (11)	McNerney J 26 (3)	Randall M 2 (4)
Connolly M....................23	Meite I .... - (2)	Sesay D...................16 (2)
Dallison T 19	Milsom R 2 (1)	Smith J 3 (1)
Doherty J 12 (6)	Morais F................... 31 (3)	Vincelot R 12
Francomb G 39 (2)	Morris G........................46	Willock M 7 (4)
Galach B.................... - (1)	N'Gala B 12 (1)	Young L....................34 (4)
Gambin L................. 21 (5)	Nathaniel-George A. 15 (15)	
German R .... - (4)	Palmer O................. 39 (1)	

League goals (51): Palmer 14, Morais 8, Nathaniel-George 6, Poleon 5, Bulman 3, Camara 3, Gambin 3, Grego-Cox 2, Maguire 1, McNerney 1, Payne 1, Smith 1, Young 1, Opponents 2
FA Cup goals (3: Palmer 2, Opponents 1. **League Cup goals (1):** Connolly 1. **League Trophy goals (2):** N'Gala 1, Poleon 1
Average home league attendance: 2,290. Player of Year: Glenn Morris

CREWE ALEXANDRA

Crewe's impressive record at Gresty Road delivered a top-half finish to continue the club progress since being relegated in 2016. No team in the division matched their 15 home victories and only runners-up Bury exceeded their 45 goals scored. The pattern was set in the opening fixture – a 6-0 win over Morecambe. They scored four times in seven minutes to defeat Crawley 6-1 after falling behind and in the final fixture dented Forest Green's chances of automatic promotion as Charlie Kirk goals in the 87th and 89th minutes brought a rousing 4-3 success. That rounded off a run of maximum points from four matches, with 11 goals scored, following disappointing local derby performance at Port Vale (0-1). The sequence lifted Crewe from 15th to 12th. Away form left plenty to be desired – the joint lowest record alongside Vale of 15 scored. included a 6-0 mauling at Colchester, one of 13 matches without a goal on their travels.

Ainley C................... 35 (8)	Lowery T 6 (9)	Reilly L 1 (2)
Bowery J................. 38 (6)	Miller S.................. 13 (16)	Richards D 4
Dale O .... - (16)	Ng P 44	Sass-Davies B.................2
Finney O 4 (13)	Nicholls A 7 (14)	Sinclair A...................4 (4)
Garratt B........................38	Nolan E 32 (1)	Sterry J 1
Green P 25 (1)	O'Connor K 5 (1)	Walker B ....- (1)
Hunt N 18 (4)	Pickering H 31 (1)	Whelan C 16
Jaaskelainen W.................4	Porter C 27 (13)	Wintle R......................46
James J 33 (5)	Ray G................... 31 (1)	
Kirk C................... 40 (2)	Raynes M 1 (4)	

League goals (60): Porter 13, Kirk 11, Bowery 8, Ainley 6, Jones 5, Miller 3, Nicholls 2, Ray 2, Sinclair 2, Dale 1, Green 1, Lowery 1, Nolan 1, Whelan 1, Wintle 1, Opponents 2
FA Cup goals: None. **League Cup goals (1):** Wintle 1. **League Trophy goals (6):** Nicholls 2, Porter 2, Bowery 1, Jones 1
Average home league attendance: 3,762. **Player of Year:** Perry Ng

EXETER CITY

Former club captain Matt Taylor led his side to within striking distance of a third successive play-off place in his first season as manager. They were in pole possession with four matches remaining, four points clear in seventh place and boasting a goal difference superior to all their rivals. But Exeter faltered at the final hurdles, notably in a 3-1 home defeat by lowly Crawley which enabled the chasing pack to crowd in. A point away to one of them, Stevenage, kept their noses ahead and there was still all to play for after Ryan Bowman, signed as the replacement for leading scorer Jayden Stockley in the winter transfer window, scored the winner against Oldham in the penultimate fixture. But despite controlling the final match at Forest Green, Exeter could do no better than a goalless draw and finished alongside Colchester and Stevenage on 70 points, one behind fast-finishing Newport who went forward to the knockout stage. Taylor had succeeded long-serving Paul Tisdale, who took his new club, MK Dons, straight back to League One, despite a 3-1 defeat on his return to St James Park.

Abrahams T	4 (12)	Hartridge A	2 (1)	Pym C	43
Boateng H	22 (6)	Holmes L	29 (5)	Stockley J	24 (1)
Bowman R	13 (5)	Jay M	10 (8)	Sweeney P	42 (1)
Brown J	3	Law N	39 (4)	Taylor J	46
Brown T	6 (2)	Martin A	20 (2)	Tillson J	13 (8)
Collins A	23 (3)	Martin L	21 (15)	Williams R	6 (4)
Croll L	11 (2)	Moxey D	37 (1)	Wilson K	12 (5)
Forte J	18 (9)	O'Shea D	26 (1)	Wilson D	3 (7)
Hamon J	3 (1)	Ogbene C	3 (11)	Woodman C	28 (4)

League goals (60): Stockley 16, Law 10, Bowman 5, Forte 5, Jay 4, Sweeney 4, Holmes 3, Martin A 3, Moxey 3, Taylor 3, Abrahams 1, Boateng 1, Collins 1, Martin L 1
FA Cup goals (2): Abrahams 1, Tillson 1. League Cup goals (1): Brown T 1. League Trophy goals (4): Forte 3 Randall J 1
Average home league attendance: 4,418. Player of Year: Nicky Law

FOREST GREEN ROVERS

The club hailed as 'the greenest in the world' lost the chance of a second promotion in three years after red cards in both legs of their play-off semi-final. Gavin Gunning was dismissed for kicking out at Jay Harris after 15 minutes of the first leg which Tranmere won 1-0. Carl Winchester received a controversial second yellow after 67 minutes of the return at New Lawn which ended 1-1. Manager Mark Cooper felt 'there was nothing in it' and commended his side for going so close. Forest Green defeated Tranmere in the 2017 National League Final to reach the Football League for the first time and beat them twice in this regular campaign. The second of those victories came during a run of 12 points gained from four successive matches in April, leaving them with a chance of going up automatically. But after leading 3-2 in the penultimate fixture at Crewe through Reece Brown, Junior Mondal and Christian Doidge, they lost 4-3 to goals in the 07th and 09th minute. Previously, the Gloucestershire team had been the last in the league to lose a game, winning four and drawing eight before conceding a stoppage-time goal in the 13th to go down 2-1 at Northampton.

Archibald T	4 (10)	James L	31 (4)	Rawson F	38
Brown R	43 (2)	Liddle B	- (2)	Reid R	20 (9)
Campbell T	10 (8)	McCoulsky S	3 (10)	Sanchez R	17
Collins L	6 (5)	McGinley N	34 (4)	Shephard L	37 (2)
Digby P	30 (7)	Mills J	44	Ward L	11 (1)
Doidge C	24 (1)	Mondal A	8 (10)	Williams G	25 (13)
Godwin-Malife U	3 (2)	Montgomery J	18	Winchester C	44 (1)
Grubb D	13 (15)	Morris R	2 (2)	Worthington M	3 (6)
Gunning G	37 (5)	Pearce I	1 (3)		

Play-offs – appearances: Brown 2, Doidge 2, Grubb 2, McGinley 2, Mills 2, Mondal 2, Rawson 2, Shephard 2, Ward 2, Winchester 2, Collins 1 (1), Gunning 1, Williams – (2), Digby – (1), James – (1) McCoulsky – (1)
League goals (68): Doidge 14, Brown 11, Reid 7, Williams 7, Shephard 5, Mills 4, Campbell 3, Grubb 3, Mondal 3, Winchester 3, Archibald 1, Collins 1, Digby 1, Gunning 1, Morris 1, Worthington 1, Opponents 2. **Play-offs – goals** (1): Mills 1
FA Cup goals: None. **League Cup goals** (3): Campbell 1, Grubb 1, Winchester 1. **League Trophy goals** (6): Grubb 2, Pearce 2, Campbell 1, Williams 1
Average home league attendance: 2,701. **Player of Year**: Reece Brown

GRIMSBY TOWN

Disciplinary problems dogged Grimsby for the second successive season. They accumulated ten red cards in all competitions, after eight in the previous campaign, but still picked up 12 points in league matches when they were down to ten men to avoid being drawn into a relegation struggle. A streak of resilience was also evident after losing Andrew Fox in the third minute of an FA Cup third round tie against Crystal Palace at Selhurst Park. Backs-to-the-wall defending kept the Premier League team at bay until the 86th minute when Jordan Ayew gave Palace a 1-0 win. Grimsby were second from bottom after a single success in the opening ten fixtures and were still finding it hard going with the approach of winter. A revival brought five wins out of six, among them 5-2 against Tranmere and 4-0 against Notts County, and they reached the top-half of the table with six goals in successive matches against Newport and Yeovil. Then it was back to grinding out results as 13 games passed with no more than one goal scored in any of them before a 2-0 success against Crewe in the final game confirmed 17th place, one better than 2018.

Burrell R .... - (4)	Grayson J 6 (2)	Rose A 2 (14)
Cardwell H 11 (8)	Hall-Johnson R 23 (5)	Rose M 15 (10)
Clifton H 30 (9)	Hendrie L 40 (1)	Russell S 3 (2)
Collins D 28 (2)	Hessenthaler J 39 (5)	Thomas W 33 (3)
Cook J 18 (6)	Hooper JJ 12 (3)	Vernam C 19 (16)
Davis H 33 (2)	McKeown J 43	Welsh J 9 (4)
Dennis K 7 (6)	Ohman L 12 (1)	Whitmore A 25 (6)
Dixon P 3	Pollock M .... - (2)	Woolford M 25 (10)
Embleton E 26 (1)	Pringle B 11 (4)	Wright M 1 (1)
Famewo A 7 (3)	Ring S 14 (1)	
Fox A 11 (1)	Robles L .... - (1)	

League goals (45): Thomas 11, Cook 4, Davis 4, Embleton 3, Rose M 3, Vernam 3, Woolford 3, Clifton 2, Grayson 2, Hendrie 2, Cardwell 1, Dennis 1, Hooper 1, Rose A 1, Whitmore 1, Opponents 3
FA Cup goals (5): Vernam 2, Clifton 1, Embleton 1, Thomas 1. **League Cup goals**: None. **League Trophy goals** (4): Cook 1, Hessenthaler 1, Hooper 1, Rose M 1
Average home league attendance: 4,430. **Player of Year**: James McKeown

LINCOLN CITY

Manager of the Year Danny Cowley led Lincoln to a second title in three seasons on the back of a record run which confirmed them as the division's outstanding side. They dictated the top of the table from the start, with five wins and a draw from the opening six fixtures, and went on to see off the challenge, in turn, from Bury, Mansfield and MK Dons. Four players, Neal Eardley, Jason Shackell, Harry Toffolo and John Akinde were in the PFA Team of the Year, with nine of leading marksman Akinde's goals coming from the penalty spot. His ninth put Lincoln on the way to a 2-0 win over MK Dons to end the home team's chance of closing the gap. They made certain of going up in a 1-1 draw against Cheltenham which extended the record sequence to 19 matches. It ended with defeat at Carlisle next time out. Three days later, a 0-0 draw against Tranmere linched the title. Celebrations fell a little flat with a 3-0 home defeat by Colchester in the final xture, completing a run of five without a victory to close with. But overall this was an impressive erformance by a club clearly on the way up.

.kinde J 41 (4)	Gordon K .... - (6)	Roberts J .... - (5)
.nderson H 39 (4)	Smith G 16	Rowe D 12 (5)
.ndrade B 39 (3)	Green M 2 (17)	Shackell J 33 (1)
ngol L .... (2)	Luque J 0 (1)	Toffolo II 46
.olger C 12 (5)	McCartan S 23 (15)	Vickers J 18
.ostwick M 45	Mensah B .... - (4)	Waterfall L 1
.hapman E 2 (3)	O'Connor M 31 (8)	Wharton S 5 (6)
.ardley H 43	O'Hara M 14 (3)	Wilson J 4 (7)
.recklington L 23 (4)	Pett T 33 (11)	
.ilks M 12	Rhead M 12 (22)	

eague goals (73): Akinde 15, Andrade 10, McCartan 7, Anderson 5, Rowe 4, Shackell 4, recklington 3, Pett 3, Toffolo 3, Bostwick 2, Eardley 2, Gordon 2, Green 2, O'Connor 2, Bolger , O'Hara 1, Rhead 1, Wharton 1, Wilson 1. Opponents 4
A Cup goals (6): Akinde 1, Anderson 1, Andrade 1, Bostwick 1, Pett 1, Rhead 1. **League Cup oals** (5): Akinde 1, Green 1, Luque 1, O'Connor 1, Shackell 1. **League Trophy goals** (6): Green , Anderson 1, McCombe J 1, Rhead 1
verage home league attendance: 9,006. **Player of Year**: Michael Bostwick

MACCLESFIELD TOWN

.ol Campbell came through what he described as 'a baptism of fire' to keep Macclesfield in e Football League against all the odds. The former Tottenham, Arsenal and England defender ompleted a successful first step into management on a nerve-shredding final day of the season. is side, starting out two points clear of Notts County, fell behind at home to Cambridge. County .en went ahead at Swindon, but Macclesfield regained the initiative with Elliott Durrell's qualiser and were safe when their rivals conceded three goals in the final 20 minutes at the ounty Ground. Campbell rated the achievement as 'up there' with the best of his playing career. .e took over approaching the midway point of the campaign when Mark Yates was sacked with .e club on the way to a English record-equalling run of 36 successive games without a victory 13 this season and 23 up to the end of their relegation from the league in 2012. Utilising his .ast experience and a network of contacts in the game, he engineered seven wins, two of them .way from home against County and Yeovil, the other side caught up in the scramble against .elegation. Victory over Exeter took them out of the bottom two for the first time, while David .itzpatrick's winner at Port Vale in the penultimate fixture proved priceless.

.rthur K 17 (4)	Jules Z 13 (1)	Ponticelli J 2 (1)
.abi B 1 (2)	Kelleher F 41 (1)	Rose M 39 (1)
.issett N 11 (8)	Lloyd R 11 (2)	Smith H 30 (9)
.ameron N 25	Lowe K 11 (2)	Stephens B 18 (4)
.ole R 11 (7)	Marsh T 18 (7)	Taylor R 9
.emetriou S 1 (1)	Martis L 1 (5)	Vincenti P 9 (7)
.urrell E 16 (1)	Maycock C 21 (6)	Welch-Hayes M 13 (10)
.vans C 10 (4)	Napa M 8 (7)	Whitaker D 16 (6)
.itzpatrick 40	Ntambwe B 6 (2)	Wilson S 21 (12)
.rimes J 13	O'Hara K 37	
.odgkiss J 17	Pearson J 20 (3)	

eague goals (48): Wilson 10, Smith 9, Rose 5, Durrell 4, Arthur 3, Fitzpatrick 3, Whitaker 3, .ameron 2, Marsh 2, Cole 1, Evans 1, Grimes 1, Kelleher 1, Pearson 1, Stephens 1, Vincenti 1

FA Cup goals (1): Stephens 1. League Cup goals (4): Grimes 1, Kelleher 1, Smith 1, Whittaker 1
League Trophy goals (7): Rose 2, Arthur 1, Blissett 1, Stephens 1, Vincenti 1, Wilson 1
Average home league attendance: 2,316. Player of Year: Kieran O'Hara

MANSFIELD TOWN

A season that promised so much fell flat in the final three weeks and ended with the sacking of manager David Flitcroft following defeat in the play-offs. His side looked a solid bet for automatic promotion after an unbeaten run of 17 matches going into the New Year was rewarded with third place. The sequence ended with a 3-2 defeat at Carlisle, followed immediately by a home loss to lowly Yeovil. But Mansfield were back on track with ten points from the next four games, then scored four against Cheltenham, Exeter and Morecambe to move into the runners-up spot behind Lincoln. With everything to play for, they lost momentum, beaten at Oldham, going down at home to Stevenage and losing a winner-takes-all final match against MK Dons, who scored the only goal in the second minute. An early strike by CJ Hamilton gave them the upper hand in the first leg of the semi-final at Newport. It was cancelled out seven minutes from the end of normal time, the return match ended goalless and Mansfield missed out when leading scorer Tyler Walker, on loan from Nottingham Forest, has his spot-kick saved in the penalty shoot-out. Flitcroft was replaced by academy manager John Dempster.

Ajose N...................... 8 (2)	Hakeem Z.................... - (1)	Rose D.................. 13 (21)
Atkinson W 4 (14)	Hamilton C....................46	Smith J 12
Benning M................ 44 (1)	Jones G................. 12 (3)	Sterling-James O..........- (1)
Bishop N................... 43 (1)	Khan O................. 15 (7)	Sweeney R 37 (1)
Butcher C 2 (10)	Logan C 17	Tomlinson W.............. 8 (4)
Davies C 5 (9)	MacDonald A............ 13 (8)	Turner B..................... 4 (4)
Elsnik T................... 12 (7)	Mellis J 33 (8)	Walker T.................. 43 (1)
Gibbens L.........................1	Olejnik B........................17	White H 18 (1)
Graham J .... - (8)	Pearce K 46	
Grant J 15 (2)	Preston M................ 38 (1)	

Play-offs – appearances: Hamilton 2, Jones 2, Logan 2, MacDonald 2, Mellis 2, Pearce 2, Rose 2, Sweeney 2, Turner 2, Walker 2, Bishop 1, Tomlinson 1, Benning – (2), Ajose – (1), Atkinson – (1), Graham – (1)
League goals (69): Walker 22, Hamilton 11, Grant 4, Pearce 4, Rose 4, Benning 3, Bishop 3, Elsnik 3, Mellis 3, Preson 3, Ajose 2, Davies 2, Khan 2, Atkinson 1, MacDonald 1, Sweeney 1
Play-offs – goals (1): Hamilton 1
FA Cup goals (1): Hamilton 1. League Cup goals (7): Walker 3, Bishop 1, Hamilton 1, Khan 1, Rose 1. League Trophy goals (7): Butcher 2, Benning 1, Blake 1, Elsnik 1, Mellis 1, Walker 1.
Average home league attendance: 4,897. Player of Year: Tyler Walker

MILTON KEYNES DONS

Paul Tisdale's side flourished, faded, then found their touch again went in mattered. In his first season in charge, the former long-serving Exeter manager led them back to League One following a second relegation in three seasons. Dons went into the final day winner-takes-all match against Mansfield with both sides disputing the third automatic promotion place on 76 points. Dons, who made an inferior goal difference, made a flying start when David Wheeler headed in Dean Lewington's corner after two minutes and successfully defended the lead after strong second half pressure which extended to eight minutes of stoppage-time because of two injuries. With Kieran Agard and Chuks Aneke one of the divison's most productive strike partnership, they were into the New Year disputing the leadership alongside Lincoln after a 6-0 victory over Cambridge. But the challenge faded with a 4-3 defeat at Bury, where a 3-1 lead was surrendered in the final 20 minutes. Five defeats in six matches forced Dons out of the top-six before Aneke's 88th minute winner at Newport, followed by a sparkling second-half performance for a 3-2 success at Carlisle, put them back in the frame.

gard K 40 (3)	Harley R 10 (4)	Pawlett P 3 (4)
neke C 26 (12)	Healey R 15 (3)	Simpson R 2 (19)
songanyi D 1 (2)	Hesketh J 13 (3)	Sow O 1 (7)
audry M 4 (1)	Houghton J 39 (5)	Walker S ....- (7)
rittain C 28 (4)	Lewington D 46	Walsh J 28 (2)
argill B 28 (1)	Martin R 18	Watson R 13 (9)
sse O 17 (9)	McGrandles C 22 (3)	Wheeler D 14 (5)
Ath L 3 (12)	Moore S 6	Williams G................27 (3)
lbey A 39	Moore-Taylor J 22 (1)	
ancox M 1	Nicholls L......................40	

ague goals (71): Agard 20, Aneke 17, Healey 8, Wheeler 4, Gilbey 3, Cisse 2, Harley 2, esketh 2, Houghton 2, Simpson 2, Walsh 2, Brittain 1, Lewington 1, Martin 1, McGrandles 1, oore-Taylor 1, Sow 1, Opponents 1
A Cup goals (1): Agard 1. **League Cup goals (3):** Asonganyi 1, Watson 1, Opponents 1. **League ophy goals (5):** Aneke 2, Agard 1, Hancox 1, Healey 1
erage home league attendance: 8,224. **Player of Year:** Alex Gilbey

ORECAMBE

r most clubs, an 18th place finish would not be acceptable. For Jim Bentley's side, it was mething of a relief after the previous season's near miss when relegation was avoided on goal fference only. Even so, it took until well into the second half of the campaign before Bentley, ngest-serving manager in the four divisions, was able lead them to safety. Morecambe kicked f with a 5-0 drubbing at Crewe, one of seven defeats in the opening eight fixtures. Then, after arting to put points on the board, they went eight without a win to share worries about the drop th Notts County, Macclesfield and Yeovil. The tide eventually turned when Aaron Collins scored e winner at Port Vale eight minutes after coming off the bench – and his team left their rivals sort it out themselves. The win was one of four in six games, including seven goals scored ainst promotion-contenders Forest Green and MK Dons. It took them nine points clear and that vantage was increased by the biggest win, 4-0 against Cheltenham, in the final home fixture.

ennett R 13 (3)	Kenyon A 24 (8)	Oswell J 7 (10)
ownsword T .... - (1)	Lavelle S.....................31	Piggott J....................... 1 (5)
llins A 11 (4)	Leitch-Smith AJ 22 (3)	Roche B..........................20
nian L 39 (4)	Mandeville L............. 28 (14)	Sinclair J.....................(1)
anston J................ 30 (5)	McKay P 2 (5)	Sutton R 14
lby S...........................(2)	Gomes C 7 (8)	Thompson G 1 (4)
ison K 25 (18)	Mills Z 38	Tutte A......................12 (6)
eming A................ 15 (4)	Mingoia P 14 (2)	Wildig A....................24 (2)
alstoad M.................26	Oates R 22 (9)	Yarney J 20 (1)
dley B.........................1	Old S 37 (2)	
gne L 1 (1)	Oliver V 21 (9)	

ague goals (54): Collins 8, Ellison 7, Leitch-Smith 6, Oates 6, Bennett 5, Cranston 4, Oliver 4, Mandeville 3, Old 2, Tutte 2, Fleming 1, Kenyon 1, Lavelle 1, Mills 1, Oswell 1, Wildig 1, ponents 1
A Cup goals: None. **League Cup goals (1):** Mandeville 1. **League Trophy goals (3):** Oliver 1, well 1, Piggott 1
erage home league attendance: 2,033. **Player of Year:** Zak Mills

EWPORT COUNTY

marathon season in league and cup ended in heartbreak with the finishing line in sight. ke Flynn's side seemed to have overcome a second yellow card for captain Mark O'Brien in the 89th minute of the Play-off Final against Tranmere. They protected a goalless scoreline in extra-time and might have had a penalty when joint leading scorer Jamille Matt went down under the challenge of Emmanuel Monthe. But their spirit was broken in the 119th minute by a Connor Jennings header which took their opponents into League Two. It proved unlucky 13 for Newport, who were on an unbeaten 12-match run after qualifying in seventh place, then defeating Mansfield on penalties in the two-leg semi-final. Matt's 87th minute goal for a 1-1 draw in the final regular game at Morecambe meant they edged out Colchester, Exeter and Stevenage by a point. Newport had lost ground during eye-catching FA Cup performances which accounted for Leicester and Middlesbrough and kept Manchester City at bay for 45 minutes before City took a grip on the fifth round tie to win 4-1. Along with League Cup and League Trophy ties, Newport's campaign stretched to 62 matches.

Amond P	43 (2)	Franks F	25	Pipe D	16 (3
Azeez A	3 (9)	Harris M	5 (11)	Poole R	20
Bakinson T	26 (4)	Hornby-Forbes T	13 (1)	Pring C	1 (6
Bennett S	36 (2)	Kennedy B	7 (3)	Randall-Hurren W	- (1
Butler D	45	Labadie J	10 (3)	Semenyo A	12 (9
Cooper C	4 (5)	Marsh-Brown K	3 (13)	Sheehan J	21 (12
Crofts A	5 (4)	Matt J	36 (7)	Townsend N	3
Day J	43	McKirdy H	2 (10)	Willmott R	29 (2
Demetriou M	45	Neufville V	1		
Dolan M	26 (6)	O'Brien M	26 (8)		

Play-offs – appearances: Amond 3, Bennett 3, Butler 3, Day 3, Demetriou 3, O'Brien 3, Matt 3, Poole 3, Sheehan 3, Willmott 3, Labadie 2 (1), Dolan 1 (2), Azeez – (3), Bakinson – (1), Crofts – (1), Marsh-Brown – (1), McKirdy – (1)
League goals (59): Amond 14, Matt 14, Demetriou 4, Butler 3, Franks 3, Semenyo 3, Bennett 2, Dolan 2, Harris 2, O'Brien 2, Willmott 2, Azeez 1, Bakinson 1, Kennedy 1, Marsh-Brown 1, McKirdy 1, Pring 1, Sheehan 1, Opponents 1. **Play-offs – goals** (1): Amond 1
FA Cup goals (12): Amond 5, Matt 3, Butler 1, Dolan 1, Willmott 1, Opponents 1. **League Cup goals (4)**: Amond 2 Matt 1, Samenyo 1. **League Trophy goals (6)**: Matt 2, Semenyo 2, Amond 1, Harris 1
Average home league attendance: 3,409. **Player of Year**: Padraig Amond

NORTHAMPTON TOWN

A dreadful start to the season ruled out any prospect of an immediate return to League Northampton had a single victory to show from the first 12 matches, costing Dean Austin his job – the fifth manager to leave since the League Two title win in 2016. Keith Curle, former in charge of Carlisle, replaced him and made a good start with 14 points from the first seven matches. Three of them came over Macclesfield, where a 5-0 victory represented the club's biggest away from home since 1987. It featured a hat-trick by Matt Crooks, who was sold to Rotherham during the winter transfer window. By then, Northampton were comfortably clear of the relegation zone, helped by a 3-0 victory over Curle's old team. They made one appearance in the top half of the table after successive wins over Stevenage, Crewe, Exeter and Newport, but couldn't hold on to it and finished 15th, having closed with a satisfying 5-2 success at Oldham, where leading scorer Andy Williams was on the mark twice.

Barnett L	4	Cox G	4 (1)	Hughes R	1
Bowditch D	9 (11)	Crooks M	19 (2)	McWilliams S	21 (4
Bridge J	17 (11)	Elsnik T	4 (5)	Morias J	7 (12
Buchanan D	37 (2)	Facey S	21 (2)	O'Toole J-J	24 (7
Goode C	17	Foley S	33 (3)	Odofin H	10 (2
Cornell D	46	Hoskins S	40 (2)	Pierre A	4

Pollock S 4 (1)	Sordell M 5 (3)	Waters B 5 (10)
Powell D 17 (18)	Taylor A 32 (1)	Williams A 26 (13)
Powell J 6 (4)	Turnbull J 30 (1)	Williams J 6 (4)
Roberts M .... - (3)	Van Veen K 20 (5)	

League goals (64): Williams A 12, Van Veen 7, Morias 6, Pierre 6, Powell D 6, Crooks 5, Hoskins 5, Bowditch 3, O'Toole 3, Bridge 2, Foley 2, Powell J 2, Waters 2, Elsnik 1, Opponents 2
FA Cup goals (2): Bridge 1, Van Veen 1. **League Cup goals** (1): Hoskins 1. **League Trophy goals** (6): Pierre 2, Van Veen 2, Crooks 1, Hoskins 1
Average home league attendance: 5,100. **Player of Year:** Aaron Pierre

NOTTS COUNTY

Plenty of long-established clubs have lost their Football League status since relegation from the game's fourth tier was introduced in 1987. But none will have found it as bruising as Notts County, the oldest professional side in the world, after 157 years in existence. County started as one of the favourites for promotion after reaching the play-offs in 2018. They finished second from bottom on a nerve-shredding final day at Swindon, where salvation beckoned then disappeared in a 3-1 defeat. Three young managers shared their demise. Kevin Nolan, who achieved fifth place in the previous campaign and reshaped his squad this time with ten summer signings, was sacked after a single point and 13 goals conceded in the opening five matches. Harry Kewell, who left Crawley to replace him, was fired ten weeks into a three-year contract following seven league and cup games without a win. In came Neal Ardley, 11 days after parting company with AFC Wimbledon, followed by seven signings in the winter transfer window. Back-to-back wins over Forest Green and Mansfield offered some comfort. So did six goals in away games against Carlisle and Stevenage. But his side were already in too deep and went into the last round of fixtures two points adrift of Macclesfield. While their rivals trailed against Cambridge, County led through a Kane Hemmings penalty at the County Ground. Swindon then scored three in the final 20 minutes and the other scoreline didn't matter. Ardley observed the old adage that the table does not lie, admitting 'We deserved to go down'.

Alessandra I 17 (9)	Gomis V 5 (5)	Palmer A 1
Barclay D 12 (1)	Hawkridge T 2 (2)	Patching W 3 (3)
Bird P 8 (4)	Hemmings K 30 (6)	Rose M 17
Boldewijn F 33 (3)	Hewitt E 23 (2)	Schofield R 17
Brisley S 17 (3)	Husin N 6 (8)	Stead J 30 (8)
Davies K 6 (1)	Jones D 13	Stubbs C 17
Denis K 13 (11)	Kellett A 4 (7)	Thomas N 14 (11)
Doyle M 17	Mackail-Smith C 11 (5)	Crawford T 1 (3)
Duffy R 17 (2)	Milsom R 37 (1)	Tootle M 22 (2)
Etete K .... - (4)	O'Brien J 18	Turley J 17 (1)
Evina C 15 (2)	Osborne S .... - (2)	Vaughan D 18 (4)
Fitzsimons R 20 (1)	Oxlade Chamberlain C ... 1 (1)	Ward E 16 (1)

League goals (48): Hemmings 14, Stead 8, Boldewijn 5, Dennis 3, Mackail-Smith 3, Alessandra 2, Hewitt 2, O'Brien 2, Barclay 1, Duffy 1, Jones 1, Kellett 1, Milsom 1, Rose 1, Thomas 1, Ward 1, Opponents 1
FA Cup goals: None. **League Cup goals** (3): Stead 2, Crawford 1. **League Trophy goals** (5): Dennis 3, Alessandra 1, Boldewijn 1
Average home league attendance: 7,357

OLDHAM ATHLETIC

Paul Scholes took a brief and controversial first step into management at Boundary Park. The former Manchester United and England midfielder declared 'the time is right' after his appointment. He won his first match, 4-1 against Yeovil, then drew three and lost three before resigning after 31 days, claiming broken promises about no interference with team selection. Club owner Abdallah Lemsagam, who said Scholes quit by text, denied there had been interference. Academy manager Pete Wild returned as caretaker, having previously been in temporary charge following the dismissal of Frankie Bunn, manager for six months. Wild, who had overseen an FA Cup third round win at Fulham, stayed for the rest of the season before he too left the club, quoting personal reasons. Oldham, relegated the previous season, looked to be on course for a place in the top-half with a late run of 14 points from six matches, but lost the last three and finished 14th after a 5-2 reversal at home against Northampton in the final fixture. The new manager is former Monaco coach Laurent Banide.

Afolayan O 4 (6)	Graham S 4 (3)	O'Grady C 28 (10)
Baxter J 13 (16)	Hamer T 27 (1)	Palmer A 1
Benteke J 2 (7)	Hunt R 32 (6)	Robinson H .... - (1)
Branger J 29 (6)	Iacovitti A 9	Stott J 3
Clarke P 42	Iversen D 42	Surridge S 10 (5)
Coke G 3 (1)	Lang C 38 (4)	Swaby-Neavin J .... - (1)
Dearnley Z 5 (4)	Lyden J 6 (4)	Sylla M 7 (8)
De la Paz, Z 3	Maouche M 26 (8)	Taylor A 14 (1)
Dummigan C 3 (3)	Miller I 10 (6)	Uche C ....- (1)
Edmundson S 45	Missilou C 40 (2)	Vera U 3 (2)
Gardner D 20	Nepomuceno G 37 (5)	

League goals (67): Lang 13, Surridge 8, O'Grady 7, Nepomuceno 6, Branger 5, Baxter 4, Maouche 4, Clarke 3, Miller 3, Edmundson 2, Gardner 2, Haymer 2, Benteke 1, Dearnley 1, Hunt 1, Iacovitti 1, Lyden 1, Missilou 1, Vera 1, Opponents 1
FA Cup goals (7): Clarke 2, Lang 2, Hunt 1, O'Grady 1, Surridge 1. **League Cup goals**: None.
League Trophy goals (8): Surridge 3, Benteke 1, Clarke 1, Lang 1, Maouche 1, Miller 1
Average home league attendance:4,364. **Player of Year**: Peter Clarke

PORT VALE

Tom Pope scored landmark goals to provide some cheer in another disappointment season for his home-town club. Pope became their record scorer at the Vale Park ground with his 56th against Newport. The captain, in his second spell at the club, later reached 100 overall from the penalty spot in the win over Northampton which removed lingering doubts about his side being drawn into a late relegation struggle for the second successive campaign. The worst home record in the division, stretching to 13 defeats when Macclesfield came away with the points to boost their own bid for survival, had left Vale with little room for manoeuvre. Neil Aspin resigned after a single victory in 12 games in all competitions, bringing in former Macclesfield and Shrewsbury manager John Askey, whose father Colin played for Vale for a decade. Askey had a single point to show from his first five games, but breathing space came with two wins in four days over Mansfield and Yeovil. A week after the season closed, owner Norman Smurthwaite sold the club to local business couple Carol and Kevin Shanahan.

Brown S 46	Harris M 3 (3)	Pugh D 1
CalveleyM .... - (1)	Howkins K 2 (1)	Quigley S 1 (10)
Clark M 39 (1)	Joyce L 30 (7)	Rawlinson C 28
Conlon T 31 (3)	Kanu I 1 (2)	Smith N 44
Crookes A 19	Kay A 21 (6)	Tonge M ....- (1)
Dodds L 2 (10)	Legge L 34 (1)	Vassell T 12 (3)
Elliott D 1 (5)	Miller R 19 (9)	Whitfield B 17 (13)
Gibbons J 13 (2)	Montano C 17 (12)	Worrall D 19 (6)
Hannant L 42 (3)	Oyeleke E 28	
Hardcastle L 2 (4)	Pope T 34 (4)	

League goals (39): Pope 11, Montano 5, Miller 4, Whitfield 4, Conlon 3, Hannant 3, Oyeleke 3, Kay 2, Kanu 1, Legge 1, Rawlinson 1, Worrall 1
FA Cup goals (1): Pope 1. **League Cup goals**: None. **League Trophy goals** (10): Miller 2, Montano 2, Pope 2, Hannant 1, Pugh 1, Quigley 1, Rawlinson 1
Average home league attendance: 4,431. **Player of Year:** Scott Brown

STEVENAGE

A stirring finish to the season was not quite enough for a play-off place. Stevenage totalled on 70 points alongside Colchester and Exeter, one behind Newport who secured the fourth spot with an 87th minutes equaliser at Morecambe. Former player Dino Maamria, in his first full season as manager, commended his players for taking 16 points and scoring 14 goals in the final six matches after falling seven points adrift with 3-0 home defeat by a Notts County side on their way out of the Football League. Kurtis Guthrie provided the spark with seven of them, two against Grimsby and Carlisle and one against Port Vale, Exeter and Mansfield. Stevenage closed by beating Cheltenham through two goals in three second-half minutes from Joe Martin and Jordan Gibson, with Guthrie having a penalty saved. Another player who made an impact was Ilias Chair, on loan from Queens Park Rangers, who scored stunning goals after 87 and 94 minutes away to champions to be Lincoln. His side retrieved a 2-0 deficit for a point and the 21-year-old went came close to completing a hat-trick.

Adebayo E....................	(2)	Gibson J...................	2 (4)	Nugent B	34
Ball J	12 (6)	Guthrie K	26 (8)	Reid A	1 (10)
Byrom J	43 (3)	Henry R	10 (8)	Revell A	35 (5)
Campbell-Ryce J.......	11 (1)	Hunt J	26 (3)	Seddon S	22 (1)
Chair I	16	Iontton A..................	10 (8)	Smyth L	(3)
Cuthbert S..................	46	Kennedy B	22 (3)	Sonupe E	9 (23)
Dieng T.......................	13	Makasi M	13 (1)	Timlin M	40 (2)
Farman P.....................	33	Martin J.....................	5	Vancooten T..............	10 (2)
Terry J	2 (10)	McKee M	1 (6)	Wildin L	39
Georgiou A	1	Newton D..................	16 (9)	Wilkinson L	8 (10)

League goals (59): Guthrie 11, Revell 7, Chair 6, Kennedy 6, Newton 6, Ball 3, Seddon 3, Sonupe 3, Byrom 2, Cuthbert 2, Reid 2, Gibson 1, Iontton 1, Martin 1, Nugent 1, Timlin 1, Wildin 1, Wilkinson 1, Opponents 1
FA Cup goals: None. **League Cup goals** (1): Ball 1. **League Trophy goals** (5): Guthrie 3, Kennedy 2
Average home league attendance: 2,716. **Player of Year:** Scott Cuthbert

SWINDON TOWN

A clear-out followed a disappointing finish to the season. Ten players were released after Swindon fell short of a play-off place in the final month for the second year running. Richie Wellens led his side to within four points of the top-seven, with a game in hand on their rivals, after a 3-1 away win over third-place Bury. All seven teams still to be faced were from mid-table downwards, but Swindon dropped points against Yeovil, Newport, Oldham, Cambridge, Crewe and Cheltenham to fall out of contention. A 3-1 victory over Notts County in the final fixture was not enough to regain a top-half spot, although the result carried huge significance for County, who were relegated from the Football League for the first time in their history. Wellens took charge when Phil Brown was sacked in November after a single win in eight matches. He became the club's fifth manager in three years. Player-coach Matt Taylor retired at the end of the season after a 20-year career spanning more than 650 games at seven clubs.

Adebayo E..................	20 (5)	Bancroft J.................	- (1)	Carroll C	15 (2)
Alzate S....................	15 (7)	Bennett K	14 (1)	Conroy D.................	26 (1)
Anderson K	36 (7)	Broadbent T.............	10 (2)	Curran T	- (1)

Diagouraga T............ 10 (2)	McCormick L.................17	Romanski J 3 (1)
Doughty M 26 (4)	McCourt J 17 (10)	Rose D 8 (2)
Dunne J................. 20 (10)	McGilp C .... - (1)	Smith M 8 (3)
House B 1 (5)	McGlashan J 12 (12)	Taylor M 29 (4)
Iandolo E.................. 8 (7)	Nelson S.........................20	Twine S 7 (7)
Knoyle K.................. 38 (4)	Pryce S..................... 1 (1)	Vigouroux L..................29
Koiki A 13 (2)	Richards M 16 (14)	Woolery K 25 (4)
Lancashire O........... 15 (5)	Robinson T 15 (1)	Woolfenden L.................32

League goals (59): Doughty 13, Robinson 7, Woolery 6, Adebayo 5, Anderson 4, Bennett 4, Richards 4, Taylor 3, Alzate 2, Pryce 2, Woolfenden 2, Carroll 1, Conroy 1, Dunne 1, McCourt 1, Romanski 1, Twine 1, Opponents 1
FA Cup goals (2): Alzate 1, Twine 1. **League Cup goals**: None. **League Trophy goals (4)**: Anderson 1, Doughty 1, Richards 1, Woolery 1
Average home league attendance: 6,390. **Player of Year**: Michael Doughty

TRANMERE ROVERS

Manager Micky Mellon was given a new contract until 2021 midway through the season after taking the club back into the Football League, then achieving solid progress in League Two. There was more – much more – to come . Tranmere reeled off seven successive wins, with just two goals conceded, to climb into the heart of the race for automatic promotion. That proved beyond them after a single victory in the remaining seven games. But there were sufficient points in the bank for a place in the play-off semi-finals, which they successfully negotiated with a spectacular 25-yard strike from Ollie Banks in the first leg against Forest Green, followed by James Norwood's 32nd goal of the season in all competitions in the return. That put Norwood level with Sergio Aguero and the chance to go in front of the Manchester City player, whose season had ended without an appearance of any kind in the FA Cup Final against Watford. It was not to be, but Norwood still celebrated after his side's 1-0 victory over Newport in the final. The match went to extra-time and looked to be heading for penalties until Connor Jennings headed in Jake Caprice's cross in the 119th minute to break the resistance of their ten-man opponents.

Akammadu F............... - (1)	Gumbs E...................... - (1)	Nelson S 4 (3)
Bakayogo Z 20 (1)	Harris J.................... 14 (7)	Norwood J 45
Banks O.................. 30 (3)	Jennings C 43 (2)	Perkins D 17
Buxton A............... 11 (5)	McCullough L.................36	Pringle B................. 12 (1)
Caprice J 40 (1)	McNulty S...................27	Ridehalgh L...............17 (1)
Cole L...................... 3 (7)	Miller I...........................2	Smith J...............21 (14)
Dagnall C.................. 1 (4)	Monthe E 42 (1)	Stockton C 13 (3)
Davies S 46	Morris K.................. 12 (2)	Sutton R 7 (2)
Ellis M................... 23 (3)	Henry D 4 (8)	Tollitt B......................1 (3)
Gilmour H................ 7 (15)	Mullin P................. 8 (14)	

Play-offs – appearances: Banks 3, Caprice 3, Davies 3, Harris 3, Jennings 3, Monthe 3, Morris 3, Nelson 3, Norwood 3, Perkins 3, Ridehalgh 3, Gilmour – (2), Buxton – (1), McNulty – (1), Pringle – (1), Smith – (1)
League goals (63): Norwood 29, Jennings 8, Mullin 5, Smith 4, Banks 3, Gilmour 3, Monthe 2, Perkins 2, Buxton 1, Harris 1, Miller 1, Morris 1, Stockton 1, Sutton 1, Opponents 1. **Play-offs – goals (3)**: Banks 1, Norwood 1, Jennings 1
FA Cup goals (8): Jennings 4, Norwood 2, Mullin 1, Smith 1. **League Cup goals (1)**: Cole 1.
League Trophy goals (3): Harris 1, Mullin 1, Stockton 1
Average home league attendance: 6,552. **Player of Year**: James Norwood

YEOVIL TOWN

Sixteen years in the Football League ended on a sour note. Players and staff were pictured on a night out after a 2-2 draw at Northampton in the penultimate game proved not enough to keep survival hopes alive. The group apologised for upsetting supporters and the club announced the matter would be 'dealt with internally.' Yeovil, who were playing in the Championship in 2014, had been offered a lifeline by two goals in seven first-half minutes from Tristan Abrahams, with a penalty, and Jake Gray. Instead, they conceded two within 10 minutes of the start of the second-half, one an own goal from Omar Sowunmi, and Macclesfield's win at Port Vale left them four points adrift, rendering the final fixture against Carlisle irrelevant. One of the youngest squads in the league started the campaign promisingly, winning 4-0 at Notts County and setting a league record with a 6-0 success at Newport. Darren Way, second longest- serving manager in the division, signed a new contract through to the summer of 2021 aiming to break a cycle of struggling to beat the drop. Almost immediately, his side hit a losing streak, slipped back into familiar territory and Way was sacked after ten defeats in 12 games. Neale Marmon, appointed caretaker for the remaining seven games, had little chance to arrest the slide.

Abrahams T.............. 11 (4)	Fisher A 26 (14)	Nelson S 12
Alcock C 4	Gafaiti A 21 (1)	Ojo D 4 (2)
Arnold D .... - (1)	Grant J.............................8	Olomola O 10 (7)
Arquin Y 22 (10)	Gray J,................... 19 (11)	Omari P 1 (8)
Baxter N 34	Green J 16 (3)	Pattison A 24 (5)
Browne R 17 (11)	Henry K .... - (4)	Rogers G 2 (2)
Cole R .... - (1)	Jaiyesimi D........................9	Santos A 15 (2)
D'Almeida S........... 33 (2)	James T 37 (1)	Seager R 2 (9)
Dickinson C........... 32 (1)	Mahmutovic E.......... 3 (1)	Sowunmi O................... 17
Dobre A 21	Worthington M 12 (3)	Warren G 24 (2)
Donnellan S 10 (1)	McDonald W.............. 8 (1)	Zoko F 16 (10)
Duffus C 9 (7)	Mugabi B 27 (5)	

League goals (41): Fisher 7, James 6, Arquin 4, Green 4, Abrahams 3, Olomola 3, Dickinson 2, Gray 2, Jaiyesimi 2, Browne 1, Almeida 1, Dobre 1, Duffus 1, Gafaiti 1, Mugabi 1, Omari 1, Seager 1

FA Cup goals (1): Fisher 1. League Cup goals: None. League Trophy goals (4): Donnellan 1, James 1, Mahmutovic 1, Opponents 1

Average home league attendance: 2,953. Player of Year: Nathan Baxter

THE THINGS THEY SAY ...

'There's a grave danger the magic of the FA Cup is being threatened' – **Malcolm Clarke**, chairman of the Football Supporters' Federation, on learning that only ten of the 32 third round ties will be played at 3pm on a Saturday.

'The manager said to make a good start and put them under pressure' – **Shane Long**, Southampton striker, takes Ralph Hasenhuttl at his word by scoring after 7.69 sec against Watford, a Premier League record.

'I talk to the players about going to war; shining their shields and drawing their sword out of its sheath' – **Tony Mowbray**, Blackburn manager, after a battling victory over Leeds.

'I live for emotion and to come back to the Premier League is emotional' – **Claudio Ranieri**, Leicester's title-winning manager on his appointment at Fulham, which proved a short-lived one.

LEAGUE CLUB MANAGERS 2019–20

Figure in brackets = number of managerial changes at club since the War. †Second spell at club

PREMIER LEAGUE

Arsenal (12)	Unai Emery	May 2018
Aston Villa (27)	Dean Smith	October 2018
Bournemouth (24)	Eddie Howe†	October 2012
Brighton (34)	Graham Potter	May 2019
Burnley (24)	Sean Dyche	October 2012
Chelsea (31)	Frank Lampard	July 2019
Crystal Palace (43)	Roy Hodgson	September 2017
Everton (20)	Marco Silva	June 2018
Leicester (31)	Brendan Rodgers	February 2019
Liverpool (14)	Jurgen Klopp	October 2015
Manchester City (30)	Pep Guardiola	May 2016
Manchester Utd (12)	Old Gunnar Solskjaer	April 2019
Newcastle (28)	Steve Bruce	July 2019
Norwich (29)	Daniel Farke	May 2017
Sheffield Utd (38)	Chris Wilder	May 2016
Southampton (29)	Ralph Hasenhuttl	December 2018
Tottenham (23)	Mauricio Pochettino	May 2014
Watford (36)	Javi Gracia	January 2018
West Ham (16)	Manuel Pellegrini	May 2018
Wolves (27)	Nuno Espirito Santo	May 2017

CHAMPIONSHIP

Barnsley (27)	Daniel Stendel	June 2018
Birmingham (29)	Pep Clotet (interim)	June 2019
Blackburn (31)	Tony Mowbray	February 2017
Brentford (34)	Thomas Frank	October 2018
Bristol City (26)	Lee Johnson	February 2016
Cardiff (31)	Neil Warnock	October 2016
Charlton (25)	Lee Bowyer	September 2018
Derby (28)	Phillip Cocu	July 2019
Fulham (34)	Scott Parker	May 2019
Huddersfield (29)	Jan Siewert	January 2019
Hull (31)	Grant McCann	June 2019
Leeds (33)	Marcelo Bielsa	June 2018
Luton (3)	Graeme Jones	May 2019
Middlesbrough (23)	Jonathan Woodgate	June 2019
Millwall (31)	Neil Harris	April 2015
Nottm Forest (27)	Sabri Lamouchi	June 2019
Preston (29)	Alex Neil	July 2017
QPR (36)	Mark Warburton	May 2019
Reading (24)	Jose Gomes	December 2018
Sheffield Wed (31)		
Stoke (26)	Nathan Jones	January 2019
Swansea (38)	Steve Cooper	June 2019
WBA (35)	Slaven Bilic	June 2019
Wigan (24)	Paul Cook	June 2017

Number of changes since elected to Football League: Wigan 1978. Since returning: Luton 2014

LEAGUE ONE

Accrington (4)	John Coleman	September 2014
AFC Wimbledon (2)	Wally Downes	December 2018
Blackpool (33)	Simon Grayson	July 2019
Bolton (23)	Phil Parkinson	June 2016

Bristol Rov (1)	Graham Coughlan	January 2019
Burton (3)	Nigel Clough	December 2015
Bury (29)	Paul Wilkinson	July 2019
Coventry (35)	Mark Robins	March 2017
Doncaster (7)	Darren Moore	July 2019
Fleetwood (5)	Joey Barton	June 2018
Gillingham (27)	Steve Evans	May 2019
Ipswich (15)	Paul Lambert	October 2018
Lincoln (-)	Danny Cowley	May 2016
MK Dons (18)	Paul Tisdale	June 2018
Oxford (4)	Karl Robinson	March 2018
Peterborough (32)	Darren Ferguson	January 2019
Portsmouth (34)	Kenny Jackett	June 2017
Rochdale (33)	Brian Barry-Murphy	April 2019
Rotherham (28)	Paul Warne	April 2017
Shrewsbury (7)	Sam Ricketts	December 2018
Southend (30)	Kevin Bond	May 2019
Sunderland (32)	Jack Ross	May 2018
Tranmere (-)	Micky Mellon	October 2016
Wycombe (10)	Gareth Ainsworth	November 2012

Number of changes since elected to Football League: Peterborough 1960, Wycombe 1993, Burton 2009, AFC Wimbledon 2011, Fleetwood 2012. Since returning: Doncaster 2003, Shrewsbury 2004, Accrington 2006, Oxford 2010, Bristol Rov 2015, Lincoln 2017, Tranmere 2018

LEAGUE TWO

Bradford (38)	Gary Bowyer	March 2019
Cambridge (3)	Colin Calderwood	December 2018
Carlisle (7)	Steven Pressley	January 2019
Cheltenham (1)	Michael Duff	September 2018
Colchester (28)	John McGreal	May 2016
Crawley (8)	Gabriele Cioffi	September 2018
Crewe (22)	David Artell	January 2017
Exeter (1)	Matt Taylor	June 2018
Forest Green (-)	Mark Cooper	May 2016
Grimsby (3)	Michael Jolley	March 2018
Leyton Orient (-)	Ross Embleton (interim)	June 2019
Macclesfield (2)	Sol Campbell	November 2018
Mansfield (4)	John Dempster	May 2019
Morecambe (1)	Jim Bentley	May 2011
Newport (5)	Mike Flynn	May 2017
Northampton (36)	Keith Curle	October 2018
Oldham (35)	Laurent Banide	June 2019
Plymouth (35)	Ryan Lowe	June 2019
Port Vale (28)	John Askey	February 2019
Salford (-)	Graham Alexander	May 2018
Scunthorpe (31)	Paul Hurst	May 2019
Stevenage (5)	Dino Maamria	March 2018
Swindon (33)	Richie Wellens	November 2018
Walsall (37)	Darrell Clarke	May 2019

Number of changes since elected to Football League: Morecambe 2007, Stevenage 2010, Crawley 2011, Forest Green 2017, Salford 2019. Since returning: Colchester 1992, Carlisle 2005, Exeter 2008, Mansfield 2013, Newport 2013, Cambridge 2014, Cheltenham 2016, Grimsby 2016, Leyton Orient 2019

MANAGERIAL CHANGES 2018–19

PREMIER LEAGUE

Brighton:	Out – Chris Hughton (May 2019); In – Graham Potter
Chelsea:	Out – Maurizio Sarri (Jun 2019); In – Frank Lampard
Fulham:	Out – Slavisa Jokanovic (Nov 2018); In – Claudio Ranieri; Out (Feb 2019); In – Scott Parker
Huddersfield:	Out – David Wagner (Jan 2019); In – Jan Siewert
Leicester:	Out – Claude Puel (Feb 2019); In – Brendan Rodgers
Manchester Utd:	Out – Jose Mourinho (Dec 2018); In – Ole Gunnar Solskjaer
Newcastle:	Out – Rafael Benitez (Jun 2019); In – Steve Bruce
Southampton:	Out – Mark Hughes (Dec 2018); In – Ralph Hasenhuttl

CHAMPIONSHIP

Aston Villa:	Out – Steve Bruce (Oct 2018); In – Dean Smith
Birmingham	Out – Garry Monk (Jun 2019); In – Pep Clotet (interim)
Brentford:	Out – Dean Smith (Oct 2018; In – Thomas Frank
Derby:	Out – Frank Lampard (Jul 2019); In – Phillip Cocu
Hull:	Out – Nigel Adkins (Jun 2019); In – Grant McCann
Ipswich:	Out – Paul Hurst (Oct 2018); In – Paul Lambert
Middlesbrough:	Out – Tony Pulis (May 2019); In – Jonathan Woodgate
Nottm Forest:	Out – Aitor Karanka (Jan 2019); In: Martin O'Neill; Out (Jun 2019); In – Sabri Lamouchi
QPR:	Out – Steve McClaren (Apr 2019); In – Mark Warburton
Reading:	Out – Paul Clement (Dec 2018); In – Jose Gomes
Sheffield Wed:	Out – Jos Luhukay (Dec 2018); In – Steve Bruce
Stoke:	Out – Gary Rowett (Jan 2019); In – Nathan Jones
Swansea:	Out – Graham Potter (May 2019); In – Steve Cooper
WBA:	Out – Darren Moore (Mar 2019); In – Slaven Bilic

LEAGUE ONE

AFC Wimbledon:	Out – Neal Ardley (Nov 2018); In – Wally Downes
Blackpool:	Out – Gary Bowyer (Aug 2018); In – Terry McPhillips; Out (Jul 2019); In – Simon Grayson
Bradford:	Out – Michael Collins (Sep 2018); In – David Hopkin; Out (Feb 2019); In – Gary Bowyer
Bristol Rov:	Out – Darrell Clarke (Dec 2018); In – Graham Coughlan
Doncaster:	Out – Grant McCann (Jun 2019); In – Darren Moore
Gillingham:	Out – Steve Lovell (Apr 2019); In – Steve Evans
Luton:	Out – Nathan Jones (Jan 2019); In – Mick Harford; Out (May 2019); In – Graeme Jones
Peterborough:	Out – Steve Evans (Jan 2019); In – Darren Ferguson
Plymouth:	Out – Derek Adams (Apr 28); In – Ryan Lowe
Rochdale:	Out – Keith Hill (Mar 20129); In – Brian Barry-Murphy
Scunthorpe:	Out – Nick Daws (Aug 2018); In – Stuart McCall; Out (Mar 2019); In – Paul Hurst
Shrewsbury:	Out – John Askey (Nov 2018); In – Sam Ricketts
Southend:	Out – Chris Powell (Mar 2019); In – Kevin Bond
Walsall:	Out – Dean Keates (Apr 2019); In – Darrell Clarke

LEAGUE TWO

Bury:	Out – Ryan Lowe (May 2019); In – Paul Wilkinson
Cambridge:	Out – Joe Dunne (Dec 2018); In – Colin Calderwood
Carlisle:	Out – John Sheridan (Jan 2019); In – Steven Pressley
Cheltenham:	Out – Gary Johnson (Aug 2018); In – Michael Duff
Crawley:	Out – Harry Kewell (Aug 2018); In – Gabriele Cioffi
Macclesfield:	Out – Mark Yates (Oct 2018); In – Sol Campbell
Mansfield:	Out – David Flitcroft (May 2019); In – John Dempster
Northampton:	Out – Dean Austin (Oct 2018); In – Keith Curle
Notts Co:	Out – Kevin Nolan (Aug 2018); In – Harry Kewell; Out (Nov 2018); In – Neal Ardley
Oldham:	Out – Frankie Bunn (Dec 2018); In – Paul Scholes; Out (Mar 2019); In – Laurent Banide
Port Vale:	Out – Neil Aspin (Jan 2019); In – John Askey
Swindon:	Out – Phil Brown (Nov 2018); In – Richie Wellens
Yeovil:	Out – Darren Way (Mar 2019); In – Darren Sarll

FOOTBALL'S CHANGING HOMES

Everton are taking another step towards a move from Goodison Park to a new stadium at Bramley-Moore Dock on the banks of the Mersey. The club have embarked on the second stage of a public consultation, with the latest designs on display for the first time. Officials will study feedback, then submit a planning application later in the year. If successful, they estimate the 52,000-seater arena could be built in three years. Without it, Everton admit they cannot hope to compete against the Premier League's top-six clubs, with revenue not even matching some teams lower in table like West Ham and Newcastle. **Wolves** unveiled long-term plans for a new side Molineux at their end-of-season awards night. In years to come, the club envisage a 50,000-plus stadium with a huge single-tier South Bank, along with redeveloped Steve Bull and Billy Wright Stands. **Manchester City** want to increase capacity at the Etihad to 63,000 by extending the North Stand into two tiers, adding 8,000 seats.

Promoted **Luton** have overcome a major hurdle to a new 17,500-seater arena on the site of an old power station, a mile from cramped and outdated Kenilworth Road. To help pay for it, the club needed approval for a new retail and leisure park near the M1, which some local retailers feared would take trade out of the town centre. Local councillors voted in favour and the Government told the club there was no need for the plans to be reviewed. **Brentford** are on course to leave Griffin Park, their home since 1904, and move into the Community Stadium, for the 2020-21 season. Situated a mile away near Kew Bridge, it will have a capacity of 17,250 and form part of a regeneration of the area, with 900 new homes, a public square and shops. The new ground is one of nine chosen for the 2021 Women's European Championship in England. It will be shared with London Irish rugby union club, who are moving from Reading's Madejski Stadium.

Queens Park Rangers have earmarked the Linford Christie Stadium, used by Thames Valley Harriers, for a move from Loftus Road, which the club believe is no longer 'sustainable' because of its size, age and not enough use on non-match days. A public survey showed 80 per cent in favour. Officials are studying options for a stadium with capacities of 45,000, 42,000 and 35,000. Another major development in west London is starting at **Fulham's** Craven Cottage, where a new two-tier, 9,000-seater Riverside Stand will increase capacity by 4,000 to 29,600. The development, costing £100m and taking two years, will include apartments and a new Thames walkway, allowing uninterrupted public access between Hammersmith and Putney bridges.

Nottingham Forest want to increase capacity at the City Ground from 30,500 to 38,000 after agreeing an extended lease with the local council. The club propose replacing the Peter Taylor Stand with a new one seating 10,000, incorporating a museum and improved facilities for disabled supporters.

EMIRATES FA CUP 2018–19

FIRST ROUND

Five non-league sides upset the rankings – three of them coming from behind to go through. They include Barnet, who defeat League One Bristol Rovers away from home with goals from Craig Robson and substitute Byron Harrison. Maidstone are also 2-1 winners as Jack Powell's free-kick and and Blair Turgott's penalty account for Macclesfield. Stockport fall behind at Yeovil, but Matty Warburton, Nyal Bell and Frank Mulhern turn the tables. Guiseley establish a 4-0 lead through Will Hatfield, Cliff Moyo, Kaine Felix and Kingsley James before Cambrdge United restore some respectability by pulling three goals back. Halifax join them with Cameron King scoring the only goal of their replay against Morecambe. Hartlepool are denied by a Tom Eaves equaliser from the penalty spot in the sixth minute of stoppage-time for Gillingham, who go on to win 4-3 in extra-time. So too are Oxford City at Tranmere after a Kabongo Tshimanga hat-trick puts them 3-2 ahead. James Norwood equalises in the 89th minute and is on the mark again in his side's victory at the second attempt. There is also heartbreak for Hampton and Richmond, who hold on to Chris Dickson's 15th minute penalty until Rob Hunt's 88th minute equaliser for Oldham and Callum Lang's 95th minute winner. Doncaster's Alfie May takes the individual honours with four goals against Chorley and there are hat-tricks for Charlton's Lyle Taylor and Chesterfield's Tom Denton.

Accrington 1 Colchester 0	Rochdale 2 Gateshead 1
Aldershot 1 Bradford 1	Scunthorpe 2 Burton 1
Alfreton 1 Fleetwood 4	Shrewsbury 1 Salford 1
Barnet 1 Bristol Rov 1	Southend 1 Crawley 1
Barnsley 4 Notts Co 0	Southport 2 Boreham Wood 0
Bromley 1 Peterborough 3	Sutton 0 Slough 0
Bury 5 Dover 0	Swindon 2 York 1
Chesterfield 1 Billericay 1	Torquay 0 Woking 1
Chorley 2 Doncaster 2	Tranmere 3 Oxford City 3
Crewe 0 Carlisle 1	Walsall 3 Coventry 2
Ebbsfleet 0 Cheltenham 0	Weston SM 0 Wrexham 2
Exeter 2 Blackpool 3	Yeovil 1 Stockport 3
Gillingham 0 Hartlepool 0	**Replays**
Grimsby 3 MK Dons 1	Billericay 1 Chesterfield 3
Guiseley 4 Cambridge Utd 3	Bradford 1 Aldershot 1
Hampton & R 1 Oldham 2	(aet, Bradford won 4-1 on pens)
Haringey 0 AFC Wimbledon 1	Bristol Rov 1 Barnet 2
Hitchin 0 Solihull 2	Charlton 5 Mansfield 0
Lincoln 3 Northampton 2	Cheltenham 2 Ebbsfleet 0
Luton 2 Wycombe 0	Crawley 2 Southend 6 (aet)
Maidenhead 0 Portsmouth 4	Doncaster 7 Chorley 0
Maidstone 2 Macclesfield 1	Forest Green 0 Oxford Utd 3
Mansfield 1 Charlton 1	Hartlepool 3 Gillingham 4 (aet)
Met Police 0 Newport 2	Halifax 1 Morecambe 0
Morecambe 0 Halifax 0	Oxford City 0 Tranmere 2
Oxford Utd 0 Forest Green 0	Salford 1 Shrewsbury 3
Plymouth 2 Stevenage 0	Slough 1 Sutton 1
Port Vale 1 Sunderland 2	(aet, Slough won 8-7 on pens)

SECOND ROUND

Jake Hyde's header at Swindon enables Woking to spring the only surprise of round two. They fly the non-league flag alongside Barnet, who edge out Stockport with a Dan Sparkes strike. Another

1-0 scoreline sees Walsall end Sunderland's run of 16 matches without defeat in all competitions, thanks to a Liam Kinsella goal. Ivan Toney scores a hat-trick for Peterborough in a 4-4 thriller at Bradford. He then misses in a penalty shoot-out, but his team go through 3-2. Accrington's win over Cheltenham marks a special day for John Coleman and Jimmy Bell, who celebrate their 1,000th match as a management team.

Accrington 3 Cheltenham 1		Solihull 0 Blackpool 0		
Barnet 1 Stockport 0		Southend 2 Barnsley 4		
Bury 0 Luton 1		Swindon 0 Woking 1		
Charlton 0 Doncaster 2		Tranmere 1 Southport 1		
Chesterfield 0 Grimsby 2		Walsall 1 Sunderland 0		
Rochdale 0 Portsmouth 1		Wrexham 0 Newport 0		
Guiseley 1 Fleetwood 2		**Replays**		
Halifax 1 AFC Wimbledon 3		Blackpool 3 Solihull 2 (aet)		
Lincoln 2 Carlisle 0		Bradford 4 Peterborough 4		
Maidstone 0 Oldham 2		(aet, Peterborough won 3-2 on pens)		
Peterborough 2 Bradford 2		Newport 4 Wrexham 0		
Plymouth 1 Oxford Utd 2		Southport 0 Tranmere 2		
Shrewsbury 1 Scunthorpe 0		Sunderland 0 Walsall 1		
Slough 0 Gillingham 1				

THIRD ROUND

A big day for the small clubs as round three shows why it remains one of the season's most eagerly anticipated weekends. The FA switch a host of ties from the traditional 3pm kick-offs to suit foreign television audiences, while top managers chop and change their line-ups with an eye on the next Premier League fixture. But nothing detracts from the way that Newport, Oldham, Gillingham, Shrewsbury and non-league Barnet upset the odds and deservedly make the headlines. After going close to embarrassing Tottenham in the previous season, Newport put out Leicester with Jamille Matt's early header and Padraig Amond's late penalty. Oldham match that 2-1 scoreline – and in some respects exceed the performance – as caretaker-manager Pete Wild's side come from behind to overcome Fulham at Craven Cottage, thanks to loanee Sam Surridge's spot-kick followed by Callum Lang's 88th minute winner. Gillingham also strike late to see off Cardiff, courtesy of Elliott List's 81st minute decider. Barnet repeat that a 1-0 result at Bramall Lane, where Shaquile Coulthirst's penalty enables manager Darren Currie to put one over his uncle, United legend Tony Currie. And Shrewsbury make light of trailing 2-0 at Stoke, James Bolton, Fejiri Okenabirhie (pen) and Josh Laurent turning the tables in the space of ten minutes. Frank Lampard, four times a winner as a player with Chelsea, sees his Derby side twice retrieve a two-goal deficit against Southampton before winning the replay on penalties. Two more teams rise to the occasion – Grimsby holding out at Crystal Palace until the 87th minute after having Andrew Fox sent off in the second minute; Lincoln giving Everton a run for their money after conceding twice in the opening 15 minutes. Elsewhere, two of the big guns record 7-0 victories. Fernando Llorente scores a hat-trick for Tottenham at Tranmere, while Manchester City have six players on the mark, along with an own goal, against Rotherham. There is another hat-trick, for Josh Magennis, as Bolton go through against Walsall. At Old Trafford, Ole Gunnar Solskjaer equals Sir Matt Busby's record of winning his first five games as Manchester United manager, his side defeating Reading.

Accrington 1 Ipswich 0		Burnley 1 Barnsley 0	
Aston Villa 0 Swansea 3		Chelsea 2 Nottm Forest 0	
Blackpool 0 Arsenal 3		Crystal Palace 1 Grimsby 0	
Bolton 5 Walsall 2		Derby 2 Southampton 2	
Bournemouth 1 Brighton 3		Everton 2 Lincoln 1	
Brentford 1 Oxford Utd 0		Fleetwood 2 AFC Wimbledon 3	
Bristol City 1 Huddersfield 0		Fulham 1 Oldham 2	

Gillingham 1 Cardiff 0
Manchester City 7 Rotherham 0
Manchester Utd 2 Reading 0
Middlesbrough 5 Peterborough 0
Millwall 2 Hull 1
Newcastle 1 Blackburn 1
Newport 2 Leicester 1
Norwich 0 Portsmouth 1
Preston 1 Doncaster 3
QPR 2 Leeds 1
Sheffield Utd 0 Barnet 1
Sheffield Wed 0 Luton 0

Shrewsbury 1 Stoke 1
Tranmere 2 Tottenham 7
WBA 1 Wigan 0
West Ham 2 Birmingham 0
Woking 0 **Watford** 2
Wolves 2 Liverpool 1
Replays
Blackburn 2 Newcastle 4 (aet)
Luton 0 Sheffield Wed 1
Southampton 2 Derby 2
(aet, Derby won 5-3 on pens)
Stoke 2 Shrewsbury 3

FOURTH ROUND

AFC Wimbledon, bottom of League One, take pride of place by beating West Ham. Two goals from Scott Wagstaff and one by Kwesi Appiah put them 3-0 ahead. Then, after the Premier League side twice reduce the arrears, Tony Sibbick's header makes sure. Millwall also upset the odds, twice coming from behind to defeat Everton, whose weakness at defending set pieces is exposed by Lee Gregory, Jake Cooper and a 94th minute winner from Murray Wallace. This success is marred by violent clashes between rival fans before kick-off. Shrewsbury look to be on the way to a famous win with goals from Greg Docherty and Luke Waterfall before Wolves cut the deficit and equalise in stoppage-time through Matt Doherty. In the replay, Doherty also has a major say with two goals as Wolves prevail 3-2. Newport substitute Matt Dolan equalises in added time at Middlesbrough and his team rise to the occasion again in the replay, goals by Robbie Willmott and Padraig Among earning a plum fifth round tie against Manchester City. There is no time to celebrate for goalkeeper Joe Day, who rushes off the pitch after hearing his wife has gone into labour – and becomes the proud father of twin girls. The day's most emotional goal celebration comes from injury-dogged Connor Wickham, on the mark for the first time since November 2016 when putting Crystal Palace on the way to victory over Tottenham, who go out three days after losing their League Cup semi-final against Chelsea. In the plum tie of the round at the Emirates, Manchester United make it eight successive wins under Ole Gunnar Solskjaer, against Arsenal.

Accrington 0 Derby 1
AFC Wimbledon 4 West Ham 2
Arsenal 1 Manchester Utd 3
Barnet 3 Brentford 3
Brighton 0 WBA 0
Bristol City 2 Bolton 1
Chelsea 3 Sheffield Wed 0
Crystal Palace 2 Tottenham 0
Doncaster 2 Oldham 1
Manchester City 5 Burnley 0
Middlesbrough 1 Newport 1

Millwall 3 Everton 2
Newcastle 0 **Watford** 2
Portsmouth 1 QPR 1
Shrewsbury 2 Wolves 2
Swansea 4 Gillingham 1
Replays
Brentford 3 Barnet 1
Newport 2 Middlesbrough 0
QPR 2 Portsmouth 0
Wolves 3 Shrewsbury 2
WBA 1 Brighton 3 (aet)

FIFTH ROUND

Manchester United take a firm grip on the top tie with headed goals from Ander Herrera and Paul Pogba, then rebuff all Chelsea's attempts to find a way back with steely defensive work after the interval. Manchester City end Newport's run, but face strong resistance until deep into the second-half when two Phil Foden goals break the League Two side. Full-back Murray Wallace, Millwall's late match winner against Everton, makes another decisive intervention, this time with the only goal after five minutes to dash AFC Wimbledon's hopes. The round's outstanding goal is scored at the end of an 80-yard run by Daniel James as Swansea come from behind to defeat Brentford 4-1. The most romantic comes from Ashley Cole in Derby's defeat by Brighton, his first in competitive English football for more than six years.

AFC Wimbledon 0 Millwall 1
Brighton 2 Derby 1
Bristol City 0 Wolves 1
Chelsea 0 Manchester Utd 2

Doncaster 0 Crystal Palace 2
Newport 1 **Manchester City** 4
QPR 0 **Watford** 1
Swansea 4 Brentford 1

SIXTH ROUND

Brighton look to be on the way out of the competition when trailing to goals from Alex Pearce and Aiden O'Brien with two minutes of normal time remaining at The Den. Instead, Jurgen Locadia pulls one back and in the fifth minute of stoppage-time a Solly March free-kick slips through David Martin's grasp. Shane Ferguson is then shown a straight red card for raking his studs down the back of Lewis Dunk's leg, Millwall surrender one of their penalty takers and lose the shoot-out 5-4. Manchester City survive the threat of an upset at Swansea – helped by the decision to limit the use of VAR to Premier League grounds. After trailing to a Matt Grimes penalty and Bersant Celina's superb finish, they level through Bernardo Silva and Sergio Aguero's penalty, which strikes a post and deflects in off goalkeeper Kristoffer Nordfeldt for an own goal. Then, Aguero's 88th minute header from an offside position is allowed. An outstanding second-half performance by Wolves is rewarded with goals from Raul Jimenez and Diogo Jota for victory against Manchester United, whose stoppage-time reply by Marcus Rashford is too little too late. Andre Gray sends Watford through 2-1 against Crystal Palace with a goal two minutes after coming off the bench.

Millwall 2 Brighton 2
(aet, Brighton won 5-4 on pens)
Swansea 2 **Manchester City** 3

Watford 2 Crystal Palace 1
Wolves 2 Manchester Utd 0

SEMI-FINALS (both at Wembley)

Two sharply-contrasting ties. Watford deliver one of the great Wembley comebacks after trailing 2-0 to goals from Matt Doherty and Raul Jimenez with the 80th minute approaching. A sublime chip from substitute Gerard Deulofeu reduces the arrears and Troy Deeney equalises with a stoppage-time penalty after being fouled by Leander Dendoncker. Deulofeu, who never quite fulfilled his potential at Barcelona, Everton and AC Milan, strikes again in extra-time to put his side in the final for the first time since 1984. Manchester City get off to a flying start with header by Gabriel Jesus, courtesy of Kevin De Bruyne's pin-point cross, after four minutes. But the expected avalanche never materialises. Brighton keep their defensive shape, restrict the scoreline to 1-0 and give City one or two anxious moments in the second half, largely through the enterprise of Anthony Knockaert. The major talking point of a disappointing match is Kyle Walker escaping with a yellow and not red after the VAR review of a thrust of his head towards Alireza Jahanbakhsh with little more than 30 minutes gone.

Manchester City 1 Brighton 0

Watford 3 Wolves 2

FINAL

Pep Guardiola, as usual, got his team selection spot-on. No Sergio Aguero, but two goals from his preferred choice Gabriel Jesus. No Kevin De Bruyne, but an influential 35 minutes off the bench which earned him the man-of-the-match award. Javi Gracia, in contrast, chose loyalty before pragmatism in continuing with Heurelho Gomes as his FA Cup goalkeeper ahead of Ben Foster, his Premier League ever-present. In the end, it made no difference to which team lifted the trophy. Instead, there was a strong argument that Foster, one of the country's finest, would have presented a greater barrier to City's attacking assault which delivered the club's unprecedented third domestic silverware of the season. He would certainly have been expected to deal more competently than the Brazilian did with Bernardo Silva's angled cross which Gabriel Jesus turned in at the far post for his side's second goal. It gave City a welcome cushion after an uncomfortable start when Gomes's compatriot Ederson rescued them in one-on-one situation with Roberto Pereyra. At least the 38-year-old prevented his side from finishing on the end of a record scoreline when keeping out a shot from John Stones. The substutute defender watched aghast, providing further evidence of City's insatiable appetite for more, a desire instilled in all his players by Guardiola in the pursuit of perfection. Watford were shellshocked, but could take credit for going this far, particularly through their comeback in the semi-finals. Supporters also did the club proud with a blaze of yellow even as the goals poured in.

MANCHESTER CITY 6 (David Silva 26, Gabriel Jesus 38, 68, De Bruyne 61, Sterling 81, 87)
WATFORD 0. Wembley (85,854); Saturday, May 18, 2019

Manchester City (4-3-3): Ederson, Walker, Kompany (capt), Laporte, Zinchenko, Gundogan (Sane 73), David Silva (Stones 79), Bernardo Silva, Mahrez (De Bruyne 55), Gabriel Jesus, Sterling. **Subs not used:** Muric, Danilo, Otamendi, Aguero. **Booked:** David Silva. **Manager:** Pep Guardiola
Watford (4-4-1-1): Gomes, Femenia, Mariappa, Cathcart, Holebas, Hughes (Cleverley 73), Capoue, Doucoure, Pereyra (Success 65), Deulofeu (Gray 65), Deeney (capt). **Subs not used:** Foster, Janmaat, Masina, Kabasele. **Booked:** Doucoure, Femenia **Manager:** Javi Gracia
Referee: K Friend (Leics). **Half-time:** 2-0

HOW THEY REACHED THE FINAL

Manchester City
Round 3: 7-0 home to Rotherham (Sterling, Foden, Gabriel Jesus, Mahrez, Otamendi, Sane, own goal)
Round 4: 5-0 home to Burnley (Gabriel Jesus, Bernardo Silva, De Bruyne, Aguero, own goal)
Round 5: 4-1 away to Newport (Foden 2, Sane, Mahrez)
Round 6: 3-2 away to Swansea (Bernardo Silva, Aguero, own goal)
Semi-final: 1-0 v Brighton (Gabriel Jesus)

Watford
Round 3: 2-0 away to Woking (Hughes, Deeney)
Round 4: 2-0 away to Newcastle (Gray, Success)
Round 5: 1-0 away to QPR (Capoue 45)
Round 6: 2-1 home to Crystal Palace (Capoue, Gray)
Semi-final: 3-2 v Wolves (Deulofeu 2, Deeney pen)

Leading scorers: 5 Amond (Newport), Gabriel Jesus (Manchester City); 4 Doherty (Wolves), Jennings (Tranmere), Raul Jimenez (Wolves), Madden (Fleetwood), May (Doncaster), Toney (Peterborough)

FINAL FACTS AND FIGURES

- Manchester City's victory was the biggest since Bury defeated Derby 6-0 in 1903 when both finalists were in the old First Division.

- Only one other side has scored six goals – Blackburn who defeated Sheffield Wednesday 6-1 in 1890.

- This was City's sixth success in the competition after previous wins in 1904 (1-0 Bolton), 1934 (2-1 Portsmouth), 1956 (3-1 Birmingham), 1969 (1-0 Leicester) and 2011 (1-0 Stoke).

- Vincent Kompany and David Silva remained from the victory over Stoke in a team managed by Roberto Mancini.

- Substitute Kevin De Bruyne was named man-of-the-match after completing 40 of 41 attempted passes, scoring his side's third goal and assisting in the fourth from Gabriel Jesus.

- Watford were making their second appearance in the final, having lost 2-0 to Everton in 1984.

- Jose Holebas was cleared to play after his red card in the last Premier League game of the season against West Ham was rescinded.

- Watford have now lost their last 11 matches against Manchester City in all competitions, conceding 38 goals. In 2017, they were beaten 6-0 in a Premier League match at Vicarage Road, Sergio Aguero scoring a hat-trick.

- Gabriel Jesus tied with Newport's Padraig Amond as the competition's leading scorer with five goals.

FA CUP FINAL SCORES & TEAMS

1872 **Wanderers 1** (Betts) Bowen, Alcock, Bonsor, Welch; Betts, Crake, Hooman, Lubbock, Thompson, Vidal, Wollaston. Note. Betts played under the pseudonym 'All Chequer' on the day of the match **Royal Engineers 0** Capt Merriman, Capt Marindin, Lieut Addison, Lieut Cresswell, Lieut Mitchell, Lieut Renny-Tailyour, Lieut Rich, Lieut George Goodwyn, Lieut Muirhead, Lieut Cotter, Lieut Bogle

1873 **Wanderers 2** (Wollaston, Kinnaird) Bowen; Thompson, Welch, Kinnaird, Howell, Wollaston, Sturgis, Rev Stewart, Kenyon-Slaney, Kingsford, Bonsor **Oxford University 0** Kirke-Smith; Leach, Mackarness, Birley, Longman, Chappell-Maddison, Dixon, Paton, Vidal, Sumner, Ottaway. March 29; 3,000; A Stair

1874 **Oxford University 2** (Mackarness, Patton) Neapean; Mackarness, Birley, Green, Vidal, Ottaway, Benson, Patton, Rawson, Chappell-Maddison, Rev Johnson **Royal Engineers 0** Capt Merriman; Major Marindin, Lieut W Addison, Gerald Onslow, Lieut Oliver, Lieut Digby, Lieut Renny-Tailyour, Lieut Rawson, Lieut Blackman Lieut Wood, Lieut von Donop. March 14; 2,000; A Stair

1875 **Royal Engineers 1** (Renny-Tailyour) Capt Merriman; Lieut Sim, Lieut Onslow, Lieut (later Sir) Ruck, Lieut Von Donop, Lieut Wood, Lieut Rawson, Lieut Stafford, Capt Renny-Tailyour, Lieut Mein, Lieut Wingfield-Stratford **Old Etonians 1** (Bonsor) Thompson; Benson, Lubbock, Wilson, Kinnaird, (Sir) Stronge, Patton, Farmer, Bonsor, Ottaway, Kenyon-Slaney. March 13; 2,000; CW Alcock. aet Replay – **Royal Engineers 2** (Renny-Tailyour, Stafford) Capt Merriman; Lieut Sim, Lieut Onslow, Lieut (later Sir) Ruck, Lieut Von Donop, Lieut Wood, Lieut Rawson, Lieut Stafford, Capt Renny-Tailyour, Lieut Mein, Lieut Wingfield-Stratford **Old Etonians 0** Capt Drummond-Moray; Kinnaird, (Sir) Stronge, Hammond, Lubbock, Patton, Farrer, Bonsor, Lubbock, Wilson, Farmer. March 16; 3,000; CW Alcock

1876 **Wanderers 1** (Edwards) Greig; Stratford, Lindsay, Chappell-Maddison, Birley, Wollaston, C Heron, G Heron, Edwards, Kenrick, Hughes **Old Etonians 1** (Bonsor) Hogg; Rev Welldon, Lyttleton, Thompson, Kinnaird, Meysey, Kenyon-Slaney, Lyttleton, Sturgis, Bonsor, Allene. March 11; 3,500; WS Rawson aet Replay – **Wanderers 3** (Wollaston, Hughes 2) Greig; Stratford, Lindsay, Chappell-Maddison, Birley, Wollaston, C Heron, G Heron, Edwards, Kenrick, Hughes **Old Etonians 0** Hogg, Lubbock, Lyttleton, Farrer, Kinnaird, (Sir) Stronge, Kenyon-Slaney, Lyttleton, Sturgis, Bonsor, Allene. March 18; 1,500; WS Rawson

1877 **Wanderers 2** (Kenrick, Lindsay) Kinnaird; Birley, Denton, Green, Heron, Hughes, Kenrick, Lindsay, Stratford, Wace, Wollaston **Oxford University 1** (Kinnaird og) Allington; Bain, Dunnell, Rev Savory, Todd, Waddington, Rev Fernandez, Otter, Parry, Rawson. March 24; 3,000; SH Wright. aet

1878 **Wanderers 3** (Kinnaird, Kenrick 2) (Sir) Kirkpatrick; Stratford, Lindsay, Kinnaird, Green, Wollaston, Heron, Wylie, Wace, Denton, Kenrick **Royal Engineers 1** (Morris) Friend; Cowan, (Sir) Morris, Mayne, Heath, Haynes, Lindsay, Hedley, (Sir) Bond, Barnet, Ruck. March 23; 4,500; SR Bastard

1879 **Old Etonians 1** (Clerke) Hawtrey; Edward, Bury, Kinnaird, Lubbock, Clerke, Pares, Goodhart, Whitfield, Chevalier, Beaufoy **Clapham Rovers 0** Birkett; Ogilvie, Field, Bailcy, Prinsep, Rawson, Stanley, Scott, Bevington, Growse, Keith Falconer. March 29; 5,000; CW Alcock

1880 **Clapham Rovers 1** (Lloyd-Jones) Birkett; Ogilvie, Field, Weston, Bailey, Stanley, Brougham, Sparkes, Barry, Ram, Lloyd-Jones **Oxford University 0** Parr; Wilson, King, Phillips, Rogers, Heygate, Rev Childs, Eyre, (Dr) Crowdy, Hill, Lubbock. April 10; 6,000; Major Marindin

1881 **Old Carthusians 3** (Page, Wynyard, Parry) Gillett; Norris, (Sir) Colvin, Prinsep, (Sir) Vintcent, Hansell, Richards, Page, Wynyard, Parry, Todd **Old Etonians 0** Rawlinson; Foley, French, Kinnaird, Farrer, Macauley, Goodhart, Whitfield, Novelli, Anderson, Chevallier. April 9; 4,000; W Pierce-Dix

1882 **Old Etonians 1** (Macauley) Rawlinson; French, de Paravicini, Kinnaird, Foley, Novelli, Dunn, Macauley, Goodhart, Chevallier, Anderson **Blackburn Rov 0** Howarth; McIntyre, Suter, Hargreaves, Sharples, Hargreaves, Avery, Brown, Strachan, Douglas, Duckworth. March 25; 6,500; JC Clegg

1883 **Blackburn Olympic 2** (Matthews, Costley) Hacking; Ward, Warburton, Gibson, Astley, Hunter, Dewhurst, Matthews, Wilson, Costley, Yates **Old Etonians 1** (Goodhart) Rawlinson; French, de Paravicini, Kinnaird, Foley, Dunn, Bainbridge, Chevallier, Anderson, Goodhart, Macauley. March 31, 8,000; Major Marindin, aet

1884 **Blackburn Rov 2** (Sowerbutts, Forrest) Arthur; Suter, Beverley, McIntyre, Forrest, Hargreaves, Brown, Inglis Sowerbutts, Douglas, Lofthouse **Queen's Park 1** (Christie) Gillespie; MacDonald, Arnott, Gow, Campbell, Allan, Harrower, (Dr) Smith, Anderson, Watt, Christie. March 29; 4,000; Major Marindin

1885 **Blackburn Rov 2** (Forrest, Brown) Arthur; Turner, Suter, Haworth, McIntyre, Forrest, Sowerbutts, Lofthouse, Douglas, Brown, Fecitt **Queen's Park 0** Gillespie; Arnott, MacLeod, MacDonald, Campbell, Sellar, Anderson, McWhammel, Hamilton, Allan, Gray. April 4; 12,500; Major Marindin

1886 **Blackburn Rov 0** Arthur; Turner, Suter, Heyes, Forrest, McIntyre, Douglas, Strachan, Sowerbutts, Fecitt, Brown **WBA 0** Roberts; Green, Bell, Horton, Perry, Timmins, Woodhall, Green, Bayliss, Loach, Bell. April 3; 15,000; Major Marindin **Replay – Blackburn Rov 2** (Sowerbutts, Brown) Arthur; Turner, Suter, Walton, Forrest, McIntyre, Douglas, Strachan, Sowerbutts, Fecitt, Brown **WBA 0** Roberts; Green, Bell, Horton, Perry, Timmins, Woodhall, Green, Bayliss, Loach, Bell. April 10; 12,000; Major Marindin

1887 **Aston Villa 2** (Hodgetts, Hunter) Warner; Coulton, Simmonds, Yates, Dawson, Burton, Davis, Albert Brown, Hunter, Vaughton, Hodgetts **WBA 0** Roberts; Green, Aldridge, Horton, Perry, Timmins, Woodhall, Green, Bayliss, Paddock, Pearson. April 2; 15,500; Major Marindin

1888 **WBA 2** (Bayliss), Woodhall) Roberts; Aldridge, Green, Horton, Perry, Timmins, Woodhall, Bassett, Bayliss, Wilson, Pearson **Preston 1** (Dewhurst) Mills-Roberts; Howarth, Holmes, Ross, Russell, Gordon, Ross, Goodall, Dewhurst, Drummond, Graham. March 24; 19,000; Major Marindin

1889 **Preston 3** (Dewhurst, Ross, Thomson) Mills-Roberts; Howarth, Holmes, Drummond, Russell, Graham, Gordon, Goodall, Dewhurst, Thompson, Ross **Wolves 0** Baynton; Baugh, Mason, Fletcher, Allen, Lowder, Hunter, Wykes, Brodie, Wood, Knight. March 30; 22,000; Major Marindin

1890 **Blackburn Rov 6** (Lofthouse, Jack Southworth, Walton, Townley 3) Horne; James Southworth, Forbes, Barton, Dewar, Forrest, Lofthouse, Campbell, Jack Southworth, Walton, Townley **Sheffield Wed 1** (Bennett) Smith; Morley, Brayshaw, Dungworth, Betts, Waller, Ingram, Woolhouse, Bennett, Mumford, Cawley. March 29; 20,000; Major Marindin

1891 **Blackburn Rov 3** (Dewar, Jack Southworth, Townley) Pennington; Brandon, Forbes, Barton, Dewar, Forrest, Lofthouse, Walton, Southworth, Hall, Townley **Notts Co 1** (Oswald) Thraves; Ferguson, Hendry, Osborne, Calderhead, Shelton, McGregror, McInnes Oswald, Locker, Daft. March 21; 23,000; CJ Hughes

1892 **WBA 3** (Geddes, Nicholls, Reynolds) Reader; Nicholson, McCulloch, Reynolds, Perry, Groves, Bassett, McLeod, Nicholls, Pearson, Geddes **Aston Villa 0** Warner; Evans, Cox, Devey, Cowan, Baird, Athersmith, Devey, Dickson, Hodgetts, Campbell. March 19; 32,810; JC Clegg

1893 **Wolves 1** (Allen) Rose; Baugh, Swift, Malpass, Allen, Kinsey, Topham, Wykes, Butcher, Griffin, Wood **Everton 0** Williams; Kelso, Howarth, Boyle, Holt, Stewart, Latta, Gordon, Maxwell, Chadwick, Milward. March 25; 45,000; CJ Hughes

1894 **Notts Co 4** (Watson, Logan 3) Toone; Harper, Hendry, Bramley, Calderhead, Shelton, Watson, Donnelly, Logan Bruce, Daft **Bolton 1** (Cassidy) Sutcliffe; Somerville, Jones , Gardiner, Paton, Hughes, Tannahill, Wilson, Cassidy, Bentley, Dickenson. March 31; 37,000; CJ Hughes

1895 **Aston Villa 1** (Chatt) Wilkes; Spencer, Welford, Reynolds, Cowan, Russell, Athersmith Chatt, Devey, Hodgetts, Smith **WBA 0** Reader; Williams, Horton, Perry, Higgins, Taggart, Bassett, McLeod, Richards, Hutchinson, Banks. April 20; 42,560; J Lewis

1896 **Sheffield Wed 2** (Spikesley 2) Massey; Earp, Langley, Brandon, Crawshaw, Petrie, Brash, Brady, Bell, Davis, Spikesley **Wolves 1** (Black) Tennant; Baugh, Dunn, Owen, Malpass, Griffiths, Tonks, Henderson, Beats, Wood, Black. April 18; 48,836; Lieut Simpson

154

1897 **Aston Villa 3** (Campbell, Wheldon, Crabtree) Whitehouse; Spencer, Reynolds, Evans, Cowan, Crabtree, Athersmith, Devey, Campbell, Wheldon, Cowan **Everton 2** (Bell, Boyle) Menham; Meechan, Storrier, Doyle, Holt, Stewart, Taylor, Bell, Hartley, Chadwick, Milward. April 10; 65,891; J Lewis

1898 **Nottm Forest 3** (Capes 2, McPherson) Allsop; Ritchie, Scott, Forman, McPherson, Wragg, McInnes, Richards, Benbow, Capes, Spouncer **Derby 1** (Bloomer) Fryer; Methven, Leiper, Cox, Goodall, Bloomer, Boag, Stevenson, McQueen. April 16; 62,017; J Lewis

1899 **Sheffield Utd 4** (Bennett, Beers, Almond, Priest) Foulke; Thickett, Boyle, Johnson, Morren, Needham, Bennett, Beers, Hedley, Almond, Priest **Derby 1** (Boag) Fryer; Methven, Staley, Cox, Paterson, May, Arkesden, Bloomer, Boag, McDonald, Allen. April 15; 73,833; A Scragg

1900 **Bury 4** (McLuckie 2, Wood, Plant) Thompson; Darroch, Davidson, Pray, Leeming, Ross, Richards, Wood, McLuckie, Sagar, Plant **Southampton 0** Robinson; Meechan, Durber, Meston, Chadwick, Petrie, Turner, Yates, Farrell, Wood, Milward. April 21; 68,945; A Kingscott

1901 **Tottenham 2** (Brown 2) Clawley; Erentz, Tait, Morris, Hughes, Jones, Smith, Cameron, Brown, Copeland, Kirwan **Sheffield Utd 2** (Priest, Bennett) Foulke; Thickett, Boyle, Johnson, Morren, Needham, Bennett, Field, Hedley, Priest, Lipsham. April 20; 110,820; A Kingscott **Replay – Tottenham 3** (Cameron, Smith, Brown) Clawley; Erentz, Tait, Morris, Hughes, Jones, Smith, Cameron, Brown, Copeland, Kirwan. **Sheffield Utd 1** (Priest) Foulke; Thickett, Boyle, Johnson, Morren, Needham, Bennett, Field, Hedley, Priest, Lipsham. April 27; 20,470; A Kingscott

1902 **Sheffield Utd 1** (Common) Foulke; Thickett, Boyle, Needham, Wilkinson, Johnson, Bennett, Common, Hedley, Priest. Lipsham **Southampton 1** (Wood) Robinson; Fry, Molyneux, Meston, Bowman, Lee, Turner, Wood Brown, Chadwick, Turner. April 19; 76,914; T Kirkham. **Replay – Sheffield Utd 2** (Hedley, Barnes) Foulke; Thickett, Boyle, Needham, Wilkinson, Johnson, Barnes, Common, Hedley, Priest, Lipsham **Southampton 1** (Brown) Robinson; Fry, Molyneux, Meston, Bowman, Lee, Turner, Wood, Brown, Chadwick, Turner. April 26; 33,068; T Kirkham

1903 **Bury 6** (Leeming 2, Ross, Sagar, Wood, Plant) Monteith; Lindsey, McEwen, Johnston, Thorpe, Ross, Richards, Wood, Sagar Leeming, Plant **Derby 0** Fryer; Methven, Morris, Warren, Goodall, May, Warrington, York, Boag, Richards, Davis. April 18; 63,102; J Adams

1904 **Manchester City 1** (Meredith) Hillman; McMahon, Burgess, Frost, Hynds, Ashworth, Meredith, Livingstone, Gillespie, Turnbull, Booth **Bolton 0** Davies; Brown, Struthers, Clifford, Greenhalgh, Freebairn, Stokes, Marsh, Yenson, White, Taylor. April 23, 61,374, AJ Barker

1905 **Aston Villa 2** (Hampton 2) George; Spencer, Miles, Pearson, Leake, Windmill, Brawn, Garratty, Hampton, Bache, Hall **Newcastle 0** Lawrence; McCombie, Carr, Gardner, Aitken, McWilliam, Rutherford, Howie, Appleyard, Veitch, Gosnell. April 15; 101,117; PR Harrower

1906 **Everton 1** (Young) Scott, Crelley, Walter Balmer, Makepeace, Taylor, Abbott, Sharp, Bolton, Young, Settle, Hardman **Newcastle 0** Lawrence; McCombie, Carr, Gardner, Aitken, McWilliam, Rutherford, Howie, Orr, Veitch, Gosnell. April 21; 75,609; F Kirkham

1907 **Sheffield Wed 2** (Stewart, Simpson) Lyall; Layton, Burton, Brittleton, Crawshaw, Bartlett, Chapman, Bradshaw, Wilson, Stewart, Simpson **Everton 1** (Sharp) Scott; Walter Balmer, Bob Balmer, Makepeace, Taylor, Abbott, Sharp, Bolton, Young, Settle, Hardman. April 20; 84,594; N Whittaker

1908 **Wolves 3** (Hunt, Hedley, Harrison) Lunn; Jones, Collins, Rev Hunt, Wooldridge, Bishop, Harrison, Shelton, Hedley, Radford, Pedley **Newcastle 1** (Howie) Lawrence; McCracken, Pudan, Gardner, Veitch, McWilliam, Rutherford, Howie, Appleyard, Speedie, Wilson. April 25; 74,697; TP Campbell

1909 **Manchester Utd 1** (Sandy Turnbull) Moger; Stacey, Hayes, Duckworth, Roberts, Bell, Meredith, Halse, J Turnbull, S Turnbull, Wall **Bristol City 0** Clay; Annan, Cottle, Hanlin, Wedlock, Spear, Staniforth, Hardy, Gilligan, Burton, Hilton. April 24; 71,401; J Mason

1910 **Newcastle 1** (Rutherford) Lawrence; McCracken, Whitson, Veitch, Low, McWilliam, Rutherford, Howie, Higgins, Shepherd, Wilson **Barnsley 1** (Tufnell) Mearns; Downs, Ness, Glendinning, Boyle, Utley, Tufnell, Lillycrop, Gadsby, Forman, Bartrop. April 23; 77,747; JT Ibbotson **Replay – Newcastle 2** (Shepherd 2, 1pen) Lawrence; McCracken, Carr, Veitch, Low, McWilliam, Rutherford, Howie, Higgins, Shepherd, Wilson **Barnsley 0** Mearns; Downs, Ness, Glendinning, Boyle, Utley, Tufnell, Lillycrop, Gadsby, Forman, Bartrop. April 28; 69,000; JT Ibbotson.

1911 **Bradford City 0** Mellors; Campbell, Taylor, Robinson, Gildea, McDonald, Logan, Speirs, O'Rourke, Devine, Thompson **Newcastle 0** Lawrence; McCracken, Whitson, Veitch, Low, Willis, Rutherford, Jobey, Stewart, Higgins, Wilson. April 22; 69,068; JH Pearson **Replay – Bradford City 1** (Speirs)

155

Mellors; Campbell, Taylor, Robinson, Torrance, McDonald, Logan, Speirs, O'Rourke, Devine, Thompson **Newcastle 0** Lawrence; McCracken, Whitson, Veitch, Low, Willis, Rutherford, Jobey, Stewart, Higgins, Wilson. April 26; 58,000; JH Pearson

1912 **Barnsley 0** Cooper; Downs, Taylor, Glendinning, Bratley, Utley, Bartrop, Tufnell, Lillycrop, Travers, Moore **WBA 0** Pearson; Cook, Pennington, Baddeley, Buck, McNeal, Jephcott, Wright, Pailor, Bowser, Shearman. April 20; 54,556; JR Shumacher **Replay – Barnsley 1** (Tufnell) Cooper; Downs, Taylor, Glendinning, Bratley, Utley, Bartrop, Harry, Lillycrop, Travers, Jimmy Moore **WBA 0** Pearson; Cook, Pennington, Baddeley, Buck, McNeal, Jephcott, Wright, Pailor, Bowser, Shearman. April 24; 38,555; JR Ochumacher. aet

1913 **Aston Villa 1** (Barber) Hardy; Lyons, Weston, Barber, Harrop, Leach, Wallace, Halse, Hampton, Stephenson, Bache **Sunderland 0** Butler; Gladwin, Ness, Cuggy, Thomson, Low, Mordue, Buchan, Richardson, Holley, Martin. April 19; 120,081; A Adams

1914 **Burnley 1** (Freeman) Sewell; Bamford, Taylor, Halley, Boyle, Watson, Nesbit, Lindley, Freeman, Hodgson, Mosscrop **Liverpool 0** Campbell; Longworth, Pursell, Fairfoul, Ferguson, McKinley, Sheldon, Metcalfe, Miller, Lacey, Nicholl. April 25; 72,778; HS Bamlett

1915 **Sheffield Utd 3** (Simmons, Fazackerly, Kitchen) Gough; Cook, English, Sturgess, Brelsford, Utley, Simmons, Fazackerly, Kitchen, Masterman, Evans **Chelsea 0** Molyneux; Bettridge, Harrow, Taylor, Logan, Walker, Ford, Halse, Thomson, Croal, McNeil. April 24; 49,557; HH Taylor

1920 **Aston Villa 1** (Kirton) Hardy; Smart, Weston, Ducat, Barson, Moss, Wallace, Kirton, Walker, Stephenson, Dorrell **Huddersfield 0** Mutch; Wood, Bullock, Slade, Wilson, Watson, Richardson, Mann, Taylor, Swann, Islip. April 24; 50,018; JT Howcroft. aet

1921 **Tottenham 1** (Dimmock) Hunter; Clay, McDonald, Smith, Walters, Grimsdell, Banks, Seed, Cantrell, Bliss, Dimmock **Wolves 0** George; Woodward, Marshall, Gregory, Hodnett, Riley, Lea, Burrill, Edmonds, Potts, Brooks. April 23; 72,805; S Davies

1922 **Huddersfield 1** (Smith pen) Mutch; Wood, Wadsworth, Slade, Wilson, Watson, Richardson, Mann, Islip, Stephenson, Billy Smith **Preston 0** Mitchell; Hamilton, Doolan, Duxbury, McCall, Williamson, Rawlings, Jefferis, Roberts, Woodhouse, Quinn. April 29; 53,000; JWP Fowler

1923 **Bolton 2** (Jack, JR Smith) Pym; Haworth, Finney, Nuttall, Seddon, Jennings, Butler, Jack, JR Smith, Joe Smith, Vizard **West Ham 0** Hufton; Henderson, Young, Bishop, Kay, Tresadern, Richards, Brown; Watson, Moore, Ruffell. April 28; 126,047; DH Asson

1924 **Newcastle 2** (Harris, Seymour) Bradley; Hampson, Hudspeth, Mooney, Spencer, Gibson, Low, Cowan, Harris, McDonald, Seymour **Aston Villa 0** Jackson; Smart, Mort, Moss, Milne, Blackburn, York, Kirton, Capewell, Walker, Dorrell. April 26; 91,695; WE Russell

1925 **Sheffield Utd 1** (Tunstall) Sutcliffe; Cook, Milton, Pantling, King, Green, Mercer, Boyle, Johnson, Gillespie, Tunstall **Cardiff 0** Farquharson; Nelson, Blair, Wake, Keenor, Hardy, Davies, Gill, Nicholson, Beadles, Evans. April 25; 91,763; GN Watson

1926 **Bolton 1** (Jack) Pym; Haworth, Greenhalgh, Nuttall, Seddon, Jennings, Butler, JR Smith, Jack, Joe Smith, Vizard **Manchester City 0** Goodchild; Cookson, McCloy, Pringle, Cowan, McMullan, Austin, Browell, Roberts, Johnson, Hicks. April 24; 91,447; I Baker

1927 **Cardiff 1** (Ferguson) Farquharson; Nelson, Watson, Keenor, Sloan, Hardy, Curtis, Irving, Ferguson, Davies, McLachlan **Arsenal 0** Lewis; Parker, Kennedy, Baker, Butler, John, Hulme, Buchan, Brain, Blythe, Hoar. April 23; 91,206; WF Bunnell

1928 **Blackburn 3** (Roscamp 2, McLean) Crawford; Hutton, Jones, Healless, Rankin, Campbell, Thornewell, Puddefoot, Roscamp, McLean, Rigby **Huddersfield 1** (Jackson) Mercer; Goodall, Barkas, Redfern, Wilson, Steele, Jackson, Kelly, Brown, Stephenson, Smith. April 21; 92,041; TG Bryan

1929 **Bolton 2** (Butler, Blackmore) Pym; Haworth, Finney, Kean, Seddon, Nuttall, Butler, McClelland, Blackmore, Gibson, Cook **Portsmouth 0** Gilfillan; Mackie, Bell, Nichol, McIlwaine, Thackeray, Forward, Smith, Weddle, Watson, Cook. April 27; 92,576; A Josephs

1930 **Arsenal 2** (James, Lambert) Preedy; Parker, Hapgood, Baker, Seddon, John, Hulme, Jack, Lambert, James, Bastin **Huddersfield 0** Turner; Goodall, Spence, Naylor, Wilson, Campbell, Jackson, Kelly, Davies, Raw, Smith. April 26; 92,488; T Crew

1931 **WBA 2** (WG Richardson 2) Pearson; Shaw, Trentham, Magee, Bill Richardson, Edwards, Glidden, Carter, WG Richardson, Sandford, Wood **Birmingham 1** (Bradford) Hibbs; Liddell, Barkas, Cringan, Morrall, Leslie, Briggs, Crosbie, Bradford, Gregg, Curtis. April 25; 92,406; AH Kingscott

1932 **Newcastle 2** (Allen 2) McInroy; Nelson, Fairhurst, McKenzie, Davidson, Weaver, Boyd, Richardson, Allen, McMenemy, Lang **Arsenal 1** (John) Moss; Parker, Hapgood, Jones, Roberts, Male, Hulme, Jack, Lambert, Bastin, John. April 23; 92,298; WP Harper

1933 **Everton 3** (Stein, Dean, Dunn) Sagar; Cook, Cresswell, Britton, White, Thomson, Geldard, Dunn, Dean, Johnson, Stein **Manchester City 0** Langtord; Cann, Dale, Busby, Cowan, Bray, Toseland, Marshall, Herd, McMullan, Eric Brook. April 29; 92,950; E Wood

1934 **Manchester City 2** (Tilson 2) Swift; Barnett, Dale, Busby, Cowan, Bray, Toseland, Marshall, Tilson, Herd, Brook **Portsmouth 1** (Rutherford) Gilfillan; Mackie, Smith, Nichol, Allen, Thackeray, Worrall, Smith, Weddle, Easson, Rutherford. April 28; 93,258; Stanley Rous

1935 **Sheffield Wed 4** (Rimmer 2, Palethorpe, Hooper) Brown; Nibloe, Catlin, Sharp, Millership, Burrows, Hooper, Surtees, Palethorpe, Starling, Rimmer **WBA 2** (Boyes, Sandford) Pearson; Shaw, Trentham, Murphy, Bill Richardson, Edwards, Glidden, Carter, WG Richardson, Sandford, Wally. April 27; 93,204; AE Fogg

1936 **Arsenal 1** (Drake) Wilson; Male, Hapgood, Crayston, Roberts, Copping, Hulme, Bowden, Drake, James, Bastin **Sheffield Utd 0** Smith; Hooper, Wilkinson, Jackson, Johnson, McPherson, Barton, Barclay, Dodds, Pickering, Williams. April 25; 93,384; H Nattrass

1937 **Sunderland 3** (Gurney, Carter, Burbanks) Mapson; Gorman, Hall, Thomson, Johnston, McNab, Duns, Carter, Gurney, Gallacher, Burbanks **Preston 1** (Frank O'Donnell) Burns; Gallimore, Andy Beattie, Shankly, Tremelling, Milne, Dougal, Beresford, Frank O'Donnell, Fagan, Hugh O'Donnell. May 1; 93,495; RG Rudd

1938 **Preston 1** (Mutch pen) Holdcroft; Gallimore, Andy Beattie, Shankly, Smith, Batey, Watmough, Mutch, Maxwell, Bob Beattie, Hugh O'Donnell **Huddersfield 0** Hesford; Craig, Mountford, Willingham, Young, Boot, Hulme, Issac, MacFadyen, Barclay, Beasley. April 30; 93,497; AJ Jewell. aet

1939 **Portsmouth 4** (Parker 2, Barlow, Anderson) Walker; Morgan, Rochford, Guthrie, Rowe, Wharton, Worrall, McAlinden, Anderson, Barlow, Parker **Wolves 1** (Dorsett) Scott; Morris, Taylor, Galley, Cullis, Gardiner, Burton, McIntosh, Westcott, Dorsett, Maguire. April 29; 99,370; T Thompson

1946 **Derby 4** (Stamps 2, Doherty, Bert Turner og) Woodley; Nicholas, Howe, Bullions, Leuty, Musson, Harrison, Carter, Stamps, Doherty, Duncan **Charlton Athletic 1** (Bert Turner) Bartram; Phipps, Shreeve, Bert Turner, Oakes, Johnson, Fell, Brown, Arthur Turner, Welsh, Duffy. April 27; 98,000; ED Smith. aet

1947 **Charlton Athletic 1** (Duffy) Bartram; Croker, Shreeve, Johnson, Phipps, Whittaker, Hurst, Dawson, Robinson, Welsh, Duffy **Burnley 0** Strong; Woodruff, Mather, Attwell, Brown, Bray, Chew, Morris, Harrison, Potts, Kippax. April 26; 99,000; JM Wiltshire. aet

1948 **Manchester Utd 4** (Rowley 2, Pearson, Anderson) Crompton; Carey, Aston, Anderson, Chilton, Cockburn, Delaney, Morris, Rowley, Pearson, Mitten **Blackpool 2** (Shimwell pen, Mortensen) Robinson; Shimwell, Crosland, Johnston, Hayward, Kelly, Matthews, Munro, Mortensen, Dick, Rickett. April 24; 99,000; CJ Barrick

1949 **Wolves 3** (Pye 2, Smyth) Williams; Pritchard, Springthorpe, Crook, Shorthouse, Wright, Hancocks, Smyth, Pye, Dunn, Mullen **Leicester 1** (Griffiths) Bradley; Jelly, Scott, Walter Harrison, Plummer, King, Griffiths, Lee, Jimmy Harrison, Chisholm, Adam. April 30; 99,500; RA Mortimer

1950 **Arsenal 2** (Lewis 2) Swindin; Scott, Barnes, Forbes, Les Compton, Mercer, Cox, Logie, Goring, Lewis, Denis Compton **Liverpool 0** Sidlow; Lambert, Spicer, Taylor, Hughes, Jones, Payne, Baron, Stubbins, Fagan, Liddell. April 29; 100,000; H Pearce

1951 **Newcastle 2** (Milburn 2) Fairbrother; Cowell, Corbett, Harvey, Brennan, Crowe, Walker, Taylor, Milburn, Jorge Robledo, Mitchell **Blackpool 0** Farm; Shimwell, Garrett, Johnston, Hayward, Kelly, Matthews, Mudie, Mortensen, Slater, Perry. April 28; 100,000; W Ling

1952 **Newcastle 1** (George Robledo) Simpson; Cowell, McMichael, Harvey, Brennan, Ted Robledo, Walker, Foulkes, Milburn, George Robledo, Mitchell **Arsenal 0** Swindin; Barnes, Smith, Forbes, Daniel, Mercer, Cox, Logie, Holton, Lishman, Roper. May 3; 100,000; A Ellis

1953 Blackpool 4 (Mortensen 3, Perry) Farm; Shimwell, Garrett, Fenton, Johnston, Robinson; Matthews, Taylor, Mortensen, Mudie, Perry **Bolton 3** (Lofthouse, Moir, Bell) Hanson; Ball, Ralph Banks, Wheeler, Barrass, Bell, Holden, Moir, Lofthouse, Hassall, Langton. May 2; 100,000; M Griffiths

1954 WBA 3 (Allen 2 [1pen], Griffin) Sanders; Kennedy, Millard, Dudley, Dugdale, Barlow, Griffin, Ryan, Allen, Nicholls, Lee **Preston 2** (Morrison, Wayman) Thompson; Cunningham, Walton, Docherty, Marston, Forbes, Finney, Foster, Wayman, Baxter, Morrison. May 1; 100,000; A Luty

1955 Newcastle 3 (Milburn, Mitchell, Hannah) Simpson; Cowell, Batty, Scoular, Stokoe, Casey, White, Milburn, Keeble, Hannah, Mitchell **Manchester City 1** (Johnstone) Trautmann; Meadows, Little, Barnes, Ewing, Paul, Spurdle, Hayes, Revie, Johnstone, Fagan. May 7; 100,000; R Leafe

1956 Manchester City 3 (Hayes, Dyson, Johnstone) Trautmann; Leivers, Little, Barnes, Ewing, Paul, Johnstone, Hayes, Revie, Dyson, Clarke **Birmingham 1** (Kinsey) Merrick; Hall, Green, Newman, Smith, Boyd, Astall, Kinsey, Brown, Murphy, Govan. May 5; 100,000; A Bond

1957 Aston Villa 2 (McParland 2) Sims; Lynn, Aldis, Crowther, Dugdale, Saward, Smith, Sewell, Myerscough, Dixon, McParland **Manchester Utd 1** (Tommy Taylor) Wood; Foulkes, Byrne, Colman, Blanchflower, Edwards, Berry, Whelan, Tommy Taylor, Charlton, Pegg. May 4; 100,000; F Coultas

1958 Bolton 2 (Lofthouse 2) Hopkinson; Hartle, Tommy Banks, Hennin, Higgins, Edwards, Birch, Stevens, Lofthouse, Parry, Holden **Manchester Utd 0** Gregg; Foulkes, Greaves, Goodwin, Cope, Crowther, Dawson, Ernie Taylor, Charlton, Viollet, Webster. May 3; 100,000; J Sherlock

1959 Nottingham Forest 2 (Dwight, Wilson) Thomson; Whare, McDonald, Whitefoot, McKinlay, Burkitt, Dwight, Quigley, Wilson, Gray, Imlach **Luton Town 1** (Pacey) Baynham; McNally, Hawkes, Groves, Owen, Pacey, Bingham, Brown, Morton, Cummins, Gregory. May 2; 100,000; J Clough

1960 Wolves 3 (McGrath og, Deeley 2) Finlayson; Showell, Harris, Clamp, Slater, Flowers, Deeley, Stobart, Murray, Broadbent, Horne **Blackburn 0** Leyland; Bray, Whelan, Clayton, Woods, McGrath, Bimpson, Dobing, Dougan, Douglas, McLeod. May 7; 100,000; K Howley

1961 Tottenham 2 (Smith, Dyson) Brown; Baker, Henry, Blanchflower, Norman, Mackay, Jones, White, Smith, Allen, Dyson **Leicester 0** Banks; Chalmers, Norman, McLintock, King, Appleton, Riley, Walsh, McIlmoyle, Keyworth, Cheesebrough. May 6; 100,000; J Kelly

1962 Tottenham 3 (Greaves, Smith, Blanchflower pen) Brown; Baker, Henry, Blanchflower, Norman, Mackay, Medwin, White, Smith, Greaves, Jones **Burnley 1** (Robson) Blacklaw; Angus, Elder, Adamson, Cummings, Miller, Connelly, McIlroy, Pointer, Robson, Harris. May 5; 100,000; J Finney

1963 Manchester Utd 3 (Law, Herd 2) Gaskell; Dunne, Cantwell, Crerand, Foulkes, Setters, Giles, Quixall, Herd, Law, Charlton **Leicester 1** (Keyworth) Banks; Sjoberg, Norman, McLintock, King, Appleton, Riley, Cross, Keyworth, Gibson, Stringfellow. May 25; 100,000; K Aston

1964 West Ham 3 (Sissons, Hurst, Boyce) Standen; Bond, Burkett, Bovington, Brown, Moore, Brabrook, Boyce, Byrne, Hurst, Sissons **Preston 2** (Holden, Dawson) Kelly; Ross, Lawton, Smith, Singleton, Kendall, Wilson, Ashworth, Dawson, Spavin, Holden. May 2; 100,000; A Holland

1965 Liverpool 2 (Hunt, St John) Lawrence; Lawler, Byrne, Strong, Yeats, Stevenson, Callaghan, Hunt, St John, Smith, Thompson **Leeds 1** (Bremner) Sprake; Reaney, Bell, Bremner, Charlton, Hunter, Giles, Storrie, Peacock, Collins, Johanneson. May 1; 100,000; W Clements. aet

1966 Everton 3 (Trebilcock 2, Temple) West; Wright, Wilson, Gabriel, Labone, Harris, Scott, Trebilcock, Young, Harvey, Temple **Sheffield Wed 2** (McCalliog, Ford) Springett; Smith, Megson, Eustace, Ellis, Young, Pugh, Fantham, McCalliog, Ford, Quinn. May 14; 100,000; JK Taylor

1967 Tottenham 2 (Robertson, Saul) Jennings; Kinnear, Knowles, Mullery, England, Mackay, Robertson, Greaves, Gilzean, Venables, Saul. Unused sub: Jones **Chelsea 1** (Tambling) Bonetti; Allan Harris, McCreadie, Hollins, Hinton, Ron Harris, Cooke, Baldwin, Hateley, Tambling, Boyle. Unused sub: Kirkup. May 20; 100,000; K Dagnall

1968 WBA 1 (Astle) Osborne; Fraser, Williams, Brown, Talbut, Kaye, Lovett, Collard, Astle Hope, Clark Sub: Clarke rep Kaye 91 **Everton 0** West; Wright, Wilson, Kendall, Labone, Harvey, Husband, Ball, Royle, Hurst, Morrissey. Unused sub: Kenyon. May 18; 100,000; L Callaghan. aet

158

1969   Manchester City 1 (Young) Dowd: Book, Pardoe, Doyle, Booth, Oakes, Summerbee, Bell, Lee, Young, Coleman. Unused sub: Connor **Leicester 0** Shilton; Rodrigues, Nish, Roberts, Woollett, Cross, Fern, Gibson, Lochhead, Clarke, Glover. Sub: Manley rep Glover 70. April 26; 100,000; G McCabe

1970   Chelsea 2 (Houseman, Hutchinson) Bonetti; Webb, McCreadie, Hollins, Dempsey, Ron Harris, Baldwin, Houseman, Osgood, Hutchinson, Cooke. Sub: Hinton rep Harris 91 **Leeds 2** (Charlton, Jones) Sprake; Madeley, Cooper, Bremner, Charlton, Hunter, Lorimer, Clarke, Jones, Giles, Gray Unused sub: Bates. April 11; 100,000; E Jennings. aet **Replay – Chelsea 2** (Osgood, Webb) Bonetti; Webb, McCreadie, Hollins, Dempsey, Ron Harris, Baldwin, Houseman, Osgood, Hutchinson, Cooke. Sub: Hinton rep Osgood 105 **Leeds 1** (Jones) Harvey; Madeley, Cooper, Bremner, Charlton, Hunter, Lorimer, Clarke, Jones, Giles, Gray Unused sub: Bates. April 29; 62,078; E Jennings. aet

1971   Arsenal 2 (Kelly, George) Wilson; Rice, McNab, Storey, McLintock Simpson, Armstrong, Graham, Radford, Kennedy, George. Sub: Kelly rep Storey 70 **Liverpool 1** (Heighway) Clemence; Lawler, Lindsay, Smith, Lloyd, Hughes, Callaghan, Evans, Heighway, Toshack, Hall. Sub: Thompson rep Evans 70. May 8; 100,000; N Burtenshaw. aet

1972   Leeds 1 (Clarke) Harvey; Reaney, Madeley, Bremner, Charlton, Hunter, Lorimer, Clarke, Jones, Giles, Gray. Unused sub: Bates **Arsenal 0** Barnett; Rice, McNab, Storey, McLintock, Simpson, Armstrong, Ball, George, Radford, Graham. Sub: Kennedy rep Radford 80. May 6; 100,000; DW Smith

1973   Sunderland 1 (Porterfield) Montgomery; Malone, Guthrie, Horswill, Watson, Pitt, Kerr, Hughes, Halom, Porterfield, Tueart. Unused sub: Young **Leeds 0** Harvey; Reaney, Cherry, Bremner, Madeley, Hunter, Lorimer, Clarke, Jones, Giles, Gray. Sub: Yorath rep Gray 75. May 5; 100,000; K Burns

1974   Liverpool 3 (Keegan 2, Heighway) Clemence; Smith, Lindsay, Thompson, Cormack, Hughes, Keegan, Hall, Heighway, Toshack, Callaghan. Unused sub: Lawler **Newcastle 0** McFaul; Clark, Kennedy, McDermott, Howard, Moncur, Smith, Cassidy, Macdonald, Tudor, Hibbitt. Sub: Gibb rep Smith 70. May 4; 100,000; GC Kew

1975   West Ham 2 (Alan Taylor 2) Day; McDowell, Tommy Taylor, Lock, Lampard, Bonds, Paddon, Brooking, Jennings, Alan Taylor, Holland. Unused sub: Gould **Fulham 0** Mellor; Cutbush, Lacy, Moore, Fraser, Mullery, Conway, Slough, Mitchell, Busby, Barrett. Unused sub: Lloyd. May 3; 100,000; P Partridge

1976   Southampton 1 (Stokes) Turner; Rodrigues, Peach, Holmes, Blyth, Steele, Gilchrist, Channon, Osgood, McCalliog, Stokes. Unused sub: Fisher **Manchester Utd 0** Stepney; Forsyth, Houston, Daly, Brian Greenhoff, Buchan, Coppell, McIlroy, Pearson, Macari, Hill. Sub: McCreery rep Hill 66. May 1; 100,000; C Thomas

1977   Manchester Utd 2 (Pearson, J Greenhoff) Stepney; Nicholl, Albiston, McIlroy, Brian Greenhoff, Buchan, Coppell, Jimmy Greenhoff, Pearson, Macari, Hill. Sub: McCreery rep Hill 81 **Liverpool 1** (Case) Clemence; Neal, Jones, Smith, Kennedy, Hughes, Keegan, Case, Heighway, Johnson, McDermott. Sub: Callaghan rep Johnson 64. May 21; 100,000; R Matthewson

1978   Ipswich Town 1 (Osborne) Cooper; Burley, Mills, Talbot, Hunter, Beattie, Osborne, Wark, Mariner, Geddis, Woods. Sub: Lambert rep Osborne 79 **Arsenal 0** Jennings; Rice, Nelson, Price, Young, O'Leary, Brady, Hudson, Macdonald, Stapleton, Sunderland. Sub: Rix rep Brady 65. May 6, 100,000, D Nippard

1979   Arsenal 3 (Talbot, Stapleton, Sunderland) Jennings; Rice, Nelson, Talbot, O'Leary, Young, Brady, Sunderland, Stapleton, Price, Rix. Sub: Walford rep Rix 83 **Manchester Utd 2** (McQueen, McIlroy) Bailey; Nicholl, Albiston, McIlroy, McQueen, Buchan, Coppell, Jimmy Greenhoff, Jordan, Macari, Thomas. Unused sub: Brian Greenhoff. May 12; 100,000; R Challis

1980   West Ham 1 (Brooking) Parkes; Stewart, Lampard, Bonds, Martin, Devonshire, Allen, Pearson, Cross, Brooking, Pike. Unused sub: Brush **Arsenal 0** Jennings; Rice, Devine, Talbot, O'Leary, Young, Brady, Sunderland, Stapleton, Price, Rix. Sub: Nelson rep Devine 61. May 10; 100,000; G Courtney

1981   Tottenham 1 (Hutchison og) Aleksic; Hughton, Miller, Roberts, Perryman, Villa, Ardiles, Archibald, Galvin, Hoddle, Crooks. Sub: Brooke rep Villa 68. **Manchester City 1** (Hutchison) Corrigan; Ranson, McDonald, Reid, Power, Caton, Bennett, Gow, Mackenzie, Hutchison Reeves. Sub: Henry rep Hutchison 82. May 9; 100,000; K Hackett. aet **Replay – Tottenham 3** (Villa 2, Crooks) Aleksic; Hughton, Miller, Roberts, Perryman, Villa, Ardiles, Archibald, Galvin, Hoddle, Crooks. Unused sub: Brooke **Manchester City 2** (Mackenzie, Reeves pen) Corrigan; Ranson, McDonald, Reid, Power, Caton, Bennett, Gow, Mackenzie, Hutchison Reeves. Sub: Tueart rep McDonald 79. May 14; 92,000; K Hackett

1982   Tottenham 1 (Hoddle) Clemence; Hughton, Miller, Price, Hazard, Perryman, Roberts, Archibald, Galvin, Hoddle, Crooks. Sub: Brooke rep Hazard 104 **Queens Park Rangers 1** (Fenwick) Hucker; Fenwick, Gillard, Waddock, Hazell, Roeder, Currie, Flanagan, Allen, Stainrod, Gregory. Sub: Micklewhite rep Allen 50. May 22; 100,000; C White. aet **Replay – Tottenham 1** (Hoddle pen) Clemence; Hughton, Miller, Price, Hazard, Perryman, Roberts, Archibald, Galvin, Hoddle, Crooks. Sub: Brooke rep Hazard 67 **Queens Park Rangers 0** Hucker; Fenwick, Gillard, Waddock, Hazell, Neill, Currie, Flanagan, Micklewhite, Stainrod, Gregory. Sub: Burke rep Micklewhite 84. May 27; 90,000; C White

1983   Manchester Utd 2 (Stapleton, Wilkins) Bailey; Duxbury, Moran, McQueen, Albiston, Davies, Wilkins, Robson, Muhren, Stapleton, Whiteside. Unused sub: Grimes **Brighton 2** (Smith, Stevens) Moseley; Ramsey, Gary A Stevens, Pearce, Gatting, Smillie, Case, Grealish, Howlett, Robinson, Smith. Sub: Ryan rep Ramsey 56. May 21; 100,000; AW Grey, aet **Replay – Manchester Utd 4** (Robson 2, Whiteside, Muhren pen) Bailey; Duxbury, Moran, McQueen, Albiston, Davies, Wilkins, Robson, Muhren, Stapleton, Whiteside. Unused sub: Grimes **Brighton 0** Moseley; Gary A Stevens, Pearce, Foster, Gatting, Smillie, Case, Grealish, Howlett, Robinson, Smith. Sub: Ryan rep Howlett 74. May 26; 100,000; AW Grey

1984   Everton 2 (Sharp, Gray) Southall; Gary M Stevens, Bailey, Ratcliffe, Mountfield, Reid, Steven, Heath, Sharp, Gray, Richardson. Unused sub: Harper **Watford 0** Sherwood; Bardsley, Price, Taylor, Terry, Sinnott, Callaghan, Johnston, Reilly, Jackett, Barnes. Sub: Atkinson rep Price 58. May 19; 100,000; J Hunting

1985   Manchester Utd 1 (Whiteside) Bailey; Gidman, Albiston, Whiteside, McGrath, Moran, Robson, Strachan, Hughes, Stapleton, Olsen. Sub: Duxbury rep Albiston 91. Moran sent off 77. **Everton 0** Southall; Gary M Stevens, Van den Hauwe, Ratcliffe, Mountfield, Reid, Steven, Sharp, Gray, Bracewell, Sheedy. Unused sub: Harper. May 18; 100,000; P Willis. aet

1986   Liverpool 3 (Rush 2, Johnston) Grobbelaar; Lawrenson, Beglin, Nicol, Whelan, Hansen, Dalglish, Johnston, Rush, Molby, MacDonald. Unused sub: McMahon **Everton 1** (Lineker) Mimms; Gary M Stevens, Van den Hauwe, Ratcliffe, Mountfield, Reid, Steven, Lineker, Sharp, Bracewell, Sheedy. Sub: Heath rep Stevens 65. May 10; 98,000; A Robinson

1987   Coventry City 3 (Bennett, Houchen, Mabbutt og) Ogrizovic; Phillips, Downs, McGrath, Kilcline, Peake, Bennett, Gynn, Regis, Houchen, Pickering. Sub: Rodger rep Kilcline 88. Unused sub: Sedgley **Tottenham 2** (Clive Allen, Mabbutt) Clemence; Hughton Thomas, Hodge, Gough, Mabbutt, Clive Allen, Paul Allen, Waddle, Hoddle, Ardiles. Subs: Gary A Stevens rep Ardiles 91; Claesen rep Hughton 97. May 16; 98,000; N Midgley. aet

1988   Wimbledon 1 (Sanchez) Beasant; Goodyear, Phelan, Jones, Young, Thorn, Gibson Cork, Fashanu, Sanchez, Wise. Subs: Cunningham rep Cork 56; Scales rep Gibson 63 **Liverpool 0** Grobbelaar; Gillespie, Ablett, Nicol, Spackman, Hansen, Beardsley, Aldridge, Houghton, Barnes, McMahon. Subs: Johnston rep Aldridge 63; Molby rep Spackman 72. May 14; 98,203; B Hill

1989   Liverpool 3 (Aldridge, Rush 2) Grobbelaar; Ablett, Staunton, Nichol, Whelan, Hansen, Beardsley, Aldridge Houghton, Barnes, McMahon. Subs: Rush rep Aldridge 72; Venison rep Staunton 91 **Everton 2** (McCall 2) Southall; McDonald, Van den Hauwe, Ratcliffe, Watson, Bracewell, Nevin, Steven, Cottee, Sharp, Sheedy. Subs: McCall rep Bracewell 58; Wilson rep Sheedy 77. May 20; 82,500; J Worrall. aet

1990   Manchester Utd 3 (Robson, Hughes 2) Leighton; Ince, Martin, Bruce, Phelan, Pallister, Robson, Webb, McClair, Hughes, Wallace. Subs: Blackmore rep Martin 88; Robins rep Pallister 93. **Crystal Palace 3** (O'Reilly, Wright 2) Martyn; Pemberton, Shaw, Gray, O'Reilly, Thorn, Barber, Thomas, Bright, Salako, Pardew. Subs: Wright rep Barber 69; Madden rep Gray 117. May 12; 80,000; A Gunn. aet **Replay – Manchester Utd 1** (Martin) Sealey; Ince, Martin, Bruce, Phelan, Pallister, Robson, Webb, McClair, Hughes, Wallace. Unused subs: Robins, Blackmore **Crystal Palace 0** Martyn; Pemberton, Shaw, Gray, O'Reilly, Thorn, Barber, Thomas, Bright, Salako, Pardew. Subs: Wright rep Barber 64; Madden rep Salako 79. May 17; 80,000; A Gunn

1991   Tottenham 2 (Stewart, Walker og) Thorstvedt; Edinburgh, Van den Hauwe, Sedgley, Howells, Mabbutt, Stewart, Gascoigne, Samways, Lineker, Paul Allen. Subs: Nayim rep Gascoigne 18; Walsh rep Samways 82. **Nottingham Forest 1** (Pearce) Crossley; Charles, Pearce, Walker, Chettle, Keane, Crosby, Parker, Clough, Glover, Woan. Subs: Hodge rep Woan 62; Laws rep Glover 108. May 18; 80,000; R Milford. aet

1992   Liverpool 2 (Thomas, Rush) Grobbelaar; Jones, Burrows, Nicol, Molby, Wright, Saunders, Houghton, Rush, McManaman, Thomas. Unused subs: Marsh, Walters **Sunderland 0** Norman; Owers,

160

Ball, Bennett, Rogan, Rush, Bracewell, Davenport, Armstrong, Byrne, Atkinson. Subs: Hardyman rep Rush 69; Hawke rep Armstrong 77. May 9; 80,000; P Don

1993   **Arsenal 1** (Wright) Seaman; Dixon, Winterburn, Linighan, Adams, Jensen, Davis, Parlour, Merson, Campbell, Wright. Subs: Smith rep Parlour 66; O'Leary rep Wright 90. **Sheffield Wed 1** (Hirst) Woods; Nilsson Worthington, Palmer, Hirst, Anderson, Waddle, Warhurst, Bright, Sheridan, Harkes. Subs: Hyde rep Anderson 85; Bart-Williams rep Waddle 112. May 15; 79,347; K Barratt. aet **Replay – Arsenal 2** (Wright, Linighan) Seaman; Dixon, Winterburn, Linighan, Adams, Jensen, Davis, Smith, Merson, Campbell, Wright. Sub: O'Leary rep Wright 81. Unused sub: Selley **Sheffield Wed 1** (Waddle) Woods; Nilsson, Worthington, Palmer, Hirst, Wilson, Waddle, Warhurst, Bright, Sheridan, Harkes. Subs: Hyde rep Wilson 62; Bart-Williams rep Nilsson 118. May 20; 62,267; K Barratt. aet

1994   **Manchester Utd 4** (Cantona 2 [2pens], Hughes, McClair) Schmeichel; Parker, Bruce, Pallister, Irwin, Kanchelskis, Keane, Ince, Giggs, Cantona, Hughes. Subs: Sharpe rep Irwin 84; McClair rep Kanchelskis 84. Unused sub: Walsh (gk) **Chelsea 0** Kharine; Clarke, Sinclair, Kjeldberg, Johnsen, Burley, Spencer, Newton, Stein, Peacock, Wise Substitutions Hoddle rep Burley 65; Cascarino rep Stein 78. Unused sub: Kevin Hitchcock (gk) May 14; 79,634; D Elleray

1995   **Everton 1** (Rideout) Southall; Jackson, Hinchcliffe, Ablett, Watson, Parkinson, Unsworth, Horne, Stuart, Rideout, Limpar. Subs: Ferguson rep Rideout 51; Amokachi rep Limpar 69. Unused sub: Kearton (gk) **Manchester Utd 0** Schmeichel; Gary Neville, Irwin, Bruce, Sharpe, Pallister, Keane, Ince, Brian McClair, Hughes, Butt. Subs: Giggs rep Bruce 46; Scholes rep Sharpe 72. Unused sub: Gary Walsh (gk) May 20; 79,592; G Ashby

1996   **Manchester Utd 1** (Cantona) Schmeichel; Irwin, Phil Neville, May, Keane, Pallister, Cantona, Beckham, Cole, Butt, Giggs. Subs: Scholes rep Cole 65; Gary Neville rep Beckham 89. Unused sub: Sharpe **Liverpool 0** James; McAteer, Scales, Wright, Babb, Jones, McManaman, Barnes, Redknapp, Collymore, Fowler. Subs: Rush rep Collymore 74; Thomas rep Jones 85. Unused sub: Warner (gk) May 11; 79,007; D Gallagher

1997   **Chelsea 2** (Di Matteo, Newton) Grodas; Petrescu, Minto, Sinclair, Lebouef, Clarke, Zola, Di Matteo, Newton, Hughes, Wise. Sub: Vialli rep Zola 89. Unused subs: Hitchcock (gk), Myers **Middlesbrough 0** Roberts; Blackmore, Fleming, Stamp, Pearson, Festa, Emerson, Mustoe, Ravanelli, Juninho, Hignett. Subs: Beck rep Ravanelli 24; Vickers rep Mustoe 29; Kinder, rep Hignett 74. May 17; 79,160; S Lodge

1998   **Arsenal 2** (Overmars, Anelka) Seaman; Dixon, Winterburn, Vieira, Keown, Adams, Parlour, Anelka, Petit, Wreh, Overmars. Sub: Platt rep Wreh 63. Unused subs: Manninger (gk); Bould, Wright, Grimandi **Newcastle 0** Given; Pistone, Pearce, Batty, Dabizas, Howey, Lee, Barton, Shearer, Ketsbaia, Speed. Subs Andersson rep Pearce 72; Watson rep Barton 77; Barnes rep Ketsbaia 85. Unused subs Hislop (gk); Albert. May 16; 79,183; P Durkin

1999   **Manchester Utd 2** (Sheringham, Scholes) Schmeichel; Gary Neville, Johnsen, May, Phil Neville, Beckham, Scholes, Keane, Giggs, Cole, Solskjaer. Subs: Sheringham rep Keane 9; Yorke rep Cole 61; Stam rep Scholes 77. Unused subs: Blomqvist, Van Der Gouw **Newcastle 0** Harper, Griffin, Charvet, Dabizas, Domi, Lee, Hamann, Speed, Solano, Ketsbaia, Shearer. Subs: Ferguson rep Hamann 46; Maric rep Solano 68; Glass rep Ketsbaia 79. Unused subs: Given (gk), Barton. May 22, 79,101, P Jones

2000   **Chelsea 1** (Di Matteo) de Goey; Melchiot Desailly, Lebouef, Babayaro, Di Matteo, Wise, Deschamps, Poyet, Weah, Zola. Subs: Flo rep Weah 87; Morris rep Zola 90. Unused subs: Cudicini (gk), Terry , Harley **Aston Villa 0** James; Ehiogu, Southgate, Barry, Delaney, Taylor, Boateng, Merson, Wright, Dublin, Carbone. Subs: Stone rep Taylor 79; Joachim rep Carbone 79; Hendrie rep Wright 88. Unused subs: Enckelman (gk); Samuel May 20; 78,217; G Poll

2001   **Liverpool 2** (Owen 2) Westerveld; Babbel, Henchoz, Hyypia, Carragher, Murphy, Hamann, Gerrard, Smicer, Heskey, Owen. Subs: McAllister rep Hamann 60; Fowler rep Smicer 77; Berger rep Murphy 77. Unused subs: Arphexad (gk); Vignal **Arsenal 1** (Ljungberg) Seaman; Dixon, Keown, Adams, Cole, Ljungberg, Grimandi, Vieira, Pires, Henry, Wiltord Subs: Parlour rep Wiltord 76; Kanu rep Ljungberg 85; Bergkamp rep Dixon 90. Unused subs. Manninger (gk), Lauren. May 12, 72,500, S Dunn

2002   **Arsenal 2** (Parlour, Ljungberg) Seaman; Lauren, Campbell, Adams, Cole, Parlour, Wiltord, Vieira, Ljungberg, Bergkamp, Henry Subs: Edu rep Bergkamp 72; Kanu rep Henry 81; Keown rep Wiltord 90. Unused subs: Wright (gk); Dixon **Chelsea 0** Cudicini; Melchiot, Desailly, Gallas, Babayaro, Gronkjaer, Lampard, Petit, Le Saux, Floyd Hasselbaink, Gudjohnsen. Subs: Terry rep Babayaro 46; Zola rep Hasselbaink 68; Zenden rep Melchiot 77. Unused subs: de Goey (gk); Jokanovic. May 4; 73,963; M Riley

2003   **Arsenal 1** (Pires) Seaman; Lauren, Luzhny, Keown, Cole, Ljungberg, Parlour, Gilberto, Pires, Bergkamp, Henry. Sub: Wiltord rep Bergkamp 77. Unused subs: Taylor (gk); Kanu, Toure, van Bronckhorst **Southampton 0** Niemi; Baird, Svensson, Lundekvam, Bridge, Telfer, Svensson, Oakley, Marsden, Beattie, Ormerod. Subs: Jones rep Niemi 66; Fernandes rep Baird 87; Tessem rep Svensson 75. Unused subs: Williams, Higginbotham. May 17; 73,726; G Barber

2004   **Manchester Utd 3** (Van Nistelrooy [2, 1 pen], Ronaldo) Howard; Gary Neville, Brown, Silvestre, O'Shea, Fletcher, Keane, Ronaldo, Scholes, Giggs, Van Nistelrooy. Subs: Carroll rep Howard, Butt rep Fletcher, Solskjaer rep Ronaldo 84. Unused subs: P Neville, Djemba-Djemba **Millwall 0** Marshall; Elliott, Lawrence, Ward, Ryan, Wise, Ifill, Cahill, Livermore, Sweeney, Harris. Subs: Cogan rep Ryan, McCammon rep Harris 74 Weston rep Wise 88. Unused subs: Gueret (gk); Dunne. May 22; 71,350; J Winter

2005   **Arsenal 0** Lehmann; Lauren, Toure, Senderos, Cole, Fabregas, Gilberto, Vieira, Pires, Reyes, Bergkamp Subs: Ljungberg rep Bergkamp 65, Van Persie rep Fabregas 86, Edu rep Pires 105. Unused subs: Almunia (gk); Campbell. Reyes sent off 90. **Manchester Utd 0** Carroll; Brown, Ferdinand, Silvestre, O'Shea, Fletcher, Keane, Scholes, Rooney, Van Nistelrooy, Ronaldo. Subs: Fortune rep O'Shea 77, Giggs rep Fletcher 91. Unused subs: Howard (gk); G Neville, Smith. **Arsenal** (Lauren, Ljungberg, van Persie, Cole, Vieira) beat Manchester Utd (Van Nistelrooy, Scholes [missed], Ronaldo, Rooney, Keane) 5-4 on penalties. May 21; 71,876; R Styles

2006   **Liverpool 3** (Gerrard 2, Cisse) Reina; Finnan, Carragher, Hyypiä, Riise, Gerrard, Xabi, Sissoko, Kewell, Cisse, Crouch. Subs: Morientes rep Kewell 48, Kromkamp rep Alonso 67, Hamman rep Crouch 71. Unused subs: Dudek (gk); Traoré **West Ham 3** (Ashton, Konchesky, Carragher (og)) Hislop; Scaloni, Ferdinand, Gabbidon, Konchesky, Benayoun, Fletcher, Reo-Coker, Etherington, Ashton, Harewood. Subs: Zamora rep Ashton 71, Dailly rep Fletcher, Sheringham rep Etherington 85. Unused subs: Walker (gk); Collins. **Liverpool** (Hamann, Hyypiä [missed], Gerrard, Riise) beat **West Ham** (Zamora [missed], Sheringham, Konchesky [missed], Ferdinand [missed]) 3-1 on penalties. May 13; 71,140; A Wiley

2007   **Chelsea 1** (Drogba) Cech, Ferreira, Essien, Terry, Bridge, Mikel, Makelele, Lampard, Wright-Phillips, Drogba, Joe Cole Subs: Robben rep J Cole 45, Kalou rep Wright-Phillips 93, A Cole rep Robben 108. Unused subs: Cudicini (gk); Diarra. **Manchester Utd 0** Van der Sar, Brown, Ferdinand, Vidic, Heinze, Fletcher, Scholes, Carrick, Ronaldo, Rooney, Giggs Subs: Smith rep Fletcher 92, O'Shea rep Carrick, Solskjaer rep Giggs 112. Unused subs: Kuszczak (gk); Evra. May 19; 89,826; S Bennett

2008   **Portsmouth 1** (Kanu) James; Johnson, Campbell, Distin, Hreidarsson, Utaka, Muntari, Mendes, Diarra, Kranjcar, Kanu. Subs: Nugent rep Utaka 69, Diop rep Mendes 78, Baros rep Kanu 87. Unused subs: Ashdown (gk); Pamarot. **Cardiff 0** Enckelman; McNaughton, Johnson, Loovens, Capaldi, Whittingham, Rae, McPhail, Ledley, Hasselbaink, Parry. Subs: Ramsey rep Whittingham 62, Thompson rep Hasselbaink 70, Sinclair rep Rae 87. Unused subs: Oakes (gk); Purse. May 17; 89,874; M Dean

2009   **Chelsea 2** (Drogba, Lampard) Cech; Bosingwa, Alex, Terry, Ashley Cole, Essien, Mikel, Lampard, Drogba, Anelka, Malouda. Subs: Ballack rep Essien 61. Unused subs: Hilario (gk), Ivanovic, Di Santo, Kalou, Belletti, Mancienne. **Everton 1** (Saha) Howard; Hibbert, Yobo, Lescott, Baines, Osman, Neville, Cahill, Pienaar, Fellaini, Saha. Subs: Jacobsen rep Hibbert 46, Vaughan rep Saha 77, Gosling rep Osman 83. Unused subs: Nash, Castillo, Rodwell, Baxter. May 30; 89,391; H Webb

2010   **Chelsea 1** (Drogba) Cech; Ivanovic, Alex, Terry, Ashley Cole, Lampard, Ballack, Malouda, Kalou, Drogba, Anelka. Subs: Belletti rep Ballack 44, J Cole rep Kalou 71, Sturridge rep Anelka 90. Unused subs: Hilario (gk), Zhirkov, Paulo Ferreira, Matic. **Portsmouth 0** James; Finnan, Mokoena, Rocha, Mullins, Dindane, Brown, Diop, Boateng, O'Hara, Piquionne. Subs: Utaka rep Boateng 73, Belhadj rep Mullins 81, Kanu rep Diop 81. Unused subs: Ashdown (gk), Vanden Borre, Hughes, Ben Haim. May 15; 88,335; C Foy

2011   **Manchester City 1** (Y Toure) Hart; Richards, Kompany, Lescott, Kolarov, De Jong, Barry, Silva, Y Toure, Balotelli, Tevez. Subs: Johnson rep Barry73, Zabaleta rep Tevez 87, Vieira rep Silva 90. Unused subs: Given (gk), Boyata, Milner, Dzeko. **Stoke 0** Sorensen; Wilkinson, Shawcross, Huth, Wilson, Pennant, Whelan, Delap, Etherington, Walters, Jones. Subs: Whitehead rep Etherington 62, Carew rep Delap 80, Pugh rep Whelan 84. Unused subs: Nash (gk), Collins, Faye, Diao. May 14; 88,643; M Atkinson

2012   **Chelsea 2** (Ramires, Drogba) Cech; Bosingwa, Ivanovic, Terry, Ashley Cole, Mikel, Lampard, Ramires, Mata, Kalou, Drogba. Subs: Meireles rep Ramires76, Malouda rep Mata 90. Unused subs: Turnbull (gk), Paulo Ferreira, Essien, Torres, Sturridge. **Liverpool 1** (Carroll) Reina; Johnson, Skrtel, Agger, Luis Enrique, Spearing, Bellamy, Henderson, Gerrard, Downing, Suarez. Subs Carroll rep Spearing 55, Kuyt rep Bellamy 78. Unused subs: Doni (gk), Carragher, Kelly, Shelvey, Rodriguez. May 5; 89,102; P Dowd

2013 Wigan 1 (Watson) Robles; Boyce, Alcaraz, Scharner, McCarthy, McArthur, McManaman, Maloney, Gomez, Espinoza, Kone. Subs: Watson rep Gomez 81. Unused subs: Al Habsi (gk), Caldwell, Golobart, Fyvie, Henriquez, Di Santo. **Manchester City 0** Hart, Zabaleta, Kompany, Nastasic, Clichy, Toure, Barry, Silva, Tevez, Nasri, Aguero. Subs: Milner rep Nasri 54, Rodwell rep Tevez 69, Dzeko rep Barry 90. Unused subs: Pantilimon (gk), Lescott, Kolarov, Garcia. Sent off Zabaleta (84). May 11; 86,254; A Marriner

2014 Arsenal 3 (Cazorla, Koscielny, Ramsey) Fabianski; Sagna, Koscielny, Mertesacker, Gibbs, Arteta, Ramsey, Cazorla, Ozil, Podolski, Giroud. Subs: Sanogo rep Podolski 61, Rosicky rep Cazorla 106, Wilshire rep Ozil 106. Unused subs: Szczesny (gk), Vermaelen, Monreal, Flamini. **Hull 2** (Chester, Davies) McGregor; Davies, Bruce, Chester, Elmohamady, Livermore, Huddlestone, Meyler, Rosenior, Quinn, Fryatt. Subs: McShane rep Bruce 67, Aluko rep Quinn 71, Boyd rep Rosenior 102. Unused subs: Harper (gk), Figueroa, Koren, Sagbo. May 17; 89,345; L Probert. aet

2015 Arsenal 4 (Walcott, Sanchez, Mertesacker, Giroud) Szczesny; Bellerin, Koscielny, Mertesacker, Monreal, Coquelin, Cazorla, Ramsey, Ozil, A Sanchez, Walcott. Subs: Wilshere rep Ozil 77, Giroud rep Walcott 77, Oxlade-Chamberlain rep A Sanchez 90. Unused subs: Ospina (gk), Gibbs, Gabriel, Flamini. **Aston Villa 0** Given; Hutton, Okore, Vlaar, Richardson, Cleverley, Westwood, Delph, N'Zogbia, Benteke, Grealish. Subs: Agbonlahor rep N'Zogbia 53, Bacuna rep Richardson 68, C Sanchez rep Westwood 71. Unused subs: Guzan (gk), Baker, Sinclair, Cole. May 30; 89,283; J Moss

2016 Manchester Utd 2 (Mata, Lingard) De Gea, Valencia, Smalling, Blind, Rojo, Carrick, Rooney, Fellaini, Mata, Martial, Rashford. Subs: Darmian rep Rojo 65, Young rep Rashford 71, Lingard rep Mata 90. Unused subs: Romero, Jones, Herrera, Schneiderlin. Smalling sent off 105 . **Crystal Palace 1** (Puncheon) Hennessey, Ward, Dann, Delaney, Souare, Cabaye, Jedinak, Zaha, McArthur, Bolasic, Wickham. Unused subs: Speroni, Adebayor, Sako, Kelly. Subs: Puncheon rep Cabaye 72, Gayle rep Wickham 86, Mariappa rep Dann 90 May 21, 88,619; M Clattenburg

2017 Arsenal 2 (Sanchez, Ramsey) Ospina, Holding, Mertesacker, Bellerin, Ramsey, Xhaka, Oxlade-Chamberlain, Sanchez, Ozil, Welbeck. Subs: Giroud rep Welbeck78, Coquelin rep Oxlade-Chamberlain 83, Elneny rep Sanchez 90. Unused subs: Cech (gk), Walcott, Iwobi, Lucas Perez. **Chelsea 0** Courtois, Azpilicueta, Luiz, Cahill, Moses, Kante, Matic, Alonso, Pedro, Diego Costa, Hazard. Subs Fabregas rep Matic 62, Willian rep Pedro 72, Batshuayi rep Diego Costa 88. Unused subs: Begovic (gk), Terry, Zouma, Ake. May 27; 89,472; A Taylor

2018 Chelsea 0 (Hazard pen) Courtois, Azpilicueta, Cahill, Rudiger, Moses, Fabregas, Kante, Bakayoko, Alonso, Hazard, Giroud. Subs: Morata rep Giroud 89, Willian rep Hazard 90. Unused subs: Caballero (gk), Barkley, Pedro, Zappacosta, Chalobah. **Manchester Utd 0** De Gea, Valencia, Smalling, Jones, Young, Herrera, Matic, Pogba, Lingard, Lingard, Sanchez, Rashford. Subs: Martial rep Lingard 73, Lukaku rep Rashford 73, Mata rep Jones 87. Unused subs: Romero (gk), Bailly, Darmian, McTominay. May 19, 87,647; M Oliver

VENUES

Kennington Oval 1872; **Lillie Bridge** 1873; **Kennington Oval** 1874 – 1892 (1886 replay at the **Racecourse Ground, Derby**); **Fallowfield**, Manchester, 1893; **Goodison Park** 1894; **Crystal Palace** 1895 – 1915 (1901 replay at **Burnden Park**; 1910 replay at **Goodison Park**; 1912 replay at **Bramall Lane**); **Old Trafford** 1915; **Stamford Bridge** 1920 – 1922; **Wembley** 1923 – 2000 (1970 replay at **Old Trafford**; all replays after 1981 at **Wembley**); **Millennium Stadium** 2001 – 2006; **Wembley** 2007 – 2019

SHARP-SHOOTER

Sheffield United's Billy Sharp became the leading scorer in English league football this century with a goal in his promotion-winning side's 3-0 victory at Wigan. It took his tally to 220, one ahead of former Southampton and Liverpool striker Rickie Lambert. Sharp netted 23 goals as United finished Championship runners-up to Norwich.

SUMMARY OF FA CUP WINS

Arsenal 13	Sheffield Wed 3	Clapham Rov 1
Manchester Utd 12	West Ham 3	Coventry 1
Tottenham 8	Bury 2	Derby 1
Chelsea 8	Nottm Forest 2	Huddersfield 1
Aston Villa 7	Old Etonians 2	Ipswich 1
Liverpool 7	Portsmouth 2	Leeds 1
Blackburn Rov 6	Preston 2	Notts Co 1
Manchester City 6	Sunderland 2	Old Carthusians 1
Newcastle 5	Barnsley 1	Oxford University 1
Everton 5	Blackburn Olympic 1	Royal Engineers 1
The Wanderers 5	Blackpool 1	Southampton 1
WBA 5	Bradford City 1	Wigan 1
Bolton 4	Burnley 1	Wimbledon 1
Sheffield Utd 4	Cardiff 1	
Wolves 4	Charlton 1	

APPEARANCES IN FINALS (Figures do not include replays)

Arsenal 20	The Wanderers* 5	Notts Co 2
Manchester Utd 20	West Ham 5	Queen's Park (Glasgow) 2
Liverpool 14	Derby 4	Watford 2
Everton 13	Leeds 4	Blackburn Olympic* 1
Newcastle 13	Leicester 4	Bradford City* 1
Chelsea 13	Oxford University 4	Brighton 1
Aston Villa 11	Royal Engineers 4	Bristol City 1
Manchester City 11	Southampton 4	Coventry* 1
WBA 10	Sunderland 4	Fulham 1
Tottenham 9	Blackpool 3	Hull 1
Blackburn Rov 8	Burnley 3	Ipswich* 1
Wolves 8	Cardiff 3	Luton 1
Bolton 7	Nottm Forest 3	Middlesbrough 1
Preston 7	Barnsley 2	Millwall 1
Old Etonians 6	Birmingham 2	Old Carthusians* 1
Sheffield Utd 6	Bury* 2	QPR 1
Sheffield Wed 6	Charlton 2	Stoke 1
Huddersfield 5	Clapham Rov 2	Wigan 1
Portsmouth 5	Crystal Palace 2	Wimbledon* 1

(* Denotes undefeated)

APPEARANCES IN SEMI-FINALS (Figures do not include replays)

30 Manchester Utd; **29** Arsenal; **26** Everton; **24** Liverpool; **23** Chelsea; **21** Aston Villa, Tottenham; **20** WBA; **18** Blackburn; **17** Newcastle; **16** Sheffield Wed; **15** Wolves; **14** Bolton, Manchester City, Sheffield Utd; **13** Derby; **12** Nottm Forest, Southampton, Sunderland; **10** Preston; **9** Birmingham; **8** Burnley, Leeds; **7** Huddersfield, Leicester, Portsmouth, Watford, West Ham; **6** Fulham, Old Etonians, Oxford University; **5** Millwall, Notts Co, The Wanderers; **4** Cardiff, *Crystal Palace, Luton, Queen's Park (Glasgow), Royal Engineers, Stoke; **3** Barnsley, Blackpool, Clapham Rov, Ipswich, Middlesbrough, Norwich, Old Carthusians, Oldham, The Swifts; **2** Blackburn Olympic, Brighton, Bristol City, Bury, Charlton, Grimsby, Hull, Reading, Swansea, Swindon, Wigan, Wimbledon; **1** Bradford City, Cambridge University, Chesterfield, Coventry, Crewe, Darwen, Derby Junction, Marlow, Old Harrovians, Orient, Plymouth Argyle, Port Vale, QPR, Rangers (Glasgow), Shropshire Wand, Wycombe, York

(*A previous and different Crystal Palace club also reached the semi-final in season 1871–72)

CARABAO EFL CUP 2018–19

FIRST ROUND

Blackpool 3 Barnsley 1
Bristol City 0 Plymouth 1
Bristol Rov 2 Crawley 1
Cambridge 1 Newport 4
Carlisle 1 Blackburn 5
Cheltenham 2 Colchester 2
(Cheltenham won 6-5 on pens)
Crewe 1 Fleetwood 1
(Fleetwood won 4-3 on pens)
Exeter 1 Ipswich 1
(Exeter won 4-2 on pens)
Grimsby 0 Rochdale 2
Leeds 2 Bolton 1
Macclesfield 1 Bradford 1
(Macclesfield won 4-2 on pens)
Mansfield 6 Accrington 1
Middlesbrough 3 Notts Co 3
(Middlesbrough won 4-3 on pens)
Millwall 0 Gillingham 0
(Millwall won 3-1 on pens)
MK Dons 3 Charlton 0
Norwich 3 Stevenage 1

Nottm Forest 1 Bury 1
(Nottm Forest won 10-9 on pens)
Oldham 0 Derby 2
Oxford 2 Coventry 0
Port Vale 0 Lincoln 4
Portsmouth 1 AFC Wimbledon 2
Preston 3 Morecambe 1
QPR 2 Peterborough 0
Reading 2 Birmingham 0
Rotherham 3 Wigan 1
Scunthorpe 1 Doncaster 2
Sheffield Utd 1 Hull 1
(Hull won 5-4 on pens)
Shrewsbury 1 Burton 2
Southend 2 Brentford 4
Sunderland 0 Sheffield Wed 2
Swindon 0 Forest Green 1
Tranmere 1 Walsall 3
WBA 1 Luton 0
Wycombe 1 Northampton 1
Yeovil 0 Aston Villa 1

SECOND ROUND

AFC Wimbledon 1 West Ham 3
Bournemouth 3 MK Dons 0
Blackburn 4 Lincoln 1
Brentford 1 Cheltenham 0
Brighton 0 Southampton 1
Burton 1 Aston Villa 0
Cardiff 1 Norwich 3
Doncaster 1 Blackpool 2
Everton 3 Rotherham 1
Fulham 2 Exeter 0
Hull 0 Derby 4
Leeds 0 Preston 2
Leicester 4 Fleetwood 0
Middlesbrough 2 Rochdale 1

Millwall 3 Plymouth 2
Nottm Forest 3 Newcastle 1
Newport 0 Oxford 3
QPR 3 Bristol Rov 1
Reading 0 Watford 2
Sheffield Wed 0 Wolves 2
Stoke 2 Huddersfield 0
Swansea 0 Crystal Palace 1
Walsall 3 Macclesfield 3
(Macclesfield won 3-1 on pens)
WBA 2 Mansfield 1
Wycombe 2 Forest Green 2
(Wycombe won 4-3 on pens)

THIRD ROUND

Arsenal 3 Brentford 1
Bournemouth 3 Blackburn 2
Blackpool 2 QPR 0
Burton 2 Burnley 1
Everton 1 Southampton 1
(Southampton won 4-3 on pens)
Liverpool 1 **Chelsea** 2
Manchester Utd 2 Derby 2
(Derby won 8-7 on pens)
Millwall 1 Fulham 3
Nottm Forest 3 Stoke 2

Oxford 0 **Manchester City** 3
Preston 2 Middlesbrough 2
(Middlesbrough won 4-3 on pens)
Tottenham 2 Watford 2
(Tottenham won 4-2 on pens)
WBA 0 Crystal Palace 3
West Ham 8 Macclesfield 0
Wolves 0 Leicester 0
(Leicester won 3-1 on pens)
Wycombe 3 Norwich 4

FOURTH ROUND

Arsenal 2 Blackpool 1
Bournemouth 2 Norwich 1
Burton 3 Nottm Forest 2
Chelsea 3 Derby 2
Leicester 0 Southampton 0

(Leicester won 6-5 on pens)
Manchester City 2 Fulham 0
Middlesbrough 1 Crystal Palace 0
West Ham 1 Tottenham 3

QUARTER-FINALS

Arsenal 0 Tottenham 2
Chelsea 1 Bournemouth 0

Leicester 1 **Manchester City** 1
(Manchester City won 3-1 on pens)
Middlesbrough 0 Burton 1

SEMI-FINALS (two legs)

Manchester City 9 Burton 0
Burton 0 **Manchester City** 1

Tottenham 1 **Chelsea** 0
Chelsea 2 Tottenham 1
(Chelsea won 4-2 on pens)

FINAL

Wembley finals have witnessed many memorable goalkeeping performances. There was none braver than Manchester City's Bert Trautmann playing on with a broken neck against Birmingham; none more spectacular than Jim Montgomery's double save from Trevor Cherry and Peter Lorimer in Sunderland's victory against Leeds. Wimbledon's Dave Beasant made history by keeping out John Aldridge's penalty for Liverpool. More recently, Petr Cech's reaction to Andy Carroll's header was a key factor in Chelsea beating Liverpool. Adding to that list of headline-makers, in sharply-contrasting circumstances, was Chelsea's world-record signing Kepa Arrizabalaga. In an unprecedented act of insubordination, he refused to be substituted near the end of extra-time in this League Cup Final, defying manager Maurizio Sarri, who was concerned about him cramping up and wanted to bring on substitute Willy Caballero. The Spaniard remained on the pitch, City won on penalties and Caballero was left wondering whether he could have influenced the outcome in the way he did when saving three spot-kicks as City lifted the trophy in the 2016 final against Liverpool. Arrizabalaga, widely condemned for his action, was fined by the club and left out of Chelsea's next Premier League match against Tottenham. It also overshadowed the performance his team who, a fortnight after losing 6-0 to City in the league, came on strongly in the second-half and with more support for Eden Hazard might have won.

CHELSEA 0 MANCHESTER CITY 0 (aet, Manchester City won 4-3 on pens)
Wembley (81,775); Sunday, February 24, 2019

Chelsea (4-3-3): Arrizabalaga, Azpilicueta (capt), Rudiger, Luiz, Emerson, Kante, Jorginho, Barkley (Loftus-Cheek 89), Pedro (Hudson-Odoi 79), Hazard, Willian (Higuain 96). **Subs not used**: Cabellero, Kovacic, Giroud, Christensen. **Booked**: Luiz, Rudiger, Jorginho. **Manager**: Maurizio Sarri
Manchester City (4-3-3): Ederson, Walker, Otamendi, Laporte (Kompany, capt, 46), Zinchenko, De Bruyne (Sane 86), Fernandinho (Danilo 90), David Silva (Gundogan 79), Bernardo Silva, Aguero, Sterling. **Subs not used**: Muric, Mahrez, Foden. **Booked**: Fernandinho, Otamendi. **Manager**: Pep Guardiola
Referee: J Moss (West Yorks)
Penalty shootout: Jorginho 0-0, Gundogan 0-1, Azpilicueta 1-1, Aguero 1-2, Emerson 2-2, Sane 2-2, Luiz 2-2, Bernardo Silva 2-3, Hazard 3-3, Sterling 3-4

HOW THEY REACHED THE FINAL
Chelsea
Round 3: 2-1 away to Liverpool (Emerson, Hazard)
Round 4: 3-2 home to Derby (Tomori og, Keogh og, Fabregas)

Quarter-finals: 1-0 home to Bournemouth (Hazard)
Semi-finals v Tottenham – first leg, 0-1 away; second leg, 2-1 home (Kante, Hazard) - won 4-2 on pens

Manchester City
Round 3: 0-0 away to Oxford (Gabriel Jesus, Mahrea, Foden)
Round 4: 2-0 home to Fulham (Diaz 2)
Quarter-finals: 1-1 away to Leicester (De Bruyne) - won 3-1 on pens
Semi-finals v Burton – first leg, 9-0 home (Gabriel Jesus 4, De Bruyne, Zinchenko, Foden, Walker, Mahrez); second leg 1-0 away (Aguero)

LEAGUE CUP – COMPLETE RESULTS

LEAGUE CUP FINALS

1961*	Aston Villa beat Rotherham 3-2 on agg (0-2a, 3-0h)
1962	Norwich beat Rochdale 4-0 on agg (3-0a, 1-0h)
1963	Birmingham beat Aston Villa 3-1 o agg (3-1h, 0-0a)
1964	Leicester beat Stoke 4-3 on agg (1-1a, 3-2h)
1965	Chelsea beat Leicester 3-2 on agg (3-2h, 0-0a)
1966	WBA beat West Ham 5-3 on agg (1-2a, 4-1h)

AT WEMBLEY

1967	QPR beat WBA (3-2)
1968	Leeds beat Arsenal (1-0)
1969*	Swindon beat Arsenal (3-1)
1970*	Man City beat WBA (2-1)
1971	Tottenham beat Aston Villa (2-0)
1972	Stoke beat Chelsea (2-1)
1973	Tottenham beat Norwich (1-0)
1974	Wolves beat Man City (2-1)
1975	Aston Villa beat Norwich (1-0)
1976	Man City beat Newcastle (2-1)
1977†	Aston Villa beat Everton (3-2 after 0-0 and 1-1 draws)
1978††	Nottm Forest beat Liverpool (1-0 after 0-0 draw)
1979	Nottm Forest beat Southampton (3-2)
1980	Wolves beat Nottm Forest (1-0)
1981†††	Liverpool beat West Ham (2-1 after 1-1 draw)

MILK CUP

1982^	Liverpool beat Tottenham (3-1)
1983*	Liverpool beat Man Utd (2-1)
1984**	Liverpool beat Everton (1-0 after *0-0 draw)
1985	Norwich beat Sunderland (1-0)
1986	Oxford Utd beat QPR (3-0)

LITTLEWOODS CUP

1987	Arsenal beat Liverpool (2-1)
1988	Luton beat Arsenal (3-2)
1989	Nottm Forest beat Luton (3-1)
1990	Nottm Forest beat Oldham (1-0)

RUMBELOWS CUP

1991	Sheffield Wed beat Man Utd (1-0)
1992	Man Utd beat Nottm Forest (1-0)

COCA-COLA CUP

1993	Arsenal beat Sheffield Wed (2-1)
1994	Aston Villa beat Man Utd (3-1)
1995	Liverpool beat Bolton (2-1)
1996	Aston Villa beat Leeds (3-0)
1997***	Leicester beat Middlesbrough (*1-0 after *1-1 draw)
1998	Chelsea beat Middlesbrough (2-0)

WORTHINGTON CUP (at Millennium Stadium from 2001)

1999	Tottenham beat Leicester (1-0)
2000	Leicester beat Tranmere (2-1)
2001	Liverpool beat Birmingham (5-4 on pens after *1-1 draw)
2002	Blackburn beat Tottenham (2-1)
2003	Liverpool beat Man Utd (2-0)

CARLING CUP (at Wembley from 2008)

2004	Middlesbrough beat Bolton (2-1)
2005	Chelsea beat Liverpool (3-2)
2006	Man Utd beat Wigan (4-0)
2007	Chelsea beat Arsenal (2-1)
2008*	Tottenham beat Chelsea (2-1)
2009	Man Utd beat Tottenham (4-1 on pens after *0-0 draw)
2010	Man Utd beat Aston Villa (2-1)
2011	Birmingham beat Arsenal (2-1)
2012	Liverpool beat Cardiff (3-2 on pens after *2-2 draw)

CAPITAL ONE CUP (at Wembley from 2013)

2013	Swansea beat Bradford (5-0)
2014	Manchester City beat Sunderland (3-1)
2015	Chelsea beat Tottenham (2-0)
2016	Manchester City beat Liverpool (3-1 on pens after *1-1 draw)

* After extra time, † First replay at Hillsborough, second replay at Old Trafford. †† Replayed at Old Trafford. ††† Replayed at Villa Park. ** Replayed at Maine Road. *** Replayed at Hillsborough

EFL CUP (at Wembley from 2017)

2017 Manchester Utd beat Southampton (3-2)

CARABAO CUP (at Wembley from 2018)

2018	Manchester City beat Arsenal (3-0)
2019	Manchester City beat Chelsea (4-3 on pens after *0-0 draw)

SUMMARY OF LEAGUE CUP WINNERS

Liverpool	8	Arsenal	2	Oxford Utd	1
Aston Villa	5	Birmingham	2	QPR	1
Manchester City	6	Norwich	2	Sheffield Wed	1
Chelsea	5	Wolves	2	Stoke	1
Manchester Utd	5	Blackburn	1	Swansea	1
Nottm Forest	4	Leeds	1	Swindon	1
Tottenham	4	Luton	1	WBA	1
Leicester	3	Middlesbrough	1		

LEAGUE CUP FINAL APPEARANCES

12 Liverpool; **9**, Chelsea, Manchester Utd; **8** Arsenal, Aston Villa, Tottenham; **7** Manchester City; **6** Nottm Forest; **5** Leicester; **4** Norwich; **3** Birmingham, Middlesbrough, WBA; **2** Bolton, Everton, Leeds, Luton, QPR, Sheffield Wed, Southampton, Stoke, Sunderland, West Ham, Wolves; **1** Blackburn, Bradford, Cardiff, Newcastle, Oldham, Oxford Utd, Rochdale, Rotherham, Swansea, Swindon, Tranmere, Wigan (Figures do not include replays)

LEAGUE CUP SEMI-FINAL APPEARANCES

17 Liverpool, Tottenham; **15** Arsenal, **14** Aston Villa, Chelsea, Manchester Utd; **11** Manchester City; **9** West Ham; **6** Blackburn, Nottm Forest; **5** Birmingham, Everton, Leeds, Leicester, Middlesbrough, Norwich; **4** Bolton, Burnley, Crystal Palace, Ipswich, Sheffield Wed, Sunderland, WBA; **3** Bristol City, QPR, Southampton, Stoke, Swindon, Wolves; **2** Cardiff, Coventry, Derby, Luton, Oxford Utd, Plymouth, Sheffield Utd, Tranmere, Watford, Wimbledon; **1** Blackpool, Bradford, Burton, Bury, Carlisle, Chester, Huddersfield, Hull, Newcastle, Oldham, Peterborough, Rochdale, Rotherham, Shrewsbury, Stockport, Swansea, Walsall, Wigan, Wycombe (Figures do not include replays)

THE THINGS THEY SAY ...

'In the first-half it was eleven lambs against eleven wolves. The wolves ate the lambs' – **Claudio Ranieri** after Fulham trailed Manchester United 3-0 at the interval.

'He is as good a penalty taker as I have ever worked with' – **Roy Hodgson**, Crystal Palace manager, after midfielder Luka Milivojevic converted a tenth successive spot-kick.

'United could sign Lionel Messi at the moment and he would struggle in this team' – **Paul Scholes**, the highest profile critic of Manchester United under Jose Mourinho.

OTHER COMPETITIONS 2018–19

FA COMMUNITY SHIELD

CHELSEA 0 MANCHESTER CITY 2 (Aguero 13, 58)
Wembley (72,724); Sunday, August 5, 2018

Chelsea (4-3-3): Caballero, Azpilicueta (capt), Rudiger, Luiz, Marcos Alonso, Fabregas (Drinkwater 60), Jorginho, Barkley, Pedro (Moses 79), Morata (Abraham 60), Hudson-Odoi (Willian 59). **Subs not used:** Bulka, Zappacosta, Christensen. **Manager:** Maurizio Sarri

Manchester City (4-3-3): Bravo, Walker, Stones (Gomes 90), Laporte (Otamendi 87), Mendy, Bernardo Silva, Fernandinho, Foden (Diaz 76), Mahrez (Gabriel Jesus 78), Aguero (Kompany capt) 80), Sane (Gundogan 46). **Subs not used:** Ederson. **Manager:** Pep Guardiola
Referee: J Moss (West Yorks). **Half-time:** 0-1

CHECKATRADE EFL TROPHY

(Three points for a group match win. One point for a drawn game after 90 minutes, then penalties with winners awarded one additional point. Group winners and runners up through to knockout stage)

NORTHERN SECTION

GROUP A

	P	W	D	L	F	A	Pts
Sunderland	3	2	1	0	4	1	8
Stoke U21	3	1	2	0	3	2	6
Carlisle	3	1	1	1	5	6	4
Morecambe	3	0	0	3	3	6	0

GROUP B

Rochdale	3	2	1	0	6	3	7
Bury	3	2	0	1	6	4	6
Leicester U21	3	0	2	1	5	6	4
Fleetwod	3	0	1	2	3	7	1

GROUP C

Accrington	3	2	0	1	8	5	6
Macclesfield	3	1	1	1	6	8	5
Blackpool	3	1	1	1	7	7	4
WBA U21	3	1	0	2	4	5	3

GROUP D

Shrewsbury	3	2	1	0	9	2	8
Man City U21	3	2	1	0	6	2	7
Crewe	3	1	0	2	6	9	3
Tranmere	3	0	0	3	3	11	0

GROUP E

Port Vale	3	3	0	0	5	1	9
Walsall	3	2	0	1	6	4	6
M'brough U21	3	1	0	2	2	5	3
Burton	3	0	0	3	1	4	0

GROUP F

Barnsley	3	2	0	1	5	3	8
Oldham	3	2	0	1	8	5	6
Everton U21	3	0	2	1	4	5	2
Bradford	3	0	1	2	3	7	2

GROUP G

Newcastle U21	3	3	0	0	8	3	9
Notts Co	3	1	0	2	5	6	3
Doncaster	3	1	0	2	5	7	3
Grimsby	3	1	0	2	4	6	3

GROUP H

Mansfield	3	3	0	0	7	4	9
Lincoln	3	0	2	1	4	5	3
Scunthorpe	3	0	2	1	3	4	3
Wolves U21	3	0	2	1	3	4	3

SOUTHERN SECTION

GROUP A

Portsmouth	3	3	0	0	8	2	6
Tottenham U21	3	1	1	1	7	4	4
Gillingham	3	1	0	2	9	3	3
Crawley	3	0	1	2	2	4	2

GROUP B

Cambridge	3	2	0	1	8	4	6
Southend	3	2	0	1	6	3	6
Colchester	3	1	0	2	3	5	3
Southampton U21	3	1	0	2	2	7	3

GROUP C

Chelsea U21	3	2	0	1	9	3	6
Newport	3	2	0	1	5	1	6
Swindon	3	2	0	1	4	4	6
Plymouth	3	0	0	3	0	10	0

GROUP D

	P	W	D	L	F	A	Pts
Exeter	3	2	1	0	4	0	8
Bristol Rov	3	2	0	1	4	2	6
Yeovil	3	1	1	1	4	2	4
West Ham U21	3	0	0	3	0	8	0

GROUP E

	P	W	D	L	F	A	Pts
Cheltenham	3	2	0	1	0	6	6
Arsenal U21	3	2	0	1	8	7	6
Forest Green	3	1	1	1	4	2	4
Coventry	3	0	1	2	1	6	2

GROUP F

	P	W	D	L	F	A	Pts
Oxford	3	2	0	1	7	2	6
Northampton	3	2	0	1	4	2	6
Wycombe	3	2	0	1	3	4	6
Fulham U21	3	0	0	3	1	7	0

GROUP G

	P	W	D	L	F	A	Pts
Swansea U21	3	2	0	1	2	5	6
AFC Wimbledon	3	1	1	1	6	3	5
Charlton	3	1	1	1	10	3	7
Stevenage	3	1	0	2	5	12	3

GROUP H

	P	W	D	L	F	A	Pts
Luton	3	2	0	1	6	3	6
Peterborough	3	1	2	0	7	6	5
Brighton U21	3	1	1	1	6	6	5
MK Dons	3	0	1	2	5	9	2

SECOND ROUND

North: Accrington 2 Lincoln 2 (Accrington won 4-2 on pens); Barnsley 3 Manchester City U21 3 (Manchester City U21 won 5-3 on pens); Mansfield 0 Bury 1; Newcastle U21 1 Macclesfield 1 (Newcastle U21 won 5-3 on pens); Port Vale 4 Stoke U21 0; Rochdale 2 Oldham 0; Shrewsbury 2 Walsall 1; Sunderland 2 Notts Co 0.

South: Cambridge 1 Northampton 1 (Northampton won 4-2 on pens); Chelsea U21 2 AFC Wimbledon 1; Cheltenham 1 Newport 1 (Cheltenham won 7-6 on pens); Exeter 0 Peterborough 2; Luton 1 Southend 1 (Southend won 4-2 on pens); Oxford 3 Tottenham U21 0; Portsmouth 2 Arsenal U21 1; Swansea U21 1 Bristol Rov 2.

THIRD ROUND

Accrington 2 Bury 4; Cheltenham 1 Oxford 1 (Oxford won 4-1 on pens); Chelsea U21 1 Peterborough 3; Northampton 1 Bristol Rov 2; Port Vale 1 Shrewsbury 1 (Port Vale won 4-3 on pens); Rochdale 2 Manchester City U21 4; Southend 0 Portsmouth 2; Sunderland 4 Newcastle U21 0.

FOURTH ROUND

Bristol Rov 3 Port Vale 0; Bury 5 Oxford 2; Portsmouth 1 Peterborough 0; Sunderland 2 Manchester City U21 0.

SEMI-FINALS

Bristol Rov 0 Sunderland 2; Bury 0 Portsmouth 3.

FINAL

PORTSMOUTH 2 (Thompson 82, Lowe 114) SUNDERLAND 2 (McGeady 38, 119) aet
(Portsmouth won 5-4 on pens)
Wembley (85,021, competition record); Sunday, March 31, 2019

Portsmouth (4-2-3-1): MacGillivray, Thompson, Burgess, Clarke, Brown, Naylor, Close (Walkes 112), Lowe, Pitman (capt), Curtis (Evans 56), Bogle (Hawkins 69). **Subs not used**: Bass, May, Vaughan, Haunstrup. **Booked**: Curtis, Evans, Lowe. **Manager**: Kenny Jackett

Sunderland (4-2-3-1): McLaughlin, O'Nien, Flanagan, Baldwin, James (Hume 88), Cattermole, Leadbitter (Wyke 94), Morgan (Gooch 73), Honeyman (capt), McGeady, Grigg (Power 77). **Subs not used**: Ruiter, McGeouch, Dunne. **Booked**: Baldwin, McGeady. **Manager**: Jack Ross

Referee: D Whitestone (Northants). **Half-time**: 0-1

BUILDBASE FA TROPHY

FIRST ROUND: Aldershot 3 Bedford 3; Altrincham 0 Stockport 1; Barnet 3 Bath 2; Barrow 1 Halifax 2; Biggleswade 2 Wealdstone 1; Boreham Wood 3 Torquay 1; Brackley 4 Hayes 2; Bromley 2 Sutton 1; Carshalton 1 Dorking 0; Chesterfield 5 Bashford 1; Dover 2 Havant 2; Eastbourne 0 Dorchester 4; Ebbsfleet 0 Dagenham 1; Fylde 5 Stratford 1; Harrogate 2 York 1; Hemel Hempstead 2 Eastleigh 1; Hereford 2 Billericay 1; Lancaster 0 Blyth 3; Leamington 0 Hartlepool 1; Leyton Orient 4 Beaconsfield 0; Maidenhad 1 Oxford 2 (aet); Salford 3 Gateshead 1; Salisbury 2 Braintree 1; Southport 0 Solihull 5; Spennynmoor 4 Barwell 0; Telford 4 Farsley 0, Truro 4 Weston SM 0; Weymouth w/o v Needham Market, Wingate 2 Dulwich 0; Woking 1 Maidstone 1; Workington 0 Ramsbottom 0; Wexham 0 Boston 0. **Replays**: Bedford 7 Aldershot 0; Havant 0 Dover 1; Maidstone 3 Woking 2; Ramsbottom 2 Workington 0

SECOND ROUND: Barnet 2 Dorchester 1; Blyth 1 Boreham Wood 0; Carshalton 4 Salisbury 1; Chesterfield 1 Bedford 0; Dover 1 Harrogate 2; Fylde 1 Biggleswade 0; Halifax 2 Solihull 2; Hartlepool1 Telford 2; Hemel Hempstead 4 Wingate 2; Hereford 1 Brackley 3; Maidstone 1 Oxford 0; Ramsbottom 2 Weymouth 2; Salford 2 Dagenham 0; Spennymoor 3 Sutton 0; Stockport 5 Truro 0; Wrexham 0 Leyton Orient 1. **Replays**: Solihull 1 Halifax 0. Weymouth 1 Ramsbottom 3

THIRD ROUND: Carshalton 3 Barnet 3; Chesterfield 0 Brackley 2; Harrogate 2 Stockport 4; Hemel Hempstead 0 Solihull 5; Leyton Orient 1 Blyth 0; Ramsbottom 5 Fylde 5; Salford 1 Maidstone 1; Spennymoor 1 Telford 2. **Replays**: Barnet 2 Carshalton 1; Fylde 4 Ramsbottom 1; Maidstone 3 Salford 0

FOURTH ROUND: Brackley 1 Leyton Orient 2; Fylde 0 Barnet 0 (aet, Fylde won 4-1 on pens); Solihull 1 Telford 2; Stockport 1 Maidstone 1. **Replay**: Maidstone 0 Stockport 3

SEMI-FINALS: First leg: Fylde 0 Stockport 0; Leyton Orient 1 Telford 0. **Second leg**: Stockport 2 Fylde 3 (Fylde won 3-2 on agg); Telford 1 Leyton Orient 2 (Leyton Orient won 3-1 on agg)

FINAL
AFC FYLDE 1 (Rowe 50) LEYTON ORIENT 0
Wembley (12,963); Sunday, May 19, 2019

AFC Fylde (4-3-1-2): Lynch, Birch (Crawford 90+3), Byrne (capt) (Brewitt 12) Tunnicliffe, Francis-Angol, Croasdale, Philliskirk, Haughton (Odusina 74), Bond, Reid, Rowe. **Subs not used**: Griffiths, Hardy. **Manager**: Dave Challinor
Leyton Orient (3-4-1-2): Brill, Ekpiteta, Coulson, Happe (Harrold 68), Turley (Maguire Drew 46), Clay, McAnuff (capt) (Lee 78), Widdowson, Brophy, Koroma, Bonne. **Subs not used**: Sargeant, Ling. **Manager**: Justin Edinburgh
Referee: A Madley (W Yorks). **Half-time**: 0-0

WELSH CUP FINAL

New Saints 3 (Draper 6, Brobbel 32, 60) **Connah's Quay** 0 – Cefn Druids

FA VASE FINAL

Chertsey 3 (Flegg 39, Baxter 105 pen, Rowe 117) **Cray Valley** 1 (Tomlin 36) – aet, Wembley

FA SUNDAY CUP FINAL

Aylesbury Flooring 3 (Deacon 77, Freshwater 87 pen, Goss 90+3) Birstall Stamford 1 (Seal 29) – ABAX Stadium, Peterborough

FINALS – RESULTS
Associated Members' Cup
1984   (Hull) Bournemouth 2 Hull 1

Freight Rover Trophy – Wembley
1985   Wigan 3 Brentford 1
1986   Bristol City 3 Bolton 0
1987   Mansfield 1 Bristol City 1
       (aet; Mansfield won 5-4 on pens)

Sherpa Van Trophy – Wembley
1988   Wolves 2 Burnley 0
1989   Bolton 4 Torquay 1

Leyland Daf Cup – Wembley
1990   Tranmere 2 Bristol Rov 1
1991   Birmingham 3 Tranmere 2

Autoglass Trophy – Wembley
1992   Stoke 1 Stockport 0
1993   Port Vale 2 Stockport 1
1994   Huddersfield 1 Swansea 1
       (aet; Swansea won 3-1 on pens)

Auto Windscreens Shield – Wembley
1995   Birmingham 1 Carlisle 0
       (Birmingham won in sudden-death
       overtime)
1996   Rotherham 2 Shrewsbury 1
1997   Carlisle 0 Colchester 0
       (aet; Carlisle won 4-3 on pens)
1998   Grimsby 2 Bournemouth 1
       (Grimsby won with golden goal in
       extra-time)
1999   Wigan 1 Millwall 0
2000   Stoke 2 Bristol City 1

LDV Vans Trophy – Millennium Stadium
2001   Port Vale 2 Brentford 1
2002   Blackpool 4 Cambridge Utd 1
2003   Bristol City 2 Carlisle 0
2004   Blackpool 2 Southend 0
2005   Wrexham 2 Southend 0

Football League Trophy – Millennium Stadium
2006   Swansea 2 Carlisle 1

Johnstone's Paint Trophy – Wembley
2007   Doncaster 3 Bristol Rov 2 (aet)
       (Millennium Stadium)
2008   MK Dons 2 Grimsby 0
2009   Luton 3 Scunthorpe 2 (aet)
2010   Southampton 4 Carlisle 1
2011   Carlisle 1 Brentford 0
2012   Chesterfield 2 Swindon 0
2013   Crewe 2 Southend 0
2014   Peterborough 3 Chesterfield 1
2015   Bristol City 2 Walsall 0
2016   Barnsley 3 Oxford 2

Checkatrade Trophy – Wembley
2017   Coventry 2 Oxford 1
2018   Lincoln 1 Shrewsbury 0

FINALS – AT WEMBLEY
Full Members' Cup (Discontinued after 1992)
1985–86   Chelsea 5 Man City 4
1986–87   Blackburn 1 Charlton 0
Simod Cup
1987–88   Reading 4 Luton 1
1988–89   Nottm Forest 4 Everton 3
Zenith Data Systems Cup
1989–90   Chelsea 1 Middlesbrough 0
1990–91   Crystal Palace 4 Everton 1
1991–92   Nottm Forest 3 Southampton 2

Anglo-Italian Cup (Discontinued after 1996
* Home club)
1970   *Napoli 0 Swindon 3
1971   *Bologna 1 Blackpool 2 (aet)
1972   *AS Roma 3 Blackpool 1
1973   *Fiorentina 1 Newcastle 2
1993   Derby 1 Cremonese 3 (at Wembley)
1994   Notts Co 0 Brescia 1 (at Wembley)
1995   Ascoli 1 Notts Co 2 (at Wembley)
1996   Port Vale 2 Genoa 5 (at Wembley)

FA Vase
At Wembley (until 2000 and from 2007)
1975   Hoddesdon 2 Epsom & Ewell 1
1976   Billericay 1 Stamford 0*
1977   Billericay 2 Sheffield 1
       (replay Nottingham after a 1-1 at
       Wembley)
1978   Blue Star 2 Barton Rov 1
1979   Billericay 4 Almondsbury Greenway 1
1980   Stamford 2 Guisborough Town 0
1981   Whickham 3 Willenhall 2*
1982   Forest Green 3 Rainworth MF Welfare 0
1983   VS Rugby 1 Halesowen 0
1984   Stansted 3 Stamford 2
1985   Halesowen 3 Fleetwood 1
1986   Halesowen 3 Southall 0
1987   St Helens 3 Warrington 2
1988   Colne Dynamoes 1 Emley 0*
1989   Tamworth 3 Sudbury 0 (replay
       Peterborough after a 1-1 at Wembley)
1990   Yeading 1 Bridlington 0 (replay
       Leeds after 0-0 at Wembley)
1991   Guiseley 3 Gresley Rov 1 (replay
       Bramall Lane Sheffield after a 4-4
       at Wembley)
1992   Wimborne 5 Guiseley 3
1993   Bridlington 1 Tiverton 0
1994   Diss 2 Taunton 1*

1995	Arlesey 2 Oxford City 1
1996	Brigg Town 3 Clitheroe 0
1997	Whitby Town 3 North Ferriby 0
1998	Tiverton 1 Tow Law 0
1999	Tiverton 1 Bedlington 0
2000	Deal 1 Chippenham 0
2001	Taunton 2 Berkhamsted 1 (Villa Park)
2002	Whitley Bay 1 Tiptree 0* (Villa Park)
2003	Brigg 2 AFC Sudbury 1 (Upton Park)
2004	Winchester 2 AFC Sudbury 0 (St Andrews)
2005	Didcot 3 AFC Sudbury 2 (White Hart Lane)
2006	Nantwich 3 Hillingdon 1 (St Andrews)
2007	Truro 3 AFC Totton 1
2008	Kirkham & Wesham (Fylde) 2 Lowestoft 1
2009	Whitley Bay 2 Glossop 0
2010	Whitley Bay 6 Wroxham 1
2011	Whitley Bay 3 Coalville 2
2012	Dunston 2 West Auckland 0
2013	Spennymoor 2 Tunbridge Wells 1
2014	Sholing 1 West Auckland 0
2015	North Shields 2 Glossop North End 1*
2016	Morpeth 4 Hereford 1
2017	South Shields 4 Cleethorpes 0
2018	Thatcham 1 Stockton 0
2019	Chertsey 3 Cray Valley 1*

* After extra-time

FA Trophy Finals

At Wembley

1970	Macclesfield 2 Telford 0
1971	Telford 3 Hillingdon 2
1972	Stafford 3 Barnet 0
1973	Scarborough 2 Wigan 1*
1974	Morecambe 2 Dartford 1
1975	Matlock 4 Scarborough 0
1976	Scarborough 3 Stafford 2*
1977	Scarborough 2 Dag & Red 1
1978	Altrincham 3 Leatherhead 1
1979	Stafford 2 Kettering 0
1980	Dag & Red 2 Mossley 1
1981	Bishop's Stortford 1 Sutton 0
1982	Enfield 1 Altrincham 0*
1983	Telford 2 Northwich 1
1984	Northwich 2 Bangor 1 (replay Stoke after a 1-1 at Wembley)
1985	Wealdstone 2 Boston 1
1986	Altrincham 1 Runcorn 0
1987	Kidderminster 2 Burton 1 (replay WBA after a 0-0 at Wembley)
1988	Enfield 3 Telford 2 (replay WBA after a 0-0 at Wembley)

1989	Telford 1 Macclesfield 0*
1990	Barrow 3 Leek 0
1991	Wycombe 2 Kidderminster 1
1992	Colchester 3 Witton 1
1993	Wycombe 4 Runcorn 1
1994	Woking 2 Runcorn 1
1995	Woking 2 Kidderminster 1
1996	Macclesfield 3 Northwich 1
1997	Woking 1 Dag & Red & Redbridge 0*
1998	Cheltenham 1 Southport 0
1999	Kingstonian 1 Forest Green 0
2000	Kingstonian 3 Kettering 2

At Villa Park

2001	Canvey 1 Forest Green 0
2002	Yeovil 2 Stevenage 0
2003	Burscough 2 Tamworth 1
2004	Hednesford 3 Canvey 2
2005	Grays 1 Hucknall 1* (Grays won 6-5 on pens)

At Upton Park

2006	Grays 2 Woking 0

At Wembley

2007	Stevenage 3 Kidderminster 2
2008	Ebbsfleet 1 Torquay 0
2009	Stevenage 2 York 0
2010	Barrow 2 Stevenage 1*
2011	Darlington 1 Mansfield 0 *
2012	York 2 Newport 0
2013	Wrexham 1 Grimsby 1 * Wrexham won 4-1 on pens
2014	Cambridge Utd 4 Gosport 0
2015	North Ferriby 3 Wrexham 3* (North Ferriby won 5-4 on pens)
2016	Halifax 1 Grimsby 0
2017	York 3 Macclesfield 2
2018	Brackley 1 Bromley 1
2019	AFC Fylde 1 Leyton Orient 0

(* Brackley won 5-4 on pens)

(*After extra-time)

FA Youth Cup Winners

Year	Winners	Runners-up	Agg
1953	Man Utd	Wolves	9-3
1954	Man Utd	Wolves	5-4
1955	Man Utd	WBA	7-1
1956	Man Utd	Chesterfield	4-3
1957	Man Utd	West Ham	8-2
1958	Wolves	Chelsea	7-6
1959	Blackburn	West Ham	2-1
1960	Chelsea	Preston	5-2
1961	Chelsea	Everton	5-3
1962	Newcastle	Wolves	2-1
1963	West Ham	Liverpool	6-5
1964	Man Utd	Swindon	5-2
1965	Everton	Arsenal	3-2

1966	Arsenal	Sunderland	5-3
1967	Sunderland	Birmingham	2-0
1968	Burnley	Coventry	3-2
1969	Sunderland	WBA	6-3
1970	Tottenham	Coventry	4-3
1971	Arsenal	Cardiff	2-0
1972	Aston Villa	Liverpool	5-2
1973	Ipswich	Bristol City	4-1
1974	Tottenham	Huddersfield	2-1
1975	Ipswich	West Ham	5-1
1976	WBA	Wolves	5-0
1977	Crystal Palace	Everton	1-0
1978	Crystal Palace	Aston Villa	*1-0
1979	Millwall	Man Utd	2-0
1980	Aston Villa	Man City	3-2
1981	West Ham	Tottenham	2-1
1982	Watford	Man Utd	7-6
1983	Norwich	Everton	6-5
1984	Everton	Stoke	4-2
1985	Newcastle	Watford	4-1
1986	Man City	Man Utd	3-1
1987	Coventry	Charlton	2-1
1988	Arsenal	Doncaster	6-1
1989	Watford	Man City	2-1
1990	Tottenham	Middlesbrough	3-2
1991	Millwall	Sheffield Wed	3-0
1992	Man Utd	Crystal Palace	6-3
1993	Leeds	Man Utd	4-1
1994	Arsenal	Millwall	5-3

1995	Man Utd	Tottenham	†2-2
1996	Liverpool	West Ham	4-1
1997	Leeds	Crystal Palace	3-1
1998	Everton	Blackburn	5-3
1999	West Ham	Coventry	9-0
2000	Arsenal	Coventry	5-1
2001	Arsenal	Blackburn	6-3
2002	Aston Villa	Everton	4-2
2003	Man Utd	Middlesbrough	3-1
2004	Middlesbrough	Aston Villa	4-0
2005	Ipswich	Southampton	3-2
2006	Liverpool	Man City	3-2
2007	Liverpool	Man Utd	††2-2
2008	Man City	Chelsea	4-2
2009	Arsenal	Liverpool	6-2
2010	Chelsea	Aston Villa	3-2
2011	Man Utd	Sheffield Utd	6-3
2012	Chelsea	Blackburn	4-1
2013	Norwich	Chelsea	4-2
2014	Chelsea	Fulham	7-6
2015	Chelsea	Man City	5-2
2016	Chelsea	Man City	4-2
2017	Chelsea	Man City	6-2
2018	Chelsea	Arsenal	7-1
2019	Liverpool	Man City	*†††1-1

†††Liverpool won 5-3 on pens
(*One match only; †Manchester Utd won 4-3 on pens, ††Liverpool won 4-3 on pens)

CHARITY/COMMUNITY SHIELD RESULTS (POST WAR)
[CHARITY SHIELD]

1948	Arsenal	Manchester Utd	4-3
1949	Portsmouth	Wolves	*1-1
1950	England World Cup XI	FA Canadian Tour Team	4-2
1951	Tottenham	Newcastle	2-1
1952	Manchester Utd	Newcastle	4-2
1953	Arsenal	Blackpool	3-1
1954	Wolves	WBA	*4-4
1955	Chelsea	Newcastle	3-0
1956	Manchester Utd	Manchester City	1-0
1957	Manchester Utd	Aston Villa	4-0
1958	Bolton	Wolves	4-1
1959	Wolves	Nottm Forest	3-1
1960	Burnley	Wolves	*2-2
1961	Tottenham	FA XI	3-2
1962	Tottenham	Ipswich Town	5-1
1963	Everton	Manchester Utd	4-0
1964	Liverpool	West Ham	*2-2
1965	Manchester Utd	Liverpool	*2-2
1966	Liverpool	Everton	1-0
1967	Manchester Utd	Tottenham	*3-3
1968	Manchester City	WBA	6-1
1969	Leeds	Manchester City	2-1
1970	Everton	Chelsea	2-1
1971	Leicester	Liverpool	1-0

1972	Manchester City	Aston Villa	1-0
1973	Burnley	Manchester City	1-0
1974	Liverpool	Leeds	1-1
	(Liverpool won 6-5 on penalties)		
1975	Derby Co	West Ham	2-0
1976	Liverpool	Southampton	1-0
1977	Liverpool	Manchester Utd	*0-0
1978	Nottm Forest	Ipswich	5-0
1979	Liverpool	Arsenal	3-1
1980	Liverpool	West Ham	1-0
1981	Aston Villa	Tottenham	*2-2
1982	Liverpool	Tottenham	1-0
1983	Manchester Utd	Liverpool	2-0
1984	Everton	Liverpool	1-0
1985	Everton	Manchester Utd	2-0
1986	Everton	Liverpool	*1-1
1987	Everton	Coventry	1-0
1988	Liverpool	Wimbledon	2-1
1989	Liverpool	Arsenal	1-0
1990	Liverpool	Manchester Utd	*1-1
1991	Arsenal	Tottenham	*0-0
1992	Leeds	Liverpool	4-3
1993	Manchester Utd	Arsenal	1-1
	(Manchester Utd won 5-4 on penalties)		
1994	Manchester Utd	Blackburn	2-0
1995	Everton	Blackburn	1-0
1996	Manchester Utd	Newcastle	4-0
1997	Manchester Utd	Chelsea	1-1
	(Manchester Utd won 4-2 on penalties)		
1998	Arsenal	Manchester Utd	3-0
1999	Arsenal	Manchester Utd	2-1
2000	Chelsea	Manchester Utd	2-0
2001	Liverpool	Manchester Utd	2-1

COMMUNITY SHIELD

2002	Arsenal	Liverpool	1-0
2003	Manchester Utd	Arsenal	1-1
	(Manchester Utd won 4-3 on penalties)		
2004	Arsenal	Manchester Utd	3-1
2005	Chelsea	Arsenal	2-1
2006	Liverpool	Chelsea	2-1
2007	Manchester Utd	Chelsea	1-1
	(Manchester Utd won 3-0 on penalties)		
2008	Manchester Utd	Portsmouth	0-0
	(Manchester Utd won 3-1 on pens)		
2009	Chelsea	Manchester Utd	2-2
	(Chelsea won 4-1 on pens)		
2010	Manchester Utd	Chelsea	3-1
2011	Manchester Utd	Manchester City	3-2
2012	Manchester City	Chelsea	3-2
2013	Manchester Utd	Wigan	2-0
2014	Arsenal	Manchester City	3-0
2015	Arsenal	Chelsea	1-0
2016	Manchester Utd	Leicester	2-1
2017	Arsenal	Chelsea	1-1
	(Arsenal won 4-1 on pens)		
2018	Manchester City	Chelsea	2-0

(Fixture played at Wembley 1974–2000 and from 2007); Millennium Stadium 2001–06; Villa Park 2012) * Trophy shared

SCOTTISH TABLES 2018–2019

LADBROKES PREMIERSHIP

				Home				Away					
		P	W	D	L	F	A	W	D	L	F	A	Gd	Pts
1	Celtic	38	17	2	0	46	7	10	4	5	31	13	57	87
2	Rangers	38	14	4	1	45	7	9	5	5	37	20	55	78
3	Kilmarnock	38	12	2	5	32	14	7	8	4	18	17	19	67
4	Aberdeen	38	9	4	6	33	27	11	3	5	24	17	13	67
5	Hibernian	38	6	9	4	28	16	8	3	8	23	23	12	54
6	Hearts	38	8	4	7	22	18	7	2	10	20	32	-8	51
7	St. Johnstone	38	8	5	6	23	21	7	2	10	15	27	-10	52
8	Motherwell	38	9	4	6	29	20	6	2	11	17	36	-10	51
9	Livingston	38	10	2	7	28	17	1	9	9	14	27	-2	44
10	Hamilton	38	5	5	9	20	34	4	1	14	8	41	-47	33
11	St Mirren	38	5	2	12	15	26	3	6	10	19	40	-32	32
12	Dundee	38	1	4	14	14	36	4	2	13	17	42	-47	21

Celtic into Champions League first qualifying round; Rangers, Kilmarnock and Aberdeen into Europa League first qualifying round
Play-offs (on agg): **Quarter-final**: Inverness 4 Ayr 2. **Semi-final**: Dundee Utd 4 Inverness 0. **Final**: St Mirren 1 Dundee Utd 1, aet, St Mirren won 2-0 pens. **Player of Year**: James Forrest (Celtic). **Manager of Year**: Steve Clarke (Kilmarnock). **PFA Team of Year**: A McGregor (Rangers), Tavernier (Rangers), Ajer (Celtic), Boyata (Celtic), Halkett (Livingston), Forrest (Celtic), C McGregor (Celtic), Brown (Celtic), Shinnie (Aberdeen), Morelos (Rangers), Kent (Rangers). **Leading scorers**: 18 Morelos (Rangers); 17 Cosgrove (Aberdeen); 15 Edouard (Celtic), Turnbull (Motherwell), 14 Tavernier (Rangers); 11 Arfield (Rangers), Brophy (Kilmarnock), Forrest (Celtic)'; 10 Naismith (Hearts); 9 Christie (Celtic), Sinclair (Celtic); 8 Defoe (Rangers), Kamberi (Hibernian), Miller (Dundee), Stewart (Kilmarnock).

LADBROKES CHAMPIONSHIP

				Home				Away					
		P	W	D	L	F	A	W	D	L	F	A	Gd	Pts
1	Ross Co	36	13	4	1	32	9	8	4	6	31	25	29	71
2	Dundee Utd	36	11	3	4	29	25	8	5	5	20	15	9	65
3	Inverness	36	5	8	5	22	23	9	6	3	26	17	8	56
4	Ayr	36	7	5	6	25	19	8	4	6	25	19	12	54
5	Morton	36	6	7	5	21	23	5	6	7	15	22	-9	46
6	Partick	36	7	3	8	25	27	5	4	9	18	25	-9	43
7	Dunfermline	36	5	3	10	13	18	6	5	7	20	22	-7	41
8	Alloa	36	6	2	10	13	21	4	7	7	26	32	-14	39
9	Queen of South	36	5	7	6	26	22	4	4	10	15	26	-7	38
10	Falkirk	36	3	7	8	19	27	6	4	8	18	22	-12	38

Play-offs (on agg): **Semi-finals**: Queen of South 5 Montrose 2. Raith 3 Forfar 2. **Final**: Queen of South 3 Raith 1. **Player of Year**: Stephen Dobbie (Queen of South). **Manager of Year**: Steven Ferguson/Stuart Kettlewell (Ross Co). **PFA Team of Year**: Fox (Ross Co), Fraser (Ross Co), Graham (Alloa), Rose (Ayr), Smith (Ayr), Doran (Inverness), Polworth (Inverness), Lindsay (Ross Co), Gardyne (Ross Co), Dobbie (Queen of South), Shankland (Ayr). **Leading scorers**: 24 Shankland (Ayr); 21 Dobbie (Queen of South); 17 McKay (Ross Co); 12 Rudden (Falkirk); Safranko (Dundee Utd); 10 Trouten (Alloa); 9 Mullin (Ross Co), Clark (Dundee Utd), Graham (Ross Co)

		P	W	D	L	F	A	W	D	L	F	A	Gd	Pts
				Home						Away				
1	Arbroath	36	11	4	3	33	21	9	6	3	30	17	25	70
2	Forfar	36	12	3	3	30	18	7	3	8	24	29	7	63
3	Raith	36	11	4	3	41	20	5	8	5	34	29	26	60
4	Montrose	36	9	4	5	29	27	6	2	10	20	23	-1	51
5	Airdrieonians	36	6	4	8	22	19	8	2	8	29	25	7	48
6	Dumbarton	36	8	5	5	33	26	4	5	9	27	34	0	46
7	East Fife	36	6	3	9	25	31	7	4	7	24	25	-7	46
8	Stranraer	36	6	4	8	24	28	5	5	8	21	29	-12	42
9	Stenhousemuir*	36	5	4	9	18	29	5	3	10	17	32	-26	37
10	Brechin	36	5	6	7	21	28	4	3	11	21	33	-19	36

*Also relegated

Play-offs (on agg): Semi-finals: Annan 4 Stenhousemuir 1. Clyde 4 Edinburgh City 0. **Final:** Clyde 2 Annan 1. **Player of Year:** Bobby Linn (Arbroath). **Manager of Year:** Dick Campbell (Arbroath). **PFA Team of Year:** McCallum (Forfar), Thomson (Arbroath), Little (Arbroath), O'Brien (Arbroath), Murray (Raith), Linn (Arbroath), Hilson (Forfar), Swankie (Arbroath), Thomas (Dumbarton), Nisbet (Raith), Baird (Forfar). **Leading scorers:** 30 Nisbet (Raith), 21 Linn (Arbroath); 16 Baird (Forfar), McGuigan (Stenhousemuir); 15 McIntosh (Airdrieonians); 14 Thomas (Dumbarton); 13 Forbes (Dumbarton), Hilson (Forfar), Gallagher (Dumbarton)

		P	W	D	L	F	A	W	D	L	F	A	Gd	Pts
				Home						Away				
1	Peterhead	36	12	4	2	27	12	12	3	3	38	17	36	79
2	Clyde*	36	12	3	3	35	18	11	2	5	28	17	28	74
3	Edinburgh City	36	11	3	4	31	15	9	4	5	27	19	27	67
4	Annan	36	10	4	4	42	21	10	2	6	28	18	31	66
5	Stirling	36	8	2	8	19	18	5	6	7	25	27	-1	47
6	Cowdenbeath	36	8	3	7	28	24	4	4	10	18	22	0	43
7	Queen's Park	36	7	6	5	24	21	4	4	10	20	26	-3	43
8	Elgin	36	7	2	9	27	35	6	2	10	25	32	-15	43
9	Albion	36	3	3	12	14	40	4	3	11	18	31	-39	27
10	Berwick**	36	3	2	13	13	40	2	2	14	14	51	-64	19

*Also promoted. **relegated

Play-offs (on agg): Semi-final: Cove 5 East Kilbride 1. **Final:** Cove 7 Berwick 0. **Player of Year:** Blair Henderson (Edinburgh City). **Manager of Year:** Danny Lennon (Clyde). **PFA Team of Year:** Currie (Clyde), Thomson (Edinburgh City), Balatoni (Edinburgh City), McNiff (Clyde), Stevenson (Peterhead), Gibson (Peterhead), Brown (Peterhead), Rankin (Clyde), Johnson (Annan), Goodwillie (Clyde), Henderson (Edinburgh City). **Leading scorers:** 30 Henderson (Edinburgh City); 17 Goodwillie (Clyde); 15 McAllister (Peterhead); 13 Sutherland (Peterhead); 12 Muir (Annan), Wallace (Annan); 11 Smith (Annan), Leitch (Peterhead), Smith (Stirling)

LADBROKES SCOTTISH LEAGUE RESULTS 2018–2019

PREMIERSHIP

	Aberdeen	Celtic	Dundee	Hamilton	Hearts	Hibernian	Kilmarnock	Livingston	Motherwell	Rangers	St Johnstone	St Mirren
Aberdeen	–	3-4	5-1	3-0	2-0	1-0	0-2	3-2	1-0	1-1	0-2	4-1
	–	0-3		0-2	2-1		0-0	1-1	3-1	2-4		2-2
Celtic	1-0	–	3-0	1-0	5-0	4-2	5-1	3-1	3-0	1-0	2-0	4-0
	0-0	–		3-0	2-1	2-0	1-0	0-0	4-1	2-1		
Dundee	0-1	0-5	–	4-0	0-3	0-3	1-2	0-0	1-3	1-1	0-2	1-1
	0-2	0-1	–	0-1	0-1	2-4	2-2		0-1			2-3
Hamilton	0-3	0-3	0-2	–	1-4	0-1	1-1	1-0	1-2	1-4	1-2	3-0
		1-1	–	1-0				3-3	1-1	0-5	2-1	1-1
											2-0	
Hearts	2-1	1-0	1-2	2-0	–	0-0	0-1	0-0	1-0	1-2	2-1	4-1
	2-1	1-2			–	1-2	0-1	0-0		1-3	2-0	1-1
Hibernian	1-1	2-0	2-2	6-0	0-1	–	3-2	1-1	3-0	0-0	0-1	2-2
	1-2	0-0		2-0	1-1	–	0-0		2-0	1-1		
	1-2					–						
Kilmarnock	1-2	2-1	3-1	1-1	0-1	3-0	–	2-0	3-1	2-1	2-0	2-1
	0-1	0-1		5-0	1-2	1-0	–		0-0	2-1	2-0	
Livingston	1-2	0-0	4-0	1-0	5-0	2-1	0-0	–	2-0	1-0	0-1	3-1
			1-2	2-0		1-2	1-0	–		0-3	3-1	1-3
			0-1					–				
Motherwell	3-0	1-1	1-0	0-1	0-1	1-0	0-1	1-1	–	3-3	0-1	0-1
			4-3	3-0	2-1			3-0	–	0-3	3-0	1-1
								3-2	–			
Rangers	0-1	1-0	4-0	1-0	3-1	1-1	1-1	3-0	7-1	–	5-1	2-0
	2-0	2-0	4-0		3-0	1-0	1-1			–	0-0	4-0
St Johnstone	1-1	0-6	1-0	4-0	2-2	1-1	0-0	1-0	1-2	1-2	–	2-0
	0-2	0-2	2-0			1-2		1-1	2-0		–	1-0
			2-0								–	
St Mirren	1-2	0-0	2-1	1-3	2-0	0-1	1-2	0-2	0-2	0-2	0-1	–
		0-2	2-1	2-0		1-3	0-1	1-0	1-2		1-1	–

	Alloa	Ayr	Dundee Utd	Dunfermline	Falkirk	Inverness	Morton	Partick	Queen of South	Ross Co
lloa	–	0-2	1-1	0-1	0-2	0-0	0-2	1-0	2-0	0-1
	–	1-3	2-1	0-1	1-2	1-2	2-1	0-2	1-0	1-0
yr	3-0	–	2-0	4-1	4-2	3-2	0-0	2-0	1-1	3-3
	1-1	–	1-0	0-1	0-1	0-1	1-1	0-1	1-0	1-3
undee Utd	4-2	0-5	–	2-3	2-1	1-1	1-1	3-1	2-0	1-5
	2-1	2-1	–	1-0	2-0	1-0	2-1	1-1	1-2	1-0
unfermline	0-0	0-0	0-2	–	0-1	0-3	3-0	1-0	0-1	1-3
	2-2	0-1	0-1	–	0-1	1-0	0-1	3-0	1-0	1-2
lkirk	2-2	0-1	0-2	0-2	–	0-1	0-0	1-1	0-3	1-1
	1-2	2-0	1-1	2-4	–	2-2	0-2	1-1	3-0	3-2
verness	2-2	0-0	1-1	2-2	2-3	–	1-1	3-2	0-0	2-2
	3-2	1-0	0-2	1-0	0-0	–	1-0	1-2	1-2	1-2
orton	0-2	1-5	1-1	1-1	1-0	1-2	–	5-1	2-2	2-1
	1-2	0-0	1-0	0-0	1-1	2-2	–	0-3	1-0	1-0
artick	2-2	0-1	1-2	2-0	2-1	0-1	1-0	–	3-2	0-2
	2-1	1-2	2-1	2-2	1-1	1-2	1-2	–	2-1	2-4
ueen of South	3-3	5-0	1-2	0-0	2-0	3-3	1-2	1-0	–	0-0
	1-2	1-1	0-1	2-1	1-1	0-2	1-1	0-3	–	4-0
ss Co	1-0	2-1	0-1	2-1	2-0	0-0	5-0	2-0	1-1	–
	2-0	3-2	1-1	1-0	2-1	2-1	2-0	0-0	4-0	–

LEAGUE ONE

	Airdrie	Arbroath	Brechin	Dumbarton	East Fife	Forfar	Montrose	Raith	Stenhousemuir	Stranraer
Airdrieonians	–	0-1	1-3	1-1	4-2	0-1	0-1	3-4	0-1	2-0
	–	3-0	0-1	2-2	0-0	1-0	1-0	1-1	0-1	3-0
Arbroath	3-1	–	2-2	3-1	1-0	3-1	2-0	0-2	5-2	3-1
	3-2	–	1-0	1-1	2-1	0-2	1-0	2-2	0-2	1-1
Brechin	0-1	1-5	–	3-2	1-0	4-0	1-3	1-1	1-2	1-1
	0-3	1-1	–	1-0	0-0	2-2	0-3	2-1	1-1	1-2
Dumbarton	1-1	1-1	4-1	–	4-0	0-2	2-1	1-5	2-1	0-1
	3-3	2-0	2-1	–	3-0	2-3	1-1	2-2	1-2	2-1
East Fife	2-1	0-3	3-1	0-2	–	1-0	0-2	2-1	2-0	3-3
	1-2	1-1	0-2	3-4	–	2-3	0-2	1-2	1-1	3-1
Forfar	1-3	2-3	1-1	3-0	0-4	–	2-1	3-2	2-0	0-0
	2-0	2-1	2-0	0-0	3-0	–	1-0	2-1	2-1	2-1
Montrose	0-3	0-4	2-1	1-0	0-2	2-2	–	3-2	3-1	1-1
	2-1	1-1	5-2	1-3	0-2	2-0	–	1-1	2-0	3-1
Raith	2-0	1-1	2-1	4-2	2-2	4-0	1-1	–	2-0	2-1
	1-0	0-1	3-2	4-1	1-2	1-1	4-1	–	5-1	2-3
Stenhousemuir	1-2	1-2	1-0	2-1	0-2	1-2	3-2	1-3	–	0-2
	1-0	1-4	1-1	2-2	1-1	0-3	1-0	1-1	–	0-1
Stranraer	1-2	0-1	0-2	3-2	0-2	2-1	2-0	1-1	2-1	–
	1-4	0-0	3-0	0-3	3-4	2-1	1-2	2-2	1-1	–

LEAGUE TWO

	Albion	Annan	Berwick	Clyde	Cowdenbeath	Edinburgh City	Elgin	Peterhead	Queen of South	Stirling
Albion	–	1-1	3-5	0-3	1-1	1-2	0-1	0-4	0-3	3-0
	–	0-2	1-1	0-1	1-0	3-2	0-3	0-2	0-4	0-5
Annan	3-1	–	4-0	1-2	0-2	1-2	1-1	1-3	3-1	2-2
	4-0	–	6-0	1-1	3-2	3-1	2-0	3-0	2-1	2-2
Berwick	2-0	0-3	–	2-3	0-3	2-2	0-3	0-5	1-2	1-0
	0-3	1-2	–	0-3	1-1	0-2	0-3	2-0	0-3	1-2
Clyde	1-0	1-0	3-3	–	2-0	0-2	4-1	1-3	2-0	1-1
	1-0	2-1	5-0	–	1-0	1-0	2-0	3-3	3-0	3-1
Cowdenbeath	1-1	1-2	4-0	1-1	–	0-2	1-2	2-4	2-0	1-0
	1-0	2-4	2-0	2-1	–	4-1	2-1	1-3	0-0	1-2
Edinburgh City	4-0	2-1	3-0	0-1	1-0	–	4-1	1-1	2-0	3-1
	3-1	1-2	1-0	1-2	2-0	–	1-1	0-0	2-0	0-1
Elgin	4-2	0-1	2-4	1-3	3-1	1-0	–	0-3	2-1	0-3
	0-2	0-1	2-0	2-1	1-4	3-3	–	1-2	2-2	3-2
Peterhead	2-1	2-1	1-0	1-0	1-0	0-1	3-0	–	1-1	4-1
	1-1	2-1	2-0	1-2	2-1	0-0	1-0	–	2-1	1-1
Queen's Park	2-0	0-0	1-0	1-0	0-0	0-2	0-4	2-0	–	1-1
	2-2	0-3	7-1	3-0	1-1	0-4	4-1	0-2	–	0-0
Stirling	1-0	1-2	3-0	0-3	2-1	0-1	5-2	0-2	1-0	–
	0-1	2-1	1-0	0-1	0-1	0-0	2-1	0-1	1-1	–

ANOTHER HISTORIC SEASON FOR CELTIC

Celtic overcame a change of manager and resisted a challenge from their biggest rivals to become the first side in Scottish football to win three successive domestic trebles. They stayed the championship course after losing Brendan Rodgers to Leicester, with Neil Lennon taking over at the club he served as a player and finishing nine points ahead of Steven Gerrard's Rangers. Celtic then came from behind to retain the Scottish Cup with two goals from Odsonne Edouard, one a penalty, against Hearts. Lennon, who was then given the job on a permanent basis, had been part of the side that won all three trophies in the 2000–01 season. Their other hat-tricks came in 1966-67 and 1968-69. This time, they won the first of the three by beating Aberdeen 1-0 in the League Cup Final thanks to a goal from Ryan Christie. Winger James Forrest added to the silverware by collecting Player of the Year awards from the PFA and the footballer writers. Forrest scored 17 goals and had 20 assists to his credit in all competitions. Four of the goals came in a 6-0 win over St Johnsone. He also made a mark on the international scene, scoring a hat-trick for Scotland against Israel, three days after netting twice against Albania. Sadly, the club's triumphs were accompanied by the loss of three players from previous glory days. Billy McNeill, captain of the first British winners of the European Cup, and Stevie Chalmers, who scored the winning goal in that final against Inter Milan in Lisbon in 1967, died within a week of each other. Harry Hood, who gained six championship medals, passed away a month later.

HOW CELTIC WON AN EIGHTH SUCCESSIVE TITLE

AUGUST 2018

4   Celtic 3 (Rogic 8, Edouard 26, Ntcham 50 pen) Livingston 1 (Robinson 90+3). Att: 58,778

11   Hearts 1 (Lafferty 56) Celtic 0. Att: 19,113

26   Celtic 1 (Boyata 63) Hamilton 0. Att: 56,044

SEPTEMBER 2018

2   Celtic 1 (Ntcham 62) Rangers 0. Att: 58,865

14   St Mirren 0 Celtic 0. Att: 7,288

23   Kilmarnock 2 (Burke 64, Findlay 90+3) Celtic 1 (Griffiths 34). Att: 10,988

29   Celtic 1 (Sinclair 63) Aberdeen 0. Att: 59,143

OCTOBER 2018

7   St Johnstone 0 Celtic 6 (Forrest 15, 30, 38, 45, Edouard 22, McGregor 84). Att: 5,993

20   Celtic 4 (Rogic 8, Ntcham 20, Edouard 70, 88) Hibernian 2 (Kamberi 63, Boyle 73). Att: 58,452

31   Dundee 0 Celtic 5 (Rogic 20, Sinclair 33 pen, Forrest 38, Edouard 45, Christie 48). Att: 7,960

NOVEMBER 2018

3   Celtic 5 (Edouard 18, 39, Benkovic 26, Forrest 65, Christie 89 pen) Hearts 0. Att: 58,831

11   Livingston 0 Celtic 0. Att: 9,016

24   Hamilton 0 Celtic 3 (Christie 13, Martin 68 og, Griffiths 82). Att: 4,688

DECEMBER 2018

Motherwell 1 (Johnson 88) Celtic 1 (Christie 13). Att: 8,433
Celtic 5 (Forrest 5, 67, Edouard 25, Lustig 35, Christie 45) Kilmarnock 1 (Brophy 52 pen). Att: 58,457
Hibernian 2 (Slivka 1, Kamberi 59) Celtic 0. Att: 18,142
Celtic 3 (Ralston 28, Sinclair 32 pen, Johnston 45) Motherwell 0. Att: 54,703
Celtic 3 (Johnston 43, 50, Benkovic 69) Dundee 0. Att: 57,234
Aberdeen 3 (May 24 pen, Cosgrove 83 pen, Ferguson 90) Celtic 4 (Sinclair 6, 76, 88, Edouard 86). Att: 20,027
Rangers 1 (Jack 31) Celtic 0. Att: 49,863

JANUARY 2019

Celtic 4 (Burke 11, 55, Sinclair 18 pen, Weah 86) St Mirren 0. Att: 54,821
Celtic 3 (McGregor 40, Christie 77, Sinclair 87) Hamilton 0. Att: 58,264
Celtic 2 (McGregor 53, Christie 55) St Johnstone 0. Att: 54,563

FEBRUARY 2019

St Johnstone 0 Celtic 2 (Forrest 78, Weah 89). Att: 6,242
Celtic 2 (Christie 24, Burke 63) Hibernian 0. Att: 56,730
Kilmarnock 0 Celtic 1 (Brown 90). Att: 11,916
Celtic 4 (Sinclair 31, Edouard 37, 88, Burke 90+1) Motherwell 1 (Ariyibi 51). Att: 58,604
Hearts 1 (Bozanic 56 pen) Celtic 2 (Forrest 36, Edouard 90+2). Att: 18,258

MARCH 2019

Celtic 0 Aberdeen 0. Att: 59,123
Dundee 0 Celtic 1 (Edouard 90+6). Att: 7,608
Celtic 2 (Edouard 27, Forrest 86) Rangers 1 (Kent 63). Att: 58,773

APRIL 2019

St Mirren 0 Celtic 2 (Weah 15, Christie 85). Att: 6,597
Celtic 0 Livingston 0. Att: 58,850
Hibernian 0 Celtic 0. Att: 19,472
Celtic 1 (Simunovic 68) Kilmarnock 0. Att: 58,851

MAY 2019

Aberdeen 0 Celtic 3 (Lustig 40, Simunovic 53, Edouard 88). Att: 15,189 (Celtic clinched title)
Rangers 2 (Tavernier 2, Arfield 63) Celtic 0. Att: 49,844
Celtic 2 (Johnston 2, 84) Hearts 1 (Mulraney 18). Att: 58,696

SCOTTISH HONOURS LIST

PREMIER DIVISION

	First	Pts	Second	Pts	Third	Pts
1975–6	Rangers	54	Celtic	48	Hibernian	43
1976–7	Celtic	55	Rangers	46	Aberdeen	43
1977–8	Rangers	55	Aberdeen	53	Dundee Utd	40
1978–9	Celtic	48	Rangers	45	Dundee Utd	44
1979–80	Aberdeen	48	Celtic	47	St Mirren	42
1980–81	Celtic	56	Aberdeen	49	Rangers	44
1981–2	Celtic	55	Aberdeen	53	Rangers	43
1982–3	Dundee Utd	56	Celtic	55	Aberdeen	55
1983–4	Aberdeen	57	Celtic	50	Dundee Utd	47
1984–5	Aberdeen	59	Celtic	52	Dundee Utd	47
1985–6	*Celtic	50	Hearts	50	Dundee Utd	47
1986–7	Rangers	69	Celtic	63	Dundee Utd	60
1987–8	Celtic	72	Hearts	62	Rangers	60
1988–9	Rangers	56	Aberdeen	50	Celtic	46
1989–90	Rangers	51	Aberdeen	44	Hearts	44
1990–1	Rangers	55	Aberdeen	53	Celtic	41
1991–2	Rangers	72	Hearts	63	Celtic	62
1992–3	Rangers	73	Aberdeen	64	Celtic	60
1993–4	Rangers	58	Aberdeen	55	Motherwell	54
1994–5	Rangers	69	Motherwell	54	Hibernian	53
1995–6	Rangers	87	Celtic	83	Aberdeen	55
1996–7	Rangers	80	Celtic	75	Dundee Utd	60
1997–8	Celtic	74	Rangers	72	Hearts	67

PREMIER LEAGUE

	First	Pts	Second	Pts	Third	Pts
1998–99	Rangers	77	Celtic	71	St Johnstone	57
1999–2000	Rangers	90	Celtic	69	Hearts	54
2000–01	Celtic	97	Rangers	82	Hibernian	66
2001–02	Celtic	103	Rangers	85	Livingston	58
2002–03	*Rangers	97	Celtic	97	Hearts	63
2003–04	Celtic	98	Rangers	81	Hearts	68
2004–05	Rangers	93	Celtic	92	Hibernian	61
2005–06	Celtic	91	Hearts	74	Rangers	73
2006–07	Celtic	84	Rangers	72	Aberdeen	65
2007–08	Celtic	89	Rangers	86	Motherwell	60
2008–09	Rangers	86	Celtic	82	Hearts	59
2009–10	Rangers	87	Celtic	81	Dundee Utd	63
2010–11	Rangers	93	Celtic	92	Hearts	63
2011–12	Celtic	93	**Rangers	73	Motherwell	62
2012–13	Celtic	79	Motherwell	63	St Johnstone	56

Maximum points: 72 except 1986–8, 1991–4 (88), 1994–2000 (108), 2001–10 (114)
* Won on goal difference. **Deducted 10 pts for administration

PREMIERSHIP

	First	Pts	Second	Pts	Third	Pts
2013–14	Celtic	99	Motherwell	70	Aberdeen	68
2014–15	Celtic	92	Aberdeen	75	Inverness	65
2015–16	Celtic	86	Aberdeen	71	Hearts	65
2016–17	Celtic	106	Aberdeen	76	Rangers	67
2017–18	Celtic	82	Aberdeen	73	Rangers	70
2018–19	Celtic	87	Rangers	78	Kilmarnock	67

	First	Pts	Second	Pts	Third	Pts
1890–1a	††Dumbarton	29	Rangers	29	Celtic	24
1891–2b	Dumbarton	37	Celtic	35	Hearts	30
1892–3a	Celtic	29	Rangers	28	St Mirren	23
1893–4a	Celtic	29	Hearts	26	St Bernard's	22
1894–5a	Hearts	31	Celtic	26	Rangers	21
1895–6a	Celtic	30	Rangers	26	Hibernian	24
1896–7a	Hearts	28	Hibernian	26	Rangers	25
1897–8a	Celtic	33	Rangers	29	Hibernian	22
1898–9a	Rangers	36	Hearts	26	Celtic	24
1899–1900a	Rangers	32	Celtic	25	Hibernian	24
1900–1c	Rangers	35	Celtic	29	Hibernian	25
1901–2a	Rangers	28	Celtic	26	Hearts	22
1902–3b	Hibernian	37	Dundee	31	Rangers	29
1903–4d	Third Lanark	43	Hearts	39	Rangers	38
1904–5a	†Celtic	41	Rangers	41	Third Lanark	35
1905–6a	Celtic	46	Hearts	39	Rangers	38
1906–7f	Celtic	55	Dundee	48	Rangers	45
1907–8f	Celtic	55	Falkirk	51	Rangers	50
1908–9f	Celtic	51	Dundee	50	Clyde	48
1909–10f	Celtic	54	Falkirk	52	Rangers	49
1910–11f	Rangers	52	Aberdeen	48	Falkirk	44
1911–12f	Rangers	51	Celtic	45	Clyde	42
1912–13f	Rangers	53	Celtic	49	Hearts	41
1913–14g	Celtic	65	Rangers	59	Hearts	54
1914–15g	Celtic	65	Hearts	61	Rangers	50
1915–16g	Celtic	67	Rangers	56	Morton	51
1916–17g	Celtic	64	Morton	54	Rangers	53
1917–18f	Rangers	56	Celtic	55	Kilmarnock	43
1918–19f	Celtic	58	Rangers	57	Morton	47
1919–20h	Rangers	71	Celtic	68	Motherwell	57
1920–1h	Rangers	76	Celtic	66	Hearts	56
1921–2h	Rangers	67	Rangers	66	Raith	56
1922–3g	Rangers	55	Airdrieonians	50	Celtic	46
1923–4g	Rangers	59	Airdrieonians	50	Celtic	41
1924–5g	Rangers	60	Airdrieonians	57	Hibernian	52
1925–6g	Celtic	58	Airdrieonians	50	Hearts	50
1926–7g	Rangers	56	Motherwell	51	Celtic	49
1927–8g	Rangers	60	Celtic	55	Motherwell	55
1928–9g	Rangers	67	Celtic	51	Motherwell	50
1929–30g	Rangers	60	Motherwell	55	Aberdeen	53
1930–1g	Rangers	60	Celtic	58	Motherwell	56
1931–2g	Motherwell	66	Rangers	61	Celtic	48
1932–3g	Rangers	62	Motherwell	59	Hearts	50
1933–4g	Rangers	66	Motherwell	62	Celtic	47
1934–5g	Rangers	55	Celtic	52	Hearts	50
1935–6g	Celtic	68	Rangers	61	Aberdeen	61
1936–7g	Rangers	61	Aberdeen	54	Celtic	52
1937–8g	Celtic	61	Hearts	58	Rangers	49
1938–9f	Rangers	59	Celtic	48	Aberdeen	46
1946–7f	Rangers	46	Hibernian	44	Aberdeen	39
1947–8g	Hibernian	48	Rangers	46	Partick	46
1948–9i	Rangers	46	Dundee	45	Hibernian	39
1949–50i	Rangers	50	Hibernian	49	Hearts	43
1950–1i	Hibernian	48	Rangers	38	Dundee	38
1951–2i	Hibernian	45	Rangers	41	East Fife	37
1952–3i	*Rangers	43	Hibernian	43	East Fife	39
1953–4i	Celtic	43	Hearts	38	Partick	35

1954–5f	Aberdeen	49	Celtic	46	Rangers	41
1955–6f	Rangers	52	Aberdeen	46	Hearts	45
1956–7f	Rangers	55	Hearts	53	Kilmarnock	42
1957–8f	Hearts	62	Rangers	49	Celtic	46
1958–9f	Rangers	50	Hearts	48	Motherwell	44
1959–60f	Hearts	54	Kilmarnock	50	Rangers	42
1960–1f	Rangers	51	Kilmarnock	50	Third Lanark	42
1961–2f	Dundee	54	Rangers	51	Celtic	46
1962–3f	Rangers	57	Kilmarnock	48	Partick	46
1963–4f	Rangers	55	Kilmarnock	49	Celtic	47
1964–5f	*Kilmarnock	50	Hearts	50	Dunfermline	49
1965–6f	Celtic	57	Rangers	55	Kilmarnock	45
1966–7f	Celtic	58	Rangers	55	Clyde	46
1967–8f	Celtic	63	Rangers	61	Hibernian	45
1968–9f	Celtic	54	Rangers	49	Dunfermline	45
1969–70f	Celtic	57	Rangers	45	Hibernian	44
1970–1f	Celtic	56	Aberdeen	54	St Johnstone	44
1971–2f	Celtic	60	Aberdeen	50	Rangers	44
1972–3f	Celtic	57	Rangers	56	Hibernian	45
1973–4f	Celtic	53	Hibernian	49	Rangers	48
1974–5f	Rangers	56	Hibernian	49	Celtic	45

*Won on goal average †Won on deciding match ††Title shared. Competition suspended 1940–46 (Second World War)

SCOTTISH TITLE WINS

Rangers	*54	Hibernian	4	Kilmarnock	1
Celtic	50	Dumbarton	*2	Motherwell	1
Aberdeen	4	Dundee	1	Third Lanark	1
Hearts	4	Dundee Utd	1	(*Incl 1 shared)

FIRST DIVISION (Since formation of Premier Division)

	First	Pts	Second	Pts	Third	Pts
1975–6d	Partick	41	Kilmarnock	35	Montrose	30
1976–7j	St Mirren	62	Clydebank	58	Dundee	51
1977–8j	*Morton	58	Hearts	58	Dundee	57
1978–9j	Dundee	55	Kilmarnock	54	Clydebank	54
1979–80j	Hearts	53	Airdrieonians	51	Ayr	44
1980–1j	Hibernian	57	Dundee	52	St Johnstone	51
1981–2j	Motherwell	61	Kilmarnock	51	Hearts	50
1982–3j	St Johnstone	55	Hearts	54	Clydebank	50
1983–4j	Morton	54	Dumbarton	51	Partick	46
1984–5j	Motherwell	50	Clydebank	48	Falkirk	45
1985–6j	Hamilton	56	Falkirk	45	Kilmarnock	44
1986–7k	Morton	57	Dunfermline	56	Dumbarton	53
1987–8k	Hamilton	56	Meadowbank	52	Clydebank	49
1988–9j	Dunfermline	54	Falkirk	52	Clydebank	48
1989–90j	St Johnstone	58	Airdrieonians	54	Clydebank	44
1990–1j	Falkirk	54	Airdrieonians	53	Dundee	52
1991–2k	Dundee	58	Partick	57	Hamilton	57
1992–3k	Raith	65	Kilmarnock	54	Dunfermline	52
1993–4k	Falkirk	66	Dunfermline	65	Airdrieonians	54
1994–5l	Raith	69	Dunfermline	68	Dundee	68
1995–6l	Dunfermline	71	Dundee Utd	67	Morton	67
1996–7l	St Johnstone	80	Airdrieonians	60	Dundee	58
1997–8l	Dundee	70	Falkirk	65	Raith	60
1998–9l	Hibernian	89	Falkirk	66	Ayr	62
1999–2000l	St Mirren	76	Dunfermline	71	Falkirk	68
2000–01l	Livingston	76	Ayr	69	Falkirk	56
2001–02l	Partick	66	Airdie	56	Ayr	52

2002–03l	Falkirk	81	Clyde	72	St Johnstone	67
2003–04l	Inverness	70	Clyde	69	St Johnstone	57
2004–05l	Falkirk	75	St Mirren	60	Clyde	60
2005–06l	St Mirren	76	St Johnstone	66	Hamilton	59
2006–07l	Gretna	66	St Johnstone	65	Dundee	53
2007–08l	Hamilton	76	Dundee	69	St Johnstone	58
2008–09l	St Johnstone	65	Partick	55	Dunfermline	51
2009–10l	Inverness	73	Dundee	61	Dunfermline	58
2010–11l	Dunfermline	70	Raith	60	Falkirk	58
2011–12l	Ross	79	Dundee	55	Falkirk	52
2012–13l	Partick	78	Morton	67	Falkirk	53

CHAMPIONSHIP

	First	Pts	Second	Pts	Third	Pts
2013–14l	Dundee	69	Hamilton	67	Falkirk	66
2014–15l	Hearts	91	Hibernian	70	Rangers	67
2015–16l	Rangers	81	Falkirk	70	Hibernian	70
2016–17l	Hibernian	71	Falkirk	60	Dundee Utd	57
2017 18l	St Mirren	74	Livingston	62	Dundee Utd	61
2018–19l	Ross Co	71	Dundee Utd	65	Inverness	56

Maximum points. a, 36, b, 44; c, 40; d 52; e, 60; f, 68; g, 76; h, 84; i, 60; j, 78; k, 88; l, 108
*Won on goal difference

SECOND DIVISION

	First	Pts	Second	Pts	Third	Pts
1921–2a	Alloa	60	Cowdenbeath	47	Armadale	45
1922–3a	Queen's Park	57	Clydebank	52	St Johnstone	50
1923–4a	St Johnstone	56	Cowdenbeath	55	Bathgate	44
1924–5a	Dundee Utd	50	Clydebank	48	Clyde	47
1925–6a	Dunfermline	59	Clyde	53	Ayr	52
1926 7a	Bo'ness	56	Raith	49	Clydebank	45
1927–8a	Ayr	54	Third Lanark	45	King'sPark	44
1928–9b	Dundee Utd	51	Morton	50	Arbroath	47
1929–30a	*LeithAthletic	57	East Fife	57	Albion	54
1930–1a	Third Lanark	61	Dundee Utd	50	Dunfermline	47
1931–2a	*E Stirling	55	St Johnstone	55	Stenhousemuir	46
1932–3c	Hibernian	55	Queen of South	49	Dunfermline	47
1933 4c	Albion	45	Dunfermline	44	Arbroath	44
1934–5c	Third Lanark	52	Arbroath	50	St Bernard's	47
1935 6c	Falkirk	59	St Mirren	52	Morton	48
1936–7c	Ayr	54	Morton	51	St Bernard's	48
1937–8c	Raith	59	Albion	48	Airdrieonians	47
1938–9c	Cowdenbeath	60	Alloa	48	East Fife	48
1946–7d	Dundee Utd	45	Airdrieonians	42	East Fife	31
1947–8e	East Fife	53	Albion	42	Hamilton	40
1948–9e	*Raith	42	Stirling	42	Airdrieonians	41
1949–50e	Morton	47	Airdrieonians	44	St Johnstone	36
1950–1e	*Queen of South	45	Stirling	45	Ayr	36
1951–2e	Clyde	44	Falkirk	43	Ayr	39
1952–3	E Stirling	44	Hamilton	43	Queen's Park	37
1953–4e	Motherwell	45	Kilmarnock	42	Third Lanark	36
1954–5e	Airdrieonians	46	Dunfermline	42	Hamilton	39
1955–6b	Queen's Park	54	Ayr	51	St Johnstone	49
1956–7b	Clyde	64	Third Lanark	51	Cowdenbeath	45
1957–8b	Stirling	55	Dunfermline	53	Arbroath	47
1958–9b	Ayr	60	Arbroath	51	Stenhousemuir	46
1959–60b	St Johnstone	53	Dundee Utd	50	Queen of South	49

	First		Second		Third	
1960–1b	Stirling	55	Falkirk	54	Stenhousemuir	50
1961–2b	Clyde	54	Queen of South	53	Morton	44
1962–3b	St Johnstone	55	E Stirling	49	Morton	48
1963–4b	Morton	67	Clyde	53	Arbroath	46
1964–5b	Stirling	59	Hamilton	50	Queen of South	45
1965–6b	Ayr	53	Airdrieonians	50	Queen of South	47
1966–7b	Morton	69	Raith	58	Arbroath	57
1967–8b	St Mirren	62	Arbroath	53	East Fife	49
1968–9b	Motherwell	64	Ayr	53	East Fife	48
1969–70b	Falkirk	56	Cowdenbeath	55	Queen of South	50
1970–1b	Partick	56	East Fife	51	Arbroath	46
1971–2b	*Dumbarton	52	Arbroath	52	Stirling	50
1972–3b	Clyde	56	Dunfermline	52	Raith	47
1973–4b	Airdrieonians	60	Kilmarnock	58	Hamilton	55
1974–5b	Falkirk	54	Queen of South	53	Montrose	53

SECOND DIVISION (MODERN)

	First	Pts	Second	Pts	Third	Pts
1975–6d	*Clydebank	40	Raith	40	Alloa	35
1976–7f	Stirling	55	Alloa	51	Dunfermline	50
1977–8f	*Clyde	53	Raith	53	Dunfermline	48
1978–9f	Berwick	54	Dunfermline	52	Falkirk	50
1979–80f	Falkirk	50	E Stirling	49	Forfar	46
1980–1f	Queen's Park	50	Queen of South	46	Cowdenbeath	45
1981–2f	Clyde	59	Alloa	50	Arbroath	50
1982–3f	Brechin	55	Meadowbank	54	Arbroath	49
1983–4f	Forfar	63	East Fife	47	Berwick	43
1984–5f	Montrose	53	Alloa	50	Dunfermline	49
1985–6f	Dunfermline	57	Queen of South	55	Meadowbank	49
1986–7f	Meadowbank	55	Raith	52	Stirling	52
1987–8f	Ayr	61	St Johnstone	59	Queen's Park	51
1988–9f	Albion	50	Alloa	45	Brechin	43
1989–90f	Brechin	49	Kilmarnock	48	Stirling	47
1990–1f	Stirling	54	Montrose	46	Cowdenbeath	45
1991–2f	Dumbarton	52	Cowdenbeath	51	Alloa	50
1992–3f	Clyde	54	Brechin	53	Stranraer	53
1993–4f	Stranraer	56	Berwick	48	Stenhousemuir	47
1994–5g	Morton	64	Dumbarton	60	Stirling	58
1995–6g	Stirling	81	East Fife	67	Berwick	60
1996–7g	Ayr	77	Hamilton	74	Livingston	64
1997–8g	Stranraer	61	Clydebank	60	Livingston	59
1998–9g	Livingston	77	Inverness	72	Clyde	53
1999–2000g	Clyde	65	Alloa	64	Ross Co	62
2000–01g	Partick	75	Arbroath	58	Berwick	54
2001–02g	Queen of South	67	Alloa	59	Forfar Athletic	53
2002–03g	Raith	59	Brechin	55	Airdrie	54
2003–04g	Airdrie	70	Hamilton	62	Dumbarton	60
2004–05g	Brechin	72	Stranraer	63	Morton	62
2005–06g	Gretna	88	Morton	70	Peterhead	57
2006–07g	Morton	77	Stirling	69	Raith	62
2007–08g	Ross	73	Airdrie	66	Raith	60
2008–09g	Raith	76	Ayr	74	Brechin	62
2009–10g	*Stirling	65	Alloa	65	Cowdenbeath	59
2010–11g	Livingston	82	*Ayr	59	Forfar	59
2011–12g	Cowdenbeath	71	Arbroath	63	Dumbarton	58
2012–13g	Queen of South	92	Alloa	67	Brechin	61

LEAGUE ONE

	First	Pts	Second	Pts	Third	Pts
2013–14g	Rangers	102	Dunfermline	63	Stranraer	51
2014–15g	Morton	69	Stranraer	67	Forfar	66
2015–16g	Dunfermline	79	Ayr	61	Peterhead	59
2016–17g	Livingston	81	Alloa	62	Airdrieonians	52
2017–18g	Ayr	76	Raith	75	Alloa	60
2018 19g	Arbroath	70	Forfar	63	Raith	60

Maximum points: a, 76; b, 72; c, 68; d, 52e, 60; f, 78; g, 108 *Won on goal average/goal difference

THIRD DIVISION (MODERN)

1994–5	Forfar	80	Montrose	67	Ross Co	60
1995–6	Livingston	72	Brechin	63	Caledonian Th	57
1996–7	Inverness	76	Forfar	67	Ross Co	77
1997–8	Alloa	76	Arbroath	68	Ross Co	67
1998–9	Ross Co	77	Stenhousemuir	64	Brechin	59
1999–2000	Queen's Park	69	Berwick	66	Forfar	61
2000–01	*Hamilton	76	Cowdenbeath	76	Brechin	72
2001–02	Brechin	73	Dumbarton	61	Albion	59
2002–03	Morton	72	East Fife	71	Albion	70
2003–04	Stranraer	79	Stirling	77	Gretna	68
2004–05	Gretna	98	Peterhead	78	Cowdenbeath	51
2005–06	*Cowdenbeath	76	Berwick	76	Stenhousemuir	73
2006–07	Berwick	75	Arbroath	70	Queen's Park	68
2007–08	East Fife	88	Stranraer	65	Montrose	59
2008–09	Dumbarton	67	Cowdenbeath	63	East Stirling	61
2009–10	Livingston	78	Forfar	63	East Stirling	61
2010–11	Arbroath	66	Albion	61	Queen's Park	59
2011–12	Alloa	77	Queen's Park	63	Stranraer	58
2012–13	Rangers	83	Peterhead	59	Queen's Park	56

LEAGUE TWO

	First	Pts	Second	Pts	Third	Pts
2013–14	Peterhead	76	Annan	63	Stirling	58
2014–15	Albion	71	Queen's Park	61	Arbroath	56
2015–16	East Fife	62	Elgin	59	Clyde	57
2016–17	Arbroath	66	Forfar	64	Annan	58
2017–18	Montrose	77	Peterhead	76	Stirling	55
2018 19	Peterhead	79	Clyde	74	Edinburgh City	67

Maximum points: 108 * Won on goal difference

RELEGATED FROM PREMIER DIVISION/PREMIER LEAGUE/PREMIERSHIP

1975–6	Dundee,	St Johnstone	1989–90	Dundee
1976–7	Kilmarnock,	Hearts	1990–1	No relegation
1977–8	Ayr,	Clydebank	1991–2	St Mirren, Dunfermline
1978 9	Hearts,	Motherwell	1992 3	Falkirk, Airdrieonians
1979–80	Dundee,	Hibernian	1993–4	St J'stone, Raith, Dundee
1980–1	Kilmarnock,	Hearts	1994–5	Dundee Utd
1981–2	Partick,	Airdrieonians	1995–6	Falkirk, Partick
1982–3	Morton,	Kilmarnock	1996–7	Raith
1983–4	St Johnstone,	Motherwell	1997–8	Hibernian
1984–5	Dumbarton,	Morton	1998–9	Dunfermline
1985–6	No relegation		1999–2000	No relegation
1986–7	Clydebank,	Hamilton	2000–01	St Mirren
1987–8	Falkirk, Dunfermline, Morton		2001–02	St Johnstone
1988 9	Hamilton		2002 03	No relegation

2003–04	Partick	2012–13	Dundee
2004–05	Dundee	2013–14	Hibernian, **Hearts
2005–06	Livingston	2014–15	St Mirren
2006–07	Dunfermline	2015–16	Dundee Utd
2007–08	Gretna	2016–17	Inverness
2008–09	Inverness	2017–18	Partick, Ross Co
2009–10	Falkirk	2018–19	Dundee
2010–11	Hamilton		
2011–12	Dunfermline, *Rangers		

*Following administration, liquidation and new club formed. **Deducted 15 points for administration

RELEGATED FROM FIRST DIVISION/CHAMPIONSHIP

1975–6	Dunfermline, Clyde	1998–9	Hamilton, Stranraer
1976–7	Raith, Falkirk	1999–2000	Clydebank
1977–8	Alloa, East Fife	2000–01	Morton, Alloa
1978–9	Montrose, Queen of South	2001–02	Raith
1979–80	Arbroath, Clyde	2002–03	Alloa Athletic, Arbroath
1980–1	Stirling, Berwick	2003–04	Ayr, Brechin
1981–2	E Stirling, Queen of South	2004–05	Partick, Raith
1982–3	Dunfermline, Queen's Park	2005–06	Brechin, Stranraer
1983–4	Raith, Alloa	2006–07	Airdrie Utd, Ross Co
1984–5	Meadowbank, St Johnstone	2007–08	Stirling
1985–6	Ayr, Alloa	2008–09	*Livingston, Clyde
1986–7	Brechin, Montrose	2009–10	Airdrie, Ayr
1987–8	East Fife, Dumbarton	2010–11	Cowdenbeath, Stirling
1988–9	Kilmarnock, Queen of South	2011–12	Ayr, Queen of South
1989–90	Albion, Alloa	2012–13	Dunfermline, Airdrie
1990–1	Clyde, Brechin	2013–14	Morton
1991–2	Montrose, Forfar	2014–15	Cowdenbeath
1992–3	Meadowbank, Cowdenbeath	2015–16	Livingston, Alloa
1993–4	Dumbarton, Stirling, Clyde, Morton, Brechin	2016–17	Raith, Ayr
		2017–18	Dumbarton, Brechin
1994–5	Ayr, Stranraer	2018–19	Falkirk
1995–6	Hamilton, Dumbarton	*relegated to Division Three for breaching insolvency rules	
1996–7	Clydebank, East Fife		
1997–8	Partick, Stirling		

RELEGATED FROM SECOND DIVISION/LEAGUE ONE

1993–4	Alloa, Forfar, E Stirling, Montrose, Queen's Park, Arbroath, Albion, Cowdenbeath	2005–06	Dumbarton
		2006–07	Stranraer, Forfar
		2007–08	Cowdenbeath, Berwick
		2008–09	Queen's Park, Stranraer
1994–5	Meadowbank, Brechin	2009–10	Arbroath, Clyde
1995–6	Forfar, Montrose	2010–11	Alloa, Peterhead
1996–7	Dumbarton, Berwick	2011–12	Stirling
1997–8	Stenhousemuir, Brechin	2012–13	Albion
1998–9	East Fife, Forfar	2013–14	East Fife, Arbroath
1999–2000	Hamilton	2014–15	Stirling
2000–01	Queen's Park, Stirling	2015–16	Cowdenbeath, Forfar
2001–02	Morton	2016–17	Peterhead, Stenhousemuir
2002–03	Stranraer, Cowdenbeath	2017–18	Queen's Park, Albion
2003–04	East Fife, Stenhousemuir	2018–19	Stenhousemuir, Brechin
2004–05	Arbroath, Berwick		

RELEGATED FROM LEAGUE TWO

2015–16	East Stirling
2018–19	Berwick

SCOTTISH PREMIERSHIP 2018–2019
(appearances and scorers)

ABERDEEN

Anderson B............. 1 (13)	Gleeson S 7 (8)	McKenna S 30
Ball D.................... 24 (7)	Halford G .... - (2)	McLennan C............ 18 (3)
Campbell D............... 1 (7)	Hoban T....................4 (1)	Ross E ....- (4)
Cerny T.....................1 (1)	Lewis J 37	Ross F 1
Considine A 33	Logan S 25 (4)	Shinnie G 36
Cosgrove S............. 29 (6)	Lowe M 31 (2)	Stewart G................ 12 (3)
Devlin M................. 16 (6)	Mackay-Steven G 19 (1)	Wilson J................ 12 (12)
Ferguson L.................. 33	May S 21 (1)	Wright S....................4 (9)
Forrester C................. 1 (4)	McGinn N 22 (5)	

League goals (57): Cosgrove 17, Ferguson 6, McGinn 5, Mackay-Steven 4, Wilson 4, Considine 3, McLennan 3, Shinnie 3, Anderson 2, Lowe 2, May 2, McKenna 2, Campbell 1, Devlin 1, Hoban 1, Stewart 1
Scottish Cup goals (12): Cosgrove 4, McGinn 3, Considine 1, Lowe 1, McLennan 1, Stewart 1, Opponents 1. **League Cup goals** (5): Mackay-Steven 2, Ferguson 1, May 1, Shinnie 1. **Europa League goals** (2): Ferguson 1, Mackay-Steven 1
Average home league attendance: 14,924. **Player of Year:** Joe Lewis

CELTIC

Ajer K...................... 23 (5)	Edouard O 22 (10)	Morgan L ....- (9)
Arzani D .... - (1)	Forrest J 31 (2)	Mulumbu Y......................1
Bain S 20	Gamboa C 1	Ntcham O 16 (4)
Bayo V .... - (1)	Gordon C 7	Ralston A 3 (1)
Benkovic F............... 17 (3)	Griffiths L 6 (5)	Rogic T................... 16 (5)
Biton N 4 (3)	Hayes J 7 (9)	Simunovic J.............. 16 (2)
Boyata D 19	Henderson E 4 (1)	Sinclair S 24 (9)
Brown S 29 (1)	Hendry J 3 (1)	Tierney K 20 (1)
Burke O 9 (5)	Izaguirre E 13 (1)	Toljan J 7 (3)
Christie R 17 (6)	Johnston M 7 (7)	Weah T.....................4 (9)
Dembele M 1	Lustig M 26 (1)	
Eboue K 1 (1)	McGregor C 33 (3)	

League goals (77): Edouard 15, Forrest 11, Christie 9, Sinclair 9, Johnston 5, Burke 4, McGregor 3, Ntcham 3, Rogic 3, Weah 3, Benkovic 2, Griffiths 2, Lustig 2, Simunovic 2, Boyata 1, Brown 1, Opponents 1
Scottish Cup goals (15): Sinclair 5, Edouard 3, Forrest 3, Brown 2, Rogic 1, Weah 1. **League Cup goals** (8): Christie 2, Griffiths 2, Dembele 1, Forrest 1, Rogic 1, Sinclair 1
Champions League goals (11): Edouard 3, Dembele 2, Forrest 2, McGregor 2, Ntcham 1, Sinclair 1. **Europa League goals** (10): Edouard 2, Griffiths 2, Ntcham 2, Ajer 1, McGregor 1, Sinclair 1, Tierney 1
Average home league attendance: 57,756. **Player of Year:** Callum McGregor

DUNDEE

Boyle A.................... 11 (2)	Deacon R 1 (4)	Horsfield J.............10 (1)
Caulker S............................2	Dieng T 16	Inniss R.................... 9 (2)
Curran C 11 (3)	Hadenius A 3	Kallman B.............. 11 (7)
Curran J 24 (10)	Hamilton J 17	Kamara G.............16 (1)
Dales A..................... 8 (2)	Henvey M .... - (1)	Kerr C 27 (1)

Kusunga G .... 22 (2) Miller K .... 21 (12) Parish E 5
Lambert J .... - (4) Moore C .... 1 (3) Ralph N 26
Madianga K .... 9 (1) Moussa S .... 4 (5) Robertson F 1
McGowan P .... 23 (7) Nabi A .... 6 (7) Robson E 12 (1)
McGowan R .... 15 Nelson A .... 9 (3) Spence L 10 (3)
Meekings J .... 4 Ngwatala E .... 7 (2) Wighton C .... - (3)
Mendy J .... 3 (3) O'Dea D .... 20 (1) Woods M 22 (2)
Miller C .... 15 (1) O'Sullivan J .... 6 (5) Wright S 11 (2)

League goals (31): Miller K 8, Nelson 4, Wright 3, Robson 2, McGowan 2, Woods 2, Boyle 1, Miller C 1, Curran 1, Kallman 1, Kerr 1, Kusunga 1, Madianga 1, Nabi 1, Ngwatala 1, Ralph 1
Scottish Cup goals (1): Curran 1. **League Cup goals** (8): Mendy 2, Moussa 2, Madianga 1, McGowan 1, Spence 1, Wighton 1
Average home league attendance: 6,024. **Player of Year**: Nathan Ralph

HAMILTON ACADEMICAL

Andreu T .... 15 (2) Keatings J .... 8 (9) Mimnaugh R 5 (3)
Bingham R .... 11 (8) Kelly S .... 3 (3) Mucha J 2
Bloomfield M .... 1 (4) Kilgallon M .... 25 Oakley G 14 (1)
Boyd S .... 10 (13) Lyon D .... 1 Ogkmpoe M 3 (3)
Brustad F .... 11 (4) MacKinnon D .... 29 Penny A 3 (5)
Cunningham R .... - (3) Marsden J .... - (1) Smith L .... - (4)
Davies S .... 5 (4) Martin S .... 26 (5) Sowah L 14 (4)
Fulton R .... 4 McGowan A .... 35 Taiwo T 12 (4)
Gogic A .... 12 (4) McMann S .... 27 (1) Tshiembe D 15 (4)
Gordon Z .... 35 (1) McMillan D .... 4 (4) Want S 9 (1)
Imrie D .... 22 (7) Miller M .... 25 (6) Woods G 32

League goals (28): Miller 5, Imrie 4, Oakley 4, Boyd 2, Davies 2, Gordon 2, McGowan 2, Andreu 1, Bingham 1, Bloomfield 1, Brustad 1, Keatings 1, MacKinnon 1, Ogkmpoe 1
Scottish Cup goals: None. **League Cup goals** (5): Miller 3, Bingham 2
Average home league attendance: 2,829

HEART OF MIDLOTHIAN

Amankwaa D .... - (2) Garuccio B .... 13 (4) Mitchell D 14 (6)
Berra C .... 25 Godinho M .... 11 (1) Morrison C 15 (10)
Bozanic O .... 15 (10) Haring P .... 26 Mulraney J 15 (6)
Brandon J .... 5 (2) Hickey A .... 1 (1) Naismith S 19
Burns B .... 3 (2) Hughes A .... 1 (4) Shaughnessy C 10
Clare S .... 23 (5) Ikpeazu U .... 15 (2) Smith C 2 (1)
Cochrane H .... 6 (2) Irving A .... 1 Smith M 28
Dikamona C .... 12 (9) Keena A .... 1 (4) Souttar J 23 (1)
Djoum A .... 30 (2) Lafferty K .... 1 (1) Vanecek D 3 (2)
Doyle C .... 9 Lee O .... 23 (8) Wighton C 8 (9)
Dunne J .... 12 MacLean S .... 17 (8) Zlamal Z 29
Edwards R .... 2 (2) McDonald A .... - (3)

League goals (42): Naismith 10, Haring 5, Bozanic 3, Djoum 3, Clare 3. Ikpeazu 3, Lee 3, MacLean 3, Dunne 2, Burns 1, Dikamona 1, Godinho 1, Lafferty 1, Morrison 1, Mulraney 1, Opponernts 1
Scottish Cup goals (12): Clare 3, Berra 2, Ikpeazu 2, Edwards 1, Keena 1, MacLean 1, Mitchell 1, Souttar 1

League Cup goals (18): Naismith 4, Ikpeazu 3, Lee 3, MacLean 3, Haring 2, Smith M 2, Garuccio 1
Averge home league attendance: 17,564. **Player of Year**: Steven Naismith

HIBERNIAN

Agyepong T 1 (8)	Hyndman E 10 (5)	Milligan M 25 (3)
Allan L 2 (4)	Johnson D .... - (1)	Murray F 2 (4)
Ambrose E 21	Kamberi F 30 (3)	Nelom M 2 (1)
Bartley M 7 (6)	Laidlaw R 1	Omeonga S 11 (4)
Bigirimana G .... - (1)	Mackie S 3 (7)	Porteous R 16
Bogdan A 17 (1)	Maclaren J 6 (6)	Shaw O 1 (15)
Boyle M 17 (1)	Mallan S 36 (1)	Slivka V 19 (10)
Gauld R 4 (1)	Marciano O 20	Spector J .... (1)
Gray D 22 (2)	Mavrias C 2	Stevenson L 33 (1)
Gullan J .... - (2)	McGinn J 1	Swanson D .... - (2)
Hanlon P 26	McGregor D 22 (2)	Whittaker S 12 (3)
Horgan D 26 (7)	McNulty M 13 (2)	

League goals (51): Kamberi 8, Mallan 7, McNulty 7, Shaw 6, Boyle 4, Gray 3, Horgan 3, Porteous 3, McGregor 2, Agyepong 1, Hanlon 1, Hyndman 1, Maclaren 1, Slivka 1, Opponents 3
Scottish Cup goals (7): Horgan 3, Kamberi 1, Mallan 1, McNulty 1, Slivka 1. **League Cup goals** (3): Gray 1, Horgan 1, Mallan 1. **Europa League goals** (16): Kamberi 4, Mallan 4, Ambrose 2, Gray 2, McGinn 2, Shaw 1, Stevenson 1
Average home league attendance: 17,740. **Player of Year**: Stevie Mallan

KILMARNOCK

Bachmann D 25	Erwin I 1	Mulumbu Y 9 (1)
Boyd K 10 (9)	Findlay S 31	Ndjoli M 5 (19)
Boyd S 16 (1)	Jones J 25 (3)	O'Donnell S 36 (1)
Broadfoot K 25 (2)	Kiltie G .... - (3)	Power A 35 (1)
Brophy E 23 (6)	MacDonald J 13	Stewart G 16
Bruce A 3 (1)	Mackay D .... - (1)	Taylor G 36
Burke C 30 (5)	McAleny C 6 (5)	Thomas D .... - (1)
Byrne J .... - (5)	McKenzie R 14 (10)	Tshibola A 21 (6)
Dicker G 30 (5)	Millar L 2 (11)	Waters C 2
Enobakhare B 2 (4)	Millen R 2 (2)	Wilson I .... - (6)

League goals (50): Brophy 11, Stewart 8, Burke 5, Jones 4, Findlay 3, McAleny 3, Boyd K 2, Ndjoli 2, Boyd S 1, Broadfoot 1, McKenzie 1, Millar 1, Millen 1, Mulumbu 1, Power 1, Taylor 1, Tshibola 1, Opponents 3
Scottish Cup goals (2): Burke 1, Findlay 1. **League Cup goals** (10): Boyd K 4, Ndjoli 3, Brophy 1, Erwin 1, Opponents 1
Average home league attendance: 6,894. **Player of Year**: Alan Power

LIVINGSTON

Brown C 4 (1)	Gallagher D 38	Lamie R 23 (2)
Brown J 1	Halkett C 34	Lawless S 29 (6)
Burns B 3 (5)	Hamilton J 2 (11)	Lawson S 16 (9)
Byrne S 29 (3)	Hardie R 13 (8)	Lithgow A 35
Cadden N 4 (8)	Jacobs K 26 (5)	McMillan J 2 (5)
De Vita R .... - (3)	Kaja E 2 (4)	Menga D 20 (5)
Erskine C 8 (2)	Kelly L 36	Miller K 2

Miller L...................... 6 (3)	Saunders S 2 (1)	Van Schaik H .... - (1)
Odofin H...................... 7 (6)	Sibbald C................16 (10)	Van Schaik H .... - (1)
Pittman S 38	Stewart R 2	Wylde G...................... - (2)
Robinson S 19 (7)	Tiffoney S 1 (6)	

League goals (42): Halkett 7, Hardie 7, Pittman 6, Lawless 3, Sibbald 3, Byrne 2, Lithgow 2, Menga 2, Robinson 2, Tiffoney 2, Erskine 1, Gallagher 1, Hamilton 1, Jacobs 1, Lawson 1, McMillan 1
Scottish Cup goals: None. League Cup goals (6): Hamilton 1, McMillan 1, Miller K 1, Miller L 1, Pittman 1
Average home league attendance: 3,664. **Player of Year:** Craig Halkett

MOTHERWELL

Aldred T 37	Frear E..................... 4 (18)	Mbulu C......................4 (2)
Ariyibi G 17	Gillespie M................26 (1)	McCormack R..............- (3)
Bigirimana G............. 12 (7)	Gorrin A 16 (4)	McHugh C................20 (8)
Bowman R 7 (9)	Grimshaw L...........30 (1)	Rose A 10 (2)
Cadden C................ 15 (5)	Hartley P.......................14	Sammon C 6 (10)
Campbell A............... 31 (4)	Hastie J 12 (1)	Scott J....................6 (6)
Carson T.......................12	Johnson D............12 (10)	Semple J....................- (3)
Donnelly L 6 (1)	Livingstone A .... - (3)	Sinclair A 5 (1)
Dunne C 23	Maguire B 1 (1)	Tait R 37 (1)
Ferguson R .... - (1)	Main C 28 (3)	Turnbull D 27 (3)

League goals (46): Turnbull 15, Hastie 6, Johnson 6, Aldred 3, Main 3, Ariyibi 2, Campbell 2, Bigirimana 1, Bowman 1, Cadden 1, Donnelly 1, Frear 1, Hartley 1, McHugh 1, Scott 1, Tait 1
Scottish Cup goals (1): Hastie 1. **League Cup goals** (14): Frear 3, Main 3, Sammon 3, Johnson 2, Bowman 1, Hartley 1, Tait 1
Average home league attendance: 5,239. **Player of Year**: David Turnbull

RANGERS

Arfield S....................28 (1)	Foderingham W 4	Middleton G 4 (11)
Atakayi S .... - (1)	Goldson C 34	Morelos A................27 (3)
Barisic B 14 (2)	Grezda E 7 (6)	Murphy J........................2
Candeias D 26 (7)	Halliday A 18 (5)	Polster M .... - (1)
Coulibaly L 14 (5)	Jack R 26 (4)	McCrorie R............... 11 (9)
Davis S 10 (4)	Kamara G 12 (1)	Rossiter J...................2 (2)
Defoe J................... 10 (7)	Katic N 16 (2)	Tavernier J 36 (1)
Dorrans G .... - (1)	Kent R 25 (2)	Umar S .... - (1)
Ejaria O 11 (3)	Lafferty K 6 (15)	Wallace L ....- (3)
Firth A........................ - (1)	McAuley G 6 (1)	Windass J....................... 1
Flanagan J 14 (2)	McGregor A................34	Worrall J 20 (3)

League goals (82): Morelos 18, Tavernier 14, Arfield 11, Defoe 8, Kent 6, Candeias 5, Jack 4, Lafferty 4, Goldson 3, Grezda 2, Middleton 2, Coulibaly 1, Halliday 1, Kamara 1, Katic 1, Ejaria 1
Scottish Cup goals (9): Morelos 4, Halliday 2, Coulibaly 1, Lafferty 1, Worrall 1. **League Cup goals** (7): Morelos 4, Middleton 2, Katic 1
Europa League goals (17): Morelos 4, Tavernier 3, Arfield 1, Candeias 1, Coulibaly 1, Ejaria 1, Goldson 1, Katic 1, Lafferty 1, Middleton 1, Murphy 1, Opponents 1
Average home league attendance: 49,564. **Player of Year**: Alfredo Morelos

ST JOHNSTONE

Alston B 10 (11)	Gordon L 10 (3)	Nydam T 1 (4)
Anderson S 2 (1)	Goss S 6	O'Halloran M 9 (5)
Bell C 4	Hamilton O .... - (1)	Scougall S .... - (1)
Callachan R 17 (7)	Hendry O 5 (7)	Ohaughnessy J 32 (1)
Clark Z 34	Kane C 14 (16)	Swanson D 6 (17)
Comrie A 1 (1)	Kennedy M 34 (2)	Tanser S 37
Craig L 33 (3)	Kerr J 37	Watt T 22 (7)
Davidson M 26 (2)	McCann A .... - (1)	Wotherspoon D 20 (9)
Easton D 1	McMillan D 7 (5)	Wright D 13 (1)
Foster R 37	Northcott J .... - (1)	

League goals (38): Kennedy 6, Alston 4, Davidson 3, Kane 3, Shaughnessy 3, Tanser 3, Watt 3, Craig 2, Hendry 2, Kerr 2, McMillan 2, Wotherspoon 2, Callachan 1, O'Halloran 1, Opponents 1
Scottish Cup goals (2): Kerr 1, Watt 1. **League Cup goals** (9): Watt 4, Hendry 1, Kennedy 1, McMillan 1, Scougall 1, Wright 1
Average home league attendance: 3,891. **Player of Year**: Jason Kerr

ST MIRREN

Baird J 31 (3)	Hodson L 19 (1)	McGinn P 34 (1)
Breadner C .... - (2)	Jackson S 22 (8)	McGinn S 31 (3)
Brock-Madsen N 3 (1)	Jamieson S .... - (2)	McShane I 4 (4)
Cooke C 3 (8)	Kellerman J 1 (2)	Mullen D 16 (7)
Corbu L 1 (2)	Jones A 14	Muzek M 13 (1)
Coulson H 5 (1)	Kirkpatrick J .... - (2)	Nazon D 6 (4)
Dreyer A 8 (2)	Kpekawa C 4	Popescu M 17
Edwards R 11 (1)	Lyness D 4	Rogers D 4
Erhahon E 19 (2)	Lyons B 14 (1)	Samson C 13
Ferdinand A 18	MacKenzie G 5	Smith C 9 (10)
Flynn R 20 (6)	MacPherson C 10 (3)	Stewart R 1
Hammill A 12 (1)	Magennis K 11 (3)	Tansey G 4 (2)
Hladky V 17	McAllister K 8 (6)	Willock M 7 (5)

Play-off appearances: Baird 2, Cooke 2, Hladky 2, Hodson 2, MacKenzie 2, Magennis 2, McAllister 2, McGinn P 2, McGinn S 2, Popescu 2, Mullen 1 (1), Flynn 1, Ferdinand – (1), Muzek – (1), Nazon – (1)
League goals (34): Jackson 6, Mullen 5, Hammill 4, Cooke 3, McGinn P 3, Magennis 2, McAllister 2, Dreyer 1, Flynn 1, Jones 1, Lyons 1, MacPherson 1, McGinn S 1, Nazon 1, Opponents 2. **Play-offs – goals** (1): Mullen 1
Scottish Cup goals (4): Cooke 1, Erhahon 1, McAllister 1, Nazon 1. **League Cup goals** (8): McGinn 2, Smith 2, Coulson 1, Kellerman 1, Mullen 1, Stewart 1
Average home league attendance: 5,351. **Player of Year**: Vaclav Hladky

BETFRED SCOTTISH LEAGUE CUP 2018–19

(Teams awarded three points for a win, one point for a drawn match after 90 minutes, then penalties with winners awarded one additional point. Eight group winners and four best runners up through to knock-out stage to join four sides competing in Europe – Celtic, Aberdeen, Hibernian and Rangers

GROUP A

	P	W	D	L	F	A	Pts
Ross Co Q	4	3	0	1	6	4	9
Arbroath	4	2	1	1	9	6	8
Alloa	4	2	1	1	9	6	8
Dundee Utd	4	1	2	1	6	3	5
Elgin	4	0	0	4	0	11	0

GROUP B

	P	W	D	L	F	A	Pts
St Johnstone Q	4	3	1	0	5	1	11
Falkirk	4	2	0	2	4	3	6
Montrose	4	2	0	2	3	4	6
Forfar	4	1	1	2	5	7	5
East Fife	4	0	2	2	2	4	2

GROUP C

	P	W	D	L	F	A	Pts
Hearts Q	4	3	1	0	13	2	9
Inverness	4	3	0	1	9	8	9
Cowdenbeath	4	2	0	2	5	10	6
Cove	4	1	0	3	3	5	3
Raith	4	0	1	3	2	7	1

GROUP D

	P	W	D	L	F	A	Pts
Dunfermline Q	4	4	0	0	14	2	12
Dundee Q	4	3	0	1	8	1	9
Brechin	4	1	1	2	3	10	4
Stirling	4	1	0	3	4	9	3
Peterhead	4	0	1	3	0	7	2

GROUP E

	P	W	D	L	F	A	Pts
Ayr Q	4	4	0	0	12	1	12
Partick Q	4	3	0	1	6	3	9
Morton	4	2	0	2	9	5	6
Stenhousemuir	4	1	0	3	4	9	3
Albion	4	0	0	4	0	13	0

GROUP F

	P	W	D	L	F	A	Pts
Livingston Q	4	3	1	0	5	1	11
Airdrieonians	4	2	1	1	9	4	7
Hamilton	4	1	2	1	5	2	6
Annan	4	2	0	2	6	5	6
Berwick	4	0	0	4	0	13	0

GROUP G

	P	W	D	L	F	A	Pts
Motherwell Q	4	3	1	0	11	2	10
Queen of South Q	4	3	0	1	12	5	9
Edinburgh City	4	1	1	2	5	12	5
Clyde	4	1	1	2	5	8	4
Stranraer	4	0	1	3	7	13	2

GROUP H

	P	W	D	L	F	A	Pts
Kilmarnock Q	4	3	1	0	9	2	10
St Mirren Q	4	1	3	0	8	2	9
Dumbarton	4	1	1	2	3	10	5
Queen's Park	4	1	1	2	4	4	4
Spartans	4	0	2	2	3	7	2

SECOND ROUND

Aberdeen 4 St Mirren 0; Dundee 0 Ayr 3; Dunfermline 0 Hearts 1; Hibernian 3 Ross Co 2; Kilmarnock 1 Rangers 3; Livingston 0 Motherwell 1; Partick 1 Celtic 3; Queen of South 2 St Johnstone 4

THIRD ROUND

Hearts 4 Motherwell 2; Hibernian 0 Aberdeen 0 (aet, Aberdeen won 6-5 on pens); Rangers 4 Ayr 0; St Johnstone 0 Celtic 1

SEMI-FINALS

Aberdeen 1 Rangers 0 (Hampden Park); Hearts 0 Celtic 3 (Murrayfield)

FINAL
CELTIC 1 (Christie 45) ABERDEEN 0
Hampden Park (50, 936); Sunday, December 2, 2018

Celtic (4-1-4-1): Bain, Lustig, Boyata (Simunovic 61), Benkovic, Tierney, McGregor, Forrest (Ntcham 86), Rogic (Brown, capt, 64), Christie, Sinclair, Edouard. **Subs not used:** Gordon, Griffiths, Gamboa, Hayes. **Booked:** Forrest, Christie, Rogic. **Manager:** Brendan Rodgers

Aberdeen (4-2-3-1): Lewis, Logan, McKenna, Considine, Lowe, Ball, Shinnie (capt), Mackay-Steven (McLennan 45), Ferguson, McGinn (Wilson 70), Cosgrove (Anderson 79). **Subs not used:** Cerny, Gleeson, Wright, May. **Booked:** Ball, Logan, Cosgrove, Ferguson. **Manager:** Derek McInnes

Referee: A Dallas. **Half-time:** 1-0

SCOTTISH LEAGUE CUP FINALS

1946	Aberdeen beat Rangers (3-2)	1985	Rangers beat Dundee Utd (1-0)
1947	Rangers beat Aberdeen (4-0)	1986	Aberdeen beat Hibernian (3-0)
1948	East Fife beat Falkirk (4-1 after 0-0 draw)	1987	Rangers beat Celtic (2-1)
1949	Rangers beat Raith Rov (2-0)	1988†	Rangers beat Aberdeen (5-3 on pens after 3-3 draw)
1950	East Fife beat Dunfermline Athletic (3-0)	1989	Rangers beat Aberdeen (3-2)
1951	Motherwell beat Hibernian (3-0)	1990†	Aberdeen beat Rangers (2-1)
1952	Dundee beat Rangers (3-2)	1991†	Rangers beat Celtic (2-1)
1953	Dundee beat Kilmarnock (2-0)	1992	Hibernian beat Dunfermline Athletic (2-0)
1954	East Fife beat Partick (3-2)	1993†	Rangers beat Aberdeen (2-1)
1955	Hearts beat Motherwell (4-2)	1994	Rangers beat Hibernian (2-1)
1956	Aberdeen beat St Mirren (2-1)	1995	Raith Rov beat Celtic (6-5 on pens after 2-2 draw)
1957	Celtic beat Partick (3-0 after 0-0 draw)	1996	Aberdeen beat Dundee (2-0)
1958	Celtic beat Rangers (7-1)	1997	Rangers beat Hearts (4-3)
1959	Hearts beat Partick (5-1)	1998	Celtic beat Dundee Utd (3-0)
1960	Hearts beat Third Lanark (2-1)	1999	Rangers beat St Johnstone (2-1)
1961	Rangers beat Kilmarnock (2-0)	2000	Celtic beat Aberdeen (2-0)
1962	Rangers beat Hearts (3-1 after 1-1 draw)	2001	Celtic beat Kilmarnock (3-0)
1963	Hearts beat Kilmarnock (1-0)	2002	Rangers beat Ayr (4-0)
1964	Rangers beat Morton (5-0)	2003	Rangers beat Celtic (2-1)
1965	Rangers beat Celtic (2-1)	2004	Livingston beat Hibernian (2-0)
1966	Celtic beat Rangers (2-1)	2005	Rangers beat Motherwell (5-1)
1967	Celtic beat Rangers (1-0)	2006	Celtic beat Dunfermline Athletic (3-0)
1968	Celtic beat Dundee (5-3)	2007	Hibernian beat Kilmarnock (5-1)
1969	Celtic beat Hibernian (6-2)	2008	Rangers beat Dundee Utd (3-2 on pens after 2-2 draw)
1970	Celtic beat St Johnstone (1-0)	2009†	Celtic beat Rangers (2-0)
1971	Rangers beat Celtic (1-0)	2010	Rangers beat St Mirren (1-0)
1972	Partick beat Celtic (4-1)	2011†	Rangers beat Celtic (2-1)
1973	Hibernian beat Celtic (2-1)	2012	Kilmarnock beat Celtic (1-0)
1974	Dundee beat Celtic (1-0)	2013	St Mirren beat Hearts (3-2)
1975	Celtic beat Hibernian (6-3)	2014	Aberdeen beat Inverness Caledonian Thistle (4-2 on pens after 0-0 draw)
1976	Rangers beat Celtic (1-0)	2015	Celtic beat Dundee Utd (2-0)
1977†	Aberdeen beat Celtic (2-1)	2016	Ross Co beat Hibernian (2-1)
1978†	Rangers beat Celtic (2-1)	2017	Celtic beat Aberdeen (3-0)
1979	Rangers beat Aberdeen (2-1)	2018	Celtic beat Motherwell (2-0)
1980	Dundee Utd beat Aberdeen (3-0 after 0-0 draw)	2019	Celtic beat Aberdeen (1-0)
1981	Dundee Utd beat Dundee (3-0)		(† After extra time; Skol Cup 1985–93, Coca-Cola Cup 1995–97, Co-operative Insurance Cup 1999 onwards)
1982	Rangers beat Dundee Utd (2-1)		
1983	Celtic beat Rangers (2-1)		
1984†	Rangers beat Celtic (3-2)		

SUMMARY OF SCOTTISH LEAGUE CUP WINNERS

Rangers	27	East Fife	3	Motherwell	1
Celtic	18	Hibernian	3	Partick	1
Aberdeen	7	Dundee Utd	2	Raith	1
Hearts	4	Kilmarnock	2	Ross Co	1
Dundee	3	Livingston	1	St Mirren	1

IRN BRU SCOTTISH CHALLENGE CUP 2018–19

First round – north: Alloa 3 Stirling 1; Cove 2 Montrose 2 (Montrose won 4-3 on pens); Cowdenbeath 1 East Fife 3; Dundee U21 2 Hibernian U21 2 (Dundee U21 won 4-3 on pens); Dundee Utd 3 St Johnstone U21 2; Elgin 1 Arbroath 1 (Arbroath won 7-6 on pens); Hearts U21 1 Ross Co 2; Inverness 1 Dunfermline 2; Inverurie 0 Formartine 1; Livingston U21 0 Forfar 0 (Livingston U21 won 5-4 on pens); Peterhead 2 Brechin 1; Raith 3 Aberdeen U21 1

First round – south: Annan 4 Celtic U21 0; Berwick 0 Airdrieonians 3; Dumbarton 2 Morton 1; East Kilbride 1 Spartans 1 (East Kilbride won 5-4 on pens); East Stirling 0 Motherwell U21 3; Edinburgh City 3 Albion 1; Hamilton U21 4 Clyde 1; Kilmarnock U21 1 St Mirren U21 2; Queen's Park 0 Ayr 0 (Queen's Park won 4-2 on pens); Rangers U21 1 Falkirk 2; Stenhousemuir 0 Queen of South 5; Stranraer 0 Partick 5

Second round: Airdrieonians 0 Sutton 1; Arbroath 3 Annan 0; Boreham Wood 0 Dunfermline 0 (Dunfermline won 6-5 on pens); Coleraine 1 Formartine 1 (Coleraine won 2-1 on pens); Dumbarton 0 Montrose 1; Dundee U21 1 Motherwell U21 2; Dundee Utd 1 Alloa 1 (Alloa won 5-4 on pens); East Fife 2 Partick 1; East Kilbride 2 Edinburgh City 3; Falkirk 0 Connah's Quay 1; New Saints 2 Queen's Park 2 (Queen's Park won 4-2 on pens); Peterhead 0 Bohemians 1; Queen of South 4 Crusaders 3; Ross Co 5 Raith 0; Sligo 4 Livingston U21 1; St Mirren U21 3 Hamilton U21 2

Third round: Arbroath 1 Edinburgh City 4; Bohemians 0 Sutton 0 (Bohemians won 4-3 on pens); Connah's Quay 2 Coleraine 0; Dunfermline 2 Alloa 2 (Alloa won 5-4 on pens); East Fife 2 Queen of South 0; Motherwell U21 2 Sligo 0; Ross Co 3 Montrose 1; St Mirren U21 2 Queen's Park 4

Quarter-finals: Edinburgh City 2 Alloa 2 (Edinburgh City won 4-3 on pens); Motherwell U21 1 Ross Co 2; Queen's Park 1 Connah's Quay 2; Bohemians v East Fife – postponed, frozen pitch, Bohemians withdrew

Semi-finals: Connah's Quay 1 Edinburgh City 1 (aet, Connah's Quay won 5-4 on pens); Ross Co 2 East Fife 1

FINAL

CONNAH'S QUAY 1 (Bakare 21) ROSS COUNTY 3 (Mullin 75, 79, Lindsay 87)
Caledonian Stadium, Inverness (3,057); Saturday, March 23, 2019
Connah's Quay (4-3-3): Danby, Holmes, Farquharson (Wignall 80), Horan (capt), Barton, Morris (Poole 66), Harrison (Phillips 88), Parker, Bakare, Wilde, Owens. **Subs not used**: Brass, Disney, Owen, Hughes. **Booked**: Holmes, Morris. **Manager**: Andy Morrison
Ross County (4-4-2): Munro, Fraser (capt), Watson, Boyle, Van der Weg, McManus (Mullin 66), Lindsay, Cowie (Spence 90+2), Gardyne (Armstrong 88), Stewart, Graham. **Subs not used**: Fox, Paton, Kelly, Grivosti. **Joint managers**: Stuart Kettlewell, Steven Ferguson
Referee: A Muir. **Half-time**: 1-0

WILLIAM HILL SCOTTISH FA CUP 2018–19

FIRST ROUND

Brora 4 Turriff 3
Burntisland 1 Cumbernauld 4
Dalbeattie 0 Kelty 0
Deveronvale 2 Bonnyrigg 1
Edusport Acad 3 Buckie 1
Forres 2 Civil Service 2
Gala 6 Lossiemouth 0
Gretna 3 Vale of Leithen 2
Huntly 1 East Stirling 4
Linlithgow 3 Fort William 0

Nairn 1 Beith 3
Rothes 4 Clachnacuddin 0
Strathspey 0 Coldstream 2
Univ Stirling 2 Keith 1
Whitehill 1 Edinburgh Univ 0
Wick 1 Auchinleck 2
Inverurie 3 Fraserburgh 4
Replays
Civil Service 2 Forres 1
Kelty 3 Dalbeattie 1

SECOND ROUND

Albion 0 Formartine 2
Beith 4 Linlithgow 0
Derwick 3 Gretna 1
Brora 6 Coldstream 0
Cove 1 Auchinleck 1
Cowdenbeath 2 Clyde 1
Cumbernauld 1 BSC Glasgow 4
Deveronvale 1 Stirling Univ 2
East Kilbride 3 Spartans 1

Edinburgh City 1 Civil Service 0
Edusport Acad 1 Fraserburgh 2
Elgin 2 Whitehill 0
Gala 2 East Stirling 0
Peterhead 3 Kelty 2
Rothes 0 Annan 1
Stirling 1 Queen's Park 2
Replay
Auchinleck 2 Cove 1

THIRD ROUND

Airdrieonians 3 Dumbarton 0
Alloa 3 Brechin 0
Arbroath 0 Stranraer 1
Beith 0 Ayr 3
Derwick 1 East Fife 2
Cowdenbeath 1 Brora 0
East Kilbride 1 Gala 0
Edinburgh City 1 Inverness 1
Forfar 2 BSC Glasgow 0
Fraserburgh 0 Auchinleck 1

Montrose 0 Annan 0
Morton 1 Peterhead 1
Queen of South 4 Formartine 1
Queen's Park 0 Raith 3
Stenhousemuir 4 Falkirk 2
Stirling Univ 0 Elgin 4
Replays
Annan 3 Montrose 4
Inverness 6 Edinburgh City 1
Peterhead 0 Morton 3

FOURTH ROUND

Aberdeen 1 Stenhousemuir 1
Auchinleck 1 Ayr 0
Celtic 3 Airdrieonians 0
Cowdenbeath 1 Rangers 3
Dundee 1 Queen of South 1
East Fife 2 Morton 1
Hearts 1 Livingston 0
Hibernian 4 Elgin 0
Inverness 4 East Kilbride 0
Kilmarnock 2 Forfar 0

Montrose 0 Dundee Utd 4
Motherwell 1 Ross Co 2
Partick 4 Stranraer 1
Raith 3 Dunfermline 0
St Johnstone 2 Hamilton 0
St Mirren 3 Alloa 2
Replays
Queen of South 3 Dundee 0
Stenhousemuir 1 Aberdeen 4

FIFTH ROUND

Aberdeen 4 Queen of South 1
Celtic 5 St Johnstone 0
East Fife 0 Partick 1
Hearts 4 Auchinleck 0
Hibernian 3 Raith 1
Kilmarnock 0 Rangers 0

Ross Co 2 Inverness 2
St Mirren 1 Dundee Utd 2
Replays
Inverness 2 Ross Co 2
(aet, Inverness won 5-4 on pens)
Rangers 5 Kilmarnock 0

Aberdeen 1 **Rangers** 1
Dundee Utd 1 **Inverness** 2
Hibernian 0 **Celtic** 2
Partick 1 **Hearts** 1

Replays
Hearts 2 Partick 1
Rangers 0 **Aberdeen** 2

SEMI-FINALS (both at Hampden Park)

Aberdeen 0 **Celtic** 3   **Hearts** 3 Inverness 0

FINAL

HEARTS 1 (Edwards 53) **CELTIC 2** (Edouard 62 pen 82)
Hampden Park (49,434): Saturday, May 25, 2019
Hearts (4-3-3): Zlamal, Smith, Souttar, Berra (capt), Hickey, Edwards, Haring (Bozanic 80), Djoum, Clare (Wighton 75), MacLean (Ikpeazu 78), Mulraney. **Subs not used**: Doyle, Shaughnessy, Burns, Cochrane. **Booked**: Zlamal, Djoum, Ikpeazu. **Manager**: Craig Levein
Celtic (4-2-3-1): Bain, Lustig, Simunovic, Ajer, Hayes (Bitton 89), Brown (capt), McGregor, Forrest, Rogic (Ntcham 70), Johnston (Sinclair 72), Edouard. **Subs not used**: De Vries, Toljan, Benkovic, Dembele. **Booked**: Bain, Brown. **Manager**: Neil Lennon
Referee: W Collum. **Half-time**: 0-0

SCOTTISH FA CUP FINALS

1874	Queen's Park beat Clydesdale (2-0)	**1899**	Celtic beat Rangers (2-0)
1875	Queen's Park beat Renton (3-0)	**1900**	Celtic beat Queen's Park (4-3)
1876	Queen's Park beat Third Lanark (2-0 after 1-1 draw)	**1901**	Hearts beat Celtic (4-3)
		1902	Hibernian beat Celtic (1-0)
1877	Vale of Leven beat Rangers (3-2 after 0-0, 1-1 draws)	**1903**	Rangers beat Hearts (2-0 after 0-0, 1-1 draws)
1878	Vale of Leven beat Third Lanark (1-0)	**1904**	Celtic beat Rangers (3-2)
1879	Vale of Leven awarded Cup (Rangers withdrew after 1-1 draw)	**1905**	Third Lanark beat Rangers (3-1 after 0-0 draw)
1880	Queen's Park beat Thornlibank (3-0)	**1906**	Hearts beat Third Lanark (1-0)
1881	Queen's Park beat Dumbarton (3-1)	**1907**	Celtic beat Hearts (3-0)
1882	Queen's Park beat Dumbarton (4-1 after 2-2 draw)	**1908**	Celtic beat St Mirren (5-1)
1883	Dumbarton beat Vale of Leven (2-1 after 2-2 draw)	**1909**	Cup withheld because of riot after two drawn games in final between Celtic and Rangers (2-2, 1-1)
1884	Queen's Park awarded Cup (Vale of Leven withdrew from Final)	**1910**	Dundee beat Clyde (2-1 after 2-2, 0-0 draws)
1885	Renton beat Vale of Leven (3-1 after 0-0 draw)	**1911**	Celtic beat Hamilton (2-0 after 0-0 draw)
		1912	Celtic beat Clyde (2-0)
1886	Queen's Park beat Renton (3-1)	**1913**	Falkirk beat Raith (2-0)
1887	Hibernian beat Dumbarton (2-1)	**1914**	Celtic beat Hibernian (4-1 after 0-0 draw)
1888	Renton beat Cambuslang (6-1)	**1915–19**	No competition (World War 1)
1889	Third Lanark beat Celtic (2-1)	**1920**	Kilmarnock beat Albion (3-2)
1890	Queen's Park beat Vale of Leven (2-1 after 1-1 draw)	**1921**	Partick beat Rangers (1-0)
1891	Hearts beat Dumbarton (1-0)	**1922**	Morton beat Rangers (1-0)
1892	Celtic beat Queen's Park (5-1)	**1923**	Celtic beat Hibernian (1-0)
1893	Queen's Park beat Celtic (2-1)	**1924**	Airdrieonians beat Hibernian (2-0)
1894	Rangers beat Celtic (3-1)	**1925**	Celtic beat Dundee (2-1)
1895	St Bernard's beat Renton (2-1)	**1926**	St Mirren beat Celtic (2-0)
1896	Hearts beat Hibernian (3-1)	**1927**	Celtic beat East Fife (3-1)
1897	Rangers beat Dumbarton (5-1)	**1928**	Rangers beat Celtic (4-0)
1898	Rangers beat Kilmarnock (2-0)	**1929**	Kilmarnock beat Rangers (2-0)
		1930	Rangers beat Partick (2-1 after 0-0 draw)
		1931	Celtic beat Motherwell (4-2 after 2-2 draw)
		1932	Rangers beat Kilmarnock (3-0 after 1-1 draw)

1933	Celtic beat Motherwell (1-0)
1934	Rangers beat St Mirren (5-0)
1935	Rangers beat Hamilton (2-1)
1936	Rangers beat Third Lanark (1-0)
1937	Celtic beat Aberdeen (2-1)
1938	East Fife beat Kilmarnock (4-2 after 1-1 draw)
1939	Clyde beat Motherwell (4-0)
1940-6	No competition (World War 2)
1947	Aberdeen beat Hibernian (2-1)
1948†	Rangers beat Morton (1-0 after 1-1 draw)
1949	Rangers beat Clyde (4-1)
1950	Rangers beat East Fife (3-0)
1951	Celtic beat Motherwell (1-0)
1952	Motherwell beat Dundee (4-0)
1953	Rangers beat Aberdeen (1-0 after 1-1 draw)
1954	Celtic beat Aberdeen (2-1)
1955	Clyde beat Celtic (1-0 after 1-1 draw)
1956	Hearts beat Celtic (3-1)
1957†	Falkirk beat Kilmarnock (2-1 after 1-1 draw)
1958	Clyde beat Hibernian (1-0)
1959	St Mirren beat Aberdeen (3-1)
1960	Rangers beat Kilmarnock (2-0)
1961	Dunfermline beat Celtic (2-0 after 0-0 draw)
1962	Rangers beat St Mirren (2-0)
1963	Rangers beat Celtic (3-0 after 1-1 draw)
1964	Rangers beat Dundee (3-1)
1965	Celtic beat Dunfermline (3-2)
1966	Rangers beat Celtic (1-0 after 0-0 draw)
1967	Celtic beat Aberdeen (2-0)
1968	Dunfermline beat Hearts (3-1)
1969	Celtic beat Rangers (4-0)
1970	Aberdeen beat Celtic (3-1)
1971	Celtic beat Rangers (2-1 after 1-1 draw)
1972	Celtic beat Hibernian (6-1)
1973	Rangers beat Celtic (3-2)
1974	Celtic beat Dundee Utd (3-0)
1975	Celtic beat Airdrieonians (3-1)
1976	Rangers beat Hearts (3-1)
1977	Celtic beat Rangers (1-0)
1978	Rangers beat Aberdeen (2-1)
1979†	Rangers beat Hibernian (3-2 after two 0-0 draws)
1980†	Celtic beat Rangers (1-0)
1981	Rangers beat Dundee Utd (4-1 after 0-0 draw)
1982†	Aberdeen beat Rangers (4-1)
1983†	Aberdeen beat Rangers (1-0)
1984†	Aberdeen beat Celtic (2-1)
1985	Celtic beat Dundee Utd (2-1)
1986	Aberdeen beat Hearts (3-0)
1987†	St Mirren beat Dundee Utd (1-0)
1988	Celtic beat Dundee Utd (2-1)
1989	Celtic beat Rangers (1-0)
1990†	Aberdeen beat Celtic (9-8 on pens after 0-0 draw)
1991†	Motherwell beat Dundee Utd (4-3)
1992	Rangers beat Airdrieonians (2-1)
1993	Rangers beat Aberdeen (2-1)
1994	Dundee Utd beat Rangers (1-0)
1995	Celtic beat Airdrieonians (1-0)
1996	Rangers beat Hearts (5-1)
1997	Kilmarnock beat Falkirk (1-0)
1998	Hearts beat Rangers (2-1)
1999	Rangers beat Celtic (1-0)
2000	Rangers beat Aberdeen (4-0)
2001	Celtic beat Hibernian (3-0)
2002	Rangers beat Celtic (3-2)
2003	Rangers beat Dundee (1-0)
2004	Celtic beat Dunfermline (3-1)
2005	Celtic beat Dundee Utd (1-0)
2006†	Hearts beat Gretna (4-2 on pens after 1-1 draw)
2007	Celtic beat Dunfermline (1-0)
2008	Rangers beat Queen of the South (3-2)
2009	Rangers beat Falkirk (1-0)
2010	Dundee Utd beat Ross Co (3-0)
2011	Celtic beat Motherwell (3-0)
2012	Hearts beat Hibernian (5-1)
2013	Celtic beat Hibernian (3-0)
2014	St Johnstone beat Dundee Utd (2-0)
2015	Inverness beat Falkirk (2-1)
2016	Hibernian beat Rangers (3-2)
2017	Celtic beat Aberdeen (2-1)
2018	Celtic beat Motherwell (2-0)
2019	Celtic beat Hearts (2-1)

† After extra time

SUMMARY OF SCOTTISH CUP WINNERS

Celtic 39, Rangers 33, Queen's Park 10, Hearts 8, Aberdeen 7, Clyde 3, Hibernian 3, Kilmarnock 3, St Mirren 3, Vale of Leven 3, Dundee Utd 2, Dunfermline 2, Falkirk 2, Motherwell 2, Renton 2, Third Lanark 2, Airdrieonians 1, Dumbarton 1, Dundee 1, East Fife 1, Inverness 1, Morton 1, Partick 1, St Bernard's 1, St Johnstone 1

BROTHERS SEE RED

Goalkeeping brothers Max and Blair Currie were both sent off in Scottish League matches on the same day last season. Max, 22, playing for Stranraer, was dismissed after clashing with an Arbroath player. Blair, 25, saw red in Clyde's game against Annan, but was cleared of violent conduct on appeal and had his red card rescinded.

VANARAMA NATIONAL LEAGUE 2018–2019

				Home				Away						
		P	W	D	L	F	A	W	D	L	F	A	GD	PTS
1	Leyton Orient	46	14	6	3	11	8	25	14	7	73	35	38	89
2	Solihull	46	12	8	3	13	3	25	11	10	73	43	30	86
3	Salford *	46	14	5	4	11	5	25	10	11	77	45	32	85
4	Wrexham	46	17	3	3	8	6	25	9	12	59	29	10	81
5	AFC Fylde	46	15	4	4	7	11	22	15	9	72	41	31	81
6	Harrogate	46	11	6	6	10	5	21	11	14	78	57	21	74
7	Eastleigh	46	11	5	7	11	3	22	8	16	62	63	-1	74
8	Ebbsfleet	46	10	3	10	8	10	18	13	15	64	50	14	67
9	Gateshead	46	9	7	7	10	2	19	9	18	52	48	4	66
10	Sutton	46	9	9	5	8	5	17	14	15	55	60	-5	65
11	Barrow	46	9	6	8	7	8	17	13	16	52	51	1	64
12	Bromley	46	11	5	7	5	7	16	12	18	68	69	-1	60
13	Barnet	46	7	8	8	9	4	16	12	18	45	50	-5	60
14	Dover	46	9	5	9	7	7	16	12	18	58	64	-6	60
15	Chesterfield	46	8	8	7	6	9	14	17	15	55	53	2	59
16	FC Halifax	46	8	11	4	5	9	13	20	13	44	43	1	59
17	Hartlepool	46	9	6	8	6	8	15	14	17	56	62	-6	59
18	Dag & Red	46	8	8	7	7	3	15	11	20	50	56	-6	56
19	Maidenhead	46	9	4	10	7	2	16	6	24	45	70	-25	54
20	Boreham	46	7	7	9	5	9	12	16	18	53	65	-12	52
21	Aldershot	46	7	6	10	4	5	11	11	24	38	67	-29	44
22	Braintree	46	6	3	14	5	5	11	8	27	48	78	-30	41
23	Havant & W	46	7	6	10	2	7	9	13	24	62	84	-22	40
24	Maidstone	46	3	4	16	6	3	9	7	30	37	82	-45	34

*also promoted

Player of Year: Josh Coulson (Leyton Orient). **Manager of Year**: Justin Edinburgh (Leyton Orient)
Leading scorers: 27 Rowe (AFC Fylde); 26 McCallum (Eastleigh); 23 Bonne (Leyton Orient); 21 Rooney (Salford); Boden (Gateshead/Chesterfield); 16 Cheek (Ebbsfleet); 15 Muldoon (Harrogate), Rutherford (Havant)
Team of Year: Brill (Leyton Orient), Hare (Eastleigh), Pearson (Wrexham), Piergianni (Salford, Jones (Barrow), McAnuff (Leyton Orient), Carter (Solihull), Osborne Solihull), Rowe (AFC Fylde), Bonne (Leyton Orient), McCallum (Eastleigh)

CHAMPIONS

1979–80	Altrincham	1994–95	Macclesfield
1980–81	Altrincham	1995–96	Stevenage
1981–82	Runcorn	1996–97*	Macclesfield
1982–83	Enfield	1997–98*	Halifax
1983–84	Maidstone	1998–99*	Cheltenham
1984–85	Wealdstone	1999–2000*	Kidderminster
1985–86	Enfield	2000–01*	Rushden
1986–87*	Scarborough	2001–02*	Boston
1987–88*	Lincoln	2002–03*	Yeovil
1988–89*	Maidstone	2003–04*	Chester
1989–90*	Darlington	2004–05*	Barnet
1990–91*	Barnet	2005–06*	Accrington
1991–92*	Colchester	2006–07*	Dagenham
1992–93*	Wycombe	2007–08*	Aldershot
1993–94	Kidderminster	2008–09*	Burton

2009–10*	Stevenage
2010–11*	Crawley
2011–2012*	Fleetwood
2012–13*	Mansfield
2013–14*	Luton
2014–15*	Barnet
2015–16*	Cheltenham
2016-17*	Lincoln
2017–18*	Macclesfield
2018–19*	Leyton Orient

*Promoted to Football League
Conference – Record
attendance: 11,085 Bristol
Rov v Alfreton, April 25, 2015

	AFC Fylde	Aldershot	Barnet	Barrow	Boreham W	Braintree	Bromley	Chesterfield	Dag & R.	Dover	Eastleigh	Ebbsfleet	Gateshead	Halifax	Harrogate	Hartlepool	Havant & W.	Leyton O	Maidenhead	Maidstone	Salford	Solihull	Sutton	Wrexham
AFC Fylde	–	3-0	1-0	2-1	3-0	1-1	2-1	0-1	1-1	4-0	0-1	2-0	1-0	0-2	1-2	4-1	6-2	1-3	2-1	2-0	0-2	3-1	2-2	2-0
Aldershot	0-0	–	2-0	1-1	1-1	1-0	3-2	0-2	2-1	2-0	0-2	0-0	2-1	3-0	2-0	1-1	2-0	1-2	0-0	0-1	0-1	0-3	2-1	0-0
Barnet	1-1	2-0	–	1-1	1-1	1-0	1-1	0-2	2-1	2-0	0-1	0-3	1-1	3-0	2-2	1-3	0-0	2-0	1-0	0-1	1-3	2-0	0-1	1-2
Barrow	1-1	1-1	3-1	–	1-2	2-1	1-1	2-1	2-1	2-0	1-2	2-1	0-1	2-4	0-1	0-0	2-2	1-0	1-0	0-1	1-3	2-0	2-2	1-2
Boreham W	1-1	1-1	1-1	1-2	–	1-1	3-2	0-1	1-0	2-3	2-1	0-0	2-2	2-4	2-0	0-1	1-3	1-0	3-1	1-0	1-3	1-2	1-2	0-0
Braintree	2-1	4-0	1-0	1-1	1-1	–	1-3	2-0	1-0	2-1	0-4	0-0	0-4	2-4	0-1	1-1	3-4	1-0	0-2	1-0	2-3	1-2	1-2	0-2
Bromley	3-2	3-0	4-4	0-2	2-4	–		3-3	0-2	2-2	5-1	1-1	1-0	2-2	1-0	4-0	4-0	2-1	0-1	4-1	0-2	0-3	2-2	0-1
Chesterfield	0-0	0-1	1-0	4-4	1-0	1-3	3-3	–	0-2	2-3	3-3	0-5	1-3	1-2	2-1	4-0	1-3	1-5	2-0	1-2	2-0	0-4	3-0	0-0
Dag & R.	2-1	1-0	1-1	1-0	1-0	2-0	1-1	2-0	–	1-3	1-3	1-2	0-1	2-1	2-1	1-2	3-1	1-2	1-3	1-2	0-0	1-1	1-0	1-2
Dover	2-1	1-0	1-2	3-0	0-2	–	0-0	0-2	1-3	–	1-2	1-3	2-1	2-3	2-3	4-3	3-1	2-0	2-0	3-1	1-4	0-2	3-0	0-1
Eastleigh	0-0	1-2	0-1	1-0	2-1	2-1	1-1	0-2	0-2	2-2	–	1-1	4-0	0-1	2-1	0-1	0-0	1-1	1-1	1-1	1-1	1-2	3-2	1-1
Ebbsfleet	1-3	3-1	1-0	3-2	4-2	0-1	1-2	1-0	0-5	0-1	1-1	–	0-1	2-3	0-1	0-1	0-0	1-0	1-2	0-1	2-0	0-0	0-0	4-2
Gateshead	0-1	2-1	1-0	1-1	0-1	2-1	0-1	3-1	1-0	3-0	0-1	0-1	–	1-1	2-3	2-1	0-0	2-0	3-0	1-0	2-1	1-2	0-0	2-1
Halifax	0-0	3-0	2-0	0-0	3-1	4-2	0-1	2-0	1-0	0-1	0-0	0-1	1-1	–	1-2	3-2	3-2	0-3	1-0	2-2	0-1	3-1	2-2	0-0
Harrogate	1-2	4-1	2-0	4-2	3-1	1-1	1-2	4-0	1-2	2-2	4-0	1-1	2-0	1-2	–	1-1	1-1	0-3	1-0	2-2	0-1	3-1	2-2	2-0
Hartlepool	1-2	1-1	1-3	2-0	1-0	2-1	2-0	0-1	1-2	0-0	2-2	3-3	2-1	2-1	2-2	–	1-1	1-2	3-2	2-2	2-1	0-1	1-2	2-3
Havant & W.	2-0	1-1	2-1	0-0	2-1	2-0	1-2	3-0	1-0	3-2	3-3	0-1	0-1	1-2	0-1	7-0	–	1-2	5-2	1-1	1-1	0-1	1-2	2-3
Leyton O	2-0	0-0	2-1	1-0	0-0	3-1	2-2	3-1	1-0	0-0	1-1	1-2	2-0	2-0	2-0	0-1	4-0	–	3-0	3-2	0-2	0-1	1-0	1-0
Maidenhead	0-6	3-1	1-1	1-0	3-1	1-1	2-0	1-1	1-0	2-0	1-1	0-1	0-1	2-2	0-1	0-1	2-1	0-2	–	3-2	0-3	1-2	0-1	2-0
Maidstone	1-1	4-0	0-0	1-2	0-2	0-1	0-1	0-3	1-3	0-2	1-1	1-1	2-4	1-2	2-1	3-0	2-1	2-1	3-2	–	0-2	2-0	2-0	1-1
Salford	0-1	4-0	0-0	3-1	2-2	1-3	3-2	1-2	2-0	4-1	2-1	1-2	1-0	2-1	3-2	3-1	3-0	1-1	3-0	1-0	–	2-2	2-0	2-0
Solihull	1-2	1-0	2-2	0-1	2-1	2-0	2-2	0-0	4-1	3-0	0-2	1-1	0-0	2-0	0-1	1-1	3-2	1-2	5-0	0-0	0-2	–	2-2	1-0
Sutton	1-2	2-1	0-0	0-4	0-3	2-2	1-1	2-0	1-1	2-2	1-1	4-2	1-1	2-1	1-2	1-2	2-2	1-0	2-2	2-1	2-1	2-2	–	1-0
Wrexham	0-0	1-0	2-0	1-0	3-1	0-2	1-0	1-0	2-2	0-1	4-1	3-1	2-1	2-1	0-2	3-1	1-0	0-2	1-0	5-1	1-0	2-2	1-0	–

NATIONAL LEAGUE NORTH

	P	W	D	L	F	A	GD	Pts
Stockport	42	24	10	8	77	36	41	82
Chorley*	42	24	9	9	83	41	42	81
Brackley	42	22	11	9	72	40	32	77
Spennymoor	42	22	10	10	78	48	30	76
Altrincham	42	20	11	11	85	56	29	71
Blyth	42	20	9	13	74	62	12	69
Bradford PA	42	18	11	13	71	61	10	65
Telford	42	17	14	11	64	55	9	65
Chester	42	16	14	12	60	62	-2	62
Kidderminster	42	17	9	16	68	62	6	60
Boston	42	17	7	18	62	60	2	58
York	42	16	10	16	58	63	-5	58
Leamington	42	13	15	14	57	60	-3	54
Southport	42	13	14	15	58	55	3	53
Alfreton	42	13	12	17	53	67	-14	51
Darlington	42	12	14	16	56	62	-6	50
Hereford	42	11	16	15	47	58	-11	49
Curzon Ashton	42	13	10	19	44	71	-27	49
Guiseley	42	9	17	16	46	60	-14	44
Ashton Utd	42	9	8	25	43	86	-43	35
FC Utd	42	8	10	24	49	82	-33	34
Nuneaton	42	4	7	31	38	96	-58	19

Play-off-Final: Chorley 0 Spennymoor 0 (aet, Chorley won 4-3 on pens)
*Also promoted

NATIONAL LEAGUE SOUTH

	P	W	D	L	F	A	GD	Pts
Torquay	42	27	7	8	93	41	52	88
Woking*	42	23	9	10	76	49	27	78
Welling	42	23	7	12	70	47	23	76
Chelmsford	42	21	9	12	68	50	18	72
Bath	42	20	11	11	58	36	22	71
Concord	42	20	13	9	69	48	21	70
Wealdstone	42	18	12	12	62	50	12	66
Billericay	42	19	8	15	72	65	7	65
St Albans	42	18	10	14	67	64	3	64
Dartford	42	18	10	14	52	58	-6	64
Slough	42	17	12	13	56	50	6	63
Oxford City	42	17	5	20	64	63	1	56
Chippenham	42	16	7	19	57	64	-7	55
Dulwich	42	13	10	19	52	65	-13	49
Hampton & R	42	13	10	19	49	66	-17	49
Hemel Hempstead	42	12	12	18	52	67	-15	48
Gloucester	42	12	11	19	35	54	-19	47
Eastbourne	42	10	12	20	52	65	-13	42
Hungerford	42	11	9	22	45	72	-27	42
Truro	42	9	12	21	63	87	-24	39
East Thurrock	42	10	7	25	42	63	-21	37
Weston SM	42	8	11	23	50	80	-30	35

Concord deducted 3 pts. **Play-off Final**: Woking 1 Welling 0
*Also promoted

OTHER LEAGUES 2018–19

JD WELSH PREMIER

	P	W	D	L	F	A	GD	Pts
New Saints	32	23	5	4	99	16	83	74
Connah's Quay	32	19	5	8	76	33	43	62
Barry	32	17	5	10	54	51	3	56
Caernarfon	32	13	7	12	45	47	-2	46
Newtown	32	13	7	12	53	56	-3	46
Bala	32	13	5	14	55	63	-8	44
Cardiff Met	32	16	3	13	53	40	13	51
Aberystwyth	32	13	5	14	44	61	-17	44
Carmarthen	32	12	6	14	49	53	-4	39
Cefn Druids	32	10	9	13	43	49	-6	39
Llandudno	32	5	7	20	33	65	-32	22
Llanelli	32	4	4	24	31	101	-70	16

Carmarthen deducted 3 pts. **League Cup Final**: Cardiff Met 2 Cambrian & Clydach 0

BOSTIK PREMIER

	P	W	D	L	F	A	GD	Pts
Dorking	42	28	9	5	87	31	56	93
Carshalton	42	21	8	13	70	49	21	71
Haringey	42	21	8	13	73	54	19	71
Tonbridge	42	21	7	14	59	46	13	70
Merstham	42	20	10	12	60	50	10	70
Folkestone	42	21	6	15	77	58	19	69
Bishop's Stortford	42	20	7	15	70	57	13	67
Leatherhead	42	19	8	15	56	42	14	65
Worthing	42	18	11	13	72	63	9	65
Enfield	42	17	10	15	76	56	20	61
Lewes	42	16	12	14	61	53	8	60
Margate	42	16	11	15	45	48	-3	59
Brightlingsea	42	16	11	15	49	54	-5	59
Bognor Regis	42	14	15	13	71	62	9	57
Hornchurch	42	12	14	16	57	59	-2	50
Potters Bar	42	13	10	19	51	56	-5	49
Corinthian	42	13	8	21	48	74	-26	47
Kingstonian	42	13	6	23	60	78	-18	45
Wingate & F	42	12	7	23	57	86	-29	43
Whitehawk	42	10	11	21	50	72	-22	41
Burgess Hill	42	9	10	23	44	91	-47	37
Harlow	42	9	7	26	53	107	-54	34

Play-off Final: Tonbridge 2 Merstham 0. **Super Play-off**: Met Police 2 Tonbridge 3 (aet) – Tonbridge also promoted

EVOSTICK SOUTH

	P	W	D	L	F	A	GD	Pts
Weymouth	42	25	11	6	96	51	45	86
Taunton	42	26	7	9	89	56	33	85
Met Police	42	22	12	8	91	64	27	78
Salisbury	42	22	11	9	97	69	28	77
Poole	42	20	10	12	84	59	25	70
Kings Langley	42	21	6	15	65	61	4	69
Harrow	42	18	9	15	97	77	20	63
Hartley	42	17	12	13	82	70	12	63
Farnborough	42	18	8	16	72	72	0	62
Chesham	42	15	14	13	54	55	-1	59
Swindon S	42	16	10	16	70	59	11	58
Beaconsfield	42	15	13	14	65	65	0	58
Merthyr	42	15	9	18	68	67	1	54
Wimborne	42	15	7	20	72	75	-3	52
Dorchester	42	14	10	18	67	75	-8	52
Hendon	42	14	10	18	64	74	-10	52
Walton	42	14	9	19	69	78	-9	51
Tiverton	42	13	12	17	65	75	-10	51
Gosport	42	15	5	22	63	70	-7	50
Basingstoke	42	14	7	21	81	82	-1	49
Frome	42	11	4	27	45	74	-29	37
Staines	42	4	0	38	40	168	-128	12

Play-off Final: Met Police 1 Poole 0. **Super Play-off**: Met Police 2 Tonbridge 3 (aet)

EVOSTICK NORTH

	P	W	D	L	F	A	GD	Pts
Farsley	40	28	6	6	82	40	42	90
South Shields	40	27	6	7	86	41	45	87
Warrington	40	25	9	6	69	33	36	84
Nantwich	40	19	12	9	70	59	11	69
Buxton	40	18	12	10	60	45	15	66
Gainsborough	40	19	8	13	53	41	12	65
Basford	40	18	7	15	82	67	15	61
Scarborough	40	18	7	15	70	56	14	61
Witton	40	16	10	14	45	41	4	58
Hyde	40	15	8	17	58	53	5	53
Whitby	40	15	4	21	48	59	-11	49
Lancaster	40	12	13	15	42	61	-19	49
Hednesford	40	13	9	18	51	63	-12	48
Stafford	40	11	14	15	62	70	-8	47
Matlock	40	12	8	20	58	79	-21	44
Bamber Bridge	40	10	12	18	62	67	-5	42
Stalybridge	40	11	9	20	46	62	16	42
Grantham	40	12	6	22	39	72	-33	42
Mickleover	40	10	11	19	37	61	-24	41
Marine	40	10	10	20	39	54	-15	40
Workington	40	8	5	27	38	73	-35	29

North Ferriby resigned – record expunged. **Play-off Final**: South Shields 1 Warrington 2. **Super Play-off**: Warrington 2 King's Lynn 3 (aet)

EVOSTICK SOUTH CENTRAL

	P	W	D	L	F	A	GD	Pts
Kettering	42	30	4	8	84	41	43	94
King's Lynn	42	23	11	8	80	41	39	80
Stourbridge	42	22	12	8	79	40	39	78
Alvechurch	42	21	10	11	66	53	13	73
Stratford	42	21	9	12	55	49	6	72
Coalville	42	20	7	15	78	66	12	67
Biggleswade	42	18	12	12	67	54	13	66
Rushall	42	17	11	14	56	49	7	62
Rushden	42	15	16	11	60	49	11	61
Royston	42	18	7	17	59	53	6	60
Needham Market	42	17	9	16	68	65	3	60
Tamworth	42	15	13	14	64	46	18	58
St Ives	42	14	13	15	36	43	-7	55
Lowestoft	42	14	9	19	55	60	-5	51
Redditch	42	14	8	20	63	79	-16	50
Barwell	42	12	13	17	55	55	0	49
Banbury	42	13	14	15	53	55	-2	49
Hitchin	42	14	6	22	50	71	-21	48
Leiston	42	12	11	19	54	73	-19	47
St Neots	42	9	9	24	32	73	-41	36
Halesowen	42	6	14	22	26	66	-40	32
Bedworth	42	3	10	29	32	91	59	19

Banbury deducted 4 pts. Royston deducted 1 pt. **Play-off Final**: King's Lynn 3 Alvechurch 0.
Super Play-off: Warrington 2 King's Lynn 3 (aet). King's Lynn also promoted

BREEDON HIGHLAND LEAGUE

	P	W	D	L	F	A	GD	Pts
Cove	34	30	3	1	100	12	88	93
Brora	34	27	4	3	99	12	87	85
Fraserburgh	34	26	1	7	125	37	88	79
Formartine	34	22	6	6	97	37	60	72
Inverurie	34	20	6	8	96	48	48	66
Forres	34	21	3	10	79	40	39	66
Wick	34	15	7	12	69	54	15	52
Buckie	34	14	7	13	72	54	18	49
Huntly	34	14	7	13	57	65	-8	49
Rothes	34	13	8	13	73	57	16	44
Nairn	34	13	3	18	61	67	-6	42
Deveronvale	34	13	2	19	55	65	-10	41
Keith	34	10	7	17	62	68	-6	37
Strathspey	34	10	3	21	47	90	-43	33
Turriff	34	9	5	20	74	91	-17	32
Clachnacuddin	34	6	6	22	44	79	-35	24
Lossiemouth	34	2	2	30	29	139	-110	8
Fort William	34	0	2	32	21	245	-224	-7

Fort William deducted 9 points. Rothes deducted 3 pts. **Cup Final**: Cove 2 Formartine 0

GEOSONIC LOWLAND LEAGUE

	P	W	D	L	F	A	GD	Pts
East Kilbride	28	23	3	2	66	12	54	72
BSC	28	18	7	3	67	29	38	61
Kelty	28	16	6	6	61	32	29	54
Spartans	28	14	9	5	63	31	32	51
Civil Service	28	15	4	9	51	38	13	49
East Stirling	28	11	6	11	57	47	10	39
Cumbernauld	28	11	6	11	40	47	-7	39
Gala	28	10	4	14	43	48	-5	34
Edusport Acad	28	9	6	13	43	52	-9	33
Univ Stirling	28	7	10	11	43	50	-7	31
Edinburgh Univ	28	7	9	12	38	54	-16	30
Gretna	28	9	2	17	42	67	-25	29
Vale of Leithen	28	8	5	15	43	74	-31	29
Dalbeattie	28	5	7	16	33	63	-30	22
Whitehill	28	2	6	20	24	70	-46	12

Selkirk resigned – record expunged. **Cup Final:** BSC 2 East Stirling 1

PREMIER LEAGUE UNDER 23

DIVISION ONE

	P	W	D	L	F	A	GD	Pts
Everton	22	12	5	5	31	14	17	41
Arsenal	22	10	7	5	48	36	12	37
Brighton	22	9	8	5	37	27	10	35
Liverpool	22	9	7	6	38	27	11	34
Blackburn	22	9	4	9	38	37	1	31
Chelsea	22	9	4	9	34	33	1	31
Derby	22	9	3	10	29	34	-5	30
Manchester City	22	9	3	10	38	48	-10	30
Tottenham	22	7	7	8	26	38	-12	28
Leicester	22	8	3	11	24	33	-9	27
West Ham	22	8	2	12	41	43	-2	26
Swansea	22	3	7	12	28	42	-14	16

Cup Final: Everton 1 Newcastle 0

DIVISION TWO

	P	W	D	L	F	A	GD	Pts
Wolves	22	13	4	5	45	22	23	43
Southampton*	22	13	4	5	37	21	16	43
Reading	22	12	4	6	45	33	12	40
Newcastle	22	13	1	8	46	37	9	40
Aston Villa	22	11	4	7	35	30	5	37
Manchester Utd	22	8	6	8	33	31	2	30
Stoke	22	7	7	8	42	37	5	28
Middlesbrough	22	6	8	8	32	36	-4	26
WBA	22	5	9	8	33	38	-5	24
Fulham	22	5	7	10	26	34	-8	22
Norwich	22	5	4	13	30	52	-22	19
Sunderland	22	2	6	14	14	47	-33	12

Play-off Final: Southampton 2 Newcastle 1

*Also promoted

WOMEN'S FOOTBALL 2018–19
ARSENAL BACK ON TOP

Arsenal overcame a catalogue of injuries to regain the Women's Super League title. England playmaker Jordan Nobbs, Swiss international Lia Walti and Scotland star Kim Little all had long spells on the sidelines. But their team never looked back after winning the first nine matches, including a 5-0 away success against defending champions Chelsea. It was the club's 15th top-flight title, but the first since 2012. Arsenal, under Australian manager Joe Montemurro, made sure of finishing ahead of Manchester City by beating Brighton 4-0 at the Amex Stadium in front of a record WSL crowd of 5,265l. Leading scorer Vivianne Miedema put them on the way and further goals came from Katie McCabe, Beth Mead and Danielle van de Donk. It was Miedema's 22nd goal of the campaign and the Dutch striker was later named the Professional Footballers' Association's Player of the Year. The football writers' award went to City's 19-goal Nikita Parris, whose club lifted the FA Cup for the second time in three years with a 3-0 win over West Ham, Keira Walsh, Georgia Stanway and Lauren Hemp scoring the goals watched by a Wembley crowd of 43,264. City completed the double, having beaten Arsenal 4-2 on penalties in the League Cup Final after a goalless draw at Bramall Lane, Sheffield.

FA SUPER LEAGUE

	P	W	D	L	F	A	GD	Pts
Arsenal	20	18	0	2	70	13	57	54
Manchester City	20	14	5	1	53	17	36	47
Chelsea	20	12	6	2	46	14	32	42
Birmingham	20	13	1	6	29	17	12	40
Reading	20	8	3	9	33	30	3	27
Bristol City	20	7	4	9	17	34	-17	25
West Ham	20	7	2	11	25	37	-12	23
Liverpool	20	7	1	12	21	38	-17	22
Brighton	20	4	4	12	16	38	-22	16
Everton	20	3	3	14	15	38	-23	12
Yeovil*	20	2	1	17	11	60	49	-3

*Deducted 10 points

CHAMPIONSHIP

	P	W	D	L	F	A	GD	Pts
Manchester Utd	20	18	1	1	98	7	91	55
Tottenham	20	15	1	4	44	27	17	46
Charlton	20	13	2	5	49	21	28	41
Durham	20	11	6	3	37	16	21	39
Sheffield Utd	20	11	1	8	35	31	4	34
Aston Villa	20	6	8	6	30	39	-9	26
Leicester	20	6	3	11	27	44	-17	21
London Bees	20	7	0	13	23	48	-25	21
Lewes	20	5	2	13	23	47	-24	17
Crystal Palace	20	3	2	15	14	44	-30	11
Milwall	20	1	2	17	14	70	-56	5

NATIONAL LEAGUE NORTH

	P	W	D	L	F	A	GD	Pts
Blackburn	24	23	0	1	115	18	97	69
Sunderland	24	15	3	6	83	36	47	48
Derby	24	15	3	6	54	35	19	48
Huddersfield	24	15	2	7	79	40	39	47
Midddlesbrough	24	13	4	7	60	41	19	43
Fylde	24	13	3	8	48	32	16	42
Stoke	24	9	6	9	59	51	8	33
Guiseley	24	9	4	11	45	48	-3	31
Nottm Forest	24	7	4	13	29	57	-28	25
Hull	24	7	2	15	41	65	-24	23
Sheffield	24	6	3	15	37	55	-18	21
Doncaster	24	4	6	14	32	75	-43	18
Bradford	24	0	0	24	12	140	-128	0

NATIONAL LEAGUE SOUTH

	P	W	D	L	F	A	GD	Pts
Coventry	22	18	3	1	80	14	66	57
Cardiff	22	16	2	4	58	26	32	50
Chichester	22	15	1	6	48	27	21	46
Oxford	22	13	2	7	56	24	32	41
Watford	22	13	1	8	43	40	3	40
Plymouth	22	11	2	9	50	54	-4	35
Loughborough	22	10	4	8	48	32	16	34
Portsmouth	22	9	1	12	41	38	3	28
MK Dons	22	6	1	15	28	52	-24	19
Gillingham	22	5	4	13	24	54	-30	19
QPR	22	2	5	15	28	69	-41	11
Basildon	22	0	2	20	17	91	-74	2

Play-off: Blackburn 3 Coventry 0

THE THINGS THEY SAY ...

'I don't know what Leroy ate before the game but maybe we should put it on the menu for everyone' – **Pep Guardiola**, Manchester City manager, after an outstanding performance by Leroy Sane against Bournemouth.

'It's the best league in the world, but the worst officials. They don't understand what is at stake' – **Neil Warnock**, Cardiff manager, after his side conceded an equaliser to Chelsea, shown to be two yards offside.

'If I knew he was this good I would have paid double' – **Jurgen Klopp**, Liverpool manager, after his £65m Brazilian goalkeeper Alisson ensured a place in the Champions League knockout stage with a stoppage-time save against Napoli.

'A deeply unpleasant but vocal minority which refuses to join us in the 21st century has shamed the great majority of our decent, well-behaved fans' – **Chelsea** statement condemning supporters for abusing Manchester City's Raheem Sterling and for anti-semitic chants during a Europa League game in Budapest.

IRISH FOOTBALL 2018–19

SSE AIRTRICITY LEAGUE OF IRELAND

PREMIER DIVISION

Dundalk	36	27	6	3	85	20	87
Cork City	36	24	5	7	71	27	77
Shamrock	36	18	8	10	57	27	62
Waterford	36	18	5	13	52	44	59
St Patrick's	36	15	5	16	51	47	50
Bohemians	36	13	9	14	52	45	48
Sligo Rov	36	12	6	18	38	50	42
Derry City	36	13	3	20	47	40	42
Limerick	36	7	6	23	25	75	27
Bray Wdrs	36	5	3	28	23	96	18

Leading scorer: 29 Patrick Hoban (Dundalk). **Player of Year:** Michael Duffy (Dundalk). **Young Player of Year:** Jamie McGrath (Dundalk). **Goalkeeper of Year:** Shane Supple (Bohemians). **Personality of Year:** Stephen Kenny (Dundalk).

FIRST DIVISION

	P	W	D	L	F	A	Pts
UCD	27	17	6	4	59	29	57
Finn Harps	27	16	6	5	46	22	54
Shelbourne	27	13	11	3	52	21	50
Drogheda	27	14	7	6	50	27	49
Longford	27	13	6	8	54	36	45
Galway	27	10	7	10	41	36	37
Cabinteely	27	9	3	15	32	45	30
Cobh	27	8	5	14	24	41	29
Wexford	27	4	5	18	23	59	17
Athlone	27	1	4	22	16	81	7

Leading scorer: 15 David O'Sullivan (Shelbourne). **Player of Year:** Gary O'Neill (UCD).

DAILY MAIL CUP FINAL

Dundalk 2 (Hoare, McEleney) **Cork City** 1 (Sadlier (pen), Aviva Stadium, November 4, 2018
Dundalk: Rogers, Gannon (Cleary), Gartland, Hoare, Massey, Shields, Mountney (McGrath), McEleney, Benson (Jarvis), Duffy, Hoban
Cork City: McNulty, McCarthy, Bennett, McLoughlin, Griffin, McCormack (Murphy), Morrissey (McNamee), Keohane (Cummins), Buckley, Sadlier, Sheppard.
Referee: N Doyle (Dublin)

EA SPORTS LEAGUE CUP FINAL

Derry City 3 (Hale, Cole, McEneff (pen) **Cobh Ramblers** 1 (Hull). Brandywell Stadium, Derry, September 10, 2018

DANSKE BANK PREMIERSHIP

	P	W	D	L	F	A	Pts
Linfield	38	26	7	5	77	27	85
Ballymena	38	24	6	8	83	47	78
Glenavon	38	20	10	8	74	46	70
Crusaders	38	20	5	13	68	55	65
Cliftonville	38	19	4	15	70	66	61
Coleraine	38	16	11	12	59	55	56
Glentoran	38	13	10	15	58	53	49
Institute	38	13	5	20	50	72	44
Dungannon	38	11	9	18	44	65	42
Warrenpoint	38	10	9	19	51	79	39
Ards	38	6	9	23	31	63	27
Newry	38	6	5	27	31	68	23

Leading scorer: 20 Joe Gormley (Cliftonville). **Manager of Year:** David Healy (Linfield). **Player of Year:** Jimmy Callacher (Linfield). **Young Player of Year:** Kofi Balmer (Ballymena). **Goalkeeper of Year:** Jonny Tuffey (Glenavon)

BLUEFIN SPORT
CHAMPIONSHIP - DIVISION ONE

	P	W	D	L	F	A	Pts
Larne	32	26	3	3	87	19	81
Carrick	32	20	4	8	59	42	64
Portadown	32	15	6	11	59	55	51
Dundela	32	13	7	12	67	60	46
Ballinamallard	32	12	3	17	39	51	39
H&W	32	11	2	19	45	68	35
Loughall	32	11	9	12	60	62	42
Dergview	32	13	3	16	51	51	42
Ballyclare	32	11	7	14	58	68	40
Knockbreda	32	10	7	15	45	63	37
PSNI	32	9	7	16	48	72	34
Limavady	32	8	8	16	45	62	32

Top six, bottom six split after 22 games
Leading scorer: 22 Martin Donnelly (Larne). **Player of the Year:** Martin Donnelly

TENNENT'S IRISH CUP FINAL

Crusaders 3 (Owens, Lowry, Clarke) **Ballinamallard** 0. Windsor Park, May 4, 2019
Crusaders: H Doherty, Burns, Coates, Lowry, Ward, Cushley (Clarke), Caddell, Forsythe, Ruddy, J Owens (Patterson), Healey
Ballinamallard: Connolly, Taheny, Smyth, Clarke, Arkinson, Campbell, McCartney, (Hume), Kelly (Warrington), Cashel, O'Reilly, McBrien (McManus)
Referee: I McNabb (Newtownabbey)

BETMCLEAN LEAGUE CUP FINAL

Linfield 1 (Waterworth) **Ballymena Utd** 0. Windsor Park, February, 19, 2019

TOALS COUNTY ANTRIM SHIELD FINAL

Crusaders 4 (Cushley 2, Coates, Forsythe) **Linfield** 3 (Stafford, Millar, Coates og). Seaview, March 12, 2019

UEFA CHAMPIONS LEAGUE 2018–19

FIRST QUALIFYING ROUND, FIRST LEG

Alashkert 0 **Celtic** 3 (Edouard 45, Forrest 81, McGregor 90). Att: 4,948. **Cork** 0 Legia Warsaw 1 (Kucharczyk 79). Att: 5,795. Ludogorets 7 (Marcelinho 25, 66, Brown 40 og, Keseru 53, Swierczok 73, 78, 80) **Crusaders** 0. Att: 4,597. Shkendija Tetovo 5 (Emini 14, Ibraimi 38, 53, 60, 66) **New Saints** 0. Att: 2,700

FIRST QUALIFYING ROUND, SECOND LEG

Celtic 3 (Dembele 8, 19 pen, Forrest 35) Alaskert 0. Att: 59,047 (Celtic won 6-0 on agg). **Crusaders** 0 Ludogorets 2 (Brown 11 og, Swierczok 65). Att: 1,116 (Ludogorets won 9-0 on agg). Legia Warsaw 3 (Kante 27, Radovic 73 pen, Lopez 89) **Cork** 0. Att: 14,576 (Legia Warsaw won 4-0 on agg). **New Saints** 4 (Ebbe 15, Redmond 30, Cabango 35, Byrne 90+6) Shkendija Tetovo 0. Att: 756 (Shkendija Tetovo won 5-4 on agg)

FIRST QUALIFYING ROUND, ON AGGREGATE

Astana 3 Sutjeska 0; Hapoel Beer Sheva 7 Flora Tallinn 2; HJK Helsinki 5 Vikingur 2; Malmo 5 Drita 0; Kukesi 1 Valletta 1 (Kukesi won on away goal); MOL Vidi 3 Dudelange 2; Red Star Belgrade 2 Spartaks Jurmala 0; Rosenborg 3 Valur Reykjavik 2; Sheriff Tiraspol 4 Torpedo Kutaisi 2; Spartak Trnava 2 Zrinjski Mostar 1; Suduva 3 Apoel Nicosia 2

SECOND QUALIFYING ROUND, FIRST LEG

Celtic 3 (Edouard 43, 75, Ntcham 46) Rosenborg 1 (Meling 16). Att: 51,184

SECOND QUALIFYING ROUND, SECOND LEG

Rosenborg 0 **Celtic** 0. Att: 14,263 (Celtic won 3-1 on agg)

SECOND QUALIFYING ROUND, ON AGGREGATE

Ajax 5 Sturm Graz 1; Astana 2 Midtjylland 1; BATE Borisov 2 HJK Helsinki 1; Dinamo Zagreb 7 Hapoel Bee Sheva 2; Malmo 2 Cluj-Napoca 1; MOL Vidi 1 Ludogorets 0 PAOK Salonica 5 Basle 1; Qarabag 3 Kukesi 0; Red Belgrade 5 Suduva 0; Shkendija Tetovo 1 Sheriff Tiraspol 0; Spartak Trnava 2 Legia Warsaw 1

THIRD QUALIFYING ROUND, FIRST LEG

Celtic 1 (McGregor 17) AEK Athens 1 (Klonaridis 44). Att: 54, 370

THIRD QUALIFYING ROUND, SECOND LEG

AEK Athens 2 (Rodrigo Galo 6, Livaja 50) **Celtic** 1 (Sinclair 78). Att: 32,300 (AEK Athens won 3-2 on agg)

THIRD QUALIFYING ROUND, ON AGGREGATE

Ajax 5 Standard Liege 2; BATE Borisov 2 Qarabag 1; Benfica 2 Fenerbahce 1; Dinamo Zagreb 3 Astana 0; Dynamo Kiev 3 Slavia Prague 1; MOL Vidi 1 Malmo 1 (MOL Vidi won on away goal); PAOK Salonica 3 Spartak Moscow 2; Red Bull Salzburg 4 Shkendija Tetovo 0; Red Star Belgrade 3 Spartak Trnava 2 (aet)

PLAY-OFFS, ON AGGREGATE

AEK Athens 3 MOL Vidi 2; Ajax 3 Dynamo Kiev 1; Benfica 5 PAOK Salonica 2; PSV Eindhoven 6 BATE Borisov 2; Red Star Belgrade 2 Red Bull Salzburg 2 (Red Star Belgrade won on away goals); Young Boys 3 Dinamo Zagreb 2

GROUP A

September 18, 2018
Club Bruges 0 **Borussia Dortmund** 1 (Pulisic 85). Att: 25,181
Monaco 1 (Grandsir 18) **Atletico Madrid** 2 (Diego Costa 31, Gimenez 45). Att. 10,575

October 3, 2018
Atletico Madrid 3 (Griezmann 28, 67, Koke 90+3) **Club Bruges** 1 (Groeneveld 39). Att: 55,742
Borussia Dortmund 3 (Larsen 51, Alcacer 72, Reus 90+2) **Monaco** 0. Att: 66,099

October 24, 2018
Borussia Dortmund 4 (Witsel 38, Guerreiro 73, 89, Sancho 83) **Atletico Madrid** 0. Att: 66,099
Club Bruges 1 (Wesley 39) **Monaco** 1 (Sylla 32). Att: 23,957

November 6, 2018
Atletico Madrid 2 (Saul 33, Griezmann 80) **Borussia Dortmund** 0. Att: 61,023
Monaco 0 **Club Bruges** 4 (Vanaken 12, 17 pen, Wesley 24, Vormer 85). Att: 8,347

November 28, 2018
Atletico Madrid 2 (Badiashile 2 og, Griezmann 24) **Monaco** 0. Att: 56,314
Borussia Dortmund 0 **Club Bruges** 0. Att: 66,099

December 11, 2018
Club Bruges 0 **Atletico Madrid** 0. Att: 25,645
Monaco 0 **Borussia Dortmund** 2 (Guerreiro 15, 88). Att: 8,731

	P	W	D	L	F	A	Pts
Borussia Dortmund Q	6	4	1	1	10	2	13
Atletico Madrid Q	6	4	1	1	9	6	13
Club Bruges	6	1	3	2	6	5	6
Monaco	6	0	1	5	2	14	1

GROUP B

September 18, 2018
Barcelona 4 (Messi 31, 77, 87, Dembele 74) **PSV Eindhoven** 0. Att: 73,462
Inter Milan 2 (Icardi 86, Vecino 90+2) **Tottenham** 1 (Eriksen 53). Att: 64,123
Tottenham (4-2-3-1): Vorm, Aurier, Sanchez, Vertonghen, Davies, Dier, Dembele, Eriksen, Lamela (Winks 72), Son Heung-min, (Lucas Moura 64), Kane (Rose 89). **Booked**: Sanchez, Vertonghen, Vorm

October 3, 2018
PSV Eindhoven 1 (Rosario 27) **Inter Milan** 2 (Nainggolan 44, Icardi 60). Att: 34,750
Tottenham 2 (Kane 52, Lamela 66) **Barcelona** 4 (Coutinho 2, Rakitic 28, Mesi 56, 90). Att: 82,137
Tottenham (4-2-3-1): Lloris, Trippier, Alderweireld, Sanchez, Davies, Winks, Wanyama (Dier 57), Lucas Moura, Lamela (Llorente 79), Son Heung-min (Sissoko 66), Kane. **Booked**: Alderweireld, Wanyama, Lamela, Kane, Dier

October 24, 2018
Barcelona 2 (Rafinha 32, Jordi Alba 83) **Inter Milan** 0. Att: 86,290
PSV Eindhoven 2 (Lozano 30, De Jong 87) **Tottenham** 2 (Lucas Moura 39, Kane 55). Att: 35,000
Tottenham (4-2-3-1): Lloris, Trippier, Alderweireld, Sanchez, Davies, Dembele (Winks 74),
Dier, Lucas Moura (Lamela 64), Erikson, Son Heung-min (Vorm 81), Kane. **Booked**: Dembele.
Sent off: Lloris (79)

November 6, 2018
Inter Milan 1 (Icardi 87) **Barcelona** 1 (Malcom 83). Att: 70,015
Tottenham 2 (Kane 78, 89) **PSV Eindhoven** 1 (De Jong 2). Att: 46,588
Tottenham (4-3-2-1): Gazzaniga, Aurier (Trippier 75), Alderweireld, Sanchez, Davies, Eriksen,
Winks, Alli, Lucas Moura (Lamela 62), Son Heung-min (Llorente 75), Kane. **Booked**: Son
Heung-min, Trippier

November 28, 2018
PSV Eindhoven 1 (De Jong 83) **Barcelona** 2 (Messi 61, Pique 70). Att: 34, 600
Tottenham 1 (Eriksen 80) **Inter Milan** 0. Att: 57,132
Tottenham (4-3-2-1): Lloris, Aurier, Alderweireld, Vertonghen, Davies, Sissoko, Winks
(Dier 87), Alli, Lamela (Eriksen 70), Lucas Moura (Son-Heung-min 62), Kane. **Booked**:
Alderweireld, Lamela, Son-Heung-Min

December 11, 2018
Barcelona 1 (Dembele 7) **Tottenham** 1 (Lucas Moura 85). Att: 69,961
Tottenham (4-2-3-1): Lloris, Walker-Peters (Lamela 61), Alderweireld, Vertonghen, Rose,
Winks (Llorente 83), Sissoko, Eriksen, Alli, Son-Heung-min (Lucas Moura 70), Kane. **Booked**:
Walker-Peters
Inter Milan 1 (Icardi 73) **PSV Eindhoven** 1 (Lozano 13). Att: 62,533

	P	W	D	L	F	A	Pts
Barcelona Q	6	4	2	0	14	5	14
Tottenham Q	6	2	2	2	9	10	8
Inter Milan	6	2	2	2	6	7	8
PSV Eindhoven	6	0	2	4	6	13	2

GROUP C

September 18, 2018
Liverpool 3 (Sturridge 30, Milner 36 pen, Firmino 90+1) **Paris SG** 2 (Meunier 40, Mbappe
83). Att: 52,478
Liverpool (4-3-3): Alisson, Alexander-Arnold, Gomez, Van Dijk, Robertson, Wijnaldum,
Henderson, Milner, Salah (Shaqiri 85), Sturridge (Firmino 72), Mane (Fabinho 90+3).
Booked: Van Dijk
Red Star Belgrade 0 **Napoli** 0. Att: 49,112

October 3, 2018
Napoli 1 (Insigne 90) **Liverpool** 0. Att: 37,057
Liverpool (4-3-3): Alisson, Alexander-Arnold, Gomez, Van Dijk, Robertson, Milner (Fabinho
76), Wijnaldum, Keita (Henderson 19), Salah, Firmino, Mane (Sturridge 89). **Booked**: Milner
Paris SG 6 (Neymar 20, 22, 81, Cavani 37, Di Maria 42, Mbappe70) **Red Star Belgrade** 1
(Marin 74). Att: 39,979

October 24, 2018
Liverpool 4 (Firmino 20, Salah 45, 51 pen, Mane 80) **Red Star Belgrade** 0. Att: 53,024
Liverpool (4-3-3): Alisson, Alexander-Arnold, Gomez, Van Dijk, Robertson (Moreno 82), Shaqiri
(Lallana 68), Fabinho, Wijnaldum, Salah (Sturridge 73), Firmino, Mane
Paris SG 2 (Rui 61 og, Di Maria 90+3) **Napoli** 2 (Insigne 29, Mertens 77). Att: 46,274

November 6, 2018
Napoli 1 (Insigne 63 pen) **Paris SG** 1 (Bernat 45). Att: 55,489
Red Star Belgrade 2 (Pavlov 22, 29) **Liverpool** 0. Att: 51,318
Liverpool (4-3-3): Alisson, Alexander-Arnold (Gomez 46), Matip, Van Dijk, Robertson, Milner,
Wijnaldum, Lallana (Origi 79), Salah, Sturridge (Firmino 46), Mane. **Booked**: Lallana

November 28, 2018
Napoli 3 (Hamsik 11, Mertens 33, 52) **Red Star Belgrade** 1 (Ben 57). Att: 44,470
Paris SG 2 (Bernat 13, Neymar 37) **Liverpool** 1 (Milner 45 pen). Att: 46,880
Liverpool (4-3-3): Alisson, Gomez, Lovren, Van Dijk, Robertson, Milner (Shaqiri 77),
Henderson, Wijnaldum (Keita 66), Salah, Firmino (Sturridge 71), Mane. **Booked**: Wijnaldum,
Gomez, Sturridge, Van Dijk, Robertson, Keita

December 11, 2018
Liverpool 1 (Salah 14) **Napoli** 0. Att: 52,015
Liverpool (4-3-3): Alisson, Alexander-Arnold (Lovren 90), Matip, Van Dijk, Robertson,
Wijnaldum, Henderson, Milner (Fabinho 85), Salah, Firmino (Keita 79), Mane. **Booked**: Van
Dijk, Salah, Robertson, Mane
Red Star Belgrade 1 (Gobeljic 56) **Paris SG** 4 (Cavani 9, Neymar 40, Marquinhos 74,
Mbappe 90)

	P	W	D	L	F	A	Pts
Paris SG Q	6	3	2	1	17	9	11
Liverpool Q	6	3	0	3	9	7	9
Napoli	6	2	3	1	7	5	9
Red Star Belgrade	6	1	1	4	5	17	4

GROUP D

September 18, 2018
Galatasaray 3 (Rodrigues 9, Derdiyok 67, Inan 90+4 pen) **Lokomotiv Moscow** 0. Att: 43,542
Schalke 1 (Embolo 64) **Porto** 1 (Otavio 75 pen). Att: 45,755

October 3, 2018
Lokomotiv Moscow 0 **Schalke** 1 (McKennie 88). Att: 21,471
Porto 1 (Marega 49) **Galatasaray** 0. Att: 42,711

October 24, 2018
Galatasaray 0 **Schalke** 0. Att: 46,667
Lokomotiv Moscow 1 (Miranchuk 38) **Porto** 3 (Marega 26 pen, Herrera 35, Corona 47). Att:
16,034

November 6, 2018
Porto 4 (Herrera 2, Marega 43, Corona 67, Otavio 90+3) **Lokomotiv Moscow** 1 (Farfan 59).
Att: 34,616
Schalke 2 (Burgstaller 4, Uth 57) **Galatasaray** 0. Att: 54,740

November 28, 2018
Lokomotiv Moscow 2 (Donk 46 og, Ignatiev 54) **Galatasaray** 0. Att: 14,037
Porto 3 (Militao 52, Corona 56, Marega 90+4) **Schalke** 1 (Bentaleb 89 pen). Att: 41,603

December 11, 2018
Galatasaray 2 (Feghouli 45 pen, Derdiyok 65) **Porto** 3 (Felipe 17, Marega 42 pen, Sergio
Oliveira 57). Att: 33,972
Schalke 1 (Schopf 90) **Lokomotiv Moscow**. Att: 48,883

	P	W	D	L	F	A	Pts
Porto Q	6	5	1	0	15	6	16
Schalke Q	6	3	2	1	6	4	11
Galatasaray	6	1	1	4	5	8	4
Lokomotiv Moscow	6	1	0	5	4	12	3

GROUP E

September 19, 2018
Ajax 3 (Tagliafico 46, 90, Van de Beek 77) **AEK Athens** 0. Att: 52,285
Benfica 0 **Bayern Munich** 2 (Lewandowski 10, Sanches 54). Att: 60,274

October 2, 2018
AEK Athens 2 (Klonaridis 53, 64) **Benfica** 3 (Seferovic 6, Grimaldo 15, Semedo 74). Att: 31,154
Bayern Munich 1 (Hummels 4) **Ajax** 1 (Mazraoui 22). Att 70,000

October 23, 2018
AEK Athens 0 **Bayern Munich** 2 (Javi Martinez 61, Lewandowski 63). Att: 61,221
Ajax 1 (Mazraoui 90+2) **Benfica** 0. Att: 52,489

November 7, 2018
Bayern Munich 2 (Lewandowski 31 pen 71) **AEK Athens** 0. Att 70,000
Benfica 1 (Jonas 29) **Ajax** 1 (Tadic 61). Att: 51,328

November 27, 2018
AEK Athens 0 **Ajax** 2 (Tadic 68 pen, 72). Att: 25,756
Bayern Munich 5 (Robben 13, 30, Lewandowski 36, 51, Ribery 76) **Benfica** 1 (Fernandes 46). Att: 70,000

December 12, 2018
Ajax 3 (Tadic 61, 82 pen, Tagliafico 90) **Bayern Munich** 3 (Lewandowski 13, 87 pen, Coman 90). Att: 52,244
Benfica 1 (Grimaldo 88) **AEK Athens** 0. Att: 33,633

	P	W	D	L	F	A	Pts
Bayern Munich Q	6	4	2	0	15	5	14
Ajax Q	6	3	3	0	11	5	12
Benfica	6	2	1	3	6	11	7
AEK Athens	6	0	0	6	2	13	0

GROUP F

September 19, 2018
Manchester City 1 (Bernardo Silva 67) **Lyon** 2 (Cornet 26, Fekir 43). Att: 40,111
Manchester City (4-3-3): Ederson, Walker, Stones, Laporte, Delph, Fernandinho, Gundogan (Sane 55), David Silva, Bernardo Silva, Gabriel Jesus (Aguero 63), Sterling (Mahrez 76).
Booked: Aguero
Shakhtar Donetsk 2 (Ismaily 27, Maycon 81) **Hoffenheim** 2 (Grillitsch 6, Nordtveit 38). Att: 28,336

October 2, 2018
Hoffenheim 1 (Belfodil 1) **Manchester City** 2 (Aguero 8, David Silva 87). Att: 24,851
Manchester City (4-3-3): Ederson, Walker, Kompany, Otamendi (Stones 64), Laporte, Fernandinho, Gundogan (Bernardo Silva 68), David Silva, Sterling (Mahrez 75), Aguero, Sane.
Booked: Otamendi, Fernandinho, Walker, David Silva, Aguero
Lyon 2 (Dembele 70, Dubois 72) **Shakhtar Donetsk** 2 (Moraes 44, 55). Played behind closed doors – previous crowd trouble

216

October 23, 2018
Hoffenheim 3 (Kramaric 32, 47, Joelinton 90+2) **Lyon** 3 (Traore 26, Ndombele 59, Depay 67). Att: 24,144
Shakhtar Donetsk 0 **Manchester City** 3 (David Silva 30, Laporte 35, Bernardo Silva 70). Att: 37,106
Manchester City (4-3-3): Ederson, Stones (Walker 80), Otamendi, Laporte, Mendy, Fernandinho, De Bruyne (Bernardo Silva 69), David Silva, Mahrez, Gabriel Jesus (Foden 87), Sterling. **Booked**: Otamendi

November 7, 2018
Lyon 2 (Fekir 19, Ndombele 28) **Hoffenheim** 2 (Kramaric 65, Kaderabek 90+2). Att: 53,850
Manchester City 6 (David Silva 13, Gabriel Jesus 24 pen, 72 pen, 90+2, Sterling 48, Mahrez 84) **Shakhtar Donetsk** 0. At: 52,286
Manchester City (4-3-3): Ederson, Walker (Danilo 61), Stones, Laporte, Zinchenko, David Silva (Gundogan 73), Fernandinho (Delph 76), Bernardo Silva, Mahrez, Gabriel Jesus, Sterling

November 27, 2018
Hoffenheim 2 (Kramaric 17, Zuber 40) **Shakhtar Donetsk** 3 (Ismaily 14, Freda 15, 90+2). Att: 22,920
Lyon 2 (Cornet 55, 81) **Manchester City** 2 (Laporte 63, Aguero 83). Att: 56,039
Manchester City (4-3-3): Ederson, Walker, Stones, Laporte, Zinchenko, Fernandinho, David Silva, Sterling, Mahrez, Aguero (Foden 90), Sane (Delph 71). **Booked**: Fernandinho, Sterling

December 12, 2018
Manchester City 2 (Sane 45, 61) **Hoffenheim** 1 (Kramaric 16). Att: 50,411
Manchester City (4-2-3-1): Ederson, Stones (Walker 46), Otamendi, Laporte, Zinchenko (Delph 64), Gundogan, Foden, Sterling, Bernardo Silva (Kompany 85), Sane, Gabriel Jesus.
Shakhtar Donetsk 1 (Moraes 22) **Lyon** 1 (Fekir 65). Att: 38,916

	P	W	D	L	F	A	Pts
Manchester City Q	6	4	1	1	16	6	13
Lyon Q	6	1	5	0	12	11	8
Shakhtar Donetsk	6	1	3	2	8	16	6
Hoffenheim	6	0	3	3	11	14	3

GROUP G

September 19, 2018
Viktoria Plzen 2 (Krmencik 39, 41) **CSKA Moscow** 2 (Chalov 49, Vlasic 90+6 pen). Att: 11,312
Real Madrid 3 (Isco 45, Bale 58, Mariano 90+1) **Roma** 0. Att: 69,251

October 2, 2018
CSKA Moscow 1 (Vlasic 2) **Real Madrid** 0. Att: 71,811
Roma 5 (Dzeko 3, 40, 90+2, Under 64, Kluivert 74) **Viktoria Plzen** 0. Att: 41,243

October 23, 2018
Real Madrid 2 (Benzema 11, Marcelo 55) **Viktoria Plzen** 1 (Hrosovsky 78). Att: 67,356
Roma 3 (Dzeko 30, 43, Under 50) **CSKA Moscow** 0. Att: 46,005

November 7, 2018
CSKA Moscow 1 (Sigurdsson 51) **Roma** 2 (Manolas 4, Pellegrini 59). Att: 64,454
Viktoria Plzen 0 **Real Madrid** 5 (Benzema 21, 37, Casemiro 23, Bale 40, Kroos 67). Att: 11,483

November 27, 2018
CSKA Moscow 1 (Vlasic 10 pen) **Viktoria Plzen** 2 (Prochazka 56 , Hejda 81). Att: 52,892
Roma 0 **Real Madrid** 2 (Bale 47, Lucas 59). Att: 59,124

December 12, 2018
Viktoria Plzen 2 (Kovarik 62, Chory 72) **Roma** 1 (Under 67). Att: 11,217
Real Madrid 0 **CSKA Moscow** 3 (Chalov 37, Schennikov 43, Sigurdsson 73). Att: 51,636

	P	W	D	L	F	A	Pts
Real Madrid Q	6	4	0	2	12	5	12
Roma Q	6	3	0	3	11	8	9
Viktoria Plzen	6	2	1	3	7	16	7
CSKA Moscow	6	2	1	3	8	9	7

GROUP H

September 19, 2018
Valencia 0 **Juventus** 2 (Pjanic 45 pen, 50 pen). Att: 46,067
Young Boys 0 **Manchester Utd** 3 (Pogba 35, 44 pen, Martial 66). Att: 31,120
Manchester Utd (4-3-3): De Gea, Dalot, Smalling, Lindelof, Shaw, Pogba (Pereira 75), Matic, Fred (Fellaini 69), Rashford (Mata 69), Lukaku, Martial. **Booked**: Fred

October 2, 2018
Juventus 3 (Dybala 5, 34, 69) **Young Boys** 0. Att: 40,961
Manchester Utd 0 **Valencia** 0. Att: 73,569
Manchester Utd (4-3-3): De Gea, Valencia, Bailly, Smalling, Shaw, Fellaini, Matic, Pogba, Sanchez (Martial 76), Lukaku, Rashford. **Booked**: Lukaku

October 23, 2018
Manchester Utd 0 **Juventus** 1 (Dybala 18). Att: 73,946
Manchester Utd (4-2-3-1): De Gea, Young, Smalling, Lindelof, Shaw, Matic, Pogba, Rashford, Mata, Martial, Lukaku. **Booked**: Young
Young Boys 1 (Hoarau 55 pen) **Valencia** 1 (Batshuayi 26). Att: 31,005

November 7 2018
Juventus 1 (Ronaldo 65) **Manchester Utd** 2 (Mata 86, Alex Sandro 90 og). Att: 41,470
Manchester Utd (4-3-3): De Gea, Young, Smalling, Lindelof, Shaw, Herrera (Mata 79), Matic, Pogba, Lingard (Rashford 70), Sanchez (Fellaini 79), Martial. **Booked**: Matic, Herrera, Martial
Valencia 3 (Santi Mina 14, 42, Carlos Soler 56) **Young Boys** 1 (Assale 37). Att: 36,480

November 27, 2018
Juventus 1 (Madzukic 59) **Valencia** 0. Att: 39,070
Manchester Utd 1 (Fellaini 90+1) **Young Boys** 0. Att: 72,876
Manchester Utd (4-3-3): De Gea, Valencia (Mata 73), Smalling, Jones, Shaw, Fred (Pogba 64), Matic, Fellaini, Lingard (Lukaku 64), Rashford, Martial. **Booked**: Matic, Valencia

December 12, 2018
Valencia 2 (Carlos Soler 17, Jones 47 og) **Manchester Utd** 1 (Rashford 87). Att: 36,544
Manchester Utd (4-3-3): Romero, Valencia, Bailly, Jones, Rojo (Young 46), Fred (Rashford 57), Fellaini, Pogba, Mata, Lukaku (Lingard 69), Pereira. **Booked**: Valencia Bailly, Rashford
Young Boys 2 (Hoarau 30 pen, 68) **Juventus** 1 (Dybala 89). Att: 30,114

	P	W	D	L	F	A	Pts
Juventus Q	6	4	0	2	9	4	12
Manchester Utd Q	6	3	1	2	7	4	10
Valencia	6	2	2	2	6	6	8
Young Boys	6	1	1	4	4	12	4

ROUND OF 16, FIRST LEG

February 12, 2019
Manchester Utd 0 **Paris SG** 2 (Kimpembe 53, Mbappe 60). Att: 75,054
Manchester Utd (4-3-3): De Gea, Young, Bailly, Lindelof, Shaw, Herrera, Matic, Pogba, Lingard, (Sanchez 45), Rashford (Lukaku 84), Martial (Mata 46). **Booked**: Pogba, Young, Lindelof, Herrera, Shaw. **Sent off**: Pogba (89)
Roma 2 (Zaniola 70, 76) **Porto** 1 (Adrian 79). Att: 51,727

February 13, 2019
Ajax 1 (Ziyech 75) **Real Madrid** 2 (Benzema 60, Marco Asensio 87). Att: 52,286
Tottenham 3 (Son Heung min 47, Vertonghen 83, Llorente 86). **Borussia Dortmund** 0. Att: 71,214
Tottenham (3-4-1-2): Lloris, Foyth, Sanchez, Alderweireld, Aurier, Winks, Sissoko (Wanyama 90+1), Vertonghen, Eriksen, Son Hueng-min (Lamela 90), Lucas Moura (Llorente 84). **Booked**: Aurier

February 19, 2019
Liverpool 0 **Bayern Munich** 0. Att: 52,250
Liverpool (4-3-3): Alisson, Alexander-Arnold, Matip, Fabinho, Robertson, Wijnaldum, Henderson, Keita (Milner 76), Salah, Firmino (Origi 76), Mane. **Booked**: Henderson
Lyon 0 **Barcelona** 0. Att: 57.889

February 20, 2019
Atletico Madrid 2 (Gimenez 78, Godin 83) **Juventus** 0. Att: 67,193
Schalke 2 (Bentaleb 38 pen, 45 pen) **Manchester City** 3 (Aguero 18, Sane 85, Sterling 90). Att: 54,417
Manchester City (4-3-3): Ederson, Walker, Fernandinho, Otamendi, Laporte, De Bruyne (Zinchenko 87), Gundogan, David Silva (Kompany 69), Bernardo Silva, Aguero (Sane 78), Sterling. **Booked**: Otamendi, Fernandinho, Ederson, **Sent off**: Otamendi (68)

ROUND OF 16, SECOND LEG

March 5, 2019
Borussia Dortmund 0 **Tottenham** 1 (Kane 49). Att: 66,099 (Tottenham won 4-0 on agg)
Tottenham (3 4 1 2): Lloris, Alderweireld, Sanchez, Vertonghen, Aurier, Sissoko, Winks (Dier 55), Davies, Eriksen (Rose 83), Son Heung-min (Lamela 71), Kane
Real Madrid 1 (Marco Asensio 70) **Ajax** 4 (Ziyech 7, Neres 18, Tadic 62, Schone 72). Att: 77,013 (Ajax won 5-3 on agg)

March 6, 2019
Paris SG 1 (Bernat 12) **Manchester Utd** 3 (Lukaku 2, 30, Rashford 90+4 pen). Att: 47,441 (agg 3-3, Manchester Utd won on away goals)
Manchester Utd (4-4-2): De Gea, Bailly (Dalot 36), Smalling, Lindelof, Shaw, Young (Greenwood 87), Fred, McTominay, Pereira (Chong 80), Rashford, Lukaku. **Booked**: Shaw
Porto 3 (Soares 26, Marega 52, Telles 117 pen) **Roma** 1 (De Rossi 31 pen). Att: 49,209 (aet, Porto won 4-3 on agg)

March 12, 2019
Juventus 3 (Ronaldo 27, 48, 86 pen) **Atletico Madrid** 0. Att: 40,884 (Juventus won 3-2 on agg)
Manchester City 7 (Aguero 35 pen, 38, Sane 42, Sterling 56, Bernardo Silva 71, Foden 78, Gabriel Jesus 84) **Schalke** 0. Att: 51,518 (Manchester City won 10-2 on agg)
Manchester City (4-3-3): Ederson, Walker, Danilo, Laporte (Delph 72), Zinchenko, Bernardo Silva, Gundogan, David Silva (Foden 64), Sterling, Aguero (Gabriel Jesus 64), Sane. **Booked**: Danilo, Zinchenko

March 13, 2019
Barcelona 5 (Messi 18 pen, 78, Coutinho 31. Pique 81, Dembele 86) **Lyon** 1 (Tousart 78).
Att: 92,346 (Barcelona won 5-1 on agg)
Bayern Munich 1 (Matip 39 og) **Liverpool** 3 (Mane 26, 84, Van Dijk 69). Att: 70,000
(Liverpool won 3-1 on agg)
Liverpool (4-3-3): Alisson, Alexander-Arnold, Matip, Van Dijk, Robertson, Wijnaldum,
Henderson (Fabinho 13), Milner (Lallana 87), Mane, Firmino (Origi 83), Salah. **Booked**:
Fabinho, Matip, Robertson

QUARTER-FINALS, FIRST LEG

April 9, 2019
Liverpool 2 (Keita 5, Firmino 26) **Porto** 0. Att: 52,465
Liverpool (4-3-3): Alisson, Alexander-Arnold, Lovren, Van Dijk, Milner, Henderson, Fabinho,
Keita, Salah, Firmino (Sturridge 82) Mane (Origi 73)
Tottenham 1 (Son Heung-min 78) **Manchester City** 0. Att: 60,044
Tottenham (4-2-3-1): Lloris, Tripper, Alderweireld, Vertonghen, Rose, Sissoko, Winks
(Wanyama 81), Eriksen, Alli (Llorente 87), Son Heung-min, Kane (Lucas Moura 58). **Booked**:
Rose
Manchester City (4-3-3): Ederson, Walker, Otamendi, Laporte, Delph, Gundogan, Fernandinho,
David Silva (De Bruyne 89), Mahrez (Sane 89), Aguero (Gabriel Jesus 71), Sterling. **Booked**:
Laporte, Mahrez

April 10, 2019
Ajax 1 (Neres 46) **Juventus** 1 (Ronaldo 45). Att: 50,396
Manchester Utd 0 **Barcelona** 1 (Shaw 12 og). Att: 74,093
Manchester Utd (3-5-2): De Gea, Smalling, Lindelof, Shaw, Young, McTominay, Fred, Pogba,
Dalot (Lingard 74), Rashford (Pereira 85), Lukaku (Martial 68). **Booked**: Shaw, Smalling,
Lingard

QUARTER-FINALS, SECOND LEG

April 16, 2019
Barcelona 3 (Messi 16, 20, Coutinho 61) **Manchester Utd** 0. Att: 96,708 (Barcelona won 4-0
on agg)
Manchester Utd (4-3-3): De Gea, Lindelof, Smalling, Jones, Young, McTominay, Fred, Pogba,
Lingard (Sanchez 80), Rashford (Lukaku 73), Martial (Dalot 65)
Juventus 1 (Ronaldo 28) **Ajax** 2 (Van de Beek 34, De Ligt 67). Att: 41,445 (Ajax won 3-2 on agg)

April 17, 2019
Manchester City 4 (Sterling 4, 21, Bernardo Silva 11, Aguero 59) **Tottenham** 3 (Son Heung-
min 7, 10, Llorente 73). Att: 53,348 (agg 4-4, Tottenham won on away goals)
Manchester City (4-3-3): Ederson Walker, Kompany, Laporte, Mendy (Sane 84), De Bruyne,
Gundogan, David Silva (Fernandinho 7), Bernardo Silva, Aguero, Sterling
Tottenham (4-1-2-1-2): Lloris, Trippier, Alderweireld, Vertonghen, Rose (Sanchez 90),
Wanyama, Sissoko (Llorente 41), Alli, Eriksen, Lucas Moura (Davies 82), Son Heung-min.
Booked: Rose, Wanyama, Sissoko, Son Heung-min
Porto 1 (Militao, 68) **Liverpool** 4 (Mane 26, Salah 65, Firmino 77, Van Dijk 84). Att: 49,117
(Liverpool won 6-1 on agg)
Liverpool (4-3-3): Allison, Alexander-Arnold (Gomez 66), Matip, Van Dijk, Robertson
(Henderson 76), Milner, Fabinho, Wijnaldum, Salah, Origi (Firmino 46), Mane. **Booked**: Mane

SEMI-FINALS, FIRST LEG

April 30, 2019
Tottenham 0 **Ajax** 1 (Van de Beek 15). Att: 60,243

Tottenham (3-4-2-1): Lloris, Alderweireld, Sanchez, Vertonghen (Sissoko 39), Trippier (Foyth 80), Eriksen, Wanyama, Rose (Davies 79), Alli, Lucas Moura, Llorente

May 1, 2019
Barcelona 3 (Suarez 26, Messi 75, 82) **Liverpool** 0. Att: 98,299
Liverpool (4-4-2): Alisson, Gomez, Matip, Van Dijk, Robertson, Milner (Origi 85), Fabinho, Keita (Henderson 24), Wijnaldum (Firmino 79), Salah, Mane. **Booked**: Fabinho

SEMI-FINALS, SECOND LEG

May 7, 2019
Liverpool 4 (Origi 7, 79, Wijnaldum 54, 56) **Barcelona** 0. Att: 55,212 (Liverpool won 4-3 on agg)
Liverpool (4-3-3): Alisson, Alexander-Arnold, Matip, Van Dijk, Robertson (Wijnaldum 46), Henderson, Fabinho, Milner, Shaqiri (Sturridge 90), Origi (Gomez 85), Mane. **Booked**: Fabinho, Matip
May 8, 2019
Ajax 2 (De Ligt 5, Ziyech 35) **Tottenham** 3 (Lucas Moura 55, 59, 90+6). Att: 53,285 (agg 3-3, Tottenham won on away goals)
Tottenham (4-2-3-1): Lloris, Trippier (Lamela 81), Alderweireld, Vertonghen, Rose (Davies 82), Wanyama (Llorente 46), Sissoko, Eriksen, Alli, Son Heung-min, Lucas Moura. **Booked**: Sissoko, Rose

FINAL

TOTTENHAM 0 LIVERPOOL 2 (Salah 2 pen, Origi 88)
Metropolitano Stadium, Madrid (63,272); Saturday, June 1, 2019
Tottenham (4-2-3-1): Lloris (capt), Trippier, Alderweireld, Vertonghen, Rose, Winks (Lucas Moura 66), Sissoko (Dier 74), Eriksen, Alli (Llorente 82), Son Heung-min, Kane. **Subs not used**: Gazzaniga, Vorm, Sanchez, Foyth, Davies, Aurier, Walker-Peters, Wanyama, Lamela. **Manager**: Mauricio Pochettino
Liverpool (4-3-3): Alisson, Alexander-Arnold, Matip, Van Dijk, Robertson, Henderson (capt) Fabinho, Wijnaldum (Milner 62), Salah, Firmino (Origi 58), Mane (Gomez 90). **Subs not used**: Mignolet, Lovren, Sturridge, Moreno, Lallana, Oxlade-Chamberlain, Shaqiri, Brewster, Kelleher. **Manager**: Jurgen Klopp
Referee: D Skomina (Slovakia). **Half-time**: 0-1

For Jurgen Klopp, the ultimate prize in club football; for Mauricio Pochettino, an honourable runners-up medal; for Divock Origi, the chance to savour his role as Liverpool's supersub, a mantle once adopted at Anfield by David Fairclough. Like Fairclough, Origi's starts have been few and far between – four in the 2018-19 Premier League season – such has been the consistency of the front three, Mohamed Salah, Roberto Firmino and Sadio Mane. But either coming off the bench, or deputising when that formidable strike force has been disrupted by injury, the Belgian can lay claim to some crucial goals. He settled the outcome of the Merseyside derby at Anfield in the sixth minute of added time; given his chance when Salah and Firmino were ruled out of the second leg of the semi-final, he netted twice in the remarkable 4-0 win over Barcelona; called into action to replace Firmino after 58 minutes of the final, Origi completed the 2-0 win over Tottenham with a flourish of his left boot. It confirmed his manager's first trophy at the club, following defeats by Real Madrid the previous season, against Sevilla in the 2016 Europa League Final and against Manchester City in the League Cup that same season. Pochettino and his players were left with the satisfaction of reaching the final of Europe's premier club competition for the first time against the odds, having taken a single point from the first three group matches, then needing to overcome a 3-0 deficit against Ajax in the semi-finals. The manager's gamble in playing Harry Kane, after the England striker missed the last month of the season, did not pay off. But it was one worth taking and in no way detracted from what Pochettino has achieved in his five years in north London, during which the club's priority has been building the new stadium, with money for new players limited.

Leading scorers: 12 Messi (Barcelona); 8 Lewandowski (Bayern Munich); 6 Aguero (Manchester City), Mareja (Porto), Ronaldo (Juventus), Tadic (Ajax); 5 Dybala (Juventus), Dzeko (Roma 5), Kane (Tottenham), Kramaric (Hoffenheim), Lucas Moura (Tottenham), Neymar (Paris SG), Salah (Liverpool), Sterling (Manchester City)

FINAL FACTS AND FIGURES

- This was Liverpool's sixth triumph in the European Cup/Champions after victories in 1977, 1978 and 1981 under Bob Paisley, 1984 with Joe Fagan as manager and 2005 when Rafael Benitez was in charge.

- Jurgen Klopp lost his two previous finals in the tournament – Liverpool's 2018 defeat by Real Madrid and Borussia Dortmund's loss to Bayern Munich at Wembley in 2013.

- Liverpool have now lifted the trophy twice as times as England's next most successful club, Manchester United, winners in 1968, 1999 and 2008.

- Liverpool moved above Barcelona and Bayern Munich to third in the overall winners' table behind Real Madrid (13) and AC Milan (7).

- Mohamed Salah's penalty, timed at 1min 48 secs, was the second fastest goal in a Champions League final after Paolo Maldini's for AC Milan (50 sec) against Liverpool in 2005.

- It was the first final without a single card being shown.

- Trent Alexander Arnold became the first player under 21 to start in successive Champions League finals.

- Tottenham were making their first appearance in Europe's premier club competition.

- The club had previously won the UEFA Cup, predecessor of the Europa League, in 1972 and 1984 and the old Cup Winners' Cup in 1963

EUROPEAN CUP/CHAMPIONS LEAGUE FINALS

1956	Real Madrid 4 Reims 3 (Paris)
1957	Real Madrid 2 Fiorentina 0 (Madrid)
1958†	Real Madrid 3 AC Milan 2 (Brussels)
1959	Real Madrid 2 Reims 0 (Stuttgart)
1960	Real Madrid 7 Eintracht Frankfurt 3 (Glasgow)
1961	Benfica 3 Barcelona 2 (Berne)
1962	Benfica 5 Real Madrid 3 (Amsterdam)
1963	AC Milan 2 Benfica 1 (Wembley)
1964	Inter Milan 3 Real Madrid 1 (Vienna)
1965	Inter Milan 1 Benfica 0 (Milan)
1966	Real Madrid 2 Partizan Belgrade 1 (Brussels)
1967	Celtic 2 Inter Milan 1 (Lisbon)
1968†	Manchester Utd 4 Benfica 1 (Wembley)
1969	AC Milan 4 Ajax 1 (Madrid)
1970†	Feyenoord 2 Celtic 1 (Milan)
1971	Ajax 2 Panathinaikos 0 (Wembley)
1972	Ajax 2 Inter Milan 0 (Rotterdam)
1973	Ajax 1 Juventus 0 (Belgrade)
1974	Bayern Munich 4 Atletico Madrid 0 (replay Brussels after a 1-1 draw Brussels)
1975	Bayern Munich 2 Leeds Utd 0 (Paris)
1976	Bayern Munich 1 St. Etienne 0 (Glasgow)
1977	Liverpool 3 Borussia Moenchengladbach 1 (Rome)

1978	Liverpool 1 Brugge 0 (Wembley)
1979	Nottm Forest 1 Malmo 0 (Munich)
1980	Nottm Forest 1 Hamburg 0 (Madrid)
1981	Liverpool 1 Real Madrid 0 (Paris)
1982	Aston Villa 1 Bayern Munich 0 (Rotterdam)
1983	SV Hamburg 1 Juventus 0 (Athens)
1984†	Liverpool 1 AS Roma 1 (Liverpool won 4-2 on penalties) (Rome)
1985	Juventus 1 Liverpool 0 (Brussels)
1986†	Steaua Bucharest 0 Barcelona 0 (Steaua won 2-0 on penalties) (Seville)
1987	Porto 2 Bayern Munich 1 (Vienna)
1988†	PSV Eindhoven 0 Benfica 0 (PSV won 6-5 on penalties) (Stuttgart)
1989	AC Milan 4 Steaua Bucharest 0 (Barcelona)
1990	AC Milan 1 Benfica 0 (Vienna)
1991†	Red Star Belgrade 0 Marseille 0 (Red Star won 5-3 on penalties) (Bari)
1992	Barcelona 1 Sampdoria 0 (Wembley)
1993	Marseille 1 AC Milan 0 (Munich)
1994	AC Milan 4 Barcelona 0 (Athens)
1995	Ajax 1 AC Milan 0 (Vienna)
1996†	Juventus 1 Ajax 1 (Juventus won 4-2 on penalties) (Rome)
1997	Borussia Dortmund 3 Juventus 1 (Munich)
1998	Real Madrid 1 Juventus 0 (Amsterdam)
1999	Manchester Utd 2 Bayern Munich 1 (Barcelona)
2000	Real Madrid 3 Valencia 0 (Paris)
2001	Bayern Munich 1 Valencia 1 (Bayern Munich won 5-4 on penalties) (Milan)
2002	Real Madrid 2 Bayer Leverkusen 1 (Glasgow)
2003†	AC Milan 0 Juventus 0 (AC Milan won 3-2 on penalties) (Manchester)
2004	FC Porto 3 Monaco 0 (Gelsenkirchen)
2005†	Liverpool 3 AC Milan 3 (Liverpool won 3-2 on penalties) (Istanbul)
2006	Barcelona 2 Arsenal 1 (Paris)
2007	AC Milan 2 Liverpool 1 (Athens)
2008†	Manchester Utd 1 Chelsea 1 (Manchester Utd won 6-5 on penalties) (Moscow)
2009	Barcelona 2 Manchester Utd 0 (Rome)
2010	Inter Milan 2 Bayern Munich 0 (Madrid)
2011	Barcelona 3 Manchester Utd 1 (Wembley)
2012†	Chelsea 1 Bayern Munich 1 (Chelsea won 4-3 on pens) (Munich)
2013	Bayern Munich 3 Borussia Dortmund 1 (Wembley)
2014†	Real Madrid 4 Atletico Madrid 1 (Lisbon)
2015	Barcelona 3 Juventus 1 (Berlin)
2016	Real Madrid 1 Atletico Madrid 1 (Real Madrid won 5-3 on pens) (Milan)
2017	Real Madrid 4 Juventus 1 (Cardiff)
2018	Real Madrid 3 Liverpool 1 (Kiev)† aet
2019	Liverpool 2 Tottenham 0 (Madrid)

● Champions League since 1993. † after extra time

THE THINGS THEY SAY ...

'If you want guarantees, buy a washing machine' – **Ralph Hasenhuttl**, Southampton manager, says nothing can be taken for granted in football.

'It would be a miracle to stay up, yes, even if we strengthen' – **Rafael Benitez**, then the Newcastle manager, whose side did preserve Premier League status.

'It's a day to relish, embrace and enjoy and it's why you put up with the bad days' – **Jack Ross**, Sunderland manager, on the League One record crowd of 46,039 for the **Boxing Day** fixture against Bradford at the Stadium Light.

UEFA EUROPA LEAGUE 2018–19

PRELIMINARY ROUND (selected results)

FIRST LEG
Cefn Druids 1 (Davies 48) Trakai 1 (Kazlauskas 86). Att: 742. Tre Fiori 3 (Mileyog 7, Procacci 32, Vassallo 36) **Bala** 0. Att: 542

SECOND LEG
Bala 1 (Burke 77) Tre Fiori 0. Att: 610 (Tre Fiori won 3-1 on agg). Trakai 1 (Bilyaletdinov 29 pen) **Cefn Druids** 0. Att: 850 (Trakai won 2-1 on agg)

FIRST QUALIFYING ROUND (selected results)

FIRST LEG
Cliftonville 0 Nordsjaelland 1 (Olsen 19). Att: 1,170. **Connah's Quay** 1 (Morris 89 pen) Shakhtyor 3 (Ngome 20, Bakaj 33, Shibun 75), Att: 577. **Derry** 0 Dinamo Minsk 2 (Galov 2, Khvashchinskiy 64). Att: 1,467. **Glenavon** 2 (Marshall 37, Daniels 59) Molde 1 (Hestad 36). Att: 631. **Hibernian** 6 (Kamberi 3 pen, 21, 48, Shaw 29, Mallan 43, 84) Runavik 1 (Knudsen 53). Att: 12,501
Levadia Tallinn 0 **Dundalk** 1 (Connolly 53). Att: 1,343. **Rangers** 2 (Murphy 23, Tavernier 90+2 pen) Shkupi 0. Att: 49,3089. **Shamrock Rov** 0 AIK 1 (Sundgren 74). Att: 2,817. Subotica 1 (Savkovic 90+6 pen) **Coleraine** 1 (McCauley 23). Att: 976

SECOND LEG
AIK 1 (Stefanelli 90+4) **Shamrock Rov** 1 (Carr 19). Att: 8,115 (aet, AIK won 2-1 on agg). **Coleraine** 0 Subotica 2 (Savkovic 33, Cecaric 90+2). Att: 976 (Subotica won 3-1 on agg). Dinamo Minsk 1 (Sachivko 28) **Derry** 2 (Roy 7, Ronan Hale 75). Att: 1,467 (Dinamo Minsk won 3-2 on agg). **Dundalk** 2 (Hoban 31, Duffy 33) Levadia Tallinn 1 (Debelko 42). Att: 1,343 (Dundalk won 3-1 on agg). Molde 5 (Hussain 29 pen, Hestad 34, 59, 90, Sarr 90+4) **Glenavon** 1 (Forren 62 og). Att: 5,750 (Molde won 6-3 on agg)
Nordsjaelland 2 (Donyoh 58, Harney 83 og) **Cliftonville** 1 (Gormley 6 pen). Att: 1,592 (Nordsjaelland won 3-1 on agg). Shakhtyor 2 (Bakaj 24 pen, Bordachev 82) **Connah's Quay** 0. Att: 2,700 (Shakhtyor won 5-1 on agg). Shkupi 0 **Rangers** 0. Att: 4,750 (Rangers won 2-0 on agg). Runavik 4 (Ambrose 1 og, Olsen 6, 35, 57) **Hibernian** 6 (McGinn 10, Stevenson 16, Gray 45, Ambrose 50, Mallan 70, 77). Att: 587 (Hibernian won 12-5 on agg).

SECOND QUALIFYING ROUND (selected results)

FIRST LEG
Aberdeen 1 (Mackay-Steven 19 pen) Burnley 1 (Vokes 80). Att: 20,313. **Dundalk** 0 AEK Larnaca 0. Att: 3,000. **Hibernian** 3 (Ambrose 64, Gray 77, Kamberi 90+3) Asteras Tripoli 2 (Kiriakopoulos 12, 35). Att: 14,148. **New Saints** 2 (Ebbe 6, Hudson 83) Lincoln Red Imps 1 (Chipolina 31). Att: 632. Olimpija 5 (Boateng 30, 68, Crnic 56, 75, Kadric 90+2) **Crusaders** 1 (Forsythe 73). Att: 2,980. Osijek 0 **Rangers** 1 (Morelos 18). Att: 7,112

SECOND LEG
AEK Larnaca 4 (Trickovski 13, 38, Tete 21, Tomas 87) **Dundalk** 0. Att: 3,991 (AEK Larnaca won 4-0 on agg). Asteras Tripoli 1 (Tsllianidis 56) **Hibernian** 1 (McGinn 44). Att: 3,870 (Hibernian won 4-3 on agg). **Burnley** 3 (Wood 6, Cork 101, Barnes 114 pen) **Aberdeen** 1 (Ferguson 27). Att: 17,404 (aet, Burnley won 4-2 on agg). **Crusaders** 1 (Heatley 41) Olimpija 1 (Kapun 15). Att: 1,080 (Olimpija won 6-2 on agg). Lincoln Red Imps 1 (Montesinos 41) **New Saints** 1 (Ebbe 82). Att: 546 (New Saints won 3-2 on agg). **Rangers** 1 (Katic 53) Osijek 1 (Barisic 89). Att: 48,202 (Rangers won 2-1 on agg)

THIRD QUALIFYING ROUND (selected results)

FIRST LEG
Basaksehir 0 **Burnley** 0. Att: 4,503. **New Saints** 0 Midtjylland 2 (Onuachu 9, 27). Att: 863.
Cork 0 Rosenborg 2 (Levi 22, 44). Att: 5,488. **Hibernian** 0 Molde 0. Att: 16,339. **Rangers** 3
(Morelos 6, Tavernier 56 pen, Coulibaly 88) Maribor 1 (Bajde 40). Att: 40,001

SECOND LEG
Burnley 1 (Cork 97) Basaksehir 0. Att: 16,583 (aet, Burnley won 1-0 on agg). Midtjylland 3
(George 16, Okosun 62, 80) **New Saints** 1 (Ebbe 22). Att: 4,368 (Midtjylland won 5-1 on
agg). Maribor 0 **Rangers** 0. Att: 11,166 (Rangers won 3-1 on agg). Molde 3 (Haland 35, 82,
Aursnes 66) **Hibernian** 0. Att: 5,554 (Molde won 3-0 on agg). Rosenborg 3 (Serbecic 26,
Soderlund 34, Trondsen 58) **Cork** 0. Att: 8,028 (Rosenborg won 5-0 on agg)

PLAY-OFFS

FIRST LEG
Olympiacos 3 (Fortounis 19, 60 pen, Bouchalakis 49) **Burnley** 1 (Wood 33 pen). Att: 25,010.
Rangers 1 (Goldson 41) Ufa 0. Att: 49,338. Suduva 1 (Verbickas 13) **Celtic** 1 (Ntcham 3).
Att: 5,100

SECOND LEG
Burnley 1 (Vydra 86) Olympiacos 1 (Podence 15). Att: 15,234 (Olympiacos won 4-2 on agg).
Celtic 3 (Griffiths 27, McGregor 53, Ajer 61) Suduva 0. Att: 44,639 (Celtic won 4-1 on agg).
Ufa 1 (Sysuev 32) **Rangers** 1 (Ejaria 9). Att: 13,186 (Rangers won 2-1 on agg)

ON AGGREGATE
AEK Larnaca 4 Trencin 1, Apollon Limassol 3 Basle 3 (Apollon Limassol won on away goals);
Astana 1 Apoel Nicosia 1 (aet, Astana won 2-1 on pens); Besiktas 4 Partizan Belgrade 1;
Bordeaux 2 Gent 0; Copenhagen 0 Atalanta 0 (aet, Copenhagen won 4-3 on pens); Dudelange
5 Cluj-Napoca 2; Genk 9 Brondby 4; Leipzig 3 Zorya 2; Ludogorets 5 Torpedo Kutaisi 0;
Malmo 4 Midtjylland 2; Qarabag 3 Sheriff Tiraspol 1; Rapid Vienna 4 Steaua Bucharest 3;
Rosenborg 5 Shkendija Tetovo 1; Sarpsborg 4 Maccabi Tel Aviv 3; Sevilla 4 Sigma Olomouc 0;
Spartak Trnava 3 Olimpija Ljubljana 1; Zenit St Petersburg 4 Molde 3

GROUP STAGE

GROUP A

Match-day 1: AEK Larnaca 0 Zurich 1 (Kololli 61 pen). Att: 3,173. Ludogorets 2 (Keseru 8,
Da Costa 31) Bayer Leverkusen 3 (Havertz 38, 69, Thelin 63). Att. 8,240
Match-day 2: Bayer Leverkusen 4 (Havertz 44, Alario 49, 88, Brandt 90+2) AEK Larnaca 2
(Trickovski 25, Raspas 90+1). Att: 23,354. Zurich 1 (Palsson 84) Ludogorets 0. Att: 7,092
Match-day 3: AEK Larnaca 1 (Roig 25 pen) Ludogorets 1 (Lukohi 7). Att: 2,631. Zurich 3
(Marchesano 44, Domgjoni 59, Odey 78) Bayer Leverkusen 2 (Bellerabi 49, 53). Att: 12,427
Match-day 4: Bayer Leverkusen 1 (Jedvaj 60) Zurich 0. Att: 16,179. Ludogorets 0 AEK
Larnaca 0. Att: 4,520
Match-day 5: Bayer Leverkusen 1 (Weiser 85) Ludogorets 1 (Nascimento 69). Att: 16,066.
Zurich 1 (Khelifi 74) AEK Larnaca 2 (Giannou 38, Trickovski 85). Att: 6,107
Match-day 6: AEK Larnaca 1 (Catala 26) Bayer Leverkusen 5 (Kohr 28, 67, Alario 41 pen,
86, Filho 78). Att: 1,584. Ludogorets 1 (Palsson 84) Zurich 0. Att: 7,092

	P	W	D	L	F	A	Pts
Bayer Leverkusen Q	6	4	1	1	16	9	13
Zurich Q	6	3	1	2	7	6	10
AEK Larnaca	6	1	2	3	6	12	5
Ludogorets	6	0	4	2	5	7	4

GROUP B

Match-day 1: Celtic 1 (Griffiths 87) Rosenborg 0. Att: 47,287. Leipzig 2 (Laimer 70, Poulsen 82). Salzburg 3 (Dabbur 20, Haidara 22, Gulbrandsen 89). Att: 24,057
Match-day 2: Rosenborg 1 (Jebali 79) Leipzig 3 (Augustin 12, Konate 54, Cunha 61). Att: 11,484. Salzburg 3 (Dabbur 55, 73 pen, Minamino 61) **Celtic** 1 (Edouard 2). Att: 24,085
Match-day 3: Leipzig 2 (Cunha 31, Bruma 35) **Celtic** 0. Att: 38,126. Salzburg 3 (Dabbur 34, 59 pen, Wolf 53) Rosenborg 0. Att: 20,639
Match-day 4: Celtic 2 (Tierney 11, Edouard 79) Leipzig 1 (Augustin 78). Att: 56,027. Rosenborg 2 (Adegbenro 52, Jensen 61) Salzburg 5 (Minamino 5, 19, 45, Gulbrandsen 37, Ovland 57 og). Att: 12,386
Match-day 5: Rosenborg 0 **Celtic** 1 (Sinclair 42). Att: 14,061. Salzburg 1 (Gulbrandsen 74) Leipzig 0. Att: 29,520
Match-day 6: Celtic 1 (Ntcham 90+5) Salzburg 2 (Dabbur 67, Gulbrandsen 77). Att: 57,578. Leipzig 1 (Cunha 47) Rosenborg 1 (Reginiussen 86). Att: 16,957

	P	W	D	L	F	A	Pts
Salzburg Q	6	6	0	0	17	6	18
Celtic Q	6	3	0	3	6	8	9
Leipzig	6	2	1	3	9	8	7
Rosenborg	6	0	1	5	4	14	1

GROUP C

Match-day 1: Copenhagen 1 (Sotiriou 63) Zenit St Petersburg 1 (Mak 43). Att: 19,005. Slavia Prague 1 (Zmrhal 35) Bordeaux 0. Att: 16,548
Match-day 2: Bordeaux 1 (Sankhare 84) Copenhagen 2 (Sotiriou 42, Skov 90+2). Att: 11,860. Zenit St Petersburg 1 (Kokorin 80) Slavia Prague 0. Att: 45,408
Match-day 3: Copenhagen 0 Slavia Prague 1 (Matousek 46). Att: 20,672. Zenit St Petersburg 2 (Dzyuba 40, Kuzyaev 85) Bordeaux 1 (Briand 26). Att: 45,723
Match-day 4: Bordeaux 1 (Kamano 35 pen) Zenit St Petersburg 1 (Zabolotny 72). Att: 8,907. Slavia Prague 0 Copenhagen 0. Att: 18,702
Match-day 5: Bordeaux 2 (De Preville 49, Kounde 90+5) Slavia Prague 0. Att: 6,311. Zenit St Petersburg 1 (Mak 59) Copenhagen 0. Att: 45,199
Match-day 6: Copenhagen 0 Bordeaux 1(Briand 73). Att: 18,209. Slavia Prague 2 (Zmrhal 32, Stoch 41) Zenit St Petersburg 0. Att: 17,748

	P	W	D	L	F	A	Pts
Zenit St Petersburg Q	6	3	2	1	6	5	11
Slavia Prague Q	6	3	1	2	4	3	10
Bordeaux	6	2	1	3	6	6	7
Copenhagen	6	1	2	3	3	5	5

GROUP D

Match-day 1: Dinamo Zagreb 4 (Sunjic 16, Hajrovic 27, 57, Olmo 60) Fenerbahce 1 (Neustadter 47). Att: 17,303. Spartak Trnava 1 (Oravec 79) Anderlecht 0. Att: 17,114
Match-day 2: Anderlecht 0 Dinamo Zagreb 2 (Hajrovic 19 pen, Gojak 68). Att: 12,137. Fenerbahce 2 (Slimani 51, 68) Spartak Trnava 0. Att: 29,622
Match-day 3: Anderlecht 2 (Bakkali 35, 49) Fenerbahce 2 (Frey 53, Kaldirim 57). Att: 13,292. Spartak Trnava 1 (Ghorbani 32) Dinamo Zagreb 2 (Gavranovic 64, Orsic 77). Played behind closed doors – previous crowd trouble
Match-day 4: Fenerbahce 2 (Valbuena 71, Frey 74) Anderlecht 0. Att: 32,789. Dinamo Zagreb 3 (Gojak 22, Kadlec 35 og, Orsic 79) Spartak Trnava 1 (Tchanturishvili 63). Att: 18,154

Match-day 5: Anderlecht 0 Spartak Trnava 0. Att: 8,063. Fenerbahce 0 Dinamo Zagreb 0. Att: 24,776

Match-day 6: Dinamo Zagreb 0 Anderlecht 0. Att: 12,170. Spartak Trnava 1 (Yilmaz 41) Fenerbahce 0. Att: 11,413

	P	W	D	L	F	A	Pts
Dinamo Zagreb Q	6	4	2	0	11	3	14
Fenerbahce Q	6	2	2	2	7	7	8
Spartak Trnava	6	2	1	3	4	7	7
Anderlecht	6	0	3	3	2	7	3

GROUP E

Match-day 1: Arsenal 4 (Aubameyang 32, 56, Welbeck 48, Ozil 74) Vorskla Poltava 2 (Ohosnalov 77, Sharpar 90+4) Att: 59,029. Sporting Lisbon 2 (Belloli 54, Cabral 88) Qarabag 0. Att: 30,098

Match-day 2: Qarabag 0 Arsenal 3 (Sokratis 4, Smith-Rowe 53, Guendouzi 79). Att: 63,412. Vorskla Poltava 1 (Kulach 10) Sporting Lisbon 2 (Montero 90, Cabral 90+3). Att: 10,082

Match-day 3: Qarabag 0 Vorskla Poltava 1 (Kulach 48). Att: 22,450. Sporting Lisbon 0 Arsenal 1 (Welbeck 77). Att: 40,784

Match-day 4: Arsenal 0 Sporting Lisbon 0. Att: 59,758. Vorskla Poltava 0 Qarabag 1 (Abdullayev 13 pen). Att: 5,479

Match-day 5: Qarabag 1 (Zoubir 14) Sporting Lisbon 6 (Bas Dost 5 pen, Fernandes 20, 75, Nani 33, Dalgo 65, 81). Att: 5,416. Vorskla Poltava 0 Arsenal 3 (Smith-Rowe 11, Ramsey 27 pen, Willock 41). Att: 7,751 (played in Kiev)

Match-day 6: Arsenal 1 (Lacazette 18) Qarabag 0. Att: 58,101. Sporting Lisbon 3 (Montero 17, Mariz Luis 35, Dalku 44 og) Vorskla Poltrava 0. Att: 25,504

	P	W	D	L	F	A	Pts
Arsenal Q	6	5	1	0	12	2	16
Sporting Lisbon Q	6	4	1	1	13	3	13
Vorskla Poltava	6	1	0	5	4	13	3
Qarabag	6	1	0	5	2	13	3

GROUP F

Match-day 1: Dudelange 0 AC Milan 1 (Higuain 59). Att: 7,983. Olympiacos 0 Real Betis 0. Att: 28,660

Match-day 2: AC Milan 3 (Cutrone 70, 79, Higuain 76) Olympiacos 1 (Guerrero 14). Att: 22,294. Real Betis 3 (Sanabria 56, Lo Celso 80, Tello 88) Att: 40,133

Match-day 3: AC Milan 1 (Cutrone 83) Real Betis 2 (Sanabria 30, Lo Celso 54). Att: 22,405. Dudelange 0 Olympiacos 2 (Torosidis 66, Jordanov 81 og). Att: 7,500

Match-day 4: Olympiacos 5 (Torosidis 6, Fortounis 15, 36, Christodoulopoulous 26, Hassan 70) Dudelange 1 (Sinani 69). Att: 24,032. Real Betis 1 (Lo Celso 12) AC Milan 1 (Suso 62). Att: 45,647

Match-day 5: AC Milan 5 (Cutrone 21, Stelvio 66 og, Calhanoglu 70, Schell 77 og, Borini 80) Dudelange 2 (Stolz 39, Turpel 49). Att: 15,521. Real Betis 1 (Canales 39) Olympiacos 0. Att: 37,722

Match-day 6: Dudelange 0 Real Betis 0. Att: 4,931. Olympiacos 3 (Cisse 60, Zapata 69 og, Fortounis 81 pen) AC Milan 1 (Zapata 71). Att: 31,010

	P	W	D	L	F	A	Pts
Real Betis Q	6	3	3	0	7	2	12
Olympiacos Q	6	3	1	2	11	6	10
AC Milan	6	3	1	2	12	9	10
Dudelange	6	0	1	5	3	16	1

GROUP G

Match-day 1: Rapid Vienna 2 (Timofeev 50 og, Murg 68) Spartak Moscow 0. Att: 21,400. Villarreal 2 (Bacca 1, Gerard 69) **Rangers** 2 (Arfield 67, Lafferty 76). Att: 15,989
Match-day 2: **Rangers** 3 (Morelos 43, 90+4, Tavernier 84 pen) Rapid Vienna 1 (Berisha 42). Att: 47,534. Spartak Moscow 3 (Ze Luis 34 pen, 82, Melgarejo 85) Villarreal 3 (Ekambi 13, Fornals 49, Cazorla 90+6 pen). Att: 21,265
Match-day 3: **Rangers** 0 Spartak Moscow 0. Att: 49,068. Villarreal 5 (Fornals 26, Ekambi 30, Barac 45 og, Antolin 63, Gerard 65) Rapid Vienna 0. Att: 14,150
Match-day 4: Rapid Vienna 0 Villarreal 0. Att: 22,100. Spartak Moscow 4 (Melgarejo 22, Goldson 35 og, Luiz Adriano 58, Hanni 59) **Rangers** 3 (Eremenko 5 og, Candeias 27, Middleton 41). Att: 22,296
Match-day 5: Spartak Moscow 1 (Ze Luis 20) Rapid Vienna 2 (Muldur 80, Schobesberger 90+1). Att: 20,739. **Rangers** 0 Villarreal 0. Att: 50,171
Match-day 6: Rapid Vienna 1 (Ljubicic 1) **Rangers** 0. Att: 23,850. Villarreal 2 (Chukwueze 11, Ekambi 46) Spartak Moscow 0. Att: 12,903

	P	W	D	L	F	A	Pts
Villarreal Q	6	2	4	0	12	5	10
Rapid Vienna Q	6	3	1	2	6	9	10
Rangers	6	1	3	2	8	8	6
Spartak Moscow	6	1	2	3	8	12	5

GROUP H

Match-day 1: Lazio 2 (Luis Alberto 14, Immobile 84 pen) Apollon Limassol 1 (Zelaya 87). Att: 11,898. Marseille 1 (Ocampos 3) Eintracht Frankfut 2 (Torro 52, Jovic 89). Played behind closed doors – previous crowd trouble
Match-day 2: Apollon Limassol 2 (Markovic 74, Zelaya 90) Marseille 2 (Payet 50, Luiz Gustavo 67). Att: 3,031. Eintracht Frankfurt 4 (Da Costa 4, 90+4, Kostic 28, Jovic 52) Lazio 1 (Parolo 23). Att: 47,000
Match-day 3: Eintracht Frankfurt 2 (Kostic 13, Haller 32) Apollon Limassol 0. Att: 47,000. Marseille 1 (Payet 86) Lazio 3 (Santos 10, Caicedo 59, Marusic 90). Att: 31,930
Match-day 4: Apollon Limassol 2 (Zelaya 71, 90+4 pen) Eintracht Frankfurt 3 (Jovic 17, Haller 55, Gacinovic 58). Att: 6,888. Lazio 2 (Parolo 45, Correa 55) Marseille 1 (Thavin 60). Att: 14,705
Match-day 5: Apollon Limassol 2 (Faupala 31, Markovic 82) Lazio 0. Att: 1,131. Eintracht Frankfurt 4 (Jovic 1, 67, Luiz Gustavo 17 og, Sarr 62 og) Marseille 0. Att: 47,000
Match-day 6: Lazio 1 (Correa 56) Eintracht Frankfurt 2 (Gacinovic 65, Haller 71). Att: 18,252. Marseille 1 (Thavin 11) Apollon Limassol 3 (Maglica 8 pen, 30, Stylianou 56). Att: 9,274

	P	W	D	L	F	A	Pts
Eintracht Frankfurt Q	6	6	0	0	17	5	18
Lazio Q	6	3	0	3	9	11	9
Apollon Limassol	6	2	1	3	10	10	7
Marseille	6	0	1	5	6	16	1

GROUP I

Match-day 1: Besiktas 3 (Babel 51, Roco 69, Lens 82) Sarpsborg 1 (Zachariassen 90+4). Att: 24,955. Genk 2 (Trossard 37, Samatta 71) Malmo 0. Att: 11,590
Match-day 2: Malmo 2 (Erkin 53 og, Rosenberg 76 pen) Besiktas 0. Att: 17,174. Sarpsborg 3 (Mortensen 5, 63, Zachariassen 54) Genk 1 (Trossard 49). Att: 7,885
Match-day 3: Besiktas 2 (Love 74, 86) Genk 4 (Samatta 23, 69, Ndongala 81, Piotrowski

83). Att: 25,209. Sarpsborg 1 (Halvorsen 87) Malmo 1 (Vindheim 79). Att: 8,022
Match-day 4: Genk 1 (Berge 87) Besiktas 1 (Quaresma 16). Att: 14,292. Malmo 1
(Antonsson 67) Sarpsborg 1 (Mortensen 63). Att: 17,601
Match-day 5: Malmo 2 (Lewicki 65, Antonsson 67) Genk 2 (Pozuelo 42, Paintsil 53). Att:
16,117. Sarpsborg 2 (Muhammed 1, Heintz 6) Besiktas 3 (Lens 62, 90, Love 66). Att: 8,022
Match-day 6: Besiktas 0 Malmo 1 (Antonsson 51): Att: 24,955. Genk 4 (Gano 2, Paintsil 5,
Berge 64, Aidoo 67) Sarpsborg 0. Att: 12,240

	P	W	D	L	F	A	Pts
Genk Q	6	3	2	1	14	0	11
Malmo Q	6	2	3	1	7	6	9
Besiktas	6	2	1	3	9	11	7
Sarpsborg	6	1	2	3	8	13	5

GROUP J

Match-day 1: Akhisarspor 0 Krasnodar 1 (Claesson 26). Att: 6,555. Sevilla 5 (Banega 8, 74
pen, Vazquez 41, Ben Yedder 49, 70). Standard Liege 1 (Djenepo 39). Att: 30,003
Match-day 2: Krasnodar 2 (Pereyra 72, Okrianshvili 88) Sevilla 1 (Nolito 43). Att. 31,346.
Standard Liege 2 (Emond 17, Djenepo 39) Akhisarspor 1 (Ayik 32). Att: 8,233
Match-day 3: Sevilla 6 (Mesa 7, Sarabia 9 pen, Lukac 35 og, Muriel 50, Promes 60, Mercado
67). Att: 29,720. Standard Liege 2 (Emond 47, Laifis 90+3) Krasnador 1 (Ari
39). Att: 8,393
Match-day 4: Akhisarspor 2 (Manu 52, Ayik 78) Sevilla 3 (Nolito 12, Muriel 38, Banega
87 pen). Att: 6,430. Krasnador 2 (Suleymanov 79, Campos 82) Standard Liege 1 (Carcela-
Gonzalez 19). Att: 21,526
Match-day 5: Krasnador 2 (Gazinskiy 48, Ari 57) Akhisarspor 1 (Serginho 24). Att: 11,008.
Standard Liege 1 (Djenepo 62) Seville 0. Att: 12,882
Match-day 6: Akhisarspor 0 Standard Liege 0. Att: 2,074. Sevilla 3 (Ben Yedder 5, 10,
Banega 49 pen) Krasnodar 0. Att: 34,114

	P	W	D	L	F	A	Pts
Sevilla Q	6	4	0	2	18	6	12
Krasnodar Q	6	4	0	2	8	8	12
Standard Liege	6	3	1	2	7	9	10
Akhisarspor	6	0	1	5	4	14	1

GROUP K

Match-day 1: Dynamo Kiev 2 (Tsygankov 11, Garmash 45) Astana 2 (Anicic 21, Murtazaev
90:6). Att: 21,783. Rennes 2 (Sarr 31, Ben Arfa 90+1 pen) Jablonec 1 (Travnik 54). Att:
20,628
Match-day 2: Astana 2 (Zainutdinov 64, Tomasov 90+1) Rennes 0. Att: 25,302. Jablonec 2
(Hovorka 33, Travnik 81) Dynamo Kiev 2 (Tsygankov 8, Garmash 14). Att: 6,077
Match-day 3: Jablonec 1 (Povazanec 4) Astana 1 (Henrique 11). Att: 4,909. Rennes 1
(Grenier 40) Dynamo Kiev 2 (Kedziora 21, Buyalsky 89). Att: 28,001
Match-day 4: Astana 2 (Henrique 18, Postnikov 88) Jablonec 1 (Zainutdinov 40 og). Att:
20,092. Dynamo Kiev 3 (Verbic 13, Mykolenko 68, Shaparenko 72) Rennes 1 (Siebatcheu
89). Att: 24,402
Match-day 5: Astana 0 Dynamo Kiev 1 (Verbic 29). Att: 26,508. Jablonec 0 Rennes 1
(Grenier 55). Att: 4,712
Match-day 6: Dynamo Kiev 0 Jablonec 1 (Dolezal 10). Att: 11,300. Rennes 2 (Sarr 68, 73)
Astana 0. Att: 24,535

	P	W	D	L	F	A	Pts
Dynamo Kiev Q	6	3	2	1	10	7	11
Rennes Q	6	3	0	3	7	8	9
Astana	6	2	2	2	7	7	8
Jablonec	6	1	2	3	6	8	5

GROUP L

Match-day 1: PAOK Salonika 0 **Chelsea** 1 (Willian 7) Att: 24,210. MOL Vidi 0 BATE Borisov 2 (Iuominen 27, Filipenko 85). Att: 14,726

Match-day 2: BATE Borisov 1 (Crespo 61 og) PAOK Salonika 4 (Prijovic 6, Rodrigues Lima 11,17, Pelekas 73). Att: 10,527. **Chelsea** 1 (Morata 70) MOL Vidi 0. Att: 39,925

Match-day 3: **Chelsea** 3 (Loftus-Cheek 2, 8, 54) BATE Borisov 1 (Rios 88). Att: 39,799. PAOK Salonika 0 MOL Vidi 2 (Huszti 12, Tavares 45). Att: 15,118

Match-day 4: BATE Borisov 0 **Chelsea** 1 (Giroud 53). Att: 13,141. MOL Vidi 1 (Milanov 50) PAOK Salonika 0. Att: 17,208

Match-day 5: BATE Borisov 2 (Signevich 22, Ivanic 85) MOL Vidi 0. Att: 8,963. **Chelsea** 4 (Giroud 27, 37, Hudson-Odoi 60, Morata 78) PAOK Salonika 0. Att: 33,933

Match-day 6: MOL Vidi 2 (Ampadu 32 og, Nego 56) **Chelsea** 2 (Willian 30, Giroud 75). Att: 19,242. PAOK Salonika 1 (Prijovic 59) BATE Borisov 3 (Skavysh 18, Signevich 42 pen, 45). Att: 13,483

	P	W	D	L	F	A	Pts
Chelsea Q	6	5	1	0	12	3	16
BATE Borisov Q	6	3	0	3	9	9	9
MOL Vidi	6	2	1	3	5	7	7
PAOK Salonika	6	1	0	5	5	12	3

ROUND OF 32, FIRST LEG

BATE Borisov 1 (Dragun 45) **Arsenal** 0. Att: 12,527. **Celtic** 0 Valencia 2 (Cheryshev 42, Sobrino 49). Att: 57,430. Club Bruges 2 (Denswil 64, Wesley 81) Salzburg 1 (Junuzovic 17). Att: 16,457. Fenerbahce 1 (Slimani 21) Zenit St Petersburg 0. Att: 36,572 Galatasaray 1 (Luyindama 54) Benfica 2 (Salvio 27 pen, Seferovic 64). Att: 42,722 Krasnodar 0 Bayer Leverkusen 0. Att: 34,827. Lazio 0 Sevilla 1 (Ben Yedder 22). Att: 19,766. Malmo 1 (Christiansen 80) **Chelsea** 2 (Barkley 30, Giroud 58). Att: 20,312 Olympiacos 2 (Hassan 9, Dias 40) Dynamo Kiev 2 (Buyalsky 27, Verbic 89). Att: 31,020. Rapid Vienna 0 Inter Milan 1 (Martinez 39 pen). Att: 23,850. Rennes 3 (Hunou 2, Garcia 9 og, Ben Arfa 45 pen) Real Betis 3 (Lo Celso 32, Sidnei 62, Lainez 90). Att: 28,656. Shakhtar Donetsk 2 (Marlow 9 pen,Taison 67) Eintracht Frankfurt 2 (Hinteregger 7, Kostic 50). Att: 13,059

Slavia Prague 0 Genk 0. Att: 18,125. Sporting Lisbon 0 Villarreal 1 (Pedraza 3). Att: 27,134. Viktoria Plzen 2 (Pernica 54, 83) Dinamo Zagreb 1 (Olmo 41). Att: 9,731. Zurich 1 (Kololli 83 pen) Napoli 3 (Insigne 11, Callejon 21, Zielinski 77). Att: 24.000

ROUND OF 32, SECOND LEG

Arsenal 3 (Volkov 4 og, Mustafi 39, Sokratis 60) BATE Borisov 0. Att: 58,812 (Arsenal won 3-1 on agg). Bayer Leverkusen 1 (Aranguiz 87) Krasnordar 1 (Suleymanov 84). Att: 16,084 (agg 1-1, Krasnodar won on away goal). Benfica 0 Galatasaray 0. Att: 49,545 (Benfica won 2-1 on agg). **Chelsea** 3 (Giroud 55, Barkley 74, Hudson-Odoi 84) Malmo 0. Att: 39,813 (Chelsea won 5-1 on agg)

Dinamo Zagreb 3 (Orsic 15, Dilaver 33, Petkovic 73) Viktoria Plzen 0. Att: 25,860 (Dinamo Zagreb won 4-2 on agg). Dynmamo Kiev 1 (Sol 32) Olympiacos 0. Att: 48,902 (Dynamo Kiev won 3-2 on agg). Eintracht Frankfurt 4 (Jovic 23, Haller 27 pen, 80, Rebic 88) Shakhtar

Donetsk 1 (Junior Moraes 63). Att: 47,000 (Eintracht Frankfurt won 6-3 on agg). Genk 1 (Trossard 10) Slavia Prague 4 (Djimsiti 23, Traore 53, Skoda 64, 68). Att: 13,688 (Slavia Prague won 4-1 on agg)
Inter Milan 4 (Vecino 11, Ranocchia 18, Perisic 80, Politano 87) Rapid Vienna 0. Att: 32,158 (Inter Milan won 5-0 on agg). Napoli 2 (Verdi 43, Ounas 75) Zurich 0. Att: 17,579 (Napoli won 5-1 on agg). Real Betis 1 (Lo Celso 41) Rennes 3 (Bensebaini 22, Hunou 30, Niang 90+4). Att: 43,623 (Rennes won 6-4 on agg). Salzburg 4 (Schlager 17, Daka 29, 43, Dabbur 90+4). Att: 24,717 (Salzburg won 4-2 on agg)
Sevilla 2 (Ben Yedder 20, Sarabia 78) Lazio 0. Att: 34,521 (Sevilla won 3-0 on agg). Valencia 1 (Gameiro 70) Celtic 0. Att: 36,619 (Valencia won 3-0 on agg). Villarreal 1 (Fornals 80) Sporting Lisbon 1 (Fernandes 45). Att: 14,098 (Villarreal won 2-1 on agg). Zenit St Petersburg 3 (Ozdoyev 4, Azmoun 37, 76) Fenerbahce 1 (Topal 43). Att: 50,448 (Zenit St Petersburg won 3-2 on agg)

ROUND OF 16, FIRST LEG

Chelsea 3 (Pedro 17, Willian 65, Hudson-Odoi 90) Dynamo Kiev 0. Att: 37,280. Dinamo Zagreb 1 (Petkovic 38 pen) Benfica 0. Att: 29,704. Eintracht Frankfurt 0 Inter Milan 0. Att: 48,000. Napoli 3 (Milik 10, Fabian 18, Onguene 68 og) Salzburg 0. Att: 32,579
Rennes 3 (Bourigeaud 43, Monreal 65 og, Sarr 88) **Arsenal** 1 (Iwobi 84). Att: 29,171. Sevilla 2 (Ben Yedder 1, Munir 28) Slavia Prague 2 (Stoch 25, Kral 39). Att: 30,698. Valencia 2 (Rodrigo 12, 24) Krasnodar 1 (Claesson 63). Att: 36,274. Zenit St Petersburg 1 (Azmoun 35) Villarreal 3 (Iborra 34, Gerard 64, Morianos 71). Att: 51,826

ROUND OF 16, SECOND LEG

Arsenal 3 (Aubameyang 5, 72, Maitland Niles 16) Rennes 0. Att: 59,453 (Arsenal won 4-3 on agg). Benfica 3 (Jonas 71, Ferro 94, Grimaldo 105) Dinamo Zagreb 0. Att: 47,808 (aet, Benfica won 3-1 on agg). Dynamo Kiev 0 **Chelsea** 5 (Giroud 5, 33, 59, Marcos Alonso 45, Hudson-Odoi 78). Att: 64,830 (Chelsea won 8-0 on agg). Inter Milan 0 Eintracht Frankfurt 1 (Jovic 5). Att: 49,000 (Eintracht Frankfurt won 1-0 on agg)
Krasnodar 1 (Suleymanov 85) Valencia 1 (Guedes 90+3). Att: 35,074 (Valencia won 3-2 on agg). Salzburg 3 (Dabbur 25, Gulbrandsen 65, Leitgeb 90+1) Napoli 1 (Milik 14). Att: 29,520 (Napoli won 4-3 on agg). Slavia Prague 4 (Ngadeu-Ngadjui 13, Soucek 46 pen, Van Buren 102, Traore 119) Sevilla 3 (Ben Yedder 44 pen, Munir 54, Vazquez 98) Att: 19,020 (aet, Slavia Prague won 6-5 on agg). Villarreal 2 (Gerard 29, Bacca 47) Zenit St Petersburg 1 (Ivanovic 90+1). Att: 14,027 (Villarreal won 5-2 on agg)

QUARTER-FINALS, FIRST LEG

Arsenal 2 (Ramsey 15, Koulibaly 25 og) Napoli 0. Att: 59,738. Benfica 4 (Felix 21 pen, 43, 54, Dias 50) Eintracht Frankfurt 2 (Jovic 40, Pacioncia 72). Att: 54,175. Slavia Prague 0 **Chelsea** 1 (Marcos Alonso 86). Att: 17,484. Villarreal 1 (Cazorla 36 pen) Valencia 3 (Guedes 6, 90+3, Wass 90). Att: 17,605

QUARTER-FINALS, SECOND LEG

Chelsea 4 (Pedro 5, 27, Deli 10 og, Giroud 17) Slavia Prague 3 (Soucek 25, Sevcik 51, 54). Att: 38,326 (Chelsea won 5-3 on agg). Eintract Frankfurt 2 (Kostic 36, Rode 67) Benfica 0. Att: 48,000 (agg 4-4, Eintracht Frankfurt won on away goals). Napoli 0 **Arsenal** 1 (Lacazette 36). Att: 39,438 (Arsenal won 3-0 on agg). Valencia 2 (Lato 13, Parejo 54) Villarreal 0. Att: 26,403 (Valencia won 5-1 on agg)

SEMI-FINALS, FIRST LEG

Arsenal 3 (Lacazette 18, 26, Aubameyang 90) Valencia 1 (Diakhaby 11). Att: 58,969. Eintracht Frankfurt 1 (Jovic 23) **Chelsea** 1 (Pedro 45). Att: 48,000

SEMI-FINALS, SECOND LEG

Chelsea 1 (Loftus-Cheek 28) Eintracht Frankfurt 1 (Jovic 49). Att: 40,853 (aet, agg 2-2, Chelsea won 4-3 on pens). Valencia 2 (Gameiro 11, 58) **Arsenal** 4 (Aubameyang 17, 69, 88, Lacazette 50). Att: 44,481 (Arsenal won 7-3 on agg)

FINAL

CHELSEA 4 (Giroud 49, Pedro 60, Hazard 65 pen, 72) ARSENAL 1 (Iwobi 69)
Olympic Stadium, Baku (51,370); Wednesday, May 29, 2019
Chelsea (4-3-3): Arrizabalaga, Azpilicueta (capt), Christensen, Luiz, Emerson, Kante, Jorginho, Kovacic (Barkley 76), Pedro (Willian 71), Giroud, Hazard (Zappacosta 89). **Subs not used:** Caballero, Marcos Alonso, Higuain, Cahill, Ampadu, Gallagher, Cumming, McEachran
Booked: Pedro, Christensen. **Manager:** Maurizio Sarri
Arsenal (3-4-1-2): Cech, Sokratis, Koscielny (capt), Monreal (Guendouzi 66), Maitland-Niles, Torreira (Iwobi 67), Xhaka, Kolasinac, Ozil (Willock 78), Lacazette, Aubameyang. **Subs not used:** Leno, Elneny, Lichtsteiner, Mustafi, Welbeck, Jenkinson, Iliev, Nketiah, Saka. **Manager:** Unai Emery
Referee: G Rocchi (Italy). **Half-time:** 0-0

Speculation about the future of manager Maurizio Sarri and star man Eden Hazard swirled around the final in distant Baku. But there was nothing uncertain about the performance of the team, whose second-half goal-rush destroyed their London rivals. With the pressure of securing a Champions League place eased by a third-place finish in the domestic campaign, Chelsea scored four times in 23 second-half minutes, Hazard taking centre stage and Olivier Giroud heading the supporting cast against his former club. The win rounded off a season of ups and downs, enabling Sarri to have the final word after facing criticism from supporters – and from beyond Stamford Bridge – over tactics and team selection. Those Arsenal fans unable to make the 2,500-mile trip were probably counting their blessings after such a poor performance. That, however, did nothing to hide UEFA's ludicrous decision to choose Azerbaijan as the venue in their desire to spread finals around Europe. Might they have learned a lesson? The victory was particularly satisfying for Giroud, a World Cup winner with France who couldn't get a game towards the end of his time at Arsenal. Admittedly, his starts with Chelsea have been limited, but there was no more prolific marksman in this tournament. A stooping header from Emerson's cross was his 11th goal, one more than Luka Jovic, of Eintract Frankfurt, Chelsea's semi-final opponents. It enabled them to break the deadlock and Giroud also won the penalty which Hazard converted for the first of his two goals.

Leading scorers: 11 Giroud (Chelsea); 10 Jovic (Eintracht Frankfurt); 8 Aubameyang (Arsenal), Ben Yedder (Sevilla), Dabbur (Salzburg); 5 Gulbrandsen (Salzburg), Haller (Eintracht Frankfurt), Lacazette (Arsenal), Lo Celso (Real Betis), Pedro (Chelsea)

FINAL FACTS AND FIGURES

- This was Chelsea's sixth European trophy, following wins in the Champions League (2012), Europa League (2013), Cup Winners' Cup (1971, 1998) and Super Cup (1998).

- Chelsea remained unbeaten throughout this tournament with a record of 12 victories and three draws.

- Olivier Giroud became the first player with an English club to score 11 goals in major European competition since Alan Shearer for Newcastle in the 2004-05 UEFA Cup, predecessor of the Europa League.

- Eden Hazard was the first with an English club to score twice in a final since Mark Hughes for Manchester United in the 1991 Cup Winners' Cup against Barcelona. (2-1)

- Arsenal have now lost their last four European finals following the 1995 Cup Winners' Cup, 2000 UEFA Cup and 2006 Champions League.

- Petr Cech, Arsenal's former Chelsea goalkeeper, was making his final appearance before retiring.

- Arsenal's Ainsley Maitland-Niles was the only English player in the starting line ups

FIFA CLUB WORLD CUP   UNITED ARAB EMIRATES 2018

QUALIFYING MATCHES

Kashima Antlers (Japan) 3 (Nagaki 49, Serginho 69 pen, Abe 84) Guadalajara (Mexico) 2 (Zaldivar 3, Silva 90+4 og). Att: 3,997. ES Tunis (Tunisia) 0 Al Ain (UAE) 3 (Ahmad 2, El Shahat 16, Bandar 60). Att: 21,333

SEMI-FINALS

Al Ain 2 (Berg 3, Caio 51) River Plate (Argentina) 2 (Borre 11, 16). Att: 21,383 (aet, Al Ain won 5 4 on pens). Real Madrid 3 (Bale 44, 53, 55) Kashima Antlers 1 (Doi 78). Att: 30,554

FINAL

REAL MADRID 4 (Modric 14, Marcos Llorente 60, Sergio Ramos 78, Nader 91 og)
AL AIN 1 (Shiotani 86)
Sports City, Abu Dhabi (40,696); Saturday, December 22, 2018
Real Madrid (4-3-3): Courtois, Daniel Carvajal, Varane, Sergio Ramos (capt), Marcelo, Modric, Marcos Llorente (Casemiro 82). Kroos (Dani Ceballos 71), Lucas Vazquez (Vinicius Junior 84), Benzema, Bale. **Booked**: Sergio Ramos. **Coach**: Santiago Solari
Al Ain (4-2-3-1): Essa, Ahmad (Bandar 64), Ahmed, Fayez, Shiotani, Yaslam, Doumbia, El Shahat, Caio, M Abdulrahman (A Abdulrahman 67), Berg (capt) (Nader 75). **Coach**: Zoran Mamic
Referee: J Marrufo (USA). **Half-time**: 1-0

EUROPEAN SUPER CUP 2018

REAL MADRID 2 (Benzema 27, Sergio Ramos 63 pen) ATLETICO MADRID 4 (Diego Costa 1, 79, Saul 98, Koke 104) - aet
Le Coq Arena, Tallinn (12,424); Wednesday, August 15, 2018
Real Madrid (4-2-3-1): Navas, Daniel Carvajal, Varane, Sergio Ramos (capt), Marcelo, Casimiro (Dani Ceballos 76), Kroos (Borjan Mayoral 102), Bale, Isco (Lucas Vazquez 83), Marco Asensio (Modric 57), Benzema. **Booked**. Marco Asensio, Marcelo, Dani Ceballos, Modric. **Coach**: Julen Lopetegui
Atletico Madrid (4-4-2): Oblak, Juanfran, Savic, Godin (capt), Lucas Hernandez, Lemar (Partey 90+1), Saul, Rodri Hernandez (Vitolo 71), Koke, Diego Costa (Gimenez 109), Griezmann (Correa 60). **Booked**: Correa, Diego Costa, Vitolo. **Coach**: Diego Simone
Referee: S Marciniak (Poland). **Half-time**: 1-1

UEFA CUP FINALS

1972   Tottenham beat Wolves 3-2 on agg (2-1a, 1-1h)
1973   Liverpool beat Borussia Moenchengladbach 3-2 on agg (3-0h, 0-2a)

1974	Feyenoord beat Tottenham 4-2 on agg (2-2a, 2-0h)
1975	Borussia Moenchengladbach beat Twente Enschede 5-1 on agg (0-0h, 5-1a)
1976	Liverpool beat Brugge 4-3 on agg (3-2h, 1-1a)
1977	Juventus beat Atletico Bilbao on away goals after 2-2 agg (1-0h, 1-2a)
1978	PSV Eindhoven beat Bastia 3-0 on agg (0-0a, 3-0h)
1979	Borussia Moenchengladbach beat Red Star Belgrade 2-1 on agg (1-1a, 1-0h)
1980	Eintracht Frankfurt beat Borussia Moenchengladbach on away goals after 3-3 agg (2-3a, 1-0h)
1981	Ipswich Town beat AZ 67 Alkmaar 5-4 on agg (3-0h, 2-4a)
1982	IFK Gothenburg beat SV Hamburg 4-0 on agg (1-0h, 3-0a)
1983	Anderlecht beat Benfica 2-1 on agg (1-0h, 1-1a)
1984	Tottenham beat Anderlecht 4-3 on penalties after 2-2 agg (1-1a, 1-1h)
1985	Real Madrid beat Videoton 3-1 on agg (3-0a, 0-1h)
1986	Real Madrid beat Cologne 5-3 on agg (5-1h, 0-2a)
1987	IFK Gothenburg beat Dundee Utd 2-1 on agg (1-0h, 1-1a)
1988	Bayer Leverkusen beat Espanol 3-2 on penalties after 3-3 agg (0-3a, 3-0h)
1989	Napoli beat VfB Stuttgart 5-4 on agg (2-1h, 3-3a)
1990	Juventus beat Fiorentina 3-1 on agg (3-1h, 0-0a)
1991	Inter Milan beat AS Roma 2-1 on agg (2-0h, 0-1a)
1992	Ajax beat Torino on away goals after 2-2 agg (2-2a, 0-0h)
1993	Juventus beat Borussia Dortmund 6-1 on agg (3-1a, 3-0h)
1994	Inter Milan beat Salzburg 2-0 on agg (1-0a, 1-0h)
1995	Parma beat Juventus 2-1 on agg (1-0h, 1-1a)
1996	Bayern Munich beat Bordeaux 5-1 on agg (2-0h, 3-1a)
1997	FC Schalke beat Inter Milan 4-1 on penalties after 1-1 agg (1-0h, 0-1a)
1998	Inter Milan beat Lazio 3-0 (one match) – Paris
1999	Parma beat Marseille 3-0 (one match) – Moscow
2000	Galatasaray beat Arsenal 4-1 on penalties after 0-0 (one match) – Copenhagen
2001	Liverpool beat Alaves 5-4 on golden goal (one match) – Dortmund
2002	Feyenoord beat Borussia Dortmund 3-2 (one match) – Rotterdam
2003	FC Porto beat Celtic 3-2 on silver goal (one match) – Seville
2004	Valencia beat Marseille 2-0 (one match) – Gothenburg
2005	CSKA Moscow beat Sporting Lisbon 3-1 (one match) – Lisbon
2006	Sevilla beat Middlesbrough 4-0 (one match) – Eindhoven
2007	Sevilla beat Espanyol 3-1 on penalties after 2-2 (one match) – Hampden Park
2008	Zenit St Petersburg beat Rangers 2-0 (one match) – City of Manchester Stadium
2009†	Shakhtar Donetsk beat Werder Bremen 2-1 (one match) – Istanbul

EUROPA LEAGUE FINALS

2010†	Atletico Madrid beat Fulham 2-1 (one match) – Hamburg
2011	Porto beat Braga 1-0 (one match) – Dublin
2012	Atletico Madrid beat Athletic Bilbao 3-0 (one match) – Bucharest
2013	Chelsea beat Benfica 2-1 (one match) – Amsterdam
2014	Sevilla beat Benfica 4-2 on penalties after 0-0 (one match) – Turin
2015	Sevilla beat Dnipro 3-2 (one match) – Warsaw
2016	Sevilla beat Liverpool 3-1 (one match) – Basle
2017	Manchester Utd beat Ajax 2-0 (one match) – Stockholm
2018	Atletico Madrid beat Marseille 3-0 (one match) – Lyon
2019	Chelsea beat Arsenal 4-1 (one match) – Baku

(† After extra-time)

FAIRS CUP FINALS
(As UEFA Cup previously known)

1958	Barcelona beat London 8-2 on agg (2-2a, 6-0h)
1960	Barcelona beat Birmingham 4-1 on agg (0-0a, 4-1h)
1961	AS Roma beat Birmingham City 4-2 on agg (2-2a, 2-0h)
1962	Valencia beat Barcelona 7-3 on agg (6-2h, 1-1a)
1963	Valencia beat Dynamo Zagreb 4-1 on agg (2-1a, 2-0h)
1964	Real Zaragoza beat Valencia 2-1 (Barcelona)
1965	Ferencvaros beat Juventus 1-0 (Turin)
1966	Barcelona beat Real Zaragoza 4-3 on agg (0-1h, 4-2a)
1967	Dinamo Zagreb beat Leeds Utd 2-0 on agg (2-0h, 0-0a)
1968	Leeds Utd beat Ferencvaros 1-0 on agg (1-0h, 0-0a)
1969	Newcastle Utd beat Ujpest Dozsa 6-2 on agg (3-0h, 3-2a)
1970	Arsenal beat Anderlecht 4-3 on agg (1-3a, 3-0h)
1971	Leeds Utd beat Juventus on away goals after 3-3 agg (2-2a, 1-1h)

CUP-WINNERS' CUP FINALS

1961	Fiorentina beat Rangers 4-1 on agg (2-0 Glasgow first leg, 2-1 Florence second leg)
1962	Atletico Madrid beat Fiorentina 3-0 (replay Stuttgart, after a 1-1 draw, Glasgow)
1963	Tottenham beat Atletico Madrid 5-1 (Rotterdam)
1964	Sporting Lisbon beat MTK Budapest 1-0 (replay Antwerp, after a 3-3 draw, Brussels)
1965	West Ham Utd beat Munich 1860 2-0 (Wembley)
1966†	Borussia Dortmund beat Liverpool 2-1 (Glasgow)
1967†	Bayern Munich beat Rangers 1-0 (Nuremberg)
1968	AC Milan beat SV Hamburg 2-0 (Rotterdam)
1969	Slovan Bratislava beat Barcelona 3-2 (Basle)
1970	Manchester City beat Gornik Zabrze 2-1 (Vienna)
1971†	Chelsea beat Real Madrid 2-1 (replay Athens, after a 1-1 draw, Athens)
1972	Rangers beat Moscow Dynamo 3-2 (Barcelona)
1973	AC Milan beat Leeds Utd 1-0 (Salonika)
1974	Magdeburg beat AC Milan 2-0 (Rotterdam)
1975	Dynamo Kiev beat Ferencvaros 3-0 (Basle)
1976	Anderlecht beat West Ham Utd 4-2 (Brussels)
1977	SV Hamburg beat Anderlecht 2-0 (Amsterdam)
1978	Anderlecht beat Austria WAC 4-0 (Paris)
1979†	Barcelona beat Fortuna Dusseldorf 4-3 (Basle)
1980†	Valencia beat Arsenal 5-4 on penalties after a 0-0 draw (Brussels)
1981	Dinamo Tbilisi beat Carl Zeiss Jena 2-1 (Dusseldorf)
1982	Barcelona beat Standard Liege 2-1 (Barcelona)
1983†	Aberdeen beat Real Madrid 2-1 (Gothenburg)
1984	Juventus beat Porto 2-1 (Basle)
1985	Everton beat Rapid Vienna 3-1 (Rotterdam)
1986	Dynamo Kiev beat Atletico Madrid 3-0 (Lyon)
1987	Ajax beat Lokomotiv Leipzig 1-0 (Athens)
1988	Mechelen beat Ajax 1-0 (Strasbourg)
1989	Barcelona beat Sampdoria 2-0 (Berne)
1990	Sampdoria beat Anderlecht 2-0 (Gothenburg)
1991	Manchester Utd beat Barcelona 2-1 (Rotterdam)
1992	Werder Bremen beat Monaco 2-0 (Lisbon)
1993	Parma beat Royal Antwerp 3-1 (Wembley)

1994	Arsenal beat Parma 1-0 (Copenhagen)
1995†	Real Zaragoza beat Arsenal 2-1 (Paris)
1996	Paris St Germain beat Rapid Vienna 1-0 (Brussels)
1997	Barcelona beat Paris St Germain 1-0 (Rotterdam)
1998	Chelsea beat VfB Stuttgart 1-0 (Stockholm)
1999	Lazio beat Real Mallorca 2-1 (Villa Park, Birmingham)

(† After extra time)

EUROPEAN SUPER CUP RESULTS

1972*	Ajax beat Rangers 6-3 on agg (3-1, 3-2)
1973	Ajax beat AC Milan 6-1 on agg (0-1, 6-0)
1974	Bayern Munich and Magdeburg did not play
1975	Dynamo Kiev beat Bayern Munich 3-0 on agg (1-0, 2-0)
1976	Anderlecht beat Bayern Munich 5-3 on agg (1-2, 4-1)
1977	Liverpool beat Hamburg 7-1 on agg (1-1, 6-0)
1978	Anderlecht beat Liverpool 4-3 on agg (3-1, 1-2)
1979	Nottm Forest beat Barcelona 2-1 on agg (1-0, 1-1)
1980	Valencia beat Nottm Forest on away goal after 2-2 agg (1-2, 1-0)
1981	Liverpool and Dinamo Tbilisi did not play
1982	Aston Villa beat Barcelona 3-1 on agg (0-1, 3-0 aet)
1983	Aberdeen beat Hamburg 2-0 on agg (0-0, 2-0)
1984	Juventus beat Liverpool 2-0 – one match (Turin)
1985	Juventus and Everton did not play
1986	Steaua Bucharest beat Dynamo Kiev 1-0 – one match (Monaco)
1987	Porto beat Ajax 2-0 on agg (1-0, 1-0)
1988	Mechelen beat PSV Eindhoven 3-1 on agg (3-0, 0-1)
1989	AC Milan beat Barcelona 2-1 on agg (1-1, 1-0)
1990	AC Milan beat Sampdoria 3-1 on agg (1-1, 2-0)
1991	Manchester Utd beat Red Star Belgrade 1-0 – one match (Old Trafford)
1992	Barcelona beat Werder Bremen 3-2 on agg (1-1, 2-1)
1993	Parma beat AC Milan 2-1 on agg (0-1, 2-0 aet)
1994	AC Milan beat Arsenal 2-0 on agg (0-0, 2-0)
1995	Ajax beat Real Zaragoza 5-1 on agg (1-1, 4-0)
1996	Juventus beat Paris St Germain 9-2 on agg (6-1, 3-1)
1997	Barcelona beat Borussia Dortmund 3-1 on agg (2-0, 1-1)
1998	Chelsea beat Real Madrid 1-0 (Monaco)
1999	Lazio beat Manchester United 1-0 (Monaco)
2000	Galatasaray beat Real Madrid 2-1 – aet, golden goal (Monaco)
2001	Liverpool beat Bayern Munich 3-2 (Monaco)
2002	Real Madrid beat Feyenoord 3-1 (Monaco)
2003	AC Milan beat Porto 1-0 (Monaco)
2004	Valencia beat Porto 2-1 (Monaco)
2005	Liverpool beat CSKA Moscow 3-1 – aet (Monaco)
2006	Sevilla beat Barcelona 3-0 (Monaco)
2007	AC Milan beat Sevilla 3-1 (Monaco)
2008	Zenit St Petersburg beat Manchester Utd 2-1 (Monaco)
2009	Barcelona beat Shakhtar Donetsk 1-0 – aet (Monaco)
2010	Atletico Madrid beat Inter Milan 2-0 (Monaco)
2011	Barcelona beat Porto 2-0 (Monaco)
2012	Atletico Madrid beat Chelsea 4-1 (Monaco)
2013	Bayern Munich beat Chelsea 5-4 on pens, aet – 2-2 (Prague)
2014	Real Madrid beat Sevilla 2-0 (Cardiff)

2015	Barcelona beat Sevilla 5-4 – aet (Tbilisi)
2016	Real Madrid beat Sevilla 3-2 – aet (Trondheim)
2017	Real Madrid beat Manchester Utd 2-1 (Skopje)
2018	Atletico Madrid beat Real Madrid 4-2 (Tallinn)

*not recognised by UEFA; from 1998 one match

INTER-CONTINENTAL CUP

Year	Winners	Runners-up	Score
1960	Real Madrid (Spa)	Penarol (Uru)	0-0 5-1
1961	Penarol (Uru)	Benfica (Por)	0-1 2-1 5-0
1962	Santos (Bra)	Benfica (Por)	3-2 5-2
1963	Santos (Bra)	AC Milan (Ita)	2-4 4-2 1-0
1964	Inter Milan (Ita)	Independiente (Arg)	0 1 2-0 1-0
1965	Inter Milan (Ita)	Independiente (Arg)	3-0 0-0
1966	Penarol (Uru)	Real Madrid (Spa)	2-0 2-0
1967	Racing (Arg)	Celtic	0-1 2-1 1-0
1968	Estudiantes (Arg)	Manchester Utd	1-0 1-1
1969	AC Milan (Ita)	Estudiantes (Arg)	3-0 1-2
1970	Feyenoord (Hol)	Estudiantes (Arg)	2-2 1-0
1971	Nacional (Uru)	Panathanaikos (Gre)	*1-1 2-1
1972	Ajax (Hol)	Independiente (Arg)	1-1 3-0
1973	Independiente (Arg)	Juventus* (Ita)	1-0 #
1974	Atletico Madrid (Spa)*	Independiente (Arg)	0-1 2-0
1975	Not played		
1976	Bayern Munich (WGer)	Cruzeiro (Bra)	2-0 0-0
1977	Boca Juniors (Arg)	Borussia Mönchengladbach* (WGer)	2-2 3-0
1978	Not played		
1979	Olimpia Asuncion (Par)	Malmö* (Swe)	1-0 2-1
1980	Nacional (Arg)	Nott'm Forest	1-0
1981	Flamengo (Bra)	Liverpool	3-0
1982	Penarol (Uru)	Aston Villa	2-0
1983	Porto Alegre (Bra)	SV Hamburg (WGer)	2-1
1984	Independiente (Arg)	Liverpool	1-0
1985	Juventus (Ita)	Argentinos Juniors (Arg)	2-2 (aet)
	(Juventus won 4-2 on penalties)		
1986	River Plate (Arg)	Steaua Bucharest (Rom)	1-0
1987	Porto (Por)	Penarol (Uru)	2-1 (aet)
1988	Nacional (Uru)	PSV Eindhoven (Hol)	1-1 (aet)
	(Nacional won 7-6 on penalties)		
1989	AC Milan (Ita)	Nacional (Col)	1-0 (aet)
1990	AC Milan (Ita)	Olimpia Asuncion (Par)	3-0
1991	Red Star (Yug)	Colo Colo (Chi)	3-0
1992	Sao Paulo (Bra)	Barcelona (Spa)	2-1
1993	Sao Paulo (Bra)	AC Milan (Ita)	3-2
1994	Velez Sarsfield (Arg)	AC Milan (Ita)	2-0
1995	Ajax (Hol)	Gremio (Bra)	0-0 (aet)
	(Ajax won 4-3 on penalties)		
1996	Juventus (Ita)	River Plate (Arg)	1-0
1997	Borussia Dortmund (Ger)	Cruzeiro (Arg)	2-0
1998	Real Madrid (Spa)	Vasco da Gama (Bra)	2-1
1999	Manchester Utd	Palmeiras (Bra)	1-0
2000	Boca Juniors (Arg)	Real Madrid (Spa)	2-1

2001	Bayern Munich (Ger)	Boca Juniors (Arg)	1-0
2002	Real Madrid (Spa)	Olimpia Ascuncion (Par)	2-0
2003	Boca Juniors (Arg)	AC Milan (Ita)	1-1
	(Boca Juniors won 3-1 on penalties)		
2004	FC Porto (Por)	Caldas (Col)	0-0

(FC Porto won 8-7 on penalties)
Played as a single match in Japan since 1980
* European Cup runners-up # One match only
Summary: 43 contests; South America 22 wins, Europe 23 wins

CLUB WORLD CHAMPIONSHIP

2005	Sao Paulo (Bra) beat Liverpool	1-0
2006	Internacional (Bra) beat Barcelona (Spa)	1-0
2007	AC Milan (Ita) beat Boca Juniors (Arg)	4-2

CLUB WORLD CUP

2008	Manchester Utd beat Liga de Quito (Ecu)	1-0
2009	Barcelona beat Estudiantes (Arg)	2-1 (aet)
2010	Inter Milan (Ita) beat TP Mazembe (DR Congo)	3-0
2011	Barcelona beat Santos (Bra)	4-0
2012	Corinthians (Bra) beat Chelsea	1-0
2013	Bayern Munich (Ger) beat Raja Casablanca (Mar)	2-0
2014	Real Madrid (Spa) beat San Lorenzo (Arg)	2-0
2015	Barcelona beat River Plate (Arg)	3-0
2016	Real Madrid beat Kashima Antlers (Jap)	4-2 (aet)
2017	Real Madrid beat Gremio (Bra)	1-0
2018	Real Madrid beat Al AIN (UAE)	4-1

THE THINGS THEY SAY ...

'A kaleidoscope of chaos' – **Jonathan Pearce**, BBC commentator, on the 3-3 draw between Bournemouth and Watford.

'I've told them not to walk out through the main entrance but find a side door to sneak through' **Chris Wilder**, Sheffield United manager, piling into his players after losing to non-league Barnet in the FA Cup.

'It was not about tonight, it was about making history and getting this far' – **Nigel Clough**, Burton manager, after a 9-0 defeat by Manchester City in the League Cup semi-finals.

EUROPEAN TABLES 2018–2019

FRANCE – LIGUE 1

	P	W	D	l	F	A	GD	Pts
Paris SG	38	29	4	5	105	35	70	91
Lille	38	22	9	7	68	33	35	75
Lyon	38	21	9	8	70	47	23	72
St Etienne	38	19	9	10	59	41	18	66
Marseille	38	18	7	13	60	52	8	61
Montpellier	38	15	14	9	53	42	11	59
Nice	38	15	11	12	30	35	-5	56
Reims	38	13	16	9	39	42	-3	55
Nimes	38	15	8	15	57	58	-1	53
Rennes	38	13	13	12	55	52	3	52
Strasbourg	38	11	16	11	58	48	10	49
Nantes	38	13	9	16	48	48	0	48
Angers	38	10	16	12	44	49	-5	46
Bordeaux	38	10	11	17	34	42	-8	41
Amiens	38	9	11	18	31	52	-21	38
Toulouse	38	8	14	16	35	57	-22	38
Monaco	38	8	12	18	38	57	-19	36
Dijon	38	9	7	22	31	60	-29	34
Caen	38	7	12	19	29	54	-25	33
Guingamp	38	5	12	21	28	68	-40	27

Leading scorers: 33 Mbappe (Paris SG); 22 Pepe (Lille); 18 Cavani (Paris SG); 16 Thauvin (Marseille); 15 Dembele (Lyon), Falcao (Monaco), Neymar (Paris SG); 14 Delort (Montpellier); 13 Bamba (Lille), Khazri (St Etienne)

Cup Final: Rennes 2 (Kimpembe 40 og, Mexer 66) Paris SG 2 (Dani Alves 13, Neymar 21) aet, Rennes won 6-5 on pens

HOLLAND – EREDIVISIE

Ajax	34	28	2	4	119	32	87	86
PSV Eindhoven	34	26	5	3	98	26	72	83
Feyenoord	34	20	5	9	75	41	34	65
Alkmaar	34	17	7	10	64	43	21	58
Vitesse Arnhem	34	14	11	9	70	51	19	53
Utrecht	34	15	8	11	60	51	9	53
Heracles	34	15	3	16	61	68	-7	48
Groningen	34	13	6	15	39	41	-2	45
Den Haag	34	12	9	13	58	63	-5	45
Willem	34	13	5	16	58	72	-14	44
Heerenveen	34	10	11	13	64	73	-9	41
VVV	34	11	8	15	47	63	-16	41
Zwolle	34	11	6	17	44	57	-13	39
Emmen	34	10	8	16	41	72	-31	38
Fortuna Sittard	34	9	7	18	50	80	-30	34
Excelsior	34	9	6	19	46	79	-33	33
De Graafschap	34	8	5	21	38	75	-37	29
Breda	34	5	8	21	29	74	-45	23

Leading scorers: 28 De Jong (PSV Eindhoven), Tadic (Ajax); 19 Dalmau (Heracles); 17 El Khayati (Den Haag), Lozano (PSV Eindhoven); 16 Huntelaar (Ajax), Lammers (Heerenveen), Van Persie (Feyenoord), Vlap (Heerenveen), Ziyech (Ajax)

Cup Final: Ajax 4 (Blind 38, Huntelaar 39, 67, Kristensen 76) Willem 0

GERMANY – BUNDESLIGA

Bayern Munich	34	24	6	4	88	32	56	78
Borussia Dortmund	34	23	7	4	81	44	37	76
Leipzig	34	19	9	6	63	29	34	66
Bayer Leverkusen	34	18	4	12	69	52	17	58
Borussia M'gladbach	34	16	7	11	55	42	13	55
Wolfsburg	34	16	7	11	62	50	12	55
Eintracht Frankfurt	34	15	9	10	60	48	12	54
Werder Bremen	34	14	11	9	58	49	9	53
Hoffenheim	34	13	12	9	70	52	18	51
Fortuna Dusseldorf	34	13	5	16	49	65	-16	44
Hertha	34	11	10	13	49	57	-8	43
Mainz	34	12	7	15	46	57	-11	43
Freiburg	34	8	12	14	46	61	-15	36
Schalke	34	8	9	17	37	55	-18	33
Augsburg	34	8	8	18	51	71	-20	32
Stuttgart	34	7	7	20	32	70	-38	28
Hannover	34	5	6	23	31	71	-40	21
Nuremberg	34	3	10	21	26	68	-42	19

Leading scorers: 22 Lewandowski (Bayern Munich); 18 Alcacer (Borussia Dortmund); 17 Havertz (Bayer Leverkusen), Jovic (Eintracht Frankfurt), Kramaric (Hoffenheim), Reus (Borussia Dortmund); 16 Belfodil (Hoffenheim), Haller (Eintracht Frankfurt), Poulsen (Leipzig), Werner (Leipzig)
Cup Final: Bayern Munich 3 (Lewandowski 29, 85, Coman 78) Leipzig 0

ITALY – SERIE A

Juventus	38	28	6	4	70	30	40	90
Napoli	38	24	7	7	74	36	38	79
Atalanta	38	20	9	9	77	46	31	69
Inter Milan	38	20	9	9	57	33	24	69
AC Milan	38	19	11	8	55	36	19	68
Roma	38	18	12	8	66	48	18	66
Torino	38	16	15	7	52	37	15	63
Lazio	38	17	8	13	56	46	10	59
Sampdoria	38	15	8	15	60	51	9	53
Bologna	38	11	11	16	48	56	-8	44
Sassuolo	38	9	16	13	53	60	-7	43
Udinese	38	11	10	17	39	53	-14	43
SPAL	38	11	9	18	44	56	-12	42
Parma	38	10	11	17	41	61	-20	41
Cagliari	38	10	11	17	36	54	-18	41
Fiorentina	38	8	17	13	47	45	2	41
Genoa	38	8	14	16	39	57	-18	38
Empoli	38	10	8	20	51	70	-19	38
Frosinone	38	5	10	23	29	69	-40	25
Chievo*	38	2	14	22	25	75	-50	17

*Deducted 3pts
Leading scorers: 26 Quagliarella (Sampdoria); 23 Zapata (Atalanta); 22 Piatek (AC Milan/Genoa); 21 Ronaldo (Juventus); 17 Milik (Napoli); 16 Caputo (Empoli), Mertens (Napoli), Pavoletti (Cagliari), Petagna (SPAL); 15 Belotti (Torino), Immobile (Lazio)
Cup Final: Lazio 2 (Milinkovic-Savic 82, Correa 90) Atalanta 0

PORTUGAL – PRIMEIRA LIGA

Benfica	34	28	3	3	103	31	72	87
Porto	34	27	4	3	74	20	54	85
Sporting Lisbon	34	23	5	6	72	33	39	74
Sporting Braga	34	21	4	9	66	37	19	67
Guimaraes	34	15	7	12	46	34	12	52
Moreirense	34	16	4	14	39	44	-5	52
Rio Ave	34	12	9	13	50	52	-2	45
Boavista	34	13	5	16	34	40	-6	44
Belenenses	34	10	13	11	42	51	-9	43
Santa Clara	34	11	9	14	43	45	-2	42
Portimonense	34	11	6	17	44	59	-15	39
Maritimo	34	12	3	19	26	44	-18	39
Setubal	34	8	12	14	28	39	-11	36
Desportivo	34	10	6	18	35	49	-14	36
Tondela	34	9	8	17	40	54	-14	35
Chaves	34	8	8	18	34	57	-23	32
Nacional	34	7	7	20	33	73	-40	28
Feirense	34	3	11	20	27	64	-37	20

Leading scorers: 23 Seferovic (Benfica); 20 Bruno Fernandes (Sporting Lisbon), 17 Rafa Silva (Benfica), 15 Bas Dost (Sporting Lisbon), Joao Felix (Benfica), Sousa (Sporting Braga), Soares (Porto); 13 Pizzi (Benfica); 12 Eduardo (Sporting Braga), To Mane (Tondela)
Cup Final: Sporting Lisbon 2 (Bruno Fernandes 45, Bas Dost 101) Porto 2 (Soares 41, Felipe 120+1) aet Sporting Lisbon won 5 4 on pens)

SPAIN – LA LIGA

Barcelona	38	26	9	3	90	36	54	87
Atletico Madrid	38	22	10	6	55	29	26	76
Real Madrid	38	21	5	12	63	46	17	68
Valencia	38	15	16	7	51	35	16	61
Getafe	38	15	14	9	48	35	13	59
Sevilla	38	17	8	13	62	47	15	59
Espanyol	38	14	11	13	48	50	-2	53
Athletic Bilbao	38	13	14	11	41	45	-4	53
Real Sociedad	38	13	11	14	45	46	-1	50
Real Betis	38	14	8	16	44	52	-8	50
Alaves	38	13	11	14	39	50	-11	50
Eibar	38	11	14	13	46	50	-4	47
Leganes	38	11	12	15	37	43	-6	45
Villarreal	38	10	14	14	49	52	-3	44
Levante	38	11	11	16	59	66	-7	44
Real Valladolid	38	10	11	17	32	51	-19	41
Celta Vigo	38	10	11	17	53	62	-9	41
Girona	38	9	10	19	37	53	-16	37
Huesca	38	7	12	19	43	65	-22	33
Rayo Vallecano	38	8	8	22	41	70	-29	32

Leading scorers: 36 Messi (Barcelona); 21 Benzema (Real Madrid), Suarez (Barcelona); 20 Aspas (Celta Vigo); 19 Stuani (Girona); 18 Ben Yedder (Sevilla); 17 Iglesias (Espanyol); 15 Griezmann (Atletico Madrid); 14 Charles (Eibar), Mata (Getafe), Molina (Getafe), De Tomas (Rayo Vallecano)
Cup Final: Valencia 2 (Gameiro 21, Rodrigo 33) Barcelona 1 (Messi 73)

BRITISH AND IRISH INTERNATIONALS
2018–19
(*denotes new cap)

EUROPEAN CHAMPIONSHIP
2020 QUALIFYING

GROUP A

ENGLAND 5 (Sterling 24, 62, 68, Kane 45 pen, Kalas 84 og) CZECH REPUBLIC 0
Wembley (82,575); Friday, March 22, 2019
England (4-3-3): Pickford, Walker, Keane, Maguire, Chilwell, Henderson, Dier (Barkley 17), Alli (*Rice 63), Sancho, Kane, Sterling (*Hudson-Odoi 70)
Czech Republic (4-2-3-1): Pavlenka, Kaderabek, Celustka, Kalas, Novak, Soucek, Pavelka, Gebre Selssie, Darida (Masopust 67), Jankto (Vydra 46), Schick (Skoda 82). **Booked:** Kaderabek, Schick
Referee: A Manuel Dias (Portugal). **Half-time:** 2-0

MONTENEGRO 1 (Vesovic 17) ENGLAND 5 (Keane 30, Barkley 39, 59, Kane 71, Sterling 81)
Podgorica (8,329); Monday, March 25, 2019
Montenegro (4-4-2): Petkovic, Stojkovic, Savic, Simic (Jovovic 74), Tomasevic, Marusic, Ivanic, Vukcevic, Vesovic (Boljevic 70), Beciraj (Jankovic 61), Mugosa. **Booked:** Boljevic
England (4-3-3): Pickford, Walker, Keane, Maguire, Rose, Barkley (Ward-Prowse 81), Rice, Alli (Henderson 64), Hudson-Odoi, Kane (Wilson 83), Sterling. **Booked:** Barkley, Henderson, Rose
Refereee: A Kulbakov (Belarus). **Half-time:** 1-2

GROUP C

NORTHERN IRELAND 2 (McGinn 56, Davis 75 pen) ESTONIA 0
Windsor Park (18,176); Thursday, March 21, 2019
Northern Ireland (4-3-3): Peacock-Farrell, Dallas, Cathcart, J Evans, Lewis, McNair, Davis, Saville, McGinn (C McLaughlin 84), K Lafferty (Magennis 76), Jones (Ferguson 81)
Estonia (5-4-1): Lepmets, Kams, Baranov, Vihmann, Tamm, Pikk, Anier (Zenjov 76), Dmitrijev (Sappinen 85), Mets, Ojamaa (Vassiljev 68), Kait. **Booked:** Tamm
Referee: I Bebek (Croatia). **Half-time:** 0-0

NORTHERN IRELAND 2 (J Evans 30, Magennis 87) BELARUS 1 (Stasevich 33)
Windsor Park (18,188); Sunday, March 24, 2019
Northern Ireland (4-3-3): Peacock-Farrell, Dallas, Cathcart, J Evans, Lewis, McNair, Davis, Saville, McGinn (Magennis 68), K Lafferty (Boyce 79), Jones (Ferguson 85)
Belarus (4-2-3-1): Klimovich, Shitov (Polyakov 73), Sivakov, Martynovich, Volodko, Maevski, Dragun, Savitski (Nekhaychik 85), Hleb (Putilo 66), Stasevich, Laptev. **Booked:** Laptev
Referee: P Raczkowski (Poland). **Half-time:** 1-1

ESTONIA 1 (Vassiljev 25) NORTHERN IRLAND 2 (Washington 77, Magennis 80)
Tallinn (8,378); Saturday, June 8, 2019
Estonia (4-2-3-1): Lepmets, Teniste (Kams 85), Vihmann, Mets, Pikk, Dmitrijev, Kait (Tamm 84), Zenjov, Vassiljev, Sinyavskiy, Sappinen (Sorga 61). **Booked:** Lepmets
Northern Ireland (4-3-3): Peacock-Farrell, Smith (Jones 64), Cathcart, J Evans, Lewis, McNair, Davis, Saville (Magennis 69), Whyte, Boyce (Washington 46), Dallas. **Booked:** Saville
Referee: F Verissimo (Portugal). **Half-time:** 1-0

BELARUS 0 NORTHERN IRELAND 1 (McNair 86)
Borisov (5,350); Tuesday, June 11, 2019

Belarus (4-2-3-1): Gutor, Shitov (Veretilo 72), Martynovich, Naumov, Polyakov, Maevski, Korzun (Kislyak 46), Kovalev, Schikavko (Laptev 58), Stasevich, Nekhajchik. **Booked:** Korzun
Northern Ireland (4-3-3): Peacock-Farrell, Smith, Cathcart, J Evans, Lewis, C Evans (Saville 70), Davis, McNair, Magennis (Dallas 56), Washington (K Lafferty 72), Jones. **Booked:** Lewis, J Evans, K Lafferty, Dallas
Referee: H Lechner (Austria). **Half-time:** 0-0

GROUP D

GIBRALTAR 0 REPUBLIC OF IRELAND 1 (Hendrick 49)
Victoria (2,015); Saturday, March 23, 2019

Gibraltar (4-1-4-1): Goldwin, Sergeant, R Chipolina, J ChipIonina, Olivero, Annersley (Priestley 64), Casciaro, Walker, Bardon, Hernandez (Pons 78), Barr. **Booked:** Casciaro, Barr
Republic of Ireland (4-4-2): Randolph, Coleman, Duffy, Keogh, Stevens, Doherty (Brady 560, Hendrick, Hourihane, McClean, Maguire (Arter 72), McGoldrick. **Booked:** McClean, Stevens
Referee: A Papapetrou (Greece). **Half-time:** 0-0

REPUBLIC OF IRELAND 1 (Hourihane 35) GEORGIA 0
Aviva Stadium (40,317). Tuesday, March 26, 2019

Republic of Ireland (4-3-3): Randolph, Coleman, Duffy, Keogh, Stevens, Hendrick, Whelan, Hourihane, Brady (O'Brien 74), McGoldrick (Doherty 81), McClean.
Georgia (4-1-4-1): Loria, Kakabadze (Okriashvili 85), Kverkvelia, Kashia, Khotcholava (Kharabadze 65), Kvekveskiri, Arveladze (Qazaishvili 73), Gvilia, Kankava, Kitelshvili, Kvilitaia. **Booked:** Kankava, Kashia
Referee: S Gözübuyuk (Holland). **Half-time:** 1-0

DENMARK 1 (Hojbjerg 76) REPUBLIC OF IRELAND 1 (Duffy 85)
Copenhagen (34,610); Friday, June 7, 2019

Denmark (4-2-3-1): Schmeichel, Dalsgaard, Kjaer, Christensen, Larsen, Schone (Hojbjerg 72), Delaney, Poulsen, Eriksen, Braithwaite (Dolberg 64), Jorgensen.
Republic of Ireland (4-5-1): Randolph, Coleman, Duffy, Keogh, Stevens, Brady (Judge 66), Hendrick, Whelan, Hourihane (Hogan 82), McClean, McGoldrick (Robinson 87). **Booked:** Hourihane
Referee: C Cakir (Turkey). **Half-time:** 0-0

REPUBLIC OF IRELAND 2 (J Chipolina 29 og, Brady 90+3) GIBRALTAR 0
Aviva Stadium (36,281); Monday, June 10

Republic of Ireland (4-4-2): Randolph, Coleman, Duffy, Keogh, Stevens, Robinson (Brady 73) Hendrick, Hourihane, McClean, McGoldrick, Hogan (Maguire 66). **Booked:** Stevens
Gibraltar (4-5-1): Goldwin, Sergeant, R Chipolina, J Chipolina, Mascarenhas-Olivero, Casciaro (Bardon 10), Hernandez (Jolly 77), Walker, Annesley, Pons (Britto 64), Barr. **Booked:** Mascarenhas-Olivero
Referee: R Petrescu (Romania). **Half-time:** 1-0

GROUP E

WALES 1 (James 5) SLOVAKIA 0
Cardiff City Stadium (31,617); Sunday March 24, 2019

Wales (4-2-3-1): Hennessey, C Roberts, Mepham, J Lawrence, B Davies, Allen, Smith, Wilson (Vaulks 87), Brooks (T Roberts 60). James (A Williams 73), Bale. **Booked:** Allen, Brooks
Slovakia (4-2-3-1): Dubravka, Pekarik (Safranko 90), Vavro, Skriniar, Hancko, Kucka, Lobotka, Rusnak, Hamsik, Mak (Stoch 69), Duda (Duris 65). **Booked:** Mak, Vavro, Lobotka, Duris, Hamsik, Stoch, Kucka
Referee: F Zwayer (Germany). **Half-time:** 1-0

CROATIA 2 (Lawrence 17 og, Perisic 48) WALES 1 (Brooks 77)
Osijek (17,061); Saturday, June 8, 2019

Croatia (4-2-3-1): Livakovic, Jedvaj, Lovren, Vida, Barisic, Modric, Brozovic, Brekalo (Pasalic 66), Kovacic (Badelj 76), Perisic (Skoric 90+3), Kramaric. **Booked:** Brekalo, Jedvaj, Lovren, Vida, Brozovic
Wales (4-3-3): Hennessey, C Roberts, Mepham, J Lawrence, B Davies, Vaulks (Ampadu 66), Allen, Smith (Brooks 65), Bale, Wilson, James (Matondo 79). **Booked:** Bale
Referee: I Kovacs (Romania). **Half-time:** 1-0

HUNGARY 1 (Patkai 80) WALES 0
Budapest (18,350); Tuesday, June 11, 2019

Hungary (4-3-3): Gulacsi, Lovrencsics, Barath, Orban, Korhut, Patkai, Nagy, Szoboszlai (Bese 83), Dzsudzsak (Kleinheisler 70), Szalai, Holender (Varga 59). **Booked:** Patkai, Nagy, Korhut
Wales (4-2-3-1): Hennessey, Gunter, A Williams, J Lawrence, Davies, Ampadu (Smith 54), Allen, Bale, Brooks (Wilson 73), T Lawrence (Vokes 79), James. **Booked:** Gunter, J Lawrence, Davies
Referee: M Jug (Slovenia). **Half-time:** 0-0

GROUP I

KAZAKHSTAN 3 (Pertsukh 6, Vorogovskiy 10, Zainutdinov 51) SCOTLAND 0
Astana (27,641); Thursday, March 21, 2019

Kazakhstan (3-5-2): Nepogodov, Vorogovskiy, Maliy, Postnikov, Yerlanov, Suyumbayev, Pertsukh, Kuat, Merkel, Zainutdinov (Muzhikov 84), Murtazaev (Turysbek 68). **Booked:** Merkel, Suyumbayev
Scotland (4-3-3): Bain, *Palmer, Bates, McKenna, Shinnie, McGinn (McTominay 70), McGregor, Armstrong, Forrest (*McNulty 81), McBurnie (Russell 61), Burke. **Booked:** Shinnie
Referee: S Jovanovic (Serbia). **Half-time:** 2-0

SAN MARINO 0 SCOTLAND 2 (McLean 4, Russell 74)
Serravalle (4,077); Sunday, March 24, 2019

San Marino (4-4-1-1): Benedettini, Battistini, Simoncini (Lunadei 86), Cevoli, Palazzi, Mularoni, E Golinucci, A Golinucci, Hirsch (Grandoni 78), Berardi, Vitaioli (Nanni 61). **Booked:** Berardi
Scotland (4-2-3-1): Bain, O'Donnell, Bates, McKenna, Robertson, McLean, C McGregor (McTominay 57), Russell, Armstrong (Forrest 71), Fraser, Paterson (McNulty 37). **Booked:** McTominay
Referee: M Schuttengruber (Austria). **Half-time:** 0-1

SCOTLAND 2 (Robertson 61, Burke 89) CYPRUS 1 (Kousoulos 87)
Hampden Park (31,277); Saturday, June 8, 2019

Scotland (4-3-3): Marshall, O'Donnell, Mulgrew, McKenna, Robertson, McGinn (McTominay 79), McLean, McGregor (Armstrong 88), Forrest, Brophy (Burke 73), Fraser. **Booked:** McGregor
Cyprus (3-1-4-2): Pardo, Kousoulos, Laifis, N Ioannou, Artymatas, Makris (Pittas 80), M Ioannou (Georgiou 66), Spoljaric (Kosti 70), Margaca, Soteriou, Efrem. **Booked:** N Ioannou, Artymatas. **Booked:** N Ioannou, Artymatas
Referee: O Nilsen (Norway). **Half-time:** 0-0
(Steve Clarke's first match as Scotland manager)

BELGIUM 3 (Lukaku 45, 57, De Bruyne 90+2) SCOTLAND 0
Brussels (50,093); Tuesday, June 11, 2019

Belgium (3-4-2-1): Courtois, Alderweireld, Kompany (Vermaelen 90), Vertonghen, Meunier, Witsel, Tielemans (Mertens 78), T Hazard (Carrasco 90+1), De Bruyne, E Hazard, Lukaku. **Booked:** De Bruyne
Scotland (4-4-2): Marshall, O'Donnell, Mulgrew, McKenna, *Taylor, Russell (Forrest 67), McTominay, McLean, C McGregor, Burke, Armstrong (Fraser 32). **Booked:** McTominay
Referee: P Ardeleanu (Czech Republic). **Half-time:** 1-0

UEFA NATIONS LEAGUE 2018–19

LEAGUE A – GROUP 4

ENGLAND 1 (Rashford 11) SPAIN 2 (Saul 13, Rodrigo 32)
Wembley (81,392); Saturday, September 8, 2018
England (3-1-4-2): Pickford, Gomez, Stones, Maguire, Henderson (Dier 64), Trippier, Alli, Lingard, Shaw (Rose 53), Rashford (Welbeck 90+4), Kane. **Booked:** Henderson, Shaw, Stones, Rose
Spain (4-3-3): De Gea, Dani Carvajal, Sergio Ramos, Nacho, Marcos Alonso (Martinez 87), Busquets, Saul, Thiago Alcantara (Sergi Roberto 80), Aspas (Marco Asensio 68), Rodrigo, Isco. **Booked:** Dani Carvajal
Referee: D Makkelie (Holland). **Half-time**: 1-2

CROATIA 0 ENGLAND 0
Rijeka; Friday, October 12, 2018 (played behind closed doors – previous crowd trouble)
Croatia (4-2-3-1): Livakovic, Jedvaj, Lovren, Vida, Pivaric, Kovacic (Badelj 73), Rakitic, Kramaric, Modric, Perisic (Pjaca 68), Rebic (Libaja 80). **Booked:** Kovacic, Lovren, Jedvaj
England (4-3-3): Pickford, Walker, Stones, Maguire, Chilwell, Henderson, Dier, Barkley, Sterling (Sancho 78), Kane, Rashford. **Booked:** Henderson, Stones, Sterling
Referee: F Brych (Germany)

SPAIN 2 (Alcacer 58, Sergio Ramos 90+7) ENGLAND 3 (Sterling 16, 38, Rashford 29)
Seville (50,355): Monday, October 15, 2018
Spain (4-3-3): De Gea, Otto, Nacho, Sergio Ramos, Marcos Alonso, Thiago Alcantara, Busquets, Saul (Alcacer 57), Aspas (Ceballos 57), Rodrigo (Morata 72), Marco Asensio. **Booked:** Sergio Ramos, Otto, Ceballos, Morata
England (4-3-3): Pickford, Trippier (Alexander-Arnold 85), Gomez, Maguire, Chilwell, Winks (Chalobah 90+1) Dier, Barkley, (Walker 76), Sterling, Kane, Rashford. **Booked:** Dier, Winks, Maguire
Referee: S Marciniak (Poland). **Half-time**: 0-3

ENGLAND 2 (Lingard 78, Kane 85) CROATIA 1 (Kramaric 57)
Wembley (78,211); Sunday, November 18, 2018
England (4-3-3): Pickford, Walker, Gomez, Stones, Chilwell, Barkley (Alli 63), Dier, Delph (Lingard 73), Sterling, Kane, Rashford (Sancho 73). **Booked:** Barkley
Croatia (4-2-3-1): Kalinic, Vrsaljko (Milic 26), Lovren, Vida, Jedvaj, Modric, Brozovic, Vlasic (Rog 79), Kramaric, Perisic, Rebic (Brekalo 46). **Booked:** Jedvaj, Brozovic, Lovren
Referee: T Sidiropoulos (Greece). **Half-time**: 0-0

LEAGUE B – GROUP 3

NORTHERN IRELAND 1 (Grigg 90+3) BOSNIA-HERZEGOVINA 2 (Duljevic 37, Saric 64)
Windsor Park (16,942); Saturday, September 8, 2018
Northern Ireland (4-3-3): Peacock-Farrell, C McLaughlin (Boyce 70), Cathcart, J Evans, Lewis, Davis, Norwood, Saville, McGinn (Ward 76), Lafferty (Grigg 69), Dallas
Bosnia-Herzegovina (4-3-3): Sehic, Besic, Sunjic, Zukanovic, Civic (Zakaric 76), Saric (Krunic 67), Cimirot, Pjanic (Bajic 83), Visca, Dzeko, Duljevic. **Booked:** Civic, Pjanic, Dzeko, Saric
Referee: P Kralovec (Czech Republic). **Half-time** 0-1

AUSTRIA 1 (Arnautovic 71) NORTHERN IRELAND 0
Vienna (22,300); Friday, October 12, 2018
Austria (4-4-2): Lindner, Lainer, Prodl, Hinteregger, Ulmer, Lazaro (Dragovic 90+1), Ilsanker, Zulj, Satitzer (Schopf 75), Arnautovic, Burgstaller (Kainz 81)
Northern Ireland (4-3-3): Peacock-Farrell, McNair, Cathcart, J Evans, Lewis, Davis, Norwood,

Saville (*Vassell 77), Dallas, Magennis (Grigg 79), Ferguson (C Evans 56). **Booked**: Peacock-Farrell, Norwood
Referee: G Kabakov (Bulgaria). **Half-time**: 0-0

BOSNIA-HERZEGOVINA 2 (Dzeko 27, 73) NORTHERN IRELAND 0
Sarajevo (11,050): Monday, October 15, 2018
Bosnia-Herzegovina (4-3-3): Sehic, Vranjes, Sunjic, Zukanovic, Civic, Besic (Cimirot 90), Pjanic, Saric, Visca (Molosevic 88), Dzeko, Duljevic (Zakaric 75). **Booked**: Duljevic, Besic
Northern Ireland (4 1 4 1): Peacock Farrell, McNair (Vassell 71), Cathcart, J Evans, Lewis, Norwood (Whyte 58), C Evans, Davis, Saville, Dallas, Boyce (Magennis 80). **Booked**: Norwood, Saville
Referee: M Gestranius (Finland). **Half-time**: 1-0

NORTHERN IRELAND 1 (C Evans 57) AUSTRIA 2 (Schlager 49, Lazaro 90+3)
Windsor Park (17,895); Sunday, November 18, 2018
Northern Ireland (4-3-3): Carson, Smith, McAuley, J Evans, Dallas, C Evans (McNair 89), Davis, Saville, McGinn (Whyte 74), Boyce (K Lafferty 74), Jones. **Booked**: McAuley
Austria (4-2-3-1): Lindner, Lainer, Dragovic, Hinteregger, Ulmer, Ilsanker (Zulj 46), Baumgartlinger, Lazaro, Schlager, Alaba, Gregoritsch (Arnautovic 71). **Booked**: Baumgartlinger, Alaba
Referee: J Lardot (Belgium). **Half-time**: 0-0

LEAGUE B – GROUP 4
WALES 4 (T Lawrence 6, Bale 18, Ramsey 37, C Roberts 55) REPUBLIC OF IRELAND 1
(S Williams 66)
Cardiff City Stadium (25,657); Thursday, September 6, 2018
Wales (4-2-3-1): Hennessey, C Roberts, A Williams, Mepham, B Davies (Dummett 81), Allen, Ampadu (Smith 67), Brooks, Ramsey, T Lawrence, Bale (T Roberts 75)
Republic of Ireland (4-4-2): Randolph, Coleman, Duffy, Clark, Ward (Stevens 61), Christie, Hourihane (S Williams 66), Hendrick, O'Dowda, *Robinson (Horgan 77), Walters. **Booked**: Clark
Referee: C Turpin (France). **Half-time**: 3-0

DENMARK 2 (Eriksen 32, 63 pen) WALES 0
Aarhus (17,506); Sunday, September 9, 2018
Denmark (4-2-3-1): Schmeichel, Dalsgaard, Jorgensen, Kjaer, Larsen, Schone, Eriksen, Delaney, Poulsen (Cornelius 86), Sisto (Fischer 46), Braithwaite **Booked**: Schmeichel
Wales (4-2-3-1): Hennessey, Gunter, Chester, Mepham, B Davies, Allen, Ampadu (T Roberts 71), C Roberts (Brooks 59), Ramsey, T Lawrence (Woodburn 79), Bale. **Booked**: B Davies, Allen
Referee: D Aytekin (Germany). **Half-time**: 1-0

REPUBLIC OF IRELAND 0 DENMARK 0
Aviva Stadium (41,220); Saturday, October 13, 2018
Republic of Ireland (3-5-1-1): Randolph, Keogh, Duffy, K Long, Doherty, Christie, Arter (Robinson 65), O'Dowda (Stevens 46), McClean, Hendrick, S Long (O'Brien 83). **Booked**: Arter, Christie, McClean, Duffy
Denmark (4-2-3-1): Schmeichel, Dalsgaard, M Jorgensen, Kjaer, Larsen, Schone, Delaney, Poulsen, Braithwaite, Sisto, Dolberg (Christiansen 79). **Booked**: Delaney
Referee: J Estrada (Spain)

REPUBLIC OF IRELAND 0 WALES 1 (Wilson 58)
Aviva Stadium (38,321); Tuesday, October 16, 2018

Republic of Ireland (3-5-2): Randolph, Keogh, Duffy, K Long (Hogan 75), Doherty, Christie, Arter, Hendrick, McClean, Robinson (Maguire 60), O'Brien (S Long 56). **Booked**: K Long, McClean, S Long
Wales (4-2-3-1): Hennessey, C Roberts, Chester, A Williams, Davies, Smith (Thomas 74), Allen, Wilson (Gunter 85), Brooks (King 87), T Lawrence, T Roberts. **Booked**: Davies
Referee: B Kuipers (Holland). **Half-time**: 0-0

WALES 1 (Bale 89) DENMARK 2 (N Jorgensen 42, Braithwaite 88)
Cardiff City Stadium (32,354); Friday, November 16, 2018
Wales (4-2-3-1): Hennessey, C Roberts, Chester (Ampadu 50), A Williams, Dummett (Gunter 39), Allen, Ramsey, Brooks, Bale, T Lawrence, T Roberts (Wilson 68). **Booked**: Dummett, Lawrence, Ampadu, A Williams
Denmark (4-2-3-1): Schmeichel, Dalsgaard, Christensen, M Jorgensen, Larsen, Schone (Lerager 79), Delaney, Poulsen, Eriksen, Braithwaite, N Jorgensen (Dolberg 70). **Booked**: Dalsgaard, Delaney, Dolberg, M Jorgensen, Schmeichel
Referee: I Kruzliak (Slovakia). **Half-time**: 0-1

DENMARK 0 REPUBLIC OF IRELAND 0
Aarhus (11,130); Monday, November 19, 2018
Denmark (4-2-3-1): Ronnow, Ankersen, M Jorgensen, Bjelland, Knudsen, Schone, Eriksen (Lerager 46), Hojbjerg, Poulsen (Gytkjaer 65), N Jorgensen, Braithwaite (Cornelius 78)
Republic of Ireland (3-5-2): Randolph, Keogh, Duffy, K Long, Coleman, Christie, Hendrick, Brady (Robinson 65), Stevens, O'Dowda (*Obafemi 80), O'Brien (Curtis 65). **Booked**: Christie
Referee: A Agayev (Azerbaijan)

LEAGUE C – GROUP 1

SCOTLAND 2 (Djimsiti 47 og, Naismith 68) ALBANIA 0
Hampden Park (17,455); Monday, September 10, 2018
Scotland (3-5-2): A McGregor, Souttar, Mulgrew, Tierney, O'Donnell, McGinn, McDonald (Armstrong 46), C McGregor (McTominay 78), Robertson, Russell (Griffiths 70), Naismith. **Booked**: Souttar, McDonald
Albania (4-3-3): Strakosha, Hysaj, Veseli (Mihaj 90+1), Djimsiti, Binaku, Xhaka, Lilaj (Manaj 66), Ndoj, Gavazaj (Prenga 46), Balaj, Memushaj. **Booked**: Ndoj, Prenga, Memushaj
Referee: M Jug (Slovenia). **Half-time**: 0-0

ISRAEL 2 (Peretz 52, Tierney og 74) SCOTLAND 1 (Mulgrew 24)
Haifa (10,234); Thursday, October 11, 2018
Israel (3-5-2): Harush, Yeini, Tibi, Ben Harush, Dasa, Peretz, Natcho, Kayal (Einbinder 82), Tawatha (Atar 76), Dabbur, Sahar (Sabar 46). **Booked**: Ben Harush, Natcho
Scotland (3-4-2-1): A McGregor, Souttar, Mulgrew (McKenna 46), Tierney, O'Donnell, McGinn, McDonald, Robertson, Russell (Forrest 67), C McGregor, Naismith (McBurnie 76). **Booked**: Souttar, Robertson. **Sent off**: Souttar (61)
Referee: D Stefanski (Poland). **Half-time**: 0-1

ALBANIA 0 SCOTLAND 4 (Fraser 14, Fletcher 45 pen, Forrest 55, 67)
Shkoder (8,632); Saturday, November 17, 2018
Albania (4-4-1-1): Berisha, Veseli, Djimsiti (Dermaku 53), Mavraj, Binaku, Uzuni, Kace (Ismajli 27), Xhaka, Grezda, Memushaj, Manaj (Balaj 62). **Booked**: Manaj, Mavraj, Grezda. **Sent off**: Mavraj (22)
Scotland (4-2-3-1): A McGregor, Paterson, Bates, McKenna, Robertson, C McGregor, Forrest, Armstrong (McTominay 61), Christie, Fraser (Russell 72), Fletcher (Phillips 68). **Booked**: Paterson, McKenna, Bates, Russell
Referee: V Bezborodov (Russia). **Half-time**: 0-2

SCOTLAND 3 (Forrest 34, 43, 64) ISRAEL 2 (Kayal 9, Zahavi 75)
Hampden Park (21,281); Tuesday, November 20, 2018
Scotland (4-3-3): A McGregor, Paterson, Bates, McKenna, Robertson, C McGregor, Armstrong (Phillips 76), Christie (Shinnie 76), Fraser, Forrest, Fletcher (McTominay 87). **Booked**: C McGregor, Phillips
Israel (3-5-2): Harush, Yeini, Taha (Cohen 67), Ben Harush, Dasa, Peretz (Saba 73), Natcho, Kayal, Tawatha (Hemed 85), Zahavi, Dabbur. **Booked**: Taha, Peretz, Ben Harush
Referee: T Welz (Germany). **Half-time**: 2-1

FRIENDLY INTERNATIONALS

SCOTLAND 0 BELGIUM 4 (Lukaku 28, E Hazard 46, Batshuayi 52, 60)
Hampden Park (20,196); Friday, September 7, 2018
Scotland (3-5-2): Gordon, *Souttar, Mulgrew (O'Donnell 67), Tierney, Fraser, McGinn (Shinnie 73), McDonald (Snodgrass 53), Armstrong (Jack 53), Robertson, C McGregor (Russell 68), Griffiths (Naismith 46)
Belgium (3-4-3): Courtois, Kompany (Vermaelen 46), Boyata, Vertonghen, T Hazard, Tielemans, Dembele (Verstaete 85), Castagne (Meunier 46), Mertens (Carrasco 46), Lukaku (Batshuayi 46), E Hazard
Referee: L Banti (Italy). **Half-time**: 0-1

ENGLAND 1 (Rashford 54) SWITZERLAND 0
King Power Stadium, Leicester (30,256); Tuesday, September 11, 2018
England (3-5-2): Butland, Walker, Tarkowski (Stones 61), Maguire, Alexander-Arnold (Trippier 68), Loftus-Cheek (Lingard 61), Dier, Delph (Henderson 68), Rose (*Chilwell 79), Welbeck (Kane 61), Rashford. **Booked**: Henderson
Switzerland (3-5-1-1): Sommer, Schar, Djourou, Akanji (Mehmedi 46), Lichtsteiner, Zakaria (Fernandes 66), Xhaka, Freuler (Zuber 67), Rodriguez (Moubandje 46), Shaqiri (Seferovic 80), Gavranovic (Ajeti 67). **Booked**: Lichtsteiner
Referee: C Turpin (France). **Half-time**: 0-0

NORTHERN IRELAND 3 (Davis 13, Dallas 42, Whyte 67) ISRAEL 0
Windsor Park (12,913); Tuesday, September 11, 2018
Northern Ireland (4-3-3): Carson (McGovern 46), McNair, Cathcart, J Evans, Lewis, Davis, C Evans (Norwood 46), Saville (Smith 71), Dallas (Ferguson 77), Grigg (Washington 65), Jones (*Whyte 65)
Israel (3-5-2): Haimov, Yeini, Tibi, Habashi (Kapiloto 46), Dasa (Bitton 65), Micha (Turgeman 59), Natcho, Peretz, Tawatha (Scheimann 40), Dabbur (Glazer 75), Hemed (Sabad 59). **Booked**: Habashi
Referee: B Nijhuis (Holland). **Half-time**: 2-0

POLAND 1 (Klich 87) REPUBLIC OF IRELAND 1 (O'Brien 53)
Wroclaw (25,455); Tuesday, September 11, 2018
Poland (4-4-2): Szczesny, Kedziora, Glik (Bednarek 59), Kaminski, Reca (Pietrzak 72), Blaszczykowski (Frankowski 81), Krychowiak (Szymanski 72), Linetty, Kurzawa (Kadzior 46), Milik, Piatek (Klich 59)
Republic of Ireland (3-5-1-1): Randolph, Keogh, Egan, K Long, Christie (Doherty 55), Hendrick (Meyler 56), S Williams (Hourihane 72), O'Dowda (Judge 89), Stevens, Robinson (Burke 63), *O'Brien (Horgan 81)
Referee: B Marhefka (Slovakia). **Half-time**: 0-0

WALES 1 (Vokes 89) SPAIN 4 (Alcacer 8, 29, Sergio Ramos 19, Bartra 74)
Principality Stadium (50,232); Thursday, October 11, 2018

Wales (3-4-1-2): Hennessey, Gunter, A Williams (Chester 46), B Davies (Richards 62), C Roberts, Ampadu (King 50), Allen (Smith 62), John (Lawrence 62), Wilson (Brooks 46), Vokes, Ramsey
Spain (4-3-3): De Gea (Arrizabalaga 46), Azpilicueta (Otto 63), Albiol, Sergio Ramos (Bartra 46), Gaya, Ceballos, Rodri, Saul (Koke 46), Suso (Rodrigo 81), Morata, Alcacer (Aspas 73)
Referee: A Taylor (England). **Half-time:** 0-0

SCOTLAND 1 (Naismith 90+3) PORTUGAL 3 (Helder Costa 43, Eder 74, Bruma 84)
Hampden Park (19,684); Sunday, October 14, 2018
Scotland (4-4-2): Gordon, O'Donnell, Hendry, McKenna, Robertson, Forrest, McGinn (Shinnie 67), Armstrong (McDonald 77), C McGregor, Naismith, McBurnie (Mackay-Steven 76)
Portugal (4-3-3): Beto (Claudio Ramos 86), Soares, Ruben Dias (Pedro Mendes 57), Neto, Kevin Rodrigues, Sergio Oliveira (Renato Sanches 56), Danilo (William Carvalho 90+1) Bruno Fernandes (Gelson Fernandes 68), Helder Costa, Eder, Bruma (Rafa Silva 90+1).
Booked: Sergio Oliveira
Referee: R Buquet (France). **Half-time:** 0-1

ENGLAND 3 (Lingard 25, Alexander-Arnold 27, Wilson 77) USA 0
Wembley (68,155); Thursday, November 15, 2018
England (4-2-3-1): Pickford (*McCarthy 46), Alexander-Arnold, Keane, *Dunk, Chilwell (Dier 58), Winks (Loftus-Cheek 70), Delph, Sancho, Alli (Henderson 58), Lingard (Rooney 58), *Wilson (Rashford 78)
USA (4-2-3-1): Guzan, Yedlin, Miazga, Brooks, Villafana (Moore 88), Trapp (Acosta 70), McKennie (Lletget 76), Pulisic, Green (Adams 62), Weah (Saief 76), Wood
Referee: Jesus Gil (Spain). **Half-time:** 2-0

REPUBLIC OF IRELAND 0 NORTHERN IRELAND 0
Aviva Stadium (31,241); Thursday, November 15, 2018
Republic of Ireland (3-5-2): Randolph, Lenihan (Christie 84), Duffy, Egan, Coleman, Hendrick, Whelan (Hourihane 36), Brady, McClean (Stevens 66), O'Dowda (*Curtis 46), Robinson (Maguire 66, Hogan 80). **Booked:** Lenihan, Hourihane
Northern Ireland (4-1-4-1): Peacock-Farrell, Smith (Ward 74), Cathcart, J Evans, Lewis, Davis, Whyte (Jones 61), C Evans (McNair 65), Saville, Dallas, Boyce (Lafferty 71). **Booked:** Saville
Referee: S Vincic (Slovenia)

ALBANIA 1 (Balaj 58 pen) WALES 0
Elbasan (3,060); Tuesday, November 20, 2018
Albania (4-1-4-1): Berisha, Hysaj, Ismajli, Veseli, Mavraj, Basha, Uzuni, Lila (Memushaj 59), Xhaka, Grezda (Lilaj 69), Balaj. **Booked:** Lila, Xhaka.
Wales (4-2-3-1): Ward, Gunter, Lockyer, *J Lawrence, C Roberts (*Freeman 76), King, Allen (Ramsey 56), Wilson, Brooks (Bale 59), *James (Woodburn 56), Vokes (*Matondo 78).
Booked: King, Gunter, Wilson, Bale
Referee: D Jakimovski (Macedonia). **Half-time:** 0-0
(Chris Gunter's record 93rd cap)

WALES 1 (Woodburn 90+2) TRINIDAD & TOBAGO 0
Racecourse Ground, Wrexham (10,326); Wednesday, March 20, 2019
Wales (4-2-3-1): Ward (*A Davies 46), Gunter, A Williams (J Lawrence 60), Dummett (John 60), Taylor, *Vaulks, Evans, T Roberts (Matondo 70), Thomas, Hedges, Woodburn. **Booked:** Evans
Trinidad & Tobago (4-3-3): Phillip, David, Bateau, Cyrus, Hodge, Hyland, George, Paul (Hackshaw 81), Garcia (Peltier 59), Plaza (Cato 46), Lewis. **Booked:** George
Referee: T Marshall (Northern Ireland). **Half-time:** 0-0

OTHER BRITISH & IRISH INTERNATIONAL RESULTS

ENGLAND

v ALBANIA

		E	A
1989	Tirana (WC)	2	0
1989	Wembley (WC)	5	0
2001	Tirana (WC)	3	1
2001	Newcastle (WC)	2	0

v ALGERIA

		E	A
2010	Cape Town (WC)	0	0

v ANDORRA

		E	A
2006	Old Trafford (EC)	5	0
2007	Barcelona (EC)	3	0
2008	Barcelona (WC)	2	0
2009	Wembley (WC)	6	0

v ARGENTINA

		E	A
1951	Wembley	2	1
1953*	Buenos Aires	0	0
1962	Rancagua (WC)	3	1
1964	Rio de Janeiro	0	1
1966	Wembley (WC)	1	0
1974	Wembley	2	2
1977	Buenos Aires	1	1
1980	Wembley	3	1
1986	Mexico City (WC)	1	2
1991	Wembley	2	2
1998†	St Etienne (WC)	2	2
2000	Wembley	0	0
2002	Sapporo (WC)	1	0
2005	Geneva	3	2

(*Abandoned after 21 mins – rain)
(† England lost 3-4 on pens)

v AUSTRALIA

		E	A
1980	Sydney	2	1
1983	Sydney	0	0
1983	Brisbane	1	0
1983	Melbourne	1	1
1991	Sydney	1	0
2003	West Ham	1	3
2016	Sunderland	2	1

v AUSTRIA

		E	A
1908	Vienna	6	1
1908	Vienna	11	1
1909	Vienna	8	1
1930	Vienna	0	0
1932	Stamford Bridge	4	3
1936	Vienna	1	2
1951	Wembley	2	2
1952	Vienna	3	2
1958	Boras (WC)	2	2
1961	Vienna	1	3
1962	Wembley	3	1
1965	Wembley	2	3
1967	Vienna	1	0
1973	Wembley	7	0
1979	Vienna	3	4
2004	Vienna (WC)	2	2
2005	Old Trafford (WC)	1	0
2007	Vienna	1	0

v AZERBAIJAN

		E	A
2004	Baku (WC)	1	0
2005	Newcastle (WC)	2	0

v BELARUS

		E	B
2008	Minsk (WC)	3	1
2009	Wembley (WC)	3	0

v BELGIUM

		E	B
1921	Brussels	2	0
1923	Highbury	6	1
1923	Antwerp	2	2
1924	West Bromwich	4	0
1926	Antwerp	5	3
1927	Brussels	9	1
1928	Antwerp	3	1
1929	Brussels	5	1
1931	Brussels	4	1
1936	Brussels	2	3
1947	Brussels	5	2
1950	Brussels	4	1
1952	Wembley	5	0
1954	Basle (WC)	4	4
1964	Wembley	2	2
1970	Brussels	3	1
1980	Turin (EC)	1	1
1990	Bologna (WC)	1	0
1998*	Casablanca	0	0
1999	Sunderland	2	1
2012	Wembley	1	0
2018	Kaliningrad (WC)	0	1
2018	St Petersburg (WC)	0	2

(*England lost 3-4 on pens)

v BOHEMIA

		E	B
1908	Prague	4	0

v BRAZIL

		E	B
1956	Wembley	4	2
1958	Gothenburg (WC)	0	0
1959	Rio de Janeiro	0	2
1962	Vina del Mar (WC)	1	3
1963	Wembley	1	1
1964	Rio de Janeiro	1	5
1969	Rio de Janeiro	1	2
1970	Guadalajara (WC)	0	1
1976	Los Angeles	0	1
1977	Rio de Janeiro	0	0
1978	Wembley	1	1
1981	Wembley	0	1
1984	Rio de Janeiro	2	0
1987	Wembley	1	1
1990	Wembley	1	0

1992	Wembley	1	1
1993	Washington	1	1
1995	Wembley	1	3
1997	Paris (TF)	0	1
2000	Wembley	1	1
2002	Shizuoka (WC)	1	2
2007	Wembley	1	1
2009	Doha	0	1
2013	Wembley	2	1
2013	Rio de Janeiro	2	2
2017	Wembley	0	0

v BULGARIA

		E	B
1962	Rancagua (WC)	0	0
1968	Wembley	1	1
1974	Sofia	1	0
1979	Sofia (EC)	3	0
1979	Wembley (EC)	2	0
1996	Wembley	1	0
1998	Wembley (EC)	0	0
1999	Sofia (EC)	1	1
2010	Wembley (EC)	4	0
2011	Sofia (EC)	3	0

v CAMEROON

		E	C
1990	Naples (WC)	3	2
1991	Wembley	2	0
1997	Wembley	2	0
2002	Kobe (Japan)	2	2

v CANADA

		E	C
1986	Vancouver	1	0

v CHILE

		E	C
1950	Rio de Janeiro (WC)	2	0
1953	Santiago	2	1
1984	Santiago	0	0
1989	Wembley	0	0
1998	Wembley	0	2
2013	Wembley	0	2

v CHINA

		E	C
1996	Beijing	3	0

v CIS
(formerly Soviet Union)

		E	CIS
1992	Moscow	2	2

v COLOMBIA

		E	C
1970	Bogota	4	0
1988	Wembley	1	1
1995	Wembley	0	0
1998	Lens (WC)	2	0
2005	New York	3	2
2018†	Moscow (WC)	1	1

(† England won 4-3 on pens)

v COSTA RICA

		E	CR
2014	Belo Horizonte (WC)	0	0
2018	Leeds	2	0

v CROATIA

		E	C
1995	Wembley	0	0
2003	Ipswich	3	1
2004	Lisbon (EC)	4	2
2006	Zagreb (EC)	0	2
2007	Wembley (EC)	2	3
2008	Zagreb (WC)	4	1
2009	Wembley (WC)	5	1
2018	Moscow (WC)	1	2
2018	Rijeka (NL)	0	0
2018	Wembley (NL)	2	1

v CYPRUS

		E	C
1975	Wembley (EC)	5	0
1975	Limassol (EC)	1	0

v CZECH REPUBLIC

		E	C
1998	Wembley	2	0
2008	Wembley	2	2
2019	Wembley (EC)	5	0

v CZECHOSLOVAKIA

		E	C
1934	Prague	1	2
1937	White Hart Lane	5	4
1963	Bratislava	4	2
1966	Wembley	0	0
1970	Guadalajara (WC)	1	0
1973	Prague	1	1
1974	Wembley (LC)	3	0
1975*	Bratislava (EC)	1	2
1978	Wembley (EC)	1	0
1982	Bilbao (WC)	2	0
1990	Wembley	4	2
1992	Prague	2	2

(* Aband 0-0, 17 mins prev day – fog)

v DENMARK

		E	D
1948	Copenhagen	0	0
1955	Copenhagen	5	1
1956	W'hampton (WC)	5	2
1957	Copenhagen (WC)	4	1
1966	Copenhagen	2	0
1978	Copenhagen (EC)	4	3
1979	Wembley (EC)	1	0
1982	Copenhagen (EC)	2	2
1983	Wembley (EC)	0	1
1988	Wembley	1	0
1989	Copenhagen	1	1
1990	Wembley	1	0
1992	Malmo (EC)	0	0
1994	Wembley	1	0
2002	Niigata (WC)	3	0
2003	Old Trafford	2	3
2005	Copenhagen	1	4
2011	Copenhagen	2	1
2014	Wembley	1	0

v EAST GERMANY

		E	EG
1963	Leipzig	2	1
1970	Wembley	3	1
1974	Leipzig	1	1
1984	Wembley	1	0

v ECUADOR

		E	Ec
1970	Quito	2	0
2006	Stuttgart (WC)	1	0
2014	Miami	2	2

v EGYPT

		E	Eg
1986	*Cairo*	*4*	*0*
1990	Cagliari (WC)	1	0
2010	Wembley	3	1

v ESTONIA

		E	Est
2007	Tallinn (EC)	3	0
2007	Wembley (EC)	3	0
2014	Tallinn (EC)	1	0
2015	Wembley (EC)	2	0

v FIFA

		E	F
1938	Highbury	3	0
1953	Wembley	4	4
1963	Wembley	2	1

v FINLAND

		E	F
1937	Helsinki	8	0
1956	Helsinki	5	1
1966	Helsinki	3	0
1976	Helsinki (WC)	4	1
1976	Wembley (WC)	2	1
1982	Helsinki	4	1
1984	Wembley (WC)	5	0
1985	Helsinki (WC)	1	1
1992	Helsinki	2	1
2000	Helsinki (WC)	0	0
2001	Liverpool (WC)	2	1

v FRANCE

		E	F
1923	Paris	4	1
1924	Paris	3	1
1925	Paris	3	2
1927	Paris	6	0
1928	Paris	5	1
1929	Paris	4	1
1931	Paris	2	5
1933	White Hart Lane	4	1
1938	Paris	4	2
1947	Highbury	3	0
1949	Paris	3	1
1951	Highbury	2	2
1955	Paris	0	1
1957	Wembley	4	0
1962	Hillsborough (EC)	1	1
1963	Paris (EC)	2	5
1966	Wembley (WC)	2	0
1969	Wembley	5	0
1982	Bilbao (WC)	3	1
1984	Paris	0	2
1992	Wembley	2	0
1992	Malmo (EC)	0	0
1997	Montpellier (TF)	1	0
1999	Wembley	0	2
2000	Paris	1	1
2004	Lisbon (EC)	1	2
2008	Paris	0	1
2010	Wembley	1	2
2012	Donetsk (EC)	1	1
2015	Wembley	2	0
2017	Paris	2	3

v GEORGIA

		E	G
1996	Tbilisi (WC)	2	0
1997	Wembley (WC)	2	0

v GERMANY/WEST GERMANY

		E	G
1930	Berlin	3	3
1935	White Hart Lane	3	0
1938	Berlin	6	3
1954	Wembley	3	1
1956	Berlin	3	1
1965	Nuremberg	1	0
1966	Wembley	1	0
1966	Wembley (WCF)	4	2
1968	Hanover	0	1
1970	Leon (WC)	2	3
1972	Wembley (EC)	1	3
1972	Berlin (EC)	0	0
1975	Wembley	2	0
1978	Munich	1	2
1982	Madrid (WC)	0	0
1982	Wembley	1	2
1985	Mexico City	3	0
1987	Dusseldorf	1	3
1990*	Turin (WC)	1	1
1991	Wembley	0	1
1993	Detroit	1	2
1996†	Wembley (EC)	1	1
2000	Charleroi (EC)	1	0
2000	Wembley (WC)	0	1
2001	Munich (WC)	5	1
2007	Wembley	1	2
2008	Berlin	2	1
2010	Bloemfontein (WC)	1	4
2012	Donetsk (EC)	1	1
2013	Wembley	0	1
2016	Berlin	3	2
2017	Dortmund	0	1
2017	Wembley	0	0

(*England lost 3-4 on pens)
(† England lost 5-6 on pens)

v GHANA

		E	G
2011	Wembley	1	1

v GREECE

		E	G
1971	Wembley (EC)	3	0
1971	Athens (EC)	2	0
1982	Salonika (EC)	3	0
1983	Wembley (EC)	0	0
1989	Athens	2	1
1994	Wembley	5	0
2001	Athens (WC)	2	0
2001	Old Trafford (WC)	2	2
2006	Old Trafford	4	0

v HOLLAND

		E	H
1935	Amsterdam	1	0
1946	Huddersfield	8	2
1964	Amsterdam	1	1
1969	Amsterdam	1	0
1970	Wembley	0	0
1977	Wembley	0	2
1982	Wembley	2	0
1988	Wembley	2	2
1988	Dusseldorf (EC)	1	3
1990	Cagliari (WC)	0	0
1993	Wembley (WC)	2	2
1993	Rotterdam (WC)	0	2
1996	Wembley (EC)	4	1
2001	White Hart Lane	0	2
2002	Amsterdam	1	1
2005	Villa Park	0	0
2006	Amsterdam	1	1
2009	Amsterdam	2	2
2012	Wembley	2	3
2016	Wembley	1	2
2018	Amsterdam	1	0
2019	Guimaraes (NL)	1	3

v HONDURAS

		E	H
2014	Miami	0	0

v HUNGARY

		E	H
1908	Budapest	7	0
1909	Budapest	4	2
1909	Budapest	8	2
1934	Budapest	1	2
1936	Highbury	6	2
1953	Wembley	3	6
1954	Budapest	1	7
1960	Budapest	0	2
1962	Rancagua (WC)	1	2
1965	Wembley	1	0
1978	Wembley	4	1
1981	Budapest (WC)	3	1
1981	Wembley (WC)	1	0
1983	Wembley (EC)	2	0
1983	Budapest (EC)	3	0
1988	Budapest	0	0
1990	Wembley	1	0
1992	Budapest	1	0
1996	Wembley	3	0
1999	Budapest	1	1
2006	Old Trafford	3	1
2010	Wembley	2	1

v ICELAND

		E	I
1982	Reykjavik	1	1
2004	City of Manchester	6	1
2016	Nice (EC)	1	2

v ISRAEL

		E	I
1986	Tel Aviv	2	1
1988	Tel Aviv	0	0
2006	Tel Aviv (EC)	0	0
2007	Wembley (EC)	3	0

v ITALY

		E	I
1933	Rome	1	1
1934	Highbury	3	2
1939	Milan	2	2
1948	Turin	4	0
1949	White Hart Lane	2	0
1952	Florence	1	1
1959	Wembley	2	2
1961	Rome	3	2
1973	Turin	0	2
1973	Wembley	0	1
1976	New York	3	2
1976	Rome (WC)	0	2
1977	Wembley (WC)	2	0
1980	Turin (EC)	0	1
1985	Mexico City	1	2
1989	Wembley	0	0
1990	Bari (WC)	1	2
1996	Wembley (WC)	0	1
1997	Nantes (TF)	2	0
1997	Rome (WC)	0	0
2000	Turin	0	1
2002	Leeds	1	2
2012*	Kiev (EC)	0	0
2012	Berne	2	1
2014	Manaus (WC)	1	2
2015	Turin	1	1
2018	Wembley	1	1

(*England lost 2-4 on pens)

v JAMAICA

		E	J
2006	Old Trafford	6	0

v JAPAN

		E	J
1995	Wembley	2	1
2004	City of Manchester	1	1
2010	Graz	2	1

v KAZAKHSTAN

		E	K
2008	Wembley (WC)	5	1
2009	Almaty (WC)	4	0

v KUWAIT

		E	K
1982	Bilbao (WC)	1	0

v LIECHTENSTEIN

		E	L
2003	Vaduz (EC)	2	0
2003	Old Trafford (EC)	2	0

v LITHUANIA

		E	L
2015	Wembley (EC)	4	0
2015	Vilnius (EC)	3	0
2017	Wembley (WC)	2	0
2017	Vilnius (WC)	1	0

v LUXEMBOURG

		E	L
1927	Luxembourg	5	2
1960	Luxembourg (WC)	9	0
1961	Highbury (WC)	4	1
1977	Wembley (WC)	5	0
1977	Luxembourg (WC)	2	0

		E	M
1982	Wembley (EC)	9	0
1983	Luxembourg (EC)	4	0
1998	Luxembourg (EC)	3	0
1999	Wembley (EC)	6	0

v MACEDONIA

		E	M
2002	Southampton (EC)	2	2
2003	Skopje (EC)	2	1
2006	Skopje (EC)	1	0
2006	Old Trafford (EC)	U	U

v MALAYSIA

		E	M
1991	Kuala Lumpur	4	2

v MALTA

		E	M
1971	Valletta (EC)	1	0
1971	Wembley (EC)	5	0
2000	Valletta	2	1
2016	Wembley (WC)	2	0
2017	Ta'Qali (WC)	4	0

v MEXICO

		E	M
1959	Mexico City	1	2
1961	Wembley	8	0
1966	Wembley (WC)	2	0
1969	Mexico City	0	0
1985	Mexico City	0	1
1986	Los Angeles	3	0
1997	Wembley	2	0
2001	Derby	4	0
2010	Wembley	3	1

v MOLDOVA

		E	M
1996	Kishinev	3	0
1997	Wembley (WC)	4	0
2012	Chisinu (WC)	5	0
2013	Wembley (WC)	4	0

v MONTENEGRO

		E	M
2010	Wembley (EC)	0	0
2011	Podgorica (EC)	2	2
2013	Podgorica (WC)	1	1
2013	Wembley (WC)	4	1
2019	Podgorica (EC)	5	1

v MOROCCO

		E	M
1986	Monterrey (WC)	0	0
1998	Casablanca	1	0

v NEW ZEALAND

		E	NZ
1991	Auckland	1	0
1991	Wellington	2	0

v NIGERIA

		E	NZ
1994	Wembley	1	0
2002	Osaka (WC)	0	0
2018	Wembley	2	1

v NORWAY

		E	NZ
1937	Oslo	6	0
1938	Newcastle	4	0
1949	Oslo	4	1
1966	Oslo	6	1
1980	Wembley (WC)	4	0
1981	Oslo (WC)	1	2
1992	Wembley (WC)	1	1
1993	Oslo (WC)	0	2
1994	Wembley	U	U
1995	Oslo	0	0
2012	Oslo	1	0
2014	Wembley	1	0

v PANAMA

		E	P
2018	Nizhny Novgorod (WC)	6	1

v PARAGUAY

		E	P
1986	Mexico City (WC)	3	0
2002	Anfield	4	0
2006	Frankfurt (WC)	1	0

v PERU

		E	P
1959	Lima	1	4
1961	Lima	4	0
2014	Wembley	3	0

v POLAND

		E	P
1966	Goodison Park	1	1
1966	Chorzow	1	0
1973	Chorzow (WC)	0	2
1973	Wembley (WC)	1	1
1986	Monterrey (WC)	3	0
1989	Wembley (WC)	3	0
1989	Katowice (WC)	0	0
1990	Wembley (EC)	2	0
1991	Poznan (EC)	1	1
1993	Chorzow (WC)	1	1
1993	Wembley (WC)	3	0
1996	Wembley (WC)	2	1
1997	Katowice (WC)	2	0
1999	Wembley (EC)	3	1
1999	Warsaw (EC)	0	0
2004	Katowice (WC)	2	1
2005	Old Trafford (WC)	2	1
2012	Warsaw (WC)	1	1
2013	Wembley (WC)	2	0

v PORTUGAL

		E	P
1947	Lisbon	10	0
1950	Lisbon	5	3
1951	Goodison Park	5	2
1955	Oporto	1	3
1958	Wembley	2	1
1961	Lisbon (WC)	1	1
1961	Wembley (WC)	2	0
1964	Lisbon	4	3
1964	Sao Paulo	1	1
1966	Wembley (WC)	2	1
1969	Wembley	1	0
1974	Lisbon	0	0

1974	Wembley (EC)	0	0
1975	Lisbon (EC)	1	1
1986	Monterrey (WC)	0	1
1995	Wembley	1	1
1998	Wembley	3	0
2000	Eindhoven (EC)	2	3
2002	Villa Park	1	1
2004	Faro	1	1
2004*	Lisbon (EC)	2	2
2006†	Gelsenkirchen (WC)	0	0
2016	Wembley	1	0

(† England lost 1–3 on pens)
(*England lost 5–6 on pens)

v REPUBLIC OF IRELAND

		E	RoI
1946	Dublin	1	0
1949	Goodison Park	0	2
1957	Wembley (WC)	5	1
1957	Dublin (WC)	1	1
1964	Dublin	3	1
1977	Wembley	1	1
1978	Dublin (EC)	1	1
1980	Wembley (EC)	2	0
1985	Wembley	2	1
1988	Stuttgart (EC)	0	1
1990	Cagliari (WC)	1	1
1990	Dublin (EC)	1	1
1991	Wembley (EC)	1	1
1995*	Dublin	0	1
2013	Wembley	1	1
2015	Dublin	0	0

(*Abandoned 27 mins – crowd riot)

v ROMANIA

		E	R
1939	Bucharest	2	0
1968	Bucharest	0	0
1969	Wembley	1	1
1970	Guadalajara (WC)	1	0
1980	Bucharest (WC)	1	2
1981	Wembley (WC)	0	0
1985	Bucharest (WC)	0	0
1985	Wembley (WC)	1	1
1994	Wembley	1	1
1998	Toulouse (WC)	1	2
2000	Charleroi (EC)	2	3

v RUSSIA

		E	R
2007	Wembley (EC)	3	0
2007	Moscow (EC)	1	2
2016	Marseille (EC)	1	1

v SAN MARINO

		E	SM
1992	Wembley (WC)	6	0
1993	Bologna (WC)	7	1
2012	Wembley (WC)	5	0
2013	Serravalle (WC)	8	0
2014	Wembley (EC)	5	0
2015	Serravalle (EC)	6	0

v SAUDI ARABIA

		E	SA
1988	Riyadh	1	1
1998	Wembley	0	0

v SERBIA-MONTENEGRO

		E	S-M
2003	Leicester	2	1

v SLOVAKIA

		E	S
2002	Bratislava (EC)	2	1
2003	Middlesbrough (EC)	2	1
2009	Wembley	4	0
2016	St Etienne (EC)	0	0
2016	Trnava (WC)	1	0
2017	Wembley (WC)	2	1

v SLOVENIA

		E	S
2009	Wembley	2	1
2010	Port Elizabeth (WC)	1	0
2014	Wembley (EC)	3	1
2015	Ljubljana (EC)	3	2
2016	Ljubljana (WC)	0	0
2017	Wembley (WC)	1	0

v SOUTH AFRICA

		E	SA
1997	Old Trafford	2	1
2003	Durban	2	1

v SOUTH KOREA

		E	SK
2002	Seoguipo	1	1

v SOVIET UNION (see also CIS)

		E	SU
1958	Moscow	1	1
1958	Gothenburg (WC)	2	2
1958	Gothenburg (WC)	0	1
1958	Wembley	5	0
1967	Wembley	2	2
1968	Rome (EC)	2	0
1973	Moscow	2	1
1984	Wembley	0	2
1986	Tbilisi	1	0
1988	Frankfurt (EC)	1	3
1991	Wembley	3	1

v SPAIN

		E	S
1929	Madrid	3	4
1931	Highbury	7	1
1950	Rio de Janeiro (WC)	0	1
1955	Madrid	1	1
1955	Wembley	4	1
1960	Madrid	0	3
1960	Wembley	4	2
1965	Madrid	2	0
1967	Wembley	2	0
1968	Wembley (EC)	1	0
1968	Madrid (EC)	2	1
1980	Barcelona	2	0
1980	Naples (EC)	2	1
1981	Wembley	1	2
1982	Madrid (WC)	0	0
1987	Madrid	4	2
1992	Santander	0	1
1996*	Wembley (EC)	0	0
2001	Villa Park	3	0
2004	Madrid	0	1

2007	Old Trafford	0	1
2009	Seville	0	2
2011	Wembley	1	0
2015	Alicante	0	2
2016	Wembley	2	2
(*England won 4-2 on pens)			
2018	Wembley (NL)	1	2
2018	Seville (NL)	3	2

v SWEDEN

		E	S
1923	Stockholm	4	2
1923	Stockholm	3	1
1937	Stockholm	4	0
1948	Highbury	4	2
1949	Stockholm	1	3
1956	Stockholm	0	0
1959	Wembley	2	3
1965	Gothenburg	2	1
1968	Wembley	3	1
1979	Stockholm	0	0
1986	Stockholm	0	1
1988	Wembley (WC)	0	0
1989	Stockholm (WC)	0	0
1992	Stockholm (EC)	1	2
1995	Leeds	3	3
1998	Stockholm (EC)	1	2
1999	Wembley (EC)	0	0
2001	Old Trafford	1	1
2002	Saitama (WC)	1	1
2004	Gothenburg	0	1
2006	Cologne (WC)	2	2
2011	Wembley	1	0
2012	Kiev (EC)	3	2
2012	Stockholm	2	4
2018	Samara (WC)	2	0

v SWITZERLAND

		E	S
1933	Berne	4	0
1938	Zurich	1	2
1947	Zurich	0	1
1949	Highbury	6	0
1952	Zurich	3	0
1954	Berne (WC)	2	0
1962	Wembley	3	1
1963	Basle	8	1
1971	Basle (EC)	3	2
1971	Wembley (EC)	1	1
1975	Basle	2	1
1977	Wembley	0	0
1980	Wembley (WC)	2	1
1981	Basle (WC)	1	2
1988	Lausanne	1	0
1995	Wembley	3	1
1996	Wembley (EC)	1	1
1998	Berne	1	1
2004	Coimbra (EC)	3	0
2008	Wembley	2	1
2010	Basle (EC)	3	1
2011	Wembley (EC)	2	2
2014	Basle (EC)	2	0
2015	Wembley (EC)	2	0
2018	Leicester	1	0

| 2019* | Guimaraes (NL) | 0 | 0 |
| (* England won 6-5 on pens) | | | |

v TRINIDAD & TOBAGO

		E	T
2006	Nuremberg (WC)	2	0
2008	Port of Spain	3	0

v TUNISIA

		E	T
1990	Tunis	1	1
1998	Marseille (WC)	2	0
2018	Volgograd (WC)	2	1

v TURKEY

		E	T
1984	Istanbul (WC)	8	0
1985	Wembley (WC)	5	0
1987	Izmir (EC)	0	0
1987	Wembley (EC)	8	0
1991	Izmir (EC)	1	0
1991	Wembley (EC)	1	0
1992	Wembley (WC)	4	0
1993	Izmir (WC)	2	0
2003	Sunderland (EC)	2	0
2003	Istanbul (EC)	0	0
2016	Etihad Stadium	2	1

v UKRAINE

		E	U
2000	Wembley	2	0
2004	Newcastle	3	0
2009	Wembley (WC)	2	1
2009	Dnipropetrovski (WC)	0	1
2012	Donetsk (EC)	1	0
2012	Wembley (WC)	1	1
2013	Kiev (WC)	0	0

v URUGUAY

		E	U
1953	Montevideo	1	2
1954	Basle (WC)	2	4
1964	Wembley	2	1
1966	Wembley (WC)	0	0
1969	Montevideo	2	1
1977	Montevideo	0	0
1984	Montevideo	0	2
1990	Wembley	1	2
1995	Wembley	0	0
2006	Anfield	2	1
2014	Sao Paulo (WC)	1	2

v USA

		E	USA
1950	Belo Horizonte (WC)	0	1
1953	New York	6	3
1959	Los Angeles	8	1
1964	New York	10	0
1985	Los Angeles	5	0
1993	Boston	0	2
1994	Wembley	2	0
2005	Chicago	2	1
2008	Wembley	2	0
2010	Rustenburg (WC)	1	1
2018	Wembley	3	0

v YUGOSLAVIA

Year	Venue	E	Y
1939	Belgrade	1	2
1950	Highbury	2	2
1954	Belgrade	0	1
1956	Wembley	3	0
1959	Belgrade	0	5
1960	Wembley	3	3
1965	Belgrade	1	1
1966	Wembley	2	0
1968	Florence (EC)	0	1
1972	Wembley	1	1
1974	Belgrade	2	2
1986	Wembley (EC)	2	0
1987	Belgrade (EC)	4	1
1989	Wembley	2	1
1937	Stockholm	4	0
1948	Highbury	4	2

Year	Venue		
1949	Stockholm	1	3
1956	Stockholm	0	0
1959	Wembley	2	3
1965	Gothenburg	2	1
1968	Wembley	3	1
1979	Stockholm	0	0
1986	Stockholm	0	1
1988	Wembley (WC)	0	0
1989	Stockholm (WC)	0	0
1992	Stockholm (EC)	1	2
1995	Leeds	3	3
1998	Stockholm (EC)	1	2
1999	Wembley (EC)	0	0
2001	Old Trafford	1	1
2002	Saltama (WC)	1	1
2004	Gothenburg	0	1
2006	Cologne (WC)	2	2

ENGLAND'S RECORD England's first international was a 0-0 draw against Scotland in Glasgow, on the West of Scotland cricket ground, Partick, on November 30, 1872 Their complete record at the start of 2019-20 is:

P	W	D	L	F	A
995	565	242	188	2172	978

ENGLAND'S 'B' TEAM RESULTS
England scores first

Year	Opponent			Year	Opponent		
1949	Finland (A)	4	0	1980	USA (H)	1	0
1949	Holland (A)	4	0	1980	Spain (H)	1	0
1950	Italy (A)	0	5	1980	Australia (H)	1	0
1950	Holland (H)	1	0	1981	Spain (A)	2	3
1950	Holland (A)	0	3	1984	N Zealand (H)	2	0
1950	Luxembourg (A)	2	1	1987	Malta (A)	2	0
1950	Switzerland (H)	5	0	1989	Switzerland (A)	2	0
1952	Holland (A)	1	0	1989	Iceland (A)	2	0
1952	France (A)	1	7	1989	Norway (A)	1	0
1953	Scotland (A)	2	2	1989	Italy (H)	1	1
1954	Scotland (H)	1	1	1989	Yugoslavia (H)	2	1
1954	Germany (A)	4	0	1990	Rep of Ireland (A)	1	4
1954	Yugoslavia (A)	1	2	1990	Czechoslovakia (H)	2	0
1954	Switzerland (A)	0	2	1990	Algeria (A)	0	0
1955	Germany (H)	1	1	1991	Wales (A)	1	0
1955	Yugoslavia (H)	5	1	1991	Iceland (H)	1	0
1956	Switzerland (H)	4	1	1991	Switzerland (H)	2	1
1966	Scotland (A)	2	2	1991	Spanish XI (A)	1	0
1957	Scotland (H)	4	1	1992	France (H)	3	0
1978	W Germany (A)	2	1	1992	Czechoslovakia (A)	1	0
1978	Czechoslovakia (A)	1	0	1992	CIS (A)	1	1
1978	Singapore (A)	8	0	1994	N Ireland (H)	4	2
1978	Malaysia (A)	1	1	1995	Rep of Ireland (H)	2	0
1978	N Zealand (A)	4	0	1998	Chile (H)	1	2
1978	N Zealand (A)	3	1	1998	Russia (H)	4	1
1978	N Zealand (A)	4	0	2006	Belarus (H)	1	2
1979	Austria (A)	1	0	2007	Albania	3	1
1979	N Zealand (H)	4	1				

GREAT BRITAIN v REST OF EUROPE (FIFA)

Year	Venue	GB	RofE	Year	Venue	GB	RofE
1947	Glasgow	6	1	1955	Belfast	1	4

SCOTLAND

v ALBANIA

		S	A
2018	Glasgow (NL)	2	0
2018	Shkoder (NL)	4	0

v ARGENTINA

		S	A
1977	Buenos Aires	1	1
1979	Glasgow	1	3
1990	Glasgow	1	0
2008	Glasgow	0	1

v AUSTRALIA

		S	A
1985*	Glasgow (WC)	2	0
1985*	Melbourne (WC)	0	0
1996	Glasgow	1	0
2000	Glasgow	0	2
2012	Edinburgh	3	1
(* World Cup play-off)			

v AUSTRIA

		S	A
1931	Vienna	0	5
1933	Glasgow	2	2
1937	Vienna	1	1
1950	Glasgow	0	1
1951	Vienna	0	4
1954	Zurich (WC)	0	1
1955	Vienna	4	1
1956	Glasgow	1	1
1960	Vienna	1	4
1963*	Glasgow	4	1
1968	Glasgow (WC)	2	1
1969	Vienna (WC)	0	2
1978	Vienna (EC)	2	3
1979	Glasgow (EC)	1	1
1994	Vienna	2	1
1996	Vienna (WC)	0	0
1997	Glasgow (WC)	2	0
(* Abandoned after 79 minutes)			
2003	Glasgow	0	2
2005	Graz	2	2
2007	Vienna	1	0

v BELARUS

		S	B
1997	Minsk (WC)	1	0
1997	Aberdeen (WC)	4	1
2005	Minsk (WC)	0	0
2005	Glasgow (WC)	0	1

v BELGIUM

		S	B
1947	Brussels	1	2
1948	Glasgow	2	0
1951	Brussels	5	0
1971	Liege (EC)	0	3
1971	Aberdeen (EC)	1	0
1974	Brugge	1	2
1979	Brussels (EC)	0	2
1979	Glasgow (EC)	1	3
1982	Brussels (EC)	2	3
1983	Glasgow (EC)	1	1
1987	Brussels (EC)	1	4
1987	Glasgow (EC)	2	0
2001	Glasgow (WC)	2	2
2001	Brussels (WC)	0	2
2012	Brussels (WC)	0	2
2013	Glasgow (WC)	0	2
2018	Glasgow	0	4
2019	Brussels (EC)	0	3

v BOSNIA

		S	B
1999	Sarajevo (EC)	2	1
1999	Glasgow (EC)	1	0

v BRAZIL

		S	B
1966	Glasgow	1	1
1972	Rio de Janeiro	0	1
1973	Glasgow	0	1
1974	Frankfurt (WC)	0	0
1977	Rio de Janeiro	0	2
1982	Seville (WC)	1	4
1987	Glasgow	0	2
1990	Turin (WC)	0	1
1998	St Denis (WC)	1	2
2011	Arsenal	0	2

v BULGARIA

		S	B
1978	Glasgow	2	1
1986	Glasgow (EC)	0	0
1987	Sofia (EC)	1	0
1990	Sofia (EC)	1	1
1991	Glasgow (EC)	1	1
2006	Kobe	5	1

v CANADA

		S	C
1983	Vancouver	2	0
1983	Edmonton	3	0
1983	Toronto	2	0
1992	Toronto	3	1
2002	Edinburgh	3	1
2017	Edinburgh	1	1

v CHILE

		S	C
1977	Santiago	4	2
1989	Glasgow	2	0

v CIS (formerly Soviet Union)

		S	C
1992	Norrkoping (EC)	3	0

v COLOMBIA

		S	C
1988	Glasgow	0	0
1996	Miami	0	1
1998	New York	2	2

v COSTA RICA

		S	C
1990	Genoa (WC)	0	1
2018	Glasgow	0	1

v CROATIA

		S	C
2000	Zagreb (WC)	1	1
2001	Glasgow (WC)	0	0
2008	Glasgow	1	1
2013	Zagreb (WC)	1	0
2013	Glasgow (WC)	2	0

v CYPRUS

		S	C
1968	Nicosia (WC)	5	0
1969	Glasgow (WC)	8	0
1989	Limassol (WC)	3	2
1989	Glasgow (WC)	2	1
2011	Larnaca	2	1
2019	Glasgow (EC)	2	1

v CZECH REPUBLIC

		S	C
1999	Glasgow (EC)	1	2
1999	Prague (EC)	2	3
2008	Prague	1	3
2010	Glasgow	1	0
2010	Prague (EC)	0	1
2011	Glasgow (EC)	2	2
2016	Prague	1	0

v CZECHOSLOVAKIA

		S	C
1937	Prague	3	1
1937	Glasgow	5	0
1961	Bratislava (WC)	0	4
1961	Glasgow (WC)	3	2
1961*	Brussels (WC)	2	4
1972	Porto Alegre	0	0
1973	Glasgow (WC)	2	1
1973	Bratislava (WC)	0	1
1976	Prague (WC)	0	2
1977	Glasgow (WC)	3	1
(*World Cup play-off)			

v DENMARK

		S	D
1951	Glasgow	3	1
1952	Copenhagen	2	1
1968	Copenhagen	1	0
1970	Glasgow (EC)	1	0
1971	Copenhagen (EC)	0	1
1972	Copenhagen (WC)	4	1
1972	Glasgow (WC)	2	0
1975	Copenhagen (EC)	1	0
1975	Glasgow (EC)	3	1
1986	Neza (WC)	0	1
1996	Copenhagen	0	2
1998	Glasgow	0	1
2002	Glasgow	0	1
2004	Copenhagen	0	1
2011	Glasgow	2	1
2016	Glasgow	1	0

v EAST GERMANY

		S	EG
1974	Glasgow	3	0
1977	East Berlin	0	1
1982	Glasgow (EC)	2	0
1983	Halle (EC)	1	2

| 1986 | Glasgow | 0 | 0 |
| 1990 | Glasgow | 0 | 1 |

v ECUADOR

		S	E
1995	Toyama, Japan	2	1

v EGYPT

		S	E
1990	Aberdeen	1	3

v ESTONIA

		S	E
1993	Tallinn (WC)	3	0
1993	Aberdeen	3	1
1996	Tallinn (WC)	*No result
1997	Monaco (WC)	0	0
1997	Kilmarnock (WC)	2	0
1998	Edinburgh (EC)	3	2
1999	Tallinn (EC)	0	0
(* Estonia absent)			
2004	Tallinn	1	0
2013	Aberdeen	1	0

v FAROE ISLANDS

		S	F
1994	Glasgow (EC)	5	1
1995	Toftir (EC)	2	0
1998	Aberdeen (EC)	2	1
1999	Toftir (EC)	1	1
2002	Toftir (EC)	2	2
2003	Glasgow (EC)	3	1
2006	Glasgow (EC)	6	0
2007	Toftir (EC)	2	0
2010	Aberdeen	3	0

v FINLAND

		S	F
1954	Helsinki	2	1
1964	Glasgow (WC)	3	1
1965	Helsinki (WC)	2	1
1976	Glasgow	6	0
1992	Glasgow	1	1
1994	Helsinki (EC)	2	0
1995	Glasgow (EC)	1	0
1998	Edinburgh	1	1

v FRANCE

		S	F
1930	Paris	2	0
1932	Paris	3	1
1948	Paris	0	3
1949	Glasgow	2	0
1950	Paris	1	0
1951	Glasgow	1	0
1958	Orebro (WC)	1	2
1984	Marseilles	0	2
1989	Glasgow (WC)	2	0
1990	Paris (WC)	0	3
1997	St Etienne	1	2
2000	Glasgow	0	2
2002	Paris	0	5
2006	Glasgow (EC)	1	0
2007	Paris (EC)	1	0
2016	Metz	0	3

v GEORGIA

		S	G
2007	Glasgow (EC)	2	1
2007	Tbilisi (EC)	0	2
2014	Glasgow (EC)	1	0
2015	Tbilisi (EC)	0	1

v GERMANY/WEST GERMANY

		S	G
1929	Berlin	1	1
1936	Glasgow	2	0
1957	Stuttgart	3	1
1959	Glasgow	3	2
1964	Hanover	2	2
1969	Glasgow (WC)	1	1
1969	Hamburg (WC)	2	3
1973	Glasgow	1	1
1974	Frankfurt	1	2
1986	Queretaro (WC)	1	2
1992	Norrkoping (EC)	0	2
1993	Glasgow	0	1
1999	Bremen	1	0
2003	Glasgow (EC)	1	1
2003	Dortmund (EC)	1	2
2014	Dortmund (EC)	1	2
2015	Glasgow (EC)	2	3

v GIBRALTAR

		S	G
2015	Glasgow (EC)	6	1
2015	Faro (EC)	6	0

v GREECE

		S	G
1994	Athens (EC)	0	1
1995	Glasgow	1	0

v HOLLAND

		S	H
1929	Amsterdam	2	0
1938	Amsterdam	3	1
1959	Amsterdam	2	1
1966	Glasgow	0	3
1968	Amsterdam	0	0
1971	Amsterdam	1	2
1978	Mendoza (WC)	3	2
1982	Glasgow	2	1
1986	Eindhoven	0	0
1992	Gothenburg (EC)	0	1
1994	Glasgow	0	1
1994	Utrecht	1	3
1996	Birmingham (EC)	0	0
2000	Arnhem	0	0
2003*	Glasgow (EC)	1	0
2003*	Amsterdam (EC)	0	6
2009	Amsterdam (WC)	0	3
2009	Glasgow (WC)	0	1
2017	Aberdeen	0	1

(*Qual Round play-off)

v HUNGARY

		S	H
1938	Glasgow	3	1
1955	Glasgow	2	4
1955	Budapest	1	3
1958	Glasgow	1	1
1960	Budapest	3	3
1980	Budapest	1	3
1987	Glasgow	2	0
2004	Glasgow	0	3
2018	Budapest	1	0

v ICELAND

		S	I
1984	Glasgow (WC)	3	0
1985	Reykjavik (WC)	1	0
2002	Reykjavik (EC)	2	0
2003	Glasgow (EC)	2	1
2008	Reykjavik (WC)	2	1
2009	Glasgow (WC)	2	1

v IRAN

		S	I
1978	Cordoba (WC)	1	1

v ISRAEL

		S	I
1981	Tel Aviv (WC)	1	0
1981	Glasgow (WC)	3	1
1986	Tel Aviv	1	0
2018	Haifa (NL)	1	2
2018	Glasgow (NL)	3	2

v ITALY

		S	I
1931	Rome	0	3
1965	Glasgow	1	0
1965	Naples (WC)	0	3
1988	Perugia	0	2
1992	Glasgow (WC)	0	0
1993	Rome (WC)	1	3
2005	Milan (WC)	0	2
2005	Glasgow (WC)	1	1
2007	Bari (EC)	0	2
2007	Glasgow (EC)	1	2
2016	Ta'Qali	0	1

v JAPAN

		S	J
1995	Hiroshima	0	0
2006	Saitama	0	0
2009	Yokohama	0	2

v KAZAKHSTAN

		S	K
2019	Astana (EC)	0	3

v LATVIA

		S	L
1996	Riga (WC)	2	0
1997	Glasgow (WC)	2	0
2000	Riga (WC)	1	0
2001	Glasgow (WC)	2	1

v LIECHTENSTEIN

		S	L
2010	Glasgow (EC)	2	1
2011	Vaduz (EC)	1	0

v LITHUANIA

		S	L
1998	Vilnius (EC)	0	0
1999	Glasgow (EC)	3	0
2003	Kaunus (EC)	0	1
2003	Glasgow (EC)	1	0

2006	Kaunas (EC)	2	1
2007	Glasgow (EC)	3	1
2010	Kaunas (EC)	0	0
2011	Glasgow (EC)	1	0
2016	Glasgow (WC)	1	1
2017	Vilnius (WC)	3	0

v LUXEMBOURG

		S	L
1947	Luxembourg	6	0
1986	Glasgow (EC)	3	0
1987	Esch (EC)	0	0
2012	Josy Barthel	2	1

v MACEDONIA

		S	M
2008	Skopje (WC)	0	1
2009	Glasgow (WC)	2	0
2012	Glasgow (WC)	1	1
2013	Skopje (WC)	2	1

v MALTA

		S	M
1988	Valletta	1	1
1990	Valletta	2	1
1993	Glasgow (WC)	3	0
1993	Valletta (WC)	2	0
1997	Valletta	3	2
2016	Ta'Qali (WC)	5	1
2017	Glasgow (WC)	2	0

v MEXICO

		S	M
2018	Mexico City	0	1

v MOLDOVA

		S	M
2004	Chisinau (WC)	1	1
2005	Glasgow (WC)	2	0

v MOROCCO

		S	M
1998	St Etienne (WC)	0	3

v NEW ZEALAND

		S	NZ
1982	Malaga (WC)	5	2
2003	Edinburgh	1	1

v NIGERIA

		S	N
2002	Aberdeen	1	2
2014	Fulham	2	2

v NORWAY

		S	N
1929	Bergen	7	3
1954	Glasgow	1	0
1954	Oslo	1	1
1963	Bergen	3	4
1963	Glasgow	6	1
1974	Oslo	2	1
1978	Glasgow (EC)	3	2
1979	Oslo (EC)	4	0
1988	Oslo (WC)	2	1
1989	Glasgow (WC)	1	1
1992	Oslo	0	0
1998	Bordeaux (WC)	1	1
2003	Oslo	0	0
2004	Glasgow (WC)	0	1
2005	Oslo (WC)	2	1
2008	Glasgow (WC)	0	0
2009	Oslo (WC)	0	4
2013	Molde	1	0

v PARAGUAY

		S	P
1958	Norrkoping (WC)	2	3

v PERU

		S	P
1972	Glasgow	2	0
1978	Cordoba (WC)	1	3
1979	Glasgow	1	1
2018	Lima	0	2

v POLAND

		S	P
1958	Warsaw	2	1
1960	Glasgow	2	3
1965	Chorzow (WC)	1	1
1965	Glasgow (WC)	1	2
1980	Poznan	0	1
1990	Glasgow	1	1
2001	Bydgoszcz	1	1
2014	Warsaw	1	0
2014	Warsaw (EC)	2	2
2015	Glasgow (EC)	2	2

v PORTUGAL

		S	P
1950	Lisbon	2	2
1955	Glasgow	3	0
1959	Lisbon	0	1
1966	Glasgow	0	1
1971	Lisbon (EC)	0	2
1971	Glasgow (EC)	2	1
1975	Glasgow	1	0
1978	Lisbon (EC)	0	1
1980	Glasgow (EC)	4	1
1980	Glasgow (WC)	0	0
1981	Lisbon (WC)	1	2
1992	Glasgow (WC)	0	0
1993	Lisbon (WC)	0	5
2002	Braga	0	2
2018	Glasgow	1	3

v QATAR

		S	Q
2015	Edinburgh	1	0

v REPUBLIC OF IRELAND

		S	RoI
1961	Glasgow (WC)	4	1
1961	Dublin (WC)	3	0
1963	Dublin	0	1
1969	Dublin	1	1
1986	Dublin (EC)	0	0
1987	Glasgow (EC)	0	1
2000	Dublin	2	1
2003	Glasgow (EC)	0	2
2011	Dublin (CC)	0	1
2014	Glasgow (EC)	1	0
2015	Dublin (EC)	1	1

v ROMANIA

		S	R
1975	Bucharest (EC)	1	1
1975	Glasgow (EC)	1	1
1986	Glasgow	3	0
1990	Glasgow (EC)	2	1
1991	Bucharest (EC)	0	1
2004	Glasgow	1	2

v RUSSIA

		S	R
1994	Glasgow (EC)	1	1
1995	Moscow (EC)	0	0

v SAN MARINO

		S	SM
1991	Serravalle (EC)	2	0
1991	Glasgow (EC)	4	0
1995	Serravalle (EC)	2	0
1995	Glasgow (EC)	5	0
2000	Serravalle (WC)	2	0
2001	Glasgow (WC)	4	0
2019	Serravalle (EC)	2	0

v SAUDI ARABIA

		S	SA
1988	Riyadh	2	2

v SERBIA

		S	Se
2012	Glasgow (WC)	0	0
2013	Novi Sad (WC)	0	2

v SLOVAKIA

		S	Sl
2016	Trnava (WC)	0	3
2017	Glasgow (WC)	1	0

v SLOVENIA

		S	SL
2004	Glasgow (WC)	0	0
2005	Celje (WC)	3	0
2012	Koper	1	1
2017	Glasgow (WC)	1	0
2017	Ljubljana (WC)	2	2

v SOUTH AFRICA

		S	SA
2002	Hong Kong	0	2
2007	Aberdeen	1	0

v SOUTH KOREA

		S	SK
2002	Busan	1	4

v SOVIET UNION (see also CIS and RUSSIA)

		S	SU
1967	Glasgow	0	2
1971	Moscow	0	1
1982	Malaga (WC)	2	2
1991	Glasgow	0	1

v SPAIN

		S	Sp
1957	Glasgow (WC)	4	2
1957	Madrid (WC)	1	4
1963	Madrid	6	2
1965	Glasgow	0	0
1975	Glasgow (EC)	1	2
1975	Valencia (EC)	1	1
1982	Valencia	0	3
1985	Glasgow (WC)	3	1
1985	Seville (WC)	0	1
1988	Madrid	0	0
2004*	Valencia	1	1
(*Abandoned after 59 mins – floodlight failure)			
2010	Glasgow (EC)	2	3
2011	Alicante (EC)	1	3

v SWEDEN

		S	Swe
1952	Stockholm	1	3
1953	Glasgow	1	2
1975	Gothenburg	1	1
1977	Glasgow	3	1
1980	Stockholm (WC)	1	0
1981	Glasgow (WC)	2	0
1990	Genoa (WC)	2	1
1995	Solna	0	2
1996	Glasgow (WC)	1	0
1997	Gothenburg (WC)	1	2
2004	Edinburgh	1	4
2010	Stockholm	0	3

v SWITZERLAND

		S	Sw
1931	Geneva	3	2
1948	Berne	1	2
1950	Glasgow	3	1
1957	Basle (WC)	2	1
1957	Glasgow (WC)	3	2
1973	Berne	0	1
1976	Glasgow	1	0
1982	Berne (EC)	0	2
1983	Glasgow (EC)	2	2
1990	Glasgow (EC)	2	1
1991	Berne (EC)	2	2
1992	Berne (WC)	1	3
1993	Aberdeen (WC)	1	1
1996	Birmingham (EC)	1	0
2006	Glasgow	1	3

v TRINIDAD & TOBAGO

		S	T
2004	Hibernian	4	1

v TURKEY

		S	T
1960	Ankara	2	4

v UKRAINE

		S	U
2006	Kiev (EC)	0	2
2007	Glasgow (EC)	3	1

v USA

		S	USA
1952	Glasgow	6	0
1992	Denver	1	0
1996	New Britain, Conn	1	2
1998	Washington	0	0
2005	Glasgow	1	1
2012	Jacksonville	1	5
2013	Glasgow	0	0

v URUGUAY

		S	U
1954	Basle (WC)	0	7
1962	Glasgow	2	3
1983	Glasgow	2	0
1986	Neza (WC)	0	0

v YUGOSLAVIA

		S	Y
1955	Belgrade	2	2
1956	Glasgow	2	0

		S	Z
1958	Vaasteras (WC)	1	1
1972	Belo Horizonte	2	2
1974	Frankfurt (WC)	1	1
1984	Glasgow	6	1
1988	Glasgow (WC)	1	1
1989	Zagreb (WC)	1	0

v ZAIRE

		S	Z
1974	Dortmund (WC)	2	0

WALES

v ALBANIA

		W	A
1994	Cardiff (EC)	2	0
1995	Tirana (EC)	1	1
2018	Elbasan	0	1

v ANDORRA

		W	A
2014	La Vella (EC)	2	1
2015	Cardiff (EC)	2	0

v ARGENTINA

		W	A
1992	Gifu (Japan)	0	1
2002	Cardiff	1	1

v ARMENIA

		W	A
2001	Yerevan (WC)	2	2
2001	Cardiff (WC)	0	0

v AUSTRALIA

		W	A
2011	Cardiff	1	2

v AUSTRIA

		W	A
1954	Vienna	0	2
1955	Wrexham	1	2
1975	Vienna (EC)	1	2
1975	Wrexham (EC)	1	0
1992	Vienna	1	1
2005	Cardiff	0	2
2008	Vienna	0	1
2013	Swansea	2	1
2016	Vienna (WC)	2	2
2017	Cardiff (WC)	1	0

v AZERBAIJAN

		W	A
2002	Baku (EC)	2	0
2003	Cardiff (EC)	4	0
2004	Baku (WC)	1	1
2005	Cardiff (WC)	2	0
2008	Cardiff (WC)	1	0
2009	Baku (WC)	1	0

v BELARUS

		W	B
1998	Cardiff (EC)	3	2
1999	Minsk (EC)	2	1
2000	Minsk (WC)	1	2
2001	Cardiff (WC)	1	0

v BELGIUM

		W	B
1949	Liege	1	3
1949	Cardiff	5	1
1990	Cardiff (EC)	3	1
1991	Brussels (EC)	1	1
1992	Brussels (WC)	0	2
1993	Cardiff (WC)	2	0
1997	Cardiff (WC)	1	2
1997	Brussels (WC)	2	3
2012	Cardiff (WC)	0	2
2013	Brussels (WC)	1	1
2014	Brussels (EC)	0	0
2015	Cardiff (EC)	1	0
2016	Lille (EC)	3	1

v BOSNIA-HERZEGOVINA

		W	B-H
2003	Cardiff	2	2
2012	Llanelli	0	2
2014	Cardiff (EC)	0	0
2015	Zenica (EC)	0	2

v BRAZIL

		W	B
1958	Gothenburg (WC)	0	1
1962	Rio de Janeiro	1	3
1962	Sao Paulo	1	3
1966	Rio de Janeiro	1	3
1966	Belo Horizonte	0	1
1983	Cardiff	1	1
1991	Cardiff	1	0
1997	Brasilia	0	3
2000	Cardiff	0	3
2006	White Hart Lane	0	2

v BULGARIA

		W	B
1983	Wrexham (EC)	1	0
1983	Sofia (EC)	0	1
1994	Cardiff (EC)	0	3
1995	Sofia (EC)	1	3
2006	Swansea	0	0
2007	Bourgas	1	0
2010	Cardiff (EC)	0	1
2011	Sofia (EC)	1	0

v CANADA

		W	C
1986	Toronto	0	2
1986	Vancouver	3	0
2004	Wrexham	1	0

v CHILE

		W	C
1966	Santiago	0	2

v CHINA

		W	C
2018	Nanning	6	0

v COSTA RICA

		W	C
1990	Cardiff	1	0
2012	Cardiff	0	1

v CROATIA

		W	C
2002	Varazdin	1	1
2010	Osijek	0	2
2012	Osijek (WC)	0	2
2013	Swansea (WC)	1	2
2019	Osijek (EC)	1	2

v CYPRUS

		W	C
1992	Limassol (WC)	1	0
1993	Cardiff (WC)	2	0
2005	Limassol	0	1
2006	Cardiff (EC)	3	1
2007	Nicosia (EC)	1	3
2014	Cardiff (EC)	2	1
2015	Nicosia	1	0

v CZECHOSLOVAKIA (see also RCS)

		W	C
1957	Cardiff (WC)	1	0
1957	Prague (WC)	0	2
1971	Swansea (EC)	1	3
1971	Prague (EC)	0	1
1977	Wrexham (WC)	3	0
1977	Prague (WC)	0	1
1980	Cardiff (WC)	1	0
1981	Prague (WC)	0	2
1987	Wrexham (EC)	1	1
1987	Prague (EC)	0	2

v CZECH REPUBLIC

		W	CR
2002	Cardiff	0	0
2006	Teplice (EC)	1	2
2007	Cardiff (EC)	0	0

v DENMARK

		W	D
1964	Copenhagen (WC)	0	1
1965	Wrexham (WC)	4	2
1987	Cardiff (EC)	1	0
1987	Copenhagen (EC)	0	1
1990	Copenhagen	0	1
1998	Copenhagen (EC)	2	1
1999	Anfield (EC)	0	2
2008	Copenhagen	1	0
2018	Aarhus (NL)	0	2
2018	Cardiff (NL)	1	2

v EAST GERMANY

		W	EG
1957	Leipzig (WC)	1	2
1957	Cardiff (WC)	4	1
1969	Dresden (WC)	1	2
1969	Cardiff (WC)	1	3

v ESTONIA

		W	E
1994	Tallinn	2	1
2009	Llanelli	1	0

v FAROE ISLANDS

		W	FI
1992	Cardiff (WC)	6	0
1993	Toftir (WC)	3	0

v FINLAND

		W	F
1971	Helsinki (EC)	1	0
1971	Swansea (EC)	3	0
1986	Helsinki (EC)	1	1
1987	Wrexham (EC)	4	0
1988	Swansea (WC)	2	2
1989	Helsinki (WC)	0	1
2000	Cardiff	1	2
2002	Helsinki (WC)	2	0
2003	Cardiff (EC)	1	1
2009	Cardiff (WC)	0	2
2009	Helsinki (WC)	1	2
2013	Cardiff	1	1

v FRANCE

		W	F
1933	Paris	1	1
1939	Paris	1	2
1953	Paris	1	6
1982	Toulouse	1	0
2017	Paris	0	2

v GEORGIA

		W	G
1994	Tbilisi (EC)	0	5
1995	Cardiff (EC)	0	1
2008	Swansea	1	2
2016	Cardiff (WC)	1	1
2017	Tbilisi (WC)	1	0

v GERMANY/WEST GERMANY

		W	G
1968	Cardiff	1	1
1969	Frankfurt	1	1
1977	Cardiff	0	2
1977	Dortmund	1	1
1979	Wrexham (EC)	0	2
1979	Cologne (EC)	1	5
1989	Cardiff (WC)	0	0
1989	Cologne (WC)	1	2
1991	Cardiff (EC)	1	0
1991	Nuremberg (EC)	1	4
1995	Dusseldorf (EC)	1	1
1995	Cardiff (EC)	1	2
2002	Cardiff	1	0
2007	Cardiff (EC)	0	2
2007	Frankfurt (EC)	0	0
2008	Moenchengladbach (WC)	0	1
2009	Cardiff (WC)	0	2

v GREECE

		W	G
1964	Athens (WC)	0	2
1965	Cardiff (WC)	4	1

v HOLLAND

		W	H
1988	Amsterdam (WC)	0	1
1989	Wrexham (WC)	1	2
1992	Utrecht	0	4
1996	Cardiff (WC)	1	3
1996	Eindhoven (WC)	1	7
2008	Rotterdam	0	2
2014	Amsterdam	0	2
2015	Cardiff	2	3

v HUNGARY

		W	H
1958	Sanviken (WC)	1	1
1958	Stockholm (WC)	2	1
1961	Budapest	2	3
1963	Budapest (EC)	1	3
1963	Cardiff (EC)	1	1
1974	Cardiff (EC)	2	0
1975	Budapest (EC)	2	1
1986	Cardiff	0	3
2004	Budapest	2	1
2005	Cardiff	2	0
2019	Budapest (EC)	0	1

v ICELAND

		W	I
1980	Reykjavik (WC)	4	0
1981	Swansea (WC)	2	2
1984	Reykjavik (WC)	0	1
1984	Cardiff (WC)	2	1
1991	Cardiff	1	0
2008	Reykjavik	1	0
2014	Cardiff	3	1

v IRAN

		W	I
1978	Tehran	1	0

v ISRAEL

		W	I
1958	Tel Aviv (WC)	2	0
1958	Cardiff (WC)	2	0
1984	Tel Aviv	0	0
1989	Tel Aviv	3	3
2015	Haifa (EC)	3	0
2015	Cardiff (EC)	0	0

v ITALY

		W	I
1965	Florence	1	4
1968	Cardiff (WC)	0	1
1969	Rome (WC)	1	4
1988	Brescia	1	0
1996	Terni	0	3
1998	Anfield (EC)	0	2
1999	Bologna (EC)	0	4
2002	Cardiff (EC)	2	1
2003	Milan (EC)	0	4

v JAMAICA

		W	J
1998	Cardiff	0	0

v JAPAN

		W	J
1992	Matsuyama	1	0

v KUWAIT

		W	K
1977	Wrexham	0	0
1977	Kuwait City	0	0

v LATVIA

		W	L
2004	Riga	2	0

v LIECHTENSTEIN

		W	L
2006	Wrexham	4	0
2008	Cardiff (WC)	2	0
2009	Vaduz (WC)	2	0

v LUXEMBOURG

		W	L
1974	Swansea (EC)	5	0
1975	Luxembourg (EC)	3	1
1990	Luxembourg (EC)	1	0
1991	Luxembourg (EC)	1	0
2008	Luxembourg	2	0
2010	Llanelli	5	1

v MACEDONIA

		W	M
2013	Skopje (WC)	1	2
2013	Cardiff (WC)	1	0

v MALTA

		W	M
1978	Wrexham (EC)	7	0
1979	Valletta (EC)	2	0
1988	Valletta	3	2
1998	Valletta	3	0

v MEXICO

		W	M
1958	Stockholm (WC)	1	1
1962	Mexico City	1	2
2012	New York	0	2
2018	Pasadena	0	0

v MOLDOVA

		W	M
1994	Kishinev (EC)	2	3
1995	Cardiff (EC)	1	0
2016	Cardiff (WC)	4	0
2017	Chisinau (WC)	2	0

v MONTENEGRO

		W	M
2009	Podgorica	1	2
2010	Podgorica (EC)	0	1
2011	Cardiff (EC)	2	1

v NEW ZEALAND

		W	NZ
2007	Wrexham	2	2

v NORWAY

		W	N
1982	Swansea (EC)	1	0
1983	Oslo (EC)	0	0
1984	Trondheim	0	1
1985	Wrexham	1	1
1985	Bergen	2	4
1994	Cardiff	1	3
2000	Cardiff (WC)	1	1

2001	Oslo (WC)	2	3
2004	Oslo	0	0
2008	Wrexham	3	0
2011	Cardiff	4	1

v PANAMA

		W	P
2017	Cardiff	1	1

v PARAGUAY

		W	P
2006	Cardiff	0	0

v POLAND

		W	P
1973	Cardiff (WC)	2	0
1973	Katowice (WC)	0	3
1991	Radom	0	0
2000	Warsaw (WC)	0	0
2001	Cardiff (WC)	1	2
2004	Cardiff (WC)	2	3
2005	Warsaw (WC)	0	1
2009	Vila-Real (Por)	0	1

v PORTUGAL

		W	P
1949	Lisbon	2	3
1951	Cardiff	2	1
2000	Chaves	0	3
2016	Lyon (EC)	0	2

v QATAR

		W	Q
2000	Doha	1	0

v RCS (formerly Czechoslovakia)

		W	RCS
1993	Ostrava (WC)	1	1
1993	Cardiff (WC)	2	2

v REPUBLIC OF IRELAND

		W	RI
1960	Dublin	3	2
1979	Swansea	2	1
1981	Dublin	3	1
1986	Dublin	1	0
1990	Dublin	0	1
1991	Wrexham	0	3
1992	Dublin	1	0
1993	Dublin	1	2
1997	Cardiff	0	0
2007	Dublin (EC)	0	1
2007	Cardiff (EC)	2	2
2011	Dublin (CC)	0	3
2013	Cardiff	0	0
2017	Dublin (WC)	0	0
2017	Cardiff (WC)	0	1
2018	Cardiff (NL)	4	1
2018	Dublin (NL)	1	0

v REST OF UNITED KINGDOM

		W	UK
1951	Cardiff	3	2
1969	Cardiff	0	1

v ROMANIA

		W	R
1970	Cardiff (EC)	0	0
1971	Bucharest (EC)	0	2

1983	Wrexham	5	0
1992	Bucharest (WC)	1	5
1993	Cardiff (WC)	1	2

v RUSSIA (See also Soviet Union)

		W	R
2003*	Moscow (EC)	0	0
2003*	Cardiff (EC)	0	1
2008	Moscow (WC)	1	2
2009	Cardiff (WC)	1	3
2016	Toulouse (EC)	3	0
(*Qual Round play-offs)			

v SAN MARINO

		W	SM
1996	Serravalle (WC)	5	0
1996	Cardiff (WC)	6	0
2007	Cardiff (EC)	3	0
2007	Serravalle (EC)	2	1

v SAUDI ARABIA

		W	SA
1986	Dahran	2	1

v SERBIA

		W	S
2012	Novi Sad (WC)	1	6
2013	Cardiff (WC)	0	3
2016	Cardiff (WC)	1	1
2017	Belgrade (WC)	1	1

v SERBIA & MONTENEGRO

		W	S
2003	Belgrade (EC)	0	1
2003	Cardiff (EC)	2	3

v SLOVAKIA

		W	S
2006	Cardiff (EC)	1	5
2007	Trnava (EC)	5	2
2016	Bordeaux (EC)	2	1
2019	Cardiff (EC)	1	0

v SLOVENIA

		W	S
2005	Swansea	0	0

v SOVIET UNION (See also Russia)

		W	SU
1965	Moscow (WC)	1	2
1965	Cardiff (WC)	2	1
1981	Wrexham (WC)	0	0
1981	Tbilisi (WC)	0	3
1987	Swansea	0	0

v SPAIN

		W	S
1961	Cardiff (WC)	1	2
1961	Madrid (WC)	1	1
1982	Valencia	1	1
1984	Seville (WC)	0	3
1985	Wrexham (WC)	3	0
2018	Cardiff	1	4

v SWEDEN

		W	S
1958	Stockholm (WC)	0	0
1988	Stockholm	1	4
1989	Wrexham	0	2
1990	Stockholm	2	4

1994	Wrexham	0	2
2010	Swansea	0	1
2016	Stockholm	0	3

v SWITZERLAND

		W	S
1949	Berne	0	4
1951	Wrexham	3	2
1996	Lugano	0	2
1999	Zurich (EC)	0	2
1999	Wrexham (EC)	0	2
2010	Basle (EC)	1	4
2011	Swansea (EC)	2	0

v TRINIDAD & TOBAGO

		W	T
2006	Graz	2	1
2019	Wrexham	1	0

v TUNISIA

		W	T
1998	Tunis	0	4

v TURKEY

		W	T
1978	Wrexham (EC)	1	0
1979	Izmir (EC)	0	1
1980	Cardiff (WC)	4	0

1981	Ankara (WC)	1	0
1996	Cardiff (WC)	0	0
1997	Istanbul (WC)	4	6

v UKRAINE

		W	U
2001	Cardiff (WC)	1	1
2001	Kiev (WC)	1	1
2015	Kiev	0	1

v URUGUAY

		W	U
1986	Wrexham	0	0
2018	Nanning	0	1

v USA

		W	USA
2003	San Jose	0	2

v YUGOSLAVIA

		W	Y
1953	Belgrade	2	5
1954	Cardiff	1	3
1976	Zagreb (EC)	0	2
1976	Cardiff (EC)	1	1
1982	Titograd (EC)	4	4
1983	Cardiff (EC)	1	1
1988	Swansea	1	2

NORTHERN IRELAND

v ALBANIA

		NI	A
1965	Belfast (WC)	4	1
1965	Tirana (WC)	1	1
1983	Tirana (EC)	0	0
1983	Belfast (EC)	1	0
1992	Belfast (WC)	3	0
1993	Tirana (WC)	2	1
1996	Belfast (WC)	2	0
1997	Zurich (WC)	0	1
2010	Tirana	0	1

v ALGERIA

		NI	A
1986	Guadalajara (WC)	1	1

v ARGENTINA

		NI	A
1958	Halmstad (WC)	1	3

v ARMENIA

		NI	A
1996	Belfast (WC)	1	1
1997	Yerevan (WC)	0	0
2003	Yerevan (EC)	0	1
2003	Belfast (EC)	0	1

v AUSTRALIA

		NI	A
1980	Sydney	2	1
1980	Melbourne	1	1
1980	Adelaide	2	1

v AUSTRIA

		NI	A
1982	Madrid (WC)	2	2
1982	Vienna (EC)	0	2

1983	Belfast (EC)	3	1
1990	Vienna (EC)	0	0
1991	Belfast (EC)	2	1
1994	Vienna (EC)	2	1
1995	Belfast (EC)	5	3
2004	Belfast (WO)	3	3
2005	Vienna (WC)	0	2
2018	Vienna (NL)	0	1
2018	Belfast(NL)	1	2

v AZERBAIJAN

		NI	A
2004	Baku (WC)	0	0
2005	Belfast (WC)	2	0
2012	Belfast (WC)	1	1
2013	Baku (WC)	0	2
2016	Belfast (WC)	4	0
2017	Baku (WC)	1	0

v BARBADOS

		NI	B
2004	Bridgetown	1	1

v BELARUS

		NI	B
2016	Belfast	3	0
2019	Belfast (EC)	2	1
2019	Borisov (EC)	1	0

v BELGIUM

		NI	B
1976	Liege (WC)	0	2
1977	Belfast (WC)	3	0
1997	Belfast	3	0

v BOSNIA-HERZEGOVINA

		NI	B-H
2018	Belfast (NL)	1	2
2018	Sarajevo (NL)	0	2

v BRAZIL

		NI	B
1986	Guadalajara (WC)	0	3

v BULGARIA

		NI	B
1972	Sofia (WC)	0	3
1973	Sheffield (WC)	0	0
1978	Sofia (EC)	2	0
1979	Belfast (EC)	2	0
2001	Sofia (WC)	3	4
2001	Belfast (WC)	0	1
2008	Belfast	0	1

v CANADA

		NI	C
1995	Edmonton	0	2
1999	Belfast	1	1
2005	Belfast	0	1

v CHILE

		NI	C
1989	Belfast	0	1
1995	Edmonton, Canada	0	2
2010	Chillan	0	1
2014	Valparaiso	0	2

v COLOMBIA

		NI	C
1994	Boston, USA	0	2

v COSTA RICA

		NI	CR
2018	San Jose	0	3

v CROATIA

		NI	C
2016	Belfast	0	3

v CYPRUS

		NI	C
1971	Nicosia (EC)	3	0
1971	Belfast (EC)	5	0
1973	Nicosia (WC)	0	1
1973	Fulham (WC)	3	0
2002	Belfast	0	0
2014	Nicosia	0	0

v CZECHOSLOVAKIA/CZECH REP

		NI	C
1958	Halmstad (WC)	1	0
1958	Malmo (WC)	2	1
2001	Belfast (WC)	0	1
2001	Teplice (WC)	1	3
2008	Belfast (WC)	0	0
2009	Prague (WC)	0	0
2016	Prague (WC)	0	0
2017	Belfast (WC)	2	0

v DENMARK

		NI	D
1978	Belfast (EC)	2	1
1979	Copenhagen (EC)	0	4
1986	Belfast	1	1
1990	Belfast (EC)	1	1
1991	Odense (EC)	1	2
1992	Belfast (WC)	0	1
1993	Copenhagen (WC)	0	1
2000	Belfast (WC)	1	1
2001	Copenhagen (WC)	1	1
2006	Copenhagen (EC)	0	0
2007	Belfast (EC)	2	1

v ESTONIA

		NI	E
2004	Tallinn	1	0
2006	Belfast	1	0
2011	Tallinn (EC)	1	4
2011	Belfast (EC)	1	2
2019	Belfast (EC)	2	0
2019	Tallinn (EC)	2	1

v FAROE ISLANDS

		NI	FI
1991	Belfast (EC)	1	1
1991	Landskrona, Sw (EC)	5	0
2010	Toftir (EC)	1	1
2011	Belfast (EC)	4	0
2014	Belfast (EC)	2	0
2015	Torshavn (EC)	3	1

v FINLAND

		NI	F
1984	Pori (WC)	0	1
1984	Belfast (WC)	2	1
1998	Belfast (EC)	1	0
1999	Helsinki (EC)	1	4
2003	Belfast	0	1
2006	Helsinki	2	1
2012	Belfast	3	3
2015	Belfast (EC)	2	1
2015	Helsinki (EC)	1	1

v FRANCE

		NI	F
1951	Belfast	2	2
1952	Paris	1	3
1958	Norrkoping (WC)	0	4
1982	Paris	0	4
1982	Madrid (WC)	1	4
1986	Paris	0	0
1988	Belfast	0	0
1999	Belfast	0	1

v GEORGIA

		NI	G
2008	Belfast	4	1

v GERMANY/WEST GERMANY

		NI	G
1958	Malmo (WC)	2	2
1960	Belfast (WC)	3	4
1961	Berlin (WC)	1	2
1966	Belfast	0	2
1977	Cologne	0	5
1982	Belfast (EC)	1	0
1983	Hamburg (EC)	1	0
1992	Bremen	1	1
1996	Belfast	1	1
1997	Nuremberg (WC)	1	1
1997	Belfast (WC)	1	3

1999	Belfast (EC)	0	3
1999	Dortmund (EC)	0	4
2005	Belfast	1	4
2016	Paris (EC)	0	1
2016	Hannover (WC)	0	2
2017	Belfast (WC)	1	3

v GREECE

		NI	G
1961	Athens (WC)	1	2
1961	Belfast (WC)	2	0
1988	Athens	2	3
2003	Belfast (EC)	0	2
2003	Athens (EC)	0	1
2014	Piraeus (EC)	2	0
2015	Belfast (EC)	3	1

v HOLLAND

		NI	H
1962	Rotterdam	0	4
1965	Belfast (WC)	2	1
1965	Rotterdam (WC)	0	0
1976	Rotterdam (WC)	2	2
1977	Belfast (WC)	0	1
2012	Amsterdam	0	6

v HONDURAS

		NI	H
1982	Zaragoza (WC)	1	1

v HUNGARY

		NI	H
1988	Budapest (WC)	0	1
1989	Belfast (WC)	1	2
2000	Belfast	0	1
2008	Belfast	0	2
2014	Budapest (EC)	2	1
2015	Belfast (EC)	1	1

v ICELAND

		NI	I
1977	Reykjavik (WC)	0	1
1977	Belfast (WC)	2	0
2000	Reykjavik (WC)	0	1
2001	Belfast (WC)	3	0
2006	Belfast (EC)	0	3
2007	Reykjavik (EC)	1	2

v ISRAEL

		NI	I
1968	Jaffa	3	2
1976	Tel Aviv	1	1
1980	Tel Aviv (WC)	0	0
1981	Belfast (WC)	1	0
1984	Belfast	3	0
1987	Tel Aviv	1	1
2009	Belfast	1	1
2013	Belfast (WC)	0	2
2013	Ramat Gan (WC)	1	1
2018	Belfast	3	0

v ITALY

		NI	I
1957	Rome (WC)	0	1
1957	Belfast	2	2
1958	Belfast (WC)	2	1
1961	Bologna	2	3

1997	Palermo	0	2
2003	Campobasso	0	2
2009	Pisa	0	3
2010	Belfast (EC)	0	0
2011	Pescara (EC)	0	3

v LATVIA

		NI	L
1993	Riga (WC)	2	1
1993	Belfast (WC)	2	0
1995	Riga (EC)	1	0
1995	Belfast (EC)	1	2
2006	Belfast (EC)	1	0
2007	Riga (EC)	0	1
2015	Belfast	1	0

v LIECHTENSTEIN

		NI	L
1994	Belfast (EC)	4	1
1995	Eschen (EC)	4	0
2002	Vaduz	0	0
2007	Vaduz (EC)	4	1
2007	Belfast (EC)	3	1

v LITHUANIA

		NI	L
1992	Belfast (WC)	2	2

v LUXEMBOURG

		NI	L
2000	Luxembourg	3	1
2012	Belfast (WC)	1	1
2013	Luxembourg (WC)	2	3

v MALTA

		NI	M
1988	Belfast (WC)	3	0
1989	Valletta (WC)	2	0
2000	Ta'Qali	3	0
2000	Belfast (WC)	1	0
2001	Valletta (WC)	1	0
2005	Valletta	1	1
2013	Ta'Qali	0	0

v MEXICO

		NI	M
1966	Belfast	4	1
1994	Miami	0	3

v MOLDOVA

		NI	M
1998	Belfast (EC)	2	2
1999	Kishinev (EC)	0	0

v MONTENEGRO

		W	M
2010	Podgorica	0	2

v MOROCCO

		NI	M
1986	Belfast	2	1
2010	Belfast	1	1

v NEW ZEALAND

		NI	NZ
2017	Belfast	1	0

v NORWAY

		NI	N
1974	Oslo (EC)	1	2
1975	Belfast (EC)	3	0
1990	Belfast	2	3
1996	Belfast	0	2
2001	Belfast	0	4
2004	Belfast	1	4
2012	Belfast	0	3
2017	Belfast (WC)	2	0
2017	Oslo (WC)	0	1

v PANAMA

		NI	P
2018	Panama City	0	0

v POLAND

		NI	P
1962	Katowice (EC)	2	0
1962	Belfast (EC)	2	0
1988	Belfast	1	1
1991	Belfast	3	1
2002	Limassol (Cyprus)	1	4
2004	Belfast (WC)	0	3
2005	Warsaw (WC)	0	1
2009	Belfast (WC)	3	2
2009	Chorzow (WC)	1	1
2016	Nice (EC)	0	1

v PORTUGAL

		NI	P
1957	Lisbon (WC)	1	1
1957	Belfast (WC)	3	0
1973	Coventry (WC)	1	1
1973	Lisbon (WC)	1	1
1980	Lisbon (WC)	0	1
1981	Belfast (WC)	1	0
1994	Belfast (EC)	1	2
1995	Oporto (EC)	1	1
1997	Belfast (WC)	0	0
1997	Lisbon (WC)	0	1
2005	Belfast	1	1
2012	Porto (WC)	1	1
2013	Belfast (WC)	2	4

v QATAR

		NI	Q
2015	Crewe	1	1

v REPUBLIC OF IRELAND

		NI	RI
1978	Dublin (EC)	0	0
1979	Belfast (EC)	1	0
1988	Belfast (WC)	0	0
1989	Dublin (WC)	0	3
1993	Dublin (WC)	0	3
1993	Belfast (WC)	1	1
1994	Belfast (EC)	0	4
1995	Dublin (EC)	1	1
1999	Dublin	1	0
2011	Dublin (CC)	0	5
2018	Dublin	0	0

v ROMANIA

		NI	R
1984	Belfast (WC)	3	2
1985	Bucharest (WC)	1	0
1994	Belfast	2	0
2006	Chicago	0	2
2014	Bucharest (EC)	0	2
2015	Belfast (EC)	0	0

v RUSSIA

		NI	R
2012	Moscow (WC)	0	2
2013	Belfast (WC)	1	0

v SAN MARINO

		NI	SM
2008	Belfast (WC)	4	0
2009	Serravalle (WC)	3	0
2016	Belfast (WC)	4	0
2017	Serravalle (WC)	3	0

v SERBIA & MONTENEGRO

		NI	S
2004	Belfast	1	1

v SERBIA

		NI	S
2009	Belfast	0	1
2011	Belgrade (EC)	1	2
2011	Belfast (EC)	0	1

v SLOVAKIA

		NI	S
1998	Belfast	1	0
2008	Bratislava (WC)	1	2
2009	Belfast (WC)	0	2
2016	Trnava	0	0

v SLOVENIA

		NI	S
2008	Maribor (WC)	0	2
2009	Belfast (WC)	1	0
2010	Maribor (EC)	1	0
2011	Belfast (EC)	0	0
2016	Belfast	1	0

v SOUTH KOREA

		NI	SK
2018	Belfast	2	1

v SOVIET UNION

		NI	SU
1969	Belfast (WC)	0	0
1969	Moscow (WC)	0	2
1971	Moscow (EC)	0	1
1971	Belfast (EC)	1	1

v SPAIN

		NI	S
1958	Madrid	2	6
1963	Bilbao	1	1
1963	Belfast	0	1
1970	Seville (EC)	0	3
1972	Hull (EC)	1	1
1982	Valencia (WC)	1	0
1985	Palma, Majorca	0	0
1986	Guadalajara (WC)	1	2
1988	Seville (WC)	0	4
1989	Belfast (WC)	0	2
1992	Belfast (WC)	0	0
1993	Seville (WC)	1	3
1998	Santander	1	4

2002	Belfast	0	5
2002	Albacete (EC)	0	3
2003	Belfast (EC)	0	0
2006	Belfast (EC)	3	2
2007	Las Palmas (EC)	0	1

v ST KITTS & NEVIS

		NI	SK
2004	Basseterre	2	0

v SWEDEN

		NI	S
1974	Solna (EC)	2	0
1975	Belfast (EC)	1	2
1980	Belfast (WC)	3	0
1981	Stockholm (WC)	0	1
1996	Belfast	1	2
2007	Belfast (EC)	2	1
2007	Stockholm (EC)	1	1

v SWITZERLAND

		NI	S
1964	Belfast (WC)	1	0
1964	Lausanne (WC)	1	2
1998	Belfast	1	0
2004	Zurich	0	0
2010	Basle (EC)	1	4
2017	Belfast (WC)	0	1
2017	Basle (WC)	0	0

v THAILAND

		NI	T
1997	Bangkok	0	0

v TRINIDAD & TOBAGO

		NI	T
2004	Port of Spain	3	0

v TURKEY

		NI	T
1968	Belfast (WC)	4	1

1968	Istanbul (WC)	3	0
1983	Belfast (EC)	2	1
1983	Ankara (EC)	0	1
1985	Belfast (WC)	2	0
1985	Izmir (WC)	0	0
1986	Izmir (EC)	0	0
1987	Belfast (EC)	1	0
1998	Istanbul (EC)	0	3
1999	Belfast (EC)	0	3
2010	Connecticut	0	2
2013	Adana	0	1

v UKRAINE

		NI	U
1996	Belfast (WC)	0	1
1997	Kiev (WC)	1	2
2002	Belfast (EC)	0	0
2003	Donetsk (EC)	0	0
2016	Lyon (EC)	2	0

v URUGUAY

		NI	U
1964	Belfast	3	0
1990	Belfast	1	0
2006	New Jersey	0	1
2014	Montevideo	0	1

v YUGOSLAVIA

		NI	Y
1975	Belfast (EC)	1	0
1975	Belgrade (EC)	0	1
1982	Zaragoza (WC)	0	0
1987	Belfast (EC)	1	2
1987	Sarajevo (EC)	0	3
1990	Belfast (EC)	0	2
1991	Belgrade (EC)	1	4
2000	Belfast	1	2

REPUBLIC OF IRELAND

v ALBANIA

		RI	A
1992	Dublin (WC)	2	0
1993	Tirana (WC)	2	1
2003	Tirana (EC)	0	0
2003	Dublin (EC)	2	1

v ALGERIA

		RI	A
1982	Algiers	0	2
2010	Dublin	3	0

v ANDORRA

		RI	A
2001	Barcelona (WC)	3	0
2001	Dublin (WC)	3	1
2010	Dublin (EC)	3	1
2011	La Vella (EC)	2	0

v ARGENTINA

		RI	A
1951	Dublin	0	1
1979*	Dublin	0	0
1980	Dublin	0	1
1998	Dublin	0	2

| 2010 | Dublin | 0 | 1 |

(*Not regarded as full int)

v ARMENIA

		RI	A
2010	Yerevan (EC)	1	0
2011	Dublin (EC)	2	1

v AUSTRALIA

		RI	A
2003	Dublin	2	1
2009	Limerick	0	3

v AUSTRIA

		RI	A
1952	Vienna	0	6
1953	Dublin	4	0
1958	Vienna	1	3
1962	Dublin	2	3
1963	Vienna (EC)	0	0
1963	Dublin (EC)	3	2
1966	Vienna	0	1
1968	Dublin	2	2
1971	Dublin (EC)	1	4

1971	Linz (EC)	0	6
1995	Dublin (EC)	1	3
1995	Vienna (EC)	1	3
2013	Dublin (WC)	2	2
2013	Vienna (WC)	0	1
2016	Vienna (WC)	1	0
2017	Dublin (WC	1	1

v BELARUS

		RI	B
2016	Cork	1	2

v BELGIUM

		RI	B
1928	Liege	4	2
1929	Dublin	4	0
1930	Brussels	3	1
1934	Dublin (WC)	4	4
1949	Dublin	0	2
1950	Brussels	1	5
1965	Dublin	0	2
1966	Liege	3	2
1980	Dublin (WC)	1	1
1981	Brussels (WC)	0	1
1986	Brussels (EC)	2	2
1987	Dublin (EC)	0	0
1997*	Dublin (WC)	1	1
1997*	Brussels (WC)	1	2
2016	Bordeaux (EC)	0	3

(*World Cup play-off)

v BOLIVIA

		RI	B
1994	Dublin	1	0
1996	East Rutherford, NJ	3	0
2007	Boston	1	1

v BOSNIA HERZEGOVINA

		RI	B-H
2012	Dublin	1	0
2015	Zenica (EC)	1	1
2015	Dublin (EC)	2	0

v BRAZIL

		RI	B
1974	Rio de Janeiro	1	2
1982	Uberlandia	0	7
1987	Dublin	1	0
2004	Dublin	0	0
2008	Dublin	0	1
2010	Arsenal	0	2

v BULGARIA

		RI	B
1977	Sofia (WC)	1	2
1977	Dublin (WC)	0	0
1979	Sofia (EC)	0	1
1979	Dublin (EC)	3	0
1987	Sofia (EC)	1	2
1987	Dublin (EC)	2	0
2004	Dublin	1	1
2009	Dublin (WC)	1	1
2009	Sofia (WC)	1	1

v CAMEROON

		RI	C
2002	Niigata (WC)	1	1

v CANADA

		RI	C
2003	Dublin	3	0

v CHILE

		RI	C
1960	Dublin	2	0
1972	Recife	1	2
1974	Santiago	2	1
1982	Santiago	0	1
1991	Dublin	1	1
2006	Dublin	0	1

v CHINA

		RI	C
1984	Sapporo	1	0
2005	Dublin	1	0

v COLOMBIA

		RI	C
2008	Fulham	1	0

v COSTA RICA

		RI	CR
2014	Chester, USA	1	1

v CROATIA

		RI	C
1996	Dublin	2	2
1998	Dublin (EC)	2	0
1999	Zagreb (EC)	0	1
2001	Dublin	2	2
2004	Dublin	1	0
2011	Dublin	0	0
2012	Poznan (EC)	1	3

v CYPRUS

		RI	C
1980	Nicosia (WC)	3	2
1980	Dublin (WC)	6	0
2001	Nicosia (WC)	4	0
2001	Dublin (WC)	4	0
2004	Dublin (WC)	3	0
2005	Nicosia (WC)	1	0
2006	Nicosia (EC)	2	5
2007	Dublin (EC)	1	1
2008	Dublin (WC)	1	0
2009	Nicosia (WC)	2	1

v CZECHOSLOVAKIA/CZECH REP

		RI	C
1938	Prague	2	2
1959	Dublin (EC)	2	0
1959	Bratislava (EC)	0	4
1961	Dublin (WC)	1	3
1961	Prague (WC)	1	7
1967	Dublin (EC)	0	2
1967	Prague (EC)	2	1
1969	Dublin (WC)	1	2
1969	Prague (WC)	0	3
1979	Prague	1	4
1981	Dublin	3	1
1986	Reykjavik	1	0
1994	Dublin	1	3
1996	Prague	0	2
1998	Olomouc	1	2
2000	Dublin	3	2
2004	Dublin	2	1

		RI	
2006	Dublin (EC)	1	1
2007	Prague (EC)	0	1
2012	Dublin	1	1

v DENMARK

		RI	D
1956	Dublin (WC)	2	1
1957	Copenhagen (WC)	2	0
1968*	Dublin (WC)	1	1
1969	Copenhagen (WC)	0	2
1969	Dublin (WC)	1	1
1978	Copenhagen (EC)	3	3
1979	Dublin (EC)	2	0
1984	Copenhagen (WC)	0	3
1985	Dublin (WC)	1	4
1992	Copenhagen (WC)	0	0
1993	Dublin (WC)	1	1
2002	Dublin	3	0
(*Abandoned after 51 mins – fog)			
2007	Aarhus	4	0
2017	Copenhagen (WC)	0	0
2017	Dublin (WC)	1	5
2018	Dublin (NL)	0	0
2018	Aarhus (NL)	0	0
2019	Copenhagen (EC)	1	1

v ECUADOR

		RI	E
1972	Natal	3	2
2007	New York	1	1

v EGYPT

		RI	E
1990	Palermo (WC)	0	0

v ESTONIA

		RI	E
2000	Dublin (WC)	2	0
2001	Tallinn (WC)	2	0
2011	Tallinn (EC)	4	0
2011	Dublin (EC)	1	1

v FAROE ISLANDS

		RI	F
2004	Dublin (WC)	2	0
2005	Torshavn (WC)	2	0
2012	Torshavn (WC)	4	1
2013	Dublin (WC)	3	0

v FINLAND

		RI	F
1949	Dublin (WC)	3	0
1949	Helsinki (WC)	1	1
1990	Dublin	1	1
2000	Dublin	0	0
2002	Helsinki	3	0

v FRANCE

		RI	F
1937	Paris	2	0
1952	Dublin	1	1
1953	Dublin (WC)	3	5
1953	Paris (WC)	0	1
1972	Dublin (WC)	2	1
1973	Paris (WC)	1	1
1976	Paris (WC)	0	2
1977	Dublin (WC)	1	0
1980	Paris (WC)	0	2
1981	Dublin (WC)	3	2

1989	Dublin	0	0
2004	Paris (WC)	0	0
2005	Dublin (WC)	0	1
2009	Dublin (WC)	0	1
2009	Paris (WC)	1	1
2016	Lyon (EC)	1	2
2018	Paris	0	2

v GEORGIA

		RI	G
2002	Tbilisi (EC)	2	1
2003	Dublin (EC)	2	0
2008	Mainz (WC)	2	1
2009	Dublin (WC)	2	1
2013	Dublin	4	0
2014	Tbilisi (EC)	2	1
2015	Dublin (EC)	1	0
2016	Dublin (WC)	1	0
2017	Tbilisi (WC)	1	1
2019	Dublin (EC)	1	0

v GERMANY/WEST GERMANY

		RI	G
1935	Dortmund	1	3
1936	Dublin	5	2
1939	Bremen	1	1
1951	Dublin	3	2
1952	Cologne	0	3
1955	Hamburg	1	2
1956	Dublin	3	0
1960	Dusseldorf	1	0
1966	Dublin	0	4
1970	Berlin	1	2
1975*	Dublin	1	0
1979	Dublin	1	3
1981	Bremen	0	3
1989	Dublin	1	1
1994	Hanover	2	0
2002	Ibaraki (WC)	1	1
2006	Stuttgart (EC)	0	1
2007	Dublin (EC)	0	0
2012	Dublin (WC)	1	6
2013	Cologne (WC)	0	3
2014	Gelsenkirchen (EC)	1	1
2015	Dublin (EC)	1	0
(*v W Germany 'B')			

v GIBRALTAR

		RI	G
2014	Dublin (EC)	7	0
2015	Faro (EC)	4	0
2019	Victoria (EC)	1	0
2019	Dublin (EC)	2	0

v GREECE

		RI	G
2000	Dublin	0	1
2002	Athens	0	0
2012	Dublin	0	1

v HOLLAND

		RI	H
1932	Amsterdam	2	0
1934	Amsterdam	2	5
1935	Dublin	3	5
1955	Dublin	1	0
1956	Rotterdam	4	1
1980	Dublin (WC)	2	1

1981	Rotterdam (WC)	2	2
1982	Rotterdam (EC)	1	2
1983	Dublin (EC)	2	3
1988	Gelsenkirchen (EC)	0	1
1990	Palermo (WC)	1	1
1994	Tilburg	1	0
1994	Orlando (WC)	0	2
1995*	Liverpool (EC)	0	2
1996	Rotterdam	1	3
(*Qual Round play-off)			
2000	Amsterdam (WC)	2	2
2001	Dublin (WC)	1	0
2004	Amsterdam	1	0
2006	Dublin	0	4
2016	Dublin	1	1

v HUNGARY

		RI	H
1934	Dublin	2	4
1936	Budapest	3	3
1936	Dublin	2	3
1939	Cork	2	2
1939	Budapest	2	2
1969	Dublin (WC)	1	2
1969	Budapest (WC)	0	4
1989	Budapest (WC)	0	0
1989	Dublin (WC)	2	0
1992	Gyor	2	1
2012	Budapest	0	0

v ICELAND

		RI	I
1962	Dublin (EC)	4	2
1962	Reykjavik (EC)	1	1
1982	Dublin (EC)	2	0
1983	Reykjavik (EC)	3	0
1986	Reykjavik	2	1
1996	Dublin (WC)	0	0
1997	Reykjavik (WC)	4	2
2017	Dublin	0	1

v IRAN

		RI	I
1972	Recife	2	1
2001*	Dublin (WC)	2	0
2001*	Tehran (WC)	0	1
(*Qual Round play-off)			

v ISRAEL

		RI	I
1984	Tel Aviv	0	3
1985	Tel Aviv	0	0
1987	Dublin	5	0
2005	Tel Aviv (WC)	1	1
2005	Dublin (WC)	2	2

v ITALY

		RI	I
1926	Turin	0	3
1927	Dublin	1	2
1970	Florence (EC)	0	3
1971	Dublin (EC)	1	2
1985	Dublin	1	2
1990	Rome (WC)	0	1
1992	Boston, USA	0	2
1994	New York (WC)	1	0
2005	Dublin	1	2
2009	Bari (WC)	1	1

2009	Dublin (WC)	2	2
2011	Liege	2	0
2012	Poznan (EC)	0	2
2014	Fulham	0	0
2016	Lille (EC)	1	0

v JAMAICA

		RI	J
2004	Charlton	1	0

v KAZAKHSTAN

		RI	K
2012	Astana (WC)	2	1
2013	Dublin (WC)	3	1

v LATVIA

		RI	L
1992	Dublin (WC)	4	0
1993	Riga (WC)	2	0
1994	Riga (EC)	3	0
1995	Dublin (EC)	2	1
2013	Dublin	3	0

v LIECHTENSTEIN

		RI	L
1994	Dublin (EC)	4	0
1995	Eschen (EC)	0	0
1996	Eschen (WC)	5	0
1997	Dublin (WC)	5	0

v LITHUANIA

		RI	L
1993	Vilnius (WC)	1	0
1993	Dublin (WC)	2	0
1997	Dublin (WC)	0	0
1997	Zalgiris (WC)	2	1

v LUXEMBOURG

		RI	L
1936	Luxembourg	5	1
1953	Dublin (WC)	4	0
1954	Luxembourg (WC)	1	0
1987	Luxembourg (EC)	2	0
1987	Luxembourg (EC)	2	1

v MACEDONIA

		RI	M
1996	Dublin (WC)	3	0
1997	Skopje (WC)	2	3
1999	Dublin (EC)	1	0
1999	Skopje (EC)	1	1
2011	Dublin (EC)	2	1
2011	Skopje (EC)	2	0

v MALTA

		RI	M
1983	Valletta (EC)	1	0
1983	Dublin (EC)	8	0
1989	Dublin (WC)	2	0
1989	Valletta (WC)	2	0
1990	Valletta	3	0
1998	Dublin (EC)	1	0
1999	Valletta (EC)	3	2

v MEXICO

		RI	M
1984	Dublin	0	0
1994	Orlando (WC)	1	2
1996	New Jersey	2	2
1998	Dublin	0	0

		RI	
2000	Chicago	2	2
2017	New Jersey	1	3

v MOLDOVA

		RI	M
2016	Chisinau (WC)	3	1
2017	Dublin (WC)	2	0

v MONTENEGRO

		RI	M
2008	Podgorica (WC)	0	0
2009	Dublin (WC)	0	0

v MOROCCO

		RI	M
1990	Dublin	1	0

v NIGERIA

		RI	N
2002	Dublin	1	2
2004	Charlton	0	3
2009	Fulham	1	1

v NORWAY

		RI	N
1937	Oslo (WC)	2	3
1937	Dublin (WC)	3	3
1950	Dublin	2	2
1951	Oslo	3	2
1954	Dublin	2	1
1955	Oslo	3	1
1960	Dublin	3	1
1964	Oslo	4	1
1973	Oslo	1	1
1976	Dublin	3	0
1978	Oslo	0	0
1984	Oslo (WC)	0	1
1985	Dublin (WC)	0	0
1988	Oslo	0	0
1994	New York (WC)	0	0
2003	Dublin	1	0
2008	Dublin	1	1
2010	Dublin	1	2

v OMAN

		RI	O
2012	Fulham	4	1
2014	Dublin	2	0
2016	Dublin	4	0

v PARAGUAY

		RI	P
1999	Dublin	2	0
2010	Dublin	2	1

v POLAND

		RI	P
1938	Warsaw	0	6
1938	Dublin	3	2
1958	Katowice	2	2
1958	Dublin	2	2
1964	Cracow	1	3
1964	Dublin	3	2
1968	Dublin	2	2
1968	Katowice	0	1
1970	Dublin	1	2
1970	Poznan	0	2
1973	Wroclaw	0	2
1973	Dublin	1	0
1976	Poznan	2	0
1977	Dublin	0	0
1978	Lodz	0	3
1981	Bydgoszcz	0	3
1984	Dublin	0	0
1986	Warsaw	0	1
1988	Dublin	3	1
1991	Dublin (EC)	0	0
1991	Poznan (EC)	3	3
2004	Bydgoszcz	0	0
2008	Dublin	2	3
2013	Dublin	2	0
2013	Poznan	0	0
2015	Dublin (EC)	1	1
2015	Warsaw (EC)	1	2
2018	Wroclaw	1	1

v PORTUGAL

		RI	P
1946	Lisbon	1	3
1947	Lisbon	0	2
1948	Lisbon	0	2
1949	Dublin	1	0
1972	Recife	1	2
1992	Boston, USA	2	0
1995	Dublin (EC)	1	0
1995	Lisbon (EC)	0	3
1996	Dublin	0	1
2000	Lisbon (WC)	1	1
2001	Dublin (WC)	1	1
2005	Dublin	1	0
2014	East Rutherford, USA	1	5

v ROMANIA

		RI	R
1988	Dublin	2	0
1990*	Genoa	0	0
1997	Bucharest (WC)	0	1
1997	Dublin (WC)	1	1
2004	Dublin	1	0

(*Rep won 5-4 on pens)

v RUSSIA (See also Soviet Union)

		RI	R
1994	Dublin	0	0
1996	Dublin	0	2
2002	Dublin	2	0
2002	Moscow (EC)	2	4
2003	Dublin (EC)	1	1
2010	Dublin (EC)	2	3
2011	Moscow (EC)	0	0

v SAN MARINO

		RI	SM
2006	Dublin (EC)	5	0
2007	Rimini (EC)	2	1

v SAUDI ARABIA

		RI	SA
2002	Yokohama (WC)	3	0

v SERBIA

		RI	S
2008	Dublin	1	1
2012	Belgrade	0	0
2014	Dublin	1	2
2016	Belgrade (WC)	2	2
2017	Dublin (WC)	0	1

v SLOVAKIA

Year	Venue	RI	S
2007	Dublin (EC)	1	0
2007	Bratislava (EC)	2	2
2010	Zilina (EC)	1	1
2011	Dublin (EC)	0	0
2016	Dublin	2	2

v SOUTH AFRICA

Year	Venue	RI	SA
2000	New Jersey	2	1
2009	Limerick	1	0

v SOVIET UNION (See also Russia)

Year	Venue	RI	SU
1972	Dublin (WC)	1	2
1973	Moscow (WC)	0	1
1974	Dublin (EC)	3	0
1975	Kiev (EC)	1	2
1984	Dublin (WC)	1	0
1985	Moscow (WC)	0	2
1988	Hanover (EC)	1	1
1990	Dublin	1	0

v SPAIN

Year	Venue	RI	S
1931	Barcelona	1	1
1931	Dublin	0	5
1946	Madrid	1	0
1947	Dublin	3	2
1948	Barcelona	1	2
1949	Dublin	1	4
1952	Madrid	0	6
1955	Dublin	2	2
1964	Seville (EC)	1	5
1964	Dublin (EC)	0	2
1965	Dublin (WC)	1	0
1965	Seville (WC)	1	4
1965	Paris (WC)	0	1
1966	Dublin (EC)	0	0
1966	Valencia (EC)	0	2
1977	Dublin	0	1
1982	Dublin (EC)	3	3
1983	Zaragoza (EC)	0	2
1985	Cork	0	0
1988	Seville (WC)	0	2
1989	Dublin (WC)	1	0
1992	Seville (WC)	0	0
1993	Dublin (WC)	1	3
2002*	Suwon (WC)	1	1
(*Rep lost 3-2 on pens)			
2012	Gdansk (EC)	0	4
2013	New York	0	2

v SWEDEN

Year	Venue	RI	S
1949	Stockholm (WC)	1	3
1949	Dublin (WC)	1	3
1959	Dublin	3	2
1960	Malmo	1	4
1970	Dublin (EC)	1	1
1970	Malmo (EC)	0	1
1999	Dublin	2	0
2006	Dublin	3	0
2013	Stockholm (WC)	0	0
2013	Dublin (WC)	1	2
2016	Paris (EC)	1	1

v SWITZERLAND

Year	Venue	RI	S
1935	Basle	0	1
1936	Dublin	1	0
1937	Berne	1	0
1938	Dublin	4	0
1948	Dublin	0	1
1975	Dublin (EC)	2	1
1975	Berne (EC)	0	1
1980	Dublin	2	0
1985	Dublin (WC)	3	0
1985	Berne (WC)	U	U
1992	Dublin	2	1
2002	Dublin (EC)	1	2
2003	Basle (EC)	0	2
2004	Basle (WC)	1	1
2005	Dublin (WC)	0	0
2016	Dublin	1	0

v TRINIDAD & TOBAGO

Year	Venue	RI	T&T
1982	Port of Spain	1	2

v TUNISIA

Year	Venue	RI	T
1988	Dublin	4	0

v TURKEY

Year	Venue	RI	T
1966	Dublin (EC)	2	1
1967	Ankara (EC)	1	2
1974	Izmir (EC)	1	1
1975	Dublin (EC)	4	0
1976	Ankara	3	3
1978	Dublin	4	2
1990	Izmir	0	0
1990	Dublin (EC)	5	0
1991	Istanbul (EC)	3	1
1999	Dublin (EC)	1	1
1999	Bursa (EC)	0	0
2003	Dublin	2	2
2014	Dublin	1	2
2018	Antalya	0	1

v URUGUAY

Year	Venue	RI	U
1974	Montevideo	0	2
1986	Dublin	1	1
2011	Dublin	2	3
2017	Dublin	3	1

v USA

Year	Venue	RI	USA
1979	Dublin	3	2
1991	Boston	1	1
1992	Dublin	4	1
1992	Washington	1	3
1996	Boston	1	2
2000	Foxboro	1	1
2002	Dublin	2	1
2014	Dublin	4	1
2018	Dublin	2	1

v YUGOSLAVIA

Year	Venue	RI	Y
1955	Dublin	1	4
1988	Dublin	2	0
1998	Belgrade (EC)	0	1
1999	Dublin (EC)	2	1

BRITISH AND IRISH INTERNATIONAL APPEARANCES SINCE THE WAR (1946–2019)

(As start of season 2019-20; in year shown 2019 = season 2018-19. *Also a pre-War international player. Totals include appearances as substitute)

ENGLAND

Agbonlahor G (Aston Villa, 2009–10)	3
Abraham T (Chelsea 2018)	2
A'Court A (Liverpool, 1958–59)	5
Adams T (Arsenal, 1987–2001)	66
Alexander-Arnold (Liverpool, 2018–19)	6
Alli D (Tottenham, 2016–18)	37
Allen A (Stoke, 1960)	3
Allen C (QPR, Tottenham, 1984–88)	5
Allen R (WBA, 1952–55)	5
Anderson S (Sunderland, 1962)	2
Anderson V (Nottm Forest, Arsenal, Manchester Utd, 1979–88)	30
Anderton D (Tottenham, 1994–2002)	30
Angus J (Burnley, 1961)	1
Armfield J (Blackpool, 1959–66)	43
Armstrong D (Middlesbrough, Southampton, 1980–4)	3
Armstrong K (Chelsea, 1955)	1
Ashton D (West Ham, 2008)	1
Astall G (Birmingham, 1956)	2
Astle J (WBA, 1969–70)	5
Aston J (Manchester Utd, 1949–51)	17
Atyeo J (Bristol City, 1956–57)	6
Bailey G (Manchester Utd, 1985)	2
Bailey M (Charlton, 1964–5)	2
Baily E (Tottenham, 1950–3)	9
Baines L (Everton, 2010–15)	30
Baker J (Hibernian, Arsenal, 1960–6)	8
Ball A (Blackpool, Everton, Arsenal, 1965–75)	72
Ball M (Everton, 2001)	1
Banks G (Leicester, Stoke, 1963–72)	73
Banks T (Bolton, 1958–59)	6
Bardsley D (QPR, 1993)	1
Barham M (Norwich, 1983)	2
Barkley R (Everton, Chelsea, 2014–19)	29
Barlow R (WBA, 1955)	1
Barmby N (Tottenham, Middlesbrough, Everton, Liverpool, 1995–2002)	23
Barnes J (Watford, Liverpool, 1983–96)	79
Barnes P (Manchester City, WBA, Leeds, 1978–82)	22
Barrass M (Bolton, 1952–53)	3
Barrett E (Oldham, Aston Villa, 1991–93)	3
Barry G (Aston Villa, Manchester City, 2000–12)	53
Barton J (Manchester City, 2007)	1
Barton W (Wimbledon, Newcastle, 1995)	3
Batty D (Leeds, Blackburn, Newcastle, Leeds, 1991–2000)	42
Baynham R (Luton, 1956)	3
Beardsley P (Newcastle, Liverpool, Newcastle, 1986–96)	59
Beasant D (Chelsea, 1990)	2
Beattie J (Southampton, 2003–04)	5
Beattie K (Ipswich, 1975–58)	9
Beckham D (Manchester Utd, Real Madrid, LA Galaxy, AC Milan 1997–2010)	115
Bell C (Manchester City, 1968–76)	48
Bent D (Charlton, Tottenham Sunderland, Aston Villa, 2006–12)	13
Bentley D (Blackburn, 2008–09)	7
Bentley R (Chelsea, 1949–55)	12
Berry J (Manchester Utd, 1953–56)	4
Bertrand R (Chelsea, Southampton, 2013–18)	19
Birtles G (Nottm Forest, 1980–81)	3
Blissett L (Watford, AC Milan, 1983–84)	14
Blockley J (Arsenal, 1973)	1
Blunstone F (Chelsea, 1955–57)	5
Bonetti P (Chelsea, 1966–70)	7
Bothroyd J (Cardiff, 2011)	1
Bould S (Arsenal, 1994)	2
Bowles S (QPR, 1974–7)	5
Bowyer L (Leeds, 2003)	1
Boyer P (Norwich, 1976)	1
Brabrook P (Chelsea, 1958–60)	3
Bracewell P (Everton, 1985–86)	3
Bradford G (Bristol Rov, 1956)	1
Bradley W (Manchester Utd, 1959)	3
Bridge W (Southampton, Chelsea, Manchester City 2002–10)	36
Bridges B (Chelsea, 1965–66)	4
Broadbent P (Wolves, 1958–60)	7
Broadis I (Manchester City, Newcastle, 1952–54)	14
Brooking T (West Ham, 1974–82)	47
Brooks J (Tottenham, 1957)	3
Brown A (WBA, 1971)	1
Brown K (West Ham, 1960)	1
Brown W (Manchester Utd, 1999–2010)	23
Bull S (Wolves, 1989–91)	13
Butcher T (Ipswich, Rangers, 1980–90)	77
Butland J (Birmingham, Stoke, 2013–19)	9
Butt N (Manchester Utd, Newcastle, 1997–2005)	39
Byrne G (Liverpool, 1963–66)	2
Byrne J (Crystal Palace, West Ham, 1962–65)	11
Byrne R (Manchester Utd, 1954–58)	33
Cahill G (Bolton, Chelsea, 2011–18)	61
Callaghan I (Liverpool, 1966–78)	4
Campbell F (Sunderland, 2012)	1
Campbell S (Tottenham, Arsenal, Portsmouth, 1996–2008)	73
Carragher J (Liverpool, 1999–2010)	38
Carrick M (West Ham, Tottenham, Manchester Utd, 2001–16)	34
Carroll A (Newcastle, Liverpool 2011–13)	9
Carson S (Liverpool, Aston Villa WBA, Bursaspor 2008–12)	4

Goddard P (West Ham, 1982) 1
Gomez J (Liverpool, 2018–19) 7
Grainger C (Sheffield Utd, Sunderland, 1956–57) 7
Gray A (Crystal Palace, 1992) 1
Gray M (Sunderland, 1999) 3
Greaves J (Chelsea, Tottenham, 1959–67) 57
Green R (Norwich, West Ham 2005–12) 12
Greenhoff F (Manchester Utd, Leeds, 1976–80) 18
Gregory J (QPR, 1983–84) 6
Guppy S (Leicester, 2000) 1

Hagan J (Sheffield Utd, 1949) 1
Haines J (WBA, 1949) 1
Hall J (Birmingham, 1956–57) 17
Hancocks J (Wolves, 1949–50) 3
Hardwick G (Middlesbrough, 1947–48) 13
Harford M (Luton, 1988–89) 2
Hargreaves O (Bayern Munich, Manchester Utd, 2002–08) 42
Harris G (Burnley, 1966) 1
Harris P (Portsmouth, 1950–54) 2
Hart J (Manchester City, 2010–18) 75
Harvey C (Everton, 1971) 1
Hassall H (Huddersfield, Bolton, 1951–54) 5
Hateley M (Portsmouth, AC Milan, Monaco, Rangers, 1984–92) 32
Haynes J (Fulham, 1955–62) 56
Heaton T (Burnley, 2016–17) 3
Hector K (Derby, 1974) 2
Hellawell M (Birmingham, 1963) 2
Henderson J (Sunderland, Liverpool, 2011–19) 51
Hendrie L (Aston Villa, 1999) 1
Henry R (Tottenham, 1963) 1
Heskey E (Leicester, Liverpool, Birmingham, Wigan, Aston Villa 1999–2010) 62
Hill F (Bolton, 1963) 2
Hill G (Manchester Utd, 1976–78) 6
Hill R (Luton, 1983–86) 3
Hinchcliffe A (Everton, Sheffield Wed, 1997–99) 7
Hinton A (Wolves, Nottm Forest, 1963–65) 3
Hirst D (Sheffield Wed, 1991–92) 3
Hitchens G (Aston Villa, Inter Milan, 1961–62) 7
Hoddle G (Tottenham, Monaco, 1980–88) 53
Hodge S (Aston Villa, Tottenham, Nottm Forest, 1986–91) 24
Hodgkinson A (Sheffield Utd, 1957–61) 5
Holden D (Bolton, 1959) 5
Holliday E (Middlesbrough, 1960) 3
Hollins J (Chelsea, 1967) 1
Hopkinson E (Bolton, 1958–60) 14
Howe D (WBA, 1958–60) 23
Howe J (Derby, 1948–49) 3
Howey S (Newcastle, 1995–96) 4
Huddlestone T (Tottenham, 2010–13) 4
Hudson A (Stoke, 1975) 2
Hudson-Odoi C (Chelsea, 2019) 2
Hughes E (Liverpool, Wolves, 1970–80) 62
Hughes L (Liverpool, 1950) 3
Hunt R (Liverpool, 1962–69) 34
Hunt S (WBA, 1984) 2

Hunter N (Leeds, 1966–75) 28
Hurst G (West Ham, 1966–72) 49

Ince P (Manchester Utd, Inter Milan, Liverool, Middlesbrough, 1993–2000) 53
Ings D (Liverpool 2016) 1

Jagielka P (Everton, 2008–17) 40
James D (Liverpool, Aston Villa, West Ham, Manchester City, Portsmouth, 1997–2010) 53
Jarvis M (Wolves, 2011) 1
Jeffers F (Arsenal, 2003) 1
Jenas J (Newcastle, Tottenham, 2003–10) 21
Jenkinson C (Arsenal, 2013) 1
Jezzard B (Fulham, 1954–56) 2
Johnson A (Crystal Palace, Everton, 2005–08) 8
Johnson A (Manchester City, 2010–13) 12
Johnson D (Ipswich, Liverpool, 1975–80) 8
Johnson G (Chelsea, Portsmouth, Liverpool, 2004–14) 54
Johnson S (Derby, 2001) 1
Johnston H (Blackpool, 1947–54) 10
Jones M (Leeds, Sheffield Utd, 1965–70) 3
Jones P (Manchester Utd, 2012–18) 27
Jones R (Liverpool, 1992–95) 8
Jones W H (Liverpool, 1950) 2

Kane H (Tottenham, 20015–19) 39
Kay A (Everton, 1963) 1
Keane M (Burnley, Everton, 2017–19) 7
Keegan K (Liverpool, Hamburg, Southampton, 1973–82) 63
Kelly M (Liverpool, 2012) 1
Kennedy A (Liverpool, 1984) 2
Kennedy R (Liverpool, 1976–80) 17
Keown M (Everton, Arsenal, 1992–2002) 43
Kevan D (WBA, 1957–61) 14
Kidd B (Manchester Utd, 1970) 2
King L (Tottenham, 2002–10) 21
Kirkland C (Liverpool, 2007) 1
Knight Z (Fulham, 2005) 2
Knowles C (Tottenham, 1968) 4
Konchesky P (Charlton, 2003–06) 2

Labone B (Everton, 1963–70) 26
Lallana A (Southampton, Liverpool, 2014–18) 34
Lambert R (Southampton, Liverpool, 2014–15) 11
Lampard F Snr (West Ham, 1973–00) 2
Lampard F Jnr (West Ham, Chelsea, 2000–14) 106
Langley J (Fulham, 1958) 3
Langton R (Blackburn, Preston, Bolton, 1947–51) 11
Latchford R (Everton, 1978–9) 12
Lawler C (Liverpool, 1971–72) 4
*Lawton T (Chelsea, Notts Co, 1947–49) 15
Lee F (Manchester City, 1969–72) 27
Lee J (Derby, 1951) 1
Lee R (Newcastle, 1995–99) 21
Lee S (Liverpool, 1983–84) 14
Lennon A (Tottenham, 2006–13) 21

Le Saux G (Blackburn, Chelsea, 1994–2001) 36
Lescott J (Everton, Manchester City, 2008–13) 26
Le Tissier M (Southampton, 1994–97) 8
Lindsay A (Liverpool, 1974) 4
Lineker G (Leicester, Everton, Barcelona, Tottenham, 1985–92) 80
Lingard J (Manchester Utd, 2017–19) 24
Little B (Aston Villa, 1975) 1
Livermore J (Tottenham, WBA, 2013–18) 7
Lloyd L (Liverpool, Nottm Forest, 1971–80) 4
Lofthouse N (Bolton, 1951–59) 33
Loftus-Cheek R (Chelsea, 2018–19) 10
Lowe E (Aston Villa, 1947) 3

Mabbutt G (Tottenham, 1983–92) 16
Macdonald M (Newcastle, 1972–76) 14
Madeley P (Leeds, 1971–77) 24
Maguire H (Leicester, 2018–19) 20
Mannion W (Middlesbrough, 1947–52) 26
Mariner P (Ipswich, Arsenal, 1977–85) 35
Marsh R (QPR, Manchester City, 1972–73) 9
Mason R (Tottenham, 2015) 1
Martin A (West Ham, 1981–87) 17
Martyn N (Crystal Palace, Leeds, 1992–2002) 23
Marwood B (Arsenal, 1989) 1
Matthews R (Coventry, 1956–57) 5
*Matthews S (Stoke, Blackpool, 1947–57) 37
McCann G (Sunderland, 2001) 1
McCarthy A (Southampton, 2019) 1
McDermott T (Liverpool, 1978–82) 25
McDonald C (Burnley, 1958–59) 8
McFarland R (Derby, 1971–77) 28
McGarry W (Huddersfield, 1954–56) 4
McGuinness W (Manchester Utd, 1959) 2
McMahon S (Liverpool, 1988–91) 17
McManaman S (Liverpool, Real Madrid, 1995–2002) 37
McNab R (Arsenal, 1969) 4
McNeil M (Middlesbrough, 1961–62) 9
Meadows J (Manchester City, 1955) 1
Medley L (Tottenham, 1951–52) 6
Melia J (Liverpool, 1963) 2
Merrick G (Birmingham, 1952–54) 23
Merson P (Arsenal, Middlesbrough, Aston Villa, 1992–99) 21
Metcalfe V (Huddersfield, 1951) 2
Milburn J (Newcastle, 1949–56) 13
Miller B (Burnley, 1961) 1
Mills D (Leeds, 2001–04) 19
Mills M (Ipswich, 1973–82) 42
Milne G (Liverpool, 1963–65) 14
Milner J (Aston Villa, Manchester City, Liverpool, 2010–16) 61
Milton A (Arsenal, 1952) 1
Moore R (West Ham, 1962–74) 108
Morley A (Aston Villa, 1982–83) 6
Morris J (Derby, 1949–50) 3
Mortensen S (Blackpool, 1947–54) 25
Mozley B (Derby, 1950) 3
Mullen J (Wolves, 1947–54) 12
Mullery A (Tottenham, 1965–72) 35
Murphy D (Liverpool, 2002–04) 9

Neal P (Liverpool, 1976–84) 50
Neville G (Manchester Utd, 1995–2009) 85
Neville P (Manchester Utd, Everton, 1996–2008) 59
Newton K (Blackburn, Everton, 1966–70) 27
Nicholls J (WBA, 1954) 2
Nicholson W (Tottenham, 1951) 1
Nish D (Derby, 1973–74) 5
Norman M (Tottenham, 1962–5) 23
Nugent D (Preston, 2007) 1

O Grady M (Huddersfield, Leeds, 1963–9) 2
Osgood P (Chelsea, 1970–74) 4
Osman L (Everton, 2013) 2
Osman R (Ipswich, 1980–84) 11
Owen M (Liverpool, Real Madrid, Newcastle, 1998–2008) 89
Owen S (Luton, 1954) 3
Oxlade-Chamberlain A (Arsenal, Liverpool, 2012–18) 32

Paine T (Southampton, 1963–66) 19
Pallister G (Middlesbrough, Manchester Utd 1988–97) 22
Palmer C (Sheffield Wed, 1992–94) 18
Parker P (QPR, Manchester Utd, 1989–94) 19
Parker S (Charlton, Chelsea, Newcastle, West Ham, Tottenham, 2004–13) 18
Parkes P (QPR, 1974) 1
Parlour R (Arsenal, 1999–2001) 10
Parry R (Bolton, 1960) 2
Peacock A (Middlesbrough, Leeds, 1962–66) 6
Pearce S (Nottm Forest, West Ham, 1987–2000) 78
Pearson Stan (Manchester Utd, 1948–52) 8
Pearson Stuart (Manchester Utd, 1976–78) 15
Pegg D (Manchester Utd, 1957) 1
Pejic M (Stoke, 1974) 4
Perry W (Blackpool, 1956) 3
Perryman S (Tottenham, 1982) 1
Peters M (West Ham, Tottenham, 1966–74) 67
Phelan M (Manchester Utd, 1990) 1
Phillips K (Sunderland, 1999–2002) 8
Phillips L (Portsmouth, 1952–55) 3
Pickering F (Everton, 1964–65) 3
Pickering N (Sunderland, 1983) 1
Pickford J (Everton, 2018–19) 19
Pilkington B (Burnley, 1955) 1
Platt D (Aston Villa, Bari, Juventus, Sampdoria, Arsenal, 1990–96) 62
Pointer R (Burnley, 1962) 3
Pope N (Burnley, 2018) 1
Powell C (Charlton, 2001–02) 5
Pye J (Wolves, 1950) 1

Quixall A (Sheffield Wed, 1954–56) 5

Radford J (Arsenal, 1969–72) 2
Ramsey A (Southampton, Tottenham, 1949–54) 32
Rashford M (Manchester Utd, 2016–19) 32
Reaney P (Leeds, 1969–71) 3

Redknapp J (Liverpool, 1996–2000) — 17
Redmond N (Southampton 2017) — 1
Reeves K (Norwich, Manchester City, 1980) — 2
Regis C (WBA, Coventry, 1982–88) — 5
Reid P (Everton, 1985–88) — 13
Revie D (Manchester City, 1955 57) — 6
Rice D (West Ham, 2019) — 3
Richards, J (Wolves, 1973) — 1
Richards M (Manchester City, 2007 12) — 13
Richardson K (Aston Villa, 1994) — 1
Richardson K (Manchester Utd, 2005–07) — 8
Rickaby S (WBA, 1954) — 1
Ricketts M (Bolton, 2002) — 1
Rimmer J (Arsenal, 1976) — 1
Ripley S (Blackburn, 1994–97) — 2
Rix G (Arsenal, 1981–84) — 17
Robb G (Tottenham, 1954) — 1
Roberts G (Tottenham, 1983–84) — 6
Robinson P (Leeds, Tottenham, 2003–08) — 41
Robson B (WBA, Manchester Utd, 1980–92) — 90
Robson R (WBA, 1958 62) — 20
Rocastle D (Arsenal, 1989–92) — 14
Rodriguez J (Southampton, 2014) — 1
Rodwell J (Everton, Manchester City, 2012–13) — 3
Rooney W (Everton, Manchester Utd, DC United, 2003–19) — 120
Rose D (Tottenham, 2016–19) — 27
Rowley J (Manchester Utd, 1949 52) — 6
Royle J (Everton, Manchester City, 1971 77) — 6
Ruddock N (Liverpool, 1995) — 1
Ruddy I (Norwich, 2013) — 1

Sadler D (Manchester Utd, 1968–71) — 4
Salako J (Crystal Palace, 1991–92) — 5
Sancho J (Borussia Dortmund, 2019) — 6
Sansom K (Crystal Palace, Arsenal, 1979 88) — 86
Scales J (Liverpool, 1995) — 3
Scholes P (Manchester Utd, 1997–2004) — 66
Scott I (Arsenal, 1947 49) — 17
Seaman D (QPR, Arsenal, 1989–2003) — 75
Sewell J (Sheffield Wed, 1952–54) — 6
Shackleton L (Sunderland, 1949–55) — 5
Sharpe L (Manchester Utd, 1991–94) — 8
Shaw G (Sheffield Utd, 1959–63) — 5
Shaw L (Southampton, Manchester Utd, 2014–19) — 1
Shawcross, R (Stoke, 2013) — 1
Shearer A (Southampton, Blackburn, Newcastle, 1992–2000) — 63
Shellito K (Chelsea, 1963) — 1
Shelvey J (Liverpool, Swansea, 2013–16) — 6
Sheringham E (Tottenham, Manchester Utd, Tottenham, 1993–2002) — 51
Sherwood T (Tottenham, 1999) — 3
Shilton P (Leicester, Stoke, Nottm Forest, Southampton, Derby, 1971–90) — 125
Shimwell E (Blackpool, 1949) — 1
Shorey N (Reading, 2007) — 2
Sillett P (Chelsea, 1955) — 3
Sinclair T (West Ham, Manchester City, 2002–04) — 12

Sinton A (QPR, Sheffield Wed, 1992–94) — 12
Slater W (Wolves, 1955 60) — 12
Smalling C (Manchester Utd, 2012–17) — 31
Smith A (Arsenal, 1989–92) — 13
Smith A (Leeds, Manchester Utd, Newcastle, 2001 06) — 19
Smith I (Arsenal, 1951–53) — 6
Smith R (Tottenham, 1961–64) — 15
Smith T (Birmingham, 1960) — 2
Smith T (Liverpool, 1971) — 1
Solanke D (Liverpool, 2018) — 1
Southgate G (Aston Villa, Middlesbrough, 1996–2004) — 57
Spink N (Aston Villa, 1983) — 1
Springett R (Sheffield Wed, 1960–66) — 33
Staniforth R (Huddersfield, 1954–55) — 8
Statham D (WBA, 1983) — 3
Stein B (Luton, 1984) — 1
Stepney A (Manchester Utd, 1968) — 1
Sterland M (Sheffield Wed, 1989) — 1
Sterling, R (Liverpool, Manchester City, 2013–19) — 51
Steven T (Everton, Rangers, Marseille, 1985–92) — 36
Stevens G (Everton, Rangers, 1985–92) — 46
Stevens G (Tottenham, 1985–86) — 7
Stewart P (Tottenham, 1992) — 3
Stiles N (Manchester Utd, 1965–70) — 28
Stone S (Nottm Forest, 1996) — 9
Stones J (Everton, Manchester City, 2014–19) — 38
Storey P (Arsenal, 1971–73) — 19
Storey-Moore I (Nottm Forest, 1970) — 1
Streten B (Luton, 1950) — 1
Sturridge D (Chelsea, Liverpool, 2012–18) — 26
Summerbee M (Manchester City, 1968–73) — 8
Sunderland, A (Arsenal, 1980) — 1
Sutton C (Blackburn, 1997) — 1
Swan P (Sheffield Wed, 1960 62) — 19
Swift F (Manchester City, 1947–79) — 19

Talbot B (Ipswich, Arsenal, 1977–80) — 6
Tambling R (Chelsea, 1963–66) — 3
Tarkowski J (Burnley, 2018–19) — 2
Taylor E (Blackpool, 1954) — 1
Taylor J (Fulham, 1951) — 2
Taylor P (Liverpool, 1948) — 3
Taylor P (Crystal Palace, 1976) — 4
Taylor T (Manchester Utd, 1953–58) — 19
Temple D (Everton, 1965) — 1
Terry J (Chelsea, 2003–13) — 78
Thomas D (QPR, 1975–76) — 8
Thomas D (Coventry, 1983) — 2
Thomas G (Crystal Palace, 1991–92) — 9
Thomas M (Arsenal, 1989–90) — 2
Thompson A (Celtic, 2004) — 1
Thompson Peter (Liverpool, 1964–70) — 16
Thompson Phil (Liverpool, 1976–83) — 42
Thompson T (Aston Villa, Preston, 1952–57) — 2
Thomson R (Wolves, 1964–65) — 8
Todd C (Derby, 1972–77) — 27
Towers A (Sunderland, 1978) — 3

Townsend A (Tottenham, Newcastle, Crystal Palace, 2014–17) 13
Trippier K (Tottenham, 2017–19) 16
Tueart D (Manchester City, 1975–77) 6

Ufton D (Charlton, 1954) 1
Unsworth D (Everton, 1995) 1
Upson M (Birmingham, West Ham, 2003–10) 21

Vardy J (Leicester, 2015–18) 26
Vassell D (Aston Villa, 2002–04) 22
Venables T (Chelsea, 1965) 2
Venison B (Newcastle, 1995) 2
Viljoen C (Ipswich, 1975) 2
Viollet D (Manchester Utd, 1960) 2

Waddle C (Newcastle, Tottenham, Marseille, 1985–92) 62
Waiters A (Blackpool, 1964–65) 5
Walcott T (Arsenal, 2006–17) 47
Walker D (Nottm Forest, Sampdoria, Sheffield Wed, 1989–94) 59
Walker I (Tottenham, Leicester, 1996–2004) 48
Walker K (Tottenham, Manchester City, 2012–19) 48
Wallace D (Southampton, 1986) 1
Walsh P (Luton, 1983–4) 5
Walters M (Rangers, 1991) 1
Ward P (Brighton, 1980) 1
Ward T (Derby, 1948) 2
Ward–Prowse J (Southampton, 2017–19) 2
Warnock S (Blackburn, Aston Villa, 2008–11) 2
Watson D (Sunderland, Manchester City, Werder Bremen, Southampton, Stoke, 1974–82) 65
Watson D (Norwich, Everton, 1984–8) 12
Watson W (Sunderland, 1950–1) 4
Webb N (Nottm Forest, Manchester Utd, 1988–92) 26
Welbeck D (Manchester Utd, Arsenal, 2011–19) 42
Weller K (Leicester, 1974) 4
West G (Everton, 1969) 3

Wheeler J (Bolton, 1955) 1
White D (Manchester City, 1993) 1
Whitworth S (Leicester, 1975–76) 7
Whymark T (Ipswich, 1978) 1
Wignall F (Nottm Forest, 1965) 2
Wilcox J (Blackburn, Leeds, 1996–2000) 3
Wilkins R (Chelsea, Manchester Utd, AC Milan, 1976–87) 84
Williams B (Wolves, 1949–56) 24
Williams S (Southampton, 1983–85) 6
Willis A (Tottenham, 1952) 1
Wilshaw D (Wolves, 1954–57) 12
Wilshere J (Arsenal, 2011–16) 34
Wilson C (Bournemouth, 2019) 3
Wilson R (Huddersfield, Everton, 1960–8) 63
Winks H (Tottenham, 2018–19) 3
Winterburn N (Arsenal, 1990–93) 2
Wise D (Chelsea, 1991–2001) 21
Withe P (Aston Villa, 1981–85) 11
Wood R (Manchester Utd, 1955–56) 3
Woodcock A (Nottm Forest, Cologne, Arsenal, 1977–86) 42
Woodgate J (Leeds, Newcastle, Middlesbrough, Tottenham, 1999–2008) 8
Woods C (Norwich, Rangers, Sheffield Wed, 1984–93) 43
Worthington F (Leicester, 1974–75) 8
Wright I (Crystal Palace, Arsenal, West Ham, 1991–99) 33
Wright M (Southampton, Derby, Liverpool, 1984–96) 45
Wright R (Ipswich, Arsenal, 2000–02) 2
Wright T (Everton, 1968–70) 11
Wright W (Wolves, 1947–59) 105
Wright–Phillips S (Manchester City, Chelsea, Manchester City, 2005–11) 36

Young A (Aston Villa, Manchester Utd, 2008–18) 39
Young G (Sheffield Wed, 1965) 1
Young L (Charlton, 2005) 7

Zaha W (Manchester Utd, 2013–14) 2
Zamora R (Fulham, 2011–12) 2

SCOTLAND

Adam C (Rangers, Blackpool, Liverpool, Stoke, 2007–15) 26
Aird J (Burnley, 1954) 4
Aitken G (East Fife, 1949–54) 8
Aitken R (Celtic, Newcastle, St Mirren, 1980–92) 57
Albiston A (Manchester Utd, 1982–6) 14
Alexander G (Preston, Burnley, 2002–10) 40
Alexander N (Cardiff, 2006) 2
Allan T (Dundee, 1974) 2
Anderson J (Leicester, 1954) 1
Anderson R (Aberdeen, Sunderland, 2003–08) 11
Anya I (Watford, Derby, 2014–18) 29
Archer J (Millwall, 2018) 1
Archibald S (Aberdeen, Tottenham, Barcelona, 1980–86) 27
Armstrong S (Celtic, Southampton, 2017–19) 15

Auld B (Celtic, 1959–60) 3

Bain S (Celtic, 2018–19) 3
Baird H (Airdrie, 1956) 1
Baird S (Rangers, 1957–58) 7
Bannan B (Aston Villa, Crystal Palace, Sheffield Wed, 2011–18) 27
Bannon E (Dundee Utd, 1980–86) 11
Bardsley P (Sunderland, 2011–14) 13
Barr D (Falkirk, 2009) 1
Bauld W (Hearts, 1950) 3
Baxter J (Rangers, Sunderland, 1961–68) 34
Beattie C (Celtic, WBA, 2006–08) 7
Bell C (Kilmarnock, 2011) 1
Bell W (Leeds, 1966) 2
Bernard P (Oldham, 1995) 2
Berra C (Hearts, Wolves, Ipswich, Hearts, 2008–18) 41

... okeren, Aberdeen, 1982–90) 26
... 1988) ?
... ampton, 1948) 1
... ers, 2013) 1
... Burnley, 1963–66) 3
Blackie, ..Hibernian, 1974 77) 7
Blair J (Blackpool, 1947) 1
Blyth J (Coventry, 1978) 2
Bone J (Norwich, 1972–73) 2
Booth S (Aberdeen, Borussia Dortmund, Iwente Enschede 1993 2002) ??
Bowman D (Dundee Utd, 1992–94) 6
Boyd G (Peterborough, Hull, 2013–14) 2
Boyd K (Rangers, Middlesbrough, 2006–11) 18
Boyd T (Motherwell, Chelsea, Celtic, 1991–2002) 72
Brand R (Rangers, 1961–62) 8
Brazil A (Ipswich, Tottenham, 1980–83) 13
Bremner D (Hibernian, 1976) 1
Bremner W (Leeds, 1965–76) 54
Drennan F (Nowcastle, 1947–54) 7
Bridcutt L (Brighton, Sunderland, 2013–16) 2
Broadfoot K (Rangers, 2009–11) 4
Brogan J (Celtic, 1971) 4
Brophy E (Kilmarnock, 2019) 1
Brown A (East Fife, Blackpool, 1950–54) 13
Brown II (Partick, 1947) 1
Brown J (Sheffield Utd, 1975) 1
Brown R (Rangers, 1947–52) 3
Brown S (Hibernian, Celtic, 2007–18) 55
Brown W (Dundee, Tottenham, 1958 66) 28
Brownlie J (Hibernian, 1971–76) 7
Bryson C (Kilmarnock, Derby, 2011–16) 3
Buchan M (Aberdeen, Manchester Utd, 1972 8) 34
Buckley P (Aberdeen, 1954–55) 3
Burchill M (Celtic, 2000) 6
Burke C (Rangers, Birmingham, 2006–14) 7
Burke O (Nottm Forest, Leipzig, WBA, 2016–19) 8
Burley C (Chelsea, Celtic, Derby, 1995 2003) 46
Burley G (Ipswich, 1979 82) 11
Burns F (Manchester Utd, 1970) 1
Burns K (Birmingham, Nottm Forest, 1974–81) 20
Burns T (Celtic, 1981–88) 8

Cadden C (Motherwell, 2018) 2
Caddis P (Birmingham, 2016) 1
Calderwood C (Tottenham, Aston Villa, 1995 2000) 36
Caldow E (Rangers, 1957–63) 40
Cairney T (Fulham, 2017–18) 3
Caldwell G (Newcastle, Sunderland, Hibernian, Wigan, 2002–13) 55
Caldwell S (Newcastle, Sunderland, Celtic, Wigan, 2001–11) 12
Callaghan T (Dunfermline, 1970) 2
Cameron C (Hearts, Wolves, 1999–2005) 28
Campbell R (Falkirk, Chelsea, 1947–50) 5
Campbell W (Morton, 1947–48) 5
Canero P (Leicester, 2004) 1
Carr W (Coventry, 1970–73) 6
Chalmers S (Celtic, 1965–67) 5
Christie R (Celtic, 2018–19) 5

Clark J (Celtic, 1966–67) 4
Clark R (Aberdeen, 1968–73) 17
Clarke S (Chelsea, 1988–94) 6
Clarkson D (Motherwell, 2008–09) 2
Collins J (Hibernian, Celtic, Monaco, Everton 1988–2000) 58
Collins R (Celtic, Everton, Leeds, 1951–65) 31
Colquhoun F (Sheffield Utd, 1972–73) 9
Colquhoun J (Hearts, 1988) 2
Combe I (Hibernian, 1948) 3
Commons K (Derby, Celtic, 2009–13) 12
Conn A (Hearts, 1956) 1
Conn A (Tottenham, 1975) 2
Connachan E (Dunfermline, 1962) 2
Connelly G (Celtic, 1974) 2
Connolly J (Everton, 1973) 1
Connor R (Dundee, Aberdeen, 1986–91) 4
Conway C (Dundee Utd, Cardiff, 2010–14) 7
Cooke C (Dundee, Chelsea, 1966–75) 16
Cooper D (Rangers, Motherwell, 1980–90) 22
Cormack P (Hibernian, 1966–72) 9
Cowan J (Morton, 1948–52) 25
Cowie D (Dundee, 1953–58) 20
Cowie D (Watford, 2010–12) 10
Cox C (Hearts, 1948) 1
Cox S (Rangers, 1948–54) 25
Craig JP (Celtic, 1968) 1
Craig J (Celtic, 1977) 1
Craig T (Newcastle, 1976) 1
Crainey S (Celtic, Southampton, Blackpool, 2002–12) 12
Crawford S (Raith, Dunfermline, Plymouth Argyle, 1995–2005) 25
Crerand P (Celtic, Manchester Utd, 1961 66) 16
Cropley A (Hibernian, 1972) ?
Cruickshank J (Hearts, 1964–76) 6
Cullen M (Luton, 1956) 1
Cumming J (Hearts, 1955–60) 9
Cummings J (Nottm Forest, 2018) ?
Cummings W (Chelsea, 2002) 1
Cunningham W (Preston, 1954–55) 8
Curran H (Wolves, 1970–71) 5

Dailly C (Derby, Blackburn, West Ham, 1997–2008) 67
Dalglish K (Celtic, Liverpool, 1972–87) 102
Davidson C (Blackburn, Leicester, Preston, 1999–2010) 19
Davidson M (St Johnstone, 2013) 1*
Davidson J (Partick, 1954–55) 8
Dawson A (Rangers, 1980–83) 5
Deans J (Celtic, 1975) 2
*Delaney J (Manchester Utd, 1947–48) 4
Devlin P (Birmingham, 2003–04) 10
Dick J (West Ham, 1959) 1
Dickov P (Manchester City, Leicester, Blackburn, 2001–05) 10
Dickson W (Kilmarnock, 1970–71) 5
Dixon P (Huddersfield, 2013) 3

283

Herd G (Clyde, 1958–61) 5

Herriot J (Birmingham, 1969–70) 8

Hewie J (Charlton, 1956 60) 19

Holt D (Hearts, 1963–64) 5

Holt G (Kilmarnock, Norwich, 2001–05) 10

Holton J (Manchester Utd, 1973–75) 15

Hope R (WBA, 1968–69) 2

Hopkin D (Crystal Palace, Leeds, 1997–2000) 7

Houliston W (Queen of the South, 1949) 3

Houston S (Manchester Utd, 1976) 1

Howie H (Hibernian, 1949) 1

Hughes J (Celtic, 1966 70) 8

Hughes R (Portsmouth, 2004–06) 5

Hughes S (Norwich, 2010) 1

Hughes W (Sunderland, 1975) 1

Humphries W (Motherwell, 1952) 1

Hunter A (Kilmarnock, Celtic, 1972 74) 4

Hunter W (Motherwell, 1960 61) 3

Husband J (Partick, 1947) 1

Hutchison D (Everton, Sunderland,
West Ham, 1999–2004) 26

Hutchison T (Coventry, 1974–76) 17

Hutton A (Rangers, Tottenham,
Aston Villa, 2007–16) 50

Imlach S (Nottm Forest, 1958) 4

Irvine B (Aberdeen, 1991–94) 9

Iwelumo C (Wolves, Burnley, 2009–11) 4

Jack R (Rangers, 2010–19) 2

Jackson C (Rangers, 1975 77) 8

Jackson D (Hibernian, Celtic, 1995–99) 28

Jardine A (Rangers, 1971–80) 38

Jarvie A (Airdrie, 1971) 3

Jess E (Aberdeen, Coventry,
Aberdeen, 1993–99) 18

Johnston A (Sunderland, Rangers,
Middlesbrough, 1999–2003) 18

Johnston L (Clyde, 1948) 2

Johnston M (Watford, Celtic, Nantes,
Rangers, 1984–92) 38

Johnston W (Rangers, WBA, 1966–78) 21

Johnstone D (Rangers, 1973 80) 14

Johnstone J (Celtic, 1965–75) 23

Johnstone R (Hibernian, Manchester City,
1951–56) 17

Jordan J (Leeds, Manchester Utd, AC Milan,
1973–82) 52

Kelly H (Blackpool, 1952) 1

Kelly J (Barnsley, 1949) 2

Kelly L (Kilmarnock, 2013) 1

Kennedy J (Celtic, 1964–65) 6

Kennedy J (Celtic, 2004) 1

Kennedy S (Rangers, 1975) 5

Kennedy S (Aberdeen, 1978–82) 8

Kenneth G (Dundee Utd, 2011) 2

Kerr A (Partick, 1955) 2

Kerr B (Newcastle, 2003–04) 3

Kingsley S (Swansea, 2016) 1

Kyle K (Sunderland, Kilmarnock, 2002–10) 10

Lambert P (Motherwell, Borussia Dortmund,
Celtic, 1995–2003) 40

Law D (Huddersfield, Manchester City,
Torino, Manchester Utd, 1959–74) 55

Lawrence T (Liverpool, 1963 69) 3

Leggat G (Aberdeen, Fulham, 1956–60) 18

Leighton J (Aberdeen, Manchester Utd,
Hibernian, Aberdeen, 1983–99) 91

Lennox R (Celtic, 1967–70) 10

Leslie L (Airdrie, 1961) 5

Levein C (Hearts, 1990–95) 16

Liddell W (Liverpool, 1947–55) 28

Linwood A (Clyde, 1950) 1

Little R (Rangers, 1953) 1

Logie J (Arsenal, 1953) 1

Long H (Clyde, 1947) 1

Lorimer P (Leeds, 1970 76) 21

Macari L (Celtic, Manchester Utd, 1972–78) 24

Macaulay A (Brentford, Arsenal, 1947–48) 7

MacDonald A (Rangers, 1976) 1

MacDougall E (Norwich, 1975–76) 7

Mackail-Smith C (Peterborough, Brighton
2011–12) 7

MacKay D (Celtic, 1959–62) 14

MacKay D (Hearts, Tottenham, 1957–66) 22

Mackay G (Hearts, 1988) 4

Mackay M (Norwich, 2004–05) 5

Mackay-Steven G (Dundee Utd, 2014) 2

MacKenzie J (Partick, 1954–56) 9

Mackie J (QPR, 2011–13) 9

MacLeod J (Hibernian, 1961) 4

MacLeod M (Celtic, Borussia Dortmund,
Hibernian, 1985–91) 20

Maguire C (Aberdeen, 2011) 2

Maloney S (Celtic, Aston Villa, Celtic,
Wigan, Chicago, Hull, 2006 16) 47

Malpas M (Dundee Utd, 1984–93) 55

Marshall D (Celtic, Cardiff, Hull, 2005–19) 29

Marshall G (Celtic, 1992) 1

Martin B (Motherwell, 1995) 2

Martin C (Derby, 2014–18) 17

Martin F (Aberdeen, 1954–55) 6

Martin N (Hibernian, Sunderland, 1965–66) 3

Martin R (Norwich, 2011–17) 29

Martis J (Motherwell, 1961) 1

Mason J (Third Lanark 1949–51) 7

Masson D (QPR, Derby, 1976–78) 17

Mathers D (Partick, 1954) 1

Matteo D (Leeds, 2001–02) 6

May S (Sheffield Wed, 2015) 1

McAllister B (Wimbledon, 1997) 3

McAllister G (Leicester, Leeds,
Coventry, 1990–99) 57

McAllister J (Livingston, 2004) 1

McArthur J (Wigan, Crystal Palace, 2011–18) 32

McAvennie F (West Ham, Celtic, 1986–88) 5

McBride J (Celtic, 1967) 2

McBurnie O (Swansea, 2018–19) 7

McCall S (Everton, Rangers, 1990–98) 40

McCalliog J (Sheffield Wed, Wolves, 1967–71) 5

McCann N (Hearts, Rangers,
Southampton, 1999–2006) 26

McCann R (Motherwell, 1959 61) 5

McClair B (Celtic, Manchester Utd, 1987–93) 30
McCloy P (Rangers, 1973) 4
McCoist A (Rangers, Kilmarnock, 1986–99) 61
McColl I (Rangers, 1950–58) 14
McCormack R (Motherwell, Cardiff, Leeds, Fulham, 2008–16) 13
McCreadie E (Chelsea, 1965–9) 23
McCulloch L (Wigan, Rangers, 2005–11) 18
McDonald J (Sunderland, 1956) 2
McDonald K (Fulham, 2018–19) 5
McEveley, J (Derby, 2008) 3
McFadden J (Motherwell, Everton, Birmingham, 2002–11) 48
McFarlane W (Hearts, 1947) 1
McGarr E (Aberdeen, 1970) 2
McGarvey F (Liverpool, Celtic, 1979–84) 7
McGeouch D (Hibernian, 2018) 2
McGhee M (Aberdeen, 1983–84) 4
McGinlay J (Bolton, 1995–97) 13
McGinn J (Hibernian, Aston Villa, 2016–19) 15
McGrain D (Celtic, 1973–82) 62
McGregor A (Rangers, Besiktas, Hull, Rangers, 2007–19) 42
McGregor C (Celtic, 2018–19) 13
McGrory J (Kilmarnock, 1965–66) 3
McInally A (Aston Villa, Bayern Munich, 1989–90) 8
McInally J (Dundee Utd, 1987–93) 10
McInnes D (WBA, 2003) 2
McKay B (Rangers, 2016) 1
Mackay–Steven G (Dundee Utd, Aberdeen, 2014–19) 2
McKean R (Rangers, 1976) 1
McKenna S (Aberdeen, 2018–19) 12
McKimmie S (Aberdeen, 1989–96) 40
McKinlay T (Celtic, 1996–98) 22
McKinlay W (Dundee Utd, Blackburn, 1994–99) 29
McKinnon R (Rangers, 1966–71) 28
McKinnon R (Motherwell, 1994–95) 3
McLaren A (Preston, 1947–48) 4
McLaren A (Hearts, Rangers, 1992–96) 24
McLaren A (Kilmarnock, 2001) 1
McLaughlin J (Hearts, 2018) 1
McLean G (Dundee, 1968) 1
McLean K (Aberdeen, Norwich, 2016–19) 8
McLean T (Kilmarnock, Rangers,1969–71) 6
McLeish A (Aberdeen, 1980–93) 77
McLintock F (Leicester, Arsenal,1963–71) 9
McManus S (Celtic, Middlesbrough,2007–11) 26
McMillan I (Airdrie, 1952–61) 6
McNamara J (Celtic, Wolves,1997–2006) 33
McNamee D (Livingston, 2004–06) 4
McNaught W (Raith, 1951–55) 5
McNaughton K (Aberdeen, Cardiff, 2002–08) 4
McNeill W (Celtic, 1961–72) 29
McNulty M (Reading, 2019) 1
McPhail J (Celtic, 1950–54) 5
McPherson D (Hearts, Rangers, 1989–93) 27
McQueen G (Leeds, Manchester Utd, 1974–81) 30

McStay P (Celtic, 1984–97) 76
McSwegan G (Hearts, 2000) 2
McTominay S (Manchester Utd, 2018–19) 9
Millar J (Rangers, 1963) 2
Miller C (Dundee Utd, 2001) 1
Miller K (Rangers, Wolves, Celtic, Derby, Rangers, Bursaspor, Cardiff, Vancouver, 2001–14) 69
Miller L (Dundee Utd, Aberdeen 2006–10) 3
Miller W (Celtic, 1946–47) 6
Miller W (Aberdeen, 1975–90) 65
Mitchell R (Newcastle, 1951) 2
Mochan N (Celtic, 1954) 3
Moir W (Bolton, 1950) 1
Moncur R (Newcastle, 1968–72) 16
Morgan L (Celtic, 2018) 2
Morgan W (Burnley, Manchester Utd, 1968–74) 21
Morris H (East Fife, 1950) 1
Morrison J (WBA, 2008–18) 46
Mudie J (Blackpool, 1957–58) 17
Mulgrew C (Celtic, Blackburn, 2012–19) 41
Mulhall G (Aberdeen, Sunderland, 1960–64) 3
Munro F (Wolves, 1971–75) 9
Munro I (St Mirren, 1979) 7
Murdoch R (Celtic, 1966–70) 12
Murphy J (Brighton, 2018) 2
Murray I (Hibernian, Rangers, 2003–06) 6
Murray J (Hearts, 1958) 5
Murray S (Aberdeen, 1972) 1
Murty G (Reading, 2004–08) 4

Naismith S (Kilmarnock, Rangers, Everton, Norwich, 2007–19) 49
Narey D (Dundee Utd, 1977–89) 35
Naysmith G (Hearts, Everton, Sheffield Utd, 2000–09) 46
Neilson R (Hearts, 2007) 1
Nevin P (Chelsea, Everton, Tranmere, 1987–96) 28
Nicholas C (Celtic, Arsenal, Aberdeen, 1983–89) 20
Nicholson B (Dunfermline, 2001–05) 3
Nicol S (Liverpool, 1985–92) 27

O'Connor G (Hibernian, Lokomotiv Moscow, Birmingham, 2002–10) 16
O'Donnell P (Motherwell, 1994) 1
O'Donnell S (Kilmarnock, 2018–19) 9
O'Hare J (Derby, 1970–72) 13
O'Neil B (Celtic, VfL Wolfsburg, Derby, Preston, 1996–2006) 7
O'Neil J (Hibernian, 2001) 1
Ormond W (Hibernian, 1954–59) 6
Orr T (Morton, 1952) 2

Parker A (Falkirk, Everton, 1955–56) 15
Parlane D (Rangers, 1973–77) 12
Palmer L (Sheffield Wed, 2019) 1
Paterson C (Hearts, Cardiff, 2016–19) 12
Paton A (Motherwell, 1952) 2
Pearson S (Motherwell, Celtic, Derby, 2004–07) 10

White J (Falkirk, Tottenham, 1959–64) 22
Whittaker S (Rangers, Norwich, 2010–16) 31
Whyte D (Celtic, Middlesbrough, Aberdeen,
1988–99) 12
Wilkie L (Dundee, 2002–03) 11
Williams G (Nottm Forest, 2002–03) 5
Wilson A (Portsmouth, 1954) 1
Wilson D (Liverpool, 2011–12) 5
Wilson D (Rangers, 1961–65) 22
Wilson I (Leicester, Everton, 1987–8) 5
Wilson M (Celtic, 2011) 1

Wilson P (Celtic, 1975) 1
Wilson R (Arsenal, 1972) 2
Wood G (Everton, Arsenal, 1978–82) 4
Woodburn W (Rangers, 1947–52) 24
Wright K (Hibernian, 1992) 1
Wright S (Aberdeen, 1993) 2
Wright T (Sunderland, 1953) 3
Yeats R (Liverpool, 1965–66) 2
Yorston H (Aberdeen, 1955) 1
Young A (Hearts, Everton, 1960–66) 8
Young G (Rangers, 1947–57) 53

WALES

Younger T (Hibernian, Liverpool, 1955–58) 24
Aizlewood M (Charlton, Leeds, Bradford City,
Bristol City, Cardiff, 1986–95) 39
Allchurch I (Swansea City, Newcastle,
Cardiff, 1951–66) 68
Allchurch L (Swansea City, Sheffield Utd,
1955–64) 11
Allen B (Coventry, 1951) 2
Allen J (Swansea, Liverpool, Stoke, 2009–19) 51
Allen M (Watford, Norwich, Millwall,
Newcastle, 1986–94) 14
Ampadu E (Chelsea, 2018–19) 8

Baker C (Cardiff, 1958–62) 7
Baker W (Cardiff, 1948) 1
Bale G (Southampton, Tottenham,
Real Madrid, 2006–19) 77
Barnard D (Barnsley, Grimsby, 1998–2004) 24
Barnes W (Arsenal, 1948–55) 22
Bellamy C (Norwich, Coventry, Newcastle,
Blackburn, Liverpool, West Ham,
Manchester City, Liverpool,
Cardiff, 1998–2014) 78
Berry G (Wolves, Stoke, 1979–83) 5
Blackmore C (Manchester Utd,
Middlesbrough, 1985–97) 39
Blake D (Cardiff, Crystal Palace, 2011–13) 14
Blake N (Sheffield Utd, Bolton, Blackburn,
Wolves, 1994–2004) 29
Bodin B (Preston, 2018) 1
Bodin P (Swindon, Crystal Palace,
Swindon, 1990–95) 23
Bowen D (Arsenal, 1955–59) 19
Bowen J (Swansea City, Birmingham, 1994–97) 2
Bowen M (Tottenham, Norwich,
West Ham, 1986–97) 41
Boyle T (Crystal Palace, 1981) 2
Bradley M (Walsall, 2010) 1
Bradshaw T (Walsall, Barnsley, 2016–18) 3
Brooks D (Sheffield Utd,
Bournemouth, 2018–19) 12
Brown J (Gillingham, Blackburn, Aberdeen,
2006–12) 3
Browning M (Bristol Rov, Huddersfield, 1996–97) 5
Burgess R (Tottenham, 1947–54) 32
Burton A (Norwich, Newcastle, 1963–72) 9

Cartwright L (Coventry, Wrexham, 1974–79) 7

Charles Jeremy (Swansea City, QPR,
Oxford Utd, 1981–87) 19
Charles John (Leeds, Juventus, Cardiff, 1950–65) 38
Charles M (Swansea City, Arsenal,
Cardiff, 1955–63) 31
Chester J (Hull, WBA, Aston Villa, 2014–19) 35
Church S (Reading, Nottm Forest, Charlton,
MK Dons 2009–16) 38
Clarke R (Manchester City, 1949–56) 22
Coleman C (Crystal Palace, Blackburn,
Fulham, 1992–2002) 32
Collins D (Sunderland, Stoke, 2005–11) 12
Collins J (Cardiff, West Ham, Aston Villa,
West Ham, 2004–17) 50
Collison J (West Ham, 2008–14) 17
Cornforth J (Swansea City, 1995) 2
Cotterill D (Bristol City, Wigan,
Sheffield Utd, Swansea,
Doncaster, Birmingham, 2006–17) 24
Coyne D (Tranmere, Grimsby, Leicester,
Burnley, Tranmere, 1996–2008) 16
Crofts A (Gillingham, Brighton, Norwich,
Brighton, Scunthorpe, 2006–18) 29
Crossley M (Nottm Forest, Middlesbrough,
Fulham, 1997–2005) 8
Crowe V (Aston Villa, 1959–63) 16
Curtis A (Swansea City, Leeds,
Southampton, Cardiff, 1976–87) 35

Daniel R (Arsenal, Sunderland, 1951–57) 21
Davies A (Manchester Utd, Newcastle,
Swansea City, Bradford City, 1983–90) 13
Davies A (Barnsley, 2019) 1
Davies A (Yeovil 2006) 1
Davies B (Swansea, Tottenham, 2013–19) 46
Davies C (Charlton, 1972) 1
Davies C (Oxford, Verona, Oldham,
Barnsley, Bolton, 2006–14) 7
Davies D (Everton, Wrexham,
Swansea City 1975–83) 52
Davies ER (Newcastle, 1953–58) 6
Davies G (Fulham, Chelsea,
Manchester City, 1980–86) 16
Davies RT (Norwich, Southampton,
Portsmouth, 1964–74) 29
Davies RW (Bolton, Newcastle, Man Utd,
Man City, Blackpool, 1964–74) 34
Davies S (Manchester Utd, 1996) 1

Pring K (Rotherham, 1966–67) 3
Pritchard H (Bristol City, 1985) 1

Ramsey A (Arsenal, 2009–19) 58
Rankmore F (Peterborough, 1966) 1
Ratcliffe K (Everton, Cardiff, 1981–93) 59
Ready K (QPR, 1997–98) 5
Reece G (Sheffield Utd, Cardiff, 1966–75) 29
Reed W (Ipswich, 1955) 2
Rees A (Birmingham, 1984) 1
Rees J (Luton, 1992) 1
Rees R (Coventry, WBA, Nottm Forest,
1965–72) 39
Rees W (Cardiff, Tottenham, 1949–50) 4
Ribeiro D (Bristol City, 2010–11) 2
Richards A (Swansea, Fulham, Cardiff, 2012–19) 14
Richards, S (Cardiff, 1947) 1
Ricketts S (Swansea, Hull, Bolton,
Wolves, 2005–14) 52
Roberts A (QPR, 1993–97) 2
Roberts C (Swansea, 2018–19) 10
Roberts D (Oxford Utd, Hull, 1973–78) 17
Roberts G (Tranmere 2000–06) 9
Roberts I (Watford, Huddersfield, Leicester,
Norwich, 1990–2002) 15
Roberts J (Arsenal, Birmingham, 1971–76) 22
Roberts J (Bolton, 1949) 1
Roberts N (Wrexham, Wigan, 2000–04) 4
Roberts P (Portsmouth, 1974) 4
Roberts S (Wrexham, 2005) 1
Roberts T (Leeds, 2019) 6
Robinson C (Wolves, Portsmouth, Sunderland,
Norwich, Toronto 2000–08) 52
Robinson J (Charlton, 1996 2002) 30
Robson-Kanu H (Reading, WBA, 2010–18) 44
Rodrigues P (Cardiff, Leicester, City
Sheffield Wed, 1965–74) 40
Rogan A (Celtic, Sunderland, Millwall, 1988–97) 18
Rouse V (Crystal Palace, 1959) 1
Rowley T (Tranmere, 1959) 1
Rush I (Liverpool, Juventus, Liverpool,
1980–96) 73
Saunders D (Brighton, Oxford Utd, Derby, Liverpool,
Aston Villa, Galatasaray, Nottm Forest, Sheffield
Utd, Benfica, Bradford City, 1986 2001) 75
Savage R (Crewe, Leicester,
Birmingham, 1996–2005) 39
Sayer P (Cardiff, 1977–8) 7
Scrine F (Swansea, 1950) 2
Sear C (Manchester City, 1963) 1
Sherwood A (Cardiff, Newport, 1947–57) 41
Shortt W (Plymouth Argyle, 1947–53) 12
Showers D (Cardiff, 1975) 2
Sidlow C (Liverpool, 1947–50) 7
Slatter N (Bristol Rov, Oxford Utd, 1983–89) 22
Smallman D (Wrexham, Everton, 1974–6) 7
Smith M (Manchester City, 2018–19) 7
Southall N (Everton, 1982–97) 92
Speed G (Leeds, Everton, Newcastle,
1990–2004) 85
Sprake G (Leeds, Birmingham,
1964–75) 37

Stansfield F (Cardiff, 1949) 1
Stevenson B (Leeds, Birmingham,
1978–82) 15
Stevenson N (Swansea, 1982–83) 4
Stitfall R (Cardiff, 1953–57) 2
Stock B (Doncaster, 2010–11) 3
Sullivan D (Cardiff, 1953–60) 17
Symons K (Portsmouth, Manchester City,
Fulham, Crystal Palace, 1992–2004) 37

Tapscott D (Arsenal, Cardiff, 1954–59) 14
Taylor G (Crystal Palace, Sheffield Utd,
Burnley, Nottm Forest, 1996–2005) 15
Taylor J (Reading, 2015) 1
Taylor N (Wrexham, Swansea,
Aston Villa, 2010–19) 42
Thatcher B (Leicester, Manchester City,
2004–05) 7
Thomas D (Swansea, 1957–58) 2
Thomas G (Leicester, 2018–19) 3
Thomas M (Wrexham, Manchester Utd,
Everton, Brighton, Stoke, Chelsea, WBA,
1977–86) 51
Thomas M (Newcastle, 1987) 1
Thomas R (Swindon, Derby, Cardiff,
1967–78) 50
Thomas S (Fulham, 1948–49) 4
Toshack J (Cardiff, Liverpool,
Swansea, 1969 80) 40
Trollope P (Derby, Fulham,
Northampton, 1997–2003) 9
Tudur Jones O (Swansea, Norwich,
Hibernian, 2008–14) 7

Van den Hauwe P (Everton, 1985–89) 13
Vaughan D (Crewe, Real Sociedad, Blackpool,
Sunderland, Nottm Forest, 20013–16) 42
Vaughan N (Newport, Cardiff, 1983–85) 10
Vaulks W (Rotherham, 2019) 3
Vearncombe G (Cardiff, 1958–61) 2
Vernon R (Blackburn, Everton, Stoke,
1957–68) 32
Villars A (Cardiff, 1974) 3
Vokes S (Wolves, Burnley, Stoke, 2008–19) 62

Walley T (Watford, 1971) 1
Walsh I (Crystal Palace, 1980–82) 18
Ward D (Bristol Rov, Cardiff, 1959–62) 2
Ward D (Notts Co, Nottm Forest, 2000–04) 5
Ward D (Liverpool, Leicester, 2016–19) 6
Watkins M (Norwich, 2010) 2
Webster C (Manchester Utd, 1957–58) 4
Weston R (Arsenal, Cardiff, 2000–05) 7
Williams A (Stockport, Swansea,
Everton, 2008–19) 86
Williams A (Reading, Wolves, Reading,
1994–2003) 13
Williams A (Southampton, 1997 98) 2
Williams D (Norwich, 1986 87) 5
Williams G (Cardiff, 1951) 1
Williams G (Derby, Ipswich, 1988–96) 13
Williams G (West Ham, 2006) 2
Williams G (Fulham, 2014–16) 7

Williams GE (WBA, 1960–69) 26
Williams GG (Swansea, 1961–62) 5
Williams HJ (Swansea, 1965–72) 3
Williams HT (Newport, Leeds, 1949–50) 4
Williams J (Crystal Palace, 2013–18) 18
Williams S (WBA, Southampton, 1954–66) 43
Wilson H (Liverpool, 2014–19) 11
Wilson J (Bristol City, 2014) 1
Witcomb D (WBA, Sheffield Wed, 1947) 3

NORTHERN IRELAND

Aherne T (Belfast Celtic, Luton, 1947–50) 4
Anderson T (Manchester Utd, Swindon,
   Peterborough, 1973–79) 22
Armstrong G (Tottenham, Watford, Real
   Mallorca, WBA, 1977–86) 63

Baird C (Southampton, Fulham, Burnley,
   WBA, Derby, 2003–16) 79
Barr H (Linfield, Coventry, 1962–63) 3
Barton A (Preston, 2011) 1
Best G (Manchester Utd, Fulham, 1964–77) 37
Bingham W (Sunderland, Luton,
   Everton, Port Vale, 1951–64) 56
Black K (Luton, Nottm Forest, 1988–94) 30
Blair R (Oldham, 1975–76) 5
Blanchflower RD (Barnsley, Aston Villa,
   Tottenham, 1950–63) 56
Blanchflower J (Manchester Utd,
   1954–58) 12
Blayney A (Doncaster, Linfield, 2006–11) 5
Bowler G (Hull, 1950) 3
Boyce L (Werder Bremen, Ross Co,
   Burton, 2011–19) 19
Braithwaite R (Linfield, Middlesbrough,
   1962–65) 10
Braniff K (Portadown, 2010) 2
Brennan R (Luton, Birmingham, Fulham,
   1949–51) 5
Briggs W (Manchester Utd, Swansea,
   1962–65) 2
Brotherston N (Blackburn, 1980–85) 27
Bruce A (Hull, 2013–14) 2
Bruce W (Glentoran, 1961–67) 2
Brunt C (Sheffield Wed, WBA, 2005–18) 65
Bryan, M (Watford, 2010) 2

Camp L (Nottm Forest, 2011–13) 9
Campbell D (Nottm Forest, Charlton,
   1987–88) 10
Campbell J (Fulham, 1951) 2
Campbell R (Crusaders, 1963–65) 2
Campbell R (Bradford City, 1982) 2
Campbell W (Dundee, 1968–70) 6
Capaldi A (Plymouth Argyle, Cardiff, 2004–08) 22
Carey J (Manchester Utd, 1947–49) 7
Carroll R (Wigan, Manchester Utd, West Ham,
   Olympiacos, Notts Co, Linfield, 1997–2017) 45
Carson J (Ipswich, 2011–13) 4
Carson S (Coleraine, 2009) 1
Carson T (Motherwell, 2018–19) 5
Casey T (Newcastle, Portsmouth, 1955–59) 12
Casement C (Ipswich, 2009) 1

Woosnam P (Leyton Orient, West Ham,
   Aston Villa, 1959–63) 17
Woodburn B (Liverpool, 2018–19) 10

Yorath T (Leeds, Coventry, Tottenham,
   Vancouver Whitecaps 1970–81) 59
Young E (Wimbledon, Crystal Palace,
   Wolves, 1990–96) 21

Caskey W (Derby, Tulsa, Roughnecks,
   1979–82) 7
Cassidy T (Newcastle, Burnley, 1971–82) 24
Cathcart C (Blackpool, Watford, 2011–19) 45
Caughey M (Linfield, 1986) 2
Clarke C (Bournemouth, Southampton,
   QPR, Portsmouth, 1986–93) 38
Cleary J (Glentoran, 1982–85) 5
Clements D (Coventry, Sheffield Wed,
   Everton, New York Cosmos,
   1965–76) 48
Clingan S (Nottm Forest, Norwich, Coventry,
   Kilmarnock, 2006–15) 39
Clyde, M (Wolves, 2005) 3
Coates C (Crusaders, 2009–11) 6
Cochrane A (Coleraine, Burnley,
   Middlesbrough, Gillingham, 1976–84) 26
Cochrane D (Leeds, 1947–50) 10
Connell T (Coleraine, 1978) 1
Coote A (Norwich, 1999–2000) 6
Cowan J (Newcastle, 1970) 1
Coyle F (Coleraine, Nottm Forest,
   1956–58) 4
Coyle L (Derry City, 1989) 1
Coyle R (Sheffield Wed, 1973–74) 5
Craig D (Newcastle, 1967–75) 25
Craigan S (Partick, Motherwell, 2003–11) 54
Crossan E (Blackburn, 1950–55) 3
Crossan J (Sparta Rotterdam,
   Sunderland, Manchester City,
   Middlesbrough, 1960–68) 24
Cunningham W (St Mirren, Leicester,
   Dunfermline, 1951–62) 30
Cush W (Glenavon, Leeds, Portadown,
   1951–62) 26

Dallas S (Crusaders, Brentford, Leeds, 2011–19) 40
D'Arcy S (Chelsea, Brentford, 1952–53) 5
Davis S (Aston Villa, Fulham, Rangers,
   Southampton, 2005–19) 111
Davison A (Bolton, Bradford City,
   Grimsby, 1996–97) 3
Dennison R (Wolves, 1988–97) 18
Devine J (Glentoran, 1990) 1
Dickson D (Coleraine, 1970–73) 4
Dickson T (Linfield, 1957) 1
Dickson W (Chelsea, Arsenal, 1951–55) 12
Doherty L (Linfield, 1985–88) 2
*Doherty P (Derby, Huddersfield,
   Doncaster, 1946–50) 6
Doherty T (Bristol City, 2003–05) 9

Donaghy M (Luton, Manchester Utd,
Chelsea, 1980–94)   91
Donnelly L (Fulham, 2014)   1
Donnelly M (Crusaders, 2009)   1
Dougan D (Portsmouth, Blackburn, Aston
Villa, Leicester, Wolves, 1958–73)   43
Douglas J (Belfast Celtic, 1947)   1
Dowd H (Glenavon, 1974)   3
Dowie I (Luton, Southampton, Crystal Palace,
West Ham, QPR, 1990–2000)   59
Duff M (Cheltenham, Burnley, 2002–12)   24
Dunlop G (Linfield, 1985–90)   4

Eglington T (Everton, 1947–49)   6
Elder A (Burnley, Stoke, 1960–70)   40
Elliott S (Motherwell, Hull, 2001–08)   38
Evans C (Manchester Utd, Hull,
Blackburn, 2009–19)   53
Evans J (Manchester Utd, WBA,
Leicester, 2007–19)   80

Farrell P (Everton, 1947–49)   7
Feeney J (Linfield, Swansea, 1947–50)   2
Feeney W (Glentoran, 1976)   1
Feeney W (Bournemouth, Luton, Cardiff,
Oldham, Plymouth 2002–12)   46
Ferguson G (Linfield, 1999–2001)   5
Ferguson S (Newcastle, Millwall, 2009–19)   39
Ferguson W (Linfield, 1966–67)   2
Ferris R (Birmingham 1950–52)   3
Fettis A (Hull, Nottm Forest, Blackburn,
1992–99)   25
Finney T (Sunderland, Cambridge Utd, 1975–00)   14
Flanagan T (Burton, 2017)   1
Fleming G (Nottm Forest, Manchester City,
Barnsley, 1987–95)   31
Forde I (Ards, 1959–61)   4

Gallogly C (Huddersfield, 1951)   2
Garrett R (Stoke, Linfield, 2009–11)   5
Gaston R (Coleraine, 1969)   1
Gault M (Linfield, 2008)   1
Gillespie K (Manchester Utd, Newcastle,
Blackburn, Leicester, Sheffield Utd,
1995–2009)   86
Gorman J (Wolves, 2010–12)   9
Gorman W (Brentford, 1947–48)   4
Graham W (Doncaster, 1951–59)   14
Gray P (Luton, Sunderland, Nancy,
Burnley, Oxford Utd, 1993–2001)   26
Grigg W (Walsall, Brentford, Wigan, 2012–19)   13
Griffin D (St Johnstone, Dundee Utd,
Stockport, 1996–2004)   29
Grigg W (Walsall, Brentford, Wigan, 2012–17)   10

Hamill R (Glentoran, 1999)   1
Hamilton B (Linfield, Ipswich, Everton,
Millwall, Swindon, 1969–80)   50
Hamilton G (Glentoran, Portadown,
2003–08)   5
Hamilton W (QPR, Burnley, Oxford Utd, 1978–86)   41
Harkin J (Southport, Shrewsbury,1968–70)   5
Harvey M (Sunderland, 1961–71)   34

Hatton S (Linfield, 1963)   2
Hazard C (Celtic, 2018)   1
Healy D (Manchester Utd, Preston, Leeds,
Fulham, Sunderland, Rangers,
Bury, 2000–13)   95
Healy F (Coleraine, Glentoran, 1982–83)   4
Hegan D (WBA, Wolves, 1970–73)   7
Hill C (Sheffield Utd, Leicester,
Trelleborg, Northampton, 1990–99)   27
Hill J (Norwich, Everton, 1959–64)   7
Hinton E (Fulham, Millwall, 1947–51)   7
Hodson L (Watford, MK Dons,
Rangers, 2011–18)   24
Holmes S (Wrexham, 2002)   1
Horlock K (Swindon, Manchester City,
1995–2003)   32
Hughes A (Newcastle, Aston Villa, Fulham,
QPR, Brighton, Melbourne,
Hearts, 1997–2018)   112
Hughes J (Lincoln, 2006)   2
Hughes M (Oldham, 2006)   2
Hughes M (Manchester City, Strasbourg,
West Ham, Wimbledon, Crystal Palace,
1992–2005)   71
Hughes P (Bury, 1987)   3
Hughes W (Bolton, 1951)   1
Humphries W (Ards, Coventry, Swansea, 1962–65)   14
Hunter A (Blackburn, Ipswich, 1970–80)   53
Hunter B (Wrexham, Reading, 1995–2000)   15
Hunter V (Coleraine, 1962)   2

Ingham M (Sunderland, Wrexham, 2005–07)   3
Irvine R (Linfield, Stoke, 1962–5)   8
Irvine W (Burnley, Preston, Brighton,
1963–72)   23

Jackson T (Everton, Nottm Forest,
Manchester Utd, 1969–77)   35
Jamison J (Glentoran, 1976)   1
Jenkins I (Chester, Dundee Utd, 1997–2000)   6
Jennings P (Watford, Tottenham,
Arsenal, Tottenham, 1964–86)   119
Johnson D (Blackburn, Birmingham,
1999–2010)   56
Johnston W (Glenavon, Oldham, 1962–66)   2
Jones J (Glenavon, 1956–57)   3
Jones J (Kilmarnock, 2018–19)   9
Jones S (Crewe, Burnley, 2003–08)   29

Keane T (Swansea, 1949)   1
Kee P (Oxford Utd, Ards, 1990–95)   9
Keith R (Newcastle, 1958–62)   23
Kelly H (Fulham, Southampton, 1950–51)   4
Kelly P (Barnsley, 1950)   1
Kennedy P (Watford, Wigan, 1999–2004)   20
Kirk A (Hearts, Boston, Northampton,
Dunfermline, 2000–10)   11

Lafferty D (Burnley, 2012–16)   13
Lafferty K (Burnley, Rangers, Sion, Palermo,
Norwich, Hearts, Rangers, 2006–19)   73
Lavery S (Everton, 2018)   1
Lawrie J (Port Vale, 2009–10)   3

Lawther W (Sunderland, Blackburn, 1960–62) — 4
Lennon N (Crewe, Leicester, Celtic, 1994–2002) — 40
Lewis J (Norwich, 2018–19) — 10
Little A (Rangers, 2009–13) — 9
Lockhart N (Linfield, Coventry, Aston Villa, 1947–56) — 8
Lomas S (Manchester City, West Ham, 1994–2003) — 45
Lund M (Rochdale, 2017) — 3
Lutton D (Wolves, West Ham, 1970–1) — 6

Magennis J (Cardiff, Aberdeen, Kilmarnock, Charlton, Bolton, 2010–19) — 44
Magill E (Arsenal, Brighton, 1962–66) — 26
Magilton J (Oxford Utd, Southampton, Sheffield Wed, Ipswich, 1991–2002) — 52
Mannus A (Linfield, St Johnstone, 2004–17) — 9
Martin C (Glentoran, Leeds, Aston Villa, 1947–50) — 6
McAdams W (Manchester City, Bolton, Leeds, 1954–62) — 15
*McAlinden J (Portsmouth, Southend, 1947–49) — 2
McArdle R (Rochdale, Aberdeen, Bradford, 2010–14) — 7
McAuley G (Lincoln, Leicester, Ipswich, WBA, Rangers, 2010–19) — 80
McBride S (Glenavon, 1991–92) — 4
McCabe J (Leeds, 1949–54) — 6
McCann G (West Ham, Cheltenham, Barnsley, Scunthorpe, Peterborough, 2002–12) — 39
McCartan S (Accrington, Bradford, 2017–18) — 2
McCarthy J (Port Vale, Birmingham, 1996–2001) — 18
McCartney G (Sunderland, West Ham) Sunderland 2002–10) — 34
McCavana T (Coleraine, 1954–55) — 3
McCleary J (Cliftonville, 1955) — 1
McClelland J (Arsenal, Fulham, 1961–67) — 6
McClelland J (Mansfield, Rangers, Watford, Leeds, 1980–90) — 53
McCourt F (Manchester City, 1952–53) — 6
McCourt P (Rochdale, Celtic, Barnsley, Brighton, Luton, 2002–16) — 18
McCoy R (Coleraine, 1987) — 1
McCreery D (Manchester Utd, QPR, Tulsa, Newcastle, 1976–90) — 67
McCrory S (Southend, 1958) — 1
McCullough L (Doncaster, 2014–18) — 6
McCullough W (Arsenal, Millwall,1961–67) — 10
McCurdy C (Linfield, 1980) — 1
McDonald A (QPR, 1986–96) — 52
McElhinney G (Bolton, 1984–85) — 6
McEvilly L (Rochdale, 2002) — 1
McFaul W (Linfield, Newcastle, 1967–74) — 6
McGarry J (Cliftonville, 1951) — 3
McGaughey M (Linfield, 1985) — 1
McGibbon P (Manchester Utd, Wigan, 1995–2000) — 7
McGinn N (Derry, Celtic, Aberdeen, 2009–19) — 57
McGivern R (Manchester City, Hibernian, Port Vale, Shrewsbury, 2009–17) — 24
McGovern M (Ross Co, Hamilton, Norwich, 2010–18) — 28

McGrath C (Tottenham, Manchester Utd 1974–79) — 21
McIlroy J (Burnley, Stoke, 1952–66) — 55
McIlroy S (Manchester Utd, Stoke, Manchester City, 1972–87) — 88
McKay W (Inverness, Wigan, 2013–16) — 11
McKeag W (Glentoran, 1968) — 2
McKenna J (Huddersfield, 1950–52) — 7
McKenzie R (Airdrie, 1967) — 1
McKinney W (Falkirk, 1966) — 1
McKnight A (Celtic, West Ham, 1988–89) — 10
McLaughlin C (Preston, Fleetwood, Millwall, 2012–19) — 35
McLaughlin J (Shrewsbury, Swansea, 1962–66) — 12
McLaughlin R (Liverpool, Oldham, 2014–18) — 5
McLean B (Motherwell, 2006) — 1
McMahon G (Tottenham, Stoke, 1995–98) — 17
McMichael A (Newcastle, 1950–60) — 40
McMillan S (Manchester Utd, 1963) — 2
McMordie E (Middlesbrough, 1969–73) — 21
McMorran E (Belfast Celtic, Barnsley, Doncaster, 1947–57) — 15
McNair P (Manchester Utd, Sunderland, Middlesbrough) — 29
McNally B (Shrewsbury, 1987–88) — 5
McPake J (Coventry, 2012) — 1
McParland P (Aston Villa, Wolves, 1954–62) — 34
McQuoid J (Millwall, 2011–12) — 5
McVeigh P (Tottenham, Norwich, 1999–2005) — 20
Montgomery F (Coleraine, 1955) — 1
Moore C (Glentoran, 1949) — 1
Moreland V (Derby, 1979–80) — 6
Morgan S (Port Vale, Aston Villa, Brighton, Sparta Rotterdam, 1972–99) — 18
Morrow S (Arsenal, QPR, 1990–2000) — 39
Mulgrew J (Linfield, 2010) — 2
Mullan G (Glentoran, 1983) — 4
Mulryne P (Manchester Utd, Norwich, 1997–2005) — 27
Murdock C (Preston, Hibernian, Crewe, Rotherham, 2000–06) — 34

Napier R (Bolton, 1966) — 1
Neill T (Arsenal, Hull, 1961–73) — 59
Nelson S (Arsenal, Brighton, 1970–82) — 51
Nicholl C (Aston Villa, Southampton, Grimsby, 1975–83) — 51
Nicholl J (Manchester Utd, Toronto, Sunderland, Rangers, WBA, 1976–86) — 73
Nicholson J (Manchester Utd, Huddersfield, 1961–72) — 41
Nolan I (Sheffield Wed, Bradford City, Wigan, 1997–2002) — 18
Norwood O (Manchester Utd, Huddersfield, Reading, Brighton, Sheffield Utd, 2011–19) — 57

O'Boyle G (Dunfermline, St Johnstone, 1994–99) — 13
O'Connor M (Crewe, Scunthorpe, Rotherham, 2008–14) — 11
O'Doherty A (Coleraine, 1970) — 2

O'Driscoll J (Swansea, 1949) 3
O'Kane W (Nottm Forest, 1970–75) 20
O'Neill C (Motherwell, 1989–91) 3
O'Neill J (Sunderland, 1962) 1
O'Neill J (Leicester, 1980–86) 39
O'Neill M (Distillery, Nottm Forest,
 Norwich, Manchester City,
 Notts Co, 1972–85) 64
O'Neill M (Newcastle, Dundee Utd,
 Hibernian, Coventry, 1989–97) 31
Owens J (Crusaders, 2011) 1

Parke J (Linfield, Hibernian, Sunderland,
 1964–68) 14
Paterson M (Scunthorpe, Burnley,
 Huddersfield, 2008–14) 22
Paton P (Dundee Utd, St Johnstone, 2014–17) 4
Patterson D (Crystal Palace, Luton,
 Dundee Utd, 1994–99) 17
Patterson R (Coleraine, Plymouth, 2010–11) 5
Peacock R (Celtic, Coleraine, 1952–62) 31
Peacock-Farrell B (Leeds, 2018–19) 9
Penney S (Brighton, 1985–89) 17
Platt J (Middlesbrough, Ballymena,
 Coleraine, 1976–86) 23

Quinn J (Blackburn, Swindon, Leicester,
 Bradford City, West Ham, Bournemouth,
 Reading, 1985–96) 46
Quinn SJ (Blackpool, WBA, Willem 11,
 Sheffield Wed, Peterborough,
 Northampton, 1996–2007) 50

Rafferty P (Linfield, 1979) 1
Ramsey P (Leicester, 1984–89) 14
Reeves B (MK Dons, 2015) 2
Rice P (Arsenal, 1969–80) 49
Robinson S (Bournemouth, Luton, 1997–2008) 7
Rogan A (Celtic, Sunderland, Millwall,
 1988–97) 18
Ross W (Newcastle, 1969) 1
Rowland K (West Ham, QPR, 1994–99) 19
Russell A (Linfield, 1947) 1
Ryan R (WBA, 1950) 1

Sanchez L (Wimbledon, 1987–89) 3
Saville G (Millwall, Middlesbrough, 2018–19) 15
Scott J (Grimsby, 1958) 2
Scott P (Everton, York, Aldershot, 1976–79) 10
Sharkey P (Ipswich, 1976) 1
Shields J (Southampton, 1957) 1
Shiels D (Hibernian, Doncaster, Kilmarnock,
 Rangers, 2006–13) 14
Simpson W (Rangers, 1951–59) 12
Sloan D (Oxford Utd, 1969–71) 2
Sloan J (Arsenal, 1947) 1
Sloan T (Manchester Utd, 1979) 3
Smith A (Glentoran, Preston, 2003–05) 18
Smith M (Peterborough, Hearts, 2016–19) 6
Smyth P (QPR, 2018) 2
Smyth S (Wolves, Stoke, 1948–52) 9
Smyth W (Distillery, 1949–54) 4
Sonner D (Ipswich, Sheffield Wed,

Birmingham, Nottm Forest,
 Peterborough, 1997–2005) 13
Spence D (Bury, Blackpool, Southend, 1975–82) 29
Sproule I (Hibernian, 2006–08) 11
*Stevenson A (Everton, 1947–48) 3
Steele J (New York Bulls, 2014) 3
Stewart A (Glentoran, Derby, 1967–69) 7
Stewart D (Hull, 1978) 1
Stewart I (QPR, Newcastle, 1982–87) 31
Stewart T (Linfield, 1961) 1

Taggart G (Barnsley, Bolton, Leicester,
 1990–2003) 51
Taylor M (Fulham, Birmingham, 1999–2012) 88
Thompson A (Watford, 2011) 2
Thompson J (Rangers, 2018) 2
Thompson P (Linfield, 2006–08) 8
Todd S (Burnley, Sheffield Wed, 1966–71) 11
Toner C (Leyton Orient, 2003) 2
Trainor D (Crusaders, 1967) 1
Tuffey J (Partick, Inverness, 2009–11) 8
Tully C (Celtic, 1949–59) 10

Uprichard W (Swindon, Portsmouth, 1952–59) 18

Vassell K (Rotherham, 2019) 2
Vernon J (Belfast Celtic, WBA, 1947–52) 17

Walker J (Doncaster, 1955) 1
Walsh D (WDA, 1947–50) 9
Walsh W (Manchester City, 1948–49) 5
Ward J (Derby, Nottm Forest, 2012–19) 35
Washington C (QPR, Sheffield Utd, 2016–19) 20
Watson P (Distillery, 1971) 1
Webb S (Ross Co, 2006–07) 4
Welsh E (Carlisle, 1966–67) 4
Whiteside N (Manchester Utd, Everton, 1982–90) 38
Whyte G (Oxford, 2019) 5
Whitley Jeff (Manchester City, Sunderland,
 Cardiff, 1997–2006) 20
Whitley Jim (Manchester City, 1998–2000) 3
Williams M (Chesterfield, Watford,
 Wimbledon, Stoke, Wimbledon,
 MK Dons, 1999–2005) 36
Williams M (Chesterfield, Watford
 Wimbledon, Stoke, Wimbledon
 MK Dons 1999–2005) 36
Williams P (WBA, 1991) 1
Wilson D (Brighton, Luton,
 Sheffield Wed, 1987–92) 24
Wilson K (Ipswich, Chelsea, Notts Co,
 Walsall, 1987–95) 42
Wilson S (Glenavon, Falkirk, Dundee,
 1962–68) 12
Winchester C (Oldham, 2011) 1
Wood T (Walsall, 1996) 1
Worthington N (Sheffield Wed, Leeds,
 Stoke, 1984–97) 66
Wright T (Newcastle, Nottm Forest, Reading,
 Manchester City, 1989–2000) 31

REPUBLIC OF IRELAND

Aherne T (Belfast Celtic, Luton, 1946–54)	16
Aldridge J (Oxford Utd, Liverpool, Real Sociedad, Tranmere, 1986–97)	69
Ambrose P (Shamrock R, 1955–64)	5
Anderson J (Preston, Newcastle, 1980–89)	16
Andrews K (Blackburn, WBA, 2009–13)	35
Arter H (Bournemouth, 2015–19)	16
Babb P (Coventry, Liverpool, Sunderland, 1994–2003)	35
Bailham E (Shamrock R, 1964)	1
Barber E (Bohemians, Birmingham, 1966)	2
Barrett G (Arsenal, Coventry, 2003–05)	6
Beglin J (Liverpool, 1984–87)	15
Bennett A (Reading, 2007)	2
Best L (Coventry, 2009–10)	7
Braddish S (Dundalk, 1978)	2
Branagan K (Bolton, 1997)	1
Bonner P (Celtic, 1981–96)	80
Boyle A (Preston, 2017)	1
Brady L (Arsenal, Juventus, Sampdoria, Inter-Milan, Ascoli, West Ham, 1975–90)	72
Brady R (QPR, 1964)	6
Brady R (Manchester Utd, Hull, Burnley, 2013–19)	45
Breen G (Birmingham, Coventry, West Ham, Sunderland, 1996–2006)	63
*Breen T (Shamrock R, 1947)	3
Brennan F (Drumcondra, 1965)	1
Brennan S (Manchester Utd, Waterford, 1965–71)	19
Browne A (Preston, 2017–18)	3
Browne W (Bohemians, 1964)	3
Bruce A (Ipswich, 2007–09)	2
Buckley L (Shamrock R, Waregem, 1984–85)	2
Burke F (Cork Ath, 1952)	1
Burke G (Shamrock Rov, Preston 2018–19)	3
Butler P (Sunderland, 2000)	1
Butler T (Sunderland, 2003)	2
Byrne A (Southampton, 1970–74)	14
Byrne J (Shelbourne, 2004–06)	2
Byrne J (QPR, Le Havre, Brighton, Sunderland, Millwall, 1985–93)	23
Byrne P (Shamrock R, 1984–86)	8
Campbell A (Santander, 1985)	3
Campbell N (St Patrick's Ath, Fortuna Cologne, 1971–77)	11
Cantwell N (West Ham, Manchester Utd, 1954–67)	36
Carey B (Manchester Utd, Leicester, 1992–94)	3
*Carey J (Manchester Utd, 1946–53)	21
Carolan J (Manchester Utd, 1960)	2
Carr S (Tottenham, Newcastle, 1999–2008)	43
Carroll B (Shelbourne, 1949–50)	2
Carroll T (Ipswich, 1968–73)	17
Carsley L (Derby, Blackburn, Coventry, Everton, 1997–2008)	39

Cascarino A (Gillingham, Millwall, Aston Villa, Chelsea, Marseille, Nancy, 1986–2000)	88
Chandler J (Leeds, 1980)	2
Christie C (Derby, Middlesbrough, Fulham, 2015–19)	22
Clark C (Aston Villa, Newcastle, 2011–19)	32
Clarke C (Stoke, 2004)	2
Clarke J (Drogheda, 1978)	1
Clarke K (Drumcondra, 1948)	2
Clarke M (Shamrock R, 1950)	1
Clinton T (Everton, 1951–54)	3
Coad P (Shamrock R, 1947–52)	11
Coffey T (Drumcondra, 1950)	1
Colfer M (Shelbourne, 1950–51)	2
Coleman S (Everton 2011–19)	53
Colgan N (Hibernian, 2002–07)	9
Conmy O (Peterborough, 1965–70)	5
Connolly D (Watford, Feyenoord, Excelsior Feyenoord, Wimbledon, West Ham, Wigan, 1996–2006)	41
Conroy G (Stoke, 1970–77)	27
Conway J (Fulham, Manchester City, 1967–77)	20
Corr P (Everton, 1949–50)	4
Courtney E (Cork Utd, 1946)	1
Cox S (WBA, Nottm Forest, 2011–14)	30
Coyle O (Bolton, 1994)	1
Coyne T (Celtic, Tranmere, Motherwell, 1992–98)	22
Crowe G (Bohemians, 2003)	2
Cummins G (Luton, 1954–61)	19
Cuneen T (Limerick, 1951)	1
Cunningham G (Man City, Bristol City, 2010–13)	4
Cunningham K (Wimbledon, Birmingham, 1996–2006)	72
Curtis D (Shelbourne, Bristol City, Ipswich, Exeter, 1956–63)	17
Curtis R (Portsmouth, 2019)	2
Cusack S (Limerick, 1953)	1
Daish L (Cambridge Utd, Coventry, 1992–96)	5
Daly G (Manchester Utd, Derby, Coventry, Birmingham, Shrewsbury, 1973–87)	48
Daly M (Wolves, 1978)	2
Daly P (Shamrock R, 1950)	1
Deacy E (Aston Villa, 1982)	4
Delaney D (QPR, Ipswich, Crystal Palace, 2008–14)	9
Delap R (Derby, Southampton, 1998–2004)	11
De Mange K (Liverpool, Hull, 1987–89)	2
Dempsey J (Fulham, Chelsea, 1967–72)	19
Dennehy J (Cork Hibernian, Nottm Forest, Walsall, 1972–77)	11
Desmond P (Middlesbrough, 1950)	4
Devine J (Arsenal, 1980–85)	13
Doherty G (Tottenham, Norwich, 2000–06)	34
Doherty M (Wolves, 2018–19)	7
Donovan D (Everton, 1955–57)	5

Donovan T (Aston Villa, 1980) 2
Douglas J (Blackburn, Leeds, 2004–08) 8
Doyle C (Shelbourne, 1959) 1
Doyle C (Birmingham, Bradford, 2007–18) 4
Doyle K (Reading Wolves, Colorado, 2006–17) 63
Doyle M (Coventry, 2004) 1
Duff D (Blackburn, Chelsea, Newcastle,
    Fulham, 1998–2012) 100
Duffy B (Shamrock R, 1950) 1
Duffy S (Everton, Blackburn, Brighton, 2014–19) 29
Dunne A (Manchester Utd, Bolton,1962–76) 33
Dunne J (Fulham, 1971) 1
Dunne P (Manchester Utd, 1965–67) 5
Dunne R (Everton, Manchester City, Aston Villa,
    2000–14) 80
Dunne S (Luton, 1953–60) 15
Dunne T (St Patrick's, 1956–57) 3
Dunning P (Shelbourne, 1971) 2
Dunphy E (York, Millwall, 1966–71) 23
Dwyer N (West Ham, Swansea, 1960–65) 14

Eccles P (Shamrock R, 1986) 1
Egan J (Brentford, Sheffield Utd, 2017–19) 4
Eglington T (Shamrock R, Everton, 1946–56) 24
Elliot R (Newcastle, 2014–16) 4
Elliott S (Sunderland, 2005–07) 9
Evans M (Southampton, 1997) 1

Fagan E (Shamrock R, 1973) 1
Fagan F (Manchester City, Derby, 1955–61) 8
Fahey K (Birmingham, 2010–13) 16
Fairclough M (Dundalk, 1982) 2
Fallon S (Celtic, 1951–55) 8
Farrell P (Shamrock R, Everton, 1946–57) 28
Farrolly G (Aston Villa, Everton, Bolton,
    1996–2000) 6
Finnan S (Fulham, Liverpool,
    Espanyol 2000–09) 53
Finucane A (Limerick, 1967–72) 11
Fitzgerald F (Waterford, 1955–6) 2
Fitzgerald P (Leeds, 1961–2) 5
Fitzpatrick K (Limerick, 1970) 1
Fitzsimons A (Middlesbrough, Lincoln,
    1950 59) 26
Fleming C (Middlesbrough, 1996–8) 10
Fogarty A (Sunderland, Hartlepool Utd,
    1960–64) 11
Folan C (Hull, 2009–10) 7
Foley D (Watford, 2000–01) 6
Foley K (Wolves, 2009–11) 8
Foley T (Northampton, 1964–67) 9
    Fullam J (Preston, Shamrock R,
    1961–70) 11
Forde D (Millwall, 2011–16) 24
Fullam J (Preston, Shamrock, 1961–70) 11

Gallagher C (Celtic, 1967) 2
Gallagher M (Hibernian, 1954) 1
Galvin A (Tottenham, Sheffield Wed,
    Swindon, 1983–90) 29
Gamble J (Cork City, 2007) 2
Gannon E (Notts Co, Sheffield Wed,
    Shelbourne, 1949–55) 14

Gannon M (Shelbourne, 1972) 1
Gavin J (Norwich, Tottenham,
    Norwich, 1950 57) 7
Gibbons A (St Patrick's Ath, 1952–56) 4
Gibson D (Manchester Utd, Everton, 2008–16) 27
Gilbert R (Shamrock R, 1966) 1
Giles C (Doncaster, 1951) 1
Giles J (Manchester Utd, Leeds,
    WBA, Shamrock R, 1960–79) 59
Given S (Blackburn, Newcastle, Manchester City,
    Aston Villa, Stoke, 1996–2016) 134
Givens D (Manchester Utd, Luton, QPR,
    Birmingham, Neuchatel, 1969–82) 56
Gleeson S (Wolves, Birmingham, 2007–17) 4
Glynn D (Drumcondra, 1952–55) 2
Godwin T (Shamrock R, Leicester,
    Bournemouth, 1949–58) 13
Goodman J (Wimbledon, 1997) 4
Goodwin J (Stockport, 2003) 1
*Gorman W (Brentford, 1947) 1
Grealish A (Orient Luton, Brighton, WBA,
    1976 86) 45
Green P (Derby, Leeds, 2010–14) 22
Gregg E (Bohemians, 1978–80) 8
Grimes A (Manchester Utd, Coventry,
    Luton, 1978–88) 18

Hale A (Aston Villa, Doncaster,
    Waterford, 1962–72) 14
Hamilton T (Shamrock R, 1959) 2
Hand E (Portsmouth, 1969–76) 20
Harte I (Leeds, Levante, 1996–2007) 64
Hartnett J (Middlesbrough, 1949 54) 2
Haverty J (Arsenal, Blackburn, Millwall,
    Celtic, Bristol Rov, Shelbourne,
    1956–67) 32
Hayes A (Southampton, 1979) 1
Hayes J (Aberdeen, 2016 17) 4
*Hayes W (Huddersfield, 1947) 2
Hayes W (Limerick, 1949) 1
Healey R (Cardiff, 1977–80) 2
Healy C (Celtic, Sunderland, 2002 04) 13
Heighway S (Liverpool, Minnesota,
    1971–82) 34
Henderson B (Drumcondra, 1948) 2
Henderson W (Brighton, Preston, 2006–08) 6
Hendrick J (Derby, Burnley, 2013–19) 49
Hennessy J (Shelbourne, St Patrick's Ath,
    1956–69) 5
Herrick J (Cork Hibernian, Shamrock R,
    1972–73) 3
Higgins J (Birmingham, 1951) 1
Hogan S (Aston Villa, 2018–19) 5
Holland M (Ipswich, Charlton, 2000–06) 49
Holmes J (Coventry, Tottenham,
    Vancouver W'caps, 1971–81) 30
Hoolahan W (Blackpool, Norwich, 2008–18) 43
Horgan D (Preston, Hibernian, 2017–19) 6
Houghton R (Oxford Utd, Liverpool,
    Aston Villa, Crystal Palace, Reading,
    1986–97) 73
Hourihane C (Aston Villa, 2017–19) 11

Moore A (Middlesbrough, 1996–97) — 8

Moran K (Manchester Utd, Sporting Gijon, Blackburn, 1980–94) — 71

Moroney T (West Ham, 1948–54) — 12

Morris C (Celtic, Middlesbrough, 1988–93) — 35

Morrison C (Crystal Palace, Birmingham, Crystal Palace, 2002–07) — 36

Moulson G (Lincoln, 1948–49) — 3

Mucklan C (Drogheda, 1978) — 1

Mulligan P (Shamrock R, Chelsea, Crystal Palace, WBA, Shamrock R, 1969–80) — 50

Munroe L (Shamrock R, 1954) — 1

Murphy A (Clyde, 1956) — 1

Murphy B (Bohemians, 1986) — 1

Murphy D (Sunderland, Ipswich, Newcastle, Nottm Forest, 2007–18) — 33

Murphy J (Crystal Palace, 1980) — 3

Murphy J (Scunthorpe, 2009–10) — 2

Murphy J (WBA, 2004) — 1

Murphy P (Carlisle, 2007) — 1

Murray I (Dundalk, 1950) — 1

Newman W (Shelbourne, 1969) — 1

Nolan E (Preston, 2009–10) — 3

Nolan R (Shamrock R, 1957–63) — 10

Obafemi M (Southampton, 2019) — 1

O'Brien Alan (Newcastle, 2007) — 5

O'Brien Andy (Newcastle, Portsmouth, 2001–07) — 26

O'Brien F (Philadelphia Forest, 1980) — 3

O'Brien J (Bolton, West Ham, 2006–13) — 5

O'Brien L (Shamrock R, Manchester Utd, Newcastle, Tranmere, 1986–97) — 16

O'Brien L (Notts Co, 1976–77) — 5

O'Byrne L (Shamrock R, 1949) — 1

O'Callaghan B (Stoke, 1979–82) — 6

O'Callaghan K (Ipswich, Portsmouth, 1981–87) — 21

O'Cearuill J (Arsenal, 2007) — 2

O'Connell A (Dundalk, Bohemians, 1967–71) — 2

O'Connor T (Shamrock R, 1950) — 4

O'Connor T (Fulham, Dundalk, Bohemians, 1968–73) — 7

O'Dowda C (Oxford, Bristol City, 2016–19) — 15

O'Dea D (Celtic, Toronto, Metalurh Donetsk, 2010–14) — 20

O'Driscoll J (Swansea, 1949) — 3

O'Driscoll S (Fulham, 1982) — 3

O'Farrell F (West Ham, Preston, 1952–59) — 9

*O'Flanagan Dr K (Arsenal, 1947) — 3

O'Flanagan M (Bohemians, 1947) — 1

O'Halloran S (Aston Villa, 2007) — 2

O'Hanlon K (Rotherham, 1988) — 1

O'Kane E (Bournemouth, Leeds, 2016–17) — 7

O'Keefe E (Everton, Port Vale, 1981–85) — 5

O'Leary D (Arsenal, 1977–93) — 68

O'Leary P (Shamrock R, 1980–1) — 7

O'Neill F (Shamrock R, 1962–72) — 20

O'Neill J (Everton, 1952–59) — 17

O'Neill J (Preston, 1961) — 1

O'Neill K (Norwich, Middlesbrough,1996–2000) — 13

O'Regan K (Brighton, 1984–85) — 4

O'Reilly J (Cork Utd, 1946) — 2

O'Shea J (Manchester Utd, Sunderland, 2002–18) — 118

Pearce A (Reading, Derby, 2013–17) — 9

Peyton G (Fulham, Bournemouth, Everton, 1977–92) — 33

Peyton N (Shamrock R, Leeds, 1957–61) — 6

Phelan T (Wimbledon, Manchester City, Chelsea, Everton, Fulham, 1992–2000) — 42

Pilkington A (Norwich, Cardiff, 2014–16) — 9

Potter D (Wolves, 2007–08) — 5

Quinn A (Sheffield Wed, Sheffield Utd, 2003–07) — 7

Quinn B (Coventry, 2000) — 4

Quinn N (Arsenal, Manchester City, Sunderland, 1986–2002) — 92

Quinn S (Hull, Reading, 2013–17) — 18

Randolph D (Motherwell, West Ham, Middlesbrough, 2013–19) — 38

Reid A (Nottm Forest, Tottenham, Charlton, Sunderland, Nottm Forest, 2004–14) — 29

Reid S (Millwall, Blackburn, 2002–09) — 23

Rice D (West Ham, 2018) — 3

Richardson D (Shamrock R, Gillingham, 1972–80) — 3

Ringstead A (Sheffield Utd, 1951–59) — 20

Robinson M (Brighton, Liverpool, QPR, 1981–86) — 24

Roche P (Shelbourne, Manchester Utd, 1972–76) — 8

Rogers E (Blackburn, Charlton, 1968–73) — 19

Rowlands M (QPR, 2004–10) — 5

Ryan G (Derby, Brighton, 1978–85) — 18

Ryan R (WBA, Derby, 1950–56) — 16

Sadlier R (Millwall, 2002) — 1

Sammon C (Derby, 2013–14) — 9

Savage D (Millwall, 1996) — 5

Saward P (Millwall, Aston Villa, Huddersfield, 1954–63) — 18

Scannell T (Southend, 1954) — 1

Scully P (Arsenal, 1989) — 1

Sheedy K (Everton, Newcastle, 1984–93) — 46

Sheridan C (Celtic, CSKA Sofia, 2010–11) — 3

Sheridan J (Leeds, Sheffield Wed, 1988–96) — 34

Slaven B (Middlesbrough, 1990–93) — 7

Sloan P (Arsenal, 1946) — 2

Smyth M (Shamrock R, 1969) — 1

St Ledger S (Preston, Leicester, 2009–14) — 37

Stapleton F (Arsenal, Manchester Utd, Ajax, Derby, Le Havre, Blackburn, 1977–90) — 71

Staunton S (Liverpool, Aston Villa, Liverpool, Crystal Palace, Aston Villa, 1989–2002) — 102

Stevens E (Sheffield Utd, 2018–19) — 10

*Stevenson A (Everton, 1947–49)	6	Walsh D (WBA, Aston Villa, 1946–54)	20
Stokes A (Sunderland, Celtic, 2007–15)	9	Walsh J (Limerick, 1982)	1
Strahan F (Shelbourne, 1964–65)	5	Walsh M (Blackpool, Everton, QPR,	
Swan M (Drumcondra, 1960)	1	Porto, 1976–85)	21
Synnott N (Shamrock R, 1978–79)	1	Walsh M (Everton, Norwich, 1982–83)	4
Taylor T (Waterford, 1959)	1	Walsh W (Manchester City, 1947–50)	9
Thomas P (Waterford, 1974)	1	Walters J (Stoke, Burnley, 2011–19)	54
Thompson J (Nottm Forest, 2004)	1	Ward S (Wolves, Burnley, 2011–19)	50
Townsend A (Norwich, Chelsea, Aston Villa,		Waters J (Grimsby, 1977–80)	2
Middlesbrough, 1989–97)	70	Westwood K (Coventry, Sunderland,	
Iraynor T (Southampton, 1954–64)	8	Sheffield Wed, 2009–17)	21
Treacy K (Preston, Burnley 2011–12)	6	Whelan G (Stoke, Aston Villa, 2009–19)	87
Treacy R (WBA, Charlton, Swindon,		Whelan R (St Patrick's Ath, 1964)	2
Preston, Shamrock R, 1966–80)	42	Whelan R (Liverpool, Southend, 1981–95)	53
Tuohy L (Shamrock R, Newcastle,		Whelan L (Manchester Utd, 1956–57)	4
Shamrock R, 1956–65)	8	Whittaker R (Chelsea, 1959)	1
Turner A (Celtic, 1963)	2	Williams D (Blackburn, 2018)	1
		Williams S (Millwall, 2018–19)	3
Vernon J (Belfast Celtic, 1946)	2	Wilson M (Stoke, Bournemouth, 2011–17)	25
Waddock G (QPR, Millwall, 1980–90)	21		

INTERNATIONAL GOALSCORERS 1946–2019

(start of season 2019–20)

ENGLAND

Rooney	53	Clarke A	10	Wright-Phillips S	6
Charlton R	49	Cole J	10	Adams	5
Lineker	48	Flowers R	10	Atyeo	5
Greaves	44	Gascoigne	10	Baily	5
Owen	40	Lee F	10	Brooking	5
Finney	30	Milburn	10	Cahill	5
Lofthouse	30	Wilshaw	10	Carter	5
Shearer	30	Beardsley	9	Edwards	5
Lampard Frank jnr	29	Bell	9	Ferdinand L	5
Platt	27	Bentley	9	Hitchens	5
Robson B	26	Hateley	9	Johnson D	5
Hurst	24	Wright I	9	Latchford	5
Mortensen	23	Ball	8	Neal	5
Crouch	22	Broadis	8	Pearce	5
Kane	22	Byrne J	8	Pearson Stan	5
Channon	21	Hoddle	8	Pearson Stuart	5
Gerrard	21	Kevan	8	Pickering F	5
Keegan	21	Sterling	8	Barkley	4
Defoe	20	Sturridge	8	Barmby	4
Peters	20	Walcott	8	Barnes P	4
Haynes	18	Anderton	7	Bent	4
Hunt R	18	Connelly	7	Bull	4
Beckham	17	Coppell	7	Dixon K	4
Lawton	16	Fowler	7	Hassall	4
Taylor T	16	Heskey	7	Lingard	4
Woodcock	16	Paine	7	Revie	4
Welbeck	16	Rashford	7	Robson R	4
Scholes	14	Vardy	7	Steven	4
Chivers	13	Young A	7	Watson Dave (Sunderland)	4
Mariner	13	Charlton J	6	Alli	3
Smith R	13	Macdonald	6	Baker	3
Francis T	12	Mullen	6	Blissett	3
Barnes J	11	Oxlade-Chamberlain	6	Butcher	3
Douglas	11	Rowley	6	Currie	3
Mannion	11	Terry	6	Dier	3
Sheringham	11	Vassell	6	Elliott	3
		Waddle	6	Francis G	3

300

Grainger	3	
Jagielka	3	
Kennedy R	3	
Lallana	3	
Lambert	3	
McDermott	3	
McManaman	3	
Matthews S	3	
Merson	3	
Morris	3	
O'Grady	3	
Peacock	3	
Ramsey	3	
Sewell	3	
Townsend	3	
Webb	3	
Wilkins	3	
Wright W	3	
Allen R	2	
Anderson	2	
Barry	2	
Bradley	2	
Broadbent	2	
Brooks	2	
Carroll	2	
Cowans	2	
Eastham	2	
Ferdinand R	2	
Froggatt J	2	
Froggatt R	2	
Haines	2	
Hancocks	2	
Hunter	2	
Ince	2	
Johnson A	2	
Keown	2	
Lee R	2	
Lee S	2	
Moore	2	
Perry	2	
Pointer	2	
Richardson	2	
Royle	2	
Smith A (1989–92)	2	
Southgate	2	
Stone	2	
Stones	2	
Taylor P	2	
Tueart	2	
Upson	2	
Wignall	2	
Wilshere	2	
Worthington	2	
A'Court	1	
Alexander-Arnold	1	
Astall	1	
Baines	1	
Beattie K	1	
Bertrand	1	

Bowles	1
Bradford	1
Bridge	1
Bridges	1
Brown	1
Campbell	1
Caulker	1
Chamberlain	1
Cole Andy	1
Crawford	1
Dixon I	1
Ehiogu	1
Goddard	1
Hirst	1
Hughes E	1
Jeffers	1
Jenas	1
Johnson G	1
Kay	1
Keane	1
Kidd	1
King	1
Langton	1
Lawler	1
Lee J	1
Lescott	1
Le Saux	1
Mabbutt	1
Maguire	1
Marsh	1
Medley	1
Melia	1
Milner	1
Mullery	1
Murphy	1
Nicholls	1
Nicholson	1
Nugent	1
Palmer	1
Parry	1
Redknapp	1
Richards	1
Sansom	1
Shackleton	1
Smalling	1
Smith A (2001–5)	1
Stiles	1
Summerbee	1
Tambling	1
Thompson Phil	1
Trippier	1
Viollet	1
Wallace	1
Walsh	1
Weller	1
Wilson	1
Wise	1
Withe	1
Wright M	1

SCOTLAND

Dalglish	30
Law	30
Reilly	22
McCoist	19
Miller K	18
McFadden	15
Johnston M	14
Collins J	12
Gilzean	12
Steel	12
Jordan	11
Collins R	10
Fletcher S	10
Johnstone R	10
Wilson D	10
Gallacher	9
McStay	9
Mudie	9
Naismith	9
St John	9
Stein	9
Brand	8
Gemmill A	8
Leggat	8
Robertson J (1978–84)	8
Boyd K	7
Dodds	7
Durie	7
Gray A	7
Maloney	7
Snodgrass	7
Wark	7
Booth	6
Brown A	6
Cooper	6
Dailly	6
Gough	6
Hutchison D	6
Liddell	6
Murdoch	6
Rioch	6
Waddell	6
Fletcher D	5
Forrest	5
Hartford	5
Henderson W	5
Macari	5
Masson	5
McAllister G	5
McQueen	5
Nevin	5
Nicholas	5
O'Hare	5
Scott A	5
Strachan	5
Young A	5
Archibald	4
Berra	4

Brown S	4	Jess	2	Johnston L	1
Caldow	4	Johnston A	2	Kyle	1

Brown S 4
Caldow 4
Crawford 4
Griffiths 4
Hamilton 4
Jackson D 4
Johnstone J 4
Lorimer 4
Mackay D 4
Mason 4
McArthur 4
McGinlay 4
McKinlay W 4
McLaren 4
O'Connor 4
Smith G 4
Souness 4
Anya 3
Baxter 3
Bremner W 3
Burley C 3
Chalmers 3
Ferguson B 3
Gibson 3
Graham G 3
Gray E 3
Greig 3
Hendry 3
Herd D 3
Lennox 3
MacDougall 3
McCann 3
McInally A 3
McNeill 3
McPhail 3
Martin C 3
Morris 3
Morrison 3
Mulgrew 3
Rhodes 3
Ritchie M 3
Robertson J (1991–5) 3
Sturrock 3
Thompson 3
White 3
Baird S 2
Bauld 2
Burke C 2
Caldwell G 2
Cameron 2
Commons 2
Flavell 2
Fleming 2
Graham A 2
Harper 2
Hewie 2
Holton 2
Hopkin 2
Houliston 2

Jess 2
Johnston A 2
Johnstone D 2
Mackie 2
McClair 2
McCormack 2
McGhee 2
McMillan 2
McManus 2
Ormond 2
Pettigrew 2
Ring 2
Robertson A (1955) 2
Robertson A (2014–16) 2
Shearer D 2
Aitken R 1
Armstrong 1
Bannon 1
Beattie 1
Bett 1
Bone 1
Boyd T 1
Brazil 1
Broadfoot 1
Buckley 1
Burke O 1
Burns 1
Calderwood 1
Campbell R 1
Clarkson 1
Combe 1
Conn A (1956) 1
Craig J 1
Curran 1
Davidson 1
Dickov 1
Dobie 1
Docherty 1
Duncan D 1
Elliott 1
Fernie 1
Fraser 1
Freedman 1
Goodwillie 1
Gray F 1
Gemmill S 1
Gemmell T (1966–71) 1
Gemmell T (1955) 1
Hanley 1
Hartley 1
Henderson J 1
Herd G 1
Holt 1
Howie 1
Hughes J 1
Hunter W 1
Hutchison T 1
Jackson C 1
Jardine 1

Johnston L 1
Kyle 1
Lambert 1
Linwood 1
Mackail-Smith 1
Mackay G 1
MacLeod 1
MacKenzie 1
McAvennie 1
McCall 1
McCalliog 1
McCulloch 1
McKimmie 1
McKinnon 1
McLean K 1
McLean T 1
McLintock 1
McSwegan 1
Miller W 1
Mitchell 1
Morgan 1
Mulhall 1
Murray J 1
Narey 1
Naysmith 1
Orr 1
Parlane 1
Phillips 1
Provan D (1980–82) 1
Quashie 1
Ritchie P 1
Sharp 1
Stewart R 1
Thornton 1
Wallace I 1
Webster 1
Weir A 1
Weir D 1
Wilkie 1
Wilson Danny 1

WALES

Bale 31
Rush 28
Allchurch I 23
Ford 23
Saunders 22
Bellamy 19
Earnshaw 16
Hughes M 16
Jones C 16
Charles John 15
Hartson 14
Ramsey 14
Toshack 13
Giggs 12
Vokes 11
James L 10
Koumas 10

Davies RT 9
Vernon 8
Flynn 7
James R 7
Speed 7
Walsh I 7
Charles M 6
Curtis A 6
Davies RW 6
Davies S 6
Griffiths A 6
Medwin 6
Pembridge 6
Clarke R 5
Leek 5
Blake 4
Coleman 4
Deacy 4
Eastwood 4
Edwards I 4
England 4
Ledley 4
Robson-Kanu 4
Tapscott 4
Thomas M 4
Allen M. 3
Bodin 3
Bowen M 3
Church 3
Collins J 3
Edwards D 3
Lawrence T 3
Melville 3
Palmer D 3
Rees R 3
Robinson J 3
Woosnam 3
Allen J. 2
Cotterill 2
Davies G 2
Durban A 2
Dwyer 2
Edwards G 2
Evans C 2
Giles D 2
Godfrey 2
Griffiths M 2
Hodges 2
Horne 2
Jones Barrie 2
Jones Bryn 2
King 2
Lowrie 2
Nicholas 2
Phillips D 2
Reece G 2
Savage 2
Slatter 2
Symons 2

Taylor N 2
Williams Ashley 2
Wilson H 2
Woodburn 2
Yorath 2
Barnes 1
Blackmore 1
Blake 1
Bowen D 1
Boyle T 1
Burgess R 1
Charles Jeremy 1
Evans I 1
Fletcher 1
Foulkes 1
Harris C 1
Hewitt R 1
Hockey 1
Huws 1
James D 1
Jones A. 1
Jones D 1
Jones J 1
Krzywicki 1
Llewollyn 1
Lovell 1
Mahoney 1
Moore G 1
Morison 1
O'Sullivan 1
Parry 1
Paul 1
Powell A 1
Powell D 1
Price P 1
Roberts C 1
Roberts P 1
Robinson O 1
Smallman 1
Vaughan 1
Williams Adrian 1
Williams GE 1
Williams GG 1
Young 1

N IRELAND

Healy 36
Lafferty K 20
Clarke 13
Armstrong 12
Davis 12
Dowie 12
Quinn JM 12
Bingham 10
Crossan J 10
McIlroy J 10
McParland 10
Best 9
McAuley 9

Whiteside 9
Dougan 8
Irvine W 8
O'Neill M (1972–85) 8
McAdams 7
Taggart C 7
Wilson S 7
Gray 6
Magennis 6
McLaughlin 6
Nicholson J 6
Wilson K 6
Cush 5
Feeney (2002–9)) 5
Hamilton W 5
Hughes M 5
Magilton 5
McIlroy S 5
Simpson 5
Smyth S 5
Walsh D 5
Anderson T 4
Elliott 4
Hamilton B 4
McCann 4
McGinn 4
McGrath 4
McMorran 4
O'Neill M (1989–96) 4
Quinn SJ 4
Ward 4
Washington 4
Brotherston 3
Brunt 3
Dallas 3
Evans J 3
Harvey M 3
Lockhart 3
Lomas 3
McDonald 3
McMordie 3
Morgan S 3
Muiryne 3
Nicholl C 3
Paterson 3
Spence D 3
Tully 3
Whitley (1997–2006) 3
Blanchflower D 3
Casey 2
Cathcart 2
Clements 2
Doherty P 2
Evans C 2
Finney 2
Gillespie 2
Grigg 2
Harkin 2
Lennon 2

HOME INTERNATIONAL RESULTS

Note: In the results that follow, WC = World Cup, EC = European Championship, CC = Carling Cup
TF = Tournoi de France For Northern Ireland read Ireland before 1921

ENGLAND V SCOTLAND

Played 114; England won 48; Scotland 41; drawn 25 Goals: England 203, Scotland 174

Year	Venue	E	S		Year	Venue		
1872	Glasgow	0	0		1921	Glasgow	0	3
1873	The Oval	4	2		1922	Birmingham	0	1
1874	Glasgow	1	2		1923	Wembley	2	2
1875	The Oval	2	2		1924	Wembley	1	1
1876	Glasgow	0	3		1925	Wembley	0	2
1877	The Oval	1	3		1926	Manchester	0	1
1878	Glasgow	2	7		1927	Glasgow	2	1
1879	The Oval	5	4		1928	Wembley	1	5
1880	Glasgow	4	5		1929	Glasgow	0	1
1881	The Oval	1	6		1930	Wembley	5	2
1882	Glasgow	1	5		1931	Glasgow	0	2
1883	Sheffield	2	3		1932	Wembley	3	0
1884	Glasgow	0	1		1933	Glasgow	1	2
1885	The Oval	1	1		1934	Wembley	3	0
1886	Glasgow	1	1		1935	Glasgow	0	2
1887	Blackburn	2	3		1936	Wembley	1	1
1888	Glasgow	5	0		1937	Glasgow	1	3
1889	The Oval	2	3		1938	Wembley	0	1
1890	Glasgow	1	1		1939	Glasgow	2	1
1891	Blackburn	2	1		1947	Wembley	1	1
1892	Glasgow	4	1		1948	Glasgow	2	0
1893	Richmond	5	2		1949	Wembley	1	3
1894	Glasgow	2	2		1950	Glasgow (WC)	1	0
1895	Goodison Park	3	0		1951	Wembley	2	3
1896	Glasgow	1	2		1952	Glasgow	2	1
1897	Crystal Palace	1	2		1953	Wembley	2	2
1898	Crystal Palace	3	1		1954	Glasgow (WC)	4	2
1899	Birmingham	2	1		1955	Wembley	7	2
1900	Glasgow	1	4		1956	Glasgow	1	1
1901	Crystal Palace	2	2		1957	Wembley	2	1
1902	Birmingham	2	2		1958	Glasgow	4	0
1903	Sheffield	1	2		1959	Wembley	1	0
1904	Glasgow	1	0		1960	Glasgow	1	1
1905	Crystal Palace	1	0		1961	Wembley	9	3
1906	Glasgow	1	2		1962	Glasgow	0	2
1907	Newcastle	1	1		1963	Wembley	1	2
1908	Glasgow	1	1		1964	Glasgow	0	1
1909	Crystal Palace	2	0		1965	Wembley	2	2
1910	Glasgow	0	2		1966	Glasgow	4	3
1911	Goodison Park	1	1		1967	Wembley (EC)	2	3
1912	Glasgow	1	1		1968	Glasgow (EC)	1	1
1913	Stamford Bridge	1	0		1969	Wembley	4	1
1914	Glasgow	1	3		1970	Glasgow	0	0
1920	Sheffield	5	4		1971	Wembley	3	1
					1972	Glasgow	1	0

1973	Glasgow	5	0
1973	Wembley	1	0
1974	Glasgow	0	2
1975	Wembley	5	1
1976	Glasgow	1	2
1977	Wembley	1	2
1978	Glasgow	1	0
1979	Wembley	3	1
1980	Glasgow	2	0
1981	Wembley	0	1
1982	Glasgow	1	0
1983	Wembley	2	0
1984	Glasgow	1	1

1985	Glasgow	0	1
1986	Wembley	2	1
1987	Glasgow	0	0
1988	Wembley	1	0
1989	Glasgow	2	0
1996	Wembley (EC)	2	0
1999	Glasgow (EC)	2	0
1999	Wembley (EC)	0	1
2013	Wembley	3	2
2014	Glasgow	3	1
2016	Wembley (WC)	3	0
2017	Glasgow (WC)	2	2
		E	W

ENGLAND v WALES

Played 102; England won 67; Wales 14; drawn 21; Goals: England 247 Wales 91

1879	The Oval	2	1
1880	Wrexham	3	2
1881	Blackburn	0	1
1882	Wrexham	3	5
1883	The Oval	5	0
1884	Wrexham	4	0
1885	Blackburn	1	1
1886	Wrexham	3	1
1887	The Oval	4	0
1888	Crewe	5	1
1889	Stoke	4	1
1890	Wrexham	3	1
1891	Sunderland	4	1
1892	Wrexham	2	0
1893	Stoke	6	0
1894	Wrexham	5	1
1895	Queens Club, London	1	1
1896	Cardiff	9	1
1897	Bramall Lane	4	0
1898	Wrexham	3	0
1899	Bristol	4	0
1900	Cardiff	1	1
1901	Newcastle	6	0
1902	Wrexham	0	0
1903	Portsmouth	2	1
1904	Wrexham	2	2
1905	Anfield	3	1
1906	Cardiff	1	0
1907	Fulham	1	1
1908	Wrexham	7	1
1909	Nottingham	2	0
1910	Cardiff	1	0
1911	Millwall	3	0
1912	Wrexham	2	0
1913	Bristol	4	3
1914	Cardiff	2	0
1920	Highbury	1	2
1921	Cardiff	0	0
1922	Anfield	1	0
1923	Cardiff	2	2
1924	Blackburn	1	2
1925	Swansea	2	1
1926	Selhurst Park	1	3
1927	Wrexham	3	3
1927	Burnley	1	2
1928	Swansea	3	2
1929	Stamford Bridge	6	0

1930	Wrexham	4	0
1931	Anfield	3	1
1932	Wrexham	0	0
1933	Newcastle	1	2
1934	Cardiff	4	0
1935	Wolverhampton	1	2
1936	Cardiff	1	2
1937	Middlesbrough	2	1
1938	Cardiff	2	4
1946	Maine Road	3	0
1947	Cardiff	3	0
1948	Villa Park	1	0
1949	Cardiff (WC)	4	1
1950	Sunderland	4	2
1951	Cardiff	1	1
1952	Wembley	5	2
1953	Cardiff (WC)	4	1
1954	Wembley	3	2
1955	Cardiff	1	2
1956	Wembley	3	1
1957	Cardiff	4	0
1958	Villa Park	2	2
1959	Cardiff	1	1
1960	Wembley	5	1
1961	Cardiff	1	1
1962	Wembley	4	0
1963	Cardiff	4	0
1964	Wembley	2	1
1965	Cardiff	0	0
1966	Wembley (EC)	5	1
1967	Cardiff (EC)	3	0
1969	Wembley	2	1
1970	Cardiff	1	1
1971	Wembley	0	0
1972	Cardiff	3	0
1972	Cardiff (WC)	1	0
1973	Wembley (WC)	1	1
1973	Wembley	3	0
1974	Cardiff	2	0
1975	Wembley	2	2
1976	Wrexham	2	1
1976	Cardiff	1	0
1977	Wembley	0	1
1978	Cardiff	3	1
1979	Wembley	0	0
1980	Wrexham	1	4
1981	Wembley	0	0

1982	Cardiff	1	0
1983	Wembley	2	1
1984	Wrexham	0	1
2004	Old Trafford (WC)	2	0

2005	Cardiff (WC)	1	0
2011	Cardiff (EC)	2	0
2011	Wembley (EC)	1	0
2016	Lens (EC)	2	1

ENGLAND v N IRELAND
Played 98; England won 75; Ireland 7; drawn 16 Goals: England 323, Ireland 81

Year	Venue	E	I
1882	Belfast	13	0
1883	Aigburth, Liverpool	7	0
1884	Belfast	8	1
1886	Whalley Range	4	0
1886	Belfast	6	1
1887	Bramall Lane	7	0
1888	Belfast	5	1
1889	Goodison Park	6	1
1890	Belfast	9	1
1891	Wolverhampton	6	1
1892	Belfast	2	0
1893	Perry Barr	6	1
1894	Belfast	2	2
1895	Derby	9	0
1896	Belfast	2	0
1897	Nottingham	6	0
1898	Belfast	3	2
1899	Sunderland	13	2
1900	Dublin	2	0
1901	Southampton	3	0
1902	Belfast	1	0
1903	Wolverhampton	4	0
1904	Belfast	3	1
1905	Middlesbrough	1	1
1906	Belfast	5	0
1907	Goodison Park	1	0
1908	Belfast	3	1
1909	Bradford PA	4	0
1910	Belfast	1	1
1911	Derby	2	1
1912	Dublin	6	1
1913	Belfast	1	2
1914	Middlesbrough	0	3
1919	Belfast	1	1
1920	Sunderland	2	0
1921	Belfast	1	1
1922	West Bromwich	2	0
1923	Belfast	1	2
1924	Goodison Park	3	1
1925	Belfast	0	0
1926	Anfield	3	3
1927	Belfast	0	2
1928	Goodison Park	2	1
1929	Belfast	3	0
1930	Bramall Lane	5	1
1931	Belfast	6	2
1932	Blackpool	1	0
1933	Belfast	3	0
1935	Goodison Park	2	1
1935	Belfast	3	1
1936	Stoke	3	1
1937	Belfast	5	1
1938	Old Trafford	7	0
1946	Belfast	7	2
1947	Goodison Park	2	2
1948	Belfast	6	2
1949	Maine Road (WC)	9	2
1950	Belfast	4	1
1951	Villa Park	2	0
1952	Belfast	2	2
1953	Goodison Park (WC)	3	1
1954	Belfast	2	0
1955	Wembley	3	0
1956	Belfast	1	1
1957	Wembley	2	3
1958	Belfast	3	3
1959	Wembley	2	1
1960	Belfast	5	2
1961	Wembley	1	1
1962	Belfast	3	1
1963	Wembley	8	3
1964	Belfast	4	3
1965	Wembley	2	1
1966	Belfast (EC)	2	0
1967	Wembley (EC)	2	0
1969	Belfast	3	1
1970	Wembley	3	1
1971	Belfast	1	0
1972	Wembley	0	1
1973	*Goodison Park	2	1
1974	Wembley	1	0
1975	Belfast	0	0
1976	Wembley	4	0
1977	Belfast	2	1
1978	Wembley	1	0
1979	Wembley (EC)	4	0
1979	Belfast	2	0
1979	Belfast (EC)	5	1
1980	Wembley	1	1
1982	Wembley	4	0
1983	Belfast	0	0
1984	Wembley	1	0
1985	Belfast (WC)	1	0
1985	Wembley (WC)	0	0
1986	Wembley (EC)	3	0
1987	Belfast	2	0
2005	Old Trafford (WC)	4	0
2005	Belfast (WC)	0	1

(*Switched from Belfast because of political situation)

SCOTLAND v WALES

Played 107; Scotland won 61; Wales 23; drawn 23; Goals: Scotland 243, Wales 124

Year	Venue	S	W
1876	Glasgow	4	0
1877	Wrexham	2	0
1878	Glasgow	9	0
1879	Wrexham	3	0
1880	Glasgow	5	1
1881	Wrexham	5	1
1882	Glasgow	5	0
1883	Wrexham	3	0
1884	Glasgow	4	1
1885	Wrexham	8	1
1886	Glasgow	4	1
1887	Wrexham	2	0
1888	Edinburgh	5	1
1889	Wrexham	0	0
1890	Paisley	5	0
1891	Wrexham	4	3
1892	Edinburgh	6	1
1893	Wrexham	8	0
1894	Kilmarnock	5	2
1895	Wrexham	2	2
1896	Dundee	4	0
1897	Wrexham	2	2
1898	Motherwell	5	2
1899	Wrexham	6	0
1900	Aberdeen	5	2
1901	Wrexham	1	1
1902	Greenock	5	1
1903	Cardiff	1	0
1904	Dundee	1	1
1905	Wrexham	1	3
1906	Edinburgh	0	2
1907	Wrexham	0	1
1908	Dundee	2	1
1909	Wrexham	2	3
1910	Kilmarnock	1	0
1911	Cardiff	2	2
1912	Tynecastle	1	0
1913	Wrexham	0	0
1914	Glasgow	0	0
1920	Cardiff	1	1
1921	Aberdeen	2	1
1922	Wrexham	1	2
1923	Paisley	2	0
1924	Cardiff	0	2
1925	Tynecastle	3	1
1926	Cardiff	3	0
1927	Glasgow	3	0
1928	Wrexham	2	2
1929	Glasgow	4	2
1930	Cardiff	4	2
1931	Glasgow	1	1
1932	Wrexham	3	2
1933	Edinburgh	2	5
1934	Cardiff	2	3
1935	Aberdeen	3	2
1936	Cardiff	1	1
1937	Dundee	1	2
1938	Cardiff	1	2
1939	Edinburgh	3	2
1946	Wrexham	1	3
1947	Glasgow	1	2
1948	Cardiff (WO)	0	1
1949	Glasgow	2	0
1950	Cardiff	3	1
1951	Glasgow	0	1
1952	Cardiff (WC)	2	1
1953	Glasgow	3	3
1954	Cardiff	1	0
1955	Glasgow	2	0
1956	Cardiff	2	2
1957	Glasgow	1	1
1958	Cardiff	3	0
1959	Glasgow	1	1
1960	Cardiff	0	2
1961	Glasgow	2	0
1962	Cardiff	3	2
1963	Glasgow	2	1
1964	Cardiff	2	3
1965	Glasgow (EC)	4	1
1966	Cardiff (EC)	1	1
1967	Glasgow	3	2
1969	Wrexham	5	3
1970	Glasgow	0	0
1971	Cardiff	0	0
1972	Glasgow	1	0
1973	Wrexham	2	0
1974	Glasgow	2	0
1975	Cardiff	2	2
1976	Glasgow	3	1
1977	Glasgow (WC)	1	0
1977	Wrexham	0	0
1977	Anfield (WC)	2	0
1978	Glasgow	1	1
1979	Cardiff	0	3
1980	Glasgow	1	0
1981	Swansea	0	2
1982	Glasgow	1	0
1983	Cardiff	2	0
1984	Glasgow	2	1
1985	Glasgow (WC)	0	1
1985	Cardiff (WC)	1	1
1997	Kilmarnock	0	1
2004	Cardiff	0	4
2009	Cardiff	0	3
2011	Dublin (CC)	3	1
2012	Cardiff (WC)	1	2
2013	Glasgow (WC)	1	2

SCOTLAND v NORTHERN IRELAND
Played 96; Scotland won 64; Northern Ireland 15; drawn 17; Goals: Scotland 258, Northern Ireland 80

Year	Venue	S	I	Year	Venue	S	I
1884	Belfast	5	0	1936	Edinburgh	2	1
1885	Glasgow	8	2	1937	Belfast	3	1
1886	Belfast	7	2	1938	Aberdeen	1	1
1887	Belfast	4	1	1939	Belfast	2	0
1888	Belfast	10	2	1946	Glasgow	0	0
1889	Glasgow	7	0	1947	Belfast	0	2
1890	Belfast	4	1	1948	Glasgow	3	2
1891	Glasgow	2	1	1949	Belfast	8	2
1892	Belfast	3	2	1950	Glasgow	6	1
1893	Glasgow	6	1	1951	Belfast	3	0
1894	Belfast	2	1	1952	Glasgow	1	1
1895	Glasgow	3	1	1953	Belfast	3	1
1896	Belfast	3	3	1954	Glasgow	2	2
1897	Glasgow	5	1	1955	Belfast	1	2
1898	Belfast	3	0	1956	Glasgow	1	0
1899	Glasgow	9	1	1957	Belfast	1	1
1900	Belfast	3	0	1958	Glasgow	2	2
1901	Glasgow	11	0	1959	Belfast	4	0
1902	Belfast	5	1	1960	Glasgow	5	1
1902	Belfast	3	0	1961	Belfast	6	1
1903	Glasgow	0	2	1962	Glasgow	5	1
1904	Dublin	1	1	1963	Belfast	1	2
1905	Glasgow	4	0	1964	Glasgow	3	2
1906	Dublin	1	0	1965	Belfast	2	3
1907	Glasgow	3	0	1966	Glasgow	2	1
1908	Dublin	5	0	1967	Belfast	0	1
1909	Glasgow	5	0	1969	Glasgow	1	1
1910	Belfast	0	1	1970	Belfast	1	0
1911	Glasgow	2	0	1971	Glasgow	0	1
1912	Belfast	4	1	1972	Glasgow	2	0
1913	Dublin	2	1	1973	Glasgow	1	2
1914	Belfast	1	1	1974	Glasgow	0	1
1920	Glasgow	3	0	1975	Glasgow	3	0
1921	Belfast	2	0	1976	Glasgow	3	0
1922	Glasgow	2	1	1977	Glasgow	3	0
1923	Belfast	1	0	1978	Glasgow	1	1
1924	Glasgow	2	0	1979	Glasgow	1	0
1925	Belfast	3	0	1980	Belfast	0	1
1926	Glasgow	4	0	1981	Glasgow (WC)	1	1
1927	Belfast	2	0	1981	Glasgow	2	0
1928	Glasgow	0	1	1981	Belfast (WC)	0	0
1929	Belfast	7	3	1982	Belfast	1	1
1930	Glasgow	3	1	1983	Glasgow	0	0
1931	Belfast	0	0	1984	Belfast	0	2
1932	Glasgow	3	1	1992	Glasgow	1	0
1933	Belfast	4	0	2008	Glasgow	0	0
1934	Glasgow	1	2	2011	Dublin (CC)	3	0
1935	Belfast	1	2	2015	Glasgow	1	0

WALES v NORTHERN IRELAND
Played 97; Wales won 45; Northern Ireland won 27; drawn 25; Goals: Wales 191 Northern Ireland 132

Year	Venue	W	I	Year	Venue	W	I
1882	Wrexham	7	1	1890	Shrewsbury	5	2
1883	Belfast	1	1	1891	Belfast	2	7
1884	Wrexham	6	0	1892	Bangor	1	1
1885	Belfast	8	2	1893	Belfast	3	4
1886	Wrexham	5	0	1894	Swansea	4	1
1887	Belfast	1	4	1895	Belfast	2	2
1888	Wrexham	11	0	1896	Wrexham	6	1
1889	Belfast	3	1	1897	Belfast	3	4
				1898	Llandudno	0	1

Year	Venue				Year	Venue		
1899	Belfast	0	1		1952	Swansea	3	0
1900	Llandudno	2	0		1953	Belfast	3	2
1901	Belfast	1	0		1954	Wrexham (WC)	1	2
1902	Cardiff	0	3		1955	Belfast	3	2
1903	Belfast	0	2		1956	Cardiff	1	1
1904	Bangor	0	1		1957	Belfast	0	0
1905	Belfast	2	2		1958	Cardiff	1	1
1906	Wrexham	4	4		1959	Belfast	1	4
1907	Belfast	3	2		1960	Wrexham	3	2
1908	Aberdare	0	1		1961	Belfast	5	1
1909	Belfast	3	2		1962	Cardiff	4	0
1910	Wrexham	4	1		1963	Belfast	4	1
1911	Belfast	2	1		1964	Swansea	2	3
1912	Cardiff	2	3		1965	Belfast	5	0
1913	Belfast	1	0		1966	Cardiff	1	4
1914	Wrexham	1	2		1967	Belfast (EC)	0	0
1920	Belfast	2	2		1968	Wrexham (EC)	2	0
1921	Swansea	2	1		1969	Belfast	0	0
1922	Belfast	1	1		1970	Swansea	1	0
1923	Wrexham	0	3		1971	Belfast	0	1
1924	Belfast	1	0		1972	Wrexham	0	0
1925	Wrexham	0	0		1973	*Goodison Park	0	1
1926	Belfast	0	3		1974	Wrexham	1	0
1927	Cardiff	2	2		1975	Belfast	0	1
1928	Belfast	2	1		1976	Swansea	1	0
1929	Wrexham	2	2		1977	Belfast	1	1
1930	Belfast	0	7		1978	Wrexham	1	0
1931	Wrexham	3	2		1979	Belfast	1	1
1932	Belfast	0	4		1980	Cardiff	0	1
1933	Wrexham	4	1		1982	Wrexham	3	0
1934	Belfast	1	1		1983	Belfast	1	0
1935	Wrexham	3	1		1984	Swansea	1	1
1936	Belfast	2	3		2004	Cardiff (WC)	2	2
1937	Wrexham	4	1		2005	Belfast (WC)	3	2
1938	Belfast	0	1		2007	Belfast	0	0
1939	Wrexham	3	1		2008	Glasgow	0	0
1947	Belfast	1	2		2011	Dublin (CC)	2	0
1948	Wrexham	2	0		2016	Cardiff	1	1
1949	Belfast	2	0		2016	Paris (EC)	1	0
1950	Wrexham (WC)	0	0		(*Switched from Belfast because of political situation)			
1951	Belfast	2	1					

THE THINGS THEY SAY ...

'Burton have had an incredible tournament. They have to be so proud' – **Pep Guardiola**, Manchester City manager, whose side completed a 10-0 aggregate victory.

'Please can I leave gaffer' – **Joe Day**, Newport goalkeeper, on hearing after his side's FA Cup win over Middlesbrough that his wife was about to give birth to twin girls.

'He sprinted off the pitch and it's the quickest I've ever seen him move' – **Mike Flynn**, Newport's manager.

'Handbags, manbags, bumbags. Some kind of bags in the tunnel' – **Sean Dyche**, Burnley manager, on an altercation between coaching staffs after the 2-2 draw against Chelsea.

'There is no sport in the world that one team, one player, always wins. When people say that, they are selling illusion. Part of the competition is you can lose' – **Pep Guardiola**, Manchester City manager.

WORLD CUP SUMMARIES 1930–2018

1930 – URUGUAY

WINNERS: Uruguay RUNNERS-UP: Argentina THIRD: USA FOURTH: Yugoslavia
Other countries taking part: Belgium, Bolivia, Brazil, Chile, France, Mexico, Paraguay, Peru, Romania. **Total entries:** 13
Venue: All matches played in Montevideo
Top scorer: Stabile (Argentina) 8 goals
Final (30/7/30): **Uruguay 4** (Dorado 12, Cea 55, Iriarte 64, Castro 89) **Argentina 2** (Peucelle 29, Stabile 35). **Att:** 90,000
Uruguay: Ballesteros; Nasazzi (capt), Mascheroni, Andrade, Fernandez, Gestido, Dorado, Scarone, Castro, Cea, Iriarte. **Argentina:** Botasso; Della Torre, Paternoster, J Evaristo, Monti, Suarez, Peucelle, Varallo, Stabile, Ferreira (capt), M Evaristo
Referee: Langenus (Belgium). **Half-time:** 1-2

1934 – ITALY

WINNERS: Italy RUNNERS-UP: Czechoslovakia THIRD: Germany FOURTH: Austria
Other countries in finals: Argentina, Belgium, Brazil, Egypt, France, Holland, Hungary, Romania, Spain, Sweden, Switzerland, USA. **Total entries:** 29 (16 qualifiers)
Venues: Bologna, Florence, Genoa, Milan, Naples, Rome, Trieste, Turin
Top scorers: Conen (Germany), Nejedly (Czechoslovakia), Schiavio (Italy), each 4 goals. **Final** (Rome, 10/6/34): **Italy 2** (Orsi 82, Schiavio 97) **Czechoslovakia 1** (Puc 70) after extra-time. **Att:** 50,000
Italy: Combi (capt); Monzeglio, Allemandi, Ferraris, Monti, Bertolini, Gualta, Meazza, Schiavio, Ferrari, Orsi. **Czechoslovakia:** Planicka (capt); Zenisek, Ctyroky, Kostalek, Cambal, Krcil, Junek, Svoboda, Sobotka, Nejedly, Puc
Referee: Eklind (Sweden). **Half-time:** 0-0 (90 mins: 1-1)

1938 – FRANCE

WINNERS: Italy RUNNERS-UP: Hungary THIRD: Brazil FOURTH: Sweden
Other countries in finals: Belgium, Cuba, Czechoslovakia, Dutch East Indies, France, Germany, Holland, Norway, Poland, Romania, Switzerland. **Total entries:** 25 (15 qualifiers)
Venues: Antibes, Bordeaux, Le Havre, Lille, Marseille, Paris, Reims, Strasbourg, Toulouse
Top scorer: Leonidas (Brazil) 8 goals
Final (Paris, 19/6/38): **Italy 4** (Colaussi 6, 36, Piola 15, 81) **Hungary 2** (Titkos 7, Sarosi 65). **Att:** 45,000
Italy: Olivieri; Foni, Rava, Serantoni, Andreolo, Locatelli, Biavati, Meazza (capt), Piola, Ferrari, Colaussi. **Hungary:** Szabo; Polgar, Biro, Szalay, Szucs, Lazar, Sas, Vincze, Sarosi (capt), Szengeller, Titkos
Referee: Capdeville (France). **Half-time:** 3-1

1950 – BRAZIL

WINNERS: Uruguay RUNNERS-UP: Brazil THIRD: Sweden FOURTH: Spain
Other countries in finals: Bolivia, Chile, England, Italy, Mexico, Paraguay, Switzerland, USA, Yugoslavia. **Total entries:** 29 (13 qualifiers)
Venues: Belo Horizonte, Curitiba, Porto Alegre, Recife, Rio de Janeiro, Sao Paulo
Top scorer: Ademir (Brazil) 9 goals
Deciding Match (Rio de Janeiro, 16/7/50): **Uruguay 2** (Schiaffino 64, Ghiggia 79) **Brazil 1** (Friaca 47). **Att:** 199,850
(For the only time, the World Cup was decided on a final pool system, in which the winners of the four qualifying groups met in a six-match series So, unlike previous and subsequent tournaments, there was no official final as such, but Uruguay v Brazil was the deciding match in the final pool)
Uruguay: Maspoli; Gonzales, Tejera, Gambetta, Varela (capt), Andrade, Ghiggia, Perez, Miguez, Schiaffino, Moran

Brazil: Barbosa; Augusto (capt), Juvenal, Bauer, Danilo, Bigode, Friaca, Zizinho, Ademir, Jair, Chico
Referee: Reader (England). **Half-time:** 0-0

1954 – SWITZERLAND

WINNERS: West Germany RUNNERS-UP: Hungary THIRD: Austria FOURTH: Uruguay
Other countries in finals: Belgium, Brazil, Czechoslovakia, England, France, Italy, Korea, Mexico, Scotland, Switzerland, Turkey, Yugoslavia. **Total entries:** 35 (16 qualifiers)
Venues: Basle, Berne, Geneva, Lausanne, Lugano, Zurich
Top scorer: Kocsis (Hungary) 11 goals
Final (Berne, 4/7/54): **West Germany 3** (Morlock 12, Rahn 17, 84) **Hungary 2** (Puskas 4, Czibor 9). **Att:** 60,000
West Germany: Turek; Posipal, Kohlmeyer, Eckel, Liebrich, Mai, Rahn, Morlock, O Walter, F Walter (capt), Schaefer. **Hungary:** Grosics; Buzansky, Lantos, Bozsik, Lorant, Zakarias, Czibor, Kocsis, Hidegkuti, Puskas (capt), J Toth
Referee: Ling (England). **Half-time:** 2-2

1958 – SWEDEN

WINNERS: Brazil RUNNERS-UP: Sweden THIRD: France FOURTH: West Germany
Other countries in finals: Argentina, Austria, Czechoslovakia, England, Hungary, Mexico, Northern Ireland, Paraguay, Scotland, Soviet Union, Wales, Yugoslavia. **Total entries:** 47 (16 qualifiers)
Venues: Boras, Eskilstuna, Gothenburg, Halmstad, Helsingborgs, Malmo, Norrkoping, Orebro, Sandviken, Stockholm, Vasteras
Top scorer: Fontaine (France) 13 goals
Final (Stockholm, 29/6/58): **Brazil 5** (Vava 10, 32, Pele 55, 88, Zagalo 76) **Sweden 2** (Liedholm 4, Simonsson 83). **Att:** 49,737
Brazil: Gilmar; D Santos, N Santos, Zito, Bellini (capt), Orlando, Garrincha, Didi, Vava, Pele, Zagallo. **Sweden:** Svensson; Bergmark, Axbom, Boerjesson, Gustavsson, Parling, Hamrin, Gren, Simonsson, Liedholm (capt), Skoglund
Referee: Guigue (France). **Half-time:** 2-1

1962 – CHILE

WINNERS: Brazil RUNNERS-UP: Czechoslovakia THIRD: Chile FOURTH: Yugoslavia
Other countries in finals: Argentina, Bulgaria, Colombia, England, Hungary, Italy, Mexico, Soviet Union, Spain, Switzerland, Uruguay, West Germany. **Total entries:** 53 (16 qualifiers)
Venues: Arica, Rancagua, Santiago, Vina del Mar
Top scorer: Jerkovic (Yugoslavia) 5 goals
Final (Santiago, 17/6/62): **Brazil 3** (Amarildo 17, Zito 69, Vava 77) **Czechoslovakia 1** (Masopust 16). **Att:** 68,679
Brazil: Gilmar; D Santos, Mauro (capt), Zozimo, N Santos, Zito, Didi, Garrincha, Vava, Amarildo, Zagallo. **Czechoslovakia:** Schroiff; Tichy, Novak, Pluskal, Popluhar, Masopust (capt), Pospichal, Scherer, Kvasnak, Kadraba, Jelinek
Referee: Latychev (Soviet Union). **Half-time:** 1-1

1966 – ENGLAND

WINNERS: England RUNNERS-UP: West Germany THIRD: Portugal FOURTH: USSR
Other countries in finals: Argentina, Brazil, Bulgaria, Chile, France, Hungary, Italy, Mexico, North Korea, Spain, Switzerland, Uruguay. **Total entries:** 53 (16 qualifiers)
Venues: Birmingham (Villa Park), Liverpool (Goodison Park), London (Wembley and White City), Manchester (Old Trafford), Middlesbrough (Ayresome Park), Sheffield (Hillsborough), Sunderland (Roker Park)
Top scorer: Eusebio (Portugal) 9 goals
Final (Wembley, 30/7/66): **England 4** (Hurst 19, 100, 120, Peters 78) **West Germany 2** (Haller 13, Weber 89) after extra-time. **Att:** 93,802

England: Banks; Cohen, Wilson, Stiles, J Charlton, Moore (capt), Ball, Hurst, Hunt, R Charlton, Peters. **West Germany:** Tilkowski; Höttges, Schnellinger, Beckenbauer, Schulz, Weber, Haller, Held, Seeler (capt), Overath, Emmerich
Referee: Dienst (Switzerland). **Half-time:** 1-1 (90 mins: 2-2)

1970 – MEXICO

WINNERS: Brazil RUNNERS-UP: Italy THIRD: West Germany FOURTH: Uruguay
Other countries in finals: Belgium, Bulgaria, Czechoslovakia, El Salvador, England, Israel, Mexico, Morocco, Peru, Romania, Soviet Union, Sweden. Total entries: 68 (16 qualifiers)
Venues: Guadalajara, Leon, Mexico City, Puebla, Toluca
Top scorer: Muller (West Germany) 10 goals
Final (Mexico City, 21/6/70): **Brazil** 4 (Pele 18, Gerson 66, Jairzinho 71, Carlos Alberto 87) **Italy** 1 (Boninsegna 38). **Att:** 107,412
Brazil: Felix; Carlos Alberto (capt), Brito, Piazza, Everaldo, Clodoaldo, Gerson, Jairzinho, Tostao, Pele, Rivelino. **Italy:** Albertosi; Burgnich, Facchetti (capt), Cera, Rosato, Bertini (Juliano 72), Domenghini, De Sisti, Mazzola, Boninsegna (Rivera 84), Riva
Referee: Glockner (East Germany). **Half-time:** 1-1

1974 – WEST GERMANY

WINNERS: West Germany RUNNERS-UP: Holland THIRD: Poland FOURTH: Brazil
Other countries in finals: Argentina, Australia, Bulgaria, Chile, East Germany, Haiti, Italy, Scotland, Sweden, Uruguay, Yugoslavia, Zaire. **Total entries:** 98 (16 qualifiers)
Venues: Berlin, Dortmund, Dusseldorf, Frankfurt, Gelsenkirchen, Hamburg, Hanover, Munich, Stuttgart
Top scorer: Lato (Poland) 7 goals
Final (Munich, 7/7/74): **West Germany** 2 (Breitner 25 pen, Muller 43) **Holland** 1 (Neeskens 2 pen). **Att:** 77,833
West Germany: Maier; Vogts, Schwarzenbeck, Beckenbauer (capt), Breitner, Bonhof, Hoeness, Overath, Grabowski, Muller, Holzenbein. **Holland:** Jongbloed; Suurbier, Rijsbergen (De Jong 69), Haan, Krol, Jansen, Van Hanegem, Neeskens, Rep, Cruyff (capt), Rensenbrink (R Van der Kerkhof 46)
Referee: Taylor (England). **Half-time:** 2-1

1978 – ARGENTINA

WINNERS: Argentina RUNNERS-UP: Holland THIRD: Brazil FOURTH: Italy
Other countries in finals: Austria, France, Hungary, Iran, Mexico, Peru, Poland, Scotland, Spain, Sweden, Tunisia, West Germany. **Total entries:** 102 (16 qualifiers)
Venues: Buenos Aires, Cordoba, Mar del Plata, Mendoza, Rosario
Top scorer: Kempes (Argentina) 6 goals
Final (Buenos Aires, 25/6/78): **Argentina** 3 (Kempes 38, 104, Bertoni 115) **Holland** 1 (Nanninga 82) after extra-time. **Att:** 77,000
Argentina: Fillol; Passarella (capt), Olguin, Galvan, Tarantini, Ardiles (Larrosa 66), Gallego, Ortiz (Houseman 74), Bertoni, Luque, Kempes. **Holland:** Jongbloed; Krol (capt), Poortvliet, Brandts, Jansen (Suurbier 73), Haan, Neeskens, W Van der Kerkhof, Rep (Nanninga 58), R Van der Kerkhof, Rensenbrink
Referee: Gonella (Italy). **Half-time:** 1-0 (90 mins: 1-1)

1982 – SPAIN

WINNERS: Italy RUNNERS-UP: West Germany THIRD: Poland FOURTH: France
Other countries in finals: Algeria, Argentina, Austria, Belgium, Brazil, Cameroon, Chile, Czechoslovakia, El Salvador, England, Honduras, Hungary, Kuwait, New Zealand, Northern Ireland, Peru, Scotland, Soviet Union, Spain, Yugoslavia. **Total entries:** 109 (24 qualifiers)
Venues: Alicante, Barcelona, Bilbao, Coruna, Elche, Gijon, Madrid, Malaga, Oviedo, Seville, Valencia, Valladolid, Vigo, Zaragoza

Top scorer: Rossi (Italy) 6 goals
Final (Madrid, 11/7/82): **Italy** 3 (Rossi 57, Tardelli 69, Altobelli 81) **West Germany** 1 (Breitner 84). **Att:** 90,089
Italy: Zoff (capt); Bergomi, Scirea, Collovati, Cabrini, Oriali, Gentile, Tardelli, Conti, Rossi, Graziani (Altobelli 18 – Causio 88). **West Germany:** Schumacher; Kaltz, Stielike, K-H Forster, B Forster, Dremmler (Hrubesch 63), Breitner, Briegel, Rummenigge (capt) (Muller 70), Fischer, Littbarski
Referee: Coelho (Brazil). **Half-time:** 0-0

1986 – MEXICO

WINNERS: Argentina RUNNERS-UP: West Germany THIRD: France FOURTH: Belgium
Other countries in finals: Algeria, Brazil, Bulgaria, Canada, Denmark, England, Hungary, Iraq, Italy, Mexico, Morocco, Northern Ireland, Paraguay, Poland, Portugal, Scotland, South Korea, Soviet Union, Spain, Uruguay. **Total entries:** 118 (24 qualifiers)
Venues: Guadalajara, Irapuato, Leon, Mexico City, Monterrey, Nezahualcoyotl, Puebla, Queretaro, Toluca
Top scorer: Lineker (England) 6 goals
Final (Mexico City, 29/6/86): **Argentina** 3 (Brown 23, Valdano 56, Burruchaga 85) **West Germany** 2 (Rummenigge 74, Voller 82). **Att:** 115,026
Argentina: Pumpido; Cuciuffo, Brown, Ruggeri, Olarticoechea, Batista, Giusti, Maradona (capt), Burruchaga (Trobbiani 89), Enrique, Valdano. **West Germany:** Schumacher; Berthold, K-H Forster, Jakobs, Brehme, Briegel, Eder, Matthaus, Magath (Hoeness 62), Allofs (Voller 45), Rummenigge (capt)
Referee: Filho (Brazil). **Half-time:** 1-0

1990 – ITALY

WINNERS: West Germany RUNNERS-UP: Argentina THIRD: Italy FOURTH: England
Other countries in finals: Austria, Belgium, Brazil, Cameroon, Colombia, Costa Rica, Czechoslovakia, Egypt, Holland, Republic of Ireland, Romania, Scotland, Spain, South Korea, Soviet Union, Sweden, United Arab Emirates, USA, Uruguay, Yugoslavia. **Total entries:** 103 (24 qualifiers)
Venues: Bari, Bologna, Cagliari, Florence, Genoa, Milan, Naples, Palermo, Rome, Turin, Udine, Verona
Top scorer: Schillaci (Italy) 6 goals
Final (Rome, 8/7/90): **Argentina** 0 **West Germany** 1 (Brehme 85 pen). **Att:** 73,603
Argentina: Goycochea; Ruggeri (Monzon 45), Simon, Serrizuela, Lorenzo, Basualdo, Troglio, Burruchaga (Calderon 53), Sensini, Maradona (capt), Dezotti **Sent-off:** Monzon (65), Dezotti (86) – first players ever to be sent off in World Cup Final. **West Germany:** Illgner; Berthold (Reuter 75), Buchwald, Augenthaler, Kohler, Brehme, Matthaus (capt), Littbarski, Hassler, Klinsmann, Voller
Referee: Codesal (Mexico). **Half-time:** 0-0

1994 – USA

WINNERS: Brazil RUNNERS-UP: Italy THIRD: Sweden FOURTH: Bulgaria
Other countries in finals: Argentina, Belgium, Bolivia, Cameroon, Colombia, Germany, Greece, Holland, Mexico, Morocco, Nigeria, Norway, Republic of Ireland, Romania, Russia, Saudi Arabia, South Korea, Spain, Switzerland, USA. **Total entries:** 144 (24 qualifiers)
Venues: Boston, Chicago, Dallas, Detroit, Los Angeles, New York City, Orlando, San Francisco, Washington
Top scorers: Salenko (Russia), Stoichkov (Bulgaria), each 6 goals
Final (Los Angeles, 17/7/94): **Brazil** 0 **Italy** 0 after extra-time; Brazil won 3-2 on pens
Att: 94,194
Brazil: Taffarel; Jorginho (Cafu 21), Aldair, Marcio Santos, Branco, Mazinho, Mauro Silva, Dunga (capt), Zinho (Viola 105), Romario, Bebeto. **Italy:** Pagliuca; Mussi (Apolloni 35), Baresi (capt), Maldini, Benarrivo, Berti, Albertini,
D Baggio (Evani 95), Donadoni, R Baggio, Massaro
Referee: Puhl (Hungary)

Shoot-out: Baresi missed, Marco Santos saved, Albertini 1-0, Romario 1-1, Evani 2-1, Branco 2-2, Massaro saved, Dunga 2-3, R Baggio missed

1998 – FRANCE

WINNERS: France RUNNERS-UP: Brazil THIRD: Croatia FOURTH: Holland

Other countries in finals: Argentina, Austria, Belgium, Bulgaria, Cameroon, Chile, Colombia, Denmark, England, Germany, Iran, Italy, Jamaica, Japan, Mexico, Morocco, Nigeria, Norway, Paraguay, Romania, Saudi Arabia, Scotland, South Africa, South Korea, Spain, Tunisia, USA, Yugoslavia. **Total entries:** 172 (32 qualifiers)

Venues: Bordeaux, Lens, Lyon, Marseille, Montpellier, Nantes, Paris (St Denis, Parc des Princes), Saint-Etienne, Toulouse

Top scorer: Davor Suker (Croatia) 6 goals

Final (Paris St Denis, 12/7/98): **Brazil** 0 **France** 3 (Zidane 27, 45, Petit 90). **Att:** 75,000
Brazil: Taffarel; Cafu, Junior Baiano, Aldair, Roberto Carlos; Dunga (capt), Leonardo (Denilson 46), Cesar Sampaio (Edmundo 74), Rivaldo; Bebeto, Ronaldo. **France:** Barthez; Thuram, Leboeuf, Desailly, Lizarazu; Karembeu (Boghossian 56), Deschamps (capt), Petit, Zidane, Djorkaeff (Viera 75); Guivarc'h (Dugarry 66) **Sent-off:** Desailly (68)
Referee: Belqola (Morocco). **Half-time:** 0-2

2002 – JAPAN/SOUTH KOREA

WINNERS: Brazil RUNNERS-UP: Germany THIRD: Turkey FOURTH: South Korea

Other countries in finals: Argentina, Belgium, Cameroon, China, Costa Rica, Croatia, Denmark, Ecuador, England, France, Italy, Japan, Mexico, Nigeria, Paraguay, Poland, Portugal, Republic of Ireland, Russia, Saudi Arabia, Senegal, Slovenia, South Africa, Spain, Sweden, Tunisia, USA, Uruguay. **Total entries:** 195 (32 qualifiers)

Venues: Japan – Ibaraki, Kobe, Miyagi, Niigata, Oita, Osaka, Saitama, Sapporo, Shizuoka, Yokohama. **South Korea** – Daegu, Daejeon, Gwangju, Incheon, Jeonju, Busan, Seogwipo, Seoul, Suwon Ulsan

Top scorer: Ronaldo (Brazil) 8 goals

Final (Yokohama, 30/6/02): **Germany** 0 **Brazil** 2 (Ronaldo 67, 79) **Att:** 69,029
Germany: Kahn (capt), Linke, Ramelow, Metzelder, Frings, Jeremies (Asamoah 77), Hamann, Schneider, Bode (Zeige 84), Klose (Bierhoff 74), Neuville. **Brazil:** Marcos, Lucio, Edmilson, Roque Junior, Cafu (capt) Kleberson, Gilberto Silva, Roberto Carlos, Ronaldinho (Juninho 85), Rivaldo, Ronaldo (Denilson 90)
Referee: Collina (Italy). **Half-time:** 0-0

2006 – GERMANY

WINNERS: Italy RUNNERS-UP: France THIRD: Germany FOURTH: Portugal

Other countries in finals: Angola, Argentina, Australia, Brazil, Costa Rica, Croatia, Czech Republic, Ecuador, England, Ghana, Holland, Iran, Ivory Coast, Japan, Mexico, Paraguay, Poland, Saudi Arabia, Serbia & Montenegro, South Korea, Spain, Sweden, Switzerland, Trinidad & Tobago, Togo, Tunisia, Ukraine, USA. **Total entries:** 198 (32 qualifiers)

Venues: Berlin, Cologne, Dortmund, Frankfurt, Gelsenkirchen, Hamburg, Hanover, Kaiserslautern, Leipzig, Munich, Nuremberg, Stuttgart

Top scorer: Klose (Germany) 5 goals

Final (Berlin, 9/7/06): **Italy** 1 (Materazzi 19) **France** 1 (Zidane 7 pen) after extra-time: Italy won 5-3 on pens. **Att:** 69,000
Italy: Buffon; Zambrotta, Cannavaro (capt), Materazzi, Grosso, Perrotta (De Rossi 61), Pirlo, Gattuso, Camoranesi (Del Piero 86), Totti (Iaquinta 61), Toni. **France:** Barthez; Sagnol, Thuram, Gallas, Abidal, Makelele, Vieira (Diarra 56), Ribery (Trezeguet 100), Malouda, Zidane (capt), Henry (Wiltord 107) **Sent-off:** Zidane (110)
Referee: Elizondo (Argentina). **Half-time:** 1-1 90 mins: 1-1
Shoot-out: Pirlo 1-0, Wiltord 1-1, Materazzi 2-1, Trezeguet missed, De Rossi 3-1, Abidal 3-2, Del Piero 4-2, Sagnol 4-3, Grosso 5-3

2010 – SOUTH AFRICA

WINNERS: Spain RUNNERS-UP: Holland THIRD: Germany FOURTH: Uruguay
Other countries in finals: Algeria, Argentina, Australia, Brazil, Cameroon, Chile, Denmark, England, France, Ghana, Greece, Honduras, Italy, Ivory Coast, Japan, Mexico, New Zealand, Nigeria, North Korea, Paraguay, Portugal, Serbia, Slovakia, Slovenia, South Africa, South Korea, Switzerland, USA. **Total entries:** 204 (32 qualifiers)
Venues: Bloemfontein, Cape Town, Durban, Johannesburg (Ellis Park), Johannesburg (Soccer City), Nelspruit, Polokwane, Port Elizabeth, Pretoria, Rustenburg
Top scorers: Forlan (Uruguay), Muller (Germany), Sneijder (Holland), Villa (Spain) 5 goals
Final (Johannesburg, Soccer City, 11/7/10): **Holland** 0 **Spain** 1 (Iniesta 116) after extra-time; **Att:** 84,490
Holland: Stekelenburg; Van der Wiel, Heitinga, Mathijsen, Van Bronckhorst (capt) (Braafheid 105), Van Bommel, De Jong (Van der Vaart 99), Robben, Sneijder, Kuyt (Elia 71), Van Persie. **Sent off:** Heitinga (109). **Spain:** Casillas (capt); Sergio Ramos, Puyol, Piquet, Capdevila, Busquets, Xabi Alonso (Fabregas 87), Iniesta, Xavi, Pedro (Jesus Navas 60), Villa (Torres 106)
Referee: Webb (England). **Half-time:** 0-0

2014 – BRAZIL

WINNERS: Germany RUNNERS-UP: Argentina THIRD: Holland FOURTH: Brazil
Other countries in finals: Algeria, Argentina, Australia, Belgium, Bosnia-Herzegovina, Brazil, Cameroon, Chile, Colombia, Costa Rica, Croatia, Ecuador, England, France, Germany, Ghana, Greece, Holland, Honduras, Iran, Italy, Ivory Coast, Japan, Mexico, Nigeria, Portugal, Russia, South Korea, Spain, Switzerland, Uruguay, USA. **Total entries:** 204 (32 qualifiers)
Venues: Belo Horizonte, Brasilia, Cuiaba, Curitiba, Fortaleza, Manaus, Natal, Porto Alegre, Recife, Rio de Janeiro, Salvador, Sao Paulo
Top scorer: Rodriguez (Colombia) 6 goals
Final (Rio de Janeiro, 13/7/14): **Germany** 1 (Gotze 113) **Argentina** 0 after extra-time; **Att:** 74,738
Germany: Neuer; Lahm (capt), Boateng, Hummels, Howedes, Kramer (Schurrle 32), Schweinsteiger, Muller, Kroos, Ozil (Mertesacker 120), Klose (Gotze 88). **Argentina:** Romero; Zabaleta, Demichelis, Garay, Rojo, Biglia, Mascherano, Perez (Gago 86), Messi (capt), Lavezzi (Aguero 46), Higuain (Palacio 78)
Referee: Rizzoli (Italy). **Half-time:** 0-0

2018 – RUSSIA

WINNERS: France RUNNERS-UP: Croatia THIRD: Belgium FOURTH: England
Other countries in finals: Argentina, Australia, Brazil, Colombia, Costa Rica, Denmark, Egypt, Germany, Iceland, Iran, Japan, Mexico, Morocco, Nigeria, Panama, Peru, Poland, Portugal, Russia, Saudi Arabia, Senegal, Serbia, Spain, South Korea, Sweden, Switzerland, Tunisia, Uruguay. **Total entries:** 209 (32 qualifiers)
Venues: Ekaterinburg, Kaliningrad, Kazan, Moscow Luzhniki, Moscow Spartak, Nizhny Novgorod, Rostov, Samara, Saransk, Sochi, St Petersburg, Volgograd
Top scorer: Kane (England) 6 goals
Final (Moscow Luzhniki, 15/7/18): **France** 4 (Mandzukic 18 og, Griezmann 38 pen, Pogba 59, Mbappe 65) **Croatia** 2 (Perisic 28, Mandzukic 69). **Att:** 78,011
France: Lloris (capt), Pavard, Varane, Umtiti, Hernandez, Pogba, Kante (Nzonzi 55), Mbappe, Griezmann, Matuidi (Tolisso 73), Giroud (Fekir 81). **Croatia:** Subasic, Vrsaljko, Lovren, Vida, Strinic (Pjaca 81), Brozovic, Rebic (Kramaric 71), Modric (capt), Rakitic, Perisic, Mandzukic
Referee: Pitana (Argentina). **Half-time:** 2-1

BRITISH AND IRISH UNDER-21
INTERNATIONALS 2018–19
EUROPEAN CHAMPIONSHIP 2019
QUALIFYING

GROUP TWO

SPAIN 1 NORTHERN IRELAND 2
Albacete (3,401): September 11, 2018
Northern Ireland: Hazard, Donnelly, Johnson, Ballard, McDonagh, Sykes, Lavery (McGonigle 61), Burns, Dunwoody (Gorman 74), Smyth, Holden (Bird 78). **Booked**: Smyth, Johnson, Lavery, Sykes, McGonigle
Scorers – Spain: Mir (90+2). **Northern Ireland**: Lavery (4), Donnelly (8 pen). **Half-time**: 0-2

ICELAND 0 NORTHERN IRELAND 1
Reykjavik (337): October 11, 2018
Northern Ireland: Hazard, Bird, Donnelly, Ballard, McDonagh, Gorman (Sykes 74), Thompson, Lavery (Parkhouse 72), Smyth, Holden (Roy 77). **Booked**: Ballard, Parkhouse
Scorer – Northern Ireland: Ballard (89). **Half-time**: 0-0

NORTHERN IRELAND 1 SLOVAKIA 0
Windsor Park (5,452): October 16, 2018
Northern Ireland: Hazard, Donnelly, Johnson, Ballard, McDonagh, Thompson (Gorman 89), Sykes, Lavery (Parkhouse 83), Burns, Roy (Dummigan 79), Smyth. **Booked**: Thompson, Sykes, Hazard
Scorer – Northern Ireland: Sykes (62). **Half-time**: 0-0

GROUP FOUR

ENGLAND 0 HOLLAND 0
Carrow Road, Norwich (16,369): September 6, 2018
England: Henderson, Konsa, Fry, Chilwell, Wan-Bissaka, Onomah (Davies 65), Cook, Sessegnon, Gray, Maddison (Solanke 76), Calvert-Lewin (Abraham 76)

SCOTLAND 3 ANDORRA 0
Tynecastle Park, Edinburgh (2,125): September 6, 2018
Scotland: Fulton, Smith, Bates, Porteous, Williamson, Ross McCrorie, Mallan (Campbell 72), Gilmour (Ferguson 78), Cadden, Johnston, Hornby (Shaw 85). **Booked**: Smith, Bates, Hornby
Scorers – Scotland: Hornby (45 pen, 69, 83). **Half-time**: 1-0

LATVIA 1 ENGLAND 2
Jelgava (1,037): September 11, 2018
England: Henderson, Kenny, Tomori, Clarke-Salter, Walker-Peters, Dowell, Davies, Mount, Solanke, Lookman (Sessegnon 64), Abraham (Calvert-Lewin 80) (Onomah 89)
Scorers – Latvia: Jurkovskis (28). **England**: Abraham (40), Mount (73). **Half-time**: 1-1

HOLLAND 1 SCOTLAND 2
Doetinchem (6,830): September 11, 2018
Scotland: Robbie McCrorie, Cadden, Bates, Porteous, Smith, Magennis, Mallan (McIntyre 78), Ross McCrorie, Johnston (Gilmour 70), Campbell (Ferguson 39), Hornby. **Booked**: Ross McCrorie, Cadden, Gilmour
Scorers – Holland: Koopmeiners (70). **Scotland**: Hornby (54, 89 pen). **Half-time**: 0-0

ENGLAND 7 ANDORRA 0
Proact Stadium, Chesterfield (7,147); October 11, 2018

England: Henderson, Kenny (Dasilva 72), Fry, Konsa, Walker-Peters, Foden, Cook, Davies, Lookman (Nelson 72), Calvert-Lewin (Solanke 72), Sessegnon. **Booked**: Calvert-Lewin, Cook
Scorers – England: Lookman (9), Konsa (28), Calvert-Lewin (45, 49 pen), Solanke (81), Nelson (90+2), Garcia (90+4 og). **Half-time**: 3-0

UKRAINE 3 SCOTLAND 1
Kiev (1,367); October 12, 2018

Scotland: Robbie McCrorie, Smith, Bates, Porteous, Taylor, Cadden, Ross McCrorie, Mallan, Campbell (Gilmour 90), Morgan, Brophy (Middleton 69)
Scorers – Ukraine: Zubkov (32, 56), Kovalenko (90+1). **Scotland**: Morgan (1). **Half-time**: 1-1

SCOTLAND 0 ENGLAND 2
Tynecastle Park, Edinburgh (4,122); October 16, 2018

Scotland: Doohan, Smith, Bates, Porteous, Taylor, Cadden, Ross McCrorie. Campbell, Shaw (Middleton 46), Morgan, Gilmour (Ferguson 61). **Booked**: Gilmour, Ross McCrorie
England: Henderson, Wan-Bissaka, Tomori, Clarke-Salter, Dasilva, Onomah (Foden 72), Dowell, Nelson (Sessegnon 73), Solanke, Barnes, Abraham (Calvert-Lewin 87)
Scorers – England: Nelson (60), Dowell (90+2). **Half-time**: 0-0

GROUP FIVE

KOSOVO 1 REPUBLIC OF IRELAND 1
Mitrovica (1.000); September 7, 2018

Republic of Ireland: O'Hara, Kane (Ronan Hale 75), Whelan, Shaughnessy, Sweeney, Charsley, Cullen, Grego-Cox, Curtis, Manning (Mulraney 75), Kinsella. **Booked**: Sweeney, Cullen, Curtis
Scorers – Kosovo: Hasani (64). **Republic of Ireland**: Curtis (82). **Half-time**: 0-0

REPUBLIC OF IRELAND 0 GERMANY 6
Tallaght Stadium, Dublin (2,325); September 11, 2018

Republic of Ireland: O'Hara, Whelan, Shaughnessy, Kinsella, Cullen, Charsley, Grego-Cox, Manning (McGrath 54), Mulraney (Quigley 87), McLoughlin (Donnellan 15) Delaney. **Booked**: O'Hara, Donnellan
Scorers – Germany: Seydel (6), Teuchert (22 pen, 66, 73 pen), Serdar (83 pen, 86). **Half-time**: 0-2

ISRAEL 3 REPUBLIC OF IRELAND 1
Acre (120): October 11, 2018

Republic of Ireland: O'Hara, Kane, Whelan, Delaney (McGrath 85), Sweeney, Charsley, Kinsella, Curtis, Cullen, Shipley (Ronan Hale 59), Grego-Cox (Mulraney 85). **Booked**: Kinsella, Curtis
Scorers – Israel: Kanichowsky (15), Plakuschenko (77), Cohen (90+7). **Republic of Ireland**: Ronan Hale (64). **Half-time**: 1-0

GERMANY 2 REPUBLIC OF IRELAND 0
Heidenheim (3,229); October 16, 2018

Republic of Ireland: Bossin, Kane (Dunne 64), Whelan, Delaney, Sweeney, Donnellan, Kinsella, McGrath, Cullen, Shipley, Ronan Hale (Grego-Cox 75). **Booked**: Kinsella, Dunne
Scorers – Germany: Serra (32), Oztunali (40). **Half-time**: 2-0

GROUP EIGHT

WALES 2 LIECHTENSTEIN 1
Bangor University (307): September 7, 2018

Wales: Pilling, Coxe, Norrington-Davies, Baker, Poole, Harries, James, Morrell, Harris (Broadhead 53), Thomas, Matondo (Babos 72). **Booked:** Morrell
Scorers – Wales: Thomas (4, 18). **Liechtenstein:** Graber (77). **Half-time:** 2-0

WALES 0 PORTUGAL 2
Bangor University (625); September 11, 2018
Wales: Pilling, Coxe, Norrington-Davies, Cooper, Harries, Baker (Babos 79), Poole, James, Morrell (Evans 74), Thomas, Broadhead (Matondo 56). **Booked:** Cooper, Coxe, Harries
Scorers – Portugal: Andre Horta (34), Joao Felix (73). **Half-time:** 0-1

ROMANIA 2 WALES 0
Cluj-Napoca (12,500); October 12, 2018
Wales: O Evans, Poole, Lewis, Cooper, Norrington-Davies, Baker (Christie-Davies 90), James, Morrell, Broadhead, Cullen (Babos 62), Harris (C Evans 62). **Booked:** Morrell, Baker
Scorers – Romania: Man (54), Puscas (70). **Half-time:** 0-0

WALES 3 SWITZERLAND 1
Rodney Parade, Newport (242); October 16, 2018
Wales: O Evans, K Davies, Harries, Poole, Lewis, Norrington-Davies, Morrell, Burton (Christie-Davies 93), C Evans, Broadhead (Babos 61), Harris (Touray 80). **Booked:** Harries, Morrell, K Davies, Norrington-Davies, Touray
Scorers – Wales: Morrell (36), C Evans (38, 87). **Switzerland:** Zeqiri (76). **Half-time:** 2-0

GROUP TABLES

(Group winners qualified for finals, along with two play-offs winners. Italy qualified as hosts)

GROUP 1

P	W	D	L	F	A	Pts
Croatia Q	10	8	1	1	31	5	25
Greece	10	8	1	1	26	5	25
Czech Rep	10	5	1	4	14	15	16
Belarus	10	4	2	4	11	14	14
Moldova	10	2	1	7	8	23	7
San Marino	10	0	0	10	1	29	0

GROUP 2

Spain Q	10	9	0	1	31	10	27
N Ireland	10	6	2	2	15	11	20
Slovakia	10	6	0	4	17	18	18
Iceland	10	3	2	5	16	19	11
Albania	10	1	4	5	9	17	7
Estonia	10	0	2	8	11	24	2

GROUP 3

Denmark Q	10	7	2	1	30	8	23
Poland Q	10	6	4	0	22	9	22
Georgia	10	3	3	4	11	19	12
Finland	10	2	3	5	13	21	9
Lithuania	10	2	2	6	7	16	8
Faroe Is	10	1	4	5	10	20	7

GROUP 4

England Q	10	8	2	0	23	4	26
Holland	10	5	3	2	21	6	18

Ukraine	10	5	2	3	18	12	17
Scotland	10	4	2	4	13	13	14
Latvia	10	0	4	6	5	18	4
Andorra	10	0	3	7	1	28	3

GROUP 5

Germany Q	10	8	1	1	33	7	25
Norway	10	4	3	3	15	13	15
Rep of Ireland	10	4	2	4	12	15	14
Israel	10	4	2	4	17	18	14
Kosovo	10	3	3	4	9	12	12
Azerbaijan	10	0	3	7	6	27	3

GROUP 6

Belgium Q	10	8	2	0	23	5	26
Sweden	10	6	2	2	19	8	20
Turkey	10	5	2	3	14	10	17
Hungary	10	3	2	5	12	14	11
Cyprus	10	2	1	7	8	23	7
Malta	10	1	1	8	8	24	4

GROUP 7

Serbia Q	10	8	2	0	23	5	26
Austria Q	10	7	1	2	25	7	22
Russia	10	6	1	3	25	13	19
Armenia	10	2	3	5	9	16	9
Macedonia	10	2	1	7	17	24	7
Gibraltar	10	1	0	9	2	36	3

GROUP 8							
Romania Q	10	7	3	0	19	4	24
Portugal	10	7	1	2	33	11	22
Bosnia-Herz	10	6	0	4	24	11	18
Wales	10	4	1	5	11	14	13
Switzerland	10	3	1	6	11	18	10
Liechtenstein	10	0	0	10	2	42	0

GROUP 9							
France Q	10	9	1	0	24	6	28
Slovenia	10	4	4	2	14	12	16
Montenegro	10	3	2	5	15	15	11
Kazakhstan	10	2	4	4	13	18	10
Bulgaria	10	2	4	4	10	11	10
Luxembourg	10	2	1	7	7	21	7

Play offs (on agg). Austria 2 Greece 0, Poland 3 Portugal 2

FRIENDLY INTERNATIONALS

ITALY 1 ENGLAND 2
Ferrara (2,700); November 15, 2018
England: Henderson, Walker-Peters, Clarke-Salter (Kelly 4), Tomori, Dasilva, Cook, Davies (Dowell 69), Gray (Nelson 63), Foden, Sessegnon (Abraham 69), Solanke (Calvert-Lewin 63).
Booked: Solanke, Davies, Abraham
Scorers – Italy: Kean (42). **England**: Solanke (8, 53). **Half-time**: 1-1

DENMARK 1 ENGLAND 5
Esbjerg (4,558); November 20, 2018
England: Henderson, Walker-Peters (Sessegnon 71), Konza, Simpson, Dasilva (Kelly 60), Dowell, Cook (Davies 72), Foden (Calvert-Lewin 60), Nelson, Solanke, Gray (Tomori 71)
Scorers – Denmark: Ingvartsen (41). **England**: Gray (31), Solanke (39, 47), Calvert-Lewin (81 86 pen). **Half-time**: 1-2

ENGLAND 1 POLAND 1
Ashton Gate, Bristol (25,119); March 21, 2019
England: Gunn, Kenny, Tomori, Kelly, Dasilva, Dowell (Choudhury 80), Maddison, Foden (Davies 73), Lookman (Barnes 72), Calvert-Lewin (Solanke 72), Nelson (Gray 72)
Scorers – England: Calvert-Lewin (13). **Poland**: Szymanski (34). **Half-time**: 1-1

SCOTLAND 0 MEXICO 0
Marbella; March 22, 2019
Scotland: Doohan, Brandon, Maguire, G Johnston, Harvie, Hastie (Miller 77), Campbell, Hornby (House 77), Turnbull (Holsgrove 55), Ross McCrorie, McAllister (M Johnson 50). **Booked**: Ross McCrorie

SCOTLAND 1 SWEDEN 2
Marbella; March 25, 2019
Scotland: Robbie McCrorie, Mackie (Brandon 46), Maguire, G Johnston, Harvie (Reading 46), Campbell, M Johnston (Shaw 72), House (Hornby 46), Holsgrove (Hastie 46), Ross McCrorie (Turnbull 72), Wilson
Scorers – Scotland: Maguire (23). **Sweden**: Asoro (7), Mbunga (38). **Half-time**: 1-2

ENGLAND 1 GERMANY 2
Vitality Stadium, Bournemouth (10,942); March 26, 2019
England: Henderson, Walker-Peters, Fry (Konsa 68), Clarke-Salter, Sessegnon (Dasilva 81), Davies (Calvert-Lewin 68), Dowell (Choudhury 68), Gray, Foden, Barnes (Lookman 81), Solanke (Maddison 81)
Scorers – England: Solanke (43). **Germany**: Dahoud (27), Uduokhai (90+1). **Half-time**: 1-1

WORLD YOUTH FESTIVAL 2019 – TOULON

GROUP A

	P	W	D	L	F	A	Pts
Japan U22 Q	3	2	0	1	8	3	6
Portugal U19	3	2	0	1	4	3	6
Chile U22	3	2	0	1	4	7	6
England U20	3	0	0	3	4	7	0

Match-day 1: England 2 (Nketiah 8, Willock 87) Portugal 3 (Marcos Paulo 21, Cardoso 39, Correira 42). **Match-day 2:** England 1 (Chalobah 38) Japan 2 (Ominami 47, Naganuma 68). **Match-day3:** Chile 2 (Jara 87, Guehi 90+2 og) England 1 (Willock 45)

GROUP B

	P	W	D	L	F	A	Pts
Brazil U22 Q	3	3	0	0	13	0	9
France U18	3	2	0	1	4	5	6
Guatemala U22	3	1	0	2	3	6	3
Qatar U22	3	0	0	3	0	9	0

GROUP C

	P	W	D	L	F	A	Pts
Republic of Ireland U21 Q	3	2	1	0	5	1	7
Mexico U22 Q	3	2	1	0	3	0	7
China U22	3	1	0	2	5	6	3
Bahrain U22	3	0	0	3	1	7	0

Match-day 1: China 1 (Li Yang 18) Republic of Ireland 4 (Elbouzedi 1, Connolly 5, Idah 56, 82). **Match-day 2:** Republic of Ireland 0 Mexico 0. **Match-day 3:** Bahrain 0 Republic of Ireland 1 (Ronan 33)

SEMI-FINALS

Brazil 2 (Paulinho 15, Cunha 47) Republic of Ireland 0. Japan 2 Mexico 2 (Japan won 5-4 on pens)

THIRD PLACE MATCH

Mexico 0 Republic of Ireland 0 (Mexico won 4-3 on pens)

FINAL

Brazil 1 Japan 1 (Brazil won 5-4 on pen) – June 15, 2019

GOLDEN OLDIES

Crystal Palace's Roy Hodgson celebrated becoming the Premier League's oldest-ever manager, at 71 years and 198 days, with a 4-1 victory at Leicester. Later in the season, he shared a 'golden oldies' fixture with Cardiff's Neil Warnock, 70, and won that one 3-2.

EUROPEAN UNDER-17 CHAMPIONSHIP
2019 – REPUBLIC OF IRELAND

GROUP A

	P	W	D	L	F	A	Pts
Belgium Q	3	1	2	0	5	2	5
Czech Republic Q	3	1	2	0	4	2	5
Republic of Ireland	3	0	3	0	3	3	3
Greece	3	0	1	2	1	6	1

Match-day 1: Republic of Ireland 1 (Everitt 58) Greece 1 (Arsenidis 90+6). Att: 4,265 (Tallaght, Dublin)
Match-day 2: Republic of Ireland 1 (Omobamidele 88) Czech Republic 1 (Sejk 63). Att: 2,613 (Waterford)
Match-day 3: Belgium 1 (Kalulika 65) Republic of Ireland 1 (Sobowale 74). Att: 4,885 (Tallaght)

GROUP B

	P	W	D	L	F	A	Pts
France Q	3	2	1	0	7	3	7
Holland Q	3	2	0	1	7	4	6
England	3	1	1	1	6	7	4
Sweden	3	0	0	3	3	9	0

Match-day 1: England 1 (Greenwood 34 pen) France 1 (Aouchiche 79). Att 1,627 (Longford)
Match-day 2: Holland 5 (Brobbey 10, 58 pen, Bannis 35, Hansen 45, Unuvar 61) England 2 (Harwood-Bellis 7, Greenwood 34 pen). Att: 2,411 (Tolka Park, Dublin)
Match-day 3: Sweden 1 (Prica 28) England 3 (Greenwood 15, Jenks 76, Sarmiento 82). Att: 522 (Whitehall, Dublin)

GROUP C

	P	W	D	L	F	A	Pts
Hungary Q	3	3	0	0	6	3	9
Portugal Q	3	2	0	1	6	4	6
Iceland	3	1	0	2	6	8	3
Russia	3	0	0	3	5	8	0

GROUP D

	P	W	D	L	F	A	Pts
Italy Q	3	3	0	0	9	3	6
Spain Q	3	2	0	1	5	4	6
Germany	3	1	0	2	4	5	3
Austria	3	0	0	3	2	8	0

Quarter-finals: Belgium 0 Holland 3; Hungary 1 Spain 1 (Spain won 5-4 on pens); France 6 Czech Republic 1; Italy 1 Portugal 0. **Semi-finals**: Holland 1 Spain 0; France 1 Italy 2
Final: Holland 4 (Hansen 20, Bannis 37, Maatsen 45, Unuvar 70) Italy 2 (Colombo 56, 89) Att: 5,952 (Tallaght Stadium, Dublin), May 19, 2019

TRANSFER TRAIL

Player	From	To	Date	£
Philippe Coutinho	Liverpool	Barcelona	1/18	142,000,000
Paul Pogba	Juventus	Manchester Utd	8/16	89,300,000
Eden Hazard	Chelsea	Real Madrid	6/19	89,000,000
Gareth Bale	Tottenham	Real Madrid	8/13	85,300,000
Cristiano Ronaldo	Manchester Utd	Real Madrid	7/09	80,000,000
Romelu Lukaku	Everton	Manchester Utd	7/17	75,000,000
Virgil van Dijk	Southampton	Liverpool	1/18	75,000,000
Kepa Arrizabalaga	Athletic Bilbao	Chelsea	8/18	71,600,000
Luis Suarez	Liverpool	Barcelona	7/14	65,000,000
Alisson	Roma	Liverpool	7/18	65,000,000
Rodri	Atletico Madrid	Manchester City	7/19	62,800,000
Riyad Mahrez	Leicester	Manchester City	7/18	60,000,000
Angel di Maria	Real Madrid	Manchester Utd	8/14	59,700,000
Christian Pulisic	Borussia Dortmund	Chelsea	7/19	58,000,000
Alvaro Morata	Real Madrid	Chelsea	7/17	57,200,000
Diego Costa	Chelsea	Atletico Madrid	1/18	57,000,000
Aymeric Laporte	Athletic Bilbao	Manchester City	1/18	57,000,000
Pierre-Emerick Aubameyang	Borussia Dortmund	Arsenal	1/18	56,000,000
Kevin De Bruyne	Wolfsburg	Manchester City	8/15	54,500,000
Tanguy Ndombele	Lyon	Tottenham	7/19	53,800,000
Oscar	Chelsea	Shanghai Shenhua	1/17	52,000,000
Benjamin Mendy	Monaco	Manchester City	7/17	52,000,000
Fred	Shakhtar Donetsk	Manchester Utd	6/18	52,000,000
Fernando Torres	Liverpool	Chelsea	1/11	50,000,000
David Luiz	Chelsea	Paris SG	6/14	50,000,000
Jorginho	Napoli	Chelsea	7/18	50,000,000
Aaron Wan-Bissaka	Crystal Palace	Manchester Utd	6/19	50,000,000
Raheem Sterling	Liverpool	Manchester City	7/15	49,000,000
Naby Keita	Leipzig	Liverpool	7/18	48,000,000
John Stones	Everton	Manchester City	8/16	47,500,000
Alexandre Lacazette	Lyon	Arsenal	7/17	46,500,000
Gylfi Sigurdsson	Swansea	Everton	8/17	45,000,000
Kyle Walker	Tottenham	Manchester City	7/17	45,000,000
Sebastien Haller	Eintracht Frankfurt	West Ham	7/19	45,000,000
Angel di Maria	Manchester Utd	Paris SG	8/15	44,300,000
Fabinho	Monaco	Liverpool	5/8	43,700,000
Bernardo Silva	Monaco	Manchester City	6/17	43,000,000
Mesut Ozil	Real Madrid	Arsenal	9/13	42,400,000
Davinson Sanchez	Ajax	Tottenham	8/17	42,000,000
Nemanja Matic	Chelsea	Manchester Utd	7/17	40,000,000
Richarlison	Watford	Everton	7/18	40,000,000
Youri Tielemans	Monaco	Leicester	7/19	40,000,000
Mateo Kovacic	Real Madrid	Chelsea	7/19	40,000,000
Tiemoue Bakayoko	Monaco	Chelsea	7/17	39,700,000
Sergio Aguero	Atletico Madrid	Manchester City	7/11	38,500,000
Thibaut Courtois	Chelsea	Real Madrid	8/18	38,000,000
Juan Mata	Chelsea	Manchester Utd	1/14	37,100,000
Leroy Sane	Schalke	Manchester City	7/16	37,000,000
Anthony Martial	Monaco	Manchester Utd	9/15	36,000,000
Felipe Anderson	Lazio	West Ham	7/18	36,000,000
Andy Carroll	Newcastle	Liverpool	1/11	35,000,000

Cesc Fabregas	Arsenal	Barcelona	8/11	35,000,000
Alexis Sanchez	Barcelona	Arsenal	7/14	35,000,000
Granit Xhaka	Borussia M'gladbach	Arsenal	6/16	35,000,000
Shkodran Mustafi	Valencia	Arsenal	8/16	35,000,000
Alex Oxlade-Chamberlain	Arsenal	Liverpool	8/17	35,000,000
Danny Drinkwater	Leicester	Chelsea	8/17	35,000,000
Ederson	Benfica	Manchester City	6/17	34,900,000
Mohamed Salah	Roma	Liverpool	7/17	34,300,000
Sadio Mane	Southampton	Liverpool	6/16	34,000,000
Michy Batshuayi	Marseille	Chelsea	7/16	33,000,000
Robinho	Real Madrid	Manchester City	9/08	32,500,000
Christian Benteke	Aston Villa	Liverpool	7/15	32,500,000
Eden Hazard	Lille	Chelsea	6/12	32,000,000
Diego Costa	Atletico Madrid	Chelsea	7/14	32,000,000
N'Golo Kante	Leicester	Chelsea	7/16	32,000,000
David Luiz	Paris SG	Chelsea	8/16	32,000,000
Eliaquim Mangala	Porto	Manchester City	8/14	31,900,000
Dimitar Berbatov	Tottenham	Manchester Utd	9/08	30,750,000
Victor Lindelof	Benfica	Manchester Utd	6/17	30,700,000
Andriy Shevchenko	AC Milan	Chelsea	5/06	30,800,000
Xabi Alonso	Liverpool	Real Madrid	8/09	30,000,000
Fernandinho	Shakhtar Donetsk	Manchester City	6/13	30,000,000
Willian	Anzhi Makhachkala	Chelsea	8/13	30,000,000
Erik Lamela	Roma	Tottenham	8/13	30,000,000
Luke Shaw	Southampton	Manchester Utd	6/14	30,000,000
Eric Bailly	Villarreal	Manchester Utd	6/16	30,000,000
Moussa Sissoko	Newcastle	Tottenham,	8/16	30,000,000
Ayoze Perez	Newcastle	Leicester	7/19	30,000,000
Islam Slimani	Sporting Lisbon	Leicester	8/16	29,700,000
Rio Ferdinand	Leeds	Manchester Utd	7/02	29,100,000
Antonio Rudiger	Roma	Chelsea	7/17	29,000,000
Ander Herrera	Athletic Bilbao	Manchester Utd	6/14	28,800,000
Nicolas Otamendi	Valencia	Manchester City	8/15	28,500,000
Juan Sebastian Veron	Lazio	Manchester Utd	7/01	28,100,000
Yaya Toure	Barcelona	Manchester City	7/10	28,000,000
Romelu Lukaku	Chelsea	Everton	7/14	28,000,000
Wilfried Bony	Swansea	Manchester City	1/15	28,000,000
Roberto Firmino	Hoffenheim	Liverpool	6/15	28,000,000
Marouane Fellaini	Everton	Manchester Utd	9/13	27,500,000
Wayne Rooney	Everton	Manchester Utd	8/04	27,000,000
Yerry Mina	Barcelona	Everton	8/18	27,200,000
Edin Dzeko	Wolfsburg	Manchester City	1/11	27,000,000
Luka Modric	Tottenham	Real Madrid	8/12	27,000,000
Cesc Fabregas	Barcelona	Chelsea	6/14	27,000,000
Gabriel Jesus	Palmeiras	Manchester City	7/16	27,000,000
Christian Benteke	Liverpool	Crystal Palace	8/16	27,000,000
Cenk Tosun	Besiktas	Everton	1/18	27,000,000
Danilo	Real Madrid	Manchester City	7/17	26,500,000
Roberto Soldado	Valencia	Tottenham	8/13	26,000,000
Henrikh Mkhitaryan	Borussua Dortmund	Manchester Utd	7/16	26,000,000
Mamadou Sakho	Liverpool	Crystal Palace	8/17	26,000,000
Lucas Torreira	Sampdoria	Arsenal	7/18	26,000,000
Marc Overmars	Arsenal	Barcelona	7/00	25,000,000
Carlos Tevez	Manchester Utd	Manchester City	7/09	25,000,000

Emmanuel Adebayor	Arsenal	Manchester City	7/09	25,000,000
Samir Nasri	Arsenal	Manchester City	8/11	25,000,000
Oscar	Internacional	Chelsea	7/12	25,000,000
Adam Lallana	Southampton	Liverpool	7/14	25,000,000
Memphis Depay	PSV Eindhoven	Manchester Utd	6/15	25,000,000
Morgan Schneiderlin	Southampton	Manchester Utd	7/15	25,000,000
Ramires	Chelsea	Jiangsu Suning	2/16	25,000,000
Georginio Wijnaldum	Newcastle	Liverpool	7/16	25,000,000
Yannick Bolasie	Crystal Palace	Everton	8/16	25,000,000
Jordan Pickford	Sunderland	Everton	6/17	25,000,000
Michael Keane	Burnley	Everton	7/17	25,000,000
Kelechi Iheanacho	Manchester City	Leicester	7/17	25,000,000
Theo Walcott	Arsenal	Everton	1/18	25,000,000
Davide Zappacosta	Torino	Chelsea	8/17	25,000,000
Jean Michael Seri	Nice	Fulham	7/18	25,000,000
Jefferson Lerma	Levante	Bournemouth	8/18	25,000,000
Arjen Robben	Chelsea	Real Madrid	8/07	24,500,000
Michael Essien	Lyon	Chelsea	8/05	24,400,000
David Silva	Valencia	Manchester City	7/10	24,000,000
James Milner	Aston Villa	Manchester City	8/10	24,000,000
Mario Balotelli	Inter Milan	Manchester City	8/10	24,000,000
Robin van Persie	Arsenal	Manchester Utd	8/12	24,000,000
Marko Arnautovic	Stoke	West Ham	7/17	24,000,000
Pablo Fornals	Villarreal	West Ham	6/19	24,000,000
Alvaro Negredo	Manchester City	Valencia	7/15	23,800,000
Davy Klaassen	Ajax	Everton	6/17	23,600,000
Juan Mata	Valencia	Chelsea	8/11	23,500,000
David Beckham	Manchester Utd	Real Madrid	7/03	23,300,000
Juan Cuadrado	Fiorentina	Chelsea	2/15	23,300,000
Didier Drogba	Marseille	Chelsea	7/04	23,200,000
Andre Schurrle	Chelsea	Wolfsburg	8/16	23,000,000
Marcos Alonso	Fiorentina	Chelsea	8/16	23,000,000
Serge Aurier	Paris SG	Tottenham	8/17	23,000,000
Lucas Moura	Paris SG	Tottenham	1/18	23,000,000
Luis Suarez	Ajax	Liverpool	1/11	22,700,000
Nicolas Anelka	Arsenal	Real Madrid	8/99	22,300,000
Andre-Frank Anguissa	Marseille	Fulham	8/18	22,300,000
Wesley	Club Bruges	Aston Villa	6/19	22,200,000
Fernando Torres	Atletico Madrid	Liverpool	7/07	22,000,000
Joleon Lescott	Everton	Manchester City	8/09	22,000,000
Stevan Jovetic	Fiorentina	Manchester City	7/13	22,000,000
Adrien Silva	Sporting Lisbon	Leicester	1/18	22,000,000
Issa Diop	Toulouse	West Ham	6/18	22,000,000
Wesley	Club Bruges	Aston Villa	6/19	22,000,000
James Maddison	Norwich	Leicester	6/18	22,000,000
Son Heung-min	Bayer Leverkusen	Tottenham	8/15	21,900,000
Baba Rahman	Augsburg	Chelsea	8/15	21,700,000
David Luiz	Benfica	Chelsea	1/11	21,300,000
Shaun Wright-Phillips	Manchester City	Chelsea	7/05	21,000,000
Nemanja Matic	Benfica	Chelsea	01/14	21,000,000
Pedro	Barcelona	Chelsea	8/15	21,000,000
Ilkay Gundogan	Borussia Dortmund	Manchester City	6/16	21,000,000
Andre Ayew	Swansea	West Ham	8/16	20,500,000
Morgan Schneiderlin	Manchester Utd	Everton	1/17	20,000,000

Lassana Diarra	Portsmouth	Real Madrid	12/08	20,000,000
Alberto Aquilani	Roma	Liverpool	8/09	20,000,000
Stewart Downing	Aston Villa	Liverpool	7/11	20,000,000
Lazar Markovic	Benfica	Liverpool	7/14	20,000,000
Dejan Lovren	Southampton	Liverpool	7/14	20,000,000
Odion Ighalo	Watford	Changchun Yatai	1/17	20,000,000
Nathan Ake	Chelsea	Bournemouth	6/17	20,000,000
Mings, Tyrone	Bournemouth	Aston Villa	7/19	20,000,000
Alfie Mawson	Swansea	Fulham	8/18	20,000,000
Kieran Trippier	Tottenham	Atletico Madrid	7/19	20,000,000

BRITISH RECORD TRANSFERS FROM FIRST £1,000 DEAL

Player	From	To	Date	£
Alf Common	Sunderland	Middlesbrough	2/1905	1,000
Syd Puddefoot	West Ham	Falkirk	2/22	5,000
Warney Cresswell	South Shields	Sunderland	3/22	5,500
Bob Kelly	Burnley	Sunderland	12/25	6,500
David Jack	Bolton	Arsenal	10/28	10,890
Bryn Jones	Wolves	Arsenal	8/38	14,500
Billy Steel	Morton	Derby	9/47	15,000
Tommy Lawton	Chelsea	Notts Co	11/47	20,000
Len Shackleton	Newcastle	Sunderland	2/48	20,500
Johnny Morris	Manchester Utd	Derby	2/49	24,000
Eddie Quigley	Sheffield Wed	Preston	12/49	26,500
Trevor Ford	Aston Villa	Sunderland	10/50	30,000
Jackie Sewell	Notts Co	Sheffield Wed	3/51	34,500
Eddie Firmani	Charlton	Sampdoria	7/55	35,000
John Charles	Leeds	Juventus	4/57	65,000
Denis Law	Manchester City	Torino	6/61	100,000
Denis Law	Torino	Manchester Utd	7/62	115,000
Allan Clarke	Fulham	Leicester	6/68	150,000
Allan Clarke	Leicester	Leeds	6/69	165,000
Martin Peters	West Ham	Tottenham	3/70	200,000
Alan Ball	Everton	Arsenal	12/71	220,000
David Nish	Leicester	Derby	8/72	250,000
Bob Latchford	Birmingham	Everton	2/74	350,000
Graeme Souness	Middlesbrough	Liverpool	1/78	352,000
Kevin Keegan	Liverpool	Hamburg	6/77	500,000
David Mills	Middlesbrough	WBA	1/79	516,000
Trevor Francis	Birmingham	Nottm Forest	2/79	1,180,000
Steve Daley	Wolves	Manchester City	9/79	1,450,000
Andy Gray	Aston Villa	Wolves	9/79	1,469,000
Bryan Robson	WBA	Manchester Utd	10/81	1,500,000
Ray Wilkins	Manchester Utd	AC Milan	5/84	1,500,000
Mark Hughes	Manchester Utd	Barcelona	5/86	2,300,000
Ian Rush	Liverpool	Juventus	6/87	3,200,000
Chris Waddle	Tottenham	Marseille	7/89	4,250,000
David Platt	Aston Villa	Bari	7/91	5,500,000
Paul Gascoigne	Tottenham	Lazio	6/92	5,500,000
Andy Cole	Newcastle	Manchester Utd	1/95	7,000,000
Dennis Bergkamp	Inter Milan	Arsenal	6/95	7,500,000
Stan Collymore	Nottm Forest	Liverpool	6/95	8,500,000
Alan Shearer	Blackburn	Newcastle	7/96	15,000,000

Nicolas Anelka	Arsenal	Real Madrid	8/99	22,500,000
Juan Sebastian Veron	Lazio	Manchester Utd	7/01	28,100,000
Rio Ferdinand	Leeds	Manchester Utd	7/02	29,100,000
Andriy Shevchenko	AC Milan	Chelsea	5/06	30,800,000
Robinho	Real Madrid	Manchester City	9/08	32,500,000
Cristiano Ronaldo	Manchester Utd	Real Madrid	7/09	00,000,000
Gareth Bale	Tottenham	Real Madrid	9/13	85,300,000
Paul Pogba	Juventus	Manchester Utd	8/16	89.300,000
Philippe Coutinho	Liverpool	Barcelona	1/18	142,000,000

• World's first £1m transfer: GuiseppeSavoldi, Bologna to Napoli, July 1975

TOP FOREIGN SIGNINGS

Player	From	To	Date	£
Neymar	Barcelona	Paris SG	8/17	198,000,000
Kylian Mbappe	Monaco	Paris SG	8/17	165,700,000
Ousmane Dembele	Borussia Dortmund	Barcelona	8/17	134,000,000
Joao Felix	Benfica	Atletico Madrid	7/19	113,000,000
Antoine Griezmann	Atletico Madrid	Barcelona	7/19	107,000,000
Cristiano Ronaldo	Real Madrid	Juventus	7/18	99,200,000
Gonzalo Higuain	Napoli	Juventus	7/16	75,300,000
Lucas Hernandez	Atletico Madrid	Bayern Munich	7/19	68,000,000
Matthijs de Ligt	Ajax	Juventus	7/19	67,500,000
Frenkie de Jong	Ajax	Barcelona	1/19	65,000,000
Luka Jovic	Eintracht Frankfurt	Real Madrid	6/19	62,000,000
Zlatan Ibrahimovic	Inter Milan	Barcelona	7/09	60,300,000
James Rodriguez	Monaco	Real Madrid	7/14	60,000,000
Kaka	AC Milan	Real Madrid	6/08	56,000,000
Edinson Cavani	Napoli	Paris SG	7/13	53,000,000
Thomas Lemar	Monaco	Atletico Madrid	6/18	52,700,000
Radamel Falcao	Atletico Madrid	Monaco	6/13	51,000,000
Neymar	Santos	Barcelona	6/13	48,600,000
Zinedine Zidane	Juventus	Real Madrid	7/01	47,200,000
Ferland Mendy	Lyon	Real Madrid	6/19	47,100,000
Hulk	Zenit St Petersburg	Shanghai SIPG	7/16	46,100,000
Eder Militao	Porto	Real Madrid	3/19	42,700,000
Vinicius Junior	Flamengo	Real Madrid	7/18	39,600,000
James Rodriguez	Porto	Monaco	5/13	38,500,000
Alex Teixeira	Shakhtar Donetsk	Jiangsu Suning	2/16	38,400,000
Joao Mario	Sporting Lisbon	Inter Milan	8/16	38,400,000
Luis Figo	Barcelona	Real Madrid	7/00	37,200,000
Javier Pastore	Palermo	Paris SG	8/11	36,600,000
Corentin Tolisso	Lyon	Bayern Munich	6/17	36,500,000
Malcom	Bordeaux	Barcelona	7/18	36,500,000
Joao Cancelo	Valencia	Juventus	7/18	36,300,000
Rodrygo	Santos	Real Madrid	6/18	36,000,000
Goncalo Guedes	Paris SG	Valencia	8/18	36,000,000
Karim Benzema	Lyon	Real Madrid	7/09	35,800,000
Julian Draxler	Wolfsburg	Paris SG	1/17	35,500,000
Arthur	Gremio	Barcelona	7/18	35,500,000
Douglas Costa	Bayern Munich	Juventus	6/18	35,200,000
Hernan Crespo	Parma	Lazio	7/00	35,000,000
Radamel Falcao	Porto	Atletico Madrid	8/11	34,700,000
Gonzalo Higuain	Real Madrid	Napoli	7/13	34,500,000

David Villa	Valencia	Barcelona	5/10	34,000,000
Thiago Silva	AC Milan	Paris SG	7/12	34,000,000
Lucas Moura	Sao Paulo	Paris SG	1/13	34,000,000
Asier Illarramendi	Real Sociedad	Real Madrid	7/13	34,000,000
Ronaldo	Inter Milan	Real Madrid	8/02	33,000,000
Thilo Kehrer	Schalke	Paris SG	8/18	33,000,000
Gianluigi Buffon	Parma	Juventus	7/01	32,600,000
Axel Witsel	Benfica	Zenit St Petersburg	8/12	32,500,000
Hulk	Porto	Zenit St Petersburg	8/12	32,000,000
Javi Martinez	Athletic Bilbao	Bayern Munich	8/12	31,600,000
Krzysztof Piatek	Genoa	AC Milan	1/19	30,900,000
Mario Gotze	Borussia Dortmund	Bayern Munich	6/13	31,500,000
Christian Vieri	Lazio	Inter Milan	6/99	31,000,000
Jackson Martinez	Atletico Madrid	Guangzhou Evergrande	2/16	31,000,000
Alessandro Nesta	Lazio	AC Milan	8/02	30,200,000

WORLD'S MOST EXPENSIVE TEENAGER
£165,700,000: Kylian Mbappe, 19, Monaco to Paris SG, August 2017

WORLD RECORD FOR 16-YEAR-OLD
£39,600,000: Vinicius Junior, Flamengo to Real Madrid, July 2018

RECORD TRIBUNAL FEE
£6.5m: Danny Ings, Burnley to Liverpool, Jun 2016

RECORD FEE BETWEEN SCOTTISH CLUBS
£4.4m: Scott Brown, Hibernian to Celtic, May 2007

RECORD NON-LEAGUE FEE
£1m: Jamie Vardy, Fleetwood to Leicester, May 2012

RECORD FEE BETWEEN NON-LEAGUE CLUBS
£275,000: Richard Brodie, York to Crawley, Aug 2010

MILESTONES

1848: First code of rules compiled at Cambridge University.

1857: Sheffield FC, world's oldest football club, formed.

1862: Notts Co (oldest League club) formed.

1863: Football Association founded – their first rules of game agreed.

1871: FA Cup introduced.

1872: First official International: Scotland 0 England 0. Corner-kick introduced.

1873: Scottish FA formed; Scottish Cup introduced.

1874: Shinguards introduced.

1875: Crossbar introduced (replacing tape).

1876: FA of Wales formed.

1877: Welsh Cup introduced.

1878: Referee's whistle first used.

1880: Irish FA founded; Irish Cup introduced.

1883: Two-handed throw-in introduced.

1885: Record first-class score (Arbroath 36 Bon Accord 0 – Scottish Cup). Professionalism legalised.

1886: International Board formed.

1887: Record FA Cup score (Preston 26 Hyde 0).

1888: Football League founded by William McGregor. First matches on Sept 8.

1889 Preston win Cup and League (first club to complete Double).

1890: Scottish League and Irish League formed.

1891: Goal-nets introduced. Penalty-kick introduced.

1892: Inter-League games began. Football League Second Division formed.

1893: FA Amateur Cup launched.

1894: Southern League formed.

1895: FA Cup stolen from Birmingham shop window – never recovered.

1897: First Players' Union formed. Aston Villa win Cup and League.

1898: Promotion and relegation introduced.

1901: Maximum wage rule in force (£4 a week). Tottenham first professional club to take FA Cup south. First six-figure attendance (110,802) at FA Cup Final

1902: Ibrox Park disaster (25 killed). Welsh League formed.

1904: FIFA founded (7 member countries).

1905: First £1,000 transfer (Alf Common, Sunderland to Middlesbrough)

1907: Players' Union revived.

1908: Transfer fee limit (£350) fixed in January and withdrawn in April.

1911: New FA Cup trophy – in use to 1991. Transfer deadline introduced.

1914: King George V first reigning monarch to attend FA Cup Final.

1916: Entertainment Tax introduced.

1919: League extended to 44 clubs.

1920: Third Division (South) formed.

1921: Third Division (North) formed.

1922: Scottish League (Div II) introduced.

1923: Beginning of football pools. First Wembley Cup Final.

1924: First International at Wembley (England 1 Scotland 1). Rule change allows goals to be scored direct from corner-kicks.

1925: New offside law.

1926: Huddersfield complete first League Championship hat-trick.

1927: First League match broadcast (radio): Arsenal v Sheffield United. First radio broadcast of Cup Final (winners Cardiff City). Charles Clegg, president of FA, becomes first knight of football.

1928: First £10,000 transfer – David Jack (Bolton to Arsenal). WR ('Dixie') Dean (Everton)

creates League record – 60 goals in season. Britain withdraws from FIFA

1930: Uruguay first winners of World Cup.

1931: WBA win Cup and promotion.

1933: Players numbered for first time in Cup Final (1-22).

1934: Sir Frederick Wall retires as FA secretary; successor Stanley Rous. Death of Herbert Chapman (Arsenal manager).

1935: Arsenal equal Huddersfield's Championship hat-trick record. Official two-referee trials.

1936: Joe Payne's 10-goal League record (Luton 12 Bristol Rov 0).

1937: British record attendance: 149,547 at Scotland v England match

1938: First live TV transmission of FA Cup Final. Football League 50th Jubilee. New pitch marking – arc on edge of penalty-area. Laws of Game re-drafted by Stanley Rous. Arsenal pay record £14,500 fee for Bryn Jones (Wolves).

1939: Compulsory numbering of players in Football League. First six-figure attendance for League match (Rangers v Celtic 118,567). All normal competitions suspended for duration of Second World War.

1945: Scottish League Cup introduced.

1946: British associations rejoin FIFA. Bolton disaster (33 killed) during FA Cup tie with Stoke. Walter Winterbottom appointed England's first director of coaching.

1947: Great Britain beat Rest of Europe 6-1 at Hampden Park, Glasgow. First £20,000 transfer – Tommy Lawton, Chelsea to Notts Co

1949: Stanley Rous, secretary FA, knighted. England's first home defeat outside British Champ. (0-2 v Eire).

1950: Football League extended from 88 to 92 clubs. World record crowd (203,500) at World Cup Final, Brazil v Uruguay, in Rio. Scotland's first home defeat by foreign team (0-1 v Austria).

1951: White ball comes into official use.

1952: Newcastle first club to win FA Cup at Wembley in successive seasons.

1953: England's first Wembley defeat by foreign opponents (3-6 v Hungary).

1954: Hungary beat England 7-1 in Budapest.

1955: First FA Cup match under floodlights (prelim round replay): Kidderminster v Brierley Hill Alliance.

1956: First FA Cup ties under floodlights in competition proper. First League match by floodlight (Portsmouth v Newcastle). Real Madrid win the first European Cup.

1957: Last full Football League programme on Christmas Day. Entertainment Tax withdrawn.

1958: Manchester United air crash at Munich. League re-structured into four divisions.

1960: Record transfer fee: £55,000 for Denis Law (Huddersfield to Manchester City). Wolves win Cup, miss Double and Championship hat-trick by one goal. For fifth time in ten years FA Cup Final team reduced to ten men by injury. FA recognise Sunday football. Football League Cup launched.

1961: Tottenham complete the first Championship–FA Cup double this century. Maximum wage (£20 a week) abolished in High Court challenge by George Eastham. First British £100-a-week wage paid (by Fulham to Johnny Haynes). First £100,000 British transfer – Denis Law, Manchester City to Torino. Sir Stanley Rous elected president of FIFA

1962: Manchester United raise record British transfer fee to £115,000 for Denis Law.

1963: FA Centenary. Season extended to end of May due to severe winter. First pools panel. English "retain and transfer" system ruled illegal in High Court test case.

1964: Rangers' second great hat-trick – Scottish Cup, League Cup and League. Football League and Scottish League guaranteed £500,000 a year in new fixtures copyright agreement with Pools. First televised 'Match of the Day' (BBC2): Liverpool 3 Arsenal 2.

1965: Bribes scandal – ten players jailed (and banned for life by FA) for match-fixing 1960–63. Stanley Matthews knighted in farewell season. Arthur Rowley (Shrewsbury) retires with record of 434 League goals. Substitutes allowed for injured players in Football League matches (one per team).

1966: England win World Cup (Wembley).

1967: Alf Ramsey, England manager, knighted; OBE for captain Bobby Moore. Celtic become first British team to win European Cup. First substitutes allowed in FA Cup Final (Tottenham v Chelsea) but not used. Football League permit loan transfers (two per club).

1968: First FA Cup Final televised live in colour (BBC2 – WBA v Everton). Manchester United first English club to win European Cup.

1970: FIFA/UEFA approve penalty shoot-out in deadlocked ties.

1971: Arsenal win League Championship and FA Cup. Sixty-six supporters die in the Ibrox Stadium disaster.

1973: Football League introduce 3 up, 3 down promotion/relegation between Divisions 1, 2 and 3 and 4-up, 4-down between Divisions 3 and 4.

1974: First FA Cup ties played on Sunday. League football played on Sunday for first time. Last FA Amateur Cup Final. Joao Havelange (Brazil) succeeds Sir Stanley Rous as FIFA president.

1975: Scottish Premier Division introduced.

1976: Football League introduce goal difference (replacing goal average) and red/yellow cards.

1977: Liverpool achieve the double of League Championship and European Cup. Don Revie defects to United Arab Emirates when England manager – successor Ron Greenwood.

1978: Freedom of contract for players accepted by Football League. PFA lifts ban on foreign players in English football. Football League introduce Transfer Tribunal. Viv Anderson (Nottm Forest) first black player to win a full England cap. Willie Johnston (Scotland) sent home from World Cup Finals in Argentina after failing dope test.

1979: First all-British £500,000 transfer – David Mills, Middlesbrough to WBA. First British million pound transfer (Trevor Francis – Birmingham to Nottm Forest). Andy Gray moves from Aston Villa to Wolves for a record £1,469,000 fee.

1981: Tottenham win 100th FA Cup Final. Liverpool first British side to win European Cup three times. Three points for a win introduced by Football League. QPR install Football League's first artificial pitch. Death of Bill Shankly, manager–legend of Liverpool 1959–74. Record British transfer – Bryan Robson (WBA to Manchester United), £1,500,000.

1982: Aston Villa become sixth consecutive English winners of European Cup. Tottenham retain FA Cup – first club to do so since Tottenham 1961 and 1962. Football League Cup becomes the (sponsored) Milk Cup.

1983: Liverpool complete League Championship–Milk Cup double for second year running. Manager Bob Paisley retires. Aberdeen first club to do Cup-Winners' Cup and domestic Cup double. Football League clubs vote to keep own match receipts. Football League sponsored by Canon, Japanese camera and business equipment manufacturers – 3-year agreement starting 1983–4. Football League agree two-year contract for live TV coverage of ten matches per season (5 Friday night, BBC, 5 Sunday afternoon, ITV).

1984: One FA Cup tie in rounds 3, 4, 5 and 6 shown live on TV (Friday or Sunday). Aberdeen take Scottish Cup for third successive season, win Scottish Championship, too. Tottenham win UEFA Cup on penalty shoot-out. Liverpool win European Cup on penalty shoot-out to complete unique treble with Milk Cup and League title (as well as Championship hat-trick). N Ireland win the final British Championship. France win European Championship – their first honour. FA National Soccer School opens at Lilleshall. Britain's biggest score this century: Stirling Alb 20 Selkirk 0 (Scottish Cup).

1985: Bradford City fire disaster – 56 killed. First £1m receipts from match in Britain (FA Cup Final). Kevin Moran (Manchester United) first player to be sent off in FA Cup Final. Celtic win 100th Scottish FA Cup Final. European Cup Final horror (Liverpool v Juventus, riot in Brussels) 39 die. UEFA ban all English clubs indefinitely from European competitions. No TV coverage at start of League season – first time since 1963 (resumption delayed until January 1986). Sept: first ground-sharing in League history – Charlton Athletic move from The Valley to Selhurst Park (Crystal Palace).

1986: Liverpool complete League and Cup double in player-manager Kenny Dalglish's first season in charge. Swindon (4th Div Champions) set League points record (102). League approve

331

reduction of First Division to 20 clubs by 1988. Everton chairman Philip Carter elected president of Football League. Death of Sir Stanley Rous (91). 100th edition of News of the World Football Annual. League Cup sponsored for next three years by Littlewoods (£2m). Football League voting majority (for rule changes) reduced from three-quarters to two-thirds. Wales move HQ from Wrexham to Cardiff after 110 years. Two substitutes in FA Cup and League (Littlewoods) Cup. Two-season League/TV deal (£6.2m):- BBC and ITV each show seven live League matches per season, League Cup semi-finals and Final. Football League sponsored by Today newspaper. Luton first club to ban all visiting supporters, as sequel are themselves banned from League Cup. Oldham and Preston install artificial pitches, making four in Football League (following QPR and Luton).

1987: League introduce play-off matches to decide final promotion/relegation places in all divisions. Re-election abolished – bottom club in Div 4 replaced by winners of GM Vauxhall Conference. Two substitutes approved for Football League 1987–8. Red and yellow disciplinary cards (scrapped 1981) re-introduced by League and FA Football League sponsored by Barclays. First Div reduced to 21 clubs.

1988: Football League Centenary. First Division reduced to 20 clubs.

1989: Soccer gets £74m TV deal: £44m over 4 years, ITV; £30m over 5 years, BBC/BSB. But it costs Philip Carter the League Presidency. Ted Croker retires as FA chief executive; successor Graham Kelly, from Football League. Hillsborough disaster: 95 die at FA Cup semi-final (Liverpool v Nottm Forest). Arsenal win closest-ever Championship with last kick. Peter Shilton sets England record with 109 caps.

1990: Nottm Forest win last Littlewoods Cup Final. Both FA Cup semi-finals played on Sunday and televised live. Play-off finals move to Wembley; Swindon win place in Div 1, then relegated back to Div 2 (breach of financial regulations) – Sunderland promoted instead. England reach World Cup semi-final in Italy and win FIFA Fair Play Award. Peter Shilton retires as England goalkeeper with 125 caps (world record). Graham Taylor (Aston Villa) succeeds Bobby Robson as England manager. International Board amend offside law (player 'level' no longer offside). FIFA make "professional foul" a sending-off offence. English clubs back in Europe (Manchester United and Aston Villa) after 5-year exile.

1991: First FA Cup semi-final at Wembley (Tottenham 3 Arsenal 1). Bert Millichip (FA chairman) and Philip Carter (Everton chairman) knighted. End of artificial pitches in Div 1 (Luton, Oldham). Scottish League reverts to 12-12-14 format (as in 1987–8). Penalty shoot-out introduced to decide FA Cup ties level after one replay.

1992: FA launch Premier League (22 clubs). Football League reduced to three divisions (71 clubs). Record TV-sport deal: BSkyB/BBC to pay £304m for 5-year coverage of Premier League. ITV do £40m, 4-year deal with Football League. Channel 4 show Italian football live (Sundays). FIFA approve new back-pass rule (goalkeeper must not handle ball kicked to him by team-mate). New League of Wales formed. Record all-British transfer, £3.3m: Alan Shearer (Southampton to Blackburn). Charlton return to The Valley after 7-year absence.

1993: Barclays end 6-year sponsorship of Football League. For first time both FA Cup semi-finals at Wembley (Sat, Sun). Arsenal first club to complete League Cup/FA Cup double. Rangers pull off Scotland's domestic treble for fifth time. FA in record British sports sponsorship deal (£12m over 4 years) with brewers Bass for FA Carling Premiership, from Aug. Brian Clough retires after 18 years as Nottm Forest manager; as does Jim McLean (21 years manager of Dundee Utd). Football League agree 3-year, £3m sponsorship with Endsleigh Insurance. Premier League introduce squad numbers with players' names on shirts. Record British transfer: Duncan Ferguson, Dundee Utd to Rangers (£4m). Record English-club signing: Roy Keane, Nottm Forest to Manchester United (£3.75m). Graham Taylor resigns as England manager after World Cup exit (Nov). Death of Bobby Moore (51), England World Cup winning captain 1966.

1994: Death of Sir Matt Busby. Terry Venables appointed England coach. Manchester United complete the Double. Last artificial pitch in English football goes – Preston revert to grass, summer 1994. Bobby Charlton knighted. Scottish League format changes to four divisions of ten clubs. Record British transfer: Chris Sutton, Norwich to Blackburn (£5m). FA announce first sponsorship of FA Cup – Littlewoods Pools (4-year, £14m deal, plus £6m for Charity Shield). Death of Billy Wright.

1995: New record British transfer: Andy Cole, Newcastle to Manchester United (£7m). First England match abandoned through crowd trouble (v Republic of Ireland, Dublin). Blackburn Champions for first time since 1914. Premiership reduced to 20 clubs. British transfer record broken again: Stan Collymore, Nottm Forest to Liverpool (£8.5m). Starting season 1995–6, teams allowed to use 3 substitutes per match, not necessarily including a goalkeeper. European Court of Justice upholds Bosman ruling, barring transfer fees for players out of contract and removing limit on number of foreign players clubs can field.

1996: Death of Bob Paisley (77), ex-Liverpool, most successful manager in English Football. FA appoint Chelsea manager Glenn Hoddle to succeed Terry Venables as England coach after Euro 96. Manchester United first English club to achieve Double twice (and in 3 seasons). Football League completes £125m, 5-year TV deal with BSkyB starting 1996–7. England stage European Championship, reach semi-finals, lose on pens to tournament winners Germany. Keith Wiseman succeeds Sir Bert Millichip as FA Chairman. Linesmen become known as 'referees' assistants'. Alan Shearer football's first £15m player (Blackburn to Newcastle). Nigeria first African country to win Olympic soccer. Nationwide Building Society sponsor Football League in initial 3-year deal worth £5.25m. Peter Shilton first player to make 1000 League appearances.

1997: Howard Wilkinson appointed English football's first technical director. England's first home defeat in World Cup (0 1 v Italy). Ruud Gullit (Chelsea) first foreign coach to win FA Cup. Rangers equal Celtic's record of 9 successive League titles. Manchester United win Premier League for fourth time in 5 seasons. New record World Cup score: Iran 17, Maldives 0 (qualifying round). Season 1997–8 starts Premiership's record £36m, 4-year sponsorship extension with brewers Bass (Carling).

1998: In French manager Arsene Wenger's second season at Highbury, Arsenal become second English club to complete the Double twice. Chelsea also win two trophies under new player-manager Gianluca Vialli (Coca-Cola Cup, Cup Winners' Cup). In breakaway from Scottish League, top ten clubs form new Premiership under SFA, starting season 1998–9. Football League celebrates its 100th season, 1998–9. New FA Cup sponsors – French insurance giants AXA (25m, 4-year deal). League Cup becomes Worthington Cup in £23m, 5-year contract with brewers Bass. Nationwide Building Society's sponsorship of Football League extended to season 2000–1.

1999: FA buy Wembley Stadium (£103m) for £320m, plan rebuilding (Aug 2000–March 2003) as new national stadium (Lottery Sports Fund contributes £110m) Scotland's new Premier League leaves 3-week mid-season break in January. Sky screen Oxford Utd v Sunderland (Div 1) as first pay-per-view match on TV. FA sack England coach Glenn Hoddle; Fulham's Kevin Keegan replaces him at £1m a year until 2003. Sir Alf Ramsey, England's World Cup-winning manager, dies aged 79. With effect 1999, FA Cup Final to be decided on day (via penalties, if necessary). Hampden Park re-opens for Scottish Cup Final after £63m refit. Alex Ferguson knighted after Manchester United complete Premiership, FA Cup, European Cup treble. Starting season 1999–2000, UEFA increase Champions League from 24 to 32 clubs. End of Cup Winners' Cup (merged into 121-club UEFA Cup). FA allow holders Manchester United to withdraw from FA Cup to participate in FIFA's inaugural World Club Championship in Brazil in January. Chelsea first British club to field an all-foreign line-up – at Southampton (Prem). FA vote in favour of streamlined 14-man board of directors to replace its 92-member council.

2000: Scot Adam Crozier takes over as FA chief executive. Wales move to Cardiff's £125m Millennium Stadium (v Finland). Brent Council approve plans for new £475m Wembley Stadium (completion target spring 2003); demolition of old stadium to begin after England v Germany (World Cup qual.). Fulham Ladies become Britain's first female professional team. FA Premiership and Nationwide League to introduce (season 2000–

01) rule whereby referees advance free-kick by 10 yards and caution player who shows dissent, delays kick or fails to retreat 10 yards. Scottish football increased to 42 League clubs in 2000–01 (12 in Premier League and 3 divisions of ten; Peterhead and Elgin elected from Highland League). France win European Championship – first time a major international tournament has been jointly hosted (Holland/ Belgium). England's £10m bid to stage 2006 World Cup fails; vote goes to Germany. England manager Kevin Keegan resigns after 1-0 World Cup defeat by Germany in Wembley's last International. Lazio's Swedish coach Sven-Goran Eriksson agrees to become England head coach.

2001: Scottish Premier League experiment with split into two 5-game mini leagues (6 clubs in each) after 33 matches completed. New transfer system agreed by FIFA/UEFA is ratified. Barclaycard begin £48m, 3-year sponsorship of the Premiership, and Nationwide's contract with the Football League is extended by a further 3 years (£12m). ITV, after winning auction against BBC's Match of the Day, begin £183m, 3-season contract for highlights of Premiership matches; BSkyB's live coverage (66 matches per season) for next 3 years will cost £1.1bn. BBC and BSkyB pay £400m (3-year contract) for live coverage of FA Cup and England home matches. ITV and Ondigital pay £315m to screen Nationwide League and Worthington Cup matches. In new charter for referees, top men can earn up to £60,000 a season in Premiership. Real Madrid break world transfer record, buying Zinedine Zidane from Juventus for £47.2m. FA introduce prize money, round by round, in FA Cup.

2002: Scotland appoint their first foreign manager, Germany's former national coach Bertie Vogts replacing Craig Brown. Collapse of ITV Digital deal, with Football League owed £178m, threatens lower-division clubs. Arsenal complete Premiership/FA Cup Double for second time in 5 seasons, third time in all. Newcastle manager Bobby Robson knighted in Queen's Jubilee Honours. New record British transfer and world record for defender, £29.1m Rio Ferdinand (Leeds to Manchester United). Transfer window introduced to British football. FA Charity Shield renamed FA Community Shield. After 2-year delay, demolition of Wembley Stadium begins. October: Adam Crozier, FA chief executive, resigns.

2003: FA Cup draw (from 4th Round) reverts to Monday lunchtime. Scottish Premier League decide to end mid-winter shut-down. Mark Palios appointed FA chief executive. For first time, two Football League clubs demoted (replaced by two from Conference). Ban lifted on loan transfers between Premiership clubs. July: David Beckham becomes record British export (Manchester United to Real Madrid, £23.3m). Biggest takeover in British football history – Russian oil magnate Roman Abramovich buys control of Chelsea for £150m. Wimbledon leave rented home at Selhurst Park, become England's first franchised club in 68-mile move to Milton Keynes.

2004: Arsenal first club to win Premiership with unbeaten record and only the third in English football history to stay undefeated through League season. Trevor Brooking knighted in Queen's Birthday Honours. Wimbledon change name to Milton Keynes Dons. Greece beat hosts Portugal to win European Championship as biggest outsiders (80-1 at start) ever to succeed in major international tournament. New contracts – Premiership in £57m deal with Barclays, seasons 2004–07. Coca-Cola replace Nationwide as Football League sponsors (£15m over 3 years), rebranding Div 1 as Football League Championship, with 2nd and 3rd Divisions, becoming Leagues 1 and 2. All-time League record of 49 unbeaten Premiership matches set by Arsenal. Under new League rule, Wrexham forfeit 10 points for going into administration.

2005: Brian Barwick, controller of ITV Sport, becomes FA chief executive. Foreign managers take all major trophies for English clubs: Chelsea, in Centenary year, win Premiership (record 95 points) and League Cup in Jose Mourinho's first season; Arsene Wenger's Arsenal win FA Cup in Final's first penalty shoot-out; under new manager Rafael Benitez, Liverpool lift European Cup on penalties after trailing 0-3 in Champions League Final. Wigan, a League club only since 1978, promoted to Premiership. In new record British-club take-over, American tycoon Malcolm Glazer buys Manchester United for £790m

Tributes are paid world-wide to George Best, who dies aged 59.

2006: Steve Staunton succeeds Brian Kerr as Republic of Ireland manager. Chelsea post record losses of £140m. Sven-Goran Eriksson agrees a settlement to step down as England coach. Steve McClaren replaces him. The Premier League announce a new 3-year TV deal worth £1.7 billion under which Sky lose their monopoly of coverage. Chelsea smash the British transfer record, paying £30.8m for Andriy Shevchenko. Clydesdale Bank replace Bank of Scotland as sponsor of the SPL.

2007: Michel Platini becomes the new president of UEFA. Walter Smith resigns as Scotland manager to return to Rangers and is replaced by Alex McLeish. The new £800m Wembley Stadium is finally completed. The BBC and Sky lose TV rights for England's home matches and FA Cup ties to ITV and Setanta. World Cup-winner Alan Ball dies aged 61. Lawrie Sanchez resigns as Northern Ireland manager to take over at Fulham. Nigel Worthington succeeds him. Lord Stevens names five clubs in his final report into alleged transfer irregularities. Steve McClaren is sacked after England fail to qualify for the European Championship Finals and is replaced by Fabio Capello. The Republic of Ireland's Steve Staunton also goes. Scotland's Alex McLeish resigns to become Birmingham manager.

2008: The Republic of Ireland follow England's lead in appointing an Italian coach – Giovanni Trapattoni. George Burley leaves Southampton to become Scotland manager. Manchester United beat Chelsea in the first all-English Champions League Final. Manchester City smash the British transfer record when signing Robinho from Real Madrid for £32.5m.

2009: Sky secure the rights to five of the six Premier League packages from 2010–13 with a bid of £1.6bn. Reading's David Beckham breaks Bobby Moore's record number of caps for an England outfield player with his 109th appearance. A British league record for not conceding a goal ends on 1,311 minutes for Manchester United's Edwin van der Sar. AC Milan's Kaka moves to Real Madrid for a world record fee of £56m. Nine days later, Manchester United agree to sell Cristiano Ronaldo to Real for £80m. Sir Bobby Robson dies aged 76 after a long battle with cancer. Shay Given and Kevin Kilbane win their 100th caps for the Republic of Ireland. The Premier League vote for clubs to have eight home-grown players in their squads. George Burley is sacked as Scotland manager and replaced by Craig Levein.

2010: npower succeed Coca-Cola as sponsors of the Football League. Portsmouth become the first Premier League club to go into administration. Chelsea achieve the club's first League and FA Cup double. Lord Triesman resigns as chairman of the FA and of England's 2018 World Cup bid. John Toshack resigns as Wales manager and is replaced by former captain Gary Speed. England is humiliated in the vote for the 2018 World Cup which goes to Russia, with the 2022 tournament awarded to Qatar.

2011: Seven club managers are sacked in a week. The transfer record between British clubs is broken twice in a day, with Liverpool buying Newcastle's Andy Carroll for £35m and selling Fernando Torres to Chelsea for £50m. Vauxhall replace Nationwide as sponsors of England and the other home nations. John Terry is restored as England captain. Football League clubs vote to reduce the number of substitutes from seven to five. Nigel Worthington steps down as Northern Ireland manager and is succeeded by Michael O'Neill. Sir Alex Ferguson completes 25 years as Manchester United manager. Manchester City post record annual losses of nearly £195m. Huddersfield set a Football League record of 43 successive unbeaten league games. Football mourns Gary Speed after the Wales manager is found dead at his home.

2012: Chris Coleman is appointed the new Wales manager. Fabio Capello resigns as manager after John Terry is stripped of the England captaincy for the second time. Roy Hodgson takes over. Rangers are forced into liquidation by crippling debts and a newly-formed club are demoted from the Scottish Premier League to Division Three. Manchester City become champions for the first time since 1968 after the tightest finish to a Premier League season. Chelsea win a penalty shoot-out against Bayern Munich in the Champions League Final. Capital One replace Carling as League Cup sponsors. Steven

Gerrard (England) and Damien Duff (Republic of Ireland) win their 100th caps. The FA's new £120m National Football Centre at Burton upon Trent is opened. Scotland manager Craig Levein is sacked.

2013: Gordon Strachan is appointed Scotland manager. FIFA and the Premier League announce the introduction of goal-line technology. Energy company npower end their sponsorship of the Football League and are succeeded by Sky Bet. Sir Alex Ferguson announces he is retiring after 26 years as Manchester United manager. Wigan become the first club to lift the FA Cup and be relegated in the same season. Chelsea win the Europa League. Ashley Cole and Frank Lampard win their 100th England caps. Robbie Keane becomes the most capped player in the British Isles on his 126th appearance for the Republic of Ireland. Scottish Football League clubs agree to merge with the Scottish Premier League. Greg Dyke succeeds David Bernstein as FA chairman. Real Madrid sign Tottenham's Gareth Bale for a world record £85.3m. Giovanni Trapatonni is replaced as Republic of Ireland manager by Martin O'Neill.

2014: Sir Tom Finney, one of the finest British players of all-time, dies aged 91. England experience their worst-ever World Cup, finishing bottom the group with a single point. Germany deliver one of the most remarkable scorelines in World Cup history – 7-1 against Brazil in the semi-finals. Manchester United announce a world-record kit sponsorship with adidas worth £750m. United break the incoming British transfer record by paying £59.7m for Real Madrid's Angel di Maria, part of a record £835m spending by Premier League clubs in the summer transfer window. England's Wayne Rooney and the Republic of Ireland's John O'Shea win their 100th caps.

2015: The Premier League sell live TV rights for 2016-19 to Sky and BT for a record £5.13bn. Bournemouth, a club on the brink of folding in 2008, win promotion to the Premier League. FIFA president Sepp Blatter resigns as a bribery and corruption scandal engulfs the world governing body. Blatter and suspended UEFA president Michel Platini are banned for eight years, reduced on appeal to six years.

2016: An inquest jury rules that the 96 Liverpool fans who died in the Hillsborough disaster of 1989 were unlawfully killed. Leicester, 5,000-1 outsiders become Premier League champions in one of the game's biggest-ever surprises. Aaron Hughes wins his 100th cap for Northern Ireland. FA Cup quarter-final replays are scrapped. England manager Roy Hodgson resigns. He is replaced by Sam Allardyce, who is forced out after one match for 'inappropriate conduct' and succeeded by Gareth Southgate. Manchester United sign Paul Pogba for a world record £89.3m.

2017 Paris Saint-Germain sign Barcelona's Neymar for a world record £198m. Managers Gordon Strachan (Scotland) and Chris Coleman (Wales) resign. Steven Davis reaches a century of Northern Ireland caps. Manchester United win the Europa League. Celtic are champions without losing a game. Arsenal win a record 13th FA Cup, Arsene Wenger for a record seventh time. Wayne Rooney retires from international football as England's record scorer with 53 goals.

2018 Manchester City become the first English champions to total 100 points. Celtic are the first in Scotland to win back-to-back domestic trebles. Alex McLeish (Scotland) and Ryan Giggs (Wales) are appointed. Arsene Wenger leaves Arsenal after 22 years as manager. A helicopter crash outside Leicester's King Power Stadium claims the lives of club owner Vichai Srivaddhanaprabha, the pilot and three others on board. Martin O'Neill is sacked as Republic of Ireland manager and replaced by Mick McCarthy, his second time in charge.

2019 Gordon Banks, England's World Cup-winning goalkeeper in 1966, dies aged 81. Tottenham open their new £1bn stadium. Manchester City achieve an unprecedented domestic treble. Celtic also make history with a third successive Scottish treble. Scotland manager Alex McLeish is sacked and replaced by Kilmarnock's Steve Clarke. For the first time, English clubs occupy all four places in the European finals - Liverpool defeating Tottenham in the Champions League and Chelsea beating Arsenal to win the Europa League.

FINAL WHISTLE – OBITUARIES 2018–19

JULY 2018

PAUL MADELEY, 73, redefined the role of a utility player in a 17-year, trophy-filled career with Leeds. He played every position bar goalkeeper as Don Revie's side rose from the old Second Division to become one of the most powerful in Europe. They also had a reputation for engaging, at times, in the darker side of the game, but that was never Madeley's forte. He played with grace and style, whether at full-back, in central defence, on the wing or leading the attack. Revie called him his Rolls Royce. Born in the Beeston district of the city, Madeley helped Leeds become champions in 1969 and 1974, ahead of Liverpool each time. He lifted the FA Cup and League Cup, with victory over Arsenal in both finals, and the Fairs Cup – forerunner of the UEFA Cup – against Ferencvaros and Juventus. There was also a European Cup Final against Bayern Munich which his team lost in 1975. In all, Madeley made 727 appearances for his only club and won 24 England caps, predominantly in defence, the first against Northern Ireland, the last against Holland.

DAVIE MCPARLAND, 83, became an influential figure in Scottish football as player and manager of Partick Thistle. In 16 seasons between 1953–69, he made 584 appearances and scored 109 goals for the club. In his first season as manager, he won promotion to the top division. The following year, Partick defeated Celtic 4-1 in the League Cup Final. McParland went on to manage Queen's Park and Hamilton, became Jock Stein's assistant at Celtic and had spells with Airdrie, Dunfermline, Motherwell and Dumbarton. Shortly before his death, he was told that Partick would be naming their new training ground after him.

JIMMY COLLINS, 80, was a Scottish inside-forward who joined Brighton from Tottenham and made 221 appearances and scored 48 goals between 1962–67. Highlight was captaining them to the keenly-contested Division Four title in 1965 when the top four teams were separated by just two points.

ALLAN BALL, 75, made a club-record 731 league and cup appearances in goal for Queen of the South between 1963–82 and in a poll was voted their greatest player. Initially an inside-forward, he switched position after replacing the injured Jim Montgomery – who went on to win the FA Cup with Sunderland – in a County Durham schools match. In later years, Ball was made an honorary director of the club, a position he held until his death.

FRED DONALDSON, 81, was part of Port Vale's Fourth Division title-winning squad of season 1958–59. The full-back spent six years at the club and also played for Exeter, Chester and Macclesfield.

JIMMY COPELAND, 76, helped Clyde back to the top flight in Scotland as runners-up to Morton in the 1963–64 season. He was previously with Montrose, Dumbarton and Kilmarnock.

AUGUST 2018

JIMMY MCILROY, 86, was one of the most skilful, influential players of his era, reaching the pinnacle of English football with Burnley and the quarter-finals of the World Cup with Northern Ireland. During 13 years at Turf Moor, after starting his career with Glentoran, the inside-forward turned down overtures from Manchester United and other big clubs while making 497 appearances and scoring 131 goals for the Lancashire side. Burnley were crowned champions in 1960, a point ahead of Wolves and two clear of Tottenham. McIlroy then scored their first goal in the European Cup against Reims before a 5-4 aggregate defeat by Hamburg in the quarter-finals. Two years later, Burnley finished runners-up to Ipswich and contested the FA Cup Final, losing 3-1 to Tottenham. He was sold, controversially, to Stoke, where he lined up alongside Stanley Matthews to win the Second Division title in 1963. McIlroy was there for three years and ended his career as player-manager of Oldham. He also had a brief spell in charge of Bolton, resigning on principle after two games when told by the board to sell players. He made 55 appearances, scoring ten goals, for Northern Ireland, who against the odds were group runners-up to West Germany in the 1958 World Cup in Sweden and defeated Czechoslovakia 2-1 in the play-offs before losing 4-0 to France in the last eight of the tournament. McIlroy received an MBE in 2011 for services to football and charity and has a stand named after him at Turf Moor.

CLIFF HUXFORD, 81, joined Southampton from Chelsea in 1959, was immediately made captain and led his new club to the Third Division title at the end of an ever-present first season. The wing-half went on to make 320 appearances, including the 1965–66 campaign when Southampton were promoted to the old first division as runners-up to Manchester City. He featured briefly the following season before moving to Exeter.

RON HUNT, 72, was a League Cup winner in 1967 with Queens Park Rangers, who retrieved a 2-0 half-time deficit to beat West Bromwich Albion 3-2 at Wembley with goals from Roger Morgan, Rodney Marsh and Mark Lazarus. The half-back also helped Rangers win the Division Three title that season, 12 points ahead of Middlesbrough. Hunt came through the ranks to make 255 appearances in ten years at his only club before retiring through injury.

DENNIS THROWER, 80, signed for Ipswich from local football in 1956 and made his debut aged 18 years and 28 days – then the club's youngest-ever player. For the next nine years the wing-half spent most of his time in the reserves as Sir Alf Ramsey led the club through the divisions to the First Division title in 1962. He then played non-league football.

TERRY BUSH, 75, spent his whole career with Bristol City, signing professional forms in 1960 making 182 appearances and scoring 45 goals in ten years at the club before having to retire through injury. His best season was 1964–65 with 16 goals in 37 league matches as City won promotion to Division Two when finishing runners up to Carlisle.

GORDON RIDDICK, 74, made more than 400 appearances between 1962–77 for six clubs – Luton, Gillingham, Charlton, Orient, Northampton and two spells at Brentford. In an era of small squads and limited resources, his main asset was the ability to play in a number of positions. Riddick retired with an ankle injury in September 1976, but returned to Brentford on a non-contract basis to help new manager Bill Dodgin before finally hanging up his boots the following February.

TED BENNETT, 93, was a goalkeeper who played as an amateur for Queens Park Rangers and represented Great Britain at the 1952 summer Olympics in Helsinki. Managed by England boss Walter Winterbottom, they were beaten 5-3 by Luxembourg in the preliminary round. Bennett, who won 11 caps as an England amateur international, later made 81 appearances as a professional for Watford before a finger injury ended his Football League career in 1955.

DAVE HARGREAVES, 64, scored a club-record 309 goals in 322 games for Accrington during their non-league days. They included 56 in 44 matches in the 1975–76 Lancashire Combination season. Hargreaves had two spells at his home-town club, either side of an injury-dogged two seasons with Blackburn.

ALAN HERCHER, 52, captained newly-formed Inverness Caledonian Thistle after the merger of Caledonian and Inverness Thistle in 1994. The midfielder, who started his career with Ross County, was a Scottish Division Three title winner in 1997 during three seasons at the new club.

SEPTEMBER 2018

KEVIN BEATTIE, 64, was described by his Ipswich manager Bobby Robson as the best England player he had ever seen. The powerful central defender joined the club at 15, progressed through the youth ranks and made his senior debut against Manchester United in 1972. Two years later, he was named PFA Young Player of the Year. Beattie made 296 appearances and scored 32 goals in ten years at the club, including the 1978 FA Cup Final when his side upset the odds to beat Arsenal 1-0 at Wembley. Injury forced him to miss the 1981 UEFA Cup Final, when Ipswich defeated the Dutch side Alkmaar 5-4 over two legs, and also restricted him to nine England caps. He later played briefly for Colchester and Middlesbrough, in addition to spells in Sweden and Norway, and was Michael Caine's body double in *Escape to Victory*, a film about a football match in a German prisoner-of-war camp.

JIM BROGAN, 74, made his Celtic debut in 1963, had to wait until the 1968-69 season for a regular place, then shared seven of the club's nine successive title triumphs under Jock Stein. The left-back also won four Scottish Cups, three League Cups and was part of the team beaten by Feyenoord in the 1970 European Cup Final. Brogan, who won four Scotland caps, made 341 appearances before spells with Coventry and Ayr.

EDDIE DAVIES, 72, invested a fortune in Bolton, enabling his home-town club to sign world-class players like Nicolas Anelka, Youri Djorkaeff and Jay Jay Okocha and become established in the Premier League under Sam Allardyce. The self-made millionaire owned the club for 13 years until 2016 when he handed over control, while writing off £171m of loans. Davies then became honorary president.

JOE CAROLAN, 81, joined Manchester United from the Home Farm club in Dublin and was part of their FA Youth Cup-winning team of 1956 which included Bobby Charlton and Alex Dawson. The full-back made his Football League debut in 1958, nine months after the Munich air disaster which claimed the lives of eight United players, and went on to make 71 appearances before joining Brighton. Carolan won two Republic of Ireland caps.

HARRY WALDEN, 77, helped Northampton to their first and only season in English football's top-flight. They finished runners-up to Newcastle in the old Second Division in 1965 and were relegated the following season. The right-winger, who joined the club from Luton in an exchange deal for Billy Hails, started and finished his career at Kettering.

GORDON PHILLIPS, 72, was an ever-present during Brentford's Fourth Division promotion-winning side in season 1971-72. The goalkeeper made 227 appearances in ten years at the club and had another two years as goalkeeping coach when returning to Griffin Park in 1990 after playing non-league football.

TOMMY BEST, 97, helped break down racial barriers at a time when non-white players were a rarity in English football. The centre forward had spells with Chester, Cardiff and Queens Park Rangers in the 1940s before finishing his career at Hereford.

BILLY NEVILLE, 83, made three appearances in West Ham's Division Two title-winning team of season 1957-58. But the forward's promising career, which included playing for the Republic of Ireland's under-23 side, was cut short when he contracted tuberculosis at the age of 22.

ERNIE BATEMAN, 89, was a centre-half who joined Watford from Hemel Hempstead in 1952, made 23 appearances for the club, then returned to non-league football with Sittingbourne.

HOWARD KENNEDY, 66, made 416 appearances and scored 102 goals for Wycombe between 1974-83 during the club's non-league days.

OCTOBER 2018

VICHAI SRIVADDHANAPRABHA, 60, was the man behind the impossible dream that came true – Leicester City winning the Premier League in season 2015-16. His death in a helicopter crash outside the King Power Stadium, was mourned throughout the city, as well as by players, officials and staff. The self-made Thai billionaire bought the club, then in the Championship, from Milan Mandaric for £39m in August 2010. He became chairman six months later and following promotion to the top-flight in 2014 pledged £180m to secure a top-five place and with it European football. Two years later, Leicester defied odds of 5,000-1 to become champions by a ten-point margin and qualify for the Champions League. The owner dismissed manager Claudio Ranieri the following season, but his widespread popularity remained undiminished. He donated £2m to building a new children's hospital and supported other local projects and charities. The bond with Leicester players was such that they flew to Bangkok for his funeral. The pilot and three others died in the crash, seconds after the helicopter took off from the stadium pitch following a match against West Ham.

SIR DOUG ELLIS, 94, was chairman of Aston Villa for 31 years and one of the pioneers of the Premier League. He had two spells in charge at Villa Park – from 1968–75, then from 1982–2006. After selling the club to American businessman Randy Lerner, he became life president. Sir Doug was knighted in 2012 for his charity work.

KEN SHELLITO, 78, served Chelsea as a player, coach and manager. He joined the club on the same day as Jimmy Greaves and was part of Tommy Docherty's Second Division promotion-winning team in season 1962–63. Shellito gained one England cap, against Czechoslovakia, and also played against the Rest of the World in a match to mark the centenary of the FA. But a knee injury forced him to retire, ending hopes of making the successful 1966 World Cup squad. He took charge of the club's youth academy and had two seasons as manager after succeeding full-back partner Eddie McCreadie. Shellito also managed Cambridge United, then coached in Malaysia and worked as a match analyst for the Asian Confederation.

GEOFF SCOTT, 61, helped two clubs secure top-flight football in successive years. The left-back went up with third-place Stoke from Division Two in 1979, thanks to victory over Notts County in their final fixture. He lost his place the following season and joined Leicester, who finished divisional champions, a point ahead of Sunderland. Scott later played for home-town club Birmingham, Charlton, Middlesbrough, Northampton and Cambridge.

TONY HOPPER, 42, played in one of the most memorable matches in Carlisle's history – the 1999 fixture against Plymouth when goalkeeper Jimmy Glass scored a 94th minute goal to keep them in the Football League. Hopper, a midfielder, spent ten years at the club and also had spells with Workington and Barrow. He died from motor neurone disease.

CHARLIE CRICKMORE, 76, was an ever-present in Notts County's Fourth Division title-winning season of 1970–71. The left-winger previously played for home-town club Hull, Bournemouth, Gillingham, Rotherham and Norwich. He was forced to retire, aged 30, in 1972 after sustaining a broken leg.

NOVEMBER 2018

DAVID STEWART, 71, played in a European Cup Final and saved a penalty on his international debut. The goalkeeper joined Leeds from Ayr as cover for David Harvey and took over when Harvey was injured in a car crash. He came in for the quarter-final against Anderlecht, the semi-final with Barcelona and kept his place for the 1975 final against Bayern Munich, who made the most of controversial refereeing decisions to win 2-0. Two years later, on his only appearance for Scotland, he kept out a spot-kick during a 1-0 defeat by East Germany. Stewart was then an ever-present in season 1980–81 for Swansea, who completed their rise to the old First Division under John Toshack with a third promotion in four seasons. He finished his career in Hong Kong.

JIM ILEY, 82, captained Newcastle on their return to the top-flight as Second Division champions in season 1964–65, a point clear of Northampton. He made 249 appearances in seven years at the club, forming a formidable half-back line with Stan Anderson and John McGrath under Joe Harvey. The England under-23 international previously played for Sheffield United, Tottenham and Nottingham Forest and ended his career as player- manager of Peterborough. He went on to manage Barnsley, Blackburn, Bury and Exeter.

JOHNNY HART, 90, served Manchester City for nearly three decades – from office boy to manager. He played from 1946–61 and was twice the club's joint leading scorer. The inside-forward helped City reach the 1955 FA Cup Final, but a broken leg sustained a week before the final ruled him out of the side beaten 3-1 by Newcastle. Hart missed out again 12 months later when they defeated Birmingham 3-1 at Wembley. He retired to take up a coaching role and succeeded Malcolm Allen as manager in 1973 – an appointment cut short by illness after six months.

GRAHAM WILLIAMS, 81, was a Wales schoolboy international, played at under-23 level, then progressed to the senior side, winning five caps in 1961–62 while at Swansea. The left winger previously played his club football at Bradford City and Everton. Williams later served home-town club Wrexham, won promotion from Division Four with Tranmere and had a spell with Port Vale.

KEVIN AUSTIN, 45, helped Swansea win two promotions – from League Two in 2005 and as League One champions in 2008. In between, he shared the club's Football League Trophy victory over Carlisle at the Millennium Stadium. Austin, who played in central defence and at left-back, also had spells with Leyton Orient, Lincoln, Barnsley, Brentford, Cambridge United, Bristol Rovers and Chesterfield. He won seven caps for Trinidad and Tobago and later worked as youth coach at Scunthorpe. He was diagnosed with pancreatic cancer in 2017.

ROGER HOY, 71, helped Crystal Palace achieve top-flight football for the first time as runners-up to Derby in the old Second Division under Bert Head in 1969. The following season, he scored the winning goal against Manchester City that kept his side up by a single point. Hoy, who could play in central defence or midfield, joined the club from Tottenham and later had spells with Luton and Cardiff.

DARREN PITCHER, 49, joined Charlton at 13, came through the youth ranks and made his senior debut in 1990. Two years later, he was part of the side that returned to The Valley against Portsmouth after the club's seven-year exile. The defensive midfielder made 204 appearances before signing for Crystal Palace, helping them reach the semi-finals of the FA Cup and League Cup in season 1994–95. A knee injury sustained against Huddersfield in 1996 ended his career. Pitcher lost a High Court claim for damages, alleging a 'negligent' tackle.

RODNEY GREEN, 79, began his career at home-town club Halifax in 1960 and played for seven other teams. They included Bradford City, where he was top scorer with 29 league goals in season 1963–64. The centre-forward also had spells at Bradford Park Avenue, Gillingham, Grimsby, Charlton, Luton, Watford and Durban in South Africa.

GEORGE YARDLEY, 76, was a self taught centre-forward after starting his career as a goalkeeper with East Fife. He had two prolific spells with Tranmere, scoring 81 goals in 149 matches. The first included promotion from Division Four in 1967. The second was interrupted the following year when he lost a kidney in a high tackle playing against Shrewsbury and spent three months in hospital. Yardley previously played for Luton and in Australia.

GORDON MORRITT, 76, combined his goalkeeping duties at home-town club Rotherham with appearances at centre-forward for the reserves. In 1964, he was in goal for a 2-2 League Cup draw against Swansea, then played up front in the replay which his side lost 2-0. He left for Durban in South Africa, returning the following season to join Doncaster. Morritt then played for Northampton, helped York gain promotion from Division Four, and spent time at Rochdale and Darlington.

BARRIE BETTS, 86, captained Manchester City in his four years at Maine Road after signing from Stockport in 1960. The right-back started his career with home-town club Barnsley and ended it at Scunthorpe. He later managed non-league Lancaster.

BILL MULLAN, 90, was a FIFA referee for ten seasons. His major matches included the second leg of the 1971 Inter-Continental Cup Final between Nacional (Uruguay) and Panathinaikos (Greece); the 1972 European Championship semi-final between Belgium and West Germany; the Olympic tournament meeting of West Germany and East Germany that year. He was also in charge of one of Scottish football's biggest upsets – Partick's 4-1 win over Celtic in the 1971 League Cup Final. After an eye injury ended his career, Mullan was appointed a referee supervisor by the Scottish FA.

DECEMBER 2018

BILL SLATER, 91, was part of the great Wolves side that won First Division titles in 1954, 1958 and 1959. He also captained them to a 3-0 win over Blackburn in the 1960 FA Cup Final. Later that year, the half-back became the only part-time player ever to win the Football Writers' Association Footballer of the Year award – at the same time as studying for a BSc degree at university. Slater also remains the last amateur to play in an FA Cup Final – for Blackpool in their 2-0 defeat by Newcastle in 1951. He won 12 full England caps, four of them at the 1958 World Cup in Sweden, made 20 appearances for the England amateur team and represented Great Britain at the 1952 Helsinki Olympics. After 339 appearances for Wolves over 11 years and a spell at Brentford, he became deputy director of the Crystal Palace Sports Centre. Public recognition came with an OBE and CBE.

PETER THOMPSON, 76, was a key figure in Bill Shankly's first great Liverpool side, a traditional left-winger who could score goals as well as create them for the likes of Roger Hunt and Ian St John. Signed from Preston in 1963, having first impressed the Anfield manager in an FA Cup tie between the clubs, he played every match in his first season as Liverpool beat Manchester United to the First Division title. They were champions again, this time ahead of Leeds, two years later. In between, there was a first FA Cup success, 2-1 against Leeds, followed by a run to the European Cup-Winners' Cup Final at Hampden Park, won 2-1 by Borussia Dortmund. Thompson made 416 appearance, scored 54 times and won 16 England caps. But he missed out on the 1966 and 1970 World Cups, with Sir Alf Ramsey reluctant to use conventional wingers. He finished his career at Bolton, retiring in 1978 after they were promoted as Second Division champions.

PETER HILL-WOOD, 82, joined the Arsenal board in 1962, became chairman in 1982 following the death of his father Denis and held the position for 31 years until stepping down through ill health. During that time the club enjoyed major league and cup successes under managers George Graham and Arsene Wenger. Hill-Wood was instrumental in the move from Highbury to the Emirates Stadium and also played a key role in the formation of the Premier League. He was succeeded in the chair by Sir Chips Keswick.

MIKE BARNARD, 85, played top-flight football and county championship cricket. He made his debut for home-town Portsmouth against Tottenham in December 1953 and helped the club finish third behind Chelsea and Wolves in the old First Division the following season, The inside-forward made 123 appearances before leaving, aged 25, to concentrate on his career with Hampshire. He helped them to a first county title in 1961 – while still turning out for non-league Chelmsford – and went on to total 9,314 runs before retiring in 1965.

COLIN BARLOW, 83, made his mark on and off the field at Manchester City. The winger scored on his debut against Chelsea in 1957 and netted 82 goals in six seasons before moving on to play for Oldham and Doncaster. He returned to Maine Road in 1994 as part of Francis Lee's takeover, serving for three years as the club's first chief executive.

BRIAN JORDAN, 86, helped Rotherham come within a whisker of promotion to the old First Division in season 1954–55. His side defeated Liverpool 6-1 at Millmoor in the final match, finished level on 54 points with Birmingham and Luton, but lost out on goal average. The centre-half spent five years at the club after starting out at Derby. He later played for Middlesbrough and York and was a part-timer throughout his career, combining football with a job in the electrical department of a local colliery.

MIKE METCALF, 79, scored 37 goals in Chester's total of 141 in Football League and cup matches in season 1964–65. His tally came during a then club-record 127 consecutive league appearances. The inside-forward signed from Wrexham after starting out in the youth ranks at Everton.

TOM BROWNLEE, 83, had a spell with Workington during their Football League days, scoring in the inaugural League Cup season of 1960–61 in a 4-2 second round defeat by Chelsea at

Stamford Bridge. The centre-forward was previously with Walsall and York and later netted 14 goals in 18 games to become Bradford City's top scorer in 1964–65.

MIKE HUGHES, 78, was a wing-half who played for Cardiff, Exeter and Chesterfield. He then managed Yeovil, leading the club to the Southern League title and to a third round FA Cup tie against Arsenal (0-3) in front of a 14,500 crowd at the old Huish ground in season 1970–71.

ROY WOOLCOTT, 72, made a single senior appearance for Tottenham, against Ipswich in 1969, spending the rest of his time at the club in the reserves. The centre forward moved on to Gillingham, then played non-league football.

JANUARY 2019

PHIL MASINGA, 49, became the first South African to play in the Premier League when he came on as a substitute for Leeds against West Ham in 1994. The striker signed from Mamelodi Sundowns and spent two years at Elland Road, scoring five goals in 31 appearances. Masinga also had spells with St Gallen in Switzerland and Salernitana and Bari in Italy, won 58 caps and scored the goal against Congo which sent South Africa through to their first World Cup in 1998. He died of cancer.

ARTHUR TURNER, 97, survived being shot down in a Wellington bomber over the Bay of Biscay during the Second World War in 1943 and three years later played in an FA Cup Final. The centre-forward was in Charlton's team beaten 4-1 by Derby in 1946 – the first amateur to feature in a Wembley final for more than two decades. All of his nine 'first class' appearances for the club came in that season's competition when he netted seven goals. Turner went on to score 100 in 164 appearances for Colchester, including their first goal in the Football League, against Swindon in August, 1950.

JOHNNY WALKER, 90, made 548 appearances in a 17-year career with three clubs. The inside-forward was leading scorer in Wolves' run to the semi-finals of the FA Cup in season 1950–51. He had five seasons at Southampton after a then record £12,000 transfer. Then, Walker played 319 matches during eight years at Reading, where he captained the side while switching position to wing half, then finally to right-back.

FREDDIE GLIDDEN, 91, won every domestic honour during 12 years with Hearts. He was the captain and last surviving member of the side that lifted the Scottish Cup in 1956 with a 3-1 victory over Celtic. A crowd of 133,000 at Hampden Park saw the club's first success in the competition for 50 years. Hearts were league champions two years later, ahead of Rangers and Celtic, and Glidden also had two League Cup trophies. The centre-half was four times a reserve for Scotland, prior to finishing his career with Dumbarton.

REG HOLLAND, 78, was part of Manchester United's successful FA Youth Cup-side of 1956. The full-back lined up alongside Bobby Charlton, Alex Dawson and Wilf McGuinness in the final against Chesterfield, who included future World Cup-winning goalkeeper Gordon Banks. After leaving the club without making the senior team, Holland helped Wrexham gain promotion from Division Four in season 1961-62, then played for Chester.

DUNCAN WELBOURNE, 78, spent 11 seasons at Watford after signing from Grimsby in 1963. He made 457 appearances, including a club-record run of 280 consecutive league matches. The full-back was part of the Division Three title-winning side in season 1968–69 and played in Watford's first FA Cup semi-final against Chelsea in 1970. He finished his career playing for and managing Southport.

MIKE HARRISON, 78, came through the youth ranks at Chelsea and made his senior debut, aged 16, at Blackpool in 1957. The following year, he scored twice in the first leg of the FA Youth Cup Final which his side lost 7-6 on aggregate against Wolves. Harrison, an England under-23 international winger, left following relegation in 1962 for Blackburn and later played for Plymouth and Luton.

DENIS HUNT, 81, made 355 appearances in a decade with Gillingham. He was part of the side that won the Fourth Division title in 1964 with a superior goal average to Carlisle after both finished on 60 points. The left-back moved to Brentford in 1968 and later managed Folkestone, Ashford and Margate.

NIGEL SADDINGTON, 53, was a centre-half who started his career at Doncaster, moved to home-town club Sunderland, then captained Carlisle. He left, aged 25, in 1991 after being diagnosed with ME and had a spell with non-league Gateshead.

FEBRUARY 2019

GORDON BANKS, 81, was well on the way to greatness during England's 1966 triumph at Wembley. Confirmation followed with an unbroken run of awards as FIFA's No 1 goalkeeper. Then, at the next World Cup in Mexico, came the moment which defined him as one of the finest of his era – and in the eyes of many the best of all-time. Banks, himself, rated a penalty save from England team-mate Geoff Hurst in a League Cup tie as better than the one which miraculously turned Pele's downward header over the bar in a group game against Brazil in Guadalajara. A sixth successive FIFA award in 1971 suggested otherwise, but it was typical of this modest, gentle man that his view never changed, no matter how many times the incident was replayed over the years. There was no happy ending to that tournament, with Banks laid low by a stomach bug and replaced by Peter Bonetti for the quarter-final against West Germany in Leon which England lost 3-2 after leading 2-0. Banks would have added to his 73 caps but for a car crash in 1972 which left him blind in one eye and also ended a Football League career spanning 632 matches. It began at Chesterfield in 1955, covered eight years at Leicester, with whom he won the League Cup against Stoke in 1964 and lost two FA Cup Finals against Tottenham (1961) and Manchester United (1963). They were followed by five years at Stoke and another League Cup success, against Chelsea, in 1972. Along the way, there was plenty of speculation about a move to a bigger club – Liverpool or Arsenal – but it came to nothing. Banks retired at 34, still in his prime, having been named Footballer of the Year by the football writers. He also had spells with Cleveland and Fort Lauderdale in the United States, Hellenic in South Africa and the Irish club St Patrick's. Later, there was one managerial job, at non-league Telford, and a coaching appointment with Port Vale. In more recent years, he sold his World Cup winner's medal for a record £124,750, carried the London Olympic torch at Wembley and was part of the Russia World Cup draw. Banks, whose official recognition, was limited to an OBE when his achievements cried out for a knighthood, was the fourth member of the successful team of 1966 to be lost, after captain Bobby Moore, Alan Ball and Ray Wilson.

FRED PICKERING, 78, scored a hat-trick on his debut for both club and country. Everton broke the British domestic transfer record when paying Blackburn £85,000 for the centre-forward, who made a flying start in their 6-1 win over Nottingham Forest in 1964. Nine goals in nine games brought an England call-up and another treble, in a 10-0 victory over the United States. Pickering was also on the mark in his two other internationals under Alf Ramsey –against Northern Ireland and Belgium. He was named in Ramsey's provisional squad for the 1966 World Cup, but had to withdraw with a knee injury sustained in an FA Cup quarter-final replay against Manchester City. Although Pickering scored 70 goals in 115 appearances for Everton, he was left out of their 1966 FA Cup Final team against Sheffield Wednesday and moved for £50,000 to Birmingham. Then came a spell with Blackpool, a return to home-town club Blackburn where he started his career as a full-back, and finally to Brighton.

IAN ROSS, 72, captained Aston Villa to league and cup honours in season 1974–75. His team gained promotion to the old First Division as runners-up to Manchester United and defeated Norwich 1-0 in the League Cup Final. The central defender previously helped Villa to the Third Division title after a £60,000 move from Liverpool in 1972. Ross later had spells with Notts County, Northampton, Peterborough and Hereford. He then coached at Wolves and was appointed caretaker-manager after the departure of John Barnwell. After that, he managed Huddersfield, two clubs in Iceland and Berwick Rangers.

ERIC HARRISON, 81, developed the careers of many Manchester United stars, including David Beckham, Ryan Giggs, Paul Scholes and Gary Neville, as youth team coach at Old Trafford. He led the Class of '92 – regarded as the best crop of young players in the English game – to the FA Youth Cup and won it again in 1995. Harrison spent 27 years at the club and was awarded an MBE in 2018. He also had four years as assistant manager of Wales alongside Mark Hughes. In his playing days, he made more than 500 appearances at Halifax, Hartlepool, Southport and two spells with Barrow.

DANNY WILLIAMS, 94, made a record 500 appearances in 15 years with home-town club Rotherham. They included promotion to the old Division Two as champions in 1951 and almost a rise to the top-flight in 1955 when his side missed out on goal average after finishing level on 54 points with champions Birmingham and runners-up Luton. The wing-half, a one-club player, went on to manage Rotherham, in addition to Swindon, Sheffield Wednesday and Mansfield. In the first of two spells at the County Ground, he led Swindon to victory over Arsenal in the 1969 League Cup Final. They also defeated Napoli in the Anglo-Italian Cup. Williams later had seven years as general manager.

MICK KENNEDY, 57, was a Republic of Ireland midfielder who helped Portsmouth reach the old First Division in season 1986–87. He was one of Alan Ball's first signings, £100,000 from Middlesbrough, and Portsmouth reached the top-flight by finishing runners up to Derby. Kennedy was sold to Bradford City for £250,000 and played for seven other clubs in a career spanning 631 matches – Halifax, Huddersfield, Leicester, Luton, Stoke, Chesterfield and Wigan. He won two Irish caps while at Fratton Park.

MATTHEW BRAZIER, 42, came through the youth ranks at Queens Park Rangers and played Premier League football in four years at Loftus Road. The midfielder moved to Fulham, then on to Cardiff, helping the club win promotion from Division Three in season 2000–01. Brazier then played for Leyton Orient before retiring in 2004. He died of cancer.

BOBBY DOYLE, 65, was a key figure in Portsmouth's Division Three title-winning side of season 1982–3. The midfielder, a £75,000 signing from Blackpool, played 44 of their 46 games. Two seasons later, Portsmouth missed out on promotion to the old First Division on goal difference. Doyle was previously with Barnsley and Peterborough and finished his career at Hull, where he was forced to retire through injury in 1987.

JOE FASCIONE, 74, joined Chelsea from Scottish junior football and had a hand in their first League Cup success in 1964–65, playing in three of the early rounds. The right-winger made a successful league debut the following season, scoring one goal and helping Barry Bridges to another in a 3-1 victory over Arsenal at Highbury. But he featured only sporadically and left for Durban in South Africa in 1969 after 34 appearances in five years.

PETER DOLBY, 78, made 365 appearances in 16 years with Shrewsbury – his only professional club. The centre-half's biggest moment came when he scored two winning goals against Everton in the fifth round of the inaugural League Cup in season 1960–61. Dolby, who was completing an engineering apprenticeship, cycled to the game and passed the Everton team coach on the way.

CLIFF MYERS, 72, was a forward who had spells with Charlton, Brentford and Torquay, along with 329 appearances for Yeovil in their non-league days. They included the 1970-71 season when Yeovil won the Southern League title and were rewarded for reaching the third round of the FA Cup with a tie against Arsenal, who won it 3-0.

GRAHAM NEWTON, 76, started as an amateur with Wolves and had spells with six other Football League clubs – Blackpool, Walsall, Coventry, Bournemouth, Port Vale and Reading. The inside-forward also played for Atlanta when they won the North American Soccer League in 1968.

JOHNNY VALENTINE, 88, made ten appearances for Rangers, all in the 1957–58 season. They included the League Cup Final against Celtic which his side lost 7-1. The centre-half joined the club from Queen's Park and later played for St Johnstone.

BARRIE BLOWER, 78, was president and former chairman of Walsall, who played a leading role in saving the club in the 1980s when successfully campaigning against ground-sharing with Wolves and Birmingham. He was also a key figure in Walsall leaving Fellows Park for the Bescot Stadium in 1990.

MARCH 2019

ERIC CALDOW, 84, captained club and country and was regarded as one of Scotland's finest full-backs. Comfortable on both defensive flanks, he made 407 appearances in 13 years with Rangers, winning five league titles, two Scottish Cups and three League Cups. He also led the side beaten 4-1 on aggregate by Fiorentina in the 1961 Cup-Winners' Cup Final. Of his 40 international caps, 29 were at left-back, 11 at right-back and 15 as captain. Caldow was an ever-present in qualifying for the 1958 World Cup and played in all three matches in the finals in Sweden against Yugoslavia, Paraguay and France. He scored in Scotland's 2-0 win over England at Hampden in 1962 and won his final cap the following year at Wembley, where he suffered a broken leg. After leaving Rangers in 1966, he played part-time for Stirling, then managed Corby and Stranraer.

TED BURGIN, 91, was one of the country's top goalkeepers during eight years at Sheffield United. He was just 5ft 9in tall, but stood out with his bravery, agility and quick feet off the line, which earned a place in the England B team. He was also a non-playing member of the squad for the 1954 World Cup in Switzerland. Burgin made 314 appearances for his home-town club and was a key figure in their Division Two title-winning side of season 1952–53. He later had spells with Doncaster and Leeds, then played 234 games for Rochdale, including the 1962 League Cup Final against Norwich, who won it 4-0 on aggregate.

BARRIE HOLE, 76, made his league debut for Cardiff at 17 in the 1959–60 season when they gained promotion to the old First Division. Hole went on to make 211 appearances, while also launching his international career which brought 30 Wales caps. The wing-half continued his club football with Blackburn and Aston Villa, then joined Swansea, his home-town club, for whom father Billy and brothers Colin and Alan also played.

KIT NAPIER, 75, was leading scorer in five of his six seasons with Brighton. He equalled Albert Munday's post-war record of 28 goals in the 1967–68 campaign and netted 19 in 1971–72 when his side won promotion from Division Three. The centre-forward's 99 goals in 291 appearances made him the club's overall leading post-war marksman until Glenn Murray reached 100 last season. Napier previously played for Blackpool, Preston, Workington and Newcastle. He left Brighton for Blackburn and finished his career with Durban in South Africa.

KEVIN RANDALL, 73, had a long association with Chesterfield, initially as a free-scoring centre-forward after joining the club from Bury in 1966. He netted 96 goals in 258 league appearances, including a Division Four title win in season 1969–70. After a move to Notts County, helping Mansfield become Division Three champions in 1977, then playing for York, Randall returned to the Recreation Ground. He had a spell as manager and was assistant to John Duncan when Chesterfield reached the semi-finals of the FA Cup in 1997. After that, he scouted and coached at Queens Park Rangers, Sheffield United, Crystal Palace, Leeds and Burnley.

DEREK LEWIN, 88, scored five goals in Bishop Auckland's three successive FA Amateur Cup Final wins, against Hendon, Corinthian Casuals in a replay and Wycombe, between 1955–57. The inside-forward made five appearances for the England amateur side and played in one of Great Britain's matches, against Bulgaria, at the 1956 Olympics in Melbourne. Two years later, following the Munich air disaster which claimed the lives of eight Manchester

United players, Lewin joined United on loan, along with team-mates Warren Bradley and Bob Hardisty. He also had spells with Oldham and Accrington.

BERNARD HALFORD, 77, became known as 'Mr Manchester City' during nearly 40 years as club secretary. He was named life president on his retirement and in 2006 became the first non-player to be elected to City's Hall of Fame.

JOHN HELLAWELL, 75, began his career with Bradford City in 1963, then played for Rotherham, Darlington and Bradford Park Avenue. The inside-forward's brother, Mike, won two England caps with Birmingham.

RON PEPLOW, 83, was an inside-forward who spent six years as a squad member at Brentford. His best season was the final one, 1960–61, with 18 appearances in all competitions. After leaving the club, he played non-league football in Kent.

GORDON HILL, 90, was a Football League referee from 1966–75. His biggest match came in his final season before compulsory retirement at 47 – the League Cup Final between Aston Villa and Norwich. He later refereed matches in the North American Soccer League.

APRIL 2019

BILLY MCNEILL, 79, crowned his career as Celtic's greatest captain with a history-making success in the 1967 European Cup Final. No British team had won club football's biggest prize and that looked likely to continue when Inter Milan, bidding for a third victory in four years, took a seventh minute lead. Instead, Tommy Gemmell equalised, Stevie Chalmers scored the winner and McNeill's side – who became known as the 'Lisbon Lions' – paved the way for more triumphs in subsequent seasons by Manchester United, Liverpool, Nottingham Forest and Aston Villa. McNeill also lifted all three domestic trophies that season during a decade in which Celtic dominated Scottish football. There were nine league titles, seven Scottish Cups and six League Cups. The imposing central defender, who joined from junior club Blantyre Victoria in 1957, made a total of 822 appearances and scored 37 goals. His last game was the Scottish Cup win over Airdrie in 1975. McNeill, capped 29 times for Scotland, continued to win trophies as a manager after starting out at Clyde and Aberdeen. He succeeded Jock Stein for the first of two spells back at Celtic which brought four titles, three Scottish Cups and a League Cup. In between, he led Manchester City to the top-flight and managed Aston Villa. McNeill received the MBE, was voted Celtic's finest captain and had a statue of him lifting the European Cup erected at Celtic Park.

STEVIE CHALMERS, 83, scored that winner in that famous match against Inter Milan, diverting a long range shot by Bobby Murdoch into the net after 85 minutes – the most important goal in the club's 131-year history. It was one of 231 the Scotland forward netted in 403 appearances during 12 years at Celtic Park. He played in four championship-winning teams, won three Scottish Cups and four League Cups. Chalmers, who scored three times in five appearances for the national team, later played for Morton and Partick Thistle. He died a week after Billy McNeill.

TOMMY SMITH, 74, grew up in the shadows of Anfield, worked as a groundsman at the stadium and went on to achieve legendary status at the heart of some of the club's biggest successes. An uncompromising midfielder-turned-central defender with a shrewd football brain, he won nine major trophies under Bill Shankly and Bob Paisley in 18 years at the club. The biggest was Liverpool's first European Cup triumph, 3-1 against Borussia Monchengladbach in the Rome final of 1977 when Smith headed his second goal from Steve Heighway's corner. It completed a season's double, with his side finishing a point ahead of Manchester City for the league title. The 'Anfield Iron', as he was known, had previously won the old First Division three times, had two UEFA Cup successes and lifted the FA Cup twice, including the club's first Wembley triumph against Leeds in 1965. Smith made 638 appearances and scored 48 goals, gained one England cap, against Wales in the Home Championship, and was awarded an MBE for his services to the game. He later played in the United States for Tampa Bay and

Los Angeles, then helped Swansea to promotion from Division Three before retiring in 1979. After that, Smith was a columnist for the *Liverpool Echo* for 35 years.

IVOR BROADIS, 96, was the oldest surviving England international, having won 14 caps when playing for Manchester City and Newcastle. He scored eight goals, two of them in a 4-4 draw with Belgium at the 1954 World Cup in Switzerland when partnering Nat Lofthouse, who also netted twice. Broadis, described by Sir Alex Ferguson as 'one of the great players in the English game,' had two spells with Carlisle. In the first, he was appointed player-manager, aged 23, and remains the youngest to hold the position in the Football League. He also played for Sunderland and finished his career in Scotland with Queen of the South.

PETER SKIPPER, 61, made 338 appearances in two spells with home-town club Hull. They included two promotions – from Division Four as runners-up in 1982–83 and two seasons later from Division Three when he scored the winner against Walsall to secure third place. Skipper, a central defender, also played for Scunthorpe, Darlington, Oldham, Walsall, Wrexham and Wigan.

GEORGE HAIGH, 103, was one of the oldest surviving professional players. He left school in 1929 to sign amateur forms with Manchester City, where he became great friends with England goalkeeper Frank Swift. The centre-back went on to play for Stockport until 1939 when World War Two effectively ended his professional career. Last season, he attended Stockport's home match against Brackley in National League North to mark Armistice Day and the 100th anniversary of the end of the Great War.

COLIN COLLINDRIDGE, 98, signed professional forms for Sheffield United in 1939, guested for Chesterfield, Notts County, Lincoln and Oldham during the War, and finally made his league debut for United, against Liverpool, at the end of the conflict in 1946. The left-winger went on to win the Third Division South title with Nottingham Forest in 1951 and finished his career with Coventry.

DAVID HARNEY, 72, started his career at Grimsby and continued it at Lincolnshire rivals Scunthorpe. There, the forward was unlucky with injuries, making a single appearance at his next club Brentford, then moving into non-league football!

MAY 2019

HARRY HOOD, 74, was the third former Celtic star to pass away in a month. He joined the club in 1969 after a second spell with Clyde and won six league titles, four Scottish Cups and the League Cup twice. Hood also had the distinction of scoring a hat-trick in an Old Firm derby, the League Cup semi-final of 1973. That feat was not repeated until Moussa Dembele netted three in a league match against Rangers in 2016. In seven years at Celtic, Hood scored 123 goals in 310 appearances. He also played for Sunderland, Motherwell and Queen of the South and had short spells as manager of Albion Rovers and Queen of the South.

ALAN SKIRTON, 80, scored Arsenal's first European goal at Highbury and was their first substitute in a competitive fixture. The winger was also leading scorer in the 1961–62 season with 19 goals in 38 First Division matches. He netted 54 in 154 appearances during six years at the club before moving to Blackpool in 1966, then on to Bristol City, Torquay, Durban in South Africa and Yeovil.

JON GITTENS, 55, played for Swindon in the controversial 1990 Second Division Play-off Final at Wembley. With Ossie Ardiles as manager, they defeated Sunderland 1-0, but the club later admitted financial irregularities and their opponents were promoted to the top division instead. Gittens, a central defender, returned to Southampton for a second spell at the club and also played for Middlesbrough on loan, Portsmouth, Torquay and Exeter.

GORDON 'FRED' NEATE, 78, served Reading as player and groundsman for more than half a century. The full-back joined the club as a 15-year-old apprentice in 1956, made his debut three years later, but suffered injuries and had to give up at 25. He was offered the job as groundsman at Elm Park and continued at the Madejski Stadium until his retirement at 68.

ALAN SMITH, 97, joined Arsenal after leaving the army in 1946. The left-winger was unable to hold down a first-team place, moved to Brentford, then played for Leyton Orient.

JUNE 2019

JUSTIN EDINBURGH, 49, died six weeks after leading Leyton Orient back to the Football League. He was taken to hospital with a cardiac arrest and passed away five days later. Edinburgh was appointed in November 2017 following a shambolic season for the club involving five different managers and a drop into non-league football for the first time in 112 years. Under new ownership, he helped restore stability, built a new squad and Orient were promoted as National League champions last season. Edinburgh previously managed Northampton and Gillingham, having been sacked at both clubs, Newport, where he won promotion, and four non-league sides. His playing career, starting at Southend, took off with a £150,000 move to Tottenham in 1990 and an FA Cup-winner's medal against Nottingham Forest the following year. There was also a League Cup Final victory over Leicester in 1999, marred by a sending-off for retaliating to a heavy challenge from Robbie Savage. After a decade at White Hart Lane, the left-back joined Portsmouth for £175,000.

JOSE ANTONIO REYES, 35, was part of Arsenal's 'Invincibles' side that went through the 2003-04 season unbeaten and won the title by 11 points from Chelsea. Arsene Wenger paid Sevilla £17m for the Spain winger midway through the campaign and he made 13 appearances, scoring two goals. The following season, Reyes was sent off seconds from the end of extra time in the FA Cup Final against Manchester United – which Arsenal won on penalties – for fouling Cristiano Ronaldo and receiving a second yellow card. In 2006, he was a late substitute in the 2-1 Champions League Final defeat by Barcelona. He played 110 times and scored 23 goals for the club, before a title-winning season on loan with Real Madrid, then featured in three Europa League wins – one with Atletico Madrid and two after rejoining Sevilla. Reyes, who won 21 international caps, also had spells with Benfica on loan, Espanyol, Cordoba and his latest club, Extremadura, in the Spanish Second Division. He died in a car crash and a minute's silence was observed before the Champions League Final between Liverpool and Tottenham.

IAN MACFARLANE, 86, was a full-back who played for Aberdeen, Chelsea and Leicester in the 1950s, then made more than 300 appearances for Yeovil. He returned to Leicester as assistant manager to Frank McLintock and later Jock Wallace, developing the careers of several promising youngsters, including Gary Lineker. MacFarlane also had spells as No 2 at Middlesbrough, Manchester City and Sunderland, managed Carlisle and was chief scout at Leeds.

LAWRIE LESLIE, 84, started his career with Hibernian and played in the 1958 Scottish Cup Final defeat by Clyde. The goalkeeper won five Scottish caps with his next club Airdrieonians, all in the 1960-61season, then joined West Ham for a £14,000 fee. Leslie moved on to Stoke, Millwall and finally Southend, where he also had a coaching role.

GEORGE DARWIN, 87, joined newly-promoted Derby in 1957, following spells with Huddersfield and Mansfield, and played a key in the new club retaining Division Two status. The inside-forward then scored 11 goals as Derby finished seventh the following season. But his wife found it difficult to settle in the city and he moved on to Rotherham, where his appearances were limited because of cartilage trouble, and he finished at Barrow and Boston.

GRAHAM BARNETT, 83, scored 20 goals in 22 appearances as Port Vale won the Fourth Division title in 1958-59. The following season, he helped them reach the fifth round of the FA Cup before losing 2-1 to Aston Villa at Vale Park, watched by a club-record crowd of 49,768. The inside-forward also played for Tranmere and Halifax, ended his career in Australia, then returned to join Vale's coaching staff.

BARRY HUGHES, 81, was born in Wales, played youth football at West Bromwich Albion, and made his name in Holland after starting as player-manager of Alkmaar. He managed several Dutch clubs, including Sparta Rotterdam and Utrecht, and while in charge of Haarlem gave a young Ruud Gullit his first professional contract.

BOBBY BROWN, 87, made a club-record 472 appearances for Workington in their Football League days after signing from Motherwell in 1956. They included a Fourth Division promotion-winning season as captain in 1963-64. The full-back's eldest son, Bobby junior, also played for the club.

JOHNNY ROBINSON, 83, signed for Bury from Leyland Motors in 1954 and spent five years at the club as a first-team regular. The outside-right then played for Oldham.

DENNIS WHITE, 70, was a full-back who helped his home-town club Hartlepool win promotion for the first time when they finished third in the old Division Four in season 1967-68.

GABRIEL JESUS ON AND OFF THE MARK

Gabriel Jesus scored one goal, assisted in another and was then sent off in Brazil's first Copa America title in 12 years. The Manchester City player left the pitch in tears after receiving a second yellow card 20 minutes from the end with his side leading Peru 2-1 in the final in Rio de Janeiro. He later apologised for kicking a water bottle and pushing a VAR monitor. Brazil overcame the loss to seal victory with a 90th minute penalty from Everton's Richarlison. Gabriel Jesus and Liverpool's Roberto Firmino scored the goals in their semi-final win over Argentina.

QUARTER-FINALS

Brazil 0 Paraguay 0 (Brazil won 4-3 on pens). Att: 44,902 (Porto Alegre). Venezuela 0 Argentina 2 (Martinez 10, Lo Celso 74). Att: 50,094 (Rio de Janeiro). Colombia 0 Chile 0 (Chile won 5-4 on pens). Sao Paolo (44,062). Uruguay 0 Peru 0 (Peru won 5-4 on pens). Att: 21,180 (Salvador)

SEMI-FINALS

Brazil 2 (Gabriel Jesus 19, Firmino 71) Argentina 0. Att: 55,947 (Belo Horizonte). Chile 0 Peru 3 (Flores 21, Yotun 38, Guerrero 90). Att: 33,058 (Porto Alegre)

FINAL

Brazil 3 (Everton 15, Gabriel Jesus 45, Richarlison 90 pen) Peru 1 (Guerrero 44 pen)
Maracana Stadium, Rio de Janeiro (69,968); Sunday, July 7, 2019
Brazil (4-2-3-1): Alisson, Dani Alves (capt), Marquinos, Thiago Silva, Alex Sandro, Arthur, Casemiro, Gabriel Jesus, Coutinho (Militao 77), Everton (Allan 90+3), Firmino (Richarlison 75). **Booked**: Gabriel Jesus, Thiagho Silva. **Sent off**: Gabriel Jesus (70). **Coach**: Tite
Peru (4-2-3-1): Gallese, Advincula, Zambrano, Abram, Trauco, Tapia (Gonzales 82), Yotun (Ruidiaz 78), Flores, Cueva, Carrillo (Polo 86), Guerrero (capt). **Booked**: Tapia, Zambrano, Advincula. **Coach**: R Gareca
Referee: R Tobar (Chile). **Half-time**: 2-1

FLYING START

Academy graduate Sol Pryce made a dream debut for Swindon in their 3-2 win over Stevenage in League Two last season. The 18-year-old scored after 18 seconds and was on the mark again in first-half stoppage-time.

RECORDS SECTION

INDEX

GOALSCORING
(†Football League pre-1992–93)

Highest: Arbroath 36 Bon Accord (Aberdeen) 0 in Scottish Cup 1, Sep 12, 1885. On same day, also in Scottish Cup 1, Dundee Harp beat Aberdeen Rov 35-0.

Internationals: France 0 England 16 in Paris, 1906 (Amateur); Ireland 0 England 13 in Belfast Feb 18, 1882 (record in UK); England 9 Scotland 3 at Wembley, Apr 15, 1961; Biggest England win at Wembley: 9-0 v Luxembourg (Euro Champ), Dec 15, 1982.

Other record wins: Scotland: 11-0 v Ireland (Glasgow, Feb 23, 1901); **Northern Ireland:** 7-0 v Wales (Belfast, Feb 1, 1930); **Wales:** 11-0 v Ireland (Wrexham, Mar 3, 1888); **Rep of Ireland:** 8-0 v Malta (Euro Champ, Dublin, Nov 16, 1983).

Record international defeats: England: 1-7 v Hungary (Budapest, May 23, 1954); **Scotland:** 3-9 v England (Wembley, Apr 15, 1961); **Ireland:** 0-13 v England (Belfast, Feb 18, 1882); **Wales:** 0-9 v Scotland (Glasgow, Mar 23, 1878); **Rep of Ireland:** 0-7 v Brazil (Uberlandia, May 27, 1982).

World Cup: Qualifying round – Australia 31 American Samoa 0, world record international score (Apr 11, 2001); Australia 22 Tonga 0 (Apr 9, 2001); Iran 19 Guam 0 (Nov 25, 2000); Maldives 0 Iran 17 (Jun 2, 1997). **Finals – highest scores:** Hungary 10 El Salvador 1 (Spain, Jun 15, 1982); Hungary 9 S Korea 0 (Switzerland, Jun 17, 1954); Yugoslavia 9 Zaire 0 (W Germany, Jun 18, 1974).

European Championship: Qualifying round – highest scorers: San Marino 0 Germany 13 (Serravalle, Sep 6, 2006). **Finals – highest score:** Holland 6 Yugoslavia 1 (quarter-final, Rotterdam, Jun 25, 2000).

Biggest England U-21 win: 9-0 v San Marino (Shrewsbury, Nov 19, 2013).

FA Cup: Preston 26 Hyde 0 1st round, Oct 15, 1887.

League Cup: West Ham 10 Bury 0 (2nd round, 2nd leg, Oct 25, 1983); Liverpool 10 Fulham 0 (2nd round, 1st leg, Sep 23, 1986). **Record aggregates:** Liverpool 13 Fulham 2 (10-0h, 3-2a), Sep 23, Oct 7, 1986; West Ham 12 Bury 1 (2-1a, 10-0h), Oct 4, 25, 1983; Liverpool 11 Exeter 0 (5-0h, 6-0a), Oct 7, 28, 1981.

League Cup – most goals in one match: 12 Reading 5 Arsenal 7 aet (4th round, Oct 30, 2012). Dagenham & Redbridge 6 Brentford 6 aet (Brentford won 4-2 on pens; 1st round, Aug 12, 2014)

Premier League (beginning 1992–93): Manchester Utd 9 Ipswich 0, Mar 4, 1995. **Record away win:** Nottm Forest 1 Manchester Utd 8 Feb 6, 1999.

Highest aggregate scores in Premier League – 11: Portsmouth 7 Reading 4, Sep 29, 2007; **10:** Tottenham 6 Reading 4, Dec 29, 2007; Tottenham 9 Wigan 1, Nov 22, 2009; Manchester Utd 8 Arsenal 2, Aug 28, 2011; Arsenal 7 Newcastle 3, Dec 29, 2012; WBA 5 Manchester Utd 5, May 19, 2013.

Big back-to-back wins: Manchester City became the first Premier League team to score five or more goals in three successive matches in the same season – beating Liverpool 5-0, Watford 6-0 and Crystal Palace 5-0 in September 2017. Chelsea also scored heavily in the last game of the 2009-10 season (Wigan 8-0) and in the first two fixtures of the following campaign (WBA 6-0, Wigan 6-0).

351

†**Football League (First Division):** Aston Villa 12 Accrington 2, Mar 12, 1892; Tottenham 10 Everton 4, Oct 11, 1958 (highest Div 1 aggregate that century); WBA 12 Darwen 0, Apr 4, 1892; Nottm Forest 12 Leicester Fosse 0, Apr 21, 1909. **Record away win:** Newcastle 1 Sunderland 9, Dec 5, 1908; Cardiff 1 Wolves 9, Sep 3, 1955; Wolves 0 WBA 8, Dec 27, 1893.

New First Division (beginning 1992–93): Bolton 7 Swindon 0, Mar 8, 1997; Sunderland 7 Oxford Utd 0, Sep 19, 1998. **Record away win:** Stoke 0 Birmingham 7, Jan 10, 1998; Oxford Utd 0 Birmingham 7, Dec 12, 1998. **Record aggregate:** Grimsby 6 Burnley 5, Oct 29, 2002; Burnley 4 Watford 7, Apr 5, 2003.

Championship (beginning 2004–05): Birmingham 0 Bournemouth 8, Oct 25, 2014. **Record away win:** Birmingham 0 Bournemouth 8, Oct 25, 2014. **Record aggregate:** Leeds 4 Preston 6, Sep 29, 2010; Leeds 3 Nottm Forest 7, Mar 20, 2012; Bristol City 5 Hull 5, Apr 21, 2018. Aston Villa 5 Nottm Forest 5, Nov 28, 2018.

†**Second Division:** Newcastle 13 Newport Co 0, Oct 5, 1946; Small Heath 12 Walsall Town Swifts 0, Dec 17, 1892; Darwen 12 Walsall 0, Dec 26, 1896; Woolwich Arsenal 12 Loughborough 0, Mar 12, 1900; Small Heath 12 Doncaster 0, Apr 11, 1903. **Record away win:** *Burslem Port Vale 0 Sheffield Utd 10, Dec 10, 1892. **Record aggregate:** Manchester City 11 Lincoln 3, Mar 23, 1895.

New Second Division (beginning 1992–93): Hartlepool 1 Plymouth Argyle 8, May 7, 1994; Hartlepool 8 Grimsby 1, Sep 12, 2003.

New League 1 (beginning 2004–05): MK Dons 7 Oldham 0, Dec 20, 2014; Oxford 0 Wigan 7, Dec 23, 2017. **Record aggregate:** Hartlepool 4 Wrexham 6, Mar 5, 2005; Wolves 6 Rotherham 4, Apr 18, 2014; Bristol City 8 Walsall 2, May 3, 2015.

†**Third Division:** Gillingham 10 Chesterfield 0, Sep 5, 1987; Tranmere 9 Accrington 0, Apr 18, 1959; Brentford 9 Wrexham 0, Oct 15, 1963. **Record away win:** Halifax 0 Fulham 8, Sep 16, 1969. **Record aggregate:** Doncaster 7 Reading 5, Sep 25, 1982.

New Third Division (beginning 1992–93): Barnet 1 Peterborough 9, Sep 5, 1998. **Record aggregate:** Hull 7 Swansea 4, Aug 30, 1997.

New League 2 (beginning 2004–05): Peterborough 7 Brentford 0, Nov 24, 2007 Shrewsbury 7 Gillingham 0, Sep 13, 2008; Crewe 7 Barnet 0, Aug 21, 2010; Crewe 8 Cheltenham 1, Apr 2, 2011; Cambridge 7 Morecambe 0, Apr 19, 2016; Luton 7 Cambridge 0, Nov 18, 2017. **Record away win:** Boston 0 Grimsby 6, Feb 3, 2007; Macclesfield 0 Darlington 6, Aug 30, 2008; Lincoln 0 Rotherham 6, Mar 25, 2011. **Record aggregate:** Burton 5 Cheltenham 6, Mar 13, 2010; Accrington 7 Gillingham 4, Oct 2, 2010.

†**Third Division (North):** Stockport 13 Halifax 0 (still joint biggest win in Football League – see Div 2) Jan 6, 1934; Tranmere 13 Oldham 4, Dec 26, 1935. (17 is highest Football League aggregate score). **Record away win:** Accrington 0 Barnsley 9, Feb 3, 1934.

†**Third Division (South):** Luton 12 Bristol Rov 0, Apr 13, 1936; Bristol City 9 Gillingham 4, Jan 15, 1927; Gillingham 9 Exeter 4, Jan 7, 1951. **Record away win:** Northampton 0 Walsall 8, Apr 8, 1947.

†**Fourth Division:** Oldham 11 Southport 0, Dec 26, 1962. **Record away win:** Crewe 1 Rotherham 8, Sep 8, 1973. **Record aggregate:** Hartlepool 10 Barrow 1, Apr 4, 1959; Crystal Palace 9 Accrington 2, Aug 20, 1960; Wrexham 10 Hartlepool 1, Mar 3, 1962; Oldham 11 Southport 0, Dec 26, 1962; Torquay 9 Newport 3, Oct 19, 1963; Shrewsbury 7 Doncaster 4, Feb 1, 1975; Barnet 4 Crewe 7, Aug 17, 1991.

Scottish Premier – Highest aggregate: 12: Motherwell 6 Hibernian 6, May 5, 2010; **11:** Celtic 8 Hamilton 3, Jan 3, 1987; Motherwell 5 Aberdeen 6, Oct 20, 1999. **Other highest team scores:** Aberdeen 8 Motherwell 0 (Mar 26, 1979); Hamilton 0 Celtic 8 (Nov 5, 1988); Celtic 9 Aberdeen 0 (Nov 6, 2010).

Scottish League Div 1: Celtic 11 Dundee 0, Oct 26, 1895. **Record away win:** Hibs 11 *Airdrie 1, Oct 24, 1959.

Scottish League Div 2: Airdrieonians 15 Dundee Wanderers 1, Dec 1, 1894 (biggest win in history of League football in Britain).

Record modern Scottish League aggregate: 12 – Brechin 5 Cowdenbeath 7, Div 2, Jan 18, 2003.

Record British score since 1900: Stirling 20 Selkirk 0 (Scottish Cup 1, Dec 8, 1984). Winger Davie Thompson (7 goals) was one of 9 Stirling players to score.

LEAGUE GOALS – BEST IN SEASON (Before restructure in 1992)

Div		Goals	Games
1	WR (Dixie) Dean, Everton, 1927–28	60	39
2	George Camsell, Middlesbrough, 1926–27	59	37
3(S)	Joe Payne, Luton, 1936–37	55	39
3(N)	Ted Harston, Mansfield, 1936–37	55	41
3	Derek Reeves, Southampton, 1959–60	39	46
4	Terry Bly, Peterborough, 1960–61	52	46

(Since restructure in 1992)

Div		Goals	Games
1	Guy Whittingham, Portsmouth, 1992–93	42	46
2	Jordan Rhodes Huddersfield 2011–12	36	40
3	Andy Morrell, Wrexham, 2002–03	34	45

Premier League – BEST IN SEASON

Andy Cole **34 goals** (Newcastle – 40 games, 1993–94); Alan Shearer **34 goals**
   (Blackburn – 42 games, 1994–95).

FOOTBALL LEAGUE – BEST MATCH HAULS

(Before restructure in 1992)

Div	Goals	
1	Ted Drake (Arsenal), away to Aston Villa, Dec 14, 1935	7
	James Ross (Preston) v Stoke, Oct 6, 1888	7
2	*Neville (Tim) Coleman (Stoke) v Lincoln, Feb 23, 1957	7
	Tommy Briggs (Blackburn) v Bristol Rov, Feb 5, 1955	7
3(S)	Joe Payne (Luton) v Bristol Rov, Apr 13, 1936	10
3(N)	Robert ('Bunny') Bell (Tranmere) v Oldham, Dec 26, 1935	
	he also missed a penalty	9
3	Barrie Thomas (Scunthorpe) v Luton, Apr 24, 1965	5
	Keith East (Swindon) v Mansfield, Nov 20, 1965	5
	Steve Earle (Fulham) v Halifax, Sep 16, 1969	5
	Alf Wood (Shrewsbury) v Blackburn, Oct 2, 1971	5
	Tony Caldwell (Bolton) v Walsall, Sep 10, 1983	5
	Andy Jones (Port Vale) v Newport Co., May 4, 1987	5
4	Bert Lister (Oldham) v Southport, Dec 26, 1962	6
	*Scored from the wing	

(Since restructure in 1992)

Div Goals

1 4 in match – John Durnin (Oxford Utd v Luton, 1992–93); Guy Whittingham
   (Portsmouth v Bristol Rov 1992–93); Craig Russell (Sunderland v Millwall, 1995–96);
   David Connolly (Wolves at Bristol City 1998–99); Darren Byfield (Rotherham at
   Millwall, 2002–03); David Connolly (Wimbledon at Bradford City, 2002–03); Marlon
   Harewood (Nottm Forest v Stoke, 2002–03); Michael Chopra (Watford at Burnley,
   2002–03); Robert Earnshaw (Cardiff v Gillingham, 2003–04). 5 in match – Paul
   Barnes (Burnley v Stockport, 1996–97); Robert Taylor (all 5, Gillingham at Burnley, 1998–
   99); Lee Jones (all 5, Wrexham v Cambridge Utd, 2001–02).

3 5 in match – Tony Naylor (Crewe v Colchester, 1992–93); Steve Butler (Cambridge Utd
   v Exeter, 1993–4); Guiliano Grazioli (Peterborough at Barnet, 1998–99).

Champ 4 in match – Garath McCleary (Nottm Forest at Leeds 2011–12); Nikola Zigic
   (Birmingham at Leeds 2011–12; Craig Davies (Barnsley at Birmingham 2012–13;
   Ross McCormack (Leeds at Charlton 2013–14), Jesse Lingard (Birmingham v Sheffield
   Wed 2013–14); Odion Ighalo (Watford v Blackpool, 2014-15); Leon Clarke (all 4,
   Sheffield Utd v Hull, 2017–18); Tammy Abraham (Aston Villa v Nottm Forest,
   2018–19).

Lge 1 **4** in match – Jordan Rhodes (all 4, Huddersfield at Sheffield Wed, 2011–12); Ellis Harrison (Bristol Rov v Northampton, 2016–17); James Vaughan (Bury v Peterborough, 2016–17).

5 in match – Juan Ugarte (Wrexham at Hartlepool, 2004–05); Jordan Rhodes (Huddersfield at Wycombe, 2011–12).

Last player to score 6 in English League match: Geoff Hurst (West Ham 8 Sunderland 0, Div 1 Oct 19,1968.

PREMIER LEAGUE – BEST MATCH HAULS

5 goals in match: Andy Cole (Manchester Utd v Ipswich, Mar 4, 1995); Alan Shearer (Newcastle v Sheffield Wed, Sep 19, 1999); Jermain Defoe (Tottenham v Wigan, Nov 22, 2009); Dimitar Berbatov (Manchester Utd v Blackburn, Nov 27, 2010), Sergio Aguero (Manchester City v Newcastle, Oct 3, 2015).

SCOTTISH LEAGUE

Div		Goals
Prem	Gary Hooper (Celtic) v Hearts, May 13, 2012	5
	Kris Boyd (Rangers) v Dundee Utd, Dec 30, 2009	5
	Kris Boyd (Kilmarnock) v Dundee Utd, Sep 25, 2004	5
	Kenny Miller (Rangers) v St Mirren, Nov 4, 2000	5
	Marco Negri (Rangers) v Dundee Utd, Aug. 23, 1997	5
	Paul Sturrock (Dundee Utd) v Morton, Nov 17, 1984	5
1	Jimmy McGrory (Celtic) v Dunfermline, Jan 14, 1928	8
1	Owen McNally (Arthurlie) v Armadale, Oct 1, 1927	8
2	Jim Dyet (King's Park) v Forfar, Jan 2, 1930 on his debut for the club	8
2	John Calder (Morton) v Raith, Apr 18, 1936	8
2	Norman Haywood (Raith) v Brechin, Aug. 20, 1937	8

SCOTTISH LEAGUE – BEST IN SEASON

Prem	Brian McClair (Celtic, 1986–87)	35
	Henrik Larsson (Celtic, 2000–01)	35
1	William McFadyen (Motherwell, 1931–32)	53
2	*Jimmy Smith (Ayr, 1927–28 – 38 appearances)	66
	(*British record)	

CUP FOOTBALL

Scottish Cup: John Petrie (Arbroath) v Bon Accord, at Arbroath, 1st round, Sep 12, 1885 — 13

FA Cup: Ted MacDougall (Bournemouth) v Margate, 1st round, Nov 20,1971 — 9

FA Cup Final: Billy Townley (Blackburn) v Sheffield Wed, at Kennington Oval, 1890; Jimmy Logan (Notts Co) v Bolton, at Everton, 1894; Stan Mortensen (Blackpool) v Bolton, at Wembley, 1953 — 3

League Cup: Frank Bunn (Oldham) v Scarborough (3rd round), Oct 25, 1989 — 6

Scottish League Cup: Willie Penman (Raith) v Stirling, Sep 18, 1948 — 6

Scottish Cup: Most goals in match since war: 10 by **Gerry Baker** (St Mirren) in 15-0 win (1st round) v Glasgow Univ, Jan 30, 1960; 9 by his brother **Joe Baker** (Hibernian) in 15-1 win (2nd round) v Peebles, Feb 11, 1961.

AGGREGATE LEAGUE SCORING RECORDS

	Goals
*Arthur Rowley (1947–65, WBA, Fulham, Leicester, Shrewsbury)	434
†Jimmy McGrory (1922–38, Celtic, Clydebank)	410

Hughie Gallacher (1921–39, Airdrieonians, Newcastle, Chelsea, Derby,

Notts Co, Grimsby, Gateshead) **387**
William ('Dixie') Dean (1923–37, Tranmere, Everton, Notts Co) **379**
Hugh Ferguson (1916–30, Motherwell, Cardiff, Dundee) **362**
● Jimmy Greaves (1957–71, Chelsea, Tottenham, West Ham) **357**
Steve Bloomer (1892–1914, Derby, Middlesbrough, Derby) **352**
George Camsell (1923–39, Durham City, Middlesbrough) **348**
Dave Halliday (1920–35, St Mirren, Dundee, Sunderland, Arsenal,
  Manchester City, Clapton Orient) **338**
John Aldridge (1979–98, Newport, Oxford Utd, Liverpool, Tranmere) **329**
Harry Bedford (1919–34), Nottm Forest, Blackpool, Derby, Newcastle,
  Sunderland, Bradford PA, Chesterfield **326**
John Atyeo (1951–66, Bristol City) **315**
Joe Smith (1908–29, Bolton, Stockport) **315**
Victor Watson (1920–36, West Ham, Southampton) **312**
Harry Johnson (1919–36, Sheffield Utd, Mansfield) **309**
Bob McPhail (1923–1939, Airdrie, Rangers) **306**

(***Rowley** scored 4 for WBA, 27 for Fulham, 251 for Leicester, 152 for Shrewsbury.

● **Greaves'** 357 is record top-division total (he also scored 9 League goals for AC Milan).
  Aldridge also scored 33 League goals for Real Sociedad. [**McGrory** scored 397 for Celtic, 13
  for Clydebank).

Most League goals for one club: 349 – Dixie Dean (Everton 1925–37); **326 – George Camsell**
  (Middlesbrough 1925–39); **315 – John Atyeo** (Bristol City 1951–66); **306 – Vic Watson**
  (West Ham 1920–35); **291 – Steve Bloomer** (Derby 1892–1906, 1910–14); **259 – Arthur**
  Chandler (Leicester 1923–35); **255 – Nat Lofthouse** (Bolton 1946–61); **251 – Arthur Rowley**
  (Leicester 1950–58).

More than 500 goals: Jimmy McGrory (Celtic, Clydebank and Scotland) scored a total of **550**
  goals in his first-class career (1922–38).

More than 1,000 goals: Brazil's **Pele** is reputedly the game's all-time highest scorer with **1,283**
  goals in 1,365 matches (1956–77), but many of them were scored in friendlies for his club,
  Santos. He scored his 1,000th goal, a penalty, against Vasco da Gama in the Maracana
  Stadium, Rio, on Nov 19, 1969. ● Pele (born Oct 23, 1940) played regularly for Santos from
  the age of 16. During his career, he was sent off only once. He played 95 'A' internationals
  for Brazil and in their World Cup-winning teams in 1958 and 1970. † Pele (Edson Arantes do
  Nascimento) was subsequently Brazil's Minister for Sport. He never played at Wembley, apart
  from being filmed there scoring a goal for a commercial. Aged 57, Pele received an 'honorary
  knighthood' (Knight Commander of the British Empire) from the Queen at Buckingham
  Palace on Dec 3, 1997

Romario (retired Apr, 2008, aged 42) scored more than 1,000 goals for Vasco da Gama,
  Barcelona, PSV Eindhoven, Valencia and Brazil (56 in 73 internationals).

MOST LEAGUE GOALS IN SEASON: DEAN'S 60

WR ('Dixie') Dean, Everton centre-forward, created a League scoring record in 1927–28 with 60
  in 39 First Division matches. He also scored three in FA Cup ties, and 19 in representative
  games, totalling 82 for the season.

George Camsell, of Middlesbrough, previously held the record with 59 goals in 37 Second
  Division matches in 1926–27, his total for the season being 75.

SHEARER'S RECORD 'FIRST'

Alan Shearer (Blackburn) is the only player to score more than 30 top-division goals in 3
  successive seasons since the War: 31 in 1993–94, 34 in 1994–95, 31 in 1995–96.

Thierry Henry (Arsenal) is the first player to score more than 20 Premier League goals in five
  consecutive seasons (2002–06). **David Halliday** (Sunderland) topped 30 First Division goals
  in 4 consecutive seasons with totals of 38, 36, 36 and 49 from 1925–26 to 1928–29.

MOST GOALS IN A MATCH

Sep 12, 1885: John Petrie set the all-time British individual record for a first-class match when, in Arbroath's 36-0 win against Bon Accord (Scottish Cup 1), he scored **13**.

Apr 13, 1936: Joe Payne set the still-existing individual record on his debut as a centre-forward, for Luton v Bristol Rov (Div 3 South). In a 12-0 win he scored **10**.

ROWLEY'S ALL-TIME RECORD

Arthur Rowley is English football's top club scorer with a total of **464 goals** for WBA, Fulham, Leicester and Shrewsbury (1947–65). There were 434 in the League, 26 FA Cup, 4 League Cup.

Jimmy Greaves is second with a total of 420 goals for Chelsea, AC Milan, Tottenham and West Ham, made up of 366 League, 35 FA Cup, 10 League Cup and 9 in Europe. He also scored nine goals for AC Milan.

John Aldridge retired as a player at the end of season 1997–98 with a career total of 329 League goals for Newport, Oxford Utd, Liverpool and Tranmere (1979–98). In all competitions for those clubs he scored 410 in 737 appearances. He also scored 45 in 63 games for Real Sociedad.

MOST GOALS IN INTERNATIONAL MATCHES

13 by **Archie Thompson** for Australia v American Samoa in World Cup (Oceania Group qualifier) at Coff's Harbour, New South Wales, Apr 11, 2001. Result: 31-0.

7 by **Stanley Harris** for England v France in Amateur International in Paris, Nov 1, 1906. Result: 15-0.

6 by **Nat Lofthouse** for Football League v Irish League, at Wolverhampton, Sep 24, 1952. Result: 7-1.

    Joe Bambrick for Northern Ireland against Wales (7-0) in Belfast, Feb 1, 1930 – a record for a Home Nations International.

    WC Jordan in Amateur International for England v France, at Park Royal, Mar 23, 1908. Result: 12-0.

    Vivian Woodward for England v Holland in Amateur International, at Chelsea, Dec 11,1909. Result: 9-1.

5 by **Howard Vaughton** for England v Ireland (Belfast) Feb 18, 1882. Result: 13-0.

    Steve Bloomer for England v Wales (Cardiff) Mar 16, 1896. Result: 9-1.

    Hughie Gallacher for Scotland against Ireland (Belfast), Feb 23, 1929. Result: 7-3.

    Willie Hall for England v Northern Ireland, at Old Trafford, Nov 16, 1938. Five in succession (first three in 3·5 mins – fastest international hat-trick). Result: 7-0.

    Malcolm Macdonald for England v Cyprus (Wembley) Apr 16, 1975. Result: 5-0.

    Hughie Gallacher for Scottish League against Irish League (Belfast) Nov 11, 1925. Result: 7-3.

    Barney Battles for Scottish League against Irish League (Firhill Park, Glasgow) Oct 31, 1928. Result: 8-2.

    Bobby Flavell for Scottish League against Irish League (Belfast) Apr 30, 1947. Result: 7-4.

    Joe Bradford for Football League v Irish League (Everton) Sep 25, 1929. Result: 7-2.

    Albert Stubbins for Football League v Irish League (Blackpool) Oct 18, 1950. Result: 6-3.

    Brian Clough for Football League v Irish League (Belfast) Sep 23, 1959. Result: 5-0.

LAST ENGLAND PLAYER TO SCORE …

3 goals: Raheem Sterling v Czech Rep (5-0) Europ Champ qual, Wembley, March 22, 2019.

4 goals: Ian Wright v San Marino (7-1), World Cup qual, Bologna, Nov 17, 1993.

5 goals: Malcolm Macdonald v Cyprus (5-0), Euro Champ qual, Wembley, Apr 16, 1975.

INTERNATIONAL TOP SHOTS

		Goals	Games
England	Wayne Rooney (2003–2019)	53	120
N Ireland	David Healy (2000–13)	36	95

		Goals	Games
Scotland	Denis Law (1958–74)	30	55
	Kenny Dalglish (1971–86)	30	102
Wales	Gareth Bale (2006–19)	31	77
Rep of Ire	Robbie Keane (1998–2017)	68	146

ENGLAND'S TOP MARKSMEN

(As at start of season 2019–20)

	Goals	Games
Wayne Rooney (2003–17)	53	120
Bobby Charlton (1958–70)	49	106
Gary Lineker (1984–92)	48	80
Jimmy Greaves (1959–67)	44	57
Michael Owen (1998–2008)	40	89
Tom Finney (1946–58)	30	76
Nat Lofthouse (1950–58)	30	33
Alan Shearer (1992–2000)	30	63
Vivian Woodward (1903–11)	29	23
Frank Lampard (2003–14)	29	106
Steve Bloomer (1895–1907)	28	23
David Platt (1989–96)	27	62
Bryan Robson (1979–91)	26	90
Geoff Hurst (1966–72)	24	49
Stan Mortensen (1947–53)	23	25
Harry Kane (2015–2019)	22	39
Tommy Lawton (1938–48)	22	23
Peter Crouch (2005–11)	22	42
Mike Channon (1972–77)	21	46
Steven Gerrard (2000–14)	21	114
Kevin Keegan (1972–82)	21	63

ROONEY'S ENGLAND RECORD

Wayne Rooney reached 50 international goals with a penalty against Switzerland at Wembley on September 8, 2015 to become England's record scorer, surpassing Bobby Charlton's mark. Charlton's record was set in 106 games, Rooney's tally in 107.

CONSECUTIVE GOALS FOR ENGLAND

Steve Bloomer scored in **10** consecutive appearances (19 goals) between Mar 1895 and Mar 1899. **Jimmy Greaves** scored **11** goals in five consecutive matches from the start of season 1960–61.

ENGLAND'S TOP FINAL SERIES MARKSMEN

Gary Lineker with 6 goals at 1986 World Cup in Mexico.
Harry Kane with 6 goals at 2018 World Cup in Russia.

ENGLAND TOP SCORERS IN COMPETITIVE INTERNATIONALS

Michael Owen 26 goals in 53 matches; **Gary Lineker** 22 in 39; **Alan Shearer** 20 in 31.

MOST ENGLAND GOALS IN SEASON

13 – **Jimmy Greaves** (1960–61 in 9 matches); **12** – **Dixie Dean** (1926–27 in 6 matches); **11** – Harry Kane (2017–18 in 11 matches); **10** – **Gary Lineker** (1990–91 in 10 matches); **10** – **Wayne Rooney** – (2008–09 in 9 matches)

MOST ENGLAND HAT-TRICKS

Jimmy Greaves 6; **Gary Lineker** 5, **Bobby Charlton** 4, **Vivian Woodward** 4, **Stan Mortensen** 3.

MOST GOALS FOR ENGLAND U-21s

13 – Alan Shearer (11 apps) Francis Jeffers (13 apps).

GOLDEN GOAL DECIDERS

The Football League, in an experiment to avoid penalty shoot-outs, introduced a new golden goal system in the 1994–95 **Auto Windscreens Shield** to decide matches in the knock-out stages of the competition in which scores were level after 90 minutes. The first goal scored in overtime ended play.

Iain Dunn (Huddersfield) became the first player in British football to settle a match by this sudden-death method. His 107th-minute goal beat Lincoln 3-2 on Nov 30, 1994, and to mark his 'moment in history' he was presented with a golden football trophy.

The AWS Final of 1995 was decided when Paul Tait headed the only goal for Birmingham against Carlisle 13 minutes into overtime – the first time a match at Wembley had been decided by the 'golden goal' formula.

First major international tournament match to be decided by sudden death was the Final of the **1996 European Championship** at Wembley in which Germany beat Czech Rep 2-1 by **Oliver Bierhoff's** goal in the 95th minute.

In the **1998 World Cup Finals** (2nd round), host country France beat Paraguay 1-0 with **Laurent Blanc's** goal (114).

France won the **2000 European Championship** with golden goals in the semi-final, 2-1 v Portugal (Zinedine Zidane pen, 117), and in the Final, 2-1 v Italy (David Trezeguet, 103).

Galatasaray (Turkey) won the **European Super Cup** 2-1 against Real Madrid (Monaco, Aug 25, 2000) with a 103rd minute golden goal, a penalty.

Liverpool won the **UEFA Cup** 5-4 against Alaves with a 117th-min golden goal, an own goal, in the Final in Dortmund (May 19, 2001).

In the **2002 World Cup Finals**, 3 matches were decided by Golden Goals: in the 2nd round Senegal beat Sweden 2-1 (Henri Camara, 104) and South Korea beat Italy 2-1 (Ahn Jung-hwan, 117); in the quarter-final, Turkey beat Senegal 1-0 (Ilhan Mansiz, 94).

France won the 2003 **FIFA Confederations Cup Final** against Cameroon (Paris, Jun 29) with a 97th-minute golden goal by Thierry Henry.

Doncaster won promotion to Football League with a 110th-minute golden goal winner (3-2) in the Conference Play-off Final against Dagenham at Stoke (May 10, 2003).

Germany won the **Women's World Cup Final** 2-1 v Sweden (Los Angeles, Oct 12, 2003) with a 98th-minute golden goal.

GOLD TURNS TO SILVER

Starting with the 2003 Finals of the UEFA Cup and Champions League/European Cup, UEFA introduced a new rule by which a silver goal could decide the winners if the scores were level after 90 minutes.

Team leading after 15 minutes' extra time win match. If sides level, a second period of 15 minutes to be played. If still no winner, result to be decided by penalty shoot-out.

UEFA said the change was made because the golden goal put too much pressure on referees and prompted teams to play negative football.

Although both 2003 European Finals went to extra-time, neither was decided by a silver goal. The new rule applied in the 2004 European Championship Finals, and Greece won their semi-final against the Czech Republic in the 105th minute.

The **International Board** decided (Feb 28 2004) that the golden/silver goal rule was 'unfair' and that from July 1 competitive international matches level after extra-time would, when necessary, be settled on penalties.

PREMIER LEAGUE TOP SHOTS (1992–2019)

Alan Shearer	260	Nicolas Anelka	125
Wayne Rooney	208	Harry Kane	125
Andy Cole	187	Dwight Yorke	123

Frank Lampard	177	Steven Gerrard	120	
Thierry Henry	175	Romelu Lukaku	113	
Sergio Aguero	164	Ian Wright	113	
Robbie Fowler	163	Dion Dublin	111	
Jermain Defoe	162	Emile Heskey	110	
Michael Owen	150	Ryan Giggs	109	
Les Ferdinand	149	Peter Crouch	108	
Teddy Sheringham	146	Paul Scholes	107	
Robin van Persie	144	Darren Bent	106	
Jimmy Floyd Hasselbaink	127	Didier Drogba	104	
Robbie Keane	126	Matt Le Tissier	100	

LEAGUE GOAL RECORDS

The highest goal-scoring aggregates in the Football League, Premier and Scottish League are:

For

	Goals	Games	Club	Season
Prem	106	38	Manchester City	2017–18
Div 1	128	42	Aston Villa	1930–31
New Div 1	108	46	Manchester City	2001–02
New Champ	99	46	Reading	2005–06
Div 2	122	42	Middlesbrough	1926–27
New Div 2	89	46	Millwall	2000–01
New Lge 1	106	46	Peterborough	2010–11
Div 3(S)	127	42	Millwall	1927–28
Div 3(N)	128	42	Bradford City	1928–29
Div 3	111	46	QPR	1961–62
New Div 3	96	46	Luton	2001–02
New Lge 2	96	46	Notts Co	2009–10
Div 4	134	46	Peterborough	1960–61
Scot Prem	105	30	Celtic	2003–04
Scot L 1	132	34	Hearts	1957–58
Scot L 2	142	34	Raith Rov	1937–38
Scot L 3 (Modern)	130	36	Gretna	2004–05

Against

	Goals	Games	Club	Season
Prem	100	42	Swindon	1993–94
Div 1	125	42	Blackpool	1930–31
New Div 1	102	46	Stockport	2001–02
New Champ	86	46	Crewe	2004–05
Div 2	141	34	Darwen	1898–99
New Div 2	102	46	Chester	1992–93
New Lge 1	98	46	Stockport	2004–05
Div 3(S)	135	42	Merthyr T	1929–30
Div 3(N)	136	42	Nelson	1927–28
Div 3	123	46	Accrington Stanley	1959–60
New Div 3	113	46	Doncaster	1997–98
New Lge 2	96	46	Stockport	2010–11
Div 4	109	46	Hartlepool Utd	1959–60
Scot Prem	100	36	Morton	1984–85
Scot Prem	100	44	Morton	1987–88
Scot L 1	137	38	Leith A	1931–32
Scot L 2	146	38	Edinburgh City	1931–32
Scot L 3 (Modern)	118	36	East Stirling	2003–04

BEST DEFENSIVE RECORDS

*Denotes under old offside law

Div	Goals Agst	Games	Club	Season
Prem	15	38	Chelsea	2004–05
1	16	42	Liverpool	1978–79
1	*15	22	Preston	1888–89
New Div 1	28	46	Sunderland	1998–99
New Champ	30	46	Preston	2005–06
2	18	28	Liverpool	1893–94
2	*22	34	Sheffield Wed	1899–1900
2	24	42	Birmingham	1947–48
2	24	42	Crystal Palace	1978–79
New Div 2	25	46	Wigan	2002–03
New Lge 1	32	46	Nottm Forest	2007–08
3(S)	*21	42	Southampton	1921–22
3(S)	30	42	Cardiff	1946–47
3(N)	*21	38	Stockport	1921–22
3(N)	21	46	Port Vale	1953–54
3	30	46	Middlesbrough	1986–87
New Div 3	20	46	Gillingham	1995–96
New Lge 2	31	46	Notts Co	2009–10
4	25	46	Lincoln	1980–81

SCOTTISH LEAGUE

Div	Goals Agst	Games	Club	Season
Prem	17	38	Celtic	2014–15
1	*12	22	Dundee	1902–03
1	*14	38	Celtic	1913–14
2	20	38	Morton	1966–67
2	*29	38	Clydebank	1922–23
2	29	36	East Fife	1995–96
New Div 3	21	36	Brechin	1995–96

TOP SCORERS (LEAGUE ONLY)

		Goals	Div
2018–19	Teemu Pukki (Norwich)	29	Champ
	James Norwood (Tranmere)	29	Lge 2
2017–18	Mohamed Salah (Liverpool)	32	Prem
2016–17	Billy Sharp (Sheffield Utd)	30	Lge 1
2015–16	Matt Taylor (Bristol Rov)	27	Lge 2
2014–15	Daryl Murphy (Ipswich)	27	Champ
2013–14	Luis Suarez (Liverpool)	31	Prem
2012–13	Tom Pope (Port Vale)	31	Lge 2
2011–12	Jordan Rhodes (Huddersfield)	36	Lge 1
2010–11	Clayton Donaldson (Crewe)	28	Lge 2
2009–10	Rickie Lambert (Southampton)	31	Lge 1
2008– 09	Simon Cox (Swindon)		
	Rickie Lambert (Bristol Rov)	29	Lge 1
2007–08	Cristiano Ronaldo (Manchester Utd)	31	Prem
2006–07	Billy Sharp (Scunthorpe)	30	Lge 1
2005–06	Thierry Henry (Arsenal)	27	Prem
2004–05	Stuart Elliott (Hull)	27	1
	Phil Jevons (Yeovil)	27	2
	Dean Windass (Bradford City)	27	1

2003–04	Thierry Henry (Arsenal)	30	Prem
2002–03	Andy Morrell (Wrexham)	34	3
2001–02	Shaun Goater (Manchester City)	28	1
	Bobby Zamora (Brighton)	28	2
2000–01	Bobby Zamora (Brighton)	28	3
1999–00	Kevin Phillips (Sunderland)	30	Prem
1998–99	Lee Hughes (WBA)	31	1
1997–98	Pierre van Hooijdonk (Nottm Forest)	29	1
	Kevin Phillips (Sunderland)	29	1
1996–97	Graeme Jones (Wigan)	31	3
1995–96	Alan Shearer (Blackburn)	31	Prem
1994–95	Alan Shearer (Blackburn)	34	Prem
1993–94	Jimmy Quinn (Reading)	35	2
1992–93	Guy Whittingham (Portsmouth)	42	1
1991–92	Ian Wright (Crystal Palace 5, Arsenal 24)	29	1
1990–91	Teddy Sheringham (Millwall)	33	2
1989–90	Mick Quinn (Newcastle)	32	2
1988–89	Steve Bull (Wolves)	37	3
1987–88	Steve Bull (Wolves)	34	4
1986–87	Clive Allen (Tottenham)	33	1
1985–86	Gary Lineker (Everton)	30	1
1984–85	Tommy Tynan (Plymouth Argyle)	31	3
	John Clayton (Tranmere)	31	4
1983–84	Trevor Senior (Reading)	36	4
1982–83	Luther Blissett (Watford)	27	1
1981–82	Keith Edwards (Hull 1, Sheffield Utd 35)	36	4
1980–81	Tony Kellow (Exeter)	25	3
1979–80	Clive Allen (Queens Park Rangers)	28	2
1978–79	Ross Jenkins (Watford)	29	3
1977–78	Steve Phillips (Brentford)	32	4
	Alan Curtis (Swansea City)	32	4
1976–77	Peter Ward (Brighton)	32	3
1975–76	Dixie McNeil (Hereford)	35	3
1974–75	Dixie McNeil (Hereford)	31	3
1973–74	Brian Yeo (Gillingham)	31	4
1972–73	Bryan (Pop) Robson (West Ham)	28	1
1971–72	Ted MacDougall (Bournemouth)	35	3
1970–71	Ted MacDougall (Bournemouth)	42	4
1969–70	Albert Kinsey (Wrexham)	27	4
1968–69	Jimmy Greaves (Tottenham)	27	1
1967–68	George Best (Manchester Utd)	28	1
	Ron Davies (Southampton)	28	1
1966–67	Ron Davies (Southampton)	37	1
1965–66	Kevin Hector (Bradford PA)	44	4
1964–65	Alick Jeffrey (Doncaster)	36	4
1963–64	Hugh McIlmoyle (Carlisle)	39	4
1962–63	Jimmy Greaves (Tottenham)	37	1
1961–62	Roger Hunt (Liverpool)	41	2
1960–61	Terry Bly (Peterborough)	52	4

100 LEAGUE GOALS IN SEASON

Manchester City, First Div Champions in 2001–02, scored 108 goals.
Bolton, First Div Champions in 1996–97, reached 100 goals, the first side to complete a century

in League football since 103 by **Northampton** (Div 4 Champions) in 1986–87.

Last League Champions to reach 100 League goals: **Manchester City** (106 in 2017–18). Last century of goals in the top division: 111 by runners-up **Tottenham** in 1962–63.

Clubs to score a century of Premier League goals in season: **Manchester City** 106 in 2017-18, **Chelsea** 103 in 2009–10, Manchester City (102) and Liverpool (101) in 2013–14.

Wolves topped 100 goals in four successive First Division seasons (1957–58, 1958–59, 1959–60, 1960–61).

In **1930–31**, the top three all scored a century of League goals: 1 Arsenal (127), 2 Aston Villa (128), 3 Sheffield Wed (102).

Latest team to score a century of League goals: Peterborough with 106 in 2010–11 (Lge 1).

100 GOALS AGAINST

Swindon, relegated with 100 goals against in 1993–94, were the first top-division club to concede a century of League goals since **Ipswich** (121) went down in 1964. Most goals conceded in the top division: 125 by **Blackpool** in 1930–31, but they avoided relegation.

MOST LEAGUE GOALS ON ONE DAY

A record of 209 goals in the four divisions of the Football League (43 matches) was set on **Jan 2, 1932:** 56 in Div 1, 53 in Div 2, 57 in Div 3 South and 43 in Div 3 North.

There were two 10-goal aggregates: Bradford City 9, Barnsley 1 in Div 2 and Coventry City 5, Fulham 5 in Div 3 South.

That total of 209 League goals on one day was equalled on **Feb 1, 1936** (44 matches): 46 in Div 1, 46 in Div 2, 49 in Div 3 South and 69 in Div 3 North. Two matches in the Northern Section produced 23 of the goals: Chester 12, York 0 and Crewe 5, Chesterfield 6.

MOST GOALS IN TOP DIV ON ONE DAY

This record has stood since **Dec 26, 1963,** when 66 goals were scored in the ten First Division matches played.

MOST PREMIER LEAGUE GOALS ON ONE DAY

47, in nine matches on **May 8, 1993** (last day of season). For the first time, all 20 clubs scored in the Premier League programme over the weekend of Nov 27-28, 2010.

FEWEST PREMIER LEAGUE GOALS IN ONE WEEK-END

10, in **10** matches on **Nov 24/25, 2001**.

FEWEST FIRST DIV GOALS ON ONE DAY

For full/near full programme: **Ten goals**, all by home clubs, in ten matches on Apr 28, 1923 (day of Wembley's first FA Cup Final).

SCORER OF LEAGUE'S FIRST GOAL

Kenny Davenport (2 mins) for Bolton v Derby, Sep 8, 1888.

VARDY'S RECORD

Jamie Vardy set a Premier League record by scoring in 11 consecutive matches for Leicester (Aug-Nov 2015). The all-time top division record of scoring in 12 successive games was set by **Jimmy Dunne** for Sheffield Utd in the old First Division in season 1931-32. **Stan Mortensen** scored in 15 successive matches for Blackpool (First Division) in season 1950-51, but that sequence included two injury breaks.

LUTON GOAL FEAST

Luton set a Football League record in season 2017–18 by scoring seven or more goals in three games before Christmas – beating Yeovil 8-2 on the opening day of the season, Stevenage 7-1 and Cambridge 7-0.

SCORERS FOR 7 PREMIER LEAGUE CLUBS

Craig Bellamy (Coventry, Newcastle, Blackburn, Liverpool, West Ham, Manchester City, Cardiff).

SCORERS FOR 6 PREMIER LEAGUE CLUBS

Les Ferdinand (QPR, Newcastle, Tottenham, West Ham, Leicester, Bolton); **Andy Cole** (Newcastle, Manchester Utd, Blackburn, Fulham, Manchester City, Portsmouth); **Marcus Bent** (Crystal Palace, Ipswich, Leicester, Everton, Charlton, Wigan); **Nick Barmby** (Tottenham, Middlesbrough, Everton, Liverpool, Leeds, Hull); **Peter Crouch** (Tottenham, Aston Villa, Southampton, Liverpool, Portsmouth, Stoke); **Robbie Keane** (Coventry, Leeds, Tottenham, Liverpool, West Ham, Aston Villa); **Nicolas Anelka** (Arsenal, Liverpool, Manchester City, Bolton, Chelsea, WBA); **Darren Bent** (Ipswich, Charlton, Tottenham, Sunderland, Aston Villa, Fulham).

SCORERS FOR 5 PREMIER LEAGUE CLUBS

Stan Collymore (Nottm Forest, Liverpool, Aston Villa, Leicester, Bradford); **Mark Hughes** (Manchester Utd, Chelsea, Southampton, Everton, Blackburn); **Benito Carbone** (Sheffield Wed, Aston Villa, Bradford, Derby, Middlesbrough); **Ashley Ward** (Norwich, Derby, Barnsley, Blackburn Bradford); **Teddy Sheringham** (Nottm Forest, Tottenham, Manchester Utd, Portsmouth, West Ham); **Chris Sutton** (Norwich, Blackburn, Chelsea, Birmingham, Aston Villa).

SCORERS IN MOST CONSECUTIVE LEAGUE MATCHES

Arsenal broke the record by scoring in 55 successive Premier League fixtures: the last match in season 2000–01, then all 38 games in winning the title in 2001–02, and the first 16 in season 2002–03. The sequence ended with a 2-0 defeat away to Manchester Utd on December 7, 2002.
Chesterfield previously held the record, having scored in 46 consecutive matches in Div 3 (North), starting on Christmas Day, 1929 and ending on December 27, 1930.

SIX-OUT-OF-SIX HEADERS

When **Oxford Utd** beat Shrewsbury 6-0 (Div 2) on Apr 23, 1996, all six goals were headers.

ALL–ROUND MARKSMEN

Alan Cork scored in four divisions of the Football League and in the Premier League in his 18-season career with Wimbledon, Sheffield Utd and Fulham (1977–95).
Brett Ormerod scored in all four divisions (2, 1, Champ and Prem Lge) for Blackpool in two spells (1997–2002, 2008–11) **Grant Holt** (Sheffield Wed, Rochdale, Nottm Forest, Shrewsbury, Norwich) has scored in four Football League divisions and in the Premier League.

CROUCH AHEAD OF THE GAME

Peter Crouch holds the record for most headed goals in the Premier League with a total of 53, ahead of Alan Shearer (46) and Dion Dublin (45).

MOST CUP GOALS

FA Cup – most goals in one season: 20 by **Jimmy Ross** (Preston, runners-up 1887–88); 15 by **Alex (Sandy) Brown** (Tottenham, winners 1900–01).
Most FA Cup goals in individual careers: 49 by **Harry Cursham** (Notts Co 1877–89); 20th century: 44 by **Ian Rush** (39 for Liverpool, 4 for Chester, 1 for Newcastle 1979–98). **Denis Law** was the previous highest FA Cup scorer in the 20th century with 41 goals for Huddersfield Town, Manchester City and Manchester Utd (1957–74).
Most FA Cup Final goals by individual: 5 by **Ian Rush** for Liverpool (2 in 1986, 2 in 1989, 1 in 1992).

HOTTEST CUP HOT-SHOT

Geoff Hurst scored 21 cup goals in season 1965–66: 11 League Cup, 4 FA Cup and 2 Cup-Winners' Cup for West Ham, and 4 in the World Cup for England.

SCORERS IN EVERY ROUND

Twelve players have scored in every round of the FA Cup in one season, from opening to Final inclusive: **Archie Hunter** (Aston Villa, winners 1887); **Sandy Brown** (Tottenham, winners 1901); **Harry Hampton** (Aston Villa, winners 1905); **Harold Blackmore** (Bolton, winners 1929); **Ellis Rimmer** (Sheffield Wed, winners 1935); **Frank O'Donnell** (Preston, beaten 1937); **Stan Mortensen** (Blackpool, beaten 1948); **Jackie Milburn** (Newcastle, winners 1951); **Nat Lofthouse** (Bolton, beaten 1953); **Charlie Wayman** (Preston, beaten 1954); **Jeff Astle** (WBA, winners 1968); **Peter Osgood** (Chelsea, winners 1970).

Blackmore and the next seven completed their 'set' in the Final at Wembley; Osgood did so in the Final replay at Old Trafford.

Only player to score in every **Football League Cup** round possible in one season: **Tony Brown** for WBA, winners 1965–66, with 9 goals in 10 games (after bye in Round 1).

TEN IN A ROW

Dixie McNeill scored for Wrexham in ten successive FA Cup rounds (18 goals): 11 in Rounds 1-6, 1977–78; 3 in Rounds 3-4, 1978–79; 4 in Rounds 3-4, 1979–80.

Stan Mortensen (Blackpool) scored 25 goals in 16 FA Cup rounds out of 17 (1946–51).

TOP MATCH HAULS IN FA CUP

Ted MacDougall scored nine goals, a record for the competition proper, in the FA Cup first round on Nov 20, 1971, when Bournemouth beat Margate 11-0. On Nov 23, 1970 he had scored six in an 8-1 first round replay against Oxford City.

Other six-goal FA Cup scorers include **George Hilsdon** (Chelsea v Worksop, 9-1, 1907–08), **Ronnie Rooke** (Fulham v Bury, 6-0, 1938–39), **Harold Atkinson** (Tranmere v Ashington, 8-1, 1952–53), **George Best** (Manchester Utd v Northampton 1969–70, 8-2 away), **Duane Darby** (Hull v Whitby, 8-4, 1996–97).

Denis Law scored all six for Manchester City at Luton (6-2) in an FA Cup 4th round tie on Jan 28, 1961, but none of them counted – the match was abandoned (69 mins) because of a waterlogged pitch. He also scored City's goal when the match was played again, but they lost 3-1.

Tony Philliskirk scored **five** when Peterborough beat Kingstonian 9-1 in an FA Cup 1st round replay on Nov 25, 1992, but had them wiped from the records.

With the score at 3-0, the Kingstonian goalkeeper was concussed by a coin thrown from the crowd and unable to play on. The FA ordered the match to be replayed at Peterborough behind closed doors, and Kingstonian lost 1-0.

● Two players have scored **ten goals** in FA Cup preliminary round matches: **Chris Marron** for South Shields against Radcliffe in Sep 1947; **Paul Jackson** when Sheffield-based club Stocksbridge Park Steels beat Oldham Town 17-1 on Aug 31, 2002. He scored 5 in each half and all ten with his feet – goal times 6, 10, 22, 30, 34, 68, 73, 75, 79, 84 mins.

QUICKEST GOALS AND RAPID SCORING

A goal in **4 sec** was claimed by **Jim Fryatt**, for Bradford PA v Tranmere (Div 4, Apr 25, 1965), and by **Gerry Allen** for Whitstable v Danson (Kent League, Mar 3,1989). **Damian Mori** scored in **4 sec** for Adelaide v Sydney (Australian National League, December 6, 1995).

Goals after **6 sec** – **Albert Mundy** for Aldershot v Hartlepool, Oct 25, 1958; **Barrie Jones** for Notts Co v Torquay, Mar 31, 1962; **Keith Smith** for Crystal Palace v Derby, Dec 12, 1964.

9.6 sec by **John Hewitt** for Aberdeen at Motherwell, 3rd round, Jan 23, 1982 (fastest goal in Scottish Cup history).

Colin Cowperthwaite reputedly scored in **3.5 sec** for Barrow v Kettering (Alliance Premier League) on Dec 8, 1979, but the timing was unofficial.

Phil Starbuck for Huddersfield **3 sec** after entering the field as 54th min substitute at home to Wigan (Div 2) on Easter Monday, Apr 12, 1993. Corner was delayed, awaiting his arrival and he scored with a header.

Malcolm Macdonald after **5 sec** (officially timed) in Newcastle's 7-3 win in a pre-season friendly at St Johnstone on Jul 29, 1972.

World's fastest goal: 2.8 sec, direct from kick-off, Argentinian **Ricardo Olivera** for Rio Negro v Soriano (Uruguayan League), December 26, 1998.

Fastest international goal: 7 sec, Christian Benteke for Belgium v Gibraltar (World Cup qual, Faro), Oct 10, 2016.

Fastest England goals: 17 sec, Tommy Lawton v Portugal in Lisbon, May 25, 1947. **27 sec, Bryan Robson** v France in World Cup at Bilbao, Spain on Jun 16, 1982; **37 sec, Gareth Southgate** v South Africa in Durban, May 22, 2003; **30 sec, Jack Cock** v Ireland, Belfast, Oct 25, 1919; **30 sec, Bill Nicholson** v Portugal at Goodison Park, May 19, 1951. **38 sec, Bryan Robson** v Yugoslavia at Wembley, Dec 13, 1989; **42 sec, Gary Lineker** v Malaysia in Kuala Lumpur, Jun 12, 1991.

Fastest international goal by substitute: 5 sec, John Jensen for Denmark v Belgium (Euro Champ), Oct 12, 1994.

Fastest goal by England substitute: 10 sec, Teddy Sheringham v Greece (World Cup qualifier) at Old Trafford, Oct 6, 2001.

Fastest FA Cup goal: 4 sec, Gareth Morris (Ashton Utd) v Skelmersdale, 1st qual round, Sep 15, 2001.

Fastest FA Cup goal (comp proper): 9.7 sec, Jimmy Kebe for Reading v WBA, 5th Round, Feb 13, 2010.

Fastest FA Cup Final goal: 25 sec, Louis Saha for Everton v Chelsea at Wembley, May 30, 2009.

Fastest goal by substitute in FA Cup Final: 96 sec, Teddy Sheringham for Manchester Utd v Newcastle at Wembley, May 22, 1999.

Fastest League Cup Final goal: 45 sec, John Arne Riise for Liverpool v Chelsea, 2005.

Fastest goal on full League debut: 7.7 sec, Freddy Eastwood for Southend v Swansea (Lge 2), Oct 16, 2004. He went on to score hat trick in 4-2 win.

Fastest goal in cup final: 4.07 sec, 14-year-old Owen Price for Ernest Bevin College, Tooting, beaten 3-1 by Barking Abbey in Heinz Ketchup Cup Final at Arsenal on May 18, 2000. Owen, on Tottenham's books, scored from inside his own half when the ball was played back to him from kick-off.

Fastest Premier League goals: 7.69 sec, Shane Long for Southampton v Watford, Apr 23, 2019. **9.82 sec, Ledley King** for Tottenham away to Bradford, Dec 9, 2000; **10.52 sec, Alan Shearer** for Newcastle v Manchester City, Jan 18, 2003; **10.54 sec Christian Eriksen** for Tottenham v Manchester Utd, Jan 31, 2018; **11.90 sec, Mark Viduka** for Leeds v Charlton, Mar 17, 2001; **12.16 sec, Dwight Yorke** for Aston Villa at Coventry, Sep 30, 1995; **12.94 sec, Chris Sutton** for Blackburn at Everton, Apr 1, 1995; **13.49 sec Kevin Nolan** for Bolton at Blackburn Jan 10, 2004; **13.52 sec. James Beattie** for Southampton at Chelsea, Aug 28, 2004; **13.64 sec Asmir Begovic** (goalkeeper) for Stoke v Southampton, Nov 2, 2013.

Fastest top-division goal: 7 sec, Bobby Langton for Preston v Manchester City (Div 1), Aug 25, 1948.

Fastest goal in Champions League: 10 sec, Roy Makaay for Bayern Munich v Real Madrid (1st ko rd), Mar 7, 2007.

Fastest Premier League goal by substitute: 9 sec, Shaun Goater, Manchester City's equaliser away to Manchester Utd (1-1), Feb 9, 2003. In Dec, 2011, Wigan's **Ben Watson** was brought off the bench to take a penalty against Stoke and scored.

Fastest goal on Premier League debut: 36 sec, Thievy Bifouma on as sub for WBA away to Crystal Palace, Feb 8, 2014.

Fastest Scottish Premiership goal: 10 sec, Kris Boyd for Kilmarnock v Ross Co, Jan 28, 2017.

Fastest-ever hat-trick: 90 sec, credited to 18-year-old **Tommy Ross** playing in a Highland match for Ross County against Nairn County on Nov 28, 1964.

Fastest goal by goalkeeper in professional football: 13 sec, Asmir Begovic for Stoke v Southampton (Prem Lge), Nov 2, 2013.

Fastest goal in Olympic Games: 14 sec, Neymar for Brazil in semi-finals v Honduras, Aug 17, 2016, Rio de Janeiro.

Fastest goal in women's football: 7 sec, Angie Harriott for Launton v Thame (Southern League, Prem Div), season 1998–99.

Fastest hat-trick in League history: 2 min 20 sec, Bournemouth's 84th-minute substitute **James Hayter** in 6-0 home win v Wrexham (Div 2) on Feb 24, 2004 (goal times 86, 87, 88 mins).

Fastest First Division hat-tricks since war: Graham Leggat, 3 goals in 3 minutes (first half) when Fulham beat Ipswich 10-1 on Boxing Day, 1963; **Nigel Clough**, 3 goals in **4 minutes** (81, 82, 85 pen) when Nottm Forest beat QPR 4-0 on Dec 13, 1987.

Fastest Premier League hat-trick: 2 min 56 sec (13, 14, 16) by **Sadio Mane** in Southampton 6, Aston Villa 1 on May 16, 2015.

Fastest international hat-trick: 2 min 35 sec, Abdul Hamid Bassiouny for Egypt in 8-2 win over Namibia in Abdallah, Libya, (African World Cup qual), Jul 13, 2001.

Fastest international hat-trick in British matches: 3.5 min, Willie Hall for England v N Ireland at Old Trafford, Manchester, Nov 16, 1938. (Hall scored 5 in 7-0 win); **3min 30 sec, Arif Erdem** for Turkey v N Ireland, European Championship qualifier, at Windsor Park, Belfast, on Sep 4, 1999.

Fastest FA Cup hat-tricks: In 3 min, Billy Best for Southend v Brentford (2nd round, Dec 7, 1968); **2 min 20 sec,** Andy Locke for Nantwich v Droylsden (1st Qual round, Sep 9, 1995).

Fastest Scottish hat-trick: 2 min 30 sec, Ian St John for Motherwell away to Hibernian (Scottish League Cup), Aug 15, 1959.

Fastest hat-trick of headers: Dixie Dean's 5 goals in Everton's 7-2 win at home to Chelsea (Div 1) on Nov 14, 1931 included 3 headers between **5th** and **15th-min.**

Scored first kick: Billy Foulkes (Newcastle) for Wales v England at Cardiff, Oct 20, 1951, in his first international match.

Preston scored six goals in **7 min** in record 26-0 FA Cup 1st round win v Hyde, Oct 15, 1887.

Notts Co scored six second-half goals in **12 min** (Tommy Lawton 3, Jackie Sewell 3) when beating Exeter 9-0 (Div 3 South) at Meadow Lane on Oct 16, 1948.

Arsenal scored six in **18 min** (71-89 mins) in 7-1 home win (Div 1) v Sheffield Wed, Feb 15, 1992.

Tranmere scored six in first **19 min** when beating Oldham 13-4 (Div 3 North), December 26, 1935.

Sunderland scored eight in **28 min** at Newcastle (9-1 Div 1), December 5, 1908. Newcastle went on to win the title.

Southend scored all seven goals in **29 min** in 7-0 win at home to Torquay (Leyland Daf Cup, Southern quarter-final), Feb 26, 1991. Score was 0-0 until 55th minute.

Plymouth scored five in first **18 min** in 7-0 home win v Chesterfield (Div 2), Jan 3, 2004.

Five in 20 min: Frank Keetley in Lincoln's 9-1 win over Halifax in Div 3 (North), Jan 16, 1932; **Brian Dear** for West Ham v WBA (6-1, Div 1) Apr 16, 1965. **Kevin Hector** for Bradford PA v Barnsley (7-2, Div 4), Nov 20, 1965.

Four in 5 min: John McIntyre for Blackburn v Everton (Div 1), Sep 16, 1922; **WG (Billy) Richardson** for WBA v West Ham (Div 1), Nov 7, 1931.

Three in 2·5 min: Jimmy Scarth for Gillingham v Leyton Orient (Div 3S), Nov 1, 1952.

Three in three minutes: Billy Lane for Watford v Clapton Orient (Div 3S), December 20, 1933; **Johnny Hartburn** for Leyton Orient v Shrewsbury (Div 3S), Jan 22, 1955; **Gary Roberts** for Brentford v Newport, (Freight Rover Trophy, South Final), May 17, 1985; **Gary Shaw** for Shrewsbury v Bradford City (Div 3), December 22, 1990.

Two in 9 sec: Jamie Bates with last kick of first half, **Jermaine McSporran** 9 sec into second half when Wycombe beat Peterborough 2-0 at home (Div 2) on Sep 23, 2000.

Premier League – fastest scoring: Four goals in 4 min 44 sec, Tottenham home to Southampton on Sunday, Feb 7, 1993.

Premier League – fast scoring away: When **Aston Villa** won 5-0 at Leicester (Jan 31, 2004), all goals scored in **18 second-half min** (50-68).

Four in 13 min by Premier League sub: Ole Gunnar Solskjaer for Manchester Utd away to Nottm Forest, Feb 6, 1999.

Five in 9 mins by substitute: Robert Lewandowski for Bayern Munich v Wolfsburg (5-1, Bundesliga), Sep 22, 2015.

FASTEST GOALS IN WORLD CUP FINAL SERIES

10.8 sec, Hakan Sukur for Turkey against South Korea in 3rd/4th-place match at Taegu, Jun 29, 2002; **15 sec, Vaclav Masek** for Czechoslovakia v Mexico (in Vina, Chile, 1962); **27 sec, Bryan Robson** for England v France (in Bilbao, Spain, 1982).

TOP MATCH SCORES SINCE WAR

By English clubs: 13-0 by Newcastle v Newport (Div 2, Oct 1946); 13-2 by Tottenham v Crewe (FA Cup 4th. Rd replay, Feb 1960); 13-0 by Chelsea v Jeunesse Hautcharage, Lux. (Cup-Winners' Cup 1st round, 2nd leg, Sep 1971).

By Scottish clubs: 20-0 by Stirling v Selkirk (S. of Scotland League) in Scottish Cup 1st round. (Dec 1984). That is the highest score in British first-class football since Preston beat Hyde 26-0 in FA Cup, Oct 1887.

MOST GOALS IN CALENDAR YEAR

91 by Lionel Messi in 2012 (79 Barcelona, 12 Argentina).

ROONEY'S DOUBLE TOP

Wayne Rooney ended season 2016–17 as top scorer for England (53) and Manchester Utd (253).

PREMIER LEAGUE LONGEST-RANGE GOALS BY OUTFIELD PLAYERS

66 yards: Charlie Adam (Stoke at Chelsea, Apr 4, 2015)
64 yards: Xabi Alonso (Liverpool v Newcastle, Sep 20, 2006)
62 yards: Maynor Figueroa (Wigan at Stoke, Dec 12, 2009)
60 yards: Wayne Rooney (Everton v West Ham, Nov 29, 2017)
59 yards: David Beckham (Manchester Utd at Wimbledon, Aug 17, 1996)
55 yards: Wayne Rooney (Manchester Utd at West Ham, Mar 22, 2014)

GOALS BY GOALKEEPERS

(Long clearances unless stated)

Pat Jennings for Tottenham v Manchester Utd (goalkeeper Alex Stepney), Aug 12, 1967 (FA Charity Shield).

Peter Shilton for Leicester v Southampton (Campbell Forsyth), Oct 14, 1967 (Div 1).

Ray Cashley for Bristol City v Hull (Jeff Wealands), Sep 18, 1973 (Div 2).

Steve Sherwood for Watford v Coventry (Raddy Avramovic), Jan 14, 1984 (Div 1).

Steve Ogrizovic for Coventry v Sheffield Wed (Martin Hodge), Oct 25, 1986 (Div 1).

Andy Goram for Hibernian v Morton (David Wylie), May 7, 1988 (Scot Prem Div).

Andy McLean, on Irish League debut, for Cliftonville v Linfield (George Dunlop), Aug 20, 1988.

Alan Paterson for Glentoran v Linfield (George Dunlop), Nov 30, 1988 (Irish League Cup Final – only instance of goalkeeper scoring winner in a senior cup final in UK).

Ray Charles for East Fife v Stranraer (Bernard Duffy), Feb 28, 1990 (Scot Div 2).

Iain Hesford for Maidstone v Hereford (Tony Elliott), Nov 2, 1991 (Div 4).

Chris Mackenzie for Hereford v Barnet (Mark Taylor), Aug 12, 1995 (Div 3).

Peter Schmeichel for Manchester Utd v Rotor Volgograd, Sep 26, 1995 (header, UEFA Cup 1).

Mark Bosnich (Aston Villa) for Australia v Solomon Islands, Jun 11, 1997 (penalty in World Cup qual – 13-0).

Peter Keen for Carlisle away to Blackpool (goalkeeper John Kennedy), Oct 24, 2000 (Div 3).

Steve Mildenhall for Notts Co v Mansfield (Kevin Pilkington), Aug 21, 2001 (free-kick inside own half, League Cup 1).

Peter Schmeichel for Aston Villa v Everton (Paul Gerrard), Oct 20, 2001 (volley, first goalkeeper to score in Premier League).

Mart Poom for Sunderland v Derby (Andy Oakes), Sep 20, 2003 (header, Div 1).

Brad Friedel for Blackburn v Charlton (Dean Kiely), Feb 21, 2004 (shot, Prem).

Paul Robinson for Leeds v Swindon (Rhys Evans), Sep 24, 2003 (header, League Cup 2).

Andy Lonergan for Preston v Leicester (Kevin Pressman), Oct 2, 2004 (Champ).

Matt Glennon for St Johnstone away to Ross Co (Joe Malin), Mar 11, 2006 (shot, Scot Div 1).

Gavin Ward for Tranmere v Leyton Orient (Glenn Morris), Sep 2, 2006 (free-kick Lge 1).

Mark Crossley for Sheffield Wed v Southampton (Kelvin Davis), Dec 23, 2006 (header, Champ).

Paul Robinson for Tottenham v Watford (Ben Foster), Mar 17, 2007 (Prem).

Adam Federici for Reading v Cardiff (Peter Enckelman), Dec 28, 2008 (shot, Champ).

Chris Weale for Yeovil v Hereford (Peter Gulacsi), Apr 21, 2009 (header, Lge 1).

Scott Flinders for Hartlepool v Bournemouth (Shwan Jalal), Apr 30, 2011 (header, Lge 1).

Iain Turner for Preston v Notts Co (Stuart Nelson), Aug 27 2011 (shot, Lge 1).

Andy Leishman for Auchinleck v Threave (Vinnie Parker), Oct 22, 2011 (Scot Cup 2).

Tim Howard for Everton v Bolton (Adam Bogdan), Jan 4, 2012 (Prem).

Asmir Begovic for Stoke v Southampton (Artur Boruc), Nov 2, 2013 (Prem).

Mark Oxley for Hibernian v Livingston (Darren Jamieson), Aug 9, 2014 (Scot Champ).

Jesse Joronen for Stevenage v Wycombe (Matt Ingram), Oct 17, 2015 (Lge 2).

Barry Roche for Morecambe v Portsmouth (Ryan Fulton), Feb 2, 2016 (header, Lge 2.)

MORE GOALKEEPING HEADLINES

Arthur Wilkie, sustained a hand injury in Reading's Div 3 match against Halifax on Aug 31, 1962, then played as a forward and scored twice in a 4-2 win.

Alex Stepney was Manchester Utd's joint top scorer for two months in season 1973–74 with two penalties.

Dundee Utd goalkeeper Hamish McAlpine scored three penalties in a ten-month period between 1976–77, two against Hibernian, home and away, and one against Rangers at Ibrox.

Alan Fettis scored twice for Hull in 1994–95 Div 2 season, as a substitute in 3-1 home win over Oxford Utd (Dec 17) and, when selected outfield, with last-minute winner (2-1) against Blackpool on May 6.

Roger Freestone scored for Swansea with a penalty at Oxford Utd (Div 2, Apr 30, 1995) and twice from the spot the following season against Shrewsbury (Aug 12) and Chesterfield (Aug 26).

Jimmy Glass, on loan from Swindon, kept Carlisle in the Football League on May 8, 1999. With ten seconds of stoppage-time left, he went upfield for a corner and scored the winner against Plymouth that sent Scarborough down to the Conference instead.

Paul Smith, Nottm Forest goalkeeper, was allowed to run through Leicester's defence unchallenged and score direct from the kick-off of a Carling Cup second round second match on Sep 18, 2007. It replicated the 1-0 score by which Forest had led at half-time when the original match was abandoned after Leicester defender Clive Clarke suffered a heart attack. Leicester won the tie 3-2.

Tony Roberts (Dagenham), is the only known goalkeeper to score from open play in the FA Cup, his last-minute goal at Basingstoke in the fourth qualifying round on Oct 27, 2001 earning a 2-2 draw. Dagenham won the replay 3-0 and went on to reach the third round proper.

The only known instance in first-class football in Britain of a goalkeeper scoring direct from a goal-kick was in a First Division match at Roker Park on Apr 14, 1900. The kick by Manchester City's **Charlie Williams** was caught in a strong wind and Sunderland keeper J. E Doig fumbled the ball over his line.

Jose Luis Chilavert, Paraguay's international goalkeeper, scored a hat-trick of penalties when his club Velez Sarsfield beat Ferro Carril Oeste 6-1 in the Argentine League on Nov 28, 1999. In all, he scored 8 goals in 72 internationals. He also scored with a free-kick from just inside his own half for Velez Sarsfield against River Plate on Sep 20, 2000.

Most goals by a goalkeeper in a League season: 5 (all penalties) by **Arthur Birch** for Chesterfield (Div 3 North), 1923–24.

When Brazilian goalkeeper **Rogerio Ceni** (37) converted a free-kick for Sao Paulo's winner (2-1) v Corinthians in a championship match on Mar 27, 2011, it was his 100th goal (56 free-kicks, 44 pens) in a 20-season career.

OWN GOALS

Most by player in one season: 5 by **Robert Stuart** (Middlesbrough) in 1934–35.

Three in match by one team: Sheffield Wed's **Vince Kenny, Norman Curtis** and **Eddie Gannon** in 5-4 defeat at home to WBA (Div 1) on Dec 26, 1952; Rochdale's **George Underwood, Kenny Boyle** and **Danny Murphy** in 7-2 defeat at Carlisle (Div 3 North), Dec 25, 1954; Sunderland's **Stephen Wright** and **Michael Proctor** (2) at home to Charlton (1-3, Prem), Feb 1, 2003;

Brighton's **Liam Bridcutt** (2) and **Lewis Dunk** in 6-1 FA Cup 5th rd defeat at Liverpool, Feb 19, 2012.; Sunderland's **Santiago Vergini, Liam Bridcutt** and **Patrick van Aanholt** in 8-0 defeat at Southampton (Prem), Oct 18, 2014.

One-man show: Chris Nicholl (Aston Villa) scored all four goals in 2-2 draw away to Leicester (Div 1), Mar 20, 1976 – two for his own side and two own goals.

Fastest own goals: 8 sec by **Pat Kruse** of Torquay, for Cambridge Utd (Div 4), Jan 3, 1977; in First Division, **16 sec** by **Steve Bould** (Arsenal) away to Sheffield Wed, Feb 17, 1990.

Late own-goal man: Frank Sinclair (Leicester) put through his own goal in the 90th minute of Premier League matches away to Arsenal (L1-2) and at home to Chelsea (2-2) in Aug 1999.

Half an own goal each: Chelsea's second goal in a 3-1 home win against Leicester on December 18, 1954 was uniquely recorded as 'shared own goal'. Leicester defenders **Stan Milburn** and **Jack Froggatt**, both lunging at the ball in an attempt to clear, connected simultaneously and sent it rocketing into the net.

Match of 149 own goals: When Adama, Champions of Malagasy (formerly Madagascar) won a League match 149-0 on Oct 31, 2002, all 149 were own goals scored by opponents Stade Olympique De L'Emryne. They repeatedly put the ball in their own net in protest at a refereeing decision.

MOST SCORERS IN MATCH

Liverpool set a Football League record with **eight** scorers when beating Crystal Palace 9-0 (Div 1) on Sep 12, 1989. Marksmen were: Steve Nicol (7 and 88 mins), Steve McMahon (18), Ian Rush (45), Gary Gillespie (56), Peter Beardsley (61), John Aldridge (67 pen), John Barnes (79), Glenn Hysen (82).

Fifteen years earlier, **Liverpool** had gone one better with **nine** different scorers when they achieved their record win, 11-0 at home to Stromsgodset (Norway) in the Cup-Winners' Cup 1st round, 1st leg on Sep 17, 1974.

Eight players scored for Swansea when they beat Sliema, Malta, 12-0 in the Cup-Winners' Cup 1st round, 1st leg on Sep 15, 1982.

Nine Stirling players scored in the 20-0 win against Selkirk in the Scottish Cup 1st Round on December 8, 1984.

Premier League record: **Seven** Chelsea scorers in 8-0 home win over Aston Villa, Dec 23, 2012. An eighth player missed a penalty.

LONG SCORING RUNS

Tom Phillipson scored in 13 consecutive matches for Wolves (Div 2) in season 1926-27, which is still an English League record. In the same season, **George Camsell** scored in 12 consecutive matches for Middlesbrough (Div 2). **Bill Prendergast** scored in 13 successive League and Cup appearances for Chester (Div 3 North) in season 1938-39.

Dixie Dean scored in 12 consecutive games (23 goals) for Everton in Div 2 in 1930-31.

Danish striker **Finn Dossing** scored in 15 consecutive matches (Scottish record) for Dundee Utd (Div 1) in 1964-65.

50-GOAL PLAYERS

With **52** goals for Wolves in 1987-78 (34 League, 12 Sherpa Van Trophy, 3 Littlewoods Cup, 3 FA Cup), **Steve Bull** became the first player to score 50 in a season for a League club since **Terry Bly** for Div 4 newcomers Peterborough in 1960-61. Bly's 54 comprised 52 League goals and 2 in the FA Cup, and included 7 hat-tricks, still a post-war League record. Bull was again the country's top scorer with 50 goals in season 1988-89: 37 League, 2 Littlewoods Cup and 11 Sherpa Van Trophy. Between Bly and Bull, the highest individual scoring total for a season was 49 by two players: **Ted MacDougall** (Bournemouth 1970-71, 42 League, 7 FA Cup) and **Clive Allen** (Tottenham 1986-87, 33 League, 12 Littlewoods Cup, 4 FA Cup).

HOT SHOTS

Jimmy Greaves was top Div 1 scorer (League goals) six times in 11 seasons: 32 for Chelsea (1958-59), 41 for Chelsea (1960-61) and, for Tottenham, 37 in 1962-63, 35 in 1963-64,

29 in 1964–65 (joint top) and 27 in 1968–69.

Brian Clough (Middlesbrough) was leading scorer in Div 2 in three successive seasons: 40 goals in 1957–58, 42 in 1958–59 and 39 in 1959–60.

John Hickton (Middlesbrough) was top Div 2 scorer three times in four seasons: 24 goals in 1967–68, 24 in 1969–70 and 25 in 1970–71.

MOST HAT-TRICKS

Nine by George Camsell (Middlesbrough) in Div 2, 1926–27, is the record for one season. Most league hat-tricks in career: 37 by **Dixie Dean** for Tranmere and Everton (1924–38).

Most top division hat-tricks in a season since last War: six by **Jimmy Greaves** for Chelsea (1960–61). **Alan Shearer** scored five hat-tricks for Blackburn in the Premier League, season 1995–96.

Frank Osborne (Tottenham) scored three consecutive hat-tricks in Div 1 in Oct–Nov 1925, against Liverpool, Leicester (away) and West Ham.

Tom Jennings (Leeds) scored hat-tricks in three successive Div 1 matches (Sep–Oct, 1926): 3 goals v Arsenal, 4 at Liverpool, 4 v Blackburn. Leeds were relegated that season.

Jack Balmer (Liverpool) scored his three hat-tricks in a 17-year career in successive Div 1 matches (Nov 1946): 3 v Portsmouth, 4 at Derby, 3 v Arsenal. No other Liverpool player scored during that 10-goal sequence by Balmer.

Gilbert Alsop scored hat-tricks in three successive matches for Walsall in Div 3 South in Apr 1939: 3 at Swindon, 3 v Bristol City and 4 v Swindon.

Alf Lythgoe scored hat-tricks in three successive games for Stockport (Div 3 North) in Mar 1934: 3 v Darlington, 3 at Southport and 4 v Wrexham.

TRIPLE HAT-TRICKS

There have been at least three **instances of 3 hat-tricks being scored for one team in a Football League match:**

Apr 21, 1909: Enoch West, Billy Hooper and **Alfred Spouncer** for Nottm Forest (12-0 v Leicester Fosse, Div 1).

Mar 3, 1962: Ron Barnes, Wyn Davies and **Roy Ambler** in Wrexham's 10-1 win against Hartlepool (Div 4).

Nov 7, 1987: Tony Adcock, Paul Stewart and **David White** for Manchester City in 10-1 win at home to Huddersfield (Div 2).

For the first time in the Premier League, **three** hat-tricks were completed on one day (Sep 23, 1995): **Tony Yeboah** for Leeds at Wimbledon; **Alan Shearer** for Blackburn v Coventry; **Robbie Fowler** with 4 goals for Liverpool v Bolton.

In the FA Cup, **Jack Carr, George Elliott** and **Walter Tinsley** each scored 3 in Middlesbrough's 9-3 first round win against Goole in Jan, 1915. **Les Allen** scored 5, **Bobby Smith** 4 and **Cliff Jones** 3 when Tottenham beat Crewe 13-2 in a fourth-round replay in Feb 1960.

HAT-TRICKS v THREE 'KEEPERS

When West Ham beat Newcastle 8-1 (Div 1) on Apr 21, 1986 **Alvin Martin** scored 3 goals against different goalkeepers: Martin Thomas injured a shoulder and was replaced, in turn, by outfield players Chris Hedworth and Peter Beardsley.

Jock Dodds of Lincoln had done the same against West Ham on Dec 18, 1948, scoring past Ernie Gregory, Tommy Moroney and George Dick in 4-3 win.

David Herd (Manchester Utd) scored against Sunderland's Jim Montgomery, Charlie Hurley and Johnny Parke in 5-0 First Division home win on Nov 26, 1966.

Brian Clark, of Bournemouth, scored against Rotherham's Jim McDonagh, Conal Gilbert and Michael Leng twice in 7-2 win (Div 3) on Oct 10, 1972.

On Oct 16, 1993 (Div 3) **Chris Pike** (Hereford) scored a hat-trick in 5-0 win over Colchester, who became the first team in league history to have two keepers sent off in the same game.

On Dec 18, 2004 (Lge 1), in 6-1 defeat at Hull, Tranmere used **John Achterberg** and **Russell Howarth,** both retired injured, and defender **Theo Whitmore.**

On Mar 9, 2008, Manchester Utd had three keepers in their 0-1 FA Cup quarter-final defeat by

Portsmouth. **Tomasz Kuszczak** came on at half-time for **Edwin van der Sar** but was sent off when conceding a penalty. **Rio Ferdinand** went in goal and was beaten by Sulley Muntari's spot-kick. Derby used three keepers in a 4-1 defeat at Reading (Mar 10, 2010, Champ). **Saul Deeney,** who took over when **Stephen Bywater** was injured, was sent off for a foul and **Robbie Savage** replaced him.

EIGHT-DAY HAT-TRICK TREBLE

Joe Bradford, of Birmingham, scored three hat-tricks in eight days in Sep 1929–30 v Newcastle (won 5-1) on the 21st, 5 for the Football League v Irish League (7-2) on the 25th, and 3 in his club's 5-7 defeat away to Blackburn on the 28th.

PREMIER LEAGUE DOUBLE HAT-TRICK

Robert Pires and **Jermaine Pennant** each scored 3 goals in Arsenal's 6-1 win at home to Southampton (May 7, 2003).

TON UP – BOTH ENDS

Manchester City are the only club to score and concede a century of League goals in the same season. When finishing fifth in the 1957–58 season, they scored 104 and gave away 100.

TOURNAMENT TOP SHOTS

Most individual goals in a World Cup Final series: 13 by **Just Fontaine** for France, in Sweden 1958. Most in European Championship Finals: 9 by **Michel Platini** for France, in France 1984.

MOST GOALS ON CLUB DEBUT

Jim Dyet scored eight in King's Park's 12-2 win against Forfar (Scottish Div 2, Jan 2, 1930). **Len Shackleton** scored six times in Newcastle's 13-0 win v Newport (Div 2, Oct 5, 1946) in the week he joined them from Bradford Park Avenue.

MOST GOALS ON LEAGUE DEBUT

Five by **George Hilsdon,** for Chelsea (9-2) v Glossop, Div 2, Sep 1, 1906. **Alan Shearer,** with three goals for Southampton (4-2) v Arsenal, Apr 9, 1988, became, at 17, the youngest player to score a First Division hat-trick on his full debut.

FOUR-GOAL SUBSTITUTE

James Collins (Swindon), sub from 60th minute, scored 4 in 5-0 home win v Portsmouth (Lge 1) on Jan 1, 2013.

CLEAN-SHEET RECORDS

On the way to promotion from Div 3 in season 1995–96, Gillingham's ever-present goalkeeper **Jim Stannard** set a clean-sheet record. In 46 matches. He achieved 29 shut-outs (17 at home, 12 away), beating the 28 by **Ray Clemence** for Liverpool (42 matches in Div 1, 1978–79) and the previous best in a 46-match programme of 28 by Port Vale (Div 3 North, 1953–54). In conceding only 20 League goals in 1995–96, Gillingham created a defensive record for the lower divisions.

Chris Woods, Rangers' England goalkeeper, set a British record in season 1986–87 by going 1,196 minutes without conceding a goal. The sequence began in the UEFA Cup match against Borussia Moenchengladbach on Nov 26, 1986 and ended when Rangers were sensationally beaten 1-0 at home by Hamilton in the Scottish Cup 3rd round on Jan 31, 1987 with a 70th-minute goal by **Adrian Sprott.** The previous British record of 1,156 minutes without a goal conceded was held by Aberdeen goalkeeper **Bobby Clark** (season 1970–01).

Manchester Utd set a new Premier League clean-sheet record of 1,333 minutes (including 14 successive match shut-outs) in season 2008–09 (Nov 15–Feb 21). **Edwin van der Sar's** personal British league record of 1,311 minutes without conceding ended when United won 2-1 at Newcastle on Mar 4, 2009.

Most clean sheets in season in top English division: **28** by **Liverpool** (42 matches) in 1978–79; **25** by **Chelsea** (38 matches) in 2004–05.

There have been three instances of clubs keeping 11 consecutive clean sheets in the Football League: **Millwall** (Div 3 South, 1925–26), **York** (Div 3, 1973–74) and **Reading** (Div 4, 1978–79). In his sequence, Reading goalkeeper **Steve Death** set the existing League shut-out record of 1,103 minutes.

Sasa Ilic remained unbeaten for over 14 hours with 9 successive shut-outs (7 in Div 1, 2 in play-offs) to equal a Charlton club record in Apr/May 1998. He had 12 clean sheets in 17 first team games after winning promotion from the reserves with 6 successive clean sheets.

Sebastiano Rossi kept a clean sheet in 8 successive away matches for AC Milan (Nov 1993–Apr 1994).

A world record of 1,275 minutes without conceding a goal was set in 1990–01 by **Abel Resino**, the Atletico Madrid goalkeeper. He was finally beaten by Sporting Gijon's Enrique in Atletico's 3-1 win on Mar 19, 1991. In international football, the record is held by **Dino Zoff** with a shut-out for Italy (Sep 1972 to Jun 1974) lasting 1,142 minutes.

LOW SCORING

Fewest goals by any club in season in Football League: 18 by **Loughborough** (Div 2, 34 matches, 1899–1900); in 38 matches 20 by **Derby** (Prem Lge, 2007–08); in 42 matches, 24 by **Watford** (Div 2, 1971–72) and **Stoke** (Div 1, 1984–85)); in 46-match programme, 27 by **Stockport** (Div 3, 1969–70).

Arsenal were the lowest Premier League scorers in its opening season (1992–93) with 40 goals in 42 matches, but won both domestic cup competitions. In subsequent seasons the lowest Premier League scorers were **Ipswich** (35) in 1993–94, **Crystal Palace** (34) in 1994–95, **Manchester City** (33) in 1995–96 and **Leeds** (28) in 1996–97 until **Sunderland** set the Premier League's new fewest-goals record with only 21 in 2002–03. Then, in 2007–08, **Derby** scored just 20.

LONG TIME NO SCORE

The world international non-scoring record was set by **Northern Ireland** when they played 13 matches and 1,298 minutes without a goal. The sequence began against Poland on Feb 13, 2002 and ended 2 years and 5 days later when David Healy scored against Norway (1-4) in Belfast on Feb 18, 2004.

Longest non-scoring sequences in Football League: 11 matches by **Coventry** in 1919–20 (Div 2); 11 matches in 1992–93 (Div 2) by **Hartlepool**, who after beating Crystal Palace 1-0 in the FA Cup 3rd round on Jan 2, went 13 games and 2 months without scoring (11 League, 1 FA Cup, 1 Autoglass Trophy). The sequence ended after 1,227 blank minutes with a 1-1 draw at Blackpool (League) on Mar 6.

In the Premier League (Oct–Jan season 1994–95) **Crystal Palace** failed to score in nine consecutive matches.

The British non-scoring club record is held by **Stirling:** 14 consecutive matches (13 League, 1 Scottish Cup) and 1,292 minutes play, from Jan 31 1981 until Aug 8, 1981 (when they lost 4-1 to Falkirk in the League Cup).

In season 1971–72, **Mansfield** did not score in any of their first nine home games in Div 3. They were relegated on goal difference of minus two.

FA CUP CLEAN SHEETS

Most consecutive FA Cup matches without conceding a goal: 11 by **Bradford City.** The sequence spanned 8 rounds, from 3rd in 1910–11 to 4th. Round replay in 1911–12, and included winning the Cup in 1911.

GOALS THAT WERE WRONGLY GIVEN

Tottenham's last-minute winner at home to Huddersfield (Div 1) on Apr 2, 1952: Eddie Baily's corner-kick struck referee WR Barnes in the back, and the ball rebounded to Baily, who crossed for Len Duquemin to head into the net. Baily had infringed the Laws by playing the ball twice, but the result (1-0) stood. Those two points helped Spurs to finish Championship runners-up; Huddersfield were relegated.

The second goal (66 mins) in **Chelsea's** 2-1 home win v Ipswich (Div 1) on Sep 26, 1970: Alan

Hudson's shot hit the stanchion on the outside of goal and the ball rebounded on to the pitch. But instead of the goal kick, referee Roy Capey gave a goal, on a linesman's confirmation. TV pictures proved otherwise. The Football League quoted from the Laws of the Game: 'The referee's decision on all matters is final.'

When **Watford's** John Eustace and **Reading's** Noel Hunt challenged for a 13th minute corner at Vicarage Road on Sep 20, 2008, the ball was clearly diverted wide. But referee Stuart Attwell signalled for a goal on the instruction on his assistant and it went down officially as a Eustace own goal. The Championship match ended 2-2.

Sunderland's 1-0 Premier League win over **Liverpool** on Oct 17, 2009 was decided by one of the most bizarre goals in football history when Darren Bent's shot struck a red beach ball thrown from the crowd and wrong-footed goalkeeper Jose Reina. Referee Mike Jones wrongly allowed it to stand. The Laws of the Game state: 'An outside agent interfering with play should result in play being stopped and restarted with a drop ball.'

Blackburn's 59th minute equaliser (2-2) in 3-3 draw away to Wigan (Prem) on Nov 19, 2011 was illegal. Morten Gamst Pedersen played the ball to himself from a corner and crossed for Junior Hoilett to net.

The Republic of Ireland were deprived of the chance of a World Cup place in the second leg of their play-off with France on Nov 18, 2009. They were leading 1-0 in Paris when Thierry Henry blatantly handled before setting up William Gallas to equalise in extra-time time and give his side a 2-1 aggregate victory. The FA of Ireland's call for a replay was rejected by FIFA.

• The most notorious goal in World Cup history was fisted in by Diego Maradona in **Argentina's** 2-1 quarter-final win over England in Mexico City on Jun 22, 1986.

ATTENDANCES

GREATEST WORLD CROWDS

World Cup, Maracana Stadium, Rio de Janeiro, Jul 16, 1950. Final match (Brazil v Uruguay) attendance 199,850; receipts £125,000.

Total attendance in three matches (including play-off) between Santos (Brazil) and AC Milan for the Inter-Continental Cup (World Club Championship) 1963, exceeded 375,000.

BRITISH RECORD CROWDS

Most to pay: 149,547, Scotland v England, at Hampden Park, Glasgow, Apr 17, 1937. This was the first all-ticket match in Scotland (receipts £24,000).

At Scottish FA Cup Final: 146,433, Celtic v Aberdeen, at Hampden Park, Apr 24, 1937. Estimated another 20,000 shut out.

For British club match (apart from a Cup Final): 143,470, Rangers v Hibernian, at Hampden Park, Mar 27, 1948 (Scottish Cup semi-final).

FA Cup Final: 126,047, Bolton v West Ham, Apr 28, 1923. Estimated 150,000 in ground at opening of Wembley Stadium.

New Wembley: 89,874, FA Cup Final, Cardiff v Portsmouth, May 17, 2008.

World Cup Qualifying ties: 120,000, Cameroon v Morocco, Yaounde, Nov 29, 1981; 107,580, Scotland v Poland, Hampden Park, Oct 13, 1965.

European Cup: 135,826, Celtic v Leeds (semi-final, 2nd leg) at Hampden Park, Apr 15, 1970.

European Cup Final: 127,621, Real Madrid v Eintracht Frankfurt, at Hampden Park, May 18, 1960.

European Cup-Winners' Cup Final: 100,000, West Ham v TSV Munich, at Wembley, May 19, 1965.

Scottish League: 118,567, Rangers v Celtic, Jan 2, 1939.

Scottish League Cup Final: 107,609, Celtic v Rangers, at Hampden Park, Oct 23, 1965.

Football League old format: First Div: 83,260, Manchester Utd v Arsenal, Jan 17, 1948 (at Maine Road); **Div 2** 70,302 Tottenham v Southampton, Feb 25, 1950; **Div 3S:** 51,621, Cardiff v Bristol City, Apr 7, 1947; **Div 3N:** 49,655, Hull v Rotherham, Dec 25, 1948; **Div 3:** 49,309, Sheffield Wed v Sheffield Utd, Dec 26, 1979; **Div 4:** 37,774, Crystal Palace v Millwall, Mar 31, 1961.

Premier League: 83,222, Tottenham v Arsenal (Wembley), Feb 10, 2018

Football League – New Div 1: 41,214, Sunderland v Stoke, Apr 25, 1998; **New Div 2:** 32,471, Manchester City v York, May 8, 1999; **New Div 3:** 22,319, Hull v Hartlepool Utd, Dec 26, 2002. **New Champs:** 52,181, Newcastle v Ipswich, Apr 24, 2010; **New Lge 1:** 46,039, Sunderland v Bradford, Dec 26, 2018; **New Lge 2:** 28,343, Coventry v Accrington, Feb 10, 2018.

In English Provinces: 84,569, Manchester City v Stoke (FA Cup 6), Mar 3, 1934.

Record for Under-21 International: 55,700, England v Italy, first match at New Wembley, Mar 24, 2007.

Record for friendly match: 104,679, Rangers v Eintracht Frankfurt, at Hampden Park, Glasgow, Oct 17, 1961

FA Youth Cup: 38,187, Arsenal v Manchester Utd, at Emirates Stadium, Mar 14, 2007.

Record Football League aggregate (season): 41,271,414 (1948–49) – 88 clubs.

Record Football League aggregate (single day): 1,269,934, December 27, 1949, previous day, 1,226,098.

Record average home League attendance for season: 75,691 by Manchester Utd in 2007–08.

Long-ago League attendance aggregates: 10,929,000 in 1906–07 (40 clubs); 28,132,933 in 1937–38 (88 clubs).

Last 1m crowd aggregate, League (single day): 1,007,200, December 27, 1971.

Record Amateur match attendance: 100,000 for FA Amateur Cup Final, Pegasus v Harwich & Parkeston at Wembley, Apr 11, 1953.

Record Cup-tie aggregate: 265,199, at two matches between Rangers and Morton, in Scottish Cup Final, 1947–48.

Abandoned match attendance records: In England – 63,480 at Newcastle v Swansea City FA Cup 3rd round, Jan 10, 1953, abandoned 8 mins (0-0), fog.

In Scotland: 94,596 v Scotland v Austria (4-1), Hampden Park, May 8, 1963. Referee Jim Finney ended play (79 minutes) after Austria had two players sent off and one carried off.

Colchester's record crowd (19,072) was for the FA Cup 1st round tie v Reading on Nov 27, 1948, abandoned 35 minutes (0-0), fog.

SMALLEST CROWDS

Smallest League attendances: 450 Rochdale v Cambridge Utd (Div 3, Feb 5, 1974); 469, Thames v Luton (Div 3 South, December 6, 1930).

Only 13 people paid to watch Stockport v Leicester (Div 2, May 7, 1921) at Old Trafford, but up to 2,000 stayed behind after Manchester Utd v Derby earlier in the day. Stockport's ground was closed.

Lowest Premier League crowd: 3,039 for Wimbledon v Everton, Jan 26, 1993 (smallest top-division attendance since War).

Lowest Saturday post-war top-division crowd: 3,231 for Wimbledon v Luton, Sep 7, 1991 (Div 1).

Lowest Football League crowds, new format – Div 1: 849 for Wimbledon v Rotherham, (Div 1) Oct 29, 2002 (smallest attendance in top two divisions since War); 1,054 Wimbledon v Wigan (Div 1), Sep 13, 2003 in club's last home match when sharing Selhurst Park; **Div 2:** 1,077, Hartlepool Utd v Cardiff, Mar 22, 1994; **Div 3:** 739, Doncaster v Barnet, Mar 3, 1998.

Lowest top-division crowd at a major ground since the war: 4,554 for Arsenal v Leeds (May 5, 1966) – fixture clashed with live TV coverage of Cup-Winners' Cup Final (Liverpool v Borussia Dortmund).

Smallest League Cup attendances: 612, Halifax v Tranmere (1st round, 2nd leg) Sep 6, 2000; 664, Wimbledon v Rotherham (3rd round), Nov 5, 2002.

Smallest League Cup attendance at top-division ground: 1,987 for Wimbledon v Bolton (2nd Round, 2nd Leg) Oct 6, 1992.

Smallest Wembley crowds for England matches: 15,628 v Chile (Rous Cup, May 23, 1989 – affected by Tube strike); 20,038 v Colombia (Friendly, Sep 6, 1995); 21,432 v Czech. (Friendly, Apr 25, 1990); 21,142 v Japan (Umbro Cup, Jun 3, 1995); 23,600 v Wales (British Championship, Feb 23, 1983); 23,659 v Greece (Friendly, May 17, 1994); 23,951 v East Germany (Friendly, Sep 12, 1984); 24,000 v N Ireland (British Championship, Apr 4, 1984); 25,756 v Colombia (Rous Cup, May 24, 1988); 25,837 v Denmark (Friendly, Sep 14, 1988).

Smallest international modern crowds: 221 for Poland v N Ireland (4-1, friendly) at Limassol, Cyprus, on Feb 13, 2002. Played at neutral venue at Poland's World Cup training base. 265 (all from N Ireland) at their Euro Champ qual against Serbia in Belgrade on Mar 25, 2011. Serbia ordered by UEFA to play behind closed doors because of previous crowd trouble.

Smallest international modern crowds at home: N Ireland: 2,500 v Chile (Belfast, May 26, 1989 – clashed with ITV live screening of Liverpool v Arsenal Championship decider); Scotland: 7,843 v N Ireland (Hampden Park, May 6, 1969); Wales: 2,315 v N Ireland (Wrexham, May 27, 1982).

Smallest attendance for post-war England match: 2,378 v San Marino (World Cup) at Bologna (Nov 17, 1993). Tie clashed with Italy v Portugal (World Cup) shown live on Italian TV.

Lowest England attendance at New Wembley. 40,181 v Norway (friendly), Sep 3, 2014

Smallest paid attendance for British first-class match: 29 for Clydebank v East Stirling, CIS Scottish League Cup 1st round, Jul 31, 1999. Played at Morton's Cappielow Park ground, shared by Clydebank. Match clashed with the Tall Ships Race which attracted 200,000 to the area.

FA CUP CROWD RECORD (OUTSIDE FINAL)

The first FA Cup-tie shown on closed-circuit TV (5th round, Saturday, Mar 11, 1967, kick-off 7pm) drew a total of 105,000 spectators to Goodison Park and Anfield. At Goodison, 64,851 watched the match 'for real', while 40,149 saw the TV version on eight giant screens at Anfield. Everton beat Liverpool 1-0.

LOWEST SEMI-FINAL CROWD

The smallest FA Cup semi-final attendance since the War was 17,987 for the Manchester Utd–Crystal Palace replay at Villa Park on Apr 12, 1995. Palace supporters largely boycotted tie after a fan died in car-park clash outside pub in Walsall before first match.

Previous lowest: 25,963 for Wimbledon v Luton, at Tottenham on Apr 9, 1988.

Lowest quarter-final crowd since the war. 6,795 for Chesterfield v Wrexham on Mar 9, 1997.

Smallest FA Cup 3rd round attendances for matches between League clubs: 1,833 for Chester v Bournemouth (at Macclesfield) Jan 5, 1991; 1,966 for Aldershot v Oxford Utd, Jan 10, 1987.

PRE-WEMBLEY CUP FINAL CROWDS

AT CRYSTAL PALACE

1895	42,560	1902	48,036	1908	74,967
1896	48,036	Replay	33,050	1909	67,651
1897	65,891	1903	64,000	1910	76,980
1898	62,017	1904	61,734	1911	69,098
1899	73,833	1905	101,117	1912	54,434
1900	68,945	1906	75,609	1913	120,028
1901	110,802	1907	84,584	1914	72,778

AT OLD TRAFFORD

1915	50,000

AT STAMFORD BRIDGE

1920	50,018	1921	72,805	1922	53,000

England women's record crowd: 45,619 v Germany, 0-3 (Wembley, Nov 23, 2014) – Karen Carney's 100th cap.

INTERNATIONAL RECORDS

MOST APPEARANCES

Peter Shilton, England goalkeeper, then aged 40, retired from international football after the 1990 World Cup Finals with the European record number of caps – 125. Previous record (119) was set by **Pat Jennings,** Northern Ireland's goalkeeper from 1964–86, who retired on his 41st birthday during the 1986 World Cup in Mexico. Shilton's England career spanned 20 seasons from his debut against East Germany at Wembley on Nov 25, 1970.

Nine players have completed a century of appearances in full international matches for England. **Billy Wright** of Wolves, was the first, retiring in 1959 with a total of 105 caps. **Bobby Charlton**, of Manchester Utd, beat Wright's record in the World Cup match against West Germany in Leon, Mexico, in Jun 1970 and **Bobby Moore**, of West Ham, overtook Charlton's 106 caps against Italy in Turin, in Jun 1973. Moore played 108 times for England, a record that stood until **Shilton** reached 109 against Denmark in Copenhagen (Jun 7, 1989). In season 2008–09, **David Beckham** (LA Galaxy/AC Milan) overtook Moore as England's most-capped outfield player. In the vastly different selection processes of their eras, Moore played 108 full games for his country, whereas Beckham's total of 115 to the end of season 2009–10, included 58 part matches, 14 as substitute and 44 times substituted. **Steven Gerrard** won his 100th cap against Sweden in Stockholm on Nov 14, 2012 and **Ashley Cole** reached 100 appearances against Brazil at Wembley on Feb 6, 2013. **Frank Lampard** played his 100th game against Ukraine in Kiev (World Cup qual) on Sep 10, 2013. **Wayne Rooney**'s 100th appearance was against Slovenia at Wembley (Euro Champ qual) on Nov 15, 2014.

Robbie Keane won his 126th Republic of Ireland cap, overtaking Shay Given's record, In a World Cup qualifier against the Faroe Islands on Jun 7, 2013. Keane scored all his team's three goals in a 3-0 win.

Kenny Dalglish became Scotland's first 100-cap international v Romania (Hampden Park, Mar 26, 1986).

World's most-capped player: Ahmed Hassan, 184 for Egypt (1995–2012).

Most-capped European player: Vitalijs Astafjevs, 167 for Latvia (1992–2010).

Most-capped European goalkeeper: Thomas Ravelli, 143 Internationals for Sweden (1981–97).

Gillian Coultard, (Doncaster Belles), England Women's captain, received a special presentation from Geoff Hurst to mark 100 caps when England beat Holland 1-0 at Upton Park on Oct 30, 1997. She made her international debut at 18 in May 1981, and retired at the end of season 1999–2000 with a record 119 caps (30 goals).

BRITAIN'S MOST-CAPPED PLAYERS

(As at start of season 2019–20)

England		Tommy Boyd	72	Mal Donaghy	91
Peter Shilton	125	**Wales**		Sammy McIlroy	88
Wayne Rooney	120	Chris Gunter	95	Maik Taylor	88
David Beckham	115	Neville Southall	92		
Steven Gerrard	114	Ashley Williams	86	**Republic of Ireland**	
Bobby Moore	108	Gary Speed	85	Robbie Keane	146
Ashley Cole	107	Wayne Hennessey	84	Shay Given	134
Bobby Charlton	106	Craig Bellamy	78	John O'Shea	118
Frank Lampard	106	Gareth Bale	77	Kevin Kilbane	110
Billy Wright	105	Joe Ledley	77	Steve Staunton	102
Scotland				Damien Duff	100
Kenny Dalglish	102	**Northern Ireland**			
Jim Leighton	91	Pat Jennings	119		
Darren Fletcher	80	Aaron Hughes	112		
Alex McLeish	77	Steven Davis	111		
Paul McStay	76	David Healy	95		

ENGLAND'S MOST-CAPPED PLAYER (either gender)

Fara Williams (Reading midfielder) with 170 appearances for England women's team to end of season 2018–19.

MOST ENGLAND CAPS IN ROW

Most consecutive international appearances: 70 by **Billy Wright,** for England from Oct 1951 to May 1959. He played 105 of England's first 108 post-war matches.

England captains most times: Billy Wright and **Bobby Moore,** 90 each.

England captains – 4 in match (v Serbia & Montenegro at Leicester Jun 3, 2003): **Michael Owen** was captain for the first half and after the interval the armband passed to **Emile Heskey** (for 15 minutes), **Phil Neville** (26 minutes) and substitute **Jamie Carragher** (9 minutes, including time added).

MOST SUCCESSIVE ENGLAND WINS

10 (Jun 1908–Jun 1909). Modern: 8 (Oct 2005–Jun 2006).

ENGLAND'S LONGEST UNBEATEN RUN

19 matches (16 wins, 3 draws), Nov 1965–Nov 1966.

ENGLAND'S TALLEST

At **6ft 7in, Peter Crouch** became England's tallest-ever international when he made his debut against Colombia in New Jersey, USA on May 31, 2005.

MOST PLAYERS FROM ONE CLUB IN ENGLAND SIDES

Arsenal supplied seven men (a record) to the England team v Italy at Highbury on Nov 14, 1934. They were: Frank Moss, George Male, Eddie Hapgood, Wilf Copping, Ray Bowden, Ted Drake and Cliff Bastin. In addition, Arsenal's Tom Whittaker was England's trainer.

Since then until 2001, the most players from one club in an England team was six from **Liverpool** against Switzerland at Wembley in Sep 1977. The side also included a Liverpool old boy, Kevin Keegan (Hamburg).

Seven **Arsenal** men took part in the England – France (0-2) match at Wembley on Feb 10, 1999. Goalkeeper David Seaman and defenders Lee Dixon, Tony Adams and Martin Keown lined up for England. Nicolas Anelka (2 goals) and Emmanuel Petit started the match for France and Patrick Vieira replaced Anelka.

Manchester Utd equalled Arsenal's 1934 record by providing England with seven players in the World Cup qualifier away to Albania on Mar 28, 2001. Five started the match – David Beckham (captain), Gary Neville, Paul Scholes, Nicky Butt and Andy Cole – and two went on as substitutes: Wes Brown and Teddy Sheringham.

INTERNATIONAL SUBS RECORDS

Malta substituted all 11 players in their 1-2 home defeat against England on Jun 3, 2000. Six substitutes by England took the total replacements in the match to 17, then an international record.

Most substitutions in match by **England:** 11 in second half by Sven-Goran Eriksson against Holland at Tottenham on Aug 15, 2001; 11 against Italy at Leeds on Mar 27, 2002; Italy sent on 8 players from the bench – the total of 19 substitutions was then a record for an England match; 11 against Australia at Upton Park on Feb 12, 2003 (entire England team changed at half-time); 11 against Iceland at City of Manchester Stadium on Jun 5, 2004,

Forty three players, a record for an England match, were used in the international against Serbia & Montenegro at Leicester on Jun 3, 2003. England sent on 10 substitutes in the second half and their opponents changed all 11 players.

The **Republic of Ireland** sent on 12 second-half substitutes, using 23 players in all, when they beat Russia 2-0 in a friendly international in Dublin on Feb 13, 2002.

First England substitute: Wolves winger **Jimmy Mullen** replaced injured Jackie Milburn (15 mins) away to Belgium on May 18, 1950. He scored in a 4-1 win.

ENGLAND'S WORLD CUP-WINNERS

At Wembley, Jul 30, 1966, 4-2 v West Germany (2-2 after 90 mins), scorers Hurst 3, Peters. Team: Banks; Cohen, Wilson, Stiles, Jack Charlton, Moore (capt), Ball, Hurst, Bobby Charlton, Hunt, Peters. Manager **Alf Ramsey** fielded that same eleven in six successive matches (an

England record): the World Cup quarter-final, semi-final and Final, and the first three games of the following season. England wore red shirts in the Final and The Queen presented the Cup to Bobby Moore. The players each received a £1,000 bonus, plus £60 World Cup Final appearance money, all less tax, and Ramsey a £6,000 bonus from the FA The match was shown live on TV (in black and white).

England's non-playing 'reserves' – there were no substitutes – also received the £1,000 bonus, but no medals. That remained the case until FIFA finally decided that non-playing members and staff of World Cup-winning squads should be given replica medals. England's 'forgotten heroes' received theirs at a reception in Downing Street on June 10, 2009 and were later guests of honour at the World Cup qualifier against Andorra at Wembley. The 11 'reserves' were: Springett, Bonetti, Armfield, Byrne, Flowers, Hunter, Paine, Connelly, Callaghan, Greaves, Eastham. Jimmy Greaves played in all three group games, against Uruguay, Mexico and France. John Connelly was in the team against Uruguay, Terry Paine against Mexico and Ian Callaghan against France.

BRAZIL'S RECORD RUN

Brazil hold the record for the longest unbeaten sequence in international football: 45 matches from 1993–97. The previous record of 31 was held by Hungary between Jun 1950 and Jul 1954.

ENGLAND MATCHES ABANDONED

May 17, 1953 v **Argentina** (Friendly, Buenos Aires) after 23 mins (0-0) – rain.
Oct 29, 1975 v **Czechoslovakia** (Euro Champ qual, Bratislava) after 17 mins (0-0) – fog. Played next day.
Feb 15, 1995 v **Rep of Ireland** (Friendly, Dublin) after 27 mins (1-0) – crowd disturbance.

ENGLAND POSTPONEMENTS

Nov 21, 1979 v **Bulgaria** (Euro Champ qual, Wembley, postponed for 24 hours – fog; Aug 10, 2011 v **Holland** (friendly), Wembley, postponed after rioting in London.
Oct 16, 2012 v **Poland** (World Cup qual, Warsaw) postponed to next day – pitch waterlogged.
The friendly against **Honduras** (Miami, Jun 7, 2014) was suspended midway through the first half for 44 minutes – thunderstorm.

ENGLAND UNDER COVER

England played indoors for the first time when they beat Argentina 1-0 in the World Cup at the Sapporo Dome, Japan, on Jun 7, 2002.

ALL-SEATED INTERNATIONALS

The first **all-seated crowd** (30,000) for a full international in Britain saw **Wales** and **West Germany** draw 0-0 at Cardiff Arms Park on May 31, 1989. The terraces were closed.

England's first all-seated international at Wembley was against Yugoslavia (2-1) on December 13, 1989 (attendance 34,796). The terracing behind the goals was closed for conversion to seating.
The first **full-house all-seated** international at Wembley was for England v Brazil (1-0) on Mar 28, 1990, when a capacity 80,000 crowd paid record British receipts of £1,200,000.

MOST NEW CAPS IN ENGLAND TEAM

6, by Sir Alf Ramsey (v Portugal, Apr 3, 1974) and **by Sven-Goran Eriksson** (v Australia, Feb 12, 2003; 5 at half-time when 11 changes made).

PLAYED FOR MORE THAN ONE COUNTRY

Multi-nationals in senior international football include: **Johnny Carey** (1938–53) – caps Rep of Ireland 29, N Ireland 7; **Ferenc Puskas** (1945–62) – caps Hungary 84, Spain 4; **Alfredo di Stefano** (1950–56) – caps Argentina 7, Spain 31; **Ladislav Kubala** (1948–58) – caps, Hungary 3, Czechoslovakia 11, Spain 19, only player to win full international honours with 3 countries. Kubala also played in a fourth international team, scoring twice for FIFA v England at Wembley in 1953. Eleven players, including **Carey**, appeared for both N Ireland and the Republic of Ireland in seasons directly after the last war.

Cecil Moore, capped by N Ireland in 1949 when with Glentoran, played for USA v England in 1953.

Hawley Edwards played for England v Scotland in 1874 and for Wales v Scotland in 1876.

Jack Reynolds (Distillery and WBA) played for both Ireland (5 times) and England (8) in the 1890s.

Bobby Evans (Sheffield Utd) had played 10 times for Wales when capped for England, in 1910–11. He was born in Chester of Welsh parents.

In recent years, several players have represented USSR and one or other of the breakaway republics. The same applies to Yugoslavia and its component states. **Josip Weber** played for Croatia in 1992 and made a 5-goal debut for Belgium in 1994.

THREE-GENERATION INTERNATIONAL FAMILY

When Bournemouth striker **Warren Feeney** was capped away to Liechtenstein on Mar 27, 2002, he became the third generation of his family to play for Northern Ireland. He followed in the footsteps of his grandfather James (capped twice in 1950) and father Warren snr. (1 in 1976).

FATHERS & SONS CAPPED BY ENGLAND

George Eastham senior (pre-war) and **George Eastham junior**; **Brian Clough** and **Nigel Clough**; **Frank Lampard snr** and **Frank Lampard jnr**; **Mark Chamberlain** and **Alex Oxlade-Chamberlain**.

FATHER & SON SAME-DAY CAPS

Iceland made father-and-son international history when they beat Estonia 3-0 in Tallin on Apr 24, 1996. **Arnor Gudjohnsen** (35) started the match and was replaced (62 mins) by his 17-year-old son **Eidur**.

LONGEST UNBEATEN START TO ENGLAND CAREER

Steven Gerrard, 21 matches (W16, D5) 2000-03.

SUCCESSIVE ENGLAND HAT-TRICKS

The last player to score a hat-trick in consecutive England matches was **Dixie Dean** on the summer tour in May 1927, against Belgium (9-1) and Luxembourg (5-2).

MOST GOALS BY PLAYER v ENGLAND

4 by **Zlatan Ibrahimovic** (Sweden 4 England 2, Stockholm, Nov 14, 2012).

POST-WAR HAT-TRICKS v ENGLAND

Nov 25, 1953, **Nandor Hidegkuti** (England 3, Hungary 6, Wembley); May 11, 1958, **Aleksandar Petakovic** (Yugoslavia 5, England 0, Belgrade); May 17, 1959, **Juan Seminario** (Peru 4, England 1, Lima); Jun 15, 1988, **Marco van Basten** (Holland 3, England 1, European Championship, Dusseldorf). Six other players scored hat-tricks against England (1878–1930).

NO-SAVE GOALKEEPERS

Chris Woods did not have one save to make when England beat San Marino 6-0 (World Cup) at Wembley on Feb 17, 1993. He touched the ball only six times.

Gordon Banks had a similar no-save experience when England beat Malta 5-0 (European Championship) at Wembley on May 12, 1971. Malta did not force a goal-kick or corner, and the four times Banks touched the ball were all from back passes.

Robert Green was also idle in the 6-0 World Cup qualifying win over Andorra at Wembley on Jun 10, 2009.

Joe Hart was untroubled in England's 5-0 win over San Marino in a World Cup qualifier at Wembley on Oct 12, 2012.

WORLD/EURO MEMBERS

FIFA has 211 member countries, **UEFA** 55

NEW FIFA PRESIDENT

The 18-year reign of FIFA president **Sepp Blatter** ended in December 2015 amid widespread allegations of corruption. He was replaced in February 2016 by Gianni Infantino, a 45-year-old Swiss-Italian lawyer, who was previously general secretary of UEFA. Under new rules, he will serve four years.

FIFA WORLD YOUTH CUP (UNDER-20)

Finals: **1977** (Tunis) Soviet Union 2 Mexico 2 (Soviet won 9-8 on pens.); **1979** (Tokyo) Argentina 3 Soviet Union 1; **1981** (Sydney) W Germany 4 Qatar 0; **1983** (Mexico City) Brazil 1 Argentina 0; **1985** (Moscow) Brazil 1 Spain 0; **1987** (Santiago) Yugoslavia 1 W Germany 1 (Yugoslavia won 5-4 on pens.); **1989** (Riyadh) Portugal 2 Nigeria 0; **1991** (Lisbon) Portugal 0 Brazil 0 (Portugal won 4-2 on pens.); **1993** (Sydney) Brazil 2 Ghana 1; **1995** (Qatar) Argentina 2 Brazil 0; **1997** (Kuala Lumpur) Argentina 2 Uruguay 1; **1999** (Lagos) Spain 4 Japan 0; **2001** (Buenos Aires) Argentina 3 Ghana 0; **2003** (Dubai) Brazil 1 Spain 0; **2005** (Utrecht) Argentina 2 Nigeria 1; **2007** (Toronto) Argentina 2 Czech Republic 1; **2009** (Cairo) Ghana 0 Brazil 0 (aet, Ghana won 4-3 on pens); **2011** (Bogota) Brazil 3 Portugal 2 (aet); **2013** (Istanbul) France 0 Uruguay 0 (aet, France won 4-1 on pens); **2015** (Auckland) Serbia 2 Brazil 1 (aet); **2017** (Suwon) England 1 Venezuela 0.

FAMOUS CLUB FEATS

Manchester City won the 2017–18 Premier League title under Pep Guardiola in record style. They became England's first champions to total 100 points and had the longest winning streak, 18 matches, in top-flight history. There were other new Premier League marks for goals scored (106), goal difference (79), overall wins (32), away victories (16), and for a 19-point gap to second-place. In season 2018–19, City made history with a domestic treble, winning the Premier League, FA Cup and League Cup.

Arsenal created an all-time English League record sequence of 49 unbeaten Premier League matches (W36, D13), spanning 3 seasons, from May 7, 2003 until losing 2-0 away to Manchester Utd on Oct 24, 2004. It included all 38 games in season 2003–04.

The Double: There have been 11 instances of a club winning the Football League/Premier League title and the FA Cup in the same season. **Preston** 1888–89; **Aston Villa** 1896–97; **Tottenham** 1960–61; **Arsenal** 1970–71, 1997–98, 2001–02; **Liverpool** 1985–86; **Manchester Utd** 1993–94, 1995–96, 1998–99; **Chelsea** 2009–10.

The Treble: Liverpool were the first English club to win three major competitions in one season when in 1983–84, Joe Fagan's first season as manager, they were League Champions, League Cup winners and European Cup winners.

Sir Alex Ferguson's **Manchester Utd** achieved an even more prestigious treble in 1998–99, completing the domestic double of Premier League and FA Cup and then winning the European Cup. In season 2008–09, they completed another major triple success – Premier League, Carling Cup and World Club Cup.

Liverpool completed a unique treble by an English club with three cup successes under Gerard Houllier in season 2000–01: the League Cup, FA Cup and UEFA Cup.

Liverpool the first English club to win five major trophies in one calendar year (Feb– Aug 2001): League Cup, FA Cup, UEFA Cup, Charity Shield, UEFA Super Cup.

As Champions in season 2001–02, **Arsenal** set a Premier League record by winning the last 13 matches. They were the first top-division club since Preston in the League's inaugural season (1888–89) to maintain an unbeaten away record.

(See Scottish section for treble feats by Rangers and Celtic).

Record Home Runs: Liverpool went 85 competitive first-team games unbeaten at home between losing 2-3 to Birmingham on Jan 21, 1978 and 1-2 to Leicester on Jan 31, 1981. They comprised 63 in the League, 9 League Cup, 7 in European competition and 6 FA Cup.

Chelsea hold the record unbeaten home League sequence of 86 matches (W62, D24) between losing 1-2 to Arsenal, Feb 21, 2004, and 0-1 to Liverpool, Oct 26, 2008.

Third to First: Charlton, in 1936, became the first club to advance from the Third to First Division in successive seasons. **Queens Park Rangers** were the second club to achieve the feat in 1968, and **Oxford Utd** did it in 1984 and 1985 as Champions of each division. Subsequently, **Derby** (1987), **Middlesbrough** (1988), **Sheffield Utd** (1990) and **Notts Co** (1991) climbed from Third Division to First in consecutive seasons.

Watford won successive promotions from the modern Second Division to the Premier League in 1997–98, 1998–99. **Manchester City** equalled the feat in 1998–99, 1999–2000. **Norwich** climbed from League 1 to the Premier League in seasons 2009–10, 2010–11. **Southampton** did the same in 2010–11 and 2011–12.

Fourth to First: Northampton , in 1965 became the first club to rise from the Fourth to the First Division. **Swansea** climbed from the Fourth Division to the First (three promotions in four seasons), 1977–78 to 1980–81. **Wimbledon** repeated the feat, 1982–3 to 1985–86. **Watford** did it in five seasons, 1977–8 to 1981–82. **Carlisle** climbed from Fourth Division to First, 1964–74.

Non-League to First: When **Wimbledon** finished third in the Second Division in 1986, they completed the phenomenal rise from non-League football (Southern League) to the First Division in nine years. Two years later they won the FA Cup.

Tottenham, in 1960–61, not only carried off the First Division Championship and the FA Cup for the first time that century but set up other records by opening with 11 successive wins, registering most First Division wins (31), most away wins in the League's history (16), and equalling Arsenal's First Division records of 66 points and 33 away points. They already held the Second Division record of 70 points (1919–20).

Arsenal, in 1993, became the first club to win both English domestic cup competitions (FA Cup and League Cup) in the same season. **Liverpool** repeated the feat in 2001. **Chelsea** did it in 2007. Chelsea achieved the FA Cup/Champions League double in May 2012.

Preston, in season 1888–89, won the first League Championship without losing a match and the FA Cup without having a goal scored against them. Only other English clubs to remain unbeaten through a League season were **Liverpool** (Div 2 Champions in 1893 94) and **Arsenal** (Premier League Champions 2003–04).

Bury, in 1903, also won the FA Cup without conceding a goal.

Everton won Div 2, Div 1 and the FA Cup in successive seasons, 1930–31, 1931–32, 1932–33.

Wolves won the League Championship in 1958 and 1959 and the FA Cup in 1960.

Liverpool won the title in 1964, the FA Cup in 1965 and the title again in 1966. In 1978 they became the first British club to win the European Cup in successive seasons. Nottm Forest repeated the feat in 1979 and 1980.

Liverpool won the League Championship six times in eight seasons (1976–83) under **Bob Paisley's** management.

Sir Alex Ferguson's **Manchester Utd** won the Premier League in 13 of its 21 seasons (1992–2013). They were runners up five times and third three times.

FA CUP/PROMOTION DOUBLE

WBA are the only club to achieve this feat in the same season (1930–31).

COVENTRY UNIQUE

Coventry are the only club to have played in the Premier League, all four previous divisions of the Football League, in both sections (North and South) of the old Third Division and in the modern Championship.

FAMOUS UPS & DOWNS

Sunderland: Relegated in 1958 after maintaining First Division status since their election to the Football League in 1890. They dropped into Division 3 for the first time in 1987.

Aston Villa: Relegated with Preston to the Third Division in 1970.

Arsenal up: When the League was extended in 1919, Woolwich Arsenal (sixth in Division Two in 1914–15, last season before the war) were elected to Division One. Arsenal have been in the top division ever since.

Tottenham down: At that same meeting in 1919 Chelsea (due for relegation) retained their place in Division One but the bottom club (Tottenham) had to go down to Division Two.

Preston and Burnley down: Preston, the first League Champions in season 1888–89, dropped into the Fourth Division in 1985. So did Burnley, also among the League's original members in 1888. In 1986, Preston had to apply for re-election.

Wolves' fall: Wolves, another of the Football League's original members, completed the fall from First Division to Fourth in successive seasons (1984–85–86).

Lincoln out: Lincoln became the first club to suffer automatic demotion from the Football League when they finished bottom of Div 4, on goal difference, in season 1986–87. They were replaced by Scarborough, champions of the GM Vauxhall Conference. Lincoln regained their place a year later.

Swindon up and down: In the 1990 play-offs, Swindon won promotion to the First Division for the first time, but remained in the Second Division because of financial irregularities.

MOST CHAMPIONSHIP WINS

Manchester Utd have been champions of England a record 20 times (7 Football League, 13 Premier League).

LONGEST CURRENT MEMBERS OF TOP DIVISION

Arsenal (since 1919), **Everton** (1954), **Liverpool** (1962), **Manchester Utd** (1975).

CHAMPIONS: FEWEST PLAYERS

Liverpool used only **14** players (five ever-present) when they won the League Championship in season 1965–66. **Aston Villa** also called on no more than 14 players to win the title in 1980–81, with seven ever-present.

UNBEATEN CHAMPIONS

Only two clubs have become Champions of England with an unbeaten record: **Preston** as the Football League's first winners in 1888–89 (22 matches) and **Arsenal**, Premier League winners in 2003–04 (38 matches).

LEAGUE HAT-TRICKS

Huddersfield created a record in 1924–25–26 by winning the League Championship three years in succession.

Arsenal equalled this hat-trick in 1933–34–35, **Liverpool** in 1982–83–84 and **Manchester Utd** in 1999–2000–01. Sir Alex Ferguson's side became the first to complete two hat-tricks (2007–08–09).

'SUPER DOUBLE' WINNERS

Since the War, there have been three instances of players appearing in and then managing FA Cup and Championship-winning teams:

Joe Mercer: Player in Arsenal Championship teams 1948, 1953 and in their 1950 FA Cup side; manager of Manchester City when they won Championship 1968, FA Cup 1969.

Kenny Dalglish: Player in Liverpool Championship-winning teams 1979, 1980, 1982, 1983, 1984, player-manager 1986, 1988, 1990: player-manager when Liverpool won FA Cup (to complete Double) 1986; manager of Blackburn, Champions 1995.

George Graham: Played in Arsenal's Double-winning team in 1971, and as manager took them to Championship success in 1989 and 1991 and the FA Cup – League Cup double in 1993.

ORIGINAL TWELVE

The original 12 members of the Football League (formed in 1888) were: **Accrington, Aston Villa, Blackburn, Bolton, Burnley, Derby, Everton, Notts Co, Preston, Stoke, WBA and Wolves.**

Results on the opening day (Sep 8, 1888): Bolton 3, Derby 6; Everton 2, Accrington 1; Preston 5, Burnley 2; Stoke 0, WBA 2; Wolves 1, Aston Villa 1. Preston had the biggest first-day crowd: 6,000. Blackburn and Notts Co did not play that day. They kicked off a week later (Sep 15) – Blackburn 5, Accrington 5; Everton 2, Notts Co 1.

Accrington FC resigned from the league in 1893 and later folded. A new club, Accrington Stanley, were members of the league from 1921 until 1962 when financial problems forced their demise. The current Accrington Stanley were formed in 1968 and gained league status in 2007.

FASTEST CLIMBS

Three promotions in four seasons by two clubs – **Swansea City**: 1978 third in Div 4; 1979 third in Div 3; 1981 third in Div 2; **Wimbledon**: 1983 Champions of Div 4; 1984 second in Div 3; 1986 third in Div 2.

MERSEYSIDE RECORD

Liverpool is the only city to have staged top-division football – through Everton and/or Liverpool – **in every season** since League football began in 1888.

EARLIEST PROMOTIONS TO TOP DIVISION POST-WAR

Mar 23, 1974, **Middlesbrough;** Mar 25, 2006, **Reading.**

EARLIEST RELEGATIONS POST-WAR

From top division: **QPR** went down from the old First Division on Mar 29, 1969; **Derby** went down from the Premier League on Mar 29, 2008, with 6 matches still to play. From modern First Division: **Stockport** on Mar 16, 2002, with 7 matches still to play; **Wimbledon** on Apr 6, 2004, with 7 matches to play.

LEAGUE RECORDS

CHAMPIONS OF ENGLAND 1888–2019

Football League and Premier league

Manchester Utd 20, Liverpool 18, Arsenal 13, Everton 9, Aston Villa 7, Chelsea 6, Manchester City 6, Sunderland 6, Newcastle 4, Sheffield Wed 4, Blackburn 3, Huddersfield 3, Leeds 3, Wolves 3, Burnley 2, Derby 2, Portsmouth 2, Preston 2, Tottenham 2, Ipswich 1, Leicester 1, Nottm Forest 1, Sheffield Utd 1, WBA 1

DOUBLE CHAMPIONS

Nine men have played in and managed League Championship-winning teams:

Ted Drake Player – Arsenal 1934, 1935, 1938. Manager – Chelsea 1955.
Bill Nicholson Player – Tottenham 1951. Manager – Tottenham 1961.
Alf Ramsey Player – Tottenham 1951. Manager – Ipswich 1962.
Joe Mercer Player – Everton 1939, Arsenal 1948, 1953. Manager – Manchester City 1968.
Dave Mackay Player – Tottenham 1961. Manager – Derby 1975.
Bob Paisley Player – Liverpool 1947. Manager – Liverpool 1976, 1977, 1979, 1980, 1982, 1983.
Howard Kendall Player – Everton 1970. Manager – Everton 1985, 1987.
Kenny Dalglish Player – Liverpool 1979, 1980, 1982, 1983, 1984. Player-manager – Liverpool 1986, 1988, 1990. Manager – Blackburn 1995.
George Graham Player – Arsenal 1971. Manager – Arsenal 1989, 1991.

CANTONA'S FOUR-TIMER

Eric Cantona played in four successive Championship-winning teams: Marseille 1990-01, Leeds 1991-92, Manchester Utd 1992–93 and 1993–94.

ARRIVALS AND DEPARTURES

The following are the Football League arrivals and departures since 1923:

Year	In	Out
1923	Doncaster	Stalybridge Celtic
	New Brighton	

1927	Torquay	Aberdare Athletic
1928	Carlisle	Durham
1929	York	Ashington
1930	Thames	Merthyr Tydfil
1931	Mansfield	Newport Co
	Chester	Nelson
1932	Aldershot	Thames
	Newport Co	Wigan Borough
1938	Ipswich	Gillingham
1950	Colchester, Gillingham	
	Scunthorpe, Shrewsbury	
1951	Workington	New Brighton
1960	Peterborough	Gateshead
1962	Oxford Utd	Accrington (resigned)
1970	Cambridge Utd	Bradford PA
1972	Hereford	Barrow
1977	Wimbledon	Workington
1978	Wigan	Southport
1987	Scarborough	Lincoln
1988	Lincoln	Newport Co
1989	Maidstone	Darlington
1990	Darlington	Colchester
1991	Barnet	
1992	Colchester	Aldershot, Maidstone (resigned)
1993	Wycombe	Halifax
1997	Macclesfield	Hereford
1998	Halifax	Doncaster
1999	Cheltenham	Scarborough
2000	Kidderminster	Chester
2001	Rushden	Barnet
2002	Boston	Halifax
2003	Yeovil, Doncaster	Exeter, Shrewsbury
2004	Chester, Shrewsbury	Carlisle, York
2005	Barnet, Carlisle	Kidderminster, Cambridge Utd
2006	Accrington, Hereford	Oxford Utd, Rushden & Diamonds
2007	Dagenham, Morecambe	Torquay, Boston
2008	Aldershot, Exeter	Wrexham, Mansfield
2009	Burton, Torquay	Chester, Luton
2010	Stevenage, Oxford Utd	Grimsby, Darlington
2011	Crawley, AFC Wimbledon	Lincoln, Stockport
2012	Fleetwood, York	Hereford, Macclesfield
2013	Mansfield, Newport	Barnet, Aldershot
2014	Luton, Cambridge Utd	Bristol Rov, Torquay
2015	Barnet, Bristol Rov	Cheltenham, Tranmere
2016	Cheltenham, Grimsby	Dagenham & Redbridge, York
2017	Lincoln, Forest Green	Hartlepool, Leyton Orient
2018	Macclesfield, Tranmere	Barnet, Chesterfield
2019	Leyton Orient, Salford	Notts Co Yeovil

Leeds City were expelled from Div 2 in Oct, 1919; Port Vale took over their fixtures.

EXTENSIONS TO FOOTBALL LEAGUE

Clubs	Season	Clubs	Season
12 to 14	1891–92	44 to 66†	1920–21
14 to 28*	1892–93	66 to 86†	1921–22

28 to 31	1893–94	86 to 88	1923–24
31 to 32	1894–95	88 to 92	1950–51
32 to 36	1898–99	92 to 93	1991–92
36 to 40	1905–06	(Reverted to 92 when Aldershot closed, Mar 1992)	

*Second Division formed. † Third Division (South) formed from Southern League clubs.
†Third Division (North) formed.
Football League reduced to 70 clubs and three divisions on the formation of the FA Premier League in 1992; increased to 72 season 1994–95, when Premier League reduced to 20 clubs.

RECORD RUNS

Arsenal hold the record unbeaten sequence in the English League – 49 Premier League matches (36 wins, 13 draws) from May 7, 2003 until Oct 24, 2004 when beaten 2-0 away to Manchester Utd. The record previously belonged to **Nottm Forest** – 42 First Division matches (21 wins, 21 draws) from Nov 19, 1977 until beaten 2-0 at Liverpool on December 9, 1978.
Huddersfield set a new Football League record of 43 League 1 matches unbeaten from Jan 1, 2011 until Nov 28, 2011 when losing 2-0 at Charlton.
Best debuts: Ipswich won the First Division at their first attempt in 1961–62.
Peterborough in their first season in the Football League (1960–01) not only won the Fourth Division but set the all time scoring record for the League of 134 goals. **Hereford** were promoted from the Fourth Division in their first League season, 1972–73.
Wycombe were promoted from the Third Division (via the play-offs) in their first League season, 1993–94. **Stevenage** were promoted from League 2 (via the play-offs) in their first League season, 2010–11. **Crawley** gained automatic promotion in their first season in 2011–12.
Record winning sequence in a season: 18 consecutive League victories by Manchester City, 2017–18, longest in English top-flight football.
Best winning start to League season: 13 successive victories in Div 3 by **Reading**, season 1985–86.
Best starts in 'old' First Division: 11 consecutive victories by **Tottenham** in 1960–61; 10 by **Manchester Utd** in 1985–86. In 'new' First Division, 11 consecutive wins by **Newcastle** in 1992–93 and by **Fulham** in 2000–01.
Longest unbeaten sequence (all competitions): 40 by **Nottm Forest,** Mar–December 1978. It comprised 21 wins, 19 draws (in 29 League matches, 6 League Cup, 4 European Cup, 1 Charity Shield).
Longest unbeaten starts to League season: 38 matches (26 wins, 12 draws) in **Arsenal's** undefeated Premier League season, 2003–04; 29 matches – **Leeds**, Div 1 1973–74 (19 wins, 10 draws); **Liverpool**, Div 1 1987–88 (22 wins, 7 draws).
Most consecutive League matches unbeaten in a season: 38 Arsenal Premier League season 2003–04 (see above); 33 **Reading** (25 wins, 8 draws) 2005–06.
Longest winning sequence in Div 1: 13 matches by **Tottenham** – last two of season 1959–60, first 11 of 1960–61.
Longest unbeaten home League sequence in top division: 86 matches (62 wins, 24 draws) by **Chelsea** (Mar 2004–Oct 2008).
League's longest winning sequence with clean sheets: 9 matches by **Stockport** (Lge 2, 2006–07 season).
Premier League – best starts to season: Arsenal, 38 games, 2003–04; **Manchester City,** 14 games, 2011–12.
Best winning start to Premier League season: 9 consecutive victories by **Chelsea** in 2005–06.
Premier League – most consecutive home wins: 20 by **Manchester City** (last 5 season 2010–11, first 15 season 2011–12).
Most consecutive away League wins in top flight: 11 by **Chelsea** (3 at end 2007–08 season, 8 in 2008–09).
Premier League – longest unbeaten away run: 27 matches (W17, D10) by **Arsenal** (Apr 5, 2003–Sep 25, 2004).
Record home-win sequences: Bradford Park Avenue won 25 successive home games in Div 3

North – the last 18 in 1926–27 and the first 7 the following season. Longest run of home wins in the top division is 21 by **Liverpool** – the last 9 of 1971–72 and the first 12 of 1972–73.

British record for successive League wins: 25 by **Celtic** (Scottish Premier League), 2003–04.

WORST SEQUENCES

Derby experienced the longest run without a win in League history in season 2007–08 – 32 games from Sep 22 to the end of the campaign (25 lost, 7 drawn). They finished bottom by a 24-pt margin. The sequence increased to 36 matches (28 lost, 8 drawn) at the start of the following season. **Macclesfield** also went 36 games without winning – 23 up to the end of the club's relegation season of 2011–12 and 13 after returning to League Two in 2018–19.

Cambridge Utd had the previous worst of 31 in 1983–84 (21 lost, 10 drawn). They were bottom of Div 2.

Longest sequence without home win: Sunderland, in the Championship, went an English record 21 games in all competitions without a victory in front of their own supporters (Dec 2016–Nov 2017).

Worst losing start to a League season : 12 consecutive defeats by **Manchester Utd** (Div 1), 1930–31.

Worst Premier League start: QPR 16 matches without win (7 draws, 9 defeats), 2012–13.

Premier League – most consecutive defeats: 20 **Sunderland** last 15 matches, 2002–03, first five matches 2005–06.

Longest non-winning start to League season: 25 matches (4 draws, 21 defeats) by **Newport**, Div 4. Worst no-win League starts since then: 16 matches by **Burnley** (9 draws, 7 defeats in Div 2, 1979–80); 16 by **Hull** (10 draws, 6 defeats in Div 2, 1989–90); 16 by **Sheffield Utd** (4 draws, 12 defeats in Div 1, 1990–91).

Most League defeats in season: 34 by **Doncaster** (Div 3) 1997–98.

Fewest League wins in season: 1 by **Loughborough** (Div 2, season 1899–1900). They lost 27, drew 6, goals 18-100 and dropped out of the League. (See also Scottish section). 1 by **Derby** (Prem Lge, 2007–08). They lost 29, drew 8, goals 20-89.

Most consecutive League defeats in season: 18 by **Darwen** (Div 1, 1898–99); 17 by **Rochdale** (Div 3 North, 1931–32).

Fewest home League wins in season: 1 by **Loughborough** (Div 2, 1899–1900), **Notts Co** (Div 1, 1904–05), **Woolwich Arsenal** (Div 1, 1912–13), **Blackpool** (Div 1, 1966–67), **Rochdale** (Div 3, 1973–74), **Sunderland** (Prem Lge, 2005–06); **Derby** (Prem Lge, 2007–08).

Most home League defeats in season: 18 by **Cambridge Utd** (Div 3, 1984–85).

Away League defeats record: 24 in row by **Crewe** (Div 2) – all 15 in 1894–95 followed by 9 in 1895–96; by **Nelson** (Div 3 North) – 3 in Apr 1930 followed by all 21 in season 1930–31. They then dropped out of the League.

Biggest defeat in Champions' season: During **Newcastle's** title-winning season in 1908–09, they were beaten 9-1 at home by Sunderland on December 5.

WORST START BY EVENTUAL CHAMPIONS

Sunderland took only 2 points from their first 7 matches in season 1912–13 (2 draws, 5 defeats). They won 25 of the remaining 31 games to clinch their fifth League title.

DISMAL DERBY

Derby were relegated in season 2007–08 as the worst-ever team in the Premier League: fewest wins (1), fewest points (11); fewest goals (20), first club to go down in March (29th).

UNBEATEN LEAGUE SEASON

Only three clubs have completed an English League season unbeaten: **Preston** (22 matches in 1888–89, the League's first season), **Liverpool** (28 matches in Div 2, 1893–94) and **Arsenal** (38 matches in Premier League, 2003–04).

100 PER CENT HOME RECORDS

Six clubs have won every home League match in a season: **Sunderland** (13 matches)' in 1891–92 and four teams in the old Second Division: **Liverpool** (14) in 1893–94, **Bury** (15) in

1894–95, **Sheffield Wed** (17) in 1899–1900 and **Small Heath,** subsequently **Birmingham** (17) in 1902–03. The last club to do it, **Brentford,** won all 21 home games in Div 3 South in 1929–30. **Rotherham** just failed to equal that record in 1946–47. They won their first 20 home matches in Div 3 North, then drew the last 3-3 v Rochdale.

BEST HOME LEAGUE RECORDS IN TOP FLIGHT

Sunderland, 1891–92 (P13, W13); **Newcastle,** 1906–07 (P19, W18, D1); **Chelsea,** 2005–06 (P19, W18, D1); **Manchester Utd,** 2010–11 (P19, W18, D1); **Manchester City,** 2011–12 (P19, W18, D1).

MOST CONSECUTIVE CLEAN SHEETS

Premier League – 14: **Manchester Utd** (2008–09); Football League – 11: **Millwall** (Div 3 South 1925–26); **York** (Div 3 1973–74); **Reading** (Div 4, 1978–79).

WORST HOME RUNS

Most consecutive home League defeats: 14 **Rochdale** (Div 3 North) seasons 1931–32 and 1932–33; 10 **Birmingham** (Div 1) 1985–86; 9 **Darwen** (Div 2) 1897–98; 9 **Watford** (Div 2) 1971–72.

Between Nov 1958 and Oct 1959 **Portsmouth** drew 2 and lost 14 out of 16 consecutive home games.

West Ham did not win in the Premier League at Upton Park in season 2002–03 until the 13th home match on Jan 29.

MOST AWAY WINS IN SEASON

Doncaster won 18 of their 21 away League fixtures when winning Div 3 North in 1946–47.

AWAY WINS RECORD

Most consecutive away League wins: 11 **Chelsea** (Prem Lge) – 8 at start of 2008–09 after ending previous season with 3.

100 PER CENT HOME WINS ON ONE DAY

Div 1 – All 11 home teams won on Feb 13, 1926 and on Dec 10, 1955. **Div 2** – All 12 home teams won on Nov 26, 1988. **Div 3,** all 12 home teams won in the week-end programme of Oct 18–19, 1968.

NO HOME WINS IN DIV ON ONE DAY

Div 1 – 8 away wins, 3 draws in 11 matches on Sep 6, 1986. **Div 2** – 7 away wins, 4 draws in 11 matches on Dec 26, 1987. **Premier League** – 6 away wins, 5 draws in 11 matches on Dec 26, 1994.

The weekend **Premier League** programme on Dec 7-8-9, 1996 produced no home win in the ten games (4 aways, 6 draws). There was again no home victory (3 away wins, 7 draws) in the week-end **Premier League** fixtures on Sep 23–24, 2000.

MOST DRAWS IN A SEASON (FOOTBALL LEAGUE)

23 by **Norwich** (Div 1, 1978–79), **Exeter** (Div 4, 1986–87). **Cardiff** and **Hartlepool** (both Div 3, 1997–98). **Norwich** played 42 matches, the others 46.

MOST DRAWS IN PREMIER LEAGUE SEASON

18 (in 42 matches) by **Manchester City** (1993–94), **Sheffield Utd** (1993–94), **Southampton** (1994–95).

MOST DRAWS IN ONE DIVISION ON A SINGLE DAY

On Sep 18, 1948 **nine** out of 11 First Division matches were drawn.

MOST DRAWS IN PREMIER LEAGUE PROGRAMME

Over the week-ends of December 2–3–4, 1995, and Sep 23–24, 2000, **seven** out of the ten matches finished level.

FEWEST DRAWS IN SEASON

In 46 matches: 3 by **Reading** (Div 3 South, 1951–52); **Bradford Park Avenue** (Div 3 North, 1956–57); **Tranmere** (Div 4, 1984–85); **Southend** (Div 3, 2002–03); in 42 matches: 2 by **Reading** (Div 3 South, 1935–36); **Stockport** (Div 3 North, 1946–47); in 38 matches: 2 by **Sunderland** (Div 1, 1908–09).

HIGHEST-SCORING DRAWS IN LEAGUE

Leicester 6, **Arsenal** 6 (Div 1 Apr 21, 1930); **Charlton** 6, **Middlesbrough** 6 (Div 2. Oct 22, 1960)

Latest **6-6** draw in first-class football was between **Tranmere** and **Newcastle** in the Zenith Data Systems Cup 1st round on Oct 1, 1991. The score went from 3-3 at 90 minutes to 6-6 after extra time, and Tranmere won 3-2 on penalties. In Scotland: **Queen of the South** 6, **Falkirk** 6 (Div 1, Sep 20, 1947).

Most recent **5-5** draws in top division: **Southampton** v **Coventry** (Div 1, May 4, 1982); **QPR** v **Newcastle** (Div 1, Sep 22, 1984); **WBA** v **Manchester Utd** (Prem Lge, May 19, 2013).

DRAWS RECORDS

Most consecutive drawn matches in Football League: 8 by **Torquay** (Div 3, 1969–70), **Middlesbrough** (Div 2, 1970–71), **Peterborough** (Div 4, 1971–72), **Birmingham** (Div 3 (1990–91), **Southampton** (Champ, 2005–06), **Chesterfield** (Lge 1, 2005–06), **Swansea** (Champ, 2008–09).

Longest sequence of draws by the same score: six 1-1 results by **QPR** in season 1957–58. **Tranmere** became the first club to play **five consecutive 0-0 League draws**, in season 1997–98. Relegated **Chesterfield** drew nine successive National League games in season 2018–19.

IDENTICAL RECORDS

There is only **one instance** of two clubs in one division finishing a season with identical records. In 1907–08, **Blackburn** and **Woolwich Arsenal** were bracketed equal 14th in the First Division with these figures: P38, W12, D12, L14, Goals 51-63, Pts. 36.

The total of **1195 goals** scored in the Premier League in season 1993–94 was repeated in 1994–95.

DEAD LEVEL

Millwall's record in Division Two in season 1973–74 was P42, W14, D14, L14, F51, A51, Pts 42.

CHAMPIONS OF ALL DIVISIONS

Wolves, Burnley and **Preston** are the only clubs to have won titles in the old Divisions 1, 2, 3 and 4. Wolves also won the Third Division North and the new Championship.

POINTS DEDUCTIONS

2000–01: Chesterfield 9 for breach of transfer regulations and falsifying gate receipts.
2002–03: Boston 4 for contractual irregularities.
2004–05: Wrexham, Cambridge Utd 10 for administration.
2005–06: Rotherham 10 for administration.
2006–07: Leeds, Boston 10 for administration; **Bury** 1 for unregistered player.
2007–08: Leeds 15 over insolvency rules; **Bournemouth, Luton, Rotherham** 10 for administration.
2008–09: Luton 20 for failing Insolvency rules, 10 over payments to agents; **Bournemouth, Rotherham** 17 for breaking administration rules; **Southampton, Stockport** 10 for administration – **Southampton** with effect from season 2009–10 **Crystal Palace** 1 for ineligible player.

2009–10: Portsmouth 9, **Crystal Palace** 10 for administration; **Hartlepool** 3 for ineligible player.

2010–11: Plymouth 10 for administration; **Hereford** 3, **Torquay** 1, each for ineligible player

2011–12: Portsmouth and **Port Vale** both 10 for administration – Portsmouth from following season.

2013–14: Coventry 10 for administration; **AFC Wimbledon** 3 for ineligible player.

2014–15: Rotherham 3 for ineligible player.

2015–16: Bury 3 for ineligible player.

2018–19: Birmingham 9 for financial irregularities; **Bolton** 12 for administration, triggered in season 2019–20.

Among previous points penalties imposed:

Nov 1990: Arsenal 2, **Manchester Utd** 1 following mass players' brawl at Old Trafford.

Dec 1996: Brighton 2 for pitch invasions by fans.

Jan 1997: Middlesbrough 3 for refusing to play Premier League match at Blackburn because of injuries and illness.

Jun 1994: Tottenham 12 (reduced to 6) and banned from following season's FA Cup for making illegal payments to players. On appeal, points deduction annulled and club re-instated in Cup.

NIGHTMARE STARTS

Most goals conceded by a goalkeeper on League debut: 13 by **Steve Milton** when Halifax lost 13-0 at Stockport (Div 3 North) on Jan 6, 1934.

Post-war: 11 by Crewe's new goalkeeper **Dennis Murray** (Div 3 North) on Sep 29, 1951, when Lincoln won 11-1.

RELEGATION ODD SPOTS

None of the Barclays Premier League relegation places in season 2004–05 were decided until the last day (Sunday, May 15). **WBA** (bottom at kick-off) survived with a 2-0 home win against Portsmouth, and the three relegated clubs were **Southampton** (1-2 v Manchester Utd), **Norwich** (0-6 at Fulham) and **Crystal Palace** (2-2 at Charlton).

In season 1937–38, **Manchester City** were the highest-scoring team in the First Division with 80 goals (3 more than Champions Arsenal), but they finished in 21st place and were relegated – a year after winning the title. They scored more goals than they conceded (77).

That season produced the **closest relegation battle** in top-division history, with only 4 points spanning the bottom 11 clubs in Div 1. **WBA** went down with **Manchester City**.

Twelve years earlier, in 1925-26, City went down to Division 2 despite totalling 89 goals – still the most scored in any division by a relegated team. Manchester City also scored 31 FA Cup goals that season, but lost the Final 1-0 to Bolton Wanderers.

Cardiff were relegated from Div 1 in season 1928-29, despite conceding fewest goals in the division (59). They also scored fewest (43).

On their way to relegation from the First Division in season 1984–85, **Stoke** twice lost ten matches in a row.

RELEGATION TREBLES

Two Football League clubs have been relegated three seasons in succession. **Bristol City** fell from First Division to Fourth in 1980–81–82 and **Wolves** did the same in 1984-85-86.

OLDEST CLUBS

Oldest Association Football Club is **Sheffield FC** (formed in 1857). The oldest Football League clubs are **Nottm Forest**, 1865; and **Sheffield Wed**, 1866.

NOTTS COUNTY RELEGATED

Notts County, formed in 1862 and the world's oldest professional club, were relegated from the Football League for the first time in season 2018–19.

FOUR DIVISIONS

In **May, 1957**, the Football League decided to re-group the two sections of the Third Division into Third and Fourth Divisions in **season 1958–59**.

The Football League was reduced to three divisions on the formation of the Premier League in **1992**. In season 2004–05, under new sponsors Coca-Cola, the titles of First, Second and Third Divisions were changed to League Championship, League One and League Two.

THREE UP – THREE DOWN

The Football League annual general meeting of Jun 1973 agreed to adopt the promotion and relegation system of three up and three down.

The **new system** came into effect in **season 1973–74** and applied only to the first three divisions; four clubs were still relegated from the Third and four promoted from the Fourth,

It was the first change in the promotion and relegation system for the top two divisions in 81 years.

MOST LEAGUE APPEARANCES

Players with more than 700 English League apps (as at end of season 2017–18)

1005 Peter Shilton 1966–97 (286 Leicester, 110 Stoke, 202 Nottm Forest, 188 Southampton, 175 Derby, 34 Plymouth Argyle, 1 Bolton, 9 Leyton Orient).

931 Tony Ford 1975–2002 (423 Grimsby, 9 Sunderland, 112 Stoke, 114 WBA, 5 Bradford City, 76 Scunthorpe, 103 Mansfield, 89 Rochdale).

840 Graham Alexander 1991–2012 (159 Scunthorpe, 152 Luton, 372 Preston, 157 Burnley)

824 Terry Paine 1956–77 (713 Southampton, 111 Hereford).

795 Tommy Hutchison 1968–91 (165 Blackpool, 314 Coventry City, 46 Manchester City, 92 Burnley, 178 Swansea). In addition, 68 Scottish League apps for Alloa 1965–68, giving career League app total of 863.

790 Neil Redfearn 1982–2004 (35 Bolton, 100 Lincoln, 46 Doncaster, 57 Crystal Palace, 24 Watford, 62 Oldham, 292 Barnsley, 30 Charlton, 17 Bradford City, 22 Wigan, 42 Halifax, 54 Boston, 9 Rochdale).

782 Robbie James 1973–94 (484 Swansea, 48 Stoke, 87 QPR, 23 Leicester, 89 Bradford City, 51 Cardiff).

777 Alan Oakes 1959–84 (565 Manchester City, 211 Chester, 1 Port Vale).

773 Dave Beasant 1980–2003 (340 Wimbledon, 20 Newcastle, 6 Grimsby, 4 Wolves, 133 Chelsea, 88 Southampton, 139 Nottm F, 27 Portsmouth, 16 Brighton).

770 John Trollope 1960–80 (all for Swindon, record total for one club).

769 David James 1990–2012 (89 Watford, 214 Liverpool, 67 Aston Villa, 91 West Ham, 93 Manchester City, 134 Portsmouth, 81 Bristol City).

764 Jimmy Dickinson 1946–65 (all for Portsmouth).

761 Roy Sproson 1950–72 (all for Port Vale).

760 Mick Tait 1974–97 (64 Oxford Utd, 106 Carlisle, 33 Hull, 240 Portsmouth, 99 Reading, 79 Darlington, 139 Hartlepool Utd).

758 Billy Bonds 1964–88 (95 Charlton, 663 West Ham).

758 Ray Clemence 1966–88 (48 Scunthorpe, 470 Liverpool, 240 Tottenham).

757 Pat Jennings 1963–86 (48 Watford, 472 Tottenham, 237 Arsenal).

757 Frank Worthington 1966–88 (171 Huddersfield Town, 210 Leicester, 84 Bolton, 75 Birmingham, 32 Leeds, 19 Sunderland, 34 Southampton, 31 Brighton, 59 Tranmere, 23 Preston, 19 Stockport).

755 Wayne Allison 1986–2008 (84 Halifax, 7 Watford, 195 Bristol City, 103 Swindon, 76 Huddersfield, 102 Tranmere, 73 Sheffield Utd, 115 Chesterfield).

749 Ernie Moss 1968–88 (469 Chesterfield, 35 Peterborough, 57 Mansfield, 74 Port Vale, 11 Lincoln, 44 Doncaster, 26 Stockport, 23 Scarborough, 10 Rochdale).

746 Les Chapman 1966–88 (263 Oldham, 133 Huddersfield Town, 70 Stockport, 139 Bradford City, 88 Rochdale, 53 Preston).

744 Asa Hartford 1967–90 (214 WBA, 260 Manchester City, 3 Nottm Forest, 81 Everton, 28 Norwich, 81 Bolton, 45 Stockport, 7 Oldham, 25 Shrewsbury).

743 Alan Ball 1963–84 (146 Blackpool, 208 Everton, 177 Arsenal, 195 Southampton, 17 Bristol Rov).

743	John Hollins 1963–84 (465 Chelsea, 151 QPR, 127 Arsenal).
743	Phil Parkes 1968–91 (52 Walsall, 344 QPR, 344 West Ham, 3 Ipswich).
737	Steve Bruce 1979–99 (205 Gillingham, 141 Norwich, 309 Manchester Utd 72 Birmingham, 10 Sheffield Utd).
734	Teddy Sheringham 1983–2007 (220 Millwall, 5 Aldershot, 42 Nottm Forest, 104 Manchester Utd, 236 Tottenham, 32 Portsmouth, 76 West Ham, 19 Colchester)
732	Mick Mills 1966–88 (591 Ipswich, 103 Southampton, 38 Stoke).
731	Ian Callaghan 1959–81 (640 Liverpool, 76 Swansea, 15 Crewe).
731	David Seaman 1982–2003 (91 Peterborough, 75 Birmingham, 141 QPR, 405 Arsenal, 19 Manchester City).
725	Steve Perryman 1969–90 (655 Tottenham, 17 Oxford Utd, 53 Brentford).
722	Martin Peters 1961–81 (302 West Ham, 189 Tottenham, 207 Norwich, 24 Sheffield Utd).
718	Mike Channon 1966–86 (511 Southampton, 72 Manchester City, 4 Newcastle, 9 Bristol Rov, 88 Norwich, 34 Portsmouth).
716	Ron Harris 1961–83 (655 Chelsea, 61 Brentford).
716	Mike Summerbee 1959–79 (218 Swindon, 357 Manchester City, 51 Burnley, 3 Blackpool, 87 Stockport).
714	Glenn Cockerill 1976–98 (186 Lincoln, 26 Swindon, 62 Sheffield Utd, 387 Southampton, 90 Leyton Orient, 40 Fulham, 23 Brentford).
705	Keith Curle 1981–2003 (32 Bristol Rov, 16 Torquay, 121 Bristol City, 40 Reading, 93 Wimbledon, 171 Manchester City, 150 Wolves, 57 Sheffield Utd, 11 Barnsley, 14 Mansfield.
705	Phil Neal 1968–89 (186 Northampton, 455 Liverpool, 64 Bolton).
705	John Wile 1968–86 (205 Peterborough, 500 WBA).
701	Neville Southall 1980–2000 (39 Bury, 578 Everton, 9 Port Vale, 9 Southend, 12 Stoke, 53 Torquay, 1 Bradford City).

● **Stanley Matthews** made 701 League apps 1932–65 (322 Stoke, 379 Blackpool), incl. 3 for Stoke at start of 1939–40 before season abandoned (war).

● Goalkeeper **John Burridge** made a total of 771 League appearances in a 28-season career in English and Scottish football (1968–96). He played 691 games for 15 English clubs (Workington, Blackpool, Aston Villa, Southend, Crystal Palace, QPR, Wolves, Derby, Sheffield Utd, Southampton, Newcastle, Scarborough, Lincoln, Manchester City and Darlington) and 80 for 5 Scottish clubs (Hibernian, Aberdeen, Dumbarton, Falkirk and Queen of the South).

LONGEST LEAGUE APPEARANCE SEQUENCE

Harold Bell, centre-half of Tranmere, was ever-present for the first nine post-war seasons (1946–55), achieving a League record of 401 consecutive matches. Counting FA Cup and other games, his run of successive appearances totalled 459.

The longest League sequence since Bell's was 394 appearances by goalkeeper **Dave Beasant** for Wimbledon, Newcastle and Chelsea. His nine-year run began on Aug 29, 1981 and was ended by a broken finger sustained in Chelsea's League Cup-tie against Portsmouth on Oct 31, 1990. Beasant's 394 consecutive League games comprised 304 for Wimbledon (1981–88), 20 for Newcastle (1988–89) and 70 for Chelsea (1989–90).

Phil Neal made 366 consecutive First Division appearances for Liverpool between December 1974 and Sep 1983, a remarkable sequence for an outfield player in top-division football.

MOST CONSECUTIVE PREMIER LEAGUE APPEARANCES

310 by goalkeeper **Brad Friedel** (152 Blackburn, 114 Aston Villa, 44 Tottenham, May 2004–Oct 2012). He played in 8 **ever-present seasons** (2004–12, Blackburn 4, Villa 3, Tottenham 1).

EVER-PRESENT DEFENCE

The **entire defence** of **Huddersfield** played in all 42 Second Division matches in season 1952–

53, namely, Bill Wheeler (goal), Ron Staniforth and Laurie Kelly (full-backs), Bill McGarry, Don McEvoy and Len Quested (half-backs). In addition, Vic Metcalfe played in all 42 League matches at outside-left.

FIRST SUBSTITUTE USED IN LEAGUE

Keith Peacock (Charlton), away to Bolton (Div 2) on Aug 21, 1965.

FROM PROMOTION TO CHAMPIONS

Clubs who have become Champions of England a year after winning promotion: **Liverpool** 1905, 1906; **Everton** 1931, 1932; **Tottenham** 1950, 1951; **Ipswich** 1961, 1962; **Nottm Forest** 1977, 1978. The first four were placed top in both seasons: Forest finished third and first.

PREMIER LEAGUE'S FIRST MULTI-NATIONAL LINE-UP

Chelsea made history on December 26, 1999 when starting their Premier League match at Southampton without a single British player in the side.

Fulham's Unique XI: In the Worthington Cup 3rd round at home to Bury on Nov 6, 2002, Fulham fielded 11 players of 11 different nationalities. Ten were full Internationals, with Lee Clark an England U–21 cap.

On Feb 14, 2005 **Arsenal** became the first English club to select an all-foreign match squad when Arsene Wenger named 16 non-British players at home to Crystal Palace (Premier League).

Fifteen nations were represented at Fratton Park on Dec 30, 2009 (Portsmouth 1 Arsenal 4) when, for the first time in Premier League history, not one Englishman started the match. The line-up comprised seven Frenchmen, two Algerians and one from each of 13 other countries.

Players from 22 nationalities (subs included) were involved in the Blackburn–WBA match at Ewood Park on Jan 23, 2011.

PREMIER LEAGUE'S FIRST ALL-ENGLAND LINE-UP

On Feb 27, 1999 **Aston Villa** (at home to Coventry) fielded the first all-English line up seen in the Premier League (starting 11 plus 3 subs).

ENTIRE HOME-GROWN TEAM

Crewe Alexandra's starting 11 in the 2-0 home win against Walsall (Lge 1) on Apr 27, 2013 all graduated from the club's academy.

THREE-NATION CHAMPIONS

David Beckham won a title in four countries: with Manchester Utd six times (1996–97–99–2000–01–03), Real Madrid (2007), LA Galaxy (2011 and Paris St Germain (2013).

Trevor Steven earned eight Championship medals in three countries: two with Everton (1985, 1987); five with Rangers (1990, 1991, 1993, 1994, 1995) and one with Marseille in 1992.

LEEDS NO WIN AWAY

Leeds, in 1992–93, provided the first instance of a club failing to win an away League match as reigning Champions.

PIONEERS IN 1888 AND 1992

Three clubs among the twelve who formed the Football League in 1888 were also founder members of the Premier League: **Aston Villa, Blackburn** and **Everton.**

CHAMPIONS (MODERN) WITH TWO CLUBS – PLAYERS

Francis Lee (Manchester City 1968, Derby 1975); **Ray Kennedy** (Arsenal 1971, Liverpool 1979, 1980, 1982); **Archie Gemmill** (Derby 1972, 1975, Nottm Forest 1978); **John McGovern** (Derby 1972, Nottm Forest 1978) **Larry Lloyd** (Liverpool 1973, Nottm Forest 1978); **Peter Withe** (Nottm

Forest 1978, Aston Villa 1981); **John Lukic** (Arsenal 1989, Leeds 1992); **Kevin Richardson** (Everton 1985, Arsenal 1989); **Eric Cantona** (Leeds 1992, Manchester Utd 1993, 1994, 1996, 1997); **David Batty** (Leeds 1992, Blackburn 1995), **Bobby Mimms** (Everton 1987, Blackburn 1995), **Henning Berg** (Blackburn 1995, Manchester Utd 1999, 2000); **Nicolas Anelka** (Arsenal 1998, Chelsea 2010); **Ashley Cole** (Arsenal 2002, 2004, Chelsea 2010); **Gael Clichy** (Arsenal 2004, Manchester City 2012); **Kolo Toure** (Arsenal 2004, Manchester City 2012); **Carlos Tevez** (Manchester Utd 2008, 2009, Manchester City 2012).

TITLE TURNABOUTS

In Jan 1996, **Newcastle** led the Premier League by 13 points. They finished runners-up to Manchester Utd.

At Christmas 1997, **Arsenal** were 13 points behind leaders Manchester Utd and still 11 points behind at the beginning of Mar 1998. But a run of 10 wins took the title to Highbury.

On Mar 2, 2003, **Arsenal**, with 9 games left, went 8 points clear of Manchester Utd, who had a match in hand. United won the Championship by 5 points.

In Mar 2002, **Wolves** were in second (automatic promotion) place in Nationwide Div 1, 11 points ahead of WBA, who had 2 games in hand. They were overtaken by Albion on the run-in, finished third, then failed in the play-offs. A year later they won promotion to the Premier League via the play-offs.

CLUB CLOSURES

Four clubs have left the Football League in mid-season: **Leeds City** (expelled Oct 1919); **Wigan Borough** (Oct 1931, debts of £20,000); **Accrington Stanley** (Mar 1962, debts £62,000); **Aldershot** (Mar 1992, debts £1.2m). **Maidstone**, with debts of £650,000, closed Aug 1992, on the eve of the season.

FOUR-DIVISION MEN

In season 1986-87, goalkeeper **Eric Nixon**, became the first player to appear in all four divisions of the Football League in one season. He served two clubs in Div 1: Manchester City (5 League games) and Southampton (4); in Div 2 Bradford City (3); in Div 3 Carlisle (16); and in Div 4 Wolves (16). Total appearances: 44.

Harvey McCreadle, a teenage forward, played in four divisions over two seasons inside a calendar year – from Accrington (Div 3) to Luton (Div 1) in Jan 1960, to Div 2 with Luton later that season and to Wrexham (Div 4) in Nov.

Tony Cottee played in all four divisions in season 2000–01, for Leicester (Premier League), Norwich (Div 1), Barnet (Div 3, player-manager) and Millwall (Div 2).

FATHERS AND SONS

When player-manager **Ian** (39) and **Gary** (18) **Bowyer** appeared together in the **Hereford** side at Scunthorpe (Div 4, Apr 21, 1990), they provided the first instance of father and son playing in the same team in a Football League match for 39 years. Ian played as substitute, and Gary scored Hereford's injury-time equaliser in a 3-3 draw.

Alec (39) and **David** (17) **Herd** were among previous father-and-son duos in league football – for Stockport, 2-0 winners at Hartlepool (Div 3 North) on May 5, 1951.

When Preston won 2-1 at Bury in Div 3 on Jan 13, 1990, the opposing goalkeepers were brothers: **Alan Kelly** (21) for Preston and **Gary** (23) for Bury. Their father, **Alan** (who kept goal for Preston in the 1964 FA Cup Final and won 47 Rep of Ireland caps) flew from America to watch the sons he taught to keep goal line up on opposite sides.

Other examples: **Bill Dodgin Snr** (manager, Bristol Rov) faced son **Bill Jnr** (manager of Fulham) four times between 1969 and 1971. On Apr 16, 2013 (Lge 1), Oldham, under **Lee Johnson**, won 1-0 at home to Yeovil, managed by his father **Gary.**

George Eastham Snr (manager) and son **George Eastham Jnr** were inside-forward partners for Ards in the Irish League in season 1954–55.

FATHER AND SON REFEREE PLAY-OFF FINALS

Father and son refereed two of the 2009 Play-off Finals. **Clive Oliver**, 46, took charge of Shrewsbury v Gillingham (Lge 2) and **Michael Oliver,** 26, refereed Millwall v Scunthorpe (Lge 1) the following day.

FATHER AND SON BOTH CHAMPIONS

John Aston snr won a Championship medal with Manchester Utd in 1952 and **John Aston jnr** did so with the club in 1967. **Ian Wright** won the Premier League title with Arsenal in 1998 and **Shaun Wright-Phillips** won with Chelsea in 2006.

FATHER AND SON RIVAL MANAGERS

When **Bill Dodgin snr** took Bristol Rov to Fulham for an FA Cup 1st Round tie in Nov 1971, the opposing manager was his son, **Bill jnr.** Rovers won 2-1. Oldham's new manager, **Lee Johnson**, faced his father **Gary's** Yeovil in a Lge 1 match in April, 2013. Oldham won 1-0.

FATHER AND SON ON OPPOSITE SIDES

It happened for the first time in FA Cup history (1st Qual Round on Sep 14, 1996) when 21-year-old **Nick Scaife** (Bishop Auckland) faced his father **Bobby** (41), who played for Pickering. Both were in midfield. Home side Bishops won 3-1.

THREE BROTHERS IN SAME SIDE

Southampton provided the first instance for 65 years of three brothers appearing together in a Div 1 side when **Danny Wallace** (24) and his 19-year-old twin brothers **Rodney** and **Ray** played against Sheffield Wed on Oct 22, 1988. In all, they made 25 appearances together for Southampton until Sep 1989.

A previous instance in Div 1 was provided by the Middlesbrough trio, **William, John** and **George Carr** with 24 League appearances together from Jan 1920 to Oct 1923.

The **Tonner** brothers, **Sam, James** and **Jack,** played together in 13 Second Division matches for Clapton Orient in season 1919–20.

Brothers **David, Donald** and **Robert Jack** played together in Plymouth's League side in 1920.

TWIN TEAM-MATES (see also Wallace twins above)

Twin brothers **David** and **Peter Jackson** played together for three League clubs (Wrexham, Bradford City and Tranmere) from 1954–62. The **Morgan** twins, **Ian** and **Roger**, played regularly in the QPR forward line from 1964–68. WBA's **Adam** and **James Chambers,** 18, were the first twins to represent England (v Cameroon in World Youth Championship, Apr 1999). They first played together in Albion's senior team, aged 19, in the League Cup 2nd. Round against Derby in Sep 2000. Brazilian identical twins **Rafael** and **Fabio Da Silva** (18) made first team debuts at full-back for Manchester Utd in season 2008– 09. Swedish twins **Martin** and **Marcus Olsson** played together for Blackburn in season 2011–12. **Josh** and **Jacob Murphy**, 19, played for Norwich in season 2013–2014.

SIR TOM DOES THE HONOURS

Sir Tom Finney, England and Preston legend, opened the Football League's new headquarters on their return to Preston on Feb 23, 1999. Preston had been the League's original base for 70 years before the move to Lytham St Annes in 1959.

SHORTENED MATCHES

The 0-0 score in the **Bradford City v Lincoln** Third Division fixture on May 11, 1985, abandoned through fire after 40 minutes, was subsequently confirmed as a result. It is the shortest officially- completed League match on record, and was the fourth of only five instances in Football League history of the score of an unfinished match being allowed to stand.

The other occasions: **Middlesbrough 4, Oldham 1** (Div 1, Apr 3, 1915), abandoned after 55 minutes when Oldham defender Billy Cook refused to leave the field after being sent off; **Barrow 7, Gillingham 0** (Div 4, Oct 9, 1961), abandoned after 75 minutes because of bad light, the match having started late because of Gillingham's delayed arrival.

A crucial **Manchester** derby (Div 1) was abandoned after 85 minutes, and the result stood, on Apr 27, 1974, when a pitch invasion at Old Trafford followed the only goal, scored for City by Denis Law, which relegated United, Law's former club.

The only instance of a first-class match in England being abandoned **'through shortage of players'** occurred in the First Division at Bramall Lane on Mar 16, 2002. Referee Eddie Wolstenholme halted play after 82 minutes because Sheffield Utd were reduced to 6 players against WBA. They had had 3 men sent off (goalkeeper and 2 substitutes), and with all 3 substitutes used and 2 players injured, were left with fewer than the required minimum of 7 on the field. Promotion contenders WBA were leading 3-0, and the League ordered the result to stand.

The last 60 seconds of **Birmingham v Stoke** (Div 3, 1-1, on Feb 29, 1992) were played behind locked doors. The ground had been cleared after a pitch invasion.

A First Division fixture, **Sheffield Wed v Aston Villa** (Nov 26, 1898), was abandoned through bad light after 79 mins with Wednesday leading 3-1. The Football League ruled that the match should be completed, and the remaining 10.5 minutes were played four months later (Mar 13, 1899), when Wednesday added another goal to make the result 4-1.

FA CUP RECORDS
(See also Goalscoring section)

CHIEF WINNERS

13 Arsenal; **12** Manchester Utd; **8** Tottenham, Chelsea; **7** Aston Villa, Liverpool; **6** Blackburn, Manchester City, Newcastle

Three times in succession: The Wanderers (1876–77–78) and Blackburn (1884–85–86).

Trophy handed back: The FA Cup became the Wanderers' absolute property in 1878, but they handed it back to the Association on condition that it was not to be won outright by any club.

In successive years by professional clubs: Blackburn (1890 and 1891); Newcastle (1951 and 1952); Tottenham (1961 and 1962); Tottenham (1981 and 1982); Arsenal (2002 and 2003); Chelsea (2009–10).

Record Final tie score: Bury 6, Derby 0 (1903); Manchester City 6 Watford 0 (2019).

Most FA Cup Final wins at Wembley: Arsenal 10, Manchester Utd 10, Chelsea 7, Tottenham 6, Liverpool 5, Manchester City 5, Newcastle 5.

SECOND DIVISION WINNERS

Notts Co (1894), Wolves (1908), Barnsley (1912), WBA (1931), Sunderland (1973), **Southampton** (1976), **West Ham** (1980). When Tottenham won the Cup in 1901 they were a Southern League club.

'OUTSIDE' SEMI-FINALISTS

Sheffield Utd. in 2014, became the ninth team from outside the top two divisions to reach the semi-finals, following **Millwall** (1937), **Port Vale** (1954), **York** (1955), **Norwich** (1959), **Crystal Palace** (1976), **Plymouth** (1984), **Chesterfield** (1997) and **Wycombe** (2001). None reached the Final.

FOURTH DIVISION QUARTER-FINALISTS

Oxford Utd (1964), Colchester (1971), Bradford City (1976), Cambridge Utd (1990).

FOURTH ROUND – NO REPLAYS

No replays were necessary in the 16 fourth round ties in January 2008 (7 home wins, 9 away). This had not happened for 51 years, since 8 home and 8 away wins in season 1956–57.

FIVE TROPHIES

The trophy which Arsenal won in 2014 was the fifth in FA Cup history. These were its predecessors:
1872–95: First Cup stolen from shop in Birmingham while held by Aston Villa. Never seen again.
1910: Second trophy presented to Lord Kinnaird on completing 21 years as FA president.
1911–91: Third trophy used until replaced ('battered and fragile') after 80 years' service.
1992–2013 Fourth FA Cup lasted 21 years – now retained at FA headquarters at Wembley Stadium.
Traditionally, the Cup stays with the holders until returned to the FA in March.

FINALISTS RELEGATED

Six clubs have reached the FA Cup Final and been relegated. The first five all lost at Wembley – **Manchester City** 1926, **Leicester** 1969, **Brighton** 1983, **Middlesbrough** 1997 and **Portsmouth** 2010. **Wigan,** Cup winners for the first time in 2013, were relegated from the Premier League three days later.

FA CUP – TOP SHOCKS

(2019 = season 2018–19; rounds shown in brackets; R = replay)

1922 (1)	Everton	0	Crystal Palace	6
1933 (3)	Walsall	2	Arsenal	0
1939 (3)	Portsmouth	4	Wolves	1
1948 (3)	Arsenal	0	Bradford PA	1
1948 (3)	Colchester	1	Huddersfield	0
1949 (4)	Yeovil	2	Sunderland	1
1954 (4)	Arsenal	1	Norwich	2
1955 (5)	York	2	Tottenham	1
1957 (4)	Wolves	0	Bournemouth	1
1957 (5)	Bournemouth	3	Tottenham	1
1958 (4)	Newcastle	1	Scunthorpe	3
1959 (3)	Norwich	3	Manchester Utd	0
1959 (3)	Worcester	2	Liverpool	1
1961 (3)	Chelsea	1	Crewe	2
1964 (3)	Newcastle	1	Bedford	2
1965 (4)	Peterborough	2	Arsenal	1
1971 (5)	Colchester	3	Leeds	2
1972 (3)	Hereford	2	Newcastle	1R
1973 (F)	Sunderland	1	Leeds	0
1975 (3)	Burnley	0	Wimbledon	1
1976 (F)	Southampton	1	Manchester Utd	0
1978 (F)	Ipswich	1	Arsenal	0
1980 (3)	Chelsea	0	Wigan	1
1980 (3)	Halifax	1	Manchester City	0
1980 (3)	West Ham	1	Arsenal	0
1981 (4)	Exeter	4	Newcastle	0R
1984 (3)	Bournemouth	2	Manchester Utd	0
1985 (4)	York	1	Arsenal	0
1986 (3)	Birmingham	1	Altrincham	2
1988 (F)	Wimbledon	1	Liverpool	0
1989 (3)	Sutton	2	Coventry	1
1991 (3)	WBA	2	Woking	4
1992 (3)	Wrexham	2	Arsenal	1
1994 (3)	Liverpool	0	Bristol City	1R
1994 (3)	Birmingham	1	Kidderminster	2
1997 (5)	Chesterfield	1	Nottm Forest	0
2001 (4)	Everton	0	Tranmere	3

2003 (3)	Shrewsbury	2	Everton	1
2005 (3)	Oldham	1	Manchester City	0
2008 (6)	Barnsley	1	Chelsea	0
2009 (2)	Histon	1	Leeds	0
2010 (4)	Liverpool	1	Reading	2R
2011 (3)	Stevenage	3	Newcastle	1
2012 (3)	Macclesfield	2	Cardiff	1
2013 (4)	Norwich	0	Luton	1
2013 (4)	Oldham	3	Liverpool	2
2013 (F)	Wigan	1	Manchester City	0
2014 (3)	Rochdale	2	Leeds	0
2015 (4)	Chelsea	2	Bradford City	4
2015 (5)	Bradford City	2	Sunderland	0
2016 (3)	Oxford	3	Swansea	2
2017 (5)	Burnley	0	Lincoln	1
2018 (5)	Wigan	1	Manchester City	0
2019 (3)	Fulham	1	Oldham	2
2019 (3)	Gillingham	1	Cardiff	0
2019 (3)	Newport	2	Leicester	1
2019 (3)	Sheffield Utd	0	Barnet	1
2019 (4)	AFC Wimbledon	4	West Ham	2

YEOVIL TOP GIANT-KILLERS

Yeovil's victories over Colchester and Blackpool in season 2000–01 gave them a total of 20 FA Cup wins against League opponents. They set another non-League record by reaching the third round 13 times.

This was Yeovil's triumphant (non-League) Cup record against League clubs: 1924–25 Bournemouth 3-2; 1934–35 Crystal Palace 3-0, Exeter 4-1; 1938–39 Brighton 2-1; 1948–49 Bury 3-1, Sunderland 2-1; 1958–59 Southend 1-0; 1960–61 Walsall 1-0; 1963–64 Southend 1-0, Crystal Palace 3-1; 1970–71 Bournemouth 1-0; 1972–73 Brentford 2-1; 1987–88 Cambridge Utd 1-0; 1991–92 Walsall 1-0; 1992–93 Torquay 5-2, Hereford 2-1; 1993–94 Fulham 1-0; 1998–99 Northampton 2-0; 2000–01 Colchester 5-1, Blackpool 1-0.

NON-LEAGUE BEST

Since League football began in 1888, three non-League clubs have reached the FA Cup Final. **Sheffield Wed** (Football Alliance) were runners-up in 1890, as were **Southampton** (Southern League) in 1900 and 1902. **Tottenham** won the Cup as a Southern League team in 1901.

Lincoln won 1-0 at Burnley on Feb 18, 2017, to become the first non-league club to reach the last eight in 103 years. Two non-league sides – **Lincoln** and **Sutton** – had reached the last 16 for the first time.

Otherwise, the furthest progress by non-League clubs has been to the 5th round on 7 occasions: **Colchester** 1948, **Yeovil** 1949, **Blyth** 1978, **Telford** 1985, **Kidderminster** 1994, **Crawley** 2011, **Luton** 2013.

Greatest number of non-League sides to reach the **3rd round** is **8** in 2009: **Barrow, Blyth, Eastwood, Forest Green, Histon, Kettering, Kidderminster** and **Torquay.**

Most to reach **Round 4: 3** in 1957 (**Rhyl, New Brighton, Peterborough**) and 1975 (**Leatherhead, Stafford** and **Wimbledon**).

Five non-League clubs reaching **round 3** in 2001 was a Conference record. They were **Chester, Yeovil, Dagenham, Morecambe** and **Kingstonian.**

In season 2002–03, **Team Bath** became the first University-based side to reach the FA Cup 1st Round since **Oxford University** (Finalists in 1880).

NON-LEAGUE 'LAST TIMES'

Last time no non-League club reached round 3: 1951. Last time only one did so: 1969 (**Kettering**).

TOP-DIVISION SCALPS

Victories in FA Cup by non-League clubs over top-division teams since 1900 include: 1900–01 (Final, replay): **Tottenham** 3 Sheffield Utd 1 (Tottenham then in Southern League); 1919–20 **Cardiff** 2, Oldham 0; Sheffield Wed 0, **Darlington** 2; 1923–24 **Corinthians** 1, Blackburn 0; 1947–48 **Colchester** 1, Huddersfield 0; 1948–9 **Yeovil** 2, Sunderland 1; 1971–72 **Hereford** 2, Newcastle 1; 1974–75 Burnley 0, **Wimbledon** 1; 1985–86 Birmingham 1, **Altrincham** 2; 1988–89 **Sutton** 2, Coventry 1; 2012–13 Norwich 0, **Luton** 1, 2016–17 Burnley 0 **Lincoln** 1.

MOST WINNING MEDALS

Ashley Cole has won the trophy seven times, with (Arsenal 2002–03–05) and Chelsea (2007–09–10–12). **The Hon Arthur Kinnaird** (The Wanderers and Old Etonians), **Charles Wollaston** (The Wanderers) and **Jimmy Forrest** (Blackburn) each earned five winners' medals. Kinnaird, later president of the FA, played in nine of the first 12 FA Cup Finals, and was on the winning side three times for The Wanderers, in 1873 (captain), 1877, 1878 (captain), and twice as captain of Old Etonians (1879, 1882).

MANAGERS' MEDALS BACKDATED

In 2010, the FA agreed to award Cup Final medals to all living managers who took their teams to the Final before 1996 (when medals were first given to Wembley team bosses). Lawrie McMenemy had campaigned for the award since Southampton's victory in 1976.

MOST WINNERS' MEDALS AT WEMBLEY

4 – **Mark Hughes** (3 for Manchester Utd, 1 for Chelsea), **Petr Cech, Frank Lampard, John Terry, Didier Drogba, Ashley Cole** (all Chelsea), **Olivier Giroud** (3 for Arsenal, 1 for Chelsea).

3 – **Dick Pym** (3 clean sheets in Finals), **Bob Haworth, Jimmy Seddon, Harry Nuttall, Billy Butler** (all Bolton); **David Jack** (2 Bolton, 1 Arsenal); **Bob Cowell, Jack Milburn, Bobby Mitchell** (all Newcastle); **Dave Mackay** (Tottenham); **Frank Stapleton** (1 Arsenal, 2 Manchester Utd); **Bryan Robson** (3 times winning captain), **Arthur Albiston, Gary Pallister** (all Manchester Utd); **Bruce Grobbelaar, Steve Nicol, Ian Rush** (all Liverpool); **Roy Keane, Peter Schmeichel, Ryan Giggs** (all Manchester Utd); **Dennis Wise** (1 Wimbledon, 2 Chelsea).

Arsenal's **David Seaman** and **Ray Parlour** have each earned 4 winners' medals (2 at Wembley, 2 at Cardiff) as have Manchester Utd's **Roy Keane** and **Ryan Giggs** (3 at Wembley, 1 at Cardiff).

MOST WEMBLEY FINALS

Nine players appeared in five FA Cup Finals at Wembley, replays excluded:

- **Joe Hulme** (Arsenal: 1927 won, 1930 won, 1932 lost, 1936 won; Huddersfield: 1938 lost).
- **Johnny Giles** (Manchester Utd: 1963 won; Leeds: 1965 lost, 1970 drew at Wembley, lost replay at Old Trafford, 1972 won, 1973 lost).
- **Pat Rice** (all for Arsenal: 1971 won, 1972 lost, 1978 lost, 1979 won, 1980 lost).
- **Frank Stapleton** (Arsenal: 1978 lost, 1979 won, 1980 lost; Manchester Utd: 1983 won, 1985 won).
- **Ray Clemence** (Liverpool: 1971 lost, 1974 won, 1977 lost; Tottenham: 1982 won, 1987 lost).
- **Mark Hughes** (Manchester Utd: 1985 won, 1990 won, 1994 won, 1995 lost; Chelsea: 1997 won).
- **John Barnes** (Watford: 1984 lost; Liverpool: 1988 lost, 1989 won, 1996 lost; Newcastle: 1998 sub, lost): – first player to lose Wembley FA Cup Finals with three different clubs.
- **Roy Keane** (Nottm Forest: 1991 lost; Manchester Utd: 1994 won, 1995 lost, 1996 won, 1999 won).
- **Ryan Giggs** (Manchester Utd: 1994 won, 1995 lost, 1996 won, 1999 won, 2007 lost).
- Clemence, Hughes and Stapleton also played in a replay, making six actual FA Cup Final appearances for each of them.
- **Glenn Hoddle** also made six appearances at Wembley: 5 for Tottenham (incl. 2 replays), in 1981 won, 1982 won and 1987 lost, and 1 for Chelsea as sub in 1994 lost.

- **Paul Bracewell** played in four FA Cup Finals without being on the winning side – for Everton 1985, 1986, 1989, Sunderland 1992

MOST WEMBLEY/CARDIFF FINAL APPEARANCES

8 by **Ashley Cole** (Arsenal: 2001 lost; 2002 won; 2003 won; 2005 won; Chelsea: 2007 won; 2009 won; 2010 won, 2012 won).

7 by **Roy Keane** (Nottm Forest: 1991 lost; Manchester Utd: 1994 won; 1995 lost; 1996 won; 1999 won; 2004 won; 2005 lost).

7 by **Ryan Giggs** (Manchester Utd): 1994 won; 1995 lost; 1996 won; 1999 won; 2004 won; 2005 lost, 2007 lost.

6 by **Paul Scholes** (Manchester Utd): 1995 lost; 1996 won; 1999 won; 2004 won; 2005 lost; 2007 lost.

5 by **David Seaman** and **Ray Parlour** (Arsenal): 1993 won; 1998 won; 2001 lost; 2002 won; 2003 won; **Dennis Wise** (Wimbledon 1988 won; Chelsea 1994 lost; 1997 won; 2000 won; Millwall 2004 lost); **Patrick Vieira** (Arsenal): 1998 won; 2001 won; 2002 won; 2005 won; (Manchester City) 2011 won.

BIGGEST FA CUP SCORE AT WEMBLEY

6-0 by Manchester City v Watford (final, May 18, 2019).

WINNING GOALKEEPER-CAPTAINS

1988 **Dave Beasant** (Wimbledon); 2003 **David Seaman** (Arsenal).

MOST WINNING MANAGERS

7 **Arsene Wenger** (Arsenal) 1998, 2002, 2003, 2005, 2014, 2015, 2017; 6 **George Ramsay** (Aston Villa) 1887, 1895, 1897, 1905, 1913, 1920; 5 **Sir Alex Ferguson** (Manchester Utd) 1990, 1994, 1996, 1999, 2004.

PLAYER-MANAGERS IN FINAL

Kenny Dalglish (Liverpool, 1986); **Glenn Hoddle** (Chelsea, 1994); **Dennis Wise** (Millwall, 2004)

DEBUTS IN FINAL

Alan Davies (Manchester Utd v Brighton, 1983); **Chris Baird** (Southampton v Arsenal, 2003); **Curtis Weston** (Millwall sub v Manchester Utd, 2004).

SEMI-FINALS AT WEMBLEY

1991 Tottenham 3 Arsenal 1, **1993** Sheffield Wed 2 Sheffield Utd 1, Arsenal 1 Tottenham 0; **1994** Chelsea 2 Luton 0, Manchester Utd 1 Oldham 1; **2000** Aston Villa beat Bolton 4 1 on pens (after 0-0), Chelsea 2 Newcastle 1; **2008** Portsmouth 1 WBA 0, Cardiff 1 Barnsley 0; **2009** Chelsea 2 Arsenal 1, Everton beat Manchester Utd 4-2 on pens (after 0-0); **2010** Chelsea 3 Aston Villa 0, Portsmouth 2 Tottenham 0; **2011** Manchester City 1 Manchester Utd 0, Stoke 5 Bolton 0; **2012** Liverpool 2 Everton 1, Chelsea 5 Tottenham 1; **2013** Wigan 2 Millwall 0, Manchester City 2 Chelsea 1; **2014** Arsenal beat Wigan 4-2 on pens (after 1-1), Hull 5 Sheffield Utd 3; **2015** Arsenal 2 Reading 1, Aston Villa 2 Liverpool 1; **2016** Manchester Utd 2 Everton 1, Crystal Palace 2 Watford 1; **2017** Arsenal 2 Manchester City 1, Chelsea 4 Tottenham 2; **2018** Chelsea 2 Southampton 0, Manchester Utd 2 Tottenham 1; **2019** Manchester City 1 Brighton 0, Watford 3 Wolves 2.

CHELSEA'S FA CUP MILESTONES

Their victory over Liverpool in the 2012 Final set the following records:
Captain **John Terry** first player to lift the trophy tour times for one club; **Didier Drogba** first to score in four Finals; **Ashley Cole** first to earn seven winner's medals (Arsenal 3, Chelsea 4); **Roberto Di Matteo** first to score for and manage the same winning club (player for Chelsea 1997, 2000, interim manager 2012).

Chelsea's four triumphs in six seasons (2007–12) the best winning sequence since Wanderers won five of the first seven competitions (1872–78) and Blackburn won five out of eight (1884–91).

FIRST ENTRANTS (1871–72)

Barnes, Civil Service, Crystal Palace, Clapham Rov, Donnington School (Spalding), Hampstead Heathens, Harrow Chequers, Hitchin, Maidenhead, Marlow, Queen's Park (Glasgow), Reigate Priory, Royal Engineers, Upton Park and Wanderers. Total 15.

LAST ALL-ENGLISH WINNERS

Manchester City, in 1969, were the last club to win the final with a team of all English players.

FA CUP FIRSTS

Out of country: Cardiff, by defeating Arsenal 1-0 in the 1927 Final at Wembley, became the first and only club to take the FA Cup out of England.

All-English Winning XI: First club to win the FA Cup with all-English XI: Blackburn Olympic in 1883. Others since: WBA in 1888 and 1931, Bolton (1958), Manchester City (1969), West Ham (1964 and 1975).

Non-English Winning XI: Liverpool in 1986 (Mark Lawrenson, born Preston, was a Rep of Ireland player).

Won both Cups: Old Carthusians won the FA Cup in 1881 and the FA Amateur Cup in 1894 and 1897. **Wimbledon** won Amateur Cup in 1963, FA Cup in 1988.

MOST GAMES NEEDED TO WIN

Barnsley played a record 12 matches (20 hours' football) to win the FA Cup in season 1911–12. All six replays (one in round 1, three in round 4 and one in each of semi-final and Final) were brought about by goalless draws.

Arsenal played 11 FA Cup games when winning the trophy in 1979. Five of them were in the 3rd round against Sheffield Wed.

LONGEST TIES

6 matches: (11 hours): Alvechurch v Oxford City (4th qual round, 1971–72). Alvechurch won 1-0.

5 matches: (9 hours, 22 mins – record for competition proper): Stoke v Bury (3rd round, 1954–55). Stoke won 3-2.

5 matches: Chelsea v Burnley (4th round, 1955–56). Chelsea won 2-0.

5 matches: Hull v Darlington (2nd round, 1960–61). Hull won 3-0.

5 matches: Arsenal v Sheffield Wed (3rd round, 1978–79). Arsenal won 2-0.

Other marathons (qualifying comp, all 5 matches, 9 hours): Barrow v Gillingham (last qual round, 1924–25) – winners Barrow; Leyton v Ilford (3rd qual round, 1924–25) – winners Leyton; Falmouth v Bideford (3rd qual round, 1973–74) – winners Bideford.

End of Cup Final replays: The FA decided that, with effect from 1999, there would be no Cup Final replays. In the event of a draw after extra-time, the match would be decided on penalties. This happened for the first time in 2005, when Arsenal beat Manchester Utd 5-4 on penalties after a 0-0 draw. A year later, Liverpool beat West Ham 3-1 on penalties after a 3-3 draw.

FA Cup marathons ended in season 1991–92, when the penalty shoot-out was introduced to decide ties still level after one replay and extra-time.

In 1932–33 **Brighton** (Div 3 South) played 11 FA Cup games, including replays, and scored 43 goals, without getting past round 5. They forgot to claim exemption and had to play from 1st qual round.

LONGEST ROUND

The longest round in FA Cup history was the **3rd round** in **1962–63**. It took 66 days to complete, lasting from Jan 5 to Mar 11, and included 261 postponements because of bad weather.

LONGEST UNBEATEN RUN

23 matches by Blackburn In winning the Cup in three consecutive years (1884–05–06), they won 21 ties (one in a replay), and their first Cup defeat in four seasons was in a first round replay of the next competition.

RE STAGED TIES

Sixth round, Mar 9, 1974: Newcastle 4, Nottm Forest 3. Match declared void by FA and ordered to be replayed following a pitch invasion after Newcastle had a player sent off. Forest claimed the hold-up caused the game to change its pattern. The tie went to two further matches at Goodison Park (0-0, then 1-0 to Newcastle).

Third round, Jan 5, 1985: Burton 1, Leicester 6 (at Derby). Burton goalkeeper Paul Evans was hit on the head by a missile thrown from the crowd and continued in a daze. The FA ordered the tie to be played again, behind closed doors at Coventry (Leicester won 1-0).

First round replay, Nov 25, 1992: Peterborough 9 (Tony Philliskirk 5), Kingstonian 1. Match expunged from records because, at 3-0 after 57 mins, Kingstonian were reduced to ten men when goalkeeper Adrian Blake was concussed by a 50 pence coin thrown from the crowd. The tie was re-staged on the same ground behind closed doors (Peterborough won 1-0).

Fifth round: Within an hour of holders Arsenal beating Sheffield Utd 2-1 at Highbury on Feb 13, 1999, the FA took the unprecedented step of declaring the match void because an unwritten rule of sportsmanship had been broken. With United's Lee Morris lying injured, their goalkeeper Alan Kelly kicked the ball into touch. Play resumed with Arsenal's Ray Parlour throwing it in the direction of Kelly, but Nwankwo Kanu took possession and centred for Marc Overmars to score the 'winning' goal. After four minutes of protests by manager Steve Bruce and his players, referee Peter Jones confirmed the goal. Both managers absolved Kanu of cheating but Arsenal's Arsene Wenger offered to replay the match. With the FA immediately approving, it was re-staged at Highbury ten days later (ticket prices halved) and Arsenal again won 2-1.

PRIZE FUND

The makeover of the FA Cup competition took off in 2001-02 with the introduction of round-by-round prize-money.

FA CUP FOLLIES

1999–2000 The FA broke with tradition by deciding the 3rd round be moved from its regular Jan date and staged before Christmas. Criticism was strong, gates poor and the 3rd round in 2000-01 reverted to the New Year. By allowing the holders Manchester Utd to withdraw from the 1999–2000 competition in order to play in FIFA's inaugural World Club Championship in Brazil in Jan, the FA were left with an odd number of clubs in the 3rd round. Their solution was a 'lucky losers' draw among clubs knocked out in round 2. Darlington, beaten at Gillingham, won it to re-enter the competition, then lost 2-1 away to Aston Villa.

HAT-TRICKS IN FINAL

There have been three in the history of the competition: **Billy Townley** (Blackburn, 1890), **Jimmy Logan** (Notts Co, 1894) and **Stan Mortensen** (Blackpool, 1953).

MOST APPEARANCES

88 by **Ian Callaghan** (79 for Liverpool, 7 for Swansea City, 2 for Crewe); **87** by **John Barnes** (31 for Watford, **51** for Liverpool, 5 for Newcastle); **86** by **Stanley Matthews** (37 for Stoke, 49 for Blackpool); **84** by **Bobby Charlton** (80 for Manchester Utd, 4 for Preston); **84** by **Pat Jennings** (3 for Watford, 43 for Tottenham, 38 for Arsenal); **84** by **Peter Shilton** for seven clubs (30 for Leicester, 7 for Stoke, **18** for Nottm Forest, 17 for Southampton, 10 for Derby, 1 for Plymouth Argyle, 1 for Leyton Orient); **82** by **David Seaman** (5 for Peterborough, 5 for Birmingham, 17 for QPR, 54 for Arsenal, 1 for Manchester City).

THREE-CLUB FINALISTS

Five players have appeared in the FA Cup Final for three clubs: **Harold Halse** for Manchester Utd (1909), Aston Villa (1913) and Chelsea (1915); **Ernie Taylor** for Newcastle (1951), Blackpool (1953) and Manchester Utd (1958); **John Barnes** for Watford (1984), Liverpool (1988, 1989, 1996) and Newcastle (1998); **Dennis Wise** for Wimbledon (1988), Chelsea (1994, 1997, 2000), Millwall (2004); **David James** for Liverpool (1996), Aston Villa (2000) and Portsmouth (2008, 2010).

CUP MAN WITH TWO CLUBS IN SAME SEASON

Stan Crowther, who played for Aston Villa against Manchester Utd in the 1957 FA Cup Final, appeared for both Villa and United in the 1957–58 competition. United signed him directly after the Munich air crash and, in the circumstances, he was given dispensation to play for them in the Cup, including the Final.

CAPTAIN'S CUP DOUBLE

Martin Buchan is the only player to have captained Scottish and English FA Cup-winning teams – Aberdeen in 1970 and Manchester Utd in 1977.

MEDALS BEFORE AND AFTER

Two players appeared in FA Cup Final teams before and after the Second World War: **Raich Carter** was twice a winner (Sunderland 1937, Derby 1946) and **Willie Fagan** twice on the losing side (Preston 1937, Liverpool 1950).

DELANEY'S COLLECTION

Scotland winger **Jimmy Delaney** uniquely earned Scottish, English, Northern Ireland and Republic of Ireland Cup medals. He was a winner with Celtic (1937), Manchester Utd (1948) and Derry City (1954) and a runner-up with Cork City (1956).

STARS WHO MISSED OUT

Internationals who never won an FA Cup winner's medal include: Tommy Lawton, Tom Finney, Johnny Haynes, Gordon Banks, George Best, Terry Butcher, Peter Shilton, Martin Peters, Nobby Stiles, Alan Ball, Malcolm Macdonald, Alan Shearer, Matthew Le Tissier, Stuart Pearce, Des Walker, Phil Neal, Ledley King.

CUP WINNERS AT NO COST

Not one member of **Bolton**'s 1958 FA Cup-winning team cost the club a transfer fee. Each joined the club for a £10 signing-on fee.

11-NATIONS LINE-UP

Liverpool fielded a team of 11 different nationalities in the FA Cup 3rd round at Yeovil on Jan 4, 2004.

HIGH-SCORING SEMI-FINALS

The **record team score** in FA Cup semi-finals is **6**: 1891–92 WBA 6, Nottm Forest 2; 1907–08 Newcastle 6, Fulham 0; 1933–34 Manchester City 6, Aston Villa 1.

Most goals in semi-finals (aggregate): 17 in 1892 (4 matches) and 1899 (5 matches). In modern times: 15 in 1958 (3 matches, including Manchester Utd 5, Fulham 3 – highest-scoring semi-final since last war); 16 in 1989–90 (Crystal Palace 4, Liverpool 3; Manchester Utd v Oldham 3-3, 2-1. All **16 goals** in those three matches were scored by **different players**.

Stoke's win against Bolton at Wembley in 2011 was the first 5-0 semi-final result since Wolves beat Grimsby at Old Trafford in 1939. In 2014, Hull defeated Sheffield Utd 5-3.

Last hat-trick in an FA Cup semi-final was scored by **Alex Dawson** for Manchester Utd in 5-3 replay win against Fulham at Highbury in 1958.

SEMI-FINAL VENUES

Villa Park has staged more such matches (55 including replays) than any other ground. Next is Hillsborough (33).

ONE IN A HUNDRED
The 2008 semi-finals included only one top-division club, Portsmouth, for the first time in 100 years – since Newcastle in 1908.

FOUR SPECIAL AWAYS
For the only time in FA Cup history, **all four quarter-finals** in season 1986–87 were won by the away team.

DRAWS RECORD
In season 1985–86, **seven** of the eight 5th round ties went to replays – a record for that stage of the competition.

SHOCK FOR TOP CLUBS
The fourth round on Jan 24, 2015 produced an astonishing set of home defeats for leading clubs. The top three in the Premier League, Chelsea, Manchester City and Southampton were all knocked out and sixth-place Tottenham also lost at home. Odds against this happening were put at 3825-1.

LUCK OF THE DRAW
In the FA Cup on Jan 11, 1947, eight of **London**'s ten Football League clubs involved in the 3rd round were drawn at home (including Chelsea v Arsenal). Only Crystal Palace played outside the capital (at Newcastle).
 In the 3rd round in Jan 1992, Charlton were the only London club drawn at home (against Barnet), but the venue of the Farnborough v West Ham tie was reversed on police instruction. So Upton Park staged Cup ties on successive days, with West Ham at home on the Saturday and Charlton (who shared the ground) on Sunday.
Arsenal were drawn away in every round on the way to reaching the Finals of 1971 and 1972. **Manchester Utd** won the Cup in 1990 without playing once at home.
The 1999 finalists, **Manchester Utd** and **Newcastle**, were both drawn at home every time in Rounds 3–6.
On their way to the semi-finals of both domestic Cup competitions in season 2002–03, **Sheffield Utd** were drawn at home ten times out of ten and won all ten matches – six in the League's Worthington Cup and four in the FA Cup.
On their way to winning the Cup in 2014, **Arsenal** did not play once outside London. Home draws in rounds 3, 4, 5 and 6 were followed by the semi-final at Wembley.

ALL TOP-DIVISION VICTIMS
The only instance of an FA Cup-winning club meeting top-division opponents in every round was provided by Manchester Utd in 1947–48. They beat Aston Villa, Liverpool, Charlton, Preston, then Derby in the semi-final and Blackpool in the Final.
In contrast, these clubs have reached the Final without playing top-division opponents on the way: West Ham (1923), Bolton (1926), Blackpool (1948), Bolton (1953), Millwall (2004).

WON CUP WITHOUT CONCEDING GOAL
1873 **The Wanderers** (1 match; as holders, exempt until Final); 1889 **Preston** (5 matches); 1903 **Bury** (5 matches). In 1966 **Everton** reached Final without conceding a goal (7 matches), then beat Sheffield Wed 3-2 at Wembley.

HOME ADVANTAGE
For the first time in FA Cup history, all eight ties in the 1992–93 5th round were won (no replays) by the **clubs drawn at home.** Only other instance of eight home wins at the last 16 stage was in 1889–90, in what was then the 2nd round.

NORTH-EAST WIPE-OUT
For the first time in 54 years, since the 4th round in Jan, 1957, the North-East's 'big three' were

knocked out on the same date, Jan 8, 2011 (3rd round). All lost to lower-division opponents – **Newcastle** 3-1 at Stevenage, **Sunderland** 2-1 at home to Notts County and **Middlesbrough** 2-1 at Burton.

FEWEST TOP-DIVISION CLUBS IN LAST 16 (5th ROUND)

5 in 1958; **6** in 1927, 1970, 1982; **7** in 1994, 2003; **8** in 2002, 2004.

SIXTH-ROUND ELITE

For the first time in FA Cup 6th round history, dating from 1926 when the format of the competition changed, all **eight quarter-finalists** in 1995–96 were from the top division.

SEMI-FINAL – DOUBLE DERBIES

There have been three instances of both FA Cup semi-finals in the same year being local derbies: **1950** Liverpool beat Everton 2-0 (Maine Road), Arsenal beat Chelsea 1-0 after 2-2 draw (both at Tottenham); **1993** Arsenal beat Tottenham 1-0 (Wembley), Sheffield Wed beat Sheffield Utd 2-1 (Wembley); **2012** Liverpool beat Everton 2-1 (Wembley), Chelsea beat Tottenham 5-1 (Wembley).

TOP CLUB DISTINCTION

Since the Football League began in 1888, there has never been an FA Cup Final in which **neither club** represented the top division.

CLUBS THROWN OUT

Bury expelled (Dec 2006) for fielding an ineligible player in 3-1 2nd rd replay win at Chester. **Droylsden** expelled for fielding a suspended player in 2-1 2nd rd replay win at home to Chesterfield (Dec 2008).

SPURS OUT – AND IN

Tottenham were banned, pre-season, from the 1994–95 competition because of financial irregularities, but were re-admitted on appeal and reached the semi-finals.

FATHER & SON FA CUP WINNERS

Peter Boyle (Sheffield Utd 1899, 1902) and **Tommy Boyle** (Sheffield Utd 1925); **Harry Johnson Snr** (Sheffield Utd 1899, 1902) and **Harry Johnson Jnr** (Sheffield Utd 1925); **Jimmy Dunn Snr** (Everton 1933) and **Jimmy Dunn Jnr** (Wolves 1949); **Alec Herd** (Manchester City 1934) and **David Herd** (Manchester Utd 1963); **Frank Lampard Snr** (West Ham 1975, 1980) and **Frank Lampard Jnr** (Chelsea 2007, 2009, 2010, 2012).

BROTHERS IN FA CUP FINAL TEAMS (modern times)

1950 **Denis and Leslie Compton** (Arsenal); 1952 **George and Ted Robledo** (Newcastle); 1967 **Ron and Allan Harris** (Chelsea); 1977 **Jimmy and Brian Greenhoff** (Manchester Utd); 1996 and 1999 **Gary and Phil Neville** (Manchester Utd).

FA CUP SPONSORS

Littlewoods Pools became the first sponsors of the FA Cup in season 1994–95 in a £14m, 4-year deal. French insurance giants **AXA** took over (season 1998–99) in a sponsorship worth £25m over 4 years. German energy company **E.ON** agreed a 4-year deal worth £32m from season 2006–07 and extended it for a year to 2011. American beer company **Budweiser** began a three-year sponsorship worth £24m in season 2011–12. The **Emirates** airline became the first title sponsor (2015-18) in a reported £30m deal with the FA. This sponsorship was extended for a further three years.

FIRST GOALKEEPER-SUBSTITUTE IN FINAL

Paul Jones (Southampton), who replaced injured Antti Niemi against Arsenal in 2003.

LEAGUE CUP RECORDS

(See also Goalscoring section)

Most winning managers: 4 Brian Clough (Nottm Forest), Sir Alex Ferguson (Manchester Utd), Jose Mourinho (3 Chelsea, 1 Manchester Utd).

Highest scores: West Ham 10 0 v Bury (2nd round, 2nd leg 1983–84; agg 12-1); Liverpool 10-0 v Fulham (2nd round, 1st leg 1986–87; agg 13-2).

Most League Cup goals (career): 49 Geoff Hurst (43 West Ham, 6 Stoke, 1960–75); 49 Ian Rush (48 Liverpool, 1 Newcastle, 1981–98).

Highest scorer (season): 12 Clive Allen (Tottenham 1986–87 in 9 apps).

Most goals in match: 6 Frank Bunn (Oldham v Scarborough, 3rd round, 1989–90).

Most winners' medals: 5 Ian Rush (Liverpool).

Most appearances in Final: 6 Kenny Dalglish (Liverpool 1978–87), Ian Rush (Liverpool 1981–95). Emile Heskey (Leicester 1997, 1999, 2000), Liverpool (2001, 2003), Aston Villa (2010)

Biggest Final win: Swansea City 5 Bradford City 0 (2013).

League Cup sponsors: Milk Cup 1981–86, Littlewoods Cup 1987–90, Rumbelows Cup 1991–92, Coca-Cola Cup 1993–98. Worthington Cup 1999–2003, Carling Cup 2003–12; Capital One Cup from season 2012–16; Carabao 2017–20..

Up for the cup, then down: In 2011, Birmingham became only the second club to win a major trophy (the Carling Cup) and be relegated from the top division. It previously happened to Norwich in 1985 when they went down from the old First Division after winning the Milk Cup.

Liverpool's League Cup records: Winners a record 8 times. **Ian Rush** only player to win 5 times. Rush also first to play in 8 winning teams in Cup **Finals at Wembley**, all with Liverpool (FA Cup 1986–89–92; League Cup 1981–82–83–84–95).

Britain's first under-cover Cup Final: Worthington Cup Final between Blackburn and Tottenham at Cardiff's Millennium Stadium on Sunday, Feb 24, 2002. With rain forecast, the retractable roof was closed on the morning of the match.

Record penalty shoot-out: Liverpool beat Middlesbrough 14-13 (3rd round, Sep 23, 2014) after 2 2. Derby beat Carlisle 14 13 (2nd round, Aug 23, 2016) after 1-1.

DISCIPLINE

SENDINGS-OFF

Season 2003–04 set an **all-time record** of 504 players sent off in English domestic football competitions. There were 58 in the Premier League, 390 Nationwide League, 28 FA Cup (excluding non-League dismissals), 22 League Cup, 2 in Nationwide play-offs, 4 in LDV Vans Trophy.

Most sendings-off in Premier League programme (10 matches): 9 (8 Sat, 1 Sun, Oct 31–Nov 1, 2009).

The 58 Premier League red cards was 13 fewer than the record English **top-division** total of 71 in 2002–03. **Bolton** were the only club in the English divisions without a player sent off in any first-team competition that season.

Worst day for dismissals in English football was Boxing Day, 2007, with **20 red cards** (5 Premier League and 15 Coca-Cola League). Three players, Chelsea's Ashley Cole and Ricardo Carvalho and Aston Villa's Zat Knight were sent off in a 4-4 draw at Stamford Bridge. Luton had three men dismissed in their game at Bristol Rov, but still managed a 1-1 draw.

Previous worst day was Dec 13, 2003, with **19 red cards** (2 Premier League and the 17 Nationwide League).

In the entire first season of post-war League football (1946–47) only 12 players were sent off, followed by 14 in 1949–50, and the total League dismissals for the first nine seasons after the War was 104.

The worst pre War total was 28 in each of seasons 1921–22 and 1922–23.

ENGLAND SENDINGS-OFF

In a total of 15 England dismissals, David Beckham and Wayne Rooney have been red-carded twice. Beckham and Steven Gerrard are the only England captains to be sent off and Robert Green the only goalkeeper.

Jun 5, 1968	**Alan Mullery**	v Yugoslavia (Florence, Euro Champ)
Jun 6, 1973	**Alan Ball**	v Poland (Chorzow, World Cup qual)
Jun 12, 1977	**Trevor Cherry**	v Argentina (Buenos Aires, friendly)
Jun 6, 1986	**Ray Wilkins**	v Morocco (Monterrey, World Cup Finals)
Jun 30, 1998	**David Beckham**	v Argentina (St Etienne, World Cup Finals)
Sep 5, 1998	**Paul Ince**	v Sweden (Stockholm, Euro Champ qual)
Jun 5, 1999	**Paul Scholes**	v Sweden (Wembley, Euro Champ qual)
Sep 8, 1999	**David Batty**	v Poland (Warsaw, Euro Champ qual)
Oct 16, 2002	**Alan Smith**	v Macedonia (Southampton, Euro Champ qual)
Oct 8, 2005	**David Beckham**	v Austria (Old Trafford, World Cup qual)
Jul 1, 2006	**Wayne Rooney**	v Portugal (Gelsenkirchen, World Cup Finals)
Oct 10, 2009	**Robert Green**	v Ukraine (Dnipropetrovsk, World Cup qual)
Oct 7, 2011	**Wayne Rooney**	v Montenegro (Podgorica, Euro Champ qual)
Sep 11, 2012	**Steven Gerrard**	v Ukraine (Wembley, World Cup qual)
Jun 4, 2014	**Raheem Sterling**	v Ecuador (Miami, friendly)

Other countries: Most recent sendings-off of players representing other Home Countries:
N Ireland – Chris Baird (European Champ qual v Hungary, Belfast, Sep 7, 2015).
Scotland – John Souttar (Nations Lge v Israel, Haifa, Oct 11, 2018).
Wales – Neil Taylor (World Cup qual v Republic of Ireland, Dublin, Mar 24, 2017).
Rep of Ireland – Shane Duffy (European Champ v France, Lyon, June 26, 2016).
England dismissals at other levels:
U-23: Stan Anderson (v Bulgaria, Sofia, May 19, 1957); **Alan Ball** (v Austria, Vienna, Jun 2, 1965); **Kevin Keegan** (v E Germany, Magdeburg, Jun 1, 1972); **Steve Perryman** (v Portugal, Lisbon, Nov 19, 1974).
U-21: Sammy Lee (v Hungary, Keszthely, Jun 5, 1981); **Mark Hateley** (v Scotland, Hampden Park, Apr 19, 1982); **Paul Elliott** (v Denmark, Maine Road, Manchester, Mar 26, 1986); **Tony Cottee** (v W Germany, Ludenscheid, Sep 8, 1987); **Julian Dicks** (v Mexico, Toulon, France, Jun 12, 1988); **Jason Dodd** (v Mexico, Toulon, May 29, 1991; 3 Mexico players also sent off in that match); **Matthew Jackson** (v France, Toulon, May 28, 1992); **Robbie Fowler** (v Austria, Kafkenberg, Oct 11, 1994); **Alan Thompson** (v Portugal, Oporto, Sep 2, 1995); **Terry Cooke** (v Portugal, Toulon, May 30, 1996); **Ben Thatcher** (v Italy, Rieti, Oct 10, 1997); **John Curtis** (v Greece, Heraklion, Nov 13, 1997); **Jody Morris** (v Luxembourg, Grevenmacher, Oct 13, 1998); **Stephen Wright** (v Germany, Derby, Oct 6, 2000); **Alan Smith** (v Finland, Valkeakoski, Oct 10, 2000); **Luke Young** and **John Terry** (v Greece, Athens, Jun 5, 2001); **Shola Ameobi** (v Portugal, Rio Maior, Mar 28, 2003); **Jermaine Pennant** (v Croatia, Upton Park, Aug 19, 2003); **Glen Johnson** (v Turkey, Istanbul, Oct 10, 2003); **Nigel Reo-Coker** (v Azerbaijan, Baku, Oct 12, 2004); **Glen Johnson** (v Spain, Henares, Nov 16, 2004); **Steven Taylor** (v Germany, Leverkusen, Oct 10, 2006); **Tom Huddlestone** (v Serbia & Montenegro, Nijmegen, Jun 17, 2007); **Tom Huddlestone** (v Wales, Villa Park, Oct 14, 2008); **Michael Mancienne** (v Finland, Halmstad, Jun 15, 2009); **Fraizer Campbell** (v Sweden, Gothenburg, Jun 26, 2009); **Ben Mee** (v Italy, Empoli, Feb 8, 2011); **Danny Rose** (v Serbia, Krusevac, Oct 16, 2012); **Andre Wisdom** (v Finland, Tampere, Sep 9, 2013); **Jack Stephens** (v Bosnia-Herz, Sarajevo, Nov 12, 2015; **Jordon Ibe** (vSwitzerland, Thun, Mar 26, 2016.
England 'B' (1): **Neil Webb** (v Algeria, Algiers, Dec 11, 1990).

MOST DISMISSALS IN INTERNATIONAL MATCHES

19 (10 Chile, 9 Uruguay), Jun 25, 1975; **6** (2 Mexico, 4 Argentina), 1956; **6** (5 Ecuador, 1 Uruguay), Jan 4, 1977 (4 Ecuadorians sent off in 78th min, match abandoned, 1-1); **5** (Holland 3, Brazil 2), Jun 6, 1999 in Goianio, Brazil.

INTERNATIONAL STOPPED THROUGH DEPLETED SIDE

Portugal v Angola (5-1), friendly international in Lisbon on Nov 14, 2001, abandoned (68 mins) because Angola were down to 6 players (4 sent off, 1 carried off, no substitutes left).

MOST 'CARDS' IN WORLD CUP FINALS MATCH

20 in Portugal v Holland quarter-final, Nuremberg, Jun 25, 2006 (9 yellow, 2 red, Portugal; 7 yellow, 2 red, Holland).

FIVE OFF IN ONE MATCH

For the first time since League football began in 1888, five players were sent off in one match (two Chesterfield, three Plymouth) in Div 2 at Saltergate on **Feb 22, 1997.** Four were dismissed (two from each side) in a goalmouth brawl in the last minute. Five were sent off on Dec 2, 1997 (4 Bristol Rov, 1 Wigan) in Div 2 match at Wigan, four in the 45th minute. The third instance occurred at Exeter on **Nov 23, 2002** in Div 3 (three Exeter, two Cambridge United) all in the last minute. On **Mar 27, 2012** (Lge 2) three Bradford players and two from Crawley were shown red cards in the dressing rooms after a brawl at the final whistle at Valley Parade.

Matches with **four** Football League club players being sent off in one match:

Jan 8, 1955: Crewe v Bradford City (Div 3 North), two players from each side.

Dec 13, 1986: Sheffield Utd (1 player) v Portsmouth (3) in Div 2.

Aug 18, 1987: Port Vale v Northampton (Littlewoods Cup 1st Round, 1st Leg), two players from each side.

Dec 12, 1987: Brentford v Mansfield (Div 3), two players from each side.

Sep 6, 1992: First instance in British first-class football of four players from one side being sent off in one match. Hereford's seven survivors, away to Northampton (Div 3), held out for a 1-1 draw.

Mar 1, 1977: Norwich v Huddersfield (Div 1), two from each side.

Oct 4, 1977: Shrewsbury (1 player), Rotherham (3) in Div 3.

Aug 22, 1998: Gillingham v Bristol Rov (Div 2), two from each side, all after injury-time brawl.

Mar 16, 2001: Bristol City v Millwall (Div 2), two from each side.

Aug 17, 2002: Lincoln (1 player), Carlisle (3) in Div 3.

Aug 26, 2002: Wycombe v QPR (Div 2), two from each side.

Nov 1, 2005: Burnley (1 player) v Millwall (3) in Championship.

Nov 24, 2007: Swindon v Bristol Rov (Lge 1), two from each side.

Mar 4, 2008: Hull v Burnley (Champ) two from each side.

Four Stranraer players were sent off away to Airdrie (Scottish Div 1) on Dec 3, 1994, and that Scottish record was equalled when four Hearts men were ordered off away to Rangers (Prem Div) on Sep 14, 1996. Albion had four players sent off (3 in last 8 mins) away to Queen's Park (Scottish Div 3) on Aug 23, 1997.

In the **Island Games** in Guernsey (Jul 2003), five players (all from Rhodes) were sent off against Guernsey for violent conduct and the match was abandoned by referee Wendy Toms.

Most dismissals one team, one match: Five players of America Tres Rios in first ten minutes after disputed goal by opponents Itaperuna in Brazilian cup match in Rio de Janeiro on Nov 23, 1991. Tie then abandoned and awarded to Itaperuna.

Eight dismissals in one match: Four on each side in South American Super Cup quarter-final (Gremio, Brazil v Penarol, Uruguay) in Oct 1993.

Five dismissals in one season – Dave Caldwell (2 with Chesterfield, 3 with Torquay) in 1987–88.

First instance of four dismissals in Scottish match: three Rangers players (all English – Terry Hurlock, Mark Walters, Mark Hateley) and Celtic's Peter Grant in Scottish Cup quarter-final at Parkhead on Mar 17, 1991 (Celtic won 2-0).

Four players (3 Hamilton, 1 Airdrie) were sent off in Scottish Div 1 match on Oct 30, 1993.

Four players (3 Ayr, 1 Stranraer) were sent off in Scottish Div 1 match on Aug 27, 1994.

In Scottish Cup first round replays on Dec 16, 1996, there were two instances of three players of one side sent off: Albion Rov (away to Forfar) and Huntly (away to Clyde).

FASTEST SENDINGS-OFF

World record – 10 sec: Giuseppe Lorenzo (Bologna) for striking opponent in Italian League match v Parma, Dec 9, 1990. Goalkeeper **Preston Edwards** (Ebbsfleet) for bringing down opponent and conceding penalty in Blue Square Premier League South match v Farnborough, Feb 5, 2011.

World record (non-professional) – 3 sec: David Pratt (Chippenham) at Bashley (British Gas Southern Premier League, Dec 27, 2008).

Domestic – 13 sec: Kevin Pressman (Sheffield Wed goalkeeper at Wolves, Div 1, Sunday, Aug 14, 2000); **15 sec: Simon Rea** (Peterborough at Cardiff, Div 2, Nov 2, 2002). **19 sec: Mark Smith** (Crewe goalkeeper at Darlington, Div 3, Mar 12, 1994). **Premier League – 72 sec: Tim Flowers** (Blackburn goalkeeper v Leeds Utd, Feb 1, 1995).

In World Cup – 55 sec: Jose Batista (Uruguay v Scotland at Neza, Mexico, Jun 13, 1986).

In European competition – 90 sec: Sergei Dirkach (Dynamo Moscow v Ghent UEFA Cup 3rd round, 2nd leg, Dec 11, 1991).

Fastest FA Cup dismissal – 52 sec: Ian Culverhouse (Swindon defender, deliberate hand-ball on goal-line, away to Everton, 3rd Round, Sunday Jan 5, 1997).

Fastest League Cup dismissal – 33 sec: Jason Crowe (Arsenal substitute v Birmingham, 3rd Round, Oct 14, 1997). Also fastest sending off on debut.

Fastest Sending-off of substitute – 0 sec: Walter Boyd (Swansea City) for striking opponent before ball in play after he went on (83 mins) at home to Darlington, Div 3, Nov 23, 1999. **15 secs: Keith Gillespie** (Sheffield Utd) for striking an opponent at Reading (Premier League), Jan 20, 2007. **90 sec: Andreas Johansson** (Wigan), without kicking a ball, for shirt-pulling (penalty) away to Arsenal (Premier League), May 7, 2006.

MOST SENDINGS-OFF IN CAREER

21	**Willie Johnston** , 1964–82 (Rangers 7, WBA 6, Vancouver Whitecaps 4, Hearts 3, Scotland 1)	
21	**Roy McDonough**, 1980–95 (13 in Football League – Birmingham, Walsall, Chelsea, Colchester, Southend, Exeter, Cambridge Utd plus 8 non-league)	
13	**Steve Walsh** (Wigan, Leicester, Norwich, Coventry)	
13	**Martin Keown** (Arsenal, Aston Villa, Everton)	
13	**Alan Smith** (Leeds, Manchester Utd, Newcastle, England U–21, England)	
12	**Dennis Wise** (Wimbledon, Chelsea, Leicester, Millwall)	
12	**Vinnie Jones** (Wimbledon, Leeds, Sheffield Utd, Chelsea, QPR)	
12	**Mark Dennis** (Birmingham, Southampton, QPR)	
12	**Roy Keane** (Manchester Utd, Rep of Ireland)	
10	**Patrick Vieira** (Arsenal)	
10	**Paul Scholes** (Manchester Utd, England)	

Most Premier League sendings-off: Patrick Vieira 9, Duncan Ferguson 8, Richard Dunne 8, Vinnie Jones 7, Roy Keane 7, Alan Smith 7. Lee Cattermole 7.

● **Carlton Palmer** holds the unique record of having been sent off with each of his five Premier League clubs: Sheffield Wed, Leeds, Southampton, Nottm Forest and Coventry.

FA CUP FINAL SENDINGS-OFF

Kevin Moran (Manchester Utd) v Everton, Wembley, 1985; **Jose Antonio Reyes** (Arsenal) v Manchester Utd, Cardiff, 2005; **Pablo Zabaleta** (Manchester City) v Wigan, Wembley 2013; **Chris Smalling** (Manchester Utd) v Crystal Palace , Wembley, 2016; **Victor Moses** (Chelsea) v Arsenal, Wembley, 2017

WEMBLEY SENDINGS-OFF

Aug 1948	**Branko Stankovic** (Yugoslavia) v Sweden, Olympic Games
Jul 1966	**Antonio Rattin** (Argentina captain) v England, World cup quarter-final
Aug 1974	**Billy Bremner** (Leeds) and **Kevin Keegan** (Liverpool), Charity Shield
Mar 1977	**Gilbert Dresch** (Luxembourg) v England, World Cup
May 1985	**Kevin Moran** (Manchester Utd) v Everton, FA Cup Final
Apr 1993	**Lee Dixon** (Arsenal) v Tottenham, FA Cup semi-final

May 1993	Peter Swan (Port Vale) v WBA, Div 2 Play-off Final
Mar 1994	Andrei Kanchelskis (Manchester Utd) v Aston Villa, League Cup Final
May 1994	Mike Wallace, Chris Beaumont (Stockport) v Burnley, Div 2 Play-off Final
Jun 1995	Tetsuji Hashiratani (Japan) v England, Umbro Cup
May 1997	Brian Statham (Brentford) v Crewe, Div 2 Play-off Final
Apr 1998	Capucho (Portugal) v England, friendly
Nov 1998	Ray Parlour (Arsenal) and Tony Vareilles (Lens), Champions League
Mar 1999	Justin Edinburgh (Tottenham) v Leicester, League Cup Final
Jun 1999	Paul Scholes (England) v Sweden, European Championship qual
Feb 2000	Clint Hill (Tranmere) v Leicester, League Cup Final
Apr 2000	Mark Delaney (Aston Villa) v Bolton, FA Cup semi-final
May 2000	Kevin Sharp (Wigan) v Gillingham, Div 2 Play-off Final
Aug 2000	Roy Keane (Manchester Utd captain) v Chelsea, Charity Shield
May 2007	Marc Tierney (Shrewsbury) v Bristol Rov, Lge 2 Play-off Final
May 2007	Matt Gill (Exeter) v Morecambe, Conf Play-off Final
May 2009	Jamie Ward (Sheffield Utd) and Lee Hendrie (Sheffield Utd) v Burnley, Champ Play-off Final (Hendrie after final whistle)
May 2009	Phil Bolland (Cambridge Utd) v Torquay, Blue Square Prem Lge Play-off Final
May 2010	Robin Hulbert (Barrow) and David Bridges (Stevenage), FA Trophy Final
Apr 2011	Paul Scholes (Manchester Utd) v Manchester City, FA Cup semi-final
Apr 2011	Toumani Diagouraga (Brentford) v Carlisle, Johnstone's Paint Trophy Final
Sep 2012	Steven Gerrard (England) v Ukraine, World Cup qual
Feb 2013	Matt Duke (Bradford) v Swansea, League Cup Final
May 2013	Pablo Zabaleta (Manchester City) v Wigan, FA Cup Final
Mar 2014	Joe Newell (Peterborough) v Chesterfield, Johnstone's Paint Trophy Final
May 2014	Gary O'Neil (QPR) v Derby, Champ Play-off Final
May 2016	Chris Smalling (Manchester Utd) v Crystal Palace, FA Cup Final
May 2017	Victor Moses (Chelsea) v Arsenal, FA Cup Final
Aug 2017	Pedro (Chelsea) v Arsenal, Community Shield
Sep 2017	Jan Vertonghen (Tottenham) v Borussia Dortmund, Champions League
May 2018	Liam Ridehalgh (Tranmere) v Boreham Wood, National League Play-off Final – after 48 secs
May 2018	Denis Odoi (Fulham) v Aston Villa, Championship Play-off Final
May 2019	Mark O'Brien (Newport) v Tranmere, Lge 2 Play-off Final

WEMBLEY'S SUSPENDED CAPTAINS

Suspension prevented four **club captains** playing at Wembley in modern finals, in successive years. Three were in FA Cup Finals – **Glenn Roeder** (QPR, 1982), **Steve Foster** (Brighton, 1983), **Wilf Rostron** (Watford, 1984). Sunderland's **Shaun Elliott** was banned from the 1985 Milk Cup Final. Roeder was banned from QPR's 1982 Cup Final replay against Tottenham, and Foster was ruled out of the first match in Brighton's 1983 Final against Manchester Utd.

RED CARD FOR KICKING BALL-BOY

Chelsea's **Eden Hazard** was sent off (80 mins) in the League Cup semi-final, second leg at Swansea on Jan 23, 2013 for kicking a 17-year-old ball-boy who refused to hand over the ball that had gone out of play. The FA suspended Hazard for three matches.

BOOKINGS RECORDS

Most players of one Football League club booked in one match is **TEN** – members of the Mansfield team away to Crystal Palace in FA Cup third round, Jan 1963. Most yellow cards for one team in Premier League match – **9** for Tottenham away to Chelsea, May 2, 2016.
Fastest bookings – 3 seconds after kick-off, **Vinnie Jones** (Chelsea, home to Sheffield Utd, FA Cup fifth round, Feb 15, 1992); 5 seconds after kick-off: **Vinnie Jones** (Sheffield Utd, away to Manchester City, Div 1, Jan 19, 1991). He was sent-off (54 mins) for second bookable offence.

FIGHTING TEAM-MATES

Charlton's **Mike Flanagan** and **Derek Hales** were sent off for fighting each other five minutes from end of FA Cup 3rd round tie at home to Southern League Maidstone on Jan 9, 1979.

Bradford City's **Andy Myers** and **Stuart McCall** had a fight during the 1-6 Premier League defeat at Leeds on Sunday, May 13, 2001.

On Sep 28, 1994 the Scottish FA suspended Hearts players **Graeme Hogg** and **Craig Levein** for ten matches for fighting each other in a pre-season 'friendly' v Raith.

Blackburn's England players **Graeme Le Saux** and **David Batty** clashed away to Spartak Moscow (Champions League) on Nov 22, 1995. Neither was sent off.

Newcastle United's England Internationals **Lee Bowyer** and **Kieron Dyer** were sent off for fighting each other at home to Aston Villa (Premier League on Apr 2, 2005).

Arsenal's **Emmanuel Adebayor** and **Nicklas Bendtner** clashed during the 5-1 Carling Cup semi-final 2nd leg defeat at Tottenham on Jan 22, 2008. Neither was sent off; each fined by their club.

Stoke's **Richardo Fuller** was sent off for slapping his captain, Andy Griffin, at West Ham in the Premier League on Dec 28, 2008.

Preston's **Jermaine Beckford** and **Eoin Doyle** clashed in the Championship game against Sheffield Wednesday on Dec 3, 2016, and were sent off.

St Johnstone's **Richard Foster** and **Danny Swanson** were dismissed for brawling in the Scottish Premier League match with Hamilton on Apr 1, 2017.

FOOTBALL'S FIRST BETTING SCANDAL

A Football League investigation into the First Division match which ended Manchester Utd 2, Liverpool 0 at Old Trafford on Good Friday, Apr 2, 1915 proved that the result had been 'squared' by certain players betting on the outcome. Four members of each team were suspended for life, but some of the bans were lifted when League football resumed in 1919 in recognition of the players' war service.

PLAYERS JAILED

Ten professional footballers found guilty of conspiracy to fraud by 'fixing' matches for betting purposes were given prison sentences at Nottingham Assizes on Jan 26, 1965.

Jimmy Gauld (Mansfield), described as the central figure, was given four years. Among the others sentenced, **Tony Kay** (Sheffield Wed, Everton & England), **Peter Swan** (Sheffield Wed & England) and **David 'Bronco' Layne** (Sheffield Wed) were suspended from football for life by the FA.

DRUGS BANS

Abel Xavier (Middlesbrough) was the first Premier League player found to have taken a performance-enchancing drug. He was banned by UEFA for 18 months in Nov 2005 after testing positive for an anabolic steroid. The ban was reduced to a year in Jul 2006 by the Court of Arbitration for Sport. **Paddy Kenny** (Sheffield Utd goalkeeper) was suspended by an FA commission for 9 months from July, 2009 for failing a drugs test the previous May. Kolo Toure (Manchester City) received a 6-month ban in May 2011 for a doping offence. It was backdated to Mar 2.

LONG SUSPENSIONS

The longest suspension (8 months) in modern times for a player in British football was imposed on two Manchester Utd players. First was **Eric Cantona** following his attack on a spectator as he left the pitch after being sent off at Crystal Palace (Prem League) on Jan 25, 1995. The club immediately suspended him to the end of the season and fined him 2 weeks' wages (est £20,000). Then, on a disrepute charge, the FA fined him £10,000 (Feb 1995) and extended the ban to Sep 30 (which FIFA confirmed as world-wide). A subsequent 2-weeks' jail sentence on Cantona for assault was altered, on appeal, to 120 hours' community service, which took the form of coaching schoolboys in the Manchester area.

On **Dec 19, 2003** an FA Commission, held at Bolton, suspended **Rio Ferdinand** from football for 8 months (plus £50,000 fine) for failing to take a random drug test at the club's training ground on Sep 23. The ban operated from Jan 12, 2004.

Aug 1974: Kevin Keegan (Liverpool) and **Billy Bremner** (Leeds) both suspended for 10 matches and fined £500 after being sent off in FA Charity Shield at Wembley.

Jan 1988: Mark Dennis (QPR) given 8-match ban after 11th sending-off of his career.

Oct 1988: Paul Davis (Arsenal) banned for 9 matches for breaking the jaw of Southampton's Glenn Cockerill.

Oct 1998: Paolo Di Canio (Sheff Wed) banned for 11 matches and fined £10,000 for pushing referee Paul Alcock after being sent off at home to Arsenal (Prem), Sep 26.

Mar 2005: David Prutton (Southampton) banned for 10 matches (plus 1 for red card) and fined £6,000 by FA for shoving referee Alan Wiley when sent off at home to Arsenal (Prem), Feb 26.

Aug 2006: Ben Thatcher (Manchester City) banned for 8 matches for elbowing Pedro Mendes (Portsmouth).

Sep 2008: Joey Barton (Newcastle) banned for 12 matches (6 suspended) and fined £25,000 by FA for training ground assault on former Manchester City team mate Ousmane Dabo.

May 2012: Joey Barton (QPR) suspended for 12 matches and fined £75,000 for violent conduct when sent off against Manchester City on final day of Premier League season.

Mar 2014: Joss Labadie (Torquay) banned for 10 matches and fined £2,000 for biting Chesterfield's Ollie Banks (Lge 2) on Feb 15, 2014.

Seven-month ban: Frank Barson, 37-year-old Watford centre half, sent off at home to Fulham (Div 3 South) on Sep 29, 1928, was suspended by the FA for the remainder of the season.

Twelve-month ban: Oldham full-back **Billy Cook** was given a 12-month suspension for refusing to leave the field when sent off at Middlesbrough (Div 1), on Apr 3, 1915. The referee abandoned the match with 35 minutes still to play, and the score (4-1 to Middlesbrough) was ordered to stand.

Long Scottish bans: Sep 1954: Willie Woodburn, Rangers and Scotland centre-half, suspended for rest of career after fifth sending-off in 6 years.

Billy McLafferty, Stenhousemuir striker, was banned (Apr 14) for 8 and a half months, to Jan 1, 1993, and fined £250 for failing to appear at a disciplinary hearing after being sent off against Arbroath on Feb 1.

Twelve-match ban: On May 12, 1994 Scottish FA suspended Rangers forward **Duncan Ferguson** for 12 matches for violent conduct v Raith on Apr 16. On Oct 11, 1995, Ferguson (then with Everton) sent to jail for 3 months for the assault (served 44 days); Feb 1, 1996 Scottish judge quashed 7 matches that remained of SFA ban on Ferguson.

On Sep 29, 2001 the SFA imposed a **17-match suspension** on Forfar's former Scottish international **Dave Bowman** for persistent foul and abusive language when sent off against Stranraer on Sep 22. As his misconduct continued, he was shown **5 red cards** by the referee.

On Apr 3, 2009, captain **Barry Ferguson** and goalkeeper **Allan McGregor** were banned for life from playing for Scotland for gestures towards photographers while on the bench for a World Cup qualifier against Iceland.

On Dec 20, 2011 Liverpool and Uruguay striker **Luis Suarez** was given an 8-match ban and fined £40,000 by the FA for making 'racially offensive comments' to Patrice Evra of Manchester Utd (Prem Lge, Oct 15).

On Apr 25, 2013 **Luis Suarez** was given a 10-match suspension by the FA for 'violent conduct' biting Chelsea defender Branislav Ivanovic, Prem Lge, Apr 21. The Liverpool player was also fined £200,000 by Liverpool. His ban covered the last 4 games of that season and the first 6 of 2013-14. On Jun 26, 2014, Suarez, while still a Liverpool player, received the most severe punishment in World Cup history – a four-month ban from 'all football activities' and £66,000 fine from FIFA for biting Giorgio Chiellini during Uruguay's group game against Italy.

On Nov 4, 2016 Rochdale's **Calvin Andrew** was banned by the FA for 12 matches – reduced to 9 on appeal – for elbowing Peter Clarke (Oldham) in the face.

On Apr 16, 2017 **Joey Barton** was banned by the FA for 18 months and fined £30,000 for breaching betting rules. The Burnley player admitted placing 1,260 bets on matches.

TOP FINES

Clubs: £49,000,000 (World record) Manchester City: May 2014 for breaking UEFA Financial

Fair Play rules (**£32,600,000** suspended subject to City meeting certain conditions over two seasons). **£42m** settlement Queens Park Rangers: Jul 2018, breaching Financial Fair Play rules; **£7.6m** Bournemouth: May 2016, for breaking Financial Fair Play rules; **£5,500,000** West Ham: Apr 2007, for breaches of regulations involving 'dishonesty and deceit' over Argentine signings Carlos Tevez and Javier Mascherano; **£3.95m**: Watford: Aug 2017, forged banking letter; **£1,500,000** (increased from original £600,000) Tottenham: Dec 1994, financial irregularities; £875,000 QPR: May 2011 for breaching rules when signing Argentine Alejandro Faurlin; **£500,000** (plus 2-year academy signings ban) Everton: Nov 2018, breaking recruitment rules; **£460,000** (plus signings ban in two transfer windows) Chelsea: Feb 2019, breaching rules relating to under-18 foreign players – club appealing; **£390,000** FA: Feb 2019, failing to police recruitment of young players; **£375,000** (reduced to £290,000 on appeal) Chelsea: May 2016, players brawl v Tottenham; **£300,000** (reduced to £75,000 on appeal) Chelsea: Jun 2005, illegal approach to Arsenal's Ashley Cole; **£300,000** (plus 2-year ban on signing academy players, part suspended) Manchester City: May 2017, approaching young players; **£225,000** (reduced to £175,000 on appeal) Tottenham: May 2016, players brawl v Chelsea; **£200,000** Aston Villa: May 2015 for fans' pitch invasion after FA Cup quarter-final v WBA; **£200,000** Leeds: Feb 2019, spying on other clubs' training sessions; **£175,000** Arsenal: Oct 2003, players' brawl v Manchester Utd; **£150,000** Leeds: Mar 2000, players' brawl v Tottenham; **£150,000** Tottenham: Mar 2000, players brawl v Leeds; **£145,000** Hull: Feb 2015, breaching Financial Fair Play rules; **£115,000** West Ham: Aug 2009, crowd misconduct at Carling Cup; v Millwall; **£105,000** Chelsea: Jan 1991, irregular payments; **£100,000** Boston Utd: Jul 2002, contract irregularities; **£100,000** Arsenal and Chelsea: Mar 2007 for mass brawl after Carling Cup Final; **£100,000** (including suspended fine) Blackburn: Aug 2007, poor disciplinary record; **£100,000** Sunderland: May 2014, breaching agents' regulations; **£100,000** Reading: Aug 2015, pitch invasion, FA Cup tie v Bradford (reduced to £40,000 on appeal); **£100,000** Chelsea: Dec 2016, players brawl v Manchester City; **£100,000** (plus 2-year ban on signing academy players, part suspended) Liverpool: Apr 2017, approaching young player; **£90,000** Brighton: Feb 2015, breaching rules on agents; **£71,000** West Ham: Feb 2015 for playing Diafra Sakho in FA Cup 4th round tie against Bristol City after declaring him unfit for Senegal's Africa Cup of Nations squad; **£65,000** Chelsea: Jan 2016, players brawl v WBA; **£62,000** Macclesfield: Dec 2005, funding of a stand at club's ground.

Players: £220,000 (plus 4-match ban) John Terry (Chelsea): Sep 2012, racially abusing Anton Ferdinand (QPR); **£150,000** Roy Keane (Manchester Utd): Oct 2002, disrepute offence over autobiography; **£100,000** (reduced to £75,000 on appeal) Ashley Cole (Arsenal): Jun 2005, illegal approach by Chelsea; **£100,000 (plus 5-match ban)** Jonjo Shelvey (Newcastle): Dec 2016, racially abusing Romain Saiss (Wolves); **£90,000** Ashley Cole (Chelsea): Oct 2012, offensive Tweet against FA; **£80,000 (plus 5-match ban)** Nicolas Anelka (WBA): Feb 2014, celebrating goal at West Ham with racially-offensive 'quenelle' gesture; **£75,000 (plus 12-match ban)** Joey Barton (QPR): May 2012, violent conduct v Manchester City; **£60,000 (plus 3-match ban)** John Obi Mikel (Chelsea): Dec 2012, abusing referee Mark Clattenburg after Prem Lge v Manchester Utd); **£60,000** Dexter Blackstock (Nottm Forest): May 2014, breaching betting rules; **£50,000** Cameron Jerome (Stoke): Aug 2013, breaching FA betting rules; **£50,000** Benoit Assou-Ekotto (Tottenham): Sep 2014, publicly backing Nicolas Anelka's controversial 'quenelle' gesture; **£45,000** Patrick Vieira (Arsenal): Oct 1999, tunnel incidents v West Ham; **£45,000** Rio Ferdinand (Manchester Utd): Aug 2012, improper comments about Ashley Cole on Twitter; **£40,000** Lauren (Arsenal): Oct 2003, players' fracas v Manchester Utd; **£40,000 (plus 8-match ban)** Luis Suarez (Liverpool): Dec 2011, racially abusing Patrice Evra (Manchester Utd); **£40,000 (plus 3-match ban)** Dani Osvaldo (Southampton): Jan 2014, violent conduct, touchline Newcastle; **£40,000** Bacary Sagna (Manchester City): Jan 2017, questioning integrity of referee Lee Mason; **£40,000 (plus 3-mtch ban)** Arsene Wenger (Arsenal): Jan 2018, abuse towards referee Mike Dean v WBA.

*In eight seasons with Arsenal (1996–2004) **Patrick Vieira** was fined a total of £122,000 by the FA for disciplinary offences.

Managers: £200,000 (reduced to £75,000 on appeal) Jose Mourinho (Chelsea): Jun 2005, illegal approach to Arsenal's Ashley Cole; **£60,000 (plus 7-match ban)** Alan Pardew (Newcastle): head-butting Hull player David Meyler (also fined £100,000 by club); **£60,000** Rafael Benitez (Newcastle): Oct 2018, talking about match referee ahead of fixture; **£58,000** Jose Mourinho (Manchester Utd): Nov 2016, misconduct involving referees Mark Clattenburg and Anthony Taylor; **£50,000** Jose Mourinho (Chelsea): Oct 2015, accusing referees of bias; **£45,000** Jurgen Klopp (Liverpool): Feb 2019, questioning integrity of referee Kevin Friend; **£40,000 (plus 1 match stadium ban)** Jose Mourinho (Chelsea): Nov 2015, abusive behaviour towards referee Jon Moss v West Ham, **£40,000 (plus 3-match Euro ban)** Arsene Wenger (Arsenal): Jan 2018, abuse towards referee Mike Dean v WBA; **£33,000 (plus 3-match Euro ban)** Arsene Wenger: Mar 2012, criticising referee after Champions League defeat by AC Milan; **£30,000** Sir Alex Ferguson (Manchester Utd): Mar 2011 criticising referee Martin Atkinson v Chelsea; **£30,000 (plus 6-match ban ((plus 6-match ban reduced to 4 on appeal);** Rui Faria (Chelsea assistant): May 2014, confronting match officials v Sunderland.

- Jonathan Barnett, Ashley Cole's agent was fined **£100,000** in Sep 2006 for his role in the 'tapping up' affair involving the player and Chelsea.
- Gillingham and club chairman Paul Scally each fined £75,000 in Jul 2015 for 'racial victimisation' towards player Mark McCammon. Club fine reduced to £50,000 on appeal.
- Leyton Orient owner Francesco Becchetti fined £40,000 and given six-match stadium ban in Jan 2016 for violent conduct towards assistant manager Andy Hessenthaler.

*£68,000 FA: May 2003, pitch invasions and racist chanting by fans during England v Turkey, Sunderland.

£50,000 FA: Dec 2014, for Wigan owner-chairman Dave Whelan, plus six-week ban from all football activity, for remarks about Jewish and Chinese people in newspaper interview.

*£250,000 FA: Dec 2016, for Leeds owner Massimo Cellino, plus 18-month ban, for breaking agent regulations (reduced to £100,000 and one year on appeal). Club fined £250,000 (reduced to £200,000 on appeal). Agent Derek Day fined £75,000 and banned for 18 months (11 months suspended).

MANAGERS

INTERNATIONAL RECORDS
(As at start of season 2019–20)

	P	W	D	L	F	A
Gareth Southgate (England appointed Sep 2016	35	19	9	7	60	28
Steve Clarke (Scotland – appointed May 2019)	2	1	0	1	2	4
Ryan Giggs (Wales – appointed Jan 2018)	13	5	1	7	16	14
Michael O'Neill (Northern Ireland – appointed Oct 2011)	66	24	17	25	69	70
Mick McCarthy (Republic of Ireland – appointed Nov 2018)	5	3	2	0	5	1

COMPLETED RECORDS

	P	W	D	L	F	A
Alex McLeish (Scotland)	12	5	0	7	14	18
Martin O'Neill (Republic of Ireland)	55	19	20	16	68	56

ENGLAND MANAGERS

		P	W	D	L
1946–62	Walter Winterbottom	139	78	33	28
1963–74	Sir Alf Ramsey	113	69	27	17
1974	Joe Mercer, caretaker	7	3	3	1
1974–77	Don Revie	29	14	8	7
1977–82	Ron Greenwood	55	33	12	10
1982–90	Bobby Robson	95	47	30	18
1990–93	Graham Taylor	38	18	13	7
1994–96	Terry Venables	23	11	11	1
1996–99	Glenn Hoddle	28	17	6	5

1999	**Howard Wilkinson**, caretaker	1	0	0	1
1999–2000	**Kevin Keegan**	18	7	7	4
2000	**Howard Wilkinson**, caretaker	1	0	1	0
2000	**Peter Taylor**, caretaker	1	0	0	1
2001–06	**Sven–Goran Eriksson**	67	40	17	10
2006–07	**Steve McClaren**	18	9	4	5
2007–12	**Fabio Capello**	42	28	8	6
2012	**Stuart Pearce**, caretaker	1	0	0	1
2012 16	**Roy Hodgson**	56	33	15	8
2016	**Sam Allardyce**	1	1	0	0

INTERNATIONAL MANAGER CHANGES

England: Walter Winterbottom 1946–62 (initially coach); **Alf Ramsey** (Feb 1963–May 1974); **Joe Mercer** (caretaker May 1974); **Don Revie** (Jul 1974–Jul 1977); **Ron Greenwood** (Aug 1977–Jul 1982); **Bobby Robson** (Jul 1982–Jul 1990); **Graham Taylor** (Jul 1990–Nov 1993); **Terry Venables**, coach (Jan 1994–Jun 1996); **Glenn Hoddle**, coach (Jun 1996–Feb 1999); **Howard Wilkinson** (caretaker Feb 1999); **Kevin Keegan coach** (Feb 1999–Oct 2000); **Howard Wilkinson** (caretaker Oct 2000); **Peter Taylor** (caretaker Nov 2000); **Sven–Goran Eriksson** (Jan 2001–Aug 2006); **Steve McClaren** (Aug 2006–Nov 2007); **Fabio Capello** (Dec 2007–Feb 2012); **Roy Hodgson** (May 2012– Jun 2016); **Sam Allardyce** (Jul-Sep 2016); **Gareth Southgate** (Sep-Nov 2016 interim, then permanent appointment).

Scotland (modern): Bobby Brown (Feb 1967–Jul 1971); **Tommy Docherty** (Sep 1971–Dec 1972); **Willie Ormond** (Jan 1973–May 1977); **Ally MacLeod** (May 1977–Sep 1978); **Jock Stein** (Oct 1978–Sep 1985); **Alex Ferguson** (caretaker Oct 1985–Jun 1986); **Andy Roxburgh**, coach (Jul 1986–Sep 1993); **Craig Brown** (Sep 1993–Oct 2001); **Berti Vogts** (Feb 2002–Oct 2004); **Walter Smith** (Dec 2004–Jan 2007); **Alex McLeish** (Jan 2007–Nov 2007); **George Burley** (Jan 2008–Nov 2009); **Craig Levein** (Dec 2009–Nov 2012); **Billy Stark** (caretaker Nov–Dec 2012); **Gordon Strachan** (Jan 2013-Oct 2017); **Malky Mackay**, (caretaker Nov 2017); **Alex McLeish** (Feb 2018–Apr 2019; **Steve Clarke** (since May 2019).

Northern Ireland (modern): Peter Doherty (1951–62); **Bertie Peacock** (1962–67); **Billy Bingham** (1967–Aug 1971); **Terry Neill** (Aug 1971–Mar 1975); **Dave Clements** (player-manager Mar 1975–1976); **Danny Blanchflower** (Jun 1976–Nov 1979); **Billy Bingham** (Feb 1980–Nov 1993); **Bryan Hamilton** Feb 1994–Feb 1998); **Lawrie McMenemy** (Feb 1998–Nov 1999); **Sammy McIlroy** (Jan 2000–Oct 2003); **Lawrie Sanchez** (Jan 2004–May 2007); **Nigel Worthington** (May 2007–Oct 2011); **Michael O'Neill** (since Oct 2011).

Wales (modern): Mike Smith (Jul 1974–Dec 1979); **Mike England** (Mar 1980–Feb 1988); **David Williams** (caretaker Mar 1988); **Terry Yorath** (Apr 1988–Nov 1993); **John Toshack** (Mar 1994, one match); **Mike Smith** (Mar 1994–Jun 1995); **Bobby Gould** (Aug 1995–Jun 1999); **Mark Hughes** (Aug 1999 – Oct 2004); **John Toshack** (Nov 2004–Sep 2010); Brian Flynn (caretaker Sep–Dec 2010); **Gary Speed** (Dec 2010–Nov 2011); **Chris Coleman** (Jan 2012-Nov 2017); **Ryan Giggs** (since Jan 2018).

Republic of Ireland (modern): Liam Tuohy (Sep 1971–Nov 1972); **Johnny Giles** (Oct 1973–Apr 1980, initially player–manager); **Eoin Hand** (Jun 1980–Nov 1985); **Jack Charlton** (Feb 1986–Dec 1995); **Mick McCarthy** (Feb 1996–Oct 2002); **Brian Kerr** (Jan 2003–Oct 2005); **Steve Staunton** (Jan 2006–Oct 2007); **Giovanni Trapattoni** (May 2008–Sep 2013); **Martin O'Neill** (Nov 2013–Nov 2018); **Mick McCarthy** (since Nov 2018)

WORLD CUP-WINNING MANAGERS

1930 Uruguay (Alberto Suppici); 1934 and 1938 Italy (Vittorio Pozzo); 1950 Uruguay (Juan Lopez Fontana); 1954 West Germany (Sepp Herberger); 1958 Brazil (Vicente Feola); 1962 Brazil (Aymore Moreira); 1966 England (Sir Alf Ramsey); 1970 Brazil (Mario Zagallo); 1974 West Germany (Helmut Schon); 1978 Argentina (Cesar Luis Menotti); 1982 Italy (Enzo Bearzot); 1986 Argentina (Carlos Bilardo); 1990 West Germany (Franz Beckenbauer); 1994 Brazil (Carlos Alberto Parreira); 1998 France (Aimee Etienne Jacquet); 2002 Brazil (Luiz Felipe Scolari); 2006 Italy (Marcello Lippi); 2010 Spain (Vicente Del Bosque); 2014 Germany

(Joachim Low); 2018 France (Didier Deschamps).

Each of the 21 winning teams had a manager/coach of that country's nationality.

YOUNGEST LEAGUE MANAGERS

Ivor Broadis, 23, appointed player-manager of Carlisle, Aug 1946; **Chris Brass**, 27, appointed player-manager of York, Jun 2003; **Terry Neill**, 28, appointed player-manager of Hull, Jun 1970; **Graham Taylor**, 28, appointed manager of Lincoln, Dec 1972.

LONGEST-SERVING LEAGUE MANAGERS – ONE CLUB

Fred Everiss, secretary–manager of WBA for 46 years (1902–48); **George Ramsay**, secretary–manager of Aston Villa for 42 years (1884–1926); **John Addenbrooke**, Wolves, for 37 years (1885–1922). Since last war: **Sir Alex Ferguson** at Manchester Utd for 27 seasons (1986–2013); **Sir Matt Busby**, in charge of Manchester Utd for 25 seasons (1945–69, 1970–71; **Dario Gradi** at Crewe for 26 years (1983–2007, 2009–11); **Jimmy Seed** at Charlton for 23 years (1933–56); **Brian Clough** at Nottm Forest for 18 years (1975–93); **Arsene Wenger** at Arsenal for 22 years (1996-2018).

LAST ENGLISH MANAGER TO WIN PREMIER LEAGUE

Howard Wilkinson (Leeds), season 1991–92.

MANAGERS WITH MORE THAN 1000 MATCHES

Sir Alex Ferguson, Sir Bobby Robson, Sir Matt Busby, Arsene Wenger, Roy Hodgson, Harry Redknapp, Alec Stock, Brian Clough, Jim Smith, Graham Taylor, Dario Gradi, Tony Pulis, Dave Bassett, Lennie Lawrence, Alan Buckley, Denis Smith, Joe Royle, Ron Atkinson, Brian Horton, Neil Warnock, Len Ashurst, Lawrie McMenemy, Graham Turner, Steve Coppell, John Toshack, Rafael Benitez, Sven Goran Eriksson, Claudio Ranieri and Carlo Ancelotti.

SHORT-TERM MANAGERS

Departed

3 days	Bill Lambton (Scunthorpe)	Apr 1959
6 days	Tommy McLean (Raith Rov)	Sep 1996
7 days	Tim Ward (Exeter)	Mar 1953
7 days	Kevin Cullis (Swansea City)	Feb 1996
8 days	Billy McKinlay (Watford)	Oct 2014
10 days	Dave Cowling (Doncaster)	Oct 1997
10 days	Peter Cormack (Cowdenbeath)	Dec 2000
13 days	Johnny Cochrane (Reading)	Apr 1939
13 days	Micky Adams (Swansea City)	Oct 1997
16 days	Jimmy McIlroy (Bolton)	Nov 1970
19 days	Martin Allen (Barnet)	Apr 2011
20 days	Paul Went (Leyton Orient)	Oct 1981
27 days	Malcolm Crosby (Oxford Utd)	Jan 1998
27 days	Oscar Garcia (Watford)	Sep 2014
28 days	Tommy Docherty (QPR)	Dec 1968
28 days	Paul Hart (QPR)	Jan 2010
31 days	Paul Scholes (Oldham)	Mar 2019
32 days	Steve Coppell (Manchester City)	Nov 1996
32 days	Darko Milanic (Leeds)	Oct 2014
34 days	Niall Quinn (Sunderland)	Aug 2006
36 days	Steve Claridge (Millwall)	Jul 2005
39 days	Paul Gascoigne (Kettering)	Dec 2005
39 days	Kenny Jackett (Rotherham)	Nov 2016
40 days	Alex McLeish (Nottm Forest)	Feb 2013
41 days	Steve Wicks (Lincoln)	Oct 1995

41 days	Les Reed (Charlton)	Dec 2006
43 days	Mauro Milanese (Leyton Orient)	Dec 2014
44 days	Brian Clough (Leeds)	Sep 1974
44 days	Jock Stein (Leeds)	Oct 1978
45 days	Paul Murray (Hartlepool)	Dec 2014
48 days	John Toshack (Wales)	Mar 1994
48 days	David Platt (Sampdoria coach)	Feb 1999
49 days	Brian Little (Wolves)	Oct 1986
49 days	Terry Fenwick (Northampton)	Feb 2003
52 days	Alberto Cavasin (Leyton Orient)	Nov 2016
54 days	Craig Levein (Raith Rov)	Oct 1996
54 days	Chris Lucketti (Bury)	Jan 2018
56 days	Martin Ling (Swindon)	Dec 2015
57 days	Henning Berg (Blackburn)	Dec 2012
59 days	Kevin Nugent (Barnet)	Apr 2017
61 days	Bill McGarry (Wolves)	Nov 1985

- In May 1984, Crystal Palace named **Dave Bassett** as manager, but he changed his mind four days later, without signing the contract, and returned to Wimbledon.
- In May 2007, **Leroy Rosenior** was reportedly appointed manager of Torquay after relegation and sacked ten minutes later when the club came under new ownership.
- **Brian Laws** lost his job at Scunthorpe on Mar 25, 2004 and was reinstated three weeks later.
- In an angry outburst after a play-off defeat in May 1992, Barnet chairman Stan Flashman sacked manager **Barry Fry** and re-instated him a day later.

EARLY-SEASON MANAGER SACKINGS

2012: Andy Thorn (Coventry) 8 days; John Sheridan (Chesterfield) 10 days; **2011:** Jim Jefferies (Hearts) 9 days; **2010** Kevin Blackwell (Sheffield Utd) 8 days; **2009** Bryan Gunn (Norwich) 6 days; **2007:** Neil McDonald (Carlisle) 2 days; Martin Allen (Leicester) 18 days; **2004:** Paul Sturrock (Southampton) 9 days; **2004:** Sir Bobby Robson (Newcastle) 16 days; **2003:** Glenn Roeder (West Ham) 15 days; **2000:** Alan Buckley (Grimsby) 10 days; **1997:** Kerry Dixon (Doncaster) 12 days; **1996:** Sammy Chung (Doncaster) on morning of season's opening League match; **1996:** Alan Ball (Manchester City) 12 days; **1994:** Kenny Hibbitt (Walsall) and Kenny Swain (Wigan) 20 days; **1993:** Peter Reid (Manchester City) 12 days; **1991:** Don Mackay (Blackburn) 14 days; **1989:** Mick Jones (Peterborough) 12 days; **1980:** Bill McGarry (Newcastle) 13 days; **1979:** Dennis Butler (Port Vale) 12 days; **1977:** George Petchey (Leyton O) 13 days; **1977:** Willie Bell (Birmingham) 16 days; **1971:** Len Richley (Darlington) 12 days.

DOUBLE DISMISSAL

Mark Hughes became the first manager to be sacked by two Premier League clubs in the same calendar year (2018) – Stoke in January and Southampton in December.

FOUR GAMES AND OUT

Frank de Boer was sacked as Crystal Palace manager after his first four Premier League matches at the start of the 2017–18 season – the competition's shortest reign in terms of games.

BRUCE'S FOUR-TIMER

Steve Bruce is the only manager to win four promotions to the Premier League – with Birmingham in 2002 and 2007 and with Hull in 2013 and 2016.

RECORD START FOR MANAGER

Russ Wilcox, appointed by Scunthorpe in Nov 2013, remained unbeaten in his first 28 league matches (14 won, 14 drawn) and took the club to promotion from League Two. It was the most successful start to a managerial career in English football, beating the record of 23 unbeaten games by Preston's William Sudell in 1889.

RECORD TOP DIVISION START

Arsenal were unbeaten in 17 league matches from the start of season 1947-48 under new manager **Tom Whittaker**.

SACKED, REINSTATED, FINISHED

Brian McDermott was sacked as Leeds manager on Jan 31, 2014. The following day, he was reinstated. At the end of the season, with the club under new ownership, he left by 'mutual consent.'

CARETAKER SUPREME

As Chelsea's season collapsed, Andre Villas-Boas was sacked in March 2012 after eight months as manager, 2012. Roberto Di Matteo was appointed caretaker and by the season's end his team had won the FA Cup and the Champions League.

MANAGER DOUBLES

Four managers have won the League Championship with different clubs: **Tom Watson**, secretary-manager with Sunderland (1892-93-95) and **Liverpool** (1901); **Herbert Chapman** with Huddersfield (1923-24, 1924-25) and Arsenal (1930-31, 1932-33); **Brian Clough** with Derby (1971-72) and Nottm Forest (1977-78); **Kenny Dalglish** with Liverpool (1985-86, 1987-88, 1989-90) and Blackburn (1994-95).

Managers to win the FA Cup with different clubs: **Billy Walker** (Sheffield Wed 1935, Nottm Forest 1959); **Herbert Chapman** (Huddersfield 1922, Arsenal 1930).

Kenny Dalglish (Liverpool) and **George Graham** (Arsenal) completed the Championship/FA Cup double as both player and manager with a single club. **Joe Mercer** won the title as a player with Everton, the title twice and FA Cup as a player with Arsenal and both competitions as manager of Manchester City.

CHAIRMAN-MANAGER

On Dec 20, 1988, after two years on the board, Dundee Utd manager **Jim McLean** was elected chairman, too. McLean, Scotland's longest-serving manager (appointed on Nov 24, 1971), resigned at end of season 1992-93 (remained chairman).

Ron Noades was chairman-manager of Brentford from Jul 1998-Mar 2001. John Reames did both jobs at Lincoln from Nov 1998-Apr 2000)

Niall Quinn did both jobs for five weeks in 2006 before appointing Roy Keane as manager of Sunderland.

TOP DIVISION PLAYER-MANAGERS

Les Allen (QPR 1968-69); **Johnny Giles** (WBA 1976-77); **Howard Kendall** (Everton 1981-82); **Kenny Dalglish** (Liverpool, 1985-90); **Trevor Francis** (QPR, 1988-89); **Terry Butcher** (Coventry, 1990-91); **Peter Reid** (Manchester City, 1990-93); **Trevor Francis** (Sheffield Wed, 1991-94); **Glenn Hoddle**, (Chelsea, 1993-95); **Bryan Robson** (Middlesbrough, 1994-97); **Ray Wilkins** (QPR, 1994-96), **Ruud Gullit** (Chelsea, 1996-98), **Gianluca Vialli** (Chelsea, 1998-2000).

FIRST FOREIGN MANAGER IN ENGLISH LEAGUE

Uruguayan **Danny Bergara** (Rochdale 1988-89).

COACHING KINGS OF EUROPE

Five coaches have won the European Cup/Champions League with two different clubs: **Ernst Happel** with Feyenoord (1970) and Hamburg (1983); **Ottmar Hitzfeld** with Borussia Dortmund (1997) and Bayern Munich (2001); **Jose Mourinho** with Porto (2004) and Inter Milan (2010); **Jupp Heynckes** with Real Madrid (1998) and Bayern Munich (2013); **Carlo Ancelotti** with AC Milan (2003, 2007) and Real Madrid (2014).

FOREIGN TRIUMPH

Former Dutch star **Ruud Gullit** became the first foreign manager to win a major English competition when Chelsea took the FA Cup in 1997.

Arsene Wenger and **Gerard Houllier** became the first foreign managers to receive recognition when they were awarded honorary OBEs in the Queen's Birthday Honours in Jun 2003 'for their contribution to English football and Franco–British relations'.

MANAGERS OF POST-WAR CHAMPIONS (*Double winners)

1947 George Kay (Liverpool); **1948** Tom Whittaker (Arsenal); **1949** Bob Jackson (Portsmouth).

1950 Bob Jackson (Portsmouth); **1951** Arthur Rowe (Tottenham); **1952** Matt Busby (Manchester Utd); **1953** Tom Whittaker (Arsenal); **1954** Stan Cullis (Wolves); **1955** Ted Drake (Chelsea); **1956** Matt Busby (Manchester Utd); **1957** Matt Busby (Manchester Utd); **1958** Stan Cullis (Wolves); **1959** Stan Cullis (Wolves).

1960 Harry Potts (Burnley); **1961** *Bill Nicholson (Tottenham); **1962** Alf Ramsey (Ipswich); **1963** Harry Catterick (Everton); **1964** Bill Shankly (Liverpool); **1965** Matt Busby (Manchester Utd); **1966** Bill Shankly (Liverpool); **1967** Matt Busby (Manchester Utd); **1968** Joe Mercer (Manchester City); **1969** Don Revie (Leeds).

1970 Harry Catterick (Everton); **1971** *Bertie Mee (Arsenal); **1972** Brian Clough (Derby); **1973** Bill Shankly (Liverpool); **1974** Don Revie (Leeds); **1975** Dave Mackay (Derby); **1976** Bob Paisley (Liverpool); **1977** Bob Paisley (Liverpool); **1978** Brian Clough (Nottm Forest); **1979** Bob Paisley (Liverpool).

1980 Bob Paisley (Liverpool); **1981** Ron Saunders (Aston Villa); **1982** Bob Paisley (Liverpool); **1983** Bob Paisley (Liverpool); **1984** Joe Fagan (Liverpool); **1985** Howard Kendall (Everton); **1986** *Kenny Dalglish (Liverpool – player/manager); **1987** Howard Kendall (Everton); **1988** Kenny Dalglish (Liverpool – player/manager); **1989** George Graham (Arsenal).

1990 Kenny Dalglish (Liverpool); **1991** George Graham (Arsenal); **1992** Howard Wilkinson (Leeds); **1993** Alex Ferguson (Manchester Utd); **1994** *Alex Ferguson (Manchester Utd); **1995** Kenny Dalglish (Blackburn); **1996** *Alex Ferguson (Manchester Utd); **1997** Alex Ferguson (Manchester Utd); **1998** *Arsene Wenger (Arsenal); **1999** *Alex Ferguson (Manchester Utd).

2000 Sir Alex Ferguson (Manchester Utd); **2001** Sir Alex Ferguson (Manchester Utd); **2002** *Arsene Wenger (Arsenal); **2003** Sir Alex Ferguson (Manchester Utd); **2004** Arsene Wenger (Arsenal); **2005** Jose Mourinho (Chelsea); **2006** Jose Mourinho (Chelsea); **2007** Sir Alex Ferguson (Manchester Utd); **2008** Sir Alex Ferguson (Manchester Utd); **2009** Sir Alex Ferguson (Manchester Utd); **2010** *Carlo Ancelotti (Chelsea); **2011** Sir Alex Ferguson (Manchester Utd); **2012** Roberto Mancini (Manchester City); **2013** Sir Alex Ferguson (Manchester Utd); **2014** Manuel Pellegrini (Manchester City); **2015** Jose Mourinho (Chelsea); **2016** Claudio Ranieri (Leicester); **2017** Antonio Conte (Chelsea); **2018** Pep Guardiola (Manchester City); **2019** Pep Guardiola (Manchester City).

WORLD NO 1 MANAGER

When **Sir Alex Ferguson**, 71, retired in May 2013, he ended the most successful managerial career in the game's history. He took Manchester United to a total of 38 prizes – 13 Premier League titles, 5 FA Cup triumphs, 4 League Cups, 10 Charity/Community Shields (1 shared), 2 Champions League wins, 1 Cup-Winners' Cup, 1 FIFA Club World Cup, 1 Inter-Continental Cup and 1 UEFA Super Cup. Having played centre-forward for Rangers, the Glaswegian managed 3 Scottish clubs, East Stirling, St Mirren and then Aberdeen, where he broke the Celtic/Rangers duopoly with 9 successes: 3 League Championships, 4 Scottish Cups, 1 League Cup and 1 UEFA Cup. Appointed at Old Trafford in November 1986, when replacing Ron Atkinson, he did not win a prize there until his fourth season (FA Cup 1990), but thereafter the club's trophy cabinet glittered with silverware. His total of 1,500 matches in charge ended with a 5-5 draw away to West Bromwich Albion. The longest-serving manager in the club's history, he constructed 4 triumphant teams. Sir Alex was knighted in 1999 and in 2012 he received the FIFA award for services to football. On retirement from management, he became a director and club ambassador. United maintained the dynasty of long-serving Scottish managers (Sir Matt Busby for 24 seasons) by appointing David Moyes, who had been in charge at Everton for 11 years.

WENGER'S LEGACY

Arsene Wenger was a virtually unknown French manager when taking over Arsenal in 1996. He left 22 years later as the most successful in the club's history. Wenger led them to three Premier League titles, including the unbeaten season in 2003-04 achieved by the team known as the 'Invincibles.' There were seven FA Cup successes, one in 2002 when Arsenal completed the Double. He was also closely involved in planning the move from Highbury to the Emirates Stadium in 2006.

THE PROMOTION MAN

Neil Warnock set a record of eight promotions when he took Cardiff back to the Premier League in 2018. In 38 years as a manager, he was also successful with Scarborough, Notts County twice, Plymouth, Huddersfield, Sheffield United and Queens Park Rangers. Warnock's achievements were marked by a special award from the League Managers' Association.

MANAGERS' EURO TREBLES

Two managers have won the European Cup/Champions League three times. **Bob Paisley** did it with Liverpool (1977,78, 81).

Carlo Ancelotti's successes were with AC Milan in 2003 and 2007 and with Real Madrid in 2014.

WINNER MOURINHO

In winning the Premier League and League Cup in 2015, Jose Mourinho embellished his reputation as Chelsea's most successful manager. Those achievements took his total of honours in two spells at the club to 8: 3 Premier League, 3 League Cup, 1 FA Cup, 1 Community Shield. Joining from Portuguese champions Porto, Mourinho was initially with Chelsea from June 2004 to September 2007. He then successfully coached Inter Milan and Real Madrid before returning to Stamford Bridge in June 2013. His Premier League triumph in 2015 was his eighth title in 11 years in four countries (England 3, Portugal 2, Italy 2, Spain 1). In his first season with Manchester Utd (2016-17), he won three trophies – League Cup, Europa League and Community Shield.

WENGER'S CUP AGAIN

Arsenal's win against Aston Villa in the 2015 Final was a record 12th success for them in the FA Cup and a sixth triumph in the competition for manager Arsene Wenger, equalling the record of George Ramsay for Villa (1887-1920). With his sixth victory in seven Finals, Wenger made history as the first manager to win the Cup in successive seasons twice (previously in 2002 and 2003). He won it for a record seventh time – in eight finals – in 2017.

RECORD MANAGER FEE

Chelsea paid Porto a record £13.25m compensation when they appointed **Andre Villas-Boas** as manager in June 2011. He lasted less than nine months at Stamford Bridge.

FATHER AND SON MANAGERS WITH SAME CLUB

Fulham: Bill Dodgin Snr 1949-53; Bill Dodgin Jnr 1968-72. **Brentford:** Bill Dodgin Snr 1953-57; Bill Dodgin Jnr 1976-80. **Bournemouth:** John Bond 1970-73; Kevin Bond 2006-08. **Derby:** Brian Clough 1967-73, Nigel Clough 2009-2013. **Bristol City.** Gary Johnson 2005-10; Lee Johnson 2016-present.

SIR BOBBY'S HAT-TRICK

Sir Bobby Robson, born and brought up in County Durham, achieved a unique hat-trick when he received the Freedom of Durham in Dec 2008. He had already been awarded the Freedom of Ipswich and Newcastle. He died in July 2009 and had an express loco named after him on the East Coast to London line.

MANAGERS WITH MOST FA CUP SUCCESSES

7 Arsene Wenger (Arsenal); **6** George Ramsay (Aston Villa); **5** Sir Alex Ferguson (Manchester Utd); **3** Charles Foweraker (Bolton), John Nicholson (Sheffield Utd), Bill Nicholson (Tottenham).

RELEGATION 'DOUBLES'

Managers associated with two clubs relegated in same season: **John Bond** in 1985–86 (Swansea City and Birmingham); **Ron Saunders** in 1985–86 (WBA – and their reserve team – and Birmingham); **Bob Stokoe** in 1986–87 (Carlisle and Sunderland); **Billy McNeill** in 1986–87 (Manchester City and Aston Villa); **Dave Bassett** in 1987–88 (Watford and Sheffield Utd); **Mick Mills** in 1989–90 (Stoke and Colchester); **Gary Johnson** in 2014-15 (Yeovil and Cheltenham)

THREE FA CUP DEFEATS IN ONE SEASON

Manager **Michael Appleton** suffered three FA Cup defeats in season 2012-13, with Portsmouth (v Notts Co, 1st rd); Blackpool (v Fulham, 3rd rd); Blackburn (v Millwall, 6th rd).

WEMBLEY STADIUM

NEW WEMBLEY

A new era for English football began in March 2007 with the completion of the new national stadium. The 90,000-seater arena was hailed as one of the world's finest – but came at a price. Costs soared, the project fell well behind schedule and disputes involving the FA, builders Multiplex and the Government were rife. The old stadium, opened in 1923, cost £750,000. The new one, originally priced at £326m in 2000, ended up at around £800m. The first international after completion was an Under-21 match between England and Italy. The FA Cup Final returned to its spiritual home after being staged at the Millennium Stadium in Cardiff for six seasons. Then, England's senior team were back for a friendly against Brazil.

DROGBA'S WEMBLEY RECORD

Didier Drogba's FA Cup goal for Chelsea against Liverpool in May 2012 meant that he had scored in all his 8 competitive appearances for the club at Wembley. (7 wins, 1 defeat). They came in: 2007 FA Cup Final (1-0 v Manchester Utd); 2008 League Cup Final (1-2 v Tottenham); 2009 FA Cup semi-final (2-1 v Arsenal); 2009 FA Cup Final (2-1 v Everton); 2010 FA Cup semi-final (3-0 v Aston Villa); 2010 FA Cup Final (1-0 v Portsmouth); 2012 FA Cup semi-final (5-1 v Tottenham); 2012 FA Cup Final (2-1 v Liverpool).

INVASION DAY

Memorable scenes were witnessed at the first **FA Cup Final at Wembley**, Apr 28, 1923, between **Bolton** and **West Ham**. An accurate return of the attendance could not be made owing to thousands breaking in, but there were probably more than 200,000 spectators present. The match was delayed for 40 minutes by the crowd invading the pitch. Official attendance was 126,047. Gate receipts totalled £27,776. The two clubs and the FA each received £6,365 and the FA refunded £2,797 to ticket-holders who were unable to get to their seats. Cup Final admission has since been by ticket only.

REDUCED CAPACITY

Capacity of the all-seated Wembley Stadium was 78,000. The last 100,000 attendance was for the 1985 FA Cup Final between Manchester Utd and Everton. Crowd record for New Wembley: 89,874 for 2008 FA Cup Final (Portsmouth v Cardiff).

WEMBLEY'S FIRST UNDER LIGHTS

Nov 30, 1955 (England 4, Spain 1), when the floodlights were switched on after 73 minutes (afternoon match played in damp, foggy conditions).
First Wembley international played throughout under lights: England 8, N Ireland 3 on evening of Nov 20, 1963 (att: 55,000).

MOST WEMBLEY APPEARANCES

59 by **Tony Adams** (35 England, 24 Arsenal); 57 by **Peter Shilton** (52 England, 3 Nottm Forest, 1 Leicester, 1 Football League X1).

WEMBLEY HAT-TRICKS

Three players have scored hat-tricks in major finals at Wembley: **Stan Mortensen** for Blackpool v Bolton (FA Cup Final, 1953), **Geoff Hurst** for England v West Germany (World Cup Final, 1966) and **David Speedie** for Chelsea v Manchester City (Full Members Cup, 1985).

ENGLAND'S WEMBLEY DEFEATS

England have lost 25 matches to foreign opponents at Wembley:

Nov 1953	3-6 v Hungary	Jun 1995	1-3 v Brazil
Oct 1959	2-3 v Sweden	Feb 1997	0-1 v Italy
Oct 1965	2-3 v Austria	Feb 1998	0-2 v Chile
Apr 1972	1-3 v W Germany	Feb 1999	0-2 v France
Nov 1973	0-1 v Italy	Oct 2000	0-1 v Germany
Feb 1977	0-2 v Holland	Aug 2007	1-2 v Germany
Mar 1981	1-2 v Spain	Nov 2007	2-3 v Croatia
May 1981	0-1 v Brazil	Nov 2010	1-2 v France
Oct 1982	1-2 v W Germany	Feb 2012	2-3 v Holland
Sep 1983	0-1 v Denmark	Nov 2013	0-2 v Chile
Jun 1984	0-2 v Russia	Nov 2013	0-1 v Germany
May 1990	1-2 v Uruguay	Mar 2016	1-2 v Holland
Sep 1991	0-1 v Germany		

A further defeat came in **Euro 96**. After drawing the semi-final with Germany 1-1, England went out 6-5 on penalties.

FASTEST GOALS AT WEMBLEY

In first-class matches: **25 sec** by **Louis Saha** for Everton in 2009 FA Cup Final against Chelsea; **38 sec** by **Bryan Robson** for England's against Yugoslavia in 1989; **42 sec** by **Roberto Di Matteo** for Chelsea in 1997 FA Cup Final v Middlesbrough; **44 sec** by **Bryan Robson** for England v Northern Ireland in 1982.

Fastest goal in **any** match at Wembley: **20 sec** by **Maurice Cox** for Cambridge University against Oxford in 1979.

FOUR WEMBLEY HEADERS

When **Wimbledon** beat Sutton 4-2 in the FA Amateur Cup Final at Wembley on May 4, 1963, Irish centre-forward **Eddie Reynolds** headed all four goals.

WEMBLEY ONE-SEASON DOUBLES

In 1989, **Nottm Forest** became the first club to win two Wembley Finals in the same season (Littlewoods Cup and Simod Cup).

In 1993, **Arsenal** made history there as the first club to win the League (Coca-Cola) Cup and the FA Cup in the same season. They beat Sheffield Wed 2-1 in both finals.

In 2012, **York** won twice at Wembley in nine days at the end of the season, beating Newport 2-0 in the FA Trophy Final and Luton 2-1 in the Conference Play-off Final to return to the Football League.

SUDDEN-DEATH DECIDERS

First Wembley Final decided on sudden death (first goal scored in overtime): Apr 23, 1995 – **Birmingham** beat Carlisle (1-0, Paul Tait 103 mins) to win Auto Windscreens Shield.

First instance of a golden goal deciding a major international tournament was at Wembley on Jun 30, 1996, when **Germany** beat the Czech Republic 2-1 in the European Championship Final with Oliver Bierhoff's goal in the 95th minute.

WEMBLEY'S MOST ONE-SIDED FINAL (in major domestic cups)

Manchester City 6 **Watford** 0 (FA Cup, May 18, 2019).

FOOTBALL TRAGEDIES

DAYS OF TRAGEDY – CLUBS

Season 1988–89 brought the worst disaster in the history of British sport, with the death of 96 Liverpool supporters (200 injured) at the **FA Cup semi-final** against Nottm Forest at **Hillsborough, Sheffield**, on Saturday, Apr 15. The tragedy built up in the minutes preceding kick-off, when thousands surged into the ground at the Leppings Lane end. Many were crushed in the tunnel between entrance and terracing, but most of the victims were trapped inside the perimeter fencing behind the goal. The match was abandoned without score after six minutes' play. The dead included seven women and girls, two teenage sisters and two teenage brothers. The youngest victim was a boy of ten, the oldest 67-year-old Gerard Baron, whose brother Kevin played for Liverpool in the 1950 Cup Final. (*Total became 96 in Mar 1993, when Tony Bland died after being in a coma for nearly four years). A two-year inquest at Warrington ended on April 26, 2016 with the verdict that the 96 were 'unlawfully killed.' It cleared Liverpool fans of any blame and ruled that South Yorkshire Police and South Yorkshire Ambulance Service 'caused or contributed' to the loss of life.

The two worst disasters in one season in British soccer history occurred at the end of 1984–85. On May 11, the last Saturday of the League season, 56 people (two of them visiting supporters) were burned to death – and more than 200 taken to hospital – when fire destroyed the main stand at the **Bradford City–Lincoln** match at Valley Parade.

The wooden, 77-year-old stand was full for City's last fixture before which, amid scenes of celebration, the club had been presented with the Third Division Championship trophy. The fire broke out just before half-time and, within five minutes, the entire stand was engulfed.

Heysel Tragedy

Eighteen days later, on May 29, at the European Cup Final between **Liverpool** and **Juventus** at the Heysel Stadium, Brussels, 39 spectators (31 of them Italian) were crushed or trampled to death and 437 injured. The disaster occurred an hour before the scheduled kick-off when Liverpool supporters charged a Juventus section of the crowd at one end of the stadium, and a retaining wall collapsed. The sequel was a 5-year ban by UEFA on English clubs generally in European competition, with a 6-year ban on Liverpool.

On May 26 1985 ten people were trampled to death and 29 seriously injured in a crowd panic on the way into the **Olympic Stadium, Mexico City** for the Mexican Cup Final between local clubs National University and America.

More than 100 people died and 300 were injured in a football disaster at **Nepal's national stadium** in Katmandu in Mar 1988. There was a stampede when a violent hailstorm broke over the capital. Spectators rushed for cover, but the stadium exits were locked, and hundreds were trampled in the crush.

In South Africa, on Jan 13 1991 40 black fans were trampled to death (50 injured) as they tried to escape from fighting that broke out at a match in the gold-mining town of Orkney, 80 miles from Johannesburg. The friendly, between top teams **Kaiser Chiefs** and **Orlando Pirates**, attracted a packed crowd of 20,000. Violence erupted after the referee allowed Kaiser Chiefs a disputed second-half goal to lead 1-0.

Disaster struck at the French Cup semi-final (May 5, 1992), with the death of 15 spectators and 1,300 injured when a temporary metal stand collapsed in the Corsican town of Bastia. The tie between Second Division **Bastia** and French Champions **Marseille** was cancelled. Monaco, who won the other semi-final, were allowed to compete in the next season's Cup-Winners' Cup.

A total of 318 died and 500 were seriously injured when the crowd rioted over a disallowed goal at the National Stadium in Lima, Peru, on May 24, 1964. **Peru** and **Argentina** were competing to play in the Olympic Games in Tokyo.

That remained **sport's heaviest death** toll until Oct 20, 1982, when (it was revealed only in Jul 1989) 340 Soviet fans were killed in Moscow's Lenin Stadium at the UEFA Cup second round first leg match between **Moscow Spartak** and **Haarlem** (Holland). They were crushed on an open stairway when a last-minute Spartak goal sent departing spectators surging back into the ground.

Among other crowd disasters abroad: Jun, 1968 – 74 died in Argentina. Panic broke out at the end of a goalless match between River Plate and Boca Juniors at Nunez, Buenos Aires, when Boca supporters threw lighted newspaper torches on to fans in the tiers below.

Feb 1974 – 49 killed in **Egypt** in crush of fans clamouring to see Zamalek play Dukla Prague Cup 1971 – 44 died in **Turkey**, when fighting among spectators over a disallowed goal (Kayseri v Siwas) led to a platform collapsing.

The then worst disaster in the history of British football, in terms of loss of life, occurred at Glasgow Rangers' ground at **Ibrox Park**, Jan 2 1971. Sixty-six people were trampled to death (100 injured) as they tumbled down Stairway 13 just before the end of the **Rangers v Celtic** New Year's match. That disaster led to the 1975 Safety of Sports Grounds legislation.

The Ibrox tragedy eclipsed even the Bolton disaster in which 33 were killed and about 500 injured when a wall and crowd barriers collapsed near a corner-flag at the **Bolton v Stoke** FA Cup sixth round tie on Mar 9 1946. The match was completed after half an hour's stoppage.

In a previous crowd disaster at **Ibrox** on Apr 5, 1902, part of the terracing collapsed during the Scotland v England international and 25 people were killed. The match, held up for 20 minutes, ended 1-1, but was never counted as an official international.

Eight leading players and three officials of **Manchester Utd** and eight newspaper representatives were among the 23 who perished in the air crash at **Munich** on Feb 6, 1958, during take-off following a European Cup-tie in Belgrade. The players were Roger Byrne, Geoffrey Bent, Eddie Colman, Duncan Edwards, Mark Jones, David Pegg, Tommy Taylor and Liam Whelan, and the officials were Walter Crickmer (secretary), Tom Curry (trainer) and Herbert Whalley (coach). The newspaper representatives were Alf Clarke, Don Davies, George Follows, Tom Jackson, Archie Ledbrooke, Henry Rose, Eric Thompson and Frank Swift (former England goalkeeper of Manchester City).

On May 14, 1949, the entire team of Italian Champions **Torino**, 8 of them Internationals, were killed when the aircraft taking them home from a match against Benfica in Lisbon crashed at Superga, near Turin. The total death toll of 28 included all the club's reserve players, the manager, trainer and coach.

On Feb 8, 1981, 24 spectators died and more than 100 were injured at a match in **Greece**. They were trampled as thousands of the 40,000 crowd tried to rush out of the stadium at Piraeus after Olympiacos beat AEK Athens 6-0.

On Nov 17, 1982, 24 people (12 of them children) were killed and 250 injured when fans stampeded at the end of a match at the Pascual Guerrero stadium in **Cali, Colombia**. Drunken spectators hurled fire crackers and broken bottles from the higher stands on to people below and started a rush to the exits.

On Dec 9, 1987, the 18-strong team squad of **Alianza Lima**, one of Peru's top clubs, were wiped out, together with 8 officials and several youth players, when a military aircraft taking them home from Puccallpa crashed into the sea off Ventianilla, ten miles from Lima. The only survivor among 43 on board was a member of the crew.

On Apr 28, 1993, 18 members of **Zambia's international squad** and 5 ZFA officials died when the aircraft carrying them to a World Cup qualifying tie against Senegal crashed into the Atlantic soon after take-off from Libreville, Gabon.

On Oct 16 1996, 81 fans were crushed to death and 147 seriously injured in the '**Guatemala Disaster**' at the World Cup qualifier against Costa Rica in Mateo Flores stadium. The tragedy happened an hour before kick-off, allegedly caused by ticket forgery and overcrowding – 60,000 were reported in the 45,000-capacity ground – and safety problems related to perimeter fencing.

On Jul 9, 1996, 8 people died, 39 injured in riot after derby match between **Libya's two top clubs** in Tripoli. Al-Ahli had beaten Al-Ittihad 1-0 by a controversial goal.

On Apr 6, 1997, 5 spectators were crushed to death at **Nigeria's national stadium** in Lagos after the 2-1 World Cup qualifying victory over Guinea. Only two of five gates were reported open as the 40,000 crowd tried to leave the ground.

It was reported from the **Congo** (Oct 29, 1998) that a bolt of lightning struck a village match, killing all 11 members of the home team Benatshadi, but leaving the opposing players from Basangana unscathed. It was believed the surviving team wore better insulated boots.

On Jan 10, 1999, eight fans died and 13 were injured in a stampede at **Egypt's Alexandria Stadium**. Some 25,000 spectators had pushed into the ground. Despite the tragedy, the cup-tie between Al-Ittihad and Al-Koroum was completed.

Three people suffocated and several were seriously injured when thousands of fans forced their way into **Liberia's national stadium** in Monrovia at a goalless World Cup qualifying match against Chad on Apr 23, 2000. The stadium (capacity 33,000) was reported 'heavily overcrowded'.

On Jul 9, 2000, 12 spectators died from crush injuries when police fired tear gas into the 50,000 crowd after South Africa scored their second goal in a World Cup group qualifier against Zimbabwe in **Harare**. A stampede broke out as fans scrambled to leave the national stadium. Players of both teams lay face down on the pitch as fumes swept over them. FIFA launched an investigation and decided that the result would stand, with South Africa leading 2-0 at the time of the 84th-minute abandonment.

On Apr 11, 2001, at one of the biggest matches of the South African season, 43 died and 155 were injured in a crush at **Ellis Park, Johannesburg**. After tearing down a fence, thousands of fans surged into a stadium already packed to its 60,000 capacity for the Premiership derby between top Soweto teams Kaizer Chiefs and Orlando Pirates. The match was abandoned at 1-1 after 33 minutes. In Jan 1991, 40 died in a crowd crush at a friendly between the same clubs at Orkney, 80 miles from Johannesburg.

On Apr 29, 2001, seven people were trampled to death and 51 injured when a riot broke out at a match between two of Congo's biggest clubs, Lupopo and Mazembe at **Lubumbashi**, southern Congo.

On May 6, 2001, two spectators were killed in Iran and hundreds were injured when a glass fibre roof collapsed at the over-crowded Mottaqi Stadium at Sari for the match between Pirouzi and Shemshak Noshahr.

On May 9, 2001, in Africa's worst football disaster, 123 died and 93 were injured in a stampede at the national stadium in **Accra, Ghana**. Home team Hearts of Oak were leading 2-1 against Asante Kotoko five minutes from time, when Asanti fans started hurling bottles on to the pitch. Police fired tear gas into the stands, and the crowd panicked in a rush for the exits, which were locked. It took the death toll at three big matches in Africa in Apr/May to 173.

On Aug 12, 2001, two players were killed by lightning and ten severely burned at a **Guatemala** Third Division match between Deportivo Culquimulilla and Pueblo Nuevo Vinas.

On Nov 1, 2002, two players died from injuries after lightning struck Deportivo Cali's training ground in **Colombia**.

On Mar 12 2004, five people were killed and more than 100 injured when spectators stampeded shortly before the Syrian Championship fixture between Al-Jihad and Al-Fatwa in **Qameshli**, Northern Syria. The match was cancelled.

On Oct 10, 2004, three spectators died in a crush at the African Zone World Cup qualifier between **Guinea** and **Morocco** (1-1) at Conakry, Guinea.

On Mar 25, 2005, five were killed as 100,000 left the Azadi Stadium, **Tehran**, after Iran's World Cup qualifying win (2-1) against Japan.

On Jun 2, 2007, 12 spectators were killed and 46 injured in a crush at the Chillabombwe Stadium, **Zambia**, after an African Nations Cup qualifier against Congo.

On Mar 29, 2009, 19 people died and 139 were injured after a wall collapsed at the Ivory Coast stadium in **Abidjan** before a World Cup qualifier against Malawi. The match went ahead, Ivory Coast winning 5-0 with two goals from Chelsea's Didier Drogba. The tragedy meant that, in 13 years, crowd disasters at club and internationals at ten different grounds across Africa had claimed the lives of 283 people.

On Jan 8, 2010, terrorists at **Cabinda**, Angola machine-gunned the Togo team buses travelling to the Africa Cup of Nations. They killed a driver, an assistant coach and a media officer and injured several players. The team were ordered by their Government to withdraw from the tournament.

On Oct 23, 2010, seven fans were trampled to death when thousands tried to force their way into the Nyayo National Stadium in **Nairobi** at a Kenya Premier League match between the Gor Mahia and AFC Leopards clubs.

On Feb 1, 2012, 74 died and nearly 250 were injured in a crowd riot at the end of the Al-Masry v Al-Ahly match in **Port Said** – the worst disaster in Egyptian sport.

On Nov 28, 2016, 71 died in the worst air crash in world football history when a charter flight carrying players, officials and staff of leading Brazilian club Chapecoense from **Bolivia** to **Colombia** hit a mountain ridge at 8,500 feet. The victims included 65 people from the club.

On Feb 8, 2019, ten young players died when fire engulfed a dormitory at the youth team training centre of one of Brazil's biggest clubs, Flamengo in Rio de Janeiro.

DAYS OF TRAGEDY – PERSONAL

Sam Wynne, Bury right-back, collapsed five minutes before half-time in the First Division match away to Sheffield Utd on Apr 30, 1927, and died in the dressing room.

John Thomson, Celtic and Scotland goalkeeper, sustained a fractured skull when diving at an opponent's feet in the Rangers v Celtic League match on Sep 5, 1931, and died the same evening.

Sim Raleigh (Gillingham), injured in a clash of heads at home to Brighton (Div 3 South) on Dec 1, 1934, continued to play but collapsed in second half and died in hospital the same night.

James Thorpe, Sunderland goalkeeper, was injured during the First Division match at home to Chelsea on Feb 1, 1936 and died in a diabetic coma three days later.

Derek Dooley, Sheffield Wed centre forward and top scorer in 1951–52 in the Football League with 46 goals in 30 matches, broke a leg in the League match at Preston on Feb.14, 1953, and, after complications set in, had to lose the limb by amputation.

John White, Tottenham's Scottish international forward, was killed by lightning on a golf course at Enfield, North London in Jul, 1964.

Tony Allden, Highgate centre-half, was struck by lightning during an Amateur Cup quarter-final with Enfield on Feb 25, 1967. He died the following day. Four other players were also struck but recovered.

Roy Harper died while refereeing the York v Halifax (Div 4) match on May 5, 1969.

Jim Finn collapsed and died from a heart attack while refereeing Exeter v Stockport (Div 4) on Sep 16, 1972.

Scotland manager **Jock Stein**, 62, collapsed and died at the end of the Wales-Scotland World Cup qualifying match (1-1) at Ninian Park, Cardiff on Sep 10, 1985.

David Longhurst, York forward, died after being carried off two minutes before half-time in the Fourth Division fixture at home to Lincoln on Sep 8, 1990. The match was abandoned (0-0). The inquest revealed that Longhurst suffered from a rare heart condition.

Mike North collapsed while refereeing Southend v Mansfield (Div 3) on Apr 16, 2001 and died shortly afterwards. The match was abandoned and re-staged on May 8, with the receipts donated to his family.

Marc-Vivien Foe, on his 63rd appearance in Cameroon's midfield, collapsed unchallenged in the centre circle after 72 minutes of the FIFA Confederations Cup semi-final against Colombia in Lyon, France, on Jun 26, 2003, and despite the efforts of the stadium medical staff he could not be revived. He had been on loan to Manchester City from Olympique Lyonnais in season 2002–03, and poignantly scored the club's last goal at Maine Road.

Paul Sykes, Folkestone Invicta (Ryman League) striker, died on the pitch during the Kent Senior Cup semi-final against Margate on Apr 12, 2005. He collapsed after an innocuous off-the-ball incident.

Craig Gowans, Falkirk apprentice, was killed at the club's training ground on Jul 8, 2005 when he came into contact with power lines.

Peter Wilson, Mansfield goalkeeping coach, died of a heart attack after collapsing during the warm-up of the League Two game away to Shrewsbury on Nov 19, 2005.

Matt Gadsby, Hinckley defender, collapsed and died while playing in a Conference North match at Harrogate on Sep 9, 2006.

Phil O'Donnell, 35-year old Motherwell captain and Scotland midfield player, collapsed when about to be substituted near the end of the SPL home game against Dundee Utd on Dec 29, 2007 and died shortly afterwards in hospital.

Vichai Srivaddhanaprabha, Leicester owner, died in a helicopter crash following the club's

Premier League match against West Ham. The pilot and three others on board also died in the crash outside the King Power Stadium, seconds after the helicopter's take-off from the pitch on Oct 27, 2018.

Emiliano Sala, Argentine striker, died in a plane crash in the English Channel on Jan 21, 2019 two days after signing for Cardiff from Nantes. The pilot of the light aircraft also died.

Jose Antonio Reyes, part of the Arsenal 'Invincibles' side that went through season 2003–04 unbeaten, died in a car crash in Spain on Jun 1, 2019.

Justin Edinburgh, Leyton Orient manager, suffered a cardiac arrest and died five days later on June 8, 2019.

GREAT SERVICE

'For services to Association Football', **Stanley Matthews** (Stoke, Blackpool and England), already a CBE, became the first professional footballer to receive a knighthood. This was bestowed in 1965, his last season. Before he retired and five days after his 50th birthday, he played for Stoke to set a record as the oldest First Division footballer (v Fulham, Feb 6, 1965).

Over a brilliant span of 33 years, he played in 886 first-class matches, including 54 full Internationals (plus 31 in war time), 701 League games (including 3 at start of season 1939–40, which was abandoned on the outbreak of war) and 86 FA Cup-ties, and scored 95 goals. He was never booked in his career.

Sir Stanley died on Feb 23, 2000, three weeks after his 85th birthday. His ashes were buried under the centre circle of Stoke's Britannia Stadium. After spending a number of years in Toronto, he made his home back in the Potteries in 1989, having previously returned to his home town, Hanley in Oct, 1987 to unveil a life-size bronze statue of himself. The inscription reads: 'Sir Stanley Matthews, CBE. Born Hanley, 1 Feb 1915.'

His name is symbolic of the beauty of the game, his fame timeless and international, his sportsmanship and modesty universally acclaimed. A magical player, of the people, for the people.' On his home-coming in 1989, Sir Stanley was made President of Stoke, the club he joined as a boy of 15 and served as a player for 20 years between 1931 and 1965, on either side of his spell with Blackpool.

In Jul 1992 FIFA honoured him with their 'Gold merit award' for outstanding services to the game.

Former England goalkeeper **Peter Shilton** has made more first-class appearances (1,387) than any other footballer in British history. He played his 1,000th. League game in Leyton Orient's 2-0 home win against Brighton on Dec 22, 1996 and made 9 appearances for Orient in his final season. He retired from international football after the 1990 World Cup in Italy with 125 caps, then a world record. Shilton kept a record 60 clean sheets for England.

Shilton's career spanned 32 seasons, 20 of them on the international stage. He made his League debut for Leicester in May 1966, two months before England won the World Cup.

His 1,387 first-class appearances comprise a record 1,005 in the Football League, 125 Internationals, 102 League Cup, 86 FA Cup, 13 for England U-23s, 4 for the Football League and 52 other matches (European Cup, UEFA Cup, World Club Championship, Charity Shield, European Super Cup, Full Members' Cup, Play-offs, Screen Sports Super Cup, Anglo-Italian Cup, Texaco Cup, Simod Cup, Zenith Data Systems Cup and Autoglass Trophy).

Shilton appeared 57 times at Wembley, 52 for England, 2 League Cup Finals, 1 FA Cup Final, 1 Charity Shield match, and 1 for the Football League. He passed a century of League appearances with each of his first five clubs: Leicester (286), Stoke (110), Nottm Forest (202), Southampton (188) and Derby (175) and subsequently played for Plymouth, Bolton and Leyton Orient.

He was awarded the MBE and OBE for services to football. At the Football League Awards ceremony in March 2013, he received the League's Contribution award.

Six other British footballers have made more than 1,000 first-class appearances:

Ray Clemence, formerly with Tottenham, Liverpool and England, retired through injury in season 1987–88 after a goalkeeping career of 1,119 matches starting in 1965–66.

Clemence played 50 times for his first club, Scunthorpe; 665 for Liverpool; 337 for Tottenham; his 67 representative games included 61 England caps.

A third great British goalkeeper, **Pat Jennings**, ended his career (1963–86) with a total of 1,098 first-class matches for Watford, Tottenham, Arsenal and N Ireland. They were made up of 757 in the Football League, 119 full Internationals, 84 FA Cup appearances, 72 League/ Milk Cup, 55 European club matches, 2 Charity Shield, 3 Other Internationals, 1 Under-23 cap, 2 Texaco Cup, 2 Anglo-Italian Cup and 1 Super Cup. Jennings played his 119th and final international on his 41st birthday, Jun 12, 1986, against Brazil in Guadalajara in the Mexico World Cup.

Yet another outstanding 'keeper, **David Seaman**, passed the 1,000 appearances milestone for clubs and country in season 2002–03, reaching 1,004 when aged 39, he captained Arsenal to FA Cup triumph against Southampton.

With Arsenal, Seaman won 3 Championship medals, the FA Cup 4 times, the Double twice, the League Cup and Cup-Winners' Cup once each. After 13 seasons at Highbury, he joined Manchester City (Jun 2003) on a free transfer. He played 26 matches for City before a shoulder injury forced his retirement in Jan 2004, aged 40.

Seaman's 22-season career composed 1,046 first-class matches: 955 club apps (Peterborough 106, Birmingham 84, QPR 175, Arsenal 564, Manchester City 26); 75 senior caps for England, 6 'B' caps and 10 at U-21 level.

Defender **Graeme Armstrong**, 42-year-old commercial manager for an Edinburgh whisky company and part-time assistant manager and captain of Scottish Third Division club Stenhousemuir, made the 1000th first team appearance of his career in the Scottish Cup 3rd Round against Rangers at Ibrox on Jan 23, 1999. He was presented with the Man of the Match award before kick-off.

Against East Stirling on Boxing Day, he had played his 864th League game, breaking the British record for an outfield player set by another Scot, Tommy Hutchison, with Alloa, Blackpool, Coventry, Manchester City, Burnley and Swansea City.

Armstrong's 24-year career, spent in the lower divisions of the Scottish League, began as a 1 match trialist with Meadowbank Thistle in 1975 and continued via Stirling Albion, Berwick Rangers, Meadowbank and, from 1992, Stenhousemuir.

Tony Ford became the first English outfield player to reach 1000 senior appearances in Rochdale's 1-0 win at Carlisle (Auto Windscreens Shield) on Mar 7, 2000. Grimsby-born, he began his 26-season midfield career with Grimsby and played for 7 other League clubs: Sunderland (loan), Stoke, WBA, Bradford City (loan), Scunthorpe, Mansfield and Rochdale. He retired, aged 42, in 2001 with a career record of 1072 appearances (121 goals) and his total of 931 League games is exceeded only by Peter Shilton's 1005.

On Apr 16, 2011, **Graham Alexander** reached 1,000 appearances when he came on as a sub for Burnley at home to Swansea. Alexander, 40, ended a 22-year career with the equaliser for Preston against Charlton (2 2, Lge 1) on Apr 28, 2012 – his 1,023rd appearance. He also played for Luton and Scunthorpe and was capped 40 times by Scotland.

RECORD FOR BARRY

Gareth Barry surpassed Ryan Giggs's record of 632 Premier League appearances in West Bromwich Albion's 2-0 defeat by Arsenal in the 2017–18 season.

GIGGS RECORD COLLECTION

Ryan Giggs (Manchester Utd) has collected the most individual honours in English football with a total of 34 prizes. They comprise: 13 Premier League titles, 4 FA Cups, 3 League Cups, 2 European Cups, 1 UEFA Super Cup, 1 Inter-Continental Cup, 1 World Club Cup, 9 Charity Shields/ Community Shields. One-club man Giggs played 24 seasons for United, making a record 963 appearances. He won 64 Wales caps and on retiring as a player, aged 40, in May 2014, became the club's assistant manager. He ended a 29-year association with the club in June 2016.

KNIGHTS OF SOCCER

Players, managers and administrators who have been honoured for their services to football:

Charles Clegg (1927), **Stanley Rous** (1949), **Stanley Matthews** (1965), **Alf Ramsey** (1967), **Matt Busby** (1968), **Walter Winterbottom** (1978) **Bert Millichip** (1991), **Bobby Charlton** (1994), Tom Finney (1998), **Geoff Hurst** (1998), **Alex Ferguson** (1999), **Bobby Robson** (2002), **Trevor Brooking** (2004), **Dave Richards** (2006), **Doug Ellis** (2011), **Kenny Dalglish** (2018).

● On Nov 6, 2014, **Karren Brady**, vice-chairman of West Ham, was elevated to the Lords as Karren, Baroness Brady, OBE, of Knightsbridge, life peer

PENALTIES

The **penalty-kick** was introduced to the game, following a proposal to the Irish FA in 1890 by William McCrum, son of the High Sheriff for Co Omagh, and approved by the International Football Board on Jun 2, 1891.

First penalty scored in a first-class match in England was by John Heath, for Wolves v Accrington Stanley (5-0 in Div 1, Sep 14, 1891).

The greatest influence of the penalty has come since the 1970s, with the introduction of the shoot-out to settle deadlocked ties in various competitions.

Manchester Utd were the first club to win a competitive match in British football via a shoot-out (4-3 away to Hull, Watney Cup semi-final, Aug 5, 1970); in that penalty contest, George Best was the first player to score, Denis Law the first to miss.

The shoot-out was adopted by FIFA and UEFA the same year (1970).

In season 1991–92, penalty shoot-outs were introduced to decide FA Cup ties still level after one replay and extra time.

Wembley saw its first penalty contest in the 1974 Charity Shield. Since then many major matches across the world have been settled in this way, including:

1976	**European Championship Final (Belgrade):** Czechoslovakia beat West Germany 5-3 (after 2-2)
1980	**Cup-Winners' Cup Final (Brussels):** Valencia beat Arsenal 5-4 (after 0-0)
1984	**European Cup Final (Rome):** Liverpool beat Roma 4-2 (after 1-1)
1984	**UEFA Cup Final:** Tottenham (home) beat Anderlecht 4-3 (2-2 agg)
1986	**European Cup Final (Seville):** Steaua Bucharest beat Barcelona 2-0 (after 0-0).
1987	**Freight Rover Trophy Final (Wembley):** Mansfield beat Bristol City 5-4 (after 1-1)
1987	**Scottish League Cup Final (Hampden Park):** Rangers beat Aberdeen 5-3 (after 3-3)
1988	**European Cup Final (Stuttgart):** PSV Eindhoven beat Benfica 6-5 (after 0-0)
1988	**UEFA Cup Final:** Bayer Leverkusen (home) beat Espanyol 3-2 after 3-3 (0-3a, 3-0h)
1990	**Scottish Cup Final (Hampden Park):** Aberdeen beat Celtic 9-8 (after 0-0)
1991	**European Cup Final (Bari):** Red Star Belgrade beat Marseille 5-3 (after 0-0)
1991	**Div 4 Play-off Final (Wembley):** Torquay beat Blackpool 5-4 (after 2-2)
1992	**Div 4 Play-off Final (Wembley):** Blackpool beat Scunthorpe 4-3 (after 1-1)
1993	**Div 3 Play-off Final(Wembley):** York beat Crewe 5-3 (after 1-1)
1994	**Autoglass Trophy Final (Wembley):** Swansea City beat Huddersfield 3-1 (after 1-1)
1994	**World Cup Final (Los Angeles):** Brazil beat Italy 3-2 (after 0-0)
1994	**Scottish League Cup Final (Ibrox Park):** Raith beat Celtic 6-5 (after 2-2)
1995	**Copa America Final (Montevideo):** Uruguay beat Brazil 5-3 (after 1-1)
1996	**European Cup Final (Rome):** Juventus beat Ajax 4-2 (after 1-1)
1996	**European U-21 Champ Final (Barcelona):** Italy beat Spain 4-2 (after 1-1)
1997	**Auto Windscreens Shield Final (Wembley):** Carlisle beat Colchester 4-3 (after 0-0)
1997	**UEFA Cup Final:** FC Schalke beat Inter Milan 4-1 (after 1-1 agg)
1998	**Div 1 Play-off Final (Wembley):** Charlton beat Sunderland 7-6 (after 4-4)
1999	**Div 2 Play-off Final (Wembley):** Manchester City beat Gillingham 3-1 (after 2-2)
1999	**Women's World Cup Final (Pasedena):** USA beat China 5-4 (after 0-0)
2000	**African Nations Cup Final (Lagos):** Cameroon beat Nigeria 4-3 (after 0-0)
2000	**UEFA Cup Final (Copenhagen):** Galatasaray beat Arsenal 4-1 (after 0-0)
2000	**Olympic Final (Sydney):** Cameroon beat Spain 5-3 (after 2-2)

2001	**League Cup Final (Millennium Stadium):** Liverpool beat Birmingham 5-4 (after 1-1)

2001   **League Cup Final (Millennium Stadium):** Liverpool beat
Birmingham 5-4 (after 1-1)
2001   **Champions League Final (Milan):** Bayern Munich beat Valencia 5-4 (after 1-1)
2002   **Euro U-21 Champ Final (Basle):** Czech Republic beat France 3-1 (after 0-0)
2002   **Div 1 Play-off Final (Millennium Stadium):** Birmingham beat Norwich 4-2 (after 1-1)
2003   **Champions League Final (Old Trafford):** AC Milan beat Juventus 3-2 (after 0-0)
2004   **Div 3 Play-off Final (Millennium Stadium):** Huddersfield beat Mansfield 4-1 (after 0-0)
2004   **Copa America Final (Lima):** Brazil beat Argentina 4-2 (after 2-2)
2005   **FA Cup Final (Millennium Stadium):** Arsenal beat Manchester Utd 5-4 (after 0-0)
2005   **Champions League Final (Istanbul):** Liverpool beat AC Milan 3-2 (after 3-3)
2006   **African Cup of Nations Final (Cairo):** Egypt beat Ivory Coast 4-2 (after 0-0)
2006   **FA Cup Final (Millennium Stadium):** Liverpool beat West Ham 3-1 (after 3-3)
2006   **Scottish Cup Final (Hampden Park):** Hearts beat Gretna 4-2 (after 1-1)
2006   **Lge 1 Play-off Final (Millennium Stadium):** Barnsley beat Swansea City 4-3 (after 2-2)
2006   **World Cup Final (Berlin):** Italy beat France 5-3 (after 1-1)
2007   **UEFA Cup Final (Hampden Park):** Sevilla beat Espanyol 3-1 (after 2-2)
2008   **Champions League Final (Moscow):** Manchester Utd beat Chelsea 6-5 (after 1-1)
2008   **Scottish League Cup Final (Hampden Park):** Rangers beat Dundee Utd 3-2 (after 2-2)
2009   **League Cup Final (Wembley):** Manchester Utd beat Tottenham 4-1 (after 0-0)
2011   **Women's World Cup Final (Frankfurt):** Japan beat USA 3-1 (after 2-2)
2012   **League Cup Final (Wembley):** Liverpool beat Cardiff 3-2 (after 2-2)
2012   **Champions League Final (Munich):** Chelsea beat Bayern Munich 4-3 (after 1-1)
2012   **Lge 1 Play-off Final (Wembley):** Huddersfield beat Sheffield Utd 8-7 (after 0-0)
2012   **Africa Cup of Nations Final (Gabon):** Zambia beat Ivory Coast 8-7 (after 0-0)
2013   **FA Trophy Final (Wembley):** Wrexham beat Grimsby 4-1 (after 1-1)
2013   **European Super Cup (Prague):** Bayern Munich beat Chelsea 5-4 (after 2-2)
2014   **Scottish League Cup Final (Celtic Park):** Aberdeen beat Inverness 4-2 (after 0-0)
2014   **Lge 1 Play-off Final (Wembley):** Rotherham beat Leyton Orient 4-3 (after 2-2)
2014   **Europa Lge Final (Turin):** Sevilla beat Benfica 4-2 (after 0-0)
2015   **Africa Cup of Nations Final (Equ Guinea):** Ivory Coast beat Ghana 9-8 (after 0-0)
2015   **Conference Play-off Final (Wembley):** Bristol Rov beat Grimsby 5-3 (after 1-1)
2015   **Lge 2 Play-off Final (Wembley):** Southend beat Wycombe 7-6 (after 1-1)
2015   **FA Trophy Final (Wembley)** North Ferriby beat Wrexham 5-4 (after 3-3)
2015   **Euro U-21 Champ Final (Prague):** Sweden beat Portugal 4-3 (after 0-0)
2015   **Copa America Final (Santiago):** Chile beat Argentina 4-1 (after 0-0)
2016   **League Cup Final (Wembley):** Manchester City beat Liverpool 3-1 (after 1-1)
2016   **Champions League Final (Milan):** Real Madrid beat Atletico Madrid 5-3 (after 1-1)
2016   **Olympic Men's Final (Rio de Janeiro):** Brazil beat Germany 5-4 (after 1-1)
2017   **Champ Play-off Final (Wembley):** Huddersfield beat Reading 4-3 (after 0-0)
2017   **Community Shield (Wembley):** Arsenal beat Chelsea 4-1 (after 1-1)
2019   **League Cup Final (Wembley):** Manchester City beat Chelsea 4-3 (after 0-0)
2019   **Football League Trophy Final (Wembley):** Portsmouth beat Sunderland 5-4 (after 2-2)

In South America In 1992, in a 26-shot competition, **Newell's Old Boys** beat America 11-10 in the Copa Libertadores.

Longest-recorded penalty contest in first-class matches was in Argentina in 1988 – from 44 shots, **Argentinos Juniors** beat Racing Club 20-19. Genclerbirligi beat Galatasaray 17-16 in a Turkish Cup-tie in 1996. Only one penalty was missed.

Highest-scoring shoot-outs in international football: **North Korea** beat Hong Kong 11-10 (after 3-3 draw) in an Asian Cup match in 1975; and **Ivory Coast** beat Ghana 11-10 (after 0-0 draw) in African Nations Cup Final, 1992.

Most penalties needed to settle an adult game in Britain: **44** in Norfolk Primary Cup 4th round replay, Dec 2000. Aston Village side **Freethorpe** beat Foulsham 20-19 (5 kicks missed). All 22 players took 2 penalties each, watched by a crowd of 20. The sides had drawn 2-2, 4-4 in a tie of 51 goals.

Penalty that took 24 days: That was how long elapsed between the award and the taking of a penalty in an Argentine Second Division match between **Atalanta** and Defensors in 2003. A riot ended the original match with 5 minutes left. The game resumed behind closed doors with the penalty that caused the abandonment. Lucas Ferreiro scored it to give Atalanta a 1-0 win.

INTERNATIONAL PENALTIES, MISSED

Four penalties out of five were missed when **Colombia** beat Argentina 3-0 in a Copa America group tie in Paraguay in Jul 1999. Martin Palmermo missed three for Argentina and Colombia's Hamilton Ricard had one spot kick saved.

In the European Championship semi-final against Italy in Amsterdam on Jun 29, 2000, **Holland** missed five penalties – two in normal time, three in the penalty contest which Italy won 3-1 (after 0-0). Dutch captain Frank de Boer missed twice from the spot.

ENGLAND'S SHOOT-OUT RECORD

England have been beaten in eight out of 11 penalty shoot-outs in major tournaments:

1990 (World Cup semi-final, Turin) 3-4 v West Germany after 1-1.
1996 (Euro Champ quarter-final, Wembley) 4-2 v Spain after 0-0.
1996 (Euro Champ semi-final, Wembley) 5-6 v Germany after 1-1.
1998 (World Cup 2nd round., St Etienne) 3-4 v Argentina after 2-2.
2004 (Euro Champ quarter-final, Lisbon) 5-6 v Portugal after 2-2.
2006 (World Cup quarter-final, Gelsenkirchen) 1-3 v Portugal after 0-0.
2007 (Euro U-21 Champ semi-final, Heerenveen) 12-13 v Holland after 1-1.
2009 (Euro U-21 Champ semi-final, Gothenburg) 5-4 v Sweden after 3-3.
2012 (Euro Champ quarter-final, Kiev) 2-4 v Italy after 0-0.
2017 (Euro-21 Champ semi-final, Tychy) 3-4 v Germany after 2-2.
2018 (World Cup round of 16, Moscow) 4-3 v Colombia after 1-1.
2019 (Nations Lge, third-place play-off, Guimaraes) 6-5 v Switzerland after 0-0

FA CUP SHOOT-OUTS

First penalty contest in the FA Cup took place in 1972. In the days of the play-off for third place, the match was delayed until the eve of the following season when losing semi-finalists Birmingham and Stoke met at St Andrew's on Aug 5. The score was 0-0 and Birmingham won 4-3 on penalties.

Highest-scoring: Preliminary round replay (Aug 30, 2005): Tunbridge Wells beat Littlehampton 16-15 after 40 spot-kicks (9 missed).

Competition proper: Scunthorpe beat Worcester 14-13 in 2nd round replay (Dec 17, 2014) after 1-1 (32 kicks).

Shoot-out abandoned: The FA Cup 1st round replay between Oxford City and Wycombe at Wycombe on Nov 9, 1999 was abandoned (1-1) after extra-time. As the penalty shoot-out was about to begin, a fire broke out under a stand. Wycombe won the second replay 1-0 at Oxford Utd's ground.

First FA Cup Final to be decided by shoot-out was in 2005 (May 21), when Arsenal beat Manchester Utd 5-4 on penalties at Cardiff's Millennium Stadium (0-0 after extra time). A year later (May 13) Liverpool beat West Ham 3-1 (3-3 after extra-time).

MARATHON SHOOT-OUT BETWEEN LEAGUE CLUBS

Highest recorded score in shoot-out between league clubs: Dagenham & Redbridge 14-13 against Leyton Orient (after 1-1) in Johnstone's Paint Trophy southern section on Sep 7, 2011

SHOOT-OUT RECORD WINNERS AND LOSERS

When **Bradford** beat Arsenal 3-2 on penalties in a League Cup fifth round tie, it was the club's ninth successive shoot-out victory in FA Cup, League Cup and Johnstone's Paint Trophy ties between Oct 2009 and Dec 2012.

Tottenham's 4-1 spot-kick failure against Basel in the last 16 of the Europa League was their seventh successive defeat in shoot-outs from Mar 1996 to Apr 2013 (FA Cup, League Cup, UEFA Cup, Europa League)

MISSED CUP FINAL PENALTIES

John Aldridge (Liverpool) became the first player to miss a penalty in an FA Cup Final at Wembley when Dave Beasant saved his shot in 1988 to help Wimbledon to a shock 1-0 win. Seven penalties before had been scored in the Final at Wembley.

Previously, **Charlie Wallace**, of Aston Villa, had failed from the spot in the 1913 Final against Sunderland at Crystal Palace, which his team won 1-0

Gary Lineker (Tottenham) had his penalty saved by Nottm Forest's Mark Crossley in the 1991 FA Cup Final.

For the first time, two spot-kicks were missed in an FA Cup Final. In 2010, Petr Cech saved from Portsmouth's **Kevin-Prince Boateng** while Chelsea's **Frank Lampard** put his kick wide.

Another miss at Wembley was by Arsenal's **Nigel Winterburn**, Luton's Andy Dibble saving his spot-kick in the 1988 Littlewoods Cup Final, when a goal would have put Arsenal 3-1 ahead. Instead, they lost 3-2.

Winterburn was the third player to fail with a League Cup Final penalty at Wembley, following **Ray Graydon** (Aston Villa) against Norwich in 1975 and **Clive Walker** (Sunderland), who shot wide in the 1985 Milk Cup Final, also against Norwich who won 1-0. Graydon had his penalty saved by Kevin Keelan, but scored from the rebound and won the cup for Aston Villa (1-0).

Derby's Martin Taylor saved a penalty from **Eligio Nicolini** in the Anglo-Italian Cup Final at Wembley on Mar 27, 1993, but Cremonese won 3-1.

LEAGUE PENALTIES RECORD

Most penalties in Football League match: Five – 4 to Crystal Palace (3 missed), 1 to Brighton (scored) in Div 2 match at Selhurst Park on Mar 27 (Easter Monday), 1989. Crystal Palace won 2-1. Three of the penalties were awarded in a 5-minute spell. The match also produced 5 bookings and a sending-off. Other teams missing 3 penalties in a match: Burnley v Grimsby (Div 2), Feb 13, 1909, Manchester City v Newcastle (Div 1), Jan 17, 1912.

HOTTEST MODERN SPOT-SHOTS

Matthew Le Tissier ended his career in season 2001–02 with the distinction of having netted 48 out of 49 first team penalties for Southampton. He scored the last 27 after his only miss when Nottm Forest keeper Mark Crossley saved in a Premier League match at The Dell on Mar 24, 1993.

Graham Alexander scored 78 out of 84 penalties in a 22-year career (Scunthorpe, Luton, Preston twice and Burnley) which ended in 2012.

SPOT-KICK HAT-TRICKS

Right-back **Joe Willetts** scored three penalties when Hartlepool beat Darlington 6-1 (Div 3N) on Good Friday 1951.

Danish international **Jan Molby's** only hat-trick in English football, for Liverpool in a 3-1 win at home to Coventry (Littlewoods Cup, 4th round replay, Nov 26, 1986) comprised three goals from the penalty spot.

It was the first such hat-trick in a major match for two years – since **Andy Blair** scored three penalties for Sheffield Wed against Luton (Milk Cup 4th round, Nov 20 1984).

Portsmouth's **Kevin Dillon** scored a penalty hat-trick in the Full Members Cup (2nd round) at home to Millwall (3-2) on Nov 4, 1986.

Alan Slough scored a hat-trick of penalties in an away game, but was on the losing side, when Peterborough were beaten 4-3 at Chester (Div 3, Apr 29, 1978).

Josh Wright's three penalties in the space of 11 minutes enabled Gillingham to come from 2-0 down to defeat his former club Scunthorpe 3-2 in League One on Mar 11, 2017.

Penalty hat-tricks in **international football: Dimitris Saravakos** (in 9 mins) for Greece v Egypt in 1990. He scored 5 goals in match. **Henrik Larsson**, among his 4 goals in Sweden's 6-0 home win v Moldova in World Cup qualifying match, Jun 6, 2001.

MOST PENALTY GOALS (LEAGUE) IN SEASON

13 out of 13 by **Francis Lee** for Manchester City (Div 1) in 1971-72. His goal total for the

season was 33. In season 1988–89, **Graham Roberts** scored 12 League penalties for Second Division Champions Chelsea. In season 2004–05, **Andrew Johnson** scored 11 Premier League penalties for Crystal Palace, who were relegated.

PENALTY-SAVE SEQUENCES

Ipswich goalkeeper **Paul Cooper** saved eight of the ten penalties he faced in 1979–80. **Roy Brown** (Notts Co) saved six in a row in season 1972–73.

Andy Lomas, goalkeeper for Chesham (Diadora League) claimed a record eighth **consecutive** penalty saves – three at the end of season 1991–92 and five in 1992–93.

Mark Bosnich (Aston Villa) saved five in two consecutive matches in 1993–94: three in Coca-Cola Cup semi-final penalty shoot-out v Tranmere (Feb 26), then two in Premier League at Tottenham (Mar 2).

MISSED PENALTIES SEQUENCE

Against Wolves in Div 2 on Sep 28, 1991, **Southend** missed their seventh successive penalty (five of them the previous season).

SCOTTISH RECORDS
(See also under 'Goals' & 'Discipline')

CELTIC SUPREME

In winning the Treble for the fourth time in 2016–17, **Celtic** rewrote the Scottish records. In the first season under **Brendan Rodgers**, previously Liverpool manager, they did not lose a domestic match, the first to stay unbeaten in the league since Rangers in 1899. They set new records for points (106), goals (106), victories (34) and for a 30-point winning margin. In 2017–18, Celtic became the first in Scotland to win back-to-back domestic trebles and stretched an unbeaten run to a British record 69 games in domestic competitions. Their 25 consecutive victories in season 2003–04 also represents a British best, while the 1966–67 record was the most successful by a British side in one season. They won the Treble and became the first to win the European Cup. Under Jock Stein, there were nine titles in a row (1966–74). In season 2018–19, Celtic completed a third successive domestic treble, this one under **Brendan Rodgers** and **Neil Lennon**, who took over when Rodgers left to become Leicester manager in late February. The club have now been champions 50 times, SFA Cup winners on 39 occasions and League Cup winners in 18 seasons.

RANGERS' MANY RECORDS

Rangers' record-breaking feats include:

League Champions: 54 times (once joint holders) – world record.

Winning every match in Scottish League (18 games, 1898–99 season).

Major hat-tricks: Rangers have completed the domestic treble (League Championship, League Cup and Scottish FA Cup) a record seven times (1948–49, 1963–64, 1975–76, 1977–78, 1992–93, 1998–99, 2002–03).

League & Cup double: 17 times.

Nine successive Championships (1989–97). Four men played in all nine sides: Richard Gough, Ally McCoist, Ian Ferguson and Ian Durrant.

115 major trophies: Championships 54, Scottish Cup 33, League Cup 27, Cup-Winners' Cup 1.

UNBEATEN SCOTTISH CHAMPIONS

Celtic and **Rangers** have each won the Scottish Championship with an unbeaten record: Celtic in 1897–98 (P18, W15, D3), Rangers in 1898–99 (P18, W18).

FORSTER'S SHUT-OUT RECORD

Celtic goalkeeper **Fraser Forster** set a record in Scottish top-flight football by not conceding a goal for 1,256 consecutive minutes in season 2013–14.

TRIO OF TOP CLUBS MISSING

Three of Scotland's leading clubs were missing from the 2014–15 Premiership season. With **Hearts** finishing bottom and **Rangers** still working their way back through the divisions after being demoted, they were joined in the second tier by **Hibernian**, who lost the play-off final on penalties to Hamilton.

SCOTTISH CUP HAT-TRICKS

Aberdeen's feat of winning the Scottish FA Cup in 1982–83–84 made them only the third club to achieve that particular hat-trick. **Queen's Park** did it twice (1874–75–76 and 1880–81–82), and **Rangers** have won the Scottish Cup three years in succession on three occasions: 1934–35–36, 1948–49–50 and 1962–63–64.

SCOTTISH CUP FINAL DISMISSALS

Five players have been sent off in the Scottish FA Cup Final: **Jock Buchanan** (Rangers v Kilmarnock, 1929); **Roy Aitken** (Celtic v Aberdeen, 1984); **Walter Kidd** (Hearts captain v Aberdeen, 1986); **Paul Hartley** (Hearts v Gretna, 2006); **Pa Kujabi** (Hibernian v Hearts, 2012); **Carl Tremarco** (Inverness v Falkirk, 2015).

HIGHEST-SCORING SHOOT-OUT

In Scottish football's highest-scoring penalty shoot out, **Stirling Albion** beat junior club Hurlford 13-12 after 28 spot-kicks in a third round replay. The tie, on Nov 8, 2014, had ended 2-2 after extra-time.

RECORD SEQUENCES

Celtic hold Britain's League record of 62 matches undefeated, from Nov 13, 1915 to Apr 21, 1917, when Kilmarnock won 2-0 at Parkhead. They won 49, drew 13 (111 points) and scored 126 goals to 26.
Greenock Morton in 1963–64 accumulated 67 points out of 72 and scored 135 goals.
Queen's Park did not have a goal scored against them during the first seven seasons of their existence (1867–74, before the Scottish League was formed).

EARLIEST PROMOTIONS IN SCOTLAND

Dundee promoted from Div 2, Feb 1, 1947; **Greenock Morton** promoted from Div 2, Mar 2, 1964; **Gretna** promoted from Div 3, Mar 5, 2005; **Hearts** promoted from Championship, Mar 21, 2015.

WORST HOME SEQUENCE

After gaining promotion to Div 1 in 1992, **Cowdenbeath** went a record 38 consecutive home League matches without a win. They ended the sequence (drew 8, lost 30) when beating Arbroath 1-0 on Apr 2, 1994, watched by a crowd of 225.

ALLY'S RECORDS

Ally McCoist became the first player to complete 200 goals in the Premier Division when he scored Rangers' winner (2-1) at Falkirk on Dec 12, 1992. His first was against Celtic in Sep 1983, and he reached 100 against Dundee on Boxing Day 1987.
When McCoist scored twice at home to Hibernian (4-3) on Dec 7, 1996, he became Scotland's record post-war League marksman, beating Gordon Wallace's 264.
Originally with St Johnstone (1978–81), he spent two seasons with Sunderland (1981–83), then joined Rangers for £200,000 in Jun 1983.
In 15 seasons at Ibrox, he scored 355 goals for Rangers (250 League), and helped them win 10 Championships (9 in succession), 3 Scottish Cups and earned a record 9 League Cup winner's medals. He won the European Golden Boot in consecutive seasons (1991–92, 1992–93).
His 9 Premier League goals in three seasons for Kilmarnock gave him a career total of 281

Scottish League goals when he retired at the end of 2000–01. McCoist succeeded Walter Smith as manager of Rangers in May 2011.

SCOTLAND'S MOST SUCCESSFUL MANAGER

Bill Struth, 30 trophies for Rangers, 1920–54 (18 Championships, 10 Scottish Cups, 2 League Cups.

SMITH'S IBROX HONOURS

Walter Smith, who retired in May, 2011, won a total of 21 trophies in two spells as Rangers manager (10 League titles, 5 Scottish Cups, 6 League Cups).

RANGERS PUNISHED

In April 2012, **Rangers** (in administration) were fined £160,000 by the Scottish FA and given a 12-month transfer ban on charges relating to their finances. The ban was later overturned in court. The club had debts estimated at around £135m and on June 12, 2012 were forced into liquidation. A new company emerged, but Rangers were voted out of the Scottish Premier League and demoted to Division Three for the start of the 2012-13 season. They returned to the top division in 2016 via three promotions in four seasons.

FIVE IN A MATCH

Paul Sturrock set an individual scoring record for the Scottish Premier Division with 5 goals in Dundee Utd's 7-0 win at home to Morton on Nov 17, 1984. **Marco Negri** equalled the feat with all 5 when Rangers beat Dundee Utd 5-1 at Ibrox (Premier Division) on Aug 23, 1997, and **Kenny Miller** scored 5 in Rangers' 7-1 win at home to St Mirren on Nov 4, 2000. **Kris Boyd** scored all Kilmarnock's goals in a 5-2 SPL win at home to Dundee Utd on Sep 25, 2004. **Boyd** scored another 5 when Rangers beat Dundee Utd 7-1 on Dec 30, 2009. That took his total of SPL goals to a record 160. **Gary Hooper** netted all Celtic's goals in 5-0 SPL win against Hearts on May 13, 2012

NEGRI'S TEN-TIMER

Marco Negri scored in Rangers' first ten League matches (23 goals) in season 1997–98, a Premier Division record. The previous best was 8 by **Ally MacLeod** for Hibernian in 1978.

DOUBLE SCOTTISH FINAL

Rangers v Celtic drew **129,643** and **120,073** people to the Scottish Cup Final and replay at Hampden Park, Glasgow, in 1963. Receipts for the two matches totalled £50,500.

MOST SCOTTISH CHAMPIONSHIP MEDALS

13 by **Sandy Archibald** (Rangers, 1918–34). Post-war record: 10 by **Bobby Lennox** (Celtic, 1966–79).

Alan Morton won **nine** Scottish Championship medals with Rangers in 1921–23–24–25–27–28–29–30–31. **Ally McCoist** played in the Rangers side that won nine successive League titles (1989–97).

Between 1927 and 1939 **Bob McPhail** helped Rangers win nine Championships, finish second twice and third once. He scored 236 League goals but was never top scorer in a single season.

TOP SCOTTISH LEAGUE SCORERS IN SEASON

Raith Rovers (Div 2) 142 goals in 1937–38; **Morton** (Div 2) 135 goals in 1963–64; **Hearts** (Div 1) 132 goals in 1957–58; **Falkirk** (Div 2) 132 goals in 1935–36; **Gretna** (Div 3) 130 goals in 2004–05.

SCOTTISH CUP – NO DECISION

The **Scottish FA** withheld their Cup and medals in 1908–09 after Rangers and Celtic played two drawn games in the Final. Spectators rioted.

FEWEST LEAGUE WINS IN SEASON

In modern times: 1 win by Ayr (34 matches, Div 1, 1966–67); **Forfar** (38 matches, Div 2, 1973–74); **Clydebank** (36 matches, Div 1, 1999–2000).

Vale of Leven provided the only instance of a British team failing to win a single match in a league season (Div 1, 18 games, 1891–92)

HAMPDEN'S £63M REDEVELOPMENT

On completion of redevelopment costing £63m **Hampden Park**, home of Scottish football and the oldest first-class stadium in the world, was re-opened full scale for the Rangers-Celtic Cup Final on May 29, 1999.

Work on the 'new Hampden' (capacity 52,000) began in 1992. The North and East stands were restructured (£12m); a new South stand and improved West stand cost £51m. The Millennium Commission contributed £23m and the Lottery Sports Fund provided a grant of £3.75m.

FIRST FOR INVERNESS

Inverness **Caledonian Thistle** won the Scottish Cup for the Highlands for the first time when beating Falkirk 2-1 in the Final on May 30, 2015.

FASTEST GOALS IN SPL

10.4 sec by **Kris Boyd** for Kilmarnock in 3-2 win over Ross Co, Jan 28, 2017; 12.1 sec by **Kris Commons** for Celtic in 4-3 win over Aberdeen, Mar 16, 2013; 12.4 sec by **Anthony Stokes** for Hibernian in 4-1 home defeat by Rangers, Dec 27, 2009.

YOUNGEST SCORER IN SPL

Fraser Fyvie, aged 16 years and 306 days, for Aberdeen v Hearts (3-0) on Jan 27, 2010.

12 GOALS SHARED

There was a record aggregate score for the SPL on May 5, 2010, when **Motherwell** came from 6-2 down to draw 6-6 with **Hibernian**.

25-POINT DEDUCTION

Dundee were deducted 25 points by the Scottish Football League in November 2010 for going into administration for the second time. It left the club on minus 11 points, but they still managed to finish in mid-table in Division One.

GREAT SCOTS

In Feb 1988, the Scottish FA launched a national **Hall of Fame**, initially comprising the first 11 Scots to make 50 international appearances, to be joined by all future players to reach that number of caps. Each member receives a gold medal, invitation for life at all Scotland's home matches, and has his portrait hung at Scottish FA headquarters in Glasgow

MORE CLUBS IN 2000

The **Scottish Premier League** increased from 10 to 12 clubs in season 2000–01. The **Scottish Football League** admitted two new clubs – Peterhead and Elgin City from the Highland League – to provide three divisions of 10 in 2000–01.

FIRST FOR EDINBURGH CITY

In May 2016, **Edinburgh City** became the first club to be promoted to Scottish League Two through the pyramid system with a 2-1 aggregate play-off aggregate win over East Stirling, whose 61 years in senior football came to an end.

NOTABLE SCOTTISH 'FIRSTS'

- The father of League football was a Scot, **William McGregor**, a draper in Birmingham. The 12-club Football League kicked off in Sep 1888, and McGregor was its first president.

- **Hibernian** were the first British club to play in the European Cup, by invitation. They reached the semi-final when it began in 1955–56.
- **Celtic** were Britain's first winners of the European Cup, in 1967.
- Scotland's First Division became the **Premier Division** in season 1975–76.
- Football's **first international** was staged at the West of Scotland cricket ground, Partick, on Nov 30, 1872: Scotland 0, England 0.
- Scotland introduced its **League Cup** in 1945–46, the first season after the war. It was another 15 years before the Football League Cup was launched.
- Scotland pioneered the use in British football of **two subs** per team in League and Cup matches.
- The world's **record football score** belongs to Scotland: Arbroath 36, Bon Accord 0 (Scottish Cup 1st rd) on Sep 12, 1885.
- The Scottish FA introduced the penalty **shoot-out** to their Cup Final in 1990.
- On Jan 22, 1994 all six matches in the **Scottish Premier Division** ended as draws.
- Scotland's new Premier League introduced a **3-week shut-down** in Jan 1999 – first instance of British football adopting the winter break system that operates in a number of European countries. The SPL ended its New Year closure after 2003. The break returned from season 2016–17.
- **Rangers** made history at home to St Johnstone (Premier League, 0-0, Mar 4, 2000) when fielding a team entirely without Scottish players.
- **John Fleck**, aged 16 years, 274 days, became the youngest player in a Scottish FA Cup Final when he came on as a substitute for Rangers in their 3-2 win over Queen of the South at Hampden Park on May 24, 2008

SCOTTISH CUP SHOCK RESULTS

1885–86	(1)	Arbroath 36 Bon Accord 0
1921–22	(F)	Morton 1 Rangers 0
1937–38	(F)	East Fife 4 Kilmarnock 2 (replay, after 1-1)
1960–61	(F)	Dunfermline 2 Celtic 0 (replay, after 0-0)
1966–67	(1)	Berwick 1 Rangers 0
1979–80	(3)	Hamilton 2 Keith 3
1984–85	(1)	Stirling 20 Selkirk 0
1984–85	(3)	Inverness 3 Kilmarnock 0
1986–87	(3)	Rangers 0 Hamilton 1
1994–95	(4)	Stenhousemuir 2 Aberdeen 0
1998–99	(3)	Aberdeen 0 Livingston 1
1999–2000	(3)	Celtic 1 Inverness 3
2003–04	(5)	Inverness 1 Celtic 0
2005–06	(3)	Clyde 2 Celtic 1
2008–09	(6)	St Mirren 1 Celtic 0
2009–10	(SF)	Ross Co 2 Celtic 0
2013–14	(4)	Albion 1 Motherwell 0

Scottish League (Coca-Cola) Cup Final
1994–95   Raith 2, Celtic 2 (Raith won 6-5 on pens)

Europa League first qualifying round
2017–18   Progres Niederkorn (Luxembourg) 2 Rangers 1 (on agg)

MISCELLANEOUS

NATIONAL ASSOCIATIONS FORMED

FA	**1863**
FA of Wales	**1876**
Scottish FA	**1873**
Irish FA	**1904**
Federation of International Football Associations (FIFA)	**1904**

NATIONAL & INTERNATIONAL COMPETITIONS LAUNCHED

FA Cup	1871
Welsh Cup	1877
Scottish Cup	1873
Irish Cup	1880
Football League	1888
Premier League	1992
Scottish League	1890
Scottish Premier League	1998
Scottish League Cup	1945
Football League Cup	1960
Home International Championship	1883–84
World Cup	1930
European Championship	1958
European Cup	1955
Fairs/UEFA Cup	1955
Cup-Winners' Cup	1960
European Champions League	1992
Olympic Games Tournament, at Shepherd's Bush	1908

INNOVATIONS

Size of Ball: Fixed in **1872**.

Shinguards: Introduced and registered by Sam Weller Widdowson (Nottm Forest & England) in **1874**.

Referee's whistle: First used on Nottm Forest's ground in **1878**.

Professionalism: Legalised in England in the summer of **1885** as a result of agitation by Lancashire clubs.

Goal-nets: Invented and patented in **1890** by Mr JA Brodie of Liverpool. They were first used in the North v South match in Jan, **1891**.

Referees and linesmen: Replaced umpires and referees in Jan, **1891**.

Penalty-kick: Introduced at Irish FA's request in the season **1891–92**. The penalty law ordering the goalkeeper to remain on the goal-line came into force in Sep, **1905**, and the order to stand on his goal-line until the ball is kicked arrived in **1929–30**.

White ball: First came into official use in **1951**.

Floodlighting: First FA Cup-tie (replay), Kidderminster Harriers v Brierley Hill Alliance, **1955**. First Football League match: Portsmouth v Newcastle (Div 1), **1956**.

Heated pitch to beat frost tried by Everton at Goodison Park in **1958**.

First soccer closed-circuit TV: At Coventry ground in Oct **1965** (10,000 fans saw their team win at Cardiff, 120 miles away).

Substitutes (one per team) were first allowed in Football League matches at the start of season **1965–66**. Three substitutes (one a goalkeeper) allowed, two of which could be used, in Premier League matches, **1992–93**. The Football League introduced three substitutes for **1993–94**.

Three points for a win: Introduced by the Football League in **1981–82**, by FIFA in World Cup games in **1994**, and by the Scottish League in the same year.

Offside law amended, player 'level' no longer offside, and 'professional foul' made sending-off offence, **1990**.

Penalty shoot-outs introduced to decide FA Cup ties level after one replay and extra time, **1991–92**.

New back-pass rule: goalkeeper must not handle ball kicked to him by team-mate, **1992**.

Linesmen became 'referees' assistants', **1998**.

Goalkeepers not to hold ball longer than 6 seconds, **2000**.

Free-kicks advanced by ten yards against opponents failing to retreat, **2000**. This experimental rule in England was scrapped in 2005).

YOUNGEST AND OLDEST

Youngest Caps

Harry Wilson (Wales v Belgium, Oct 15, 2013)	**16 years 207 days**
Norman Whiteside (N Ireland v Yugoslavia, Jun 17, 1982)	**17 years 41 days**
Theo Walcott (England v Hungary, May 30, 2006)	**17 years 75 days**
Johnny Lambie (Scotland v Ireland, Mar 20, 1886)	**17 years 92 days**
Jimmy Holmes (Rep of Ireland v Austria, May 30, 1971)	**17 years 200 days**

Youngest England scorer: Wayne Rooney (17 years, 317 days) v Macedonia, Skopje, Sep 6, 2003.

Youngest scorer on England debut: Marcus Rashford (18 years, 208 days) v Australia, Sunderland, May 27, 2016.

Youngest England hat-trick scorer: Theo Walcott (19 years, 178 days) v Croatia, Zagreb, Sep 10, 2008.

Youngest England captains: Bobby Moore (v Czech., Bratislava, May 29, 1963), 22 years, 47 days; Michael Owen (v Paraguay, Anfield, Apr 17, 2002), 22 years, 117 days.

Youngest England goalkeeper: Jack Butland (19 years, 158 days) v Italy, Bern, Aug 15, 2012

Youngest England players to reach 50 caps: Michael Owen (23 years, 6 months) v Slovakia at Middlesbrough, Jun 11, 2003; Bobby Moore (25 years, 7 months) v Wales at Wembley, Nov 16, 1966.

Youngest player in World Cup Final: Pele (Brazil) aged 17 years, 237 days v Sweden in Stockholm, Jun 12, 1958.

Youngest player to appear in World Cup Finals: Norman Whiteside (N Ireland v Yugoslavia in Spain – Jun 17, 1982, age 17 years and 42 days.

Youngest First Division player: Derek Forster (Sunderland goalkeeper v Leicester, Aug 22, 1964) aged 15 years, 185 days.

Youngest First Division scorer: At 16 years and 57 days, schoolboy Jason Dozzell (substitute after 30 minutes for Ipswich at home to Coventry on Feb 4, 1984). Ipswich won 3-1 and Dozzell scored their third goal.

Youngest Premier League player: Matthew Briggs (Fulham sub at Middlesbrough, May 13, 2007) aged 16 years and 65 days.

Youngest Premier League scorer: James Vaughan (Everton, home to Crystal Palace, Apr 10, 2005), 16 years, 271 days.

Youngest Premier League captain: Lee Cattermole (Middlesbrough away to Fulham, May 7, 2006) aged 18 years, 47 days.

Youngest player sent off in Premier League: Wayne Rooney (Everton, away to Birmingham, Dec 26, 2002) aged 17 years, 59 days.

Youngest First Division hat-trick scorer: Alan Shearer, aged 17 years, 240 days, in Southampton's 4-2 home win v Arsenal (Apr 9, 1988) on his full debut. Previously, Jimmy Greaves (17 years, 309 days) with 4 goals for Chelsea at home to Portsmouth (7-4), Christmas Day, 1957.

Youngest to complete 100 Football League goals: Jimmy Greaves (20 years, 261 days) when he did so for Chelsea v Manchester City, Nov 19, 1960.

Youngest players in Football League: Reuben Noble-Lazarus (Barnsley 84th minute sub at Ipswich, Sep 30, 2008, Champ) aged 15 years, 45 days; Mason Bennett (Derby at Middlesbrough, Champ, Oct 22, 2011) aged 15 years, 99 days; Albert Geldard (Bradford PA v Millwall, Div 2, Sep 16, 1929) aged 15 years, 158 days; Ken Roberts (Wrexham v Bradford Park Avenue, Div 3 North, Sep 1, 1951) also 15 years, 158 days.

Youngest Football League scorer: Ronnie Dix (for Bristol Rov v Norwich, Div 3 South, Mar 3, 1928) aged 15 years, 180 days.

Youngest player in Scottish League: Goalkeeper Ronnie Simpson (Queens Park) aged 15 in 1946.

Youngest player in FA Cup: Andy Awford, Worcester City's England Schoolboy defender, aged 15 years, 88 days when he substituted in second half away to Boreham Wood (3rd qual round) on Oct 10, 1987.

Youngest player in FA Cup proper: Luke Freeman, Gillingham substitute striker (15 years, 233 days) away to Barnet in 1st round, Nov 10, 2007.

Youngest FA Cup scorer: Sean Cato (16 years, 25 days), second half sub in Barrow Town's 7-2 win away to Rothwell Town (prelim rd), Sep 3, 2011.

Youngest Wembley Cup Final captain: Barry Venison (Sunderland v Norwich, Milk Cup Final, Mar 24, 1985 – replacing suspended captain Shaun Elliott) – aged 20 years, 220 days.

Youngest FA Cup-winning captain: Bobby Moore (West Ham, 1964, v Preston), aged 23 years, 20 days.

Youngest FA Cup Final captain: David Nish aged 21 years and 212 days old when he captained Leicester against Manchester City at Wembley on Apr 26, 1969.

Youngest FA Cup Final player: Curtis Weston (Millwall sub last 3 mins v Manchester Utd, 2004) aged 17 years, 119 days.

Youngest FA Cup Final scorer: Norman Whiteside (Manchester Utd v Brighton, 1983 replay, Wembley), aged 18 years, 19 days.

Youngest FA Cup Final managers: Stan Cullis, Wolves (32) v Leicester, 1949; Steve Coppell, Crystal Palace (34) v Manchester Utd, 1990; Ruud Gullit, Chelsea (34) v Middlesbrough, 1997.

Youngest player in Football League Cup: Chris Coward (Stockport) sub v Sheffield Wed, 2nd Round, Aug 23, 2005, aged 16 years and 31 days.

Youngest Wembley scorer: Norman Whiteside (Manchester Utd v Liverpool, Milk Cup Final, Mar 26, 1983) aged 17 years, 324 days.

Youngest Wembley Cup Final goalkeeper: Chris Woods (18 years, 125 days) for Nottm Forest v Liverpool, League Cup Final on Mar 18, 1978.

Youngest Wembley FA Cup Final goalkeeper: Peter Shilton (19 years, 219 days) for Leicester v Manchester City, Apr 26, 1969.

Youngest senior international at Wembley: Salomon Olembe (sub for Cameroon v England, Nov 15, 1997), aged 16 years, 342 days.

Youngest winning manager at Wembley: Stan Cullis, aged 32 years, 187 days, as manager of Wolves, FA Cup winners on April 30 1949.

Youngest scorer in full international: Mohamed Kallon (Sierra Leone v Congo, African Nations Cup, Apr 22, 1995), reported as aged 15 years, 192 days

Youngest English player to start a Champions League game: Phil Foden (Manchester City v Shakhtar Donetsk, Dec 6, 2017) aged 17 years, 192 days

Youngest English scorer in Champions League: Alex Oxlade-Chamberlain (Arsenal v Olympiacos, Sep 28, 2011) aged 18 years 1 month, 13 days

Youngest player sent off in World Cup Final series: Rigobert Song (Cameroon v Brazil, in USA, Jun 1994) aged 17 years, 358 days.

Youngest FA Cup Final referee: Kevin Howley, of Middlesbrough, aged 35 when in charge of Wolves v Blackburn, 1960.

Youngest player in England U-23 team: Duncan Edwards (v Italy, Bologna, Jan 20, 1954), aged 17 years, 112 days.

Youngest player in England U-21 team: Theo Walcott (v Moldova, Ipswich, Aug 15, 2006), aged 17 years, 152 days.

Youngest player in Scotland U-21 team: Christian Dailly (v Romania, Hampden Park, Sep 11, 1990), aged 16 years, 330 days.

Youngest player in senior football: Cameron Campbell Buchanan, Scottish-born outside right, aged 14 years, 57 days when he played for Wolves v WBA in War-time League match, Sep 26, 1942.

Youngest player in peace-time senior match: Fanini Cullis (Blackpool v Kilmarnock, Anglo Scottish Cup quarter-final 1st leg, Sep 9, 1980) aged 14 years, 323 days.

World's youngest player in top division match: Centre-forward Fernando Rafael Garcia, aged 13, played for 23 minutes for Peruvian club Juan Aurich in 3-1 win against Estudiantes on May 19, 2001.

Oldest player to appear in Football League: New Brighton manager Neil McBain (51 years, 120 days) as emergency goalkeeper away to Hartlepool (Div 3 North, Mar 15, 1947).

Other oldest post-war League players: Sir Stanley Matthews (Stoke, 1965, 50 years, 5 days); Peter Shilton (Leyton Orient 1997, 47 years, 126 days); Kevin Poole (Burton, 2010, 46 years, 291 days); Dave Beasant (Brighton 2003, 44 years, 46 days); Alf Wood (Coventry, 1958, 43 years, 199 days); Tommy Hutchison (Swansea City, 1991, 43 years, 172 days).

Oldest Football League debutant: Andy Cunningham, for Newcastle at Leicester (Div 1) on Feb 2, 1929, aged 38 years, 2 days.

Oldest post-war debut in English League: Defender David Donaldson (35 years, 7 months, 23 days) for Wimbledon on entry to Football League (Div 4) away to Halifax, Aug 20, 1977.

Oldest player to appear in First Division: Sir Stanley Matthews (Stoke v Fulham, Feb 6, 1965), aged 50 years, 5 days – on that his last League appearance, the only 50-year-old ever to play in the top division.

Oldest players in Premier League: Goalkeepers John Burridge (Manchester City v QPR, May 14, 1995), 43 years, 5 months, 11 days; Alec Chamberlain (Watford v Newcastle, May 13, 2007) 42 years, 11 months, 23 days; Steve Ogrizovic (Coventry v Sheffield Wed, May 6, 2000), 42 years, 7 months, 24 days; Brad Friedel (Tottenham v Newcastle, Nov 10, 2013) 42 years, 4 months, 22 days; Neville Southall (Bradford City v Leeds, Mar 12, 2000), 41 years, 5 months, 26 days. Outfield: Teddy Sheringham (West Ham v Manchester City, Dec 30, 2006), 40 years, 8 months, 28 days; Ryan Giggs (Manchester Utd v Hull, May 6, 2014), 40 years, 5 months, 7 days; Gordon Strachan (Coventry City v Derby, May 3, 1997), 40 years, 2 months, 24 days.

Oldest player for British professional club: John Ryan (owner-chairman of Conference club Doncaster, played as substitute for last minute in 4-2 win at Hereford on Apr 26, 2003), aged 52 years, 11 months, 3 weeks.

Oldest FA Cup Final player: Walter (Billy) Hampson (Newcastle v Aston Villa on Apr 26, 1924), aged 41 years, 257 days.

Oldest captain and goalkeeper in FA Cup Final: David James (Portsmouth v Chelsea, May 15, 2010) aged 39 years, 287 days.

Oldest FA Cup Final scorers: Bert Turner (Charlton v Derby, Apr 27, 1946) aged 36 years, 312 days. Scored for both sides. Teddy Sheringham (West Ham v Liverpool, May 13, 2006) aged 40 years, 41 days. Scored in penalty shoot-out.

Oldest FA Cup-winning team: Arsenal 1950 (average age 31 years, 2 months). Eight of the players were over 30, with the three oldest centre-half Leslie Compton 37, and skipper Joe Mercer and goalkeeper George Swindin, both 35.

Oldest World Cup-winning captain: Dino Zoff, Italy's goalkeeper v W Germany in 1982 Final, aged 40 years, 92 days.

Oldest player capped by England: Stanley Matthews (v Denmark, Copenhagen, May 15, 1957), aged 42 years, 103 days.

Oldest England scorer: Stanley Matthews (v N Ireland, Belfast, Oct 6, 1956), aged 41 years, 248 days.

Oldest British international player: Billy Meredith (Wales v England at Highbury, Mar 15, 1920), aged 45 years, 229 days.

Oldest 'new caps': Goalkeeper Alexander Morten, aged 41 years, 113 days when earning his only England Cap against Scotland on Mar 8, 1873; Arsenal centre-half Leslie Compton, at 38 years, 64 days when he made his England debut in 4-2 win against Wales at Sunderland on Nov 15, 1950. **For Scotland:** Goalkeeper Ronnie Simpson (Celtic) at 36 years, 186 days v England at Wembley, Apr 15, 1967.

Oldest scorer in Wembley Final: Chris Swailes, 45, for Morpeth in 4-1 win over Hereford (FA Vase), May 22, 2016.

Longest Football League career: This spanned 32 years and 10 months, by Stanley Matthews (Stoke, Blackpool, Stoke) from Mar 19, 1932 until Feb 6, 1965.

Shortest FA Cup-winning captain: 5ft 4in – Bobby Kerr (Sunderland v Leeds, 1973).

KANTE'S PEAK

N'Golo Kante became the first player in English football to win back-to-back titles with different clubs while playing a full season with each – Leicester (2015-16), Chelsea (2016–17).

SHIRT NUMBERING

Numbering players in Football League matches was made compulsory in 1939. Players wore numbered shirts (1-22) in the FA Cup Final as an experiment in 1933 (Everton 1-11 v Manchester City 12-22).

Squad numbers for players were introduced by the Premier League at the start of season 1993–94. They were optional in the Football League until made compulsory in 1999–2000.

Names on shirts: For first time, players wore names as well as numbers on shirts in League Cup and FA Cup Finals, 1993.

SUBSTITUTES

In **1965**, the Football League, by 39 votes to 10, agreed that **one substitute** be allowed for an injured player at any time during a League match. First substitute used in Football League: Keith Peacock (Charlton), away to Bolton in Div 2, Aug 21, 1965.

Two substitutes per team were approved for the League (Littlewoods) Cup and FA Cup in season 1986–87 and two were permitted in the Football League for the first time in 1987–88.

Three substitutes (one a goalkeeper), two of which could be used, introduced by the Premier League for 1992–93. The Football League followed suit for 1993–94.

Three substitutes (one a goalkeeper) were allowed at the World Cup Finals for the first time at US '94.

Three substitutes (any position) introduced by Premier League and Football League in 1995–96.

Five named substitutes (three of which could be used) introduced in Premier League in 1996–97, in FA Cup in 1997–98, League Cup in 1998–99 and Football League in 1999–2000.

Seven named substitutes for Premier League, FA Cup and League Cup in 2008–09. Still only three to be used. Football League adopted this rule for 2009–10, reverted to five in 2011–12 and went back to seven for the 2012–13 season.

First substitute to score in FA Cup Final: Eddie Kelly (Arsenal v Liverpool, 1971). The **first recorded use** of a substitute was in 1889 (Wales v Scotland at Wrexham on Apr 15) when Sam Gillam arrived late – although he was a Wrexham player – and Allen Pugh (Rhostellyn) was allowed to keep goal until he turned up. The match ended 0-0.

When **Dickie Roose**, the Welsh goalkeeper, was injured against England at Wrexham, Mar 16, 1908, **Dai Davies** (Bolton) was allowed to take his place as substitute. Thus Wales used 12 players. England won 7-1.

END OF WAGE LIMIT

Freedom from the maximum wage system – In force since the formation of the Football League in 1888 – was secured by the Professional Footballers' Association in 1961. About this time Italian clubs renewed overtures for the transfer of British stars and Fulham's **Johnny Haynes** became the first British player to earn £100 a week.

THE BOSMAN RULING

On Dec 15, 1995 the **European Court of Justice** ruled that clubs had no right to transfer fees for out-of-contract players, and the outcome of the 'Bosman case' irrevocably changed football's player-club relationship. It began in 1990, when the contract of 26-year-old **Jean-Marc Bosman**, a midfield player with FC Liege, Belgium, expired. French club Dunkirk wanted him but were unwilling to pay the £500,000 transfer fee, so Bosman was compelled to remain with Liege. He responded with a lawsuit against his club and UEFA on the grounds of 'restriction of trade', and after five years at various court levels the European Court of Justice ruled not only in favour of Bosman but of all professional footballers.

The end of restrictive labour practices revolutionised the system. It led to a proliferation of transfers, rocketed the salaries of elite players who, backed by an increasing army of agents, found themselves in a vastly improved bargaining position as they moved from team to team, league to league, nation to nation. Removing the limit on the number of foreigners clubs could field brought an increasing ratio of such signings, not least in England and Scotland.

Bosman's one-man stand opened the way for footballers to become millionaires, but ended his own career. All he received for his legal conflict was 16 million Belgian francs (£312,000) in compensation, a testimonial of poor reward and martyrdom as the man who did most to change the face of football.

By 2011, he was living on Belgian state benefits, saying: 'I have made the world of football rich and shifted the power from clubs to players. Now I find myself with nothing.'

INTERNATIONAL SHOCK RESULTS

1950	USA 1 England 0 (World Cup).
1953	England 3 Hungary 6 (friendly).
1954	Hungary 7 England 1 (friendly)
1966	North Korea 1 Italy 0 (World Cup).
1982	Spain 0, Northern Ireland 1; Algeria 2, West Germany 1 (World Cup).
1990	Cameroon 1 Argentina 0; Scotland 0 Costa Rica 1; Sweden 1 Costa Rica 2 (World Cup).
1990	Faroe Islands 1 Austria 0 (European Champ qual).
1992	Denmark 2 Germany 0 (European Champ Final).
1993	USA 2 England 0 (US Cup tournament).
1993	Argentina 0 Colombia 5 (World Cup qual).
1993	France 2 Israel 3 (World Cup qual).
1994	Bulgaria 2 Germany 1 (World Cup).
1994	Moldova 3 Wales 2; Georgia 5 Wales 0 (European Champ qual).
1995	Belarus 1 Holland 0 (European Champ qual).
1996	Nigeria 4 Brazil 3 (Olympics).
1998	USA 1 Brazil 0 (Concacaf Gold Cup).
1998	Croatia 3 Germany 0 (World Cup).
2000	Scotland 0 Australia 2 (friendly).
2001	Australia 1 France 0; Australia 1, Brazil 0 (Confederations Cup).
2001	Honduras 2 Brazil 0 (Copa America).
2001	Germany 1 England 5 (World Cup qual).
2002	France 0 Senegal 1; South Korea 2 Italy 1 (World Cup).
2003:	England 1 Australia 3 (friendly)
2004:	Portugal 0 Greece 1 (European Champ Final).
2005:	Northern Ireland 1 England 0 (World Cup qual).
2014:	Holland 5 Spain 1 (World Cup).
2014:	Brazil 1 Germany 7 (World Cup).
2016	England 1 Iceland 2 (European Champ)
2018	South Korea 2 Germany 0 (World Cup)

GREAT RECOVERIES – DOMESTIC FOOTBALL

On Dec 21, 1957, **Charlton** were losing 5-1 against Huddersfield (Div 2) at The Valley with only 28 minutes left, and from the 15th minute, had been reduced to ten men by injury, but they won 7-6, with left-winger Johnny Summers scoring five goals. **Huddersfield** (managed by Bill Shankly) remain the only team to score six times in a League match and lose. On Boxing Day, 1927 in Div 3 South, **Northampton** won 6-5 at home to Luton after being 1-5 down at half-time.

Season 2010–11 produced a Premier League record for **Newcastle**, who came from 4-0 down at home to Arsenal to draw 4-4. Previous instance of a team retrieving a four-goal deficit in the top division to draw was in 1984 when Newcastle trailed at QPR in a game which ended 5-5.

In the 2012-13 League Cup, **Arsenal** were 0-4 down in a fourth round tie at Reading, levelled at 4-4 and went on to win 7-5 in extra-time.

MATCHES OFF

Worst day for postponements: Feb 9, 1963, when 57 League fixtures in England and Scotland were frozen off. Only 7 Football League matches took place, and the entire Scottish programme was wiped out.

Other weather-hit days:

Jan 12, 1963 and Feb 2, 1963 – on both those Saturdays, only 4 out of 44 Football League matches were played.

Jan 1, 1979 – 43 out of 46 Football League fixtures postponed.

Jan 17, 1987 – 37 of 45 scheduled Football League fixtures postponed; only 2 Scottish matches survived.

Feb 8–9, 1991 – only 4 of the week-end's 44 Barclays League matches survived the freeze-up (4 of

the postponements were on Friday night). In addition, 11 Scottish League matches were off.
Jan 27, 1996 – 44 Cup and League matches in England and Scotland were frozen off.
On the weekend of Jan 9, 10, 11, 2010, 46 League and Cup matches in England and Scotland were victims of the weather. On the weekend of Dec 18-21, 2010, 49 matches were frozen off in England and Scotland.

Fewest matches left on one day by postponements was during the Second World War – Feb 3, 1940 when, because of snow, ice and fog only one out of 56 regional league fixtures took place. It resulted Plymouth Argyle 10, Bristol City 3.

The Scottish Cup second round tie between Inverness Thistle and Falkirk in season 1978–79 was **postponed 29 times** because of snow and ice. First put off on Jan 6, it was eventually played on Feb 22. Falkirk won 4-0.

Pools Panel's busiest days: Jan 17, 1987 and Feb 9, 1991 – on both dates they gave their verdict on 48 postponed coupon matches.

FEWEST 'GAMES OFF'

Season 1947-48 was the best since the war for English League fixtures being played to schedule. Only six were postponed.

LONGEST SEASON

The latest that League football has been played in a season was **Jun 7, 1947** (six weeks after the FA Cup Final). The season was extended because of mass postponements caused by bad weather in mid-winter.

The latest the FA Cup competition has been completed was in season 2014–15 when Arsenal beat Aston Villa 4-0 in the Final on May 30, kick-off 5.30pm

Worst winter hold-up was in season 1962–63. The Big Freeze began on Boxing Day and lasted until Mar, with nearly 500 first-class matches postponed. The FA Cup 3rd round was the longest on record – it began with only three out of 32 ties playable on Jan 5 and ended 66 days and 261 postponements later on Mar 11. The Lincoln-Coventry tie was put off 15 times. The Pools Panel was launched that winter, on Jan 26, 1963.

HOTTEST DAYS

The Nationwide League kicked off season 2003-04 on Aug 9 with pitch temperatures of 102 degrees recorded at Luton v Rushden and Bradford v Norwich. On the following day, there was a pitch temperature of 100 degrees for the Community Shield match between Manchester Utd and Arsenal at Cardiff's Millennium Stadium. Wembley's pitch-side thermometer registered 107 degrees for the 2009 Chelsea-Everton FA Cup Final.

FOOTBALL LEAGUE NAME CHANGE

From the start of the 2016-17 season, the Football League was renamed the English Football League, as part of a corporate and competition rebranding.

FOOTBALL ASSOCIATION SECRETARIES/CHIEF EXECUTIVES

1863–66 Ebenezer Morley; 1866–68 **Robert Willis**; 1868–70 **RG Graham**; 1870–95 **Charles Alcock** (paid from 1887); 1895–1934 **Sir Frederick Wall**; 1934-62 **Sir Stanley Rous**; 1962–73 **Denis Follows**; 1973–89 **Ted Croker** (latterly chief executive); 1989–99 **Graham Kelly** (chief executive); 2000–02 **Adam Crozier** (chief executive); 2003–04 **Mark Palios** (chief executive); 2005–08: **Brian Barwick** (chief executive); 2009-10 **Ian Watmore** (chief executive); 2010-15 **Alex Horne** (chief executive); 2015–19 **Martin Glenn** (chief executive); 2019 **Mark Bullingham** (chief executive).

FOOTBALL'S SPONSORS

Football League: Canon 1983–86; Today Newspaper 1986–87; Barclays 1987–93; Endsleigh Insurance 1993–96; Nationwide Building Society 1996–2004; Coca-Cola 2004–10; npower 2010–14; Sky Bet from 2014.

League Cup: Milk Cup 1982–86; Littlewoods 1987–90; Rumbelows 1991-92; Coca-Cola 1993–

98; Worthington 1998–2003; Carling 2003–12; Capital One 2012–16; Carabao from 2017.
Premier League: Carling 1993–2001; Barclaycard 2001–04; Barclays 2004–16.
FA Cup: Littlewoods 1994–98; AXA 1998–2002; E.ON 2006–11; Budweiser 2011–15; Emirates (title sponsor) from 2015.

NEW HOMES FOR CLUBS

Newly-constructed League grounds in England since the war: 1946 Hull (Boothferry Park); 1950 Port Vale (Vale Park); 1955 Southend (Roots Hall); 1988 Scunthorpe (Glanford Park); 1990 Walsall (Bescot Stadium); 1990 Wycombe (Adams Park); 1992 Chester (Deva Stadium); 1993 Millwall (New Den); 1994 Huddersfield (McAlpine Stadium); 1994 Northampton (Sixfields Stadium); 1995 Middlesbrough (Riverside Stadium); 1997 Bolton (Reebok Stadium); 1997 Derby (Pride Park); 1997 Stoke (Britannia Stadium); 1997 Sunderland (Stadium of Light); 1998 Reading (Madejski Stadium); 1999 Wigan (JJB Stadium); 2001 Southampton (St Mary's Stadium); 2001 Oxford Utd (Kassam Stadium); 2002 Leicester (Walkers Stadium); 2002 Hull (Kingston Communications Stadium); 2003 Manchester City (City of Manchester Stadium); 2003 Darlington (New Stadium); 2005 Coventry (Ricoh Arena); Swansea (Stadium of Swansea, Morfa); 2006 Arsenal (Emirates Stadium); 2007 Milton Keynes Dons (Stadium: MK); Shrewsbury (New Meadow); 2008 Colchester (Community Stadium); 2009 Cardiff City Stadium; 2010 Chesterfield (b2net Stadium), Morecambe (Globe Arena); 2011 Brighton (American Express Stadium); 2012 Rotherham (New York Stadium). 2016 West Ham (Olympic Stadium).

NATIONAL FOOTBALL CENTRE

The FA's new £120m centre at St George's Park, Burton upon Trent, was opened on Oct 9, 20012 by the Duke of Cambridge, president of the FA. The site covers 330 acres, has 12 full-size pitches (5 with undersoil heating and floodlighting). There are 5 gyms, a 90-seat lecture theatre, a hydrotherapy unit with swimming pool for the treatment of injuries and two hotels. It is the base for England teams, men and women, at all levels.

GROUND-SHARING

Manchester Utd played their home matches at **Manchester City's** Maine Road ground for 8 years after Old Trafford was bomb-damaged in Aug 1941. **Crystal Palace** and **Charlton** shared Selhurst Park (1985–91); **Bristol Rov** and **Bath City** (Twerton Park, Bath, 1986–96); **Partick Thistle** and **Clyde** (Firhill Park, Glasgow, 1986–91; in seasons 1990–01, 1991–92 **Chester** shared **Macclesfield's** ground (Moss Rose).
Crystal Palace and **Wimbledon** shared Selhurst Park, from season 1991–92, when **Charlton** (tenants) moved to rent Upton Park from **West Ham**, until 2003 when Wimbledon relocated to Milton Keynes. **Clyde** moved to Douglas Park, **Hamilton Academical's** home, in 1991–92. **Stirling Albion** shared **Stenhousemuir's** ground, Ochilview Park, in 1992–93. In 1993–94, **Clyde** shared **Partick's** home until moving to Cumbernauld. In 1994–95, **Celtic** shared Hampden Park with **Queen's Park** (while Celtic Park was redeveloped); **Hamilton** shared **Partick's** ground. **Airdrie** shared **Clyde's** Broadwood Stadium. **Bristol Rov** left **Bath City's** ground at the start of season 1996–97, sharing Bristol Rugby Club's Memorial Ground. **Clydebank** shared **Dumbarton's** Boghead Park from 1996–97 until renting **Greenock Morton's** Cappielow Park in season 1999–2000. **Brighton** shared **Gillingham's** ground in seasons 1997–98, 1998–99. **Fulham** shared **QPR's** home at Loftus Road in seasons 2002–03, 2003–04, returning to Craven Cottage in Aug 2004. **Coventry** played home fixtures at Northampton in season 2013–14, returning to their own ground, the Ricoh Arena, in Sept 2014.
Inverness Caledonian Thistle moved to share **Aberdeen's** Pittodrie Stadium in 2004–05 after being promoted to the SPL; **Gretna's** home matches on arrival in the SPL in 2007–08 were held at Motherwell and Livingston. Stenhousemuir (owners) share Ochilview with East Stirling (tenants).

ARTIFICIAL TURF

QPR were the first British club to install an artificial pitch, in 1981. They were followed by **Luton**

in 1985, and **Oldham** and **Preston** in **1986**. QPR reverted to grass in 1988, as did Luton and promoted Oldham in season 1991–92 (when artificial pitches were banned in Div 1). **Preston** were the last Football League club playing 'on plastic' in 1993–94, and their Deepdale ground was restored to grass for the start of 1994–95.
Stirling were the **first Scottish club** to play on plastic, in season 1987–88.

DOUBLE RUNNERS-UP

There have been nine instances of clubs finishing runner-up in **both the League Championship** and **FA Cup** in the same season: 1928 Huddersfield; 1932 Arsenal; 1939 Wolves; 1962 Burnley; 1965 and 1970 Leeds; 1986 Everton; 1995 Manchester Utd; 2001 Arsenal.

CORNER-KICK RECORDS

Not a single corner-kick was recorded when **Newcastle** drew 0–0 at home to **Portsmouth** (Div 1) on Dec 5, 1931.
The record for **most corners** in a match for one side is believed to be **Sheffield Utd's 28** to **West Ham's 1** in Div 2 at Bramall Lane on Oct 14, 1989. For all their pressure, Sheffield Utd lost 2–0.
Nottm Forest led **Southampton** 22–2 on corners (Premier League, Nov 28, 1992) but lost the match 1–2.
Tommy Higginson (Brentford, 1960s) once passed back to his own goalkeeper from a corner kick.
When **Wigan** won 4–0 at home to Cardiff (Div 2) on Feb 16, 2002, all four goals were headed in from corners taken by N Ireland international **Peter Kennedy**.
Steve Staunton (Rep of Ireland) is believed to be the only player to score direct from a corner in **two** Internationals.
In the 2012 Champions League Final, **Bayern Munich** forced 20 corners without scoring, while **Chelsea** scored from their only one.

SACKED AT HALF-TIME

Leyton Orient sacked **Terry Howard** on his 397th appearance for the club – at half-time in a Second Division home defeat against Blackpool (Feb 7, 1995) for 'an unacceptable performance'. He was fined two weeks' wages, given a free transfer and moved to Wycombe.
Bobby Gould resigned as **Peterborough**'s head coach at half-time in their 1–0 defeat in the LDV Vans Trophy 1st round at Bristol City on Sep 29, 2004.
Harald Schumacher, former Germany goalkeeper, was sacked as Fortuna Koln coach when they were two down at half-time against Waldhof Mannheim (Dec 15, 1999). They lost 5–1.

MOST GAMES BY 'KEEPER FOR ONE CLUB

Alan Knight made 683 League appearances for Portsmouth, over 23 seasons (1978–2000), a record for a goalkeeper at one club. The previous holder was Peter Bonetti with 600 League games for Chelsea (20 seasons, 1960–79).

PLAYED TWO GAMES ON SAME DAY

Jack Kelsey played full-length matches for both club and country on Wednesday Nov 26, 1958. In the afternoon he kept goal for Wales in a 2–2 draw against England at Villa Park, and he then drove to Highbury to help Arsenal win 3–1 in a prestigious floodlit friendly against Juventus.
On the same day, winger **Danny Clapton** played for England (against Wales and Kelsey) and then in part of Arsenal's match against Juventus.
On Nov 11, 1987, **Mark Hughes** played for Wales against Czechoslovakia (European Championship) in Prague, then flew to Munich and went on as substitute that night in a winning Bayern Munich team, to whom he was on loan from Barcelona.
On Feb 16, 1993 goalkeeper **Scott Howie** played in Scotland's 3–0 U-21 win v Malta at Tannadice Park, Dundee (ko 1.30pm) and the same evening played in Clyde's 2–1 home win v Queen of South (Div 2).
Ryman League **Hornchurch**, faced by end-of-season fixture congestion, played **two matches** on the same night (May 1, 2001). They lost 2–1 at home to Ware and drew 2–2 at Clapton.

RECORD LOSS

Manchester City made a record loss of £194.9m in the 2010–11 financial year.

FIRST 'MATCH OF THE DAY'

BBC TV (recorded highlights): Liverpool 3, Arsenal 2 on Aug 22, 1964. **First complete match to be televised:** Arsenal 3, Everton 2 on Aug 29, 1936. **First League match televised in colour:** Liverpool 2, West Ham 0 on Nov 15, 1969.

'MATCH OF THE DAY' – BIGGEST SCORES

Football League: Tottenham 9, Bristol Rov 0 (Div 2, 1977–78). **Premier League:** Nottm Forest 1, Manchester Utd 8 (1998–99); Portsmouth 7 Reading 4 (2007–08).

FIRST COMMENTARY ON RADIO

Arsenal 1 Sheffield Utd 1 (Div 1) broadcast on BBC, Jan 22, 1927.

OLYMPIC FOOTBALL WINNERS

1908 Great Britain (in London); **1912** Great Britain (Stockholm); **1920** Belgium (Antwerp); **1924** Uruguay (Paris); **1928** Uruguay (Amsterdam); **1932** No soccer in Los Angeles Olympics; **1936** Italy (Berlin); **1948** Sweden (London); **1952** Hungary (Helsinki); **1956** USSR (Melbourne); **1960** Yugoslavia (Rome); **1964** Hungary (Tokyo); **1968** Hungary (Mexico City); **1972** Poland (Munich); **1976** E Germany (Montreal); **1980** Czechoslovakia (Moscow); **1984** France (Los Angeles); **1988** USSR (Seoul); **1992** Spain (Barcelona); **1996** Nigeria (Atlanta); **2000** Cameroon (Sydney); **2004** Argentina (Athens); **2008** Argentina (Beijing); **2012** Mexico (Wembley); **2016** Brazil (Rio de Janeiro).

Highest scorer in Final tournament: Ferenc Bene (Hungary) 12 goals, 1964.

Record crowd for Olympic Soccer Final: 108,800 (France v Brazil, Los Angeles 1984).

MOST AMATEUR CUP WINS

Bishop Auckland set the FA Amateur Cup record with 10 wins, and in 1957 became the only club to carry off the trophy in three successive seasons. The competition was discontinued after the Final on Apr 20, 1974. (Bishop's Stortford 4, Ilford 1, at Wembley).

FOOTBALL FOUNDATION

This was formed (May 2000) to replace the **Football Trust**, which had been in existence since 1975 as an initiative of the Pools companies to provide financial support at all levels, from schools football to safety and ground improvement work throughout the game.

SEVEN-FIGURE TESTIMONIALS

The first was **Sir Alex Ferguson's** at Old Trafford on Oct 11, 1999, when a full-house of 54,842 saw a Rest of the World team beat Manchester Utd 4-2. United's manager pledged that a large percentage of the estimated £1m receipts would go to charity.

Estimated receipts of £1m and over came from testimonials for **Denis Irwin** (Manchester Utd) against Manchester City at Old Trafford on Aug 16, 2000 (45,158); **Tom Boyd** (Celtic) against Manchester Utd at Celtic Park on May 15, 2001 (57,000) and **Ryan Giggs** (Manchester Utd) against Celtic on Aug 1, 2001 (66,967).

Tony Adams' second testimonial (1-1 v Celtic on May 13, 2002) two nights after Arsenal completed the Double, was watched by 38,021 spectators at Highbury. Of £1m receipts, he donated £500,000 to Sporting Chance, the charity that helps sportsmen/women with drink, drug, gambling problems.

Sunderland and a Republic of Ireland XI drew 0-0 in front of 35,702 at the Stadium of Light on May 14, 2002. The beneficiary, **Niall Quinn**, donated his testimonial proceeds, estimated at £1m, to children's hospitals in Sunderland and Dublin, and to homeless children in Africa and Asia.

A record testimonial crowd of 69,591 for **Roy Keane** at Old Trafford on May 9, 2006 netted more than £2m for charities in Dublin, Cork and Manchester. Manchester Utd beat Celtic 1-0, with Keane playing for both teams.

Alan Shearer's testimonial on May 11, 2006, watched by a crowd of 52,275 at St James' Park, raised more than £1m. The club's record scorer, in his farewell match, came off the bench in stoppage time to score the penalty that gave Newcastle a 3-2 win over Celtic. Total proceeds from his testimonial events, £1.64m, were donated to 14 charities in the north-east.

Ole Gunnar Solskjaer, who retired after 12 years as a Manchester Utd player, had a crowd of 68,868, for his testimonial on Aug 2, 2008 (United 1 Espanyol 0). He donated the estimated receipts of £2m to charity, including the opening of a dozen schools in Africa.

Liverpool's **Jamie Carragher** had his testimonial against Everton (4-1) on Sep 4, 2010. It was watched by a crowd of 35,631 and raised an estimated £1m for his foundation, which supports community projects on Merseyside.

Gary Neville donated receipts of around £1m from his testimonial against Juventus (2-1) in front of 42,000 on May 24, 2011, to charities and building a Supporters' Centre near Old Trafford.

Paul Scholes had a crowd of 75,000 for his testimonial, Manchester United against New York Cosmos, on Aug 5, 2011. Receipts were £1.5m.

Steven Gerrard, Liverpool captain, donated £500,000 from his testimonial to the local Alder Hey Children's Hospital after a match against Olympiacos was watched by a crowd of 44,362 on Aug 3, 2013. Gerrard chose the Greek champions because he scored a special goal against them in the season Liverpool won the 2005 Champions League.

Wayne Rooney's match against Everton on Aug 3, 2016, raised £1.2m, which the Manchester United captain donated to local children's charities.

WHAT IT USED TO COST

Minimum admission to League football was one shilling in 1939 After the war, it was increased to 1s 3d in 1946; 1s 6d in 1951; 1s 9d in 1952; 2s in 1955; 2s 6d; in 1960; 4s in 1965; 5s in 1968; 6s in 1970; and 8s (40p) in 1972 After that, the fixed minimum charge was dropped.

Wembley's first Cup Final programme in 1923 cost three pence (1¼p in today's money). The programme for the 'farewell' FA Cup Final in May, 2000 was priced £10.

FA Cup Final ticket prices in 2011 reached record levels – £115, £85, £65 and £45.

WHAT THEY USED TO EARN

In the 1930s, First Division players were on £8 a week (£6 in close season) plus bonuses of £2 win, £1 draw. The maximum wage went up to £12 when football resumed post-war in 1946 and had reached £20 by the time the limit was abolished in 1961.

EUROPEAN TROPHY WINNERS

European Cup/Champions League: 13 Real Madrid, **7** AC Milan; **6** Liverpool; **5** Barcelona, Bayern Munich; **4** Ajax; **3** Inter Milan, Manchester Utd; **2** Benfica, Juventus, Nottm Forest, Porto; **1** Aston Villa, Borussia Dortmund, Celtic, Chelsea, Feyenoord, Hamburg, Marseille, PSV Eindhoven, Red Star Belgrade, Steaua Bucharest

Cup-Winners' Cup: 4 Barcelona; **2** Anderlecht, Chelsea, Dynamo Kiev, AC Milan, **1** Aberdeen, Ajax, Arsenal, Atletico Madrid, Bayern Munich, Borussia Dortmund, Dynamo Tbilisi, Everton, Fiorentina, Hamburg, Juventus, Lazio, Magdeburg, Manchester City, Manchester Utd, Mechelen, Paris St Germain, Parma, Rangers, Real Zaragoza, Sampdoria, Slovan Bratislava, Sporting Lisbon, Tottenham, Valencia, Werder Bremen, West Ham.

UEFA Cup: 3 Barcelona, Inter Milan, Juventus, Liverpool, Valencia; **2** Borussia Moenchengladbach, Feyenoord, Gothenburg, Leeds, Parma, Real Madrid, Sevilla, Tottenham; **1** Anderlecht, Ajax, Arsenal, Bayer Leverkusen, Bayern Munich, CSKA Moscow, Dynamo Zagreb, Eintracht Frankfurt, Ferencvaros, Galatasaray, Ipswich, Napoli, Newcastle, Porto, PSV Eindhoven, Real Zaragoza, Roma, Schalke, Shakhtar Donetsk, Zenit St Petersburg.

Europa League: 3 Sevilla, Atletico Madrid; **2** Chelsea; **1** Manchester Utd, Porto.

● The Champions League was introduced into the European Cup in 1992–93 to counter the threat of a European Super League. The UEFA Cup became the Europa League, with a new format, in season 2009–10.

BRITAIN'S 37 TROPHIES IN EUROPE

Euro Cup/Champs Lge (14)	Cup-Winners' Cup (10)	Fairs/UEFA Cup/Europa Lge (13)
1967 Celtic	1963 Tottenham	1968 Leeds
1968 Manchester Utd	1965 West Ham	1969 Newcastle
1977 Liverpool	1970 Manchester City	1970 Arsenal
1978 Liverpool	1971 Chelsea	1971 Leeds
1979 Nottm Forest	1972 Rangers	1972 Tottenham
1980 Nottm Forest	1983 Aberdeen	1973 Liverpool
1981 Liverpool	1985 Everton	1976 Liverpool
1982 Aston Villa	1991 Manchester Utd	1981 Ipswich
1984 Liverpool	1994 Arsenal	1984 Tottenham
1999 Manchester Utd	1998 Chelsea	2001 Liverpool
2005 Liverpool		2013 Chelsea
2008 Manchester Utd		2017 Manchester Utd
2012 Chelsea		2019 Chelsea
2019 Liverpool		

ENGLAND'S EUROPEAN RECORD

England had an unprecedented clean sweep of finalists in the two European club competitions in season 2018–19, with Liverpool defeating Tottenham in the Champions League and Chelsea beating Arsenal in the Europa League.

END OF CUP-WINNERS' CUP

The **European Cup-Winners' Cup**, inaugurated in 1960–61, terminated with the 1999 Final. The competition merged into a revamped **UEFA Cup**.

From its inception in 1955, the **European Cup** comprised only championship-winning clubs until 1998–99, when selected runners-up were introduced. Further expansion came in 1999–2000 with the inclusion of clubs finishing third in certain leagues and fourth in 2002.

EUROPEAN CLUB COMPETITIONS – SCORING RECORDS

European Cup – record aggregate: 18-0 by Benfica v Dudelange (Lux) (8-0a, 10-0h), prelim rd, 1965–66.

Record single-match score: 11-0 by Dinamo Bucharest v Crusaders (rd 1, 2nd leg, 1973-74 (agg 12-0).

Champions League – record single-match score: Liverpool 8-0 v Besiktas, Group A qual (Nov 6, 2007).

Highest match aggregate: 13 – Bayern Munich 12 Sporting Lisbon 1 (5-0 away, 7-1 at home, 1st ko rd, 2008–09)

Cup-Winners' Cup – *record aggregate: 21-0 by Chelsea v Jeunesse Hautcharage (Lux) (8-0a, 13-0h), 1st rd, 1971–72.

Record single-match score: 16-1 by Sporting Lisbon v Apoel Nicosia, 2nd round, 1st leg, 1963–64 (aggregate was 18-1).

UEFA Cup (prev Fairs Cup) – *Record aggregate: 21-0 by Feyenoord v US Rumelange (Lux) (9-0h, 12-0a), 1st round, 1972–73.

Record single-match score: 14-0 by Ajax Amsterdam v Red Boys (Lux) 1st rd, 2nd leg, 1984–85 (aggregate also 14-0).

Record British score in Europe: 13-0 by **Chelsea** at home to Jeunesse Hautcharage (Lux) in Cup-Winners' Cup 1st round, 2nd leg, 1971–72. Chelsea's overall 21-0 win in that tie is highest aggregate by British club in Europe.

Individual scoring record for European tie (over two legs): 10 goals (6 home, 4 away) by **Kiril Milanov** for Levski Spartak in 19-3 agg win Cup-Winners' Cup 1st round v Lahden Reipas, 1976–77. Next highest: **8** goals by **Jose Altafini** for AC Milan v US Luxembourg (European Cup, prelim round, 1962–63, agg 14-0) and by **Peter Osgood** for Chelsea v Jeunesse Hautcharage (Cup-Winners' Cup, 1st round 1971–72, agg 21-0). Altafini and Osgood each scored 5 goals at home, 3 away.

Individual single-match scoring record in European competition: **6** by **Mascarenhas** for Sporting Lisbon in 16-1 Cup-Winner's Cup 2nd round, 1st leg win v Apoel, 1963–64; and by **Lothar Emmerich** for Borussia Dortmund in 8-0 CWC 1st round, 2nd leg win v Floriana 1965–66; and by **Kiril Milanov** for Levski Spartak in 12-2 CWC 1st round, 1st leg win v Lahden Reipas, 1976–77.

Most goals in single European campaign: 15 by **Jurgen Klinsmann** for Bayern Munich (UEFA Cup 1995–96).

Most goals by British player in European competition: 30 by **Peter Lorimer** (Leeds, in 9 campaigns).

Most individual goals in Champions League match: 5 by **Lionel Messi** (Barcelona) in 7-1 win at home to Bayer Leverkusen in round of 16 second leg, 2011–12.

Most European Cup goals by individual player: 49 by **Alfredo di Stefano** in 58 apps for Real Madrid (1955–64).

(*Joint record European aggregate)

First European treble: Clarence Seedorf became the first player to win the European Cup with three clubs: Ajax in 1995, Real Madrid in 1998 and AC Milan in 2003.

EUROPEAN FOOTBALL – BIG RECOVERIES

In the most astonishing Final in the history of the European Cup/Champions League, **Liverpool** became the first club to win it from a 3-0 deficit when they beat AC Milan 3-2 on penalties after a 3-3 draw in Istanbul on May 25, 2005. Liverpool's fifth triumph in the competition meant that they would keep the trophy.

The following season, **Middlesbrough** twice recovered from three-goal aggregate deficits in the **UEFA Cup**, beating Basel 4-3 in the quarter finals and Steaua Bucharest by the same scoreline in the semi-finals. In 2010, **Fulham** beat Juventus 5-4 after trailing 1-4 on aggregate in the second leg of their Europa League, Round of 16 match at Craven Cottage.

Two Scottish clubs have won a European tie from a 3-goal, first leg deficit: **Kilmarnock** 0-3, 5-1 v Eintracht Frankfurt (Fairs Cup 1st round, 1964–65); **Hibernian** 1-4, 5-0 v Napoli (Fairs Cup 2nd Round, 1967–68).

English clubs have three times gone out of the **UEFA Cup** after leading 3-0 from the first leg: 1975–76 (2nd Rd) **Ipswich** lost 3-4 on agg to Bruges, 1976–77 (quarter-final) **QPR** lost on penalties to AEK Athens after 3-3 agg; 1977–78 (3rd round) **Ipswich** lost on penalties to Barcelona after 3-3 agg.

On Oct 16, 2012, Sweden recovered from 0-4 down to draw 4-4 with Germany (World Cup qual) in Berlin.

● In the **1966 World Cup quarter-final** (Jul 23) at Goodison Park, North Korea led Portugal 3-0, but Eusebio scored 4 times to give **Portugal** a 5-3 win.

RONALDO'S EURO CENTURY

Cristiano Ronaldo became the first player to reach a century of goals in European club competitions when scoring twice for Real Madrid away to Bayern Munich on Apr 12, 2017. He reached the hundred in 143 matches (84 for Real, 16 for Manchester Utd) in the Champions League (97), UEFA Super Cup (2) and Champions League qualifying round (1).

RECORD COMEBACK

The greatest turnaround in Champions League history took place in a round of 16 match on Mar 8, 2017. **Barcelona**, 0-4 down to Paris St Germain, won the return leg 6-1, scoring three goals in the last seven minutes.

HEAVIEST ENGLISH-CLUB DEFEATS IN EUROPE

(Single-leg scores)

Champions League: Porto 5 Leicester 0 (group, Dec 6, 2016)
European Cup: Artmedia Bratislava 5, **Celtic** 0 (2nd qual round), Jul 2005 (agg 5-4); Ajax 5, **Liverpool** 1 (2nd round), Dec 1966 (agg 7-3); Real Madrid 5, **Derby** 1 (2nd round), Nov 1975 (agg 6-5).
Cup-Winners' Cup: Sporting Lisbon 5, **Manchester Utd** 0 (quarter-final), Mar 1964 (agg 6-4).
Fairs/UEFA Cup: Bayern Munich 6, **Coventry** 1 (2nd round), Oct 1970 (agg 7-3). **Combined**

London team lost 6-0 (agg 8-2) in first Fairs Cup Final in 1958. Barcelona 5, **Chelsea** 0 in Fairs Cup semi-final play-off, 1966, in Barcelona (after 2-2 agg).

SHOCK ENGLISH CLUB DEFEATS

1968–69 (Eur Cup, 1st round): **Manchester City** beaten by Fenerbahce, 1-2 agg.
1971–72 (CWC, 2nd round): **Chelsea** beaten by Atvidaberg on away goals.
1993–94 (Eur Cup, 2nd round): **Manchester Utd** beaten by Galatasaray on away goals.
1994–95 (UEFA Cup, 1st round): **Blackburn** beaten by Trelleborgs, 2-3 agg.
2000–01 (UEFA Cup, 1st round): **Chelsea** beaten by St Gallen, Switz 1-2 agg.

PFA FAIR PLAY AWARD (Bobby Moore Trophy from 1993)

1988	Liverpool	2003	Crewe
1989	Liverpool	2004	Crewe
1990	Liverpool	2005	Crewe
1991	Nottm Forest	2006	Crewe
1992	Portsmouth	2007	Crewe
1993	Norwich	2008	Crewe
1994	Crewe	2009	Stockport
1995	Crewe	2010	Rochdale
1996	Crewe	2011	Rochdale
1997	Crewe	2012	Chesterfield
1998	Cambridge Utd	2013	Crewe
1999	Grimsby	2014	Exeter
2000	Crewe	2015	Exeter
2001	Hull	2016	Walsall
2002	Crewe	2017	Bradford City

RECORD MEDAL SALES

At Sotherby's in London on Nov 11, 2014, the FA Cup winner's medal which **Sir Stanley Matthews** earned with Blackpool in 1953 was sold for £220,000 – the most expensive medal in British sporting history. At the same auction, **Ray Wilson's** 1966 World Cup winner's medal fetched £136,000, while **Jimmy Greaves**, who was left out of the winning England team, received £44,000 for the medal the FA belatedly awarded him in 2009

West Ham bought (Jun 2000) the late **Bobby Moore's** collection of medals and trophies for £1.8m at Christie's auction. It was put up for sale by his first wife Tina and included his World Cup-winner's medal.

A No. 6 duplicate red shirt made for England captain **Bobby Moore** for the 1966 World Cup Final fetched £44,000 at an auction at Wolves' ground in Sep, 1999. Moore kept the shirt he wore in that Final and gave the replica to England physio Harold Shepherdson.

Sir Geoff Hurst's 1966 World Cup-winning shirt fetched a record £91,750 at Christie's in Sep, 2000. His World Cup Final cap fetched £37,600 and his Man of the Match trophy £18,800. Proceeds totalling £274,410 from the 129 lots went to Hurst's three daughters and charities of his choice, including the Bobby Moore Imperial Cancer Research Fund.

In Aug, 2001, Sir Geoff sold his World Cup-winner's medal to his former club West Ham Utd (for their museum) at a reported £150,000.

'The **Billy Wright** Collection' – caps, medals and other memorabilia from his illustrious career – fetched over £100,000 at Christie's in Nov, 1996.

At the sale in Oct 1993, trophies, caps and medals earned by **Ray Kennedy**, former England, Arsenal and Liverpool player, fetched a then record total of £88,407. Kennedy, suffering from Parkinson's Disease, received £73,000 after commission. The PFA paid £31,080 for a total of 60 lots – including a record £16,000 for his 1977 European Cup winner's medal – to be exhibited at their Manchester museum. An anonymous English collector paid £17,000 for the medal and plaque commemorating Kennedy's part in the Arsenal Double in 1971.

Previous record for one player's medals, shirts etc collection: £30,000 (**Bill Foulkes**, Manchester

Utd in 1992). The sale of **Dixie Dean**'s medals etc in 1991 realised £28,000.

In Mar, 2001, **Gordon Banks**' 1966 World Cup-winner's medal fetched a new record £124,750. TV's Nick Hancock, a Stoke fan, paid £23,500 for **Sir Stanley Matthews**'s 1953 FA Cup-winner's medal. He also bought one of Matthews's England caps for £3,525 and paid £2,350 for a Stoke Div 2 Championship medal (1963).

Dave Mackay's 1961 League Championship and FA Cup winner's medals sold for £18,000 at Sotherby's. Tottenham bought them for their museum.

A selection of England World Cup-winning manager **Sir Alf Ramsey**'s memorabilia – England caps, championship medals with Ipswich etc. – fetched more than £80,000 at Christie's. They were offered for sale by his family, and his former clubs Tottenham and Ipswich were among the buyers.

Ray Wilson's 1966 England World Cup-winning shirt fetched £80,750. Also in Mar, 2002, the No. 10 shirt worn by **Pele** in Brazil's World Cup triumph in 1970 was sold for a record £157,750 at Christies. It went to an anonymous telephone bidder.

In Oct, 2003, **George Best**'s European Footballer of the Year (1968) trophy was sold to an anonymous British bidder for £167,250 at Bonham's. It was the then most expensive item of sporting memorabilia ever auctioned in Britain.

England captain **Bobby Moore**'s 1970 World Cup shirt, which he swapped with Pele after Brazil's 1-0 win in Mexico, was sold for £60,000 at Christie's in Mar, 2004.

Sep, 2004: England shirt worn by tearful **Paul Gascoigne** in 1990 World Cup semi-final v Germany sold at Christie's for £28,680. At same auction, shirt worn by Brazil's **Pele** in 1958 World Cup Final in Sweden sold for £70,505.

May, 2005: The **second FA Cup** (which was presented to winning teams from 1896 to 1909) was bought for £420,000 at Christie's by Birmingham chairman David Gold, a world record for an item of football memorabilia. It was presented to the National Football Museum, Preston. At the same auction, the World Cup-winner's medal earned by England's **Alan Ball** in 1966 was sold for £164,800.

Oct, 2005: At auction at Bonham's, the medals and other memorabilia of Hungary and Real Madrid legend **Ferenc Puskas** were sold for £85,000 to help pay for hospital treatment.

Nov, 2006: A ball used in the 2006 World Cup Final and signed by the winning **Italy** team was sold for £1.2m (a world record for football memorabilia) at a charity auction in Qatar. It was bought by the Qatar Sports Academy.

Feb, 2010: A pair of boots worn by **Sir Stanley Matthews** in the 1953 FA Cup Final was sold at Bonham's for £38,400.

Oct, 2010: Trophies and memorabilia belonging to **George Best** were sold at Bonham's for £193,440. His 1968 European Cup winner's medal fetched £156,000.

Oct–Nov 2010: **Nobby Stiles** sold his 1966 World Cup winner's medal at an Edinburgh auction for a record £188,200. His old club, Manchester Utd, also paid £40,300 for his 1968 European Cup medal to go to the club's museum at Old Trafford. In London, the shirt worn by Stiles in the 1966 World Cup Final went for £75,000. A total of 45 items netted £424,438. **George Cohen** and **Martin Peters** had previously sold their medals from 1966.

Oct 2011: **Terry Paine** (who did not play in the Final) sold his 1966 World Cup medal for £27,500 at auction.

Mar 2013: **Norman Hunter** (Leeds and England) sold his honours' collection on line for nearly £100,000

Nov 2013: A collection of **Nat Lofthouse's** career memorabilia was sold at auction for £100,000. Bolton Council paid £75,000 for items including his 1958 FA Cup winner's medal to go on show at the local museum.

LONGEST UNBEATEN CUP RUN

Liverpool established the longest unbeaten Cup sequence by a Football League club: 25 successive rounds in the League/Milk Cup between semi-final defeat by Nottm Forest (1-2 agg) in 1980 and defeat at Tottenham (0-1) in the third round on Oct 31, 1984. During this period Liverpool won the tournament in four successive seasons, a feat no other Football League club has achieved in any competition.

BIG HALF-TIME SCORES

Tottenham 10, Crewe 1 (FA Cup 4th round replay, Feb 3, 1960; result 13-2); Tranmere 8, Oldham 1 (Div 3N., Dec 26, 1935; result 13-4); **Chester City 8, York 0** (Div 3N., Feb 1, 1936; result 12-0; believed to be record half-time scores in League football).

Nine goals were scored in the first half – **Burnley 4, Watford 5** in Div 1 on Apr 5, 2003. Result: 4-7.

Stirling Albion led Selkirk 15-0 at half-time (result 20-0) in the Scottish Cup 1st round, Dec 8, 1984.

World record half-time score: **16-0** when **Australia** beat **American Samoa** 31-0 (another world record) in the World Cup Oceania qualifying group at Coff's Harbour, New South Wales, on Apr 11 2001.

● On Mar 4 1933 **Coventry** beat QPR (Div 3 South) 7-0, having led by that score at half-time. This repeated the half-time situation in Bristol City's 7-0 win over Grimsby on Dec 26, 1914.

TOP SECOND-HALF TEAM

Most goals scored by a team in one half of a League match is **11. Stockport** led Halifax 2-0 at half-time in Div 3 North on Jan 6 1934 and won 13-0.

FIVE NOT ENOUGH

Last team to score **5** in League match and lose: **Burton**, beaten 6-5 by Cheltenham (Lge 2, Mar 13, 2010).

LONG SERVICE WITH ONE CLUB

Bill Nicholson, OBE, was associated with Tottenham for 67 years – as a wing-half (1938–55), then the club's most successful manager (1958–74) with 8 major prizes, subsequently chief advisor and scout. He became club president, and an honorary freeman of the borough, had an executive suite named after him at the club, and the stretch of roadway from Tottenham High Road to the main gates has the nameplate Bill Nicholson Way. He died, aged 85, in Oct 2004.

Ted Bates, the Grand Old Man of Southampton with 66 years of unbroken service to the club, was awarded the Freedom of the City in Apr, 2001. He joined Saints as an inside-forward from Norwich in 1937, made 260 peace-time appearances for the club, became reserve-team trainer in 1953 and manager at The Dell for 18 years (1955–73), taking Southampton into the top division in 1966. He was subsequently chief executive, director and club president. He died in Oct 2003, aged 85.

Bob Paisley was associated with Liverpool for 57 years from 1939, when he joined them from Bishop Auckland, until he died in Feb 1996. He served as player, trainer, coach, assistant-manager, manager, director and vice-president. He was Liverpool's most successful manager, winning 13 major trophies for the club (1974–83).

Dario Gradi, MBE, stepped down after completing 24 seasons and more than 1,000 matches as manager of Crewe (appointed Jun 1983). Never a League player, he previously managed Wimbledon and Crystal Palace. At Crewe, his policy of finding and grooming young talent has earned the club more than £20m in transfer fees. He stayed with Crewe as technical director, and twice took charge of team affairs again following the departure of the managers who succeeded him, Steve Holland and Gudjon Thordarson.

Ronnie Moran, who joined Liverpool in as a player 1952, retired from the Anfield coaching staff in season 1998–99.

Ernie Gregory served West Ham for 52 years as goalkeeper and coach. He joined them as boy of 14 from school in 1935, retired in May 1987.

Ryan Giggs played 24 seasons for Manchester Utd (1990-2014), then became assistant manager under Louis van Gaal.

Ted Sagar, Everton goalkeeper, 23 years at Goodison Park (1929–52, but only 16 League seasons because of war).

Alan Knight, goalkeeper, played 23 seasons (1977–2000) for his only club, Portsmouth.

Sam Bartram was recognised as one of the finest goalkeepers never to play for England, apart from unofficial wartime games. He was with Charlton from 1934–56

Jack Charlton, England World Cup winner, served Leeds from 1952–73.
Roy Sproson, defender, played 21 League seasons for his only club, Port Vale (1950–71).
John Terry had a 22-year association with Chelsea from 1994–2017.

TIGHT AT HOME

Fewest home goals conceded in League season (modern times): 4 by **Liverpool** (Div 1, 1978–9); 4 by **Manchester Utd** (Premier League, 1994–95) – both in 21 matches.

VARSITY MATCH

First played in 1873, this is the game's second oldest contest (after the FA Cup). Played 135, Oxford 53 wins, Cambridge 50, draws 32. Goals: Oxford 218, Cambridge 208. The latest match, at The Hive, Barnet, was drawn 1-1, with Cambridge winning 5-3 on penalties.

TRANSFER WINDOW

This was introduced to Britain in Sep 2002 via FIFA regulations to bring uniformity across Europe (the rule previously applied in a number of other countries).
The transfer of contracted players is restricted to two periods: Jun 1–Aug 31 and Jan 1–31).
On appeal, Football League clubs continued to sign/sell players (excluding deals with Premier League clubs).

PROGRAMME PIONEERS

Chelsea pioneered football's magazine-style programme by introducing a 16-page issue for the First Division match against Portsmouth on Christmas Day 1948. It cost sixpence (2.5p). A penny programme from the 1909 FA Cup Final fetched £23,500 at a London auction in May, 2012.

FOOTBALL POOLS

Littlewoods launched them in 1923 with capital of £100. Coupons (4,000 of them) were first issued outside Manchester United's ground, the original 35 investors staking a total of £4 7s 6d (pay-out £2 12s). Vernons joined Littlewoods as leading promoters. The Treble Chance, leading to bonanza dividends, was introduced in 1946 and the Pools Panel began in January 1963 to counter mass fixture postponements caused by the Big Freeze winter.
But business was hard hit by the launch of the National Lottery in 1994. Dividends slumped, the work-force was cut severely and in June 2000 the Liverpool-based Moores family sold Littlewoods Pools in a £161m deal. After 85 years, the name Littlewoods disappeared from Pools betting in August 2008. The New Football Pools was formed. Vernons and Zetters continued to operate in their own name under the ownership of Sportech. The record prize remains the £2,924,622 paid to a syndicate in Worsley, Manchester, in November 1994.

WORLD'S OLDEST FOOTBALL ANNUAL

Now in its 133rd edition, this publication began as the 16-page Athletic News Football Supplement & Club Directory in 1887. From the long-established Athletic News, it became the Sunday Chronicle Annual in 1946, the Empire News in 1956, the News of the World & Empire News in 1961 and the News of the World Annual from 1965 until becoming the Nationwide Annual in 2008.

PREMIER LEAGUE CLUB DETAILS AND SQUADS 2019–20

(at time of going to press)

ARSENAL

Ground: Emirates Stadium, Highbury, London, N5 1BU
Telephone: 0207 619 5003. **Club nickname:** Gunners
Capacity: 60,260. **Colours:** Red and white. **Main sponsor:** Emirates
Record transfer fee: £56m to Borussia Dortmund for Pierre-Emerick Aubameyang, Jan 20018
Record fee received: £35m from Barcelona for Cesc Fabregas, Aug 2011; £35m from Liverpool for Alex Oxlade-Chamberlain, Aug 2017
Record attendance: Highbury: 73,295 v Sunderland (Div 1) Mar 9, 1935. Emirates Stadium: 60,161 v Manchester Utd (Prem Lge) Nov 3, 2007. Wembley: 73,707 v Lens (Champ Lge) Nov 25, 1998
League Championship: Winners 1930–31, 1932–33, 1933–34, 1934–35, 1937–38, 1947–48, 1952–53, 1970–71, 1988–89, 1990–91, 1997–98, 2001–02, 2003–04
FA Cup: Winners 1930, 1936, 1950, 1971, 1979, 1993, 1998, 2002, 2003, 2005, 2014, 2015, 2017
League Cup: Winners 1987, 1993
European competitions: Winners Fairs Cup 1969–70; Cup-Winners' Cup 1993–94
Finishing positions in Premier League: 1992–93 10th, 1993–94 4th, 1994–95 12th, 1995–96 5th, 1996–97 3rd, 1997–98 1st, 1998–99 2nd, 1999–2000 2nd, 2000–01 2nd, 2001–02 1st, 2002–03 2nd, 2003–04 1st, 2004–05 2nd, 2005–06 4th, 2006–07 4th, 2007–08 3rd, 2008–09 4th, 2009–10 3rd, 2010–11 4th, 2011–12 3rd, 2012–13 4th, 2013–14 4th, 2014–15 3rd, 2015–16 2nd, 2016–17 5th, 2017–18 6th, 2018–19 5th
Biggest win: 12-0 v Loughborough (Div 2) Mar 12, 1900
Biggest defeat: 0-8 v Loughborough (Div 2) Dec 12, 1896
Highest League scorer in a season: Ted Drake 42 (1934–35)
Most League goals in aggregate: Thierry Henry 175 (1999–2007) (2012)
Longest unbeaten League sequence: 49 matches (2003–04)
Longest sequence without a League win: 23 matches (1912–13)
Most capped player: Thierry Henry (France) 81

Name	Height ft in	Previous club	Birthplace	Birthdate
Goalkeepers				
Iliev, Dejan	6.4	Belastica	Strumica, Mace	25.02.95
Leno, Bernd	6.3	Bayer Leverkusen	Bietigehm-Bissingen, Ger	04.03.92
Martinez, Damian	6.4	Independiente	Mar del Plata, Arg	02.09.92
Defenders				
Bellerin, Hector	5.10	Barcelona	Barcelona, Sp	19.03.95
Chambers, Calum	6.0	Southampton	Petersfield	20.01.95
Holding, Rob	6.0	Bolton	Tameside	12.09.95
Jenkinson, Carl	6.1	Charlton	Harlow	08.02.92
Kolasinac, Sead	6.0	Schalke	Karlsruhe, Ger	20.06.93
Koscielny, Laurent	6.1	Lorient	Tulle, Fr	10.09.85
Mavropanos, Konstantinos	6.4	Giannina	Athens, Gre	11.12.97
Monreal, Nacho	5.10	Malaga	Pamplona, Sp	26.02.86
Mustafi, Shkodran	6.1	Valencia	Bad Hersfeld, Ger	17.04.92
Sokratis	6.1	Borussia Dortmund	Kalamata, Gre	09.06.88
Midfielders				
Elneny, Mohamed	5.11	Basle	El-Mahalla, Egy	11.07.92
Guendouzi, Matteo	6.1	Lorient	Poissy, Fr	14.04.99

Maitland-Niles, Ainsley	5.10	–	Goodmayes	29.08.97
Mkhitaryan, Henrikh	5.10	Man Utd	Yerevan, Arm	21.01.89
Ozil, Mesut	5.11	Real Madrid	Gelsenkirchen, Ger	15.10.88
Suarez, Denis	5.10			
Smith Rowe, Emile	6.0	–	Croydon	28.07.2000
Torreira, Lucas	5.6	Sampdoria	Fray Bentos, Uru	11.02.96
Xhaka, Granit	6.1	Borussia M'gladbach	Basle, Swi	27.09.92
Forwards				
Aubameyang, Pierre-Emerick	6.2	Borussia Dortmund	Laval, Fr	18.06.89
Iwobi, Alex	5.11	–	Lagos, Nig	03.05.96
Lacazette, Alexandre	5.9	Lyon	Lyon, Fr	28.05.91
Martinelli, Gabriel	5.11	Ituano	Guarulhos, Br	18.06.01
Nelson, Reiss	5.9	–	Elephant and Castle	10.12.99
Nketiah, Eddie	5.9	–	Lewisham	30.05.99
Willock, Joe	5.10	–	Waltham Forest	20.08.99

ASTON VILLA

Ground: Villa Park, Trinity Road, Birmingham, B6 6HE
Telephone: 0333 323 1874. **Club nickname:** Villans
Capacity: 42,682. **Colours:** Claret and blue. **Main sponsor:** W88
Record transfer fee: £22m to Club Bruges for Wesley, Jun 2019
Record fee received: £32.5m from Liverpool for Christian Benteke, Jul 2015
Record attendance: 76,588 v Derby (FA Cup 6) Mar 2, 1946
League Championship: Winners 1893–94, 1895–96, 1896–97, 1898–99, 1899–1900, 1909–10, 1980–81
FA Cup: Winners 1887, 1895, 1897, 1905, 1913, 1920, 1957
League Cup: Winners 1961, 1975, 1977, 1994, 1996
European competitions: Winners European Cup 1981–82; European Super Cup 1982
Finishing positions in Premier League: 1992–93 2nd, 1993–94 10th, 1994–95 18th, 1995–96 4th, 1996–97 5th, 1997–98 7th, 1998–99 6th, 1999–2000 6th, 2000–01 8th, 2001–02 8th, 2002–03 16th, 2003–04 6th, 2004–05 10th, 2005–06 16th, 2006–07 11th, 2007–08 6th, 2008–09 6th, 2009–10 6th, 2010–11 9th, 2011–12 16th, 2012–13th 15th, 2013–14 15th, 2014–15 17th, 2015–16 20th
Biggest win: 12-2 v Accrington (Div 1) Mar 12, 1892; 11-1 v Charlton (Div 2) Nov 24, 1959; 10-0 v Sheffield Wed (Div 1) Oct 5, 1912, v Burnley (Div 1) Aug 29, 1925. Also: 13-0 v Wednesbury (FA Cup 1) Oct 30, 1886
Biggest defeat: 0-8 v Chelsea (Prem Lge) Dec 23, 2012
Highest League scorer in a season: 'Pongo' Waring 49 (1930–31)
Most League goals in aggregate: Harry Hampton 215 (1904–15)
Longest unbeaten League sequence: 15 matches (1897, 1909–10) and 1949
Longest sequence without a League win: 19 matches (2015–16)
Most capped player: Steve Staunton (Republic of Ireland) 64

Goalkeepers				
Nyland, Orjan	6.3	Ingolstadt	Kristiansund, Nor	10.09.90
Steer, Jed	6.3	Norwich	Norwich	23.09.92
Defenders				
Bree, James	5.10	Barnsley	Wakefield	11.10.97
Chester, James	5.11	WBA	Warrington	23.01.89
Guilbert, Frederic	5.10	Caen	Valognes, Fr	24.12.94
Hause, Kortney	6.3	Wolves	Goodmayes	16.07.95
Konsa, Ezri	6.0	Brentford	Newham	23.10.97
Mings, Tyrone	6.3	Bournemouth	Bath	13.03.93
Taylor, Neil	5.9	Swansea	St Asaph	07.02.89

Midfielders

Bjarnason, Birkir	6.0	Basle	Akureyri, Ice	27.05.88
El Ghazi, Anwar	6.2	Lille	Barendrecht, Hol	03.05.95
Elmohamady, Ahmed	5.11	Hull	Basyoun, Egy	09.09.87
Grealish, Jack	5.9	–	Solihull	10.09.95
Green, Andre	5.11	–	Solihull	26.07.98
Hourihane, Conor	6.0	Barnsley	Cork, Ire	02.02.91
Jota	5.11	Birmingham	Pobra do Caraminal, Sp	16.06.91
Lansbury, Henri	6.0	Nottm Forest	Enfield	12.10.90
McGinn, John	5.10	Hibernian	Glasgow	18.10.94
Targett, Matt	6.0	Southampton	Eastleigh	18.09.95
Tshibola, Aaron	6.3	Reading	Newham	02.01.95

Forwards

Davis, Keinan	6.3	–	Stevenage	13.02.98
Hepburn-Murphy, Russell	5.8	–	Birmingham	28.08.98
Hogan, Scott	5.11	Brentford	Salford	13.04.92
Kodjia, Jonathan	6.2	Bristol City	St Denis, Fr	22.10.89
Wesley	6.2	Club Bruges	Juiz de Fora, Br	26.11.96

BOURNEMOUTH

Ground: Vitality Stadium, Dean Court, Bournemouth BH7 7AF
Telephone: 0344 576 1910. **Club nickname:** Cherries
Capacity: 11,329. **Colours:** Red and black. **Main sponsor:** M88
Record transfer fee: £25 to Levante for Jefferson Lerma, Aug 2018
Record fee received: £20m from Aston Villa for Tyrone Mings, July 2019
Record attendance: 28,799 v Manchester Utd (FA Cup 6) Mar 2, 1957
FA Cup: Sixth round 1957
League Cup: Fifth round 2014
Finishing position in Premier League: 2015–16 16th, 2016–17 9th, 2017–18 12th, 2018–19 14th
Biggest win: 8-0 v Birmingham (Champ) Oct 15, 2014. Also: 11-0 v Margate (FA Cup 1) Nov20, 1971
Biggest defeat: 0-9 v Lincoln (Div 3) Dec 18, 1982
Highest League scorer in a season: Ted MacDougall 42 (1970–71)
Most League goals in aggregate: Ron Eyre 202 (1924–33)
Longest unbeaten League sequence: 18 (1982)
Longest sequence without a League win: 14 (1974)
Most capped player: Gerry Peyton (Republic of Ireland) 7

Goalkeepers

Begovic, Asmir	6.5	Chelsea	Trebinje, Bos	20.06.87
Boruc, Artur	6.4	Southampton	Siedice, Pol	20.02.80
Travers, Mark	6.3	–	Maynooth, Ire	18.05.99

Defenders

Ake, Nathan	5.11	Chelsea	The Hague, Hol	18.02.95
Cook, Steve	6.1	Brighton	Hastings	19.04.91
Daniels, Charlie	5.10	Leyton Orient	Harlow	07.09.86
Francis, Simon	6.0	Charlton	Nottingham	16.02.85
Kelly, Lloyd	5.10	Bristol City	Bristol	01.10.98
Mepham, Chris	6.3	Brentford	Hammersmith	05.11.97
Rico, Diego	6.0	Leganes	Burgos, Sp	23.02.93
Simpson, Jack	5.10	–	Weymouth	08.01.97
Smith, Adam	5.11	Tottenham	Leystonstone	29.04.91

Midfielders

Arter, Harry	5.9	Woking	Eltham	28.12.89
Brooks, David	5.8	Sheffield Utd	Warrington	08.07.97
Cook, Lewis	5.9	Leeds	Leeds	03.02.97
Fraser, Ryan	5.4	Aberdeen	Aberdeen	24.02.94
Gosling, Dan	5.10	Newcastle	Brixham	02.02.90
Ibe, Jordon	5.7	Liverpool	Bermondsey	08.12.95
Lerma, Jefferson	5.10	Levante	Cerrito, Col	25.10.94
Stanislas, Junior	6.0	Burnley	Eltham	26.11.89
Surman, Andrew	5.11	Norwich	Johannesburg, SA	20.08.86

Forwards

King, Josh	5.11	Blackburn	Oslo, Nor	15.01.92
Mousset, Lys	6.0	Le Havre	Montivilliers, Fr	08.12.96
Solanke, Dominic	6.1	Liverpool	Reading	14.09.97
Surridge, Sam	6.3	–	Slough	28.07.98
Wilson, Callum	5.11	Coventry	Coventry	27.02.92

BRIGHTON AND HOVE ALBION

Ground: American Express Community Stadium, Village Way, Brighton BN1 9BL
Telephone: 0344 324 6282. **Club nickname:** Seagulls
Capacity: 30,666. **Colours.** Blue and white. **Main sponsor:** American Express
Record transfer fee: £17m to Alkmaar for Alireza Jahanbakhsh, Jul 2018
Record fee received: £8m from Leicester for Leonardo Ulloa, July 2014
Record attendance: Goldstone Ground: 36,747 v Fulham (Div 2) Dec 27, 1958; Withdean Stadium: 8,729 v Manchester City (League Cup 2) Sep 24, 2008; Amex Stadium: 30,634 v Liverpool (Prem Lge) Dec 2, 2017
League Championship: 13th1981–92
FA Cup: Runners-up 1983
League Cup: Fifth round 1979
Finishing position in Premier League: 2017–18 15th, 2018–19 17th
Biggest win: 10-1 v Wisbech (FA Cup 1) Nov 13, 1965
Biggest defeat: 0-9 v Middlesbrough (Div 2) Aug 23, 1958
Highest League scorer in a season: Peter Ward 32 (1976–77)
Most League goals in aggregate: Tommy Cook 114 (1922–29)
Longest unbeaten League sequence: 22 matches (2015)
Longest sequence without a League win: 15matches (1972–73)
Most capped player: Shane Duffy (Republic of Ireland) 24

Goalkeepers

Button, David	6.3	Fulham	Stevenage	27.02.89
Ryan, Mathew	6.1	Valencia	Plumpton, Aus	08.04.92

Defenders

Balogun, Leon	6.3	Mainz	Berlin, Ger	28.06.88
Bernardo	6.1	Leipzig	Sao Paulo, Bra	14.05.95
Bong, Gaetan	6.2	Wigan	Sakbayeme, Cam	25.04.88
Burn, Dan	6.7	Wigan	Blyth	09.05.92
Clarke, Matt	5.11	Portsmouth	Ipswich	22.09.96
Duffy, Shane	6.4	Blackburn	Derry	01.01.92
Dunk, Lewis	6.4	–	Brighton	1.11.91
Montoya, Martin	5.9	Valencia	Barcelona, Sp	04.04.91

Midfielders

Bissouma, Yves	6.0	Lille	Issia, Iv C	30.08.96
Gross, Pascal	6.0	Ingolstadt	Mannheim, Ger	15.06.91
Izquierdo, Jose	5.8	Club Bruges	Pereira, Col	07.07.92

Kayal, Beram	5.10	Celtic	Jadeidi, Isr	02.05.88
Knockaert, Anthony	5.8	Standard Liege	Roubaix, Fr	20.11.91
March, Solly	5.11	–	Eastbourne	20.07.94
Propper, Davy	6.1	PSV Eindhoven	Arnhem, Hol	02.09.91
Stephens, Dale	5.7	Charlton	Bolton	12.06.89
Forwards				
Andone, Florin	5.11	Dep La Coruna	Botosani, Rom	11.04.93
Gyokeres, Viktor	6.2	Brommapojkarna	Sweden	04.06.98
Jahanbakhsh, Alireza	5.11	Alkmaar	Jirandeh, Ira	11.08.93
Locadia, Jurgen	6.1	PSV Eindhoven	Emmen, Hol	07.11.93
Murray, Glenn	6.1	Bournemouth	Maryport	25.09.83
Trossard, Leandro	5.8	Genk	Waterschei, Bel	04.12.94

BURNLEY

Ground: Turf Moor, Harry Potts Way, Burnlety BB10 4BX
Telephone: 0871 221 1882. **Club nickname:** Clarets
Capacity: 21,944. **Colours:** Claret and blue. **Main sponsor:** LoveBet
Record transfer fee: £15m to Leeds for Chris Wood, Aug 2017, £15m to Middlesbrough for Ben Gibson, Aug 2018
Record fee received: £25m from Everton for Michael Keane, Jul 2017
Record attendance: 54,775 v Huddersfield (FA Cup 3) Feb 23, 1924
League Championship: Winners 1920–21, 1959–60
FA Cup: Winners 1914
League Cup: Semi-finals 1961, 1969, 1983, 2009
European competitions: European Cup quarter-finals 1960–61
Finishing positions in Premier League: 2014–15 19th, 2016–17 16th, 2017–18 7th, 2018–19 15th
Biggest win: 9-0 v Darwen (Div 1) Jan 9, 1892, v Crystal Palace (FA Cup 2) Feb 10, 1909, v New Brighton (FA Cup 4) Jan 26, 1957, v Penrith (FA Cup 1) Nov 17, 1984
Biggest defeat: 0-10 v Aston Villa (Div 1) Aug 29, 1925, v Sheffield Utd (Div 1) Jan 19, 1929
Highest League scorer in a season: George Beel 35 (1927–28)
Highest League scorer in aggregate: George Beel 178 (1923–32)
Longest unbeaten League sequence: 30 matches (1920–21)
Longest sequence without a League win: 24 matches (1979)
Most capped player: Jimmy McIlroy (Northern Ireland) 51

Goalkeepers				
Heaton, Tom	6.1	Bristol City	Chester	15.04.86
Pope, Nick	6.3	Charlton	Cambridge	19.04.92
Defenders				
Bardsley, Phil	5.11	Stoke	Salford	28.06.85
Gibson, Ben	6.1	Middlesbrough	Nunthorpe	05.01.93
Long, Kevin	6.2	Cork	Cork, Ire	18.08.90
Lowton, Matthew	5.11	Aston Villa	Chesterfield	09.06.89
Mee, Ben	5.11	Man City	Sale	23.09.89
Taylor, Charlie	5.9	Leeds	York	18.09.93
Midfielders				
Brady, Robbie	5.10	Norwich	Dublin, Ire	14.01.92
Cork, Jack	6.1	Swansea	Carshalton	25.06.89
Gudmundsson, Johann Berg	6.1	Charlton	Reykjavik, Ice	27.10.90
Hendrick, Jeff	6.1	Derby	Dublin, Ire	31.01.92
Lennon, Aaron	5.5	Everton	Leeds	16.04.87
McNeil, Dwight	6.1	–	Rochdale	22.11.99
Tarkowski, James	6.1	Brentford	Manchester	19.11.92

| Westwood, Ashley | 5.7 | Aston Villa | Nantwich | 01.04.90 |

Forwards

Barnes, Ashley	6.0	Brighton	Bath	31.10.89
Rodriguez, Jay	6.1	WBA	Burnley	29.07.89
Wood, Chris	6.3	Leeds	Auckland, NZ	07.12.91
Vydra, Matej	5.11	Derby	Chotebor, Cz	01.05.92

CHELSEA

Ground: Stamford Bridge Stadium, London SW6 1HS
Telephone: 0371 811 1955. **Club nickname:** Blues
Capacity: 42,332. **Colours:** Blue. **Main sponsor:** Yokohama Tyres
Record transfer fee: £71.6m to Athletic Bilbao for Kepa Arrizabalaga, Aug 2018
Record fee received: £88.5m from Real Madrid for Eden Hazard, Jun 2019
Record attendance: 82,905 v Arsenal (Div 1) Oct 12, 1935
League Championship: Winners 1954–55, 2004–05, 2005–06, 2009–10, 2014–15, 2016–17
FA Cup: Winners 1970, 1997, 2000, 2007, 2009, 2010, 2012, 2018
League Cup: Winners 1965, 1998, 2005, 2007, 2015
European competitions: Winners Champions League 2011–12; Cup-Winners' Cup 1970–71, 1997–98; Europa League 2012–13, 2018–19; European Super Cup 1998
Finishing positions in Premier League: 1992–93 11th, 1993–94 14th, 1994–95 11th, 1995–96 11th, 1996–97 6th, 1997–98 4th, 1998–99 3rd, 1999–2000 5th, 2000–01 6th, 2001–02 6th, 2002–03 4th, 2003–04 2nd, 2004–05 1st, 2005–06 1st, 2006–07 2nd, 2007–08 2nd, 2008–09 3rd, 2009–10 1st, 2010–11 2nd, 2011–12 6th, 2012–13 3rd, 2013–14 3rd, 2014–15 1st, 2015–16 10th, 2016–17 1st, 2017–18 5th, 2018–19 3rd
Biggest win: 8-0 v Aston Villa (Prem Lge) Dec 23, 2012. Also: 13-0 v Jeunesse Hautcharage, (Cup-Winners' Cup 1) Sep 29, 1971
Biggest defeat: 1-8 v Wolves (Div 1) Sep 26, 1953; 0-7 v Leeds (Div 1) Oct 7, 1967, v Nottm Forest (Div 1) Apr 20, 1991
Highest League scorer in a season: Jimmy Greaves 41 (1960–61)
Most League goals in aggregate: Bobby Tambling 164 (1958–70)
Longest unbeaten League sequence: 40 matches (2004–05)
Longest sequence without a League win: 21 matches (1987–88)
Most capped player: Frank Lampard (England) 104

Goalkeepers

Arrizabalaga, Kepa	6.2	Athletic Bilbao	Ondarroa, Sp	03.10.94
Caballero, Willy	6.1	Man City	Santa Elena, Arg	28.09.81
Eduardo	6.2	Dinamo Zagreb	Mirandela, Port	19.09.82

Defenders

Alonso, Marcos	6.2	Fiorentina	Madrid, Sp	28.12.90
Azpilicueta, Cesar	5.10	Marseille	Pamplona, Sp	28.08.89
Christensen, Andreas	6.2	Brondby	Lillerod, Den	10.04.96
Emerson	5.9	Roma	Santos, Br	03.08.94
Luiz, David	6.3	Paris SG	Diadema, Br	22.04.87
Rudiger, Antonio	6.3	Roma	Berlin, Ger	03.03.93
Zappacosta, Davide	6.1	Torino	Sora, It	11.06.92
Zouma, Kurt	6.3	St Etienne	Lyon, Fr	27.10.94

Midfielders

Barkley, Ross	6.2	Everton	Liverpool	05.12.93
Jorginho	5.11	Napoli	Imbituba, Bra	20.12.91
Kante, N'Golo	5.7	Leicester	Paris, Fr	29.03.91
Kenedy	6.0	Fluminense	Santa Rita, Bra	08.02.96
Kovacic, Mateo	5.10	Real Madrid	Linz, Aut	06.05.94
Loftus-Cheek, Ruben	6.3	–	Lewisham	23.01.96

Moses, Victor	5.10	Wigan	Lagos, Nig	12.12.90
Pedro	5.6	Barcelona	Santa Cruz, Ten	28.07.87
Willian	5.9	Anzhi Makhachkala	Ribeirao Pires, Br	09.08.88
Forwards				
Batshuayi, Michy	6.0	Marseille	Brussels, Bel	02.10.93
Giroud, Olivier	6.4	Arsenal	Chambery, Fr	30.09.86
Hudson-Odoi, Callum	6.0	–	Wandsworth	07.11.00

CRYSTAL PALACE

Ground: Selhurst Park, Whitehorse Lane, London SE25, 6PU
Telephone: 0208 768 6000. **Club nickname:** Eagles
Capacity: 25,486. **Colours:** Red and blue. **Main sponsor:** ManBetX
Record transfer fee: £27m to Liverpool for Christian Benteke, Aug 2016
Record fee received: £50m from Manchester Utd for Aaron Wan-Bissaka, Jun 2019
Record attendance: 51,482 v Burnley (Div 2), May 11, 1979
League Championship: 3rd 1990–91
FA Cup: Runners-up 1990, 2016
League Cup: Semi-finals 1993, 1995, 2001, 2012
Finishing positions in Premier League: 1992–93 20th, 1994–95 19th, 1997–98 20th, 2004–05 18th, 2013–14 11th, 2014–15 10th, 2015–16 15th, 2016–17 14th, 2017–18 11th, 2018–19 12th
Biggest win: 9-0 v Barrow (Div 4) Oct 10, 1959
Biggest defeat: 0-9 v Liverpool (Div 1) Sep 12, 1989. Also: 0-9 v Burnley (FA Cup 2 rep) Feb 10, 1909
Highest League scorer in a season: Peter Simpson 46 (1930–31)
Most League goals in aggregate: Peter Simpson 153 (1930–36)
Longest unbeaten League sequence: 18 matches (1969)
Longest sequence with a League win: 20 matches (1962)
Most capped player: Wayne Hennessey (Wales) 43

Goalkeepers				
Guaita, Vicente	6.3	Getafe	Torrente, Sp	10.01.87
Henderson, Stephen	6.3	Nottingham Forest	Dublin, Ire	02.05.88
Hennessey, Wayne	6.5	Wolves	Bangor, Wal	24.01.87
Defenders				
Dann, Scott	6.2	Blackburn	Liverpool	14.02.87
Kelly, Martin	6.3	Liverpool	Whiston	27.04.90
Kouyate, Cheikhou	6.4	West Ham	Dakar, Sen	21.12.89
Sakho, Mamadou	6.2	Liverpool	Paris, Fr	13.02.90
Schlupp, Jeffrey	5.8	Leicester	Hamburg, Ger	23.12.92
Souare, Pape	5.10	Lille	Mbao, Sen	06.06.90
Tomkins, James	6.3	West Ham	Basildon	29.03.89
Van Aanholt, Patrick	5.9	Sunderland	Hertogenbosch, Hol	29.08.90
Ward, Joel	6.2	Portsmouth	Emsworth	29.10.89
Midfielders				
McArthur, James	5.7	Wigan	Glasgow	07.10.87
Meyer, Max	5.8	Schalke	Oberhausen, Ger	18.09.95
Milivojevic, Luka	6.0	Olympiacos	Kragujevac, Serb	07.04.91
Townsend, Andros	6.0	Newcastle	Leytonstone	16.07.91
Forwards				
Benteke, Christian	6.3	Liverpool	Kinshasa, DR Cong	03.12.90
Sorloth, Alexander	6.4	Midtjylland	Trondheim, Nor	05.12.95
Wickham, Connor	6.3	Sunderland	Colchester	31.03.93
Zaha, Wilfried	5.10	Man Utd	Abidjan, Iv C	10.11.92

EVERTON

Ground: Goodison Park, Liverpool L4 4EL
Telephone: 0151 556 1878. **Club nickname:** Toffees
Capacity: 39,221. **Colours:** Blue and white. **Main sponsor:** SportPesa
Record transfer fee: £45m to Swansea for Gylfi Sigurdsson, Aug 2017
Record fee received: £75m from Manchester Utd for Romelu Lukaku, Jul 2017
Record attendance: 78,299 v Liverpool (Div 1) Sep 18, 1948
League Championship: Winners 1890–91, 1914–15, 1927–28, 1931–31, 1938–39,
1962–63, 1969–70, 1984–85, 1986–87
FA Cup: Winners 1906, 1933, 1966, 1984, 1995
League Cup: Runners-up 1977, 1984
European competitions: Winners Cup-Winners' Cup 1984–85
Finishing positions in Premier League: 1992–93 13th, 1993–94 17th, 1994–95 15th,
1995–96 6th 1996–97 15th 1997–98 17th 1998–99 14th, 1999–2000 13th, 2000–01
16th, 2001–02 15th, 2002–03 7th, 2003–04 17th, 2004–05 4th, 2005–06 11th, 2006–07
6th, 2007–08 5th, 2008–09 5th, 2009–10 8th, 20010–11 7th, 2011–12 7th, 2012–13 6th,
2013–14 5th, 2014–15 11th, 2015–16 11th, 2016–17 7th, 2017–18 8th, 2018–19 8th
Biggest win: 9–1 v Manchester City (Div 1) Sep 3, 1906, v Plymouth (Div 2) Dec 27, 1930.
Also: 11-2 v Derby (FA Cup 1) Jan 18, 1890
Biggest defeat: 0–7 v Portsmouth (Div 1) Sep 10, 1949, v Arsenal (Prem Lge) May 11, 2005
Highest League scorer in a season: Ralph 'Dixie' Dean 60 (1927–28)
Most League goals in aggregate: Ralph 'Dixie' Dean 349 (1925–37)
Longest unbeaten League sequence: 20 matches (1978)
Longest sequence without a League win: 14 matches (1937)
Most capped player: Neville Southall (Wales) 92

Goalkeepers

Lossl, Jonas	6.5	Huddersfield	Kolding, Den	01.02.89
Pickford, Jordan	6.1	Sunderland	Washington, Co Dur	07.03.94
Stekelenburg, Maarten	6.6	Fulham	Haarlem, Hol	22.09.82

Defenders

Baines, Leighton	5.7	Wigan	Liverpool	11.12.84
Coleman, Seamus	5.10	Sligo	Donegal, Ire	11.10.88
Digne, Lucas	5.10	Barcelona	Meaux, Fr	20.07.93
Holgate, Mason	5.11	Barnsley	Doncaster	22.10.96
Keane, Michael	6.3	Burnley	Stockport	11.01.93
Mina, Yerry	6.4	Barcelona	Guachene, Col	23.09.94

Midfielders

Bernard	5.5	Shakhtar Donetsk	Belo Horizonte, Br	08.09.92
Davies, Tom	5.11	–	Liverpool	30.06.98
Delph, Fabian	5.9	Manchester City	Bradford	21.11.89
Gomes, Andre	6.2	Barcelona	Crijo, Port	30.07.93
Gueye, Idrissa	5.9	Aston Villa	Dakar, Sen	26.09.89
Schneiderlin, Morgan	5.11	Man Utd	Zellwiller, Fr	08.11.89
Sigurdsson, Gylfi	6.1	Swansea	Hafnarfjordur, Ice	08.09.89

Forwards

Calvert-Lewin, Dominic	6.2	Sheffield Utd	Sheffield	16.03.97
Lookman, Ademola	5.9	Charlton	Wandsworth	20.10.97
Richarlison	5.10	Watford	Nova Venecia, Br	10.05.97
Tosun, Cenk	6.0	Besiktas	Wetzlar, Ger	07.06.91
Walcott, Theo	5.8	Arsenal	Newbury	16.03.89

LEICESTER CITY

Ground: King Power Stadium, Filbert Way, Leicester, LE2 7FL
Telephone: 0344 815 5000. **Club nickname:** Foxes
Capacity: 32,242. **Colours:** Blue and white. **Main sponsor:** King Power
Record transfer fee: £40m to Monaco for Youri Tielemans, Jul 2019
Record fee received: £60m from Manchester City for Riyad Mahrez, Jul 2018
Record attendance: Filbert Street: 47,298 v. Tottenham (FA Cup 5) Feb 18, 1928; King Power Stadium 32,148 v Newcastle (Prem Lge) Dec 26, 2003. Also: 32,188 v Real Madrid (friendly) Jul 30, 2011
League Championship: Winners 2015–16
FA Cup: Runners-up 1949, 1961, 1963, 1969
League Cup: Winners 1964, 1997, 2000
European competitions: Champions League quarter-finals 2016–17
Finishing positions in Premier League: 1994–95 21st, 1996–97 9th, 1997–98 10th, 1998–9 10th, 1999–2000 8th, 2000–01 13th, 2001–02 20th, 2003–04 18th, 2014–15 14th, 2015–16 1st, 2016–17 12th, 2017–18 9th, 2018–19 9th
Biggest win: 10-0 v Portsmouth (Div 1) Oct 20, 1928. Also: 13-0 v Notts Olympic (FA Cup) Oc 13, 1894
Biggest defeat (while Leicester Fosse): 0-12 v Nottm Forest (Div 1) Apr 21, 1909
Highest League scorer in a season: Arthur Rowley 44 (1956–57)
Most League goals in aggregate: Arthur Chandler 259 (1923–35)
Longest unbeaten League sequence: 23 matches (2008–09)
Longest sequence without a League win: 19 matches (1975)
Most capped player: Andy King (Wales) 50

Goalkeepers				
Jakupovic, Eldin	6.3	Hull	Sarajevo, Bos	02.10.84
Schmeichel, Kasper	6.0	Leeds	Copenhagen, Den	05.11.86
Ward, Danny	6.4	Liverpool	Wrexham	22.06.93
Defenders				
Caglar Soyuncu	6.1	Freiburg	Izmir, Tur	23.05.96
Chilwell, Ben	5.10	–	Milton Keynes	21.12.96
Evans, Jonny	6.2	WBA	Belfast	02.01.88
Fuchs, Christian	6.1	Schalke	Neunkirchen, Aut	07.04.86
Justin, James	6.3	Luton	Luton	11.07.97
Maguire, Harry	6.2	Hull	Sheffield	05.03.93
Morgan, Wes	6.1	Nottm Forest	Nottingham	21.01.84
Ricardo Pereira	5.9	Porto	Lisbon, Port	06.10.93
Midfielders				
Adrien Silva	5.9	Sporting Lisbon	Angouleme, Fr	15.03.89
Albrighton, Mark	6.1	Aston Villa	Tamworth	18.11.89
Amartey, Daniel	6.0	Copenhagen	Accra, Gh	01.12.94
Choudhury, Hamza	5.10	–	Loughborough	01.10.97
Ghezzal, Rachid	6.0	Monaco	Decines, Fr	09.05.92
Gray, Demarai	5.10	Birmingham	Birmingham	28.06.96
Maddison, James	5.10	Norwich	Coventry	23.11.96
Mendy, Nampalys	5.6	Nice	La Seyne, Fr	23.06.92
Ndidi, Wilfred	6.0	Genk	Lagos, Nig	16.12.96
Tielemans, Youri	5.10	Monaco	Sint-Pieters, Bel	07.05.97
Forwards				
Ayoze Perez	5.11	Newcastle	Santa Cruz, Ten	23.07.93
Barnes, Harvey	5.9	–	Burnley	09.12.97
Hirst, George	6.3	Leuven	Sheffield	15.02.99
Iheanacho, Kelechi	6.2	Man City	Owerri, Nig	03.10.96
Vardy, Jamie	5.10	Fleetwood	Sheffield	11.01.87

LIVERPOOL

Ground: Anfield, Liverpool L4 OTH
Telephone: 0151 263 2361. **Club nickname:** Reds or Pool
Capacity: 53,394. **Colours:** Red. **Main sponsor:** Standard Chartered
Record transfer fee: £75 to Southampton for Virgil van Dijk Jan 2018
Record fee received: £142m from Barcelona for Philippe Coutinho, Jan 2018
Record attendance: 61,905 v Wolves, (FA Cup 4), Feb 2, 1952
League Championship: Winners 1900–01, 1905–06, 1921–22, 1922–23, 1946–47,
1963–64, 1965–66, 1972–73, 1975–76, 1976–77, 1978–79, 1979–80, 1981–82,
1982–83, 1983–84, 1985–86, 1987–88, 1989–90
FA Cup: Winners 1965, 1974, 1986, 1989, 1992, 2001, 2006
League Cup: Winners 1981, 1982, 1983, 1984, 1995, 2001, 2003, 2012
European competitions: Winners European Cup/Champions League 1976–77, 1977–78, 1980–81, 1983 84, 2004–05, 2018–19; UEFA Cup 1972–73, 1975–76, 2000–01; European Super Cup 1977, 2001, 2005
Finishing positions in Premier League: 1992–93 6th, 1993–94 8th, 1994–95 4th, 1995–96 3rd, 1996–97 4th, 1997–98 3rd, 1998–99 7th, 1999–2000 4th, 2000–01 3rd, 2001–02 2nd, 2002–03 5th, 2003 04 4th, 2004–05 5th, 2005–06 3rd, 2006–07 3rd, 2007 08 4th, 2008–09 2nd, 2009–10 7th, 2010–11 6th, 2011–12 8th, 2012–13 7th, 2013–14 2nd, 2014–15 6th, 2015–16 8th, 2016–17 4th, 2017–18 4th, 2018–19 2nd
Biggest win: 10-1 v Rotherham (Div 2) Feb 18, 1896. Also: 11-0 v Stromsgodset (Cup-Winners' Cup 1) Sep 17, 1974
Biggest defeat: 1-9 v Birmingham (Div 2) Dec 11, 1954
Highest League scorer in a season: Roger Hunt 41 (1961–62)
Most League goals in aggregate: Roger Hunt 245 (1959–69)
31 matches (1907–09))
Longest sequence without a League win: 14 matches (1953–54))
Most capped player: Steven Gerrard (England) 114

Goalkeepers				
Alisson	6.4	Roma	Novo Hamburgo, Bra	02.10.92
Mignolet, Simon	6.4	Sunderland	Sint-Truiden, Bel	06.08.88
Defenders				
Alexander-Arnold, Trent	5.10	–	Liverpool	07.10.98
Clyne, Nathaniel	5.9	Southampton	Stockwell	05.04.91
Gomez, Joe	6.1	Charlton	Catford	23.05.97
Lovren, Dejan	6.2	Southampton	Zenica, Bos	05.07.89
Matip, Joel	6.5	Schalke	Bochum, Ger	08.08.91
Robertson, Andrew	5.10	Hull	Glasgow	11.03.94
Van den Berg, Sepp	6.2	FC Zwolle	Zwolle, Hol	20.12.01
Van Dijk, Virgil	6.4	Southampton	Breda, Hol	08.07.91
Midfielders				
Fabinho	6.2	Monaco	Campinas, Bra	23.10.93
Henderson, Jordan	5.10	Sunderland	Sunderland	17.06.90
Keita, Naby	5.8	Leipzig	Conakry, Guin	10.02.95
Lallana, Adam	5.10	Southampton	Bournemouth	10.05.88
Milner, James	5.11	Man City	Leeds	04.01.86
Oxlade-Chamberlain, Alex	5.11	Arsenal	Portsmouth	15.08.93
Shaqiri, Xherdan	5.7	Stoke	Gjilan, Kos	10.10.91
Wijnaldum, Georginio	5.9	Newcastle	Rotterdam, Hol	11.11.90
Forwards				
Firmino, Roberto	6.0	Hoffenheim	Maceio, Br	02.10.91
Mane, Sadio	5.9	Southampton	Sedhiou, Sen	10.04.92
Origi, Divock	6.1	Lille	Ostend, Bel	18.04.95

| Salah, Mohamed | 5.9 | Roma | Basyoun, Egy | 15.06.92 |
| Woodburn, Ben | 5.11 | – | Nottingham | 15.10.99 |

MANCHESTER CITY

Ground: Etihad Stadium, Etihad Campus, Manchester M11 3FF
Telephone: 0161 444 1894. **Club nickname:** City
Capacity: 55,017. **Colours:** Sky blue and white. **Main sponsor:** Etihad
Record transfer fee: £62.8m to Atletico Madrid for Rodri, Jul 2019
Record fee received: £25m from Leicester for Kelechi Iheanacho, Jul 2017
Record attendance: Maine Road: 84,569 v Stoke (FA Cup 6) Mar 3, 1934 (British record for any game outside London or Glasgow). Etihad Stadium: 54,693 v Leicester (Prem Lge) February 6, 2016
League Championship: Winners 1936–37, 1967–68, 2011–12, 2013–14, 2017–18, 2018–19
FA Cup: Winners 1904, 1934, 1956, 1969, 2011, 2019
League Cup: Winners 1970, 1976, 2014, 2016, 2018, 2019
European competitions: Winners Cup-Winners' Cup 1969–70
Finishing positions in Premier League: 1992–93 9th, 1993–94 16th, 1994–95 17th, 1995–96 18th, 2000–01: 18th, 2002–03 9th, 2003–04 16th, 2004–05 8th, 2005–06 15th, 2006–07 14th, 2007–08 9th, 2008–09 10th, 2009–10 5th, 2010–11 3rd, 2011–12 1st, 2012–13 2nd, 2013–14 1st, 2014–15 2nd, 2015–16 4th, 2016–17 3rd, 2017–18 1st, 2018–19 1st
Biggest win: 10-1 v Huddersfield (Div 2) Nov 7, 1987. Also: 10-1 v Swindon (FA Cup 4) Jan 29, 193
Biggest defeat: 1-9 v Everton (Div 1) Sep 3, 1906
Highest League scorer in a season: Tommy Johnson 38 (1928–29)
Most League goals in aggregate: Tommy Johnson, 158 (1919–30)
Longest unbeaten League sequence: 22 matches (1946–47) and (2017–18)
Longest sequence without a League win: 17 matches (1979–80)
Most capped player: Joe Hart (England) 63

Goalkeepers

Bravo, Claudio	6.1	Barcelona	Viluco, Chil	13.04.83
Ederson	6.2	Benfica	Osasco, Br	17.08.93
Defenders				
Angelino	5.10	PSV Eindhoven	Coristanco, Sp	04.01.97
Danilo	6.0	Real Madrid	Bicas, Br	15.07.91
Laporte, Aymeric	6.3	Athletic Bilbao	Agen, Fr	27.05.94
Mangala, Eliaquim	6.2	Porto	Colombes, Fr	13.02.91
Mendy, Benjamin	6.0	Monaco	Longjumeau, Fr	17.07.94
Otamendi, Nicolas	6.0	Valencia	Buenos Aires, Arg	12.02.88
Stones, John	6.2	Everton	Barnsley	28.05.94
Walker, Kyle	6.0	Tottenham	Sheffield	28.05.90
Zinchenko, Oleksandr	5.9	FC Ufa	Radomysli, Ukr	15.12.96
Midfielders				
De Bruyne, Kevin	5.11	Wolfsburg	Drongen, Bel	28.06.91
Fernandinho	5.10	Shakhtar Donetsk	Londrina, Br	04.05.85
Foden, Phil	5.7	–	Stockport	28.05.00
Gundogan, Ilkay	5.11	Borussia Dortmund	Gelsenkirchen, Ger	24.10.90
Mahrez, Riyad	5.10	Leicester	Sarcelles, Fr	21.02.91
Rodri	6.3	Atletico Madrid	Madrid, Sp	23.06.96
Silva, Bernardo	5.8	Monaco	Lisbon, Port	10.08.94
Silva, David	5.7	Valencia	Arguineguin, Sp	08.01.86
Forwards				
Aguero, Sergio	5.8	Atletico Madrid	Quilmes, Arg	02.06.88

Gabriel Jesus	5.9	Palmeiras	Sao Paulo, Br	03.04.97
Sane, Leroy	6.0	Schalke	Essen, Ger	11.01.96
Sterling, Raheem	5.7	Liverpool	Kingston, Jam	08.12.94

MANCHESTER UNITED

Ground: Old Trafford Stadium, Sir Matt Busby Way, Manchester, M16 0RA
Telephone: 0161 868 8000. **Club nickname:** Red Devils
Capacity: 74,879. **Colours:** Red and white. **Main sponsor:** Chevrolet
Record transfer fee: £89.3m to Juventus for Paul Pogba, Aug 2016
Record fee received: £80m from Real Madrid for Cristiano Ronaldo, Jun 2009
Record attendance: 75,811 v Blackburn (Prem Lge), Mar 31, 2007. Also: 76,962 Wolves v Grimsby (FA Cup semi-final) Mar 25, 1939. Crowd of 83,260 saw Manchester Utd v Arsenal (Div 1) Jan 17, 1948 at Maine Road – Old Trafford out of action through bomb damage
League Championship: Winners 1907–08, 1910–11, 1951 52, 1955–56, 1956–7, 1964–65, 1966–67, 1992–93, 1993–94, 1995 96, 1996–97, 1998–99, 1999–2000, 2000–01, 2002–03, 2006–07, 2007–08, 2008–09, 2010–11, 2012 13
FA Cup: Winners 1909, 1948, 1963, 1977, 1983, 1985, 1990, 1994, 1996, 1999, 2004, 2016
League Cup: Winners 1992, 2006, 2009, 2010, 2017
European competitions: Winners European Cup/Champions League 1967–68, 1998–99, 2007–08; Cup-Winners' Cup 1990–91; European Super Cup 1991; Europa League 2016–17
World Club Cup: Winners 2008
Finishing positions in Premier League: 1992–93 1st, 1993–94 1st, 1994–95 2nd, 1995–96 1st, 1996–97 1st, 1997–98 2nd, 1998–99 1st, 1999–2000 1st, 2000–01 1st, 2001–02 3rd, 2002 03 1st, 2003–04 3rd, 2004–05 3rd, 2005–06 2nd, 2006–07 1st, 2007 08 1st, 2008–09 1st, 2009–10 2nd, 2010–11 1st, 2011–12 2nd, 2012–13 1st, 2013–14 7th, 2014–15 4th, 2015–16 5th, 2016–17 6th, 2017–18 2nd, 2018–19 6th
Biggest win: As Newton Heath: 10-1 v Wolves (Div 1) Oct 15, 1892. As Manchester Utd: 9-0 v Ipswich (Prem Lge), Mar 4, 1995. Also: 10-0 v Anderlecht (European Cup prelim rd) Sep 26, 1956
Biggest defeat: 0-7 v Blackburn (Div 1) Apr 10, 1926, v Aston Villa (Div 1) Dec 27, 1930, v Wolves (Div 2) 26 Dec, 1931
Highest League scorer in a season: Dennis Viollet 32 (1959–60)
Most League goals in aggregate: Bobby Charlton 199 (1956 73)
Longest unbeaten League sequence: 29 matches (1998–99)
Longest sequence without a League win: 16 matches (1930)
Most capped player: Sir Bobby Charlton (England) 106

Goalkeepers

De Gea, David	6.4	Atletico Madrid	Madrid, Sp	07 11 90
Romero, Sergio	6.4	Sampdoria	Bernardo, Arg	22.02.87
Defenders				
Bailly, Eric	6.1	Villarreal	Bingerville, Iv C	12.04.94
Dalot, Diogo	6.1	Porto	Braga, Port	18.03.99
Darmian, Matteo	6.0	Torino	Legnano, It	02.12.89
Jones, Phil	5.11	Blackburn	Blackburn	21.02.92
Lindelof, Victor	6.2	Benfica	Vasteras, Swe	17.07.94
Rojo, Marcos	6.2	Sporting Lisbon	La Plata, Arg	20.03.90
Shaw, Luke	6.1	Southamptonn	Kingston upon Thames	12 07.95
Smalling, Chris	6.1	Fulham	Greenwich	22.11.89
Tuanzebe, Axel	6.1		DR Cong	14.11.97
Wan-Bissaka, Aaron	6.0	Crystal Palace	Croydon	26.11.97
Young, Ashley	5.10	Aston Villa	Stevenage	09.07.85
Midfielders				
Fred	5.7	Shakhtar Donetsk	Belo Horizonte, Bra	05.03.93
James, Daniel	5.8	Swansea	Beverley	10.11.97

Mata, Juan	5.7	Chelsea	Burgos, Sp	28.04.88
Matic, Nemanja	6.4	Chelsea	Sabac, Serb	01.08.88
McTominay, Scott	6.4	–	Lancaster	08.12.96
Pereira, Andreas	5.10	PSV Eindhoven	Duffel, Bel	01.01.96
Pogba, Paul	6.3	Juventus	Lagny-sur-Marne, Fr	15.03.93
Forwards				
Lingard, Jesse	6.2	–	Warrington	15.12.92
Lukaku, Romelu	6.3	Everton	Antwerp, Bel	13.05.93
Martial, Anthony	5.11	Monaco	Massy, Fr	05.12.95
Rashford, Marcus	6.0	–	Wythensawe	31.10.97
Sanchez, Alexis	5.7	Arsenal	Tocopilla, Chil	19.12.88

NEWCASTLE UNITED

Ground: St James' Park, Newcastle-upon-Tyne, NE1 4ST
Telephone: 0844 372 1892. **Club nickname:** Magpies
Capacity: 52,305. **Colours:** Black and white. **Main sponsor:** Fun88
Record attendance: 68,386 v Chelsea (Div 1) Sep 3, 1930
Record transfer fee: £20.5m to Atlanta for Miguel Almiron, Jan 2019
Record fee received: £35m from Liverpool for Andy Carroll, Jan 2011
League Championship: Winners 1904–05, 1906–07, 1908–09, 1926–27
FA Cup: Winners: 1910, 1924, 1932, 1951, 1952,1955
League Cup: Runners-up 1976
European competitions: Winners Fairs Cup 1968–69; Anglo-Italian Cup 1972–73
Finishing positions in Premier League: 1993–94 3rd, 1994–95 6th, 1995–96 2nd, 1996–97 2nd, 1997–98 13th, 1998–99 13th, 1999–2000 11th, 2000–01 11th, 2001–02 4th, 2002–03 3rd, 2003–04 5th, 2004–05 14th, 2005–06 7th, 2006–07 13th, 2007–08 12th, 2008–09 18th, 2010–11 12th, 2011–12 5th, 2012–13 16th, 2013–14 10th, 2014–15 15th, 2015–16 18th, 2017–18 10th, 2018–19 13th
Biggest win: 13-0 v Newport (Div 2) Oct 5, 1946
Biggest defeat: 0-9 v Burton (Div 2) Apr 15, 1895
Highest League scorer in a season: Hughie Gallacher 36 (1926–27)
Most League goals in aggregate: Jackie Milburn 177 (1946–57)
Longest unbeaten League sequence: 14 matches (1950)
Longest sequence without a League win: 21 matches (1978)
Most capped player: Shay Given (Republic of Irelnd) 83

Goalkeepers				
Darlow, Karl	6.1	Nottm Forest	Northampton	08.10.90
Dubravka, Martin	6.3	Sparta Prague	Zilina, Slovak	15.01.89
Elliot, Rob	6.3	Charlton	Chatham	30.04.86
Woodman, Freddie	6.2	Crystal Palace	Croydon	04.03.97
Defenders				
Clark, Ciaran	6.2	Aston Villa	Harrow	26.09.89
Dummett, Paul	6.0	–	Newcastle	26.09.91
Fernandez, Federico	6.3	Swansea	Tres Algarrobos, Arg	21.02.89
Lascelles, Jamaal	6.2	Nottm Forest	Derby	11.11.93
Lejeune, Florian	6.3	Eibar	Paris, Fr	20.05.91
Manquillo, Javier	6.0	Atletico Madrid	Madrid, Sp	05.05.94
Schar, Fabian	6.2	Dep La Coruna	Wil, Switz	20.12.91
Yedlin, DeAndre	5.9	Tottenham	Seattle, US	09.07.93
Midfielders				
Almiron, Miguel	5.9	Atlanta	Asuncion, Par	10.02.94
Atsu, Christian	5.8	Chelsea	Ada Foah, Gh	10.01.92
Hayden, Isaac	6.1	Arsenal	Chelmsford	22.03.95

Ki Sung-Yeung	6.2	Swansea	Gwangju, S Kor	24.01.89
Murphy, Jacob	5.10	Norwich	Wembley	24.02.95
Ritchie, Matt	5.8	Bournemouth	Gosport	10.09.89
Shelvey, Jonjo	6.0	Swansea	Romford	27.02.92
Forwards				
Gayle, Dwight	5.10	Crystal Palace	Walthamstow	20.10.90
Joselu	6.3	Stoke	Stuttgart, Ger	27.03.90
Muto, Yoshinori	5.10	Mainz	Tokyo, Jap	15.07.92

NORWICH CITY

Ground: Carrow Road, Norwich NR1 1JE
Telephone: 01603 760760. **Club nickname:** Canaries
Capacity: 27,244. **Colours:** Yellow and green. **Main sponsor:** LeoVegas
Record transfer fee: £8.5m to Everton for Steven Naismith, Jan 2016
Record fee received: £22m from Leicester for James Maddison, Jun 2018
Record attendance: 43,984 v Leicester (FA Cup 6), Mar 30, 1963
League Championship: 3rd 1993
FA Cup: semi finals 1959, 1989, 1992
League Cup: Winners 1962, 1985
European competitions: UEFA Cup rd 3 1993 94
Finishing positions in Premier League: 1992–93 3rd, 1993–94 12th,1994–95 20th, 2004–05 19th, 2011–12 12th, 2012–13 11th, 2013–14 18th, 2015–16 19 th
Biggest win: 10-2 v Coventry (Div3S) Mar 15, 1930
Biggest defeat: 2-10 v Swindon (Southern Lge) Sep 5, 1908
Highest League scorer in a season: Ralph Hunt 31 (1955–56)
Most League goals in aggregate: Johnny Gavin 122 (1945–54, 55–58)
Longest unbeaten League sequence: 20 matches (1950)
Longest sequence without a League win: 25 matches (1956 57)
Most capped player: Wes Hoolahan (Republic of Ireland) 42

Goalkeepers

Fahrmann, Ralf	6.5	Schalke (loan)	Chemnitz, Ger	27.09.88
Krul, Tim	6.3	Brighton	Den Haag, Hol	03.04.88
McGovern, Michael	6.3	Hamilton	Enniskillen	12.07.84
Defenders				
Aarons, Max	5.10	Luton	Hammersmith	04.01.00
Adshead, Daniel	5.7	Rochdale	Manchester	02.09.01
Byram, Sam	5.11	West Ham	Thurrock	16.09.93
Cantwell, Todd	6.0	–	Dereham	27.02.98
Godfrey, Ben	6.0	Middlesbrough	York	1501.98
Hanley, Grant	6.2	Newcastle	Dumfries	20.11.91
Heise, Philip	6.0	Dynamo Dresden	Dusseldorf, Ger	20.06.91
Husband, James	5.11	Middlesbrough	Leeds	03.01.94
Klose, Timm	6.4	Wolfsburg	Frankfurt, Ger	09.05.88
Lewis, Jamal	5.10	–	uton	25.01.98
Zimmermann, Christoph	6.4	Borussia Dortmund	Dusseldorf, Ger	12.01.93
Midfielders				
Buendia, Emiliano	5.8	Getafe	Mar del Plata, Arg	25.12.96
Hernandez, Onel	5.8	Braunschweig	Moron, Cub	01.12.93
Leitner, Moritz	5.9	Augsburg	Munchen, Ger	08.12.92
McLean, Kenny	6.0	Aberdeen	Rutherglen	08.01.92
Roberts, Patrick	5.8	Man City (loan)	Kingston	05.02.97
Stiepermann, Marco	6.3	Bochum	Dortmund, Ger	09.02.91
Tettey, Alexander	5.11	Rennes	Accra, Gh	04.04.86
Thompson, Louis	5.11	Swindon	Bristol	19.12.94

Trybull, Tom	5.11	Den Haag	Berlin, Ger	09.03.93
Vrancic, Mario	6.1	Darmstadt	Slavonski Brod, Croa	23.05.89
Forwards				
Drmic, Josip	6.0	Borussia M'gladbach	Freienbach, Switz	08.08.92
Pukki, Teemu	5.11	Brondby	Kotka, Fin	29.03.90
Srbeny, Dennis	6.3	Paderborn	Berlin, Ger	05.05.94

SHEFFIELD UNITED

Ground: Bramall Lane, Sheffield S2 4SU
Telephone: 0114 253 7200. **Club nickname:** Blades
Capacity: 32,702. **Colours:** Red and white, **Main sponsor:** Union Standard Group
Record attendance: 68,287 v Leeds (FA Cup 5) Feb 15, 1936
Record transfer fee: £8m to Preston for Callum Robinson, July 2019
Record fee received: £11.1m from Bournemouth for David Brooks, Jul 2018
League Championship: Winners 1897.98
FA Cup: Winners 1899, 1902, 1915, 1925
League Cup: Semi-finals 2003, 2015
Finishing positions in Premier League: 1992–93 14th, 1993–94 20th, 2006–07 18th
Biggest win: 10-0 v Burslem Port Vale (Div 2) Dec 10, 1892
Biggest defeat: 0-13 v Bolton (FA Cup 2) Feb 1, 1890
Highest League scorer in a season: Jimmy Dunne 41 (1930–31)
Most League goals in aggregate: Harry Johnson 205 (1919–30)
Longest unbeaten League sequence: 22 matches (1899–1900)
Longest sequence without a League win: 19 matches (1975–76)
Most capped player: BillyGillespie (Northern Ireland) 25

Goalkeepers				
Henderson, Dean	6.3	Man Utd (loan)	Whitehaven	12.03.97
Moore, Simon	6.3	Cardiff	Sandown, IOW	19.05.90
Defenders				
Baldock, George	5.9	MK Dons	Buckingham	09.03.93
Basham, Chris	5.11	Blackpool	Hebburn	18.02.88
Egan, John	6.2	Brentford	Cork, Ire	20.10.92
Freeman, Kieron	6.1	Derby	Bestwood	21.03.92
Jagielka, Phil	5.11	Everton	Manchester	17.08.82
Lundstram, John	5.11	Oxford	Liverpool	18.02.94
O'Connell, Jack	6.3	Brentford	Liverpool	29.03.94
Stearman, Richard	6.2	Fulham	Wolverhampton	19.08.87
Stevens, Enda	6.0	Portsmouth	Dublin, Ire	09.07.90
Midfielders				
Duffy, Mark	5.9	Birmingham	Liverpool	07.10.85
Fleck, John	5.7	Coventry	Glasgow	24.08.91
Freeman, Luke	5.10	QPR	Dartford	22.03.92
Morrison, Ravel	5.9	Ostersunds	Wythenshawe	02.02.93
Norwood, Oliver	5.11	Brighton	Burnley	12.04.91
Forwards				
Clarke, Leon	6.2	Bury	Birmingham	10.02.85
Holmes, Ricky	6.2	Charlton	Uxbridge	19.06.87
McGoldrick, David	6.1	Ipswich	Nottingham	29.11.87
Robinson, Callum	5.10	Preston	Northampton	02.02.95
Sharp, Billy	5.9	Leeds	Sheffield	05.02.86

SOUTHAMPTON

Ground: St Mary's Stadium, Britannia Road, Southampton, SO14 5FP

Telephone: 0845 688 9448. **Club nickname:** Saints
Capacity: 32,384. **Colours:** Red and white. **Main sponsor:** LD Sports
Record transfer fee: £19.1m to Monaco for Guido Carrillo, Jan 2018
Record fee received: £75m from Liverpool for Virgil van Dijk, Jan 2018
Record attendance: The Dell: 31,044 v Manchester Utd (Div 1) Oct 8, 1969. St Mary's: 32,363 v Coventry (Champ) Apr 28, 2012
League Championship: Runners-up 1983–84
FA Cup: Winners 1976
League Cup: Runners-up 1979, 2017
European competitions: Fairs Cup rd 3 1969–70; Cup-Winners' Cup rd 3 1976–77
Finishing positions in Premier League: 1992–93 18th, 1993–94 18th, 1994–5 10th, 1995–96 17th, 1996–97 16th, 1997–98 12th, 1998–99 17th, 1999–200 15th, 2000–01 10th, 2001–02 11th, 2002–03 8th, 2003–04 12th, 2004–05 20th, 2012–13 14th, 2013–14 8th, 2014–15 7th, 2015–16 6th, 2016–17 8 th, 2017–18 17th, 201819 16 th
Biggest win: 8-0 v Northampton (Div 3S) Dec 24, 1921, v Sunderland (Prem Lge) Oct 18, 2014
Biggest defeat: 0-8 v Tottenham (Div 2) Mar 28, 1936, v Everton (Div 1) Nov 20, 1971
Highest League scorer in a season: Derek Reeves 39 (1959–60)
Most League goals in aggregate: Mick Channon 185 (1966–82)
Longest unbeaten League sequence: 19 matches (1921)
Longest unbeaten League sequence: 20 matches (1969)
Most capped player: Steven Davis (Northern Ireland)) 59

Goalkeepers

Forster, Fraser	6.7	Celtic	Hexham	17.03.88
Gunn, Angus	6.5	Man City	Norwich	22.01.96
McCarthy, Alex	6.4	Crystal Palace	Guildford	03.12.89

Defenders

Bednarek, Jan	6.2	Lech Poznan	Slupca, Pol	12.04.96
Bertrand, Ryan	5.10	Chelsea	Southwark	05.08.89
Hoedt, Wesley	6.2	Lazio	Alkmaar, Hol	06.03.94
Soares, Cedric	5.8	Sporting Lisbon	Singen, Ger	31.08.91
Stephens, Jack	6.1	Plymouth	Torpoint	27.01.94
Valery, Yan	5.11	Rennes	Champigny, Fr	22.02.99
Vestergaard, Jannik	6.6	Borussia M'gladbach	Copenhagen, Den	03.08.92
Yoshida, Maya	6.2	Venlo	Nagasaki, Jap	24.08.88

Midfielders

Armstrong, Stuart	6.0	Celtic	Inverness	30.03.92
Djenepo, Moussa	5.10	Standard Liege	Bamako, Mali	15.06.98
Elyounoussi, Mohamed	5.10	Basle	Al Hoceima, Mor	04.08.94
Hojbjerg, Pierre-Emile	6.1	Bayern Munich	Copenhagen, Den	05.08.95
Lemina, Mario	6.1	Juventus	Libreville, Gab	01.09.93
Redmond, Nathan	5.8	Norwich	Birmingham	06.03.94
Romeu, Oriol	6.0	Chelsea	Ulldecona, Sp	24.09.91
Sims, Joshua	5.9	–	Yeovil	28.03.97
Ward-Prowse, James	5.8	–	Portsmouth	01.11.94

Forwards

Adams, Che	5.10	Birmingham	Leicester	13.07.96
Ings, Danny	5.10	Liverpool	Winchester	16.03.92
Long, Shane	5.10	Hull	Gortnahoe, Ire	22.01.87
Obafemi, Michael	5.7	–	Dublin, Ire	06.07.00

TOTTENHAM HOTSPUR

Ground: Tottenham Hotspur Stadium, High Road , Tottenham N17 0BX
Telephone: 0344 499 5000. **Club nickname:** Spurs

Capacity: 62,062. **Colours:** White. **Main sponsor:** AIA
Record transfer fee: £54m to Lyon for Tanguy Ndombele, Jul 2019
Record fee received: £85.3m from Real Madrid for Gareth Bale, Aug 2013
Record attendance: White Hart Lane: 75,038 v Sunderland (FA Cup 6) Mar 5, 1938. Wembley 85,512 v Bayer Leverkusen (Champs Lge group) Nov 2, 2016. Tottenham Hotspur Stadium: 60,243 v Ajax (Champs Lge semi-final) Apr 29, 2019
League Championship: Winners 1950–51, 1960–61
FA Cup: Winners 1901, 1921, 1961, 1962, 1967, 1981, 1982, 1991
League Cup: Winners 1971, 1973, 1999, 2008
European competitions: Winners Cup-Winners' Cup 1962–63; UEFA Cup 1971–72, 1983–84
Finishing positions in Premier League: 1992–93 8th, 1993–94 15th, 1994–95 7th, 1995–96 8th, 1996–97 10th, 1997–98 14th, 1998–99 11th, 1999–2000 10th, 2000–01 12th, 2001–02 9th, 2002–03 10th, 2003–04 14th, 2004–05 9th, 2005–06 5th, 2006–07 5th, 2007–08 11th, 2008–09 8th, 2009–10 4th, 2010–11 5th, 2011–12 4th, 2012–13 5th, 2013–14 6th, 2014–15 5th, 2015–16 3rd, 2016–17 2nd, 2017–18 3rd, 2018–19 4th
Biggest win: 9-0 v Bristol Rov (Div 2) Oct 22, 1977. Also: 13-2 v Crewe (FA Cup 4 replay) Feb 3, 1960
Biggest defeat: 0-7 v Liverpool (Div 1) Sep 2, 1979. Also: 0-8 v Cologne (Inter Toto Cup) Jul 22, 1995
Highest League scorer in a season: Jimmy Greaves 37 (1962–63)
Most League goals in aggregate: Jimmy Greaves 220 (1961–70)
Longest unbeaten League sequence: 22 matches (1949)
Longest sequence without a League win: 16 matches (1934–35)
Most capped player: Pat Jennings (Northern Ireland) 74

Goalkeepers

Gazzaniga, Paulo	6.5	Southampton	Murphy, Arg		02.01.92
Lloris, Hugo	6.2	Lyon	Nice, Fr		26.12.86

Defenders

Alderweireld, Toby	6.2	Atletico Madrid	Antwerp, Bel	02.03.89
Aurier, Serge	5.9	Paris SG	Ouragahio, Iv C	24.12.92
Davies, Ben	5.6	Swansea	Neath	24.04.93
Dier, Eric	6.2	Sporting Lisbon	Cheltenham	15.01.94
Foyth, Juan	5.10	Estudiantes	La Plata, Arg	12.01.98
Rose, Danny	5.8	Leeds	Doncaster	02.07.90
Sanchez, Davinson	6.2	Ajax	Caloto, Col	12.06.96
Vertonghen, Jan	6.2	Ajax	Sint-Niklaas, Bel	24.04.87
Walker-Peters, Kyle	5.8	–	Edmonton	13.04.97

Midfielders

Alli, Dele	6.1	MK Dons	Milton Keynes	11.04.96
Dembele, Mousa	6.1	Fulham	Wilrijk, Bel	16.07.87
Eriksen, Christian	5.10	Ajax	Middelfart, Den	14.02.92
Lamela, Erik	6.0	Roma	Buenos Aires, Arg	04.03.92
Lucas Moura	5.8	Paris SG	Sao Paulo, Br	13.08.92
Ndombele, Tanguy	5.11	Lyon	Longjumeau, Fr	28.12.96
Nkoudou, Georges-Kevin	5.8	Marseille	Versailles, Fr	13.02.95
Onomah, Josh	5.11	–	Enfield	27.04.97
Sissoko, Moussa	6.2	Newcastle	Le Blanc-Mesnil, Fr	16.08.89
Wanyama, Victor	6.2	Southampton	Nairobi, Ken	25.06.91
Winks, Harry	5.10	–	Hemel Hempstead	02.02.96

Forwards

Janssen, Vincent	5.11	Alkmaar	Heesch, Hol	15.06.94
Kane, Harry	6.2	–	Walthamstow	28.07.93
Llorente, Fernando	6.5	Swansea	Pamplona, Sp	26.02.85
Son Heung-Min	6.1	Bayer Leverkusen	Chuncheon, S Kor	08.07.92

WATFORD

Ground: Vicarage Road Stadium, Vicarage Road, Watford WD18 0ER
Telephone: 01923 496000. **Club nickname:** Hornets
Capacity: 21,000. **Colours:** Yellow and black. **Main sponsor:** Sportsbet
Record transfer fee: £10.6m to Burnley for Andre Gray, Aug 2017
Record fee received: £40m from Everton for Richarlison, Jul 2018
Record attendance: 34,099 v Manchester Utd (FA Cup 4 rep) Feb 3, 1969
League Championship: Runners-up 1982–83
FA Cup: Runners-up 1984
League Cup: Semi-finals 1979, 2005
European competitions: UEFA Cup rd 3 1983–84
Finishing positions in Premier League: 1999–2000 20th, 2006–07 20th, 2015–16 13th, 2016–17 17th, 2017–18 14th, 2018–19 11th
Biggest win: 8-0 v Sunderland (Div 1) Sep 25, 1982. Also: 10-1 v Lowestoft (FA Cup 1) Nov 27, 1926
Biggest defeat: 0-10 v Wolves (FA Cup 1 replay) Jan 24, 1912
Highest League scorer in a season: Cliff Holton 42 (1959–60)
Most League goals in aggregate: Luther Blissett 148 (1976–83; 1984–88, 1991–92)
Longest unbeaten League sequence: 22 matches (1996–97)
Longest sequence without a League win: 19 matches (1971–72)
Most capped players: John Barnes (England) 31, Kenny Jackett (Wales) 31

Goalkeepers

Bachmann, Daniel	6.3	Stoke	Vienna, Aut	09.07.94
Foster, Ben	6.2	WBA	Leamington	03.04.03
Gomes, Heurelho	6.2	PSV Eindhoven	Joao Pinheiro, Br	15.12.81

Defenders

Cathcart, Craig	6.2	Blackpool	Belfast	06.02.89
Dawson, Craig	6.2	WBA	Rochdale	06.05.90
Femenia, Kiko	5.9	Alaves	Sanet Negrals, Sp	02.02.91
Holebas, Jose	6.1	Roma	Aschaffenburg, Ger	27.06.84
Janmaat, Daryl	6.1	Newcastle	Leidschendam, Hol	22.07.89
Kabasele, Christian	6.1	Genk	Lubumbashi, DR Cong	24.02.91
Mariappa, Adrian	5.11	Crystal Palace	Harrow	03.10.86
Masina, Adam	6.2	Bologna	Khouribga, Mor	02.01.94
Navarro, Marc	6.2	Espanyol	Barcelona, Sp	02.07.95
Prodl, Sebastian	6.4	Werder Bremen	Graz, Aut	21.06.87
Wilmot, Ben	6.2	Stevenage	Stevenage	04.11.99

Midfielders

Capoue, Etienne	6.2	Tottenham	Niort, Fr	11.07.88
Chalobah, Nathaniel	6.1	Chelsea	Freetown, SLeone	12.12.94
Cleverley, Tom	5.10	Everton	Basingstoke	12.08.89
Doucoure, Abdoulaye	6.0	Rennes	Meulan, Fr	01.01.93
Hughes, Will	6.1	Derby	Weybridge	07.04.95
Lukebakio, Dodi	6.2	Anderlecht	Asse, Bel	24.09.97
Pereyra, Roberto	6.0	Juventus	San Miguel, Arg	07.01.91
Quina, Domingos	5.10	West Ham	Bissau, Guin-Biss	18.11.99
Sema, Ken	5.10	Ostersunds	Norrkoping, Swe	30.09.93

Forwards

Deeney, Troy	6.0	Walsall	Birmingham	29.06.88
Gray, Andre	5.10	Burnley	Wolverhampton	26.06.91
Okaka, Stefano	6.1	Anderlecht	Castiglione, It	09.08.89
Success, Isaac	6.0	Granada	Benin City, Nig	07.01.96

WEST HAM UNITED

Ground: Queen Elizabeth Olympic Park, London E20 2ST
Telephone: 0208 548 2748. **Club nickname:** Hammers
Capacity: 60,000. **Colours:** Claret and blue. **Main sponsor:** Betway
Record transfer fee: £45m to Eintracht Frankfurt for Sebastien Haller, July 2019
Record fee received: £25m from Marseille for Dimitri Payet, Jan 2017
Record attendance: Upton Park: 43,322 v Tottenham (Div 1) Oct 17, 1970. Olympic Stadium: 59,988 v Everton (Prem Lge) Mar 30, 2019
League Championship: 3rd 1985–86
FA Cup: Winners 1964, 1975, 1980
League Cup: Runners-up 1966, 1981
European competitions: Winners Cup-Winners' Cup 1964–65
Finishing positions in Premier League: 1993–94 13th, 1994–95 14th, 1995–96 10th, 1996–97 14th, 1997–98 8th, 1998–99 5th, 1999–2000 9th, 2000–01 15th, 2001–02 7th, 2002–03 18th, 2005–06 9th, 2006–07 15th, 2007–08 10th, 2008–09: 9th, 2009 10 17th, 2010–11 20th, 2012–13 10th, 2013–14 13th, 2014–15 12th, 2015–16 7th, 2016–17 11th, 2017–18 13th, 2018–19 10th
Biggest win: 8-0 v Rotherham (Div 2) Mar 8, 1958, v Sunderland (Div 1) Oct 19, 1968. Also: 10-0 v Bury (League Cup 2) Oct 25, 1983
Biggest defeat: 0-7 v Barnsley (Div 2) Sep 1, 1919, v Everton (Div 1) Oct 22, 1927, v Sheffield Wed (Div 1) Nov 28, 1959
Highest League scorer in a season: Vic Watson 42 (1929–30)
Most League goals in aggregate: Vic Watson 298 (1920–35)
Longest unbeaten League sequence: 27 matches (1980–81)
Longest sequence without a League win: 17 matches (1976)
Most capped player: Bobby Moore (England) 108

Goalkeepers

Fabianski, Lukasz	6.3	Swansea	Kostrzyn, Pol	18.04.85
Martin, David	6.2	Millwall	Romford	22.01.86
Roberto	6.3	Espanyol	Madrid, Sp	10.02.86

Defenders

Balbuena, Fabian	6.2	Corinthians	Ciudad del Este, Par	23.08.91
Cresswell, Aaron	5.7	Ipswich	Liverpool	15.12.89
Diop, Issa	6.4	Toulouse	Toulouse	09.01.97
Fredericks, Ryan	5.8	Fulham	Potters Bar	10.10.92
Masuaku, Arthur	5.11	Olympiacos	Lille, Fr	07.11.93
Ogbonna, Angelo	6.3	Juventus	Cassino, It	23.05.88
Oxford, Reece	6.3	Tottenham	Edmonton	16.12.98
Rice, Declan	6.1	–	London	14.01.99
Zabaleta, Pablo	5.10	Man City	Buenos Aires, Arg	16.01.85

Midfielders

Antonio, Michail	5.11	Nottm Forest	Wandsworth	28.03.90
Cullen, Josh	5.9	–	Westcliff-on-Sea	07.04.96
Diangana, Grady	5.11	–	DR Congo	19.04.98
Fornals, Pablo	5.10	Villarreal	Castellon, Sp	22.02.96
Lanzini, Manuel	5.6	Al Jazira	Ituzaingo, Arg	15.02.93
Noble, Mark	5.11	–	West Ham	08.05.87
Obiang, Pedro	6.1	Sampdoria	Alcala, Sp	27.03.92
Sanchez, Carlos	6.0	Fiorentina	Quibdo, Col	06.02.86
Snodgrass, Robert	6.0	Hull	Glasgow	07.09.87
Wilshere, Jack	5.8	Arsenal	Stevenage	01.01.92

Forwards

Arnautovic, Marko	6.4	Stoke	Vienna, Aut	19.04.89

Haller, Sebastien	6.3	Eintracht Frankfurt	Ris Orangis, Fr	22.06.94
Hernandez, Javier	5.9	Bayer Leverkusen	Guadalajara, Mex	01.06.88
Hugill, Jordan	6.0	Preston	Middlesbrough	04.06.92
Xande Silva	5.10	Guimaraes	Porto, Port	16.03.97
Yarmolenko, Andriy	6.2	Borussia Dortmund	St Petersburg, Rus	23.10.89

WOLVERHAMPTON WANDERERS

Ground: Molineux Stadium, Waterloo Road, Wolverhampton WV1 4QR
Telephone: 0871 222 1877. **Club nickname:** Wolves
Capacity: 32,050. **Colours:** Yellow and black. **Main sponsor:** ManBetX
Record attendance: 61,315 v Liverpool (FA Cup 5) Feb 11, 1939
Record transfer fee: £30m to Benfica for Raul Jimenez, Apr 2019
Record fee received: £14m from Sunderland for Steven Fletcher, Aug 2012
Record attendance: 61,315 v Liverpool (FA Cup 5), Feb 11, 1935
League Championship: Winners 1953-54, 1957-58, 1958-59
FA Cup: Winners 1893, 1908, 1949, 1960
League Cup: Winners 1974, 1980
European competitions: UEFA Cup runners-up 1971-72
Finishing positions in Premier League: 2003-04 20th, 2009-10 15th, 2003-04 20th, 2011-12 20th, 2018-19 7th
Biggest win: 10-1 v Leicester (Div 2) Apr 15, 1938. Also: 14-0 v Crosswell's Brewery (FA Cup 2) Nov 13, 1886
Biggest defeat: 1-10 v Newton Heath (Div 1) Oct 15, 1892
Highest League scorer in a season: Dennis Westcott 38 (1946-47)
Most League goals in aggregate: Steve Bull 250 (1986-90)
Longest unbeaten League sequence: 20 matches (1923-24)
Longest sequence without a League win: 19 matches (1984-85)
Most capped player: Billy Wright (England) 105

Goalkeepers

Norris, Will	6.5	Cambridge	Watford	12.08.93
Rui Patricio	6.2	Sporting Lisbon	Marrazes, Port	15.02.88
Ruddy, John	6.4	Norwich	St Ives, Camb	24.10.86

Defenders

Bennett, Ryan	6.2	Norwich	Orsett	06.03.90
Boly, Willy	6.2	Porto	Melun, Fr	03.02.91
Coady, Conor	6.1	Huddersfield	St Helens	25.02.93
Doherty, Matt	5.11	–	Dublin, Ire	16.01.92
Jonny	5.9	Atletico Madrid	Vigo, Sp	03.03.94
Kilman, Max	5.10	Maidenhead	Kensington	23.05.97
Ruben Vinagre	5.9	Monaco	Charneca, Port	09.04.99

Midfielders

Dendoncker, Leander	6.2	Anderlecht	Passendale, Bel	15.04.95
Diogo Jota	5.10	Atletico Madrid	Porto	04.12.96
Gibbs-White, Morgan	5.11	–	Stafford	27.01.00
Joao Moutinho	5.7	Monaco	Portimao, Port	08.09.86
Ruben Neves	6.0	Porto	Mozelos, Port	13.03.97
Saiss, Romain	6.3	Angers	Bourg-de-Peage, Fr	26.03.90
Zyro, Michal	6.2	Legia Warsaw	Warsaw, Pol	20.09.92

Forwards

Bonatini, Leo	6.1	Al-Hilal	Belo Horizonte, Br	28.03.94
Mir, Rafael	6.1	Valencia	Murcia, Sp	18.06.97
Raul Jimenez	6.2	Benfica	Tepeji del Rio, Mex	05.05.91
Traore, Adama	5.10	Middlesbrough	L'Hospitalet, Sp	25.01.96

CHAMPIONSHIP

BARNSLEY

Ground: Oakwell Stadium, Barnsley S71 1ET
Telephone: 01226 211211. **Club nickname:** Tykes
Colours: Red and white. **Capacity:** 23,009
Record attendance: 40,255 v Stoke (FA Cup 5) Feb 15, 1936

Goalkeepers				
Collins, Brad	6.0	Chelsea	Southampton	18.02.97
Radlinger, Samuel	6.6	Hannover	Ried, Aut	07.11.92
Walton, Jack	6.1	–	Bury	23.04.98
Defenders				
Andersen, Mads Juel	6.4	Horsens	Albertsund, Den	27.12.97
Cavare, Dimitri	6.1	Rennes	Poite-a-Pitre, Guad	05.02.95
Diaby, Bambo	6.1	Lokeren	Mataro, Sp	17.12.97
Halme, Aapo	6.5	Leeds	Helsinki, Fin	22.05.98
Pinillos, Dani	6.0	Cordoba	Logrono, Sp	22.10.92
Sibbick, Toby	6.0	AFC Wimbledon	Isleworth	23.05.99
Williams, Ben	5.10	Blackburn	–	31.03.99
Williams, Jordan	5.10	Huddersfield	Huddersfield	22.10.99
Midfielders				
Bahre, Mike-Steven	5.10	Hannover	Garbsen, Ger	10.08.95
Dougall, Kenny	6.0	Sparta Rotterdam	Brisbane, Aus	07.05.93
Green, Jordan	5.6	Yeovil	New Cross	22.02.95
McGeehan, Cameron	5.11	Luton	Kingston upon Thames	06.04.95
Mowatt, Alex	5.10	Leeds	Doncaster	13.02.95
Styles, Callum		Burnley	Bury	28.03.00
Thomas, Luke	5.8	Derby	Soudley	19.02.99
Wilks, Mallik	5.10	Leeds	Leeds	15.12.98
Forwards				
Adeboyejo, Victor	5.11	Leyton Orient	Ibadan, Nig	12.01.98
Brown, Jacob	5.10	–	Halifax	10.04.98
Moore, Kieffer	6.5	Ipswich	Torquay	08.08.92
Thiam, Mamadou	5.11	Dijon	Aubervilliers, Fr	20.03.95
Woodrow, Cauley	6.1	Fulham	Hemel Hempstead	02.12.94

BIRMINGHAM CITY

Ground: St Andrew's, Birmingham B9 4NH
Telephone: 0844 557 1875. **Club nickname:** Blues
Colours: Blue and white. **Capacity:** 30,016
Record attendance: 66,844 v Everton (FA Cup 5) Feb 11, 1939

Goalkeepers				
Camp, Lee	6.1	Cardiff	Derby	22.08.84
Stockdale, David	6.3	Brighton	Leeds	28.09.85
Trueman, Connal	6.1	–	Birmingham	26.03.96
Defenders				
Colin, Maxime	5.11	Brentford	Arras, Fr	15.11.91

Crowley, Dan	5.9	Willem II	Coventry	03.08.97
Dacres-Cogley, Joshua	5.9	–	–	12.03.96
Dean, Harlee	5.10	Brentford	Basingstoke	26.07.91
Grounds, Jonathan	6.1	Oldham	Thornaby	02.02.88
Harding, Wes	5.11	–	Leicester	20.10.96
Kieftenbeld, Maikel	5.11	Groningen	Lemelerveld, Hol	26.06.90
Lakin, Charlie	5.11	Walsall	Solihull	08.05.99
O'Keefe, Corey	6.0	–	Birmingham	05.06.98
Pedersen, Kristian	6.2	Union Berlin	Ringsted, Den	04.08.94
Roberts, Marc	6.0	Barnsley	Wakefield	26.07.90
Midfielders				
Davis, David	5.8	Wolves	Smethwick	20.02.91
Gardner, Craig	5.10	WBA	Solihull	25.11.86
Gardner, Gary	6.2	Aston Villa	Solihull	29.06.92
Maghoma, Jacques	5.11	Sheffield Wed	Lubumbashi, DR Cong	23.10.87
Mrabti, Kerim	5.9	Djurgardens	Nacka, Swe	20.05.94
Solomon-Otabor, Viv	5.9	–	London	02.01.96
Forwards				
Jutkiewicz, Lukas	6.1	Burnley	Southampton	20.03.89
Vassell, Isaac	5.8	Luton	Newquay	09.09.93

BLACKBURN ROVERS

Ground: Ewood Park, Blackburn BB2 4JF
Telephone: 0871 702 1875. Rovers
Colours: Blue and white. **Capacity:** 31,367
Record attendance: 62,522 v Bolton (FA Cup 6) Mar 2, 1929

Goalkeepers				
Fisher, Andrew	6.0	–	Wigan	12.02.98
Leutwiler, Jayson	6.4	Shrewsbury	Neuchatel, Switz	25.04.89
Defenders				
Bell, Amari'i	5.11	Fleetwood	Burton	05.05.94
Dennett, Elliott	6.01	Norwich	Telford	18.12.88
Caddis, Paul	5.7	Birmingham	Irvine	19.04.88
Lenihan, Darragh	5.10	Belvedere	Dunboyne, Ire	16.03.94
Mulgrew, Charlie	6.3	Celtic	Glasgow	06.03.86
Nyambe, Ryan	6.0	–	Katima, Nam	04.12.97
Wharton, Scott	–	–	Blackburn	03.10.97
Williams, Derrick	6.2	Bristol City	Waterford, Ire	17.01.93
Midfielders				
Buckley, John	5.8	–	Manchester	13.10.99
Dack, Bradley	5.8	Gillingham	Greenwich	31.12.93
Downing, Stewart	6.0	Middlesbrough	Middlesbrough	22.07.84
Evans, Corry	5.11	Hull	Belfast	30.07.90
Gladwin, Ben	6.3	QPR	Reading	08.06.92
Johnson, Bradley	5.10	Derby	Hackney	28.04.87
Rodwell, Jack	6.2	Sunderland	Southport	11.03.91
Rothwell, Joe	6.1	Oxford	Manchester	11.01.95
Smallwood, Richie	5.11	Rotherham	Redcar	29.12.90
Travis, Lewis	6.0	Liverpool	Whiston	16.10.97
Forwards				
Armstrong, Adam	5.8	Newcastle	Newcastle	10.02.97
Brereton, Ben	6.0	Nottm Forest	Blythe Bridge	18.04.99
Chapman, Harry	5.10	Middlesbrough	Hartlepool	15.11.97

Graham, Danny	6.1	Sunderland	Gateshead	12.08.85
Nuttall, Joe	6.0	Aberdeen	Bury	27.11.97
Gallagher, Sam	6.4	Southampton	Crediton	15.09.95
Samuel, Dominic	6.0	Reading	Southwark	01.04.94

BRENTFORD

Ground: Griffin Park, Braemar Road, Brentford TW8 0NT
Telephone: 0845 345 6442. **Club nickname:** Bees
Colours: Red, white and black. **Capacity:** 12,763
Record attendance: 38,678 v Leicester (FA Cup 6) Feb 26, 1949

Goalkeepers

| Daniels, Luke | 6.4 | Scunthorpe | Bolton | 05.01.88 |
| Raya, David | 6.0 | Blackburn | Barcelona, Sp | 15.09.95 |

Defenders

Carroll, Canice	6.0	Oxford	Oxford	26.01.99
Clarke, Josh	5.8	–	Walthamstow	05.07.94
Dalsgaard, Henrik	6.3	Zulte Waregem	Roum, Den	27.07.89
Field, Tom	5.10	–	Kingston upon Thames	14.03.97
Henry, Rico	5.8	Walsall	Birmingham	08.07.97
Jansson, Pontus	6.5	Leeds	Arlov, Swe	13.02.91
Jeanvier, Julian	6.0	Reims	Clichy, Fr	31.03.92
Pinnock, Ethan	6.2	Barnsley	Lambeth	29.05.93

Midfielders

Canos, Sergi	5.9	Norwich	Nules, Sp	02.02.97
Dasilva, Josh	6.0	Arsenal	Ilford	23.10.98
Jensen, Mathias	5.10	Celta Vigo	Jerslev, Den	01.01.96
Marcondes, Emiliano	6.0	Nordsjaelland	Hvidovre, Den	09.03.95
Maupay, Neal	5.7	St Etienne	Versailles, Fr	14.08.96
Mokotjo, Kamo	5.7	Twente	Odendaalsrus, SA	11.03.91
Norgaard, Christian	6.1	Fiorentina	Copenhagen, Den	10.03.94
Ogbene, Chiedozie	5.9	Limerick	Enugu, Nig	01.05.97
Sawyers, Romaine	5.9	Walsall	Birmingham	02.11.91

Forwards

Benrahma, Said	5.8	Nice	Temouchent, Alg	10.08.95
Shaibu, Justin	6.0	Koge	Denmark	28.10.97
Watkins, Ollie	5.10	Exeter	Torbay	30.12.95

BRISTOL CITY

Ground: Ashton Gate, Bristol BS3 2EJ
Telephone: 0871 222 6666. **Club nickname:** Robins
Colours: Red and white. **Capacity:** 27,000
Record attendance: 43,335 v Preston (FA Cup 5) Feb 16, 1935

Goalkeepers

Bentley, Daniel	6.2	Brentford	Basildon	13.07.93
Gilmartin, Rene	6.5	Colchester	Dublin	31.05.87
Maenpaa, Niki	6.3	Brighton	Espoo, Fin	23.01.85

Defenders

Baker, Nathan	6.3	Aston Villa	Worcester	23.04.91
Dasilva, Jay	5.7	Chelsea	Luton	22.04.98
Hunt, Jack	5.9	Sheffield Wed	Rothwell	06.12.90
Kalas, Tomas	6.0	Chelsea	Olomouc, Cz	15.05.93
Moore, Taylor	6.1	Lens	Walthamstow	12.05.97

| Webster, Adam | 6.3 | Ipswich | Chichester | 04.01.95 |
| Wright, Bailey | 5.10 | Preston | Melbourne, Aus | 28.07.92 |

Midfielders

Adelakun, Hakeeb	6.0	Scunthorpe	Hackney	11.06.96
Brownhill, Josh	5.10	Preston	Warrington	19.12.95
Eliasson, Niclas	5.9	Norrkoping	Sweden	07.12.95
O'Dowda, Callum	5.11	Oxford	Oxford	23.04.95
Pack, Marlon	6.2	Cheltenham	Portsmouth	25.03.91
Rowe, Tommy	5.11	Doncaster	Manchester	01.05.89
Smith, Korey	6.0	Oldham	Hatfield	31.01.91
Szmodics, Sammie	5.7	Colchester	Colchester	24.09.95
Walsh, Liam	5.8	Everton	Huyton	15.09.97

Forwards

Diedhiou, Famara	6.2	Angers	Saint-Louis, Sen	15.12.92
Paterson, Jamie	5.9	Nottm Forest	Coventry	20.12.91
Taylor, Matty	5.9	Bristol Rov	Oxford	30.03.90
Weimann, Andreas	6.2	Derby	Vienna, Aut	05.08.91
Watkins, Marley	6.1	Norwich	Lewisham	17.10.90

CARDIFF CITY

Ground: Cardiff City Stadium, Leckwith Road, Cardiff CF11 8AZ
Telephone: 0845 365 1115. **Club nickname**: Bluebirds
Colours: Blue. **Capacity**: 33,300
Record attendance: Ninian Park: 62,634 Wales v England, Oct 17, 1959; Club: 57,893 v Arsenal (Div 1) Apr 22, 1953. Cardiff City Stadium: 33,280 (Wales v Belgium) Jun 12, 2015. Club: 33,082 v Liverpool (Prem Lge) Apr 21, 2019

Goalkeepers

Day, Joe	6.0	Newport	Brighton	13.08.90
Etheridge, Neil	6.3	Walsall	Enfield	07.02.90
Murphy, Brian	6.1	Portsmouth	Waterford, Ire	07.05.83
Smithies, Alex	6.3	QPR	Huddersfield	05.03.90

Defenders

Bamba, Sol	6.3	Leeds	Ivry sur Seine, Fr	13.01.85
Bennett, Joe	5.10	Aston Villa	Rochdale	28.03.90
Connolly, Matthew	6.2	QPR	Barnet	24.09.07
Cunningham, Greg	6.0	Preston	Carnmore, Ire	31.01.91
Manga, Bruno	6.1	Lorient	Libreville, Gab	16.07.88
Morrison, Sean	6.1	Reading	Plymouth	08.01.91
Nelson, Curtis	6.0	Oxford	Newcastle-under-Lyme	21.05.93
Peltier, Lee	5.11	Huddersfield	Liverpool	11.12.86
Richards, Jazz	6.1	Fulham	Swansea	12.04.91

Midfielders

Bacuna, Leandro	6.2	Reading	Groningen, Hol	21.08.91
Damour, Loic	5.11	Bourg-Peronnas	Chantilly, Fr	08.01.91
Hoilett, Junior	5.8	QPR	Brampton, Can	05.06.90
Mendez-Laing, Nathaniel	5.10	Rochdale	Birmingham	15.04.92
Murphy, Josh	5.9	Norwich	Wembley	24.02.95
Paterson, Callum	6.0	Hearts	London	13.10.94
Ralls, Joe	6.0	–	Aldershot	13.10.93
Reid, Bobby	5.7	Bristol City	Bristol	02.02.93
Vaulks, Will	5.11	Rotherham	Wirral	13.09.93

Forwards

| Bogle, Omar | 6.3 | Wigan | Birmingham | 26.07.92 |

Madine, Gary	6.3	Bolton	Gateshead	24.08.90
Ward, Danny	5.11	Rotherham	Bradford	09.12.90
Zohore, Kenneth	6.3	Kortrijk	Copenhagen, Den	31.01.94

CHARLTON ATHLETIC

Ground: The Valley, Floyd Road, London SE7 8BL
Telephone: 0208 333 4000. **Club nickname:** Addicks
Colours: Red and white. **Capacity:** 27,111
Record attendance: 75,031 v Aston Villa (FA Cup 5) Feb 12, 1938

Goalkeepers

| Amos, Ben | 6.3 | Bolton | Macclesfield | 10.04.90 |
| Phillips, Dillon | 6.2 | – | Hornchurch | 11.06.95 |

Defenders

Lockyer, Tom	6.1	Bristol Rov	Cardiff	03.12.94
Page, Lewis	5.10	West Ham	Enfield	20.05.96
Pearce, Jason	5.11	Wigan	Hillingdon	06.12.87
Purrington, Ben	5.9	Rotherham	Exeter	05.05.96
Sarr, Naby	6.5	Sporting Lisbon	Marseille, Fr	13.08.93
Solly, Chris	5.8	–	Rochester	20.01.90

Midfielders

Aneke, Chuks	6.3	MK Dons	Newham	03.07.93
Dijksteel, Anfernee	6.0	–	Holland	27.10.96
Forster-Caskey, Jake	5.10	Brighton	Southend	05.04.94
Lapslie, George	5.9	–	Waltham Forest	05.09.97
Maloney, Taylor	5.9	–	Gravesend	21.01.99
Pratley, Darren	6.0	Bolton	Barking	22.04.85

Forwards

| Bonne, Macauley | 5.11 | Leyton Orient | Ipswich | 26.10.95 |
| Taylor, Lyle | 6.2 | AFC Wimbledon | Greenwich | 29.03.90 |

DERBY COUNTY

Ground: Pride Park, Derby DE24 8XL
Telephone: 0871 472 1884. **Club nickname:** Rams
Colours: White and black. **Capacity:** 33,597
Record attendance: Baseball Ground: 41,826 v Tottenham (Div 1) Sep 20, 1969; Pride Park: 33,597 (England v Mexico) May 25, 2011; Club: 33,475 v Rangers (Ted McMinn testimonial) May 1, 2006

Goalkeepers

Carson, Scott	6.3	Wigan	Whitehaven	03.09.85
Mitchell, Jonathan	6.2	Newcastle	Hartlepool	24.11.94
Roos, Kelle	6.5	Nuneaton	Rijkevoort, Hol	31.05.92

Defenders

Davies, Curtis	6.2	Hull	Waltham Forest	15.03.85
Forsyth, Craig	6.0	Watford	Carnoustie	24.02.89
Keogh, Richard	6.2	Coventry	Harlow	11.08.86
Lowe, Max	5.9	–	Birmingham	11.05.97
Malone, Scott	6.2	Huddersfield	Rowley Regis	25.03.91
Shinnie, Graeme	5.9	Aberdee,	Aberdeen	04.08.91
Wisdom, Andre	6.1	Liverpool	Leeds	09.05.93

Midfielders

| Anya, Ikechi | 5.7 | Watford | Glasgow | 03.01.88 |
| Butterfield, Jacob | 5.11 | Huddersfield | Bradford | 10.06.90 |

Dowell, Kieran	5.10	Everton (loan)	Ormskirk	10.10.97
Evans, George	6.1	Reading	Cheadle	13.12.94
Holmes, Duane	5.6	Scunthoprpe	Columbus, US	06.11.94
Huddlestone, Tom	6.1	Hull	Nottingham	28.12.86
Ledley, Joe	6.0	Crystal Palace	Cardiff	23.01.87
Thorne, George	6.2	WBA	Chatham	04.01.93

Forwards

Bennett, Mason	5.10	–	Shirebrook	15.07.96
Blackman, Nick	6.1	Reading	Whitefield	11.11.89
Jozefzoon, Florian	5.9	Brentford	Saint-Laurent, Fr Gui	09.01.91
Lawrence, Tom	5.10	Leicester	Wrexham	13.01.94
Marriott, Jack	5.9	Peterborough	Beverley	09.09.84
Martin, Chris	5.10	Norwich	Beccles	04.11.88
Waghorn, Martyn	5.10	Ipswich	South Shields	23.01.93

FULHAM

Ground: Craven Cottage, Stevenage Road, Lndon SW6 6HH
Telephone: 0870 442 1222. **Club nickname:** Cottagers
Colours: White and black. **Capacity:** 25,700 (reduced this season):
Record attendance: 49,335 v Millwall (Div 2) Oct 8, 1938

Goalkeepers

| Bettinelli, Marcus | 6.4 | Simpeleen | Camberwell | 24.05.92 |
| Fabri | 6.1 | Besiktas | Las Palmas, Sp | 31.12.87 |

Defenders

Bryan, Joe	5.7	Bristol Oity	Bristol	17.09.93
Christie, Cyrus	6.2	Middlesbrough	Coventry	30.09.92
Le Marchand, Maxime	5.11	Nice	Saint-Malo, Fr	11.10.89
Mawson, Alfie	6.2	Swansea	Hillingdon	19.01.94
Odoi, Denis	5.10	Lokeren	Leuven, Bel	27.05.88
Ream, Tim	6.1	Bolton	St Louis, US	05.10.87
Sessegnon, Ryan	5.10		Roehampton	18.05.00

Midfielders

Cairney, Tom	6.0	Blackburn	Nottingham	20.01.91
Ivan Cavaleiro	5.9	Wolves (loan)	Vila Franca de Xira, Por	18.10.93
Cisco, Ibrahima	6.0	Standard Liege	Liege, Bel	28.02.94
Edun, Tayo	5.10	–	Islington	14.05.98
Johansen, Stefan	6.0	Celtic	Vardo, Nor	08.01.91
Kebano, Neeskens	5.11	Genk	Montereau, Fr	10.03.92
McDonald, Kevin	6.2	Wolves	Carnoustie	04.11.88
Seri, Jean Michael	5.7	Nice	Grand-Bereby, Iv C	19.07.91
Zambo Anguissa, Andre-Frank	6.1	Marseille	Yaounde, Cam	16.11.95

Forwards

Ayite, Floyd	5.9	Bastia	Bordeaux, Fr	15.12.88
Fonte, Rui	5.11	Braga	Penafiel, Port	23.04.90
Kamara, Aboubakar	5.10	Amiens	Gonesse, Fr	07.03.95
Mitrovic, Aleksandar	6.3	Newcastle	Smederevo, Serb	16.09.94

HUDDERSFIELD TOWN

Ground: John Smith's Stadium, Huddersfield HD1 6PX
Telephone: 0870 444 4677. **Club nickname:** Terriers.
Colours: Blue and white. **Capacity:** 24,169.
Record attendance: Leeds Road: 67,037 v Arsenal (FA Cup 6) Feb 27, 1932; John Smith's Stadium: 24,426 v Manchester Utd (Prem Lge), Oct 21, 2017

Goalkeepers

Coleman, Joel	6.4	Oldham	Bolton	06.09.95
Grabara, Kamil	6.5	Liverpool (loan)	Ruda Slaska, Pol	08.01.99
Hamer, Ben	6.4	Leicester	Taunton	20.11.87

Defenders

Elphick, Tommy	5.11	Aston Villa	Brighton	07.09.87
Hadergjonaj, Florent	6.0	Ingolstadt	Langnau, Switz	31.07.94
Kongolo, Terence	6.2	Monaco	Fribourg, Switz	14.02.94
Jorgensen, Mathias	6.3	FC Copenhagen	Copenhagen, Den	23.04.90
Schindler, Christopher	6.2	1860 Munich	Munich, Ger	29.04.90

Midfielders

Bacuna, Juninho	5.10	Groningen	Groningen, Hol	07.08.97
Billing, Philip	6.4	–	Esbjerg, Den	11.06.96
Brown, Reece	5.9	Forest Green	Dudley	03.03.96
Hogg, Jonathan	5.7	Watford	Middlesbrough	06.12.88
Mooy, Aaron	5.11	Man City	Sydney, Aus	15.09.90
Pritchard, Alex	5.8	Norwich	Orsett	03.05.93
Sabiri, Abdelhamid	6.0	Nuremberg	Goulmima, Mor	28.11.96
Stankovic, Jon Gorenc	6.3	Borussia Dortmund	Ljubljana, Sloven	14.01.96
Van La Parra, Rajiv	5.11	Wolves	Rotterdam, Hol	04.06.91

Forwards

Diakhaby, Adama	6.1	Monaco	Ajaccio, Fr	05.07.96
Grant, Karlan	6.0	Charlton	Greenwich	19.12.97
Kachunga, Elias	5.10	Ingolstadt	Haan, Ger	22.04.92
Koroma, Josh	5.10	Leyton Orient	Southwark	09.11.98
Mbenza, Isaac	6.2	Montpellier	Saint-Dennis, Fr	08.03.96
Mounie, Steve	6.3	Montpellier	Parakin, Benin	29.09.94
Quaner, Collin	6.3	Union Berlin	Dusseldorf, Ger	18.06.91

HULL CITY

Ground: KCOM Stadium, Anlaby Road, Hull, HU3 6HU
Telephone: 01482 504 600. **Club nickname:** Tigers
Capacity: 25,404. **Colours:** Amber and black
Record attendance: Boothferry Park: 55,019 v Manchester Utd (FA Cup 6) Feb 26, 1949. KC Stadium: 25,030 v Liverpool (Prem Lge) May 9, 2010. Also: 25,280 (England U21 v Holland) Feb 17, 2004

Goalkeepers

Ingram, Matt	6.3	QPR	High Wycombe	18.12.93
Long, George	6.4	Sheffield Utd	Sheffield	05.11.93

Defenders

Burke, Reece	6.2	West Ham	Newham	02.09.96
De Wijs, Jordy	6.2	PSV Eindhoven	Kortrijk, Bel	08.01.95
Kingsley, Stephen	5.10	Swansea	Stirling	23.07.94
Lichaj, Eric	5.10	Nottm Forest	Downers Grove, US	17.11.88
MacDonald, Angus	6.2	Barnsley	Winchester	15.10.92
Mckenzie, Robbie	6.1	–	Hull	25.09.98

Midfielders

Batty, Daniel	5.11	–	Pontefract	10.12.97
Grosicki, Kamil	5.11	Rennes	Szczecin, Pol	08.06.88
Henriksen, Markus	6.2	Alkmaar	Trondheim, Nor	25.07.92
Irvine, Jackson	6.2	Burton	Melbourne, Aus	07.03.93
Milinkovic, David	5.11	Genoa	Antibes, Fr	20.05.94
Stewart, Kevin	5.7	Liverpool	Enfield	07.09.93

Toral, Jon	6.1	Arsenal	Reus, Sp	05.02.95
Forwards				
Bowen, Jarrod	5.9	Hereford	Leominster	20.12.96
Campbell, Fraizer	5.11	Crystal Palace	Huddersfield	13.09.87
Dicko, Nouha	5.8	Wolves	Paris, Fr	14.05.92
Cuves, Tom	6.4	Gillingham	Liverpool	14.01.92

LEEDS UNITED

Ground: Elland Road, Leeds LS11 0ES
Telephone. 0871 334 1919. **Club nickname:** Whites
Colours: White. **Capacity:** 37,900
Record attendance: 57,892 v Sunderland (FA Cup 5 rep) Mar 15, 1967

Goalkeepers				
Casilla, Kiko	6.3	Real Madrid	Alcover, Sp	02.10.86
Peacock-Farrell, Bailey	6.2	–	Darlington	29.10.96
Defenders				
Ayling, Luke	6.1	Bristol City	Lambeth	25.08.91
Berardi, Gaetano	5.11	Sampdoria	Sorengo, Swi	21.08.88
Cooper, Liam	6.0	Chesterfield	Hull	30.08.91
Douglas, Barry	5.9	Wolves	Glasgow	04.09.89
Helder Costa	5.10	Wolves (loan)	Luandra, Ang	12.01.94
Pearce, Tom	6.1	Everton	Ormskirk	12.04.98
White, Ben	6.0	Brighton (loan)	Poole	08.11.97
Midfielders				
Alioski, Ezgjan	5.8	Lugano	Prilep, Maced	12.02.92
Dallas, Stuart	6.0	Brentford	Cookstown	19.04.91
Forshaw, Adam	6.1	Middlesbrough	Liverpool	08.10.91
Harison, Jack	5.9	Man City (loan)	Stoke	20.11.96
Hernandez, Pablo	5.8	Al-Arabi	Castellon, Sp	11.04.85
Klich, Mateusz	6.0	FC Twente	Tarnow, Pol	13.06.90
McCarron, Liam	5.9	Carlisle	Preston	07.03.01
Phillips, Kalvin	6.10	–	Leeds	02.12.95
Roberts, Tyler	5.11	WBA	Gloucester	12.01.99
Forwards				
Bamford, Patrick	6.1	Middlesbrough	Grantham	05.09.93
Clarke, Jack	6.2	Tottenham (loan)	York	23.11.00
Roofe, Kemar	5.10	Oxford	Walsall	06.01.93

LUTON TOWN

Ground: Kenilworth Road, Maple Road, Luton LU4 8AW
Telephone: 01582 411622. **Club nickname:** Hatters
Colours: Orange and black. **Capacity:** 10,226
Record attendance: 30,069 v Blackpool (FA Cup 6) Mar 4, 1959

Goalkeepers				
Shea, James	5.11	AFC Wimbledon	Islington	16.06.91
Stech, Marek	6.5	Sparta Prague	Prague, Cz	28.01.90
Defenders				
Bradley, Sonny	6.4	Plymouth	Hull	13.09.91
Cranie, Martin	6.0	Sheffield Utd	Yeovil	26.09.86
Galloway, Brendan	6.1	Everton	Harare, Zim	17.03.96
Jones, Lloyd	6.3	Liverpool	Plymouth	07.10.95
Moncur, George	5.9	Barnsley	Swindon	18.08.93

Pearson, Matty	6.3	Barnsley	Keighley	03.08.93
Potts, Dan	5.8	West Ham	Romford	13.04.94
Rea, Glen	6.1	Brighton	Brighton	03.09.94
Sheehan, Alan	5.11	Bradford	Athlone, Ire	14.09.86
Stacey, Jack	5.11	Reading	Ascot	06.04.96
Midfielders				
Berry, Luke	5.9	Cambridge	Cambridge	12.07.92
McManaman, Callum	5.9	Wigan	Huyton	25.04.91
Ruddock, Pelly	5.9	West Ham	Hendon	17.07.93
Shinnie, Andrew	5.11	Birmingham	Aberdeen	17.07.89
Tunnicliffe, Ryan	6.0	Millwall	Heywood	30.12.92
Forwards				
Collins, James	6.2	Crawley	Coventry	01.12.90
Cornick, Harry	5.11	Bournemouth	Poole	06.03.95
Hylton, Danny	6.0	Oxford	Camden	25.02.89
Jervis, Jake	6.3	Plymouth	Birmingham	17.09.91
Lee, Elliot	5.11	Barnsley	Durham	16.12.94
LuaLua Kazenga	5.11	Sunderland	Kinshasa, DR Cong	10.12.90

MIDDLESBROUGH

Ground: Riverside Stadium, Middlesbrough, TS3 6RS
Telephone: 0844 499 6789. **Club nickname:** Boro
Capacity: 35,100. **Colours:** Red
Record attendance: Ayresome Park: 53,596 v Newcastle (Div 1) Dec 27, 1949; Riverside Stadium: 35,000 (England v Slovakia) Jun 11, 2003. Club: 34,836 v Norwich (Prem Lge) Dec 28, 2004

Goalkeepers				
Mejias, Tomas	6.4	Omonia Nicosia	Madrid	30.01.89
Randolph, Darren	6.1	West Ham	Bray, Ire	12.05.87
Defenders				
Ayala, Daniel	6.3	Norwich	El Saucejo, Sp	07.11.90
Flint, Aden	6.2	Bristol City	Pinxton	11.07.89
Friend, George	6.0	Doncaster	Barnstaple	19.10.87
Fry, Dael	6.0	–	Middlesbrough	30.08.97
McNair, Paddy	6.0	Sunderland	Ballyclare	27.04.95
Shotton, Ryan	6.3	Birmingham	Stoke	30.09.88
Midfielders				
Clayton, Adam	5.9	Huddersfield	Manchester	14.01.89
Howson, Jonny	5.11	Norwich	Leeds	21.05.88
Johnson, Marvin	5.10	Oxford	Birmingham	01.12.90
Saville, George	5.10	Millwall	Camberley	01.06.93
Tavernier, Marcus	5.10	Newcastle	Leeds	22.03.99
Wing, Lewis	6.1	Shildon	Newton Aycliffe	23.05.95
Forwards				
Assombalonga, Britt	5.10	Nottm Forest	Kinshasa, DR Cong	06.12.92
Braithwaite, Martin	5.11	Toulouse	Esbjerg, Den	05.06.91
Fletcher, Ashley	6.1	West Ham	Keighley	02.10.95
Gestede, Rudy	6.4	Aston Villa	Nancy, Fr	10.10.88

MILLWALL

Ground: The Den, Zampa Road, London SE16 3LN
Telephone: 0207 232 1222. **Club nickname:** Lions
Colours: Blue. **Capacity:** 20,146

Record attendance: The Den: 48,672 v Derby (FA Cup 5) Feb 20, 1937. New Den: 20,093 v Arsenal (FA Cup 3) Jan 10, 1994

Goalkeepers

Fielding, Frank	6.0	Bristol City	Blackburn	04.04.88
Sandford, Ryan	6.2	–	Lambeth	21.02.99

Defenders

Cooper, Jake	6.4	Reading	Bracknell	03.02.95
Hutchinson, Shaun	6.2	Fulham	Newcastle	23.11.90
Meredith, James	6.1	Bradford	Albury, Aus	04.04.88
Pearce, Alex	6.2	Derby	Wallingford	09.11.88
Romeo, Mahlon	5.10	Gillingham	Westminster	19.09.95
Wallace, Murray	6.2	Scunthorpe	Glasgow	10.01.93

Midfielders

Ferguson, Shane	5.11	Newcastle	Derry	12.07.91
Leonard, Ryan	6.1	Sheffield Utd	Plymouth	24.05.92
Mahoney, Connor	5.9	Bournemouth	Blackburn	12.02.97
Oyedinma, Fred	6.1		Plumstead	24.11.96
Saville, George	5.9	Wolves	Camberley	01.06.93
Skalak, Jiri	5.9	Brighton	Pardubice, Cz	12.03.92
Thompson, Ben	5.10	–	Sidcup	03.10.95
Wallace, Jed	5.10	Wolves	Reading	26.03.94
Williams, Shaun	6.0	MK Dons	Dublin, Ire	19.09.86

Forwards

Bodvarsson, Jon Dadi	6.3	Reading	Selfoss, Ice	25.05.92
Bradshaw, Tom	5.10	Barnsley	Shrewsbury	27.07.92
O'Brien, Aiden	5.8	–	Islington	04.10.93
Smith, Matt	6.6	QPR	Birmingham	07.06.89

NOTTINGHAM FOREST

Ground: City Ground, Pavilion Road, Nottingham NG2 5FJ
Telephone: 0115 982 4444. **Club nickname:** Forest
Colours: Red and white. **Capacity:** 30,576
Record attendance: 49,946 v Manchester Utd (Div 1) Oct 28, 1967

Goalkeepers

Muric, Arijanet	6.6	Man City (loan)	Schlieren, Switz	07.11.98
Pantilimon, Costel	6.8	Watford	Bacau, Rom	01.02.87
Steele, Luke	6.2	Bristol City	Peterborough	24.09.84

Defenders

Benalouane, Yohan	6.2	Leicester	Bagnols-sur-Ceze, Fr	28.03.87
Darikwa, Tendayi	6.2	Burnley	Nottingham	13.12.91
Dawson, Michael	6.2	Hull	Northallerton	18.11.83
Figueiredo, Tobias	6.2	Sporting CP	Satao, Port	02.02.94
Hefele, Michael	6.3	Huddersfield	Pfaffenhofen, Ger	01.09.90
Milosevic, Alexander	6.4	AIK	Rissne, Swe	30.01.92
Robinson, Jack	5.7	QPR	Warrington	01.09.93
Worrall, Joe	6.4	–	Hucknall	10.01.97

Midfielders

Adomah, Albert	6.1	Aston Villa	Lambeth	13.12.87
Ameobi, Sammy	6.4	Bolton	Newcastle	01.05.92
Ariyibi, Gboly	6.0	Chesterfield	Arlington, US	18.01.95
Bridcutt, Liam	5.9	Leeds	Reading	08.05.89
Cash, Matty	6.1	–	Slough	07.08.97

Guedioura, Adlene	6.0	Middlesbrough	La Roche, Fr	12.11.85
Joao Carvalho	5.8	Benfica	Castanheira, Port	09.03.97
Lolley, Joe	5.10	Huddersfield	Redditch	25.08.92
Osborn, Ben	5.10	–	Derby	05.08.94
Tiago Silva	5.8	Feirense	Lisbon, Port	02.06.93
Watson, Ben	5.10	Watford	Camberwell	09.07.85
Yacob, Claudio	5.11	WBA	Carcarana, Arg	18.07.87
Yates, Ryan	6.3	–	Lincoln	21.11.97
Forwards				
Appiah, Arvin	5.7	–	Amsterdam, Hol	05.01.01
Clough, Zach	5.8	Bolton	Manchester	08.03.95
Cummings, Jason	5.10	Hibernian	Edinburgh	19.12.95
Grabban, Lewis	6.0	Bournemouth	Croydon	12.01.88
Murphy, Daryl	6.2	Newcastle	Waterford, Ire	15.03.83
Walker, Tyler	5.11	–	Nottingham	17.10.96

PRESTON NORTH END

Ground: Deepdale, Sir Tom Finney Way, Preston PR1 6RU
Telephone: 0844 856 1964. **Club nickname:** Lilywhites
Colours: White and navy. **Capacity:** 23,404
Record attendance: 42,684 v Arsenal (Div 1) Apr 23, 1938

Goalkeepers				
Ripley, Connor	6.3	Middlesbrough	Middlesbrough	13.02.93
Rudd, Declan	6.3	Norwich	Diss	16.01.91
Defenders				
Bauer, Patrick	6.4	Charlton	Backnang, Ger	28.10.92
Clarke, Tom	5.11	Huddersfield	Halifax	21.12.87
Davies, Ben	5.11	–	Barrow	11.08.95
Earl, Joshua	6.4	–	Southport	24.10.98
Fisher, Darnell	5.9	Rotherham	Reading	04.04.94
Hughes, Andrew	5.11	Peterborough	Cardiff	05.06.92
Huntington, Paul	6.2	Yeovil	Carlisle	17.09.87
Rafferty, Joe	6.0	Rochdale	Liverpool	06.10.93
Storey, Jordan	6.2	Exeter	Yeovil	02.09.97
Midfielders				
Browne, Alan	5.8	Cork	Cork, Ire	15.04.95
Ginnelly, Josh	5.8	Walsall	Coventry	24.03.97
Harrop, Josh	5.9	Man Utd	Stockport	15.12.95
Johnson, Daniel	5.8	Aston Villa	Kingston, Jam	08.10.92
Ledson, Ryan	5.9	Oxford	Liverpool	19.08.97
Pearson, Ben	5.5	Man Utd	Oldham	04.01.95
Potts, Brad	6.2	Barnsley	Hexham	07.03.94
Forwards				
Barkhuizen, Tom	5.11	Preston	Blackpool	04.07.93
Burke, Graham	5.11	Shamrock Rov	Dublin, Ire	21.09.93
Gallagher, Paul	6.0	Leicester	Glasgow	09.08.84
Maguire, Sean	5.9	Cork	Luton	01.05.94
Moult, Louis	6.0	Motherwell	Stoke	14.05.92
Nugent, David	5.11	Derby	Liverpool	02.05.85
Simpson, Connor	6.5	Hartlepool	Guisborough	24.01.00
Stockley, Jayden	6.3	Exeter	Poole	15.09.93

QUEENS PARK RANGERS

Ground: Loftus Road Stadium, South Africa Road, London W12 7PA
Telephone: 0208 743 0262. **Club nickname:** Hoops
Colours: Blue and white. **Capacity:** 18,360
Record attendance: 35,353 v Leeds (Div 1) 27 Apr, 1974

Goalkeepers

Kelly, Liam	6.3	L:ivingston	Glasgow	23.01.96
Lumley, Joe	6.4	Tottenham	Harlow	15.02.95

Defenders

Ball, Dominic	6.1	Rotherham	Welwyn Garden City	02.08.95
Barbet, Yoann	62	Brentford	Libourne, Fr	10.05.93
Furlong, Darnell	5.11	–	Luton	31.10.95
Hall, Grant	6.4	Tottenham	Brighton	29.10.91
Kakay, Osman	5.11	–	Westminster	25.08.97
Leistner, Toni	6.3	Union Berlin	Dresden, Ger	19.08.90
Masterson, Conor	6.1	Liverpool	Cellbridge, Ire	08.09.98
Rangel, Angel	5.11	Swansea	Tortosa, Sp	28.10.82
Wallace, Lee	6.1	Rangers	Edinburgh	01.08.87

Midfielders

Amos, Luke	5.11	Tottenham (loan)	Welwyn Garden City	23.02.97
Luongo, Massimo	5.10	Swindon	Sydney, Aus	25.09.92
Manning, Ryan	5.11	Galway	Galway, Ire	14.06.96
Osayi-Samuel, Bright	5.9	Blackpool	Okija, Nig	01.02.97
Scowen, Josh	5.10	Barnsley	Enfield	28.03.93
Smyth, Paul		Linfield	Belfast	10.09.97

Forwards

Chair, Ilias	5.4	Lierse	Belgium	30.10.97
Eze, Eberechi	5.8	Millwall	Greenwich	29.06.98
Oteh, Aramide	5.9	Tottenham	Lewisham	10.09.98
Shodipo, Olamide	5.10	–	Leixlip, Ire	05.07.97
Walker, Lewis	6.0	Derby	Nottingham	14.04.99

READING

Ground: Madejski Stadium, Junction 11 M4, Reading RG2 OFL
Telephone: 0118 968 1100. **Club nickname:** Royals
Colours: Blue and white. **Capacity:** 24,200
Record attendance: Elm Park: 33,042 v Brentford (FA Cup 5) Feb 19, 1927; Madejski Stadium: 24,184 v Everton (Prem Lge) Nov 17, 2012

Goalkeepers

Joao Virginia	6.3	Everton (loan)	Faro, Port	10.10.99
Walker, Sam	6.6	Colchester	Gravesend	02.10.91

Defenders

Blackett, Tyler	6.1	Man Utd	Manchester	02.04.94
Gunter, Chris	5.11	Nottm Forest	Newport	21.07.89
Moore, Liam	6.1	Leicester	Leicester	31.01.93
Obita, Jordan	5.11	–	Oxford	08.12.93
Richards, Omar	–	Fulham	Lewisham	15.02.98
Watson, Tennai	6.0	–	Hillingdon	04.03.97
Yiadom, Andy	5.11	Barnsley	Holloway	02.12.91

Midfielders

Barrett, Josh	5.11		Oxford	21.06.98

McCleary, Garath	5.11	Nottm Forest	Bromley	15.05.87
Meyler, David	6.2	Hull	Cork, Ire	29.05.89
Popa, Adrian	5.7	Steaua Bucharest	Bucharest, Rom	24.07.88
Rinomhota, Andy	5.9	Portchester	Leeds	21.04.97
Swift, John	6.0	Chelsea	Portsmouth	23.06.95

Forwards

Baldock, Sam	5.8	Brighton	Bedford	15.03.89
Barrow, Modou	5.10	Swansea	Banjul, Gam	13.10.92
Loader, Danny	6.0	Wycombe	Reading	28.08.00
Meite, Yakou	6.1	Paris SG	Paris, Fr	11.02.96
McNulty, Marc	5.10	Coventry	Edinburgh	14.09.92

SHEFFIELD WEDNESDAY

Ground: Hillsborough, Sheffield, S6 1SW
Telephone: 0871 995 1867. **Club nickname:** Owls
Colours: Blue and white. **Capacity:** 39,812
Record attendance: 72,841 v Manchester City (FA Cup 5) Feb 17, 1934

Goalkeepers

| Dawson, Cameron | 6.0 | Sheffield Utd | Sheffield | 07.07.95 |
| Westwood, Keiren | 6.1 | Sunderland | Manchester | 23.10.84 |

Defenders

Baker, Ashley	–	Cardiff	Bridgend	30.10.96
Borner, Julian	6.2	Arminia Bielefield	Weimar, Ger	21.01.91
Fox, Morgan	6.1	Charlton	Chelmsford	21.09.93
Hutchinson, Sam	6.0	Chelsea	Windsor	03.08.89
Iorfa, Dominic	6.4	Wolves	Southend	24.06.95
Lees, Tom	6.1	Leeds	Warwick	18.11.90
Odubajo, Moses	5.10	Brentford	Greenwich	28.07.93
Palmer, Liam	6.2	–	Worksop	19.09.91
Penney, Matt	5.10	–	Chesterfield	11.02.98
Thorniley, Jordan	5.11	Everton	Warrington	24.11.96
Van Aken, Joost	6.4	Heerenveen	Haarlem, Hol	13.05.94

Midfielders

Bannan, Barry	5.11	Crystal Palace	Airdrie	01.12.89
Harris, Kadeem	5.9	Cardiff	Westminster	08.06.93
Lee, Kieran	6.1	Oldham	Tameside	22.06.88
Pelupessy, Joel	5.11	Heracles	Nijverdal, Hol	15.05.93
Reach, Adam	6.1	Middlesbrough	Gateshead	03.02.93

Forwards

Fletcher, Steven	6.1	Sunderland	Shrewsbury	26.03.87
Forestieri, Fernando	5.8	Watford	Rosario, Arg	15.01.90
Lucas Joao	6.4	Nacional	Luanda, Ang	04.09.93
Nuhiu, Atdhe	6.6	Rapid Vienna	Prishtina, Kos	29.07.89
Rhodes, Jordan	6.1	Middlesbrough	Oldham	05.02.90
Winnall, Sam	5.9	Barnsley	Wolverhampton	19.01.91

STOKE CITY

Ground: bet365 Stadium, Stanley Matthews Way, Stoke-on-Trent ST4 7EG
Telephone: 01782 367598. **Club nickname:** Potters
Colours: Red and white. **Capacity:** 30,183.
Record attendance: Victoria Ground: 51,380 v Arsenal (Div 1) Mar 29, 1937. bet365 Stadium: 30,022 v Everton (Prem Lge) Mar 17, 2018

Goalkeepers

Butland, Jack	6.4	Birmingham	Bristol	10.03.93
Davies, Adam	6.1	Barnsley	Rintein, Ger	17.07.92
Federici, Adam	6.2	Bournemouth	Nowra, Aus	31.01.85

Defenders

Batth, Danny	6.3	Wolves	Brierley Hill	21.09.90
Bauer, Moritz	5.11	Rubin Kazan	Winterthur, Switz	25.01.92
Collins, Nathan	6.4	Cherry Orchard	Leixlip, Ire	30.04.01
Edwards, Tom	5.9	–	Stafford	22.01.99
Lindsay, Liam	6.3	Barnsley	Paisley	12.10.95
Martins Indi, Bruno	6.1	Porto	Barreiro, Port	08.02.92
Pieters, Erik	6.1	PSV Eindhoven	Tiel, Hol	07.08.88
Shawcross, Ryan	6.3	Man Utd	Chester	04.10.87
Smith, Tommy	6.1	Huddersfield	Warrington	14.04.92
Tymon, Josh	5.10	Hull	Hull	22.05.99
Ward, Stephen	5.11	Burnley	Dublin, Ire	20.08.85

Midfielders

Allen, Joe	5.7	Liverpool	Carmarthen	14.03.90
Clucas, Sam	5.10	Swansea	Lincoln	25.09.90
Cousins, Jordan	5.10	QPR	Greenwich	06.03.94
Imbula, Giannelli	6.1	Porto	Vilvoorde, Bel	12.09.92
Ince, Tom	5.10	Huddersfield	Stockport	30.01.92
McClean, James	5.11	WBA	Derry	22.04.89
Ndiaye, Badou	5.11	Galatasaray	Dakar, Sen	27.10.90
Powell, Nick	6.0	Wigan	Crewe	23.03.94
Sorenson, Lasse	6.1	Esbjerg	Vejen, Den	21.10.99
Verlinden, Thibaud	5.8	Standard Liege	Brussels, Bel	09.07.99
Woods, Ryan	5.8	Brentford	Norton Canes	13.12.93

Forwards

Afobe, Benik	6.0	Wolves	Waltham Forest	12.02.93
Biram Diouf, Mame	6.1	Hannover	Dakar, Sen	16.12.87
Campbell, Tyrese	6.0	Man City	Cheadle Hulme	28.12.99
Gregory, Lee	6.2	Millwall	Sheffield	26.08.88
Krkic, Bojan	5.7	Barcelona	Linyola, Sp	28.08.90
Vokes, Sam	5.11	Burnley	Lymington	21.10.89

SWANSEA CITY

Ground: Liberty Stadium, Morfa, Swansea SA1 2FA
Telephone: 01792 616600. **Club nickname:** Swans
Colours: White. **Capacity:** 20,972.
Record attendance: Vetch Field: 32,796 v Arsenal (FA Cup 4) Feb 17, 1968. Liberty Stadium: 20,972 v Liverpool (Prem Lge) May 1, 2016

Goalkeepers

Benda, Steven	6.3	1860 Munich	Stuttgart, Ger	01.10.98
Mulder, Erwin	6.4	Heerenveen	Pannerden, Hol	03.03.89
Nordfeldt, Kristoffer	6.1	Heerenveen	Stockholm, Swe	23.06.89

Defenders

Bidwell, Jake	6.1	QPR	Southport	21.03.93
Harries, Cian	6.1	Coventry	Birmingham	01.04.97
John, Declan	5.10	Rangers	Merthyr Tydfil	30.06.95
Naughton, Kyle	5.10	Tottenham	Sheffield	11.11.88
Roberts, Connor	5.10	–	Neath	23.09.95
Rodon, Joe	6.4	–	Llangyfelach	22.10.97
Van der Hoorn, Mike	6.3	Ajax	Almere, Hol	15.10.92

Midfielders

Baker-Richardson , Courtney	6.1	Leamingtopn	Coventry	05.12.95
Byers, George	5.11	Watford	Ilford	29.05.96
Carroll, Tom	5.10	Tottenham	Watford	28.05.92
Celina, Bersant	5.11	Man City	Prizren, Kos	09.09.96
Dhanda, Yan	5.8	Liverpool	Birmingham	14.12.98
Dyer, Nathan	5.10	Southampton	Trowbridge	29.11.87
Fulton, Jay	5.10	Falkirk	Bolton	04.04.94
Grimes, Matt	5.10	Exeter	Exeter	16.07.95
McKay, Barrie	5.9	Nottm Forest	Paisley	30.12.94
Montero, Jefferson	5.7	Morelia	Babahoyo, Ec	01.09.89
Routledge, Wayne	5.7	Newcastle	Sidcup	07.01.85

Forwards

Asoro, Joel	5.9	Sunderland	Stockholm, Swe	27.04.99
Ayew, Andre	5.10	West Ham	Seclin, Fr	17.12.89
Ayew, Jordan	6.0	Aston Villa	Marseille, Fr	11.09.91
Borja	6.3	Atletico Madrid	Madrid, Sp	25.08.92
McBurnie, Oliver	6.2	Bradford	Leeds	04.06.96

WEST BROMWICH ALBION

Ground: The Hawthorns, Halfords Lane, West Bromwich B71 4LF
Telephone: 0871 271 1100. **Club nickname:** Baggies
Colours: Blue and white. **Capacity:** 26,500.
Record attendance: 64,815 v Arsenal (FA Cup 6) Mar 6, 1937

Goalkeepers

Bond, Jonathan	6.4	Reading	Hemel Hempstead	19.05.93
Johnstone, Sam	6.4	Man Utd	Preston	25.03.93

Defenders

Bartley, Kyle	6.1	Swansea	Stockport	22.05.91
Gibbs, Kieran	5.10	Arsenal	Lambeth	26.09.89
Hegazi, Ahmed	6.4	Al Ahly	Ismailia, Egy	25.01.91
Nyom, Allan	6.2	Watford	Neuilly-sur-Seine, Fr	10.05.88
Townsend, Conor	5.6	Scunthorpe	Hessle	04.03.93

Midfielders

Brunt, Chris	6.1	Sheffield Wed	Belfast	14.12.84
Burke, Oliver	6.2	Leipzig	Kircaldy	07.04.97
Field, Sam	5.11	–	Stourbridge	08.05.98
Harper, Rekeem	6.0	–	Birmingham	08.03.00
Krovinovic, Filip	5.10	Benfica (loan)	Zagreb, Cro	29.08.95
Leko, Jonathan	6.0	–	Kinshasa, DR Cong	24.04.99
Livermore, Jake	6.0	Hull	Enfield	14.11.89
Phillips, Matt	6.0	QPR	Aylesbury	13.03.91

Forwards

Edwards, Kyle	5.9	–	Dudley	17.02.98
Robson-Kanu, Hal	6.0	Reading	Acton	21.05.89
Rondon, Salomon	6.2	Zenit St Petersburg	Caracas, Ven	16.09.89

WIGAN ATHLETIC

Ground: DW Stadium, Robin Park, Wigan WN5 0UZ
Telephone: 01942 774000. **Club nickname:** Latics
Colours: Blue and white. **Capacity:** 25,023
Record attendance: Springfield Park: 27,526 v Hereford (FA Cup 2) Dec 12, 1953;
DW Stadium: 25,133 v Manchester Utd (Prem Lge) May 11, 2008

Goalkeepers

Jones, Jamie	6.2	Stevenage	Kirkby	18.02.89
Marshall, David	6.3	Hull	Glasgow	05.03.85

Defenders

Dunkley, Chey	6.2	Oxford	Wolverhampton	13.02.92
Fox, Danny	6.0	Nottm Forest	Winsford	29.05.86
Kipre, Cedric	6.3	Motherwell	Paris, Fr	09.12.96
Robinson, Antonee	6.0	Everton	Milton Keynes	08.08.97

Midfielders

Byrne, Nathan	5.11	Wolves	St Albans	05.06.92
Evans, Lee	6.1	Sheffield Utd	Newport	24.07.94
Jacobs, Michael	5.9	Wolves	Rothwell	04.11.91
Lopes, Leonardo	5.7	Peterborough	Lisbon, Por	30.11.98
Morsy, Sam	5.9	Chesterfield	Wolverhampton	10.09.91
Naismith, Kai	6.1	Portsmouth	Glasgow	18.02.92
Pilkington, Anthony	6.0	Cardiff	Blackburn	06.06.88
Roberts, Gary	5.10	Portsmouth	Chester	18.03.84

Forwards

Garner, Joe	5.10	Ipswich	Blackburn	12.04.88
Massey, Gavin	5.10	Leyton Orient	Watford	14.10.92
Windass, Josh	5.9	Rangers	Hull	09.01.94

LEAGUE ONE

ACCRINGTON STANLEY

Ground: Wham Stadium, Livingstone Road, Accrington BB5 5BX
Telephone: 0871 434 1968. **Club nickname:** Stanley
Colours: Red and white. **Capacity:** 5,500
Record attendance: 5,397 v Derby (FA Cup 4) Jan 26, 2019

Goalkeepers

Evtimov, Dimitar	6.3	Burton	Shumen, Bul	07.09.93

Defenders

Barclay, Ben	6.2	Brighton	Altrincham	07.10.96
Conneely, Seamus	6.1	Sligo	Lambeth	09.07.88
Hughes, Mark	6.3	Stevenage	Kirkby	09.12.86
Callum Johnson	—	Middlesbrough	Yarm	23.10.96
Francis-Angol, Zaine	5.8	Fylde	Waltham Forest	30.06.93
Maguire, Joe	5.11	Fleetwood	Manchester	18.01.96
Ogle, Reagan	5.9	—	Australia	29.03.99
Rodgers, Harvey	5.11	Fleetwood	York	20.10.96
Sykes, Ross	6.5	—	Burnley	26.03.99

Midfielders

Clark, Jordan	6.0	Shrewsbury	Hoyland	22.09.93
Finley, Sam	5.8	Fylde	Liverpool	04.08.92
McConville, Sean	5.11	Chester	Burscough	06.03.89
Pritchard, Joe	5.8	Bolton	Watford	10.09.96
Sherif, Lamine Kaba	6.0	Leicester	Conakry, Guin	27.01.99
Sousa, Erico	5.7	Tranmere	Vale da Amoreira, Por	12.03.95

Forwards

Kee, Billy	5.9	Scunthorpe	Leicester	01.12.90
Mangan, Andy	5.9	Bala	Liverpool	30.08.86
Zanzala, Offrande	6.1	Derby	Brazzaville, Cong	08.11.96

AFC WIMBLEDON

Ground: Kingsmeadow, Kingston Road, Kingston upon Thames KT1 3PB
Telephone: 0208 547 3528. **Club nickname:** Dons
Colours: Blue. **Capacity:** 4,850
Record attendance: 4,870 v Accrington (Lge 2 play-off semi-final 1st leg) May 14, 2016

Goalkeepers

Trott, Nathan	6.1	West Ham (loan)	Bermuda	21.11.98
Tzanev, Nik	6.5	Brentford	Wellington, NZ	23.12.96

Defenders

Kalambay, Paul	6.0	–	Dulwich	09.07.99
McDonald, Rod	6.3	Coventry	Crewe	11.04.92
Nightingale, Will	6.1	–	Wandsworth	02.08.95
O'Neill, Luke	6.0	Gillingham	Slough	20.08.91
Thomas, Terell	6.0	Wigan	Redbridge	13.10.97

Midfielders

Hartigan, Anthony	5.10	–	Kingston u Thames	27.01.00
Kaja, Egli	5.10	Kingstonian	Albania	26.07.97
McLoughlin, Shane	5.9	Ipswich	Castleisland, Ire	01.03.97
Pinnock, Mitch	6.3	Dover	Gravesend	12.12.94
Wagstaff, Scott	5.9	Gillingham	Maidstone	31.03.90
Wordsworth, Anthony	6.1	Southend	Camden	03.01.89

Forwards

Appiah, Kwesi	5.11	Crystal Palace	Thamesmead	12.08.90
Folivi, Michael	6.0	Watford (loan)	Wembley	25.02.98
Pigott, Joe	6.2	Maidstone	Maidstone	24.11.93
Wood, Tommy	6.2	Burnley	Hillingdon	26.11.98

BLACKPOOL

Ground: Bloomfield Road, Blackpool FY1 6JJ
Telephone: 0871 622 1953. **Club nickname:** Seasiders
Colours: Tangerine and white. **Capacity:** 17,338
Record attendance: 38,098 v Wolves (Div 1) Sep 17, 1955

Goalkeepers

Boney, Myles	5.11	–	Blackpool	01.02.98
Howard, Mark	6.0	Bolton	Southwark	21.09.86
Mafoumbi, Christoffer	6.5	Free State	Roubaix, Fr	03.03.94

Defenders

Anderton, Nick	6.2	Barrow	Preston	22.04.96
Bola, Marc	6.1	Arsenal	Greenwich	09.12.97
Edwards, Ryan	5.11	Plymouth	Liverpool	07.10.93
Nottingham, Michael	6.4	Salford	Birmingham	14.04.89
Tilt, Curtis	6.4	Wrexham	Walsall	04.08.91
Turton, Ollie	5.11	Crewe	Manchester	06.12.92

Midfielders

Devitt, Jamie	5.10	Carlisle	Dublin, Ire	06.07.90
Feeney, Liam	6.0	Blackburn	Hammersmith	21.01.87
Guy, Callum	5.10	Derby	Nottingham	25.11.96
Kaikai, Sullay	6.0	Breda	Southwark	26.08.95
Pritchard, Harry	5.9	Maidenhead	High Wycombe	14.09.92
Ryan, Jimmy	5.10	Fleetwood	Maghull	06.09.88
Spearing, Jay	5.6	Bolton	Wallasey	25.11.88

Thompson, Jordan	5.9	Rangers	Belfast	03.01.97
Tollitt , Ben	6.1	Tranmere	Liverpool	30.11.94
Virtue, Matty	5.10	Liverpool	Epsom	02.05.97
Forwards				
Delfouneso, Nathan	6.1	Swindon	Birmingham	02.02.91
Gnanduillet, Armand	6.3	Leyton Orient	Angers, Fr	13.02.92
Hardie, Ryan	6.2	Rangers	Stranraer	17.03.97
Yussuf, Adi	6.1	Solihull	Zanzibar, Tanz	20.02.92

BOLTON WANDERERS

Ground: University of Bolton Stadium, Burnden Way, Lostock, Bolton BL6 6JW
Telephone: 0844 871 2932. **Club nickname:** Trotters
Colours: White and navy. **Capacity:** 28,723
Record attendance: Burnden Park: 69,912 v Manchester City (FA Cup 5) Feb 18, 1933.
Macron Stadium: 28,353 v Leicester (Prem Lge) Dec 28, 2003

Goalkeepers				
Alnwick, Ben	6.2	Peterborough	Prudhoe	01.01.87
Matthews, Remi	6.1	Norwich	Gorleston	10.02.94
Defenders				
Hobbs, Jack	6.3	Nottm Forest	Portsmouth	18.08.88
Muscatt, Joseph	5.10	Tottenham	Whipps Cross	15.12.97
Olkowski, Pawel	6.1	Cologne	Ozimek, Pol	13.02.90
Taylor, Andrew	5.10	Wigan	Hartlepool	01.08.86
Wheater, David	6.5	Middlesbrough	Redcar	14.02.87
Wilson, Marc	6.2	Sunderland	Aghagallon	17.08.87
Midfielders				
Buckley, Will	6.0	Sunderland	Oldham	12.08.88
Earing, Jack	6.0	–	Bury	21.01.99
Lowe, Jason	5.10	Birmingham	Wigan	02.09.91
Murphy, Luke	6.2	Leeds	Macclesfield	21.10.89
O'Neil, Gary	5.8	Bristol City	Beckenham	18.05.83
Oztumer, Erhun	5.3	Walsall	Greenwich	29.05.91
Forwards				
Magennis, Josh	6.2	Charlton	Bangor, NI	15.08.90

BRISTOL ROVERS

Ground: Memorial Stadium, Filton Avenue, Horfield, Bristol B37 OBF
Telephone: 0117 909 6648. **Club nickname:** Pirates
Colours: Blue and white. **Capacity:** 12,011
Record attendance: Eastville: 38,472 v Preston (FA Cup 4) Jan 30, 1960. Memorial Stadium:
12,011 v WBA (FA Cup 6) Mar 9, 2008

Goalkeepers				
Jaakkola, Anssi	6.5	Reading	Kemi, Fin	13.03.87
Van Stappershoef, Jordi	6.0	Volendam	Amsterdam, Hol	10.03.96
Defenders				
Craig, Tony	6.0	Millwall	Greenwich	20.04.85
Davies, Tom	5.11	Coventry	Warrington	18.04.92
Hare, Josh	6.0	Eastleigh	Canterbury	12.08.94
Holmes-Dennis, Tareiq	5.10	Huddersfield	Farnborough	31.10.95
Kelly, Michael	5.11	Leicester	Kilmarnock	03.11.97
Kilgour, Alfie	5.10	–	Bath	18.05.98
Leahy, Luke	5.10	Walsall	Coventry	19.11.92
Little, Mark	6.1	Bolton	Worcester	20.08.88

| Menayesse, Rollin | 6.3 | Western SM | Kinshasa, DR Cong | 04.12.97 |

Midfielders

Bennett, Kyle	5.5	Portsmouth	Telford	09.09.90
Matthews, Sam	5.10	Bournemouth	Poole	01.03.97
Sercombe, Liam	5.10	Oxford	Exeter	25.04.90
Upson, Ed	5.10	MK Dons	Bury St Edmunds	21.11.89

Forwards

Clarke-Harris, Jonson	6.0	Coventry	Leicester	20.07.94
Mensah, Bernard	5.8	Aldershot	Hounslow	29.12.94
Nichols, Tom	5.10	Peterborough	Taunton	28.08.93
Reilly, Gavin	5.11	St Mirren	Dumfries	10.05.93
Rodman, Alex	6.2	Shrewsbury	Sutton Coldfield	15.12.87
Smith, Tyler	5.10	Sheffield Utd (loan)	Sheffield	04.12.98

BURTON ALBION

Ground: Pirelli Stadium, Princess Way, Burton upon Trent DE13 AR
Telephone: 01283 565938. **Club nickname:** Brewers
Colours: Yellow and black. **Capacity:** 6,912
Record attendance: 6,746 v Derby (Champ),Aug 26, 2016

Goalkeepers

| Bywater, Stephen | 6.3 | Kerala | Oldham | 07.06.81 |
| O'Hara, Kieran | 6.3 | Man Utd (loan) | Manchester | 22.04.96 |

Defenders

Anderson, Jevan	6.1	Formartine	Aberdeen	03.03.00
Brayford, John	5.8	Sheffield Utd	Stoke	29.12.87
Buxton, Jake	5.11	Wigan	Sutton-in-Ashfield	04.03.85
Hutchinson, Reece	5.8	–	Birmingham	14.04.00
Nartey, Richard	6.0	Chelsea (loan)	Hammersmith	06.09.98
Wallace, Kieran	6.1	Matlock	Nottingham	26.01.95

Midfielders

Daniel, Colin	5.11	Peterboroughl	Nottingham	15.02.88
Fox, Ben	5.11	–	Burton	01.02.98
Fraser, Scott	6.0	Dundee Utd	Dundee	30.03.95
Harness, Marcus	6.0	–	Coventry	01.08.94
O'Toole, John-Joe	6.2	Northampton	Harrow	30.09.88
Quinn, Stephen	5.6	Reading	Dublin, Ire	01.04.86
Sbarra, Joe	5.10	–	Lichfield	21.12.98
Templeton, David	5.10	Hamilton	Glasgow	07.01.89

Forwards

Akins, Lucas	6.0	Stevenage	Huddersfield	25.02.89
Boyce, Liam	6.1	Ross Co	Belfast	08.04.91
Sordell, Marvin	5.10	Coventry	Harrow	17.02.91

BURY

Ground: Gigg Lane, Bury BL9 9HR
Telephone: 08445 790009. **Club nickname:** Shakers
Colours: White and blue. **Capacity:** 11,640
Record attendance: 35,000 v Bolton (FA Cup 3) Jan 9, 1960

Goalkeepers

| Moloney, Scott | 6.3 | – | Ashton-u-Lyne | 05.02.01 |

Defenders

| Edwards, Phil | 5.9 | Burton | Bootle | 08.11.85 |
| Miller, Tom | 5.11 | Carlisle | Ely | 29.06.90 |

O'Connell, Eoghan	6.2	Celtic	Cork, Ire	13.08.95
Shotton, Saul	6.1	–	Stoke	10.11.00
Thompson, Adam	6.2	Southend	Harlow	28.09.92
Skarz, Joe	6.0	Oxford	Huddersfield	13.07.89
Midfielders				
Dawson, Stephen	5.6	Scunthorpe	Dublin, Ire	04.12.85
Forwards				
Archer, Jordan	6.3	Maidenhead	Bedworth	11.11.93
Beckford, Jermaine	6.2	Preston	Ealing	09.12.83
Bunn, Harry	5.9	Huddersfield	Oldham	21.11.92
Moore, Byron	6.0	Bristol Rov	Stoke	24.08.88

COVENTRY CITY

Ground: St Andrew's, Birmingham B9 4NH (ground sharing).
Telephone: 02476 992326. **Club nickname:** Sky Blues
Colours: Sky blue. **Capacity:** 30,016
Record attendance: Highfield Road: 51,455 v Wolves (Div 2) Apr 29, 1967. Ricoh Arena:
31,407 v Chelsea (FA Cup 6), Mar 7, 2009

Goalkeepers				
Marosi, Marko	6.3	Doncaster	Slovakia	23.10.93
Wilson, Ben	6.1	Bradford	Stanley	09.08.92
Defenders				
Brown, Junior	5.9	Shrewsbury	Crewe	07.05.89
Dabo, Fankaty	5.11	Chelsea	Southwark	11.10.95
Hyam, Dom	6.2	Reading	Dundee	20.12.95
Mason, Brandon	5.9	Watford	Westminster	30.09.97
McFadzean, Kyle	6.1	Burton	Sheffield	28.02.87
Pask, Josh	6.2	West Ham	Waltham Forest	01.11.97
Midfielders				
Allasssani, Reise	5.8	Dulwich Hamlet	London	03.01.96
Allen, Jamie	5.11	Burton	Rochdale	29.01.95
Bayliss, Tom	6.0	–	Leicester	06.04.99
Jones, Jodi	5.10	Dagenham	Bow	22.10.97
Kelly, Liam	5.10	Leyton Orient	Milton Keynes	10.02.90
Rose, Michael	5.11	Ayr	Aberdeen	11.10.95
Shipley, Jordan	6.0	–	Leamington Spa	26.09.97
Wakefield, Charlie	6.1	Chelsea	Worthing	10.04.98
Westbrooke, Zain	5.11	Brentford	Chertsey	28.10.96
Forwards				
Bakayoko, Amadou	6.3	Walsall	Sierra Leone	01.01.96
Biamou, Maxime	6.1	Sutton	Creteil, Fr	13.11.90
Chaplin, Conor	5.10	Portsmouth	Worthing	16.02.97
Hiwula, Jordy	5.10	Huddersfield	Manchester	21.09.94
Jobello, Wesley	5.10	Ajaccio	Gennevilliers, Mart	23.01.94
Kastaneer, Gervane	6.2	Breda	Rotterdam, Hol	09.06.96

DONCASTER ROVERS

Ground: Keepmoat Stadium, Stadium Way, Doncaster DN4 5JW
Telephone: 01302 764664. **Club nickname:** Rovers
Colours: Red and white. **Capacity:** 15,231
Record attendance: Belle Vue: 37,149 v Hull (Div 3 N) Oct 2, 1948. Keepmoat Stadium:
15,001 v Leeds (Lge 1) Apr 1, 2008

Goalkeepers

Jones, Louis	6.1	–	Doncaster	12.10.98
Lawlor, Ian	6.4	Man City	Dublin, Ire	27.10.94

Defenders

Anderson, Tom	6.3	Burnley	Burnley	02.09.93
James, Reece	6.0	Sunderland	Bacup	07.11.93
Wright, Joe	6.4	Huddersfield	Monk Fryston	26.02.95

Midfielders

Amos, Danny	5.11		Sheffield	22.12.99
Blair, Matty	5.10	Mansfield	Warwick	30.11.87
Coppinger, James	5.7	Exeter	Middlesbrough	10.01.81
Crawford, Ali	5.8	Hamilton	Lanark	30.07.91
Halliday, Brad	5.11	Cambridge	Redcar	10.07.95
Madger Gomes	5.10	NK Istra	Alicante, Sp	01.02.97
Sadlier, Kieran	6.0	Cork	Haywards Heath	14.09.9
Whiteman, Ben	6.0	Sheffield Utd	Rochdale	17.06.96

Forwards

Marquis, John	6.1	Millwall	Lewisham	16.05.92
May, Alfie	5.10	Hythe	Gravesend	02.07.93
Taylor, Paul	5.11	Bradford	Liverpool	04.10.87

FLEETWOOD TOWN

Ground: Highbury Stadium, Park Avenue, Fleetwod FY7 6TX
Telephone: 01253 775080. **Club nickname:** Fishermen
Colours: Red and white. **Capacity:** 5,311
Record attendance: 5,194 v York (Lge 2 play-off semi-final, 2nd leg) May 16, 2014

Goalkeepers

Cairns, Alex	6.0	Rotherham	Doncaster	04.01.93

Defenders

Andrew, Danny	5.11	Doncaster	Holbeach	23.12.90
Coyle, Lewie	5.8	Leeds (loan)	Hull	15.10.95
Eastham, Ashley	6.3	Rochdale	Preston	22.03.91
Jones, Gethin	5.10	Everton	Perth, Aus	13.10.95
Morgan, Craig	6.0	Wigan	Flint	16.06.85

Midfielders

Coutts, Paul	6.1	Sheffield Utd	Aberdeen	22.07.88
Dempsey, Kyle	5.10	Huddersfield	Whitehaven	17.09.95
Grant, Bobby	5.11	Blackpool	Litherland	01.07.90
Marney, Dean	5.11	Burnley	Barking	31.01.84
Morris, Josh	5,0	Scunthorpe	Preston	30.09.91
Rossiter, Jordan	5.10	Rangers (loan)	24.03.97	
Sowerby, Jack	5.9	–	Preston	23.03.95
Wallace, James	5.11	Tranmere	Liverpool	19.12.91
Wallace, Ross	5.7	Sheffield Wed	Dundee	23.05.85

Forwards

Biggins, Harrison	–	Stocksbridge	Sheffield	15.03.96
Burns, Wes	5.8	Bristol City	Cardiff	23.11.94
Hunter, Ashley	5.10	Ilkeston	Derby	29.09.95
Madden, Paddy	6.0	Scunthorpe	Dublin, Ire	04.03.90

GILLINGHAM

Ground: Mems Priestfield Stadium, Redfern Avenue, Gillingham ME7 4DD
Telephone: 01634 300000. **Club nickname:** Gills

Colours: Blue and white. **Capacity:** 11,582
Record attendance: 23,002 v QPR (FA Cup 3) Jan 10, 1948

Goalkeepers

Bonham, Jack	6.4	Brentford	Stevenage	14.09.93

Defenders

Ehmer, Max	6.2	QPR	Frankfurt, Ger	03.02.92
Fuller, Barry	5.10	AFC Wimbledon	Ashford, Kent	25.09.84
Garmston, Bradley	5.11	WBA	Chorley	18.01.94
Jones, Alfie	5.11	Southampton (loan)	Bristol	07.10.97
Ogilvie, Connor	6.1	Tottenham	Waltham Abbey	14.02.96
Zakuani, Gabriel	6.1	Northampton	Kinshasa, DR Cong	31.05.86

Midfielders

Byrne, Mark	5.9	Newport	Dublin, Ire	09.11.88
Charles-Cook, Regan	5.9	Charlton	Lewisham	14.02.97
Cisse, Ousseynou	6.4	MK Dons	Suresnes, Fr	07.04.91
Hodson, Lee	5.11	Rangers	Borehamwood	02.10.91
List, Elliott	5.10	Crystal Palace	Camberwell	12.05.97
O'Keefe, Stuart	5.8	Cardiff	Norwich	04.03.91
Oldaker, Darren	5.9	QPR	London	01.04.99
Rees, Josh	5.9	Bromley	Hemel Hempstead	04.10.93
Reilly, Callum	6.1	Bury	Warrington	03.10.93
Simpson, Aaron	5.9	–	Croydon	17.06.99
Stevenson, Bradley	6.0	–	Canterbury	12.09.98
Thomas, Nathan	5.9	Sheffield Utd (loan)	Ingleby Barwick	27.09.94
Willock, Matty	5.8	Man Utd	Waltham Forest	20.08.96

Forwards

Hanlan, Brandon	6.0	Charlton	Chelsea	31.05.97
Ndjoli, Mikael	6.0	Bournemouth (loan)	London	08.09.98

IPSWICH TOWN

Ground: Portman Road, Ipswich IP1 2DA
Telephone: 01473 400500. **Club nickname:** Blues/Town
Colours: Blue and white. **Capacity:** 30,300
Record attendance: 38,010 v Leeds (FA Cup 6) Mar 8, 1975

Goalkeepers

Bialkowski, Bartosz	6.0	Notts Co	Braniewo, Pol	06.07.87
Holy, Tomas	6.9	Gillingham	Rychnov, Cz	10.12.91

Defenders

Chambers, Luke	5.11	Nottm Forest	Kettering	29.08.85
Donacien, Janoi	6.0	Accrington	Castries, St Luc	03.11.93
El Mizouni, Idris	5.10	–	Paris, Fr	26.09.00
Emmanuel, Josh	6.0	West Ham	London	18.08.97
Garbutt, Luke	5.10	Everton (loan)	Harrogate	21.05.93
Kenlock, Myles	6.1	–	Croydon	29.11.96
Nsiala, Toto	6.4	Shrewsbury	Kinshasa, DR Cong	25.03.92
Nydam, Tristan	5.8	–	Harare, Zim	06.11.99
Woolfenden, Luke	6.1	–	Ipswich	21.10.98

Midfielders

Bishop, Ed	5.11	–	Cambridge	15.07.96
Downes, Flynn	5.10	–	Brentwood	20.01.99
Dozzell, Andre	5.10	–	Ipswich	02.05.99
Edwards, Gwion	5.9	Peterborough	Lampeter	01.04.93
Huws, Emyr	5.10	Cardiff	Llanelli	30.09.93

Judge, Alan	6.0	Brentford	Dublin, Ire	11.11.88
Nolan, Jon	5.10	Shrewsbury	Huyton	22.04.92
Roberts, Jordan	6.1	Crawley	Watford	05.01.94
Rowe, Danny	6.0	Macclesfield	Wythenshawe	09.03.92
Skuse, Cole	5.9	Bristol City	Bristol	29.03.86
Forwards				
Jackson, Kayden	5.11	Accrington	Bradford	22.02.94
Norwood, James	5.10	Tranmere	Eastbourne	05.09.90
Sears, Freddie	5.10	Colchester	Hornchurch	27.11.89

LINCOLN CITY

Ground: Sincil Bank Stadium, Lincoln LN5 8LD
Telephone: 01522 880011. **Club nickname:** Imps
Colours: Red and white. **Capacity:** 10,130
Record attendance: 23,196 v Derby (League Cup 4) Nov 15, 1967

Goalkeepers				
Gilks, Matt	6.1	Scunthorpe	Rochdale	04.06.82
Smith, Grant	6.1	Boreham Wood	Reading	20.11.93
Vickers, Josh	6.0	Swansea	Basildon	01.12.95
Defenders				
Bolger, Cian	6.4	Fleetwood	Cellbridge, Ire	12.03.92
Eardley, Neal	5.11	Northampton	Llandudno	06.11.88
Habergham, Sam	6.0	Braintree	Doncaster	20.02.92
Shackell, Jason	6.4	Derby	Stevenage	27.09.83
Toffolo, Harry	6.0	Millwall	Welwyn Garden City	19.08.95
Wilson, James	6.2	Sheffield United	Newport	26.02.89
Midfielders Anderson, Harry	5.7	Peterborough	Slough	09.01.97
Bostwick, Michael	6.1	Peterborough	Greenwich	17.05.88
Chapman, Ellis	6.1	–	Lincoln	08.01.01
Frecklington, Lee	5.8	Rotherham	Lincoln	08.09.85
Grant, Jorge	5.10	Nottm Forest	Banbury	19.12.94
Morrell, Joe	6.1	Bristol City (loan)	Ipswich	03.01.97
O'Connor, Michael	6.1	Notts Co	Belfast	06.10.87
Payne, Jack	5.6	Huddersfield	Tower Hamlets	25.10.94
Forwards				
Akinde, John	6.2	Barnet	Gravesend	08.07.89
Bruno Andrade	5.9	Boreham Wood	Viseu, Port	02.10.93
Pett, Tom	5.8	Stevenage	Potters Bar	03.12.91
Rhead, Matt	6.4	Mansfield	Stoke	31.05.84

MILTON KEYNES DONS

Ground: stadiummk, Stadium Way West, Milton Keynes MK1 1ST
Telephone: 01908 622922. **Club nickname:** Dons
Colours: White. **Capacity:** 30,500
Record attendance: 28,127 v Chelsea (FA Cup 4) Jan 31, 2016

Goalkeepers				
Moore, Stuart	6.2	Swindon	Sandown, IOW	08.09.94
Nicholls, Lee	6.3	Wigan	Huyton	05.10.92
Defenders				
Brittain, Callum	5.10	–	Bedford	12.03.98
Cargill, Baily	6.2	Bournemouth	Winchester	05.07.95
Lewington, Dean	5.11	Wimbledon	Kingston upon Thames	18.05.84

Martin, Russell	6.1	Walsall	Brighton	04.01.86
Moore-Taylor, Jordan	5.10	Exeter	Exeter	21.01.94
Poole, Regan	5.10	Man Utd	Cardiff	18.06.98
Walsh, Joe	5.11	Crawley	Cardiff	13.05.92
Williams, George	5.9	Barnsley	Hillingdon	14.04.93
Midfielders				
Boateng, Hiram	6.0	Exeter	Wandsworth	08.01.96
Dickenson, Brennan	6.0	Colchester	Ferndown	26.02.93
Gilbey, Alex	6.0	Wigan	Dagenham	09.12.94
Harley, Ryan	5.9	Exeter	Bristol	22.01.85
Houghton, Jordan	6.0	Chelsea	Chertsey	09.11.95
Kasumu, David	5.11	–	Lambert	05.10.99
McGrandles, Conor	6.0	Norwich	Falkirk	24.09.95
Forwards				
Agard, Kieran	5.10	Bristol City	Newham	10.10.89
Asonganyi, Dylan	–	–	Sheffield	10.12.00
Bowery, Jordan	6.1	Crewe	Nottingham	02.07.91
Healey, Rhys	5.11	Cardiff	Manchester	06.12.94
Mason, Joe	5.10	Wolves	Plymouth	13.05.91
Nombe, Sam	5.11	–	Croydon	22.10.98

OXFORD UNITED

Ground: Kassam Stadium, Grenoble Road, Oxford OX4 4XP
Telephone: 01865 337500. **Club nickname:** U's
Colours: Yellow. **Capacity:** 12,500
Record attendance: Manor Ground: 22,750 v Preston (FA Cup 6) Feb 29, 1964. Kassam
Stadium: 12,243 v Leyton Orient (Lge 2) May 6, 2006

Goalkeepers				
Eastwood, Simon	6.2	Blackburn	Luton	26.06.89
Stevens, Jack	6.2	–	–	02.08.97
Defenders				
Dickie, Rob	6.3	Reading	Wokingham	03.03.96
Long, Sam	5.10	–	Oxford	16.01.95
McMahon, Tony	5.10	Bradford	Bishop Auckland	24.03.86
Mousinho, John	6.1	Burton	Isleworth	30.04.86
Midfielders				
Brannagan, Cameron	5.11	Liverpool	Manchester	09.05.96
Fosu, Tarique	5.8	Charlton	Wandsworth	05.11.95
Hanson, Jamie	6.3	Derby	Burton upon Trent	10.11.95
Henry, James	6.1	Wolves	Reading	10.06.89
Rodriguez, Alex	6.1	Motherwell	Tenerife, Sp	01.08.93
Ruffels, Josh	5.10	Coventry	Oxford	23.10.93
Forwards				
Hall, Rob	6.2	Bolton	Aylesbury	20.10.93
Mackie, Jamie	5.11	QPR	Dorking	22.09.85
Whyte, Gavin	5.10	Crusaders	Belfast	31.01.96

PETERBOROUGH UNITED

Ground: Abax Stadium, London Road, Peterborough PE2 8AL
Telephone: 01733 563947. **Club nickname:** Posh
Colours: Blue and white. **Capacity:** 14,319
Record attendance: 30,096 v Swansea (FA Cup 5) Feb 20, 1965

Goalkeepers

O'Malley, Conor	6.3	St Patrick's	Westport, Ire	01.08.94
Pym, Christy	5.11	Exeter	Exeter	24.04.95

Defenders

Beevers, Mark	6.4	Bolton	Barnsley	21.11.89
Bennett, Rhys	6.3	Mansfield	Manchester	01.09.91
Butler, Dan	5.9	Newport	Cowes	26.08.94
Cartwright, Sam	6.1	–	Huntngdon	08.07.00
Cooke, Callum	5.8	Middlesbrough	Peterlee	21.02.97
Kent, Frankie	6.2	Colchester	Romford	21.11.95
Mason, Niall	5.11	Doncaster	Bromley	10.01.97
Naismith, Jason	6.2	Ross Co	Paisley	25.06.94

Midfielders

Boyd, George	5.10	Sheffield Wed	Chatham	02.10.85
Cooper, George	5.9	Crewe	Warrington	02.11.96
Dembele, Siriki	5.8	Grimsby	Ivory Coast	07.09.96
O'Hara, Mark	6.4	Dundee	Barrhead	12.12.95
Reed, Louis	5.8	Sheffield Utd	Barnsley	25.07.97
Tasdemir, Serhat	5.11	Fylde	Blackburn	21.07.00
Ward, Joe		Woking	Chelmsford	22.08.95
Woodyard, Alex	5.9	Lincoln	Gravesend	03.05.93

Forwards

Eisa, Mo	6.0	Bristol City	Khartoum, Sud	12.07.94
Godden, Matt	6.1	Stevenage	Canterbury	29.07.91
Kanu, Idris	6.0	Aldershot	London	05.12.99
Maddison, Marcus	5.11	Gateshead	Durham	26.09.93
Toney, Ivan	5.10	Newcastle	Northampton	16.03.96

PORTSMOUTH

Ground: Fratton Park, Frogmore Road, Portsmouth, PO4 8RA
Telephone: 0239 273 1204. **Club nickname:** Pompey
Colours: Blue and white. **Capacity:** 20,700
Record attendance: 51,385 v Derby (FA Cup 6) Feb 26, 1949

Goalkeepers

Bass, Alex	6.2	–	Southampton	01.04.98
McGee, Luke	6.2	Tottenham	Edgware	02.09.95
MacGillivray, Craig	6.2	Shrewsbury	Harrogate	12.01.93

Defenders

Bolton, James	6.0	Shrewsbury	Stone	13.08.94
Brown, Lee	6.0	Bristol Rov	Farnborough	10.08.90
Burgess, Christian	6.5	Peterborough	Barking	07.10.91
Casey, Matt	6.5	–	Southampton	13.11.99
Downing, Paul	6.1	Blackburn	Taunton	26.10.91
Haunstrup, Brandon	5.8	–	Waterlooville	26.10.96
Naylor, Tom	6.0	Burton	Sutton-in-Ashfield	28.06.91
Raggett, Sean	6.6	Norwich (loan)	Gillingham	25.01.94
Thompson, Nathan	5.10	Swindon	Chester	22.04.91
Walkes, Anton	6.2	Tottenham	Lewisham	08.02.97
Whatmough, Jack	6.0	–	Gosport	19.08.96

Midfielders

Cannon, Andy	5.9	Rochdale	Tameside	14.03.96
Close, Ben	5.9	–	Portsmouth	08.08.96
Dennis, Louis	6.1	Bromley	Hendon	09.10.92

Evans, Gareth	6.0	Fleetwood	Macclesfield	26.04.88
Lowe, Jamal	6.0	Hampton	Harrow	21.07.94
McCrorie, Ross	6.3	Rangers (loan)	Dailly	18.03.98
Morris, Bryn	6.0	Shrewsbury	Hartlepool	25.04.96
Williams, Ryan	5.8	Rotherham	Perth, Aus	28.10.93
Forwards				
Curtis, Ronan	6.0	Derry	Donegal	29.03.96
Harrison, Ellis	5.11	Ipswich	Newport	29.01.94
Hawkins, Oliver	6.3	Dagenham	Ealing	08.04.92
Pitman, Brett	6.0	Ipswich	St Helier, Jer	03.01.88

ROCHDALE

Ground: Crown Oil Arena, Wilbutts Lane, Rochdale OL11 5DS
Telephone: 01706 644648. **Club nickname:** Dale
Colours: Blue and black. **Capacity:** 10,249
Record attendance: 24,231 v Notts Co (FA Cup 2) Dec 10, 1949

Goalkeepers				
Lillis, Josh	6.0	Scunthorpe	Derby	24.06.87
Wade, Bradley	5.11	–	Gloucester	03.07.00
Defenders				
Delaney, Ryan	6.0	Burton	Wexford, Ire	06.09.96
McLaughlin, Ryan	6.0	Blackpool	Belfast	30.09.94
McNulty, Jim	6.0	Bury	Liverpool	13.02.85
Norrington-Davies, Rhys	5.11	Sheffield Utd (loan)	Riyadh	22.04.99
Midfielders				
Camps, Callum	5.11	–	Stockport	14.03.96
Done, Matt	5.10	Sheffield Utd	Oswestry	22.07.88
Dooley, Stephen	5.11	Coleraine	Ballymoney	19.10.91
Keohane, Jimmy	5.11	Cork	Aylesbury	22.01.91
Morley, Aaron	–		Bury	27.02.00
Rathbone, Oliver	5.11	Man Utd	Blackburn	10.10.96
Thompson, Joe	6.0	Carlisle	Rochdale	05.03.89
Forwards				
Andrew, Calvin	6.2	York	Luton	19.12.86
Henderson, Ian	5.10	Colchester	Thetford	24.01.85
Pyke, Rekeil	5.10	Huddersfield (loan)	Leeds	01.09.97
Wilbraham, Aaron	6.3	Bolton	Knutsford	21.10.79

ROTHERHAM UNITED

Ground: New York Stadium, New York Way, Rotherham S60 1AH
Telephone: 08444 140733. **Club nickname:** Millers
Colours: Red and white. **Capacity:** 12,021
Record attendance: Millmoor: 25,170 v Sheffield Wed (Div 2) Jan 26, 1952 and v Sheffield Wed (Div 2) Dec 13, 1952; Don Valley Stadium: 7,082 v Aldershot (Lge 2 play-off semi-final, 2nd leg) May 19, 2010; New York Stadium: 11,758 v Sheffield Utd (Lge 1) Sep 7, 2013

Goalkeepers				
Bilboe, Laurence	6.3	–	Walsall	21.02.98
Price, Lewis	6.3	Sheffield Wed	Bournemouth	19.07.84
Defenders				
Ajayi, Semi	6.4	Cardiff	Crayford	09.11.93
Hinds, Akeem	6.1	–	Sheffield	26.12.98
Ihiekwe, Michael	6.1	Tranmere	Liverpool	29.11.92

Jones, Billy	5.11	Sunderland	Shrewsbury	24.03.87
Mattock, Joe	6.0	Sheffield Wed	Leicester	15.05.90
Olosunde, Matthew	6.1	Man Utd	Philadelphia, US	07.03.98
Robertson, Clark	6.2	Blackpool	Aberdeen	05.09.93
Wood, Richard	6.3	Charlton	Ossett	05.07.85
Midfielders				
Barlaser, Dan	5.10	Newcastle (loan)	Gateshead	18.01.97
Crooks, Matt	6.1	Northampton	Leeds	20.01.94
Forde, Anthony	5.9	Walsall	Ballingarry, Ire	16.11.93
MacDonald, Shaun	6.1	Wigan	Swansea	17.06.88
Taylor, Jon	5.11	Peterborough	Liverpool	20.07.92
Wiles, Ben	5.8	–	Rotherham	17.04.99
Forwards				
Kayode, Joshua	6.3	–	Lagos, Nig	04.05.00
Ladapo, Freddie	6.0	Plymouth	Romford	01.02.93
Lamy, Julien	6.1	Plabennecois	France	06.11.99
Morris, Carlton	6.2	Norwich (loan)	Cambridge	16.12.95
Procter, Jamie	6.2	Bolton	Preston	25.03.92
Smith, Michael	6.4	Bury	Wallsend	17.10.91
Vassell, Kyle	6.0	Blackpool	Milton Keynes	07.02.93

SHREWSBURY TOWN

Ground: Montgomery Waters Meadow, Oteley Road, Shrewsbury SY2 6ST
Telephone: 01743 289177. **Club nickname:** Shrews
Colours: Blue and yellow. **Capacity:** 9,875
Record attendance: Gay Meadow: 18,917 v Walsall (Div 3) Apr 26, 1961. Greenhous Meadow:
10,210 v Chelsea (Lge Cup 4) Oct 28, 2014

Goalkeepers				
Gregory, Cameron	6.3	–	Sutton Coldfield	20.01.00
Murphy, Joe	6.2	Bury	Dublin, Ire	21.08.81
Defenders				
Beckles, Omar	6.3	Accrington	Kettering	19.10.91
Ebanks-Landell, Ethan	6.2	Wolves	West Bromwich	16.12.92
Golbourne, Scott	5.8	Bristol City	Bristol	29.02.88
Love, Donald	5.10	Sunderland	Rochdale	`02.12.94
Pierre, Aaron	6.1	Northampton	Southall	17.02.93
Sears, Ryan	5.11	–	Newtown	30.12.98
Vincelot, Romain	5.10	Crawley	Poitiers, Fr	29.10.85
Waterfall, Luke	6.2	Lincoln	Sheffield	30.07.90
Williams, Ro-Shaun	6.0	Man Utd	Manchester	03.09.98
Midfielders				
Barnett, Ryan	5.11	–	Shrewsbury	23.09.99
Edwards, Dave	5.11	Reading	Pontesbury	03.02.85
Eisa, Abo	6.1	Wealdstone	Khartoum, Sud	05.01.96
Giles, Ryan	5.11	Wolves (loan)	Telford	26.01.00
Laurent, Josh	6.2	Wigan	Leystonstone	06.05.95
McCormick, Luke	5.9	Chelsea (loan)	Bury St Edmunds	21.01.99
Norburn, Ollie	6.1	Tranmere	Bolton	26.10.92
Walker, Brad	6.1	Crewe	Billingham	25.04.96
Whalley, Shaun	5.9	Luton	Whiston	07.08.87
Forwards				
John-Lewis, Lenell	5.10	Newport	Hammersmith	17.05.89
Morison, Steve	6.2	Millwall (loan)	Enfield	29.08.83

Okenabirhie, Fejiri	5.10	Dagenham	Hendon	25.02.96
Rowland, James	5.6	WBA	Walsall	03.12.01
Taylor, Kian	5.0	Leicester	Leicester	10.01.01
Udoh, Daniel	6.1	AFC Telford	Lagos, Nig	30.08.96

SOUTHEND UNITED

Ground: Roots Hall, Victoria Avenue, Southend SS2 6NQ
Telephone: 01702 304050. **Club nickname:** Shrimpers
Colours: Blue and white. **Capacity:** 12,392
Record attendance: 31,090 v Liverpool (FA Cup 3) Jan 10, 1979

Goalkeepers
| Bishop, Nathan | 6.1 | – | Hillingdon | 15.10.99 |
| Oxley, Mark | 6.2 | Hibernian | Sheffield | 28.09.90 |

Defenders
Demetriou, Jason	5.11	Walsall	Newham	18.11.87
Ferdinand, Anton	6.0	Reading	Peckham	18.02.85
Kiernan, Rob	6.1	Rangers	Rickmansworth	13.01.91
Kyprianou, Harry	6.0	Watford	Enfield	16.03.97
Lennon, Harry	6.3	Charlton	Romford	16.12.94
Ralph, Nathan	5.9	Dundee	Great Dunmow	14.02.93
White, John	6.0	Colchester	Colchester	25.07.86

Midfielders
Dieng, Timothee	6.2	Bradford	Grenoble, Fr	09.04.92
Hyam, Luke	5.10	Ipswich	Ipswich	24.10.91
Kightly, Michael	5.11	Burnley	Basildon	24.01.86
Klass, Michael	5.9	–	Hammersmith	09.02.99
Mantom, Sam	5.9	Scunthorpe	Stourbridge	20.02.92
McLaughlin, Stephen	5.10	Nottm Forest	Donegal, Ire	14.06.90
Milligan, Mark	5.10	Hibernian	Sydney, Aus	04.08.85
Yearwood, Dru	5.9	–	Harlow	17.02.00

Forwards
Cox, Simon	5.11	Reading	Reading	28.04.87
Goodship, Brandon	6.2	Weymouth	Poole	22.09.94
Hopper, Tom	6.1	Scunthorpe	Boston	14.12.93
Humphrys, Stephen	6.1	Fulham	Oldham	15.09.97
Robinson, Theo	5.10	Lincoln	Birmingham	22.01.89

SUNDERLAND

Ground: Stadium of Light, Sunderland SR5 1SU
Telephone: 0871 911 1200. **Club nickname:** Black Cats
Capacity: 48,707. **Colours:** Red and white
Record attendance: Roker Park: 76,118 v Derby (FA Cup 6 rep) Mar 8, 1933. Stadium of Light: 48,353 v Liverpool (Prem Lge) Apr 13, 2002

Goalkeepers
| Burge, Lee | 6.0 | Coventry | Hereford | 09.01.93 |
| McLaughlin, Jon | 6.3 | Hearts | Edinburgh | 09.09.87 |

Defenders
Baldwin, Jack	6.1	Peterborough	Barking	30.06.93
Flanagan, Tom	6.2	Burton	Hammersmith	21.10.91
Hume, Denver	5.10	–	Newbiggin	11.08.98
Loovens, Glenn	6.2	Sheffield Wed	Doetinchem, Hol	22.10.83
McLaughlin, Conor	6.0	Millwall	Belfast	26.07.91

Oviedo, Bryan	5.8	Everton	San Jose, C Rica	18.02.90
Ozturk, Alim	6.3	Boluspor	Alkmaar, Hol	17.11.92
Willis, Jordan	5.11	Coventry	Coventry	24.08.94
Midfielders				
Cattermole, Lee	5.10	Wigan	Stockton	21.03.88
Gooch, Lynden	5.8	–	Santa Cruz, US	24.12.95
Honeyman, George	5.8	–	Prudhoe	02.09.94
Leadbitter, Grant	5.9	Middlesbrough	Chester-le-Street	07.01.86
Maguire, Chris	5.8	Bury	Dollahill	16.01.89
McGeady, Aiden	5.11	Everton	Paisley	04.04.86
McGeouch, Dylan	5.10	Hibernian	Glasgow	15.01.93
O'Nien, Luke	5.9	Wycombe	Hemel Hempstead	21.11.94
Power, Max	5.11	Wigan	Birkenhead	27.07.93
Forwards				
Grigg, Will	5.11	Wigan	Solihull	03.07.91
Watmore, Duncan	5.9	Altrincham	Cheadle Hulme	08.03.94
Wyke, Charlie	5.11	Bradford	Middlesbrough	06.12.92

TRANMERE ROVERS

Ground: Prenton Park, Prenton Road, West Birkenhead CH42 9PY
Telephone: 0871 221 2001. **Club nickname:** Rovers
Colours: White. **Capacity:** 16,567
Record attendance: 24,424 v Stoke (FA Cup 4) Feb 5, 1972

Goalkeepers				
Davies, Scott	6.0	Fleetwood	Blackpool	27.02.87
Pilling, Luke	5.11	–	Birkenhead	25.07.97
Defenders				
Bakayogo, Zoumana	5.9	Crewe	Paris, Fr	17.08.86
Buxton, Adam	6.1	Portsmouth	Liverpool	12.05.92
Ellis, Mark	6.2	Carlisle	Plymouth	30.09.88
Caprice, Jake	5.11	Leyton Orient	Lambeth	11.11.92
Monthe, Manny	6.1	Forest Green	Cameroon	26.01.95
Nelson, Sid	6.1	Millwall	Lewisham	01.01.96
Ray, George	6.0	Crewe	Warrington	03.10.93
Ridehalgh, Liam	5.10	Huddersfield	Halifax	20.04.91
Woods, Calum	5.11	Bradford	Liverpool	05.02.87
Midfielders				
Banks, Ollie	6.3	Oldham	Rotherham	21.09.92
Blackett-Taylor, Corey	5.8	Aston Villa	Erdington	23.09.97
Gilmour, Harvey	5.11	Sheffield Utd	Sheffield	15.12.98
Harris, Jay	5.7	Wrexham	Liverpool	15.04.87
Jennings, Connor	6.0	Wrexham	Manchester	29.10.91
Morris, Kieron	5.10	Walsall	Hereford	03.06.94
Perkins, David	5.6	Rochdale	Heysham	21.06.82
Potter, Darren	5.10	Rotherham	Liverpool	21.12.84
Forwards				
Dagnall, Chris	5.8	Bury	Liverpool	15.04.86
Miller, Ishmael	6.3	Oldham	Moston	05.03.87
Mullin, Paul	5.10	Swindon	Liverpool	06.11.94
Payne, Stefan	5.10	Bristol Rov	Lambeth	10.08.91
Ponticelli, Jordan	5.11	Coventry (loan)	Nuneaton	10.09.98

WYCOMBE WANDERERS

Ground: Adams Park, Hillbottom Road, High Wycombe HP12 4HJ
Telephone: 01494 472100. **Club nickname:** Chairboys
Colours: Light and dark blue. **Capacity:** 10,300
Record attendance: 10,000 v Chelsea (friendly) July 13, 2005

Goalkeepers

Allsop, Ryan	6.3	Bournemouth	Birmingham	17.06.92
Yates, Cameron	6.0	Leicester	Edinburgh	14.02.99

Defenders

El-Abd, Adam	6.0	Shrewsbury	Brighton	11.09.84
Jacobson, Joe	5.11	Shrewsbury	Cardiff	17.11.86
Jombati, Sido	6.1	Cheltenham	Lisbon, Por	20.08.87
McCarthy, Jason	6.1	Barnsley	Southampton	07.11.95
Stewart, Anthony	6.0	Crewe	Lambeth	18.09.92

Midfielders

Bloomfield, Matt	5.8	Ipswich	Felixstowe	08.02.84
Freeman, Nick	5.11	Biggleswade	Stevenage	07.11.95
Gape, Dominic	5.11	Southampton	Burton Bradstock	09.09.94
Pattison, Alex	6.0	Middlesbrough	Darlington	06.09.97
Thompson, Curtis	5.7	Notts Co	Nottingham	02.09.93

Forwards

Akinfenwa, Adebayo	6.0	Wimbledon	Islington	10.05.82
Kashket, Scott	5.9	Leyton Orient	Chigwell	25.02.96
Mackail-Smith, Craig	5.10	Luton	Watford	25.02.84
Samuel, Alex	5.9	Stevenage	Neath	20.09.95

LEAGUE TWO

BRADFORD CITY

Ground: Northern Commercials Stadium, Valley Parade, Bradford BD8 7DY
Telephone: 01274 773355. **Club nickname:** Bantams
Colours: Yellow and claret. **Capacity:** 25,136
Record attendance: 39,146 v Burnley (FA Cup 4) Mar 11, 1911

Goalkeepers

Hornby, Sam	6.2	Port Vale	Sutton Coldfield	14.02.95
O'Donnell, Richard	6.2	Northampton	Sheffield	12.09.88

Defenders

French, Tyler	6.1	Sudbury	Bury St Edmunds	28.04.00
Hanley, Adam	5.10	Salt Lake	Knoxville, US	14.06.94
Longridge, Jackson	6.0	Dunfermline	Glasgow	12.04.95
Mellor, Kelvin	6.2	Blackpool	Crewe	25.01.91
O'Connor, Paudie	6.3	Leeds	Limerick, Ire	14.07.97
Richards-Everton, Ben	6.4	Accrington	Birmingham	17.10.91
Riley, Joe	5.10	Man Utd	Blackpool	06.12.96
Wood, Connor	5.11	Leicester	Harlow	17.07.96

Midfielders

Akpan, Hope	6.0	Burton	Liverpool	14.08.91
Anderson, Jermaine	5.11	Peterborough	Camden	16.05.96
Devine, Danny	5.11	–	Bradford	04.09.97
Gibson, Jordan	5.10	Rangers	Birmingham	26.02.98

Ismail, Zeli	5.9	Walsall	Kukes, Alb	12.12.93
O'Connor, Anthony	6.2	Aberdeen	Cork, Ire	25.10.92
Palmer, Matt	5.10	Rotherham (loan)	Derby	01.08.93
Reeves, Jake	5.7	AFC Wimbledon	Greenwich	30.05.93
Scannell, Sean	5.9	Huddersfield	Croydon	21.03.89

Forwards

Donaldson, Clayton	6.1	Bolton	Bradford	07.02.84
Doyle, Eoin	6.0	Preston	Dublin, Ire	12.03.88
McCartan, Shay	5.10	Accrington	Newry	18.05.94
Patrick, Omari	6.1	Barnsley	Slough	24.05.96
Vaughan, James	5.11	Wigan	Birmingham	14.07.88

CAMBRIDGE UNITED

Ground: Abbey Stadium, Newmarket Road, Cambridge CB5 8LN
Telephone: 01223 566500. **Club nickname:** U's
Colours: Yellow and black. **Capacity:** 9,617
Record attendance: 14,000 v Chelsea (friendly) May 1, 1970

Goalkeepers

Burton, Callum	6.2	Hull	Newport, Salop	15.08.96
Mitov, Dimitar	6.2	Charlton	–	22.01.97

Defenders

Darling, Harry	5.11	–	Cambridge	08.08.99
Davies, Leon	5.11	–	Cambridge	22.11.99
John, Louis	6.3	Sutton	Croydon	19.04.94
Knoyle, Kyle	5.10	Swindon	Newham	24.09.96
O'Neil, Liam	5.11	Chesterfield	Cambridge	31.07.93
Taft, George	6.3	Mansfield	Leicester	29.07.93
Taylor, Greg	6.1	Luton	Bedford	15.01.90

Midfielders

Deegan, Gary	5.9	Shrewsbury	Dublin, Ire	28.09.87
Hannant, Luke	5.11	Port Vale	Great Yarmouth	04.11.93
Lambe, Reggie	5.9	Carlisle	Hamilton, Berm	04.02.91
Lewis, Paul	6.1	Macclesfield	Liverpool	17.12.94

Forwards

Dunk, Harrison	6.0	Bromley	London	25.10.90
Ibehre, Jabo	6.2	Carlisle	Islington	28.01.83
Knibbs, Harvey	6.1	Aston Villa	–	26.04.99
Knowles, Tom	6.0	–	Cambridge	27.09.98
Maris, George	5.11	Barnsley	Sheffield	06.03.96

CARLISLE UNITED

Ground: Brunton Park, Warwick Road, Carlisle CA1 1LL
Telephone: 01228 526237. **Club nickname:** Cumbrians
Colours: Blue and white. **Capacity:** 17,949
Record attendance: 27,500 v Birmingham City (FA Cup 3) Jan 5, 1957, v Middlesbrough (FA Cup 5) Jan 7, 1970

Goalkeepers

Collin, Adam	6.2	Notts Co	Penrith	09.12.84
Gray, Louis	6.1	Nuneaton	Wrexham	11.08.95

Defenders

Branthwaite, Jarrad	6.2	–	Carlisle	27.06.02
Iredale, Jack	6.1	Morton	Greenock	02.05.96

Knight-Percival, Nat	6.0	Bradford	Cambridge	31.03.87
Elliott, Christie	6.2	Partick	Jarrow	26.05.91
Webster, Byron	6.4	Scunthorpe	Sherburn	31.03.87
Midfielders				
Bridge, Jack	5.10	Northampton	Southend	21.09.95
Etuhu, Kelvin	6.1	Bury	Kano, Nig	30.05.88
Jones, Mike	6.0	Oldham	Birkenhead	15.08.87
Scougall, Stefan	5.7	St Johnstone	Edinburgh	07.12.92
Forwards				
Hope, Hallam	5.11	Bury	Manchester	17.03.94
Kerr, Keighan	5.11	–	Carlisle	20.11.00
McKirdy, Harry	5.9	Aston Villa	London	29.03.97
Mellish, Jon	6.2	Gateshead	South Shields	19.09.97

CHELTENHAM TOWN

Ground: Jonny-Rocks Stadium, Whaddon Road, Cheltenham GL52 5NA
Telephone: 01242 573558. **Club nickname:** Robins
Colours: Red and black. **Capacity:** 7,066
Record attendance: 8,326 v Reading (FA Cup 1) Nov 17, 1956

Goalkeepers				
Flinders, Scott	6.4	Macclesfield	Rotherham	12.06.86
Lovett, Rhys	6.2	Rochdale	Birmingham	15.06.97
Defenders				
Bowry, Daniel	6.1	Charlton	London	29.04.98
Boyle, Will	6.2	Huddersfield	Garforth	01.09.95
Broom, Ryan	5.10	Bristol Rov	Newport	04.09.96
Debayo, Josh	6.0	Leicester	Hendon	17.10.96
Hussey, Chris	6.0	Sheffield Utd	Hammersmith	02.01.89
Long, Sean	5.10	Lincoln	Dublin	02.05.95
Raglan, Charlie	6.0	Oxford	Wythenshawe	28.04.93
Midfielders				
Addai, Alex	5.10	Merstham	Stepney	20.12.93
Campbell, Tahvon	5.8	Forest Green	Birmingham	10.01.97
Clements, Chris	5.9	Grimsby	Birmingham	06.02.90
Ince, Rohan	6.3	Brighton	Whitechapel	08.11.92
Thomas, Conor	6.1	ATK	Coventry	29.10.93
Tozer, Ben	6.1	Newport	Plymouth	01.03.90
Forwards				
Lloyd, George	5.8	–	Gloucester	11.02.00
Reid, Reuben	6.0	Forest Green	Bristol	26.07.88
Varney, Luke	5.11	Burton	Leicester	28.09.82

COLCHESTER UNITED

Ground: Weston Homes Community Stadium, United Way, Colchester CO4 5HE
Telephone: 01206 755100. Club nickname: U's
Colours: Blue and white. Capacity: 10,105
Record attendance: Layer Road:19,072 v Reading (FA Cup 1) Nov 27, 1948.
Community Stadium: 10,064 v Norwich (Lge 1) Jan 16, 2010

Goalkeepers				
Barnes, Dillon	6.4	Bedford	Enfield	08.04.96
Gerken, Dean	6.2	Ipswich	Southend	04.08.85
Defenders				

Collinge, Danny	6.2	Stuttgart	–	09.04.98
Eastman, Tom	6.3	Ipswich	Colchester	21.10.91
James, Cameron	6.0	–	Chelmsford	11.02.98
Jackson, Ryan	5.9	Gillingham	Streatham	31.07.90
Kensdale, Ollie	6.2	–	Colchester	20.04.00
Prosser, Luke	6.3	Southend	Enfield	28.05.88
Sowunmi, Omar	6.6	Yeovil	Colchester	07.11.95
Vincent-Young, Kane	5.11	Tottenham	Camden	15.03.96
Weaire, Matthew	6.2	Brighton	Denmark	20.08.01
Midfielders				
Comley, Brandon	5.11	QPR	Islington	18.11.95
Cowan-Hall, Paris	5.8	Wycombe	Hillingdon	05.10.90
Fernandes, Michael	5.11	Farnborough	–	24.06.99
Gambin, Luke	5.7	Luton	Sutton	16.03.93
Lapslie, Tom	5.6	–	Waltham Forest	05.10.95
Pell, Harry	6.4	Cheltenham	Tilbury	21.10.91
Saunders, Sam	5.8	Wycombe	Erith	29.08.83
Senior, Courtney	5.9	Brentford	Croydon	11.02.98
Stevenson, Ben	6.0	Wolves	Leicester	23.03.97
Forwards				
Brown, Jevani	5.9	Cambridge	Letchworth	16.10.94
Norris, Luke	6.1	Swindon	Stevenage	03.06.93
Nouble, Frank	6.3	Newport	Lewisham	24.09.91

CRAWLEY TOWN

Ground: Checkatrade Stadium, Winfield Way, Crawley RH11 9RX
Telephone: 01293 410000. **Club nickname:** Reds
Colours: Red. **Capacity:** 6,134
Record attendance: 5,880 v Reading (FA Cup 3) Jan 5, 2013

Goalkeepers				
Luyambula, Michael	6.2	Birmingham (loan)	DR Congo	08.06.99
Morris, Glenn	6.0	Gillingham	Woolwich	20.12.83
Defenders				
Dallison, Tom	6.1	Falkirk	Romford	02.02.96
Doherty, Josh	5.10	Ards	Newtonards	15.03.96
McNerney, Joe	6.4	Woking	Chertsey	24.01.90
Midfielders				
Allarakhia, Tarryn	5.10	–	Redbridge	17.10.97
Bulman, Dannie	5.8	AFC Wimbledon	Ashford, Surrey	24.01.79
Ferguson, Nathan	6.2	Dulwich Hamlet	Walthamstow	10.12.95
Francomb, George	6.0	AFC Wimbledon	Hackney	08.09.91
Morais, Filipe	5.9	Bolton	Benavente, Por	21.11.85
Nathaniel-George, Ashley	5.10	Hendon	London	14.06.95
Payne, Josh	6.0	Eastleigh	Basingstoke	25.11.90
Powell, Jack	5.10	Maidstone	Canning Town	29.01.94
Sesay, David	6.1	Watford	Brent	18.09.98
Smith, Jimmy	6.1	Stevenage	Newham	07.01.87
Young, Lewis	5.9	Bury	Stevenage	27.09.89
Forwards				
Bloomfield, Mason	6.2	Norwich (loan)	Westminster	06.11.96
Camara, Panutche	6.1	Dulwich Hamlet	Guin-Bassau	28.02.97
Galach, Brian	5.9	Aldershot	Waltham Forest	16.05.01
German, Ricky	5.11	Hendon	Harlesden	13.01.99

Grego-Cox, Reece	5.7	Woking	Hammersmith	02.11.96
Lubula, Beryly	5.10	Birmingham	DR Congo	08.01.98
Meite, Ibrahim	6.1	Cardiff	Roehampton	01.06.96
Nadesan, Ashley	6.2	Fleetwood	Redhill	09.09.94
Palmer, Ollie	6.5	Lincoln	Epsom	21.01.92
Poleon, Dominic	6.2	Bradford	Newham	07.09.93

CREWE ALEXANDRA

Ground: Alexandra Stadium, Gresty Road, Crewe CW2 6EB
Telephone: 01270 213014. **Club nickname:** Railwaymen
Colours: Red and white. **Capacity:** 10,066
Record attendance: 20,000 v Tottenham (FA Cup 4) Jan 30, 1960

Goalkeepers
| Jaaskelainen, Will | 6.0 | Bolton | Bolton | 25.07.98 |
| Richards, David | 6.0 | Bristol City | Abergavenny | 31.12.93 |

Defenders
Hunt, Nicky	6.1	Notts Co	Westhoughton	03.09.83
Lancashire, Olly	6.1	Swindon	Basingstoke	13.12.88
Ng, Perry	5.11	–	Liverpool	27.04.96
Nolan, Eddie	6.0	Blackpool	Waterford, Ire	05.08.88
Sass-Davies, Billy	6.1	–	Abergele	17.02.00

Midfielders
Ainley, Callum	5.8	–	Middlewich	02.11.97
Finney, Oliver	5.7	–	Stoke	15.12.97
Green, Paul	5.9	Oldham	Pontefract	10.04.83
Jones, James	5.9	–	Winsford	01.02.96
Kirk, Charlie	5.7	–	Winsford	24.12.97
Lowery, Tom	–	–	Holmes Chapel	31.12.97
Pickering, Harry	–	–	Chester	29.12.98
Powell, Daniel	6.2	Northampton	Luton	12.03.91
Wintle, Ryan	5.6	Alsager	Newcastle-under-Lyme	13.06.97

Forwards
Dale, Owen	5.9	–	Warrington	01.11.98
Miller, Shaun	5.10	Carlisle	Alsager	25.09.87
Porter, Chris	6.1	Colchester	Wigan	12.12.83
Reilly, Lewis	5.11	–	Liverpool	07.07.99

EXETER CITY

Ground: St James Park, Stadium Way, Exeter EX4 6PX
Telephone: 01392 411243. **Club nickname:** Grecians
Colours: Red and white. **Capacity:** 8,830
Record attendance: 20,984 v Sunderland (FA Cup 6 replay) Mar 4, 1931

Goalkeepers
| Maxted, Jonny | 6.0 | Accrington | Tadcaster | 26.10.93 |
| Ward, Lewis | 6.5 | Reading | – | 05.03.97 |

Defenders
Brown, Troy	6.1	Cheltenham	Croydon	17.09.90
Cundy, Robbie	6.5	Bristol City (loan)	Oxford	30.05.97
Martin, Aaron	6.3	Oxford	Newport, IOW	29.09.89
Moxey, Dean	5.11	Bolton	Exeter	14.01.86
Sweeney, Pierce	5.11	Reading	Dublin, Ire	11.09.94
Warren, Gary	5.11	Yeovil	Bristol	16.08.84

| Woodman, Craig | 5.9 | Brentford | Tiverton | 22.12.82 |

Midfielders

Atangana, Nigel	6.2	Cheltenham	Corbeil-Essonnes, Fr	09.09.89
Holmes, Lee	5.9	Preston	Mansfield	02.04.87
Law, Nicky	5.10	Bradford	Plymouth	29.03.88
Martin, Lee	5.10	Gillingham	Taunton	09.02.87
Parkes, Tom	6.3	Carlisle	Sutton-in-Ashfield	15.01.92
Randall, Joel	5.10	–	Salisbury	01.11.99
Sparkes, Jack	5.9	–	Exeter	29.09.00
Taylor, Jake	5.10	Reading	Ascot	01.12.91
Tillson, Jordan	6.0	Bristol Rov	Bath	05.03.93
Williams, Randell	5.9	Watford	Lambeth	30.12.96

Forwards

Ajose, Nicky	5.7	Charlton	Bury	07.10.91
Bowman, Ryan	6.2	Motherwell	Carlisle	30.11.91
Fisher, Alex	6.3	Yeovil	Westminster	30.06.90
Forte, Jonathan	6.0	Notts Co	Sheffield	25.07.86
Jay, Matt	5.10	–	Torbay	27.02.96

FOREST GREEN ROVERS

Ground: New Lawn, Another Way, Nailsworth GL6 OFG
Telephone: 01453 835291. **Club nickname:** Green Devils
Capacity: 5,140. **Record attendance:** 4,836 v Derby (FA Cup 3, Jan 3, 2009)

Goalkeepers

| Montgomery, James | 6.2 | Gateshead | Sunderland | 20.04.94 |
| Smith, Adam | 6.0 | Bristol Rov | Sunderland | 23.11.92 |

Defenders

Bernard, Dom	6.0	Birmingham	Gloucester	29.03.97
Kitching, Liam	6.1	Leeds	Harrogate	01.10.99
McGinley, Nathan	6.3	Middlesbrough	Middlesbrough	15.09.96
Mills, Joseph	5.9	Perth Glory	Swindon	30.10.89
Mills, Matt	6.3	Pune City	Swindon	14.07.86
Rawson, Farrend	6.2	Derby	Nottingham	11.07.96
Shephard, Liam	5.10	Peterborough	Pentre	22.11.94

Midfielders

Adams, Ebou	5.11	Ebbsfleet	Greenwich	15.01.96
Allen, Taylor	6.0	Nuneaton	–	16.06.00
Cooper, Charlie	5.9	Birmingham	Stockton	01.05.97
Dawson, Kevin	5.11	Cheltenham	Dublin, Ire	30.06.90
Grubb, Dayle	6.0	Weston SM	Weston SM	24.07.91
James, Lloyd	5.11	Exeter	Bristol	16.02.88
Morton, James	5.11	Bristol City (loan)	Bristol	22.04.99
Winchester, Carl	6.0	Cheltenham	Belfast	12.04.93

Forwards

Collins, Aaron	6.1	Morecambe	Newport	27.05.97
Junior Mondal	5.10	Normanby	Whitby	27.03.97
McCoulsky, Shawn	6.0	Bristol City	Lewisham	06.01.97
Williams, George	5.8	Fulham	Milton Keynes	07.09.95

GRIMSBY TOWN

Ground: Blundell Park, Cleethorpes DN35 7PY
Telephone: 01472 605050 **Colours:** Black and white. **Capacity:** 9,052
Record attendance: 31,651 v Wolves (FA Cup 5) 20 February, 1937

Goalkeepers

McKeown, James	6.1	Peterborough	Birmingham	24.07.89
Russell, Sam	6.0	Forest Green	Middlesbrough	04.10.82

Defenders

Davis, Harry	6.2	St Mirren	Burnley	24.09.91
Gibson, Liam	6.1	Newcastle (loan)	Stanley	25.04.97
Hendrie, Luke	6.2	Shrewsbury	Leeds	27.08.94
Hewitt, Elliott	5.11	Notts Co	Bodelwyddan	30.05.94
Ohman, Ludvig	6.3	Brommapojkarna	Umea, Swe	10.09.91
Pollock, Mattie	6.3	Leeds	Redhill	21.09.00
Ring, Sebastian	5.10	Orebro SK	Orebro, Swe	18.04.95

Midfielders

Clifton, Harry	5.11	–	Grimsby	12.06.98
Cook, Jordan	5.9	Luton	Sunderland	20.03.90
Hessenthaler, Jake	5.10	Gillingham	Gravesend	20.04.90
Whitehouse, Elliott	5.11	Lincoln	Worksop	27.10.93
Wright, Max	5.8	–	Grimsby	06.04.98

Forwards

Duckley, Brandon	6.2	–	Grimsby	21.09.00
Cardwell, Harry	6.2	Reading	Beverley	23.10.96
Green, Matt	6.1	Salford	Bath	02.01.87
Hanson, James	6.4	AFC Wimbledon	Bradford	09.11.87
Rose, Akeem	5.10	–	Jamaica	27.11.98
Ugbo, Moses	6.1	Al-Ain	Nigeria	07.02.91
Vernam, Charles	5.9	Derby	Lincoln	08.10.96

LEYTON ORIENT

Ground: Breyer Group Stadium, Brisbane Road, London E10 5NF
Telephone: 0208 926 1111. **Club nickname:** O's
Colours: Red. **Capacity:** 9,217
Record attendance: 34,345 v West Ham (FA Cup 4) Jan 25, 1964

Goalkeepers

Brill, Dean	6.2	Colchester	Luton	02.12.85
Sargeant, Sam	6.0		Greenwich	23.09.97

Defenders

Coulson, Josh	6.3	Cambridge Utd	Cambridge	28.01.89
Ekpiteta, Marvin	6.4	East Thurrock	Enfield	26.08.95
Happe, Dan	–	–	Tower Hamlets	28.09.98
Judd, Myles	5.10	–	Redbridge	03.02.99
Ling, Sam	5.9	Dagenham	Broxbourne	17.12.96
Turley, Jamie	6.0	Notts Co	Reading	07.04.90
Widdowson, Joe	6.0	Dagenham	Forest Gate	29.03.89

Midfielders

Brophy, James	5.10	Swindon	Brent	25.07.94
Clay, Craig	5.11	Motherwell	Nottingham	05.05.92
Dayton, James	5.8	Cheltenham	Enfield	12.12.88
Gorman, Dale	5.11	Stevenage	Letterkenny, Ire	28.06.96
Maguire-Drew, Jordan	5.11	Brighton	Crawley	19.09.97
McAnuff, Jobi	5.11	Stevenage	Edmonton	09.11.81
Wright, Josh	6.0	Bradford	Bethnal Green	06.11.89

Forwards

Alabi, James	6.0	Stoke	Southwark	08.11.94
Angol, Lee	6.2	Shrewsbury	Sutton	04.08.94

| Harrold Matt | 6.1 | Crawley | Leyton | 25.07.84 |
| Wilkinson, Conor | 6.2 | Dagenham | Croydon | 23.01.95 |

MACCLESFIELD TOWN

Ground: Moss Rose Stadium, London Road, Macclesfield SK11 7SP
Telephone: 01625 264686. **Club nickname:** Silkmen
Colours: Blue and white. **Capacity:** 6,335
Record attendance: 9,003 v Winsford (Cheshire Senior Cup 2) Feb 14, 1948

Goalkeepers

Idem, Manny	6.2	Aston Villa	Lambeth	06.12.98
Defenders				
Cameron, Nathan	6.2	Bury	Birmingham	21.11.91
Evans, Callum	5.10	Forest Green	Bristol	11.10.95
Fitzpatrick, David	5.10	Southport	Manchester	28.02.90
Jules, Zak	6.3	Shrewsbury	Islington	02.07.97
McCourt, Jak	5.10	Swindon	Liverpool	06.07.95
Welch-Hayes, Miles	5.11	Bath	Oxford	25.10.96
Pearson, James	6.1	Kidderminster	Sheffield	19.01.93
Vassell, Theo	6.1	Port Vale	Stoke	02.01.97
Midfielders				
Durrell, Elliot	5.10	Chester	Shrewsbury	31.07.89
Ntambue, Brice	6.0	Partick	Brussels, Bel	29.04.93
Osadebe, Emmanuel	6.2	Cambridge	Dundalk, Ire	01.10.96
Rose, Michael	5.10	Morecambe	Salford	28.07.82
Stephens, Ben	5.8	Stratford	Leicester	09.08.97
Vincenti, Peter	6.2	Coventry	St Peter, Jer	07.07.86
Forwards				
Blyth, Jacob	6.3	Barrow	Nuneaton	14.08.92
Ironside, Joe	5.11	Kidderminster	Middlesbrough	16.10.93
Wilson, Scott	6.1	Eastleigh	Bristol	11.01.93

MANSFIELD TOWN

Ground: One Call Stadium, Quarry Lane, Mansfield NG18 5DA
Telephone: 01623 482482. Club nickname: Stags
Colours: Amber and blue. **Capacity:** 6,335
Record attendance: 24,467 v Nottm Forest (FA Cup 3) Jan 10, 1953

Goalkeepers

Logan, Conrad	6.2	Rochdale	Ramelton, Ire	18.04.86
Olejnik, Bobby	6.0	Exeter	Vienna, Aut	26.11.86
Defenders				
Benning, Malvind	5.10	Walsall	Sandwell	02.11.93
Gibbens, Lewis	6.0	–	Leicester	10.11.99
Pearce, Krystian	6.2	Torquay	Birmingham	05.01.90
Preston, Matt	6.0	Swindon	Birmingham	16.03.95
Sweeney, Ryan	6.5	Stoke	Kingston	15.04.97
White, Hayden	6.1	Peterborough	Greenwich	15.04.95
Midfielders				
Bishop, Neal	6.0	Scunthorpe	Stockton	07.08.81
Donohue, Dion	5.10	Portsmouth	Anglesey	26.08.93
Khan, Otis	5.9	Yeovil	Ashton-under-Lyne	05.09.95
MacDonald, Alex	5.7	Oxford	Warrington	14.04.90
Mellis, Jacob	5.11	Bury	Nottingham	08.01.91

| Smith, Alistair | 6.2 | Hull | Beverley | 19.05.99 |
| Tomlinson, Willem | 5.11 | Blackburn | Burnley | 27.01.98 |

Forwards

Cook, Andy	6.1	Walsall	Bishop Auckland	18.10.90
Davies, Craig	6.2	Oldham	Burton	09.01.86
Graham, Jordan	6.2	Oxford Utd	Peterborough	30.12.97
Hamilton CJ	5.7	Sheffield Utd	Harrow	23.03.95
Law, Jason	5.10	Carlton	Nottingham	26.04.99
Maynard, Nicky	5.11	Bury	Winsford	11.12.86
Rose, Danny	5.10	Bury	Barnsley	10.12.93
Sterling-James, Omari	5.10	Solihull	Birmingham	15.09.93

MORECAMBE

Ground: Globe Arena, Christie Way, Westgate, Morecambe LA4 4TB
Telephone: 01524 411797. **Club nickname:** Shrimps
Colours: Red and white. **Capacity:** 6,476
Record attendance: Christie Park: 9,234 v Weymouth (FA Cup 3) Jan 6, 1962. Globe Arena: 5,003 v Burnley (League Cup 2) Aug 24, 2010

Goalkeepers

| Halstead, Mark | 6.3 | Southport | Blackpool | 17.09.90 |
| Roche, Barry | 6.4 | Chesterfield | Dublin, Ire | 06.04.82 |

Defenders

Brewitt, Tom	6.1	AFC Fylde	Liverpool	11.02.97
Conlan, Luke	5.11	Burnley	Portaferry	31.10.94
Cranston, Jordan	5.11	Cheltenham	Wednesfield	11.11.93
Lavelle, Sam	6.0	Bolton	Blackpool	03.10.96
Old, Steve	6.3	GAIS	Palmerston, NZ	17.02.86
Sutton, Ritchie	6.0	Tranmere	Stoke	29.04.86

Midfielders

Brownsword, Tyler	5.11	–	South Shields	31.12.99
Ellison, Kevin	6.0	Rotherham	Liverpool	23.02.79
Fleming, Andy	5.11	Wrexham	Liverpool	05.10.87
Jagne, Lamin	5.7	Preston	Newham	28.10.07
Kenyon, Alex	6.0	Stockport	Euxton	17.07.92
O'Sullivan, John	5.11	Blackpool	Dublin, Ire	18.09.93
Tutte, Andrew	5.9	Bury	Liverpool	21.09.90
Wildig, Aaron	5.9	Shrewsbury	Hereford	15.04.92

Forwards

Hawley, Kyle	5.10	–	Oldham	11.05.00
Howard, Michael	6.1	Preston	Southport	17.10.99
Leitch-Smith AJ	5.11	Shrewsbury	Crewe	06.03.90
Oates, Rhys	6.2	Hartlepool	Pontefract	04.12.94
Stockton, Cole	6.1	Tranmere	Huyton	13.03.94

NEWPORT COUNTY

Ground: Rodney Parade, Newport NP19 0UU
Telephone: 01633 670690. **Club nickname:** Exiles
Colours: Amber and black. **Capacity:** 7,850
Record attendance: Somerton Park: 24,268 v Cardiff (Div 3S) Oct 16, 1937. Rodney Parade: 9,836 v Tottenham (FA Cup 4) Jan 27, 2018

Goalkeepers

| King, Tom | 6.1 | Millwall | Plymouth | 09.03.95 |

Townsend, Nick	5.11	Barnsley	Solihull	01.11.94
Defenders				
Bennett, Scott	5.10	Notts Co	Newquay	30.11.90
Demetriou, Mickey	6.2	Shrewsbury	Dorrington	12.03.90
Howkins, Kyle	6.4	WBA	Walsall	04.05.96
Leadbitter, Daniel	6.1	Bristol Rov	Newcastle	07.10.90
O'Brien, Mark	5.11	Luton	Dublin, Ire	20.11.92
Stojsavljevic, Lazar	6.1	Millwall	Serbia	05.05.98
Midfielders				
Collins, Lewis	5.10	–	Newport	09.05.01
Dolan, Matt	5.9	Yeovil	Hartlepool	11.02.93
Haynes, Ryan	6.1	Shrewsbury	Northampton	27.09.95
Labadie, Joss	6.3	Dagenham	Croydon	30.08.90
Marsh-Brown, Keanu	6.1	Forest Green	Hammersmith	10.08.92
Sheehan, Josh	6.0	Swansea	Pembrey	30.03.95
Willmott, Robbie	5.9	Chelmsford	Harlow	16.05.90
Forwards				
Amond, Padraig	5.11	Hartlepool	Carlow, Ire	15.04.88
Azeez, Ade	6.0	Cambridge	Orpington	08.01.94
Matt, Jamille	6.1	Blackpool	Jamaica	20.10.89
Touray, Momodou	5.11	–	Gambia	30.07.99
Whitely, Corey	5.10	Ebbsfleet	Enfield	11.07.91

NORTHAMPTON TOWN

Ground: Sixfields Stadium, Upton Way, Northampton NN5 5QA
Telephone: 01604 683700. **Club nickname:** Cobblers
Colours: Claret and white. **Capacity:** 7,750
Record attendance: County Ground: 24,523 v Fulham (Div 1) Apr 23, 1966. Sixfields Stadium: 7,798 v Manchester Utd (Lge Cup 3) Sep 21, 2016

Goalkeepers				
Arnold, Steve	6.1	Shrewsbury	Welham Green	22.08.89
Cornell, David	6.0	Oldham	Swansea	28.03.91
Defenders				
Barnett, Leon	6.1	Bury	Luton	30.11.85
Goode, Charlie	6.5	Scunthorpe	Watford	03.08.95
Hall-Johnson, Reece	5.9	Grimsby	Aylesbury	09.05.95
Hughes, Ryan	6.4	–	Burton	24.04.01
Martin, Joe	6.0	Stevenage	Dagenham	29.11.88
Turnbull, Jordan	6.1	Coventry	Trowbridge	30.10.94
Williams, Jay	6.2	–	Northampton	04.10.00
Midfielders				
Adams, Nicky	5.10	Bury	Bolton	16.10.83
Lines, Chris	6.2	Bristol Rov	Bristol	30.11.85
McCormack, Alan	5.8	Luton	Dublin, Ire	10.01.84
McWilliams, Shaun	5.11	–	Northampton	14.08.98
Watson, Ryan	6.1	MK Dons	Crewe	07.07.93
Forwards				
Hoskins, Sam	5.8	Yeovil	Dorchester	04.02.93
Morias, Junior	5.8	Peterborough	Kingston, Jam	04.07.95
Oliver, Vadaine	6.1	Morecambe	Sheffield	21.10.91
Smith, Harry	6.5	Macclesfield	Chatham	18.05.95
Waters, Billy	5.9	Cheltenham	Epsom	15.10.94
Williams, Andy	5.10	Doncaster	Hereford	14.08.86

OLDHAM ATHLETIC

Ground: Boundary Park, Oldham OL1 2PA
Telephone: 0161 624 4972. **Club nickname:** Latics
Colours: Blue and white. **Capacity:** 13,500
Record attendance: 47,761 v Sheffield Wed (FA Cup 4) Jan 25, 1930

Goalkeepers

Zeus de la Paz	6.2	Cincinnati	Nijmegen, Hol	11.03.95
Woods, Gary	6.0	Hamilton	Kettering	01.10.90
Zabret, Gregor	6.2	Swansea (loan)	Ljubljana, Sloven	18.08.95

Defenders

Hamer, Tom	6.2	–	Bolton	16.11.99
Iacovitti, Alex	6.3	Nottm Forest	Nottingham	02.09.97
Mills, Zak	5.10	Morecambe	Peterborough	28.05.92
Sefil, Sonhy	6.4	Lyon-Duchere	Schoelcher, Mart	16.06.94
Stott, Jamie	6.1	–	Failsworth	22.12.97

Midfielders

Coke, Giles	5.11	Chesterfield	Westminster	03.06.86
Maouche, Mohamed	5.11	Tours	Ambilly, Fr	10.01.93
Missilou, Christopher	5.11	Le Puy	Auxerre, Fr	18.07.92
Nepomuceno, Gevaro	5.9	Maritimo	Tilburg, Hol	10.11.92
Sylla, Mohamad	6.2	L'Entente	Ivry, Fr	01./12.93

Forwards

Benteke, Jonathan	6.1	Omonia Nicosia	Liege, Bel	28.04.95
Branger, Johan	6.0	Dieppe	Sens, Fr	05.07.93
O'Grady, Chris	6.1	Chesterfield	Nottingham	25.01.86

PLYMOUTH ARGYLE

Ground: Home Park, Plymouth PL2 3DQ
Telephone: 01752 562561. **Club nickname:** Pilgrims
Colours: Green and white. **Capacity:** 16,388
Record attendance: 43,596 v Aston Villa (Div 2) Oct 10, 1936

Goalkeepers

Cooper, Michael	–	–	Exeter	08.10.99
Palmer, Alex	6.3	WBA (loan)	Kidderminster	10.08.96

Defenders

Aimson, Will	5.10	Bury	Christchurch	01.01.94
Canavan, Niall	6.3	Rochdale	Leeds	11.04.91
Edwards, Joe	5.9	Walsall	Gloucester	31.10.90
Moore, Tafari	5.10	Arsenal	Kilburn	05.07.97
Riley, Joe	6.0	Shrewsbury	Salford	13.10.91
Sawyer, Gary	6.0	Leyton Orient	Bideford	05.07.85
Smith-Brown, Ashley	5.10	Man City	Manchester	31.03.96
Wootton, Scott	6.2	MK Dons	Birkenhead	12.09.91

Midfielders

Fox, David	5.10	Crewe	Leek	13.12.83
Grant, Conor	5.9	Everton	Fazakerley	18.04.95
Jephcott, Luke	5.10	–	Truro	26.01.00
Mayor, Danny	6.0	Bury	Leyland	18.10.90
McFadzean, Callum	5.11	Bury	Sheffield	16.01.94
Sarcevic, Antoni	6.0	Shrewsbury	Manchester	13.03.92

Forwards

Dyson, Callum	6.2	Everton	Fazakerley	19.09.96
Fletcher, Alex	5.10	–	Newton Abbot	09.02.99
Grant, Joel	6.0	Exeter	Acton	26.08.87
Taylor, Ryan	6.2	Oxford	Rotherham	04.05.88
Telford, Dom	5.9	Bury	Burnley	05.12.96

PORT VALE

Ground: Vale Park, Hamil Road, Burslem, Stoke-on-Trent ST6 1AW
Telephone: 01782 655800. **Club nickname:** Valiants
Colours: Black and white. **Capacity:** 18,947
Record attendance: 49,768 v Aston Villa (FA Cup 5) Feb 20, 1960

Goalkeepers

Brown, Scott	6.1	Wycombe	Wolverhampton	26.04.85

Defenders

Crookes, Adam	6.0	Nottm Forest	Lincoln	18.11.97
Gibbons, James	5.9	–	Stoke	16.03.98
Kennedy, Kieran	6.0	Wrexham	Manchester	23.09.93
Legge, Leon	6.1	Cambridge	Hastings	28.04.85
Rawlinson, Connell	6.1	New Saints	Chester	22.10.91
Smith, Nathan	6.0	–	Madeley	03.04.96

Midfielders

Burgess, Scott	5.10	Bury	Warrington	12.08.97
Conlon, Tom	5.9	Stevenage	Stoke	03.02.96
Joyce, Luke	5.11	Carlisle	Bolton	09.07.87
Lloyd, Ryan	5.10	Macclesfield	Newcastle-u-Lyme	01.02.94
Montano, Cristian	5.11	Bristol Rov	Cali, Col	11.12.91
Oyeleke, Manny	5.9	Aldershot	Wandsworth	24.12.92
Whitfield, Ben	5.5	Bournemouth	Bingley	28.02.96

Forwards

Amoo, David	5.10	Cambridge	Southwark	13.04.91
Bennett, Richie	6.4	Carlisle	Oldham	23.03.91
Cullen, Mark	5.9	Blackpool	Stakeford	21.04.92
Pope, Tom	6.3	Bury	Stoke	27.08.85
Worrall, David	6.0	Millwall	Manchester	12.06.90

SALFORD CITY

Ground: Peninsula Stadium, Moor Lane, Salford M7 3PZ
Telephone: 0161 792 6287. **Club nickname:** Ammies
Colours: Red and white. **Capacity:** 5,106

Goalkeepers

Crocombe, Max	6.4	Carlisle	Auckland, NZ	12.08.93
Letheren, Kyle	6.2	Plymouth	Llanelli	26.12.87
Neal, Chris	6.2	Fleetwood	St Albans	23.10.85

Defenders

Hogan, Liam	6.0	Gateshead	Salford	08.02.89
Jones, Dan	6.0	Barrow	Bishop Auckland	14.12.94
Jones, James	6.4	Chester	Shrewsbury	16.02.99
Piergianni, Carl	6.1	South Melbourne	Peterborough	03.05.92
Pond, Nathan	6.3	Fleetwood	Presron	05.01.85
Touray, Ibou	5.10	Nantwich	Liverpool	24.12.94
Wiseman, Scott	6.0	Chesterfield	Hull	09.10.85

Midfielders

Name		Club		
Glynn, Kieran		Woking	–	14.12.97
Jones, Joey	6.1	Eastleigh	Hull	15.04.94
Maynard, Lois	6.2	Tranmere	Cheetham Hill	22.01.89
Shelton, Mark	5.11	Alfreton	Nottingham	12.09.96
Threlkeld, Oscar	5.11	Beveren	Bolton	15.12.94
Towell, Richie	5.8	Brighton	Dublin, Ire	17.07.91
Walker, Tom	6.0	FC United	Salford	12.12.95
Whitehead, Danny	5.10	Macclesfield	Manchester	23.10.93

Forwards

Name		Club		
Beesley, Jake	6.1	Chesterfield	Sheffield	02.12.96
Dieseruvwe, Emmanuel	6.5	Kidderminster	Leeds	20.02.95
Gaffney, Rory	6.0	Bristol Rov	Tuam, Ire	23.10.89
Lloyd, Danny	5.8	Peterborough	Liverpool	03.12.91
Rodney, Devante	5.10	Hartlepool	Manchester	19.05.98
Rooney, Adam	5.10	Aberdeen	Dublin	21.04.88

SCUNTHORPE UNITED

Ground: Glanford Park, Doncaster Road, Scunthorpe DN15 8TD
Telephone: 0871 221 1899. **Club nickname:** Iron
Colours: Claret and blue. **Capacity:** 9,183
Record attendance: Old Show Ground: 23,935 v Portsmouth (FA Cup 4) Jan 30, 1954. Glanford Park: 8,921 v Newcastle (Champ) Oct 20, 2009

Goalkeepers

Name		Club		
Eastwood, Jake	6.1	Sheffield Utd (loan)	Sheffield	03.10.96
Watson, Rory	6.3	Hull	York	05.02.96

Defenders

Name		Club		
Burgess, Cameron	6.4	Fulham	Aberdeen	21.10.95
Butler, Andy	6.0	Doncaster	Doncaster	04.11.83
Butroid, Lewis	5.9	–	Gainsborough	17.09.98
Clarke, Jordan	6.0	Coventry	Coventry	19.11.91
Horsfield, James	5.10	Breda	Stockport	30.11.95
McArdle, Rory	6.1	Bradford	Sheffield	01.05.87
McGahey, Harrison	6.1	Rochdale	Preston	26.09.95
Ntlhe, Kgosi	5.9	Rochdale	Protoria, SA	21.02.94
Perch, James	6.0	QPR	Mansfield	28.09.85

Midfielders

Name		Club		
Colclough, Ryan	6.0	Wigan	Burslem	27.12.94
Dales, Andy	5.11	Dundee	Derby	13.11.94
El-Mhanni, Yasin	5.10	Newcastle	Shepherd's Bush	26.10.95
Hallam, Jordan	5.8	Sheffield Utd	Sheffield	06.10.98
Hammill, Adam	5.11	St Mirren	Liverpool	25.01.88
Lewis, Clayton	5.7	Auckland	Wellington NZ	12.02.97
Lund, Matthew	6.0	Burton	Manchester	21.11.90
Songo'o, Yann	6.2	Plymouth	Yaounde, Cam	19.11.91
Sutton, Levi	5.11	–	Scunthorpe	24.03.96

Forwards

Name		Club		
Gilliead, Alex	6.0	Shrewsbury	Shotley Bridge	11.02.96
Novak, Lee	6.0	Charlton	Newcastle	28.09.88
Olomola, Olufela	5.7	Southampton	London	05.09.97
Van Veen, Kevin	6.0	Northampton	Eindhoven, Hol	01.06.91
Wootton, Kyle	6.2	–	Epworth	11.10.96

STEVENAGE

Ground: Lamex Stadium, Broadhall Way, Stevenage SG2 8RH
Telephone: 01438 223223. **Club nickname:** Boro
Colours: White and red. **Capacity:** 6,920
Record attendance: 8,040 v Newcastle (FA Cup 4) January 25, 1998

Goalkeepers

Farman, Paul	6.5	Lincoln	North Shields	02.11.89
Defenders				
Cuthbert, Scott	6.2	Luton	Alexandria, Scot	15.06.87
Denton, Tyler	5.10	Leeds	Dewsbury	06.09.95
Henry, Ronnie	5.11	Luton	Hemel Hempstead	02.01.84
Nugent, Ben	6.5	Gillingham	Welwyn Garden City	29.11.92
Stokes, Chris	6.1	Bury	Trowbridge	08.03.91
Vancooten, Terence	6.1	Reading	Kingston u Thames	29.12.97
Wildin, Luther	5.10	Nuneaton	Leicester	03.12.97
Midfielders				
Byrom, Joel	6.0	Mansfield	Oswaldtwistle	14.09.86
Carter, Charlie	6.1	Chesterfield	London	25.10.96
Digby, Paul	6.3	Forest Green	Sheffield	02.02.95
Iontton, Arthur	6.0	–	Enfield	16.12.00
Parrett, Dean	5.9	Gillinghham	Hampstead	16.11.91
Sonupe, Emmanuel	5.11	Kidderminster	Denmark Hill	21.03.96
Forwards				
Georgiou, Andronicos	5.11	–	Enfield	28.10.99
Guthrie, Kurtis	6.3	Colchester	Jersey	21.04.93
Kennedy, Ben	5.10	–	Belfast	12.01.97
Newton, Dan	5.10	Tamworth	Liverpool	01.02.98
Reid, Alex	6.3	Fleetwood	Birmingham	06.09.95
Revell, Alex	6.3	Northampton	Cambridge	07.07.83
White, Joe	6.0	Dagenham	Camden	16.01.99

SWINDON TOWN

Ground: County Ground, County Road, Swindon SN1 2ED
Telephone: 0871 423 6433. **Club nickname:** Robins
Colours: Red and white. **Capacity:** 15,728
Record attendance: 32,000 v Arsenal (FA Cup 3) Jan 15, 1972

Goalkeepers

Henry, Will	6.0	Bristol City	Bristol	06.07.98
McCormick, Luke	6.0	Plymouth	Coventry	15.08.83
Defenders				
Baudry, Mathieu	6.2	MK Dons	Le Havre, Fr	24.02.88
Broadbent, Tom	6.3	Bristol Rov	Basingstoke	15.02.92
Fryers, Zeki	6.0	Barnsley	Manchester	09.09.92
Hunt, Rob	5.8	Oldham	Dagenham	07.07.95
Reid, Tyler	5.11	Swansea	Luton	02.09.97
Midfielders				
Curran, Taylor	6.0	Southend	Redbridge	07.07.00
Diagouraga, Toumani	6.2	Fleetwood	Paris, Fr	10.06.87
Doughty, Michael	6.1	Peterborough	Westminster	20.11.92
Iandolo, Ellis	5.10	–	Chatham	22.08.97
May, Adam	6.0	Portsmouth (loan)	Southampton	06.12.97

McGlashan, Jermaine	5.7	Southend	Croydon	14.04.88
McGilp, Cameron	5.11	Birmingham	Glasgow	08.02.98
Rose, Danny	5.8	Portsmouth	Bristol	21.02.88
Twine, Scott	5.9	–	Swindon	14.07.99
Forwards				
Anderson, Keshi	5.10	Crystal Palace	Luton	06.04.95
Woolery, Kaiyne	5.10	Wigan	Hackney	11.01.95
Yates, Jerry	5.9	Rotherham (loan)	Doncaster	10.11.96

WALSALL

Ground: Banks's Stadium, Bescot Crescent, Walsall WS1 4SA
Telephone: 01922 622791. **Club nickname:** Saddlers
Colours: Red and white. **Capacity:** 11,300
Record attendance: Fellows Park: 25,453 v Newcastle (Div 2) Aug 29, 1961. Banks's
Stadium: 11,049 v Rotherham (Div 1) May 10, 2004

Goalkeepers				
Roberts, Liam	6.0		Walsall	24.11.94
Rose, Jack	6.3	Southampton (loan)	Solihull	31.01.95
Defenders				
Clarke, James	6.0	Bristol Rov	Aylesbury	17.11.89
Cockerill-Mollett, Callum	5.10	–	Leicester	15.01.99
Facey, Shay	5.10	Northampton	Stockport	07.01.95
Norman, Cameron	6,.2	Oxford	Norwich	12.10.95
Pring, Cameron	6.1	Bristol City (loan)	Cheltenham	22.01.98
Roberts, Kory	6.1		Birmingham	17.12.97
Sadler, Mat	5.11	Shrewsbury	Birmingham	26.02.85
Scarr, Dan	6.2	Birmingham	Bromsgrove	24.12.94
Midfielders				
Dobson, George	6.1	Sparta Rotterdam	Harold Wood	15.11.97
Guthrie, Danny	5.9	Mitra Kukar	Shrewsbury	18.04.87
Hardy, James	5.9	AFC Fylde	Stockport	11.05.96
Kiersey, Jack	5.10	Everton	Manchester	26.09.98
Kinsella, Liam	5.9	–	Colchester	23.02.96
McDonald, Wes	5.9	Birmingham	Lambeth	04.05.97
Sinclair, Stuart	5.8	Bristol Rov	Houghton Conquest	09.11.87
Forwards				
Adebayo, Elijah	6.4	Fulham	Brent	07.01.98
Candlin, Mitchel	6.0	–	Stafford	08.06.00
Ferrier, Morgan		Boreham Wood	London	15.11.94
Gordon, Josh	5.10	Leicester	Stoke	19.01.95

SCOTTISH PREMIERSHIP SQUADS 2019–20

(at time of going to press)

ABERDEEN

Ground: Pittodrie Stadium, Pittodrie Street, Aberdeen AB24 5QH. **Capacity:** 22,199.
Telephone: 01224 650400. **Manager:** Derek McInnes. **Colours:** Red and white. Nickname: Dons
Goalkeepers: Tomas, Cerny, Joe Lewis, Danny Rogers
Defenders: Andrew Considine, Michael Devlin, Jon Gallagher (loan), Greg Leigh (loan), Shaleum
Logan, Scott McKenna, Ash Taylor
Midfielders: Craig Bryson, Dean Campbell, Lewis Ferguson, Stephen Gleeson, Funso Ojo, Ethan
Ross, Miko Virtanen
Forwards: Bruce Anderson, Sam Cosgrove, Ryan Hedges, Curtis Main, Stevie May, Niall
McGinn, Connor McLennan, James Wilson, Scott Wright

CELTIC

Ground: Celtic Park, Glasgow G40 3RE. **Capacity:** 60,832. **Telephone:** 0871 226 1888
Manager: Neil Lennon. **Colours:** Green and white. **Nickname:** Bhoys
Goalkeepers: Scott Bain, Craig Gordon, Conor Hazard
Defenders: Kristoffer Ajer, Boli Bolingoli, Jack Hendry, Christopher Jullien, Calvin Miller,
Anthony Ralston, Jozo Simunovic, Kieran Tierney
Midfielders: Daniel Arzani, Nir Bitton, Scott Brown, Ryan Christie, James Forrest, Jonny Hayes,
Mikey Johnston, Eboue Kouassi, Callum McGregor, Lewis Morgan, Olivier Ntcham, Tom Rogic,
Maryan Shved, Scott Sinclair
Forwards: Vakoun Issouf Bayo, Odsonne Edouard. Leigh Griffiths

HAMILTON ACADEMICAL

Ground: New Douglas Park, Hamilton ML3 0FT. **Capacity:** 6,000. **Telephone:** 01698 368652.
Manager: Brian Rice. **Colours:** Red and white. **Nickname:** Accies
Goalkeepers: Owain Fon Williams, Ryan Fulton, Kyle Gourlay
Defenders: Brian Easton, Alex Gogic, Markus Fjortoft, Johnny Hunt, Aaron McGowan, Ciaran
McKenna, Scott McMann, Shaun Want
Midfielders: Blair Alston, Jack Breen, Will Collar, Ronan Hughes, Darian MacKinnon, Scott
Martin, Reegan Mimnaugh, Lewis Smith
Forwards: Korede Adedoyin (loan), Steven Boyd, Ross Cunningham, Steve Davies, Mickel
Miller, George Oakley, Marios Ogkmpoe, Andy Winter

HEART OF MIDLOTHIAN

Ground: Tynecastle Stadium, McLeod Street Edinburgh EH11 2NL. **Capacity:** 20,099.
Telephone: 0871 663 1874. **Manager:** Craig Levein. **Colours:** Maroon and white. **Nickname:**
Jam Tarts
Goalkeepers: Colin Doyle, Zdenek Zlamal
Defenders: Christophe Berra, Jamie Brandon, Bobby Burns, Clevid Dikamona, Ben Garuccio,
Craig Halkett, Michael Smith, John Souttar
Midfielders: Oliver Bozanic, Sean Clare, Harry Cochrane, Ryan Edwards, Peter Haring, Olly Lee,
Anthony McDonald, Lewis Moore, Callumn Morrison, Jake Mulraney, Josh Vela, Jamie Walker
Forwards: Uche Ikpeazu, Steven MacLean, Steven Naismith, Craig Wighton,
Connor Washington,

HIBERNIAN

Ground: Easter Road Stadium, Albion Place, Edinburgh EH7 5QG. **Capacity:** 20,451.
Telephone: 0131 661 2159. **Manager:** Paul Heckingbottom. **Colours:** Green and whote.
Nickname: Hibees

Goalkeepers: Ofir Marciano, Chris Maxwell (loan)
Defenders: David Gray, Paul Hanlon, Adam Jackson, Tom James, Sean Mackie, Darren McGregor, Ryan Porteous, Lewis Stevenson, Steven Whittaker
Midfielders: Scott Allan, Daryl Horgan, Stevie Mallan, Fraser Murray, Joe Newell, Vykintas Slivka
Forwards: Martin Boyle, Christian Doidge, Jamie Gullan, Florian Kamberi, Oli Shaw

KILMARNOCK

Ground: Rugby Park, Kilmarnock KA 1 2DP. **Capacity:** 18,128. **Telephone:** 01563 545300
Manager: Angelo Alessio. **Colours:** Blue and white. **Nickname:** Killie
Goalkeepers: Laurentiu Branescu (loan), Jamie MacDonald, Devlin MacKay
Defenders: Kirk Broadfoot, Alex Bruce, Stuart Findlay, Ross Millen, Stephen O'Donnell, Greg Taylor, Calum Waters
Midfielders: Chris Burke, Mohamed El Makrini, Gary Dicker, Adam Frizzell, Alan Power, Dom Thomas, Iain Wilson
Forwards: Eamonn Brophy, Innes Cameron, Greg Kiltie, Rory McKenzie

LIVINGSTON

Ground: Tony Macaroni Arena, Alderstone Road, Livingston EH54 7DN. Capacity: 10,000
Telephone: 01506 417000. **Manager:** Gary Holt. **Colours:** Gold and black. **Nickname:** Livvy's Lions
Goalkeepers: Matija Sarkic (loan), Ross Stewart
Defenders: Nicky Devlin, Steve Lawson, Ricki Lamie, Alan Lithgow, Jack McMillan, Hakeem Odoffin, Cec Pepe, Ibrahima Savane, Henk van Schaik
Midfielders: Marvin Bartley, Cameron Blues, Robbie Crawford, Rafaele Keaghan Jacobs, Steven Lawless, Scott Pittman, Scott Robinson, Craig Sibbald, Scott Tiffoney, Gregg Wylde
Forwards: Lyndon Dykes, Chris Erskine, Dolly Menga, Lee Miller, Aymen Souda

MOTHERWELL

Ground: Fir Park, Firpark Street, Motherwell ML1 2QN. **Capacity:** 13,742. **Telephone:** 01698 333333. **Manager:** Stephen Robinson. **Colours:** Claret and amber. **Nickname:** Well
Goalkeepers: Trevor Carson, Rohan Ferguson, Mark Gillespie
Defenders: Jake Carroll, Liam Donnelly, Charles Dunne, Declan Gallagher, Liam Grimshaw, Peter Hartley, Christian Ilic, Adam Livingstone, Barry Maguire, Richard Tait
Midfielders: Allan Campbell, Mohamed El Makrini, Liam Polworth, Sherwin Seedorf, Casper Sloth, Craig Tanner, David Turnbull
Forwards: Devante Cole (loan), De Vita, Craig Henderson, Jermaine Hylton, Danny Johnson, Chris Long, Jamie Semple, James Scott

RANGERS

Ground: Ibrox Park, Edmison Drive, Glasgow G51 2XD. **Capacity:** 50,411
Telephone: 0871 702 1972. **Manager:** Steven Gerrard. **Colours:** Blue. **Nickname:** Gers
Goalkeepers: Jak Alnwick, Andy Firth, Wes Foderingham, Allan McGregor
Defenders: Borna Barisic, George Edmundson, Jon Flanaghan, Connor Goldson, Filip Helander, Nikola Katic, Matt Polster, James Tavernier
Midfielders: Scott Arfield, Joe Aribo, Daniel Candeias, Steven Davis, Greg Docherty, Graham Dorrans, Andy Halliday, Jason Holt, Ryan Jack, Glen Kamara
Forwards: Joe Dodoo, Eros Grezda, Jordan Jones, Alfredo Morelos, Jamie Murphy, Sheyi Ojo (loan), Greg Stewart

ROSS COUNTY

Ground: Global Energy Stadium, Victoria Park, Jubilee Road, Dingwall IV15 9QZ.: 10,673
Telephone: 01738 459090. **Managers:** Steven Ferguson, Stuart Kettlewell. **Colours:** Blue and

white. **Nickname**: Staggies
Goalkeepers: Nathan Baxter (loan), Ross Laidlaw
Defenders: Joe Chalmers, Liam Fontaine, Marcus Fraser, Tom Grivosti, Sean Kelly, Callum Morris, Kenny van der weg, Keith Watson
Midfielders: Daniel Armstrong, Don Cowie, Ross Draper, Michael Gardyne, Davis Keillor-Dunn, Jamie Lindsay, Josh Mullin, Harry Paton, Simon Power (loan), Lewis Spence, Blair Spittal, Iain Vigurs
Forwards: Brian Graham, Billy McKay, Ross Stewart

ST JOHNSTONE

Ground: McDiarmid Park, Crieff Road, Perth PH1 2SJ. **Capacity**: 10,673. **Telephone**: 01738 459090. **Manager**: Tommy Wright. **Colours**: Blue and white. **Nickname**: Saints
Goalkeepers: Zander Clark, Elliott Parish, Ross Sinclair
Defenders: Steven Anderson, Wallace Duffy, Richard Foster, Liam Gordon, Jason Kerr, Scott Tanser
Midfielders: Ross Callachan, Liam Craig, Murray Davidson, Ali McCann, Kyle McClean, Danny Swanson, David Wotherspoon, Drey Wright
Forwards: Callum Hendry, Chris Kane, Matty Kennedy, David McMillan, Michael O'Halloran

ST MIRREN

Ground: Simple Digital Arena Greenhill Road, Paisley PA3 IRU. **Capacity**: 8,023
Telephone: 0141 889 2558. **Manager**: .Jim Goodwin. **Colours**: Black and white. **Nickname**: Buddies
Goalkeepers: Vaclav Hladky, Dean Lyness
Defenders: Jack Baird, Gary MacKenzie, Paul McGinn
Midfielders: Tony Andreu, Oan Djorkaeff, Ethan Erhahon, Ryan Flynn, Scott Glover, Jim Kellerman, Cameron MacPherson, Kyle Magennis, Stephen McGinn, Greg Tansey, Jamie Walker
Forwards: Cody Cooke, Danny Mullen

ENGLISH FIXTURES 2019–2020
Premier League and Football League

Friday 2 August
Championship
Luton v Middlesbrough

Saturday 3 August
Championship
Barnsley v Fulham
Blackburn v Charlton
Brentford v Birmingham
Millwall v Preston
Nottm Forest v WBA
Reading v Sheff Wed
Stoke v QPR
Swansea v Hull
Wigan v Cardiff

League One
AFC Wimbledon v Rotherham
Blackpool v Bristol Rov
Burton v Ipswich
Bury v MK Dons
Coventry v Southend
Doncaster v Gillingham
Lincoln v Accrington
Peterborough v Fleetwood
Shrewsbury v Portsmouth
Sunderland v Oxford
Tranmere v Rochdale
Wycombe v Bolton

League Two
Salford v Stevenage
Bradford v Cambridge
Carlisle v Crawley
Colchester v Port Vale
Crewe v Plymouth
Exeter v Macclesfield
Forest Green v Oldham
Leyton Orient v Cheltenham
Morecambe v Grimsby
Newport v Mansfield
Northampton v Walsall
Scunthorpe v Swindon

Sunday 4 August
Championship
Bristol City v Leeds

Monday 5 August
Championship
Huddersfield v Derby

Friday 9 August
Premier League
Liverpool v Norwich

Saturday 10 August
Premier League
West Ham v Man City
Bournemouth v Sheff Utd
Burnley v Southampton
Crystal Palace v Everton
Watford v Brighton
Tottenham v Aston Villa

Championship
Birmingham v Bristol City
Cardiff v Luton
Charlton v Stoke
Derby v Swansea
Fulham v Blackburn
Hull v Reading
Leeds v Nottm Forest
Middlesbrough v Brentford
Preston v Wigan
QPR v Huddersfield
Sheff Wed v Barnsley
WBA v Millwall

League One
Accrington v Bury
Bolton v Coventry
Bristol Rov v Wycombe
Fleetwood v AFC Wimbledon
Gillingham v Burton
Ipswich v Sunderland
MK Dons v Shrewsbury
Oxford v Peterborough
Portsmouth v Tranmere
Rochdale v Doncaster
Rotherham v Lincoln
Southend v Blackpool

League Two
Cambridge v Newport
Cheltenham v Scunthorpe
Crawley v Salford
Grimsby v Bradford
Macclesfield v Leyton Orient
Mansfield v Morecambe
Oldham v Crewe
Plymouth v Colchester
Port Vale v Northampton
Stevenage v Exeter
Swindon v Carlisle
Walsall v Forest Green

Sunday 11 August
Premier League
Leicester v Wolves
Man Utd v Chelsea
Newcastle v Arsenal

Friday 16 August
Championship
Huddersfield v Fulham

Saturday 17 August
Premier League
Arsenal v Burnley
Aston Villa v Bournemouth
Brighton v West Ham
Everton v Watford
Man City v Tottenham
Norwich v Newcastle
Southampton v Liverpool

Championship
Barnsley v Charlton
Blackburn v Middlesbrough
Brentford v Hull
Bristol City v QPR
Luton v WBA
Millwall v Sheff Wed
Nottm Forest v Birmingham
Stoke v Derby
Swansea v Preston
Wigan v Leeds

League One
AFC Wimbledon v Accrington
Blackpool v Oxford
Burton v Rotherham
Bury v Gillingham
Coventry v Bristol Rov
Doncaster v Fleetwood
Lincoln v Southend
Peterborough v Ipswich
Shrewsbury v Rochdale
Sunderland v Portsmouth
Tranmere v Bolton
Wycombe v MK Dons

League Two
Bradford v Oldham
Carlisle v Mansfield
Colchester v Cambridge
Crewe v Walsall
Exeter v Swindon
Forest Green v Grimsby
Leyton Orient v Stevenage
Morecambe v Cheltenham
Newport v Plymouth
Northampton v Macclesfield
Salford v Port Vale
Scunthorpe v Crawley

Sunday 18 August
Premier League

Chelsea v Leicester
Sheff Utd v Crystal Palace

Championship
Reading v Cardiff

Monday 19 August
Premier League
Wolves v Man Utd

Tuesday 20 August
Championship
Birmingham v Barnsley
Derby v Bristol City
Hull v Blackburn
Middlesbrough v Wigan
Sheff Wed v Luton

League One
Accrington v Shrewsbury
Bristol Rov v Tranmere
Fleetwood v Wycombe
Gillingham v Blackpool
Ipswich v AFC Wimbledon
MK Dons v Lincoln
Oxford v Burton
Portsmouth v Coventry
Rochdale v Sunderland
Rotherham v Bury
Southend v Peterborough
Bolton v Doncaster

League Two
Cambridge v Scunthorpe
Cheltenham v Carlisle
Crawley v Crewe
Grimsby v Colchester
Macclesfield v Morecambe
Mansfield v Leyton Orient
Oldham v Exeter
Plymouth v Salford
Port Vale v Forest Green
Stevenage v Bradford
Swindon v Northampton
Walsall v Newport

Wednesday 21 August
Championship
Cardiff v Huddersfield
Charlton v Nottm Forest
Fulham v Millwall
Leeds v Brentford
Preston v Stoke
QPR v Swansea
WBA v Reading

Friday 23 August
Premier League
Aston Villa v Everton

Saturday 24 August
Premier League
Brighton v Southampton
Liverpool v Arsenal
Man Utd v Crystal Palace
Norwich v Chelsea
Sheff Utd v Leicester
Watford v West Ham
Wolves v Burnley

Championship
Barnsley v Luton
Blackburn v Cardiff
Charlton v Brentford
Derby v WBA
Fulham v Nottm Forest
Huddersfield v Reading
Hull v Bristol City
Middlesbrough v Millwall
Preston v Sheff Wed
QPR v Wigan
Stoke v Leeds

League One
Bolton v Ipswich
Bristol Rov v Oxford
Coventry v Gillingham
Doncaster v Lincoln
Fleetwood v Accrington
MK Dons v Peterborough
Portsmouth v Rotherham
Rochdale v Blackpool
Shrewsbury v Burton
Sunderland v AFC Wimbledon
Tranmere v Bury
Wycombe v Southend

League Two
Bradford v Forest Green
Cambridge v Oldham
Carlisle v Salford
Cheltenham v Swindon
Colchester v Northampton
Grimsby v Port Vale
Leyton Orient v Crawley
Macclesfield v Scunthorpe
Mansfield v Stevenage
Morecambe v Exeter
Newport v Crewe
Plymouth v Walsall

Sunday 25 August
Premier League
Bournemouth v Man City
Tottenham v Newcastle
Championship
Swansea v Birmingham

Friday 30 August
Championship
Cardiff v Fulham

Saturday 31 August
Premier League
Burnley v Liverpool
Chelsea v Sheff Utd
Crystal Palace v Aston Villa
Leicester v Bournemouth
Man City v Brighton
Newcastle v Watford
Southampton v Man Utd
West Ham v Norwich

Championship
Birmingham v Stoke
Brentford v Derby
Bristol City v Middlesbrough
Leeds v Swansea
Luton v Huddersfield
Millwall v Hull
Nottm Forest v Preston
Reading v Charlton
Sheff Wed v QPR
WBA v Blackburn
Wigan v Barnsley

League One
Accrington v MK Dons
AFC Wimbledon v Wycombe
Blackpool v Portsmouth
Burton v Bristol Rov
Bury v Doncaster
Gillingham v Bolton
Ipswich v Shrewsbury
Lincoln v Fleetwood
Oxford v Coventry
Peterborough v Sunderland
Rotherham v Tranmere
Southend v Rochdale

League Two
Crawley v Cheltenham
Crewe v Bradford
Exeter v Mansfield
Forest Green v Newport
Northampton v Plymouth
Oldham v Colchester
Port Vale v Cambridge
Salford v Leyton Orient
Scunthorpe v Carlisle
Stevenage v Macclesfield
Swindon v Morecambe
Walsall v Grimsby

Sunday 1 September
Premier League
Arsenal v Tottenham
Everton v Wolves

Saturday 7 September

League One

Bolton v Bury
Bristol Rov v Accrington
Coventry v Blackpool
Doncaster v Rotherham
Fleetwood v Oxford
MK Dons v AFC Wimbledon
Portsmouth v Southend
Rochdale v Ipswich
Shrewsbury v Peterborough
Sunderland v Burton
Tranmere v Gillingham
Wycombe v Lincoln

League Two

Bradford v Northampton
Cambridge v Forest Green
Carlisle v Exeter
Cheltenham v Stevenage
Colchester v Walsall
Grimsby v Crewe
Leyton Orient v Swindon
Macclesfield v Crawley
Mansfield v Scunthorpe
Morecambe v Salford
Newport v Port Vale
Plymouth v Oldham

Friday 13 September

League One

Burton v Coventry

Saturday 14 September

Premier League

Brighton v Burnley
Liverpool v Newcastle
Man Utd v Leicester
Norwich v Man City
Sheff Utd v Southampton
Tottenham v Crystal Palace
Wolves v Chelsea

Championship

Barnsley v Leeds
Blackburn v Millwall
Charlton v Birmingham
Derby v Cardiff
Fulham v WBA
Huddersfield v Sheff Wed
Hull v Wigan
Middlesbrough v Reading
Preston v Brentford
QPR v Luton
Stoke v Bristol City
Swansea v Nottm Forest

League One

Accrington v Sunderland
AFC Wimbledon v Shrewsbury

Blackpool v MK Dons
Bury v Portsmouth
Gillingham v Wycombe
Ipswich v Doncaster
Lincoln v Bristol Rov
Oxford v Tranmere
Peterborough v Rochdale
Rotherham v Bolton
Southend v Fleetwood

League Two

Crawley v Mansfield
Crewe v Cambridge
Exeter v Leyton Orient
Forest Green v Colchester
Northampton v Newport
Oldham v Grimsby
Port Vale v Plymouth
Salford v Cheltenham
Scunthorpe v Morecambe
Stevenage v Carlisle
Swindon v Macclesfield
Walsall v Bradford

Sunday 15 September

Premier League

Bournemouth v Everton
Watford v Arsenal

Monday 16 September

Premier League

Aston Villa v West Ham

Tuesday 17 September

League One

Bristol Rov v Gillingham
Coventry v AFC Wimbledon
Doncaster v Blackpool
Fleetwood v Bury
MK Dons v Ipswich
Portsmouth v Burton
Rochdale v Lincoln
Shrewsbury v Southend
Sunderland v Rotherham
Tranmere v Peterborough
Wycombe v Accrington
Bolton v Oxford

League Two

Carlisle v Forest Green
Cheltenham v Bradford
Crawley v Plymouth
Exeter v Port Vale
Leyton Orient v Crewe
Macclesfield v Newport
Mansfield v Cambridge
Morecambe v Walsall
Salford v Grimsby
Scunthorpe v Oldham
Stevenage v Northampton
Swindon v Colchester

Friday 20 September

Premier League

Southampton v Bournemouth

Saturday 21 September

Premier League

Burnley v Norwich
Crystal Palace v Wolves
Everton v Sheff Utd
Leicester v Tottenham
Man City v Watford
Newcastle v Brighton

Championship

Birmingham v Preston
Brentford v Stoke
Bristol City v Swansea
Cardiff v Middlesbrough
Leeds v Derby
Luton v Hull
Millwall v QPR
Nottm Forest v Barnsley
Reading v Blackburn
Sheff Wed v Fulham
WBA v Huddersfield
Wigan v Charlton

League One

Accrington v Blackpool
AFC Wimbledon v Bristol Rov
Bolton v Sunderland
Bury v Coventry
Doncaster v Peterborough
Fleetwood v Rochdale
Gillingham v Ipswich
Lincoln v Oxford
MK Dons v Southend
Rotherham v Shrewsbury
Tranmere v Burton
Wycombe v Portsmouth

League Two

Bradford v Carlisle
Cambridge v Swindon
Colchester v Leyton Orient
Crewe v Salford
Forest Green v Stevenage
Grimsby v Macclesfield
Newport v Exeter
Northampton v Crawley
Oldham v Morecambe
Plymouth v Cheltenham
Port Vale v Mansfield
Walsall v Scunthorpe

Sunday 22 September

Premier League

Arsenal v Aston Villa
Chelsea v Liverpool
West Ham v Man Utd

Friday 27 September
League One
Blackpool v Lincoln
Burton v Bury

Saturday 28 September
Premier League
Aston Villa v Burnley
Bournemouth v West Ham
Chelsea v Brighton
Crystal Palace v Norwich
Leicester v Newcastle
Sheff Utd v Liverpool
Tottenham v Southampton
Wolves v Watford

Championship
Barnsley v Brentford
Blackburn v Luton
Charlton v Leeds
Derby v Birmingham
Fulham v Wigan
Huddersfield v Millwall
Hull v Cardiff
Middlesbrough v Sheff Wed
Preston v Bristol City
QPR v WBA
Stoke v Nottm Forest
Swansea v Reading

League One
Bristol Rov v Rotherham
Coventry v Doncaster
Ipswich v Tranmere
Oxford v Gillingham
Peterborough v AFC Wimbledon
Portsmouth v Bolton
Rochdale v Wycombe
Shrewsbury v Fleetwood
Southend v Accrington
Sunderland v MK Dons

League Two
Carlisle v Oldham
Cheltenham v Crewe
Crawley v Walsall
Exeter v Grimsby
Leyton Orient v Port Vale
Macclesfield v Colchester
Mansfield v Plymouth
Morecambe v Northampton
Salford v Forest Green
Scunthorpe v Bradford
Stevenage v Cambridge
Swindon v Newport

Sunday 29 September
Premier League
Everton v Man City

Monday 30 September
Premier League
Man Utd v Arsenal

Tuesday 1 October
Championship
Blackburn v Nottm Forest
Hull v Sheff Wed
Leeds v WBA
Middlesbrough v Preston
Reading v Fulham
Stoke v Huddersfield
Wigan v Birmingham

Wednesday 2 October
Championship
Barnsley v Derby
Brentford v Bristol City
Cardiff v QPR
Charlton v Swansea
Luton v Millwall

Saturday 5 October
Premier League
Brighton v Tottenham
Burnley v Everton
Liverpool v Leicester
Man City v Wolves
Norwich v Aston Villa
Southampton v Chelsea
Watford v Sheff Utd
West Ham v Crystal Palace

Championship
Birmingham v Middlesbrough
Bristol City v Reading
Derby v Luton
Fulham v Charlton
Huddersfield v Hull
Millwall v Leeds
Nottm Forest v Brentford
Preston v Barnsley
QPR v Blackburn
Sheff Wed v Wigan
Swansea v Stoke
WBA v Cardiff

League One
Accrington v Oxford
AFC Wimbledon v Rochdale
Bolton v Blackpool
Bury v Bristol Rov
Doncaster v Portsmouth
Fleetwood v Ipswich
Gillingham v Southend
Lincoln v Sunderland
MK Dons v Burton
Rotherham v Coventry
Tranmere v Shrewsbury
Wycombe v Peterborough

League Two
Bradford v Swindon
Cambridge v Macclesfield
Colchester v Stevenage
Crewe v Exeter
Forest Green v Crawley
Grimsby v Mansfield
Newport v Carlisle
Northampton v Leyton Orient
Oldham v Cheltenham
Plymouth v Scunthorpe
Port Vale v Morecambe
Walsall v Salford

Sunday 6 October
Premier League
Arsenal v Bournemouth
Newcastle v Man Utd

Saturday 12 October
League One
Blackpool v Rotherham
Bristol Rov v MK Dons
Burton v Bolton
Coventry v Tranmere
Ipswich v Wycombe
Oxford v Doncaster
Peterborough v Lincoln
Portsmouth v Gillingham
Rochdale v Accrington
Shrewsbury v Bury
Southend v AFC Wimbledon
Sunderland v Fleetwood

League Two
Carlisle v Crewe
Cheltenham v Newport
Crawley v Colchester
Exeter v Forest Green
Leyton Orient v Walsall
Macclesfield v Port Vale
Mansfield v Oldham
Morecambe v Bradford
Salford v Cambridge
Scunthorpe v Northampton
Stevenage v Grimsby
Swindon v Plymouth

Friday 18 October
League One
Lincoln v Shrewsbury
Tranmere v Southend

Saturday 19 October
Premier League
Aston Villa v Brighton
Bournemouth v Norwich
Chelsea v Newcastle
Crystal Palace v Man City
Everton v West Ham

Leicester v Burnley
Man Utd v Liverpool
Sheff Utd v Arsenal
Tottenham v Watford
Wolves v Southampton

Championship
Barnsley v Swansea
Blackburn v Huddersfield
Brentford v Millwall
Cardiff v Sheff Wed
Charlton v Derby
Hull v QPR
Leeds v Birmingham
Luton v Bristol City
Middlesbrough v WBA
Reading v Preston
Stoke v Fulham
Wigan v Nottm Forest

League One
Accrington v Ipswich
AFC Wimbledon v Portsmouth
Bolton v Rochdale
Bury v Blackpool
Doncaster v Bristol Rov
Fleetwood v Burton
Gillingham v Peterborough
MK Dons v Coventry
Rotherham v Oxford
Wycombe v Sunderland

League Two
Bradford v Crawley
Cambridge v Exeter
Colchester v Morecambe
Crewe v Swindon
Forest Green v Mansfield
Grimsby v Leyton Orient
Newport v Scunthorpe
Northampton v Salford
Oldham v Macclesfield
Plymouth v Carlisle
Port Vale v Stevenage
Walsall v Cheltenham

Tuesday 22 October
Championship
Birmingham v Blackburn
Millwall v Cardiff
Preston v Leeds
QPR v Reading
Sheff Wed v Stoke
Swansea v Brentford
WBA v Barnsley

League One
Blackpool v Wycombe
Bristol Rov v Bolton
Burton v AFC Wimbledon
Ipswich v Rotherham

Oxford v Bury
Peterborough v Accrington
Portsmouth v Lincoln
Rochdale v MK Dons
Shrewsbury v Gillingham
Southend v Doncaster
Sunderland v Tranmere

League Two
Bradford v Port Vale
Cambridge v Grimsby
Carlisle v Northampton
Cheltenham v Macclesfield
Crewe v Colchester
Mansfield v Salford
Morecambe v Forest Green
Newport v Crawley
Oldham v Walsall
Plymouth v Leyton Orient
Scunthorpe v Exeter
Swindon v Stevenage

Wednesday 23 October
Championship
Bristol City v Charlton
Derby v Wigan
Fulham v Luton
Huddersfield v Middlesbrough
Nottm Forest v Hull

League One
Coventry v Fleetwood

Saturday 26 October
Premier League
Arsenal v Crystal Palace
Brighton v Everton
Burnley v Chelsea
Liverpool v Tottenham
Man City v Aston Villa
Newcastle v Wolves
Norwich v Man Utd
Southampton v Leicester
Watford v Bournemouth
West Ham v Sheff Utd

Championship
Birmingham v Luton
Huddersfield v Barnsley
Hull v Derby
Middlesbrough v Fulham
Millwall v Stoke
Nottm Forest v Reading
Preston v Blackburn
QPR v Brentford
Sheff Wed v Leeds
Swansea v Cardiff
WBA v Charlton

League One
Accrington v Gillingham
Bristol Rov v Portsmouth

Burton v Blackpool
Bury v AFC Wimbledon
Fleetwood v MK Dons
Lincoln v Bolton
Oxford v Rochdale
Peterborough v Coventry
Rotherham v Wycombe
Shrewsbury v Sunderland
Southend v Ipswich
Tranmere v Doncaster

League Two
Colchester v Newport
Crawley v Swindon
Exeter v Plymouth
Forest Green v Crewe
Grimsby v Cheltenham
Leyton Orient v Carlisle
Macclesfield v Bradford
Northampton v Cambridge
Port Vale v Oldham
Salford v Scunthorpe
Stevenage v Morecambe
Walsall v Mansfield

Sunday 27 October
Championship
Bristol City v Wigan

Saturday 2 November
Premier League
Arsenal v Wolves
Aston Villa v Liverpool
Bournemouth v Man Utd
Brighton v Norwich
Crystal Palace v Leicester
Everton v Tottenham
Man City v Southampton
Sheff Utd v Burnley
Watford v Chelsea
West Ham v Newcastle

Championship
Barnsley v Bristol City
Blackburn v Sheff Wed
Brentford v Huddersfield
Cardiff v Birmingham
Charlton v Preston
Derby v Middlesbrough
Fulham v Hull
Leeds v QPR
Luton v Nottm Forest
Reading v Millwall
Stoke v WBA
Wigan v Swansea

League One
AFC Wimbledon v Lincoln
Blackpool v Peterborough
Bolton v Fleetwood

Coventry v Accrington
Doncaster v Burton
Gillingham v Rotherham
Ipswich v Bury
MK Dons v Tranmere
Portsmouth v Oxford
Rochdale v Bristol Rov
Sunderland v Southend
Wycombe v Shrewsbury

League Two
Bradford v Exeter
Cambridge v Crawley
Carlisle v Macclesfield
Cheltenham v Forest Green
Crewe v Port Vale
Mansfield v Colchester
Morecambe v Leyton Orient
Newport v Salford
Oldham v Northampton
Plymouth v Grimsby
Scunthorpe v Stevenage
Swindon v Walsall

Saturday 9 November
Premier League
Burnley v West Ham
Chelsea v Crystal Palace
Liverpool v Man City
Newcastle v Bournemouth
Norwich v Watford
Southampton v Everton
Tottenham v Sheff Utd
Wolves v Aston Villa

Championship
Barnsley v Stoke
Birmingham v Fulham
Cardiff v Bristol City
Hull v WBA
Leeds v Blackburn
Millwall v Charlton
Nottm Forest v Derby
Preston v Huddersfield
QPR v Middlesbrough
Reading v Luton
Sheff Wed v Swansea
Wigan v Brentford

Sunday 10 November
Premier League
Leicester v Arsenal
Man Utd v Brighton

Saturday 16 November
League One
Blackpool v AFC Wimbledon
Bolton v MK Dons
Bristol Rov v Sunderland
Burton v Southend

Bury v Peterborough
Coventry v Rochdale
Doncaster v Shrewsbury
Gillingham v Lincoln
Oxford v Ipswich
Portsmouth v Fleetwood
Rotherham v Accrington
Tranmere v Wycombe

League Two
Colchester v Bradford
Crawley v Morecambe
Exeter v Cheltenham
Forest Green v Plymouth
Grimsby v Newport
Leyton Orient v Scunthorpe
Macclesfield v Mansfield
Northampton v Crewe
Port Vale v Carlisle
Salford v Swindon
Stevenage v Oldham
Walsall v Cambridge

Saturday 23 November
Premier League
Arsenal v Southampton
Aston Villa v Newcastle
Bournemouth v Wolves
Brighton v Leicester
Crystal Palace v Liverpool
Everton v Norwich
Man City v Chelsea
Sheff Utd v Man Utd
Watford v Burnley
West Ham v Tottenham

Championship
Blackburn v Barnsley
Brentford v Reading
Bristol City v Nottm Forest
Charlton v Cardiff
Derby v Preston
Fulham v QPR
Huddersfield v Birmingham
Luton v Leeds
Middlesbrough v Hull
Stoke v Wigan
Swansea v Millwall
WBA v Sheff Wed]

League One
Accrington v Bolton
AFC Wimbledon v Gillingham
Fleetwood v Tranmere
Ipswich v Blackpool
Lincoln v Bury
MK Dons v Rotherham
Peterborough v Burton
Rochdale v Portsmouth
Shrewsbury v Bristol Rov
Southend v Oxford

Sunderland v Coventry
Wycombe v Doncaster

League Two
Carlisle v Cambridge
Cheltenham v Colchester
Crawley v Exeter
Crewe v Morecambe
Leyton Orient v Forest Green
Newport v Oldham
Northampton v Grimsby
Plymouth v Bradford
Salford v Macclesfield
Scunthorpe v Port Vale
Swindon v Mansfield
Walsall v Stevenage

Tuesday 26 November
Championship
Cardiff v Stoke
Fulham v Derby
Huddersfield v Swansea
Luton v Charlton
Millwall v Wigan
Reading v Leeds

Wednesday 27 November
Championship
Blackburn v Brentford
Hull v Preston
Middlesbrough v Barnsley
QPR v Nottm Forest
Sheff Wed v Birmingham
WBA v Bristol City

Saturday 30 November
Premier League
Burnley v Crystal Palace
Chelsea v West Ham
Leicester v Everton
Liverpool v Brighton
Newcastle v Man City
Southampton v Watford
Tottenham v Bournemouth
Wolves v Sheff Utd

Championship
Barnsley v Hull
Birmingham v Millwall
Brentford v Luton
Bristol City v Huddersfield
Charlton v Sheff Wed
Derby v QPR
Leeds v Middlesbrough
Nottm Forest v Cardiff
Preston v WBA
Stoke v Blackburn
Swansea v Fulham
Wigan v Reading

Sunday 1 December
Premier League
Man Utd v Aston Villa
Norwich v Arsenal

Tuesday 3rd December
Premier League
Arsenal v Brighton
Burnley v Man City
Leicester v Watford
Sheff Utd v Newcastle
Wolves v West Ham
Man Utd v Tottenham

Wednesday 4 December
Premier League
Chelsea v Aston Villa
Southampton v Norwich
Crystal Palace v Bournemouth
Liverpool v Everton

Saturday 7 December
Premier League
Aston Villa v Leicester
Bournemouth v Liverpool
Brighton v Wolves
Everton v Chelsea
Man City v Man Utd
Newcastle v Southampton
Norwich v Sheff Utd
Tottenham v Burnley
Watford v Crystal Palace
West Ham v Arsenal

Championship
Blackburn v Derby
Cardiff v Barnsley
Fulham v Bristol City
Huddersfield v Leeds
Hull v Stoke
Luton v Wigan
Middlesbrough v Charlton
Millwall v Nottm Forest
QPR v Preston
Reading v Birmingham
Sheff Wed v Brentford
WBA v Swansea

League One
Blackpool v Fleetwood
Bolton v AFC Wimbledon
Bristol Rov v Southend
Burton v Lincoln
Bury v Wycombe
Doncaster v MK Dons
Gillingham v Sunderland
Oxford v Shrewsbury
Portsmouth v Peterborough
Rotherham v Rochdale
Tranmere v Accrington

League Two
Bradford v Newport
Cambridge v Plymouth
Colchester v Salford
Exeter v Northampton
Forest Green v Scunthorpe
Grimsby v Swindon
Macclesfield v Crewe
Mansfield v Cheltenham
Morecambe v Carlisle
Oldham v Leyton Orient
Port Vale v Walsall
Stevenage v Crawley

Sunday 8 December
League One
Coventry v Ipswich

Tuesday 10 December
Championship
Bristol City v Millwall
Charlton v Huddersfield
Leeds v Hull
Nottm Forest v Middlesbrough
Preston v Fulham
Stoke v Luton

Wednesday 11 December
Championship
Barnsley v Reading
Birmingham v QPR
Brentford v Cardiff
Derby v Sheff Wed
Swansea v Blackburn
Wigan v WBA

Saturday 14 December
Premier League
Arsenal v Man City
Burnley v Newcastle
Chelsea v Bournemouth
Crystal Palace v Brighton
Leicester v Norwich
Liverpool v Watford
Man Utd v Everton
Sheff Utd v Aston Villa
Southampton v West Ham
Wolves v Tottenham

Championship
Barnsley v QPR
Birmingham v WBA
Brentford v Fulham
Bristol City v Blackburn
Charlton v Hull
Derby v Millwall
Leeds v Cardiff
Nottm Forest v Sheff Wed
Preston v Luton
Stoke v Reading

Swansea v Middlesbrough
Wigan v Huddersfield

League One
Accrington v Portsmouth
AFC Wimbledon v Doncaster
Fleetwood v Gillingham
Ipswich v Bristol Rov
Lincoln v Tranmere
MK Dons v Oxford
Peterborough v Bolton
Rochdale v Bury
Shrewsbury v Coventry
Southend v Rotherham
Sunderland v Blackpool
Wycombe v Burton

League Two
Carlisle v Grimsby
Cheltenham v Cambridge
Crawley v Port Vale
Crewe v Mansfield
Leyton Orient v Bradford
Newport v Stevenage
Northampton v Forest Green
Plymouth v Morecambe
Salford v Exeter
Scunthorpe v Colchester
Swindon v Oldham
Walsall v Macclesfield

Saturday 21 December
Premier League
Aston Villa v Southampton
Bournemouth v Burnley
Brighton v Sheff Utd
Everton v Arsenal
Man City v Leicester
Newcastle v Crystal Palace
Norwich v Wolves
Tottenham v Chelsea
Watford v Man Utd
West Ham v Liverpool

Championship
Blackburn v Wigan
Cardiff v Preston
Fulham v Leeds
Huddersfield v Nottm Forest
Hull v Birmingham
Luton v Swansea
Middlesbrough v Stoke
Millwall v Barnsley
QPR v Charlton
Reading v Derby
Sheff Wed v Bristol City
WBA v Brentford

League One
Blackpool v Shrewsbury
Bolton v Southend
Bristol Rov v Peterborough

Burton v Rochdale
Bury v Sunderland
Coventry v Lincoln
Doncaster v Accrington
Gillingham v MK Dons
Oxford v Wycombe
Portsmouth v Ipswich
Rotherham v Fleetwood
Tranmere v AFC Wimbledon

League Two
Bradford v Salford
Cambridge v Leyton Orient
Colchester v Carlisle
Exeter v Walsall
Forest Green v Swindon
Grimsby v Scunthorpe
Macclesfield v Plymouth
Mansfield v Northampton
Morecambe v Newport
Oldham v Crawley
Port Vale v Cheltenham
Stevenage v Crewe

Thursday 26 December
Premier League
Aston Villa v Norwich
Bournemouth v Arsenal
Chelsea v Southampton
Crystal Palace v West Ham
Everton v Burnley
Leicester v Liverpool
Man Utd v Newcastle
Sheff Utd v Watford
Tottenham v Brighton
Wolves v Man City

Championship
Barnsley v WBA
Blackburn v Birmingham
Brentford v Swansea
Cardiff v Millwall
Charlton v Bristol City
Hull v Nottm Forest
Leeds v Preston
Luton v Fulham
Middlesbrough v Huddersfield
Reading v QPR
Stoke v Sheff Wed
Wigan v Derby

League One
Blackpool v Accrington
Bristol Rov v AFC Wimbledon
Burton v Tranmere
Coventry v Bury
Ipswich v Gillingham
Oxford v Lincoln
Peterborough v Doncaster
Portsmouth v Wycombe
Rochdale v Fleetwood

Shrewsbury v Rotherham
Southend v MK Dons
Sunderland v Bolton

League Two
Carlisle v Bradford
Cheltenham v Plymouth
Crawley v Northampton
Exeter v Newport
Leyton Orient v Colchester
Macclesfield v Grimsby
Mansfield v Port Vale
Morecambe v Oldham
Salford v Crewe
Scunthorpe v Walsall
Stevenage v Forest Green
Swindon v Cambridge

Saturday 28 December
Premier League
Arsenal v Chelsea
Brighton v Bournemouth
Burnley v Man Utd
Liverpool v Wolves
Man City v Sheff Utd
Newcastle v Everton
Norwich v Tottenham
Southampton v Crystal Palace
Watford v Aston Villa
West Ham v Leicester

Sunday 29 December
Championship
Birmingham v Leeds
Bristol City v Luton
Derby v Charlton
Fulham v Stoke
Huddersfield v Blackburn
Millwall v Brentford
Nottm Forest v Wigan
Preston v Reading
QPR v Hull
Sheff Wed v Cardiff
Swansea v Barnsley
WBA v Middlesbrough

League One
Accrington v Burton
AFC Wimbledon v Oxford
Bolton v Shrewsbury
Bury v Southend
Doncaster v Sunderland
Fleetwood v Bristol Rov
Gillingham v Rochdale
Lincoln v Ipswich
MK Dons v Portsmouth
Rotherham v Peterborough
Tranmere v Blackpool
Wycombe v Coventry

League Two
Bradford v Mansfield
Cambridge v Morecambe
Colchester v Exeter
Crewe v Scunthorpe
Forest Green v Macclesfield
Grimsby v Crawley
Newport v Leyton Orient
Northampton v Cheltenham
Oldham v Salford
Plymouth v Stevenage
Port Vale v Swindon
Walsall v Carlisle

Wednesday 1 January
Premier League
Arsenal v Man Utd
Brighton v Chelsea
Burnley v Aston Villa
Liverpool v Sheff Utd
Man City v Everton
Newcastle v Leicester
Norwich v Crystal Palace
Southampton v Tottenham
Watford v Wolves
West Ham v Bournemouth

Championship
Birmingham v Wigan
Bristol City v Brentford
Derby v Barnsley
Fulham v Reading
Huddersfield v Stoke
Millwall v Luton
Nottm Forest v Blackburn
Preston v Middlesbrough
QPR v Cardiff
Sheff Wed v Hull
Swansea v Charlton
WBA v Leeds
League One
Accrington v Rochdale
AFC Wimbledon v Southend
Bolton v Burton
Bury v Shrewsbury
Doncaster v Oxford
Fleetwood v Sunderland
Gillingham v Portsmouth
Lincoln v Peterborough
MK Dons v Bristol Rov
Rotherham v Blackpool
Tranmere v Coventry
Wycombe v Ipswich

League Two
Bradford v Morecambe
Cambridge v Mansfield
Colchester v Crawley
Crewe v Carlisle
Forest Green v Exeter
Grimsby v Salford

Newport v Cheltenham
Northampton v Stevenage
Oldham v Scunthorpe
Plymouth v Swindon
Port Vale v Macclesfield
Walsall v Leyton Orient

Saturday 4 January
League One
Blackpool v Bolton
Bristol Rov v Bury
Burton v MK Dons
Coventry v Rotherham
Ipswich v Fleetwood
Oxford v Accrington
Peterborough v Wycombe
Portsmouth v Doncaster
Rochdale v AFC Wimbledon
Shrewsbury v Tranmere
Southend v Gillingham
Sunderland v Lincoln

League Two
Carlisle v Newport
Cheltenham v Oldham
Crawley v Forest Green
Exeter v Crewe
Leyton Orient v Northampton
Macclesfield v Cambridge
Mansfield v Grimsby
Morecambe v Port Vale
Salford v Walsall
Scunthorpe v Plymouth
Stevenage v Colchester
Swindon v Bradford

Saturday 11 January
Premier League
Aston Villa v Man City
Bournemouth v Watford
Chelsea v Burnley
Crystal Palace v Arsenal
Everton v Brighton
Leicester v Southampton
Man Utd v Norwich
Sheff Utd v West Ham
Tottenham v Liverpool
Wolves v Newcastle

Championship
Barnsley v Huddersfield
Blackburn v Preston
Brentford v QPR
Cardiff v Swansea
Charlton v WBA
Hull v Fulham
Leeds v Sheff Wed
Luton v Birmingham
Middlesbrough v Derby
Reading v Nottm Forest

Stoke v Millwall
Wigan v Bristol City

League One
Blackpool v Bury
Bristol Rov v Doncaster
Burton v Fleetwood
Coventry v MK Dons
Ipswich v Accrington
Oxford v Rotherham
Peterborough v Gillingham
Portsmouth v AFC Wimbledon
Rochdale v Bolton
Shrewsbury v Lincoln
Southend v Tranmere
Sunderland v Wycombe

League Two
Carlisle v Plymouth
Cheltenham v Walsall
Crawley v Bradford
Exeter v Cambridge
Leyton Orient v Grimsby
Macclesfield v Oldham
Mansfield v Forest Green
Morecambe v Colchester
Salford v Northampton
Scunthorpe v Newport
Stevenage v Port Vale
Swindon v Crewe

Saturday 18 January
Premier League
Arsenal v Sheff Utd
Brighton v Aston Villa
Burnley v Leicester
Liverpool v Man Utd
Man City v Crystal Palace
Newcastle v Chelsea
Norwich v Bournemouth
Southampton v Wolves
Watford v Tottenham
West Ham v Everton

Championship
Birmingham v Cardiff
Bristol City v Barnsley
Derby v Hull
Fulham v Middlesbrough
Huddersfield v Brentford
Millwall v Reading
Nottm Forest v Luton
Preston v Charlton
QPR v Leeds
Sheff Wed v Blackburn
Swansea v Wigan
WBA v Stoke

League One
Accrington v Southend
AFC Wimbledon v Peterborough

Bolton v Portsmouth
Bury v Burton
Doncaster v Coventry
Fleetwood v Shrewsbury
Gillingham v Oxford
Lincoln v Blackpool
MK Dons v Sunderland
Rotherham v Bristol Rov
Tranmere v Ipswich
Wycombe v Rochdale

League Two
Bradford v Scunthorpe
Cambridge v Stevenage
Colchester v Macclesfield
Crewe v Cheltenham
Forest Green v Salford
Grimsby v Exeter
Newport v Swindon
Northampton v Morecambe
Oldham v Carlisle
Plymouth v Mansfield
Port Vale v Leyton Orient
Walsall v Crawley

Tuesday 21 January
Premier League
Aston Villa v Watford
Bournemouth v Brighton
Everton v Newcastle
Leicester v West Ham
Sheff Utd v Man City
Wolves v Liverpool
Man Utd v Burnley

Wednesday 22 January
Premier League
Chelsea v Arsenal
Crystal Palace v Southampton
Tottenham v Norwich

Friday 24 January
League One
Southend v Bury

Saturday 25 January
Championship
Barnsley v Preston
Blackburn v QPR
Brentford v Nottm Forest
Cardiff v WBA
Charlton v Fulham
Hull v Huddersfield
Leeds v Millwall
Luton v Derby
Middlesbrough v Birmingham
Reading v Bristol City
Stoke v Swansea
Wigan v Sheff Wed

League One

Blackpool v Tranmere
Bristol Rov v Fleetwood
Burton v Accrington
Coventry v Wycombe
Ipswich v Lincoln
Oxford v AFC Wimbledon
Peterborough v Rotherham
Portsmouth v MK Dons
Rochdale v Gillingham
Shrewsbury v Bolton
Sunderland v Doncaster

League Two

Carlisle v Walsall
Cheltenham v Northampton
Crawley v Grimsby
Exeter v Colchester
Leyton Orient v Newport
Macclesfield v Forest Green
Mansfield v Bradford
Morecambe v Cambridge
Salford v Oldham
Scunthorpe v Crewe
Stevenage v Plymouth
Swindon v Port Vale

Tuesday 28 January
League One

Accrington v Peterborough
AFC Wimbledon v Burton
Bury v Oxford
Doncaster v Southend
Fleetwood v Coventry
Gillingham v Shrewsbury
Lincoln v Portsmouth
MK Dons v Rochdale
Rotherham v Ipswich
Tranmere v Sunderland
Wycombe v Blackpool
Bolton v Bristol Rov

League Two

Bradford v Cheltenham
Cambridge v Salford
Colchester v Swindon
Crewe v Leyton Orient
Forest Green v Carlisle
Grimsby v Stevenage
Newport v Macclesfield
Northampton v Scunthorpe
Oldham v Mansfield
Plymouth v Crawley
Port Vale v Exeter
Walsall v Morecambe

Friday January 31
Championship

Cardiff v Reading

Saturday 1 February
Premier League

Bournemouth v Aston Villa
Burnley v Arsenal
Crystal Palace v Sheff Utd
Leicester v Chelsea
Liverpool v Southampton
Man Utd v Wolves
Newcastle v Norwich
Tottenham v Man City
Watford v Everton
West Ham v Brighton

Championship

Birmingham v Nottm Forest
Charlton v Barnsley
Derby v Stoke
Fulham v Huddersfield
Hull v Brentford
Leeds v Wigan
Middlesbrough v Blackburn
Preston v Swansea
QPR v Bristol City
Sheff Wed v Millwall
WBA v Luton

League One

Accrington v AFC Wimbledon
Bolton v Tranmere
Bristol Rov v Coventry
Fleetwood v Doncaster
Gillingham v Bury
Ipswich v Peterborough
MK Dons v Wycombe
Oxford v Blackpool
Portsmouth v Sunderland
Rochdale v Shrewsbury
Rotherham v Burton
Southend v Lincoln

League Two

Cambridge v Colchester
Cheltenham v Morecambe
Crawley v Scunthorpe
Grimsby v Forest Green
Macclesfield v Northampton
Mansfield v Carlisle
Oldham v Bradford
Plymouth v Newport
Port Vale v Salford
Stevenage v Leyton Orient
Swindon v Exeter
Walsall v Crewe

Friday 7 February
Championship

Bristol City v Birmingham

League One

Lincoln v Rotherham

Saturday 8 February
Premier League

Arsenal v Newcastle
Aston Villa v Tottenham
Brighton v Watford
Chelsea v Man Utd
Everton v Crystal Palace
Man City v West Ham
Norwich v Liverpool
Sheff Utd v Bournemouth
Southampton v Burnley
Wolves v Leicester

Championship

Barnsley v Sheff Wed
Blackburn v Fulham
Brentford v Middlesbrough
Huddersfield v QPR
Luton v Cardiff
Millwall v WBA
Nottm Forest v Leeds
Reading v Hull
Stoke v Charlton
Swansea v Derby
Wigan v Preston

League One

AFC Wimbledon v Fleetwood
Blackpool v Southend
Burton v Gillingham
Bury v Accrington
Coventry v Bolton
Doncaster v Rochdale
Peterborough v Oxford
Shrewsbury v MK Dons
Sunderland v Ipswich
Tranmere v Portsmouth
Wycombe v Bristol Rov

League Two

Bradford v Grimsby
Carlisle v Swindon
Colchester v Plymouth
Crewe v Oldham
Exeter v Stevenage
Forest Green v Walsall
Leyton Orient v Macclesfield
Morecambe v Mansfield
Newport v Cambridge
Northampton v Port Vale
Salford v Crawley
Scunthorpe v Cheltenham

Tuesday 11 February
Championship

Barnsley v Birmingham
Blackburn v Hull
Brentford v Leeds
Nottm Forest v Charlton
Swansea v QPR
Wigan v Middlesbrough

League One

AFC Wimbledon v Ipswich
Blackpool v Gillingham
Burton v Oxford
Bury v Rotherham
Coventry v Portsmouth
Doncaster v Bolton
Lincoln v MK Dons
Peterborough v Southend
Shrewsbury v Accrington
Sunderland v Rochdale
Tranmere v Bristol Rov
Wycombe v Fleetwood

League Two

Bradford v Stevenage
Carlisle v Cheltenham
Colchester v Grimsby
Crewe v Crawley
Exeter v Oldham
Forest Green v Port Vale
Leyton Orient v Mansfield
Morecambe v Macclesfield
Newport v Walsall
Northampton v Swindon
Salford v Plymouth
Scunthorpe v Cambridge

Wednesday 12 February
Championship
Bristol City v Derby
Huddersfield v Cardiff
Luton v Sheff Wed
Millwall v Fulham
Reading v WBA
Stoke v Preston

Saturday 15 February
Premier League
Arsenal v Everton
Burnley v Bournemouth
Chelsea v Tottenham
Crystal Palace v Newcastle
Leicester v Man City
Liverpool v West Ham
Man Utd v Watford
Sheff Utd v Brighton
Southampton v Aston Villa
Wolves v Norwich

Championship
Birmingham v Brentford
Cardiff v Wigan
Charlton v Blackburn
Derby v Huddersfield
Fulham v Barnsley
Hull v Swansea
Leeds v Bristol City
Middlesbrough v Luton

Preston v Millwall
QPR v Stoke
Sheff Wed v Reading
WBA v Nottm Forest

League One
Accrington v Lincoln
Bolton v Wycombe
Bristol Rov v Blackpool
Fleetwood v Peterborough
Gillingham v Doncaster
Ipswich v Burton
MK Dons v Bury
Oxford v Sunderland
Portsmouth v Shrewsbury
Rochdale v Tranmere
Rotherham v AFC Wimbledon
Southend v Coventry

League Two
Cambridge v Bradford
Cheltenham v Leyton Orient
Crawley v Carlisle
Grimsby v Morecambe
Macclesfield v Exeter
Mansfield v Newport
Oldham v Forest Green
Plymouth v Crewe
Port Vale v Colchester
Stevenage v Salford
Swindon v Scunthorpe
Walsall v Northampton

Saturday 22 February
Championship
Barnsley v Middlesbrough
Birmingham v Sheff Wed
Brentford v Blackburn
Bristol City v WBA
Charlton v Luton
Derby v Fulham
Leeds v Reading
Nottm Forest v QPR
Preston v Hull

League One
Accrington v Rotherham
AFC Wimbledon v Blackpool
Fleetwood v Portsmouth
Ipswich v Oxford
Lincoln v Gillingham
MK Dons v Bolton
Peterborough v Bury
Rochdale v Coventry
Shrewsbury v Doncaster
Southend v Burton
Sunderland v Bristol Rov
Wycombe v Tranmere

League Two
Carlisle v Morecambe
Cheltenham v Mansfield
Crawley v Stevenage
Crewe v Macclesfield
Leyton Orient v Oldham
Newport v Bradford
Northampton v Exeter
Plymouth v Cambridge
Salford v Colchester
Scunthorpe v Forest Green
Swindon v Grimsby
Walsall v Port Vale

Sunday 23 February
Championship
Swansea v Huddersfield
Wigan v Millwall

Tuesday 25 February
Championship
Cardiff v Nottm Forest
Fulham v Swansea
Huddersfield v Bristol City
Luton v Brentford
QPR v Derby
WBA v Preston

Wednesday 26 February
Championship
Blackburn v Stoke
Hull v Barnsley
Middlesbrough v Leeds
Millwall v Birmingham
Reading v Wigan
Sheff Wed v Charlton

Saturday 29 February
Premier League
Aston Villa v Sheff Utd
Bournemouth v Chelsea
Brighton v Crystal Palace
Everton v Man Utd
Man City v Arsenal
Newcastle v Burnley
Norwich v Leicester
Tottenham v Wolves
Watford v Liverpool
West Ham v Southampton

Championship
Blackburn v Swansea
Cardiff v Brentford
Fulham v Preston
Huddersfield v Charlton
Hull v Leeds
Luton v Stoke
Middlesbrough v Nottm Forest
Millwall v Bristol City

QPR v Birmingham
Reading v Barnsley
Sheff Wed v Derby
WBA v Wigan

League One

Blackpool v Ipswich
Bolton v Accrington
Bristol Rov v Shrewsbury
Burton v Peterborough
Bury v Lincoln
Coventry v Sunderland
Doncaster v Wycombe
Gillingham v AFC Wimbledon
Oxford v Southend
Portsmouth v Rochdale
Rotherham v MK Dons
Tranmere v Fleetwood

League Two

Bradford v Plymouth
Cambridge v Carlisle
Colchester v Cheltenham
Exeter v Crawley
Forest Green v Leyton Orient
Grimsby v Northampton
Macclesfield v Salford
Mansfield v Swindon
Morecambe v Crewe
Oldham v Newport
Port Vale v Scunthorpe
Stevenage v Walsall

Saturday 7 March
Premier League

Arsenal v West Ham
Burnley v Tottenham
Chelsea v Everton
Crystal Palace v Watford
Leicester v Aston Villa
Liverpool v Bournemouth
Man Utd v Man City
Sheff Utd v Norwich
Southampton v Newcastle
Wolves v Brighton

Championship

Barnsley v Cardiff
Birmingham v Reading
Brentford v Sheff Wed
Bristol City v Fulham
Charlton v Middlesbrough
Derby v Blackburn
Leeds v Huddersfield
Nottm Forest v Millwall
Preston v QPR
Stoke v Hull
Swansea v WBA
Wigan v Luton

League One

Accrington v Tranmere
AFC Wimbledon v Bolton
Fleetwood v Blackpool
Ipswich v Coventry
Lincoln v Burton
MK Dons v Doncaster
Peterborough v Portsmouth
Rochdale v Rotherham
Shrewsbury v Oxford
Southend v Bristol Rov
Sunderland v Gillingham
Wycombe v Bury

League Two

Carlisle v Colchester
Cheltenham v Port Vale
Crawley v Oldham
Crewe v Stevenage
Leyton Orient v Cambridge
Newport v Morecambe
Northampton v Mansfield
Plymouth v Macclesfield
Salford v Bradford
Scunthorpe v Grimsby
Swindon v Forest Green
Walsall v Exeter

Saturday 14 March
Premier League

Aston Villa v Chelsea
Bournemouth v Crystal Palace
Brighton v Arsenal
Everton v Liverpool
Man City v Burnley
Newcastle v Sheff Utd
Norwich v Southampton
Tottenham v Man Utd
Watford v Leicester
West Ham v Wolves

Championship

Blackburn v Bristol City
Fulham v Brentford
Huddersfield v Wigan
Hull v Charlton
Luton v Preston
Middlesbrough v Swansea
Millwall v Derby
QPR v Barnsley
Reading v Stoke
Sheff Wed v Nottm Forest
WBA v Birmingham

League One

Blackpool v Sunderland
Bolton v Peterborough
Bristol Rov v Ipswich
Burton v Wycombe
Bury v Rochdale
Coventry v Shrewsbury

Doncaster v AFC Wimbledon
Gillingham v Fleetwood
Oxford v MK Dons
Portsmouth v Accrington
Rotherham v Southend
Tranmere v Lincoln

League Two

Bradford v Leyton Orient
Cambridge v Cheltenham
Colchester v Scunthorpe
Exeter v Salford
Forest Green v Northampton
Grimsby v Carlisle
Macclesfield v Walsall
Mansfield v Crewe
Morecambe v Plymouth
Oldham v Swindon
Port Vale v Crawley
Stevenage v Newport

Sunday 15 March
Championship

Cardiff v Leeds

Tuesday 17 March
Championship

Barnsley v Millwall
Brentford v WBA
Bristol City v Sheff Wed
Charlton v QPR
Derby v Reading

League Two

Colchester v Crewe
Crawley v Newport
Exeter v Scunthorpe
Forest Green v Morecambe
Grimsby v Cambridge
Leyton Orient v Plymouth
Macclesfield v Cheltenham
Northampton v Carlisle
Port Vale v Bradford
Salford v Mansfield
Stevenage v Swindon
Walsall v Oldham

Wednedsday 18 March
Championship

Birmingham v Hull
Leeds v Fulham
Nottm Forest v Huddersfield
Preston v Cardiff
Stoke v Middlesbrough
Swansea v Luton
Wigan v Blackburn

Saturday 21 March
Premier League

Burnley v Watford
Chelsea v Man City

Leicester v Brighton
Liverpool v Crystal Palace
Man Utd v Sheff Utd
Newcastle v Aston Villa
Norwich v Everton
Southampton v Arsenal
Tottenham v West Ham
Wolves v Bournemouth

Championship
Barnsley v Blackburn
Birmingham v Huddersfield
Cardiff v Charlton
Hull v Middlesbrough
Leeds v Luton
Millwall v Swansea
Nottm Forest v Bristol City
Preston v Derby
QPR v Fulham
Reading v Brentford
Sheff Wed v WBA
Wigan v Stoke

League One
Accrington v Doncaster
AFC Wimbledon v Tranmere
Fleetwood v Rotherham
Ipswich v Portsmouth
Lincoln v Coventry
MK Dons v Gillingham
Peterborough v Bristol Rov
Rochdale v Burton
Shrewsbury v Blackpool
Southend v Bolton
Sunderland v Bury
Wycombe v Oxford

League Two
Bradford v Macclesfield
Cambridge v Northampton
Carlisle v Leyton Orient
Cheltenham v Grimsby
Crewe v Forest Green
Mansfield v Walsall
Morecambe v Stevenage
Newport v Colchester
Oldham v Port Vale
Plymouth v Exeter
Scunthorpe v Salford
Swindon v Crawley

Saturday 28 March
League One
Accrington v Coventry
Bristol Rov v Rochdale
Burton v Doncaster
Bury v Ipswich
Fleetwood v Bolton
Lincoln v AFC Wimbledon
Oxford v Portsmouth

Peterborough v Blackpool
Rotherham v Gillingham
Shrewsbury v Wycombe
Southend v Sunderland
Tranmere v MK Dons

League Two
Colchester v Mansfield
Crawley v Cambridge
Exeter v Bradford
Forest Green v Cheltenham
Grimsby v Plymouth
Leyton Orient v Morecambe
Macclesfield v Carlisle
Northampton v Oldham
Port Vale v Crewe
Salford v Newport
Stevenage v Scunthorpe
Walsall v Swindon

Saturday 4 April
Premier League
Arsenal v Norwich
Aston Villa v Wolves
Bournemouth v Newcastle
Brighton v Man Utd
Crystal Palace v Burnley
Everton v Leicester
Man City v Liverpool
Sheff Utd v Tottenham
Watford v Southampton
West Ham v Chelsea

Championship
Blackburn v Leeds
Brentford v Wigan
Bristol City v Cardiff
Charlton v Millwall
Derby v Nottm Forest
Fulham v Birmingham
Huddersfield v Preston
Luton v Reading
Middlesbrough v QPR
Stoke v Barnsley
Swansea v Sheff Wed
WBA v Hull

League One
AFC Wimbledon v Bury
Blackpool v Burton
Bolton v Lincoln
Coventry v Peterborough
Doncaster v Tranmere
Gillingham v Accrington
Ipswich v Southend
MK Dons v Fleetwood
Portsmouth v Bristol Rov
Rochdale v Oxford
Sunderland v Shrewsbury
Wycombe v Rotherham

League Two
Bradford v Colchester
Cambridge v Walsall
Carlisle v Port Vale
Cheltenham v Exeter
Crewe v Northampton
Mansfield v Macclesfield
Morecambe v Crawley
Newport v Grimsby
Oldham v Stevenage
Plymouth v Forest Green
Scunthorpe v Leyton Orient
Swindon v Salford

Thursday 9 April
League One
Bury v Tranmere

Friday 10 April
Championship
Birmingham v Swansea
Brentford v Charlton
Bristol City v Hull
Cardiff v Blackburn
Leeds v Stoke
Luton v Barnsley
Millwall v Middlesbrough
Nottm Forest v Fulham
Reading v Huddersfield
Sheff Wed v Preston
WBA v Derby
Wigan v QPR

League One
Accrington v Fleetwood
AFC Wimbledon v Sunderland
Blackpool v Rochdale
Burton v Shrewsbury
Gillingham v Coventry
Ipswich v Bolton
Lincoln v Doncaster
Oxford v Bristol Rov
Peterborough v MK Dons
Rotherham v Portsmouth
Southend v Wycombe

League Two
Crawley v Leyton Orient
Crewe v Newport
Exeter v Morecambe
Forest Green v Bradford
Northampton v Colchester
Oldham v Cambridge
Port Vale v Grimsby
Salford v Carlisle
Scunthorpe v Macclesfield
Stevenage v Mansfield
Swindon v Cheltenham
Walsall v Plymouth

Saturday 11 April
Premier League
Burnley v Sheff Utd
Chelsea v Watford
Leicester v Crystal Palace
Liverpool v Aston Villa
Man Utd v Bournemouth
Newcastle v West Ham
Norwich v Brighton
Southampton v Man City
Tottenham v Everton
Wolves v Arsenal

Monday 13 April
Championship
Barnsley v Wigan
Blackburn v WBA
Charlton v Reading
Derby v Brentford
Huddersfield v Luton
Hull v Millwall
Middlesbrough v Bristol City
Preston v Nottm Forest
QPR v Sheff Wed
Stoke v Birmingham
Swansea v Leeds

League One
Bristol Rov v Burton
Coventry v Oxford
Doncaster v Bury
Fleetwood v Lincoln
MK Dons v Accrington
Portsmouth v Blackpool
Rochdale v Southend
Shrewsbury v Ipswich
Sunderland v Peterborough
Tranmere v Rotherham
Wycombe v AFC Wimbledon

League Two
Bradford v Crewe
Cambridge v Port Vale
Carlisle v Scunthorpe
Cheltenham v Crawley
Colchester v Oldham
Grimsby v Walsall
Leyton Orient v Salford
Macclesfield v Stevenage
Mansfield v Exeter
Morecambe v Swindon
Newport v Forest Green
Plymouth v Northampton

Tuesday 14 April
Championship
Fulham v Cardiff

League One
Bolton v Gillingham

Saturday 18 April
Premier League
Arsenal v Leicester
Aston Villa v Man Utd
Bournemouth v Tottenham
Brighton v Liverpool
Crystal Palace v Chelsea
Everton v Southampton
Man City v Newcastle
Sheff Utd v Wolves
Watford v Norwich
West Ham v Burnley

Championship
Birmingham v Charlton
Brentford v Preston
Bristol City v Stoke
Cardiff v Derby
Leeds v Barnsley
Luton v QPR
Millwall v Blackburn
Nottm Forest v Swansea
Reading v Middlesbrough
Sheff Wed v Huddersfield
WBA v Fulham
Wigan v Hull

League One
Accrington v Bristol Rov
AFC Wimbledon v MK Dons
Blackpool v Coventry
Burton v Sunderland
Bury v Bolton
Gillingham v Tranmere
Ipswich v Rochdale
Lincoln v Wycombe
Oxford v Fleetwood
Peterborough v Shrewsbury
Rotherham v Doncaster
Southend v Portsmouth

League Two
Crawley v Macclesfield
Crewe v Grimsby
Exeter v Carlisle
Forest Green v Cambridge
Northampton v Bradford
Oldham v Plymouth
Port Vale v Newport
Salford v Morecambe
Scunthorpe v Mansfield
Stevenage v Cheltenham
Swindon v Leyton Orient
Walsall v Colchester

Saturday 25 April
Premier League
Aston Villa v Crystal Palace
Bournemouth v Leicester
Brighton v Man City
Liverpool v Burnley
Man Utd v Southampton
Norwich v West Ham
Sheff Utd v Chelsea
Tottenham v Arsenal
Watford v Newcastle
Wolves v Everton

Championship
Barnsley v Nottm Forest
Blackburn v Reading
Charlton v Wigan
Derby v Leeds
Fulham v Sheff Wed
Huddersfield v WBA
Hull v Luton
Middlesbrough v Cardiff
Preston v Birmingham
QPR v Millwall
Stoke v Brentford
Swansea v Bristol City

League One
Bolton v Rotherham
Bristol Rov v Lincoln
Coventry v Accrington
Doncaster v Ipswich
Fleetwood v Southend
MK Dons v Blackpool
Portsmouth v Bury
Rochdale v Peterborough
Shrewsbury v AFC Wimbledon
Sunderland v Accrington
Tranmere v Oxford
Wycombe v Gillingham

League Two
Bradford v Walsall
Cambridge v Crewe
Carlisle v Stevenage
Cheltenham v Salford
Colchester v Forest Green
Grimsby v Oldham
Leyton Orient v Exeter
Macclesfield v Swindon
Mansfield v Crawley
Morecambe v Scunthorpe
Newport v Northampton
Plymouth v Port Vale

Saturday 2 May
Premier League
Arsenal v Liverpool
Burnley v Wolves
Chelsea v Norwich
Crystal Palace v Man Utd
Everton v Aston Villa
Leicester v Sheff Utd
Man City v Bournemouth
Newcastle v Tottenham
Southampton v Brighton
West Ham v Watford

Championship
Birmingham v Derby
Brentford v Barnsley
Bristol City v Preston
Cardiff v Hull
Leeds v Charlton
Luton v Blackburn
Millwall v Huddersfield
Nottm Forest v Stoke
Reading v Swansea
Sheff Wed v Middlesbrough
WBA v QPR
Wigan v Fulham

Sunday 3 May
League One
Accrington v Wycombe
AFC Wimbledon v Coventry

Blackpool v Doncaster
Burton v Portsmouth
Bury v Fleetwood
Gillingham v Bristol Rov
Ipswich v MK Dons
Lincoln v Rochdale
Oxford v Bolton
Peterborough v Tranmere
Rotherham v Sunderland
Southend v Shrewsbury

Saturday 9 May
Premier League
Aston Villa v Arsenal
Bournemouth v Southampton
Brighton v Newcastle
Liverpool v Chelsea
Man Utd v West Ham

Norwich v Burnley
Sheff Utd v Everton
Tottenham v Leicester
Watford v Man City
Wolves v Crystal Palace

Sunday 17 May
Premier League
Arsenal v Watford
Burnley v Brighton
Chelsea v Wolves
Crystal Palace v Tottenham
Everton v Bournemouth
Leicester v Man Utd
Man City v Norwich
Newcastle v Liverpool
Southampton v Sheff Utd
West Ham v Aston Villa

SCOTTISH FIXTURES 2019–2020
Premiership Championship League One and League Two

Friday 2 August
Championship
Dunfermline v Dundee

Saturday 3 August
Premiership
Aberdeen v Hearts
Celtic v St Johnstone
Hibernian v St Mirren
Livingston v Motherwell
Ross Co v Hamilton

Championship
Alloa v Partick
Arbroath v Queen of South
Ayr v Morton
Dundee Utd v Inverness

League One
Airdrieonians v Forfar
Clyde v East Fife
Dumbarton v Raith
Peterhead v Falkirk
Stranraer v Montrose

League Two
Brechin v Annan
Cove v Edinburgh City
Elgin v Cowdenbeath
Stenhousemuir v Albion Rovers
Stirling v Queen's Park

Sunday 4 August
Premiership
Kilmarnock v Rangers

Friday 9 August
Championship
Partick v Dundee Utd

Saturday 10 August
Premiership
Hamilton v Kilmarnock
Hearts v Ross Co
Motherwell v Celtic
Rangers v Hibernian
St Johnstone v Livingston
St Mirren v Aberdeen

Championship
Dundee v Ayr
Inverness v Arbroath
Morton v Alloa
Queen of South v Dunfermline

League One
East Fife v Peterhead
Falkirk v Dumbarton
Forfar v Stranraer
Montrose v Airdrieonians
Raith v Clyde

League Two
Albion Rovers v Cove
Annan v Elgin
Cowdenbeath v Stirling
Edinburgh City v Brechin
Queen's Park v Stenhousemuir

Saturday 17 August
League One
Airdrieonians v Clyde
Falkirk v Montrose
Forfar v East Fife

Peterhead v Dumbarton
Stranraer v Raith

League Two
Annan v Albion Rovers
Brechin v Queen's Park
Cove v Cowdenbeath
Edinburgh City v Stirling
Elgin v Stenhousemuir

Friday 23 August
Championship
Morton v Partick

Saturday 24 August
Premiership
Celtic v Hearts
Hamilton v Motherwell
Hibernian v St Johnstone
Kilmarnock v Aberdeen
Ross Co v Livingston

Championship
Alloa v Arbroath
Ayr v Queen of South
Dundee v Inverness
Dunfermline v Dundee Utd

League One
Clyde v Falkirk
Dumbarton v Stranraer
East Fife v Airdrieonians
Peterhead v Forfar
Raith v Montrose

League Two
Albion Rovers v Brechin
Cowdenbeath v Annan
Queen's Park v Elgin

Stenhousemuir v Edinburgh City
Stirling v Cove

Sunday 25 August
Premiership
St Mirren v Rangers

Friday 30 August
Championship
Dundee Utd v Dundee
Inverness v Morton

Saturday 31 August
Premiership
Aberdeen v Ross Co
Hearts v Hamilton
Livingston v St Mirren
Motherwell v Hibernian
St Johnstone v Kilmarnock

Championship
Arbroath v Dunfermline
Partick v Ayr
Queen of South v Alloa

League One
Airdrieonians v Falkirk
East Fife v Raith
Forfar v Clyde
Montrose v Dumbarton
Stranraer v Peterhead

League Two
Albion Rovers v Stirling
Annan v Stenhousemuir
Cove v Queen's Park
Cowdenbeath v Brechin
Elgin v Edinburgh City

Sunday 1 September
Premiership
Rangers v Celtic

Friday 13 September
Championship
Arbroath v Partick

Saturday 14 September
Premiership
Aberdeen v St Johnstone
Hamilton v Celtic
Hearts v Motherwell
Kilmarnock v Hibernian
Rangers v Livingston
Ross Co v St Mirren

Championship
Ayr v Dundee Utd
Dundee v Alloa

Dunfermline v Inverness
Queen of South v Morton

League One
Clyde v Stranraer
Dumbarton v Airdrieonians
Falkirk v Forfar
Montrose v East Fife
Raith v Peterhead

League Two
Brechin v Cove
Edinburgh City v Annan
Queen's Park v Albion Rovers
Stenhousemuir v Cowdenbeath
Stirling v Elgin

Saturday 21 September
Premiership
Celtic v Kilmarnock
Hibernian v Hearts
Livingston v Aberdeen
Motherwell v Ross Co
St Johnstone v Rangers
St Mirren v Hamilton

Championship
Alloa v Ayr
Dundee Utd v Arbroath
Inverness v Queen of South
Morton v Dundee
Partick v Dunfermline

League One
Airdrieonians v Raith
East Fife v Dumbarton
Forfar v Montrose
Peterhead v Clyde
Stranraer v Falkirk

League Two
Albion Rovers v Edinburgh City
Annan v Stirling
Elgin v Cove
Queen's Park v Cowdenbeath
Stenhousemuir v Brechin

Friday 27 September
Championship
Queen of South v Dundee

Saturday 28 September
Premiership
Hamilton v Livingston
Hibernian v Celtic
Kilmarnock v Ross Co
Rangers v Aberdeen
St Johnstone v Motherwell
St Mirren v Hearts

Championship
Arbroath v Ayr
Dundee Utd v Morton
Dunfermline v Alloa
Inverness v Partick

League One
Airdrieonians v Stranraer
Dumbarton v Clyde
Falkirk v East Fife
Forfar v Raith
Montrose v Peterhead

League Two
Brechin v Elgin
Cove v Annan
Cowdenbeath v Albion Rovers
Edinburgh City v Queen's Park
Stirling v Stenhousemuir

Friday 4 October
Championship
Alloa v Dundee Utd

Saturday 5 October
Premiership
Aberdeen v Hibernian
Hearts v Kilmarnock
Livingston v Celtic
Motherwell v St Mirren
Rangers v Hamilton
Ross Co v St Johnstone

Championship
Ayr v Inverness
Dundee v Arbroath
Morton v Dunfermline
Partick v Queen of South

League One
Clyde v Montrose
Dumbarton v Forfar
East Fife v Stranraer
Peterhead v Airdrieonians
Raith v Falkirk

League Two
Albion Rovers v Elgin
Brechin v Stirling
Cowdenbeath v Edinburgh City
Queen's Park v Annan
Stenhousemuir v Cove

Saturday 19 October
Premiership
Celtic v Ross Co
Hamilton v Hibernian
Hearts v Rangers
Kilmarnock v Livingston
Motherwell v Aberdeen
St Mirren v St Johnstone

Championship
Arbroath v Morton
Dundee v Partick
Dunfermline v Ayr
Inverness v Alloa
Queen of South v Dundee Utd

League One
Airdrieonians v Montrose
Clyde v Raith
East Fife v Forfar
Falkirk v Peterhead
Stranraer v Dumbarton

Friday 25 October
Championship
Ayr v Dundee

Saturday 26 October
Premiership
Aberdeen v Celtic
Hibernian v Ross Co
Kilmarnock v St Mirren
Livingston v Hearts
Rangers v Motherwell
St Johnstone v Hamilton

Championship
Alloa v Queen of South
Dundee Utd v Dunfermline
Morton v Inverness
Partick v Arbroath

League One
Dumbarton v Peterhead
Falkirk v Clyde
Forfar v Airdrieonians
Montrose v Stranraer
Raith v East Fife

League Two
Annan v Brechin
Cove v Albion Rovers
Edinburgh City v Stenhousemuir
Elgin v Queen's Park
Stirling v Cowdenbeath

Tuesday 29 October
Championship
Alloa v Dundee
Dundee Utd v Partick
Dunfermline v Arbroath
Morton v Ayr
Queen of South v Inverness

Wednesday 30 October
Premiership
Celtic v St Mirren
Hamilton v Aberdeen

Hibernian v Livingston
Motherwell v Kilmarnock
Ross Co v Rangers
St Johnstone v Hearts

Friday 1 November
Championship
Dundee v Morton

Saturday 2 November
Premiership
Aberdeen v Kilmarnock
Hamilton v Ross Co
Hearts v Celtic
Motherwell v Livingston
Rangers v St Johnstone
St Mirren v Hibernian

Championship
Arbroath v Alloa
Ayr v Partick
Dunfermline v Queen of South
Inverness v Dundee Utd

League One
Airdrieonians v Dumbarton
East Fife v Montrose
Forfar v Falkirk
Peterhead v Raith
Stranraer v Clyde

League Two
Brechin v Edinburgh City
Cowdenbeath v Cove
Elgin v Annan
Stenhousemuir v Queen's Park
Stirling v Albion Rovers

Saturday 9 November
Premiership
Celtic v Motherwell
Hearts v St Mirren
Kilmarnock v Hamilton
Livingston v Rangers
Ross Co v Aberdeen
St Johnstone v Hibernian

Championship
Alloa v Dunfermline
Arbroath v Inverness
Dundee v Dundee Utd
Partick v Morton
Queen of South v Ayr

League One
Clyde v Peterhead
Dumbarton v East Fife
Falkirk v Airdrieonians
Montrose v Forfar
Raith v Stranraer

League Two
Albion Rovers v Stenhousemuir
Annan v Cowdenbeath
Cove v Stirling
Edinburgh City v Elgin
Queen's Park v Brechin

Saturday 16 November
Championship
Ayr v Dunfermline
Dundee Utd v Queen of South
Inverness v Dundee
Morton v Arbroath
Partick v Alloa

League One
Dumbarton v Falkirk
East Fife v Clyde
Peterhead v Montrose
Raith v Forfar
Stranraer v Airdrieonians

League Two
Cove v Brechin
Cowdenbeath v Queen's Park
Edinburgh City v Albion Rovers
Stenhousemuir v Elgin
Stirling v Annan

Saturday 23 November
Premiership
Celtic v Livingston
Hamilton v Rangers
Hibernian v Motherwell
Kilmarnock v Hearts
St Johnstone v Aberdeen
St Mirren v Ross Co

Saturday 30 November
Premiership
Aberdeen v St Mirren
Hibernian v Kilmarnock
Livingston v Hamilton
Motherwell v St Johnstone
Rangers v Hearts
Ross Co v Celtic

Saturday 30 November
Championship
Alloa v Inverness
Ayr v Arbroath
Dundee v Queen of South
Dunfermline v Partick
Morton v Dundee Utd

League One
Airdrieonians v East Fife
Clyde v Dumbarton
Falkirk v Stranraer
Forfar v Peterhead
Montrose v Raith

League Two
Albion Rovers v Cowdenbeath
Annan v Cove
Brechin v Stenhousemuir
Elgin v Stirling
Queen's Park v Edinburgh City

Wednesday 4 December
Premiership
Aberdeen v Rangers
Celtic v Hamilton
Hearts v Livingston
Kilmarnock v St Johnstone
Ross Co v Hibernian
St Mirren v Motherwell

Saturday 7 December
Premiership
Hamilton v St Mirren
Hibernian v Aberdeen
Livingston v Kilmarnock
Motherwell v Hearts
Rangers v Ross Co
St Johnstone v Celtic

Championship
Arbroath v Dundee
Dundee Utd v Alloa
Dunfermline v Morton
Inverness v Ayr
Queen of South v Partick

League One
Clyde v Forfar
Dumbarton v Montrose
East Fife v Falkirk
Peterhead v Stranraer
Raith v Airdrieonians

League Two
Albion Rovers v Queen's Park
Cowdenbeath v Elgin
Edinburgh City v Cove
Stenhousemuir v Annan
Stirling v Brechin

Saturday 14 December
Premiership
Aberdeen v Hamilton
Celtic v Hibernian
Hearts v St Johnstone
Motherwell v Rangers
Ross Co v Kilmarnock
St Mirren v Livingston

Championship
Arbroath v Dundee Utd
Ayr v Alloa
Dundee v Dunfermline
Morton v Queen of South
Partick v Inverness

League One
Airdrieonians v Peterhead
Falkirk v Raith
Forfar v Dumbarton
Montrose v Clyde
Stranraer v East Fife

League Two
Annan v Edinburgh City
Brechin v Cowdenbeath
Cove v Stenhousemuir
Elgin v Albion Rovers
Queen's Park v Stirling

Saturday 21 December
Premiership
Celtic v Aberdeen
Hamilton v Hearts
Hibernian v Rangers
Kilmarnock v Motherwell
Livingston v Ross Co
St Johnstone v St Mirren

Championship
Alloa v Morton
Dundee Utd v Ayr
Inverness v Dunfermline
Partick v Dundee
Queen of South v Arbroath

League One
Clyde v Airdrieonians
Montrose v Falkirk
Peterhead v East Fife
Raith v Dumbarton
Stranraer v Forfar

League Two
Albion Rovers v Annan
Cowdenbeath v Stenhousemuir
Elgin v Brechin
Queen's Park v Cove
Stirling v Edinburgh City

Saturday 28 December
Championship
Ayr v Queen of South
Dundee Utd v Dundee
Dunfermline v Alloa
Inverness v Arbroath
Morton v Partick

League One
Airdrieonians v Falkirk
Dumbarton v Stranraer
East Fife v Raith
Forfar v Montrose
Peterhead v Clyde

League Two
Annan v Queen's Park
Brechin v Albion Rovers

Cove v Elgin
Edinburgh City v Cowdenbeath
Stenhousemuir v Stirling

Sunday 29 December
Premiership
Celtic v Rangers
Hearts v Aberdeen
Livingston v Hibernian
Motherwell v Hamilton
St Johnstone v Ross Co
St Mirren v Kilmarnock

Saturday 4 January
Championship Alloa v Partick
Arbroath v Morton
Dundee v Inverness
Dunfermline v Ayr
Queen of South v Dundee Utd

League One
Airdrieonians v Forfar
Clyde v Stranraer
Falkirk v Dumbarton
Montrose v East Fife
Raith v Peterhead

League Two
Albion Rovers v Stirling
Brechin v Cove
Cowdenbeath v Annan
Elgin v Edinburgh City
Queen's Park v Stenhousemuir

Saturday 11 January
Championship
Alloa v Arbroath
Dundee v Ayr
Inverness v Queen of South
Morton v Dunfermline
Partick v Dundee Utd

League One
Dumbarton v Clyde
East Fife v Airdrieonians
Forfar v Raith
Peterhead v Falkirk
Stranraer v Montrose

League Two
Annan v Elgin
Cowdenbeath v Albion Rovers
Edinburgh City v Queen's Park
Stenhousemuir v Brechin
Stirling v Cove

Saturday 18 January
League Two
Albion Rovers v Edinburgh City
Annan v Stirling
Brechin v Queen's Park

Cove v Cowdenbeath
Elgin v Stenhousemuir

Wednesday 22 January
Premiership
Aberdeen v Motherwell
Hibernian v Hamilton
Kilmarnock v Celtic
Livingston v St Johnstone
Rangers v St Mirren
Ross Co v Hearts

Saturday 25 January
Premiership
Celtic v Ross Co
Hamilton v Livingston
Hearts v Rangers
Motherwell v Hibernian
St Johnstone v Kilmarnock
St Mirren v Aberdeen

Championship
Arbroath v Partick
Ayr v Inverness
Dundee Utd v Morton
Dunfermline v Dundee
Queen of the South v Alloa

League One
Airdrieonians v Stranraer
Clyde v East Fife
Falkirk v Forfar
Peterhead v Dumbarton
Raith v Montrose

League Two
Cove v Annan
Cowdenbeath v Brechin
Queen's Park v Albion Rovers
Stenhousemuir v Edinburgh City
Stirling v Elgin

Saturday 1 February
Premiership
Hamilton v Celtic
Hibernian v St Mirren
Kilmarnock v Ross Co
Livingston v Motherwell
Rangers v Aberdeen
St Johnstone v Hearts

Championship
Dundee Utd v Arbroath
Inverness v Alloa
Morton v Dundee
Partick v Ayr
Queen of the South v Dunfermline

League One
Airdrieonians v Raith

East Fife v Dumbarton
Forfar v Clyde
Montrose v Peterhead
Stranraer v Falkirk

League Two
Albion Rovers v Cove
Annan v Stenhousemuir
Brechin v Elgin
Edinburgh City v Stirling
Queen's Park v Cowdenbeath

Wednesday 5 February
Premiership
Aberdeen v St Johnstone
Hearts v Kilmarnock
Motherwell v Celtic
Rangers v Hibernian
Ross Co v Livingston
St Mirren v Hamilton

Saturday 8 February
League Two
Albion Rovers v Brechin
Edinburgh City v Annan
Elgin v Cove
Stenhousemuir v Cowdenbeath
Stirling v Queen's Park

Wednesday 12 February
Premiership
Celtic v Hearts
Hamilton v Aberdeen
Hibernian v Ross Co
Kilmarnock v Rangers
Livingston v St Mirren
St Johnstone v Motherwell

Saturday 8 February
League One
Clyde v Montrose
Dumbarton v Airdrieonians
Falkirk v East Fife
Peterhead v Forfar
Stranraer v Raith

Saturday 15 February
Premiership
Aberdeen v Celtic
Hearts v Hamilton
Kilmarnock v Hibernian
Motherwell v St Mirren
Rangers v Livingston
Ross Co v St Johnstone

Championship
Alloa v Dundee Utd
Arbroath v Queen of South
Ayr v Morton
Dundee v Partick

Dunfermline v Inverness

League One
Airdrieonians v Clyde
East Fife v Peterhead
Forfar v Stranraer
Montrose v Dumbarton
Raith v Falkirk

League Two
Brechin v Annan
Cove v Edinburgh City
Cowdenbeath v Stirling
Queen's Park v Elgin
Stenhousemuir v Albion Rovers

Saturday 22 February
Premiership
Aberdeen v Ross Co
Celtic v Kilmarnock
Hamilton v Motherwell
Hibernian v Livingston
St Johnstone v Rangers
St Mirren v Hearts

Championship
Arbroath v Ayr
Dundee Utd v Inverness
Morton v Alloa
Partick v Dunfermline
Queen of the South v Dundee

League One
Dumbarton v Forfar
East Fife v Stranraer
Falkirk v Montrose
Peterhead v Airdrieonians
Raith v Clyde

League Two
Annan v Albion Rovers
Cove v Queen's Park
Edinburgh City v Brechin
Elgin v Cowdenbeath
Stirling v Stenhousemuir

Saturday 29 February
Championship
Alloa v Ayr
Dundee v Arbroath
Dunfermline v Dundee Utd
Inverness v Partick
Queen of the South v Morton

League One
Clyde v Falkirk
Dumbarton v Raith
Forfar v East Fife
Montrose v Airdrieonians
Stranraer v Peterhead

League Two
Albion Rovers v Elgin
Brechin v Stirling
Cowdenbeath v Edinburgh City
Queen's Park v Annan
Stenhousemuir v Cove

Tuesday 3 March
Championship
Ayr v Dundee Utd
Dundee v Alloa
Inverness v Morton
Partick v Queen of South

Wednesday 4 March
Premiership
Hibernian v Hearts
Kilmarnock v Aberdeen
Livingston v Celtic
Motherwell v Ross Co
Rangers v Hamilton
St Mirren v St Johnstone

Championship
Arbroath v Dunfermline

Saturday 7 March
Premiership
Aberdeen v Hibernian
Celtic v St Mirren
Hamilton v Kilmarnock
Hearts v Motherwell
Ross Co v Rangers
St Johnstone v Livingston

Championship
Alloa v Inverness
Ayr v Dundee
Dundee Utd v Partick
Dunfermline v Queen of South
Morton v Arbroath

League One
Airdrieonians v East Fife
Clyde v Dumbarton
Falkirk v Peterhead
Montrose v Stranraer
Raith v Forfar

League Two
Annan v Cowdenbeath
Cove v Brechin
Edinburgh City v Albion Rovers
Elgin v Stirling
Stenhousemuir v Queen's Park

Saturday 14 March
Premiership
Hibernian v St Johnstone
Kilmarnock v St Mirren

Livingston v Hearts
Motherwell v Aberdeen
Rangers v Celtic
Ross Co v Hamilton

Championship
Arbroath v Inverness
Dundee v Dunfermline
Morton v Dundee Utd
Partick v Alloa
Queen of the South v Ayr

League One
Dumbarton v Falkirk
East Fife v Montrose
Forfar v Airdrieonians
Peterhead v Raith
Stranraer v Clyde

League Two
Albion Rovers v Queen's Park
Cowdenbeath v Cove
Edinburgh City v Stenhousemuir
Elgin v Brechin
Stirling v Annan

Saturday 21 March
Premiership
Celtic v St Johnstone
Hamilton v Hibernian
Hearts v Ross Co
Livingston v Aberdeen
Motherwell v Kilmarnock
St Mirren v Rangers

Championship
Ayr v Partick
Dundee Utd v Alloa
Dunfermline v Morton
Inverness v Dundee
Queen of the South v Arbroath

League One
Airdrieonians v Dumbarton
Clyde v Peterhead
Falkirk v Stranraer
Montrose v Forfar
Raith v East Fife

League Two
Annan v Edinburgh City
Brechin v Cowdenbeath
Cove v Albion Rovers
Queen's Park v Stirling
Stenhousemuir v Elgin

Saturday 28 March
Championship
Alloa v Dunfermline
Arbroath v Dundee Utd
Dundee v Queen of the South

Inverness v Ayr
Partick v Morton

League One
East Fife v Clyde
Forfar v Falkirk
Peterhead v Montrose
Raith v Airdrieonians
Stranraer v Dumbarton

League Two
Annan v Brechin
Cowdenbeath v Stenhousemuir
Edinburgh City v Cove
Elgin v Queen's Park
Stirling v Albion Rovers

Saturday 4 April
Premiership
Aberdeen v Hearts
Hibernian v Celtic
Kilmarnock v Livingston
Rangers v Motherwell
Ross Co v St Mirren
St Johnstone v Hamilton

Championship
Alloa v Dundee
Ayr v Dunfermline
Dundee Utd v Queen of South
Morton v Inverness
Partick v Arbroath

League One
Clyde v Forfar
Dumbarton v Peterhead
Falkirk v Airdrieonians
Montrose v Raith
Stranraer v East Fife

League Two
Albion Rovers v Annan
Brechin v Stenhousemuir
Cove v Elgin
Queen's Park v Edinburgh City
Stirling v Cowdenbeath

Saturday 11 April
Championship
Ayr v Alloa
Dundee v Morton
Dunfermline v Arbroath
Inverness v Dundee Utd
Queen of the South v Partick

League One
Airdrieonians v Montrose
East Fife v Forfar
Falkirk v Clyde
Peterhead v Stranraer
Raith v Dumbarton

League Two
Annan v Cove
Brechin v Albion Rovers
Cowdenbeath v Queen's Park
Edinburgh City v Elgin
Stenhousemuir v Stirling

Saturday 18 April
Championship
Alloa v Queen of South
Arbroath v Dundee
Dundee Utd v Dunfermline
Morton v Ayr
Partick v Inverness

League One
Clyde v Raith
Dumbarton v East Fife
Forfar v Peterhead
Montrose v Falkirk
Stranraer v Airdrieonians

League Two
Albion Rovers v Cowdenbeath

Cove v Stenhousemuir
Elgin v Annan
Queen's Park v Brechin
Stirling v Edinburgh City

Saturday 25 April
Championship
Alloa v Morton
Ayr v Arbroath
Dundee v Dundee Utd
Dunfermline v Partick
Queen of the South v Inverness

League One
Airdrieonians v Peterhead
East Fife v Falkirk
Forfar v Dumbarton
Montrose v Clyde
Raith v Stranraer

League Two
Edinburgh City v Cowdenbeath
Elgin v Albion Rovers
Queen's Park v Cove

Stenhousemuir v Annan
Stirling v Brechin

Saturday 2nd May
Championship
Arbroath v Alloa
Dundee Utd v Ayr
Inverness v Dunfermline
Morton v Queen of South
Partick v Dundee

League One
Clyde v Airdrieonians
Dumbarton v Montrose
Falkirk v Raith
Peterhead v East Fife
Stranraer v Forfar

League Two
Albion Rovers v Stenhousemuir
Annan v Queen's Park
Brechin v Edinburgh City
Cove v Stirling
Cowdenbeath v Elgin

NATIONAL LEAGUE
Premier fixtures 2019–2020

Saturday 3 August
Aldershot v Fylde
Barnet v Yeovil
Chesterfield v Dover
Chorley v Bromley
Dag & Red v Woking
Eastleigh v Notts Co
Ebbsfleet v Halifax
Harrogate v Solihull
Hartlepool v Sutton
Stockport v Maidenhead
Torquay v Boreham Wood
Wrexham v Barrow

Tuesday 6 August
Barrow v Harrogate
Boreham Wood v Wrexham
Bromley v Ebbsfleet
Dover v Dag & Red
Fylde v Chorley
Halifax v Hartlepool
Maidenhead v Chesterfield
Notts Co v Stockport
Solihull v Torquay
Sutton v Barnet
Woking v Aldershot
Yeovil v Eastleigh

Saturday 10 August
Barrow v Eastleigh
Boreham Wood v Chesterfield
Bromley v Torquay
Dover v Wrexham

Fylde v Ebbsfleet
Halifax v Dag & Red
Maidenhead v Hartlepool
Notts Co v Barnet
Solihull v Aldershot
Sutton v Chorley
Woking v Harrogate
Yeovil v Stockport

Tuesday 1
3 August
Aldershot v Bromley
Barnet v Dover
Chesterfield v Woking
Chorley v Solihull
Dag & Red v Boreham Wood
Eastleigh v Sutton
Ebbsfleet v Yeovil
Harrogate v Notts Co
Hartlepool v Fylde
Stockport v Barrow
Torquay v Maidenhead
Wrexham v Halifax

Saturday 17 August
Aldershot v Halifax
Barnet v Chesterfield
Barrow v Yeovil
Boreham Wood v Sutton
Dag & Red v Harrogate
Dover v Torquay
Fylde v Woking
Hartlepool v Bromley

Maidenhead v Chorley
Notts Co v Wrexham
Solihull v Ebbsfleet
Stockport v Eastleigh

Saturday 24 August
Bromley v Boreham Wood
Chesterfield v Barrow
Chorley v Hartlepool
Eastleigh v Dag & Red
Ebbsfleet v Notts Co
Halifax v Fylde
Harrogate v Stockport
Sutton v Dover
Torquay v Aldershot
Woking v Solihull
Wrexham v Barnet
Yeovil v Maidenhead

Monday 26 August
Aldershot v Sutton
Barnet v Torquay
Barrow v Halifax
Boreham Wood v Ebbsfleet
Dag & Red v Yeovil
Dover v Woking
Fylde v Harrogate
Hartlepool v Wrexham
Maidenhead v Bromley
Notts Co v Chorley
Solihull v Eastleigh
Stockport v Chesterfield

Saturday 31 August
Bromley v Fylde
Chesterfield v Dag & Red
Chorley v Boreham Wood
Eastleigh v Barnet
Ebbsfleet v Aldershot
Halifax v Solihull
Harrogate v Dover
Sutton v Maidenhead
Torquay v Hartlepool
Woking v Barrow
Wrexham v Stockport
Yeovil v Notts Co

Tuesday 3 September
Barnet v Aldershot
Barrow v Hartlepool
Chesterfield v Halifax
Dag & Red v Bromley
Dover v Ebbsfleet
Eastleigh v Boreham Wood
Harrogate v Chorley
Notts Co v Solihull
Stockport v Fylde
Woking v Torquay
Wrexham v Maidenhead
Yeovil v Sutton

Saturday 7 September
Aldershot v Barrow
Boreham Wood v Dover
Bromley v Chesterfield
Chorley v Stockport
Ebbsfleet v Eastleigh
Fylde v Barnet
Halifax v Yeovil
Hartlepool v Woking
Maidenhead v Dag & Red
Solihull v Wrexham
Sutton v Notts Co
Torquay v Harrogate

Saturday 14 September
Barnet v Maidenhead
Barrow v Solihull
Chesterfield v Torquay
Dag & Red v Hartlepool
Dover v Chorley
Eastleigh v Bromley
Harrogate v Boreham Wood
Notts Co v Halifax
Stockport v Aldershot
Woking v Ebbsfleet
Wrexham v Sutton
Yeovil v Fylde

Saturday 21 September
Aldershot v Wrexham
Boreham Wood v Stockport
Bromley v Notts Co
Chorley v Woking

Ebbsfleet v Barrow
Fylde v Eastleigh
Halifax v Barnet
Hartlepool v Dover
Maidenhead v Harrogate
Solihull v Yeovil
Sutton v Chesterfield
Torquay v Dag & Red

Tuesday 24 September
Aldershot v Yeovil
Boreham Wood v Notts Co
Bromley v Woking
Chorley v Barrow
Ebbsfleet v Barnet
Fylde v Wrexham
Halifax v Harrogate
Hartlepool v Chesterfield
Maidenhead v Dover
Solihull v Stockport
Sutton v Dag & Red
Torquay v Eastleigh

Saturday 28 September
Barnet v Solihull
Barrow v Maidenhead
Chesterfield v Aldershot
Dag & Red v Chorley
Dover v Halifax
Eastleigh v Hartlepool
Harrogate v Sutton
Notts Co v Fylde
Stockport v Torquay
Woking v Boreham Wood
Wrexham v Ebbsfleet
Yeovil v Bromley

Saturday 5 October
Boreham Wood v Solihull
Bromley v Barrow
Chesterfield v Eastleigh
Chorley v Aldershot
Dag & Red v Barnet
Dover v Notts Co
Harrogate v Ebbsfleet
Hartlepool v Yeovil
Maidenhead v Halifax
Sutton v Stockport
Torquay v Fylde
Woking v Wrexham

Tuesday 8 October
Aldershot v Dover
Barnet v Bromley
Barrow v Boreham Wood
Eastleigh v Maidenhead
Ebbsfleet v Torquay
Fylde v Chesterfield
Halifax v Chorley
Notts Co v Dag & Red
Solihull v Sutton

Stockport v Hartlepool
Wrexham v Harrogate
Yeovil v Woking

Saturday 12 October
Aldershot v Hartlepool
Barnet v Woking
Barrow v Dover
Eastleigh v Chorley
Ebbsfleet v Maidenhead
Fylde v Sutton
Halifax v Boreham Wood
Notts Co v Torquay
Solihull v Bromley
Stockport v Dag & Red
Wrexham v Chesterfield
Yeovil v Harrogate

Saturday 26 October
Boreham Wood v Fylde
Bromley v Halifax
Chesterfield v Notts Co
Chorley v Yeovil
Dag & Red v Wrexham
Dover v Stockport
Harrogate v Aldershot
Hartlepool v Barnet
Maidenhead v Solihull
Sutton v Ebbsfleet
Torquay v Barrow
Woking v Eastleigh

Tuesday 29 October
Boreham Wood v Aldershot
Bromley v Stockport
Chesterfield v Yeovil
Chorley v Ebbsfleet
Dag & Red v Barrow
Dover v Eastleigh
Harrogate v Barnet
Hartlepool v Solihull
Maidenhead v Fylde
Sutton v Halifax
Torquay v Wrexham
Woking v Notts Co
Latest news

Saturday 2 November
Aldershot v Maidenhead
Barnet v Chorley
Barrow v Sutton
Eastleigh v Harrogate
Ebbsfleet v Chesterfield
Fylde v Dover
Halifax v Torquay
Notts Co v Hartlepool
Solihull v Dag & Red
Stockport v Woking
Wrexham v Bromley
Yeovil v Boreham Wood